Fifty Years of Television

Fifty Years of Television

A Guide to Series and Pilots, 1937–1988

Vincent Terrace

Cornwall Books
New York • London • Toronto

Cornwall Books
440 Forsgate Drive
Cranbury, NJ 08512

Cornwall Books
25 Sicilian Avenue
London WC1A 2QH, England

Cornwall Books
P.O. Box 39, Clarkson Pstl. Stn.
Mississauga, Ontario
Canada L5J 3X9

The paper used in this publication meets the
requirements of the American National Standard for
Permanence of Paper for Printed Library Materials Z39.48-1984.

Library of Congress Cataloging-in-Publication Data

Terrace, Vincent, 1948–
    Fifty years of television.

    Includes index.
    1. Television programs—United States—Catalogs.
    I. Title.   II. Title: 50 years of television.
    PN1992.3.U5T47   1991   791.45′75′0973   87-47835
    ISBN 0-8453-4811-6

SECOND PRINTING

PRINTED IN THE UNITED STATES OF AMERICA

Contents

Preface

Fifty Years of Television is the first and only guide to fifty years of series, pilot films, and experimental programs broadcast from 1937 through 1988. Each of the more than 4,800 titles included is arranged alphabetically with a brief, yet comprehensive storyline, a complete cast list, and the show's producer, air date, running time, network (ABC, CBS, DuMont, Fox, NBC, PBS), Syndication (Syn.), and cable (CBN, Disney, HBO, Showtime, TBS, TEC [The Entertainment Channel], USA) information.

In addition to providing a quick reference guide to entertainment series and thirty- and sixty-minute pilot films, *Fifty Years of Television* provides a wealth of never-before published and very rare information concerning the unaired pilots to regular series—for example, the original casts of "Mr. Terrific" (with Alan Young as the superhero); "The Munsters" (with Joan Marshall as Herman's wife); and "That Girl" (with Ted Bessell as Ann's agent, Don Bluesky). Also included is the first-time publication of some virtually unknown and long-time forgotten series (e.g., "The Adventures of Patches," the 1954 "Blondie," and "Jackson and Jill").

A great deal of information on both older and new shows has been compiled from actual viewings and will contradict information that appears elsewhere (e.g., *TV Guide* and press releases). Because there are numerous occurrences of these discrepancies (e.g., "Hong Kong"), please keep in mind that the information that appears here is most likely from the actual program and not from press releases, *TV Guide,* or press kits.

Excluded from this book are 90- and 120-minute pilot films (TV movies), miniseries, daytime serials, specials, and sports and news programs.

The author would like to thank the following people for their help in making this book possible: Lloyd Friedman, Barry Gillam, Alvin H. Marill, Steve Eberly, and Robert (Bob) Reed.

Fifty Years of Television is a nostalgic, memory-jogging guide to the more than 4,800 programs that have been broadcast over the past fifty years. It provides access to the total world of entertainment programing in one easy-to-use quick reference guide.

Fifty Years of Television

The Abbott and Costello Show

Comedy; 30 min; Syn. 1952

The antics of Bud Abbott and Lou Costello, two unemployed comedians, as they attempt to find work and enjoy a more comfortable life.

Bud Abbott	Himself
Lou Costello	Himself
Hillary Brooke	Herself
Sidney Fields	Himself
Mike the Cop	Gordon Jones
Stinky	Joe Besser
Mr. Bacciagalupe	Joe Kirk
Mrs. Bronson	Renie Riano
	Sarah Haden
Mrs. Crumcake	Elvia Allman
Short Bald Man	Bobby Barbar
Bingo the Chimp	Bingo

Producer: Pat Costello, Alex Gottlieb, Jean Yarbrough

The Abbott and Costello Show

Cartoon; 5½ min; Syn. 1966

An animated series that involves comedians Bud Abbott and Lou Costello in a variety of predicaments.

Bud Abbott	Himself
Lou Costello	Stan Irwin

Producer: William Hanna, Joseph Barbera

ABC Album

Anthology; 30 min; ABC 4/12/53 to 6/28/53

Various dramatic and comedic productions featuring such stars as Wendell Corey, Geraldine Fitzgerald, Janis Paige, Neva Patterson, Sheila Bond, Alan Webb and Robert Preston. Also known as "Plymouth Playhouse."

Host: Donald Cook

Producer: Herbert Brodkin

ABC Fun Fit

Health; 5 min; ABC 9/7/85 to 9/6/86

Exercises geared to children with Olympic gymnist champion Mary Lou Retton.

Hostess: Mary Lou Retton

Assistants: Melissa Kern, Ericka Pazcoquin, Bradley Kane, Efrain Bracero

Producer: Eleanor Riger

ABC-Powers Charm School

Women; 30 min; ABC 10/2/46 to 12/25/46

A program of beauty tips and fashion advice.

Hostess: Peggy Allenby

Regulars: Pat Hosley, John Robert Powers, Walter Herlihy

Producer: Harvey Marlowe

ABC Stage '67

Anthology; 60 min; ABC 9/14/66 to 5/11/67

A series of original television productions (music, comedy, and drama). Stars include Carol Lynley, Donald O'Connor, Phyllis Newman, Douglas Fairbanks Jr., Fred Clark, Arlene Golonka, Anne Bancroft, Eddie Foy Jr., Michael Redgrave, Dick Shawn, Lee Grant, Redd Foxx, Larry Blyden, David Frost, Sidney Poitier, and Diahann Carroll. Various producers.

Abe Burrows Almanac

Variety; 30 min; CBS 1/4/50 to 3/29/50

A live program of music and comedy featuring performances by guests.

Host: Abe Burrows

Music: Milton DeLugg

Producer: Abe Burrows, Alan Dinehart

Abe Lincoln in Illinois

Experimental; 2 hrs; NBC 4/15/45

The story, based on the Robert E. Sherwood play, follows Abraham Lincoln from his backwoods law practice to the Presidency.

Abraham Lincoln	Stephen Courtleigh
Mary Todd	Mary Michaels

Producer: Edward Sobol

About Faces

Game; 30 min; ABC 1/4/60 to 6/30/61

The object calls for two players, each presented with clues concerning incidents in their past lives, to associate their relationships. The first player to do so wins merchandise prizes.

Host: Ben Alexander

Producer: Joe Landis

The Academy

Comedy Pilot; 30 min; NBC 3/31/82

The antics of a group of mischievous cadets at the Stone Military Academy. Aired as a segment of "The Facts of Life."

Major Tim Dorsey	David Ackroyd
Cadet Buzz Ryan	Jimmy Baio
Cadet George Knight	Peter Frechette
Cadet Alfred Webster	John P. Navin Jr.
Cadet Chip Nelson	David Hubbard

Producer: Jack Elinson, Jerry Mayer

The Academy II

Comedy Pilot; 30 min; NBC 12/8/82

A second "Facts of Life" pilot about the antics of the male cadets at the Stone Military Academy in Peekskill, N.Y.

Major Tim Dorsey	David Ackroyd
Cadet Buzz Ryan	Jimmy Baio
Cadet George Knight	Peter Frechette
Cadet Alfred Webster	John P. Navin Jr.
Cadet Hank Barton	Ben Marley
Cadet Chip Nelson	David Raynr

Producer: Jack Elinson, Jerry Mayer

Academy Theatre

Anthology; 30 min; NBC 7/25/49 to 9/12/49

A series of eight live plays that feature such performers as Anne Jackson, Emily Lawrence, Mark Roberts, Peter Wynn, Jack Davis, Peter Pagan, Michael Higgins, Shirley Dale and Richard Newton.

Acapulco

Adventure; 30 min; NBC 2/27/61 to 4/24/61

Gregg Miles and Patrick Malone, Korean war vets dissatisfied with life in the States, retreat to Mexico's Acapulco where their adventures as do-gooders are depicted.

Gregg Miles	James Coburn
Patrick Malone	Ralph Taeger
Chloe	Allison Hayes
Mr. Carver	Telly Savalas
Bobby Troup	Himself

Producer: John Robinson

Accidental Family

Comedy; 30 min; NBC 9/15/67 to 1/5/68

In an attempt to keep his son, Sandy, night club comedian Jerry Webster agrees to raise him in a non-show business atmosphere. When Jerry finds that he cannot evict Susannah Kramer, a pretty divorcee renting his San Fernando farm house, he and Susannah agree to share the home. Stories relate the problems that befall an "Accidental Family."

Jerry Webster	Jerry Van Dyke
Susannah Kramer	Lois Nettleton
Sandy Webster	Teddy Quinn
Tracy Kramer	
(Susannah's	
daughter)	Susan Benjamin
Ben McGrath	
(Susannah's uncle)	Ben Blue
Marty Warren	
(Jerry's agent)	Larry D. Mann

Producer: Sheldon Leonard

Accused

Drama; 30 min; ABC 12/10/58 to 9/30/59

Reenactments of actual courtroom cases.

Judge	Edgar Allan Jones Jr.
Substitute Judge	William Gwinn
Bailiff	Tim Farrell
Clerk	Jim Hodson
Reporter	Violet Gilmore

Producer: Selig J. Seligman

Ace

Comedy Pilot; 30 min; ABC 7/26/76

The adventures of Edward R. Ace, an eccentric private detective who, in the pilot, seeks to stop a security leak in a large corporation.

Edward R. Ace	Bob Dishy
Gloria Ross	Rae Allen
Janet Slade	Barbara Brownell
Mr. Mason	Dick Van Patten
Alice Slade	Ruth Manning
Mr. Strutt	Liam Dunn

Producer: Larry White

Ace Crawford, Private Eye

Comedy; 30 min; CBS 3/15/83 to 4/19/83

The exploits of Ace Crawford, an inexperienced private detective who stumbles upon and solves crimes quite by accident.

Ace Crawford	Tim Conway
Toomey	Joe Regalbuto
Inch	Billy Barty
Luana	Shera Danese
Lt. Fanning	Dick Christie
Mello	Bill Henderson

Producer: Philip Weltman, Ron Clark

Aces Up

Comedy Pilot; 30 min; CBS 3/29/74

The comic escapades of Jose and Raul, the owners of the Ace Moving and Hauling Service.

Jose	Jose Perez
Raul	Raul Julia
Parmejian	Ron Feinberg
Father	Ron Steinberg
Daughter	Carol Bagdasarian
Son	Paul Michael Glaser

Producer: Sheldon Leonard, Danny Arnold

Acrobat Ranch

Variety; 30 min; ABC 8/19/50 to 5/12/51

A program of circus variety acts with Jack Stillwell (as Uncle Tim) and Billy and Valerie Alberts (as Tumbling Tim and Flying Flo).

Across the Board

Game; 30 min; ABC 6/1/59 to 10/9/59

Object: For players to complete crossword puzzles from a series of picture and word clues.

Host: Ted Brown

Act II

Comedy Pilot; 30 min; NBC 9/3/87

The story of Meg Prescott, a Broadway actress who gives up her career to marry Ben Madison, a widower with three children (Laura, Zan, and Jimmy). The unsold series was to relate her misadventures as she moves from New York to begin a new life in Santa Fe, New Mexico.

Meg Madison	Sandy Duncan
Ben Madison	Charles Frank
Laura Madison	Cami Cooper
Zan Madison	Hayley Carr
Jimmy Madison	Joel Carlson
Dede	Miriam Byrd-Netherly

Theme Vocal ("Over My Head"): Sandy Duncan.

Producer: Michael Filerman, Janis Hirsch.

Action Autographs

Variety; 15 min; ABC 4/24/49 to 1/8/50

Celebrities' homemade films are showcased.

Host: Jack Brand, Ed Prentiss

Producer: Jack Brand, Marge Bishop

Action in the Afternoon

Western; 30 min; CBS 2/2/53 to 1/29/54

A live series, set in 1890s Montana (Huberle), that focuses on the lives of its citizens with a comparison of values then and in 1953.

Cast: Jack Valentine, Elaine Watts, John Zacherle, Phil Sheridan, Creighton Stewart, Kris Keegan, Jack V. Harriss Forest

Narrator: Blake Ritter

Actor's Hotel

Comedy; 30 min; ABC 9/25/51 to 5/13/52

The story of Carlo Corelli, the proprietor of a small rural boarding house.

Carlo Corelli	William Edmunds
Uncle Antonio	Alan Dale

Actor's Studio

Anthology; 30 min; ABC 9/26/48 to 10/26/49
          CBS 11/1/49 to 5/13/52

A live series, based on the works of noted authors, that is produced by the Actor's Studio, a non-profit organization of professional performers.

Recurring Players: Kim Hunter, George Reeves, Cloris Leachman, Steven Hill, Tom Ewell, Jocelyn Brando

Producer: Donald Davis, Hume Cronyn

Adam-12

Crime Drama; 30 min; NBC 9/21/68 to 8/26/75

The daily assignments of Los Angeles patrol car (Adam-12) police officers Pete Malloy and Jim Reed.

Off. Pete Malloy	Martin Milner
Off. Jim Reed	Kent McCord
Sgt. MacDonald	William Boyett
Off. Ed Wells	Gary Crosby
Sgt. Jerry Miller	Jack Hogan
Radio Dispatcher	Sharon Claridge
Lt. Tom Aston	Art Balinger
Marilyn Wells	Christina Sinatra
Betty Wells	Barbara Baldavin
Jean Reed	Mikki Jamison
	Kristin Nelson
D.A. Paul Ryan	Robert Conrad
Capt. Grant	Art Balinger
Officer Woods	Fred Stromsoe
Officer Walters	William Stevens

Producer: Herman S. Saunders, Tom Williams

Adams Apple

Crime Drama Pilot; 60 min; CBS 8/23/86

The exploits of Toni Adams, a beautiful detective working out of New York City.

Toni Adams	Sydney Walsh
Tricia Hammond	Carolyn Seymour
Janice Eaton	Cherry Jones
Marcy Potts	Kasi Lemmons
Jeff Chapman	John Furey
Dora Adams	Lois Smith
Danny Marshall	Terrence Mann
Bernadette Pasco	Polly Draper
Garth Russell	Keith Szarabajka

Producer: Frank Abatemarco, Andrew Gottlieb

Adams House

Comedy Pilot; 30 min; CBS 7/14/83

Events in the life of Chris Bennett, a social worker with the Adams House Community Center in Chicago.

Chris Bennett	Karen Valentine	Judge Fairbrother	Charlie Ruggles
Jennifer Bennett	Shelby Balik	Jake Hollander	Charles Bickford
Michael Purcell	Mark Shera	Burke O'Hara	Kenneth Tobey
Gilbert Spencer	Earl Boen	Ben Solomon	Gene Raymond
Mr. Webster	Byrne Piven	Joe Dominic	John Larkin
Frank Gallagher	Lloyd Nolan	Clay Maitland	Dennis Morgan
Lauren Drucker	Lili Haydn	Deke Barron	Edward Binns

Producer: Allan Katz

Adams of Eagle Lake

Crime Drama; 60 min; ABC 8/23/75 to 8/30/75

A two episode series about the exploits of Sam Adams, the sheriff of a small resort town called Eagle Lake.

Sam Adams	Andy Griffith
Margaret Kelly	Abby Dalton
Off. Jerry Troy	Nick Nolte
Off. Jubal Hammond	Iggie Wolfington
Monty	Paul Winchell

Producer: Richard O. Linke, Walter Grauman, Charles Stewart

Adam's Rib

Comedy; 30 min; ABC 9/14/73 to 12/28/73

Comic incidents in the lives of Adam Bonner, an Assistant D.A., and his wife, Amanda, a prosecuting attorney with the Los Angeles firm of Kipple, Kipple and Smith.

Adam Bonner	Ken Howard
Amanda Bonner	Blythe Danner
Kip Kipple	Edward Winter
Grace Peterson	Dena Dietrich
Francis Donahue	Norman Bartold
Bailiff	Fred Sylter
Court Reporter	Virginia Hawkins

Producer: Peter H. Hunt, William Froug

Adamsburg, U.S.A.

Drama Pilot; 60 min; NBC 4/23/63

Incidents in the lives of the people of Adamsburg, a small American town, as seen through the eyes of a kindly judge (Fairbrother). Aired as a segment of "The Dick Powell Theater."

The Addams Family

Comedy; 30 min; ABC 9/18/64 to 9/2/66

Events in the lives of the Addams family, eccentric residents of a macabre house in an unnamed town on North Cemetery Ridge.

Morticia Addams	Carolyn Jones
Gomez Addams	John Astin
Wednesday Addams	Lisa Loring
Pugsley Addams	Ken Weatherwax
Uncle Fester	Jackie Coogan
Grandmama Addams	Blossom Rock
Lurch	Ted Cassidy
Ophelia Frump	Carolyn Jones
Cousin Itt	Felix Silla
	Roger Arravo
Mother Lurch	Ellen Corby
Mr. Briggs	Rolfe Sedan
Thing	Itself

Producer: David Levy, Nat Perrin, Harry Browar

The Addams Family

Cartoon; 30 min; NBC 9/8/73 to 8/30/75

The misadventures of the Addams family as they leave Cemetery Ridge and embark on a motor tour of America.

Morticia Addams	Janet Waldo
Gomez Addams	Lennie Weinrib
Wednesday Addams	Cindy Henderson
Pugsley Addams	Jodie Foster
Uncle Fester	Jackie Coogan
Lurch	Ted Cassidy
Grandmama Addams	Janet Waldo

Producer: William Hanna, Joseph Barbera

Adderly

Comedy Adventure; 70 min; CBS 9/24/86 (Premiere)

The exploits of V. H. Adderly, an agent for the Bureau of Miscellaneous Affairs, a somewhat useless government agency.

V. H. Adderly	Winston Reckert
Mona	Dixie Seatly
Melville Greenspan	Jonathan Welsh
Major Clack	Ken Pogue

Producer: Robert Cooper, Jerry Golod

The Admiral Broadway Revue

Variety; 60 min; NBC 1/28/49 to 6/3/49

A musical comedy revue, sponsored by Admiral, that features lavish production numbers and top name guest stars.

Host: Sid Caesar

Regulars: Imogene Coca, Marge and Gower Champion, Mary McCarty, Roy Atwill, Bobby Van, Loren Welch

Orchestra: Charles Sanford

Producer: Max Liebman

Adorn Playhouse

A CBS Summer series (5/13/58 to 7/1/58) of repeat dramas from "The Schlitz Playhouse of Stars."

The Adventure of the Three Garridebs

Experimental; 30 min; NBC 11/27/37

The first known appearance of Sherlock Holmes on TV, which relates his efforts to find a man with the odd name of Garrideb to fill the conditions of an eccentric's will. Written by Thomas Hutchinson and produced by NBC Radio City Television Test Station.

Sherlock Holmes	Louis Hector
Dr. John Watson	William Podmore

Adventure Theatre

Anthology; 60 min; NBC 6/16/56 to 8/18/56

A British produced series of suspense dramas hosted by Paul Douglas and produced by Edward J. and Harry Lee Danziger.

Adventure Theatre

Repeats of dramas from "The Schlitz Playhouse of Stars." Aired on CBS from 7/21/61 to 9/22/61.

The Adventurer

Adventure; 30 min; Syn. 1972

The exploits of Gene Bradley, a wealthy businessman turned U.S. government espionage agent.

Gene Bradley	Gene Barry
Mr. Parminter	Barry Morse
Diane Marsh	Catherine Schell
Gavin Jones	Garrick Hagon

Producer: Monty Berman

Adventures at Scott Island

See "Harbourmaster."

Adventures in Paradise

Adventure; 60 min; ABC 10/5/59 to 4/1/62

The original format relates the adventures of Adam Troy, skipper of the schooner Tiki, as he roams the South Pacific seeking cargo and passengers. The revised format (last season) follows Troy's adventures as the owner of the Bali Miki Hotel.

Adam Troy	Gardner McKay
Oliver Kee	Weaver Levy
Clay Baker	James Holden
Chris Parker	Guy Stockwell
Trader Penrose	George Tobias
Bulldog Lovey	Henry Slate
Renee	Linda Lawson
Insp. Bouchard	Marcel Hillaire

Producer: Dominick Dunne, Richard Goldstone, Art Wallace

Adventures in Rainbow Country

Adventure; 30 min; Syn. 1972

The adventures of Billy Williams, a teenage boy growing up amid the challenge of the land around Lake Huron in Ontario, Canada.

Billy Williams	Stephen Cottier
Nancy Williams	Lois Maxwell
Hannah Williams	Susan Conway
Pete Gawa	Buckley Patawabano
Dennis Mogubgub	Wally Koster

Producer: Ralph C. Ellis, William Davidson

The Adventures of a Jungle Boy

Adventure; 30 min; Syn. 9/57

The exploits of Boy, the orphaned survivor of a plane crash, as he and Dr. Laurence, a research scientist, battle evil in Africa.

Boy	Michael Carr
	Hartley
Dr. Laurence	Ronald Adams

Adventures of a Model

Comedy Pilot; 30 min; NBC 8/19/58

The story of Marilyn Woods, a beautiful fashion model living in New York City.

Marilyn Woods	Joanne Dru
Ralph Carter	John Emery
Roger Boone	William Redfield
Texan	Roland Winters
Woman	Nancy Kulp

Producer: Norman Tokar

The Adventures of Black Beauty

Adventure; 30 min; Syn. 1972

The series, set in Hertfordshire, England, 1877, follows the adventures of Victoria Gordon and her horse, Black Beauty.

Victoria Gordon	Judi Bowker
Dr. James Gordon	William Lucas
Kevin Gordon	Roderick Shaw
Amy Winthrop	Charlotte Mitchell
Jenny Gordon	Stacy Dorning
Ned Lewis	Michael Cobert
Mr. Armstrong	Michael Armstrong

Producer: Paul Knight, Sidney Cole

The Adventures of Blinkey

Children; 15 min; Syn. 1952

While wandering through an enchanted forest, a young boy (Blinkey) is transformed into a marionette and transported to a land of puppets. The series relates his adventures as he seeks a way to again become human.

Voice of Blinkey	Michael Mann

Producer: Murray King

The Adventures of Captain Hartz

Adventure; 15 & 30 min; Syn. 1953

The series, sponsored by Hartz Mountain Pet Foods, relates the adventures of Captain Hartz, a pilot, as he explores jungles.

Captain Hartz	Philip Lord
	Ned Locke
His Sidekick	Jerry Givney

The Adventures of Champion

Adventure; 30 min; CBS 9/30/55 to 2/3/56

The series, set in the Southwest during the 1880s, follows the adventures of 12-year-old Ricky North and his horse, Champion.

Ricky North	Barry Curtis
Sandy North	Jim Bannon
Will Calhoun	Francis MacDonald
Sheriff Powers	Ewing Mitchell

Theme Vocal ("Champion the Wonder Horse"): Frankie Laine

Producer: Gene Autry, Eric Jenson, Louis Gray

The Adventures of Colonel Flack

Comedy; 30 min; DuMont 10/7/53 to 7/2/54
Syn. 1958

The story of a retired colonel (Humphrey Flack) and his companion (Garvey) and their efforts to help the needy. See also "Colonel Humphrey Flack." Also known as "The Fabulous Fraud" and "The Imposter."

Humphrey Flack	Alan Mowbray
Uthas P. Garvey	Frank Jenks

Producer: Wilbur Stark, Jerry Layton

The Adventures of Con Sawyer and Hucklemary Finn

Comedy Pilot; 30 min; ABC 9/7 & 9/14/85

A variation of Mark Twain's classic stories about the adventures of Connie "Con"

Sawyer and "Huckle" Mary Finn, two pretty, but mischievous girls living in modern-day Mississippi.

Con Sawyer	Drew Barrymore
Hucklemary Finn	Brandy Ward
Pamela Sawyer	Pat Richardson
Charlie Riley	James Rebhorn
Capt. Sawyer	James Naughton
Sarah	Terri Hanauer
Skeezer	Alan North
Rocco	M. Emmet Walsh

Producer: Diane Silver, Doro Bacharach

The Adventures of Cyclone Malone

A syndicated (1950) puppet series about a western character called Cyclone Malone (voiced by Ross Jones). Produced by Carl Hittleman, Ann Davis, and Dorothy Novis.

The Adventures of Dr. Fu Manchu

Adventure; 30 min; Syn. 1/56

The story of Dr. Fu Manchu, an evil Chinese physician who commands Subtly, an organization through which he attempts to destroy good by provoking tension between East and West. Based on the character created by Sax Rohmer.

Dr. Fu Manchu	Glen Gordon
Lia Elthram	Laurette Luez
Dennis Nyland	
Smith	Lester Stevens
Dr. Jack Petrie	Clark Hovat
Malik	Lester Matthews
Karameneh	Carla Balenda
Dr. Fu Manchu*	John Carradine
Dennis Nyland	
Smith*	Sir Cedric Hardwicke

*Stars of a 1950 NBC pilot.

The Adventures of Ellery Queen

Crime Drama; 30 min;	DuMont 10/19/50 to 12/6/51
	ABC 12/16/51 to 11/26/52
	Syn. 1954

The investigations of Ellery Queen, a gentleman detective and writer living in New York City. Also known as "Mystery Is My Business." See also "Ellery Queen" and "The Further Adventures of Ellery Queen."

Ellery Queen	Richard Hart
	Lee Bowman
	Hugh Marlowe
Insp. Richard Queen	Florenz Ames
Nikki Porter	Charlotte Keane

Producer: Norman & Irving Pincus

The Adventures of the Galaxy Rangers

Cartoon; 30 min; Syn. 9/86

The exploits of the Galaxy Rangers, crime fighters who battle evil throughout the universe.

Voices: Maia Danziger, Laura Dean, Earl Hammond, Hubert Kelly, Henry Mandell, Alexander Marshall, Corinne Orr, Jerry Orbach.

Producer: Abe Mandell

The Adventures of Gulliver

Cartoon; 30 min; ABC 9/14/69 to 9/5/70

When Lemuel Gulliver, the hero of Jonathan Swift's "Gulliver's Travels," fails to return home, his son, Gary, begins a search to find him. Stories, set on the island of Lilliput, relate Gary's efforts to find his father.

Gary Gulliver	Jerry Dexter
Flurtacia	Ginny Tyler
Eager	Jerry Dexter
Bunko	Allan Melvin
Edgar	Herb Vigran
King Pomp/Captain	
Leach	John Stephenson
Tag	Don Messick

Producer: William Hanna, Joseph Barbera

The Adventures of Hiram Holiday

Comedy; 30 min; NBC 10/3/56 to 2/28/57

When a mild-mannered proof reader (Hiram Holiday) corrects a mistake that could have meant a law suit for his paper, he is awarded with a trip around the world. Stories relate his adventures as he attempts to help people in trouble.

Hiram Holiday	Wally Cox
Joel Smith	Ainslee Pryor

Producer: Philip Rapp

The Adventures of Hoppity Hopper from Foggy Bogg

Cartoon; 30 min; Syn. 1962
ABC 9/12/64 to 10/2/65

The escapades of Hoppity Hopper (a frog), Uncle Waldo (a fox), and Fillmore (a bear).

Hoppity Hopper	Chris Allen
Uncle Waldo	Hans Conried
Fillmore	Bill Scott
Narrator	Paul Frees

Producer: Jay Ward

The Adventures of Huckleberry Finn

Adventure; 60 min; PBS 2/10/86 to 3/3/86

The adventures of Huckleberry Finn and Tom Sawyer, two rambunctious boys living in 1844 St. Petersburg, Missouri.

Huckleberry Finn	Patrick Day
Tom Sawyer	Eugene Oakes
Widow Douglas	Sada Thompson
Miss Watson	Anne Shropshire
Pap Finn	Frederic Forrest
Jim	Samm-Art Williams
The King	Barnard Hughes
Aunt Polly	Hula Drake
Sally Phelps	Geraldine Page
Mrs. Loftus	Lillian Gish
Blind Negress	Butterfly McQueen
Billy	Jason Hankins
Sheriff	Richard Niehaus
Rev. Spragprevgue	David Watters
Agnes	Amy Hause
Hannah	Roberta Wooten
Mrs. Spragprevgue	Harriet Martell

Producer: William Perry

The Adventures of Jim Bowie

Adventure; 30 min; ABC 9/7/56 to 8/29/58

New Orleans during the 1830s and the adventures of Jim Bowie, the legendary frontiersman-pioneer and inventor of the Bowie Knife, as he crusades for justice.

Jim Bowie	Scott Forbes
Rezin Bowie	Peter Hanson
Maw Bowie	Minerva Urecal
Francois	Paul Playdon
Marie	Joyce Vanderveen
Madeline Duprez	Marilyn Saris
James Audubon	Robert Cornthwaite
Justinian Tubbs	William Schallert
Pres. Andrew Jackson	Leslie Kimmel
George Freiwald	Ken Sherman

Theme Vocal ("Adventurin' Man''): Ken Darby and the King's Men

Producer: Louis F. Edelman, William H. Wright

The Adventures of Jonny Quest

Cartoon; 30 min; ABC 9/18/64 to 9/9/65

The global expeditions of Dr. Benton Quest and his young son, Jonny, as they search for the answers to scientific mysteries.

Benton Quest	John Stephenson
Jonny Quest	Tim Matthieson (Tim Matheson)
Roger Bannon	Mike Road
Hadji	Danny Bravo
Bandit	Don Messick

Producer: William Hanna, Joseph Barbera

The Adventures of Judge Roy Bean

See "Judge Roy Bean."

The Adventures of Kit Carson

Western; 30 min; Syn. 1956

The exploits of Christopher "Kit" Carson, an 1880s frontiersman, and his Mexican sidekick, El Toro.

Kit Carson	Bill Williams
El Toro	Bill Diamond

The Adventures of Long John Silver

Adventure; 30 min; Syn. 1956

The story of Long John Silver, the notorious 18th-century pirate, as he defends the Crown against warring marauders and battles the Spanish for the acquisition of land.

Long John Silver Robert Newton
Hawkins Kit Taylor
Purity Pinker Connie Gilchrist
Gov. Strong Harvey Adams
Mendoza Lloyd Berrell
Patch Grant Taylor
Israel Hands Rodney Taylor
Billy Bowledge Henry Gilbert

Producer: Mark Evans, Joseph Kaufman

The Adventures of Nick Carter

Crime Drama Pilot; 90 min; ABC 2/20/72

The exploits of Nick Carter, a tough private detective working out of New York City at the turn of the century. The pilot relates Nick's efforts to locate a missing playboy's wife.

Nick Carter Robert Conrad
Capt. Dan Keller Neville Brand
Bess Tucker Shelley Winters
Otis Duncan Broderick Crawford
Hallelujah Harry Pat O'Brien
Joyce Jordan Laraine Stephens
Roxy O'Rourke Brooke Bundy
Neal Duncan Pernell Roberts

Producer: Stanley Kallis

The Adventures of Noah Beery Jr.

Adventure; 15 min; Syn. 1954

Actor Noah Beery Jr. in varied adventures with emphasis placed on a situation and its solution.

Producer: Jerry Courneya

The Adventures of Oky Doky

Children; 30 min; DuMont 11/4/48 to 5/26/49

The program, presided over by a puppet (Oky Doky), features game contests and performances by juvenile stars.

Hostess Wendy Barrie
Oky Doky's Voice Dayton Allen

Producer: Frank Bunetta

The Adventures of Ozzie and Harriet

Comedy; 30 min; ABC 10/3/52 to 9/3/66

Events in the day-to-day lives of the Nelson family: parents Ozzie and Harriet and their children Dave and Ricky. See also "Ozzie's Girls."

Ozzie Nelson Himself
Harriet Nelson Herself
Ricky Nelson Himself
Dave Nelson Himself
Kris Nelson Kristen Harmon
June Nelson June Blair
Tracy Nelson Herself
Thorny Thornberry Don DeFore
Joe Randolph Lyle Talbot
Clara Randolph Mary Jane Croft
Herb Darby Parley Baer
Doc Williams Frank Cady
Wally Dipple Skip Young
Ginger Charlene Salerno
Herb Dunkel Joseph Kearns
Connie Harper Constance Harper
Happy Hotpoint* Mary Tyler Moore
Ralph Dobson Francis DeSales
Don Kelly Joe Flynn
Fred James Stacy

Producer: Robert Angus, Bill Lewis, Ozzie Nelson, Leo Penn

*The dancing elf in 1955 Hotpoint Appliance commercials.

The Adventures of Patches

Children; 30 min; Syn. 1951

A puppet series about the amazing adventures of an orphaned hobo boy named Patches and his friend, Wacky Rabbit.

Patches Don Messick
Wacky Rabbit Larry Harmon

Producer: Charles Shows

The Adventures of Pollyana

Drama Pilot; 60 min; CBS 4/10/82

The escapades of Pollyana Harrington, a pretty twelve-year-old orphan, now the ward of her aunt, who possesses the uncanny knack of bringing out the best in people.

Pollyana Harrington	Patsy Kensit
Polly Harrington	Shirley Jones
Herman Chilton	Edward Winter
Marylee	Roxana Zal
Mrs. Leveler	Lucille Benson
Cora Spencer	Stacey Nelkin
Angelica	Beverly Archer
Johnny Muller	John Putch
Mrs. Tarkell	Gretchen Wyler
Mr. Muller	John Randolph
Rev. Tull	Nicholas Hammond

Producer: William Robert Yates

The Adventures of Pow Wow

A syndicated (1957) five minute cartoon about a young Indian boy (Pow Wow) learning about life. Produced by Sam Singer.

The Adventures of Rin Tin Tin

Adventure; 30 min; ABC 10/15/54 to 9/22/61

During a patrol, the Fighting Blue Devils of the 101st Cavalry discover two survivors of an Apache raid: a young boy named Rusty and his dog, Rin Tin Tin. When brought back to Fort Apache, they are unofficially adopted by Lt. Rip Masters. Stories, set in Arizona during the 1880s, relate Rusty's efforts to assist the cavalry in maintaining the peace.

Corporal Rusty	Lee Aaker
Lt. Rip Masters	James L. Brown
Sgt. Aloysius "Biff" O'Hara	Joe Sawyer
Cpl. Randy Boone	Rand Brooks
Col. Barker	John Hoyt
Cpl. Carson	Tommy Farrell
Cpl. Clark	Hal Hopper
Maj. Swanson	William Forrest

Producer: Herbert B. Leonard, Fred Briskin

The Adventures of Robin Hood

Adventure; 30 min; CBS 9/26/55 to 9/22/58

The exploits of Robin Hood, the 11th-century English outlaw who robbed from the rich to give to the poor, as he battles the evils of Prince John and the Sheriff of Nottingham.

Robin Hood	Richard Greene
Maid Marian	
Fitzwater	Bernadette O'Farrell
	Patricia Driscoll
Prince John	Donald Pleasence
	Herbert Gregg
Friar Tuck	Alexander Gauge
Little John	Archie Duncan
Will Scarlet	Paul Eddington
	Ronald Howard
Sir Richard	Ian Hunter
Edgar	Alfie Bass
Lady Guineveve	Gillian Sterrett
King Arthur	Peter Asher
Queen Eleanor	Jill Esmond

Producer: Hannah Weinstein

The Adventures of Sherlock Holmes

Mystery; 60 min; PBS 3/14/85 to 4/25/85
2/8/86 to 3/8/86

The cases of Sherlock Holmes, a consulting detective and master of deductive reasoning, as he helps the police solve baffling crimes. See also "The Adventure of the Three Garridebs" and "Sherlock Holmes."

Sherlock Holmes	Jeremy Brett
Dr. John H. Watson	David Burke
Mrs. Hudson	Rosalie Williams
Insp. Lestrade	Colin Jeavons
Prof. Moriarty	Eric Porter
Mycroft Holmes	Charles Gray

Producer: Michael Cox

The Adventures of Sir Francis Drake

Adventure; 30 min; NBC 6/24/62 to 9/9/62

The exploits of Sir Francis Drake, a 16th-century admiral of the Queen's Navy, as he defends the Crown against marauders.

Sir Francis Drake	Terrence Morgan
Queen Elizabeth I	Jean Kent
Mendoza	Roger Delgado
Richard Trevelyan	Patrick McLaughlen
Earl of Lennox	Ewan Roberts
John Drake	Michael Crawford

Producer: Anthony Bushell

The Adventures of Sir Lancelot

Adventure; 30 min; NBC 9/24/56 to 9/16/57
ABC 10/1/57 to 9/26/58

The adventures of Sir Lancelot du Lac, a Knight of King Arthur's Round Table, and the paramour of Queen Guinevere during England's 12th century.

Sir Lancelot	William Russell
Queen Guinevere	Jane Hylton
Merlin	Cyril Smith
King Arthur	Ronald Leigh-Hunt
Squire Brian	Robert Scroggins
Sir Gwayne	Andrew Crawford
Sir Kay	Brian Worth

Producer: Hannah Weinstein, Sidney Cole

The Adventures of Superboy

Adventure Pilot; 30 min; Unaired (Produced in 1961)

The adventures of Clark Kent, alias Superboy, as he attends Smallville High School. See also "The Adventures of Superman" and "The Adventures of Superpup."

Clark Kent	Johnny Rockwell
Lana Lang	Bonny Henning
Fred Drake	Ross Elliott
Martha Kent	Monty Margetts
Shorty Barnes	Richard Reeves
Miss Gibbs	Yvonne White
Jake Ferde	Stacy Harris
Mr. Edlund	Ray Walker

Producer: Whitney Ellsworth

The Adventures of Superman

Adventure; 30 min; Syn. 1953–1957

Moments before the destruction of the doomed planet Krypton, the baby Kal-El is placed in a rocket by his father (Jor-El) and mother (Lara). The ship lands on Earth where its infant passenger is found and raised by Eben and Martha Kent, a farm couple who name him Clark. Many years later, Clark, who possesses amazing powers, decides to use his abilities to help mankind. Episodes relate Clark's battle, as Superman, against evil. See also "The Adventures of Superboy" and "The Adventures of Superpup."

Clark Kent	George Reeves
Lois Lane	Phyllis Coates
	Noel Neill
Jimmy Olsen	Jack Larson
Perry White	John Hamilton
Insp. Bill Henderson	Robert Shayne
Prof. J. J. Pepperwinkle	Phillips Tead
Jor-El	Robert Rockwell
Lara	Aline Towne
Eben Kent	Tom Fadden
Martha Kent	Dina Nolan
Clark (as a boy)	Stuart Randall

Producer: Whitney Ellsworth, Robert Maxwell, Bernard Luber

The Adventures of Superpup

Adventure Pilot; 30 min; Unaired (Produced in 1958)

An unsold and never aired series idea that relates the exploits of Bark Bent, alias Superpup, as a reporter for the "Daily Beagle." The program features actors dressed as dogs. See also "The Adventures of Superboy" and "The Adventures of Superman."

Bark Bent	Billy Curtis
Pamela Poodle	Ruth Delfino
Perry Bite	Angelo Rossitto
Sgt. Beagle	Frank Delfino
Prof. Sheepdip	Harry Monty
Sheepdip's dupe	Sandie Delfino

Producer: Whitney Ellsworth

The Adventures of Teddy Ruxpin

Cartoon Pilot; 30 min; Syn. 3/87

The exploits of Teddy Ruxpin, a lovable teddy bear, and his friend, Grubby, as they travel throughout the world seeking adventure.

Voices: Phil Barron, John Stocker, Will Ryan, John Koensgen, Robert Bockstael, Pier Kohl, Holly Larocque, Abby Hagyard

Producer: Jean Chalopin, Andy Heyward, Alison Clayton

The Adventures of the Scarlet Pimpernel

Adventure; 30 min; Syn. 6/56

The exploits of Sir Percy Blakeney, a man of wealth who adopts the guise of The Scarlet Pimpernel to aid the oppressed in 1790s England.

Percy Blakeney	Marius Goring
Percy's Aide	Patrick Troughton
Madame Tussaud	Susan Richmond
Robespierre	Anthony Newlands
Police Heavy	Stanley Van Beers

Producer: Marius Goring

The Adventures of the Sea Hawk

Adventure; 30 min; Syn. 1/59

The adventures of John Hawk, commander of the schooner "Sea Hawk," a floating electronics lab.

John Hawk	John Howard
His Assistant	John Lee

Producer: Eugene Solow, Brewster Morgan

Adventures of the Seaspray

Adventure; 30 min; Syn. 9/68

The exploits of John Wells, an Australian writer and skipper of the schooner "Seaspray," as he roams the South Pacific seeking story material.

John Wells	Walter Brown
Sue Wells	Susanne Haworth
Mike Wells	Gary Gray
Noah Wells	Rodney Pearlman
Willyum	Leoni Lesinawai

Producer: Roger Mirams

The Adventures of Tugboat Annie

See "Tugboat Annie."

The Adventures of Uncle Mistletoe

See "Uncle Mistletoe."

The Adventures of William Tell

Adventure; 30 min; Syn. 1957

The story of William Tell, leader of the Forest Cantons in 14th-century Switzerland, as he attempts to free his country from the rule of the Austrian Empire.

William Tell	Conrad Phillips
Walter Tell	Richard Rogers
Hedda Tell	Jennifer Jayne
The Bear	Nigel Green
Gessler	Willoughby Goddard

Producer: Ralph Smart, Lester Arliss

Adventuring with the Chopper

Comedy Pilot; 30 min; NBC 8/7/76

The misadventures of Arnold "The Chopper" Jackson and Leonard Jones, two dim-witted private detectives.

Arnold Jackson	Harrison Page
Leonard Jones	Antonio Fargas
Cousin Bea	Ketty Lester
Lt. Hoover	Lawrence Cook

Producer: Norman Steinberg

A.E.S. Hudson Street

Comedy; 30 min; ABC 3/16/78 to 4/20/78

A satirization of medical shows as seen through the antics of the poorly equipped Adult Emergency Service Hospital on Hudson Street in New York City.

Dr. Tony Menzies	Gregory Sierra
	F. Murray Abraham*
Nurse Rosa Santiago	Rosana Soto
Nurse Rhonda Todd	Julienne Wells
J. Powell Karbo	Stefan Gierasch
	Irwin C. Watson*
Foshko	Susan Peretz
Stanke	Ralph Manza
Dr. Gloria Manners	Barrie Youngfellow
Dr. Jerry Miller	Bill Cort
Nurse Sawyer	Margaret Avery
	Barbara O. Jones*
Nurse Newton	Ray Stewart

Producer: Danny Arnold, Roland Kibbee

*Role in the pilot (4/21/77).

The Affairs of China Smith

Adventure; 30 min; Syn. 1952

The exploits of China Smith, an American soldier of fortune living in Singapore. Also titled "China Smith" and "The New Adventures of China Smith."

William "China"
    Smith   Dan Duryea

Producer: Arthur Pierson

African Patrol

Adventure; 30 min; Syn. 1957

The exploits of Inspector Paul Derek, chief of
the African Patrol, as he battles crime in Africa.

Paul Derek	John Bentley
Allan (a doctor)	Brian Epson
Sergeant	Tony Blain
Police Officer	John Stewart
Police Officer	Ian Young

Producer: Hal Klein

The African Queen

Adventure Pilot; 60 min; CBS 3/18/77

The adventures of Charlie Allnot, captain of
"The African Queen," a decrepit boat that
traverses the Ulanga River during World War
I.

Charlie Allnot	Warren Oates
Rosie Sayer	Mariette Hartley
Jogana	Johnny Sekka
Lt. Biedemeyer	Wolf Roth
Sgt. Abuttu	Clarence Thomas
Maj. Strauss	Alfred Polsen

Producer: Mark Carliner, Len Kaufman

After George

Comedy Pilot; 30 min; CBS 6/6/83

Before his untimely death in a car accident,
George Roberts electronically rigs his personality into the home he and his wife, Susan,
share. The unsold series was to relate Susan's
efforts to live a normal life while attempting
to contend with George's alter ego—their
house.

Susan Roberts	Susan Saint James
Voice of George	Richard Schaal
Cal Sloane	Joel Brooks
Marge	Susan Ruttan
Rose	Allyn Ann McLerie
Walt	John Reilly

Producer: Fred Freeman, Lawrence J. Cohen

AfterMash

Comedy; 30 min; CBS 9/26/83 to 10/30/84

A spin-off from "M*A*S*H" wherein Sherman Potter becomes head of the General Pershing V.A. Hospital, and Maxwell Klinger
and Father Mulcahy become staff members.
Stories relate their experiences working with
veterans.

Sherman Potter	Harry Morgan
Maxwell Klinger	Jamie Farr
Father Francis	
Mulcahy	William Christopher
Soon-Lee Klinger	Rosalind Chao
Mildred Potter	Barbara Townsend
	Anne Pitoniak
Mike D'Angelo	John Chappell
Wally Wainwright	Peter Michael Goetz
Alma Cox	Brandis Kemp
Dr. Gene Pfeiffer	Jay O. Sanders
Dr. Boyer	David Ackroyd
Bob Scannell	Pat Cranshaw
Nurse Freeman	Patricia Gaul
Bonnie Hornback	Wendy Schaal

Producer: Burt Metcalfe

Aggie

Comedy; 30 min; Syn. 12/57

The misadventures of Aggie, an American
fashion buyer living in England.

Aggie	Joan Shawlee
Her boyfriend	Christopher Lee

Producer: Michael Sadlier

Air Time '57

Variety; 30 min; ABC 12/27/56 to 4/4/57

Performances by members of the U.S. Air
Force Reserve.

Host: Vaughn Monroe, Merv Griffin

Orchestra: Bobby Hackett, Elliott Alexander

Airwolf

Adventure; 60 min; CBS 1/22/84 to 7/23/86

Fearing that Dr. Moffet, creator and possessor of an awesome attack helicopter (Airwolf), will sell it to an enemy nation, Michael
Archangel, head of "The Firm," asks pilot

Stringfellow Hawke to retrieve it. Hawke agrees, but only if the U.S. government searches for his brother, Saint John, who is missing in Vietnam. When Hawke retrieves Airwolf he decides to keep it, forcing the government to do what they promised. Episodes relate Hawke's exploits as he uses Airwolf to assist Michael whenever the need arises. See the following title also.

Stringfellow Hawke	Jan-Michael Vincent
Dominic Santini	Ernest Borgnine
Michael Archangel	Alex Cord
Caitlin O'Shannessy	Jean Bruce Scott
Gabrielle	Belinda Bauer
Marella	Deborah Pratt
Amanda	Kandace Kuehl
Saint John Hawke	Chris Connelly
Dr. Moffet	David Hemmings

Producer: Donald P. Bellisario, Bernard L. Kowalski

Airwolf

Adventure; 60 min; USA 1/23/87 (Premiere)

A revised version of the previous title which relates the adventures of the futuristic attack helicopter, Airwolf's new crew: Saint John Hawke, the brother of Stringfellow; Jo Santini, Dominic's niece; Mike Rivers, a pilot; and Jason Locke, an agent for "The Firm," who sides with Saint John and agrees to keep Airwolf's location a secret. Stories relate the group's exploits as they use Airwolf to help the government in times of need.

Saint John Hawke	Barry Van Dyke
Jo Santini	Michele Scarabelli
Mike Rivers	Geraint Wyn Davies
Jason Locke	Anthony Sherwood

Producer: Michael MacMillan, Steve Ecclesine, Arthur L. Annecharico

A.K.A. Pablo

Comedy; 30 min; ABC 3/6/84 to 4/17/84

The misadventures of Paul Rivera (known as Pablo to his family), a struggling young comedian.

Paul Rivera	Paul Rodriquez
Jose Sanchez	Hector Elizondo
Domingo Rivera	Joe Santos
Rosa Maria Rivera	Katy Juardo
Sylvia Rivera	Alma Cuervo
Lucia Rivera-DelGato	Martha Velez
Hector DelGato	Arnoldo Santana
Manuel Rivera	Bert Rosario
Anna Maria DelGato	Claudia Gonzales
Susan DelGato	Martha Gonzales
Thomas DelGato	Marco Lopez
Mario DelGato	Beto Lovato
Elena DelGato	Michelle Smith

Producer: Norman Lear, Jack Elinson, Rick Mintz

The Al Morgan Show

Variety; 30 min; DuMont 9/5/49 to 8/30/51

A Chicago-based program of music and songs with Al Morgan and the music of the Billy Chandler Trio. Produced by Don Cook.

The Al Pearce Show

A daily CBS program (2/11/52 to 9/26/52) of music and songs with Al Pearce.

The Alan King Show

Comedy Pilot; 30 min; CBS 7/12/86

Feeling that his life is unfulfilled, Wall Street tycoon Alan Cooper leaves his business to teach practical business philosophy at Burbridge University. The unsold series was to relate his experiences.

Alan Cooper	Alan King
Nan Cooper	Dina Merrill
Samantha Cooper	Sarah Jessica Parker
Cassandra Cooper	Lisa Rieffel
Abby	Catherine Keener
John Emerson	Paxton Whitehead
Kit Henderson	Max Cantor
Miss Kemper	Robin Menken

Producer: Emily Levine, Deanne Barkley

The Alan Young Show

Variety; 30 min; CBS 4/6/50 to 6/21/53

A weekly series of music, songs, and comedy sketches.

Host: Alan Young

Regulars: Polly Bergen, Dawn Adams, Ben Wright, Joseph Kearns, David Alpert, Mabel Paige, Phillips Tead, Jane Hollar, Jean Mahoney, Tom Mahoney, Jerry Antes

Orchestra: Lud Gluskin

Producer: Ralph Levy, Richard Linkroum

The Alaskans

Adventure; 60 min; ABC 10/4/59 to 9/25/60

Originally, the adventures of Rocky Shaw, Silky Harris, and Reno McKee as they search for gold in Alaska during the 1890s. Later, Rocky's experiences as a saloon singer, and Silky and Reno's exploits as swindlers, are depicted.

Rocky Shaw	Dorothy Provine
Silky Harris	Roger Moore
Reno McKee	Jeff York
Nifty Cronin	Ray Danton
Fantan	Frank DeKova
Soapie Smith	John Dehner

Producer: William T. Orr, Harry Tatelman, Barry Ingster

The Alcoa/Goodyear Theatre

Anthology; 30 min; NBC 9/29/58 to 5/23/60

A series of varying presentations, sponsored alternately by Alcoa and Goodyear. Produced by Winston O'Keefe, William Sackheim, James Fonda, and Richard Alan Simmons.

The Alcoa Hour

Anthology; 60 min; NBC 10/16/55 to 9/22/57

Top quality dramas sponsored by the Alcoa Corporation. Produced by Alex Segal, Herbert Brodkin, Vincent M. Fennelly, and Gene Roddenberry.

Alcoa Premiere

Anthology; 60 min; ABC 10/10/61 to 9/12/63

A series of first rate dramas, sponsored by Alcoa, and featuring such stars as Lloyd Bridges, Carroll O'Connor, Jane Wyatt, Ernest Borgnine, Peggy Ann Garner, John For-

sythe, Lee Marvin, Shelley Winters, Ed Nelson, and David Wayne.

Host: Fred Astaire

Producer: Hal Hudson, Peter Tewksbury, George Schaefer, Alex Segal

Alcoa Presents

See "One Step Beyond."

The Aldrich Family

Comedy; 30 min; NBC 10/2/49 to 5/29/53

Events in the lives of the Aldrich family: Sam, the district attorney (in the town of Centerville); his wife, Alice; their daughter, Mary; and their mischievous teenage son, Henry.

Henry Aldrich	Robert Casey
	Richard Tyler
	Henry Girard
	Kenneth Nelson
	Bobby Ellis
Sam Aldrich	House Jameson
Alice Aldrich	Lois Wilson
	Nancy Carroll
	Barbara Robbins
Mary Aldrich	Mary Malone
	June Dayton
Homer Brown	Jackie Kelk
	Robert Barry
	Jackie Grimes
Kathleen	Marcia Henderson
Mr. Brown	Howard Smith
Mrs. Brown	Leona Powers

Producer: Roger Kay, Ed Duerr, Ralph Warren

Alec Templeton Time

A DuMont program (6/3/55 to 8/26/55) of music and song with blind pianist Alec Templeton.

Alex and the Doberman Gang

Crime Drama Pilot; 60 min; NBC 4/11/80

Following the death of a carnival performer, private detective Alex Parker inherits five smart Doberman pinschers. The unsold series was to relate Alex's efforts to solve crimes with the help of the dogs.

Alex Parker	Jack Stauffer
Barney	Taurean Blacque
Denise	Lane Binkley
Susan Hamilton	Martha Smith
Myers	Alan Gibbs
Preacher	Don Starr

Producer: Harve Bennett, Harris Katleman

Alexander the Great

Drama Pilot; 60 min; ABC 1/26/68

The pilot episode for a proposed series based on stories from the Bible. The pilot tells of the historic battle of Issus in which Alexander's Greek forces met the opposing Persian army.

Alexander	William Shatner
Karonos	John Cassavetes
Antigonus	Joseph Cotten
Attalos	Simon Oakland
Ada	Ziva Rodann
Cleander	Adam West

Producer: Phil Karlson

ALF

Comedy; 30 min; NBC 9/22/86 (Premiere)

While using his shortwave radio, electronic hobbyist Willie Tanner's signal interfers with the frequency of an alien craft. The craft, manned by Gordon Schumway of Melmack, crashes into Willie's garage and maroones the Alien Life Force (ALF). Stories depict ALF's adventures as he moves in with the Tanners.

Willie Tanner	Max Wright
Kate Tanner	Anne Schedeen
Lynn Tanner	Andrea Elson
Brian Tanner	Benji Gregory
Raquel Ochmonek	Liz Sheridan
Gordon Ochmonek	John LaMotta
Alf's voice	Paul Fusco
Dorothy (Kate's mother)	Anne Meara

Producer: Paul Fusco, Tom Patchett

ALF

Cartoon; 30 min; NBC 9/26/87 (Premiere)

An extension series based on the live action "ALF." The program relates ALF's adventures on his home planet, Melmac, where, before the planet blew up, he was known as Gordon Schumway.

Gordon Schumway	Paul Fusco

Other Voices: Prunella Gillis, Len Carlson, Greg Morton, Peggy Mahon, Thick Wilson, Dan Hennessey, Don Francks

Producer: Bernie Brillstein, Andy Heyward, Haim Saban

The Alfred and Josephine Butler Show

Experimental; 30 min; NBC 7/28/39

Dance instruction by professional dancers Alfred and Josephine Butler. Produced and directed by Edward Sobol.

Alfred Hitchcock Presents

A weekly series of mystery and suspense stories hosted by Alfred Hitchcock. The series began on CBS as "Alfred Hitchcock Presents" (30 minutes, 10/2/55 to 9/25/60), switched to NBC (9/27/60 to 9/18/62), reverted back to CBS (as "The Alfred Hitchcock Hour," 9/20/62 to 9/18/64) and ended its run on NBC (10/5/64 to 9/6/65). On 5/12/85 NBC aired a two hour "Alfred Hitchcock Presents" pilot that served as the basis for a new "Alfred Hitchcock Presents" (NBC, 30 minutes 9/29/85 to 7/26/86) that presented adaptations of stories originally aired on the prior series. Alfred Hitchcock is again seen as the host, this time with appropriate computer colored openings from the original series. New episodes of the 1985 NBC series premiered on the U.S.A. cable network on January 24, 1987.

Alfred of the Amazon

Comedy Pilot; 30 min; CBS 7/31/67

The exploits of Alfred of the Amazon, a bumbling jungle adventurer and plantation owner who fights injustice in his spare time.

Alfred	Wally Cox
Willy	Allan Melvin
Simba	Mako
Jennifer	Susan Oden
Dr. Schwimmer	Paul Hartman
Herr Futterman	Leon Askin

Producer: Arne Rosen, Gene Reynolds.

Alias Mike Hercules

Crime Drama Pilot; 30 min; ABC 7/31/56

The exploits of Mike Hercules, a tough San Francisco-based detective.

Mike Hercules	Hugh Beaumont
Vivian Harding	Anne Kimbel
Birdie Hackett	Ellen Corby
Lydia Tremaine	Marie Windsor
Professor	Reginald Denney
Charlie	Victor Sen Yung
Walter Harding	Roy Roberts

Producer: Hal Roach Jr.

Alias Smith and Jones

Western; 60 min; ABC 1/21/71 to 1/13/73

Seeking to end their life of crime, outlaws Jed Curry and Hannibal Hayes approach the governor and are given a provisional amnesty. Stories relate their adventures, adopting the aliases of Thaddeus Jones (Curry) and Joshua Smith (Hayes) as they roam the Kansas Territory (of the 1890s) seeking to stray from trouble long enough (12 months) to earn full pardons.

Jed Curry	Ben Murphy
Hannibal Hayes	Peter Duel
	Roger Davis
Sheriff Lom Travers	James Drury
	Mike Road
Harry Briscoe	J. D. Cannon
Wheat	Earl Holliman
Lobo	Read Morgan
Kyle	Dennis Fimple
Clementine Hale	Sally Field
Big Mac McCreedy	Burl Ives
Silky O'Sullivan	Walter Brennan
Blackjack Jenny	Ann Sothern
Georgette Sinclair	Michele Lee
Winford Fletcher	Rudy Vallee

Producer: Roy Huggins, Jo Swerling Jr.

Alice

Comedy; 30 min; CBS 9/29/76 to 3/19/85

Following the death of her husband, Alice Hyatt and her son, Tommy, relocate to Phoenix, Arizona, where Alice acquires a job as a waitress in Mel's Diner. Stories relate Alice's adventures as she struggles to support herself and Tommy, and her attempts to achieve a long-awaited dream of becoming a singer. See also "Flo."

Alice Hyatt	Linda Lavin
Mel Sharples	Vic Tayback
Flo Castleberry	Polly Holliday
Vera Gorman	Beth Howland
Tommy Hyatt	Alfred Lutter*
	Philip McKeon
Belle DuPree	Diane Ladd
Jolene Hunnicutt	Celia Weston
Henry	Marvin Kaplan
Earl Hicks	Dave Madden
Andy	Pat Cranshaw
Carrie Sharples	Martha Raye
Chloe	Ruth Buzzi
Elliott Novack	Charles Levin
Doug	Doug Robinson
Chuck	Duane Campbell

Theme Vocal ("There's a New Girl in Town"): Linda Lavin

Producer: David Susskind, William P. D'Angelo, Ray Allen, Harvey Bullock, Madelyn Davis, Bob Carroll Jr.

*Pilot role (8/31/76).

The Alice Pearce Show

A quarter-hour program (ABC, 1949) of music and comedy with comedienne Alice Pearce.

Alive and Well

Magazine; 60 min; Syn. 9/84

A daily program of health tips and advice.

Host: Mike Jerrick, Marion Ross, Linda Arkin

Regulars: Cathy Rigby, Joanne Carson

Producer: James E. Thompson, Lisa Kridos

Alkali Ike

Comedy; 15 min; CBS 4/17/50 to 5/11/50

Puppet antics with ventriloquist Al Robinson and his dummy Alkali Ike. The program, produced by Beverly Fite, features The Slim Jackson Quartet.

All Aboard

Variety; 15 min; CBS 10/19/52 to 1/11/53

The antics of Jimmy Morton, the dummy of ventriloquist Skeets Minton. Produced by Lester Lewis and featuring Junie Keegan.

All About Barbara

Comedy Pilot; 30 min; CBS 9/2/63

The story of Barbara Adams, an entertainer who gives up the stage to marry James Hadley, a small town college professor.

Barbara Adams	Barbara Nichols
James Hadley	William Bishop
Ray Biddle	Willard Waterman
Albert Murdock	Larry Keating
Sybil Murdock	Shirley Mitchell

Producer: Quinn Martin

All About Faces

Game; 30 min; Syn. 1971

The object calls for players to predict the outcomes of unsuspecting people caught in prearranged situations.

Host: Richard Hayes

Regulars: Glenda Jones, Ken Deas, Andy Kunkel

Producer: Dan Enright, David B. Fein

All About Music

Variety; 30 min; ABC 4/7/57 to 4/21/57

A three week interim series that explores three fields of music: Calypso, American Folk, and Jazz.

Cast: Johnny Banacuda, Helen Ferguson, Pearl Gonzalez, Susan Reed, Buzz Miller, Bruce King, Lawrence Winters, Rudy Tronto, Gomez Delappe, The Nelle Fisher Dancers

Music: The King Carib Stud Band, Al Rickey Orchestra, Paul Whiteman Orchestra

All About Us

Magazine; 30 min; Syn. 10/85

A series of programs that focus on unusual and interesting people.

Host: Ron Hendron

Regulars: Dr. Joyce Brothers, Michael Reagan, Saundra Sharp, David Sparks

Producer: Dan Enright, Chris Pye

All Around Town

Interview; 15 min; CBS 6/18/51 to 8/7/52

Interviews with people from all walks of life.

Host: Mike Wallace, Buff Cobb

Producer: Hal Purdy

All in One

Variety; 30 min; ABC 12/27/52 to 4/2/53

A live series, hosted by George DeWitt, that features performances by guest comics.

All in the Family

Comedy Pilot; 30 min; NBC 3/28/60

The story of a wealthy family who must learn to live with sudden poverty when their wealth is lost through bad investments. See also "I Remember Caviar."

Maggie Randall	Patricia Crowley
Caroline Randall	Lurene Tuttle
Eric Randall	Edward Mallory
Ansol Pryor	Henry Hull
David	Adam West
Kitty	Sue Ane Langdon
Bertha	Alma Murphy

Producer: Harry Ackerman, Winston O'Keefe

All in the Family

Comedy; 30 min; CBS 1/12/71 to 9/16/79

Events in the lives of the Bunker family: Archie, a bigoted, loud-mouthed, dock foreman; Edith, his honest but dim-witted wife; Gloria, their beautiful, liberal-minded daughter; and Mike, Gloria's idealistic husband and Archie's constant source of aggravation. See also: "Archie Bunker's Place," "The Jeffersons," and "Maude."

Archie Bunker	Carroll O'Connor	Archie Bunker	Carroll O'Connor
Edith Bunker	Jean Stapleton	Edith Bunker	Jean Stapleton
Gloria Stivic	Sally Struthers	Gloria	Candice Azzara
Mike Stivic	Rob Reiner	Mike	Chip Oliver
Joey Stivic	Corey Miller		
	Jason Drager		

Producer: Norman Lear

Barney Hefner	Allan Melvin
George Jefferson	Sherman Hemsley
Louise Jefferson	Isabel Sanford
Lionel Jefferson	Mike Evans
Henry Jefferson	Mel Stewart
Irene Lorenzo	Betty Garrett
Frank Lorenzo	Vincent Gardenia
Bert Munson	Billy Halop
Jerome "Stretch"	
Cunningham	James Cromwell
Teresa Betancourt	Liz Torres
Stephanie Mills	Danielle Brisebois
Harry Snowden	Jason Wingreen
Blanche Hefner	Estelle Parsons
Maude Findley	Beatrice Arthur
Walter Findley	Bill Macy
Carol	Marcia Rodd
Floyd Mills	Marty Brill
Tommy Kelsey	Brandon Dillon
	Bob Hastings
	Frank Maxwell
Fred Bunker	Richard McKenzie
Casimir Stivic	Michael Conrad

Producer: Norman Lear, Woody Kling, Hal Kanter, Mort Lachman, Don Nichol

All in the Family

The original, unaired pilot for the series (prior title). In 1967, Norman Lear produced a pilot based on the British series "Till Death Do Us Part" (about an argumentative father and his son-in-law). When ABC rejected it, a second pilot was taped. Carroll O'Connor and Jean Stapleton repeated their roles as Archie and Edith, but new actors were chosen for the roles of Mike and Gloria (see cast). When ABC again rejected it, Lear abandoned the idea. Two years later, CBS approached Lear with a firm commitment to tape thirteen episodes. O'Connor and Stapleton again played Archie and Edith and Sally Struthers and Rob Reiner were cast as Gloria and Mike in what would become a landmark series. This and the previous pilot became the series first episode (a surprise anniversary party for Archie becomes an argument when Mike and Gloria accuse him of being a bigot).

All Is Forgiven

Comedy; 30 min; NBC 3/20/86 to 8/23/86

While being interviewed for the position of associate producer on the TV soap opera, "All Is Forgiven," the producer quits and Paula Russell, a former ad agency commercials producer, is hired to replace him. Stories relate Paula's efforts to cope with her new job and a marriage (to Matt) as well.

Paula Russell	Bess Armstrong
Matt Russell	Terence Knox
Sonia Russell	Shawnee Smith
Nicolette Bingham	Carol Kane
Cecile Porter-	
Lindsey	Judith-Marie Bergan
Wendell Branch	Bill Wiley
Sherry Levy	Debi Richter
Lorraine Elder	Valerie Landsburg
Oliver Royce	David Alan Grier

Producer: Ian Praiser, Howard Gewirtz, Kimberly Hill

The All New Let's Make a Deal

Game; 30 min; Syn. 9/85

A revised version of "Let's Make a Deal," which see for format.

Host: Monty Hall

Producer: Stefan Hatos, Monty Hall

The All New Newlywed Game

Game; 30 min; Syn. 9/85

A revised version of "The Newlywed Game," which see for format.

Host: Bob Eubanks

Announcer: Bob Hilton

Producer: Chuck Barris, Walt Case

The All New Popeye Hour

Cartoon; 55 min; CBS 9/9/78 to 9/5/81

Segments: "Popeye" (the adventures of the sailor who receives incredible strength from spinach), and "Dinky Dog" (about a family plagued by the antics of a mischievous dog).

Popeye	Jack Mercer
Olive Oyl	Marilyn Schreffler
Bluto	Allan Melvin
Sea Hag	Marilyn Schreffler
Wimpy	Daws Butler
Uncle Dudley	Frank Nelson
Sandy	Jackie Joseph
Monica	Julie Bennett
Dinky Dog	Frank Welker

Producer: William Hanna, Joseph Barbera

All Night Radio

Comedy Pilot; 30 min; HBO 10/26/82

Comical events in the lives of people who listen to "All Night Radio," a Los Angeles music program hosted by Mack and Jamie.

Mack	Mack Dryden
Jamie	Jamie Alcroft
Prof. Bowzer	Jon Bauman
Ronny	Scott McGinnis
Luca	Richard Molinare
Dora	Donna Seigel
Junior	Michael Wyle
Lory	Elayne Heilveil
Mr. Worthington	Jack Riley
Mark	Denny Evans

Producer: Rocco Urbisci, Tom Steele

All Star Anything Goes

Game; 30 min; Syn. 9/77

Celebrities compete in various outlandish games for fun.

Host: Bill Boggs

Score Girl: Judy Abercrombie

Commentator: Jim Healy

Producer: Bob Banner, Beryl Vertue, Sam Riddle

All Star Blitz

Game; 30 min; ABC 4/8/85 to 12/20/85

One player (two compete) selects one of four celebrity guests. The celebrity is then asked a question. If the player correctly determines whether or not the celebrity's answer is correct, he receives a clue to the identity of a person, place, or thing. Players alternate turns and the first contestant to identify the mystery subject wins a merchandise prize.

Host: Peter Marshall

Regular: Abby Dalton

Producer: Noreen Conlin, Art Alisi

The All Star Revue

Variety; 60 min; NBC 10/4/50 to 4/18/53

Variety programs that are tailored to the talents of its guest hosts, including Martha Raye, Ed Wynn, Danny Thomas, Jimmy Durante, Victor Borge, Ezio Pinza, Spike Jones, Paul Winchell, Jane Froman, Jack Carson, George Jessel, and Bob Hope.

Orchestras: Allen Roth, Lou Bring, Milton DeLugg, Roy Bargy, George Bassman, Les Brown

Producers: Leo Morgan, Sid Smith, Ezra Stone, Joseph Stanley, Coby Ruskin, James V. Kern, Sam Fuller, Ernest D. Glucksman, Peter Barnum

All Star Secrets

Game; 30 min; NBC 1/8/79 to 8/10/79

A true secret, relating to one of five celebrities is read. The player who correctly guesses the subject of the secret wins prizes.

Host: Bob Eubanks

Announcer: Charlie O'Donnell

Producer: Bob Eubanks, Michael Hill

The All Star Summer Revue

Variety; 60 min; NBC 6/28/52 to 8/30/52

Performances by new and established entertainers with hosts Carl Ballantine and Oliver Wakefield, regulars Georgia Gibbs and The Paul Steffin Dancers, and the orchestra of Dean Elliot.

All That Glitters

Satire; 30 min; Syn. 4/77

An off-beat series that focuses on a society where women are the workers and men the housekeepers and secretaries.

Christina Stockwood	Lois Nettleton
Nancy Langston	Anita Gillette
L. W. Carruthers	Barbara Baxley
Andrea Martin	Louise Shaffer
Linda Murkland	Linda Gray
Peggy Horner	Vanessa Brown
Joan Hamlyn	Jessica Walter
Grace Smith	Marte Boyle Slout
Bert Stockwood	Chuck McCann
Glenn Langston	Wes Parker
Michael McFarland	David Haskell
Dan Kincaid	Gary Sandy

Producer: Viva Knight, Stephanie Sils

All Together Now

Comedy Pilot; 30 min; NBC 6/30/84

Events in the lives of a middle-aged couple (Elly and Walt) and their children, Linda and Kip.

Elly Parker	Barbara Barrie
Walt Parker	Peter Michael Goetz
Linda Parker	Joan Cusack
Kip Parker	Tom Byrd
Grandpa Ed	Don Porter
Viola	Betty Kean
Tony Kunkel	Robert Prescott

Producer: Deidre Fay, Stuart Wolpert

All's Fair

Comedy; 30 min; CBS 9/20/76 to 8/15/77

The relationship between a 49-year-old conservative newspaper columnist (Richard) and a beautiful 29-year-old free-lance photographer (Charlotte).

Richard Barrington	Richard Crenna
Charlotte Drake	Bernadette Peters
Al Brooks	J. A. Preston
Ginger Livingston	Judith Kahan
Lucy Daniels	Lee Chamberlain
Wayne Joplin	Jack Dodson
Barbara Murray	Salome Jens
Lanny Wolf	Michael Keaton

Producer: Rod Parker, Bob Weiskopf, Bob Schiller

Allan

Comedy Pilot; 30 min; NBC 8/23/71

The misadventures of a hard working father (Harold) and his lazy, hippie son (Allan).

Harold Fisher	Lou Jacobi
Allan Fisher	Mark Jennings
Blanche Fisher	Florence Halop
Doris	Barbara Press
Alice	Brioni Farrell

Allen Ludden's Gallery

A syndicated (1969) series of music and chatter with Allen Ludden as host. Produced by Jerome Reeves and Roger Ailes.

Allison Sidney Harrison

Crime Drama Pilot; 60 min; NBC 8/19/83

The adventures of Allison Sidney Harrison, a teenage girl who teams with her detective father (David) to solve crimes.

Allison Harrison	Katy Kurtzman
David Harrison	Ted Danson
Pat Rosetti	Don Calfa
Joyce	Ellen Travolta
Lt. Jesse Herman	James McEachin
Valerie Parker	Elaine Joyce
Clarisse Spencer	Cynthia Harris
Walt Spencer	Granville Van Dusen
Art Appraiser	Hans Conried
Sgt. Beatty	Charles Hallahan
The Dean	Macon McCalman
Steve Malloy	Corbin Bernsen
Det. Davis	Dan Leegant
Karate Teacher	Stanley Ralph Ross
Doorman	Billy Swan
Jimmy	Clyde Katsau

Producer: Leon & Dian Tokatyan, John Cutts

'Allo 'Allo

Comedy; 30 min; Syn. 10/86

A World War II comedy about a French restaurant owner (Rene) who offers his establishment (Cafe Rene) as a place of refuge for the British as they battle the Germans.

Rene	Gorden Kaye
Edith (his wife)	Carmen Silvera
Maria (waitress)	Vickie Michelle
Michelle (resistance fighter)	Kristen Cooke
Yvette (Rene's mistress)	Francesca Gonshaw
Edith's mother	Rose Hill
Colonel Von Strom	Richard Marner
Col. Von Klinckerhoff	Richard Gibson
Helga (Colonel's assistant)	Kim Hartman

Producer: David Croft

Almost American

Comedy Pilot; 30 min; NBC 4/1/81

The experiences of Catherine Armstrong, a teacher who instructs foreign students studying for their naturalization tests.

Catherine Armstrong	Maureen McNamara
Milosh Dubrowski	Bob Ari
Ming-Lee Chang	Rosalind Chao
Rudy	Richard Yniquez
Kristen	Anne Bjorn
Kwame Botulo	Ernie Hudson

Producer: Budd Grossman, Howard Leeds, John Maxwell Anderson

Almost Anything Goes

Game; 30 min; ABC 7/31/75 to 5/9/76

Three six member teams compete in various stunt contests for prizes.

Host: Charlie Jones, Lynn Shakelfrod, Sam Riddle

Producer: Bob Banner, Beryl Vertue

Almost Heaven

Comedy Pilot; 30 min; ABC 12/28/78

The antics of a group of deceased souls, regulated to the Heavenly Crisis and Conscience Center, who must perform good deeds before they can enter Heaven.

Lydia	Eva Gabor
Danny	Jay Leno
Bridget	Ellen Regan
Randall	Richard Roat
George	Larry Gelman
Dave	Robert Hays
Annie	Laurie Heinemann
Margie	Anne Schedeen

Producer: Dale McRaven, David Pollock, Elias Davis

Almost Home

Comedy Pilot; 30 min; ABC 2/21/86

The story of Jake Tyler, a singer who relinquishes his career to care for a group of orphans.

Jake Tyler	Mac Davis
Charlie Sands	Norman Fell
Theo Gabler	Allyn Ann McLerie
P.J.	Billy Lombardo
Michael	Larry O. Williams
Sandy	Shannon Lynch
Mandy	Robin Lynch

Producer: Steve and Madeline Sunshine, James O'Keefe

Aloha Paradise

Comedy-Drama; 60 min; ABC 2/18/81 to 4/29/81

Brief incidents in the lives of people who vacation at Paradise Village, a resort in Hawaii.

Sydney Chase	Debbie Reynolds
Curtis Shaw	Bill Daily
Fran Linhart	Patricia Klous
Richard Bean	Stephen Shortridge

Producer: Aaron Spelling, Douglas S. Cramer

Alone at Last

Comedy Pilot; 30 min; NBC 6/24/80

Comic events in the lives of the Elliotts, a family of four living in California.

Gregg Elliott	Bill Daily
Laurie Elliott	Virginia Vestoff
Nancy Elliott	Kerry Sherman
Michael Elliott	Michael Horton
Agnes Bernoski	Francine Beers
Jack Bernoski	Martin Garner
Sherry	Elaine Joyce

Producer: Bob Sweeney, Edward H. Feldman

Alone at Last

Comedy Pilot; 30 min; NBC 9/3/80

A second pilot about the day-to-day lives of the Elliott family.

Larry Elliott	Eugene Roche
Maureen Elliott	Susan Bay
Nancy Elliott	Lilibet Stern
Michael Elliott	Dana Carvey
Agnes Bernoski	Florence Halop
Jack Bernoski	Martin Garner

Producer: Larry Rosen, Larry Tucker

Along the Barbary Coast

Crime Drama Pilot; 60 min; NBC 2/27/61

The exploits of Pete Bishop, a private detective based on San Francisco's Barbary Coast.

Pete Bishop	Jerome Thor
Trixie Cochran	Barbara Stanwyck
Sam Verner	Richard Eastham

Producer: Louis F. Edelman

Alumni Fun

Game; 30 min; ABC 1/20/63 to 4/28/63
CBS 1/12/64 to 5/7/66

Celebrity college alumni compete in a series of question and answer rounds with all winnings being donated to their alumni.

Host: Peter Lind Hayes, Clifton Fadiman

Producer: John P. Cleary

Alvin and the Chipmunks

Cartoon; 30 min; NBC 9/17/83 (Premiere)

An update of "The Alvin Show" which continues to depict the antics of Alvin, Theodore and Simon, the singing Chipmunks.

Dave Seville	Ross Bagdasarian
Chipmunks	Ross Bagdasarian

Producer: Joe Ruby, Ken Spears

The Alvin Show

Cartoon; 30 min; CBS 10/4/61 to 9/12/62

The misadventures of Dave Seville, the manager of Alvin, Theodore and Simon, the famous singing Chipmunks. Other segments: "The Adventures of Clyde Crashcup" (a wacky inventor) and "Sinbad Jr." (a mighty sailor).

Dave/Chipmunks	Ross Bagdasarian
Clyde	Shepard Menken
Sinbad	Tim Matthieson
Salty	Mel Blanc

Producer: Herbert Klynn

Always April

Comedy Pilot; 30 min; CBS 2/23/61

The adventures of April Fleming, a beautiful aspiring actress.

April Fleming	Susan Silo
Guinevere Fleming	Constance Bennett
David Fleming	John Emery
Erskine Wild	Marty Ingels
Nettie	Elmira Sessions

Producer: Arthur Hoffe

Amanda Fallon

Drama Pilot; 60 min; NBC 3/5/72

The work of Amanda Fallon, a Los Angeles-based pediatrician. In the first pilot, Amanda attempts to help a young boy with bleeding ulcers.

Amanda Fallon	Jane Wyman
Vic Wheelwright	Mike Farrell
Nurse Crawford	Lillian Lehman
Dee Merlino	Lynnette Mettey
Peter Merlino	Jim Davis
Cory Merlino	Ron Howard

Producer: Jack Laird

Amanda Fallon

Drama Pilot; 60 min; NBC 5/4/73

A second pilot about the work of Amanda Fallon, a pediatrician. The story relates Amanda's attempts to help a pregnant teenage girl.

Amanda Fallon	Jane Wyman
Joyce Cummings	Laurie Prange
Carol Steadman	Kathleen Nolan
Mr. Cummings	Leslie Nielsen
Emory	Pat O'Brien

Producer: Jack Laird

Amanda's

Comedy; 30 min; ABC 1/10/83 to 5/26/83

The comic efforts of Amanda Cartwright, the owner of Amanda's By the Sea, to run a hotel fraught with problems.

Amanda Cartwright	Beatrice Arthur
Zachary Cartwright	Kevin McCarthy
Marty Cartwright	Fred McCarren
Arlene Cartwright	Simone Griffeth
Earl Nash	Rick Hurst
Aldo	Tony Rosato
Clifford Mundy	Keene Curtis

Producer: Len Rosenberg, Elliott Schoenman

An Amateur's Guide to Love

Comedy Pilot; 30 min; CBS 8/8/71

The results of unsuspecting individuals caught in prearranged romantic situations.

Host: Joe Flynn

Producer: Ed Simmons

The Amateur's Guide to Love

Game; 30 min; CBS 3/27/72 to 6/23/72

The object calls for celebrity guests to predict the outcome of unsuspecting individuals caught in prearranged romantic situations.

Host: Gene Rayburn

Regular: Barbara Crosby

Announcer: Kenny Williams

Producer: Merrill Heatter, Bob Quigley

The Amazing Chan and the Chan Clan

Cartoon: 30 min; CBS 9/9/72 to 9/22/74

The investigations of Charlie Chan, the famous Chinese detective, who receives the sometimes unwanted assistance of his ten children.

Charlie Chan	Keye Luke
Henry Chan	Robert Ito
Stanley Chan	Stanley Wong
	Lennie Weinrib
Suzie Chan	Virginia Ann Lee
	Cherylene Lee
Alan Chan	Brian Tochi
Anne Chan	Leslie Kumamoto
	Jodie Foster
Tom Chan	Michael Takamoto
	John Gunn
Flip Chan	Jay Jay Jue
	Gene Andrusco
Nancy Chan	Debbie Jue
	Beverly Kushida
Mimi Chan	Leslie Kawai
	Cherylene Lee
Scooter Chan	Robin Toma
	Michael Morgan
Chu Chu (dog)	Don Messick

Producer: William Hanna, Joseph Barbera

The Amazing Dunninger

Human Interest; 30 min; Syn. 1968

The mind-reading abilities of mentalist Joseph Dunninger.

Host: Hank Stohl, Bob Delaney

Announcer: Bob Delaney

The Amazing Mr. Malone

Crime Drama; 30 min; CBS 9/24/51 to 3/10/52

A live series about the investigations of John J. Malone, a criminal attorney.

John J. Malone	Lee Tracy

Producer: Edgar & Edward Peterson

The Amazing Polgar

Human Interest; 10 min; CBS 9/16/49 to 10/21/49

Demonstrations of psychic phenomena with psychologist Franz J. Polgar.

Announcer: Cy Harrice

Producer: Charles Lewin

The Amazing Spider-Man

Adventure; 60 min; CBS 4/5/78 to 7/6/79

After being bitten by a radioactive spider, "New York Bugle" newspaper photographer Peter Parker discovers that the venom has become a part of his system and he has absorbed the power and ability of a living spider. Stories relate Peter's battle against crime as the mysterious Spider-Man.

Peter/Spider-Man	Nicholas Hammond
Spider-Man (stunts)	Fred Waugh
J. Jonah Jameson	Robert F. Simon
	David White*
Capt. Barbera	Michael Pataki
Rita Conway	Chip Fields
Julie Masters	Ellen Bry
Peter's Aunt May	Irene Tedrow

Producer: Charles Fries, Daniel Goodman

*TV Movie role (9/14/77).

Amazing Stories

Anthology; 30 min; NBC 9/29/85 to 5/15/87

A series of unusual stories that combine elements of fantasy, amazement, irony, and comedy. The program, developed by Steven Spielberg, features top name directors and well-known performers.

Caveman (in program open): Ray Walston

Performers Include: Loni Anderson, Dom DeLuise, Drew Barrymore, Amy Irving, Sid Caesar, Penny Peyser, Kathleen Lloyd, Polly Holliday, June Lockhart, John Lithgow, Shawn Weatherly, Jamie Rose, Beau Bridges, Natalie Gregory, Helen Shaver, Abbe Lane, Gail Edwards, Milton Berle, Christopher Lloyd, and Charles Durning

Directors Include: Burt Reynolds, Clint Eastwood, Joan Darling, Martin Scorsese, William Dear, Steven Spielberg, Donald Petrie, Irving Kershner, Bob Clark, and Timothy Hutton

Producer: Steven Spielberg, David E. Vogel, Joshua Brand

"Amazing Stories" Theme Song: Johnny Williams

The Amazing Tales of Hans Christian Andersen

Anthology; 30 min; Syn. 1954

An early color series of stories based on tales by Hans Christian Andersen and performed by Gene and George Sheldon.

The Amazing Three

Cartoon; 30 min; Syn. 1967

The exploits of three celestial beings and Earthling Kenny Carter as they battle evil. The Japanese series is produced by Osamu Tezuka.

The Amazing World of Kreskin

A syndicated (1971) series that features feats of mind reading, E.S.P., and sleight of hand by mentalist Kreskin.

Amen

Comedy; 30 min; NBC 9/27/86 (Premiere)

The conflicts that ensue when Ernest Frye, Deacon of the First Community Church of Philadelphia, and the newly appointed Reverend Gregory fail to come to terms on exaclty how the church should be run.

Deacon Ernest Frye	Sherman Hemsley
Rev. Reuben Gregory	Clifton Davis
Sister Amelia	Roz Ryan
Sister Casietta	Barbara Montgomery
Thelma Frye	Anna Maria Horsford
Lorenzo Hollingsworth	Franklyn Seales
Marvin Russell	Willie Walton
Rolly Forbes	Jester Hariston

Producer: Ed Weinberger, David Lloyd

America

Magazine; 60 min; Syn. 9/85

A daily program of people, places, events and current trends.

Host: Sarah Purcell, McLean Stevenson, Stuart Damon

Announcer: Charlie O'Donnell, Rod Roddy

Regulars: Dale Harimoto, Erma Bombeck, Dr. Ruth Westheimer

Producer: Woody Fraser, Susan Winston

America Alive

Variety; 60 min; NBC 7/24/78 to 1/5/79

A daily series of music, news, and celebrity interviews.

Host: Jack Linkletter, Janet Langhart

Producer: Woody Fraser, Susan Winston, Kenny Price

America 2-Night

Satire; 30 min; Syn. 7/78

A spoof of variety programs as seen through the outrageous antics of Barth Gimble, host of the United Broadcasting System's "America 2-Night," a talk show that features well-known celebrities as well as grotesque people.

Barth Gimble	Martin Mull
Jerry Hubbard	Fred Willard
Happy Kyne	Frank DeVol
William "Bud" Prize	Ken Mars

Producer: Alan Thicke

America 2100

Comedy Pilot; 30 min; ABC 7/24/79

One hundred and twenty years after comics Chester Barnes and Phil Keese were accidentally frozen alive, scientists discover a process that allows them to thaw out. The unsold series was to relate their adventures in the year 2100.

Dr. Karen Harland	Karen Valentine
Chester Barnes	Jon Cutler
Phil Keese	Mark King
Voice of Max	Sid Caesar

Producer: Austin and Irma Kalish

American Bandstand

Variety; 60 min; ABC 10/7/57 (Premiere)

Music and entertainment geared to teenagers. The program originally premiered locally in Philadelphia (over WFIL-TV) in October

1952. Ron Joseph and Lee Stewart were the hosts from 1952–1956. Dick Clark became the host in August of 1956.

Host: Dick Clark

Producer: Dick Clark, Judy Price, Barry Glazer, Larry Klein

The American Dream

Drama; 60 min; ABC 4/26/81 to 6/10/81

Hoping to find their idea of the American Dream, the Novack family move from the suburb of Arlington Heights, Chicago, to an interracial inner-city. Stories relate their experiences in new surroundings.

Donna Novack	Karen Carlson
Danny Novack	Stephen Macht
Casey Novack	Tim Waldrip
Todd Novack	Michael Hershewe
Jennifer Novack	Andrea Smith
Abe Berlowitz	Hans Conried
Sam Whittier	John McIntire

Theme Vocal ("Chasin' the American Dream"): Jim Gilstrap

Producer: Mace Neufeld, Jerry Thorpe, William Blinn

The American Girls

Drama; 60 min; CBS 9/23/78 to 11/10/78

The assignments of Rebecca Tompkins and Amy Waddell, reporters for the TV magazine series "The American Report."

Rebecca Tompkins	Priscilla Barnes
Amy Waddell	Debra Clinger
Francis X. Casey	David Spielberg
Jason Cook	William Prince

Producer: Harve Bennett, Harris Katleman

American Minstrels

Variety; 30 min; ABC 1/13/49 to 3/17/49

Comedy sketches based on vaudeville routines with host Jack Carter and regulars Mary Small, Estelle Sloan, Jimmy Burrell, and Pick and Pat.

American Song

Variety; 15 min; NBC 4/21/48 to 4/25/49

Performances by folk artists with host Paul Arnold and regulars Ray Harrison and Nellie Fisher.

Americana

Game; 30 min; NBC 12/8/47 to 7/4/49

Two teams of high school students compete in an American history quiz.

Host: John Mason Brown, Ben Grauer

Americans

Drama; 60 min; NBC 1/23/61 to 9/11/61

The Civil War-time activities of Ben Canfield, a Union Loyalist, and his brother, Jeff, a Confederate with the Virginia Militia.

Ben Canfield	Darryl Hickman
Jeff Canfield	Dick Davalos

Producer: Frank Telford

The Ames Brothers Show

Variety; 15 min; Syn. 1955

Music and songs with Ed, Vic, Joe, and Gene Ames, a quartet of popular singers during the 1950s. With Cheerio Meredith and the orchestra of Harry Geller. Produced by Bill Ficks.

America's Top Ten

Variety; 30 min; Syn. 5/80

A weekly series, hosted by Casey Kasem, that spotlights the top ten singles as reported by "Billboard" magazine. Produced by Syd Vinnedge and Tony Scotti.

The Amos and Andy Show

Comedy; 30 min; CBS 6/28/51 to 6/11/53

The story of three men: Andrew Halt Brown, the naive president of the Fresh Air Taxi Cab Company of America; Amos Jones, his level-headed partner; and George "Kingfish" Stevens, an inept con artist.

Andrew Halt Brown	Spencer Williams Jr.
George Stevens	Tim Moore
Amos Jones	Alvin Childress
Sapphire Stevens	Ernestine Wade
Mama	Amanda Randolph
Lightnin'	Horace Stewart
Algonquin J. Calhoun	Johnny Lee
Ruby Jones	Jane Adams
Madame Queen	Lillian Randolph

Producer: James Fonda, Freeman Gosden, Charles Correll

Amos Burke, Secret Agent

Crime Drama; 60 min; ABC 9/15/65 to 1/12/66

The exploits of Amos Burke, a former police captain turned U.S. government undercover agent. A spin-off from "Burke's Law."

Amos Burke	Gene Barry
The Man	Carl Benton Reid

Producer: Aaron Spelling

Amos Burke: Who Killed Julie Greer?

Crime Drama Pilot; 60 min; ABC 9/26/61

The pilot episode for "Burke's Law," which aired on "The Dick Powell Show." The story of Amos Burke, an L.A.P.D. inspector who, in the pilot, attempts to solve the murder of a model.

Amos Burke	Dick Powell
Julie Greer	Carolyn Jones
Phil Winslow	Dean Jones
George Townsend	Nick Adams
Judge Hanson	Ralph Bellamy
Dr. Coombs	Edgar Bergen
Fairchild	Jack Carson

Producer: Aaron Spelling

Amy Prentiss

Crime Drama; 90 min; NBC 12/1/74 to 7/6/75

The exploits of Amy Prentiss, a chief of detectives with the San Francisco Police Department.

Amy Prentiss	Jessica Walter
Jill Prentiss	Helen Hunt
Sgt. Tony Russell	Steve Sandor
Det. Roy Pena	Art Metrano
Joan Carter	Gwen Mitchell
Chief Dempsey	M. Emmet Walsh

Producer: Cy Chermak

And Everything Nice

Women; 30 min; DuMont 3/15/49 to 1/2/50

A program of beauty tips and advice with Maxine Barat.

And Here's the Show

Variety; 30 min; NBC 7/9/55 to 9/24/55

A weekly series of music and comedy.

Host: Ransom Sherman

Regulars: Jonathan Winters, Kay O'Grady, Tommy Knox, Stephanie Antler, The Double Daters

Announcer: Bob LeMond

Orchestra: John Scott Trotter

Producer: Bob Finkel

And They All Lived Happily Ever After

Comedy Pilot; 30 min; CBS 8/4/81

Events in the lives of the Westcott family: parents Liz and Paul, and their children Lorraine (married), Timmie (separated) and Matt.

Liz Westcott	Rue McClanahan
Paul Westcott	Dick Latessa
Lorraine Hofstedter	Maggie Roswell
Timmie Gordon	Wendy Goldman
Matt Westcott	Larry Cedar
Ted Hofstedter	James Staley
Ernie Gordon	Sandy Hackett

Producer: Hal Cooper, Rod Parker

Anderson and Company

Comedy Pilot; 30 min; NBC 5/12/69

The misadventures of Marshall Anderson, head of the Anderson and Company Department Store, and the father of a large family.

Marshall Anderson	Fred Gwynne
Augusta Anderson	Abby Dalton
Amanda Anderson	Cynthia Eilbacher
Alfa Anderson	Heather Harrison
Adrienne Anderson	Robin Eccles
Anstruther Anderson	Nick Beauvy
Amory Anderson	Ray Dimas
Ansford Anderson	Teddy Eccles
Artanza Anderson	Sean Kelly
Apollo Anderson	Leig Nervik

The Andros Targets

Crime Drama; 30 min; CBS 1/31/77 to 5/16/77

The exploits of Mike Andros, an investigative reporter for "The New York Forum," a crusading newspaper.

Mike Andros	James Sutorius
Sandi Farrell	Pamela Reed
Norman Kale	Alan Mixon
Chet Reynolds	Roy Poole
Wayne Hillman	Ted Beniades

Producer: Bob Sweeney, Larry Rosen

Andy

Variety; 30 min; Syn. 9/76

A weekly program of music and song.

Host: Andy Williams

Regular: Wayland Flowers

Orchestra: George Wyle

Producer: Pierre Cossette

The Andy Griffith Show

Comedy; 30 min; CBS 10/3/60 to 9/16/68

The simple pleasures and trying times of Andy Taylor, sheriff of Mayberry, North Carolina. The pilot aired on "The Danny Thomas Show" on 2/15/60. See also "Gomer Pyle, U.S.M.C." and "Mayberry R.F.D."

Andy Taylor	Andy Griffith
Deputy Barney Fife	Don Knotts
Opie Taylor	Ron Howard
Bee Taylor	Frances Bavier
Ellie Walker	Elinor Donahue
Helen Crump	Aneta Corsaut
Mary Simpson	Sue Ane Langdon
Thelma Lou	Betty Lynn
Otis Campbell	Hal Smith
Howard Sprague	Jack Dodson
Floyd Lawson	Howard McNear
Gomer Pyle	Jim Nabors
Goober Pyle	George Lindsey
Warren Ferguson	Jack Burns
Ernest T. Bass	Howard Morris
Sam Jones	Ken Berry
Millie Swanson	Arlene Golonka
Brisco Darling	Denver Pyle
Emma Brand	Cheerio Meredith
Mike Jones	Buddy Foster
Martha Clark	Mary Lansing
Charlene Darling	Maggie Peterson
Mayor Pike	Dick Elliott
Mayor Stoner	Parley Baer
Mary Simpson	
(later)	Julie Adams
Irene Fairchild	Nina Shipman
Rose	Mary Treen
Leon	Clint Howard

Producer: Sheldon Leonard, Aaron Ruben, Richard O. Linke, Bob Ross

The Andy Williams-June Valli Show

Variety; 15 min; NBC 7/2/57 to 9/5/57

A program of music and song with singers Andy Williams and June Valli and the orchestra of Alvy West.

The Andy Williams Show

Variety; 60 min; CBS 7/7/59 to 9/22/59

A weekly series of music and songs.

Host: Andy Williams

Regulars: Jane Tallman, Michael Storm, Rae Whiting, Marilyn Jackson, Cynthia Stone, Jayne Turner

Orchestra: Jack Kane

Producer: Perry Lafferty

The Andy Williams Show

Variety; 60 min; NBC 9/20/69 to 7/17/71

Music, songs, and light comedy.

Host: Andy Williams

Regulars: Charlie Callas, Irwin Corey, Janos Prohaska, The Jaime Rogers Singers, The Earl Brown Dancers

Orchestra: Mike Post

Producer: Alan Bernard, Andy Williams

Andy's Gang

Children; 30 min; NBC 8/20/55 to 6/28/58

Music, songs, stories, and comedy set against the background of a clubhouse. Originally titled "The Buster Brown TV Show with Smilin' Ed McConnell and the Buster Brown Gang" (9/23/50 to 8/4/51) and then "Smilin' Ed McConnell and His Gang" (8/11/51 to 8/13/55).

Ed McConnell	Himself
Andy Devine	Himself
Gunga	Nino Marcel
Rama	Vito Scotti
Marajah	Lou Krugman
Froggie the Gremlin	Ed McConnell
	Frank Ferrin
Midnight the Cat/	
Grandie the Piano	June Foray
Teacher	Billy Gilbert

Producer: Frank Ferrin

Angel

Comedy; 30 min; CBS 10/6/60 to 9/20/61

During a business trip to France, architect John Smith meets and later marries a beautiful French girl named Angel. Stories relate Angel's misadventures as she struggles to adjust to the American way of life.

Angel Smith	Annie Farge
John Smith	Marshall Thompson
Susie	Doris Singleton
George	Don Keefer

Producer: Jess Oppenheimer, Edward H. Feldman

Angie

Comedy; 30 min; ABC 2/8/79 to 10/23/80

While working in the Liberty Coffee Shop in Philadelphia, Angie Falco, a poor waitress, meets, falls in love with, and later marries Brad Benson, a wealthy pediatrician. Stories relate incidents in Angie's life as she struggles to adjust to a new life style.

Angie Falco	Donna Pescow
Brad Benson	Robert Hays
Marie Falco	Debralee Scott
Theresa Falco	Doris Roberts
Joyce Benson	Sharon Spelman
Hillary Benson	Tammy Lauren
Di Di Malloy	Diane Robin
Randall Benson	John Randolph
Gianni	Tim Thomerson
Connie	Tessa Richards
Phipps	Emory Bass
Hector	Richard Beauchamp

Theme Vocal ("Different Worlds"): Maureen McGovern

Producer: Garry K. Marshall, Leonora Thuna

Animal Crack-Ups

Game Pilot; 30 min; ABC 3/28/87

Amusing films of animals coupled with a game show for charity. Four celebrity guests have to answer questions based on the activities of animals seen in tape clips. The player with the highest score (most correct answers) wins $2500 for his favorite wildlife charity.

Host: Alan Thicke

Guests: Allysa Milano, Mary Hart, JM J. Bullock, Christopher Hewitt

Assistant: Debbie Bartlett

Animal Voices: Ron Lucas

Producer: Vin DiBona, Bill Armstrong

Ann in Blue

Comedy Pilot; 30 min; ABC 8/8/74

The story of Ann Neal, the head of a four-woman police unit in New York City.

Sgt. Ann Neal	Penny Fuller
Off. Bea Russo	Mary Elaine Monte
Off. Liz Jensen	Maybeth Hart
Off. Jessie Waters	Hattie Winston

Producer: Danny Arnold

The Ann Sothern Show

Comedy; 30 min; CBS 10/6/58 to 9/25/61

The misadventures of Katy O'Connor, assistant manager of the Bartley House Hotel.

Katy O'Connor	Ann Sothern
Jason Maculey	Ernest Truex
James Devery	Don Porter
Flora Maculey	Reta Shaw
Olive Smith	Ann Tyrrell
Dr. Delbart Gray	Louis Nye
Woody	Ken Berry
Paul Martine	Jacques Scott
Johnny Wallace	Jack Mullavey
Oscar Pudney	Jesse White

Producer: Richard Whorf, Devery Freeman, Desi Arnaz

Anna and the King

Comedy-Drama; 30 min; CBS 9/17/72 to 12/31/72

Seeking to educate his children, the King of Siam commissions an American teacher (Anna Owens) to instruct them. Stories, set in Siam in 1862, relate Anna's experiences as she attempts to introduce Western culture to the King and his children.

King of Siam	Yul Brynner
Anna Owens	Samantha Eggar
Louis Owens	Eric Shea
Prince Kralahome	Keye Luke
Prince Chulalongkorn	Brian Tochi
Lady Thiang	Lisa Lu
Princess Serena	Rosalind Chao

Producer: Gene Reynolds

Anne of Green Gables

Drama; 60 min; PBS 2/16/86 to 3/2/86

A beautifully enacted series about Anne Shirley, an orphan girl who yearns for a home and love. Her experiences with Matthew and Marilla, the elderly brother and sister who adopt her, is the focal point of the program. (The title refers to Marilla's home, Green Gables).

Anne Shirley	Megan Follows
Marilla Cuthbert	Colleen Dewhurst
Matthew Cuthbert	Richard Farnsworth
Diana Barry	Schulyer Grant
Gilbert Blythe	Jonathan Crombie
Mrs. Barry	Rosemary Radcliffe
John Barry	Robert Collins
Rachel Lynde	Patricia Hamilton

Producer: Kevin Sullivan

Annette

Drama Serial; 30 min; ABC 2/6/58 to 3/6/58

A "Mickey Mouse Club" serial about the experiences of Annette McCleod, a pretty country girl who comes to live with relatives in the big city.

Annette McCleod	Annette Funicello
Archie McCleod	Richard Deacon
Lila McCleod	Sylvia Field
Katie	Mary Wickes
Laura Rogan	Roberta Shore
Stephen Abernathy	Tim Considine
Val Abernathy	Doreen Tracy
Mike Martin	David Stollery
Jet Maypen	Judy Nugent
Corey	Shelley Fabares
Madge	Cheryl Holdridge
Kitty	Sharon Baird
Steady Ware	Ruby Lee

Theme Song ("Annette"): Jimmie Dodd

Producer: Walt Disney, Bill Walsh

Annie Flynn

Comedy Pilot; 30 min; CBS 1/21/78

The story of Annie Flynn, a former nurse trying to succeed in medical school.

Annie Flynn	Barrie Youngfellow
C.C.	Carol Potter
Elliott Hoag	Harvey Lewis
Hoyt Kosloff	Louis Guss
Paul Lucas	Charles Frank
Sherry	Lisa Loring

Producer: Coleman Mitchell, Geoffrey Neigher

Annie Oakley

Western; 30 min; Syn. 1/54

Following the death of their parents, Annie Oakley, a pretty sharpshooter, and her young brother, Tagg, are taken in by their uncle, the sheriff of Diablo County, Arizona. Stories, set in the early 1900s, relate Annie's exploits as she uses her expertise with a gun to help Deputy Lofty Craig maintain the peace.

Annie Oakley	Gail Davis
Deputy Lofty Craig	Brad Johnson
Tagg Oakley	Jimmy Hawkins
Chet Osgood	Stanley Adams
Marge Hardy	Virginia Lee
Bess Murdock	Nancy Hale
Tom Conrad	Fess Parker
Tom Jennings	William Fawcett
Elroy	Isa Ashdown
Penny	Judy Nugent
Priscilla Bishop	Nita Talbot
Gloria Marshall	Sally Fraser
Curley Dawes	Roscoe Ates
Alias Annie Oakley (Annie's outlaw double)	Nan Leslie
Mary Farnsworth	Wendy Drew
Deborah Scott	Nancy Hale
Jim	Bob Woodward
Pete	Larry Reeves

Producer: Armand Schaefer, Colbert Clark, Louis Gray

The Anniversary Game

Game; 30 min; Syn. 1/69

Three husband and wife teams compete. One member of each team is involved in a specific situation. The teammate must predict the outcome to score points. The highest scorers receive prizes.

Host: Al Hamel

Announcer: Dean Webber

Another April

Comedy Pilot; 30 min; CBS 3/7/74

Events in the life of April Moss, a liberal-minded divorcee struggling to find peace in her conservative parents' home.

April Moss	Leslie Charleson
Marion Weston	Barnard Hughes
Ruth Weston	Elizabeth Wilson
Brenda Sanders	Ellen Weston
Howard Sanders	Will MacKenzie
Dennis Weber	Howard Hesseman

Producer: Lawrence Kasha, Lew Gallo

Another Day

Comedy; 30 min; CBS 4/8/78 to 4/29/78

Incidents in the lives of Don and Ginny Gardner, a couple whose lives are complicated by their jobs, their children and Don's outspoken mother.

Don Gardner	David Groh
Ginny Gardner	Joan Hackett
Kelly Gardner	Lisa Lindgren
Mark Gardner	Al Eisenmann
Olive Gardner	Hope Summers

Producer: James Komack

Another Day, Another Dollar

Comedy Pilot; 30 min; NBC 9/21/59

A would-be series about the misadventures of Augie Adams, a good-natured toy salesman. See also "How's Business?"

Augie Adams	Jack Carson
Joyce Adams	Jean Gillespie
Robbie Adams	Flip Mark
John Burke	Jesse White

Producer: William Sackheim

Another Man's Shoes

Comedy Pilot; 30 min; CBS 5/28/84

Following the death of his brother, Dwayne Schneider moves to Florida to care for his orphaned niece and nephew (Lori and Keith). There, he acquires a job as the maintenance man for an arcade run by Jackie Cahill. The unsold pilot, a proposed spin-off from "One Day At a Time," was to relate Dwayne's misadventures.

Dwayne Schneider	Pat Harrington Jr.
Lori Schneider	Natalie Klinger
Keith Schneider	Corey Feldman
Jackie Cahill	Candice Azzara
Cassie	Darian Mathias
Madame Zorina	Ruth Kobart

Producer: Dick Bensfield, Perry Grant

Anson and Lorrie

Variety Pilot; 60 min; NBC 9/19/81

A program of music and songs with hosts Anson Williams and Lorrie Mahaffey (his wife). With regulars Jeff Altman, Andrea Martin, Davey Dillon, and Darrow Igus. Produced by Alvin J. Tenzer and orchestrations by Dennis McCarthy.

The Answer Man

Game Pilot; 15 min; DuMont 9/26/46

Based on the radio program in which the Answer Man (host) responds to questions asked of him by the studio audience.

Host: Herbert Mitchell

Producer: Benjamin R. Parker

Answer Yes or No

Game; 30 min; NBC 4/30/50 to 7/23/50

A celebrity panel must predict whether or not a contestant would involve himself with a specific situation dilemma.

Host: Moss Hart

Panelists: Arlene Francis, Jane Pickens, Peter Lind Hayes, Mary Healy

Anybody Can Play

Game; 30 min; ABC 7/6/58 to 12/8/58

The object calls for players to guess (through probe rounds) objects possessed by celebrity guests.

Host: George Fenneman

Assistant: Judy Bamber

Anyone Can Win

Game; 30 min; CBS 7/14/53 to 9/1/53

The object calls for players to guess the identities of celebrities whose identities are concealed via makeup.

Host: Al Capp

Panelists: Patsy Kelly, Ilka Chase, Jimmy Dykes

Producer: Everett Rosenthal

Anything For Love

Comedy Pilot; 30 min; NBC 8/7/85

The story of Dot and Elaine, two Dayton, Ohio beauticians wrestling with the problems of work, men and family.

Dot Bailey	Lauren Tewes
Elaine Monty	Vicki Lawrence
Allison Bailey	Christa Denton
Timmy Bailey	Leaf Phoenix
Cleo	Marsha Warfield
Jenny	Rebecca Arthur
Randy Howard	Mark Harrison
Larry Worth	Paul Gleason
Helen Worth	Jennifer Savidge

Producer: Sy Rosen, Douglas Aragno, Phil Doran

Anything For Money

Crime Drama Pilot; 60 min; ABC 4/16/57

The first of two pilots for "77 Sunset Strip" (see also "Girl on the Run"). The exploits of Stuart Bailey, a private detective working out of California.

Stuart Bailey	Efrem Zimbalist Jr.
Glen Callister	Barton MacLane
Eileen Callister	Margaret Hayes
Madden	Richard Webb
Betty Callister	Joanna Barnes

Producer: Roy Huggins

Anything For Money

Game; 30 min; Syn. 9/84

The object calls for players to determine if people, caught in prearranged situations, went along with or refused to become a part of the setup.

Host: Fred Travalena

Announcer: Johnny Gilbert

Producer: David Fein, Tracy Gross

Anything You Can Do

Game; 30 min; Syn. 1971

Two three-member teams compete in various timed stunts with the team performing the overall lowest time the winner.

Host: Gene Wood, Don Harron

Announcer: Bill Luxton

Producer: Don Reid

Anywhere, U.S.A.

Anthology; 30 min; ABC 11/9/52 to 12/14/52

Edward Dowling and Robert Preston as doctors in stories based on the often neglected health problems of people. Produced by Victor Weingarter.

The Apartment House

Comedy Pilot; 30 min; CBS 9/5/64

Events in the life of Wally Weaver, the harassed manager of the Zimmerman Arms Apartment House.

Wally Weaver	George Gobel
Marge Weaver	Sue Ane Langdon
Billie	Jane Withers
Fred MacMurray	Himself
Steve Allen	Himself

Producer: Josef Shaffel

An Apartment in Rome

Comedy Pilot; 30 min; CBS 8/22/64

A would-be series about Debbie and Steve Adams, a young couple struggling to survive in Rome on what the husband makes as an artist.

Debbie Adams	Susan Oliver
Steve Adams	Allen Case
Uncle Howard	Howard St. John
Aunt Ethel	Lurene Tuttle

Producer: Sol Saks

Apartment 2-C

Comedy Pilot; 30 min; HBO 8/21/85

An "R" rated pilot about George Carlin, a writer whose work is constantly interrupted by bizarre people. Contains strong adult language.

George Carlin	George Carlin
Biff Doyle	Pat McCormick
Lois Bromfield	Herself
Patty Dunbar	Lucy Webb
Girl Scout	Kelly Carlin
Toki	Blake Clarke
Bobby	Bob Goldthwait

Producer: Bernard Carlin, Molly Miles

Apartment 3-C

A syndicated (1949) fifteen-minute comedy that relates incidents in the lives of a young newlywed couple (John and Barbara Gay, who portray themselves).

Apple Pie

Comedy; 30 min; ABC 9/23/78 to 10/7/78

Seeking to acquire a family, a lonely woman (Ginger-Nell Hollyhock) places a newspaper ad requesting a family. Stories relate the adventures of the newly formed Hollyhocks when Ginger-Nell acquires a husband (Fast Eddie), two children (Anna Marie and Junior) and a grandfather.

Ginger-Nell Hollyhock	Rue McClanahan
Fast Eddie Barnes	Dabney Coleman
Grandpa Hollyhock	Jack Gilford
Anna Marie Hollyhock	Caitlin O'Heaney
Junior Hollyhock	Derrell Maury

Producer: Charlie Hauck

Apple's Way

Drama; 60 min; CBS 2/10/74 to 1/12/75

Hoping to relive the fascination of his childhood and give his children the opportunity to experience the wonders of nature, George Apple uproots his family and moves to the small town of Appleton, Iowa. Stories relate the experiences of the six member Apple family.

George Apple	Ronny Cox
Barbara Apple	Frances Lee McCain
Paul Apple	Vincent Van Patten
Patricia Apple	Franny Michel
	Kristy McNichol
Cathy Apple	Patti Cohoon
Aldon Apple	Malcolm Atterbury

Producer: Lee Rich, Earl Hamner

Appointment with Adventure

A series of half-hour dramas based on the experiences of ordinary people. Produced by David Susskind and broadcast on CBS from 4/3/55 to 4/1/56.

Aquaman

Cartoon; 7 min; Syn. 9/70

The exploits of Aquaman, ruler of the Seven Seas, as he battles evil.

Aquaman	Ted Knight
Mera	Diana Maddox
Aqualad	Jerry Dexter

The Aquanauts

Adventure; 30 min; CBS 9/14/60 to 3/1/61

The exploits of Drake Andrews, Larry Lahr, and Mike Madison, salvage divers based in Hawaii. See also "Malibu Run."

Drake Andrews	Keith Larsen
Larry Lahr	Jeremy Slate
Mike Madison	Ron Ely

Producer: Ivan Tors

Archer

Crime Drama; 60 min; NBC 1/30/75 to 3/14/75

The cases of Lew Archer, a private detective based in Melrose, California.

Lew Archer	Brian Keith
Lt. Barney Brighton	John P. Ryan

Producer: Jack Miller, Leonard B. Kaufman

Archie

Comedy Pilot; 60 min; ABC 12/19/76

The adventures of the Archie Gang, teenagers who live in the mythical town of Riverdale.

Archie Andrews	Dennis Bowen
Betty Cooper	Audrey Landers
Veronica Lodge	Hilary Thompson
Reggie Mantle	Mark Winkworth
Jughead Jones	Derrel Maury
Moose	Jim Boelsen
Midge	Susan Blu
Big Ethel	Tifni Twitchell
Mr. Andrews	Gordon Jump
Miss Grundy	Jane Lambert
Mr. Weatherbee	Byron Webster

Producer: James Komack, George Yanok

Archie Bunker's Place

Comedy; 30 min; CBS 9/23/79 to 9/21/83

A spin-off from "All in the Family" that continues to depict events in the life of Archie Bunker, now the owner of Archie Bunker's Place, a bar in Astoria, Queens, N.Y.

Archie Bunker	Carroll O'Connor
Murray Klein	Martin Balsam
Stephanie Mills	Danielle Brisebois
Billie Bunker	Denise Miller
Barney Hefner	Allan Melvin
Harry Snowden	Jason Wingreen
Veronica Rooney	Anne Meara
Edgar Van Ranseleer	Bill Quinn
Jose	Abraham Alvarez
Raoul	Joe Rosario
Ellen Canby	Barbara Meek
Gary Rabinowitz	Barry Gordon
Polly Swanson	Janet MacLachlan
Ed Swanson	Mel Bryant

Producer: Mort Lachman

The Archie Comedy Hour

Cartoon; 60 min; CBS 9/13/69 to 9/4/71

The animated antics of the Archie Gang, high school students in the town of Riverdale.

Archie Andrews	Dallas McKennon
Betty Cooper	Jane Webb
Veronica Lodge	Jane Webb
Jughead Jones	Howard Morris
Reggie Mantle	Dallas McKennon

Producer: Norm Prescott, Lou Scheimer

The Archie Situation Comedy Musical Variety Show

Comedy Pilot; 60 min; ABC 8/5/78

A second pilot, based on the 1942 "Archie" comic strip, about the antics of a group of teenagers in Riverdale. See also "Archie."

Archie Andrews	Dennis Bowen
Betty Cooper	Audrey Landers
Veronica Lodge	Hilary Thompson
Reggie Mantle	Mark Winkworth
Jughead Jones	Derrel Maury
Midge	Susan Blu
Moose	Jim Boelsen
Mr. Weatherbee	Byron Webster
Miss Grundy	Jane Lambert
Mr. Andrews	Gordon Jump

Producer: James Komack, George Yanok

Are You Positive?

Game; 30 min; NBC 7/6/52 to 8/24/52

Celebrity panelists attempt to identify well known personalities from their baby pictures.

Host: Bill Stern, Frank Coniff

Panelists: Jimmy Cannon, Frank Frisch, Lefty Gomez

The Arena

Comedy Pilot; 30 min; ABC 6/27/86

The misadventures of Max Harrison, the manager of The Arena, an old sports facility fraught with problems.

Max Harrison	Ted Bessell
Lorraine Lemelle	Teresa Ganzel
Gus Leodas	Jimmy Briscoe
Cannonball Reghetti	Kevin Scannell
Johnny Vega	Mario Lopez
Bernie Sagowitz	Lou Jacobi
Dolores	Linda Thompson-Jenner
Sidney	H. B. Haggerty
Sheldon	Jay S. York

Producer: Paul Junger Witt, Tony Thomas

Ark II

Adventure; 30 min; CBS 9/11/76 to 8/25/79

The efforts of three scientists to "bring the hope of the new future to mankind" after the Earth falls ruin to pollution in the year 2476.

Jonah	Terry Lester
Ruth	Jean Marie Hon
Samuel	Jose Flores

Producer: Norm Prescott, Lou Scheimer

Arlene Dahl's Beauty Spot

A daily five minute women's program (ABC 9/27/65 to 6/24/66) of beauty tips and advice with actress Arlene Dahl.

The Arlene Francis Show

Variety; 30 min; NBC 8/12/57 to 2/21/58

Music and interviews with hostess Arlene Francis and the music of the Norman Paris Trio.

Armchair Detective

Game; 30 min; CBS 7/6/49 to 9/28/49

Object: For players to solve criminal cases based on partial reenactments of the actual crime.

Det. Jonas Flint	Cy Kendall
Insp. Harrison	Jerome Sheldon
Mr. Crime Attorney	H. Allen Smith
Mr. Crime Investigator	John Milton Kennedy

Producer: Mike Stokey

The Armstrong Circle Theatre

Anthology; 60 min; NBC 1/6/50 to 6/25/57
CBS 10/2/57 to 8/28/63

A series of quality dramas, sponsored by Armstrong, and featuring such stars as Cara Williams, Anne Jackson, Cloris Leachman, Grace Kelly, Leslie Nielsen, Jackie Cooper, Ed Begley, James Dean, Joanne Woodward, Darren McGavin, Lois Nettleton, Elizabeth Montgomery, and Patty Duke.

Host: Nelson Case, Douglas Edwards, Ron Cochran, Henry Hamilton

Producer: Robert Costello, Jacqueline Babbin, Ralph Nelson, George Simpson, Selig Alkon

Arnie

Comedy; 30 min; CBS 9/19/70 to 9/9/72

When a new department is created at the Continental Flange Company, dock foreman Arnie Nuvo is chosen to run it. Stories relate Arnie's misadventures as he attempts to run his new department.

Arnie Nuvo	Herschel Bernardi
Lillian Nuvo	Sue Ane Langdon
Andrea Nuvo	Stephanie Steele
Richard Nuvo	Del Russell
Hamilton Majors	Roger Bowen
Julius	Tom Pedi
Neil Ogilvie	Herbert Voland
Fred Springer	Olan Soule
Felicia Farfas	Elaine Shore
Randy Robinson	Charles Nelson Reilly

Producer: E. Duke Vincent, Bruce Johnson, David Swift

Arnold's Closet Revue

Comedy Pilot; 30 min; NBC 8/30/71

Blackouts and sketches that satirize everyday life.

Host: Arte Johnson

Regulars: Joyce Bulifant, Bonnie Boland, Jim Connell, Joan Gerber, Chuck McCann, Fred Smoot, Frank Welker

Producer: George Schlatter

Around the World in 80 Days

Cartoon; 30 min; NBC 9/9/72 to 9/1/73

In an attempt to win the hand of the lovely Belinda Maze, adventurer Phineas Fogg accepts her father's challenge to travel around the world within eighty days. Stories relate Fogg's efforts to complete the trip despite the efforts of the evil Mr. Fix to delay him.

Phineas Fogg	Alastair Duncan
Jean Pasepartout	Ross Higgins
Mister Fix	Max Obestein

Producer: Walter Hucker

Arrest and Trial

Crime Drama; 90 min; ABC 9/15/63 to 9/13/64

Two interwoven series that relate police apprehension methods in "The Arrest" and the courtroom hearing in "The Trial."

Sgt. Nick Anderson	Ben Gazzara
John Egan	Chuck Connors
Jerry Miller	John Kerr
Dan Kirby	Roger Perry
Janet Okada	Jo Anne Miya
Mitchell Harris	Don Galloway

Producer: Frank P. Rosenberg

Art and Mrs. Bottle

Experimental; 80 min; NBC 9/14/39

The romantic escapades of a middle-class English family.

Mother	Ann Revere
Father	Jake Gray
Daughter	Katherine Emery
Son	Tom Speidel
Artist	Carl Gose
Maid	Dorothy Matthews

Producer: Donald Davis

The Art Ford Show

Game; 30 min; NBC 7/28/51 to 9/15/51

The object calls for three disc jockeys, playing for home viewers, to answer questions based on songs.

Host: Art Ford

Assistant: Arlene Cunningham

Panelists: Fred Robbins, Johnny Syme, Hal Moore

Music: The Archie Koty Trio

Producer: Ray Buffum

The Art Linkletter Show

Variety; 30 min; NBC 12/29/69 to 9/25/70

A daily series of music, songs, and chatter with Art Linkletter and his son Jack, and regulars Carl Reiner and Joyce Meadows. Produced by John Guedel.

Art Linkletter's House Party

Variety; 30 min; CBS 9/1/52 to 9/5/69

A long-running CBS daytime series of music, interviews, and audience participation with Art Linkletter, announcer Jack Slattery, and the music of the Muzzy Marcellino Trio. Produced by John Guedel.

Arthur Godfrey and Friends

Variety; 60 min; CBS 1/12/49 to 6/6/56

An informal program of music, songs, comedy and chatter.

Host: Arthur Godfrey

Regulars: Pat Boone, Marion Marlowe, Janette Davis, Julius LaRosa, Johnny Nash, Lu Ann Simms, Allen Case, Carmel Quinn, Dottie Schwartz, The McGuire Sisters, The Chordettes, The Mariners

Music: Archie Bleyer, Neil Hefti

Arthur Godfrey and His Ukulele

Variety; 30 min; CBS 4/4/50 to 6/30/50

An informal program of music and chatter with Arthur Godfrey and the Archie Bleyer Orchestra.

The Arthur Godfrey Show

Variety; 60 min; CBS 9/23/58 to 2/24/59

A casual program of music and chatter.

Host: Arthur Godfrey

Regulars: Johnny Nash, Lani Nill

Announcer: Tony Marvin

Orchestra: Dick Hyman

Arthur Godfrey Time

Variety; 30 min; CBS 1/7/52 to 4/24/59

Arthur Godfrey as host of a casual program of music and chatter. Produced by Will Roland.

Arthur Godfrey's Talent Scouts

Variety; 30 min; CBS 12/6/48 to 7/21/58

Performances by undiscovered professional talent.

Host: Arthur Godfrey

Vocalists: The Holidays

Orchestra: Archie Bleyer

Announcer: Tony Marvin

Producer: Irving Mansfield, Jack Carney

Arthur Murray's Dance Party

A weekly program of dance music, instruction and contests. Aired on ABC, CBS, DuMont and NBC on various dates from 7/20/50 through 9/6/60.

Hostess: Kathryn Murray

Regulars: Arthur Murray, Joyce Bulifant, Bil and Cora Baird, Arnold Stang, Teresa Brewer, Victor Borge, Lauritz Melchoir, Fran Warren, Jeri Gale, Mary Beth Hughes, Jack Norton, David Street

Announcer: Ted Brown

Orchestra: Ray Carter, Emil Coleman, Stanley Melba

Producer: Arthur Murray, Howard Barnes, West Hooker

Ask Me Another

Game; 30 min; NBC 7/3/52 to 9/25/52

Object: For players to identify sports figures through indirect question-and-answer rounds.

Host: Joe Boland

Panel: Kay Westfall, Tom Duggan, Warren Brown

The Asphalt Cowboy

Crime Drama Pilot; 60 min; NBC 12/7/80

The exploits of Max Culpepper, owner of the Culpepper Security Service, as he attempts (in the pilot) to solve the murder of a friend.

Max Culpepper	Max Baer
Molly Culpepper	Lory Walsh
Rosie Culpepper	Robin Dearden
Meg Culpepper	Lori Lowe
Sgt. Brown	Noah Beery
Lt. Lassiter	James Luisi
Charles Van Heuran	Richard Denning
Annie Van Heuran	Jennifer Holmes
Rita	Kathy Shea

Producer: Michael Fisher

The Asphalt Jungle

Crime Drama; 60 min; ABC 4/2/61 to 9/29/61

The assignments of detectives attached to The Metropolitan Squad, a crime busting unit of the N.Y.P.D.

Matthew Gower	Jack Warden
Gus Honochek	Arch Johnson
Danny Keller	Bill Smith

Producer: Arthur Lewis

Assignment: Earth

Science Fiction Pilot; 60 min; NBC 3/29/68

The story of Gary Seven, a human trained by aliens to protect mankind from itself. Aired on "Star Trek."

Gary Seven	Robert Lansing
Roberta Lincoln	Teri Garr

Producer: Gene Roddenberry

Assignment: Foreign Legion

Anthology; 30 min; Syn. 9/57

Merle Oberon as a correspondent reporting incidents in the lives of the men of the French Foreign Legion during World War II. Produced by Anthony Bartley.

Assignment: Manhunt

Varying stories of police work in action. Produced by Julian Claman and broadcast on NBC from 7/14/51 to 8/23/52.

Assignment: Underwater

Adventure; 30 min; Syn. 9/60

The story of Bill Greer, an ex-marine turned owner of the "Lively Lady," a charter boat for hire.

Bill Greer	Bill Williams
Patty Greer (his daughter)	Diane Mountford

Music: Alec Compinsky

Producer: Bernard Glasser, Mort Zarcoff

Assignment: Vienna

Adventure; 60 min; ABC 9/28/72 to 6/9/73

The series, set in Vienna, Austria, tells the story of Jake Webster, a U.S. government agent who poses as the owner of Jake's Bar and Grill, as he helps people in trouble. Aired on "The Men."

Jake Webster	Robert Conrad
	Roy Scheider*
Maj. Bernard	
Caldwell	Charles Cioffi
	Richard Basehart*
Insp. Hoffman	Anton Diffring

Producer: Eric Bercovici, Jerry Ludwig

*TV Movie role (4/30/72, "Assignment: Munich").

The Associates

Comedy; 30 min; ABC 9/23/79 to 4/17/80

The misadventures of the legal staff of the Bass and Marshall law offices in Manhattan.

Emerson Marshall	Wilfrid Hyde-White
Sara James	Shelley Smith
Leslie Dunn	Alley Mills
Tucker Kerwin	Martin Short
Eliot Streeter	Joseph Regalbuto
Johnny Danko	Tim Thornton

Theme Vocal ("Wall Street Blues"): B. B. King

Producer: James L. Brooks, Stan Daniels, Ed Weinberger

Astro Boy

Cartoon; 30 min; Syn. 9/63

When his wife and son are killed in a car accident, Dr. Boynton builds an indestructible robot (Astro Boy) for companionship. When the robot fails to mature, Boynton sells it to a circus. Shortly after, Dr. Elefun acquires it and instills it with human qualities. Eventually Dr. Elefun creates his robot sister, Astro Girl. Stories relate their battle against evil. The first Japanese-produced series to become a hit in the U.S.

Astro Boy/Astro Girl	Billie Lou Watt
Dr. Elefun	Ray Owens

Producer: Osamu Tezuka

The Astronaut Show

Cartoon; 30 min; Syn. 9/65

The story of a friendly alien who is sent to Earth to help mankind.

Astronaut	Dayton Allen
Oscar/Luno/Tim/	
Gadmouse	Bob McFadden

Producer: Bill Weiss

The Astronauts

Comedy Pilot; 30 min; CBS 8/11/82

The experiences of three astronauts assigned to Scilab, an earth-orbiting NASA probe.

Roger Canfield	Granville Van Dusen
Jennifer Tate	Brianne Leary
David Ackroyd	Bruce Davison
Col. Michael Booker	McLean Stevenson
Scotty	Nathan Cook

Producer: Rod Parker, Hal Cooper

The A-Team

Adventure; 60 min; NBC 1/23/83 to 3/8/87

In Vietnam in 1972, a crack military unit (the A-Team) is arrested and imprisoned on false charges. Shortly after, they escape and retreat to the Los Angeles underground. There, they establish themselves as soldiers of fortune and, though still wanted by the military, aid people who are unable to turn to the authorities for help.

Three years later, the team is captured, tried, and convicted. Through a clever maneuver, the team (Hannibal, B.A., and Peck) escape and find a chance for freedom when a retired general (Stockwell) offers them a full pardon if they will perform certain missions for the government. Stories relate their exploits as they encompass their military skills to accomplish their missions.

John "Hannibal" Smith	George Peppard
Bosco "B.A." Baracus	Mr. T (Lawrence Tero)
Templeton Peck (Faceman)	Tim Dunigan
	Dirk Benedict
H. M. Murdock	Dwight Schultz
Amy Allen	Melinda Culea
Tawnia Baker	Marla Heasley
Gen. Hunt Stockwell	Robert Vaughn
Frankie Santana	Eddie Velez
Col. Roderick Decker	Lance LeGault
Col. Lynch	William Lucking
Captain Crane	Carl Franklin

Producer: Stephen J. Cannell

At Ease

Comedy Pilot; 30 min; CBS 9/7/76

The story of Sgt. Henry Rumsey, a 27-year Army veteran, as he struggles to bridge the generation gap that exists between himself and his young recruits.

Sgt. Henry Rumsey	Dick O'Neill
Agnes Rumsey	Peg Shirley
Stacy Rumsey	Kathleen Beller
Cpl. Harvey Green	Danny Goldman
Lt. Block	Kenneth Gilman
Pvt. Albert Franklin	Roy Applegate

Producer: Jay Benson

At Ease

Comedy; 30 min; ABC 3/4/83 to 7/15/83

The antics of Tyrone Valentine, a conniving sergeant (at Camp Tar Creek, Texas) as he attempts to profit from his hitch in the Army.

Sgt. Tyrone Valentine	Jimmie Walker
Pvt. Tony Baker	David Naughton
Maj. Hawkins	Richard Jaeckel
Col. Clarence Clapp	Roger Bowen
Pvt. Maxwell	Josh Mostel
Cpl. Lola Grey	Jourdan Fremin
Pvt. Cardinal	John Vargas
Cpl. Wessel	George Wyner

Producer: Aaron Spelling, Douglas S. Cramer

The At Home Show

Variety; 15 min; CBS 9/14/49 to 6/7/50
ABC 8/30/51 to 9/21/52

Earl Wrightson as the host of a program of music and songs with the Norman Paris Trio.

The At Liberty Club

Variety; 15 min; NBC 6/25/48 to 9/16/48

A weekly songfest with Parisian singer Jacqueline Turner and regulars Shara DeVries and Gordon Gaines. Produced by E. Roger Muir.

At the Movies

A syndicated (1982) movie review series with hosts Roger Ebert and Gene Siskel (1982–86) and Rex Reed and Bill Harris (1986–).

At Your Service

Comedy Pilot; 30 min; CBS 8/3/64

The story of James Devlin, the owner of a tourist service bureau in Paris that helps Americans in trouble.

James Devlin	Van Johnson
Michel	Marcel Dalio
Gloria Miles	Jan Sterling
Penny Miles	Judi Meredith

Producer: Gene Kelly

At Your Service

Comedy Pilot; 30 min; NBC 8/1/84

Would-be series about the staff of a wealthy woman who take charge of her mansion when she is away.

Barbara Stonehill	Barbara Rush
Jerry Bianco	Derek McGrath
Audrey Ritter	Megan Gallagher
Dwayne	Garrett Morris
Albert Vogel	Joseph Maher
Theresa	Maria DuVall
Susan Ottinger	Susan Kellerman

Producer: Gary Nardino, David Lloyd

The Atom Ant/Secret Squirrel Show

Cartoon; 30 min; NBC 10/2/65 to 9/7/68

The adventures of Atom Ant, the world's mightiest insect, and Secret Squirrel, an undercover agent.

Atom Ant	Howard Morris
	Don Messick
Secret Squirrel	Mel Blanc
Morocco Mole	Paul Frees

Producer: William Hanna, Joseph Barbera

The Atom Squad

Adventure; 15 min; NBC 7/6/53 to 1/22/54

The exploits of the Atom Squad, a secret organization established to combat cosmic invaders.

Steve Elliott	Bob Hastings
Assistant	Bob Courtleigh
Assistant	Bram Nossem

Producer: Adrian Samish

Auction Aire

Game; 30 min; ABC 9/30/49 to 6/23/50

Audience members bid for expensive merchandise items via an auction.

Host: John Gregson

Assistant: Rebel Randall

Producer: Paul Masterson, Ralph Nelson

Aunt Jenny's Real Life Stories

Drama Pilot; 30 min; CBS 11/20/45

Dramas based on real life stories as told by a kindly woman (Aunt Jenny).

Aunt Jenny	Eve Spencer
Calvin	Bill Adams

Producer: Worthington Miner

Automan

Adventure; 60 min; ABC 12/15/83 to 4/9/84

Walter Nebicher, head of the computer department of the L.A.P.D., creates Automan, a three-dimensional holographic image that is designed to be the perfect sleuth. The force for good created by Walter is accompanied by Cursor, a glowing hexagon that chases beautiful women and creates whatever Automan

requests. Stories relate Walter and Automan's battle against crime.

Off. Walter Nebicher	Desi Arnaz Jr.
Automan	Chuck Wagner
Off. Roxanne	
Caldwell	Heather McNair
Lt. Jack Curtis	Robert Lansing
Capt. E. G. Boyd	Gerald S.
	O'Loughlin
Walter's landlady	Gloria LeRoy
Girl Cursor Eyes in	
Opening Theme	Angela Aames

Producer: Glen A. Larson, Larry Brody

The Avenger

Unaired Pilot; 30 min; Produced in 1950

The story of Jim Brandon, a chemist who battles crime via a diffusion capsule he invented that cloaks him a black light of invisibility.

Jim Brandon	Malcolm Thorne

The Avengers

Adventure; 60 min; ABC 3/28/66 to 9/1/66
1/20/67 to 9/1/67
1/10/68 to 9/15/69

When drug dealers kill his fiancée, Dr. David Keel sets out to find her murderers. During his investigation, he meets John Steed, a Ministry agent who is seeking the same culprits. The two form a partnership and set out to avenge crimes.

One year later, following Keel's departure, anthropologist Catherine Gale returns to England when her husband is killed in Kenya. There, she takes a position with the British Museum and, although an amateur, is teamed with the professional John Steed to battle evil and help the victims of crime.

Shortly after Catherine resigns, Steed becomes involved in a minor car accident with Emma Peel, a beautiful, wealthy widow who teams with him for the sheer love of adventure. When Emma's husband Peter, a test pilot believed to have been killed in a crash, returns to her, Steed is teamed with Tara King, a shapely agent. Stories relate their adventures as they avenge crimes against the British government.

John Steed	Patrick Macnee
Emma Peel	Diana Rigg
Tara King	Linda Thorson
Mother (Steed's superior)	Patrick Newell
Rhonda (Mother's aide)	Rhonda Parker
Catherine Gale*	Honor Blackman
David Keel*	Ian Hendry

Producer: Leonard White, Julian Wintle, Brian Clemens, Albert Fennell

*Video-taped black and white episodes not seen in the U.S. (1961–65).

Award Theatre

A syndicated (1958) series of repeat dramas from "Alcoa Theatre."

Away We Go

Variety; 60 min; CBS 6/3/67 to 9/2/67

A weekly series of music and comedy with hosts Buddy Greco and George Carlin and the orchestra of Allyn Ferguson.

Baby Crazy

Comedy Pilot; 30 min; ABC 8/19/66

The midsadventures of Joan Terry, the nurse-receptionist for a young pediatrician (Peter Cooper).

Joan Terry	Joan Blondell
Dr. Peter Cooper	James Stacy
Jennie Winton	Lynn Loring
Charles Norwood	Gavin MacLeod
Jimmy	Ronnie Dapo
Linda Jayne	Pamelyn Ferdin

The Baby Game

Game; 30 min; ABC 12/4/67 to 7/12/68

Object: For players to predict the reactions of children to specific situations.

Host: Richard Hayes

Baby, I'm Back!

Comedy; 30 min; CBS 1/30/78 to 8/12/78

Seven years after deserting his family, Ray Ellis returns home seeking to regain his wife (Olivia) and children's (Angie and Jordan) love. Stories relate Ray's efforts to prove he can be a good husband.

Ray Ellis	Demond Wilson
Olivia Ellis	Denise Nicholas
Angie Ellis	Kim Fields
Jordan Ellis	Tony Holmes
Luzelle Carter	Helen Martin
Col. Wallace Dickey	Ed Hall

Producer: Charles Fries, Sandy Krinski

Baby Makes Five

Comedy; 30 min; ABC 4/1/83 to 4/29/83

The story of Eddie and Jennie Riddle, a married couple with five children, numerous expenses and a limited income, as they struggle to make ends meet.

Eddie Riddle	Peter Scolari
Jennie Riddle	Louise Williams
Laura Riddle	Emily Moultrie
Annie Riddle	Brandy Gold
Michael Riddle	Andre Gower
Blanche Riddle	Janis Paige

Producer: Mort Lachman, Sy Rosen

Bachelor at Law

Comedy Pilot; 30 min; CBS 6/5/73

The story of Ben Sikes, a recent law school graduate, as he begins his career as an attorney.

Ben Sikes	John Ritter
Ellen Brandon	Sarah Kennedy
Matthew Brandon	Harold Gould
Gloria Farrell	Betsy Von Furstenburg
Mr. Woodward	Bill Zuckert
Mrs. Woodward	Kathleen O'Malley

Producer: Ed Weinberger

Bachelor Father

Comedy; 30 min; CBS 9/15/57 to 6/11/58
NBC 6/18/58 to 9/19/61
ABC 10/3/61 to 9/25/62

Following the death of her parents in a car accident, 13-year-old Kelly becomes the ward of her uncle Bentley, a sophisticated bachelor attorney living in Beverly Hills. Stories relate

Bentley's efforts to raise his orphaned niece. See also "New Girl in His Life."

Bentley Gregg	John Forsythe
Kelly Gregg	Noreen Corcoran
Peter Tong	Sammee Tong
Howard Meechim	Jimmy Boyd
Ginger	Bernadette Winters
Vickie	Alice Backus
Kitty Devereaux	Shirley Mitchell
	Jane Nigh
Kitty Marsh	Sue Ane Langdon
Connie	Sally Mansfield
Chuck Forrest	Pat McCaffrie
Gloria (later Lila)	Cheryl Holdridge
Charlie Fong	Victor Sen Yung
Frank Curtis	Harry Von Zell
Warren Dawson	Aaron Kincaid

Producer: Everett Freeman, Harry Ackerman, Robert Sparks

Back the Fact

Game; 30 min; ABC 10/22/53 to 11/26/53

Object: For players to back the facts they are relaying during interviews if an offstage voice interrupts them and asks for proof of a statement.

Host: Joey Adams

Co-Host: Hope Lange

Announcer: Carl Caruso

Producer: Jack Barry, Dan Enright, Fred W. Friendly

Back Together

Comedy Pilot; 30 min; CBS 1/25/84

When the late Herkie Burke is classified alive by a celestial computer, he is forced to remain on earth until a correction can be made. The unsold series was to relate Herkie's antics as he spends his interim period with friends Elliott and Anne Harrington.

Herkie Burke	Paul Provenza
Elliott Harrington	Jamie Widdoes
Anne Harrington	Gracie Harrison
Dora Holloway	Lisa Jane Persky
Mr. Christopher	Richard Hamilton

Producer: Charlie Hauck

B.A.D. Cats

Crime Drama; 60 min; ABC 1/14/80 to 2/8/80

The exploits of Ocee James, Samantha Jensen, and Nick Donovan, members of the Burglary Auto Detail, Commercial Auto Thefts division of the L.A.P.D.

Ocee James	Steven Hanks
Samantha Jensen	Michelle Pfeiffer
Nick Donovan	Asher Brauner
Capt. Eugene Nathan	Vic Morrow
Rodney Washington	Jimmie Walker
Ma	LaWanda Page

Producer: Aaron Spelling, Douglas S. Cramer

The Bad News Bears

Comedy; 30 min; CBS 3/24/79 to 7/26/80

The antics of the W. Wendell Weaver School Bears, an undisciplined Little League baseball team.

Morris Buttermaker	Jack Warden
Emily Rappant	Catherine Hicks
Roy Turner	Philip R. Allen
Amanda Wurlitzer	Tricia Cast
Tanner Boyle	Meeno Peluce
Rudi Stein	Billy Jacoby
Regi Tower	Corey Feldman
Timothy Lupus	Shane Butterworth
Ahmad Abdual Rahim	Christoff St. John
Mike Engelberg	J. Brennan Smith
Kelly Leak	Gregg Forrest
Josh Matthews	Rad Daly

Producer: Arthur Silver, Bob Brunner

Baffle

Game; 30 min; NBC 3/26/73 to 3/29/74

Object: For players to identify phrases via letters that are placed on a board by their teammate. Players who identify phrases in the least amount of time win.

Host: Dick Enberg

Announcer: Kenny Williams

Baggy Pants and the Nitwits

Cartoon; 30 min; NBC 9/10/77 to 10/28/79

The "Baggy Pants" segment relates the antics of a Charlie Chaplin-like hobo cat; "The Nitwits" tells of Tyrone, a semi-retired super hero struggling to battle crime.

Tyrone	Arte Johnson
Gladys	Ruth Buzzi

Producer: David DePatie, Friz Freleng

Bailey's Comets

Cartoon; 30 min; NBC 9/8/73 to 1/26/74

The adventures of the Bailey's Comets roller derby team as they compete in a contest to win $1,000,000.

Voices: Sarah Kennedy, Don Messick, Daws Butler, Karen Smith, Robert Holt, Frank Welker

Producer: Friz Freleng, David DePatie

The Baileys of Balboa

Comedy; 30 min; CBS 9/24/64 to 4/1/65

The bickering relationship between Sam Bailey, captain of a decrepit charter boat ("The Island Princess"), and Cecil Wyntoon, commodore of the high-class Balboa Beach Yachting Club.

Sam Bailey	Paul Ford
Cecil Wyntoon	John Dehner
Barbara Wyntoon	Judy Carne
Jim Bailey	Les Brown Jr.
Buck Singleton	Sterling Holloway

Producer: Bob Sweeney

Baker's Dozen

Comedy; 30 min; CBS 3/17/82 to 3/31/82

The experiences of Terry Munson and Mike Locasale, lovers and police officers with the Anti Crime Unit of the N.Y.P.D.

Off. Terry Munson	Cindy Weintraub
Off. Mike Locasale	Ron Silver
Capt. Florence Baker	Doris Belack
Off. Otis Kelly	Alan Weeks
Off. Harry Schoendorf	Sam McMurray

Producer: Nick Arnold, Larry Gross

Balance Your Budget

Game; 30 min; CBS 10/18/52 to 5/2/53

Object: For housewives to win their yearly household budget by answering a series of questions.

Host: Bert Parks

Assistant: Lynn Connor

Producer: Louis Cowan, Peter Arnell

Ball Four

Comedy; 30 min; CBS 9/22/76 to 10/27/76

A satire on major league baseball as seen through the antics of the Washington Americans, a disorganized team.

Jim Barton	Jim Bouton
Rayford Plunkett	Marco St. John
Ben Rhinelander	Ben Davidson
C. B. Travis	Sam Wright
Orlando Lopez	Jamie Tirelli
Harold Pinkney	Bill McCutceson
Cap Capogrosso	Jack Somack
Bill Westlake	David-James Carroll
Lenny "Birdman" Siegel	Lennie Schultz

Producer: Don Segall

The Banana Company

Comedy Pilot; 30 min; CBS 8/25/77

The misadventures of a group of W.W. II combat correspondents (the Banana Company) who go to outrageous lengths to acquire stories.

Maj. Platt	Ted Gehring
Capt. Harry Gill	John Reilly
Peebles	Gailard Sartain
Segal	Sam Chew Jr.
Muldoon	Ron Masak

Producer: Carroll O'Connor

The Banana Splits Adventure Hour

Cartoon; 60 min; NBC 9/7/68 to 9/5/70

The overall title for: "The Banana Splits" (antics of Fleegle, Bingo, Drooper and Snorky); "The Micro Venture" (Prof. Carter explores the microscopic world); "Danger Island" (live segment about archeologist Irwin

Hayden); "The Three Musketeers" (D'Artagnan and the exploits of the Three Musketeers); "The Hillbilly Bears" (a family of backwoods bears); and "The Arabian Knights" (animated legends).

Fleegle	Paul Winchell
Bingo	Daws Butler
Drooper	Allan Melvin
Snorky	Don Messick
Prof. Carter	Don Messick
Irwin Hayden	Frank Aletter
Leslie Hayden	Ronne Troup
Link Simmons	Jan-Michael Vincent
D'Artagnan	Bruce Watson
Porthos	Barney Phillips
Aramis	Don Messick
Athos	Jonathan Harris
Paw Rugg	Henry Corden
Maw Rugg/Flora Rugg	Jean VanderPyl
Shagg Rugg	Don Messick

Producer: William Hanna, Joseph Barbera

Banacek

Crime Drama; 90 min; NBC 9/13/72 to 9/3/74

The exploits of Thomas Banacek, an insurance investigator who recovers stolen merchandise for ten percent of its value.

Thomas Banacek	George Peppard
Felix Mulholland	Murray Matheson
Jay Drury	Ralph Manza
Carlie Kirkland	Christine Belford

Producer: George Eckstein

Bandstand

A live daytime variety series (NBC 7/30/56 to 11/23/56) with host Bert Parks and the music of Tex Beneke.

Bank on the Stars

Game; 30 min; CBS 6/20/53 to 5/8/54
NBC 5/15/54 to 8/21/54

Object: For players to answer questions based on film clips.

Host: Jack Paar, Bill Cullen, Jimmy Nelson

Banyon

Crime Drama; 60 min; NBC 9/15/72 to 1/12/73

The exploits of Miles C. Banyon, a detective in Los Angeles in 1937.

Miles C. Banyon	Robert Forster
Sgt. Peter McNeil	Richard Jaeckel
Peggy Revere	Joan Blondell
Abby Graham	Julie Gregg

Producer: Quinn Martin

Barbapapa

Cartoon; 30 min; Syn. 1981

The adventures of a family of creatures who grow from the ground and are able to change their forms.

Narrator: Allen Swift

Voices: Ann Costello, Alexander Marshall, Allen Swift

Producer: Annette Tilson

The Barbara Eden Show

Comedy Pilot; 30 min; ABC 5/21/73

The story of Barbara Norris, a beautiful divorcee who writes a TV soap opera.

Barbara Norris	Barbara Eden
Matthew Norris	Moosie Drier
Brad Newton	Joe Flynn
Barry Michaels	Lyle Waggoner
Ralph Green	Roger Perry

Producer: Michael Ansara

Barbara Mandrell and the Mandrell Sisters

Variety; 60 min; NBC 11/18/80 to 6/26/82

An entertaining series featuring Barbara Mandrell and her sisters Louise and Irlene.

Hostess: Barbara, Louise, and Irlene Mandrell

Regulars: Georgi Irene, Melanie Gaffin, Jackie Joseph, Bill Kirchenbauer, The Krofft Puppets

Orchestra: Dennis McCarthy

Producer: Sid & Marty Krofft

The Barbara McNair Show

A weekly variety program (Syn. 1969) with singer Barbara McNair, her announcer Ronald Long, and the Coleridge Parkinson Orchestra. Produced by David Winters and Jorn Winter.

The Barbara Rush Show

Comedy Pilot; 30 min; CBS 7/9/65

The story of Barbara Warren, a housewife who struggles to support her medical student husband by working as a public stenographer.

Barbara Warren	Barbara Rush
Matt Warren	Bob Fortier
Marsden	Alan Napier

Producer: Tony Owen

The Barbara Stanwyck Theatre

Anthology; 30 min; NBC 9/19/60 to 9/11/61

A series of varying productions featuring such stars as Yvonne Craig, Susan Oliver, Lloyd Nolan, Vic Morrow, Milton Berle, Anna May Wong, Robert Culp, Joan Blondell, and Peter Falk.

Hostess: Barbara Stanwyck

Producer: Louis F. Edelman, William Wright

The Barbary Coast

Adventure; 60 min; ABC 9/8/75 to 1/9/76

The exploits of Jeff Cable, an agent for the governor of California, and Cash Canover, owner of the Golden Gate casino, as they battle crime on San Francisco's notorious Barbary Coast of the 1880s.

Jeff Cable	William Shatner
Cash Canover	Dennis Cole*
	Doug McClure
Moose Moran	Richard Kiel
Thumbs	Dave Turner
Brandy	Francine York
Rusty	Brooke Mills
Flame	Bobbi Jordan

Producer: Cy Chermak, Douglas Heyes

*TV Movie role (5/4/75).

Barbie and the Rockers

Cartoon Pilot; 60 min; Syn. 12/87

A proposed series, based on the Barbie doll toy, that follows the adventures of Barbie, a fabulously successful rock singer, and her group, The Rockers (Ken, Didi, Diva, and Derek).

Barbie	Sharon Lewis

Other Voices: John Stocker, Veena Sood, Debbie Lick, Nikki Sharp, Lynn Johnson, John Payne, Victoria Langston, Catherine Mead

Producer: Andy Heyward, Haim Saban

Bare Essence

Drama; 60 min; NBC 2/15/83 to 6/13/83

The power, intrigue, and romance behind the scenes of a conglomerate (Kellcro) that ventures into international perfume manufacturing.

Patricia "Tyger" Hayes	Genie Francis
Ava Marshall	Lee Grant*
	Jessica Walter
Bobbi Rowan	Linda Evans*
	Jennifer O'Neill
Barbara Fisher	Donna Mills*
	Jamie Lyn Bauer
Chase Marshall	Bruce Boxleitner*
	Al Corley
Hadden Marshall	John Dehner
Margaret Marshall	Susan French
Niko Theophilis	Ian McShane
Sean Benedict	Michael Woods
Laura Parker	Penny Fuller
Muffin	Wendy Fuller
Kathy	Laura Berneau

Producer: Walter Grauman

*TV Movie role (CBS, 10/4 & 10/5/82).

Barefoot in the Park

Comedy; 30 min; ABC 9/24/70 to 1/14/71

The story of Paul and Corie Bratter, newlyweds struggling to survive the difficult first years of marriage. Based on the movie.

Paul Bratter	Scoey Mitchlll
Corie Bratter	Tracy Reed
Honey Robinson	Nipsey Russell
Mabel Bates	Thelma Carpenter
Arthur Kendricks	Harry Holcombe
Mr. Velasquez	Vito Scotti

Producer: William P. D'Angelo

Barefoot in the Park

Comedy Pilot; 30 min; Unaired; Produced in 1969

The original pilot for the prior series, which see for storyline. An edited version of the pilot aired as "Love and the Good Deal" on "Love, American Style" (11/24/69).

Corie Bratter	Skye Aubrey
Paul Bratter	Philip Clarke
Corie's Mother	Jane Wyatt
Mr. Velasco	Hans Conried
Lewis	Norman Fell
Harry	Frank Campanella
Armand	Felix Locher

Producer: Garry K. Marshall

Baretta

Crime Drama; 60 min; ABC 1/17/75 to 6/1/78

The exploits of Tony Baretta, an undercover police detective in an unidentified eastern city.

Tony Baretta	Robert Blake
Billy Truman	Tom Ewell
Insp. Schiller	Dana Elcar
Lt. Hal Brubaker	Edward Glover
Rooster	Michael D. Roberts
Mimi Ames	Sharon Cintron
Det. Foley	John Ward
Fats	Chino Williams
Fred (cockatoo)	Lala

Theme Vocal ("Keep Your Eye on the Sparrow"): Sammy Davis Jr.

Producer: Bernard L. Kowalski, Anthony Spinner

The Barkleys

Cartoon; 30 min; NBC 9/9/72 to 9/1/73

The life of Arnie Barkley, an opinionated, loudmouthed bus driver.

Arnie Barkley	Henry Corden
Agnes Barkley	Joan Gerber
Terri Barkley	Julie McWhirter
Chester Barkley	Steve Lewis
Roger Barkley	Gene Andrusco

Producer: Friz Freleng, David DePatie

Barnaby Jones

Crime Drama; 60 min; CBS 1/23/73 to 9/4/80

The exploits of Barnaby Jones, a Los Angeles-based private detective who is also an investigator for the California Maridian Insurance Company.

Barnaby Jones	Buddy Ebsen
Betty Jones	Lee Meriwether
J. R. Jones	Mark Shera
Lt. John Biddle	John Carter
Lt. Joe Taylor	Vince Howard
Various Roles	Bonnie Ebsen

Producer: Quinn Martin, Philip Saltzman

Barney and Me

Comedy Pilot; 30 min; NBC 3/19/73

In an attempt to boost his faltering ratings, kiddie show host Pete Richards incorporates a talking bear named Barney into the program. The unsold series was to relate Pete's misadventures as a kid show host.

Pete Richards	Soupy Sales
Sue	Udana Power
Jungle Johnny	Joey Forman
Barney	Janos Prohaska
Barney's Voice	Shepard Menkin

Producer: Arthur Jacobs

Barney Blake, Police Reporter

Crime Drama; 30 min; NBC 4/22/48 to 7/8/48

The exploits of Barney Blake, a New York City police reporter.

Barney Blake	Gene O'Donnell
Jennifer Allen	Judy Parrish

Producer: Wynn Wright

Barney Miller

Comedy; 30 min; ABC 1/23/75 to 9/9/82

Events in the life of Barney Miller, chief of detectives of the 12th Precinct in New York's Greenwich Village. See also "Fish."

Barney Miller	Hal Linden
Elizabeth Miller	Abby Dalton
	Barbara Barrie
Rachel Miller	Anne Wyndham
David Miller	Michael Tessier
Sgt. Phil Fish	Abe Vigoda
Bernice Fish	Florence Stanley
Sgt. Stan "Wojo" Wojehowich	Max Gail
Det. Chano Amengual	Gregory Sierra
Sgt. Nick Yemana	Jack Soo
Det. Ron Harris	Ron Glass
Insp. Frank Luger	James Gregory
Det. Janet Wentworth	Linda Lavin
Det. Battista	June Gable
Sgt. Arthur Dietrich	Steve Landesberg
Off. Carl Levitt	Ron Carey
Det. Mike Lovatti	Art Metrano
Arnold Ripner	Alex Henteloff

Producer: Danny Arnold, Theodore J. Flicker

The Baron

Mystery; 60 min; ABC 1/20/66 to 7/14/66

The story of John Mannering, an American antique dealer who investigates crimes associated with the art world.

John Mannering	Steve Forrest
Cordelia Winfield	Sue Lloyd
Templeton Greene	Colin Gordon
David Marlowe	Paul Ferris

Producer: Monty Berman

Barrier Reef

Adventure; 30 min; NBC 9/11/71 to 9/2/72

The explorations of the biologists assigned to study Australia's Great Barrier Reef.

Chet King	Joe James
Kip King	Ken James
Tracy Dean	Rowena Wallace
Elizabeth Hanna	Ihab Nafa
Diana Parker	Elli MacLure
Elizabeth Grant	Susanna Brett
Steve Goba	Howard Hopkins

Bat Masterson

Western; 30 min; NBC 10/8/58 to 9/21/61

Events in the life of William Barclay "Bat" Masterson, a wandering law enforcer during the 1880s.

Bat Masterson	Gene Barry

Announcer: Bill Baldwin

Producer: Andy White, Frank Pittman

Batfink

Cartoon; 5 min; Syn. 9/66

The exploits of Batfink as he and Karate battle evil.

Batfink	Frank Buxton
Karate	Len Maxwell

Producer: Hal Seeger

Batman

Adventure; 30 min; ABC 1/12/66 to 3/14/68

Shortly after his parents are killed by gangsters, young Bruce Wayne vows to avenge their deaths by battling crime. Years later, after constructing a great crime lab beneath Wayne Manor, Bruce adopts the secret alias of Batman. Sometime later, when the parents of young Dick Grayson are killed during a circus high wire act, Bruce adopts the orphaned boy. When Dick learns of Bruce's crusade, he joins Batman as Robin, the Boy Wonder. Years later, Barbara Gordon, daughter of Police Commissioner Gordon, decides to wage her own war on crime and adopts the secret alias of Batgirl. Stories relate the trio's exploits as they battle crime in Gotham City.

Bruce Wayne	Adam West	Batman	Adam West
Dick Grayson	Burt Ward	Robin	Burt Ward
Barbara Gordon	Yvonne Craig	Batgirl	Melendy Britt
Alfred Pennyworth	Alan Napier	Isis	Diane Pershing
Harriet Cooper	Madge Blake	Hercules	Bob Denison
Commissioner		Merlin/Sinbad/	
Gordon	Neil Hamilton	Samurai	Michael Bell
Chief O'Hara	Stafford Repp	Manta	Joe Stern
Mayor John		Moray	Joan Van Ark
Lindseed	Byron Keith	Micro Woman	Kim Hamilton
Millie Lindseed	Jean Byron	Super Stretch	Ty Henderson
The Penguin*	Burgess Meredith	Web Woman	Linda Gary
The Joker*	Cesar Romero		
The Riddler*	Frank Gorshin		
	John Astin		

Producer: Norm Prescott, Lou Scheimer

Catwoman*	Julie Newmar
	Lee Meriwether
	Eartha Kitt
Egghead*	Vincent Price
Mr. Freeze*	George Sanders
	Eli Wallach
The Siren*	Joan Collins
Louie the Lilac*	Milton Berle
King Tut*	Victor Buono
Marsha*	Carolyn Jones
The Archer*	Art Carney
Dr. Cassandra	Ida Lupino
Cabala*	Howard Duff
Lola Lasagne*	Ethel Merman
The Mad Hatter*	David Wayne
Ma Parker*	Shelley Winters
The Bookworm*	Roddy McDowall
Nora Clavicle*	Barbara Rush
Shame*	Cliff Robertson
Sophie Starr*	Kathleen Crowley

Narrator: William Dozier

Producer: William Dozier, Howie Horwitz

*Recurring criminals.

Batman and the Super Seven

Cartoon; 60 min; NBC 9/27/80 to 9/5/81

The overall title for: "Batman" and Robin as they battle evil in Gotham City; "Isis and the Freedom Force" (Goddess Isis and Hercules, Merlin, Sinbad and Super Samurai battle evil); "Manta and Moray" (two underwater crime fighters); "Micro Woman and Super Stretch" (two super heroes battling crime); and "Web Woman" (about a girl endowed by aliens with the power of all insects to battle evil).

Battle of the Ages

Game; 30 min; DuMont 1/1/52 to 6/17/52
                CBS 9/6/52 to 11/29/52

The Show Business Veterans vs. The Youngsters in a series of talent contests.

Host: John Reed King, Morey Amsterdam

Announcer: Norman Brokenshire, Arthur Van Horn

Producer: Norman Livingston, Roger Kay

Battle of the Planets

Cartoon; 30 min; Syn. 9/78

The exploits of G-Force, a defense organization, as they battle Zoltar, an alien seeking to control the universe.

7-Zark-7	Alan Young
Zoltar	Keye Luke
Mark	Casem Kasem
Princess	Janet Waldo
Keop/Jason	Ronnie Schell
Tiny	Alan Dinehart

Producer: Jameson Brewer

Battlestar Galactica

Science Fiction; 60 min; ABC 9/17/78 to 4/29/79

When the war-like mechanical Cylons defeat humans, the survivors of a far away galaxy board the battlestar spaceship Galactica and begin a search for their thirteenth colony—Earth. Stories relate their search and efforts to battle the pursuing Cylons. See also "Galactica 1980."

Commander Adama	Lorne Greene
Captain Apollo	Richard Hatch
Athena	Maren Jensen
Lt. Starbuck	Dirk Benedict
Lt. Boomer	Herb Jefferson Jr.
Col. Tigh	Terry Carter
Sgt. Jolly	Tony Swartz
Boxey	Noah Hathaway
Cassiopea	Laurette Spang
Sheba	Anne Lockhart
Baltar	John Colicos
Cylon Leader's Voice	Patrick Macnee
Imperious Leader	Dick Durock

Producer: Glen A. Larson, Leslie Stevens

Battlestars

Game; 30 min; NBC 10/26/81 to 4/23/82

Object: For players to win six triangle spaces by calling on celebrities and either agreeing or disagreeing with their answers.

Host: Alex Trebek

Announcer: Rod Roddy

Producer: Merrill Heatter

The Baxters

Drama; 30 min; Syn. 9/79

The first half dramatizes events in the lives of the Baxters, a five-member family living in St. Louis. The second fifteen minutes features a discussion with a studio audience on the particular program's theme.

Nancy Baxter	Anita Gillette
Fred Baxter	Larry Keith
Naomi Baxter	Derin Altay
Jonah Baxter	Chris Peterson
Rachel Baxter	Terri Lynn Wood

Producer: Norman Lear

The Baxters

Drama; 30 min; Syn. 9/80

A revised version of the previous title, which see for format.

Jim Baxter	Sean McCann
Suzie Baxter	Terry Tweed
Alison Baxter	Marianne McIsaac
Lucy Baxter	Megan Follows
Greg Baxter	Sammy Snyders

Producer: Chet Collier

The Bay City Amusement Company

Comedy Pilot; 30 min; NBC 7/28/77

The antics of the staff of "The Bay City Amusement Company," a locally produced, San Francisco TV series.

Ann	Barrie Youngfellow
Howie	Pat McCormick
Gail	June Gable
Bradshaw	Ted Gehring
Alan	Dennis Howard
Warren	Jim Scott
Clifford	Terry Kiser

Producer: Norman Steinberg

Bay City Blues

Comedy-Drama; 60 min; NBC 10/25/83 to 11/15/83

The off-the-field activities of the Bluebirds, a Bay City, California, minor league baseball team.

John Nuckles	Perry Lang
Ozzie Peoples	Bernie Casey
Terry St. Marie	Patrick Cassidy
Angelo Carbone	Dennis Franz
Lynwood Scott	Larry Flash Jenkins
Rocky Padillo	Ken Olin
Lee Jacoby	Tony Spiridakis
Deejay Cunningham	Mykel T. Williamson
Vic Kresky	Jeff McCracken
Bird	Marco Rodriquez
Joe Rohner	Michael Nouri
Lynn Holtz	Sheree North
Judy Nuckles	Michele Greene
Ray Holtz	Pat Corley

Producer: Steven Bochco, Gregory Hoblit

The Bay City Rollers Show

Variety; 60 min; ABC 11/4/78 to 1/27/79

Music, songs, and comedy with the Bay City Rollers rock group and regulars Billie Hayes,

Jay Robinson, Billy Barty, Paul Gale, Patty Maloney, Louise Duart, Micky McMeel, and Van Snowden. Produced by Alvin J. Tenzer, Sid and Marty Krofft.

The B. B. Beegle Show

Variety Pilot; 30 min; Syn. 1/80

An unsold series in which fifty-one puppets were to join guests in comedy sketches.

Pilot Hosts: Joyce DeWitt, Arte Johnson

Puppet Voices: Michael Bell, Marilyn Schreffler, Norman Grohmann

Producer: Joseph Barbera

The Beach Girls

Comedy Pilot; 30 min; Syn. 12/77

The story of three aspiring singers (Ginny, Sue, and Abby) as they seek fame as the singing Beach Girls.

Ginny Day	Rita Wilson
Sue Albright	Kim O'Brien
Abby Graham	Ava Lazar
Sonny Pink	Don Calfa

Producer: Joseph Barbera

The Beachcomber

Adventure; 30 min; Syn. 1961

Pressured by society, businessman John Lackland leaves San Francisco and retreats to Amura, an island in the South Pacific. Stories relate John's adventures as he becomes a beachcomber and searches for the meaning of life.

John Lackland	Cameron Mitchell
Captain Huckabee	Don Megowan
Andrew Crippen	Sebastain Cabot
	Edmond Mills
Tarmu	Jerry Summers

Producer: Nat Perrin, Robert Stambler

Beacon Hill

Drama; 60 min; CBS 8/25/75 to 11/4/75

A serial about the Lassiters, a powerful Boston family of the 1920s, and their servants, Irish immigrants who live with them.

Benjamin Lassiter	Stephen Elliott
Mary Lassiter	Nancy Marchand
Emily Bullock	DeAnn Mears
Trevor Bullock	Ray Cooper
Betsy Bullock	Linda Purl
Maude Palmer	Maeve McGuire
Richard Palmer	Edward Herrmann
Rosamond Lassiter	Kitty Wynn
Robert Lassiter	David Dukes
Fawn Lassiter	Kathryn Walker
Mr. Hacker	George Rose
Emmaline Hacker	Beatrice Straight
William Piper	Richard Ward
Brian Mallory	Paul Rudd
Kate	Lisa Pelikan

Producer: Beryl Vertue, Jacqueline Babbin

The Bean Show

Variety Pilot; 30 min; CBS 9/7/64

A proposed series of music and comedy sketches.

Host: Orson Bean

Regulars: Avery Schreiber, Mina Kolb, Richard Schaal, Arlene Golonka

Orchestra: Jack Elliott

Beane's of Boston

Comedy Pilot; 30 min; CBS 5/5/79

The antics of the staff of the Beane's of Boston Department Store.

Frank Beane	Tom Poston
John Peacock	John Hillerman
Mae Slocombe	Charlotte Rae
Franklyn Beane	George O'Hanlon Jr.
Shirley Brahms	Lorna Patterson
George Humphries	Alan Sues

Producer: Garry K. Marshall, Tony Marshall

The Beany and Cecil Show

Cartoon; 30 min; Syn. 1961
ABC 12/27/64 to 10/23/66

The adventures of Beany, a small boy, and his sidekick, Cecil the sea serpent.

Voices: Daws Butler, Don Messick, Joan Gerber, Bob Clampett

Creator-Producer: Bob Clampett

Bearcats!

Adventure; 60 min; CBS 9/16/71 to 12/30/71

The adventures of Hank Brackett and Johnny Reach, troubleshooters who roam America's Southwest in 1914.

Hank Brackett	Rod Taylor
Johnny Reach	Dennis Cole

Producer: David Freidkin, Mort Fine

Beat the Clock

Game; 30 min; CBS 3/25/50 to 9/12/58
ABC 10/13/58 to 9/26/62

Object: For contestants to perform stunts by beating the amount of time on a sixty-second ticking clock.

Host: Bud Collyer

Assistant: Roxanne Rosedale, Beverly Bentley

Beat the Clock

Game; 30 min; Syn. 9/69

Object: For players, usually married couples, to perform stunts and beat the amount of time shown on a ticking clock.

Host: Jack Narz, Gene Wood

Assistants: Diane Mead, Gail Sheldon, Betsy Hirst, Ellen Singer, Linda Somer

Beat the Clock

Game; 30 min; CBS 9/17/79 to 2/1/80

Object: For contestants to perform stunts before the amount of time on a ticking clock expires.

Host: Monty Hall

Announcer: Jack Narz

Beat the Odds

Game; 30 min; Syn. 1969

Object: For players to supply words based on two letters that are given. The first player to score 100 points receives that amount in cash.

Host: Johnny Gilbert

Announcer: Bill Baldwin

The Beatles

Cartoon; 30 min; ABC 9/25/65 to 9/27/69

Animated adventures based on the songs and lives of the Beatles.

John Lennon/George Harrison	Paul Frees
Ringo Starr/Paul McCartney	Lonie Percival

Producer: Arthur Rankin Jr., Jules Bass

The Beautiful Phyllis Diller Show

Variety; 60 min; NBC 9/15/68 to 12/22/68

Various comedy skits that satirize world problems.

Hostess: Phyllis Diller

Regulars: Norm Crosby, Rip Taylor, Dave Willock, Bob Jellison

Orchestra: Jack Elliott

Producer: Bob Finkel

Beauty and the Beast

Fantasy; 60 min; CBS 9/25/87 (Premiere)

One night, while waiting for a cab, N.Y. corporate lawyer Catherine Chandler is attacked and left for dead by thugs. She is found by a kindly man-beast (Vincent) who takes her to his subterranean world beneath Manhattan. There, Catherine is nursed back to health by Vincent and his Father, an apparent doctor who found Vincent as an infant and adopted him. Upon recovering, Catherine returns to her world (where she joins the D.A.'s office) with a promise to keep Vincent and his world a secret. Stories relate Catherine's experiences as she investigates cases—and receives the secret help of Vincent, who can preceive when she is in danger.

Catherine Chandler	Linda Hamilton
Vincent	Ron Perlman
Father	Roy Dotrice
Charles Chandler	John McMartin
Joseph Maxwell	Jay Acovone
Eddie	Ren Woods
Isaac Stubbs	Ron O'Neal

Producer: Paul Junger Witt, Tony Thomas, Ron Koslow

Bedtime Stories

Game; 30 min; Syn. 6/79

Object: For married couples to predict the highest-scoring responses to questions asked of 100 people. Correct guesses score $500.

Host: Al Lohman, Roger Barkley

Announcer: Kenny Williams, Johnny Gilbert

Producer: Merrill Heatter, Bob Quigley

Behind Closed Doors

Anthology; 30 min; NBC 10/2/58 to 4/9/59

Tales of international intrigue, hosted by Bruce Gordon as Commander Matson. Produced by Sam Gallu.

Behind the Screen

Drama; 30 min; CBS 10/9/81 to 1/8/82

The private and professional lives of those associated with "Generations," a fictional TV soap opera.

Evan Hammer	Mel Ferrer
Janie-Claire Willow	Janine Turner
Gerry Holmby	Joshua Bryant
Dory Holmby	Loyita Chapel
Brian Holmby	Michael Sabatino
Sally Dundee	Catherine Parks
Lynette Porter	Debbi Morgan
Zina Willow	Joanne Linville
Bobby Danzig	Bruce Fairbairn
Merritt Madison	Warren Stevens

Producer: David Jacobs, Michael Filerman

Believe It Or Not

Anthology; 30 min; NBC 3/1/49 to 9/28/50

Dramas based on Robert Ripley's "Believe It Or Not" newspaper column. On 1/4/50, it became a program of horror yarns based on true incidents.

Host: Robert L. Ripley, Robert St. John

Producer: Vic McLeod, Douglas Stoner, Harry Herrmann

Bell, Book, and Candle

Comedy Pilot; 30 min; NBC 9/9/76

The adventures of a beautiful young witch (Gillian).

Gillian Holroyd	Yvette Mimieux
Alex Brandt	Michael Murphy
Aunt Enid	Doris Roberts
Nicky Holroyd	John Pleshette
Lois	Bridget Hanley

Producer: Bruce Lansbury

Belle Starr

Western Pilot; 30 min; CBS 6/6/58

The story of Belle Starr, a lawless woman of the Old West who, despite her outlaw reputation, fights for right.

Belle Starr	Abby Dalton
John Carter	John Forsythe
Col. Taylor	Staats Cotsworth
Gus Garner	Claude Akins

Producer: Frank P. Rosenberg

Ben Blue's Brothers

Comedy Pilot; 30 min; CBS 6/28/65

The antics of four brothers: a henpecked industrialist; an ex-vaudevillian; a Navy man; and a Charlie Chaplin-like mute.

All Four Brothers	Ben Blue
Their mother	Ruth McDevitt

Also: Jane McGowan, Yvette Vickers

Producer: Jerry Stagg

Ben Casey

Drama; 60 min; ABC 10/2/61 to 3/21/66

The story of Ben Casey, a neurosurgeon at County General Hospital.

Dr. Ben Casey	Vince Edwards
Dr. David Zorba	Sam Jaffe
Dr. Daniel Freeland	Franchot Tone
Dr. Maggie Graham	Bettye Ackerman
Nurse Willis	Jeanne Bates
Dr. Ted Hoffman	Harry Landers
Nick Kanavaras	Nick Dennis
Dr. Terry McDaniel	Jim McMullan
Dr. Harold Jansen	Maurice Manson
	John Zaremba
Dr. Mike Rogers	Ben Piazza
Dr. David McMillan	Leo Penn
Stanley Schultz	James Dunn
Jane Hancock	
(patient)	Stella Stevens

"Ben Casey" Theme Song: David Victor

Producer: James E. Moser, Matthew Rapf, Wilton Schiller, Jack Laird

Ben Hecht's Tales of the City

Anthology; 30 min; CBS 6/25/53 to 9/17/53

Dramas hosted by and based on the stories of Ben Hecht. Produced by William Dozier and also known as "Tales of the City."

Ben Vereen . . . Comin' At Ya

Variety; 60 min; NBC 8/7/75 to 8/28/75

A program of music, songs, and comedy.

Host: Ben Vereen

Regulars: Arte Johnson, Avery Schreiber, Lola Falana, Liz Torres, Lee Lund

Orchestra: Jack Elliott, Allyn Ferguson

Producer: Jaime Rogers, Jean McAvoy

Bender

Crime Drama Pilot; 60 min; CBS 9/12/79

The exploits of Harry Bender, the police chief of Tamarisk Wells, a rich California resort town.

Harry Bender	Harry Guardino
Bert Arkins	Nicholas Coster
Wade Rawlings	Joe Burke
Joanne Clark	Susan Damante Shaw
R. J. Phillips	Stephen Elliott

Producer: Carroll O'Connor

Benji, Zax, and the Alien Prince

Children; 30 min; CBS 9/17/83 to 9/1/84

Ubi, prince of the planet Antaz, and his droid, Zax, escape from the evil Zanu and land on Earth. They meet and befriend Benji, the famous movie dog. Stories relate Benji's efforts to protect Ubi from the soldiers (Darah and Khyber) Zanu has dispatched to capture Ubi.

Ubi	Chris Burton
Darah	Angie Bolling
	Anna Holbrook
Khyber	Joe Rainer
	Dallas Miles
Zanu	Ken Miller
Zax's Voice	Ric Spiegel
Benji	Benji

Producer: Joseph Barbera

The Benny Hill Show

Comedy; 30 min; Syn. 1979

A series of adult-oriented comedy sketches culled from "The Benny Hill Show," a British series of comedy specials.

Host: Benny Hill

Regulars Include: Jackie Wright, Henry McGee, Bob Todd, Sue Bond, Diana Darvey, Samantha Stevens, Nicholas Parsons, Connie Georges, The Lady Birds, Hill's Angels

Producer: Denis Spencer

The Benny Rubin Show

Variety; 30 min; NBC 4/29/49 to 6/24/49

Guest acts are interwoven around the antics of Benny Rubin, the owner of a theatrical agency.

Benny Rubin	Himself
Vinnie	Vinnie Monte

Regulars: Jackie Coogan, Edith Fellows, Lois and Lillian Bernard

Orchestra: Rex Maupin

Producer: Jerry Rosen

Benson

Comedy; 30 min; ABC 9/13/79 to 8/30/86

Events in the life of Benson DuBois, the butler to Gene Gatling, the governor of Capitol City. Later episodes relate Benson's experiences as the budget director of the state. A spin-off from "Soap."

Benson DuBois	Robert Guillaume
Gene Gatling	James Noble
Katie Gatling	Missy Gold
Gretchen Krauss	Inga Swenson
Marcie Hill	Caroline McWilliams
Denise Stevens	Didi Conn
Clayton Endicott	Rene Auberjonois
Peter Downey	Ethan Phillips
John Taylor	Lewis J. Stalden
Mrs. Cassidy	Billie Bird
Sen. Diane Hartford	Donna LaBrie
Katie's Cousin	
Laura	Tracey Gold
Gene's Sister Libby	Dorothy Green
Benson's Brother	
Russell	Tim Reid

Producer: Tony Thomas, Paul Junger Witt, John Rich, Susan Harris

Be Our Guest

Variety; 30 min; CBS 1/27/60 to 6/1/60

The program spotlights the unknown or unusual talents of celebrities.

Host: George DeWitt, Keefe Brasselle

Vocalist: Mary Ann Mobley

Producer: Al Singer, Perry Cross

The Berenstain Bears

Cartoon; 30 min; CBS 9/14/85 (Premiere)

The adventures of the forest-dwelling Bear family, residents of the city of Beartown.

Mama Bear	Ruth Buzzi
Papa Bear	Brian Cummings
Sister Bear	Christina Lange
Brother Bear	David Mendenhall
Ratfish Ralph	Frank Welker

Producer: Buzz Potamkin

Berringer's

Drama; 60 min; NBC 1/5/85 to 3/16/85

Serial-type episodes that focus on the passions and conflicts of the Berringers, owners of the New York-based Berringer's Department Store.

Simon Berringer	Sam Wanamaker
Paul Berringer	Ben Murphy
Shane Bradley	Yvette Mimieux
Cammie Springer	Leslie Hope
Gloria Berringer	Andrea Marcovicci
Stacey Russell	Jonelle Allen
Laurel Hayes	Laura Ashton
Barbara Berringer	Anita Morris
Melodie Hughes	Claudia Christian
John Higgins	Jeff Conaway
Danny Krucek	Jack Scalia
Rinaldi	Cesar Romero

Producer: David Jacobs

Bert D'Angelo/Superstar

Crime Drama; 60 min; ABC 2/21/76 to 7/10/76

The exploits of Bert D'Angelo, a tough L.A.P.D. cop whose impressive record of arrests have earned him the nickname "Superstar."

Bert D'Angelo	Paul Sorvino
Det. Larry Johnson	Robert Pine
Capt. Jack Breen	Dennis Patrick

Producer: Quinn Martin

The Bert Parks Show

Variety; 30 min; NBC 11/1/50 to 1/11/52
                        CBS 1/14/52 to 6/26/52

A daily program of music and interviews with host Bert Parks and regulars Betty Ann Grove, Bobby Sherwood, Marianne McCormick, Jean Swain, and Harold Lang. Music by the Bobby Sherwood Quintet and produced by Sherman Marks, Mary Harris, and Louis Cowan.

Best Friends

Comedy Pilot; 30 min; CBS 7/19/77

The misadventures of a group of teenagers from varying backgrounds.

Nick	James Canning
Kathy	Sherry Hursey
Arthur	Bill Henry Douglas
Mountain Man	Gary Epp
Gypsy	Barry Pearl
Maggie	Gloria LeRoy
Big O	Ray Sharkey

Producer: Alan Sacks

The Best in Mystery

Polly Bergen as the hostess of a series of repeat anthology dramas (NBC 7/16/54 to 9/3/54).

The Best in Mystery

Drama; 60 min; NBC 7/13/56 to 8/31/56

The adventures of Willie Dante, a former gambler turned owner of the Dante's Inferno night club in San Francisco. Culled from episodes of "Four Star Playhouse."

Willie Dante	Dick Powell
Jackson	Alan Mowbray
Monte	Herb Vigran
Lt. Waldo	Regis Toomey

The Best of Groucho

The syndicated title for "You Bet Your Life" (which see).

Best of the Post

A 1959 syndicated series of dramas, hosted by John Conte and based on stories from "The Saturday Evening Post." Produced by Robert J. Enders.

The Best of Times

Variety Pilot; 60 min; ABC 7/13/81

Observations on teen life as seen through the eyes of actual teenagers.

Crispin	Crispin Glover
Julie	Julie Piekarski
Jill	Jill Schoelen
Nick	Nicholas Coppola

Kevin	Kevin Cortes
Lisa	Lisa Hope Ross
David	David Rambo
Janet	Janet Robin
Mr. O'Reilly	Jackie Mason
Crispin's mother	Betty Glover

Producer: George Schlatter

The Best of Times

Comedy Pilot; 30 min; CBS 8/29/83

The day-to-day activities of a group of students at U.S. Grant High School.

Pete Falcone	Robert Romanus
Robin DuPree	Krista Errickson
Patti Eubanks	Hallie Todd
Dewey Cooper	Chris Nash
Neil Hefernan	Leif Green
Peggy Falcone	Arlene Golonka
Howlin' Joe	Whitman Mayo
Kim Sedgwick	Denise Galick

Producer: Bob Comfort, Rick Kellard

Best of the West

Comedy; 30 min; ABC 9/10/81 to 8/23/82

Dissatisfied with life in Philadelphia, Sam Best heads west and settles in Copper Creek, Montana (in 1865), a town that is run by the insidious Parker Tillman. When fate intervenes and Sam is forced to face a vicious gunfighter, he is elected marshal. Episodes depict Sam's inept attempts to uphold the law.

Sam Best	Joel Higgins
Elvira Best	Carlene Watkins
Daniel Best	Meeno Peluce
Parker Tillman	Leonard Frey
Jerome "Doc" Kullens	Tom Ewell
Laney Gibbs	Valri Bromfield
Frog Rothchild Jr.	Tracey Walter
Rudy	Pat Ast
Mayor	Malcolm McClaman
The Calico Kid	Christopher Lloyd
Lamont Devereaux	Andy Griffith
Lily Devereaux	Eve Brent Ashe

Producer: Earl Pomerantz, David Lloyd

The Best Years

Comedy Pilot; 30 min; NBC 8/4/69

The misadventures of Walt Randolph, a widowed father, as he struggles to raise three beautiful daughters.

Walt Randolph	Craig Stevens
Nancy Randolph	Brooke Bundy
Kim Randolph	Robyn Millan
Charlotte Randolph	Susan Joyce
Dempster	Peter Brown
Tracy	Marion Moses

Better Days

Comedy; 30 min; CBS 10/1/86 to 10/29/86

When his parents decide to divorce, Brian McGuire is sent to live with his grandfather in Brooklyn. Stories relate Brian's antics as he attempts to adjust to life in New York, having previously lived in Beverly Hills.

Brian McGuire	Raphael Sbarge
Harry Clooney	Dick O'Neill
Harriet Winners	Randee Heller
Luther Kane	Chip McCallister
Snake	Guy Killum
Dean	Randall Batinkoff

Producer: Jeff Freilich, Stuart Sheslow, Arthur Silver

The Better Sex

Game; 30 min; ABC 7/18/77 to 1/13/78

Two teams compete, male vs. female. One player faces his opponents and responds to a question that is asked. The opponents must either agree or disagree with the answer. An incorrect guess defeats one player. The first team to defeat all his opposing players wins.

Host: Sarah Purcell, Bill Anderson

Announcer: Gene Wood

Producer: Mark Goodson, Bill Todman

The Betty Crocker Star Matinee

Variety; 30 min; ABC 11/3/51 to 4/26/52

Betty Crocker, the General Mills homemaking expert, demonstrates kitchen techniques, answers viewer mail, interviews celebrities, and hosts dramatic vignettes.

Betty Crocker	Adelaide Hawley

Producer: Tom Hicks, Al C. Ward

The Betty Hutton Show

Comedy; 30 min; CBS 10/1/59 to 6/30/60

Following the death of one of her customers, manicurist Goldie Appleby finds that she is the beneficiary of his will, head of his 60-million dollar estate, and the guardian of his three motherless children. Stories relate Goldie's efforts to run the estate and care for the Strickland children (Patricia, Nicky, and Roy).

Goldie Appleby	Betty Hutton
Patricia Strickland	Gigi Perreau
Nicky Strickland	Richard Miles
Roy Strickland	Dennis Joel
Lorna	Joan Shawlee
Rosemary	Jean Carson
Hollister	Gavin Muir

Producer: Marvin Marx

The Betty White Show

Variety; 30 min; NBC 2/8/54 to 12/31/54

Music, songs, and interviews with hostess Betty White, announcer Del Sharbutt, and the music of Frank DeVol and his orchestra.

The Betty White Show

Variety; 30 min; ABC 2/5/58 to 4/30/58

A program of music and songs with hostess Betty White and regulars John Dehner, Chill Wills, Reta Shaw, and Peter Leeds. With the announcing of Johnny Jacobs and the orchestra of Frank DeVol.

The Betty White Show

Comedy; 30 min; CBS 9/12/77 to 1/9/78

The story of Joyce Whitman, a mediocre actress who stars in "Undercover Woman," a second rate series directed by her estranged husband (John).

Joyce Whitman	Betty White
John Elliott	John Hillerman
Mitzi Maloney	Georgia Engel
Fletcher Huff	Barney Phillips
Hugo Muncy	Charles Cyphers
Tracy Garrett	Caren Kaye
Doug Porterfield	Alex Henteloff

Producer: Ed Weinberger, Stan Daniels

Between the Lines

Comedy Pilot; 30 min; ABC 7/7/80

The antics of the staff of the "Back Bay Mainline," an underground newspaper published in Boston.

Harry	Kristoffer Tabori
Abbie	Susan Krebs
Stanley	Sandy Helberg
Lynn	Nancy Lane
Frank	Squire Fridell
Max	Adam Arkin
Perfect Teacher	Gino Conforti

Producer: Philip Mandelker, Patricia Nardo

Beulah

Comedy; 30 min; CBS 10/10/50 to 9/22/53

Comic events in the life of Beulah, maid to attorney Harry Henderson and his family.

Beulah	Ethel Waters
	Hattie McDaniel
	Louise Beavers
Harry Henderson	William Post Jr.
	David Bruce
Alice Henderson	Ginger Jones
	Jane Frazee
Donnie Henderson	Clifford Sales
	Stuffy Singer
Oriole	Butterfly McQueen
	Ruby Dandridge
Bill Jackson	Dooley Wilson
	Ernest Whitman

Producer: Roland Reed

The Beverly Hillbillies

Comedy; 30 min; CBS 9/26/62 to 9/7/71

While hunting for food, Jed Clampett, a poor Ozark mountaineer, discovers oil on his property. Suddenly wealthy, he and his kin move to Beverly Hills where their adventures as they attempt to adjust to the sophisticated life are depicted.

Jed Clampett	Buddy Ebsen
Daisy "Granny" Moses	Irene Ryan
Elly Mae Clampett	Donna Douglas
Jethro Bodine	Max Baer
Milburn Drysdale	Raymond Bailey
Margaret Drysdale	Harriet MacGibbon
Jane Hathaway	Nancy Kulp
Pearl Bodine	Bea Benaderet
John Brewster	Frank Wilcox
Isabel Brewster	Lisa Seagram
Lester Flatt	Himself
Earl Scruggs	Himself
Gladys Flatt	Joi Lansing
Louise Scruggs	Midge Ware
Homer Winch	Paul Winchell
Dash Riprock	Larry Pennell
Mark Templeton	Roger Torrey
Homer Crachit	Percy Helton
Sonny Drysdale	Louis Nye
Shifty Shafer	Phil Silvers
Flo Shafer	Kathleen Freeman
Dr. Roy Clayburn	Fred Clark
Ravenscott	Arthur Porter
Janet Trego	Sharon Tate

Theme Vocal ("The Ballad of Jed Clampett"): Jerry Scoggins

Producer: Al Simon, Paul Henning, Joseph DePew, Mark Tuttle

Beverly Hills Buntz

Comedy; 30 min; NBC 11/5/87 (Premiere)

Following the demise of the series "Hill Street Blues," Detective Norman Buntz and his companion, Sid the Snitch, leave the "Hill" and head for Beverly Hills. There Buntz becomes a private detective (owner of Norman Buntz Investigations). Stories relate the less-than-honorable investigations of a sleazy detective and his partner.

Norman Buntz	Dennis Franz
Sid "The Snitch"	
Thurston	Peter Jurasik
Rebecca Griswald	
(Buntz's business	
neighbor)	Eve Gordon*
	Dana Wheeler-Nicholson

Producer: Michael Vittes, Jeffrey Lewis, David Milch

*Role in the original, never telecast pilot.

Bewitched

Comedy; 30 min; ABC 9/17/64 to 7/1/72

Events in the life of Samantha, a beautiful witch who marries a mortal (Darrin) and her efforts to live life as an average American housewife and later mother.

Samantha Stevens	Elizabeth Montgomery
Darrin Stevens	Dick York
	Dick Sargent
Endora	Agnes Moorehead
Maurice	Maurice Evans
Larry Tate	David White
Louise Tate	Irene Vernon
	Kasey Rogers
Gladys Kravitz	Sandra Gould
Abner Kravitz	George Tobias
Harriet Kravitz	Mary Grace Canfield
Tabitha Stevens	Erin Murphy
	Diane Murphy
Adam Stevens	David Lawrence
	Greg Lawrence
Aunt Clara	Marion Lorne
Dr. Bombay	Bernard Fox
Uncle Arthur	Paul Lynde
Esmeralda	Alice Ghostley
Cousin Serina	Elizabeth Montgomery
Betty	Marcia Wallace
	Samantha Scott
	Jean Blake
	Samantha Hathaway
Howard McMahon	Leon Ames
	Gilbert Roland
Margret McMahon	Louise Sorel
Apothecary	Bernie Kopell
Aunt Enchantra	Estelle Winwood
Aunt Hepzibah	Jane Connell
Cousin Edgar	Arte Johnson

Frank Stevens	Robert F. Simon
	Roy Roberts
Phyllis Stevens	Mabel Albertson
Aunt Hagatha	Reta Shaw

Producer: Harry Ackerman, William Asher

Beyond Westworld

Adventure; 60 min; CBS 3/5/80 to 3/19/80

When Simon Quaid feels that the robots he created for the futuristic playground Westworld are being misused, he reprograms them for evil. Stories relate Delos Corporation agent John Moore's efforts to stop Quaid and his reign of terror.

Simon Quaid	James Wainwright
John Moore	Jim McMullan
Pamela Williams	Connie Sellecca
Joseph Oppenheimer	William Jordan
Jan	Mo Lauren
Laura Garvey	Judith Chapman
Foley	Stewart Moss
	Severn Darden
Gunfighter (program open)	Alex Kubik
Gunfighter's Opponent	Edward Coch Jr.
Dance Hall Girl	Cassandra Peterson

Producer: Lou Shaw, Leonard B. Kaufman

Beyond Witch Mountain

Adventure Pilot; 60 min; CBS 2/20/82

Aliens, forced to leave their planet when it collides with the sun, land on Earth and establish a base in Witch Mountain. Later, Tia and Tony leave the safety of their colony to search for others of their kind. During their trek, they befriend Jason O'Day, an earthling who rescues them from Bolt, a billionaire who is seeking the alien children for the amazing powers they possess. The unsold series was to relate Jason's efforts to protect Tia and Tony from Bolt.

Jason O'Day	Eddie Albert
Tia	Tracey Gold
Tony	Andy Freeman
Aristotle Bolt	Efrem Zimbalist Jr.
Deranian	J. D. Cannon
Uncle Bene	Noah Beery Jr.

Producer: William Robert Yates

The Bickersons

An early 1950s syndicated comedy series that relates incidents in the lives of John and Blanche Bickerson, a quarrelsome husband and wife. Based on the radio series.

Blanche Bickerson	Frances Langford
John Bickerson	Lew Parker

Producer: Philip Rapp

Bid N' Buy

Game; 30 min; CBS 7/1/58 to 9/23/58

Object: For players to bid for clues and identify the silhouette of an unknown object.

Host: Bert Parks

Announcer: Bill Rogers

Producer: Robert Stivers

Biff Baker, U.S.A.

Adventure; 30 min; CBS 11/6/52 to 3/26/53

The exploits of Biff and Louise Baker, husband and wife export buyers who secretly work for the U.S. government.

Biff Baker	Alan Hale Jr.
Louise Baker	Randy Stuart

Producer: Allan Miller

Big Bend Country

Drama Pilot; 60 min; CBS 8/27/81

The adventures of Ian McGregor, a battle-weary Confederate soldier who brings his family to Big Bend, Tennessee (1865) to begin a new life.

Ian McGregor	James Keach
Mary McGregor	Dorothy Fielding
Davey McGregor	Robert MacNaughton
Donny McGregor	Johnny Graves
Sam Purdy	Stefan Gierasch
Minerva Purdy	Anne Haney
Sarah Marden	Wendy Fuller

Producer: Norman Rosemont

The Big Brain

Comedy Pilot; 30 min; CBS 8/19/63

The misadventures of Lester Belstrip, an inventor whose creations are less than perfect.

Lester Belstrip	Frank Aletter
Ellen	Ellen McRae (Ellen Burstyn)
Seymour	George Niese
Adele	Evelyn Ward

Producer: Jess Oppenheimer

Big City Boys

Comedy Pilot; 30 min; CBS 4/11/78

When his sister and brother-in-law receive three years for tax evasion, Harry Buckman, a disorganized P.R. man, receives custody of their son, Peter. The unsold series was to relate their misadventures.

Harry Buckman	Austin Pendleton
Peter	Christopher Barnes
Emily	Laurie Heinemann
Susan	Francesca Bill

Producer: Frank Konigsberg, Bruce Paltrow

Big City Comedy

Comedy; 30 min; Syn. 9/80

Comedy skits that satirize city life.

Host: John Candy

Regulars: Audrey Neenan, Patty Oakley, Tim Kazurinski, Donald Mont

Producer: Toby Martin

The Big Easy

Crime Drama Pilot; 60 min; NBC 8/15/82

The exploits of Jake Rubidoux, a tough New Orleans-based detective.

Jake Ribidoux	William Devane
Gloria Shenar	Ja'net DuBois
Walker Garrett	Nicholas Pryor
Lt. Frank Medley	Lane Smith
Cynthia Hayes	Mary Crosby
Lorri Fitzgerald	Barbara Babcock

Producer: Dan Curtis

Big Eddie

Comedy; 30 min; CBS 8/23/75 to 11/7/75

The story of "Big" Eddie Smith, a gambler turned owner of the Big E Sports Arena.

Eddie Smith	Sheldon Leonard
Honey Smith	Sheree North
Ginger Smith	Quinn Cummings
Monty Valentine	Billy Sands
Jessie Smith	Alan Oppenheimer
Raymond McKay	Ralph Wilcox
Too Late	Lonnie Shorr
No Marbles	Cliff Pellow

Producer: Bill Persky, Sam Denoff

Big Foot and Wild Boy

Adventure; 30 min; ABC 9/10/77 to 8/11/79

The crime-fighting exploits of the legendary man-beast Big Foot and his foundling Wild Boy.

Big Foot	Ray Young
Wild Boy	Joseph Butcher
Suzie	Monika Ramirez
Cindy	Yvonne Regaldo

Producer: Sid and Marty Krofft

The Big Game

Game; 30 min; NBC 6/14/58 to 9/12/58

Two players each set three play animals on a board that is concealed from the other. When a player correctly answers a question, he attempts to "shoot" his opponent's animals by calling a position (as in "Battleships"). The first player to "shoot" his opponent's animals wins.

Host: Tom Kennedy

Producer: Jackson Stanley

Big Hawaii

Drama; 60 min; NBC 9/21/77 to 11/30/77

The lives of the Fears, the wealthy owners of the Paradise Ranch in Ohana, Hawaii.

Barrett Fears	John Dehner
Mitch Fears	Cliff Potts
Karen "Kete" Fears	Lucia Strasler
Oscar Kalahani	William Lucking
Anita Kalahani	Josie Oliver
Lulu	Elizabeth Smith
Garfield	Moe Keale
Kimo	Remi Abellira

Producer: Perry Lafferty

Big John

Crime Drama Pilot; 60 min; NBC 12/3/83

The exploits of "Big" John Corbin, a detective with the Manhattan 4th Precinct of the N.Y.P.D.

Det. John Corbin	Dale Robertson
Frank Novaricchi	Joey Travolta
Capt. Hawkins	Dick Anthony Williams
Katherine Corbin	Kaaren Lee
Marcia Corbin	Natalie Klinger
Alicia Bridgeport	Tracy Scoggins

Producer: George Reeves, Fred Silverman

Big John, Little John

Comedy; 30 min; NBC 9/11/76 to 9/3/77

While in Florida, science teacher John Martin finds a small spring in the Ponce DeLeon National Park and drinks from it. Later, the middle-aged John unpredictably reverts to the 12-year-old Little John. Stories relate John's efforts to cope with and find a cure for his problem.

Big John Martin	Herb Edelman
Little John Martin	Robbie Rist
Marjorie Martin	Joyce Bulifant
Ricky Martin	Mike Darnell
Bertha Bottomley	Olive Dunbar
Valerie	Cari Anne Warder
Homer	Christoff St. John

Producer: William P. D'Angelo, Harvey Bullock, Ray Allen, Sherwood Schwartz

The Big Party for Revlon

Variety; 90 min; CBS 10/8/59 to 12/31/59

A variety series in which guests gather at a pre-selected celebrity's home for an informal party. Sponsored by Revlon.

Hostess: Barbara Britton

Producer: Perry Lafferty

The Big Payoff

Game; 30 min; NBC 12/31/51 to 3/27/53
CBS 3/30/53 to 10/23/59

A combination of music, songs, and audience participation for prizes.

Host: Bert Parks, Randy Merriman, Mort Lawrence, Robert Paige

Hostess: Bess Myerson, Constance Bennett

Regulars: Denise Lor, Betty Ann Grove, Susan Sayers, Dori Ann Grey

Producer: Walt Framer, Sid Tamber

The Big Record

A variety series, hosted by Patti Page, in which top music entertainers perform. Produced by Lester Gottlieb, Lee Cooley, and Jack Philbin, and broadcast on CBS from 9/18/57 to 6/11/58.

Big Shamus, Little Shamus

Crime Drama; 60 min; CBS 9/29/79 to 10/6/79

The cases of Arnie Sutter, house detective at the Atlantic City Ansonia Hotel, and his 13-year old son and assistant, Max.

Arnie Sutter	Brian Dennehy
Max Sutter	Doug McKeon
George Korman	George Wyner
Stephanie Marsh	Kathryn Leigh Scott
Jingles Lodestar	Cynthia Sikes
Jerry Wilson	Ty Henderson
Lt. Tom Grainger	Dennis Cole

Producer: Sam H. Rolfe, Lee Rich

Big Shots in America

Comedy Pilot; 30 min; NBC 6/20/85

The story of Jovan "Joey" Shagula, a Russian-born immigrant who has become a janitor in Brooklyn and who hopes to one day make a fortune and become a big shot.

Jovan Shagula	Joe Mantegna
Enci Shagula	Keith Szarabajka
Dave	Dan Vitale
Cara	Christine Baranski
Mrs. Cohen	Helen Hanft
Mr. Pipski	Irving Metzman

Producer: Bernie Brillstein

The Big Show

Variety; 90 min; NBC 3/4/80 to 5/27/80

Performances by top talent from around the world. Guest hosts include Barbara Eden, Marie Osmond, Mariette Hartley, Sarah Purcell, Shirley Jones, Tony Randall, Steve Allen and Dean Martin.

Regulars: Mimi Kennedy, Edie McClurg, Joe Baker, Charlie Hill, Owen Sullivan

Orchestra: Nick Perito

Producer: Nick Vanoff

The Big Showdown

Game; 30 min; ABC 12/23/74 to 7/4/75

Object: For contestants to reach established point values by answering questions. Winners roll two dice (containing the words "Show" and "Down"). If "Show Down" is rolled, they win $10,000.

Host: Jim Peck

Co-Host: Heather Cunningham

Announcer: Dan Daniels

Producer: Don Lipp, Ron Greenberg

The Big Story

Anthology; 30 min; NBC 9/16/49 to 6/28/57

Dramatizations based on actual newspaper stories.

Host: William Sloane, Ben Grauer, Norman Rose, Burgess Meredith

Producer: Bernard Prockter, Everett Rosenthal

The Big Surprise

Human Interest; 30 min; NBC 10/8/55 to 4/2/57

A person, chosen for an act of kindness, receives prizes for performing an unselfish deed.

Host: Jack Barry, Mike Wallace

Producer: Steve Carlin

The Big Top

Variety; 60 min; CBS 7/1/50 to 9/21/57

American and foreign circus acts perform.

Ringmaster: Jack Sterling

Clown: Ed McMahon, Chris Keegan

Circus Dan: Dan Lurie

Regulars: Lott and Joe Anders

Producer: Charles Vanda, Paul Ritts, Glen Bernard

Big Town

Crime Drama; 30 min; CBS 10/5/50 to 9/16/54
                NBC   10/11/54   to
                10/2/56

The story-gathering assignments of Big Town, U.S.A. "Illustrated Press" newspaper reporters Steve Wilson and Lorelei Kilbourne.

Steve Wilson	Patrick McVey
	Mark Stevens
Lorelei Kilbourne	Margaret Hayes
	Mary K. Wells
	Jane Nigh
	Beverly Tyler
	Trudy Wroe
	Julie Stevens
Diane Walker	Doe Averdon
Charlie Anderson	Barry Kelly
Lt. Tom Gregory	John Doucette

Producer: Lloyd Gross, Mark Stevens, Charles Robinson

The Big Valley

Western; 60 min; ABC 9/12/65 to 5/19/69

The exploits of the Barkleys, cattle ranchers in the San Joaquin Valley in Stockton, California, in the late 1870s.

Victoria Barkley	Barbara Stanwyck
Jarrod Barkley	Richard Long
Nick Barkley	Peter Breck
Audra Barkley	Linda Evans
Heath Barkley	Lee Majors
Eugene Barkley	Charles Briles
Silas	Napoleon Whiting

"The Big Valley" theme music by George Duning

Producer: Arthur Gardner, Jules Levy, Arnold Laven

The Bil Baird Show

A children's variety series featuring the creations of puppeteers Bil and Cora Baird (also the stars). CBS 8/4/53 to 10/22/53.

The Bill Cosby Show

Comedy; 30 min; NBC 9/14/69 to 8/31/71

The story of Chet Kincaid, athletic coach at Richard Allen Holmes High School in Los Angeles.

Chet Kincaid	Bill Cosby
Marsha Patterson	Joyce Bulifant
Brian Kincaid	Lee Weaver
Verna Kincaid	Olga James
	Dee Dee Young
Roger Kincaid	Donald Livingston
Rose Kincaid	Lillian Randolph
	Beah Richards
Chet's Father	Fred Pickard
Tom Bennett	Robert Rockwell

Producer: Bill Cosby, Marvin Miller

The Bill Cullen Show

Variety; 15 min; CBS 2/12/53 to 5/14/53

A Thursday morning program of music and chatter with Bill Cullen, Betty Brewer and the Milton DeLugg Trio.

The Bill Dana Show

Comedy; 30 min; NBC 9/22/63 to 1/17/65

The story of Jose Jimenez, a bewildered Latin American bellboy at New York's Park Central Hotel.

Jose Jimenez	Bill Dana
Byron Glick	Don Adams
Mr. Phillips	Jonathan Harris
Susie	Maggie Peterson
Eddie	Gary Crosby

Theme Song: "Jose Ole" by Earle Hagen

Producer: Sheldon Leonard, Danny Thomas

The Bill Goodwin Show

Variety; 30 min; NBC 9/11/51 to 3/27/52

A twice-weekly series of music and interviews with Bill Goodwin, Eileen Barton, Roger Dann and the music of the Joe Bushkin Trio. Produced by Louis Cowan, Sherman Marks.

Billboard's Disco Party

A music series, hosted by Donna Summer, that surveys the top-selling records. Syndicated in 1968. Produced by Sheldon Riss.

Billy

Comedy; 30 min; CBS 2/26/79 to 4/28/79

The story of Billy Fisher, a 19-year-old who prefers his colorful fantasies to life's realities.

Billy Fisher	Steve Guttenberg
Alice Fisher	Peggy Pope
George Fisher	James Gallery
Billy's Grandma	Paula Trueman
Mr. Shadrock	Michael Alaimo

Producer: John Rich

The Billy Bean Show

Comedy; 30 min; ABC 1951

The misadventures of Billy Bean, a clumsy soda jerk in a small town corner drugstore.

Billy Bean	Arnold Stang
His Girlfriend	Billie Lou Watt
His Boss	Phillips Tead

Producer: Jeffrey Hayden

Billy Boone and Cousin Kibb

Children; 30 min; CBS 7/9/50 to 8/27/50

Cartoon strips, drawn by Cousin Kibb, that follows the adventures of Billy Boone.

Cousin Kibb	Carroll Colby
Suzy	Patti Milligan

Producer: Judy Dupuy

The Billy Crystal Comedy Hour

Variety; 60 min; NBC 1/30/82 to 2/27/82

A weekly series of music, songs, and comedy sketches.

Host: Billy Crystal

Regulars: Paula Myers, Will Wheaton, Jane Anderson, Phyllis Katz, Michael McManus, Sal Viscuso

Announcer: John Harlan

Orchestra: Van Dyke Parks

Producer: Buddy Morra

The Billy Daniels Show

Variety; 15 min; ABC 10/5/56 to 12/28/56

Music and songs with singer Billy Daniels and the music of the Benny Payne Trio.

Billy Rose's Playbill

Anthology; 30 min; NBC 10/3/50 to 3/27/51

Dramas, hosted by Billy Rose, and based on stories appearing in the newspaper column, "Pitching Horseshoes." Produced by Jed Harris.

The Bing Crosby Show

Comedy; 30 min; ABC 9/14/64 to 6/14/65

The story of Bing Collins, a former singer-musician turned building engineer.

Bing Collins	Bing Crosby
Ellie Collins	Beverly Garland
Joyce Collins	Carol Faylen
Janice Collins	Diane Sherry
Willie Walters	Frank McHugh

Orchestra: John Scott Trotter

Producer: Steven Gethers

The Bionic Six

Cartoon; 30 min; Syn. 4/86

The futuristic story of six people, brought together by fate, who are able to transform themselves into indestructible crime fighters via a special wrist transformer device. Stories relate the exploits of the Bionic Six (Bionic One, Bionic Two, I.Q., J.D., Sport One, and Fluffy) as they battle the evils of Dr. Scarab and his henchmen.

Voices: Norman Bernard, Carol Bilger, Bobbi Block, Jim MacGeorge, Alan Oppenheimer, Hal Rayle, Neil Ross, Brian Tochi, Frank Welker

Producer: Yutaka Fujioka, Sachiko Tsuneda, Gerrard Baldwin

The Bionic Woman

Adventure; 60 min; ABC 1/14/76 to 5/4/77
                      NBC 9/10/77 to 9/2/78

When tennis pro Jaime Sommers is critically injured in a skydiving accident, Oscar Goldman of the O.S.I. authorizes a bionic operation to save her life. Stories relate Jaime's assignments as she uses her amazing abilities (bionic legs, right arm, and ear) on behalf of the O.S.I. (Office of Scientific Intelligence). A spin-off from "The Six Million Dollar Man."

Jaime Sommers	Lindsay Wagner
Oscar Goldman	Richard Anderson
Dr. Rudy Wells	Martin E. Brooks
Janet Callahan	Jennifer Darling
Mark Russell	Sam Chew Jr.
Jim Elgin	Ford Rainey
Helen Elgin	Martha Scott
Chris Williams	Christopher Stone
Dr. Michael Marchetti	Rick Lenz
Andrew (student)	Robbie Rist
Pam (student)	Robin Harlan
Stacy (student)	Stacy O'Brien
Mark (student)	Robbie Wolcott

Producer: Kenneth Johnson, Harve Bennett

Birdman and the Galaxy Trio

Cartoon; 30 min; NBC 9/9/67 to 12/27/68

The exploits of Ray Randall, alias Birdman, a daring defender of justice, and the Galaxy Trio (Vapor Man, Galaxy Girl, and Meteor Man) as they perform good deeds throughout the universe.

Birdman	Keith Andes
Falcon 7	Don Messick
Birdboy	Dick Beals
Vapor Man	Don Messick
Galaxy Girl	Virginia Eiler
Meteor Man	Ted Cassidy

Producer: William Hanna, Joseph Barbera

The Biskitts

Cartoon; 30 min; CBS 9/17/83 to 9/1/84

The adventures of the Biskitts, puppies only a dog biscuit high, as they strive to protect the treasures of Biskitt Castle.

Voices: Dick Beals, Peter Cullen, Jennifer Darling, Marshall Efron, Henry Gibson, Darryl Hickman, Ken Mars, B. J. Ward

Producer: William Hanna, Joseph Barbera

Bizarre

Comedy Pilot; 30 min; ABC 3/30/79

Unusual and bizarre comedy sketches.

Host: Richard Dawson

Regulars: Tanya Boyd, Melissa Steinberg, Nancy Steen, George Allen

Producer: Bob Einstein, Allan Blye

Bizarre

Comedy; 30 min; SHO 1980–1986

A series of adult-oriented comedy sketches. Contains nudity and strong language.

Host: John Byner

Featured: Bob Einstein, Billy Barty

Producer: Bob Einstein, Allan Blye, Perry Rosemond

B. J. and the Bear

Adventure; 60 min; NBC 2/10/79 to 8/1/81

The exploits of B. J. (Billie Joe) McKay, a trucker who will haul anything anywhere for $1.50 a mile. Later episodes depict B. J.'s efforts to start his own business, Bear Enterprises (named after his simian companion). See also "The Misadventures of Sheriff Lobo."

B. J. McKay — Greg Evigan
Sheriff Elroy Lobo — Claude Akins
Deputy Perkins — Mills Watson
Deputy Birdie
  Hawkins — Brian Kerwin
Sheriff Masters — Richard Deacon
Deputy Beauregard
  Wiley — Slim Pickens
Deputy Wilhelmina
  Johnson — Conchata Ferrell
Bullits — Joshua Shelley
Capt. John Cain — Ed Lauter
Deputy Higgins — Otto Felix
Tommy — Janet Louise
  Johnson
Stacy — Susan Woollen
Capt. Rutherford T.
  Grant — Murray Hamilton
Jeannie "Stacks"
  Campbell — Judy Landers
Teri Garrison — Candi Brough
Geri Garrison — Randi Brough
Samantha Smith — Barbra Horan
Callie Everett — Linda McCullough
Cindy Grant — Sherilyn Wolter
Angie Cartwright — Sheila DeWindt
Lt. Jim Steiger — Eric Server
Snow White — Laurette Spang
Honey — Angela Aames
Leather — Carlene Watkins
Sal — Julie Gregg
Clancy — Spray Rosso
Angel — Daryln Ann Lindley
Chattanooga — Sonia Manzano
Dixie — Liberty Godshall
Manny — Bert Rosario
Jack Benedict — Charles Napier
Jason T. Willard — Jock Mahoney
Dave Chaffey — Neil Zevnik
Nick — John Dullaghan
Deke — Steve Reisch
Fred Tipton — Henry Jones
Hatsie Tipton — Rosemary DeCamp
Stilts — Penny Peyser
Pogo Lil — Anne Lockhart
Bear — Sam

Theme Vocal ("B. J. and the Bear"): Greg
  Evigan

Producer: Glen A. Larson, Michael Sloan,
  and John Peyser

Black Bart

Comedy Pilot; 30 min; CBS 4/4/75

The story of Black Bart, an Old West sheriff
in the bigoted town of Paris, Arizona.

Black Bart — Lou Gossett
Reb Jordan — Steve Landesberg
Belle Buzzer — Millie Slavin
Fern Malaga — Noble Willingham
Jennifer — Brooke Adams

Producer: Mark Tuttle

The Black Robe

Anthology; 30 min; NBC 5/18/49 to 4/6/50

Dramatizations based on actual police night
court cases.

Judge — Frankie Thomas Sr.
Court Clerk — John Green

Producer: Phillips H. Lord

Black Saddle

Western; 30 min; ABC 1/10/59 to 9/28/60

The exploits of Clay Culhane, an ex-gunfighter turned lawyer in Latigo, New Mexico,
during the 1860s.

Clay Culhane — Peter Breck
Nora Travers — Anna-Lisa
Marshal Gib Scott — Russell Johnson

"Black Saddle" Theme Song: Jerry Goldsmith

Producer: Hal Hudson, Anthony Ellis

The Black Sheep Squadron

Adventure; 60 min; NBC 9/21/76 to 9/1/78

The exploits of Major Gregory "Pappy" Boy-
ington, a daring air ace and commander of the
VMF 214 Black Sheep, an undisciplined
fighter squadron based on Bella La Cava in
the South Pacific during W.W. II.

Maj. Gregory Boyington	Robert Conrad
Gen. Thomas Moore	Simon Oakland
Col. Carl Lard	Dana Elcar
Capt. James Gutterman	James Whitmore Jr.
Lt. Joseph Wiley	Robert Ginty
Lt. Jerry Bragg	Dirk Blocker
Capt. Lawrence Casey	W. K. Stratton
Lt. Robert Anderson	John Larroquette
Lt. Robert Boyle	Jake Mitchell Larry Manetti
Lt. Donald French	Jeff MacKay
Lt. Hutch	Joey Aresco
Lt. Jeb Pruitt	Jeb Adams
Sgt. Andy Micklin	Red West
Pvt. Stan Richards	Steve Richmond
Nurse Nancy Gilmore	Nancy Conrad
Nurse Samantha Green	Denise DuBarry
Nurse Dottie Dickson	Katherine Cannon
Nurse Sue Webster	Brianne Leary
Nurse Ellie Farrell	Kathy McCullem
Nurse Ann Wilson	Leslie Charleson
Nurse Cheryl Stone	Sharon Ullrick
Capt. T. Harachi	Byron Chung

Producer: Stephen J. Cannell

Blacke's Magic

Mystery; 60 min; NBC 1/8/86 to 6/11/86

After a near fatal accident while performing a stunt, famed illusionist Alexander Blacke decides to retire. A short time later, while attending a magician's convention, Blacke witnesses the death of a friend who dies from a gunshot wound while submerged in ten feet of water. Determined to solve the murder, Alexander contacts his father, a retired con artist named Leonard Blacke. Together, with Alexander's knowledge of magic and Leonard's genius for the con, they find the killer. With both Alexander and Leonard finding a new excitement in life, they decide to team and use their unique skills to help the police solve baffling crimes. Stories relate their exploits.

Alexander Blacke	Hal Linden
Leonard Blacke	Harry Morgan
Lt. Hank Wallenstein	Stephen Macht
Laurie Blacke	Claudia Christian
Ted Byrnes	Mark Shera

Producer: Peter S. Fischer, Robert F. O'Neill, Douglas Benton

Blackstar

Cartoon; 30 min; CBS 9/12/81 to 2/4/84

During a test flight, U.S. astronaut John Blackstar is drawn through a black hole and marooned on the planet Zagar. Stories relate his exploits as he helps the friendly Trolletts battle the evil Overlord.

John Blackstar	George DiCenzo

Additional Voices: Linda Gary, Alan Oppenheimer

Producer: Norm Prescott, Lou Scheimer

Blake's 7

Science Fiction; 60 min; Syn. 1986

The series is set in a future time when the Earth's surface has been transformed into a radioactive wasteland by a holocaustic war. The inhabitants are now forced to live in domed cities that are controlled by the Federation, a ruthless dictatorship whose power extends to various colonies in the galaxy. The series follows the efforts of Roj Blake and a group of dissidents as they attempt to free humanity from the control of the Federation.

Roj Blake	Gareth Thomas
Jenna Stannis	Sally Knyvette
Kerr Avon	Paul Darrow
Cally	Jan Chappell
Dayna Mellanby	Josette Simon
Vila Restal	Michael Keating
Olag Gan	David Jackson
Del Tarrant	Steven Pacey
Soolin	Glynis Barber
Servalan	Jacqueline Pearce
Cmdr. Travis	Brian Croucher

Producer: David Maloney, Vere Lorrimer

Blank Check

Game; 30 min; NBC 1/6/75 to 7/4/75

One player secretly selects one of five numbers. If a challenger fails to guess the number, that number becomes the fourth digit of a four digit blank check. When a challenger guesses the number, he becomes the new check writer. The player who writes the largest check wins.

Host: Art James

Co-Host: Judy Rich

Announcer: Johnny Jacobs

Producer: Jack Barry

Blankety Blanks

Game; 30 min; ABC 4/21/75 to 6/27/75

Object: For players to unscramble mystery phrases from a series of clues. The highest scorers receive cash prizes.

Host: Bill Cullen

Producer: Bob Stewart

Blansky's Beauties

Comedy; 30 min; ABC 2/12/77 to 6/27/77

The misadventures of Nancy Blansky, the den mother to ten beautiful show girls at the seedy Las Vegas Oasis Hotel.

Nancy Blansky	Nancy Walker
Joey DeLuca	Eddie Mekka
Anthony DeLuca	Scott Baio
Bambi Benton	Caren Kaye
Sunshine Akalino	Lynda Goodfriend
Hillary Prentiss	Taaffee O'Connell
Misty Karamazov	Jill Owens
Arkansas Baits	Rhonda Bates
Bridget Muldoon	Elaine Bolton
Sylvia Silver	Antoinette Yuskis
Jackie Outlaw	Gerri Reddick
Gladys Littlefeather	Shirley Kirkes
Lovely Carson	Bond Gideon
Stubs Wilmington	George Pentecost
Arnold Takahashi	Pat Morita

Theme Vocal ("I Want It All"): Cyndi Grecco

Producer: Garry K. Marshall

Blind Date

Game; 30 min; ABC 5/5/49 to 9/20/51
NBC 6/7/52 to 7/19/52
DuMont 6/9/53 to 9/15/53

Two men, seated on one side of a wall, telephone a girl (seated on the other side) and attempt to talk her into accepting a date with him. Based on voice, personality and answers to prepared questions, the girl chooses the man she would like to date.

Host: Melvyn Douglas, Jan Murray

Hostess: Arlene Francis

Producer: Bernard L. Schubert, Richard Lewis

The Blinkins

Cartoon Pilot; 30 min; Syn. 4/86

The adventures of the Blinkins, fireflys who struggle to keep their forest bright and beautiful and protect it from Mr. Slime, an alligator who detests beauty.

Mr. Ben	Burgess Meredith
Grog the Frog	Paul Williams
Mr. Slime	Henry Gibson
Flashy	Tracey Gold
Shady	Missy Gold
Twinkle	Brandy Gold

Producer: Harvey Harrison

Bliss

Comedy Pilot; 30 min; ABC 6/28/84

The clash between Kate Bliss, a former corporate executive who believes that the Bliss Chocolate Company should be run as a high-powered operation, and Harry Bliss, her father, the founder, who believes in a casual, relaxed operation.

Harry Bliss	George Kennedy
Kate Bliss	Diane Stilwell
Bo	Chris Sarandon
Fritz	Allan Miller
Marvin Shefter	Philip Sterling
Eleanor	Anne Haney
Velma	Barbara Babcock

Producer: Chip and Doug Keyes

Blockbusters

Game; 30 min; NBC 1/5/87 to 5/1/87

A board with twenty letters of the alphabet is displayed. One player (two compete) selects a letter and must answer a question that begins with that letter. The first player to correctly answer five questions and fill a row (either across or up and down) wins the round. The first player to win two rounds is the champion.

Host: Bill Rafferty

Announcer: Rich Jeffries

Producer: Robert Sherman, Diana Janaver

Blondie

Comedy Pilot; 30 min; Unaired (Produced in 1952)

The first known attempt to bring the Depression-era comic strip to television. The original, unaired video misadventures of Dagwood Bumstead, a bumbling architect, and his level-headed wife, Blondie.

Blondie Bumstead	Jeff Donnell
Dagwood Bumstead	John Harvey

Blondie

Comedy; 30 min; Syn. 1954

A virtually unknown "Blondie" series that relates events in the lives of the Bumstead family: Dagwood, an architect for the J. C. Dithers Construction Company; his wife, Blondie; and their children, Cookie and Alexander. See the following two titles also.

Blondie Bumstead	Pamela Britton
Dagwood Bumstead	Hal LeRoy
Cookie Bumstead	Mimi Gibson
Alexander Bumstead	Stuffy Singer
J. C. Dithers	Robert Burton
Cora Dithers	Isabel Withers
Tootsie Woodley	Robin Raymond
Mr. Beasley	Lucien Littlefield

Producer: Hal Roach Jr.

Blondie

Comedy; 30 min; NBC 1/4/57 to 9/27/57

A second series about the antics of a bumbling architect (Dagwood) and his level-headed wife (Blondie). See the prior and following title also.

Blondie Bumstead	Pamela Britton
Dagwood Bumstead	Arthur Lake
Cookie Bumstead	Ann Barnes
Alexander Bumstead	Stuffy Singer
Julius C. Dithers	Florenz Ames
Cora Dithers	Lela Bliss
	Elvia Allman
Herb Woodley	Hal Peary
Harriet Woodley	Lois Collier
	Hollis Irving
Eloise	Pamela Duncan

Producer: Hal Roach Jr., William Harmon

Blondie

Comedy; 30 min; CBS 9/26/68 to 1/9/69

A color version of the prior "Blondie" titles, which see for storyline.

Blondie Bumstead	Patricia Harty
Dagwood Bumstead	Will Hutchins
Cookie Bumstead	Pamelyn Ferdin
Alexander Bumstead	Peter Robbins
Julius C. Dithers	Jim Backus
Cora Dithers	Henny Backus
Tootsie Woodley	Bobbi Jordan

Producer: Al Brodax

Blondie and Dagwood

Cartoon; 30 minutes; CBS 5/15/87

The first animated TV adaptation of the comic strip. The updated (to 1987) story finds Blondie taking a job when hubby Dagwood, the bumbling architect, loses his job.

Blondie Bumstead	Loni Anderson
Dagwood Bumstead	Frank Welker
Cookie Bumstead	Ellen Gerstel
Alexander Bumstead	Ike Eisenman
J. C. Ditchers	Alan Oppenheimer
Cora Dithers	Russi Taylor
Daisy	Pat Fraley

Producer: Hank Saroyan

The Blue Angel

Variety; 30 min; CBS 7/6/54 to 10/12/54

A musical revue, set in New York's Blue Angel Supper Club, with host Orson Bean, vocalist Polly Bergen, and the music of the Norman Paris Trio.

The Blue Angels

Adventure; 30 min; Syn. 1960

The experiences of the pilots and crew of the Blue Angels, four precision U.S. Naval jets.

Arthur Richards	Dennis Cross
Russ MacDonald	Mike Galloway
Wilbur Scott	Warner Jones
Hank Bertelli	Don Gordon
Zeke Powers	Robert Knapp
Cort Ryker	Ross Elliot

Producer: Sam Gallu

Blue Jeans

Comedy Pilot; 30 min; ABC 7/26/80

The story of Vickie, Jimmy, Miles and Beethoven, four teenagers who comprise the rock group Blue Jeans.

Vickie Gardner	Elissa Leeds
Jimmy Scanlon	Paul Provenza
Miles Savatini	Charles Fleischer
Beethoven Zwirko	Jay Fenichel

Producer: Jerry Wintraub

The Blue Knight

Crime Drama; 60 min; CBS 12/17/75 to 10/20/76

The exploits of William "Bumper" Morgan, a veteran Los Angeles cop.

Off. William Morgan	George Kennedy
Carrie Williamson	Barbara Rhoades
Sgt. Newman	Philip Pine
Wimpy	John Steadman

Producer: Lee Rich, Philip Capice

Blue Light

Adventure; 30 min; ABC 1/12/66 to 8/31/66

During World War II, David March, an agent for Blue Light Control, pretends to renounce his American citizenship and poses as a traitor. He accomplishes his mission when he joins the ranks of the German High Command. Episodes relate David's suicide mission to destroy the Third Reich from within.

David March	Robert Goulet
Suzanne Duchard	Christine Carera

Producer: Walter Grauman, Buck Houghton

Blue Skies

Comedy Pilot; Unaired; Produced in 1987

The story of Annie and Frank, a newlywed couple with three children (from previous marriages) who move from New York to Oregon to begin new lives.

Annie Cobb	Season Hubley
Frank Cobb	Tom Wopat
Sarah Cobb	Alyson Croft
Charley Cobb	Danny Gerard
Zoe Cobb	Kim Hauser
Henry Cobb	Pat Hingle

Producer: Nigel McKeand

Blue Thunder

Adventure; 60 min; ABC 4/16/84 to 7/9/84

The exploits of The Blue Thunder Unit of the L.A.P.D., a crime-fighting team that incorporates an awesome state-of-the-art helicopter (Blue Thunder).

Frank Chaney	James Farentino
Clinton "Jafo" Wonderlove	Dana Carvey
Capt. Ed Braddock	Sandy McPeak
Off. Richard "Ski" Butowski	Dick Butkus
Off. Lyman "Bubba" Kelsey	Bubba Smith
Off. J. J. Douglas	Ann Cooper

Producer: Roy Huggins

Blues by Bargy

A variety series featuring singer-pianist Jean Bargy. CBS 1/24/49 to 7/6/50.

Bob & Carol & Ted & Alice

Comedy; 30 min; ABC 9/26/73 to 11/7/73

The lives of two families: the Sanders, a young, progressive couple; and the Hendersons, their neighbors, an older, conservative couple.

Bob Sanders	Robert Urich
Carol Sanders	Anne Archer
Ted Henderson	David Spielberg
Alice Henderson	Anita Gillette
Elizabeth Henderson	Jodie Foster
Sean Sanders	Brad Savage

Producer: M. J. Frankovich, James Henerson

The Bob and Ray Show

Comedy; 30 min; NBC 11/25/51 to 9/28/53

A series of vignettes by master comedians Bob and Ray.

Hosts: Bob Elliott, Ray Goulding

Regulars: Audrey Meadows, Cloris Leachman, Marion Brash, Charles Wood

Announcer: Bob Denton, Durward Kirby, Charles Wood

The Bob Crane Show

Comedy; 30 min; NBC 3/6/75 to 6/19/75

The story of Bob Wilcox, a 42-year-old executive who quits his insurance salesman job to pursue a medical career (at the City Medical School of University Hospital in Los Angeles).

Bob Wilcox	Bob Crane
Ellie Wilcox	Trisha Hart
Pam Wilcox	Erica Petal
Ernest Busso	Ronny Graham
Lyle Ingersoll	Jack Fletcher
Jerry Mallory	James Sutorius
Marvin Sussman	Todd Susman

Producer: Martin Cohan, Norman S. Powell

The Bob Crosby Show

A series of music and songs with Bob Crosby and regulars Joan O'Brien, Cathy Crosby and The Modernaires. CBS 9/14/53 to 8/30/57.

The Bob Crosby Show

A Summer series of music and songs with Host Bob Crosby, regulars Gretchen Wyler, The Clay Warnick Singers, The Peter Gennero Dancers and the orchestra of Carl Hoff. NBC 6/14/58 to 9/6/58.

The Bob Cummings Show

Comedy; 30 min; CBS 10/5/61 to 3/1/62

The romantic misadventures of Bob Carson, a bachelor-pilot fraught with money problems.

Bob Carson	Bob Cummings
Lionel	Murvyn Vye
Henrietta Gregory	Roberta Shore

Producer: Bob Finkel, William Frye

The Bob Hope Chrysler Theatre

Anthology; 60 min; NBC 10/4/63 to 9/6/67

A weekly series of quality dramatizations sponsored by the Chrysler Corporation.

Host: Bob Hope

Producer: Jack Laird, Frank P. Rosenberg, Jo Swerling Jr., Richard Collins, Dick Berg, Bert Mulligan, Rod Amateau, Gordon Oliver

The Bob Howard Show

Music and songs with singer-pianist Bob Howard. Produced by Bob Stevens and broadcast on CBS from 7/26/48 to 12/12/50.

The Bob Newhart Show

Variety; 30 min; NBC 10/11/61 to 6/13/62

A program of music and comedy with host Bob Newhart, regulars Jackie Joseph, Mickey Manners, June Ericson, Abby Albin, Pearl Shear, Ken Berry, Joe Flynn, Kay Westfall, and the orchestra of Paul Weston. Produced by Roland Kibbee. Announcer: Dan Sorkin.

The Bob Newhart Show

Comedy; 30 min; CBS 9/16/72 to 9/2/78

Events in the life of Bob Hartley, a Chicago-based psychologist. See also "Newhart."

Bob Hartley	Bob Newhart
Emily Hartley	Suzanne Pleshette
Howard Borden	Bill Daily
Jerry Robinson	Peter Bonerz
Carol Kester	Marcia Wallace
Margaret Hoover	Patricia Smith
Larry Bondaurant	Will MacKenzie
Elliott Carlin	Jack Riley
Michele Nardo	Renne Lippin
Victor Gianelli	Noam Pitlik
Edgar Vickers	Lucien Scott
Lillian Bakerman	Florida Friebus
Margaret Hoover	Patricia Smith
Dr. Bernie Tupperman	Larry Gelman
Howard Borden Jr.	Moosie Drier
Ellen Hartley	Pat Finley
Herb Hartley	Barnard Hughes
Martha Hartley	Martha Scott
Corneilius "Junior" Harrison	John Randolph
Aggie Harrison	Ann Rutherford
Cliff Murdock	Tom Poston
Lois Borden	Alice Borden
Debbie	Heather Menzies
Mrs. Peterson	Toni Lamond

Producer: Tom Patchett, Jay Tarses, David Davis, Lorenzo Music

The Bob Smith Show

Variety; 30 min; NBC 9/2/48 to 6/30/49

Music, songs, new talent discoveries, and game contests with host Bob Smith, regulars Eve Young, Bob Wren, Johnny Guarnieri, and Enoch Light and the Light Brigade Orchestra. Produced by Rod Erickson and Edward Keane.

Bobbie Gentry's Happiness Hour

Variety; 60 min; NBC 6/5/74 to 6/26/74

A Summer series of music and songs.

Hostess: Bobbie Gentry

Regulars: Valri Bromfield, Michael Greer, Earl Pomerantz

Orchestra: Jack Elliott, Allyn Ferguson

Producer: Frank Peppiatt

The Bobby Darin Amusement Company

Variety; 60 min; NBC 7/27/72 to 9/7/72
1/19/73 to 4/27/73

A program of music, songs and comedy. Also titled "The Bobby Darin Show" (in 1973).

Host: Bobby Darin

Regulars: Kathy Cahill, Dorrie Thompson, Dick Bakalyan, Geoff Edwards, Tony Amato, Steve Landesberg, Charlene Wong, Rip Taylor, Sarah Frankboner, The Jimmy Joyce Singers

Announcer: Roger Carroll

Orchestra: Eddie Karam

Producer: Saul Ilson, Ernest Chambers

The Bobby Goldsboro Show

Variety; 30 min; Syn. 1973

A program of music and comedy with host Bobby Goldsboro and Peter Cullen as the voice of puppets Calvin Calaveris (a frog) and Jonathan Rebel (a dog). Music by Robert Montgomery and Tim Tappan.

Bobby Jo and the Big Apple Goodtime Band

Comedy Pilot; 30 min; CBS 3/31/72

The story of Bobby Jo, a pretty, but naive singer who heads a country and western rock group called The Big Apple Goodtime Band.

Bobby Jo	Season Hubley
Cousin Jack	Forrest Tucker
Augie	Robert Walden
Jeff	John Bennett Perry
Virgil	Ed Begley Jr.
Brian	Michael Gray

Producer: Paul Junger Witt

Bobby Parker and Company

Comedy Pilot; 30 min; CBS 4/22/74

The story of Bobby Parker, a man whose hangups follow him around in imaginary form.

Bobby Parker	Ted Bessell
His Wife	Marj Dusay
His Mother	Joan Blondell
His Father	Tom D'Andrea
His Psychiatrist	Tom Poston
His Policeman	Noam Pitlik

Producer: Bill Persky

The Bobby Vinton Show

Variety; 30 min; Syn. 9/75

A program of music and songs with host Bobby Vinton and regulars Arte Johnson, Billy Van, Freeman King, and Jack Duffy. Music by Jimmy Dale and produced by Allan Blye and Chris Bearde.

Bobo Hobo and His Traveling Troupe

A syndicated (1953) series of miniature musicals for children with Bobo Hobo (a puppet voiced by Brett Morrison). Produced by Lorraine Lester.

Body Electric

Health; 30 min; PBS Syn. 6/86

The program combines dance with the benefits of aerobic exercise.

Hostess: Margaret Richard

Dancers: P. D. Baskin, Guy Davis, Liz Kelly, Nancy Kunkei, Deborah O'Neil, Kelly Watson, Mark Sontag, Kelly Watson

Producer: Pat Keating

Body Language

Game; 30 min; CBS 6/4/84 to 1/3/86

Object: For players to guess words that are pantomimed by their teammates.

Host: Tom Kennedy

Announcer: Johnny Olsen

Producer: Robert Sherman

The Bold Ones

Drama; 60 min; NBC 9/14/69 to 1/9/73

The overall title for four rotating series (which see): "The Doctors," "The Law Enforcers," "The Lawyers," and "The Senator."

Bold Venture

Adventure; 30 min; Syn. 9/59

When adventurer Slate Shannon is called to the bedside of a dying friend (Duvall), he agrees to become the guardian of his daughter, Sailor. Shortly after, when Slate becomes bored with his lifestyle, he leaves the states and retreats to Trinidad, where he purchases a hotel ("Shannon's Place") and a sixty-foot sloop ("The Bold Venture"). Stories relate Slate's adventures as he begins a charter service and attempts to help people in trouble.

Slate Shannon	Dane Clark
Sailor Duvall	Joan Marshall
King Moses	Bernie Gozier

Slate's Girl Crew: Joyce Taylor, Barbara Wilson, Narda Onyx, Jerry Bender

Bon Voyage

Game; 30 min; ABC 4/24/49 to 8/26/49

Object: For players to identify geographical locations through stills and rhyming clues.

Host: John Weigel

Producer: Alan Fishburn

Bonanza

Western; 60 min; NBC 9/12/59 to 1/16/73

The exploits of the Cartwrights as they struggle to maintain the Ponderosa, a thousand-mile timberland ranch in Virginia City, Nevada, during the mid-1800s.

In March of 1988, the syndicated TV movie, "Bonanza: The Next Generation," continued the saga of the Cartwrights with a new cast: John Ireland as Aaron, the late Ben's brother and head of the Ponderosa; Barbara Anderson as Annabelle, the wife of Little Joe (killed in action while serving with the Rough Riders), Brian A. Smith as Josh, Hoss's bastard son, and Michael Landon Jr. as Benji, Little Joe's son.

Ben Cartwright	Lorne Greene
Adam Cartwright	Pernell Roberts
Hoss Cartwright	Dan Blocker
"Little" Joe	
Cartwright	Michael Landon
Hop Sing	Victor Sen Yung
Jamie Cartwright	Mitch Vogel
Sheriff Roy Coffee	Ray Teal
Deputy Clem Poster	Bing Russell
Mr. Canaday	David Canary
Griff King	Tim Matheson
Dusty Rhodes	Lou Frizzell

"Bonanza" Theme by David Rose

Producer: David Dortort, Richard Collins, Robert Blees

Bonino

Comedy; 30 min; NBC 9/12/53 to 12/26/53

Feeling that he has become a stranger to his six children, opera singer Babbo Bonino decides to relinquish his career and become a full time father. Stories relate his efforts to raise his motherless children.

Babbo Bonino	Ezio Pinza
Andrew Bonino	Van Dyke Parks
Doris Bonino	Lenka Peterson
Edward Bonino	Conrad Janis
Jerry Bonino	Chet Allen
Francesca Bonino	Gaye Huston
Carlo Bonino	Oliver Andes
Martha	Mary Wickes
Rusty	Mike Kellin

Producer: Fred Coe

Bonkers

Comedy; 30 min; Syn. 9/78

A weekly series of music and comedy.

Host: Bill, Mark, and Brett Hudson

Regulars: Bob Monkhouse, Linda Cunningham, Jack Burns

Music: Jack Parnell

Producer: Thomas M. Battista

The Book of Lists

Human Interest; 60 min; CBS 5/4/82 to 5/25/82

Unusual facts, trivia, and comedy skits.

Host: Bill Bixby, Leslie Uggams, Cloris Leachman, Lorna Patterson

Regulars: Dennis Burkley, Renny Temple, Lucy Webb, Janet McMillan, Teresa Colleran, Jeff DeHart

Announcer: John Harlan

Music: Les Brown

Producer: Mort Lachman

Boone

Drama; 60 min; NBC 9/26/83 to 8/11/84

The series, set in Trinity, Tennessee, in 1953, tells of Boone Sawyer, a 17-year-old who yearns to become a singer, but faces opposition from his parents—his mother, who wants him to be a preacher; and his father, who wants him to be a mechanic in the family-owned gas station.

Boone Sawyer	Thomas Byrd
Faye Sawyer	Elizabeth Huddle
Merit Sawyer	Barry Corbin
Susannah Sawyer	Kitty Moffat
Lorie Sawyer	Amanda Peterson
Rome Holly	Greg Webb
Link Sawyer	William Edward Phipps
Dolly Sawyer	Ronnie Claire Edwards
Banjo	Julie Anne Haddock
Boone's Cousin	
Geneva	Karlene Crockett
Norman	Chris Hebert

Producer: Lee Rich, Earl Hamner

Boots and Saddles

Adventure; 30 min; Syn. 1957

The life and times of the men and officers of the American Fifth Cavalry during the 1870s.

Capt. Shank Adams	Jack Pickard
Scout Luke	
Cummings	Michael Hinn
Lt. Col. Hayes	Patrick McVey
Lt. Kelly	Gardner McKay
Lt. Binning	Dave Willock
Sgt. Bullock	John Anderson

Border Pals

Comedy Pilot; 60 min; ABC 8/17/81

During a card game, Norbert Bibey, an American Sheriff in Moose County, Montana, and Douglas MacDonald, Superintendent of the British Columbia Mounted Police in Lake Canusa, each accuse the other of cheating and vow never to speak to each other again. The unsold series was to relate the efforts of their staffs to devise ways to end the feud.

Norbert Bibey	Hugh Gillin
Douglas MacDonald	Graham Jarvis
Juliette "Gigi"	
Marais	Katherine Baumann
Kelly Morgan	Reid Smith
Sgt. Maj. Radcliffe	Frank O'Brien
Dusty Griffith	Gerald Prendergast
Lucas Jordan	T. K. Carter
Joe Cincinnati	Marc Lawrence

Producer: Rod Amateau

The Boris Karloff Mystery Playhouse

Anthology; 30 min; ABC 9/22/49 to 12/15/49

A short-lived series of mystery dramas, hosted by Boris Karloff, and also known as "Starring Boris Karloff." Announcer: George Gunn. Produced by Alex Segal.

Born Free

Adventure; 60 min; NBC 9/9/74 to 12/30/74

The story of George Adamson, a game warden in Kenya, East Africa. Based on the feature film.

George Adamson	Gary Collins
Joy Adamson	Diana Muldaur
Makedde	Hal Frederick
Nuru	Peter Lukoye

Producer: David Gerber

Born to the Wind

Drama; 60 min; NBC 8/19/82 to 9/5/82

The series, set in 1825, follows the lives of a tribe of Plains Indians who call themselves "The People."

Painted Bear	Will Sampson
Low Wolf	A Martinez
Lost Robe	Henry Darrow
Star Fire	Rose Portillo
One Feather	Dehl Berti
White Bull	Emilio Delgado
Two Hawks	Guillermo San Juan
Broken Foot	Ned Romero
Arrow Woman	Cynthia Avila
Night Eyes	Claudio Martinez

Producer: Edgar J. Scherick, Daniel H. Blatt

Bosom Buddies

Comedy; 30 min; ABC 11/27/80 to 8/5/82

The original format relates the adventures of Henry Desmond and Kip Wilson, an ad agency copyrighter and artist, who disguise themselves as women (Hildegarde Desmond and Buffy Wilson) to live in a hotel for women only (the Susan B. Anthony) when they are evicted and have no place else to go. The revised format relates their misadventures when they begin their own ad agency (60 Seconds Street) and drop the masquerade.

Henry/Hildegarde	Peter Scolari
Kip/Buffy	Tom Hanks
Ruth Dunbar	Holland Taylor
Amy Cassidy	Wendie Jo Sperber
Sonny Lumet	Donna Dixon
Isabelle Hammond	Telma Hopkins
Lillian Sinclair	Lillian Bronson

Producer: Edward K. Milkis, Thomas L. Miller, William Boyett

Boss Lady

Comedy; 30 min; NBC & DuMont 7/15/52 to 9/23/52

The story of Gwen F. Allen, the owner-operator of The Hillendale Homes Construction Company in California.

Gwen Allen	Lynn Bari
Jeff Standish	Nicholas Joy
Mr. Allen	Glenn Langan
Chester Allen	Charles Smith
Aggie	Lee Patrick
Roger	Richard Gaines

Producer: Jack Wrather, Robert Mann

Boston and Kilbride

Crime Drama Pilot; 60 min; CBS 3/3/79

The exploits of Tom Boston and Jim Kilbride, freewheeling private eyes.

Tom Boston	Tom Selleck
Jim Kilbride	James Whitmore Jr.
Jill Miller	Jamie Lyn Bauer
Armand Beller	Don Ameche
Louise	Lane Bradbury
Toby	Kathryn Leigh Scott
C. Donald Devlin	William Daniels

Producer: Stephen J. Cannell

Boston Blackie

Crime Drama; 30 min; Syn. 1951

The exploits of Boston Blackie, a thief turned private detective.

Boston Blackie	Kent Taylor
Mary Wesley	Lois Collier
Insp. Faraday	Frank Orth

Producer: Paul Landers

The Boston Terrier

Crime Drama Pilot; 60 min; NBC 4/10/62

The exploits of A. Dunster Lowell, a Harvard-educated private detective. The first pilot relates Lowell's efforts to solve the murders of several mobsters. Aired on "The Dick Powell Show."

A. Dunster Lowell	Robert Vaughn
Prof. Mumford	John McGiver
Lt. Duffy Cardoza	Robert J. Wilke
Sally Paine	Diana Millay
Julia	Bennye Gatteys
Otis Coots	Russell Collins

Producer: Dick Powell, Blake Edwards

The Boston Terrier

Crime Drama Pilot; 30 min; ABC 6/11/63

A second pilot about Boston-based detective A. Dunster Lowell. The story relates Lowell's efforts to find a missing socialite.

A. Dunster Lowell	Robert Vaughn
Millie Curtin	Elizabeth Montgomery
Lt. Clarence McKenzie	Stanley Adams
Josiah Bowditch	John Hoyt
Lt. Foley	Paul Comi
Mrs. Dee	Helen Wallace

Producer: Blake Edwards

The Bounder

Comedy Pilot; 30 min; CBS 7/7/84

The story of Howard Bender, a charming ex-con who seeks an easy life and easy money.

Howard Bender	Michael McKean
Bonnie Slater	Jeannetta Arnette
Charles Slater	Richard Masur
Laura Spencer	Francine Tacker

Producer: Barbara Corday

The Bounder

Comedy; 30 min; Syn. 9/85

A British series about Howard Booth, a charming con artist who seeks an easy life and easy money.

Howard Booth	Peter Bowles
Mary	Rosalind Ayres
Trevor	George Cole
Laura Miles	Ilsa Blair

Producer: Vernon Lawrence

The Bounty Hunter

Western Pilot; 30 min; CBS 3/7/57

The pilot for "Wanted: Dead Or Alive," which relates the exploits of bounty hunter Josh Randall. Aired on "Trackdown."

Josh Randall	Steve McQueen
Hoby Gilman	Robert Culp
Janette York	Jean Willes
Sheriff	Ken McDonald

Producer: Vincent M. Fennelly

Bourbon Street Beat

Mystery; 60 min; ABC 10/5/59 to 9/26/60

The exploits of Cal Calhoun and Rex Randolph, private detectives based in New Orleans.

Cal Calhoun	Andrew Duggan
Rex Randolph	Richard Long
Melody Lee Mercer	Arlene Howell
Ken Madison	Van Williams
The Baron	Eddie Cole
Lusti Weather	Nita Talbot

Producer: William T. Orr, Charles Hoffman, Harry Tatelman

Bowzer

Comedy Pilot; 30 min; Syn. 1/81

The misadventures of Bowzer J. Bowzer, the proprietor of the Chez Bowzer, a shabby, near-bankrupt night club.

Bowzer J. Bowzer	Jon Bauman
Victoria	Susan Lawrence
Barney Sheldon	Bruce Kirby
Jason	Tony Christopher
Barbi Benton	Herself

Producer: Pierre Cossette

The Boys

Comedy Pilot; 30 min; NBC 7/6/70

The antics of Jud and Billy, two boys growing up in a small Wisconsin town.

Jud Thomas	Mitch Vogel
Billy	Mark Kearney
Willis Bickett	William Schallert
Theater owner	Dabbs Greer

Producer: Jim Parker

The Boys

Comedy Pilot; 30 min; CBS 5/16/74

The misadventures of comedy writers Eddie Ryan and Harry Rufkin.

Eddie Ryan	Tim Conway
Harry Rufkin	Herb Edelman
Cassie	Esther Sutherland
Alice	Gwynne Gilford
Vicki	Phyllis Davis

Producer: Bill Persky, Sam Denoff

The Boys in Blue

Crime Drama Pilot; 60 min; CBS 9/9/84

The activities of patrol car officers with the Prospect Division of the L.A.P.D.

Off. Danny Harris	Dean Paul Martin
Off. Jeff Martin	Gregg Henry
Off. Grace Carpenter	Maggie Cooper
Capt. Sid Bender	Murray Hamilton
Sgt. Hernandez	Luis Avalos
Off. Don Mutuccie	Vince McKewin
Lt. Shenk	Garret Graham
Rena	Ruth Britt

Producer: David Gerber

Bozo the Clown

The program, set at a circus big top, features game contests, cartoons, circus acts, and sketches geared to children. Basically, the entire program is produced by stations who purchase the syndicated format from its creator, Larry Harmon. The idea was first syndicated in 1959. In 1966 (through 1967) 130 episodes were produced for syndication with Frank Avruch as Bozo in "Bozo's Big Top Circus Show." In 1972, 185 additional half-hours were produced. The series, titled "Bozo's Place," related teaching concepts to children. In addition to Frank Avruch as Bozo, Peter Barth played the ringmaster and Ruth Carlson, A. Del Grosso, and Ed Spinney were the regulars. Produced by Larry Harmon.

Bracken's World

Drama; 60 min; NBC 9/19/69 to 1/1/71

A behind-the-scenes look at movie making as seen through the eyes of John Bracken, the head of Century Studios.

John Bracken	Leslie Nielsen
Sylvia Caldwell	Eleanor Parker
Anne Frazer	Bettye Ackerman
Kevin Grant	Peter Haskell
Marjorie Grant	Madlyn Rhue
Laura Dean	Elizabeth Allen
Davey Evans	Dennis Cole
Rachel Holt	Karen Jensen
Paulette Douglas	Linda Harrison
Diane Waring	Laraine Stephens
Tom Hutson	Stephen Oliver

Theme Vocal ("Worlds") by The Lettermen

Producer: Del Reisman

Braddock

Crime Drama Pilot; 60 min; CBS 7/22/68

The exploits of Braddock, a private detective with Braddock and Tratner Investigations in Los Angeles.

Braddock	Tom Simcox
Tratner	Stephen McNally
Louise Tratner	Karen Steele
Lawrence	Lloyd Bochner
Marie	Kathy Kersh
Mongol	Tom Reese
Lt. MacMillan	John Doucette
Victoria	Laura Lindsay
Gilmore	Don Marshall
Hitchaess	Arthur Adams
Beverly	Colette Jackson
Cop	Robert Sampson
Man	Charles Macauley

Producer: Paul Monash

The Brady Brides

Comedy; 30 min; NBC 3/6/81 to 4/17/81

Events in the lives of the newlywed Brady sisters (Marcia and Jan) as both set up housekeeping in the same home to save on expenses.

Marcia Logan	Maureen McCormick
Jan Covington	Eve Plumb
Wally Logan	Jerry Houser
Philip Covington	Ron Kuhlman
Alice Franklin	Ann B. Davis

Producer: Sherwood Schwartz, Warren Murray

The Brady Bunch

Comedy; 30 min; ABC 9/26/69 to 8/30/74

The story of Mike Brady, a widower with three sons, who marries Carol Martin, a widow with three daughters, and their adventures as they begin a new life together.
See also: "The Brady Brides," "The Brady Bunch Hour," "The Brady Girls Get Married," and "The Brady Kids."

Mike Brady	Robert Reed
Carol Brady	Florence Henderson
Alice Nelson	Ann B. Davis
Marcia Brady	Maureen McCormick
Jan Brady	Eve Plumb
Cindy Brady	Susan Olsen
Gregg Brady	Barry Williams
Peter Brady	Christopher Knight
Bobby Brady	Michael Lookinland
Oliver	Robbie Rist
Sam Franklin	Allan Melvin

Producer: Sherwood Schwartz, Howard Leeds, Lloyd J. Schwartz

The Brady Bunch Hour

Variety; 60 min; ABC 1/23/77 to 5/24/77

The fictional Brady family in songs, dances and comedy sketches.

Mike Brady	Robert Reed
Carol Brady	Florence Henderson
Marcia Brady	Maureen McCormick
Jan Brady	Geri Reischl
Cindy Brady	Susan Olsen
Gregg Brady	Barry Williams
Peter Brady	Christopher Knight
Bobby Brady	Michael Lookinland
Alice Nelson	Ann B. Davis

Producer: Sid and Marty Krofft

The Brady Girls Get Married

Comedy; 30 min; NBC 2/6/81 to 2/20/81

Continued events in the lives of the now-grown Brady girls, Marcia and Jan, as they prepare for marriage (Marcia to Wally, a toy designer; and Jan to Philip, a chemistry teacher).

Marcia Brady	Maureen McCormick
Jan Brady	Eve Plumb
Wally Logan	Jerry Houser
Philip Covington	Ron Kuhlman

Producer: Sherwood Schwartz

The Brady Kids

Cartoon; 30 min; ABC 9/9/72 to 8/31/74

The misadventures of the Brady children as they attempt to solve their own problems.

Marcia Brady	Maureen McCormick
Jan Brady	Eve Plumb
Cindy Brady	Susan Olsen
Gregg Brady	Barry Williams
Peter Brady	Christopher Knight
Bobby Brady	Michael Lookinland
Moptop (dog)	Larry Storch

Producer: Sherwood Schwartz

Brains and Brawn

Game; 30 min; NBC 9/13/58 to 12/27/58

Two teams compete: The Brain (who answer difficult questions) and The Brawn (who perform physical-dexterity feats). The team that is best at solving its portion wins.

Host: Fred Davis, Jack Lescoulie

Branagan and Mapes

Comedy Pilot; 30 min; CBS 8/1/83

The story of an L.A. ad man (Dan) and his attempts to raise his three stepchildren (Gussie, Logan, and Theresa) after the sudden death of his wife.

Dan Branagan	Don Murray
Gussie Mapes	Dana Hill
Logan Mapes	Brett Johnson
Theresa Mapes	Rebecca Sweet
Barney Sutter	Bruce Kirby
Aunt Cathy	Judith Kahan

Producer: Charlie Hauck

Branded

Adventure; 30 min; NBC 1/24/65 to 9/4/66

During the Battle of Bitter Creek, Army captain Jason McCord is knocked unconscious and left for dead by the Commanche Indians. When the military brass refuses to believe his story, Jason is branded a coward and dishonorably discharged. Stories, set in the 1870s, relate Jason's efforts to clear his name.

Jason McCord	Chuck Connors
Ann Williams	Lola Albright
Gen. Joshua McCord	John Carradine
Pres. Ulysses S. Grant	William Bryant

Producer: Andrew J. Fenady, Cecil Baker

Brave Eagle

Western; 30 min; CBS 9/28/55 to 6/6/56

The hardships of the American Indian as seen through the eyes of Brave Eagle, a young Cheyenne Chief.

Brave Eagle	Keith Larsen
Keena	Keena Nomleena
Morning Star	Kim Winona
Smokey Joe	Bert Wheeler
Black Cloud	Pat Hogan

Producer: Arthur Rush, Mike North

Bravo Duke

Adventure Pilot; 30 min; CBS 7/30/65

The story of a man, known only as Duke, who operates Duke's Cantina (a gambling house in Mexico) and helps American's in distress.

Duke	Gerald Mohr
Lisa	Kathleen Crowley
Constantine	Sebastian Cabot
Manuel	Jay Novello

Producer: Douglas Heyes

Bravo Two

Adventure Pilot; 30 min; CBS 3/25/77

The exploits of Wiley and Bud, the crew of the Bravo Two patrol boat, a unit of the Los Angeles Harbor Police.

Wiley Starrett	Bruce Fairbairn
Bud Wizzer	David Gilliam
Lt. O'Brien	James Hampton
T. J. Phillips	Cooper Huckabee
Mrs. Morgan	Lynn Carlin
Eddie Morgan	Matthew Laborteaux

Producer: Lee Rich, Philip Capice

Break the Bank

Game; 30 min; ABC 10/22/48 to 9/23/49
NBC 10/5/49 to 1/9/52
CBS 6/3/52 to 10/19/52
NBC 3/30/53 to 9/18/53
ABC 1/31/54 to 6/20/56

Players attempt to win the money in a jackpot by answering eight difficult questions in a row.

Host: Bert Parks, Bud Collyer

Assistant: Janice Wolfe, Janice Gilbert

Producer: Ed Wolf, Joe Rubin

Break the Bank

Game; 30 min; ABC 4/12/76 to 7/23/76

One player selects one box from nine that are displayed. A celebrity, representing the box, is asked a question. If the player correctly agrees (or disagrees) with the answer, he wins that box and money.

Host: Tom Kennedy, Jack Barry

Announcer: Johnny Jacobs, Ernie Anderson

Producer: Jack Barry, Dan Enright

Break the Bank

Game; 30 min; Syn. 9/85

Two married couples compete in a question and answer session wherein the first couple to score $2,000 is the winner. The couple then attempts to solve puzzles for bank cards. If the couple wins a card that says "Break the Bank" they receive a large cash prize.

Host: Gene Rayburn, Joe Farago

Assistant: Kandice Keuhl

Announcer: Michael Hanks

Producer: Richard S. Kline, Gary Cox

Break the $250,000 Bank

Game; 30 min; NBC 10/9/56 to 1/29/57

The same basic format as the first "Break the Bank" that also allows a player to have an expert assist in answering the questions.

Host: Bert Parks

Announcer: Johnny Olsen

Producer: Joe Rubin

Breakaway

A daily magazine series (syndicated 9/83) of celebrity interviews and news reports with Monte Markham, Martha Lambert, and Norman Mark. Produced by Jorn Winther and Sanford Feldman.

Breakfast in Hollywood

A morning variety series, hosted by Johnny Dugan, that features music, game contests and interviews. NBC 1/11/54 to 2/5/54.

Breakfast Party

A morning program of music and songs with Mel and Eileen Martin. Music by The Bell Airs Trio. NBC 1/7/52 to 5/23/52.

Breaking Away

Comedy-Drama; 60 min; ABC 11/29/80 to 7/6/81

The experiences of four high school grads as they attempt to find a place for themselves in the adult world.

Dave Stohler	Shaun Cassidy
Mike Carnahan	Tom Wiggins
Cyril	Thom Bray
Moocher	Jackie Earle Haley
Evelyn Stohler	Barbara Barrie
Ray Stohler	Vincent Gardenia
Nancy	Shelly Brammer
Paulina	Dominique Dunne

Producer: Herbert B. Leonard, Peter Yates

Breaking Point

Drama; 60 min; ABC 9/16/63 to 9/7/64

The work of Dr. Edward Raymer, director of the psychiatric clinic at York Hospital in Los Angeles.

Dr. Edward Raymer	Eduard Franz
Dr. McKinley	
Thompson	Paul Richards

Theme: "The Theme from Breaking Point" by David Raksin

Producer: George Lefferts

Brenda Starr

Drama Pilot; 90 min; NBC 5/8/76

The adventures of Brenda Starr, a crusading journalist who, in the pilot, becomes involved with murder and voodoo.

Brenda Starr	Jill St. John
A. J. Livwright	Sorrell Booke
Roger Randall	Jed Allan
Lance O'Toole	Victor Buono
Kentucky Smith	Marcia Strassman
Carlos Varga	Joel Fabiani

Producer: Paul Mason

Brenda Starr, Reporter

Drama Pilot; 30 min; Syn. 1/79

The exploits of Brenda Starr, a reporter for "The Daily Flash," as she attempts to help free a hostage from a madman.

| Brenda Starr | Sherry Jackson |
| A. J. Livwright | Shelly Berman |

Producer: Jerry Harrison

Brenner

Crime Drama; 30 min; CBS 6/6/59 to 9/18/59

The story of Roy Brenner, head of the Confidential Squad, a special crime-busting unit of the N.Y.P.D., and his son, Ernie, a patrolman.

Lt. Roy Brenner	Edward Binns
Off. Ernie Brenner	James Broderick
Capt. Laney	Joe Sullivan

Producer: Herbert Brodkin

Bret Maverick

Western; 60 min; NBC 12/1/81 to 8/24/82

A continuation of the "Maverick" series wherein Bret Maverick finally decides to settle down (in Sweetwater, Arizona) after he wins the Lazy Ace Ranch and the Red Ox Saloon in a poker game. Stories relate his experiences as a rancher and saloon owner.

Bret Maverick	James Garner
Mary Lou Springer	Darleen Carr
Philo Sandine	Stuart Margolin
Tom Guthrie	Ed Bruce
Elijah Crow	Ramon Bieri
Rodney	David Knell
Mitchell Dowd	John Shearin
Cy Whitaker	Richard Hamilton
Kate Hanrahan	Marj Dusay
Jasmine DuBois	Simone Griffeth
Jack	Jack Garner
Bank Teller	Norman Mailer
Hotel desk clerk	Eldon Quick
Estelle Springer	Priscilla Morrill

Theme Vocal ("Maverick Didn't Come Here to Lose"): Ed Bruce

Producer: Meta Rosenberg

Brian and Sylvia

Comedy Pilot; 30 min; NBC 3/25/81

The problems of an interracial marriage as seen through the experiences of Sylvia, a black TV newscaster (Ch. 9 in Buffalo, N.Y.), and Brian, her white husband, a counselor in a youth center. Aired on "The Facts of Life."

Sylvia Parker	Rosanne Katon
Brian Parker	Richard Dean Anderson
Ethel	Ja'net DuBois
Ray	Anthony Holland

Producer: Jack Elinson, Rita Dillon

The Brian Keith Show

See "The Little People."

Bride and Groom

Human Interest; 30 min; CBS 1/25/51 to 10/9/53
NBC 12/7/53 to 8/27/54
NBC 7/1/57 to 1/10/58

Telecasts of actual wedding ceremonies from a chapel in New York.

Host: Byron Palmer, Robert Paige, Phil Hanna, Frank Parker, John Nelson

Producer: John Reddy, John Masterson, John Nelson

Bridges to Cross

Drama; 60 min; CBS 4/24/86 to 6/12/86

The story gathering assignments of Tracy Bridges and Peter Cross, a divorced couple who share a personal rivalry as the reporter-columnists of "Bridges to Cross," a column for "World Week" magazine.

Tracy Bridges	Suzanne Pleshette
Peter Cross	Nicholas Surovy
Norman Parks	Roddy McDowall
Maria Talbot	Eva Gabor
Morris Kane	Jose Ferrer

Producer: Christopher Beaumont, William Blinn, Joel Rogosin

Bridget Loves Bernie

Comedy; 30 min; CBS 9/16/72 to 9/8/73

Bridget Fitzgerald, a Catholic school teacher, and Bernie Steinberg, a Jewish cab driver, meet, fall in love, and marry. Stories relate their attempts to overcome family opposition by bridging the ethnic gap that exists in their lives.

Bridget Fitzgerald	Meredith Baxter
Bernie Steinberg	David Birney
Walter Fitzgerald	David Doyle
Amy Fitzgerald	Audra Lindley
Sam Steinberg	Harold J. Stone
Sophie Steinberg	Bibi Osterwald
Moe Plotnic	Ned Glass
Michael Fitzgerald	Robert Sampson

Producer: Douglas S. Cramer

Brief Pause for Murder

Anthology Pilot; 30 min; CBS 11/21/46

A proposed series of murder mysteries. The pilot tells of a radio announcer (David Manners) who seeks the perfect way to dispose of his two-timing wife (Mary Patton). Produced by Philip Booth.

Bring 'Em Back Alive

Adventure; 60 min; CBS 9/24/82 to 6/21/83

The series, set in the Far East in 1939, relates the adventures of big game trapper and collector Frank Buck.

Frank Buck	Bruce Boxleitner
Gloria Marlowe	Cindy Morgan
Ali	Clyde Kusatsu
H.H.	Ron O'Neal
Edward Ridley-Jones	Roger Newman
Myles	Sean McClory
G. B. Von Turgo	John Zee

Producer: Jay Bernstein, Larry Thompson, Frank Cardea

Bringing Up Buddy

Comedy; 30 min; CBS 10/10/60 to 9/25/61

Events in the life of Buddy Flower, a bachelor investment broker whose life is plagued by his two meddlesome aunts, Violet and Iris.

Buddy Flower	Frank Aletter
Violet Flower	Enid Markey
Iris Flower	Doro Merande

Producer: Joe Connelly, Bob Mosher

Britt Ekland's Juke Box

Britt Ekland as the host of a syndicated (1979) series that features performances by the top names in music.

Broadside

Comedy; 30 min; ABC 9/20/64 to 9/5/65

The World War II adventures of four beautiful WAVES (Ann, Molly, Roberta, and Selma) as they attempt to run a motor pool on the male dominated South Pacific island of Ranakai. A spin-off from "McHale's Navy."

Lt. Ann Morgan	Kathleen Nolan
Molly McGuire	Lois Roberts
Roberta Love	Joan Staley
Selma Kowalski	Sheila James
Cmdr. Rogers Adrian	Edward Andrews
Lt. Maxwell Trotter	Dick Sargent
Marion Botnick	Jimmy Boyd
Nicky	Don Edmonds

Producer: Edward J. Montagne

Broadway Open House

Variety; 60 min; NBC 5/22/50 to 8/24/51

TV's first late night series of music, songs, and comedy (broadcast from 11 p.m. to Midnight).

Host: Jerry Lester, Morey Amsterdam, Jack E. Leonard

Regulars: Jennie "Dagmar" Lewis, Barbara Nichols, David Street, Ray Malone, Helen Wood, Elaine Dunn, Maureen Cannon, Marion Colby, Andy Roberts, Buddy Greco

Announcer: Wayne Howell

Orchestra: Milton DeLugg

Producer: Vic McLeod, Ray Buffum, Doug Coulter

Broadway to Hollywood

Variety; 30 min; DuMont 7/20/49 to 7/15/54

A program of music and interviews with hosts George Putnam, Bill Slater, and Conrad Nagel, and regulars Dorothy Claire, Jerry Wayne, and Earl Berton. Music by the Al Logan Trio.

Brock Callahan

Crime Drama Pilot; 30 min; CBS 8/11/59

The exploits of Brock Callahan, a Beverly Hills-based private detective.

Brock Callahan	Ken Clark
Jan Barrett	Randy Stewart
Lt. Larry Pascal	Richard Shannon
Linda Hollander	Barbara Darrow

Producer: James Fonda

Broken Arrow

Western; 30 min; ABC 9/23/58 to 9/20/60

In an attempt to stop the constant Indian attacks on Pony Express Riders, U.S. Army Captain Tom Jeffords decides to confront Apache Chief Cochise and accomplish through talk what weapons cannot. Mutual respect leads to an understanding and the Broken Arrow, the Indian symbol of friendship. Stories, set in Arizona during the 1870s, tells the story of Tom Jeffords as an Indian Agent to the Apache Indians.

Tom Jeffords	John Lupton
Cochise	Michael Ansara
Marshal Stuart Randall	Russ Bender
Duffield	Tom Fadden

Producer: Mel Epstein

Bronco

Western; 60 min; ABC 9/23/58 to 9/20/60

The exploits of Bronco Layne, an ex-Confederate Army captain, as he wanders throughout Texas during the 1860s.

Bronco Layne	Ty Hardin
Toothy Thompson	Jack Elam

Producer: William T. Orr, Arthur Silver, Charles Hoffman

Bronk

Crime Drama; 60 min; CBS 9/21/75 to 7/18/76

The exploits of Alex "Bronk" Bronkov, a police lieutenant operating under special assignment for the mayor of Ocean City, California.

Lt. Alex Bronkov	Jack Palance
Ellen Bronkov	Dina Ousley
Mayor Pete Santori	Joseph Mascolo
Sgt. John Webster	Tony King
Harry Mark	Henry Beckman

Producer: Carroll O'Connor, Bruce Geller

The Bronx Zoo

Drama; 60 min; NBC 3/19/87 to 5/6/87

Seeking a man to run Benjamin Harrison High School, an unruly institution in the Bronx (N.Y.), the board of education assigns Joe Danzig, a tough but dedicated teacher as its principal. Stories relate Joe's efforts to turn the school around and see that his students get an education. Based on the series "Making the Grade."

Joe Danzig	Edward Asner
Sara Newhouse	Kathryn Harrold
Mary Caitlin	
Callahan	Kathleen Beller
Harry Burns	David Wilson
Jack Felspar	Nicholas Pryor
Connie Delvecchio	Linda Thorson
Gus Butterfield	Mykel T. Williamson
Victor Ginelli	Peter Hobbs
Trudy Burgess	Mitzi Hoag
Carol Danzig	Janet Carroll

Producer: Patricia Jones, Donald Reiker, Mel Erros

Brother Rat

Experimental; 70 min; NBC 9/6/39

An early, and perhaps the first TV adaptation of a Broadway play. The humorous story of Bing Edwards (played by Lyle Bettger) and his mischievous school pals. Also cast: Anna Franklin, Tom Ewell, Juliet Forbes, Frederick DeWilde, Marjorie Davies, and Owen Martin. Produced by Edward Sobol.

The Brothers

Comedy; 30 min; CBS 10/2/56 to 9/7/57

Inexperienced and desperately in need of money, brothers Harvey and Gilmore Box pool their resources and purchase a photography studio in San Francisco. Stories relate their efforts to succeed in business.

Harvey Box	Gale Gordon
Gilmore Box	Bob Sweeney
Marilee Dorf	Nancy Hadley
Carl Dorf	Oliver Blake
Sam Box	Howard McNear
Barbara	Barbara Billingsley
Barrington Steele	Robin Hughes
Dr. Margaret Kleeb	Ann Morriss
Hazel	Mary Lansing
Lester	Rodney Bell

Producer: Edward H. Feldman

Brothers

Comedy Pilot; 30 min; CBS 7/30/80

The story of Michael and Allan Radford, two adopted and unlikely brothers (one Jewish, the other Irish) who pick up their lives together after many years of separation.

Michael Radford	Charles Levin
Allan Radford	James O'Sullivan
Sheri Radford	Dori Brenner
Horatio Beckett	Bobby Ramsen
Lee On Wong	James Hong
Rhonda	Jeanetta Arnette

Producer: Ric Podell

Brothers

Comedy; 30 min; SHO 7/13/84 (Premiere)

Incidents in the lives of three brothers; Lou Waters, the eldest; Joe, the middle brother, and Cliff, the youngest, a gay.

Cliff Waters	Paul Regina
Joe Waters	Robert Walden
Lou Waters	Brandon Maggart
Penny Waters	Hallie Todd

Producer: Stu Silver, Greg Antonacci

Brothers and Sisters

Comedy; 30 min; NBC 1/21/79 to 4/6/79

The high jinks between Pi Nu Fraternity and Gamma Delta Iota, its sister sorority at the Larry Krandall College.

Larry Krandall	William Windom
Suzi Cooper	Mary Crosby
Mary Lee	Amy Johnston
Isabel	Susan Gotton
Margie	Jana Hill
Yoko	Marilyn Tokuda
Checko Sabolick	Chris Lemmon
Stanley Zipper	Jon Cutler
Ronald Holmes	Randy Brooks
Harlan Ramsey	Larry Anderson
Hattie	LaWanda Page

Producer: Arthur Silver, Bob Brunner

The Brothers Brannagan

Crime Drama; 30 min; Syn. 1960

The exploits of brothers Mike and Bob Brannagan, private detectives based in Phoenix, Arizona.

Mike Brannagan	Steve Dunne
Bob Brannagan	Mark Roberts
Sally Ross	
(secretary)	Rebecca Wells

Producer: Wilbur Stark

Brown Sugar

Documentary; 60 min; PBS Syn. 2/86

A well-produced series that recalls, via clips, stills, and photographs, the personal and professional lives of black female entertainers.

Host: Billy Dee Williams

Producer: Donald Bogle

Bruce Forsyth's Hot Streak

Game; 30 min; ABC 1/6/86 to 4/5/86

Two five-member teams compete in a game wherein one member must get the next to identify specific words via indirect clues.

Host: Bruce Forsyth

Announcer: Gene Wood

Producer: Robert Noah

The Buccaneers

Adventure; 30 min; CBS 9/22/56 to 9/14/57

The exploits of Dan Tempest, a buccaneer in the 1720s, as he battles the injustice of Spanish rule. Also known as "Dan Tempest."

Capt. Dan Tempest	Robert Shaw
Lt. Beamish	Peter Hammond
Gov. Woods Rogers	Alec Clunes
Blackbeard	Terrence Cooper
Gaff	Brian Rawlinson
Paula Meadows	Jane Griffith

Producer: Hannah Weinstein

Buchanan High School

Drama; 30 min; Syn. 10/85

Incidents in the lives of the staff members of "The Bugle," the newspaper of fictional Buchanan High School.

Nicki Peck	Sherry Hursey
Luigi McNeil	Ike Eisenmann
Clark Prescott	Bruno Kirby
Ernie Tuttle	Al Eisenmann

Producer: Elwood Kieser

Buck James

Drama; 60 min; ABC 9/27/87 (Premiere)

The story of Frank "Buck" James, a crack, no-nonsense surgeon and head of the trauma section of a large university hospital in Texas (Holloman Hospital).

Frank James	Dennis Weaver
Jenny James	Shannon Wilcox
Dinah James	Elena Stiteler
Clint James	Jon Maynard Pennell
Dr. Rebecca Meyer	Alberta Watson
Vittorio	Dehl Berti
Henry Carliner	John Collum

Producer: Robert Fuisz, William Storke

Buck Rogers in the 25th Century

Adventure; 30 min; ABC 4/15/50 to 1/30/51

While surveying a mine (in 1919) U.S. Air Corps veteran Buck Rogers is trapped and rendered unconscious by a gas when the roof from behind him caves in. When the earth shifts and fresh air awakens Buck, he discovers that it is the year 2430. Stories relate Buck's exploits as he joins Lt. Wilma Deering and scientist Dr. Huer in their battle against evil.

Buck Rogers	Kem Dibbs
	Robert Pastene
	Earl Hammond*
Lt. Wilma Deering	Lou Prentis
	Eva Marie Saint*
Dr. Huer	Harry Southern
Black Barney Wade	Harry Kingston

*Stars of the never-telecast pilot version.

Buck Rogers in the 25th Century

Adventure; 60 min; NBC 9/27/79 to 8/20/81

In 1987, while manning the last NASA space probe, a freak accident alters Ranger III's trajectory and freezes the life support systems of its pilot, William "Buck" Rogers. After 500 years in space, Buck awakens to a world still rebuilding itself after a holocaustic war. The first format relates Buck's exploits as he battles evil on behalf of the Earth Federation. The revised format follows Buck as he explores the universe in the spaceship Searcher.

Capt. Buck Rogers	Gil Gerard
Lt. Wilma Deering	Erin Gray
Dr. Elias Huer	Tim O'Connor
Twiki	Felix Silla
Twiki's Voice	Mel Blanc
Dr. Theopolis's	
Voice	Eric Server
Princess Ardella	Pamela Hensley
Kane	Henry Silva
	Michael Ansara
Dr. Goodfellow	Wilfrid Hyde-White
Adm. Isaac Asimov	Jay Garner
Hawk	Thom Christopher
Crichton's Voice	Jeff David

Producer: Glen A. Larson, Leslie Stevens, Bruce Lansbury

Buckskin

Western; 30 min; NBC 7/3/58 to 9/25/58

The story of Annie O'Connell, a widow and the owner of a hotel in Buckskin, Montana, during the 1880s.

Annie O'Connell	Sallie Brophy
Jody O'Connell	Tommy Nolan
Sheriff Tom Sellers	Mike Road
Ben Newcombe	Michael Lipton

Producer: Robert Bassler

Buffalo Bill

Comedy; 30 min; NBC 6/2/83 to 4/5/84

The misadventures of Bill Bittinger, the egotistical, sharp-tongued host of "The Buffalo Bill Show" (a talk show on WBFL, Ch. 12 in Buffalo, N.Y.).

Bill Bittinger	Dabney Coleman
Jo Jo White	Joanna Cassidy
Karl Shub	Max Wright
Wendy Killian	Geena Davis
Woody Deschler	John Fiedler
Tony	Meshach Taylor
Newdell Spriggs	Charles Robinson
Melanie Wayne	Pippa Pearthree

Producer: Tom Patchett, Jay Tarses

Buffalo Bill Jr.

Western; 30 min; Syn. 1955

The story of Buffalo Bill Jr. and his sister, Calamity, as they maintain law and order in Wileyville, Texas (1890s).

Buffalo Bill Jr.	Dick Jones
Calamity	Nancy Gilbert
Judge Ben Wiley	Harry Cheshire

Producer: Armand Schaefer

The Buffalo Billy Show

Children; 30 min; CBS 10/22/50 to 1/14/51

A puppet series about Buffalo Billy, a young adventurer, as he journeys West with a wagon train.

Voices/Puppeteers: Don Messick, Joan Gardner, Bob Clampett, Walker Edmiston, Chris Allen

Producer: Eric Jansen

The Buffalo Soldiers

Western Pilot; 60 min; NBC 5/26/79

The exploits of the U.S. Army's 10th Cavalry, a mostly black unit patrolling the West of the 1860s.

Col. Frank	
O'Connor	John Beck
Sgt. Joshua	
Haywood	Stan Shaw
Caleb Holiday	Richard Lawson
Willie	Hilly Hicks
Oakley	Ralph Wilcox
Pvt. Wright	Charles Robinson
Renegade	L. Q. Jones
Girl	Angel Tompkins
Girl	Marla Pennington

Producer: Douglas Netter, Jim Byrnes

Buford and the Ghost

Cartoon; 30 min; NBC 2/3/79 to 9/1/79

"Buford" relates the crime-solving exploits of Buford the bloodhound and his human assistants Cindy and Woody. "The Galloping Ghost" tells of Nugget Nose, a prospector's ghost who haunts a dude ranch in modern times.

Buford	Frank Welker	Barbara Thackery	Joyce Van Patten
Cindy Mae	Pat Parris	Jackson Conway	Miles Chapin
Woody	David Landsberg	Gary Holmes	Jeff Altman
Nugget Nose	Frank Welker	Holly Compton	Jo Jacobson
Fenwick Fuddy	Hal Peary	V. Ogelthorpe	Gregory Itzin
Wendy	Marilyn Schreffler	Charles Medwick	Armen Shimerman
		Minister of Bulba	Gailard Sartain
		Hampton Frazer	Lyle Waggoner

Producer: William Hanna, Joseph Barbera

Producer: Greg Strangis

The Bugaloos

Comedy; 30 min; NBC 9/12/70 to 9/2/72

The evil Benita Bizarre's misguided attempts to destroy the disgusting goodness of the Bugaloos, a group of human-looking, singing insects who protect Tranquility Forest from evil.

Benita Bizarre	Martha Raye
Bugaloo Joy	Caroline Ellis
Bugaloo Harmony	Wayne Laryea
Bugaloo IQ	John McIndoe
Firefly Sparky	Billy Barty
Tweeter	Van Snowden
Woofer	Joy Campbell
Flunky Rat	Sharon Baird

Producer: Si Rose, Sid and Marty Krofft

The Buick Circus Hour

Musical Drama; 60 min; NBC 10/7/52 to 6/16/53

Circus variety acts coupled with the story of an aging clown and his attempts to help a young singer (Kim) who has just joined the troupe.

Clown	Joe E. Brown
Kim O'Neill	Dolores Gray
Ringmaster	Frank Gallop
Bill Southern	John Riatt

Orchestra: Victor Young

Producer: John C. Wilson

Bulba

Comedy Pilot; 30 min; ABC 8/3/81

The antics of the staff members of the U.S. Embassy on Bulba, a tiny island in the Indian Ocean.

Bullseye

Game; 30 min; Syn. 9/80

A player pushes a button that stops three spinning wheels. The first two wheels reveal a category topic and a money amount. The player must answer the number of questions specified by the third wheel to win the money.

Host: Jim Lange

Announcer: Jay Stewart, Charlie O'Donnell

The Bullwinkle Show

Cartoon; 30 min; ABC 9/20/64 to 9/2/73

Segments: "Rocky and Bullwinkle" (the adventures of Rocky the Flying Squirrel and his dim-witted friend Bullwinkle J. Moose); "Dudley Do-Right" (a simple-minded Canadian Mountie); "Peabody's Improbable History" (Peabody the Dog and Sherman the Boy travel back in time to help famous people); "Aesop's Fables" and "Fractured Fairy Tales."

Rocky	June Foray
Bullwinkle	Bill Scott
Boris Badenov	Paul Frees
Natasha Fataly	June Foray
Dudley Do-Right	Bill Scott
Snidley Whiplash	Hans Conried
Insp. Ray K.	
Fenwick	Paul Frees
Nell Fenwick	June Foray
Mr. Peabody	Bill Scott
Sherman	Walter Tetley
Aesop	Charlie Ruggles
Aesop's Son	Daws Butler
Fairy Tales Narrator	Edward Everett Horton

Producer: Jay Ward, Bill Scott

Bumpers

Comedy Pilot; 30 min; NBC 5/16/77

The misadventures of Joey Webber, a Detroit car assembly-line worker.

Joey Webber	Richard Masur
Rozzie Webber	Stephanie Faracy
Murphy	Jack Riley
Andy	Michael McManus
Jennifer	Zane Buzby
Ernie Stapp	Brian Dennehy

Producer: Charlotte Brown, David Davis

Bunco

Crime Drama Pilot; 60 min; NBC 1/13/77

The exploits of Ben Gordean and Ed Walker, detectives with the Bunco Division of the L.A.P.D.

Ben Gordean	Tom Selleck
Ed Walker	Robert Urich
Off. Frankie Dawson	Donna Mills
Lt. Hyatt	Milt Kogan
Yousha	Arte Johnson
Winky	Will Geer

Producer: Lee Rich, Philip Capice

Bungle Abbey

Comedy Pilot; 30 min; NBC 5/31/81

The misadventures of a group of Benevolence Monks assigned to the San Fernando Abbey founded by Brother Bungle (hence the title).

The Abbott	Gale Gordon
Brother Charles	Charlie Callas
Brother Hush	Guy Marks
Brother Virgil	Graham Jarvis
Brother Gino	Gino Conforti
Brother Peter	Peter Palmer
Brother Antony	Antony Alda

Producer: Lucille Ball

Burke's Law

Mystery; 60 min; ABC 9/20/63 to 8/31/65

The cases of Amos Burke, a multimillionaire police captain and head of the Homicide Division of the L.A.P.D. See also "Amos Burke, Secret Agent."

Amos Burke	Gene Barry
Det. Tim Tillson	Gary Conway
Det. Lester Hart	Regis Toomey
Henry	Leon Lontoc
Sgt. Ames	Eileen O'Neill
Lt. Joe Nolan	Barry Kelly

"Burke's Law" theme by Herschel Burke Gilbert

Producer: Aaron Spelling

The Bureau

Comedy Pilot; 30 min; NBC 7/26/76

The exploits of Peter Davlin, the inept chief of The Bureau, a government investigation unit.

Peter Davlin	Henry Gibson
Kate Peterson	Barbara Rhoades
Paul Browning	Richard Gilliland
Charlie Sunglasses	Arnold Stang
"Combat" Cummings	Beeson Carroll
Agent Butterfield	John Lawlor

Producer: Gerald I. Isenberg

The Burns and Schreiber Comedy Hour

Variety; 60 min; ABC 6/30/73 to 9/1/73

Low-key, physical comedy with the team of Burns and Schreiber.

Hosts: Jack Burns, Avery Schreiber

Regulars: Teri Garr, Fred Willard, Gloria Mills, Pat Proft, Frank Welker, Robert Ito

Orchestra: Jack Elliott, Allyn Ferguson

Producer: Bernie Brillstein

Bus Stop

Drama; 60 min; ABC 10/1/61 to 3/25/62

Stories of lost and troubled people who stop at the Sherwood Bus Depot and Diner in Sunrise, Colorado, and their attempts to overcome their difficulties.

Grace Sherwood	Marilyn Maxwell
Elma Gahringer	Joan Freeman
Will Mayberry	Rhodes Reason
Glenn Wagner	Richard Anderson

Producer: William Self

The Busters

Adventure Pilot; 60 min; CBS 5/28/78

The story of Chad Kimbrough and Albie McRae, cowboys who team to tackle the professional rodeo circuit.

Chad Kimbrough	Bo Hopkins
Albie McRae	Brian Kerwin
Wister Kane	Slim Pickens
Marti Hamilton	Devon Ericson
Joanna Bailey	Susan Howard

Producer: Stu Erwin, Jim Byrnes

Busting Loose

Comedy; 30 min; CBS 1/17/77 to 11/16/77

Events in the life of Lenny Markowitz, a 24-year-old who decides to cut the apron strings and begin his own life.

Lenny Markowitz	Adam Arkin
Sam Markowitz	Jack Kruschen
Pearl Markowitz	Pat Carroll
Melody Feebeck	Barbara Rhoades
Vinnie Mordabito	Greg Antonacci
Alan Simmonds	Stephen Nathan
Woody Warshaw	Paul Sylvan
Ralph Kabell	Paul B. Brice
Raymond St. Williams	Ralph Wilcox
Jackie Gleason	Louise Williams

Producer: Mark Rothman, Lowell Ganz

Bustin' Loose

Comedy; 30 min; Syn. 9/87

Following a run-in with the law, Sonny Barnes is assigned by a judge to do community service: Keep house for Mimi Shaw, a social worker struggling to raise four foster children. Stories relate Sonny's misadventures as he uses his carefree attitude to help Mimi raise the kids (Sue Anne, Trish, Rudley, and Nicky).

Sonny Barnes	Jimmie Walker
Mimi Shaw	Vonetta McGee
Sue Anne	Marie Lynn Wise
Trish	Tyren Perry
Rudley	Larry Williams
Nicky	Aaron Lohr

Producer: Topper Carew, Allan Manings

But Mother!

Comedy Pilot; 30 min; NBC 6/27/79

The relationship between a former madam (Billie) and her estranged daughter (Sharon) as they attempt to begin a new life together.

Billie Barkley	Dena Dietrich
Sharon Barkley	Amy Johnston
Trixie	Gloria LeRoy
Harold	Philip Bruns
Carl	Allan Rich

Producer: Bob Schiller, Bob Weiskopf

Butch and Billy and Their Bang Bang Western Movies

Children; 5 min; Syn. 1961

Cartoon characters Butch and Billy Bang Bang host and narrate the cliffhanging adventures of Bronco Bill, an Old West lawman.

Bronco Bill	Bob Cust
Butch Bang Bang	Danny Krieger
Billy Bang Bang	Stevie Krieger

Butch Cassidy and the Sundance Kids

Cartoon; 30 min; NBC 9/8/73 to 8/31/74

The exploits of Butch Cassidy and the Sundance Kids, government agents who pose as a rock group with the World Wide Talent Agency.

Voices: Ross Martin, Hans Conried, Pamela Peters, Virginia Gregg, Mickey Dolenz, Henry Corden, Ronnie Schell

Producer: William Hanna, Joseph Barbera

Butterflies

Comedy Pilot; 30 min; NBC 8/1/79

Comical incidents in the life of Rea Parkinson, a very attractive housewife who feels that her life is a drudge. See the following title also.

Rea Parkinson	Jennifer Warren
Ben Parkinson	John McMartin
Russell Parkinson	Craig Wasson
Adam Parkinson	Robert Doran
Leonard Dean	Jim Hutton

Producer: Roger Gimbel, Tony Converse

Butterflies

Comedy; 30 min; Syn. 6/82

The story of Ria Parkinson, a very pretty 40-year-old housewife who worries about growing old and becoming a drudge. Produced by the BBC.

Ria Parkinson	Wendy Craig
Ben Parkinson	Geoffrey Palmer
Russell Parkinson	Andre Hall
Adam Parkinson	Nicholas Lyndhurst
Ruby	Joyce Windsor
Leonard Dunn	Bruce Montague

Producer: Gareth Gwenlan

Buzzy Wuzzy

A fifteen-minute ABC comedy series featuring the antics of Imogene Coca and Jerry Bergen. Broadcast from 11/17/47 to 12/8/48.

Byline—Betty Furness

Mystery; 30 min; ABC 11/4/51 to 12/16/51

A series of five live mysteries in which Betty Furness plays a reporter who attempts to solve crimes. Produced by George Quint and Hal Davis.

By Popular Demand

Variety; 30 min; CBS 7/2/50 to 9/22/50

Arlene Francis and Robert Alda as hosts of a program featuring performances by undiscovered talent. Music by Harry Sosnik.

The Cabot Connection

Adventure Pilot; 60 min; CBS 5/10/77

The exploits of Marcus Cabot, a jet-set socialite who works as an undercover agent for the U.S. government.

Marcus Cabot	Craig Stevens
Olivia Cabot	Catherine Shirriff
Muffin Cabot	Jane Actman
Stephen Kordiak	Chris Robinson
Harold O'Hara	Warren Kemmerling
Essie	Matilda Calnan
Dolly Foxworth	Gloria DeHaven
Brom Loomis	Dirk Benedict

Producer: Barry Weitz

Cactus Jim

Edited versions of theatrical westerns with Clarence Hartzell and later Bill Bailey as the host (Cactus Jim). NBC 10/31/49 to 10/26/51.

Cade's County

Drama; 60 min; CBS 9/19/71 to 9/4/72

The story of Sheriff Sam Cade and his attempts to maintain the law in Madrid County, a southwestern community.

Sam Cade	Glenn Ford
J. J. Jackson	Edgar Buchanan
Arlo Pritchard	Taylor Lacher
Rudy Davillo	Victor Campos
Pete	Peter Ford
Joanie Little Bird	Sandra Ego
Kitty Ann Sundown	Betty Ann Carr

Producer: David Gerber

Caesar's Hour

Variety; 60 min; NBC 9/27/54 to 5/25/57

A program of music and comedy with host Sid Caesar and regulars Carl Reiner, Howard Morris, Nanette Fabray, Janet Blair, Ellen Parker, Earl Wild, Sondra Dell, Virginia Curtis, Cliff Norton and Shirl Conway.

Announcer: Vaughn Monroe, Joe DeSantis

Orchestra: Bernard Green

Producer: Leo Morgan

Cafe De Paris

Music and songs set in a Paris night club with hostess Sylvie St. Clair and the music of The Stan Free Trio. DuMont 1/17/49 to 3/4/49.

Cagney and Lacey

Crime Drama; 60 min; CBS 3/25/82 (Premiere)

The realistic story of Chris Cagney and Mary Beth Lacey, undercover police women with the 14th Precinct of the New York Police Department.

Det. Chris Cagney	Loretta Swit*
	Meg Foster
	Sharon Gless
Det. Mary Beth	
Lacey	Tyne Daly
Lt. Albert Samuels	Al Waxman
Sgt. Mark Petrie	Carl Lumbly
Det. Victor Isbecki	Jefferson Mapin*
	Martin Kove
Det. Paul LaGuardia	Sidney Klute
Harvey Lacey	Roland Hunter*
	John Karlen
Harvey Lacey Jr.	Jamie Dick*
	Tony LaTorre
Michael Lacey	Evan Routbard*
	Troy Slaten
Sgt. Ronald Coleman	Harvey Atkin
Det. Manny	
Esposito	Robert Hegyes
Charlie Cagney	Dick O'Neill
Claudia Petrie	Suzanne Stone
	Jonelle Allen
	Vonetta McGee
Alice (Mary Beth's	
daughter)	Dana & Paige
	Bardolh
	Michele Sepe
Sgt. Dory McKenna	Barry Primus
Thelma Samuels	
(Albert's wife)	Barbara Tarbuck
Brian Cagney	
(Chris's brother)	David Ackroyd
Brigit Cagney	
(Brian's daughter)	Amanda Wyss
Muriel Lacey	
(Harvey's mother)	Penny Santon

Producer: Barney Rosenzweig, Terry Louise Fisher

*TV Movie roles (10/8/81).

Cain's Hundred

Crime Drama; 60 min; NBC 9/19/61 to 9/10/62

Nicholas Cain, a former underworld attorney, teams with the federal authorities in an attempt to bring the nation's top one hundred criminals to justice.

| Nicholas Cain | Peter Mark Richman |

"Theme from Cain's Hundred" by Jerry Goldsmith

Producer: Paul Monash

California Fever

Comedy-Drama; 60 min; CBS 9/25/79 to 12/11/79

The day-to-day lives of a group of teenagers who find fun at Sunset Beach in California.

Vince Butler	Jimmy McNichol
Laurie	Michele Tobin
Ross Whitman	Marc McClure
Rick	Lorenzo Lamas
Vickie	Ruth Cox
Pattie	Heidi Bohay
Lucille	April Clough
Mary Butler	Barbara Tarbuck

Theme Vocal ("California Fever"): Jimmy McNichol

Producer: Paul R. Picard, Mel Swope

The Californians

Western; 30 min; NBC 9/24/57 to 9/6/59

The story of two men, Dion Patrick (episodes 1–22) and Matt Wayne (episodes 23–69), and their attempts to establish a system of law and order in San Francisco during the 1850s.

Dion Patrick	Adam Kennedy
Matt Wayne	Richard Coogan
Jack McGivern	Sean McClory
Martha McGivern	Nan Leslie
R. Jeremy Pitt	Art Fleming
Sam Brennan	Herbert Rudley
Wilma Fansler	Carole Matthews

Producer: Louis F. Edelman

Call Holme

Comedy Pilot; 30 min; NBC 4/24/72

The story of Fabian Holme, a private detective who uses his mastery of disguises to apprehend criminals.

Fabian Holme	Arte Johnson
Miss Musky	Arlene Golonka
Lt. Frank Hayward	Jim Hutton
Phadera Hayes	Linda Cristal
Lester Faulkner	Noel Harrison
Nora Benedict	Hermione Baddeley
Avery Crest	Vic Tayback

Producer: Douglas S. Cramer

Call Mr. D

See "Richard Diamond, Private Detective."

Call My Bluff

Game; 30 min; NBC 3/29/65 to 9/24/65

Object: For players to determine the correct definitions of obscure words.

Host: Bill Leyden

Producer: Mark Goodson, Bill Todman

Call of the West

A syndicated (1969) series of repeat episodes that originally aired on "Death Valley Days." Hosted by John Payne.

Call to Danger

Adventure Pilot; 30 min; CBS 12/10/61

The story of Robert Hale, a U.S. Treasury Department agent, who recruits citizens to help solve crimes (stolen currency plates in this pilot, broadcast on "G.E. Theatre").

Robert Hale	Lloyd Nolan
Johnny Henderson	Larry Blyden
Audrey Henderson	Grace Lee Whitney
Andre Kellman	Edward Andrews
Joseph Kane	Paul Mazursky
Paul Wilkens	Ed Peck

Call to Danger

Adventure Pilot; 60 min; CBS 7/1/68

The story of Jim Kingsley, chief of National Resources, a government agency that recruits citizens with special skills to solve crimes (in the pilot: to retrieve plates for the one dollar bill).

Jim Kingsley	Peter Graves
Paul Wilkens	James Gregory
John Henderson	Daniel J. Travanti
Andrae Kellman	Albert Paulsen
Joseph Kane	William Smithers
Rita Henderson	Laurel Goodwin

Call to Glory

Drama; 60 min; ABC 8/13/84 to 2/12/85

The series, set in the 1960s, relates incidents in the lives of Air Force colonel Raynor Sar-nac, his family, and the men and women of the 4080th Strategic Reconnaissance Wing.

Col. Raynor Sarnac	Craig T. Nelson
Vanessa Sarnac	Cindy Pickett
Jackie Sarnac	Elisabeth Shue
Wesley Sarnac	David Hollander
R. H. Sarnac	Gabriel Damon
Carl Sarnac	Keenan Wynn
Patrick Thomas	Thomas O'Brien
Tom Bonelli	David Lain Baker
Elly Thomas	Kathleen Lloyd
Gen. Hampton	J. D. Cannon
Gen. Mike Thornton	G. D. Spradlin
Jerry Thomas	Joe Hacker

Producer: Jon Avent, Steve Tisch

Callahan

Comedy Pilot; 30 min; ABC 9/9/82

The story of Callahan, curator of the Regis Historical Foundation in New York City, and Rachel Bartlett, his assistant, as they attempt to expose the frauds who profit from faking relics.

Callahan	Hart Bochner
Rachel Bartlett	Jamie Lee Curtis
Marcus Vex	John Harkins
Phloti	John Moschitta Jr.

Producer: Tom Werner, Marcy Carsey

Calling Dr. Storm, M.D.

Comedy Pilot; 30 min; NBC 8/25/77

Events in the life of Jim Storm, a resident surgeon at All Fellows Hospital.

Dr. Jim Storm	Larry Linville
Patti Storm	Sharon Spelman
Paul Storm	Stephen Parr
Dr. Ilko Stendak	Bruce Gordon
Vanessa Stendak	Mary Louise Weller
Maggie Barbour	Marian Mercer

Producer: Stirling Silliphant

Calling Miss Peters

Comedy Pilot; 30 min; NBC 4/25/60

The romantic adventures of Connie Peters, a salesgirl in the Gracious Living department of Cooksins Department Store, and Eddie Rock-well, her secret lover,* the floor manager of

Gracious Living. Aired as "Marked Down for Connie" on "The Alcoa/Goodyear Theatre."

Connie Peters	Elinor Donahue
Eddie Rockwell	Tony Travis
Mr. Vosburgh	
(manager)	Alan Hewitt
Stella (salesgirl)	Shirley O'Neal
Ann (salesgirl)	Beverly Allyson
Billie (salesgirl)	Ann Robinson
Mr. Cramer	Howard McNear
Miss Williams	Alice Backes

Producer: Edward Buzzell, Harry Ackerman

*Store policy forbids employees dating each other.

Calling Terry Conway

Comedy Pilot; 30 min; NBC 7/3/56

The misadventures of Terry Conway, a Las Vegas hotel public relations director.

Terry Conway	Ann Sheridan
Stan	Philip Ober
Pearl McGrath	Una Merkel

Calucci's Department

Comedy; 30 min; CBS 9/14/73 to 12/28/73

The harassed life of Joe Calucci, a soft-hearted office supervisor for the N.Y. State Unemployment Department.

Joe Calucci	James Coco
Shirley Balukis	Candice Azzara
Ramon Gonzales	Jose Perez
Oscar Cosgrove	Jack Fletcher
Elaine P. Fusco	Peggy Pope
Jack Woods	Bill Lazarus
Mitzi Gordon	Rosetta LeNoir
Walter Frohler	Bernard Wexler

Producer: Nick Arnold

Calvin and the Colonel

Cartoon; 30 min; ABC 10/3/61 to 9/22/62

The antics of Calvin Burnside, a not-too-bright bear, and his friend Montgomery J. Klaxon, a cunning fox.

Montgomery J.	
Klaxon	Freeman Gosden
Calvin Burnside	Charles Correll
Maggie Bell Klaxon	Virginia Gregg
Sue	Beatrice Kay
Oliver Wendell	
Klutch	Paul Frees

Producer: Joe Connelly, Bob Mosher

Cambridge Circus

Comedy Pilot; 30 min; Syn. 2/65

Comedy skits with five graduates of England's Cambridge University who write and perform their own material.

Cast: Jonathan Lynn, Tim Brooke-Taylor, Jo Kendall, Bill Oddie, David Hatch.

Cameo Theatre

Anthology; 30 min; NBC 5/16/50 to 8/21/55

Live dramas that feature such performers as Ilona Massey, James Drury, Chester Morris, Sam Wanamaker, Rita Gam, Jan Miner, Constance Bennett, Karen Sharpe, Ed Begley, Judy Parrish, Mildred Natwick, Patricia Breslin, Ernest Truex, Richard Carlson and Mary K. Wells. Produced by Albert McCleery.

Cameo Theatre

A syndicated (1959) series of dramas that originally aired on "Matinee Theatre."

Camouflage

Game; 30 min; ABC 1/9/61 to 11/16/62

Object: For players to find hidden objects in camouflaged cartoon drawings.

Host: Don Morrow

Music: Paul Taubman

Camouflage

Game; 30 min; Syn. 2/80

A revised version of the above title, which see for format.

Host: Tom Campbell

Announcer: Johnny Jacobs

Music: Milton DeLugg

Producer: Chuck Barris

Camp Grizzly

Comedy Pilot; 30 min; ABC 6/30/80

Life at Uncle Bernie's Camp Grizzly, a run-down summer camp with incompetent counselors and decrepit facilities.

Uncle Bernie	Carl Ballantine
Missy	Hilary Thompson
Nick Nickerson	Richard Cox
Furman	Demetre Phillips
Garafala	Jay Fenichel

Producer: Nick Vanoff

Camp Runamuck

Comedy; 30 min; NBC 9/17/65 to 9/2/66

The antics of the counselors of the slipshodly run Camp Runamuck Summer Boys Camp and the impeccably maintained Camp Divine Girls Camp.

Commander Wivenhoe	Arch Johnson
Caprice Yeudelman	Nina Wayne
Mahala May Gruenecker	Alice Nunn
Counselor Spiffy	Dave Ketchum
Counselor Pruitt	Dave Madden
Counselor Malden	Mike Wagner
Counselor Doc Joslyn	Leonard J. Stone
	Frank DeVol
Eulalia Divine	Hermione Baddeley
Counselor Nadine Smith	Beverly Adams
Counselor Ivy	Carol Anderson

Producer: David Swift

Camp Wilderness

Adventure; 30 min; Syn. 12/80

The adventures of a group of teenagers (members of Camp Wilderness) as they explore the natural wonders of the United States.

Counselors: Franci Hogle, Stefan Hayes

Campers: Ruth Ingersoll, Matt Boston, Lisa Catalli, Nora Lester, Phil Catalli, Jeff Kurtz, Korry Blakemor, Steve Abbott

Producer: David Jackson

The Campbell Television Soundstage

Anthology; 30 min; NBC 7/10/53 to 9/3/54

A series of quality dramas, sponsored by the Campbell Soup Company, and featuring such stars as James Dean, Henry Hull, Jean Gillespie, Betsy Von Furstenberg, Jack Lemmon, Walter Matthau, E. G. Marshall, Betsy Palmer, Patricia McCormack, Eileen Heckart, Darren McGavin, Elliott Reid, Janice Rule, and Carl Reiner.

Campo 44

Comedy Pilot; 30 min; NBC 9/9/67

The World War II antics of the American and British residents of Campo 44, an Italian prisoner-of-war camp.

Flickinger	Philip Abbott
Wellington	Jim Dawson
Bergamo	Dino Fazio
Berry	Fred Smoot
Barracutti	Vito Scotti

Producer: Buzz Kulik

Can Do

Game; 30 min; NBC 11/26/56 to 12/31/56

Object: For players to determine, through question and answer rounds, whether or not celebrities can perform certain stunts.

Host: Robert Alda

Can You Top This?

Game; 30 min; ABC 10/3/50 to 3/26/51

A joke, submitted by a home viewer and told by the Joke Teller is rated from zero to one hundred. A panel of three comedians then attempts to beat the score with a joke in the same category. The home viewer receives money for each panelist who fails to beat the established score.

Host: Ward Wilson

Joke Teller: Edward Ford

Panelists: Harry Hersfield, Joe Laurie Jr., Peter Donald

Producer: Edward Ford

Can You Top This?

Game; 30 min; Syn. 9/70

A revised version of the previous title, which see for format.

Host: Wink Martindale

Joke Teller: Dick Gautier, Richard Dawson

Regular Panelist: Morey Amsterdam

Candid Camera

Comedy; 30 min; ABC 12/5/48 to 8/15/49
CBS 9/12/49 to 8/19/51
ABC 8/27/51 to 8/22/56

Ordinary people, confronted with prearranged situations, are filmed by hidden cameras and caught in the act of being themselves. Based on the radio program "Candid Microphone." When first broadcast on TV, the series was also titled "Candid Microphone" and featured host Allen Funt as "Candid Mike."

Host: Allen Funt

Regular: Jerry Lester

Announcer: Ken Roberts

Producer-Creator: Allen Funt

Candid Camera

Comedy; 30 min; CBS 10/2/60 to 9/3/67

A revised version of the previous title, which see for format.

Host: Allen Funt

Co-Host: Arthur Godfrey, Durward Kirby, Bess Myerson

Regulars: Fannie Falgg, Marilyn Van De Bur, Dorothy Collins, Joey Faye, Betsy Palmer, Marge Green, Tom O'Malley, Thelma Pellmige

Producer: Allen Funt, Bob Banner

Candid Camera

Comedy; 30 min; Syn. 1974 to 1980

The filmed (and taped) reactions of people caught in prearranged, ludicrous situations by hidden cameras.

Host: Allen Funt

Co-Host: John Bartholomew Tucker, Phyllis George, Jo Ann Pflug, Betsy Palmer

Regulars: Fannie Flagg, Sheila Burnett

Producer: Allen Funt

Candid Kids

Comedy Pilot; 30 min; NBC 3/16/85

A proposed juvenile version of "Candid Camera." Children, placed in prearranged situations, are caught in the act of being themselves.

Host: Allen Funt

Co-Host: Nancy McKeon

Producer: Allen Funt, Thomas Lynch

The Canned Film Festival

Comedy; 90 min; Syn. 6/86

When the Majestic Theatre begins to suffer from a lack of movie goers, Laraine Potter hits on the idea to screen the best of the worst films ever made. The series, set in a movie theatre, features a cast performing skits between acts of films so bad that many have never before seen the light of TV.

Laraine Potter
(Hostess)   Laraine Newman

Regulars: F. Richards Ford, Laura Galusha, Patrick Garner, Phil Nee, Kathryn Rossetter

Producer: Jeff Lewenda, Michael Yudin

Cannon

Crime Drama; 60 min; CBS 9/14/71 to 9/19/76

The exploits of Frank Cannon, a highly paid (and overweight) private detective.

Frank Cannon — William Conrad
Lt. Rea Eiler — Kathryn Reynolds
Lt. Ed Misner — Andy Romano

Producer: Quinn Martin

Cannonball

Adventure; 30 min; Syn. 1958

The adventures of Mike "Cannonball" Malone and Jerry Austin, drivers for the International Transport Trucking Company.

Mike Malone — Paul Birch
Jerry Austin — William Campbell

Producer: Rudy E. Abel, Robert Maxwell

Capitol Capers

Variety; 15 min; NBC 8/1/49 to 9/7/49

A live program of music and songs from Washington, D.C. with host Glenn Archer and the music of the Cliff Quartet.

Cap'n Ahab

Comedy Pilot; 30 min; CBS 9/3/65

At the reading of a will, Tillie Meeks and her distant cousin, Maggie Feeney, inherit money, a New York townhouse, and a 97-year-old parrot named Cap'n Ahab. The unsold series was to relate Tillie and Maggie's efforts to keep their inheritance by living together and caring for Cap'n Ahab.

Tillie Meeks — Judy Canova
Maggie Feeney — Jaye P. Morgan
Battersea — Don Porter
Angelo — Sid Gould
Miss Langdon — Francine York
Emcee — Eddie Quillan

Producer: Hal Kanter; Director: Richard Crenna

Capsule Mysteries

Glenn Langan (as Inspector Drew) in a three and one-half minute syndicated (1951) series in which a complete mystery is presented and solved.

Captain America

Adventure Pilot; 2 hrs; CBS 1/19/79

When Steve Rogers, the son of a famous World War II scientist, is critically injured in an accident, he is given a special serum (FLAG—Full Latent Ability Gain) developed by his father. The serum saves Steve's life and endows him with superhuman abilities (which he uses as Captain America to battle evil). The first pilot relates Steve's efforts to stop a madman who is threatening to destroy the world with a neutron bomb.

Steve Rogers — Reb Brown
Dr. Simon Mills — Len Birman
Dr. Wendy Day — Heather Menzies
Lou Brackett — Steve Forrest
Harley — Lance LeGault
Sandrini — Joseph Ruskin

Producer: Allan Balter

Captain America

Adventure Pilot; 60 min; CBS 11/23 and 11/24/79

A second pilot (see above title) about the exploits of a daring crime fighter. The story relates Captain America's (alias Steve Rogers) efforts to locate a kidnapped scientist who possesses the ability to accelerate the aging process.

Steve Rogers — Reb Brown
Dr. Simon Mills — Len Birman
Dr. Wendy Day — Connie Sellecca
Miguel — Christopher Lee
Yolanda — Lana Wood
Prof. Ilson — Christopher Cary
June Cullen — June Dayton

Producer: Allan Balter

The Captain and Tennille

Variety; 60 min; ABC 9/20/76 to 3/14/77

A weekly program of music and songs.

Host: Toni Tennille, Daryl Dragon

Regulars: Melissa Tennille, Billy Barty, Dave Shelley, Damian London, Jerry Trent, Joan Lawrence, Milton Frome

Orchestra: Lenny Stack

Producer: Dick Clark, Mace Neufeld, Alan Bernard

Captain Billy's Mississippi Music Hall

Variety; 30 min; CBS 8/16/48 to 11/26/48

Comedy, music, songs and dramatic vignettes set against the background of a paddle-wheel showboat.

Capt. Billy Bryant	Ralph Dunne

Regulars: Virginia Gibson, Johnny Downs, Bibi Osterwald, Juanita Hall, Betty Brewer, George Jason

Orchestra: Vic Smalley, John Gart

Producer: Paul Killiam, Allen Ducovny

Captain Caveman and the Teen Angels

Cartoon; 30 min; ABC 3/8/80 to 6/21/80

While exploring a cave, Taffy, Brenda and Dee Dee, three beautiful girls known as the Teen Angels, release and befriend a prehistoric caveman they find frozen in a block of ice. Stories relate their battle against crime.

Captain Caveman	Mel Blanc
Taffy Dare	Laurel Page
Brenda Chance	Marilyn Schreffler
Dee Dee Sykes	Vernee Watson

Producer: William Hanna, Joseph Barbera

Captain David Grief

Adventure; 30 min; Syn. 10/57

The exploits of David Grief, captain of a sloop, as he roams the West Indies.

David Grief	Maxwell Reed
Anura	Maureen Hingert

Producer: Duke Goldstone

Captain Gallant of the Foreign Legion

Adventure; 30 min; NBC 2/13/55 to 2/7/57

The exploits of Michael Gallant, a captain with the French Foreign Legion in North Africa.

Michael Gallant	Buster Crabbe
Cuffy Sanders	Cullen Crabbe
Pvt. Fuzzy Knight	Fuzzy Knight
Sgt. DuVal	Gilles Queant
Carla	Norma Eberhardt

Producer: Gilbert A. Ralston

Captain Kangaroo

Children; 60 min; CBS 10/30/55 to 12/8/84

An entertaining series that helps children understand their rapidly changing world through sketches, cartoons and songs.

Captain Kangaroo	Bob Keeshan
Mr. Green Jeans	Lumpy Brannum
Debbie	Debbie Weems
Cosmo	Cosmo F. Allegretti
Mr. Baxter	James E. Wall
Banana Man	A. Robbins
Participation Segment Host	Bill Cosby

Captain Midnight

Adventure; 30 min; CBS 9/4/54 to 4/28/56

The exploits of Jim Albright, alias Captain Midnight and the leader of the Secret Squadron, as he battles the sinister forces of evil. Also known as "Jet Jackson, Flying Commando."

Captain Midnight	Richard Webb
Ichabod "Ickky" Mudd	Sid Melton
Aristotle "Tut" Jones	Olan Soule
Chuck Ramsey	Renee Beard

Producer: George Bilson

Captain Nice

Comedy; 30 min; NBC 1/9/67 to 9/4/67

While working in the lab, police chemist Carter Nash develops Super Juice, a liquid that transforms him into Captain Nice, an heroic crime fighter. Stories relate Carter's battle against crime in Big Town, U.S.A.

Carter Nash	William Daniels
Sgt. Candy Cane	Ann Prentiss
Mrs. Nash	Alice Ghostley
Chief Segal	Bill Zuckert
Mayor Finny	Liam Dunn
Mr. Nash	Byron Foulger

Produced by Buck Henry and Jay Sandrich

Captain Power and the Soldiers of the Future

Science Fiction; 30 min; Syn. 9/87

In the year 2147 a war between man and machine begins. As the machines begin to defeat humans, the evil Lord Dread, leader of the Volcanian Empire, creates Bio-Dreads to seek out and destroy all remaining humans. To combat Lord Dread, mankind creates a new breed of warrior—the Soldiers of the Future. Stories, enhanced by computer animation, relate the efforts of one freedom force leader, Captain Power, and his soldiers to defeat Lord Dread.

Capt. Jonathan Power	Tim Dunigan
Lt. Matthew Ellis	Sven-Ole Thorsen
Cpl. Jennifer Chase	Jessica Steen
Maj. Matthew Masterson	Peter MacNeill
Sgt. Michael Baker	Maurice Dean Wint
Lord Dread	David Hamblin

Producer: Gary Goodard, Tony Christopher, Douglas Netter.

Captain Safari of the Jungle Patrol

Adventure; 30 min; CBS 5/21/55 to 8/13/55

The adventures of a jungle explorer (Captain Safari) whose expeditions unfold through a magic TV screen.

Capt. Safari	Randy Knight
Sylvester	Zippy the Chimp

Announcer: Randy Kraft

Producer: Louis Freedman

Captain Scarlet and the Mysterons

Marionettes; 30 min; Syn. 1967

While Spectrum, an organization established to safeguard the world, explores Mars, the Mysterons, its inhabitants, believe their world is being attacked and declare war on Earth. Episodes relate Spectrum's battle against the never-seen Mysterons war of attrition.

Captain Scarlet	Francis Matthews
Colonel White	Donald Gray
Captain Grey	Paul Maxwell
Captain Blue	Ed Bishop
Captain Ochre	Jeremy Wilkins
Captain Magenta	Gary Files
Lt. Green	Cy Grant
Dr. Fawn	Charles Tingwell
Symphony Angel	Jana Hill
Melody Angel	Sylvia Anderson
Destiny Angel	Liz Morgan
Rhapsody Angel	Liz Morgan
Harmony Angel	Shin-Lian
Mysteron Voice	Donald Gray

Producer: Gerry Anderson

Captain Video and His Video Rangers

Adventure; 30 min; DuMont 6/27/49 to 8/16/57

The exploits of Captain Video, a scientific genius who possesses amazing electronic weapons, as he battles the people dangerous to the safety and peace of the universe.

Captain Video	Richard Coogan
	Al Hodge
The Video Ranger	Don Hastings
Dr. Pauli	Hal Conklin
	Stephen Elliott
Clipper Evans	Grant Sullivan
Commissioner Carey	Jack Orsen
	Ben Lackland
Tobor the Robot	Dave Ballard
Ranger Carter	Nat Polen
Nargola	Ernest Borgnine
Ranger Colt	Kenneth Nelson
Ranger Rogers	Fred Scott

Producer: Olga Druce, Frank Telford, Al Hodge, James L. Caddington

Captain Z-Ro

Adventure; 30 min; Syn. 1955

Captain Z-Ro, the inventor of a time machine, establishes a day of crisis in the life of an individual. Jet, his assistant, is sent back in time to resolve the situation.

Captain Z-Ro	Roy Steffins
Jet	Bobby Trumbull

Producer: Henry Brown

Captured

A syndicated (1954) series of repeat episodes from "Gangbusters." Hosted by Chester Morris.

Car 54, Where Are You?

Comedy; 30 min; NBC 9/17/61 to 9/8/63

The antics of Gunther Toody and Francis Muldoon, bumbling police officers (assigned to Car 54) with the 53rd Precinct in the Bronx, N.Y.

Off. Gunther Toody	Joe E. Ross
Off. Francis Muldoon	Fred Gwynne
Capt. Martin Block	Paul Reed
Lucille Toody	Beatrice Pons
Off. Leo Schnauzer	Al Lewis
Sylvia Schnauzer	Charlotte Rae
Off. Ed Nicholson	Hank Garrett
Sgt. Sol Abrams	Nathaniel Frey
Off. Rodrigues	Jack Healy
Off. Anderson	Nipsey Russell
Off. O'Hara	Al Henderson
Off. Steinmetz	Joseph Warren
Off. Kissel	Bruce Kirby
Off. McBride	Jimmy Little
Mrs. Bronson	Molly Picon
Mrs. Muldoon	Ruth Masters
Peggy Muldoon	Helen Parker
Cathy Muldoon	Nancy Donohue
Al	Carl Ballantine
Rose	Martha Greenhouse
Claire Block	Louise Kirtland
	Patricia Bright
Charlie the drunk	Larry Storch

Producer: Nat Hiken

Car Wash

Comedy Pilot; 30 min; NBC 5/24/79

The antics of the crew of the Great American Car Wash, a Los Angeles garage, gas station and car wash.

Last Chance	Stuart Pankin
Frank Ravelli	Danny Aiello
Charlie	Hilary Beane
Rocky	Matt Landers
Viva	Pepe Serna
Floyd	T. K. Carter
Lloyd	John Anthony Bailey

Producer: Leonard B. Stern

The Cara Williams Show

Comedy; 30 min; CBS 9/23/64 to 9/10/65

The story of Cara Wilton, a secretary, and Frank Bridges, an efficiency expert, employees of Fenwick Diversified Industries, Inc., who marry against company rules and struggle to keep their marriage a secret.

Cara Wilton	Cara Williams
Frank Bridges	Frank Aletter
Damon Burkhardt	Paul Reed
Fletcher Kincaid	Jack Sheldon
Mary Hamilmyer	Jeanne Arnold
Mr. Fenwick	Edward Everett Horton
Martha Burkhardt	Hermione Baddeley
	Reta Shaw

Theme Song, "Cara's Theme" by Kenyon Hopkins

Producer: Keefe Brasselle, Phil Sharpe

The Carmel Myers Show

A series of celebrity interviews hosted by Carmel Myers, a famous star of silent pictures. ABC 6/26/51 to 2/21/52.

Card Sharks

Game; 30 min; NBC 4/22/78 to 10/23/81

A question, based on a survey of 100 people, is stated. The player (two compete) who comes closest to predicting the number of people who said yes, plays high-low card. The first card of five playing cards is shown. The player has to predict whether the next card will be higher or lower. The first player to correctly predict his line of cards wins. See also "The New Card Sharks."

Host: Jim Perry

Hostess: Becky Price, Linda Hocks

Announcer: Gene Wood

Producer: Jonathan Goodson, Chester Feldman

The Care Bears Family

Cartoon; 30 min; ABC 9/13/86 (Premiere)

The story of a family of bears who join forces to prevent Mr. Beastly from destroying all love and feeling in the world.

Tenderheart Bear	Jim Henshaw
Grumpy Bear	Bob Dermer
Brave Heart Lion	Dan Hennessey
Mr. Beastly	John Stocker

Producer: Michael Hirsh

Caribe

Crime Drama; 60 min; ABC 2/17/75 to 8/11/75

The story of Ben Logan and Mark Walters, Miami-based police agents who tackle special crime-fighting assignments in the Caribbean.

Lt. Ben Logan	Stacy Keach
Sgt. Mark Walters	Carl Franklin
Capt. Ed Rawlings	Robert Mandan

Producer: Quinn Martin

Carlton Your Doorman

Cartoon Pilot; 30 min; CBS 5/21/80

The story of Carlton, a New York City doorman who seeks to better his position in life. Based on the never-seen (only heard) doorman on the "Rhoda" series.

Carlton	Lorenzo Music
Charles Shaftman	Jack Somack
Mrs. Shaftman	Lucille Meredith
Carlton's mother	Lurene Tuttle
Darlene	Kay Cole

Producer: Lorenzo Music, Barton Dean

Carol

Comedy Pilot; 30 min; CBS 2/1/67

The misadventures of Carol Chase, a beautiful, but slightly dizzy secretary to a real estate broker (William Ogelthorpe).

Carol Chase	Elaine Joyce
William Ogelthorpe	Richard Deacon
Lillian Grant	Emmaline Henry
Harry Grant	Cliff Norton
Mark Allen	George Furth

Producer: Paul Henning

Carol Burnett and Company

Variety; 60 min; CBS 8/18/79 to 9/8/79

Music, song and comedy with hostess Carol Burnett and regulars Tim Conway, Vicki Lawrence, Ken Mars and Craig Richard Nelson. Music by Peter Matz. Produced by Joe Hamilton.

Carol Burnett and Friends

A syndicated (1977) series of half-hour programs culled from "The Carol Burnett Show."

The Carol Burnett Show

Variety; 60 min; CBS 9/11/67 to 8/9/78

A weekly series of music, songs and comedy sketches.

Hostess: Carol Burnett

Regulars: Lyle Waggoner, Vicki Lawrence, Tim Conway, Dick Van Dyke, Shirley Kirkes, April Nevins, Vivian Bonnell

Orchestra: Harry Zimmerman, Peter Matz

Producer: Joe Hamilton

The Carol Channing Show

Comedy Pilot; 30 min; Unaired (Produced for CBS in 1967)

Seeking to further her career as an actress, Carol Hunnicutt leaves Indiana and heads for New York. The unsold pilot relates Carol's first experiences in Manhattan. The only known series attempt for Miss Channing.

Carol Hunnicutt	Carol Channing
Florence Thatcher	Jane Dulo
Leon Thatcher	Richard Deacon

Producer: Desi Arnaz

Carolyn

Comedy Pilot; 30 min; NBC 8/7/56

The story of Carolyn Daniels, an actress who becomes the guardian of three children after the death of her best friend.

Carolyn Daniels	Celeste Holm
Elizabeth	Patricia Morrow
Candy	Susan Hawkins
Buster	Jimmy Hawkins
Smattering	Parley Baer
Miss Tuttle	Jeanette Nolan
Reporter	Kay Walker

The Carolyn Gilbert Show

A 15-minute program of music and song with Carolyn Gilbert. ABC 1/15/50 to 7/30/50.

Carson's Comedy Classics

A syndicated (9/85) series of comedy highlights from "The Tonight Show Starring Johnny Carson." Written, produced and directed by Kenneth J. Koerner. Announcer: Ed McMahon.

Carter Country

Comedy; 30 min; ABC 9/15/77 to 8/23/79

The bickering relationship between Roy Mobey, a white, old-fashioned police chief (of Clinton Corners, Georgia), and Curtis Baker, his sergeant, an urban, black, N.Y.P.D. officer.

Chief Roy Mobey	Victor French
Sgt. Curtis Baker	Kene Holliday
Mayor Teddy	
Burnside	Richard Paul
Off. Jasper DeWitt	Harvey Vernon
Off. Cloris Phebus	Barbara Cason
Off. Harley Puckett	Guich Koock
Lucille Banks	Vernee Watson

Producer: Bud Yorkin, Saul Turteltaub, Bernie Orenstein, Austin and Irma Kalish

Cartoon Teletales

Children; 30 min; ABC 11/14/48 to 9/24/50

An artist (Charles Luchsinger) draws line sketches to illustrate the yarns spun by Jack Luchsinger. Produced by Barry Schloes.

Cartoonsville

Cartoon; 30 min; ABC 4/6/63 to 9/28/63

Paul Winchell as the host of several theatrical cartoons ("The Cat," "Goodie the Gremlin," "Jeepers Creepers" and "Scatt Skit").

Cartune-O

Game; 30 min; DuMont 1950

Object: For players to guess song titles via clues drawn by an artist.

Host: Holland Engle, Lee Bennett

Regulars: Nancy Wright, Peggy Taylor, The Temptones

Artist: Arv Miller

Orchestra: Robert Trendler

Casablanca

Drama; 60 min; ABC 9/27/55 to 4/24/56

The story of Rick Blaine, the owner of the Cafe Americain (in Casablanca), as he helps people in trouble by offering his bar as a place of refuge. Aired on "Warner Brothers Presents."

Rick Blaine	Charles McGraw
Sam	Clarence Muse
Ilsa Lund Laszlo	Anita Ekberg
Victor Laszlo	Peter Van Eyck
Captain Renaud	Marcel Dalio

Producer: Joel Robinson

Casablanca

Drama; 60 min; NBC 4/10/83 to 9/3/83

A second series about Rick Blaine, the owner of Rick's Cafe Americain in Nazi-occupied French Morocco in 1941, as he assists people in trouble.

Rick Blaine	David Soul
Sam	Scatman Crothers
Sacha	Ray Liotta
Louie Ranault	Hector Elizondo
Maj. Henrich	
Strasser	Patrick Horgan
Ferrari	Reuben Bar-Yotam
Lt. Heinz	Kai Wulff
Carl	Arthur Malet

Producer: David L. Wolper, Harold Gast

Casanova

Drama; 60 min; Syn. 5/81

The story, which contains nudity, uses flashbacks to recall the life of Giovanni Cassanova, an 18th-century Italian lover and poet.

Giovanni Cassanova	Frank Finlay
Christina	Zienia Merton
Lorenzo	Norman Rossington
Barbarina	Christine Noonan
Rose	Julie Cornelius
Nanan	Bridget Bates
Anna	Carolyn Bowbesvlo
Columbia	Rowan Wylie
Helena	Elaine Donnelly

The Case of the Dangerous Robin

Mystery; 30 min; Syn. 1961

The story of Robin Scott and Phyllis Collier, insurance investigators, as they attempt to expose people who defraud insurance companies.

Robin Scott	Rick Jason
Phyllis Collier	Jean Blake

Theme Song ("Robin's Theme") by David Rose

The Casebusters

Comedy Pilot; 60 min; ABC 5/25/86

The exploits of Allie and Jamie Donahue, sister and brother amateur sleuths who help their grandfather (Sam), a security service owner, solve crimes.

Sam Donahue	Pat Hingle
Allie Donahue	Virginia Keehne
Jamie Donahue	Noah Hathaway
Anthony Zubrowski	Gary Riley
Capt. Harry Fogel	Arthur Taxier
Loretta Bonner	Sharon Barr

Producer: John Garbett

The Cases of Eddie Drake

Crime Drama; 30 min; DuMont 3/6/52 to 5/29/52

The story of Eddie Drake, a private detective who receives assistance from Karen Gayle, a psychologist who is writing a book on criminal behavior.

Eddie Drake	Don Haggerty
Karen Gayle	Patricia Morrison

Producer: Harlan Thompson, Herbert L. Strock

Casey Jones

Adventure; 30 min; Syn. 1957

The series, set in Jackson, Tennessee (1890s) tells the story of John Luther "Casey" Jones, engineer of the Illinois Central Railroad's Cannonball Express.

Casey Jones	Alan Hale Jr.
Alice Jones	Mary Lawrence
Casey Jones Jr.	Bobby Clark
Red Rock	Eddy Waller
Wallie Simms	Dub Taylor
Sam Peachpit	Pat Hogan
Mr. Carter	Paul Keast

Producer: Harold Green

Cash and Carry

Game; 30 min; DuMont 6/20/46 to 7/1/47

Dennis James as the host of a show, set in a grocery store, and in which contestants answer questions that are attached to the labels of the sponsor's product (Libby's Foods).

Casper and Friends

Cartoon; 6 to 8 min; Syn. 1963

The title for various Harvey Films theatrical cartoons produced between 1946 and 1959. Included: "Casper the Friendly Ghost," "Herman and Katnip," "Little Audry" and "Baby Huey."

Casper	Mae Questel
	Norma McMillan
	Gwen Davis
	Cecil Roy
Little Audry	Mae Questel
Baby Huey	Syd Raymond
Herman	Arnold Stang
Katnip	Syd Raymond

Casper and the Angels

Cartoon; 30 min; NBC 9/22/79 to 9/20/80

The exploits of Casper the Friendly Ghost as he and Minnie and Maxie, two 21st-century Space Patrol Women, attempt to maintain the peace in outer space.

Casper	Julie McWhirter
Officer Minnie	Laurel Page
Officer Maxie	Dian McCannon
Hairy Scary	John Stephenson

Producer: William Hanna, Joseph Barbera

Cass Malloy

Comedy Pilot; 30 min; CBS 7/21/82

The story of Cass Malloy, a wife and mother who, after the untimely death of her husband, replaces him as the sheriff of Burr County, Indiana.

Cass Malloy	Caroline McWilliams
Colleen Malloy	Amanda Wyss
Nona Malloy	Heather Hobbs
Jim Malloy	Corey Feldman
Max Rosencrantz	George Wyner
Tina Marie Nelson	Dianne Kay
Off. Woody Freeman	Glynn Turman
Off. Alvin Dimsky	Dick Butkus

Producer: Karen Mack, Gary Adelson

Cassie and Company

Crime Drama; 60 min; NBC 1/29/82 to 8/20/82

The exploits of Cassie Holland, a beautiful Los Angeles private detective who uses her expertise as a former criminologist to solve crimes.

Cassie Holland	Angie Dickinson
Lyman Shackelford	John Ireland
Meryl Foxx	Dori Brenner
Mike Holland	Alex Cord
Benny Silva	A Martinez

Producer: Nigel and Evan Mckeand

Castle Rock

Gothic Drama Pilot; 73 min; CBS 7/31/81

The story of Celena McKenna, an Irish girl who becomes involved in the supernatural existences of the Stratton family, when she becomes governess to ten-year-old Annabell. (The title refers to the Stratton's home.)

Celena McKenna	Cyndi Girling
Michael Stratton	James Burge
Annabell Stratton	Tangie Beaudin
Alice Somers	Margaret Phillips
Joan Donahue	Tedde Moore
Simon Donahue	Dave Nichols
Jeanette Stewart	Linda Mason Greene
Elizabeth Stratton	Janet Lynn Greene

Producer: Mel and Ethel Brez

Cat Ballou

Comedy Pilot; 30 min; NBC 9/5/71

The adventures of Cat Ballou, a beautiful Old West heroine. In the first pilot (see next title), Cat attempts to start a school.

Cat Ballou	Lesley Ann Warren
Kid Sheleen	Jack Elam
Jackson Two Bears	Tom Nardini
Sheriff	Joel Higgins
Land Developer	Laurie Main
Clay	Bo Hopkins

Cat Ballou

Comedy Pilot; 30 min; NBC 9/6/71

The comical adventures of Cat Ballou, the rather unorthodox Old West heroine, as she (in the second pilot) hires Kid Sheleen, the intoxicated ex-gunfighter, to protect her from a land-hungry rancher.

Cat Ballou	Jo Ann Harris
Kid Sheleen	Forrest Tucker
Jackson Two Bears	Lee J. Casey
Rancher	Harry Morgan
Clay	Bryan Montgomery
Spider Levinsky	Jim Luisi
Indian Chief	Jay Silverheels

Catalina C-Lab

Adventure Pilot; 60 min; NBC 1/3/82

The exploits of the oceanographers attached to the Gamma Foundation, a marine research center off California's Catalina Island.

Dr. Matt Jennings	Bruce Weitz
Christy Jennings	Melora Hardin
Rick Guthrie	Jeff Daniels
Johnny Silver	Gary Prendergast
Valerie Ono	Nani Asing
Dwight Purdy III	Steve Vinovitch
Tom Whitehead	Malachy McCourt

Producer: Marty Katz

Catch Phrase

Game; 30 min; Syn. 9/85

Object: For players to identify computer-generated catch phrases in return for money.

Host: Art James

Assistant: Shana Forman

Announcer: John Harlan

Producer: Steve Radosh

Catch 22

Comedy Pilot; 30 min; ABC 5/21/73

The World War II antics of an Air Force base that is staffed by an assortment of odd people.

Captain Yossarian	Richard Dreyfuss
Colonel Cathcart	Dana Elcar
Colonel Korn	Stewart Moss
Milo Minderbinder	Andy Jarrell
Lt. McWatt	Frank Welker
Nurse Duckett	Susan Zenor

Producer: Richard Bluel

The Cattanooga Cats

Cartoon; 60 min; ABC 9/6/69 to 9/4/71

Segments: "The Cattanooga Cats" (antics of Chessie, Kitty Jo, Scootz, Groovey and Country, a feline rock group); "It's the Wolf" (Mildew Wolf's efforts to catch Lambsey the lamb); "Around the World in 79 Days" (Phineas Fogg Jr.'s efforts to circle the globe); "Auto Cat and Motor Mouse" (a cat who is determined to beat a mouse in an auto race).

Chessie/Kitty Jo	Julie Bennett
Groovey	Casey Kasem
Scootz	Jim Begg
Country	Bill Calloway
Mildew Wolf	Paul Lynde
Lambsey	Daws Butler
Bristol Hound	Allan Melvin
Phineas Fogg Jr.	Bruce Watson
Jenny Trent	Janet Waldo
Happy	Don Messick
Crumdon	Daws Butler
Motor Mouse	Dick Curtis
Auto Cat	Marty Ingels

Producer: William Hanna, Joseph Barbera

Cavalcade of America

A series of dramas based on the people and events that have shaped America. The 60-minute program began on NBC on 10/1/52 and ended 6/24/53. ABC revised it on 9/29/53 and it ran until 4/30/57. In 1955 it was titled "DuPont Presents the Cavalcade Theatre" and finally "The DuPont Theatre" (1956–57).

Cavalcade of Bands

Variety; 60 min; DuMont 1/17/50 to 9/25/51

The music and performers of the Big Band era.

Host: Fred Robbins, Warren Hull, Ted Steele, Buddy Rogers

Regulars: Marsha Van Dyke, The Mellolarks, The Clark Brothers

Cavalcade of Stars

Variety; 60 min; DuMont 6/4/49 to 9/26/52

A series of variety programs tailored to its rotating hosts (Jack Carter, Jackie Gleason, Jerry Lester, and Larry Storch). Produced by Joseph Cates and Jack Hurdle with the announcing of Jack Lescoulie and the orchestra of Sammy Spear.

The Cavanaughs

Comedy; 30 min; CBS 12/1/86 to 3/9/87

Events in the lives of the Cavanaughs, an Irish Catholic family living in Boston.

Francis Cavanaugh	Barnard Hughes
Katherine "Kit" Cavanaugh	Christine Ebersole
Charles Cavanaugh Sr.	Peter Michael Goetz
Mary Margaret Cavanaugh	Mary Tanner
Father Charles Cavanaugh Jr.	John Short
Kevin Cavanaugh	Matt Shakeman
John Cavanaugh	Scott Curtis

Producer: Leonard Goldberg, Deborah Aal, Robert Moloney

The C. B. Bears

Cartoon; 60 min; CBS 9/10/77 to 1/28/78

Segments: "The C. B. Bears" (about three crime-fighting bears, Hustle, Boogie and Bump); "Blast-off Buzzard and Crazy Legs" (a hungry buzzard's efforts to catch a meal: Crazy Legs the snake); "Heyyyyy, It's the King" (antics of a 1950s type, hip-talking lion); "Posse Impossible" (an Old West sheriff's misguided efforts to uphold the law); "Shake, Rattle and Roll" (three ghosts who run the Haunted Inn); "Undercover Elephant" (a government agent and his assistant Loud Mouse).

Hustle	Daws Butler
Bump	Henry Corden
Boogie	Chuck McCann
Charlie	Susan Davis
The King	Lennie Weinrib
Skids	Marvin Kaplan
Yukayuka	Lennie Weinrib
Big H	Sheldon Allman
Sheriff	William Woodson
Deputy Stick	Daws Butler
Deputy Blubber	Chuck McCann
Shake	Paul Winchell
Rattle	Lennie Weinrib
Roll	Joe E. Ross
Undercover Elephant	Daws Butler
Loud Mouse	Bob Hastings

Producer: William Hanna, Joseph Barbera

The CBS Cartoon Theatre

Cartoon; 30 min; CBS 6/13/56 to 9/5/56

A theatrical cartoon series featuring "Heckle and Jeckle," "Gandy Goose" and "Little Roguefort."

Host	Dick Van Dyke
Heckle/Jeckle	Dayton Allen
	Ron Halee
Gandy Goose	Arthur Kay
Little Roguefort	Tom Morrison

The CBS Newcomers

Variety; 60 min; CBS 7/21/71 to 9/6/71

Performances by new talent discoveries.

Host: Dave Garroway

Regulars: Rex Allen Jr., Cynthia Clawson, Peggy Sears, Rodney Winfield, Joey Garya, David Arlen, Paul Perez, Gay Perkins

Orchestra: Nelson Riddle

Producer: Bill Hobin

CBS Storybreak

Cartoon; 30 min; CBS 3/30/85 to 1/18/86

Adaptations of children's literature, hosted by Bob Keeshan, and designed to encourage children to read.

Celanese Theatre

A series of live dramas, broadcast from New York, and sponsored by the Celanese Corporation of America. Produced by A. Burke Crotty and Alex Segal. ABC 10/3/51 to 6/25/52.

Celebrity Billiards

A game in which Minnesota Fats (Rudolph Wanderone Jr.) challenges celebrities to various games of billiards. Syn. 1967.

Celebrity Bowling

Game; 30 min; Syn. 1971

Four celebrities (two teams of two) play a ten frame game for selected studio audience members.

Host: Jed Allan

Assistant: Bobby Cooper, Bill Buneta, Dave Davis, Sherry Kominsky

Celebrity Charades

Game; 30 min; Syn. 1979

Two four-member celebrity teams compete. One player performs a charade, which his teammates must guess. Each player performs a charade and the team with the lowest total guessing time wins.

Host: Jay Johnson

Regulars: Judy Landers, Lani O'Grady, Vernee Watson, Jamie Farr, Robert Mandan, Judy Norton-Taylor, Jon Bowman

Announcer: Dick Patterson

Producer: David Fein

Celebrity Challenge of the Sexes

Game; 30 min; CBS 1/31/78 to 2/28/78

Male and female TV personalities are pitted against one another in various athletic contests.

Host: Tom Brookshire

Female Coach: Barbara Rhoades

Male Coach: McLean Stevenson

Judge: Jim Tunney

Celebrity Cooks

A Canadian produced series (syndicated in 1978) that features celebrities preparing their favorite recipes. Hosted by Bruno Gerussi.

The Celebrity Game

Game; 30 min; CBS 4/5/64 to 9/13/64
4/18/65 to 9/9/65

Object: For players to predict how a panel of nine celebrities answered specific questions.

Host: Carl Reiner

Producer: Merrill Heatter, Bob Quigley

Celebrity Playhouse

A syndicated (1955) series of dramas that originally aired on "Schlitz Playhouse of Stars."

Celebrity Revue

Interviews and performances by celebrities with hosts Carole Taylor and Tommy Banks. Syndicated in 1976.

Celebrity Sweepstakes

Game; 30 min; NBC 4/1/74 to 10/10/76

Object: For a player to select one celebrity (from six) and predict whether or not he was able to correctly answer a question that was previously asked. A correct guess scores points and the player with the highest score wins.

Host: Jim McKrell

Regulars: Carol Wayne, Joey Bishop, Buddy Hackett

Announcer: Bill Armstrong

Producer: Ralph Andrews, Burt Sugarman

Celebrity Talent Scouts

Variety; 60 min; CBS 8/1/60 to 9/26/60

Sam Levinson as the host of a program wherein celebrities present undiscovered talent. Music by Harry Sosnik and produced by Irving Mansfield.

Celebrity Time

Variety; 30 min; CBS 11/20/48 to 1/27/49
ABC 4/3/49 to 3/26/50
CBS 4/2/50 to 9/21/52

A potpourri of music, interviews and game contests. Also known as "The Eyes Have It," "Stop, Look and Listen" and "Riddle Me This."

Host: Conrad Nagel, Ralph McNair, Douglas Edwards, Paul Gallico

Regulars: Ilka Chase, John Daly, Kyle Mac-Donnell, Kitty Carlisle, Mary McCarty, Jane Wilson, Herman Hickman

Producer: Fred Rosen, Steve Alexander

Center Stage

A Summer series (ABC 6/1/54 to 9/21/54) of dramas that aired on other anthology programs.

The Centurions

Cartoon; 30 min; Syn. 9/86

The exploits of Crystal Kane and the Centurions, Max Ray, Jake Rockwell and Ace McCloud, as they defend Earth against the evil Doc Terror and Hacker.

Voices: Pat Farley, Neilson Ross, Vince Edwards, Diane Pershing, Jennifer Darling, Bill Martin, Mona Marshall, John Stephenson, Alan Oppenheimer, Frank Welker

Producer: Joe Ruby, Ken Spears

Chain Letter

Game; 30 min; NBC 7/4/66 to 10/14/66

A category topic is presented to two two-member teams. One player gives a word that corresponds with the subject. The next player must give a word that ends with the last letter of that word. The player who fails to do so breaks the chain and the opposing team scores points. The team with the highest point score is the winner.

Host: Jan Murray

Producer: Stefan Hatos

Chain Reaction

Game; 30 min; NBC 1/14/80 to 6/20/80

A board that contains eight boxes is revealed. Six boxes conceal a word that relates to the words shown in the first and last box. The object calls for players to suggest letters and guess the words that are hidden.

Host: Bill Cullen

Substitute Host: Geoff Edwards

Semi-Regulars: Lois Nettleton, Soupy Sales, Nipsey Russell, Debralee Scott, Joanna Gleason

Announcer: Johnny Gilbert

Producer: Bob Stewart

Chalk One Up for Johnny

Drama Pilot; 60 min; ABC 4/8/62

Dissatisfied with life in California, Johnny Pace, a famous politician, retreats to the island of Kauai, where he and his wife,

Jeanette, open a hotel. The unsold series, broadcast on "Follow the Sun," was to relate the Paces efforts to help people in trouble.

Johnny Pace	Lee Tracy
Jeanette Pace	Rosemary DeCamp
Jennifer	Joanne Gilbert
Theodore	Lew Gallo

Producer: Ellis Kadison

Challenge of the GoBots

Cartoon; 30 min; Syn. 5/85

The exploits of the GoBots, robots who are able to change their forms, as they battle evil in outer space.

Voices: Rene Auberjonois, Candy Brown, Peter Cullen, Bob Holt, Marilyn Lighthouse, Sparky Marcus, Gail Mathius, Brock Peters, Lou Richards, Robert Ridgely, Kelly Ward, Frank Welker

Producer: Joe Ruby, Ken Spears

The Chamber Music Society of Lower Basin Street

A program of swing music with host Orson Bean, vocalist Martha Lou Harp and the music of Henry Levine's Dixieland Octet. ABC 9/14/48 to 9/22/51; NBC 6/15/52 to 8/31/52

Chameleon

Comedy Pilot; 30 min; ABC 7/18/86

When she feels that her mother is being fleeced by a weight loss clinic, Violet Kingsley disguises herself as an overweight woman and goes undercover in an attempt to expose the company. The investigation so impresses Morton Waterman, owner of WGGK-TV, Channel 8, that he hires her as the investigator for the station's pompous consumer editor, Wes Bushnell (host of "The Bushnell Report"). The unsold series was to relate Violet's misadventures as she goes undercover to expose rackets.

Violet Kingsley	Madeline Kahn
Hannah Kingsley	Nina Foch
Morton Waterman	Henry Jones
Wes Bushnell	George Wyner
Lucas Hanlon	Frederick Coffin
Neil Hanlon	Taliesin Jaffe
June	Priscilla Morrill
Dr. Brickman	Hamilton Camp

Producer: Gary Nardino, David Lloyd

Champagne and Orchids

A program of music and song with Adrienne Meyerberg. Announcing by Robert Turner. DuMont 9/6/48 to 1/10/49.

The Champions

Adventure; 60 min; NBC 5/26/68 to 9/9/68

While attempting to escape from enemy agents, Nemesis operatives Sharron Macready, Craig Stirling and Richard Barrett crash into the Himalayas when their plane is struck by gunfire. The lifeless agents are found by a mysterious old man and taken to a lost city. There, they are healed and endowed with amazing powers. Stories relate Sharron, Craig and Richard's exploits as they battle the enemies of the free world.

Sharron Macready	Alexandra Bastedo
Craig Stirling	Stuart Damon
Richard Barrett	William Gaunt
W. L. Tremayne	Anthony Nicholls

Producer: Monty Berman

Chance of a Lifetime

Variety; 30 min; ABC 9/20/50 to 8/20/53
                   DuMont 9/11/53 to 6/17/55
                   ABC 7/3/55 to 6/23/56

In the original format, players have to identify persons, places or objects from clues that are provided by comics or singers. In the revised format, undiscovered professional talent performs in the hope of winning $1,000.

Host: Dennis James, John Reed King

Regulars: Denise Darcel, Russell Arms, Liza Palmer, Dick Collier

Orchestra: Bernard Leighton

Producer: Robert Jennings, Lou Sposa

Change at 125th Street

Comedy Pilot; 30 min; CBS 3/28/74

The story of John Morse, a black Harvard graduate who acquires an executive position in an all-white Wall Street banking firm.

John Morse	Ron Glass
Eloise Morse	Roxie Roker
Harriet Morse	Chip Fields
Uncle Herbert	Vernon Washington
Kip	Terry Kiser
Mr. Murray	Franklin Cover

Producer: Robert Precht

Channing

Drama; 60 min; ABC 9/18/63 to 4/8/64

The story of Joseph Howe, an English professor at mythical Channing University.

Joseph Howe	Jason Evers
Dean Fred Baker	Henry Jones
Assist. Dean Ryder	Marion Ross
Lori Moore*	Suzanne Pleshette
Nancy Kyle*	Dawn Wells
Larry Franklin*	Keir Dullea
Lynn Walton*	Joey Heatherton
Kathy O'Reardon*	Yvonne Craig
Prof. Paul Stafford	Leslie Nielsen
Prof. John Miller	Leo G. Carroll

Producer: Jack Laird, Stanley Rubin

*Students

Characters

Comedy Pilot; 30 min; NBC 10/26/80

Events in the lives of Carol and Jack, acting students at Chicago's Workshop.

Carol Goodman	Maggie Roswell
Jack Elmdorf	Philip Charles MacKenzie
Lelia Flynn	Marcia Wallace
Steve Tucker	Terry Lester

Producer: Ken Levine, David Isaacs

Charade Quiz

Game; 30 min; DuMont 12/4/47 to 6/23/49

Object: For players to identify charades, submitted by home viewers and enacted by a stock company.

Host: Bill Slater

Panelists: Minna Bess Lewis, Herb Polesie, Jackson Beck, Bob Shepard

Regulars: Sandra Poe, Allan Frank, Eileen Fenwick, Richard Seff

Charge Account

Game; 30 min; NBC 9/5/60 to 9/28/62

Object: For players to purchase expensive merchandise items through money that is earned on the program (via making the most three and four letter words from sixteen letters that are shown).

Host: Jan Murray

Assistant: Maureen Arthur, Morgan Schmitter

Announcer: Bill Wendell

Music: Milton DeLugg

The Charles Boyer Theatre

A syndicated (1953) series of dramas with host and frequent star, Charles Boyer.

Charles in Charge

Comedy; 30 min; CBS 10/3/84 to 7/24/85

The story of Charles, a college student who, in return for room and board, becomes the live-in helper for Jill and Stan Pembroke, a busy professional couple with three mischievous kids (Lila, Douglas, and Jason). See the following title also.

Charles	Scott Baio
Jill Pembroke	Julie Cobb
Stan Pembroke	James Widdoes
Lila Pembroke	April Lerman
Douglas Pembroke	Jonathan Ward
Jason Pembroke	Michael Pearlman
Gwendolyn Pierce	Jennifer Runyon
Buddy Lembeck	Willie Aames
Kim	Samantha Smith
Linda	Jade Chin
Heather	Allisun Sturges
Valerie	Betsy Chasse
Irene Pembroke	Rue McClanahan

Producer: Al Burton, Jane Startz

Charles in Charge

Comedy; 30 min; Syn. 1/87

A revised version of the prior title. When he returns from a two week vacation, Charles finds that the Pembrokes have moved to Seattle and have sublet the house to the Powell family (Ellen and her children Jamie, Sarah, and Adam). When Charles learns that Ellen's husband is a Navy commander stationed in the South Seas, he accepts Ellen's offer to live with them (while he attends college) and help her care for the kids. Stories relate Charles's misadventures as he attempts to care for two very pretty sisters and one mischievous boy.

Charles	Scott Baio
Ellen Powell	Sandra Kerns
Jamie Powell	Nicole Eggert
Sarah Powell	Josie Davis
Adam Powell	Alexander Polinsky
Buddy Lembeck (Charles's friend)	Willie Aames
Walter Powell (Ellen's father-in-law)	James Callahan
Jill Pembroke (first episode)	Lisa Donovan
Jason Pembroke (first episode)	Michael Pearlman
Gloria (Buddy's grandmother)	Betsy Palmer

Producer: Al Burton, Jane Startz, Michael Jacobs

Charlie and Company

Comedy; 30 min; CBS 9/18/85 to 4/25/86

The misadventures of Charlie Richmond, an administrative assistant with the Chicago Department of Highways, as he struggles to cope with life at work and at home.

Charlie Richmond	Flip Wilson
Diana Richmond	Gladys Knight
Lauren Richmond	Fran Robinson
Charlie Richmond	Christoff St. John
Robert Richmond	Jaleel White
Walter Simpson	Ray Girardin
Milton Biberman	Richard Karron
Miguel Santana	Eddie Velez
Ronald Sandler	Kip King

Theme Vocal ("We're Family") by Gladys Knight

Charlie Angelo

Comedy Pilot; 30 min; CBS 8/28/62

The story of Charlie Angelo, an angel who has been assigned to earth to promote good and discourage evil.

Charlie Angelo	James Komack
Dan Devlin	Larry Storch
Chico Hernandez	Bernard Kates
Tony	Robert Carricart
Thief	Len Lesser
George	Ben Wright

Producer: Jackie Cooper

The Charlie Brown and Snoopy Show

Cartoon; 30 min; CBS 9/17/83 (Premiere)

The misadventures of the Peanuts Gang (Charlie Brown, his dog, Snoopy, and friends Lucy, Peppermint Patty, Schroeder, Linus, Sally and Pig Pen).

Charlie Brown	Brian Kesten
Lucy	Angela Lee
Snoopy	Bill Melendez

Additional voices: Victoria Vargas, Heather Tolkin, Michael Dockery

Producer: Lee Mendelson, Bill Melendez

The Charlie Chaplin Comedy Theatre

A syndicated (1966) series of excerpts from various Charlie Chaplin comedy shorts of the 1920s. Produced by Vernon P. Becker.

The Charlie Farrell Show

Comedy; 30 min; CBS 7/2/56 to 9/24/56

The story of Charlie Farrell, a retired film star who operates the Racquet Club, a Palm Springs vacation resort.

Charlie Farrell	Himself
Dad Farrell	Charles Winninger
Sherman Hull	Richard Deacon
Rodney Farrell	Jeff Silver
Mrs. Papernow	Kathryn Card
Chef Pierre	Leon Askin
Doris Mayfield	Anna Lee

Producer: Gordon B. Hughes

Charlie Wild, Private Detective

Crime Drama; 30 min; CBS 12/22/50 to 6/27/51
ABC 9/11/51 to 3/4/52
DuMont 3/13/52 to 6/19/52

The exploits of Charlie Wild, a New York-based private detective.

Charlie Wild	Kevin O'Morrison
	John McQuade
Effie Perrine	Cloris Leachman

Producer: Herbert Brodkin

Charlie's Angels

Crime Drama; 60 min; ABC 9/22/76 to 8/19/81

The exploits of Sabrina Duncan, Jill Munroe and Kelly Garrett, three beautiful private detectives employed by Charlie Townsend, the never-seen head of Townsend Investigations.

Sabrina Duncan	Kate Jackson
Jill Munroe	Farrah Fawcett
Kelly Garrett	Jaclyn Smith
Kris Munroe (replaced Jill)	Cheryl Ladd
Tiffany Wells (replaced Sabrina)	Shelley Hack
Julie Rogers (replaced Tiffany)	Tanya Roberts
John Bosley	David Doyle
Charlie's Voice	John Forsythe

Producer: Aaron Spelling, Leonard Goldberg

Charmed Lives

Comedy Pilot; 30 min; ABC 5/13/86

The story of Lauren Sullivan, a beautiful San Francisco photographer turned model. Aired on "Who's the Boss?"

Lauren Sullivan	Donna Dixon
Joyce Columbus	Fran Drescher
Angela Bower	Judith Light
Mickey Day	John Kapelos
Frank Vionelli	John Randolph

The Charmings

Comedy; 30 min; ABC 3/20/87 to 4/24/87

Once upon a time, when a vain queen (Lillian) is told by her magic mirror that her beautiful stepdaughter, Snow White, is the fairest of all, she casts an evil spell that backfires and puts her, Snow White, her husband, Prince Charming, their children Thomas and Cory, and a dwarf (Luther) to sleep for 1000 years. As the series begins, the Charmings have awakened and purchased a home in present-day Burbank. Stories relate the Charmings efforts to adjust to life in 1987.

Snow White	
Charming	Caitlin O'Heaney
	Carol Huston
Prince Eric	
Charming	Christopher Rich
Lillian White	Judy Parfitt
Thomas Charming	Brandon Call
Cory Charming	Garette Ratliff
Sally Miller	
(neighbor)	Dori Brenner
Don Miller (Sally's	
husband)	Paul Eiding
Voice of Lillian's	
Mirror	Paul Winfield
Luther	Cork Hubbert

Producer: Prudence Fraser, Robert Sternin

Charo and the Sergeant

Comedy Pilot; 30 min; ABC 8/24/76

The story of Charo, a beautiful Spanish entertainer, who marries a U.S. Marine sergeant (Hank) and her efforts to adjust to the American way of life.

Charo Palmer	Charo
Sgt. Hank Palmer	Tom Lester
Sgt. Norman Turkel	Noam Pitlik
Chaplain	Dick Van Patten

Producer: Aaron Ruben, John Rich

Chase

Crime Drama; 60 min; NBC 9/11/73 to 9/4/74

The exploits of Chase, L.A.P.D. undercover agents who tackle the cases left unsolved by homicide, robbery and burglary.

Capt. Chase Reddick	Mitchell Ryan
Sgt. Sam MacCray	Wayne Maunder
Off. Steve Baker	Michael Richardson
Off. Fred Sing	Brian Fong
Insp. Frank Dawson	Albert Reed
Off. Ed Rice	Gary Crosby

Producer: Jack Webb

The Cheap Detective

Comedy Pilot; 30 min; NBC 6/3/80

The story of Eddie Krowder, a Los Angeles private eye who charges $19.95 a day, plus expenses.

Eddie Krowder	Flip Wilson
Inez Krowder	Paula Kelly
Ricky	Richard Beaucamp
Ralph Garvey	Murray Hamilton
Arloe Fairweather	Michael Keenan

Producer: Edward H. Feldman

The Cheap Show

Game; 30 min; Syn. 9/78

A question is read to two celebrity guests. One member of one team (two two-member teams compete) chooses the celebrity he feels has the right answer. If he is correct, he receives a cheap prize and one of his opponent's teammates is punished (doused with water or hit with harmless foods). If he is incorrect, his teammate is punished.

Host: Dick Martin

Wanda the Hostess: Janelle Price

Polly the Prize Lady: Shirl Bernheim

Purveyor of Punishment: Joe Baker, Billy Beck

Producer: Chris Bearde, Bob Wood

The Cheaters

Mystery; 30 min; Syn. 1960

The investigations of John Hunter, a detective for the London-based Eastern Insurance Company.

John Hunter	John Ireland
Walter Allen	Robert Ayres

Check It Out

Comedy; 30 min; USA 9/85 (Premiere)

The misadventures of Howard Bannister, the harassed manager of Cobb's, a supermarket in Canada.

Howard Bannister	Don Adams
Edna Mosley	Dinah Christie
Marleen	Kathleen Laskey
Jennifer Woods	Tonya Williams
Alf Scully	Henry Beckman
Jack Christian	Jeff Pustil
Murray Amhearst	Simon Reynolds
Leslie	Aaron Schwartz
Mrs. Cobb	Barbara Hamilton

Checking In

Comedy; 30 min; CBS 4/9/81 to 4/30/81

A spin-of from "The Jeffersons" wherein their maid, Florence Johnston, takes a leave of absence to work as the executive housekeeper at the St. Frederick Hotel in New York City.

Florence Johnston	Marla Gibbs
Lyle Block	Larry Linville
Elena Beltran	Liz Torres
Betty	Ruth Brown
Earl Bellamy	Patrick Collins
Hank Sabatino	Robert Costanzo
Dennis	Charles Fleischer

Producer: Jay Moriarity, Mike Mulligan

Checkmate

Mystery; 60 min; CBS 9/17/60 to 9/19/62

The cases of Don Corey and Jed Sills, detectives with the San Francisco-based Checkmate, Incorporated.

Don Corey	Anthony George
Jed Sills	Doug McClure
Carl Hyatt	Sebastian Cabot
Chris Devlin	Jack Betts

Producer: Dick Berg, Maxwell Shane

The Cheer Television Theatre

A five week interim series (NBC 5/30/54 to 6/27/54) of dramatic stories sponsored by Cheer soap powder.

The Cheerleaders

Comedy Pilot; 30 min; NBC 8/2/76

The misadventures of three beautiful high school cheerleaders (Snowy, B. J. and Beverly).

Snowy	Kathleen Cody
B. J.	Debbie Zip
Beverly	Teresa Medaris
Margie	Mary Kay Place
Dorothy Snow	Susan Quick
Terry Sears	Robin Mattson
Janis	Janis Lynn
Howard	Darel Glaser
Doris	Rita Wilson
Joe King	Ronald Roy

Director: Richard Crenna

Cheers

Comedy; 30 min; NBC 9/30/82 (Premiere)

The activities of the staff and clientele of Cheers, a Boston bar.

Sam Malone	Ted Danson
Diane Chambers	Shelley Long
Carla Tortelli	Rhea Perlman
Ernie Pantusso	Nicholas Colasanto
Cliff Claven	John Ratzenberger
Norm Peterson	George Wendt
Nick Tortelli	Dan Hedaya
Frasier Crane	Kelsey Grammer
Woody Boyd	Woody Harrelson
Loretta Tortelli	Jean Kasem
Hester Crane	Nancy Marchand
Dr. Ludlow	James Karen
Janet Eldridge	Kate Mulgrew
Cliff's mother	Frances Sternhagen
Cliff's father	Dick O'Neill
Harry Gillies	Harry Anderson
Helen Chambers	Glynis Johns
Lisa Pantusso	Allyce Beasley
Rebecca Howe	Kirstie Alley

Theme Vocal ("Where Everybody Knows Your Name"): Gary Portnoy

Producer: Glen Charles, Les Charles, Ken Levine, David Isaacs

Cher

Variety; 60 min; CBS 2/16/75 to 1/4/76

A weekly program of music and songs with hostess Cher and featuring the Tony Charmoli Dancers. Music by Jimmy Dale and produced by George Schlatter.

The Cherokee Trail

Western Pilot; 60 min; CBS 11/28/81

Events in the life of Mary Breydon, the manager of Cherokee Station, a stopover point for the Overland Express Stage Lines in Cherokee, Colorado (1864).

Mary Breydon	Cindy Pickett
Peggy Breydon	Tina Yothers
Matty Maginnis	Mary Larkin
Temple Boone	David Hayward
Scant Luther	Victor French
Ridge Fenton	Richard Farnsworth

Producer: Douglas Netter

Chester the Pup

Children; 15 min; ABC 10/7/50 to 9/30/51

Art Whitfield narrates the on-air cartoon sketches (drawn by Sid Stone) of Chester the puppy. Producer: Franklyn Dyson.

The Chesterfield Supper Club

Variety; 15 min; NBC 12/24/48 to 5/28/50

A program of music and songs sponsored by Chesterfield cigarettes.

Host: Perry Como

Regulars: Geri, Margie and Bea Fontaine

Announcer: Martin Block

Orchestra: Mitchell Ayres

Producer: Bob Moss, Richard Berger

Chevrolet On Broadway

Variety; 15 min; NBC 7/17/56 to 9/13/56

Music and songs with hosts Gisele MacKenzie, Janet Blair, and Fred Waring, and regulars the Mellolarks. With the orchestra of Hal Hastings and the announcing of Bill Wendell.

The Chevrolet Tele-Theatre

Anthology; 30 min; NBC 9/27/48 to 6/26/50

A series of live dramas under the sponsorship of Chevrolet. Produced by Fred Coe, Vic McLeod, Owen Davis Jr.

The Chevron Hall of Stars

A syndicated (1956) series of quality dramas produced by Warren Lewis.

The Chevy Mystery Show

Walter Slezak and later Vincent Price as hosts of a series of repeat mystery stories. NBC 5/29/60 to 9/23/60.

The Chevy Summer Show

Edie Admas, Janet Blair and John Raitt as the hosts of a Summer series of music, songs and light comedy. With regulars Dan Rowan, Dick Martin, Dorothy Kirsten, Stan Freberg, and the orchestra of Harry Zimmerman. NBC 6/22/58 to 9/28/58.

Cheyenne

Western; 60 min; ABC 9/20/56 to 8/30/63

The exploits of Cheyenne Bodie, a frontier scout, learned in both the ways of the White Man and the Cheyenne Indian, as he roams throughout the West of the 1860s.

Cheyenne Bodie	Clint Walker
Toothy Thompson	Jack Elam

Producer: Arthur Silver, Roy Huggins, William T. Orr

Chez Paree Revue

A 1950 DuMont program of music and songs with host Jim Dimitri, regulars Joyce Sellers, Dave Dursten, the Mellolarks, and the orchestra of Cee Davidson.

Chicago Story

Crime Drama: 90 min; NBC 3/6/82 to 8/27/82

The lives of a group of Chicago-based doctors, lawyers and police officers who ban together to solve crimes.

Dr. Judith Bergstrom	Maud Adams
Lawyer Lou Pellegrino	Vincent Baggetta
Lawyer Megan Powers	Molly Cheek
Off. Joe Gilland	Dennis Franz
Dr. Maxwell Carson	Kristoffer Tabori
Off. Frank Wajorski	Daniel Hugh-Kelly
Off. O. Z. Tate	Richard Lawson
D.A. Kenneth A. Dutton	Craig T. Nelson
Anne Gilland (Joe's Wife)	Connie Foster
Lt. Rossei	John Mahoney
Dr. Pauline Caldwell	Pauline Brailsford

Producer: Eric Bercovici

Theme Vocal ("Chicago") by Linda Clifford

The Chicago Teddy Bears

Comedy; 30 min; CBS 9/17/71 to 12/17/71

The clash that exists between Linc McCray and his cousin "Big" Nick Marr, rival night club owners in Chicago during the 1920s.

Linc McCray	Dean Jones
"Big" Nick Marr	Art Metrano
Uncle Latzi	John Banner
Marvin	Marvin Kaplan
Duke	Mickey Shaughnessy
Dutch	Huntz Hall
Lefty	Jamie Farr
Julius	Mike Mazurki

Producer: Jerry Thorpe

Chicago 212

Drama Pilot; 30 min; CBS 4/30/57

The story of Ed McCook, an inspector for the Chicago Fire Department.

Ed McCook	Frank Lovejoy
Arsonist	Roy Thinnes
Mickey	Tomi Thurston
Keno	Franklyn McCormick

Producer: Don Sharpe, Warren Lewis

Chicagoland Mystery Players

Crime Drama; DuMont 9/18/49 to 7/30/50

The story of Jeffrey Hall, a criminologist with the Chicago Police Department, as he attempts to solve baffling crimes.

Jeffrey Hall	Gordon Urquhart
Sgt. Holland	Bob Smith

Producer: J. E. Faraghan

Chico and the Man

Comedy; 30 min; NBC 9/13/74 to 7/28/78

The bickering relationship between Ed Brown, the honest but cynical owner of a Los Angeles garage, and his partner, Chico Rodriquez, a cheerful young Mexican-American.

Ed Brown	Jack Albertson
Chico Rodriquez	Freddie Prinze
Louie Wilson	Scatman Crothers
Della Rogers	Della Reese
Reverend Bemis	Ronny Graham
Rudy	Rodolfo Hoyos
Mabel	Bonnie Boland
Raul Garcia	Gabriel Melgar
Raul's Aunt Charo	Charo
Monica	Julie Hill

Producer: James Komack

Theme Vocal ("Chico and the Man") by Jose Feliciano

The Children's Corner

Children; 30 min; NBC 8/20/55 to 4/28/56

Music, songs and puppet adventures designed to instill learning abilities in children.

Hostess: Josie Carey

Voices/Puppeteer: Fred Rogers

The Children's Hour

Performances by juvenile talent acts with host Ed Herlihy. NBC 1/30/49 to 5/26/51.

The Children's Hour

Hour-long films for children with hostess Maureen O'Sullivan. Produced by Hal Roach Jr. and syndicated in 1951.

Children's Sketch Book

Stories for children, told by Edith Skinner, and illustrated by Lisi Weil. NBC 1/7/50 to 2/4/50.

Child's Play

Game; 30 min; CBS 9/20/82 to 9/16/83

Object: For players to determine the words children are seen describing.

Host: Bill Cullen

Announcer: Gene Wood

Producer: Jonathan Goodson, Chester Feldman

China Smith

See "The Affairs of China Smith."

Chips

Crime Drama; 60 min; NBC 9/15/77 to 7/18/83

The exploits of Francis "Ponch" Poncherello and Jon Baker, members of the California Highway Patrol (Chips).

Off. Francis Poncherello	Erik Estrada
Off. Jon Baker	Larry Wilcox
Sgt. Joe Getraer	Robert Pine
Off. Bonnie Clark	Randi Oakes
Off. Kathy Linehan	Tina Gayle
Off. Arthur Grossman	Paul Linke
Off. Bariczu	Brodie Greer
Harlan (mechanic)	Lou Wagner
Off. Steve McLeish	Bruce Jenner
Off. Bruce Penhall	Bruce Penhall
Off. Sindy Cahill	Brianne Leary
Off. Robert Nelson	Tom Reilly
Sgt. Murdock	Lawrence Cook
Off. Ben Cantrell	Rawn Hutchinson

Producer: Cy Chermak, Paul Mason

Theme Song ("CHIPS") by John Parker

The Chisholms

Western; 60 min; CBS 1/19/80 to 3/15/80

The saga of the pioneering Chisholm family as they travel by wagon train from Wyoming to California to seek a new life. Based on the miniseries (12 hrs; CBS 3/29/79 to 4/19/79).

Hadley Chisholm	Robert Preston
Minerva Chisholm	Rosemary Harris
Will Chisholm	Ben Murphy
Bonnie Sue Chisholm	Stacey Nelkin*
	Delta Burke
Annabelle Chisholm	Susan Swift*
Bo Chisholm	James Van Patten
Gideon Chisholm	Brian Kerwin*
	Brett Cullen
Elizabeth Chisholm	Glynnis O'Connor*
Kewedinok Chisholm	Sandra Griego*
	Victoria Racimo
Cooper Hawkins	Mitchell Ryan
Lester Hackett	Reid Smith
Mercy Howell	Susan Swift
Betsy O'Neal	Devon Ericson
Frank O'Neal	Guich Koock
Jeremy O'Neal	Les Lannom
Enos	Donald Moffat

Producer: Alan Landsburg

*Miniseries role.

The Chopped Liver Brothers

Comedy Pilot; 30 min; ABC 5/6/77

The antics of Tom Van Brocklin and Jay Luckman, two struggling stand-up comics.

Tom Van Brocklin	Tom Patchett
Jay Luckman	Jay Tarses
Sally Van Brocklin	Gwynne Gilford
Mr. Ruth	Philip Bruns
Kelso	Michael Pataki

Producer: Tom Patchett, Jay Tarses

Chopper One

Adventure; 30 min; ABC 1/17/74 to 7/11/74

The exploits of Gil Foley and Don Burdick, helicopter pilots (of Chopper One) with the West California Police Department.

Off. Gil Foley	Dirk Benedict
Off. Don Burdick	Jim McMullan
Capt. Ted McKeegan	Ted Hartley
Mitch (mechanic)	Lou Frizzell

Producer: Aaron Spelling, Leonard Goldberg

Choose Up Sides

Game; 30 min; NBC 1/7/56 to 3/31/56

Two teams of children compete in various game contests. The best performing team receives prizes.

Host: Gene Rayburn, Dean Miller

Producer: Mark Goodson, Bill Todman

A Christmas for Boomer

Drama Pilot; 60 min; NBC 12/6/79

The pilot for "Here's Boomer," about an adorable stray dog. The pilot relates Boomer's experiences with the Sinclairs, the first family to temporarily adopt him.

Dan Sinclair	Lawrie Driscoll
Marsha Sinclair	Margie Impert
Jaime Sinclair	Gillian Grant
Johnny Sinclair	Jonathan Ward
Helen Sinclair	Harriet Nelson
Lila Manchester	Joyce Van Patten
Dorothy	Sheree North
Jack	Larry Linville

Producer: A. C. Lyles

The Chrysler Medallion Theatre

Anthology; 30 min; CBS 7/11/53 to 4/3/54

Dramatic stories, sponsored by Chrysler, and featuring such stars as Ronald Reagan, Henry Fonda, Jack Lemmon, Janet Gaynor, Eddie Albert, Charlie Ruggles, Charlton Heston, June Havoc, Claude Rains, Diana Douglas, Jan Sterling, Leslie Nielsen and Roddy McDowall. Produced by William Spier.

The Chuck Barris Rah-Rah Show

Variety; 60 min; NBC 2/28/78 to 4/11/78

Performances by professional and amateur talent acts.

Host: Chuck Barris

Regulars: Jaye P. Morgan

Announcer: Johnny Jacobs

Music: Milton DeLugg

Producer: Chuck Barris, Gene Banks

Chuck Norris Karate Kommandos

Cartoon Pilot; 30 min; Syn 9/86

The exploits of Chuck Norris, a special agent for the President, as he uses his ingenuity and skills as a Samurai warrior, to battle evil.

Chuck Norris   Himself

Voices: Robert Ito, Sam Fontana, Robert Ridgely, Kathy Garver, Mona Marshall, Linda Gary, Alan Oppenheimer

Producer: Joe Ruby, Ken Spears

The Chuckle Heads

A syndicated (1963) five minute series of re-edited comedy silents from the 1920s. Produced by Adrian Weiss.

Cimarron City

Western; 30 min; NBC 10/11/58 to 9/16/60

Events in the growth of Cimarron City (Oklahoma, 1890s) as seen through the eyes of Matthew Rockford, a benevolent cattle baron.

Matthew Rockford	George Montgomery
Beth Purcell	Audrey Totter
Lane Temple	John Smith
Alice Purdy	Claire Carleton
Burt Purdy	Fred Sherman
Tiny Budinger	Dan Blocker
Art Simpson	Stuart Randall

Producer: Richard Lewis

Cimarron Strip

Western; 90 min; CBS 9/7/67 to 9/19/68

The exploits of Jim Crown, a U.S. Marshal in Cimarron City, Oklahoma during the 1880s.

Jim Crown	Stuart Whitman
Dulcey Coopersmith	Jill Townsend
Francis Wilde	Randy Boone
Deputy MacGregor	Percy Herbert

Producer: Philip Leacock

Circle

A syndicated (1960) series of music and songs with hosts Barbara McNair and Lonnie Sattin and the music of Richard Hayman and Richard Wess.

The Circle Family

Comedy-Drama Pilot; NBC 7/29/82

Events in the day-to-day lives of the Circle family, the owners of a motor court.

Hearst Circle	Max Baer
Betsy Circle	Sarah Torgov
Roxy Circle	Sydney Penny
Dakota Circle	Roberto Ramon
Hemi Circle	Granger Hines
Q. P. Circle	Barrett Oliver
Grandpa Circle	Morgan Woodward
Adrian Tweed	Ben Piazzi
Lili Boyd	Betty Kennedy
Registrar	Linda Kaye Henning

Producer: Cy Chermak

Circle of Fear

Anthology; 60 min; NBC 1/5/73 to 6/22/73

Supernatural-based tales with such stars as Susan Dey, Janet Leigh, Kim Darby, Louise Sorel, Martin Sheen, Patty Duke, Tab Hunter, Barry Nelson, Frank Converse, Rory Calhoun and Bridget Hanley. A spin-off from "Ghost Story" and produced by William Castle.

Circus Boy

Adventure; 30 min; NBC 9/23/56 to 9/8/57
ABC 9/19/57 to 9/11/58

The struggles endured by the Champion Circus as it travels throughout the frontier of the latter 19th-century. (The title refers to Corky, water boy to Bimbo the elephant.)

Big Tim Champion	Robert Lowery
Corky	Mickey Braddock
Joey the Clown	Noah Beery Jr.
Pete	Guinn Williams
Circus Jack	Andy Clyde
Little Tom	Billy Barty
Circus Barker	Eddie Marr

Producer: Herbert B. Leonard

Circus of the 21st Century

A syndicated (1979) series of circus variety acts with hosts Sherisse Laurence and Cal Dodd.

Circus Time

Paul Winchell as host to a series of circus variety acts. With Betty Ann Grove and the music of Ralph Herman. ABC 10/4/56 to 6/27/57.

The Cisco Kid

Western; 30 min; Syn. 1950

The exploits of the Cisco Kid and his partner, Pancho, as they fight for justice in the New Mexico territory during the 1890s.

The Cisco Kid	Duncan Renaldo
Pancho	Leo Carrillo

Producer: Walter Schwimmer

Cities Service Band of America

A simulcast of the radio program, featuring the 48-piece Band of America. With Host Ford Bond and the musical direction of Paul LaValle. NBC 10/17/49 to 1/9/50.

Citizen Soldier

A syndicated (1957) anthology series about Americans in combat during World War II and the Korean War. Also known as "The Big Attack." Produced by R. W. Alcorn with the music of Bert Grund.

The City

Drama Pilot; 60 min; ABC 8/1/86

The life of a city (unidentified) as seen through the experiences of its mayor (Luger), police chief (Pittman) and the people who report its happenings.

Chet Luger	Chris Sarandon
Chris Racine	Season Hubley
Otis Pittman	Georg Stanford Brown
Stewart Moffitt	Fritz Weaver
Bear Werner	M. Emmet Walsh
Carey Brock	Gary Swanson
Mae Thayer	Dana Delany
Rudy Broadbeck	Louis Giambalvo
Gretchen	Mary Jackson

Producer: William Blinn

City Assignment

See "Big Town."

City Detective

Crime Drama; 30 min; Syn. 1953

The exploits of Bart Grant, a lieutenant with the N.Y.P.D.

Lt. Bart Grant	Rod Cameron

Producer: Blake Edwards

City Hospital

Drama; 30 min; ABC 4/19/51 to 11/3/51
CBS 3/25/52 to 10/1/53

Incidents in the lives of patients at New York Hospital as seen through the eyes of Dr. Barton Crane, the medical director.

Dr. Barton Crane	Melville Ruick
Dr. Kate Morrow	Ann Burr

Announcer: John Cannon

Producer: Walter Selden, Wendy Sanford

City of Angels

Crime Drama; 60 min; NBC 2/3/76 to 8/24/76

The exploits of Jake Axminster, a hard-boiled private detective in Los Angeles during the 1930s.

Jake Axminster	Wayne Rogers
Marsha	Elaine Joyce
Lt. Murray Quint	Clifton James
Lester	Timmie Rogers
Michael Brimm	Philip Sterling

Producer: Jo Swerling Jr., Roy Huggins

Class of '55

Drama Pilot; 30 min; Unaired; Produced in 1972

A proposed series that was to recall and update the lives of members of the 1955 graduating class of an unidentified college. The pilot focuses on the life of Peter Giddings, a now successful New York lawyer.

Peter Giddings	Alan Alda
Christina	Louise Lasser
Jonathan Spaulding	Gary Conway
Photographer	Jamie Farr

Producer: James L. Brooks, David Seltzer

Classic Concentration

Game; 30 min; NBC 5/4/87 (Premiere)

A revised version of "Concentration." One player (two compete) selects two numbers from twenty-five numbers that are displayed on a game board. Two prizes are revealed. If they match, two puzzle parts are revealed (if not, the opponent receives a turn and the prizes return to numbers). The first player to solve the concealed rebus puzzle wins those prizes that he has matched.

Host: Alex Trebek

Model: Diana Taylor

Announcer: Gene Wood

Producer: Mark Goodson

The Claudette Colbert Show

Comedy Pilot; 30 min; NBC 9/30/58

The story of Elizabeth Harper, a newly elected Washington, D.C. congresswoman.

Elizabeth Harper	Claudette Colbert
Paul Harper	Leif Erickson
Susie Harper	Shelley Fabares
Billy Harper	Eric Anderson
Miss Hoper	Maudie Pritchard

Producer-Director: Norman Tokar

Claudia: The Story of a Marriage

Comedy-Drama; 30 min; NBC 1/6/52 to 3/30/52

Events in the lives of the newlywed Naughtons: David, an architect, and his naive, 18-year-old wife, Claudia.

Claudia Naughton	Joan McCracken
David Naughton	Hugh Riley
Mrs. Brown	Margaret Wycherly
Julia Naughton	Faith Brook
Harley Naughton	Alex Clark

Producer: Carol Irwin

The Cliff Dwellers

Drama Pilot; 60 min; ABC 8/28/66

The story of a group of college graduates (Highcliffe College, class of 1956) who have remained friends and are now living in New York.

Jonathan Murray	Hal Holbrook
Annie Navasky	Carol Rossen
Frank Saxon	Bert Convy
Jerry Wexler	Lee Allen
William Canning	James Beck
Stacy Robbins	Robert Hooks
Linda Murry	Beverlee McKinsey
Teddy Saxton	Terrence Logan

Producer-Director: Boris Sagal

The Cliff Edwards Show

Variety; 15 min; CBS 5/23/49 to 9/19/49

Music, songs and homespun humor with comedian Cliff Edwards. Produced by Franklin Heller. Music by the Tony Mottola Trio.

Cliffhangers

Serial; 60 min; NBC 2/27/79 to 5/1/79

The title for three adventure serials. See "The Curse of Dracula," "The Secret Empire" and "Stop Susan Williams."

The Cliffwood Avenue Kids

Comedy; 30 min; Syn. 1977

The adventures of a group of pre-teen children who are members of the Cliffwood Avenue Club.

Poindexter	Poindexter Yothers
Samwich	J. Brennan Smith
	Kevin King Cooper
Melora	Melora Hardin
Tara	Tara Talboy
Jeremy	Jeremy Lawrence
Sheldon	Kris Marquis
Andre	Andre Broudie

Producer: Win Opie

Climax!

Anthology; 60 min; CBS 10/7/54 to 6/26/58

A series of quality suspense dramas, hosted by Mary Costa and William Lundigan, and produced by Eva Wolas, Martin Manulis, Bretagne Windust, and Anthony Barr.

Clinic on 18th Street

Crime Drama Pilot; 30 min; NBC 3/13/74

The story of Abe Strayhorn, Lynn Carmichael and Gino Bardi, agents for M.F.C.P. (Major Frauds and Consumer Protection), a unit of the Los Angeles D.A.'s office that investigates frauds.

D.A. Abe Strayhorn	Ed Nelson
Lynn Carmichael	Sharon Gless
Gino Bardi	Frank Sinatra Jr.
Marian Fenton	Virginia Vincent
Don Bates	Kenneth Tobey
Elroy Guntham	Dick Haymes

Producer: Jack Webb

Cloak of Mystery

Repeat episodes of "The Alcoa Theatre" and "The General Electric Theatre." Broadcast on NBC from 5/11/65 to 8/8/65.

The Clock

Anthology; 30 min; CBS 5/16/49 to 8/31/51
ABC 10/17/51 to 1/9/52

Suspense dramas about people who attempt to overcome a crisis before time runs out. Produced by William Spier, Herbert Swope Jr., Lawrence Schwab, and Ernest Walling.

Club Celebrity

Variety; 30 min; NBC 2/2/50 to 3/29/50

Music and comedy with hostess Ginny Simms, announcer Harry Von Zell, and regulars Jill Richards, Greg Mitchell, Betty Bligh and the Tune Tailors. Music by Dick Peterson.

Club Embassy

Comedy; 15 min; NBC 10/7/52 to 12/23/52

Bob and Ray (Bob Elliott, Ray Goulding) as the stars of an offbeat program of comedy. Regulars: Audrey Meadows, Florian ZaBach and Julia Meade.

Club Embassy

Variety; 15 min; NBC 12/30/52 to 6/23/53

Music and songs with hosts Mindy Carson and Connie Russell and the music of The Embassy Quartet.

Club Oasis

A variety program with two formats: Originally (9/28/57 to 5/24/58) it was a bi-weekly series that featured a different guest performer each week. From 6/7/58 to 9/6/58, Spike Jones became the host of a program of music and comedy. Regulars: Helen Grayco, Joyce Jameson, Billy Barty, Georgia Rock and Carl Fontana. Music by The City Slickers.

Club 7

Performances by new talent discoveries with hosts Johnny Thompson and Rony Bavaar and the orchestra of Bobby Byrne. ABC 8/13/48 to 9/24/51

Club 60

A live, color series of music and songs with hosts Don Sherwood, Dennis James and Howard Miller and the orchestra of Joseph Gallichio. Regulars are Mike Douglas, Nancy Wright, Barbara Becker and The Mellolarks. NBC 2/11/57 to 1/10/58. Also known as "The Howard Miller Show (9/57 to 1/58).

The Clue Club

Cartoon; 30 min; CBS 8/14/76 to 9/2/79

The story of four teens (Pepper, Larry, D. D. and Dotty) and two dogs (Woofer and Wimper) and their efforts to solve crimes.

Pepper	Patricia Stich
Larry	David Jolliffe
D. D.	Bob Hastings
Dotty	Tara Talbot
Woofer/Wimper	Paul Winchell

Producer: William Hanna, Joseph Barbera

Clutch Cargo

Cartoon; 5 min; Syn. 3/59

The exploits of adventurer Clutch Cargo and his companions Spinner (a boy) and Paddlefoot (a dog).

Clutch Cargo	Richard Cotting
Spinner/Paddlefoot	Margaret Kerry

Producer-Director: Dick Brown

Cobina

Experimental: 30 min; NBC 6/16/39

A variety experiment with singer Cobina Wright Jr. Produced by Edward Sobol.

Co-Ed Fever

Comedy Pilot; 30 min; CBS 2/4/79

The misadventures that occur when the all-girl Baxter University in Connecticut becomes a co-educational college.

Sandi	Heather Thomas
Melba	Jillian Kesner
Hope	Tracey Phillips
Elizabeth	Cathryn O'Neil
Maria	Alexa Kenin
Tucker Davis	David Keith
Doug	Christopher S. Nelson
Gobo	Michael Pasternak
Mrs. Selby	Jane Rose

Producer: Martin Ransohoff

The Code of Jonathan West

Western Pilot; 30 min; CBS 4/17/60

The exploits of Jonathan "Preach" West, a fighting man with principals, who roams throughout the West of the late 1860s righting wrongs. Broadcast as "Aftermath" on "G.E. Theatre."

Jonathan West	Fess Parker
Ernie ("Galoot")	Sammy Jackson
Hardy Couter	James Best
Sarah Couter	Maureen Dawson
Bessie Couter	Gina Gillespie
Gordon	John Hambreck
Murray	Stephen Joyce
Old Timer	Burt Mustin

Music: Fred Steiner

Producer: Harry Tatelman

Code R

Adventure; 60 min; CBS 1/21/77 to 6/10/77

The work of the Emergency Services, an organization that combines police, fire and ocean rescue services into the Code R rescue forces (based off Southern California's Channel Island).

Walt Robinson	Tom Simcox
Rick Wilson	James Houghton
George Baker	Martin Kove
Suzy	Suzanne Reed
Ted Milbank	Ben Davidson
Harry	W. T. Zacha

Producer: Ed Self

Code Red

Adventure; 60 min; ABC 11/1/81 to 9/12/82

The exploits of the fire fighters of Batallion 6, Station Number 1, of the Los Angeles City Fire Department.

Capt. Joe Rorchek	Lorne Greene
Ann Rorchek	Julie Adams
Ted Rorchek	Andrew Stevens
Haley Green	Martina Deignan
Chris Rorchek	Sam J. Jones
Al Martelli	Jack Lindine
Mike Benton	Joe Maross
Danny Blake	Adam Rich

Producer: Irwin Allen

Code 3

Anthology; 30 min; Syn. 3/56

Stories of police work in action as seen through the eyes of George Barnett, the assistant sheriff of Los Angeles County.

Sheriff Barnett	Richard Travis
Sgt. Murchison	Denver Pyle
Lt. Bill Hollis	Fred Wynn

Producer: Hal Roach Jr.

Code 3

Drama Pilot; Unaired; Produced in 1972

The exploits of the doctors and nurses attached to Code 3 Emergency Medicine Division of the U.C.L.A. Medical Center.

Dr. John Ogden	John Cypher
Dr. Pat Loeb	Craig Littler
Dr. Dan Brewster	James McMullen
Nurse Marge Nelson	Barbara Barrie
Nurse Anne Linden	Jean Fowler
Julie	Anne Archer

Producer: Douglas S. Cramer, W. L. Baums

Music: Elmer Bernstein

Coke Time With Eddie Fisher

Variety; 15 min; NBC 4/29/53 to 2/20/57

Music and songs with host Eddie Fisher and regulars Jaye P. Morgan, Don Ameche, Fred Robbins and The Echos. Musical direction by Axel Stordahl and Carl Hoff. Sponsored by Coca-Cola.

The Colbys

Drama; 60 min; ABC 11/21/85 to 3/26/87

A spin-off from "Dynasty" that relates the intrigues surrounding members of the Colbys, a family born to wealth and power, and their attempts to maintain their position in the financial world.

Jason Colby	Charlton Heston
Constance Colby	Barbara Stanwyck
Jeff Colby	John James
Sable Scott Colby	Stephanie Beacham
Monica Colby	Tracy Scoggins
Miles Colby	Maxwell Caulfield
Bliss Colby	Claire Yarlett
Francesca Scott Colby	Katharine Ross
Fallon Carrington Colby	Emma Samms
Garrett Boydston	Ken Howard
Zachary Powers	Ricardo Montalban
Hutch Corrigan	Joseph Campanella
Sean McAllister	Charles Van Eman
L. B.	Ashely Mutrux
Sylvia Heywood	June Lockhart
Channing Carlen Colby	Kim Morgan Greene
Cash Cassidy	James Houghton
Kolya Rostov	Adrian Paul
Adrienne Cassidy	Shanna Reed
Hoyt Parker	Michael Parks
Billy Erskine	John Dehner
Georginna Sinclair	Nana Visitor
Anna Rostov	Anna Levine
Sacha Malenkov	Judson Scott

Producer: Aaron Spelling, Richard & Esther Shapiro

The Colgate Comedy Hour

Variety; 60 min; NBC 9/10/50 to 12/25/55

A lavish series of comedy spectaculars featuring top name guests and various hosts (including Abbott and Costello, Dean Martin and Jerry Lewis, Donald O'Connor, Judy Canova, Jimmy Durante, Bob Hope, Eddie Cantor, Robert Paige and Gordon MacRae).

Orchestra: Al Goodman, Dick Stabile, Charles Dent

Producer: Ernest D. Glucksman, Sid Kuller, Bud Yorkin, Edward Sobol, Sam Fuller, Jack Hurdle, Charles Friedman

Colgate Theatre

Pilot Films; 30 min; NBC 8/19/58 to 10/7/58

See the following titles for information: "Adventures of a Model," "The Claudette Colbert Show," "Fountain of Youth," "If You Knew Tomorrow," "McCreedy's Woman," "Strange Counsel" and "Tonight in Havana."

Coliseum

A series of circus variety acts with guest hosts. Produced by Joseph Cates. 60 min; CBS 1/26/67 to 6/1/67.

The College Bowl

Variety; 30 min; ABC 10/2/50 to 3/26/51

Performances by the youthful clientele of The College Bowl, the campus soda fountain of a small university.

Host: Chico Marx

Regulars: Mike Douglas, Evelyn Ward, Paula Huston, Jimmy Brock, Lee Lindsay, Stanley Prager, Barbara Ruick, Joan Holloway, Vickie Barrett, Kenny Buffert

Producer: Martin Gosch

Colonel Bleep

Cartoon; 30 min; Syn. 9/57

When Dr. Destructo, an evil scientist from the planet Pheutora, begins to wreck havoc in outer space, Colonel Bleep and his space deputies Squeak the Puppet and Scratch the Caveman, are assigned to capture him. Stories, which feature non-speaking characters, relate Colonel Bleep's efforts to apprehend Dr. Destructo.

Producer: Richard H. Ulman, Robert Bachanan

Colonel Humphrey Flack

See "Adventures of Colonel Flack."

Colonel Humphrey J. Flack

Comedy Pilot; 30 min; ABC 5/31/53

The pilot for "The Adventures of Colonel Flack," about a retired army colonel turned modern-day Robin Hood.

Col. Humphrey J. Flack	Frank McHugh
Girl	Constance Ford

Producer: Herbert Brodkin

Colonel March of Scotland Yard

Crime Drama; 30 min; Syn. 1957

The exploits of Colonel Perceval Clovis Adelbart March, a British inspector, and head of Department D-3, the Office of Queens Complaints of the New Scotland Yard.

Col. Perceval March	Boris Karloff
Insp. Ames	Ewan Roberts
Insp. Gordon	Eric Pohlmann

Producer: Leslie Gilliat

Colonel Stoopnagle's Stoop

Comedy Pilot; 30 min; CBS 6/23/48

The exchange of conversation between Colonel Lemuel Q. Stoopnagle and the friends and neighbors who just happen to drop by his home.

Col. Lemuel Stoopnagle	F. Chase Taylor

Also: Richard Collier, Dave Ballard, Eda Heineman

Producer: Arthur Moore

Colorado C.I.

Crime Drama Pilot; 60 min; CBS 5/26/78

The story of brothers Mark and Pete Gunnison, members of the Criminal Investigation Unit of the Colorado Police Department.

Mark Gunnison	John Elerick
Pete Gunnison	Marshall Colt
Hoyt Gunnison	L. Q. Jones
Chris Morrison	Laurette Spang
Carla Winters	Christine Belford
David Royce	David Hedison
Piper Collins	Christine DeLisle
Capt. Cochran	Van Williams
Kessler	John Karlen

Producer: Philip Saltzman

Colossus

Drama Pilot; 60 min; NBC 3/12/63

Events in the lives of Eric Tegman and John Michael Reardon, immigrants struggling to begin new lives in California's San Fernando Valley in 1912. Aired on "The Dick Powell Show."

Eric Tegman	William Shatner
John Reardon	Robert Brown
Dan Corbett	Frank Overton
Ruth Corbett	Geraldine Brooks
Kathy Quire	Joan Staley

Producer: Dick Powell, Richard Alan Simmonds

Colt .45

Western; 30 min; ABC 10/18/57 to 10/10/62

In an attempt to stem the rising lawlessness on the frontier during the 1880s, the government recruits Christopher Colt to pose as a salesman for the Colt .45 repeater. Stories relate his attempts to maintain the law as he travels throughout the West.

Christopher Colt	Wade Preston
Sam Colt Jr.	Donald May

Producer: William T. Orr

Columbo

Crime Drama; Various (90 min to 2 hrs); NBC 9/15/71 to 9/1/78

The exploits of Philip* Columbo, an underpaid and untidy detective with the Central Homicide Division of the L.A.P.D. The character of Columbo first appeared on "The Chevy Mystery Show" episode "Enough Rope (7/31/60) with Bert Freed as Columbo.

Lt. Columbo	Peter Falk
Capt. Sampson	Bill Zuckert

Producer: Richard Levinson, William Link

*Although not associated with having a first name, he has been called Philip in some episodes. See also "Kate Loves a Mystery" and "Mrs. Columbo."

The Columnist

Comedy Pilot; 30 min; ABC 6/28/85

The story of Barrie Shepherd, a beautiful unmarried columnist who covers the single scene for her newspaper column "The Single Life."

Barrie Shepherd	Jan Smithers
John	Derek McGrath
Doris	Mary Long
Leslie	Joanna Schellenberg
Rocky	Sean Thompson

Producer: Al Rogers, Miles Dale

Combat

Drama; 60 min; ABC 10/2/62 to 8/29/67

The World War II activities of the men of K Company (Second Platoon of the U.S. Infantry) from their D-Day landing to victory one year later.

Lt. Gil Hanley	Rick Jason
Sgt. Chip Saunders	Vic Morrow
William "Wildman" Kirby	Jack Hogan
Caje	Pierre Jalbert
Littlejohn	Dick Peabody
Billy Nelson	Tom Lowell
Doc	Conlan Carter
	Stephen Rogers
Braddock	Shecky Greene
McCall	William Bryant

Producer: Selig J. Seligman

"Combat" theme by Leonard Rosenman

Combat Sergeant

Drama; 30 min; ABC 6/29/56 to 9/27/56

A World War II series about the Allied Forces battle against Rommel's Afrika Korps.

Sgt. Nelson	Michael Thomas
WAC Cpl. Harbin	Mara Corday
Gen. Harrison	Cliff Clark
Cpl. Murphy	Frank Marlowe

Come a Running

Comedy Pilot; 30 min; CBS 9/16/63

The story of David Latham, a young doctor struggling to establish a practice in the country, having just relocated from the city.

David Latham	Linden Chiles
Edie	Ruth Hussey
Alice Watson	Sherry Jackson
David Watson	Andrew Prine
Aunt Josie	Reta Shaw
Ernie Watson	Alan Hale Jr.
Pharmacist	Stu Erwin
Susan	Susan Seaforth

Theme Vocal ("Come a Running"): Bing Crosby

Producer: Harry Tatelman

Comeback

A syndicated (1979) series in which host James Whitmore profiles people who, after reaching the zenith of their careers, fell from those heights and then fought their way back to the top.

The Comeback Story

Interview; 30 min; ABC 10/23/53 to 2/5/54

The program recalls the lives of one-time famous personalities.

Host: George Jessel

Hostess: Arlene Francis

Producer: Louis Cowan

Comedy Break

Comedy; 30 min; Syn. 9/85

Skits, guest comics and clips from vintage TV series (reedited for laughs).

Host: Mack Dryden, Jamie Alcroft

Regulars: Bobbie Eakes, Julia Farey, Rebecca Ryan, Heidi Sterner, Cece Worrall, Suzy Zarow

Producer: Bob Booker, Barbara Booker, Jeffrey Barron

The Comedy Factory

Pilot Films; 30 min; ABC 6/21/85 to 8/9/85

See the following titles: "The Columnist," "Fast Food," "Harry and the Kids," "It Takes Two" (pilot version), "Max and Me," "Modern Times" and "The Second Time Around."

Comedy of Horrors

Comedy Pilot; 30 min; CBS 9/1/81

One night in Beacon House, a small honeymoon hotel located on a desolate road on the North Carolina coast, a beautiful woman is murdered by her fiendish husband. The woman's spirit, who is unable to rest, resolves to haunt Beacon House and protect the innocent and pure of heart. The unsold series, set many years later at Beacon House, was to relate incidents in the lives of the people who stay at the hotel.

The Host	Patrick Macnee
Molly Sutherland	Deborah Harmon
Danny Logan	Walter Olkewicz
Eileen Mannings	Jo DeWinter
Gregory	Vincent Schiavelli
Dr. Landreaux	Richard Roat
Female Ghost	Ivana Moore
Pamela Soames	Patricia Conwell
Michael Soames	Kip Niven

Producer: John Boni, Harry Colomby

Comedy Playhouse

Pilot Films; 30 min; CBS 8/1/71 to 9/5/71

For information, see the following: "Eddie," "Elke," "My Wives Jane," and "Shepherd's Flock."

Comedy Preview

Pilot Films; 30 min; ABC 8/19/70 to 9/2/70

See the following titles: "The Murdocks and the McClays," "Prudence and the Chief," and "Three for Tahiti."

The Comedy Shop

Comedy; 30 min; Syn. 1978

Norm Crosby as the host of a program that features performances by guest comics. Produced by Paul Roth.

Comedy Spot

Pilot Films; 30 min; CBS 7/5/60 to 9/20/60

For information, see "Coogan's Reward," "Full Speed Anywhere," "Head of the Family," "Meet the Girls," "The Sky's the Limit," "Tom, Dick and Harry" and "Welcome to Washington."

Host: Art Gilmore

Comedy Spotlight

Rebroadcasts of comedies that aired on "G.E. Theatre." CBS 7/25/61 to 9/19/61.

Comedy Tonight

Comedy; 60 min; CBS 7/5/70 to 8/23/70

Skits that satirize everyday life.

Host: Robert Klein

Regulars: Madeline Kahn, Laura Greene, Lynn Lipton, Jerry Lacy, Barbara Cason, Marty Barris, Peter Boyle, Judy Graubart, Bonnie Enten, Macintyre Dixon

Orchestra: Jack Elliott, Allyn Ferguson

Producer: Joseph Cates

The Comedy Zone

Comedy; 60 min; CBS 8/17/84 to 9/7/84

A program of adult and unique comedy sketches. Guests host, including Steve Allen, Zohra Lambert, Andrea Martin, Penny Marshall, Bonnie Franklin, Patty Duke, Mariette Hartley, Jane Curtin and Robert Klein.

Regulars: Audrie Neenan, Bill Randolph, Anne Lange, Mark Linn-Baker, Joe Mantegna and Bob Gunton

Announcer: Dick Tufeld

Producer: Gladys Rackmil, Joseph Cates

Commando Cody

Adventure; 30 min; NBC 7/16/55 to 10/8/55

The exploits of Jeff King, alias Commando Cody, Sky Marshal of the Universe, as he battles evil doers.

Jeff King	Judd Holdren
Joan Albright	Aline Towne
Ted Richards	William Schallert
Retik	Greg Grey
	Richard Crane
Dr. Varney	Peter Brocco
Baylor	Lyle Talbot

Producer: Franklin Adreon

Concentration

Game; 30 min; NBC 8/25/58 to 3/23/73

A board with thirty numbered, three sided wedges is displayed. One player chooses two numbers. The wedges rotate and reveal prizes. If they match, the wedges rotate and reveal two puzzle parts. A non match costs a player his turn and the wedges rotate back to numbers. The object is for players to match prizes and reveal puzzle parts. The first player to identify the puzzle wins what prizes he has uncovered.

Host: Hugh Downs, Jack Barry, Art James, Bill Mazer, Ed McMahon, Bob Clayton

Announcer: Wayne Howell, Art James, Bob Clayton

Concentration

Game; 30 min; Syn. 1973

A revised version of the above title, which see for format.

Host: Jack Barry

Announcer: Johnny Olsen

Music: Edd Kalehoff

Concrete Cowboys

Adventure; 60 min; CBS 2/7/81 to 3/21/81

The adventures of J. D. Reed and Will Ewbanks, two vagabond cowboys.

J. D. Reed	Jerry Reed
Will Ewbanks	Tom Selleck*
	Geoffrey Scott

Producer: Ernie Frankel

Theme Vocal ("Breaking Loose") by Jerry Reed

*Role in the CBS TV movie, 10/17/79.

Condo

Comedy; 30 min; ABC 2/10/83 to 6/9/83

The story of James Kirkridge, a textbook WASP, and Jesse Rodriquez, an upwardly mobile Hispanic, condominium neighbors who find themselves on opposite sides of almost every issue.

James Kirkridge	McLean Stevenson
Margaret "Kiki" Kirkridge	Brooke Alderson
Scott Kirkridge	Mark Schubb
Billy Kirkridge	Marc Price
Jesse Rodriquez	Luis Avalos
Maria Rodriquez	Yvonne Wilder
Linda Rodriquez	Julie Carmen
Jose Montoya	James Victor

Producer: Paul Junger Witt, Tony Thomas, John Rich

Theme Vocal ("Condo") by Drake Frye

The Coneheads

Cartoon Pilot; 30 min; NBC 10/14/83

Shortly after they are sent to Earth to capture humans for slave labor on the planet Remulak, Beldar and Prymaat Conehead become marooned. Shortly after they establish a home for themselves in New Jersey, a daughter, Connie is born to them. The unsold series was to relate their attempts to adjust to life on Earth. Based on "Saturday Night Live" sketches.

Beldar Conehead	Dan Aykroyd
Prymaat Conehead	Jane Curtin
Connie Conehead	Laraine Newman
Myrtle	Cynthia Adler
Barry	Tom Davis

Producer: Lorne Michaels, Arthur Rankin Jr., Jules Bass

Confidential File

Filmed dramatizations of newspaper stories with host Paul Coates. Syndicated in 1955 and also known as "Paul Coates' Confidential File."

Confidential for Women

A drama, then discussion of problems faced by women with hostess Jane Wyatt and commentator Dr. Theodore Rubin. ABC 3/18/66 to 7/8/66.

Confidentially Yours

Drama Pilot; 30 min; CBS 4/10/60

The story of Barnaby Hooke, a newspaper reporter-columnist. Aired as "Mystery at Malibu" on "G.E. Theatre."

Barnaby Hooke	Dan Duryea
Olga Lemaire	Audrey Totter
Tony Warren	Dianne Foster
Reggie Lemaire	Tyler McDuff

Producer: Richard Irving

Conflict

Anthology; 60 min; ABC 9/18/56 to 5/28/57

Dramas of people whose lives are suddenly changed by unexpected and unfavorable circumstances. Aired on "Warner Brothers Presents."

Host: Gig Young

Producer: Jack Barry, Paul Stewart

Congressional Investigator

Drama; 30 min; Syn. 1959

The series, set in Washington, D.C., dramatizes stories behind the Fifth Amendment as seen through the activities of a team of U.S. government investigators as they seek evidence for Congressional hearings.

Investigators: Edward Stroll, Marion Collier, Stephen Roberts, William Masters

The Contender

Drama; 60 min; CBS 4/3/80 to 5/1/80

Events in the life of Johnny Captor, an amateur boxer who forsakes his college studies for a chance at fame in the ring.

Johnny Captor	Marc Singer
George Beifus	Moses Gunn
Jill Cyndon	Katherine Cannon
Brian Captor	Alan Stock
Alma Captor	Louise Latham
Missy Dinwitte	Tina Andrews
Lou Waverly	Susan Walden
Mike Captor	Art Lund
Killer Dinwitte	Albert Myles
Harry	Don Gordon

Producer: Jon Epstein

Constantinople

Variety Pilot; 30 min; ABC 7/25/77

A fast-paced program of music and song featuring guest performers.

Pilot Guests: Tina Turner, Lance LeGault, The Manhattan Transfer, John Valenti, Doug Kershaw

Producer: Grant Tinker

Contest Carnival

Variety; 30 min; NBC 1/3/54 to 12/18/55

Performances by aspiring circus acts and new talent discoveries.

Host: Phil Sheridan

Regulars: Henry Levin, Joanie Coale, Gene Crane

Producer: Charles Vanda, Robert A. Forrest

The Continental

Women; 30 min; ABC 10/11/52 to 1/6/53

A suave and sophisticated man, known as The Continental (Renzo Cesana) romances members of the female audience via soft music (by the Tony Mottola Trio), poetry, and conversation. Produced by Renzo Cesana.

Continental Showcase

Jim Backus as the host of a variety series that presents entertainers from around the world. CBS 6/11/66 to 9/10/66.

Convoy

Drama; 60 min; NBC 9/17/65 to 12/10/65

The World War II saga of a convoy of two hundred heavily armed American ships slowly heading for Europe.

Cmdr. Dan Talbot	John Gavin
Capt. Ben Foster	John Larch
Chief Steve Kirkland	Linden Chiles
Lt. Richard O'Connell	James Callahan

Producer: Frank Price

Coogan's Reward

Comedy Pilot; 30 min; CBS 8/20/65

The story of Willie Coogan, a World War II combat correspondent who dislikes covering the war in the field.

Willie Coogan	Tony Randall
Cpl. Konstanti	Alan Carney
Ben Moore	Robert Gist
Girl	Roxanne Berail

Producer: Winston O'Keefe

Cool and Lam

Crime Drama Pilot; 30 min; Unaired; Produced in 1957

The light-hearted exploits of Bertha Cool, the penny-pinching co-owner of the L.A.-based Cool and Lam Investigations, and Donald Lam, her shrewd investigator. Based on the stories by Erle Stanley Gardner.

Bertha Cool	Beany Venuta
Donald Lam	Billy Pearson
Elsie	Judith Bess Jones
Flo Mortinson	Sheila Bromley
John Harvard	Don Megowan
Erle Stanley Gardner	Himself

Producer: Gail Patrick Jackson, Edmund Hartmann

Cool McCool

Cartoon; 30 min; NBC 9/10/66 to 8/31/68

The less than spectacular exploits of Cool McCool, a secret agent who has waged a war on crime.

Cool McCool	Chuck McCann
Harry McCool	Bob McFadden
Additional Voices	Carol Corbett

Producer: Al Brodax

Cool Million

Crime Drama; 90 min; NBC 10/25/72 to 7/11/73

The exploits of Jefferson Keyes, a U.S. government agent turned private detective, who charges one million dollars and guarantees results or refunds the money.

Jefferson Keyes	James Farentino
Tony Baylor	Ed Bernard
Elena	Adele Mara

Producer: Roy Huggins, Jo Swerling Jr.

The Cop and the Kid

Comedy; 30 min; NBC 12/4/75 to 3/4/76

The story of Frank Murphy, a tough bachelor police officer (with the 6th Division of the L.A.P.D.), as he attempts to care for Lucas Adams, an orphan who is now his ward.

Off. Frank Murphy	Charles Durning
Lucas Adams	Tierre Turner
Mary Goodhew	Sharon Spelman
Brigid Murphy	Patsy Kelly
Sgt. Zimmerman	William Preston
Shortstuff	Eric Laneuville

Producer: Jerry Davis

Cops

Comedy Pilot; 30 min; CBS 6/5/73

The story of Sonny Miglio, a hardboiled city police captain, as he struggles to adjust to a new position in a quiet suburban precinct.

Capt. Sonny Miglio	Vincent Gardenia
Det. Dennis Till	Bruce Davison
Sgt. Monroe Dupree	Scoey Mitchlll
Det. Ed Carter	Britt Leach
Capt. Irving Ho	Pat Morita
Wanda Burke	Ruth Roman
Benny the Squealer	Stuart Margolin

Producer: Meta Rosenberg

Corky and White Shadow

Adventure Serial; 30 min; ABC 1/30/56 to 2/24/56

A "Mickey Mouse Club" serial about a young girl (Corky Brady) and her German Shepherd dog (White Shadow) and their efforts to capture an outlaw.

Corky Brady	Darlene Gillespie
Matt Brady	Buddy Ebsen
Uncle Dan	Lloyd Corrigan

Producer: Walt Disney, Bill Walsh

Coronado 9

Crime Drama; 30 min; Syn. 1960

The exploits of Dan Adams, a private detective working out of San Diego's Coronado Peninsula.

Dan Adams   Rod Cameron

Producer: Richard Irving

Coronet Blue

Mystery; 60 min; CBS 5/29/67 to 9/4/67

Michael Alden, a shooting victim, awakens in a hospital room to learn that he is suffering from amnesia. Unaware of who his attackers were, or the reason for the attempt on his life, he remembers only two words, "Coronet Blue." Episodes relate Alden's attempts to uncover the meaning of "Coronet Blue"— unaware that he is being followed and will be killed if he comes close to discovering who he is. An ending was never filmed.

Michael Alden   Frank Converse
Brother Anthony   Brian Medford
Max Spier   Joe Silver

Producer: Herbert Brodkin

The Corner Bar

Comedy; 30 min; ABC 6/21/72 to 8/23/72

The misadventures of Harry Grant, the owner of Grant's Toomb, a restaurant-bar on 137 Amsterdam Avenue in N.Y.C.

Harry Grant   Gabriel Dell
Meyer Shapiro   Shimen Ruskin
Mary Ann   Langhorne Scruggs
Phil Bracken   Bill Fiore
Peter Panama   Vincent Schiavelli
Fred Costello   J. J. Barry
Joe   Joe Keyes

Producer: Alan King, Howard Morris

The Corner Bar

Comedy; 30 min; ABC 8/3/73 to 9/7/73

A revised version of the previous title. The story of Mae and Frank, co-owners of The Corner Bar, as they struggle to run it amid numerous staff and clientele problems.

Mae   Anne Meara
Frank Flynn   Eugene Roche
Meyer Shapiro   Shimen Ruskin
Fred Costello   J. J. Barry
Phil Bracken   Bill Fiore
Donald Hooten   Ron Carey

Producer: Alan King, Howard Morris

Cos (The Bill Cosby Show)

Variety; 60 min; ABC 9/19/76 to 10/31/76

A weekly series of monologues, music, and comedy sketches.

Host: Bill Cosby

Regulars: Jeff Altman, Marion Ramsey, Tim Thomerson, Pat Delaney, Willie Bobo, Buzzy Linhart

Announcer: John Wilson

Orchestra: Stu Gardner

Producer: Chris Bearde

The Cosby Show

Comedy: 30 min; NBC 9/20/84 (Premiere)

Events in the lives of the Huxtable family: Cliff, a pediatrician; Clair, his wife, a lawyer; and their children Denise, Sondra, Vanessa, Theodore, and Rudy.

Cliff Huxtable   Bill Cosby
Clair Huxtable   Phylicia Rashad
                         (Phylicia Ayers-
                         Allen)
Denise Huxtable   Lisa Bonet
Sondra Huxtable   Sabrina LeBeauf
Vanessa Huxtable   Tempestt Bledsoe
Theodore Huxtable   Malcolm-Jamal
                         Warner
Rudy Huxtable   Keshia Knight
                         Pulliam
Russell Huxtable   Earle Hyman
Anna Huxtable   Clarice Taylor
Peter Chiara   Peter Costa
Walter
  ("Cockroach")   Carl Payne

Producer: Marcy Carsey, Tom Werner, Earl Pomerantz

Cosmopolitan Theatre

Anthology; 60 min; DuMont 10/2/51 to 12/25/51

Adaptations of stories appearing in "Cosmopolitan" magazine. Stars include E. G. Marshall, John Forsythe, Marsha Hunt, Betty Field, Lon Chaney Jr., Lee Tracy, Bethel Leslie and Tom Ewell.

Producer: Sherman Marks, Albert McCleery, Louis Cowan

The Couch

Comedy Pilot; 30 min; CBS 10/16/85

The misadventures of Liz and Leo Greene, an affluent couple who go to all lengths to impress people with their idea of class. In the pilot, Leo and Liz attempt to get an antique couch to impress the parents of their daughter's fiance. The pilot for "Leo and Liz in Beverly Hills"; broadcast on "George Burns Comedy Week."

Leo Greene	Harvey Korman
Liz Greene	Valerie Perrine
Mitzie Greene	Carrie Fisher
Richardson	Bronson Pinchot
Mr. Winthrop	Parker Whitman
Wife	Susan Powell

Producer: Carl Gottlieb

The Count of Monte Cristo

Adventure; 30 min; Syn. 1956

Edmond Dantes, falsely accused of treason, is imprisoned in the Chateau d'if. When he learns of a buried treasure, he escapes and retreats to Monte Carlo. There, he uncovers the treasure and establishes himself as a powerful figure for justice. Stories, set in 18th-Century France, relate his battle against corruption.

Edmond Dantes	George Dolenz
Princess Anne	Faith Domergue
Jacopo	Nick Cravat
Mario	Fortunio Bonanova
Minister Bonjean	Leslie Bradley

Producer: Hal Roach Jr. Leon Fromkess

Counterattack: Crime in America

Human Interest; 60 min; ABC 5/2/82 to 5/23/82

An unusual program that reenacts actual crimes to illustrate crime-prevention tips and increase viewer awareness of potential crime situations.

Host: George Kennedy

Reporters: Terence McNally, Pam Galloway, Frank Wheaton

Producer: Robert Guenette

Counterpoint

A series of dramas, produced by Bernard Girard, that were made especially for syndication in 1952. Stars include Gloria Jean, Barbara Billingsley, Hayden Rorke, Lee Marvin, Elisabeth Fraser, Jeff Donnell, Raymond Burr and Gloria Saunders.

Counterspy

Adventure; 30 min; Syn. 1958

The exploits of David Harding, a U.S. government counterintelligence agent. Based on the radio series.

David Harding	Don Megowan

A Country Happening

Comedy Pilot; 30 min; NBC 9/8/69

An unsold series of skits that take an off-center look at the world in which we live.

Host: Roy Rogers, Dale Evans

Guests: Bobby Goldsboro, Jody Miller, Michael Landon, Glen Ash

Producer: Greg Garrison, Don Van Atta

County Fair

A program of music and songs with host Bert Parks, the announcing of Kenny Williams, and the music of the Bill Gale Band. Broadcast on NBC from 9/22/58 to 9/25/59.

A Couple of Joes

Variety; 55 min; ABC 8/5/49 to 7/12/50

Music, songs, and comedy with two men named Joe.

Host: Joe Rosenfield, Joe Bushkin

Regulars: Pat Harrington Jr., Warren Hull, Joan Barton, Allyn Edwards

Announcer: Tom Shirley

Orchestra: Mike Reilly, Milton DeLugg

Producer: Richard Gordon, Alan Kent

Courageous Cat

Cartoon; 5 min; Syn. 1961

The efforts of Courageous Cat and Minute Mouse to uphold the law in crime-ridden Empire City.

Courageous Cat	Robert McFadden
Minute Mouse	Robert McFadden

Music: Johnny Holiday

Producer: Sam Singer

Court-Martial

Drama; 60 min; ABC 4/8/66 to 9/2/66

World War II courtroom dramas in which attorneys David Young and Frank Whitaker (attached to the Judge Advocate General's Office in England) defend American military personnel.

Maj. Frank Whitaker	Peter Graves
Capt. David Young	Bradford Dillman
Wendy	Diene Clare
Sgt. John MacCaskey	Kenneth J. Warren

Producer: Richard Irving

The Court of Last Resort

Crime Drama; 30 min; NBC 10/4/57 to 4/11/58

The program, designed to help people falsely accused of a crime, details actual case histories through the investigations of detective Sam Larsen and the courtroom defenses of Erle Stanley Gardner.

Erle Stanley Gardner	Paul Birch
Sam Larsen	Lyle Bettger

Producer: Elliott Lewis, Jules Goldstone

The Courtship of Eddie's Father

Comedy-Drama; 30 min; ABC 9/17/69 to 6/14/72

The relationship between Tom Corbett, editor of "Tomorrow" magazine, and his 6-year-old son, Eddie.

Tom Corbett	Bill Bixby
Eddie Corbett	Brandon Cruz
Mrs. Livingston	Miyoshi Umeki
Cissy Drummond	Tippi Hedren
Norman Tinker	James Komack
Tina Rickles	Kristina Holland
Joey Kelley	Jodie Foster

Theme Vocal ("Best Friend") by Nilsson

Producer: James Komack

Cousins

Comedy Pilot; 30 min; ABC 8/10/76

The comic adventures of Gail Raymond and Barbara Donohue, secretaries in a large New York ad agency.

Gail Raymond	Lisa Mordente
Barbara Donohue	Dee Dee Rescher
Leonard Mandorf	David Ogden Stiers
Alan Peters	Ray Buktenica

Producer: Patricia Nardo, Gloria Banta

Cover Story

Profile; 30 min; Syn. 9/86

A series of celebrity profiles in which the stars talk about their personal and professional lives. Produced and directed by Rift Fournier.

Cover Up

Adventure; 60 min; CBS 9/22/84 to 7/6/85

The exploits fo Dani Reynolds and Mac Harper (later Jack Stryker), U.S. government espionage agents who pose as a fashion photographer and her model.

Dani Reynolds	Jennifer O'Neill
Mac Harper	Jon-Erik Hexum
Jack Stryker	Antony Hamilton
Henry Towler	Richard Anderson
Rick	Mykel T. Williams
Gretchen (model)	Ingrid Anderson
Billie (model)	Irena Ferris
Ashley (model)	Dana Sparks
Terri (model)	Terri Wynn
Rachel (model)	Rosemarie Thomas
	Sheree Wilson

Producer: Glen A. Larson

Cowboy G-Men

Western; 30 min; Syn. 1952

The exploits of Pat Gallagher and Stoney Crockett, U.S. government undercover agents patrolling California during the 1880s.

Pat Gallagher	Russell Hayden
Stoney Crockett	Jackie Coogan

Producer: Henry Donovan, Lesley Selander

Cowboy in Africa

Adventure; 60 min; ABC 9/11/67 to 9/16/68

The adventures of rodeo rider Jim Sinclair as he helps game rancher Howard Hayes establish an animal preserve in Kenya, East Africa.

Jim Sinclair	Chuck Connors
John Henry	Tom Nardini
Howard Hayes	Ronald Howard
Samson	Gerald B. Edwards

Producer: Andy White, George M. Cahan

Cowboy Theatre

Monty Hall as the host of an hour series of edited theatrical westerns of the 1930s and 40s. DuMont 9/15/56 to 3/9/57.

The Cowboys

Western; 30 min; ABC 2/6/74 to 8/14/74

When he is unable to find drovers to herd his cattle to Dodge City, Will Andersen, owner of the Longhorn Ranch in Spanish Wells, New Mexico, hires seven children to help him. When Will is killed by rustlers, the kids and a range cook (Mr. Nightlinger) decide to remain with Kate, Will's widow, and help her run the ranch. Stories, set in the 1870s, relate their experiences. Based on the feature film.

Mr. Nightlinger	Moses Gunn
Kate Andersen	Diana Douglas
Marshal Bill Winter	Jim Davis
Slim (child)	Robert Carradine
Cimmaron (child)	A Martinez
Homer (child)	Kerry McLane
Steve (child)	Clint Howard
Jim (child)	Sean Kelly
Hardy (child)	Mitch Brown
Weedy (child)	Clay O'Brien

Producer: David Dortort, John Hawkins

Cowboys and Injuns

An informal children's series, hosted by Rex Bell, in which Indian and cowboy folklore is explained. ABC 10/15/50 to 12/31/50.

C.P.O. Sharkey

Comedy; 30 min; NBC 12/1/76 to 7/28/78

A satirical look at Navy life as seen through the eyes of Steve Sharkey, a Chief Petty Officer at the San Diego Naval Training Center.

C.P.O. Sharkey	Don Rickles
C.P.O. Robinson	Harrison Page
Captain Quinlan	Elizabeth Allen
Capt. Buckner	Richard X. Slattery
Drill Sgt. Pruitt	Peter Isacksen
Recruit Leon Sholnick	David Landsberg
Recruit Kowalski	Tom Ruben
Recruit Shimokawa	Evan Kim
Recruit Mignone	Barry Pearl

Producer: Aaron Ruben

The Cracker Brothers

Comedy Pilot; 60 min; NBC 9/14/84

Skits that relate the misadventures of Mark, Kevin and Derek Cracker, three brothers who will do anything for a laugh.

Mark Cracker	Mark King
Kevin Cracker	Kevin Scannell
Derek Cracker	Derek McGrath

Regulars: Melinda Naud, Angela Aames, Pat McCormick, Jane Bowers, Nancy Roberts, Lauren-Marie Taylor, Cassandra Gava

Producer: Sid and Marty Krofft

Craig Kennedy, Criminologist

Crime Drama; 30 min; Syn. 1952

The story of Craig Kennedy, a criminologist who uses scientific deduction to solve crimes.

Craig Kennedy	Donald Woods

Producer: Adrian Weiss

Crash Corrigan's Ranch

A children's program of musical acts and sketches with host Ray "Crash" Corrigan. Broadcast on ABC from 7/15/50 to 9/29/50.

Crash Island

Comedy Pilot; 60 min; NBC 4/11/81

A plane, carrying Ohio school children to Honolulu, is damaged during an electrical storm. The plane crashes into the ocean and its occupants escape to a nearby desert island from which there is no escape. The story relates their attempts to begin a new life on the island.

Happy Burleson (pilot)	Greg Mullavey
Meadowlark (mechanic)	Meadowlark Lemon
Ceci (stewardess)	Jenny Sherman
Warren Bundy (coach)	Warren Berlinger
Tina (Warren's assistant)	Sheila DeWindt
Kazi Yamamora (Japanese soldier)	Pat Morita
Sandy*	Penelope Sudrow
Kris*	Lisa Lindgren
Heather*	Heather Hobbs
Susan*	Elizabeth Ringwald
Chubby*	Paul Jarnagin Jr.
Harry*	Jeffrey Knootz
Larry*	Gregory Knootz
Brett*	Bradley Liberman
Fred*	Rusty Gilligan
Mark*	Danie Wade Dalton
Angie*	Cjon Damitri Patterson
Jeff*	Jeff Kirkland

Producer: Don Nelson, Arthur Alsberg

*The kids.

Crazy Dan

Comedy Pilot; 60 min; NBC 7/19/86

A satirical spoof of police dramas as seen through the exploits of "Crazy" Dan Gatlin, a single-minded, unorthodox L.A. police detective who will get his man by any means possible.

Dan Gatlin	John Beck
Off. Bonnie Raines	Mary Crosby
Captain Walker	John Hancock
James Fields	Vincent Schiavelli
Ricco Ritter	Lloyd Bochner
Hamilton	Stuart Margolin
Wednesday	Pat Carroll
Lila	Shannon Tweed
Hood	Sid Haig
Lawyer	Terry Kiser

Producer: Glen A. Larson

Crazy Like a Fox

Comedy-Crime Drama; 60 min; CBS 12/30/84 to 9/4/86

The story of Harry Fox, a San Francisco-based private detective who incorporates his skills as a con artist to apprehend criminals.

Harry Fox	Jack Warden
Harrison K. Fox	John Rubinstein
Cindy Fox	Penny Peyser
Josh Fox	Robbie Kiger
Allison	Lydia Lei

Producer: Roger Shulman, John Baskin, George Schenck, Frank Cardea

Crime Photographer

Crime Drama; 30 min; CBS 4/19/51 to 6/5/52

The exploits of Casey, a press-photographer for the "Morning Express," a crusading New York Newspaper. Also known as "Casey, Crime Photographer."

Casey	Richard Carlyle
	Darren McGavin
Ann Williams	Jan Miner
Ethelbert	John Gibson
	Cliff Hall
Capt. Bill Logan	Bernard Lenrow
Jack Lipman	Archie Smith

Announcer: Ken Roberts

The Blue Note Cafe Musicians: The Tony Mottola Trio

Music: Morton Gould

Producer: Charles Russell, Martin Manulis

Crime Reporter

See "Big Town."

Crime Story

Crime Drama; 60 min; NBC 9/18/86 to 3/13/87

The series, set in Chicago during the 1960s, follows the relationship between Mike Torello, a no-nonsense cop with the Major Crime Unit; Ray Luca, a rising mobster; and David Abrams, a lawyer who is the son of a former gangster. (Later episodes are set in Las Vegas.)

Lt. Mike Torello	Dennis Farina
Julie Torello	Darlene Fluegel
Sgt. Danny Krychek	Bill Smithrovich
David Abrams	Steve Lang
Ray Luca	Anthony Denison
Frank Holman	Ted Levine
Pernell Randall	John Snyder
Max Goldman	Andrew Dice Clay
Pauli Taglia	John Santucci
Inger	Patricia Carboneau
Noah Ganz	Ray Serra
Bartoli	Jon Polito
Hector Lincoln	Ving Rhames
June Lincoln	Kim Staunton
Susan Terry	Pam Grier
Det. Walter Clemmons	Paul Butler
Det. Joey Indelli	William Campbell
Det. Nate Grossman	Steve Ryan

Producer: Michael Mann

Theme Vocal ("Runaway"): Del Shannon

Crime Syndicated

Dramas based on the files of the Senate Crime Investigating Committee and hosted by Rudolph Halley. CBS 9/18/51 to 6/23/53.

Crime with Father

Crime Drama; 30 min; ABC 8/31/51 to 1/25/52

The story of Chris Riland, the beautiful daughter of the N.Y.P.D. homicide bureau chief (Jim Riland) as she helps her father solve crimes.

Capt. Jim Riland	Rusty Lane
Chris Riland	Peggy Lobbin

Producer: Wilbur Stark

Crimes of Passion

Crime Drama; 60 min; Syn. 9/76

Dramatizations based on French criminal records of crimes of passion.

Judge	Anthony Newlands
Saval (defense)	Daniel Moynihan
Lacan (prosecutor)	John Phillips

Producer: Ian Fordyce

Crisis

Interview-Game; 30 min; NBC 10/5/49 to 12/28/49

A person who faced a real crisis tells his story, but stops before the climax. A group of actors, who are unaware of what the outcome was, attempt to ad-lib the climax. The player reveals the outcome and receives prizes.

Host: Adrian Spies

Assistant: Arthur Peterson, Bob Cunningham

Producer: Norman Felton

Crisis

Drama Pilot; 60 min; CBS 9/2/68

The work of Frank Chandler, head of the Crisis Clinic of the Los Angeles Board of Welfare, an around-the-clock psychiatric service.

Dr. Frank Chandler	Carl Betz
Lisa Edwards	Susan Strasberg
Dan Gardner	Billy Dee Williams
Jerry Taylor	Roger Perry
June Fielding	Davey Davison
Phyllis Edwards	Joan Kerr

Producer: Adrian Samish, Quinn Martin

Crisis

Repeats of dramas that originally aired on "The Bob Hope Chrysler Theatre" and "The Kraft Suspense Theatre." Syndicated 1971.

Cross Current

See "Foreign Intrigue."

Crossroads

Anthology; 30 min; ABC 10/7/55 to 9/27/55

Dramatizations based on the experiences of men of the clergy. Stars include Rod Cameron, Yvonne Lime, Stephen McNally, Patricia Crowley, Alan Hale Jr., Vincent Price, Phyllis Coates, Elinor Donahue, Lee Van Cleef, Maureen O'Sullivan, Victor Jory and Richard Jaeckel.

Producer: Joe Harry Brown, Herbert F. Stewart

The Cross-Wits

Game; 30 min; Syn. 12/75 and 9/86

Object: For players to fill in a crossword puzzle by calling positions and guessing the word that fills the space.

Host (1975): Jack Clark

Host (1986): David Sparks

Producer (1975): Ralph Edwards

Producer (1986): Philip Mayer, Norman Checkor

Crown Theatre with Gloria Swanson

Anthology; 30 min; Syn. 1953

Dramas, produced especially for syndication, and hosted by actress Gloria Swanson.

Producer: Bernard Girard, Harve Foster, Richard Dorso, Albert Lopez

Crunch and Des

Adventure; 30 min; Syn. 1955

The exploits of Crunch Adams and Des Smith, the owner-operators of the "Poseidon," a charter service for hire. Also known as "Charter Boat" and "Deep Sea Adventures."

Crunch Adams	Forrest Tucker
Des Smith	Sandy Kenyon
Sari Adams	Joanne Bayes

Producer: Burton Benjamin, Perry Lafferty

The Crusader

Adventure; 30 min; CBS 10/7/55 to 12/28/56

The exploits of Matt Anders, a crusading free-lance magazine writer.

Matt Anders	Brian Keith

Producer: Richard Lewis

Crusader Rabbit

Cartoon; 5 min; Syn. 1949 to 1951; 1957 to 1958

Serial-like adventures of Crusader Rabbit and Rags the Tiger. 195 episodes aired in 1949–51; 260 episodes 1957–58.

Crusader Rabbit	Lucille Bliss
	Ge Ge Pearson
Rags the Tiger	Vern Louden
Narrator	Roy Whaley

Producer: Jay Ward

The Crystal Room

A program of music and songs with Maggi McNellis. ABC 8/15/48 to 9/12/48.

Curiosity Shop

Children; 60 min; ABC 9/11/71 to 9/9/73

Sketches, cartoons and songs are used to explain various aspects of the adult world to children.

Gittel the Witch	Barbara Minkus
Pam	Pamelyn Ferdin
Gerard	John Levin
Ralph	Kerry MacLane
Cindy	Jerelyn Fields

Producer: Chuck Jones

The Curse of Dracula

Serial; 20 min; NBC 2/27/79 to 5/1/79

A "Cliffhangers" segment about Kurt von Helsing and Mary Gibbons and their efforts to destroy Count Dracula, the 512-year-old vampire who is now posing as a European History professor at San Francisco's Southbay College.

Count Dracula	Michael Nouri
Kurt von Helsing	Stephen Johnson
Mary Gibbons	Carol Baxter
Amanda Gibbons	Louise Sorel
Antoinette	Antoinette Stella
Christine	Bever-Leigh Banfield

Producer: Kenneth Johnson

Curtain Call Theatre

Anthology; 30 min; NBC 6/20/52 to 9/26/52

Dramas based on classical and contemporary short stories and featuring such stars as James Dunn, Boris Karloff, Jack Palance, Robert Preston, Louise Larabee, Priscilla Gillette, Miriam Hopkins, John Forsythe, Ilona Massey, Wendell Corey, Maureen Stapleton and Paul Ford.

Producer: Worthington Miner, Frank Wisbar

Custer

See the original title, "The Legend of Custer," for information.

Cut

Game; 30 min; DuMont 6/4/49 to 6/18/49

A group of actors perform a skit which suggests a person, place or thing. An operator places a random telephone call. If the viewer can identify the subject, he wins a prize.

Host: Carl Caruso

Producer: Jerry Layton, Wilbur Stark

Cutter to Houston

Drama; 60 min; CBS 10/1/83 to 12/31/83

Events in the lives of Beth Gilbert, Andy Fenton, and Hal Wexler, young doctors battling disease in Cutter, a small Texas town.

Dr. Beth Gilbert	Shelley Hack
Dr. Andy Fenton	Jim Metzler
Dr. Hal Wexler	Alec Baldwin
Nurse Connie Buford	K Callan
Nurse Patty Alvarez	Susan Styles
Mayor Warren Jarvis	Noble Willingham
Dorothy Jarvis	Georgann Johnson
Dr. Easley	Percy Rodrigues

Theme Song ("Cutter to Houston"): James DiPasquale

Producer: Michael Rhodes, Gerald W. Abrams

The D.A.

Crime Drama; 30 min; NBC 9/17/71 to 1/7/72

The exploits of Paul Ryan, a Los Angeles County District Attorney.

Paul Ryan	Robert Conrad
H. M. "Staff" Stafford	Harry Morgan
Katy Benson	Julie Cobb
Bob Ramerez	Ned Romero
Charlotte	Sonja Dunson

Producer: Jack Webb

The D.A.'s Man

Crime Drama; 30 min; NBC 1/3/59 to 8/29/59

The investigations of Shannon, a detective who works anonymously for the New York District Attorney's office.

Shannon	John Compton
Al Bonacorsi	Ralph Manza

Producer: Frank LaTourette

Daddy's Girl

Comedy Pilot; 30 min; CBS 6/19/73

The story of a widowed father (Bob) and his efforts to raise his young daughter (Flossie).

Bob Randall	Eddie Albert
Flossie Randall	Dawn Lyn
Diane	Della Reese
Aunt Mary	Helen Page Camp
Bennett	Alan Oppenheimer

Producer: Jay Sommers

Dads

Comedy; 30 min; ABC 12/5/86 to 2/6/87

Rick Armstrong and Louis Mangotti, best friends since high school and now single fathers, combine forces and decide to share a Philadelphia house to save on expenses. The male version of "Kate and Allie" relates the efforts of both families to live together.

Rick Armstrong	Barry Bostwick
Louis Mangotti	Carl Weintraub
Kelly Armstrong	Skye Bassett
Ken Mangotti	Eddie Castrodad
Allan Mangotti	Jason Naylor

Producer: Jeff Harris, Mark Waxman

The Daffy/Speedy Show

Cartoon; 30 min; NBC 9/12/81 to 9/11/82

Various Warner Brothers cartoons, including the misadventures of Daffy Duck and Speedy Gonzales.

Daffy and Speedy	Mel Blanc

Additional Voices: June Foray, Larry Storch, Larry Mann

Announcer: Casey Kasem

Producer: Hal Geer

Dagmar's Canteen

Variety; 15 min; NBC 3/22/52 to 6/14/52

Interviews with and performances by members of the U.S. Armed forces.

Hostess: Jennie "Dagmar" Lewis

Regulars: Joey Faye, Ray Malone, Jeanie Lewis

Orchestra: Milton DeLugg

The Dakotas

Western; 60 min; ABC 1/17/63 to 9/9/63

The exploits of U.S. Marshal Frank Regan as he attempts to maintain law and order in the post-Civil War Dakotas. See also "A Man Called Regan."

Marshal Frank Regan	Larry Ward
Deputy Del Stark	Chad Everett
Deputy J. D. Smith	Jack Elam
Deputy Vance Porter	Michael Green

Producer: William T. Orr

Daktari

Adventure; 60 min; CBS 1/11/66 to 1/15/69

The story of Daktari (Swahili for Doctor) Marsh Tarcy, director of the Wameru Game Preserve Center in Africa, as he attempts to protect endangered wildlife.

Dr. Marsh Tracy	Marshall Thompson
Paula Tracy	Cheryl Miller
Warden Headley	Hadley Mattingley
Jack Dane	Yale Sommers
Jenny Jones	Erin Moran
Bert Jason	Ross Hagen

Producer: Ivan Tors

Dallas

Drama; 60 min; CBS 4/2/78 (Premiere)

The drives, ambitions, passions, and personal conflicts of the oil-and-cattle-rich Ewings, owners of the Ewing Oil Company in Dallas, and the Southfork Ranch in Braddock, Texas. See also "Knots Landing."

John "Jock" Ewing	Jim Davis
Eleanor Ewing	Barbara Bel Geddes
	Donna Reed
J. R. Ewing	Larry Hagman
Bobby Ewing	Patrick Duffy
Sue Ellen Ewing	Linda Gray
Pamela Barnes	Victoria Principal
Lucy Ewing	Charlene Tilton
Jamie Ewing	Jenilee Harrison
Willard "Digger" Barnes	David Wayne
	Keenan Wynn
Cliff Barnes	Ken Kercheval
Ray Krebs	Steve Kanaly
Valene Ewing	Joan Van Ark
Gary Ewing	Ted Shackelford
Kristin Shepard	Mary Crosby
Donna Culver	Susan Howard
Liz Craig	Barbara Babcock

Casey Denault
Nicholas Pearce
Lisa
Kimberly
Kay Lloyd
Paul Morgan
April Stevens
Connie
Vaughn Leland
Ann McFadden
Nicholas
Wes Parmalee
Patricia Shepard
Max Flowers
Earl Johnson
Holly Harwood
Jack
Muriel Gillis
Linda
Jenna Wade

John Ross Ewing III

Clayton Farlow
Steve "Dusty"
    Farlow
Mitch Cooper
Arliss Cooper
Afton Cooper
Marilee Stone
Lady Jessica
    Montford
Peter Richards
Clint Ogden
Jeremy Wendell
Katherine
    Wentworth
Mark Graison
Charlene Wade
Matt Cantrell
Angelica Nero

Andrew Stevens
Jack Scalia
Amy Stock
Leigh Taylor-Young
Karen Kopins
Glenn Corbett
Sheree J. Wilson
Michele Scarabelli
Dennis Patrick
Rosemary Forsyth
George Chakaris
Steve Forrest
Martha Scott
Denny Miller
Donegan Smith
Lois Chiles
Dack Rambo
Karlene Crockett
Melody Anderson
Francine Tacker
Priscilla Presley
Tyler Banks
Omri Katz
Howard Keel

Jared Martin
Leigh McCloskey
Anne Francis
Audrey Landers
Fern Fitzgerald

Alexis Smith
Christopher Atkins
Monte Markham
William Smithers

Morgan Brittany
John Beck
Shalane McCall
Marc Singer
Barbara Carrera

Producer: Philip Capice, Lee Rich

Dalton's Code of Vengeance

Adventure; 60 min; NBC 7/27/86 to 8/24/86

The exploits of David Dalton, a ruthless Vietnam vet who wanders across the country and helps people in deep trouble.

David Dalton   Charles Taylor

Producer: Robert Vincent O'Neil, Alex Beaton

The Damon Runyon Theatre

Anthology; 30 min; CBS 4/16/55 to 6/30/56

Dramatizations based on stories by Damon Runyon. Stars include Beverly Garland, Fay Wray, Dorothy Lamour, Jackie Coogan, Broderick Crawford, Wayne Morris, Gale Robbins, John Carradine, Rick Jason, Hugh O'Brian, Scott Brady, Sid Melton and Irene Hervey.

Host: Donald Woods

Dan August

Crime Drama; 60 min; ABC 9/23/70 to 9/9/71

The exploits of Dan August, a detective lieutenant with the Santa Luisa, California, Police Department.

Dan August   Burt Reynolds
Sgt. Charles Wilentz   Norman Fell
Chief George
    Untermeyer   Richard Anderson
Sgt. John Rivera   Ned Romero
Katy Grant   Ena Hartman

Producer: Quinn Martin

Dan Raven

Crime Drama; 30 min; NBC 9/23/60 to 1/6/61

The exploits of Dan Raven, a detective lieutenant with the Hollywood Sheriff's Office.

Dan Raven   Skip Homeier
Sgt. Burke   Dan Barton
Perry Levitt   Quinn Redeker

Dan Temptest

See "The Buccaneers."

Dance Fever

Contest; 30 min; Syn. 9/79

Five couples compete in a 90 second dancing segment wherein they perform their own specialty dances. Each act is judged and rated by a panel of three celebrity guests. The highest scoring act receives a cash prize and returns to compete again.

Host: Deney Terrio, Adrian Zmed

Assistants (Motion): Cindy Millican, Jeannie Thompson, Deborah Johnson, Debbie Harris

Regulars: Janet Jones, Freeman King, Stacy Thatcher, Cindy Scoggins, Cynthia Tucker

Producer: Stan Harris, Paul Gilbert

The Dance Show

Variety; 60 min; Syn. 1/84

Townsend Coleman and Cal DuPree as hosts of a series of music videos, interviews and live rock performances.

Dancin' to the Hits

Music; 30 min; Syn. 9/86

Lorenzo Lamas as the host of a series that features the Sweet Dreams Dancers performing to a medley of the week's top 40 hits. Produced by Bruce Gowers and Carol Rosenstein.

Dancing Party

See "The Lawrence Welk Show."

Danger

Anthology; 30 min; CBS 9/26/50 to 5/31/55

Dramas that explore the art of murder. Stars include E. G. Marshall, John Forsythe, Lee Grant, Paul Newman, Peggy Ann Garner, Carroll Baker, Barbara Nichols, James Dean, Art Carney, Cloris Leachman, Chester Morris, Anthony Quinn, Rod Steiger, Joan Bennett, Anne Jackson, Jack Lemmon, Grace Kelly, Jack Palance.

Producer: William Dozier, Charles Russell, Martin Ritt, Stanley Niss

Danger Man

Adventure; 30 min; CBS 4/5/61 to 9/13/61

The story of John Drake, a special investigator for NATO. See also "Secret Agent" and "The Prisoner."

John Drake   Patrick McGoohan

Producer: Sidney Cole

Danger Mouse

Cartoon; 30 min; Syn. 9/86

A British cartoon about the exploits of daring crime fighters Danger Mouse and his assistant, Penfold.

Danger Mouse   Jason Terry
Penfold   Terry Scott
Colonel K   Edward Kelsey

Producer: Brian Cosgrove

Dangerous Assignment

Adventure; 30 min; Syn. 1952

The exploits of Steve Mitchell, a troubleshooter who investigates crimes on behalf of the U.S. government.

Steve Mitchell   Brian Donlevy

Daniel Boone

Adventure; 60 min; NBC 9/24/64 to 9/10/70

Events in the life of Daniel Boone, the legendary 19th-century frontiersman and pioneer.

Daniel Boone   Fess Parker
Rebecca Boone   Patricia Blair
Jemima Boone   Veronica Cartwright
Israel Boone   Darby Hinton
Yadkin   Albert Salmi
Mingo   Ed Ames
Cincinnatus   Dallas McKennon
Josh Clements   Jimmy Dean
Gabe Cooper   Roosevelt Grier
Gideon   Don Pedro Colley
Cully   James Wainwright

Producer: Aaron Spelling, Aaron Rosenberg

Theme Vocal ("Daniel Boone"): The Imperials

Danny and the Mermaid

Comedy Pilot; 30 min; CBS 5/17/78

While in an underwater observer, student oceanographer Danny Stevens sees and later befriends Aqua, a beautiful mermaid. The would-be series was to depict Danny's misadventures as he attempts to learn about the sea from Aqua and conceal her presence from his mentor, Professor Stoneman.

Aqua	Harlee McBride
Danny Stevens	Patrick Collins
Professor Stoneman	Ray Walston
Turtle	Rick Fazel

Producer: Ivan Tors

The Danny Kaye Show

Variety; 60 min; CBS 9/25/63 to 6/7/67

Music, songs and comedy sketches.

Host: Danny Kaye

Regulars: Harvey Korman, Joyce Van Patten, Vikki Car, Victoria Meyerink, Laurie Ichino

Announcer: Bern Bennett

Orchestra: Paul Weston

Producer: Perry Lafferty

The Danny Thomas Hour

Anthology; 60 min; NBC 9/11/67 to 9/9/68

Varying presentations, including drama, comedy and musical, with host Danny Thomas. Produced by Aaron Spelling and Danny Thomas.

The Danny Thomas Show

See "Make Room for Daddy."

Dante

Drama; 30 min; NBC 10/3/60 to 4/10/61

The story of Willie Dante, a former gambler turned owner of the San Francisco-based Dante's Inferno night club. See also "The Best in Mystery."

Willie Dante	Howard Duff
Stewart Styles	Alan Mowbray
Biff	Tom D'Andrea

Darkroom

Anthology; 60 min; ABC 11/27/81 to 1/15/82

Tales of the supernatural with host James Coburn. Performers include Helen Hunt, Quinn Cummings, Samantha Eggar, Ronny Cox, David Carradine, Mary Frann, Richard Anderson, Cyndy Garvey, Andrew Prine, Anne Lockhart, Misty Rowe, Eugene Roche, Gloria DeHaven, June Lockhart, and Claude Akins. Produced by Peter S. Fischer, Christopher Crowe, and Robert F. O'Neill.

Dark Shadows

Gothic Serial; 30 min; ABC 6/27/66 to 4/2/71

The experiences of Victoria Winters, a young woman who becomes the governess to David Collins, a ten-year-old boy whose family is involved with the world of the Supernatural. The syndicated version of the series begins with the introduction of Barnabas Collins, a modern-day vampire who returns from the dead to terrorize the fishing village of Collinsport.

Barnabas Collins	Jonathan Frid
Victoria Winters	Alexandra Moltke
	Betsy Durkin
	Carolyn Groves
Elizabeth Collins	Joan Bennett
Carolyn Stoddard	Nancy Barrett
Roger Collins	Louis Edmonds
Maggie Evans	Kathryn Leigh Scott
Angelique Collins	Lara Parker
Willie Loomis	John Karlen
David Collins	David Henesy
Dr. Julia Hoffman	Grayson Hall
Joe Haskell	Joel Crothers
Peter Bradford	Roger Davis
Elliot Stokes	Thayer David
Burke Devlin	Anthony George
	Mitchell Ryan
Sam Evans	David Ford
Nicholas Blair	Humbert A. Astredo

Producer: Dan Curtis, Robert Costello

Dastardly and Muttley in Their Flying Machines

Cartoon; 30 min; CBS 9/13/69 to 9/3/71

The World War I adventures of Dick Dastardly, an enemy of the Allies, as he attempts to win the war for his unnamed country by intercepting the vital messages of Yankee Doodle Pigeon, the American courier.

Dick Dastardly	Paul Winchell
Muttley (his dog)	Don Messick
The General	Paul Winchell
Klunk and Zilly	Don Messick

Producer: William Hanna, Joseph Barbera

A Date with the Angels

Comedy; 30 min; ABC 5/10/57 to 1/29/58

Events in the hectic lives of marrieds Gus and Vickie Angel.

Gus Angel	Bill Williams
Vickie Angel	Betty White
George Clemson	Roy Engle
Wilma Clemson	Natalie Masters
George Neise	Karl Koening
Dottie Neise	Joan Banks
Adam Henshaw	Russell Hicks
Mary Henshaw	Isabel Elsom
Mr. Finley	Burt Mustin
Roger Finley	Richard Deacon

Producer: Don Fedderson

A Date with Judy

Comedy; 30 min; ABC 6/2/51 to 9/30/53

The misadventures of Judy Foster, a pretty, unpredictable high school girl with a knack for finding trouble.

Judy Foster	Patricia Crowley
	Mary Lynn Beller
Melvyn Foster	Judson Rees
	John Gibson
Dora Foster	Anna Lee
	Flora Campbell
Randolph Foster	Gene O'Donnell
Oogie Pringle	Jimmie Sommers

Producer: Aleen Leslie

Dateline: Hollywood

Magazine; 30 min; ABC 4/3/67 to 9/29/67

A daily program of celebrity interviews and industry news with hosts Joanna Barnes and Rona Barrett.

The Dating Game

Game; 30 min; ABC 10/6/66 to 7/6/73

Object: For a young woman to question three bachelors and choose the one she would like to have as a date. Also played in reverse. See also "The New Dating Game."

Host: Jim Lange

Announcer: Johnny Jacobs

Producer: Chuck Barris

Daughters

Comedy Pilot; 30 min; NBC 7/20/77

The story of a widowed cop and his efforts to raise three daughters.

Dominick	Michael Constantine
Cookie	Judy Landers
Diane	Olivia Barash
Terry	Robin Groves
Aunt Rosa	Julie Bovasso

Producer: Paul Junger Witt, Tony Thomas, Susan Harris

Dave Allen at Large

A syndicated (1975) series of sketches that spoof everyday life.

Host: Dave Allen

Regulars: Jacqueline Clarke, Susan Baker, Ronnie Brody, Ralph Watson, Robert East, Paul McDowell

Dave and Charley

Comedy; 15 min; NBC 1/7/52 to 3/28/52

The antics of a senile oldster (Charlie) and his companion Dave, an unemployed file clerk.

Charlie Weaver	Cliff Arquette
Dave	Dave Willock

The Dave Garroway Show

Variety; 30 min; NBC 10/2/53 to 6/25/54

A casual program of music, songs and chatter with host Dave Garroway and regulars Jill Corey, Jack Haskell, Cliff Norton and Shirley Hammer. Music by Skitch Henderson.

David Brenner's Night Life

Variety; 30 min; Syn. 9/86

A nightly program of music and comedy coupled with celebrity interviews.

Host: David Brenner

Announcer: Dan Ingram

Orchestra: Billy Preston

Producer: Bob Teschler

David Cassidy—Man Undercover

Crime Drama; 60 min; NBC 11/2/78 to 8/2/79

The exploits of Dan Shay, an undercover agent with the L.A.P.D.

Dan Shay	David Cassidy
Joanne Shay	Wendy Rastatter
Cindy Shay	Elizabeth Reddin
Sgt. Walt Abrams	Simon Oakland
Paul Sanchez	Michael A. Saleido
T. J.	Ray Vitte

Producer: David Gerber

The David Frost Revue

Satire; 30 min; Syn. 1971

Sketches and blackouts based on topical issues.

Host: David Frost

Regulars: Jack Gilford, Marcia Rodd, Cleavon Little, Lynn Lipton, George S. Irving, Larry Moss, Jim Catusi

Producer: David Frost, Marc Merson

The David Frost Show

A syndicated (1969–72) series of celebrity interviews with host David Frost.

The David Letterman Show

Variety; 60 min; NBC 6/23/80 to 10/24/80

A weekday series of music, comedy and celebrity interviews.

Host: David Letterman

Regulars: Edie McClurg, Valri Bromfield, Kim Carney, Edwin Newman, Wil Shriner, Bob Sarlatte, Paul Kelly

Announcer: Bill Wendell

The David Niven Theatre

Anthology; 30 min; NBC 4/7/59 to 9/15/59

Original dramas that feature such stars as Fay Wray, Anne Francis, Barry Nelson, James Best, Eddie Bracken, Julie London, Eddie Albert, Frank Lovejoy, Carolyn Jones and Dan Duryea.

Host: David Niven

Producer: Vincent M. Fennelly

The David Steinberg Show

Variety; 60 min; CBS 7/19/72 to 8/16/72

A Summer series of comedy sketches and blackouts.

Host: David Steinberg

Announcer: Bill Thompson

Orchestra: Artie Butler

Producer: Bob Booker, George Foster

Davy and Goliath

Cartoon; 15 min; Syn. 1961

A religious oriented series about the adventures of young Davy Hanson and his talking dog, Goliath. Characters are animated clay figures.

Voices: Richard Belah, Hal Smith, Nancy Wible, Norma MacMillan

Producer: Arthur Clokey

Davy Crockett

A five-part chronicle of Davy Crockett, a legendary frontiersman-pioneer of the early 1800s. Episodes: "Davy Crockett, Indian Fighter" (12/15/54); "Davy Crockett Goes to Congress" (1/26/55); "Davy Crockett at the Alamo" (2/23/55); "Davy Crockett's Keelboat Race" (11/16/55); and "Davy Crockett and the River Pirates" (12/14/55). Aired on "Disneyland."

Davy Crockett	Fess Parker
George Russell	Buddy Ebsen
Polly Crockett	Helen Stanley
Billy Crockett	Eugene Brindle
Johnny Crockett	Ray Whiteside
Thimbelrig	Hans Conried
Bustedluck	Nick Cravat
Mike Fink	Jeff York
Red Stick	Pat Hogan
Big Foot Mason	Mike Mazurki

Producer: Bill Walsh

Day by Day

Comedy Pilot; Unaired; 30 min; Produced in 1973

Events in the day-to-day lives of the Farraday family: Mort and Annie (parents) and their mischievous children, Richie and Donald.

Mort Farraday	Murray Hamilton
Annie Farraday	Pippa Scott
Richie Farraday	Mitch Vogel
Donald Farraday	Ike Eisenmann
Athena	Cynthia Eilbacher
Loretta	Elaine Giftos

Producer: E. Duke Vincent, Bruce Johnson

Day in Court

Drama; 30 min; ABC 10/13/58 to 6/24/65

Dramatizations of actual criminal and civil court hearings. Judge: Edgar Allan Jones Jr., William Gwinn.

Producer: Selig J. Seligman

Day to Day

Comedy Pilot; 30 min; CBS 8/28/87

Events in the lives of Judith, Shirley, and Hope, three different sisters who never forget they are family. The pilot relates the sisters efforts to arrange a 35th wedding anniversary for their parents (Walter and Jean).

Judith Lumley	Linda Purl
Hope Lumley	Noelle Parker
Shirley Rovitch	Deborah Harmon
Walter Lumley	Darren McGavin
Jean Lumley	K Callan
Mike Rovitch	Cliff Potts
Diane Rovitch	Jenny Beck
Carrie Rovitch	Jessica Puscas
Uncle Bob	Pat Corley
Aunt Sue	Diane Stilwell

Producer: Leonard Hill, Robert O'Connor

A Day with Doodles

A syndicated (1965) series of comedy skits with Doodles Weaver (as himself) attempting to cope with life's endless problems.

Daydreaming with Laraine

A daily series of music, interviews, chatter and dramatic vignettes. Broadcast as "Daydreaming with Laraine" from 5/5/51 to 8/18/51, and as "The Laraine Day Show" from 5/17/51 to 7/19/51. Aired on ABC.

Hostess: Laraine Day

Vocalist: Ruth Woodner

Music: The Bill Harrington Trio

The Days and Nights of Molly Dodd

Comedy-Drama; 30 min; NBC 5/23/87 (Premiere)

The story of Molly Dodd, an attractive, divorced woman in her thirties, as she attempts to make life as meaningful as possible while realizing that her biological clock is ticking.

Molly Dodd	Blair Brown
Fred Dodd	William Converse-Roberts
Florence	Allyn Ann McLerie
Davey	James Greene
Dennis	Victor Garber
Birmanyi	Kabir Bedi

The Dayton Allen Show

A syndicated (1961) series of comical advice with comedian Dayton Allen. Produced by Mark Lipsky.

D.C. Cop

Crime Drama Pilot; 60 min; CBS 8/27/86

Feeling a need to become part of the action, newspaper reporter Michael Halsey resigns and becomes a detective with the Washington, D.C., P.D. The unsold series was to relate Halsey's exploits as he uses his journalistic experience to solve crimes.

Michael Halsey	Cotter Smith
Deborah Matheson	Carolyn McCormick
Chief Nathan Jackson	Robert Hooks
Cliff Dickerson	Mario Van Peebles
Lucas Adams	Kyle T. Heffner
Maxwell Vane	Fritz Weaver
Molly St. Clair	Nancy Stafford

Producer: Dick Berg

D.C. Follies

Comedy Pilot; 30 min; Syn. 4/87

A proposed series in which puppets that resemble celebrities and politicians frequent a Washington bar (D.C. Follies) to relate events in their everyday lives to its bartender (Fred). Puppets are the creations of Sid and Marty Krofft.

Host (as Fred): Fred Willard

Voices: Louise Duart, Joe Alaskey, John Roarke

Guest: Tom Poston

Producer: Sid and Marty Krofft

Deadline

A syndicated (1959) series of dramas that depict the work of newspapermen. Hosted by Paul Stewart and produced by Arnold Perl.

Deadline for Action

ABC network repeats (2/8/59 to 9/20/59) of the Dane Clark segments of "Wire Service" (which see).

Dealer's Choice

Game: 30 min; Syn; 1/74

The format involves players in various gambling situations. Players with the highest chip score are the winners.

Host: Bob Hastings, Jack Clark

Assistant: Jane Nelson

Producer: Ralph Edwards

The Dean Jones Show

Comedy Pilot; 30 min; CBS 7/2/65

The story of a swinging bachelor (Alec) who tries to mend his ways and set an example for his visiting 15-year-old sister (Bunny).

Alec Tate	Dean Jones
Bunny Tate	Robyn Millan
Cappy Skidmore	Jay C. Flippen
Sherry	Diane McBain
Bev Ferguson	Ann Jillian
Miss Malloy	Christine White

Producer: Hank Gerson

Dean Martin's Celebrity Roast

Comedy; 60 min; NBC 2/8/74 to 1/19/79

Celebrities from various aspects of the entertainment world are honored via a comical roast. Presented as a series of specials.

Host: Dean Martin

Regulars: Nipsey Russell, Foster Brooks, Ruth Buzzi, Milton Berle, Orson Welles, LaWanda Page, Rich Little, Charlie Callas, Red Buttons, Don Rickles, Georgia Engel

Orchestra: Les Brown

Producer: Greg Garrison

Dean Martin's Comedy World

Comedy; 60 min; NBC 6/6/74 to 8/8/74

Performances by new comedy talent with hosts Jackie Cooper, Barbara Feldon and Nipsey Russell. Produced by Greg Garrison

Dean Martin Presents Music Country, U.S.A.

Variety; 60 min; NBC 7/26/73 to 9/6/73

Performances by new and established country and western artists.

Regulars: Loretta Lynn, Donna Fargo, Mac Davis, Jerry Reed, Lynn Anderson, Kris Kristofferson, Tammy Wynette, Ray Stevens, Tom T. Hall, Marty Robbins

Orchestra: Jonathan Lucas

Producer: Greg Garrison

Dean Martin Presents the Golddiggers

Variety; 60 min; NBC 6/20/68 to 9/12/68

Music and comedy featuring the Golddiggers, twelve talented young ladies assembled by producer Greg Garrison.

Hosts: Joey Heatherton, Frank Sinatra Jr.

Regulars: Paul Lynde, Barbara Heller, Stu Gilliam, Gail Martin, Avery Schreiber, Stanley Myron Handleman

Orchestra: Les Brown

Producer: Greg Garrison

Dean Martin Presents the Golddiggers

Variety; 60 min; NBC 7/17/69 to 9/11/69

The music, songs and dances of the 1930s and 40s.

Hosts: Gail Martin, Paul Lynde, Lou Rawls

Regulars: Darleen Carr, The Golddiggers, Stanley Myron Handleman, Tommy Tune, Albert Brooks, Joyce Ames, Allison McKay

Orchestra: Les Brown

Producer: Greg Garrison

Dean Martin Presents the Vic Damone Show

Variety; 60 min; NBC 6/22/67 to 9/7/67

Music and songs with singer Vic Damone, regulars Gail Martin and Carol Lawrence, and the music of Les Brown. Produced by Greg Garrison.

The Dean Martin Show

Variety; 60 min; NBC 9/16/65 to 5/24/74

A weekly series of music, songs and comedy sketches.

Host: Dean Martin

Regulars: Dom DeLuise, Tom Bosley, Marian Mercer, Nipsey Russell, Rodney Dangerfield, Lou Jacobi, Kay Medford, Ken Lane, The Golddiggers, Jayne Kennedy, Tara Leigh, Helen Funai

Announcer: Frank Barton

Orchestra: Les Brown

Producer: Greg Garrison

Dear Detective

Crime Drama; 60 min; CBS 3/28/79 to 4/18/79

The exploits of Kate Hudson, a detective sergeant with the L.A.P.D.

Det. Kate Hudson	Brenda Vaccaro
Lisa Hudson	Jet Yardum
Richard Weyland	Arlen Dean Snyder
Det. Chuck Morris	Jack Ging
Capt. Mike Gorcey	M. Emmet Walsh

Producer: Roland Kibbee, Dean Hargrove

Dear Mom, Dear Dad

Comedy Pilot; 30 min; NBC 5/18/59

The misadventures of Bunty Perkins, a mischievous college freshman (at Boyden University). Aired as "Boyden vs. Bunty" on "Alcoa Theatre."

Bunty Perkins	Robert Trumbull
The Dean	Raymond Bailey
Amy Porter	Kathy Reed
Galen Lawrence	Bert Convy
Bill Davidson	Jimmy Bates

Producer: Winston O'Keefe

Dear Penelope and Peter

Comedy Pilot; 30 min; ABC 5/19/86

The misadventures of Judy and Ben Berlin, marrieds who write the "Dear Penelope and Peter" advice-to-the-lovelorn column for a New York newspaper.

Judy Berlin	Melinda Culea
Ben Berlin	Rex Smith
Cliff	Terrence McGovern
Wilbur Smith	Iggie Wolfington
Diana	Melissa Harrison
Mr. Collins	Eric Bullock

Producer: Gordon Farr

Dear Phoebe

Comedy; 30 min; NBC 9/10/54 to 9/2/55

The story of Bill Hastings, an ex-college professor who is employed as Phoebe Goodheart, the male advice-to-the-lovelorn columnist for the Los Angeles "Daily Blade."

Bill Hastings	Peter Lawford
Mickey Riley	Marcia Henderson
Mr. Fosdick	Charles Lane
Humphrey Humpsteader	Josef Corey

Producer: Alex Gottlieb

Dear Teacher

Comedy Pilot; 30 min; NBC 7/17/81

The experiences of Annie Cooper, a pretty sixth grade school teacher.

Annie Cooper	Melinda Culea
Fran Ohlmeyer	Rebecca York
Karen Lipner	Nan Martin
Todd Goodwin	David Hollander
Heidi Prince	Rachel Jacobs
Cece Taft	LaShana Dendy
Gloria	Sydney Penny
Steve Goodwin	Ted Danson

Producer: Roger Schulman, John Baskin

Death Valley Days

Anthology; 30 min; Syn. 1952

Western dramatizations that depict incidents in the lives of the people who lived, worked and journeyed throughout Nevada and California during the latter 1800s.

Host: Stanley Andrews (1952–64)
      Ronald Reagan (1964–67)
      Robert Taylor (1967–69)
      Dale Robertson (1969–72)

The Debbie Reynolds Show

Comedy; 30 min; NBC 9/16/69 to 9/8/70

Events in the lives of the Thompsons: Jim, a sportswriter for the Los Angeles "Sun," and Debbie, his wife, who longs for a career as a newspaper feature writer.

Debbie Thompson	Debbie Reynolds
Jim Thompson	Don Chastain
Charlotte Landers	Patricia Smith
Bob Landers	Tom Bosley
Bruce Landers	Bobby Riha

Producer: Jess Oppenheimer

Theme Vocal ("With a Little Love"): Debbie Reynolds

December Bride

Comedy; 30 min; CBS 10/4/54 to 9/24/59

The trials and tribulations of marrieds Matt and Ruth Henshaw; and the romantic misadventures of Lily Ruskin, Ruth's mother, a widow who lives with them.

Lily Ruskin	Spring Byington
Ruth Henshaw	Frances Rafferty
Matt Henshaw	Dean Miller
Hilda Crocker	Verna Felton
Peter Porter	Harry Morgan

Producer: Marvin Marx, Fred DeCordova

Decoy

Crime Drama; 30 min; Syn. 1957

The undercover assignments of Patricia "Casey" Jones, an undercover police woman with the 16th Precinct of the N.Y.P.D.

Off. Patricia Jones	Beverly Garland
Lt. Harris (a.k.a. Torry)	Frank Campanella
Det. "Mac" McGowan	Bill Quinn
Captain Doyle	Edward Holmes
Lt. Kendall	John Newton

Producer: Everett Rosenthal

The Defender

Drama Pilot; 60 min; CBS 2/25 and 3/4/57

The pilot for "The Defenders." The story of Walter and Kenneth Pearson, a father and son legal team. Aired on "Studio One."

Walter Pearson	Ralph Bellamy
Kenneth Pearson	William Shatner
Francis Toohey	Martin Balsam
Joseph Gordon	Steve McQueen

Producer: Herbert Brodkin

The Defenders

Drama; 60 min; CBS 9/16/61 to 9/9/65

A critically acclaimed series about Lawrence Preston, a seasoned attorney, and his son, Kenneth, a recent law school graduate (and his partner in the New York law firm of Preston and Preston). The series, created by Reginald Rose, was unique for its time as it tackled important issues while at the same time showing the "heroes" being capable of losing as well as winning a case.

Lawrence Preston	E. G. Marshall
Kenneth Preston	Robert Reed
Helen Davidson	Barbara Bolton*
	Polly Rowles
Joan Miller	Rosemary Forsyth
Frances Preston (Lawrence's wife)	Meg Mundy*

Producer: Herbert Brodkin

*Roles in the original, never-televised 1960 pilot. The edited, aired version of the pilot (then titled "Death Across the Street") was broadcast as the third episode of the series (with the Bolton and Mundy roles cut).

Defenders of the Earth

Cartoon; 30 min; Syn. 4/86

The exploits of Flash Gordon, Mandrake the Magician, Lother, and the Phantom, comic book heroes who join forces to safeguard the Earth from evil.

Voices: William Callaway, Adam Carl, Ron Feinberg, Buster Jones, Loren Lester, Sarah Partridge, Diane Pershing, Lou Richards, Peter Mark Richman, Dion Williams.

Producer: Margaret Loesch, Lee Gunther, Bruce Paisner

Degrassi Junior High

Drama; 30 min; PBS Syn. 9/87

Realistic events in the daily lives of a group of students who attend Canada's mythical Degrassi Junior High School.

Stephanie Kaye	Nicole Stoffman
Melanie	Sara Ballingall
Arthur Kobalewscuy	Duncan Waugh
Yick	Siluck Saysanasy
Caitlin Ryan	Stacie Mistysyn
Voula Grivogiannis	Niki Kemeny
Joey Jeremiah	Pat Mastroianni
Suzie Rivera	Sarah Charlesworth
L.D.	Amanda Cook
Snake	Stefan Brogren
Wheels	Neil Hope
Christine (Spike)	Amanda Stepto
Heather	Angela Deiseach
Erica	Maureen Deiseach
Mr. Raditch	Daniel Woods
Ms. Avery	Michelle Goodeve

Producer: Linda Schuyler, Kate Taylor.

Deja View

Variety Pilot; 60 min; Syn. 12/85

A proposed series of music videos based on the songs of the 1960s.

Host: John Sebastian

Guests: Teri Garr, Harry Dean Stanton, Graham Nash, William Daniels

Producer: Syd Vinnedge, Tony Scotti

Deja Vu

Variety Pilot; 60 min; Syn. 7/87

A second pilot (see prior title) of music videos based on 1960s songs.

Narration Host: Peter Fornatle

Guests: Teri Garr, Bronson Pinchot, Michael Pare, John Sebastian, Sly Stone

Producer: Syd Vinnedge, Tony Scotti

The Dell O'Dell Show

Female magician Dell O'Dell as host of a program that spotlights guest magicians. Broadcast on ABC from 9/14/51 to 12/14/51.

Della

A syndicated (1970) variety series with singer Della Reese, co-host Sandy Baron, and the music of H. B. Barnum. Produced by Rocco Urbisci.

The Delora Bueno Show

See "Flight to Rhythm."

The Delphi Bureau

Crime Drama; 60 min; ABC 10/5/72 to 9/1/73

The assignments of Glenn Garth Gregory, an investigator for the Delphi Bureau, an agency responsible only to the President and whose function is to protect the national security. Aired on "The Men."

Glenn Garth Gregory	Laurence Luckinbill
Sybil Van Loween	Celeste Holm
	Anne Jeffreys

Producer: Sam H. Rolfe

Delta House

Comedy; 30 min; ABC 1/18/79 to 4/28/79

The antics of the students who comprise the Delta House fraternity of Faber College in 1962. Based on "National Lampoon's Animal House."

Jim "Blotto"
  Blutarski — Josh Mostel
Kent "Flounder"
  Dorfman — Stephen Furst
Robert Hoover — James Widdoes
Eric "Otter"
  Stratton — Peter Fox
Larry "Pinto"
  Kruger — Richard Seer
Daniel "D-Day" Day — Bruce McGill
Dean Vernon
  Wormer — John Vernon
Marion Wormer — Gloria DeHaven
Doug Niedermeyer — Gary Cookson
Muffy Jones — Wendy Goldman
Bombshell — Michelle Pfeiffer
Mr. Jennings — Peter Kastner
Mandy Pepridge — Susanna Dalton
Greg Marmalaide — Brian Patrick Clarke

Producer: Matty Simmons, Ivan Reitman

Delvecchio

Crime Drama; 60 min; CBS 9/9/76 to 7/17/77

The story of Dominick Delvecchio, a detective with the Washington Heights division of the L.A.P.D.

Dominick
  Delvecchio — Judd Hirsch
Det. Paul Shonski — Charles Haid
Lt. Macavan — Michael Conrad
Thomas Delvecchio — Mario Gallo
Assistant D.A.
  Dorfman — George Wyner

Producer: William Sackheim

Dempsey and Makepeace

Crime Drama; 60 min; Syn. 9/85

The exploits of James Dempsey, a tough New York lieutenant on exchange with London's New Scotland Yard, and Harriet "Harry" Makepeace, a beautiful British undercover cop.

Lt. James Dempsey — Michael Brandon
Sgt. Harriet
  Makepeace — Glynis Barber
Chief Gordon
  Spikings — Ray Smith

Producer: Nick Elliott

The Dennis Day Show

See "The R.C.A. Victor Show."

Dennis James' Carnival

Music, songs and comedy with host Dennis James, regulars Dagmar, Victoria Rone, and the music of Lew White. CBS 10/3/48 to 11/7/48.

The Dennis James Show

Interviews, discussions and audience participation with hosts Dennis James and Julia Meade. ABC 2/8/52 to 8/2/54.

The Dennis James Sports Parade

Experimental; 30 min; DuMont 9/38

The first known sports series wherein guests are interviewed and demonstrate their skills.

Host: Dennis James

Producer: Dr. Allen B. DuMont

The Dennis O'Keefe Show

Comedy; 30 min; CBS 9/22/59 to 6/7/60

Events in the life of Hal Towne, an L.A. newspaperman who writes the "All About Towne" column.

Hal Towne — Dennis O'Keefe
Randy Towne — Ricky Kelman
Sarge — Hope Emerson
Karen Hadley — Eloise Hardt
Elliot — Eddie Ryder

Producer: Lee Hafner

Dennis the Menace

Comedy; 30 min; CBS 10/4/59 to 9/22/63

The antics of Dennis Mitchell, a very mischievous young boy.

Dennis Mitchell	Jay North
Henry Mitchell	Herbert Anderson
Alice Mitchell	Gloria Henry
George Wilson	Joseph Kearns
Martha Wilson	Sylvia Field
John Wilson	Gale Gordon
Eloise Wilson	Sara Seeger
Tommy Anderson	Billy Booth
Seymour Williams	Robert John Pitman
Margaret Wade	Jeannie Russell
Sgt. Theodore Mooney	George Cisar
Lucy Elkins	Irene Tedrow
Joey McDonald	Gil Smith
Esther Cathcart	Mary Wickes
Mr. Quigley	Willard Waterman
Mr. Dorfman	Robert B. Williams
Lawrence Finch	Charles Lane

Producer: Harry Ackerman, Winston O'Keefe, James Fonda

Dennis the Menace

Cartoon; 30 min; Syn. 9/86

The animated antics of Dennis Mitchell, a very mischievous young boy.

Dennis Mitchell	Brennan Thicke
Henry Mitchell	Brian George
Alice Mitchell	Louise Vallance
George Wilson	Phil Hartman

Additional voices: Marilyn Lightstone, Jeannie Elias

Producer: Christopher Hallowell, Jean Chalopin, Andy Heyward

Department S

Mystery; 60 min; Syn. 1971

The investigations of Jason King, Annabell Hurst and Stewart Sullivan, the top operatives of Department S, a special branch of Interpol that resolves baffling crimes.

Jason King	Peter Wyngarde
Annabell Hurst	Rosemary Nicols
Stewart Sullivan	Joel Fabiani
Sir Curtis Seretse	Dennis Alaba Peters

Producer: Monty Berman

The Deputy

Western; 30 min; NBC 9/12/59 to 9/16/61

The story of Marshal Simon Fry as he attempts to maintain the law in Silver City, Arizona, during the 1880s.

Simon Fry	Henry Fonda
Deputy Clay McCord	Allen Case
Fran McCord	Betty Lou Keim
Sgt. Trasker	Read Morgan
Herk Lamson	Wallace Ford

Producer: Roland Kibbee

Deputy Dawg

Cartoon; 30 min; Syn. 1960

The antics of Deputy Dawg, a simple-minded Mississippi lawman.

| Deputy Dawg | Dayton Allen |

The Des O'Connor Show

Variety; 60 min; NBC 6/24/70 to 9/21/70
                      6/2/71 to 9/1/71

A Summer series of music, songs and comedy sketches.

Host: Des O'Connor

Regulars: Connie Stevens, Charlie Callas, Jack Douglas, Joe Baker, The Mike Sammes Singers

Orchestra: Jack Parnell

Designing Women

Comedy; 30 min; CBS 9/29/86 (Premiere)

Hoping to succeed in the business world, four women pool their resources and begin Sugarbakers, an Atlanta-based decorating firm. Stories relate their misadventures.

Julia Sugarbaker	Dixie Carter
Suzanne Sugarbaker	Delta Burke
Mary Jo Shively	Annie Potts
Charlene Winston	Jean Smart
Anthony Bouvier	Meshach Taylor
Perky Sugarbaker	Louise Latham

Producer: Harry Thomason, Linda Bloodworth Thomason

The Desilu Playhouse

Anthology; 60 min; CBS 10/13/58 to 6/10/60

Quality productions that feature such stars as Cara Williams, Dina Merrill, Anna Maria Alberghetti, Lloyd Bridges, Piper Laurie, Keenan Wynn, E. G. Marshall, Phyllis Coates, Claire Trevor, Jane Russell, Buddy Ebsen, Cameron Mitchell, Joseph Cotten and Lloyd Nolan.

Host: Desi Arnaz

Commercial Spokeswoman: Betty Furness

Producer: Desi Arnaz

Destiny

Francis L. Sullivan as host of a network (CBS) series of repeat anthology dramas. 7/5/57 to 9/27/57; 7/18/58 to 9/26/58.

Destry

Western; 60 min; ABC 2/14/64 to 5/9/64

The saga of Harrison Destry, the peace-loving son of a rugged gunfighter, as he seeks to clear his name, having been framed and falsely accused of robbery.

Harrison Destry	John Gavin

Producer: Frank Telford

Detect and Collect

Game Pilot; 30 min; DuMont 9/26/46

Object: For players to answer questions, ranging from easy to difficult, in return for cash prizes.

Host: Lew Lehr

Producer: Harvey Marlowe

The Detective

Comedy Pilot; 30 min; NBC 10/12/75

The exploits of Dennis O'Finn, a not-too-bright private detective.

Dennis O'Finn	Larry Hagman
Miss Bessie	Hope Summers
Miss Hiddy-Lou	Helen Kleeb
Miss Amantha	Helen Craig
Miss Birdie	Shirley O'Hara

Producer: Jules Irving

Detective in the House

Comedy-Mystery; 60 min; CBS 3/15/85 to 4/19/85

Longing for a career as a detective, mechanical engineer Press Wyman resigns to pursue his dream. Stories relate his efforts to divide his time between his career as a detective and a house husband who must care for three kids while his wife resumes her role as a school teacher.

Press Wyman	Judd Hirsch
Diane Wyman	Cassie Yates
Deborah Wyman	Mandy Ingber
Todd Wyman	Meeno Peluce
Dunc Wyman	R. J. Williams
Nick Turner	Jack Elam

Theme Vocal ("What Are You Waitin' For?"): Jon Joyce

Producer: Gary Adelson, Gil Grant

Detective in the House

Comedy-Mystery; 60 min; Unaired Pilot (Produced in 1985)

The original pilot about Press Wyman, a detective who must care for his three kids while his wife resumes her role as a school teacher. See prior title also.

Press Wyman	David Steinberg
Diane Wyman	Caroline McWilliams
Deborah Wyman	Heather Hobbs
Todd Wyman	Meeno Peluce
Dunc Wyman	Brandon Call
Nick Turner	Jack Elam

Producer: Mitch Ackerman

Writer: Gil Grant

Director: Harry Harris

Detective School

Comedy; 30 min; ABC 7/31/79 to 11/24/79

The antics of a group of aspiring gumshoes at the Los Angeles-based Hannigan Detective School and Agency.

Nick Hannigan	James Gregory
Maggie Ferguson	Melinda Naud
Teresa Cleary	Jo Ann Harris
Eddie Dawkins	Randolph Mantooth
Robert Redford	Douglas V. Fowley
Charlene Jenkins	LaWanda Page
Leo Frack	Pat Proft

Producer: Bernie Kukoff, Jeff Harris

The Detectives

Crime Drama; ABC 10/16/59 to 9/22/61 (30 min)
9/29/61 to 9/21/62 (60 min)

The exploits of Matt Holbrook, head of an elite team of N.Y.P.D. plainclothes detectives who battle the criminal element.

Capt. Matt Holbrook	Robert Taylor
Lt. Johnny Russo	Tige Andrews
Sgt. Steve Nelson	Adam West
Sgt. Chris Ballard	Mark Goddard
Reporter Lisa Bonay	Ursula Thiess
Lt. Otto Lindstrom	Russell Thorson
Lt. Jim Conway	Lee Farr

Producer: Jules Levy, Arthur Gardner, Arnold Laven

Detective's Diary

See "Saber of London."

The Detective's Wife

Crime Drama; 30 min; CBS 7/7/50 to 10/6/50

The story of Adam Conway, an N.Y.P.D. detective whose assignments are complicated by the intervention of Connie, his well-meaning but trouble-prone wife.

Adam Conway	Donald Curtis
Connie Conway	Lynn Bari

Devlin

Cartoon; 30 min; ABC 9/7/74 to 2/15/76

The story of Ernie, Todd and Sandy Devlin, orphans who support themselves as a motorcycle stunt team.

Ernie Devlin	Michael Bell
Todd Devlin	Mickey Dolenz
Sandy Devlin	Michele Robinson

Producer: William Hanna, Joseph Barbera

The Devlin Connection

Crime Drama; 60 min; NBC 10/2/82 to 12/25/82

The story of Brian Devlin, a former detective, now director of the Performing Arts Center in Los Angeles, and Nick, his son, a private detective who works as a racquet ball pro at a health club.

Brian Devlin	Rock Hudson
Nick Corsella	Jack Scalia
Lauren Dean	Leigh Taylor-Young
Lt. Earl Borden	Louis Giambalvo
Otis Barnes	Herb Jefferson Jr.

Producer: Jerry Thorpe, John Wilder

D.H.O.

Drama Pilot; 60 min; ABC 6/17/73

The story of Sam Delaney, a doctor who runs a District Health Office and who is responsible twenty-four hours a day, seven days a week, for the health of the people of his community.

Dr. Sam Delaney	Frank Converse
Dr. Levine	Luther Adler
Dr. Bianca Pearson	Ruby Dee
Axel Thorson	Ed Grover
Mr. Randall	Jack Weston
Milo	Richard Gere

Producer: Herman Rush

Dhondo

Adventure Pilot; 60 min; Unaired (Produced for CBS in 1967)

The adventures of Rham, an India elephant boy, and his American friend, David Stuart, an architectual engineer, as they help good defeat evil.

David Stuart	Jim Beck
Rham	Gerald Michenaud
Susan Eden	Anna Capri
P. K. Dunne	Jamie Farr

Producer: Leon Benson

Diagnosis: Danger

Drama Pilot; 60 min; CBS 3/1/63

The story of Dr. Daniel Dana, an officer with the county health service of a large metropolitan hospital. Aired on "The Alfred Hitchcock Hour."

Dr. Daniel Dana	Michael Parks
Dr. Simon Oliver	Charles McGraw
Dr. Paul Mackey	Rupert Crosse
Dr. Norman Abrams	Allen Joseph
Sheriff Judd	Berkeley Harris

Producer: Roland Kibbee, Gordon Hessler

Diagnosis: Unknown

Crime Drama; 60 min; CBS 7/5/60 to 9/20/60

The exploits of Dr. Daniel Coffee, the head of the pathology unit of a large New York hospital, as he uses scientific technology to solve crimes.

Dr. Daniel Coffee	Patrick O'Neal
Doris Hudson	Phyllis Newman
Dr. Motilal Mookerji	Cal Bellini
Capt. Max Ritter	Chester Morris
Link	Martin Houston

The Diahann Carroll Show

Variety; 60 min; CBS 8/14/76 to 9/4/76

A program of music, song and dance with singer-actress Diahann Carroll. Orchestrations by H. B. Barnum. Produced by Robert DeLeon

Dial 999

Crime Drama; 30 min; Syn. 1958

The exploits of Michael Maguire, a Royal Canadian Mounted Policeman assigned to study British crime detection methods at the New Scotland Yard in London.

| Insp. Michael Maguire | Robert Beatty |

The Diamond Head Game

Game: 30 min; Syn. 1/75

Eight players compete in a series of question-and-answer rounds that are designed to eliminate seven contestants. The remaining player is placed in a glass room wherein thousands of bills are blown around by an air machine. The bills the player is able to collect within fifteen seconds are his prizes.

Host: Bob Eubanks

Assistant: Jane Nelson

Announcer: Jim Thompson

Producer: Randall Freer, Ed Fishman

Diamonds

Crime Drama; 70 min; CBS 9/22/87 (Premiere)

Following the cancellation of their TV series ("Diamonds"), its stars, Mike and Christina, become "real" detectives when they open their own agency—Two of Diamonds, Confidential Investigations. Stories relate their light-hearted efforts to solve crimes.

Mike Devitt	Nicholas Campbell
Christina Towne	Peggy Smithhart
Sgt. Lou Gianetti	Tony Rosato

Producer: Sonny Grosso, Larry Jacobson

Diana

Comedy; 30 min; NBC 9/10/73 to 1/7/74

Events in the life of Diana Smythe, a young divorcee newly arrived in New York from London, as she begins work as a fashion illustrator at Buckley's Department Store.

Diana Smythe	Diana Rigg
Norman Brodnik	David Sheiner
Norma Brodnik	Barbara Barrie
Howard Tolbrook	Richard B. Shull
Holly Green	Carol Androsky
Marshall Tyler	Robert Moore
Jeff Harmon	Richard Mulligan
Smitty	Liam Dunn

Producer: Leonard B. Stern

The Diana Rigg Show

Comedy Pilot; 34 min; Unaired (Produced for NBC in 1973)

The original, unaired pilot for "Diana" (above title). The original concept follows thirty-year-old Diana Smythe as she relocates from London to New York to become the assistant dress designer to Mr. Vincent, the head designer at Sue Ellen Frocks. The pilot, titled "The Lady Comes Across," was written by Sam Bobrick, Ron Clark, and Leonard B. Stern (also the director).

Diana Smythe	Diana Rigg
Rodney Brodnik	David Sheiner
Norma Brodnik	Nanette Fabray
Mr. Vincent	Philip Proctor
Holly Green	Carol Androsky
Smitty	Liam Dunn
Gerald Honig	Bernie Kopell

Producer: Leonard B. Stern

The Diane Doxee-Jimmy Blaine Show

Music and songs with singer Diane Doxee and pianist Jimmy Blaine. ABC 8/6/50 to 9/24/50.

Dick and the Duchess

Comedy; 30 min; CBS 9/28/57 to 5/16/58

The cases of Dick Starrett, a London-based insurance claims detective, who receives the sometimes unwanted assistance of his wife, Jane, a British Duchess.

Dick Starrett	Patrick O'Neal
Jane Starrett	Hazel Court
Insp. Stark	Michael Shepley
Peter Jamison	Richard Wattis
Mathilda	Beatrice Valley

Producer: Sheldon Reynolds

The Dick Cavett Show

Celebrity interviews with host Dick Cavett. ABC 5/26/69 to 9/19/69.

The Dick Cavett Show

Variety; 60 min; CBS 8/16/75 to 9/6/75

A weekly series of music and comedy sketches with host Dick Cavett and regulars Leigh French, Imogene Coca and Marshall Efron. Produced by Carole and Bruce Hart.

Dick Clark Presents the Rock and Roll Years

Variety; 60 min; ABC 11/28/73 to 1/9/74

The music and personalities of the 1950s, 60s, and 70s.

Host: Dick Clark

Producer: Dick Clark, Bill Lee

The Dick Clark Saturday Night Beechnut Show

Variety; 30 min; ABC 2/15/58 to 9/10/60

Performances by rock and roll personalities with host Dick Clark. Sponsored by Beechnut chewing gum.

Dick Clark's Live Wednesday

Variety; 60 min; NBC 9/20/78 to 12/27/78

A live Wednesday evening program of celebrity interviews and performances.

Host: Dick Clark

Announcer: Jerry Bishop

Orchestra: Lenny Stack

Producer: Dick Clark, Bill Lee

Dick Clark's Nighttime

A syndicated (1985) weekly series that features performances by guest comics, celebrities, and musicians. Hosted and produced by Dick Clark.

Dick Clark's World of Talent

Variety; 30 min; ABC 9/27/59 to 12/20/60

Performances by young talent hopefuls and discussions of their merits with a professional guest panel.

Host: Dick Clark

Producer: Irving Mansfield

The Dick Powell Show

Anthology; 60 min; NBC 9/26/61 to 9/17/63

A series of quality dramatic productions. Also known as "Hollywood Showcase" when syndicated in 1966 with June Allyson as host.

Host: Dick Powell

Substitute Host: Robert Mitchum, James Stewart, Robert Taylor

Hostess: June Allyson

Producer: Dick Powell, Aaron Spelling, Ralph Nelson

Dick Powell's Zane Grey Theatre

See "Zane Grey Theatre."

The Dick Van Dyke Show

Comedy; 30 min; CBS 10/3/61 to 9/7/66

Events in the lives of the Petrie family: Rob, head writer of the fictitious "Alan Brady Show," his beautiful wife, Laura, and their son, Richie. See also "Head of the Family."

Rob Petrie	Dick Van Dyke
Laura Petrie	Mary Tyler Moore
Richie Petrie	Larry Matthews
Buddy Sorrell	Morey Amsterdam
Sally Rogers	Rose Marie
Mel Cooley	Richard Deacon
Alan Brady	Carl Reiner
Jerry Helper	Jerry Paris
Millie Helper	Ann Morgan Guilbert
Freddie Helper	Peter Oliphant David Fresco
Feona "Pickles" Sorrell	Barbara Perry Joan Shawlee
Stacy Petrie	Jerry Van Dyke
Herman Glimcher	Bill Idelson
Sol Pomeroy	Marty Ingels Allan Melvin

Producer: Carl Reiner, Sheldon Leonard, Ronald Jacobs

Dick Tracy

Crime Drama; 30 min; ABC 9/11/50 to 2/12/51

The exploits of Dick Tracy, a dauntless plainclothes detective with the N.Y.P.D.

Dick Tracy	Ralph Byrd
Sam Catchem	Joe Devlin
Tess Trueheart	Angela Greene
Chief Murphy	Dick Elliott

Producer: Dick Moore

The Dick Tracy Show

Cartoon; 5 min; Syn. 9/61

The adventures of police detective Dick Tracy. Programs are designed to include a local market host serving as "The Chief." Other characters: Hemlock Holmes, Joe Jitsu, Speedy Gonzalez, Heap O'Calorie, Sketch Paree and the Mole, Prune Face and Itchy, Flattop and Bee Bee Eyes, Stooge Villa and Mumbles, and The Brow and Oodles.

Dick Tracy   Everett Sloane

Other Voices: Mel Blanc, Paul Frees, Benny Rubin

Producer: Peter DeMet, Henry Saperstein

Did You Hear About Josh and Kelly?!

Comedy Pilot; 30 min; CBS 10/13/80

Shortly after their divorce, Josh Fowler and Kelly Porter discover that they still love each other. The unsold series was to relate their misadventures when they decide to live together so each can pursue his own career without the hassles of a marriage.

Josh Fowler	Dennis Dugan
Kelly Porter	Jane Daly
Rick Mannings	Jimmy Samuels
Jennifer Mannings	Denise Galik

Producer: Rod Parker, Hal Cooper

Diff'rent Strokes

Comedy; 30 min; NBC 11/3/78 to 8/31/85
ABC 9/27/85 to 3/21/86

Following the death of his housekeeper, Park Avenue millionaire Phillip Drummond adopts her two young boys, Arnold and Willis, when he finds they have no relations and will be sent to an orphanage. Stories relate the adventures of the newly formed Drummond and Jackson families. See also "The Facts of Life."

Philip Drummond	Conrad Bain
Kimberly	
Drummond	Dana Plato
Arnold Jackson	Gary Coleman
Willis Jackson	Todd Bridges
Maggie McKinney-	
Drummond	Dixie Carter
	Mary Ann Mobley
Sam McKinney	Danny Cooksey
Edna Garrett	Charlotte Rae
Adelaide Brubaker	Nedra Volz
Pearl Gallagher	Mary Jo Catlett
Dudley Ramsey	Shavar Ross
Charlene DuPrey	Janet Jackson
Robbie	Stephen Mond
Lisa	Nikki Swasey
Sophia	Dody Goodman
Miss Chung	Rosalind Chao

Producer: Budd Grossman, Howard Leeds, John Maxwell Anderson

A Different World

Comedy; 30 min; NBC 9/24/87 (Premiere)

A spin-off from "The Cosby Show" which relates Denise Huxtable's experiences as a freshman at her parents alma mater, Hillman College in Georgia.

Denise Huxtable	Lisa Bonet
Jaleesa	Dawnn Lewis
Maggie Vincent	Marisa Tomei
Dwayne Wayne	Kadeem Harrison
Whitley Gilbert	Jasmine Guy
Stevie Rollins	Loretta Devine

Producer: Thad Mumford, George Crosby, Lissa Levin, Anne Beatts.

Dinah!

Variety; 60 min; Syn. 10/74

A daily series of celebrity interviews with Dinah Shore. Music by John Rodby and produced by Henry Jaffe and Carolyn Raskin.

Dinah and Friends

Variety; 60 min; Syn. 9/79

Celebrity interviews with hostess Dinah Shore and co-hosts Fernando Lamas, Paul Williams, Charles Nelson Reilly, and Don Meredith. Announcing by Johnny Jacobs with the music of the John Rodby Group. Produced by Henry Jaffe and Fred Tatashore.

Dinah and Her New Best Friends

Variety; 60 min; CBS 6/5/76 to 7/31/76

A Summer series of music, songs, and comedy sketches.

Hostess: Dinah Shore

Regulars: Diana Canova, Dee Dee Rescher, Leland Palmer, Mike Neun, Gary Mule Deer, Bruce Kimmel, Michael Preminger, Avie Falana

Music: Ian Bernard

Producer: Henry Jaffe, Carolyn Raskin, Rita Scott

The Dinah Shore Chevy Show

Variety; 15 min; NBC 11/7/51 to 7/12/56

A casual program of music and songs under the sponsorship of Chevrolet.

Hostess: Dinah Shore

Regulars: The Skylarks, The Notables

Announcer: Art Baker

Orchestra: Vic Schoen, Harry Zimmerman

Producer: Bob Henry

The Dinah Shore Show

Variety; 30 min; NBC 9/20/56 to 7/18/57

A weekly series of music and songs

Hostess: Dinah Shore

Regulars: Joe Hamilton, Jackie Joslin, Earl Brown, Gilda Maiken, George Becker

Announcer: Art Baker

Orchestra: Harry Zimmerman

Producer: Alan Handley, Bob Banner

Dinah's Place

Variety; 30 min; NBC 8/30/70 to 7/26/74

A daily series of interviews, cooking, health tips, decorating ideas and songs.

Hostess: Dinah Shore

Regulars: Karen Valentine, David Horowitz, Lyle Waggoner, Jerry Baker

Music: John Rodby

Diner

Comedy-Drama Pilot; 30 min; CBS 8/8/83

The activities of five young men who gather at the Fells Point Diner in Baltimore to discuss the ways of the world. Based on the movie.

Modell	Paul Reiser
Fenwick	James Spader
Eddie	Michael Binder
Shrevie	Max Cantor
Boogie	Michael Badsen
Elyse	Alison LaPlaca
Beth	Mandy Kaplan

Producer: Jerry Weintraub, Barry Levinson

Dinner Date

Variety; 15 min; DuMont 1/28/50 to 7/29/50

A relaxed program of music and song with the hosting and orchestra of Vincent Lopez.

Dinner Date with Vincent Lopez

Variety; 15 min; DuMont; 3/7/49 to 7/22/50

Music and songs from New York's Hotel Taft with host Vincent Lopez and regulars Ann Warren and Lee Russell.

Dione Lucas' Cooking School

A program of cooking instruction with hostess Dione Lucas. Originally titled "To the Queen's Taste" and broadcast on CBS from 2/25/48 to 12/29/49.

Dirty Sally

Western; 30 min; CBS 1/11/74 to 7/19/74

While traveling to California, Sally Ferguson, an aging collector of prairie junk, befriends Cyrus Pike, a young outlaw she soon regards as the son she never had. Stories, set in the 1880s, relate their adventures as they head for the gold hills of California.

Sally Fergus	Jeanette Nolan
Cyrus Pike	Dack Rambo

Producer: John Mantley

Dirty Work

Comedy-Crime Drama Pilot; 60 min; CBS 6/6/85

After a succession of jobs that fail to excite her, Nadine Leevanhoek acquires the position of file clerk to George Wylie, a private detective who will take any job as long as it means money. The unsold series was to relate Nadine's adventures as she attempts to run the Wylie Detective Agency when George, wanted by the mob and police, goes undercover.

Nadine Leevanhoek	Kerrie Keane
George Wylie	Louis Giambalvo
Cheryl Burke	Teresa Ganzel
Lt. Jack Hill	Dorian Harewood
Commander Leevanhoek	William Windom
Jeannie Leevanhoek	Diana Douglas

Producer: Seth Freeman

Disney's Adventures of the Gummi Bears

Cartoon; 30 min; NBC 9/14/85 (Premiere)

The adventures of a group of talking bears who live in a medieval English forest.

Voices: June Foray, Bob Holt, Christian Jacobs, Katie Leigh, Lorenzo Music, Noelle North, Will Ryan, Michael Rye, Bill Scott, Paul Winchell

Producer: Arthur Vitello

Diver Dan

Children; 7 min; Syn. 10/60

The live-action, serial-like adventures of Diver Dan, a fearless ocean explorer.

Diver Dan	Frank Freda
Miss Minerva (Mermaid)	Suzanne Turner

And: Allen Swift as the voice of: Baron Barracuda, Trigger Fish, Finley Haddock, Skipper Kipper, Scout Fish, Sam the Sawfish, Goldie Goldfish, Hermit Crab, Glow Fish, Seabiscuit, Gabby the Crab

Producer: Hal Tunis, Louis Kellman

Divorce Court

A syndicated (1957) series of dramatized divorce hearings with Voltaire Perkins as the judge and the commentary of Bill Walsh and Colin Mayer.

Divorce Court

A syndicated (1984) series of dramatizations based on actual divorce court records. William Keene portrays the judge and Jim Peck is the court reporter.

Do It Yourself

Comedy; 30 min; NBC 6/26/55 to 9/18/55

Humor combined with straight advice on home repair projects.

Instructor Dave	Dave Willock
Charley Weaver (aide)	Cliff Arquette
Mary (aide)	Mary McAdoo
Steve (aide)	Stephen Woolton

Producer: Bob Henry

The Do-It-Yourself Show

Instruction; 30 min; PBS Syn. 1985

An interesting, well-coordinated series of tips and how to information concerning home repair and maintenance.

Hosts: Kirk Burbick, Avian Rogers

Producer: David Brayton

Do Not Disturb

Comedy Pilot; 30 min; CBS 3/20/60

The story of Arthur Marks, a writer who works at home but seldom finds the peace and quiet he needs to write.

Arthur Marks	David Wayne
Irene Marks	Peggy Knudsen
Andy Marks	Scott Davey
Andrea	Andrea King
Miss Burdick	Irene Vernon

Do You Trust Your Wife?

See "Who Do You Trust?"

Dobie Gillis

Comedy; 30 min; CBS 9/29/59 to 9/18/63

The story of Dobie Gillis, the romantic son of a grocery store owner, and Maynard G. Krebs, a beatnik, two friends seeking to find their place in society. See also "Whatever Happened to Dobie Gillis."

Dobie Gillis	Dwayne Hickman
Maynard G. Krebs	Bob Denver
Thalia Menninger	Tuesday Weld
Zelda Gilroy	Sheila James
Herbert T. Gillis	Frank Faylen
Winnie Gillis	Florida Friebus
Chatsworth Osborne Jr.	Steve Franken
Clarissa Osborne	Doris Packer
Davey Gillis	Darryl Hickman
Duncan Gillis	Bobby Diamond
Leander Pomfritt	William Schallert
Ruth Adams/ Imogene Burkhart	Jean Byron
Jerome Krebs	Michael J. Pollard
Milton Armitage	Warren Beatty
Trembly	David Bond
Dean Magruder	Raymond Bailey
Lt. Meriwether	Richard Claire
Mr. Millfloss	Lee Goodman
Charlie Wong	Marvin Kaplan James Yagi Johnny Lee
Riff Ryan	Tommy Farrell
Maude Pomfritt	Joyce Van Patten
Clarice Armitage	Doris Packer
Edwina Kagel	Lynn Loring
Dean Hollister	Addison Richards Paul Tripp
Osborne Chauffeur	Angelo DeMeo

Producer: Martin Manulis, Joel Kane, Guy Scarpitta

Doc

Comedy Pilot; 30 min; NBC 7/28/69

The story of Jason Fillmore, an elderly doctor in the sleepy town of Stubbville, and his young assistant, Orville Truebody, a bumbling klutz.

Dr. Jason Fillmore	Forrest Tucker
Dr. Orville Truebody	Rick Lenz
Amy Fillmore	Margaret Ann Peterson
Nurse Tillie	Mary Treen

Producer: Jay Sommers

Doc

Comedy; 30 min; CBS 9/13/75 to 8/14/76

The story of Joe Bogert, a G.P. who lives in a rundown New York neighborhood and strives to treat his patients with dignity.

Dr. Joe Bogert	Barnard Hughes
Annie Bogert	Elizabeth Wilson
Laurie Fenner	Judith Kahan
Fred Fenner	John Harkins
Beatrice Tully	Mary Wickes
Gwen Bogert	Linda Kelsey
Fred Fenner Jr.	Tom Blaylock
Michael Fenner	Moosie Drier
Happy Miller	Irwin Corey
Ben Goldman	Herbie Faye

Producer: Ed Weinberger, Stan Daniels

Doc

Comedy; 30 min; CBS 9/25/76 to 10/30/76

A revised version of the previous title wherein Dr. Joe Bogert becomes the medical director of the hectic and free New York Westside Community Clinic.

Dr. Joe Bogert	Barnard Hughes
Nurse Janet Scott	Audra Lindley
Teresa Ortega	Lisa Mordente
Stanley Moss	David Ogden Stiers
Dr. Woody Henderson	Ray Vitte

Producer: Ed Weinberger, Stan Daniels

Doc Corkle

Comedy; 30 min; NBC 10/5/52 to 10/19/52

The story of Doc Corkle, a dentist beset with financial problems.

Doc Corkle	Eddie Mayehoff
Laurie Corkle	Connie Marshall
Nellie Corkle	Hope Emerson
Pop Corkle	Chester Conklin
Winfield Dill	Arnold Stang
Melinda	Billie Burke

Producer: Lou Place

Doc Elliot

Drama; 60 min; ABC 10/10/73 to 8/14/74

Dissatisfied with his medical practice at Bellevue Hospital, Benjamin Elliot retreats to Southern Colorado's Alora Valley, where he hopes to find the true meaning of being a doctor. Stories relate his attempts to help people desperately in need of a doctor.

Benjamin Elliot	James Franciscus
Barney Weeks	Noah Beery Jr.
Margaret "Mags" Brimble	Neva Patterson
Eldred McCoy	Bo Hopkins

Producer: Lee Rich

Doc Holliday

Western Pilot; 30 min; CBS 3/14/58

The exploits of "Doc" John H. Holliday, the famed gunman and doctor, as he travels throughout the Old West. Aired as "Man of Fear" on "Zane Grey Theatre."

Doc Holliday	Dewey Martin
Julie Brand	Julie Adams
Lee Brand	Arthur Franz
Sheriff	Brett King

Producer: Hal Hudson

The Doctor

Anthology; 30 min; NBC 8/24/52 to 6/28/53

Dramas of people confronted with mentally disturbing situations as seen through the eyes of a general practitioner. Also known as "The Visitor."

Doctor	Warner Anderson

Producer: Marion Parsonnet

Doctor Christian

Drama; 30 min. Syn. 1956

Following his Uncle Paul's retirement, young Mark Christian assumes control of his practice in River's End, Minnesota. Stories relate the problems faced by a young doctor in a small town. Based on the radio series.

Dr. Mark Christian	Macdonald Carey
Dr. Paul Christian	Jean Hersholt

Nurses: Jan Shepard, Cynthia Baer, Kay Faylen

Producer: Maurice Unger

Doctor Dan

Comedy Pilot; 30 min; CBS 4/22/74

The story of Dan Morgan, a Los Angeles-based child psychologist.

Dr. Dan Morgan	Jackie Cooper
Elaine Morgan	Barbara Stuart
Joyce Morgan	Heather Menzies
Adam Morgan	Willie Aames
Chris Morgan	Robert Reiser
Dr. Viola Nickerson	Madeleine Sherwood
Lisa	Patti Cohoon

Producer-Director: Jackie Cooper

Doctor Dolittle

Cartoon; 30 min; NBC 9/12/70 to 9/2/72

The world travels of Dr. John Dolittle, a veterinarian who possesses the ability to talk to and understand animals.

Dr. John Dolittle	Robert Holt
Tommy Stubbins	Hal Smith
Sam Scurvy	Lennie Weinrib
Animal Voices	Don Messick
	Barbara Towers

Producer: David DePatie, Friz Freleng

Doctor Fix-Um

A program of household tips and advice with Arthur Youngquist. ABC 5/3/49 to 8/6/50.

Doctor Fu Manchu

See "The Adventures of Dr. Fu Manchu."

Doctor Hudson's Secret Journal

Drama; 30 min; Syn. 1955

The problems faced by Dr. Wayne Hudson, a neurosurgeon at Wayne Memorial Hospital, as he pioneers new methods of treatment.

Dr. Wayne Hudson	John Howard
His daughter	Cheryl Galloway
Mrs. Grady	Olive Blakeney

Producer: Eugene Solow, Brewster Morgan

Doctor in the House

Comedy; 30 min; Syn. 1971

The antics of seven young medical students at England's Saint Swithin's Teaching Hospital.

Michael Upton	Barry Evans
Duncan Waring	Robin Newdell
Paul Collier	George Layton
Dick Stuart-Clark	Geoffrey Davis
Huw Evans	Martin Shaw
Danny Wholey	Jonathan Lynn
Dave Briddock	Simon Cuff
Sir Geoffrey Loftus	Ernest Clark

Doctor I.Q.

Game; 30 min; ABC 11/4/53 to 10/10/54
            12/15/58 to 3/23/59

Object: For contestants to answer a series of questions that are posed to him by Dr. I.Q., the mental banker.

Dr. I.Q.: James McLain, Jay Owen, Tom Kennedy

Assistant: Mimi Walters, Kay Christopher, Tom Reddy, Ed Michaels, Arthur Fleming, George Ansbro

Doctor Kildare

Drama; NBC 9/27/61 to 9/9/65 (60 min)
            9/13/65 to 8/29/66 (30 min)

The story of James Kildare, a young intern (later resident physician) at Blair General Hospital. See also "Young Dr. Kildare."

Dr. James Kildare	Richard Chamberlain
Dr. Leonard Gillespie	Raymond Massey
Nurse Zoe Lawton	Lee Kurty
Dr. Thomas Gerson	Jud Taylor
Dr. Simon Agurski	Eddie Ryder
Dr. Kapish	Ken Berry
Nurse Conant	Jo Helton
Nurse Sain	Jean Innes

Producer: Norman Felton, Herbert Hirschman, David Victor

Doctor Mike

Drama Pilot; 30 min; CBS 8/18/59

The experiences of Mike Grant, a young doctor in a large metropolitan hospital.

Dr. Mike Grant	Keith Andes
Dr. Sam Talbert	Lewis Martin
Mary Barker	Mary Adams
Alex Bartos	Joe DeSantis
Anna Bartos	Greta Granstedt

Producer: Harold Greene

Doctor Shrinker

Comedy; 15 min; ABC 9/11/76 to 9/3/77

When their plane crashes on a remote island, B. J., Brad and Gordie are captured by Dr. Shrinker, a mad scientist who reduces them to a height of six inches. Stories relate the trio's efforts to regain their normal height. Aired on "The Krofft Supershow."

Dr. Shrinker	Jay Robinson
B. J.	Susan Lawrence
Brad	Teddy Eccles
Gordie	Jeff McKay
Hugo	Billy Barty

Producer: Sid and Marty Krofft

Doctor Simon Locke

Drama; 30 min; Syn. 1971

The story of Andrew Sellers and Simon Locke, doctors struggling to help the people of Dixon Mills, a poor Canadian community. See also "Police Surgeon."

Dr. Simon Locke	Sam Groom
Dr. Andrew Sellers	Jack Albertson
Nurse Louise Wynn	Nuala Fitzgerald
Chief Dan Palmer	Len Birman

Producer: Wilton Schiller

Doctor Snuggles

Cartoon; 30 min; Syn. 9/81

The story of Dr. Snuggles, an ingenious vet who uses his fantastic inventions to help people and animals.

Dr. Snuggles	Peter Ustinov

Other Voices: Owen Griffiths, John Challis

Producer: Jeffrey O'Kelly

Dr. Strange

Fantasy Pilot; 90 min; CBS 9/6/78

The story of Stephen Strange, a sorcerer who poses as a psychiatrist and who uses his magical powers to battle evil.

Dr. Stephen Strange	Peter Hooten
Wong (his aide)	Clyde Kusatsu
Morgan Le Fay	Jessica Walter
The Nameless One	David Hooks
The Ancient One	Michael Ansara
Clea Lake	Eddie Benton
Dr. Frank Taylor	Philip Sterling

Producer: Philip DeGuere, Alex Beaton

The Doctor was a Lady

Comedy Pilot; 30 min; NBC 3/27/58

The misadventures of a married couple with conflicting careers: Fran, the wife, a doctor, and Paul, her husband, a real estate broker. Aired on "The Jane Wyman Theatre."

Dr. Fran Mitchell	Frances Bergen
Paul Mitchell	Keith Andes
Paula Mitchell	Wendy Winkleman

Producer: William Asher

Doctor Who

Science Fiction; Various (30 min to 3 hrs); Syn. 1973 (Produced in England; 1963-Current)

When they are cut off from their planet and unable to return to it (Gallifrey), a Time Lord (The Doctor) and his granddaughter (Susan) take refuge in 20th-century England. Five months later, when Barbara and Ian, two of Susan's teachers (at the Coal Hill School) become suspicious of her actions, they follow her to a junkyard (at 76 Totter's Lane). There they encounter The Doctor and his time traveling machine, the TARDIS (Time and Relative Dimension in Space). Shortly after, when Ian and The Doctor become involved in a scuffle, the TARDIS is launched and sent into time. Thus began The Doctor's amazing adventures as he travels to the past, present, and futures of various planets to safeguard their beings from evil. See also "K-9 and Company."

The Doctor	William Hartnell
	Patrick Troughton
	Jon Pertwee
	Tom Baker
	Peter Davison
	Colin Baker
	Peter Cushing*
Companions (in order):	
Susan Foreman	Carole Ann Ford
Barbara Wright	Jacqueline Hill
Ian Chesterton	William Russell
Vicki	Maureen O'Brien
Katariva	Jean Marsh
Polly	Anneke Wells
Jamie McCrimmon	Frazer Hines
Victoria Waterfield	Deborah Watling
Zoe Herriet	Wendy Padbury
Elizabeth Shaw	Caroline John
Jo Grant	Katy Manning
Sarah Jane Smith	Elisabeth Sladen
Harry Sullivan	Ian Marter
Leela	Louise Jameson
Romana	Mary Tamm
	Lalla Ward
Adric	Matthew Waterhouse
Tegan	Janet Fielding
Nissa	Sarah Sutton
Perpugilliam (Peri) Brown	Nicola Bryant
Also:	
Brigadier Alastier Leftbridge-Stewart	Nicholas Courtney
Capt. Mike Yates	Richard Franklin
The Master	Roger Delgado
	Peter Pratt
	Anthony Ainley
K-9's Voice	John Leeson
	David Brierley

Producer: Verity Lambert, Graham Williams, Barry Letts

*The Doctor in theatrical features.

The Doctors

Drama; 60 min; NBC 9/14/69 to 6/22/73

The work of Dr. Benjamin Craig, founder of the Benjamin Craig Medical Research Center in Los Angeles, and his proteges Ted Stuart and Paul Hunter. Aired as a segment of "The Bold Ones."

Dr. Benjamin Craig	E. G. Marshall
Dr. Ted Stuart	John Saxon
Dr. Paul Hunter	David Hartman
Dr. Paul Cohen	Robert Walden
Nurse Robbins	Sally Kemp
Dr. Lee Williams	Michael Baseleon
Nurse Tate	Pat Anderson

Producer: Cy Chermak, Herbert Hirschman

The Doctors and the Nurses

See "The Nurses"

Doctors Hospital

Drama; 60 min; NBC 9/10/75 to 1/14/76

The experiences of Dr. Jake Goodwin, chief of neurosurgery at Lowell Memorial Hospital.

Dr. Jake Goodwin	George Peppard
Dr. Norah Purcell	Zohra Lampert
Dr. Felipe Ortega	Victor Campos
Nurse Connie Kimbrough	Elisabeth Brooks
Dr. Janos Varga	Albert Paulsen

Producer: Matthew Rapf

Doctors' Private Lives

Drama; 60 min; ABC 3/5/79 to 4/26/79

The private and professional lives of the doctors at the cardiovascular unit of City Hospital in California.

Dr. Jeffrey Latimer	John Gavin
Dr. Michael Wise	Ed Nelson
Dr. Sheila Castle	Gwen Humble
Dr. Rick Calder	Randolph Powell
Nurse Diane Curtis	Eddie Benton
Mona Wise	Elinor Donahue
Kenny Wise	Leigh McCloskey
	Philip Levien
Frances Latimer	Barbara Anderson

Producer: David Gerber, Matthew Rapf

Dodo—The Kid from Outer Space

A syndicated (1965) cartoon series about Dodo, from the atomic planet Hena Hydro, who is sent to Earth to assist Professor Fingers with his research. The five minute episodes are produced by John Halas and Joy Batchelor.

Dog and Cat

Crime Drama; 60 min; ABC 3/5/77 to 5/14/77

In an attempt to test the feasibility of male and female squad car teams, the L.A.P.D. teams J. Z. Kane, a beautiful female officer, with Jack Ramsey, a tough sergeant. Stories relate the exploits of the experimental dog and cat team.

Off. J. Z. Kane	Kim Basinger
Sgt. Jack Ramsey	Lou Antonio
Lt. Art Kipling	Matt Clark

Producer: Robert Gordon, Lawrence Singer

A Dog's Life

Comedy Pilot; 30 min; NBC 6/15/79

Actors, dressed as dogs, present man as seen through the eyes of his best friend.

McGurk	Barney Martin
Iris	Beej Johnson
Tucker	Charles Martin Smith
Camille	Sherry Lynn
Spike	Hamilton Camp
Turk	Michael Huddleston

Producer: Charlie Hauck

Dollar a Second

Game; 30 min; DuMont 9/20/53 to 6/14/54
NBC 7/4/54 to 8/22/54
ABC 10/1/54 to 6/24/55
NBC 7/5/55 to 8/23/55
ABC 9/2/55 to 8/31/56
NBC 6/22/57 to 9/28/57

Contestants compete in a series of rapid fire question and answer rounds with dollars being awarded for each second of correct responses.

Host: Jan Murray

Assistant: Patricia White, Bernard Martin, Stuart Mann

Announcer: Ken Roberts, Terry O'Sullivan

Producer: Jess Kimmel, Mike Dutton, Dave Brown

The $1.98 Beauty Show

Game; 30 min; Syn. 9/78

A spoof of beauty pageants wherein six females compete in contests of beauty, poise, talent and swimwear for the title "The $1.98 beauty of the Week" and the top prize—a $1.98 in cash!

Host: Rip Taylor

Assistant: Larry Spencer

Announcer: Johnny Jacobs

Producer: Chuck Barris

Dolly

Variety; 30 min; Syn. 9/76

A charming program of music and songs with hostess Dolly Parton and the orchestra of Jerry Whitehurst. Produced by Bill Graham and Reg Dunlap.

Dolly

Variety; 60 min; ABC 9/27/87 (Premiere)

A well-produced, sparkling hour of music, songs, and light comedy.

Hostess: Dolly Parton

Producer: Sandy Gallin, Don Mischer

Music Director: Velton Bunch

The Dom DeLuise Show

Variety; 60 min; CBS 5/1/68 to 9/18/68

Music, songs and comedy sketches.

Host: Dom DeLuise

Regulars: Marian Mercer, Carol Arthur, Peggy March, Dick Lynn, Paul Dooley, Bill McCutcheon, The June Taylor Dancers

Announcer: Johnny Olsen

Orchestra: Sammy Spear

Producer: Rod Parker

The Dom DeLuise Show

Comedy; 30 min; Syn. 9/87

The series, set at Dom's Barber Shop in Hollywood, relates the antics of its owner (Dom)

as he interreacts with an assortment of odd neighborhood characters.

Dominick DeLuca	Dom DeLuise
George	George Wallace
Maureen	Maureen Murphy
Penny	Angela Aames
Rosa DeLuca	Lauren Woodland
Blanche	Lois Foraker
Charlie Tyler	Charlie Callas
Michael	Michael Chambers

Producer: Greg Garrison, Lee Hale, Janet Tighe

Domestic Life

Comedy; 30 min; CBS 1/4/84 to 9/11/84

The story of Martin Crane, a TV commentator (of Seattle's "Domestic Life Report" on KMRT-TV, Ch. 8) whose ideal commentary world varies greatly from his actual world.

Martin Crane	Martin Mull
Candy Crane	Judith-Marie Bergan
Didi Crane	Megan Follows
Harold Crane	Christian Brackett-Zika
Cliff Hamilton	Robert Ridgely
Jane Funakubo	Mie Hunt
Enid Hamilton	Allyn Ann McLerie
Amy Hamilton	Sandra Alexander
Sally Dwyer	Tina Yothers
KMRT Floor Manager	Jeffrey A. Thomas

Theme Vocal ("Domestic Life"): Wendy Hass-Mull, Martin Mull

Producer: Steve Martin

Dominic's Dream

Comedy Pilot; 30 min; CBS 3/28/74

Seeking to fulfill a life time dream of living in suburban Los Angeles, Dominic and Anita Bente begin by packing up and leaving New York. Stories relate their misadventures as they begin a new life in California.

Dominic Bente	Joseph Mascolo
Anita Bente	Rita Moreno
Marie Bente	Toni Kalem
Crystal Hendrickson	Marjorie Battles
Jess Hendrickson	Burt Heyman
Mark Hendrickson	Dennis Kort

Producer: William P. D'Angelo, Garry K. Marshall

The Don Adams Screen Test

Game; 30 min; Syn. 9/75

Two players are each teamed with a guest celebrity and perform a scene from a movie. The best performer receives a part in a film.

Host: Don Adams

Announcer: Dick Tufeld

Producer: Don Adams

The Don Ameche Theatre

A syndicated (1958) series in which Don Ameche hosts repeat anthology series dramas.

The Don Ho Show

Variety; 30 min; ABC 10/25/76 to 3/4/77

A daily series of music and songs from Hawaii with host Don Ho and the orchestra of Johnny Todd. Produced by Bob Banner and Brad Lachman.

The Don Knotts Show

Variety; 60 min; NBC 9/15/70 to 7/6/71

Music, songs, and comedy sketches.

Host: Don Knotts

Regulars: Elaine Joyce, John Dehner, Gary Burghoff, Ken Mars, Mickey Deems, Frank Welker, Bob Williams, Eddy Carroll

Announcer: Dick Tufeld

Orchestra: Nick Perito

Producer: Nick Vanoff

The Don Lane Show

An Australian series of celebrity interviews with host Don Lane. Syndicated to the U.S. in 1980.

Don McNeill's TV Club

Variety; 30 min; ABC 9/13/50 to 2/25/55

A daily program of music, song, comedy and conversation. Based on radio's "The Breakfast Club."

Host: Don McNeill

Regulars: Fran Allison, Johnny Desmond, Sam Cowling, Eileen Parker, Cliff Peterson, Patsy Lee, Lois Weaver, Jack Owen

Orchestra: Eddie Ballantine

The Don Rickles Show

Variety; 30 min; ABC 9/27/68 to 1/31/69

Don Rickles as the host of a weekly series of music and comedy. With the music of Vic Mizzy and the announcing of Pat McCormick.

The Don Rickles Show

Comedy; 30 min; CBS 1/14/72 to 5/26/72

The misadventures of Don Robinson, an account executive with the advertising firm of Kingston, Cohen, and Vanderpool, as he struggles to survive the mechanizations of a computerized society.

Don Robinson	Don Rickles
Barbara Robinson	Louise Sorel
Janie Robinson	Erin Moran
Tyler Benedict	Robert Hogan
Jean Benedict	Joyce Van Patten
Audrey	Judy Cassmore
Conrad Musk	Barry Gordon
Arthur Kingston	Edward Andrews

Producer: Sheldon Leonard

The Donald O'Connor Show

Variety; 60 min; NBC 10/9/54 to 9/10/55

A weekly series of music, songs and comedy.

Host: Donald O'Connor

Regulars: Regina Gleason, Sid Miller, Joyce Smight, Jan Arvan, Joyce Holden, Laurette Luez, Olan Soule, Nestor Paiva, Eileen Janssen

Orchestra: Al Goodman

Producer: Ernest D. Glicksman

The Donald O'Connor Show

A syndicated (1968) interview series with host Donald O'Connor, announcer Joyce Jameson, and the music of the Alan Copeland Orchestra.

The Donna Fargo Show

Variety; 30 min; Syn. 9/78

Performances by country and western artists.

Hostess: Donna Fargo

Announcer: Harrison Henderson

Orchestra: Bob Rozario

Producer: Tom Biener

The Donna Reed Show

Comedy; 30 min; ABC 9/24/58 to 9/3/66

Events in the lives of the Stone family: Alex, a pediatrician; his wife, Donna; and their children, Mary, Jeff, and Tricia (adopted).

Donna Stone	Donna Reed
Dr. Alex Stone	Carl Betz
Mary Stone	Shelley Fabares
Jeff Stone	Paul Petersen
Tricia	Patty Petersen
David Kelsey	Bob Crane
Midge Kelsey	Ann McCrea
Smitty	Daryl Richard
Karen	Janet Landgard
Bibi Barnes	Candy Moore
Herbie Bailey	Tommy Ivo
Celia Wilgus	Kathleen Freeman
Wilbur Wilgus	Howard McNear
Susanna	Sandy Descher
Scotty Simpson	Jerry Hawkins
Donna's Uncle Fred	Rhys Williams
Donna's Aunt Belle	Gladys Hurlbut
David's Goddaughter Louise	Marlo Thomas

Theme Song ("Happy Days"): William Loose, John Seely

Producer: Tony Owen, William Roberts

Donny and Marie

Variety; 60 min; ABC 1/23/76 to 1/19/79

A charming hour of music, songs, and comedy sketches.

Hosts: Marie and Donny Osmond

Regulars: Paul Lynde, Sharon Baird, Jim Connell, Van Snowden, Patty Maloney, The Osmond Brothers

Orchestra: Bob Rozario, Tommy Oliver

Producer: Raymond Katz, Sid & Marty Krofft

Announcer: George Fenneman, George Benedict, Wayne Osmond

Don's Musical Playhouse

Variety; 30 min; ABC 7/5/51 to 10/4/51

The lives and struggles of a group of performers as seen through the eyes of the stage manager of a summer theatre. Also known as "The Don Ameche Show."

Stage Manager   Don Ameche

Regulars: Betty Brewer, Dorothy Greener, The June Graham Dancers, The Don Large Chorus

Orchestra: Bernard Green

Producer: Felix Jackson

Don't Call Me Charlie

Comedy; 30 min; NBC 9/21/62 to 1/25/63

The story of Judson McKay, a backwoods Iowa veterinarian, now stationed at a U.S. Army Veterinary post in Paris, who refuses to let the sophistication of Europe change his square, innocent ways. The title is derived from Charles Baker, a colonel who detests being called "Charlie."

Pvt. Judson McKay	Josh Peine
Col. Charles Baker	John Hubbard
Sgt. Wozniah	Cully Richard
Patricia Perry	Linda Lawson
Gen. Steele	Alan Napier
Cpl. Lefkowitz	Arte Johnson
Selma Yossarian	Louise Glenn

Producer: Don McGuire

Don't Call Us

Comedy Pilot; 30 min; CBS 8/13/76

The misadventures of two brothers (Marty and Larry) as they attempt to run the Talent Unlimited Theatrical Agency in Philadelphia.

Larry King	Jack Gilford
Marty King	Allan Miller
Rene Patterson	Leland Palmer
Jackie Nakamura	Richard Narita
Tolanda	Tina Louise
Sylvia	Patty Maloney
Lloyd	Billy Barty

Producer: Ed Weinberger, Stan Daniels

The Doodles Weaver Show

Variety; 30 min; NBC 6/9/51 to 9/1/51

Music, songs and comedy with host Doodles Weaver, regulars Lois Weaver, Rex Marshall, Marian Colby and Peanuts Mann, and the music of Milton DeLugg.

The Dooley Brothers

Comedy Pilot; 30 min; CBS 7/31/79

The exploits of George and Bill Dooley, two bumbling Old West brothers who dispense justice to all deserving individuals.

George Dooley	Garrett Brown
Bill Dooley	Robert Pierce
Jack Black	John Myhers
Cool Sam Bennett	Dub Taylor
Lucy Bennett	Shelley Long

Producer: Arnold Margolin

Doorway to Danger

Adventure; 30 min; NBC 7/4/52 to 8/28/53

A spin-off from "The Door With No Name." The U.S. government's battle against international intrigue as seen through the secret missions of undercover agents.

Chief John Randolph	Roland Winters
	Raymond Bramley
Agent Doug Carter	Stacy Harris

Narrator: Westbrook Van Voorhis

Announcer: Ernest Chapell

Producer: Walter Selden

Doorway to Fame

Variety; 30 min; DuMont 3/7/49 to 7/11/49

Originally, performances by undiscovered talent; later, a low-budget anthology wherein actors performed against a black backdrop (with scenes superimposed by a second camera trained on sets or paintings).

Host: Johnny Olsen

Producer: Lou Dahlman, George Scheck

The Door With No Name

Adventure; 30 min; NBC 7/6/51 to 8/17/51

Dramas based on the secret activities of The Door With No Name, an unidentified portal in Washington, D.C., through which presumably pass the most intrepid of spies and spy fighters.

Chief John Randolph	Melville Ruick
Agent Doug Carter	Grant Richards

Narrator: Westbrook Van Voorhis

Doris Day's Best Friends

Actress-singer Doris Day chatting with various show business friends and discussing her work with and dedication to animals. Premiered on the CBN cable network in 1985.

The Doris Day Show

Comedy; 30 min; CBS 9/24/68 to 9/3/73

Dissatisfied with life in the city, widowed singer Doris Martin relinquishes her career and returns to her father's ranch in Mill Valley, California, to raise her two sons. One year later, Doris acquires a job as the executive secretary to Michael Nicholson, editor of "Today's World" magazine. During the final two seasons, the format changed to depict the life of Doris Martin as a glamorous general news reporter for "Today's World."

Doris Martin	Doris Day
Buck Webb (her father)	Denver Pyle
Billy Martin (her son)	Philip Brown
Toby Martin (her son)	Todd Starke
Leroy B. Simpson	James Hampton
Aggie Thompson	Fran Ryan
Juanita	Naomi Stevens
Michael Nicholson	McLean Stevenson
Cyril Bennett	John Dehner
Myrna Gibbons	Rose Marie
Jackie Parker	Jackie Joseph
Ron Harvey	Paul Smith
Willard Jarvis	Billy DeWolfe
Angie Pallucci	Kaye Ballard
Louis Pallucci	Bernie Koppel
Dr. Peter Lawrence	Peter Lawford
Jonathan Rusk	Patrick O'Neal

Theme Vocal ("Que Sera Sera"): Doris Day

Producer: Terry Melcher, Doris Day, Bob Sweeney, Norman Paul

Dorothy

Comedy; 30 min; CBS 8/8/79 to 8/29/79

The story of Dorothy Banks, a former Broadway star turned music and drama teacher at Connecticut's Hannah Huntley School for Girls.

Dorothy Banks	Dorothy Loudon
Burton Foley	Russell Nype
Lorna Cathcart	Priscilla Morrill
T. Jack Landis	Kenneth Gilman
Hannah Huntley	Irene Tedrow
Cissy	Elissa Leeds
Meredith	Susan Brecht
Frankie	Linda Manz
Margo	Michele Greene

Producer: Madelyn Davis, Bob Carroll Jr.

Dotto

Game; 30 min; CBS 1/6/58 to 8/29/58

Object: For players to connect dots and identify the person, place or object that is represented by fifty such dots.

Host: Jack Narz

Announcer: Wayne Howell

The Dotty Mack Show

Variety; 15 min; DuMont 2/16/53 to 8/25/53
ABC 9/3/53 to 9/3/56

Dotty Mack as the host of a program that features her and a cast (Bob Braum, Colin Male) pantomiming the hit songs of famous singers.

Double Dare

Crime Drama; 60 min; CBS 4/10/85 to 5/22/85

When Billy Diamond, a suave thief is caught red handed, he elects to work undercover for the San Francisco Police Department rather than spend twenty years in jail. Stories relate his attempts to solve baffling crimes.

Billy Diamond	Billy Dee Williams
Ken Sisko	Ken Wahl
Lt. Samantha	
Warner	Jennifer Warren
	Janet Carroll
Sylvester	Joseph Maher

Producer: Leo Tokatyan

Double Exposure

Game; 30 min; CBS 3/13/61 to 9/29/61

Object: For players to identify a personality or event that is hidden under a jigsaw puzzle. Each correct answer to a question removes a puzzle part and reveals a cash amount. The first player to identify the subject receives the money amounts he uncovered.

Host: Steve Dunne

The Double Life of Henry Phyfe

Comedy; 30 min; ABC 1/13/66 to 9/1/66

When U-31, a foreign spy, is killed by a hit-and-run before he is able to divulge information to the CIA, Henry Phyfe, a mild-mannered accountant and U-31's exact double, is recruited to replace him. Stories relate Henry's reluctant efforts to carry out U-31's missions.

Henry Phyfe	Red Buttons
Sub Chief Gerald B.	
Hannahan	Fred Clark
Judy	Zeme North
Florence Kimball	Marge Redmond
Mr. Hamble	Parley Baer
Agent Sandy	Rob Kilgallen
Agent Larry	Ed Faulkner

Music: Vic Mizzy

Producer: Luther Davis

Double or Nothing

Game; 30 min; CBS 10/6/52 to 7/3/53

Five players, working as a team, start with a specific money amount. Each player is individually questioned and wagers money on his ability to give the correct response. The final cash earnings are divided between the players.

Host: Bert Parks

Assistant: Joan Meinch

Announcer: Bob Williams

Double Talk

Game; 30 min; ABC 8/18/86 to 12/19/86

Object: For players to unscramble double talk words (e.g., "Crack the Cubes" means "Break the Ice") and score the most points to win the game and money.

Host: Henry Polic II

Producer: Anne Marie Schmitt, David Stewart

Double Trouble

Comedy; 30 min; NBC 4/4/84 to 9/5/84

Events in the lives of Kate and Allison Foster, two beautiful and identical teenage twins living in Des Moines, Iowa.

Allison Foster	Jean Sagal
Kate Foster	Liz Sagal
Art Foster	Donnelly Rhodes
Beth McConnell	Patricia Richardson

Producer: Bernie Orenstein, Saul Turteltaub

Double Trouble

Comedy; 30 min; NBC 12/1/84 to 4/20/85

A revised version of the previous title, which picks up the lives of twins Kate and Allison Foster as they leave Iowa for careers in New York City: Kate as an actress and Allison as a fashion designer.

Allison Foster	Jean Sagal
Kate Foster	Liz Sagal
Margo Foster	Barbara Barrie
Billy Batalato	Jonathan Schmock
Charles Kincade	James Vallely
Max	Bobby Ramsen
Mr. Arrechia	Michael D. Roberts
Aileen Lewis	Ann-Marie Johnson

Producer: Judith Allison

Doug Re Mi

Game; 30 min; NBC 2/24/58 to 12/30/60

Object: For players to identify song titles after hearing the first three notes. If they are unable, they bid for the next note. Highest bidders hear the next note and win cash if they identify the song.

Host: Gene Rayburn

Douglas Fairbanks Jr. Presents

Anthology; 30 min; Syn. 1/53 to 3/57

Dramas of people caught in unusual circumstances. Hosted by Douglas Fairbanks Jr. and featuring both known, but mostly non-name performers.

Produced by Lance Comfort, Douglas Fairbanks Jr.

Down and Out in Beverly Hills

Comedy; 30 min; FOX 4/26/87 (Premiere)

Feeling down on his luck, Jerry Baskin, a former businessman turned bum, decides to end it all by drowning himself in the Beverly Hills swimming pool of millionaire hanger manufacturer Dave Whiteman. Dave spots Jerry, saves his life, and offers to let him live with him and his family. Stories focus on Jerry's antics as he tries to teach the Whiteman's the true meaning of existence.

Jerry Baskin	Tim Thomerson
Dave Whiteman	Hector Elizondo
Barbara Whiteman (his wife)	Anita Morris
Jenny Whiteman (daughter)	Eileen Seeley
Max Whiteman (son)	Evan Richards
Carmen (their maid)	April Ortiz
Duchess (Jerry's friend)	Susan Kellerman
Matisse	Mike the Dog

Producer: Howard Gewirtz, Richard Rosenstock, Don Van Atta

Down Home

Comedy Pilot; 30 min; CBS 9/10/65

The story of Hardy Madison, a struggling newspaper editor in a small town (Freedom).

Hardy Madison	Pat Buttram
Emma Madison	Sarah Haden
Warren Bullard	Jack Orrinson
Late	El Brendel

Producer-Director: Hal Kanter

Down Home

Drama Pilot; 60 min; CBS 8/16/78

Hoping to find a more meaningful life, Priscilla and Nate Simmons move from Detroit to a small Southern town. The unsold series was to relate their efforts to achieve their dream.

Priscilla Simmons	Madge Sinclair
Nate Simmons	Robert Hooks
Darlene Simmons	Tia Rance
Nate Simmons Jr.	Kevin Hooks
Highpockets Simmons	Eric Hooks
Aunt Velvet	Beah Richards
Sheriff	Andrew Duggan
Joe Mayfield	Lincoln Kilpatrick
Helen Mayfield	Beverly Hope Atkinson

Producer: Philip Barry

Downtown

Crime Drama; 60 min; CBS 9/27/86 to 12/27/86

Faced with the problem of what to do with four troublesome parolees, the L.A.P.D. assigns them to John Forney, an undercover detective who reluctantly accepts the job. Stories relate John's adventures as the parole officer to Terry, Jesse, Harriet, and Dennis.

Det. John Forney	Michael Nouri
Terry Corsaro	Blair Underwood
Harriet Conover	Millicent Martin
Jesse Smith	Mariska Hagitay
Dennis Shothoffer	Robert Englund
Delia Bonnert	Virginia Capers
Lt. Kiner	David Paymer

Producer: Ron Samuels, Reuben Leder

Down You Go

Game; 30 min; DuMont 5/30/51 to 5/27/55
　　　　　CBS 6/18/55 to 9/3/55
　　　　　ABC 9/15/55 to 6/14/56
　　　　　NBC 6/16/56 to 9/8/56

Object: For panelists to suggest letters of the alphabet and guess the slogan, quotation, or phrase that is indicated by a line of dashes. If an incorrect letter is posed, that player is disqualified and five dollars is awarded to the sender (home viewer) of the phrase.

Host: Dr. Bergen Evans, Bill Cullen

Panelists: Jayne Mansfield, Arthur Treacher, Toni Gilman, Frances Couglin, Carmelita Pope, Jimmy Nelson, Patricia Cutts, Fran Allison, Basil Davenport, Boris Karloff, Hildy Parks, Jean Kerr, Phil Rizzuto

Producer: Louis Cowan, Joseph Stuhl, Barry McKinley

Dragnet

Crime Drama; 30 min; NBC 12/16/51 to 9/6/59

A realistic look at police work in action as seen through the cases of Joe Friday, a sergeant with the L.A.P.D. Also known as "Badge 714."

Sgt. Joe Friday	Jack Webb
Sgt. Ben Romero	Barton Yarborough
Sgt. Ed Jacobs	Barney Phillips
Off. Frank Smith	Herb Ellis
	Ben Alexander
Ann Baker	Dorothy Abbott

Producer: Jack Webb, Stanley Meyer, Mike Meshekoff, Herman Canfield

Announcer: Hal Gibney, George Fenneman

"The Dragnet Theme" song by: Walter Schumann

Dragnet

Crime Drama; 30 min; NBC 1/12/67 to 9/10/70

A revised version of the previous title. The cases of Joe Friday and Bill Gannon, plainclothes officers with the L.A.P.D.

Sgt. Joe Friday	Jack Webb
Off. Bill Gannon	Harry Morgan
Ellen Gannon	Randy Stuart
Captain Nelson	Clark Hovat
	Len Wayland
	Byron Morrow
Captain Brown	Art Ballinger

Announcer: George Fenneman

Narrator: Jack Webb

Producer-Director: Jack Webb

Dragon's Lair

Cartoon; 30 min; ABC 9/8/84 to 8/31/85

The series, set in the medieval kingdom of Ethelfred, relates the exploits of Dick the Darling as he battles the evil dragon Singe.

Voices: Arthur Berghardt, Fred Travalena, Bob Sarlatte, Ellen Gerstel, Marilyn Schreffler, Peter Cullen

Producer: Joe Ruby, Ken Spears

Drak Pack

Cartoon; 30 min; CBS 9/6/80 to 9/12/82

In an attempt to atone for the sins of their ancestors, Dracula Jr. (Drak), Frankenstein Jr. (Frankie), and Wolfman Jr. (Howler) form a pack to battle the evils of Dr. Dred, a madman who seeks to control the world. Stories relate their efforts to defeat Dr. Dred.

Drak Jr.	Jerry Dexter
Frankie/Howler	Bill Callaway
Big D (Dracula)	Alan Oppenheimer
Dr. Dred	Hans Conried
Vampira	Julie McWhirter
Mummy Man	Chuck McCann
Toad/Fly	Don Messick

Producer: William Hanna, Joseph Barbera

Draw Me a Laugh

Game; 30 min; ABC 1/15/49 to 2/5/49

A cartoon is drawn from an idea submitted by a home viewer. The gag line, but not the cartoon idea, is given to a player (who must draw a sketch for the gag line). If the player's sketch is judged funnier than the artist's, he wins a prize.

Host: Walter Hurley

Cartoonist: Mel Casson

Regulars: Oscar Brand, Jay Irving

Producer: Milton Kirents

Draw to Win

Game; 30 min; CBS 4/22/52 to 6/10/52

Object: For panelists to identify persons, places, or objects from an artist's sketches. Failure to do so awards the sender (home viewer) $25.

Host: Henry Morgan

Panelists: Eve Hunter, Abner Dean, Bill Holman, Sid Hoff

Producer: Joel O'Brien, Winston O'Keefe

Dream Girl of '67

Contest; 30 min; ABC 12/19/66 to 12/29/67

A daily beauty program wherein twenty girls (five per day) compete in contests of beauty, charm and talent. Weekly winners (chosen from the Monday through Thursday daily competition) return at a later date to compete for the "Dream Girl of '67" title and various prizes.

Host: Dick Stewart, Wink Martindale, Paul Petersen

Producer: Chuck Barris, Gene Banks

Dream Girl U.S.A.

Contest; 30 min; Syn. 9/86

A weekly program in which four girls compete in contests of beauty, figure and form, talent, and personality for the title "Dream Girl of 1987." Weekly winners return at a later date to compete in a final competition.

Host: Ken Howard

Announcer: Danny Dark

Regulars: The Kevin Carlisle Dancers

Producer: Ernest Chambers, Michael Seligman

Dream House

Game; 30 min; ABC 4/1/68 to 1/2/70

Three couples compete for their dream house via a series of question and answer rounds wherein winners receive one room of furniture. Couples receive their dream house by winning seven straight games.

Host: Mike Darrow

Announcer: Chet Gould

Producer: Don Reid

Dream House

Game; 30 min; NBC 4/4/83 to 6/29/84

Object: For couples to win their dream house by answering questions and acquiring rooms of furniture. The couple that wins seven straight games acquires the needed amount of furniture and a dream house.

Host: Bob Eubanks

Hostess: Deborah Bartlett

Announcer: Johnny Gilbert

Producer: Don Reid

Dreams

Comedy; 30 min; CBS 10/3/84 to 10/31/84

The story of Gino, Martha, Phil, Albert and Lisa, five young adults struggling to make it as the rock band Dreams.

Gino Minnelli	John Stamos
Martha Spino	Jami Gertz
Lisa Copley	Valerie Stevenson
Phil Taylor	Cain Devore
Morris Weiner	Albert Macklin
Frank Franconi	Ron Karabatsos
Louise Franconi	Sandy Freeman
Torpedo	Bill Henderson

Producer: Jon Peters

Dribble

Comedy Pilot; 30 min; NBC 8/21/80

The antics of an unnamed professional basketball team.

Anne Harrelson	Dee Wallace
Coach Red Arnold	Dan Frazier
John Raider	Joseph Hacker
Lou Jamison	Julius J. Carry III
Pete Terry	Larry Anderson
Will Herb	Edward Edwards
Ginny Jamison	Vernee Watson
Sarabeth Herb	Amy Stryker

Producer: Linda Bloodworth

Droodles

Game; 30 min; NBC 6/21/54 to 9/17/54

Object: For panelists to identify nonsense drawings either drawn by the host or submitted by home viewers.

Host: Roger Price

Panelists: Carl Reiner, Denise Lor, Marc Connelly

The Duck Factory

Comedy; 30 min; NBC 4/12/84 to 7/11/84

When Skip Tarkenton, a young animator, applies for a job with Buddy Winkler Productions, he finds not only the job he sought, but the added task of producing the "The Dippy Duck Show," a Saturday morning cartoon series produced by the rundown studio. Stories relate the antics of the staff of "The Dippy Duck Show."

Skip Tarkenton	Jim Carrey
Brooks Carmichael	Jack Gilford
Sherry Winkler	Teresa Ganzel
Aggie Aylesworth	Julie Payne
Andrea Lewin	Nancy Lane
Marty Fenneman	Jay Tarses
Wally Wooster	Don Messick
Roland Culp	Clarence Gilyard Jr.

Producer: Allan Burns, Rod Daniel

Theme Song ("The Duck Factory Theme"): Mark Vieha

The Dudley Do-Right Show

Cartoon; 30 min; ABC 4/27/69 to 9/6/70

The relentless efforts of Dudley Do-Right, a fumbling, simple-minded North Canadian Mounted Policeman, to capture the evasive and evil Snidley Whiplash.

Dudley Do-Right	Bill Scott
Insp. Ray K.	
Fenwick	Paul Frees
Nell Fenwick	June Foray
Snidley Whiplash	Hans Conried

Producer: Jay Ward, Bill Scott

Duet

Comedy; 30 min; FOX 4/19/87 (Premiere)

While catering her former fiance's wedding, Laura Kelly (owner of Laura's Cornucopia), and Ben Coleman, a mystery story writer, meet and fall in love. The series follows their ups and downs as they begin a serious relationship.

Laura Kelly	Mary Page Keller
Ben Coleman	Matthew Laurance
Jane Kelly	Jodi Thelen
Richard	Chris Lemmon
Linda	Alison LaPlaca

Producer: Susan Seeger, Ruth Bennett

Duffy

Comedy Pilot; 30 min; CBS 5/6/77

The story of Duffy, a nondescript dog with almost human qualities who is the adopted mascot of a junior high school.

Cliff Sellers	Fred Grandy
Thomas N. Tibbles	Roger Bowen
Marty Carter	Lane Binkley
Happy Jack	George Wyner
Nick	John Sheldon
Craig	John Herbsleb

Producer: George Eckstein

Duffy's Tavern

Comedy; 30 min; NBC 4/5/54 to 9/3/54

The story of Archie, a con artist who operates and manages Duffy's Tavern, a rundown restaurant-bar on Third Avenue in New York City, for the never-seen Mr. Duffy.

Archie	Ed Gardner
Clifton Finnegan	Alan Reed
Miss Duffy	Patte Chapman
Charley	Jimmy Conlin
Clayton	William Fawcett

Producer: Hal Roach Jr.

The Duke

Comedy; 30 min; NBC 7/2/54 to 9/24/54

When prize fighter Duke Zenlee (a.k.a. Duke London) believes he is meant for the finer things in life, he quits the ring and opens a night club. Stories relate Duke's efforts to enjoy his new life, despite his former trainer's (Johnny) efforts to get him back into the ring.

Duke	Paul Gilbert
Gloria	Phyllis Coates
Johnny	Allen Jenkins
Rudy Cromwell	Claude Stroud
Sam Marco	Sheldon Leonard

Producer: William Harmon

The Duke

Crime Drama; 60 min; NBC 3/5/79 to 5/18/79

The exploits of Oscar "Duke" Ramsey, a retired boxer turned Chicago private detective.

Duke Ramsey	Robert Conrad
Joe Cadillac	Larry Manetti
Sgt. Mick O'Brien	Red West
Dedra	Patricia Conwell
Eddie	Ed O'Bradovich

Producer: Stephen J. Cannell

The Dukes

Cartoon; 30 min; CBS 2/5/83 to 11/5/83

In an attempt to pay the mortgage on their farm, the Duke cousins (Daisy, Coy, and Vance) enter a world auto race to raise the money. Stories relate their attempts to beat their evil landlord, Boss Hogg, who is seeking to win the race, the Dukes farm, and the prize money.

Daisy Duke	Catherine Bach
Uncle Jesse Duke	Denver Pyle
Coy Duke	Byron Cherry
Vance Duke	Christopher Mayer
Boss Hogg	Sorrell Booke
Roscoe Coltrane	James Best
Bo Duke	John Schneider
Luke Duke	Tom Wopat

Producer: William Hanna, Joseph Barbera

The Dukes of Hazzard

Comedy; 60 min; CBS 1/26/79 to 2/8/85

Events in the lives of the Duke Cousins (Bo, Luke and Daisy) as they attempt to ferret out evil in Hazzard County, Georgia. See also "The Dukes" and "Enos."

Bo Duke	John Schneider
Luke Duke	Tom Wopat
Daisy Duke	Catherine Bach
Jesse Duke	Denver Pyle
Jefferson Davis "Boss" Hogg	Sorrell Booke
Roscoe Coltrane	James Best
Coy Duke	Byron Cherry
Vance Duke	Christopher Mayer
Cooter Davenport	Ben Jones
Deputy Enos Strate	Sonny Shroyer
B. B. Davenport	Mickey Jones
Deputy Cletus Hogg	Rick Hurst
Sheriff Buster Moon	James Hampton
Hughie Hogg	Jeff Altman
Lulu Hogg	Peggy Rea
Balladeer	Waylon Jennings
Miz Tisdale	Nedra Volz
Roscoe's Aunt Clara	Mary Treen
Cooter's Daughter Nancylou	Kim Richards
Doc Appleby	Parley Baer
Jesse's Cousin Jeb	Christopher Hensel
Jesse's Cousin Holly	Miriam Byrd Nethery
Holly's Daughter Laurie	Lori Lethin

Theme Vocal ("Good Ol' Boys"): Waylon Jennings

Producer: Joseph Gantman, Hy Averback, Paul R. Picard, Rod Amateau

The Dumplings

Comedy; 30 min; NBC 1/28/76 to 3/24/76

The story of Joe and Angela Dumpling, the overweight owners of the Dumplings Luncheonette on the ground floor of the New York-based Bristol Oil Company.

Joe Dumpling	James Coco
Angela Dumpling	Geraldine Brooks
Stephanie	Marcia Rodd
Frederick Steele	George Furth
Charles Sweetzer	George S. Irving
Norah McKenna	Jane Connell
Cully	Mort Marshall

Producer: Don Nicholl, Bernie West, Michael Ross

Dundee and the Culhane

Western; 60 min; CBS 9/6/67 to 12/13/67

The story of a trail-riding British lawyer (Dundee) and his partner (the Culhane) as they battle injustice in the West of the 1870s.

Dundee	John Mills
The Culhane	Rick Falk*
	Sean Garrison

Producer: Sam H. Rolfe, David Victor

*The Culhane in the original, unaired pilot.

Dungeons and Dragons

Cartoon; 30 min; CBS 9/17/83 to 9/6/86

While riding an amusement park attraction called Dungeons and Dragons, six youngsters are mysteriously transported to a fantasy world of wizards and warriors. There, they are granted special powers and learn from the Wizard Master that they are needed to battle the evil Venger; but to return to their time, they must play out a dangerous and complicated game. Stories follow their efforts to return home.

Hank	Willie Aames
Eric	Donny Most
Sheila	Katie Leigh
Diana	Toni Gayle Smith
Presto	Adam Rich
Bobby	Ted Field
Dungeon Master	Sidney Miller
Venger	Peter Cullen

Producer: David DePatie

Dunninger and Winchell

Variety; 30 min; CBS 10/14/48 to 7/7/49
                        NBC 10/5/49 to 12/28/49

Comedy with ventriloquist Paul Winchell and feats of mind reading with mentalist Joseph Dunninger. Also known as "The Bigelow Show."

The Dunninger Show

The mind reading abilities of mentalist Joseph Dunninger. First syndicated in 1953, the series also aired on NBC (9/24/54 to 9/10/55) and on ABC (5/9/56 to 10/10/56).

The DuPont Show of the Month

Anthology; 90 min; CBS 9/29/57 to 3/21/61

Varying programs, including dramas, comedies, musicals and adaptations from books and Broadway. Sponsored by DuPont.

Producer: David Susskind, Paul Gregory, Ralph Nelson, Audrey Geller, Richard Lewine, Lewis Warren

The DuPont Show of the Week

Anthology; 60 min; NBC 9/17/61 to 9/6/64

Varying presentations, including variety programs, musicals, dramas, comedies and Broadway adaptations. Sponsored by DuPont.

Producer: David Susskind, Ralph Nelson, Julian Claman, John Aaron, Jacqueline Babbin, William Nichols, Jesse Zousmer, Eugene Burr, Jack Philbin, Louis Freedman

Dusty

Crime Drama Pilot; 60 min; NBC 7/24/83

The story of Dusty, a Los Angeles cabbie who longs to be a private detective.

Dusty	Saul Rubinek
Tim Halloran	Gerald S. O'Loughlin
Slugger	Nancy McKeon
Lt. Harry Beathoven	Hank Garrett

Producer: Lee Rich, Marc Merson

Dusty's Trail

Comedy; 30 min; Syn. 9/73

Shortly after a wagon train, destined for California (1880s) begins its journey, a wagon and stage are separated from the main body and lost. Stories relate the efforts of the wagon master to get his passengers to California.

Mr. Callahan	Forrest Tucker
Dusty	Bob Denver
Lulu	Jeannine Riley
Betsy	Lori Saunders
Carter Brookhaven	Ivor Francis
Daphne Brookhaven	Lynn Wood
Andy	Bill Cort

Producer: Sherwood Schwartz

Dynasty

Drama; 60 min; ABC 1/12/81 (Premiere)

The conflicts, passions, drives, and tensions of the Carringtons, a powerful, rich, and greedy Colorado oil family. See also "The Colbys."

Blake Carrington	John Forsythe
Krystle Carrington	Linda Evans
Fallon Carrington	Pamela Sue Martin Emma Samms
Alexis Colby	Joan Collins
Cecil Colby	Lloyd Bochner
Jeff Colby	John James
Steven Carrington	Al Corley Jack Coleman
Joseph Anders	Lee Bergere
Kirby Anders	Kathleen Beller
Matthew Blaisdel	Bo Hopkins
Claudia Blaisdel	Pamela Bellwood
Lindsay Blaisdel	Katy Kurtzman
Andrew Laird	Peter Mark Richman
Mark Jennings	Geoffrey Scott
Sammy Jo Dean	Heather Locklear
Adam Carrington	Gordon Thomson
Dominique Devereaux	Diahann Carroll
Brady Lloyd	Billy Dee Williams
Amanda	Catherine Oxenberg
Tracy Kendall	Deborah Adair
Peter DeVilbis	Helmut Berger
Farnsworth "Dex" Dexter	Michael Nader
Chris Deegen	Grant Goodeve
Ted Dinard	Mark Withers
Lady Ashley Mitchell	Ali MacGraw
Rashid Ashmed	John Saxon
Daniel Reece	Rock Hudson
Neal McVane	Paul Burke
King Galen	Joel Fabiani
Ben Carrington	Christopher Cazenove
Leslie Carrington	Terri Garber
Clay Fallmont	Ted McGinely
Prince Michael	Michael Traed
Joel Abrigore	George Hamilton
Shawn Rowan	James Healey
Wayne Northrup	Michael Cullen
Sarah Curtis	Cassie Yates
Nicole Simpson	Susan Scannell
Yuri	Carl Strano
Elena	Kerry Armstrong
Luke Fuller	William Campbell
Danny	Jamison Sampley
Krystina	Jessica Player
Caress Morell	Kate O'Mara
Jackie Devereaux	Troy Beyer

Producer: Aaron Spelling, Richard & Esther Shapiro

The Earl Wrightson Show

Variety; 15 min; ABC 11/27/48 to 2/21/52

Music and songs with Earl Wrightson and Betty Jane Watson. Produced by Gil Fates with the music of the Buddy Weed and Norman Paris Trios.

Earn Your Vacation

Game; 30 min; CBS 5/23/54 to 9/5/54

Object: For players to win their dream vacation by selecting a category and answering questions of ascending difficulty.

Host: Johnny Carson

Assistant: Jackie Loughery, Millie Sinclair

The Earthlings

Comedy Pilot; 30 min; ABC 7/5/84

During the first flight of a passenger shuttle, the engines malfunction and maroon the "Destiny" in outer space. The unsold series was to relate the efforts of the crew and passengers to repair the craft and return to Earth.

Capt. Jim Adams	Mike Connors
Cal	Dan Hedaya
Sally	Robin Dearden
Dr. Noah Greene	Charles Hill
Jane Lassiter	Ilene Graff
D.J. Young	Michael D. Roberts
Simon Ganes	James Cromwell
Jaza	Leonard Frey
Zet	Debbie Carrington
Voice of Bobbo	G.W. Bailey

Producer: Reinhold Weege

East Side/West Side

Drama; 60 min; CBS 9/30/63 to 9/14/64

The problems of coping with the poor, the aged and the homeless of New York as seen through the eyes of Neil Brock, a Manhattan social worker.

Neil Brock	George C. Scott
Freida "Hecky" Hechlinger	Elizabeth Wilson
Jane Foster	Cicely Tyson
Charles Hanson	Linden Chiles

Producer: David Susskind

Easy Aces

Comedy; 30 min; DuMont 12/14/49 to 6/7/50

Events in the lives of the Aces: Jane, a scatterbrained wife, and Goodman, her husband, the recipient of her antics.

Goodman Ace	Himself
Jane Ace	Herself
Dorothy	Betty Garde

Announcer: Ken Roberts

Producer: Goodman Ace

Easy Does It . . . Starring Frankie Avalon

Variety; 60 min; CBS 8/25/76 to 9/15/76

A Summer program of music and songs with host Frankie Avalon, regulars Annette Funicello, Tim Reid, and Susan Nesbitt, and the orchestra of Vic Glaser. Produced by Dick Clark, Bill Lee, and Robert Arthur.

Easy Street

Comedy; 30 min; NBC 9/13/86 to 5/27/87

Following her husband's death, L.K. McGuire, a beautiful showgirl, inherits a Beverly Hills mansion but must share it with her snooty in-laws (Eleanor and Quentin). Stories relate the changes that occur when L.K. invites her estranged Uncle Bully and his friend Ricardo to live with her and liven up the dreary mansion.

L.K. McGuire	Loni Anderson
Alvin "Bully" Stevenson	Jack Elam
Ricardo Williams	Lee Weaver
Eleanor Standard	Dana Ivey
Quentin Standard	James Cromwell
Bobby (butler)	Arthur Malet

Producer: Hugh Wilson

The Ed Sullivan Show

Variety; 60 min; CBS 9/25/55 to 9/6/71

A lavish entertainment series featuring the top names in entertainment. Broadcast as "Toast of the Town" from 6/10/48 to 9/18/55.

Host: Ed Sullivan

Commercial Spokeswoman: Julia Meade

Regulars: Jim Henson's Muppets, The Hugh Lambert Dancers, The Toastettes Chorus Line

Announcer: Ralph Paul

Orchestra: Ray Bloch

Producer: Jack Meegan, Ed Sullivan, Robert Precht, Jack McGeehan, Marlo Lewis, Stu Erwin Jr., Ken Campbell

The Ed Wynn Show

Variety; 30 min; CBS 10/6/49 to 7/4/50

A weekly series of music, songs and comedy sketches.

Host: Ed Wynn

Regulars: Edith Praf, Ben Wrigley, The Merrill Dancers

Announcer: Robert LeMond

Orchestra: Lud Gluskin

Producer: Harlan Thompson

The Ed Wynn Show

Comedy; 30 min; NBC 9/25/58 to 1/1/59

The story of John Beamer, a retired, widowed businessman, and his efforts to raise his orphaned granddaughters, Laurie and Midge.

John Beamer	Ed Wynn
Laurie Beamer	Jacklyn O'Donnell
Midge Beamer	Sherry Alberoni
Ernie Henshaw	Herb Vigran
Mayor Brandon	Clarence Straight

Producer: Gary Simpson

Eddie

Comedy Pilot; 30 min; CBS 9/5/71

The dealings of Eddie Skinner, a private patrolman in the posh El Dorado Estates in Bel Air, California.

Eddie Skinner	Phil Silvers
Chief Pike	Fred Clark
Patrolman Callahan	Frank Faylen
Sylvia	Joanna Barnes
Mr. Milburn	Edward Andrews
Mrs. Milburn	Patricia Barry

Producer: Irving Pincus

The Eddie Albert Show

Variety; 30 min; CBS 3/2/53 to 5/8/53

Music and comedy with host Eddie Albert and singer Ellen Hanley. Music by the Norman Paris Trio. Produced by Franklin Heller.

Eddie and Herbert

Comedy Pilot; 30 min; CBS 5/30/77

The relationship between two blue collar workers: Eddie, who is pompous and opinionated, and Herbert, who is naive and worships Eddie.

Eddie Scanlon	Jeffrey Tambor
Herbert Draper	James Cromwell
Madge Scanlon	Marilyn Meyer
Corine Draper	Candice Azzara

Producer: Perry Lafferty

The Eddie Cantor Comedy Theatre

A syndicated (1955) series of music and comedy with Eddie Cantor and regulars Helen O'Connell, Billie Burke, Ralph Peters, Frank Jenks and Pierre Watkin. Orchestra: Ray Anthony.

The Eddie Capra Mysteries

Crime Drama; 60 min; NBC 9/22/78 to 1/12/79

The exploits of Eddie Capra, an attorney with the Los Angeles firm of Devlin, Linkman, and O'Brien.

Eddie Capra	Vincent Baggetta
Lacey Brown	Wendy Phillips
J.J. Devlin	Ken Swofford
Harvey Mitchell	Michael Horton
Jennie Brown	Seven Ann McDonald
Lynn	Lynn Toping

Producer: Peter S. Fischer

The Eddie Condon Show

Variety; 30 min; NBC 1/1/49 to 6/24/50

Performances by jazz musicians with hosts Eddie Condon and Carl Reiner, regulars Joe Bushkin, Billy Butterfield, Sidney Becket, and Peewee Russell, and the orchestra of Eddie Condon.

The Eddie Fisher Show

Variety; 60 min; NBC 9/24/57 to 3/17/59

An hour of music and song that alternates with "The George Gobel Show."

Host: Eddie Fisher

Regulars: George Gobel, Debbie Reynolds, Erin O'Brien, The Johnny Mann Singers

Orchestra: Buddy Bregman

The Eddy Arnold Show

Variety; 15 min; CBS 7/14/52 to 8/22/52
NBC 7/7/53 to 10/1/53

Country and western music with host Eddy Arnold, regulars Chet Atkins and the Dickens Sisters, and the music of Paul Mitchell's Quintet.

Eddy Arnold Time

Variety; 30 min; NBC 4/20/56 to 7/19/56

Performances by country and western artists with host Eddy Arnold, regulars Betty Johnson and the Gordonaires Quartet, and the Russ Case Orchestra.

The Edison Twins

Comedy-Mystery; 30 min; DIS 3/3/84 (Premiere)

The adventures of Ann and Tom Edison, twin teenage sleuths who apply scientific principals to solve crimes.

Ann Edison	Marnie McPhail
Tom Edison	Andrew Sabiston
Paul Edison	Sunny Thraser

The Edward Arnold Theatre

A syndicated (1954) series of dramas produced for syndication with host Edward Arnold.

Egan

Crime Drama Pilot; 30 min; ABC 9/18/73

The exploits of Eddie Egan, a former N.Y.P.D. detective turned private investigator.

Eddie Egan	Eugene Roche
Capt. Walter Jones	Dabney Coleman
Det. Burke	Glenn Corbett
J.R. King	John Anderson
Phil Califano	Del Monroe

Producer: Thomas L. Miller

The Egg and I

Comedy; 15 min; CBS 9/3/51 to 8/1/52

The misadventures of Bob and Betty MacDonald as they struggle to operate a run-down chicken farm in Cape Flattery, New York.

Betty MacDonald	Patricia Kirkland
Bob MacDonald	Frank Craven
Jed Simmons	Grady Sutton
Ma Kettle	Doris Rich
Pa Kettle	Frank Twedell

Producer: Montgomery Ford

Eight Is Enough

Comedy-Drama; 60 min; ABC 3/15/77 to 8/29/81

Events in the day-to-day lives of the Bradfords, a ten-member family living at 1436 Oak Street in Sacramento, California.

On October 18, 1987, NBC aired "Eight Is Enough: A Family Reunion," a TV movie that reunited the cast of "Eight Is Enough" (with the exception of Betty Buckley). Since the series ended, Tom had become managing editor of the "Sacramento Register"; Abby (played by Mary Frann), owns a restaurant, The Delta Supper Club; Mary, now a doctor, is married to Chuck (Jonathan Perpich); Susan and Merle are the parents of Sandy (Amy Gibson); Tommy is a struggling singer; Elizabeth has married Mark (Peter Nelson) and owns a car restoration business; David, an architect, is still divorced from Janet, a lawyer; Joanie is married to Jean Pierre (Paul Rosilli), a film director; Nancy has married a sheep rancher (Jeb, played by Chris McDonald); and Nicholas is attending college.

Tom Bradford	Dick Van Patten
Joan Bradford	Diana Hyland
Sandra "Abby"	
Bradford	Betty Buckley
Mary Bradford	Lani O'Grady
Joanie Bradford	Laurie Walters
Nancy Bradford	Kimberly Beck
	Dianne Kay
Elizabeth Bradford	Connie Needham
David Bradford	Mark Hamill
	Grant Goodeve
Tommy Bradford	Chris English
	Willie Aames
Nicholas Bradford	Adam Rich
Donna	Lucy Saroyan
	Jennifer Darling
Dr. Craig Maxwell	Michael Thoma
Daisy Maxwell	Virginia Vincent
Janet McCarther	Joan Prather
Merle Stockwell	Brian Patrick Clarke
Ernie Fields	Michael Goodrow
Jill Cassidy	Michele Greene
Elliott Randolph	John Karen
Jeffrey Trout	Nicholas Pryor
Ms. Chovick	Kate Woodville
Vivian (Aunt V)	Janis Paige
Jeremy Andreddi	Ralph Macchio

Producer: Lee Rich, Philip Capice

Theme Vocal ("Eight Is Enough"): Grant Goodeve

The 87th Precinct

Crime Drama; 60 min; NBC 9/25/61 to 9/10/62

The day-to-day activities of the detectives attached to New York's 87th Police Precinct.

Det. Steve Carella	Robert Lansing
Det. Bert Kling	Ron Harper
Det. Meyer Meyer	Norman Fell
Det. Roger Havilland	Gregory Walcott
Teddy Carella	
(Steve's wife)	Gena Rowlands
Sarah Meyer	
(Meyer's wife)	Ruth Storey
Norma Meyer	
(Meyer's daughter)	Andrea Margolis
Buckey Meyer	
(Meyer's son)	Larry Adare

Producer: Hubbell Robinson

Eischied

Crime Drama; 60 min; NBC 9/21/79 to 7/29/80

The exploits of Earl Eischied, Chief of Detectives of the N.Y.P.D.

Earl Eischied	Joe Don Baker
Edward Parks	Eddie Egan
Det. Rick Alessi	Vincent Bufano
Det. Carol Wright	Suzanne Lederer
Capt. John Finnerty	Alan Oppenheimer
Irene Stefan	Laraine Stephens
Sgt. Jim Kimbrough	Alan Fudge

Producer: David Gerber, Matthew Rapf

Electra Woman and Dyna Girl

Adventure; 15 min; ABC 9/11/76 to 9/3/77

The exploits of Laurie and Judy, reporters for "Newsmaker" magazine, who become the crime-fighting Electra Woman and Dyna Girl through Crimescope, an amazing computer complex. Aired on "The Krofft Supershow."

Laurie	Deidre Hall
Judy	Judy Strangis
Frank Heflin	Norman Alden

Producer: Sid and Marty Krofft

The Eleventh Hour

Drama; 60 min; NBC 10/3/62 to 9/9/64

The work of Theodore Bassett, a New York psychiatrist, as he attempts to help people overcome by the turmoil of human emotion.

Dr. Theodore	
Bassett	Wendell Corey
Dr. Paul Graham	Jack Ging
Dr. L. Richard	
Starke	Ralph Bellamy
Receptionist	Marge McNally

Producer: Norman Felton

Elfego Baca

A "Walt Disney Presents" series about the exploits of Elfego Baca, a sheriff, then lawyer, who battles for justice in Socorro County, New Mexico, during the 1880s.

Elfego Baca	Robert Loggia
Sheriff Morgan	Robert F. Simon
Zangano	Leonard Strong
Lucita	Valerie Allen
Ross Mantee	Skip Homeier
Suzanna	Beverly Garland
Shadrock	Brian Keith
Don Estevan	Ramon Navarro

Producer: Walt Disney, James Pratt

The Elgin Hour

Anthology; 60 min; NBC 10/6/54 to 6/14/55

A series of live dramas broadcast from New York and sponsored by Elgin watches. Produced by Herbert Brodkin and featuring such stars as Kathleen Nolan, June Lockhart, E.G. Marshall, Polly Bergen, Louis Jourdan, Brian Keith, Theodore Bikel, Boris Karloff, Richard Kiley, Dorothy Gish, Janet Blair, Jack Lord, and Roddy McDowall.

Elke

Comedy Pilot; 30 min; CBS 8/22/71

The story of a beautiful German girl (Elke) who marries an American doctor (Peter) and her attempts to adjust to the American way of life.

Elke Stefan	Elke Sommer
Peter Stefan	Peter Bonerz
Peter's mother	Kay Medford
Dodie Stefan	Debi Storm
Charlie Stefan	Paul Petersen

Producer-Director-Writer: Melville Shevelson

The Ellen Burstyn Show

Comedy; 30 min; ABC 9/21/86 to 11/15/86

Events in the life of Ellen Brewer, a college professor whose Baltimore Brownstone is also home to her recently separated daughter, Molly (and son Nick), and her mother, Sydney.

Ellen Brewer	Ellen Burstyn
Molly	Megan Mullally
Sydney Brewer	Elaine Stritch
Nick	Jesse Tendler
Tom Hines (student)	Barry Sobel
Carrie (student)	Winifred Freeman
Michael Selkirk (student)	Matt Mulhern
Maria (student)	Maria Strova
Dean Morton (college head)	Roscoe Lee Brown

Theme Vocal ("Nothing in the World Like Love"): Rita Coolidge

Producer: Norman Steinberg

Ellery Queen

Mystery; 60 min; NBC 9/11/75 to 9/19/76

New York City in 1947 and the exploits of Ellery Queen, a detective and writer who helps his father, Inspector Richard Queen, solve crimes.

Ellery Queen	Jim Hutton
Insp. Richard Queen	David Wayne
Sgt. Velie	Tom Reese
Frank Flannigan	Ken Swofford
Simon Brimmer	John Hillerman

Producer: Richard Levinson, William Link

Elvira's Movie Macabre

Movies; 2 hrs; Syn. 1983

Non-classic horror films are showcased with the comical hosting of Elvira, the beautiful Mistress of Horror.

Elvira	Cassandra Peterson
The Breather	John Paragon

"Elvira's Theme" music by Mark Pierson

Emerald Point, N.A.S.

Drama; 60 min; CBS 9/26/83 to 3/12/84

The experiences of the men and women stationed at Southern California's Emerald Point Naval Air Station base.

Admiral Thomas
 Mallory — Dennis Weaver
Celia Warren — Susan Dey
Kay Mallory — Stephanie Dunnam
Ensign Leslie
 Mallory — Doran Clark
Lt. Cmdr. Jack
 Warren — Charles Frank
Harlan Adams — Patrick O'Neal
 — Robert Vaughn
Hilary Adams — Sela Ward
Lt. Glen Matthews — Andrew Stevens
Deanna Kincaid — Jill St. John
Maggie Farrell — Maud Adams
Yuri Bukharin — Robert Loggia
Lt. Alexi
 Gorichenko — Michael Carven

Producer: Esther and Richard Shapiro

"Emerald Point" theme by Bill Conti

Emergency!

Drama; 60 min; NBC 1/22/72 to 12/31/78

The work of the paramedics of Squad 51 (Rescue Division) of the L.A. County Fire Department and the staff of Rampart Hospital.

Dr. Kelly Brackett — Robert Fuller
Dr. Joe Early — Bobby Troup
Nurse Dixie McCall — Julie London
Fireman Roy DeSoto — Kevin Tighe
Fireman John Gage — Randolph Mantooth
Captain Henderson — Dick Hammer
Captain Stanley — Michael Norell
Batallion Chief — Art Balinger
Fireman Marco
 Lopez — Marco Lopez
Fireman Chet Kelly — Tim Donnelly
Fireman Mike
 Woiski — Jack Kruschen
Fireman Stoker — Mike Stoker
Nurse Carol
 Williams — Lillian Lehman

Producer: Jack Webb, Robert Cinader

Emergency!

Drama; 2 hrs; NBC 6/26/79 to 7/3/79

The work of John Gage and Roy DeSoto as visiting paramedics with the 87th Rescue Unit of the San Francisco Fire Department.

Fireman John Gage — Randolph Mantooth
Fireman Roy DeSoto — Kevin Tighe
Medic Laurie
 Campbell — Deirdre Lenihan
Medic Gail Warren — Patricia McCormack
Capt. Pete Delaney — Paul Sylvan
Medic Joe Marshall — Jordan Suffin
Nurse Ellen Ankers — Jacki Murphy
Dr. DeRoy — John DeLancie

Producer: Robert A. Cinader

Emergency Plus Four

Cartoon; 30 min; NBC 9/8/73 to 9/4/76

The rescue operations of firemen John Gage and Roy DeSoto as they, assisted by four children, help people trapped in life-and-death situations.

Roy DeSoto — Kevin Tighe
John Gage — Randolph Mantooth
Sally — Sarah Kennedy
 — Carol Harper
Matt — David Jolliffee
 — Matthew Harper
Jason — Donald Fullilove
 — Jason Phillips
Randy — Peter Haas
 — Randy Alrich

Producer: Fred Calvert

Empire

Drama; 60 min; NBC 9/25/62 to 9/17/63
 ABC 3/22/64 to 9/6/64

The story of Jim Redigo, foreman of the half-million acre Garrett Ranch in Santa Fe, New Mexico. See also "Redigo."

Jim Redigo — Richard Egan
Lucia Garrett — Anne Seymour
Connie Garrett — Terry Moore
Tal Garrett — Ryan O'Neal
Paul Moreno — Charles Bronson
Chuck — Warren Vanders

Producer: William Sackheim

Empire

Comedy; 30 min; CBS 1/4/84 to 2/1/84

The misadventures of Ben Christian, the naive head of research and development for Empire Industries, a New York conglomorate run by double-dealing, paranoid executives.

Ben Christian	Dennis Dugan
Calvin Cromwell	Patrick Macnee
Jack Willow	Richard Masur
Jackie Willow	Christine Belford
Edward Roland	Michael McGuire
Arthur Broaderick	Dick O'Neill
Roger Martinson	Howard Platt
T. Howard Daniels	Edward Winter
Meredith Blake	Caren Kaye
Peggy	Maureen Arthur
Amelia Lapidus	Francine Tacker

Producer: Lawrence J. Cohen, Fred Freeman

Encounter

Anthology; 60 min; ABC & CBC 10/5/58 to 11/2/58

A short-lived effort to simulcast a live Canadian series on American TV. The programs: "Breakthrough" (10/5); "End of Summer" (10/12); "The Flower in the Rock" (10/19); "Depth Three-Hundred" (10/26); and "Men Don't Make Passes" (11/2).

End of the Rainbow

Human Interest; 30 min; NBC 1/11/58 to 2/15/58

A preselected subject is given the opportunity to realize a lifetime ambition, regain a sound footing in business, or be provided with an unexpected opportunity for success.

Host: Art Baker

Producer: Ralph Edwards

The Engelbert Humperdinck Show

Variety; 60 min; ABC 1/21/70 to 9/19/70

Music, songs, and light comedy with singer Engelbert Humperdinck. With the Irving Davies Dancers and the Jack Parnell Orchestra.

Enigma

Adventure Pilot; 60 min; CBS 5/27/77

The exploits of Andrew Icarus, an agent for the Caribbean-based crime-fighting organization Triangle.

Andrew Icarus	Scott Hylands
Maurice Mockcastle	Guy Doleman
Miranda Larawa	Barbara O. Jones
Mei San Gow	Soon-Teck Oh
Dora Herren	Melinda Dillon
Idi Ben Youref	Percy Rodrigues
Kate Valentine	Sherry Jackson
Colonel Valentine	Jim Davis

Producer: Sam H. Rolfe

Enos

Crime Drama; 60 min; CBS 11/20/80 to 9/19/81

When Georgia Deputy Enos Strate single-handley captures two of America's most wanted felons, he is recruited by the L.A.P.D. and teamed with Turk Adams. Stories relate their case investigations on behalf of the Metro Squad's Division 8. A spin-off from "The Dukes of Hazzard."

Off. Enos Strate	Sonny Shroyer
Off. Turk Adams	Samuel E. Wright
Lt. Jacob Broggi	John Dehner
Capt. Dempsey	John Milford
Sgt. Theodore Kick	Leo V. Gordon

Producer: Rod Amateau

Ensign O'Toole

Comedy; 30 min; NBC 9/23/62 to 9/15/63

The World War II misadventures of the men and officers of the Navy destroyer USS Appleby.

Ensign O'Toole	Dean Jones
CPO Homer Nelson	Jay C. Flippen
Lt. Rex St. John	Jack Mullavey
Lt. Cmdr. Virgil Stoner	Jack Albertson
Gabby DiJulio	Harvey Lembeck
Howard Spicer	Beau Bridges
Claude White	Robert Sorrells

Producer: Hy Averback, Bob Claver

The Entertainers

Variety; 60 min; CBS 9/25/64 to 3/27/65

Music, song, dance and comedy presented in the style of a revue.

Host: Bob Newhart, Carol Burnett, Caterina Valente

Regulars: John Davidson, Art Buchwald, Tessie O'Shea, Jack Burns, Dom DeLuise, Tony Hendra, Nick Ullet

Orchestra: Harry Zimmerman

Producer: Joe Hamilton

Entertainment Tonight

Magazine; 30 min; Syn. 9/14/84 (Premiere)

A daily series of entertainment news.

Hostess: Marjorie Wallace, Dixie Whatley, Mary Hart, Leeza Gibbons

Host: Tom Hallick, Ron Hendren, Robb Weller, Steve Edwards, Steve Tesh

Reporters (include): Robin Leach, Leonard Harris, Leonard Maltin, Catherine Mann, Rona Barrett, Barbara Howar, Scott Osborn, Joyce Jillson, Maureen Reagan, Lee Leonard, Dick Shoemaker, Ann Simon, Bobby Colomby, Katie Kelly

The Equalizer

Crime Drama; 60 min; CBS 9/18/85 (Premiere)

The exploits of Robert McCall, a former government agent turned one-man security force who helps people facing insurmountable odds.

Robert McCall	Edward Woodward
Scott McCall	William Zabka
Control	Robert Lansing
Det. Isadore Smalls	Ron O'Neal
Lt. Jeff Burnett	Steven Williams
Kay McCall	Sandy Dennis
Jason Masur	Saul Rubinek
Mickey	Keith Szarabajka
Sterno	Irving Metzman
Brahms	Jerry Stiller

"The Equalizer" theme by Stewart Copeland

Producer: Michael Sloan, Haywood Gould

E/R

Comedy; 30 min; CBS 9/16/84 to 7/24/85

Comical incidents in the life of Howard Sheinfeld, a divorced ear-nose-and throat specialist who moonlights as a doctor in the emergency room of Chicago's Clark Street Hospital.

Dr. Howard Sheinfeld	Elliott Gould
Dr. Eve Sheridan	Marcia Strassman
	Mary McDonnell
Nurse Joan Thor	Conchata Ferrell
Nurse Julie Williams	Lynne Moody
Maria Amarda	Shuko Akune
Off. Fred Burdock	Bruce A. Young
Nurse Cory Smith	Corinne Bohrer
Dr. Thomas Esqueval	Luis Avalos
Phyllis Sheinfeld	Patch MacKenzie
Sheila Sheinfeld	Karen Black
Jenny Sheinfeld	Pamela Segall
Harold Stickley	Jason Alexander

Producer: Bernie Orenstein, Saul Turteltaub

The Ern Westmore Show

Beauty tips and advice for women with Ern Westmore, Betty Westmore and Dick Hyde. ABC 8/7/55 to 9/11/55.

Ernie in Kovacsland

Comedy; 15 min; NBC 5/14/51 to 6/29/51

A live comedy series from Philadelphia that spotlights the comic talent of Ernie Kovacs. With regulars Edie Adams and Hugh Price and the Harry Sosnik Orchestra.

The Ernie Kovacs Show

Comedy; 30 min; NBC 12/12/55 to 9/10/56

Sketches and blackouts that spotlights the genius of Ernie Kovacs. See also "The New Ernie Kovacs Show."

Host: Ernie Kovacs

Regulars: Edie Adams, Matt Dennis, Kenny Delmar, Harry Lascoe, Al Keith

Announcer: Bill Wendell

Music: Artie Koty

Producer: Barry Shear, Perry Cross, Jack Hein

Ernie, Madge and Artie

Comedy Pilot; 30 min; ABC 8/15/74

The story of a ghost (Ernie) who comes back to haunt his wife (Madge) and her new husband (Artie) following Madge's remarriage.

Madge	Cloris Leachman
Artie	Dick Van Patten
Ernie	Frank Sutton
Blanche	Susan Sennett
Charlie	William Molloy

The Errol Flynn Theatre

Anthology; 30 min; DuMont 3/22/57 to 7/26/57

Dramatizations featuring Errol Flynn as both host and frequent performer. Produced by Marcel Leduc and Norman Williams.

Escapade

Adventure Pilot; 60 min; CBS 5/19/78

The exploits of Joshua Rand, a U.S. government agent who receives his orders from a computer named Oz.

Joshua Rand	Granville Van Dusen
Suzy	Morgan Fairchild
Paula	Janice Lynde
Wences	Alex Henteloff
Arnold Tolliver	Len Birman

Producer: Philip Saltzman

Escape

Anthology; 30 min; CBS 1/5/50 to 3/30/50

Live dramas that relate the plight of people caught in life and death situations.

Narrator: William Conrad

Announcer: Jack McCoy, Elliott Lewis

Producer: Wyllis Cooper

Escape

Anthology; 30 min; NBC 2/11/73 to 4/1/73

True stories of people caught in life and death situations.

Narrator: Jack Webb

Producer: Jack Webb, Robert A. Cinader

Escape

Anthology Pilot; 30 min; Syn. 3/81

A proposed series of dramas about famous escapees. The pilot dramatizes the escape of Billy Hayes, an American convicted of drug possession, from a Turkish prison.

Host/Narrator	James Coburn
Billy Hayes	Randy Shepard

Producer: Abe Lowenstein

E.S.P.

Game; 30 min; ABC 7/11/58 to 8/1/58

Two people, screened by psychiatrists, are tested to determine their degree of E.S.P.

Host: Vincent Price

Consultant: Carroll B. Nash

Producer: George Wolfe, Leo Morgan

E.S.P.

Anthology; 30 min; ABC 8/8/58 to 8/22/58

A revised version of the previous title which presents stories of people endowed with extrasensory perception.

Host: Vincent Price

Producer: George Wolfe, Leo Morgan

Espionage

Anthology; 60 min; NBC 10/2/63 to 9/2/64

Dramas based on the activities of international undercover agents. Produced by Herbert Brodkin and featuring such stars as Millicent Martin, George Grizzard, Jim Backus, Bradford Dillman, Steven Hill, Madlyn Rhue, Chester Morris, and Joseph Campanella.

Ethel and Albert

Comedy; 30 min; NBC 4/25/53 to 12/25/54
CBS 6/20/55 to 9/26/55
ABC 10/14/55 to 7/6/56

Events in the lives of Ethel and Albert Arbuckle, a happily married couple who live in the small town of Sandy Harbor.

Ethel Arbuckle	Peg Lynch
Albert Arbuckle	Alan Bunce
Aunt Eva	Margaret Hamilton

Producer: William Hamilton, Walter Hart, Thomas Leob

The Ethel Barrymore Theatre

Anthology; 30 min; DuMont 9/21/54 to 12/14/56

A series of dramas hosted by veteran actress Ethel Barrymore. Produced by William Calihan Jr.

Ethel Is an Elephant

Comedy Pilot; 30 min; CBS 6/18/80

Enroute to his home, photographer Eugene Henderson crosses the path of Ethel, an abandoned baby elephant. Eugene removes a painful nail from Ethel's foot and soon finds himself with a new pet when she follows him home. The unsold series was to relate Eugene's misadventures as the owner of a half-ton elephant in Manhattan.

Eugene Henderson	Todd Susman
Dr. Diane Taylor	Liberty Godshall
Howard Dimitri	Steven Peterman
Harold Brainer	Ed Barth

Producer: Bob Sweeney, Edward H. Feldman

The Ethel Waters Show

Experimental; 60 min; NBC 6/14/39

A program of music and songs. The first known program to star a black performer.

Hostess: Ethel Waters

Guests: Georgette Harvey, Fred Washington, Ollie Barber, Georgia Buck, Philip Leob, Joey Faye, Edith Gresham

Announcer: George Hicks

Producer: Edward Sobol

The Eva Gabor Show

Actress Eva Gabor as host of a women's program of music, chatter and beauty tips. ABC 11/10/50 to 10/22/51.

The Eve Arden Show

Comedy; 30 min; CBS 9/17/57 to 3/25/58

The story of Liza Hammond, a widowed traveling lecturer, as she struggles to divide her time between work and her twin daughters, Jenny and Mary.

Liza Hammond	Eve Arden
Jenny Hammond	Gail Stone
Mary Hammond	Karen Greene
George Howell	Allyn Joslyn
Nora	Frances Bavier

Producer: Robert Sparks

The Eve Arden Show

Comedy Pilot; 30 min; CBS 7/20/64

The misadventures of Claudia Cooper, the London branch manager of the T.J. Gitting Travel Agency.

Claudia Cooper	Eve Arden
Marsha Cooper	Cindy Carol
T.J. Gitting	Howard Smith
Bertie Barrington	Jeremy Lloyd
Tillie	Ambrosine Philpots
Katie	Katy Greenwood

Producer: Harry Ackerman

The Eve Hunter Show

A daily series of celebrity interviews with Eve Hunter. NBC 10/10/51 to 3/28/52.

Evel Knievel

Adventure Pilot; 30 min; CBS 3/29/74

The exploits of thrill-seeker Evel Knievel.

Evel Knievel	Sam Elliott
Gene Ray Stone	Gary Barton
Tracy Butler	Karen Philipp
Darrell Pettet	Michael Anderson Jr.
Jack Decataur	Nobel Willingham

Producer: Robert E. Relyea

Evening at the Improv

Comedy; 60 min; Syn. 9/81

Performances by established and new comedy talent. Taped at the Improv Club in L.A.

Host: Budd Friedman

Regulars: Donnie Archibald, Carrie Carrington, Gina Hecht, Jack Knight, Mark Goldstein, Julie Brown, Barbara Gannon, Marilyn Jones, Terrence McGovern

Music: John Lombardo

The Everglades

Adventure; 30 min; Syn. 1961

The exploits of Lincoln Vail, a law enforcement officer with the Everglades County Police Patrol in Florida.

Lincoln Vail	Ron Hayes
Chief Anderson	Gordon Cosell

Producer: Jack Herzberg

The Everly Brothers Show

Variety; 60 min; ABC 7/8/70 to 9/16/70

Music and comedy with hosts Phil and Don Everly, regulars Dick Clair, Jenna McMahon, Joel Higgins and Ruth McDevitt, and the orchestra of Jack Elliott and Allyn Ferguson.

Every Stray Dog and Kid

Comedy-Drama Pilot; 60 min; NBC 9/21/81

When her sister is killed in an accident involving the car she stole, Bobbi Marshall, serving time for auto theft, vows to make an honest living as a writer and care for other kids. Upon her release, she is placed in charge of four juvenile offenders (Jenny, Tommy, Normie and Cathy). The would-be series was to relate Bobbi's efforts to care for her charges.

Bobbi Marshall	Maureen Anderman
Sgt. Mike Pirelli	Bruce Weitz
Jenny Baxter	Denise Miller
Tommy Ryan	Jackie Earle Haley
Cathy Aronson	Kris McKeon
Normie Taylor	Patrick J. Peterson
Geri Balin	Rita Taggart
Mrs. Braverman	Toni Gilman

Producer: Steven Bochco

Everyday

Variety; 60 min; Syn. 1978

A daily program of music, songs, and comedy sketches.

Hosts: Stephanie Edwards, John Bennett Perry

Regulars: Annie Bloom, Murray Langston, Emily Levine, Tom Chapin, Judy Gibson, Robert Corff

Producer: David Saltzman, Viva Knight

Everything Goes

Variety; 60 min; Syn. 9/73

Music, songs and celebrity interviews with hosts Norm Crosby and Tom O'Malley, regulars Mike Darrow (also announcer) and Katherine McKenna, and the orchestra of Moe Kaufman.

Everything Happens to Me

Comedy Pilot; 30 min; CBS 3/27/61

The pilot for "The Joey Bishop Show." The story of Joey Mason, a Hollywood press agent. Aired on "The Danny Thomas Show."

Joey Mason	Joey Bishop
Pop Mason	Billy Gilbert
Mom (Sylvia) Mason	Madge Blake

Producer: Sheldon Leonard

Everything's Archie

Cartoon; 30 min; CBS 9/8/73 to 1/26/74

The antics of the Archie Gang, teenagers who live in fictional Riverdale.

Archie Andrews	Dallas McKennon
Betty Cooper	Jane Webb
Veronica Lodge	Jane Webb
Jughead Jones	Howard Morris
Reggie Mantle	Dallas McKennon

Producer: Norm Prescott, Lou Scheimer

Everything's Relative

Comedy; 30 min; CBS 10/3/87 to 11/7/87

The misadventures of Julian Beeby, a product tester, and Scott Beeby, a construction worker, two brothers who share a Manhattan apartment. Focal point of the series is their mother's constant intervention in their lives.

Julian Beeby	Jason Alexander
Scott Beeby	John Bolger
Rae Beeby	Anne Jackson
Emily	Gina Hecht
Betsy	Kim Morgan Green
Aunt Rhoda	Peggy Cass

Producer: Maurice Duke, David Deben.

The Evil Touch

Anthology; 30 min; Syn. 1973

Stories of people who are driven to evil through frustration.

Host: Anthony Quayle

Producer: Mende Brown

Ewoks

Cartoon; 30 min; ABC 9/7/85 (Premiere)

The futuristic adventures of the Ewoks, creatures from the "Star Wars" films, as they battle evil.

Kneesaa	Cree Summer Francks
Wicket	Jim Kenshar

Additional Voices: Alan Fawcett, Myra Friend, Mellany Brown, Leane Coffee, Anthony Parr, Erik Peterson, Richard Donat

Producer: Mikki Herman

Exciting People, Exotic Places

Magazine Pilot; 60 min; Syn. 1/85

The program explores the world's most celebrated personalities and most intriguing locales.

Host: Pam Dawber

Guests: Brooke Shields, Persis Khambatta

Producer: Robin Leach, Al Masini

Executive Suite

Drama; 60 min; CBS 9/20/76 to 2/11/77

The problems that befall members of the California-based Cardway Corporation.

Don Walling	Mitchell Ryan
Helen Walling	Sharon Acker
Brian Walling	Leigh McCloskey
Stacy Walling	Wendy Phillips
Howard Rutledge	Stephen Elliott
Mark Desmond	Richard Cox
Yvonne Holland	Trisha Noble
Astrid Rutledge	Gwyda DonHowe
Glory Dalessio	Joan Prather
Summer Johnson	Brenda Sykes
Hilary Madison	Madlyn Rhue
Anderson Galt	William Smithers
Malcolm Gibson	Percy Rodrigues
Elly Gibson	Pauline Myers
	Kim Hamilton
Sharon Cody	Joanna Barnes
Nick Kaslow	Scott Marlowe
David Valerio	Ricardo Montalban

Producer: Norman Felton, Stanley Rubin, Rita Lakin

Expedition: Danger

Adventure; 30 min; Syn. 1/85

The real life adventures of Stan Brock, an adventurer who pits his strength against the perils of the jungle. Filmed in Brazil.

Stan Brock	Himself
Nadjama	Nadjama Iataleze
Peter Tors	Himself
Tracy	Tracy St. John

Producer: M. B. Scott, James Aubrey

Expert Witness

Crime Drama Pilot; 30 min; NBC 5/22/58

The story of Dan Wilder, a scientific detective who possesses a mobile crime lab and travels across the country to help where he is needed. Aired as "Hide and Seek" on "The Jane Wyman Theatre."

Dan Wilder	Everett Sloane
Joe Sackett	Richard Erdman
Joe McHale	Louis Jean Heydt
Sheriff	James Westerfield

Expose

Crime Drama Pilot; 60 min; NBC 12/27/63

The exploits of Anita King, a beautiful U.S. government undercover agent. Aired as "Corridor 400'' on "The Bob Hope Chrysler Theatre.''

Anita King	Suzanne Pleshette
Ralph Traven	Theodore Bikel
Donald Guthrie	Andrew Duggan
Frank Mancini	Joseph Campanella
Gene Farrell	Frank Overton

Eye Guess

Game; 30 min; NBC 1/3/66 to 9/26/69

A board, which contains eight numbered answers, is revealed for eight seconds. At the end of the time, the answers are hidden by overlaying numbers. A question that relates to one of the hidden answers is read. A player calls on a number; if it contains the correct answer, he scores one point. Seven points wins the game and merchandise prizes.

Host: Bill Cullen

Announcer: Don Pardo, Jack Clark

Eye to Eye

Crime Drama; 60 min; ABC 3/21/85 to 5/2/85

When her detective father is murdered, Tracy Doyle convinces her father's former partner (Oscar) to help her solve the crime. Resolving the crime, Tracy and Oscar decide to remain partners. Stories relate their adventures as private detectives.

Oscar Poole	Charles Durning
Tracy Doyle	Stephanie Faracy
Diane	Rita Taggart
Det. Ernie Rowen	James Carrington

Producer: Rich Eustis, Michael Elias

Eye Witness

Anthology; 30 min; NBC 3/20/53 to 6/29/53

Live dramas about people who witness accidents or crimes and come forward to testify.

Host-Narrator: Richard Carlson

Producer: Robert Montgomery

The Eyes Have It

Game; 30 min; NBC 11/20/48 to 6/19/49

Object: For players to identify a famous person or place from a portion of a picture (which may be seen in an extreme close-up, at an unusual angle, or at a particular focus.)

Host: Douglas Edwards, Ralph McNair

The Eyes of Texas

Crime Drama Pilot; 60 min NBC 5/24/80 (1st pilot); 7/5/80 (2nd pilot)

The exploits of Heather Fern and Caroline Capoty, private eyes for Texas International, a two-bit investigative organization run by Mort Jarvis (first pilot) and Helen Jarvis (Mort's widow, second pilot). Aired on "B.J. and the Bear.''

Heather Fern	Rebecca Reynolds
Caroline Capoty	Lorrie Mahaffey
Caroline (second	
pilot)	Heather Thomas
Mort Jarvis	Roger C. Carmel
Helen Jarvis	Eve Arden

Producer: Glen A. Larson

The Ezio Pinza Show

See "The R.C.A. Victor Show.''

The Fabulous Dr. Fable

Crime Drama Pilot; 60 min; ABC 6/17/73

The story of Justin Fable, an eccentric diagnostician and teacher with an uncanny knack for preceiving ailments that are the results of criminal actions.

Dr. Justin Fable	W.B. Brydon
June Fable	Jane Elliot
Lt. DeLusso	Jack Ging
Elliott Borden	William Daniels
Marilla	Cynthia Hall

Producer: Rick Rosenberg

The Fabulous Funnies

Cartoon; 30 min; NBC 9/9/78 to 9/1/79

Various aspects of the world are explained to children via adaptations of Sunday comic strips.

Voices: June Foray, Robert Holt, Jayne Hamil, Alan Oppenheimer

Producer: Norm Prescott, Lou Scheimer

The Face Is Familiar

Game; 30 min; CBS 5/7/66 to 9/3/66

Object: For players to identify famous personalities who are shown in scrambled photographs.

Host: Jack Whitaker

Producer: Bob Stewart

Face of Danger

A CBS series (4/18/59 to 5/30/59) of dramas originally broadcast on other anthology series.

Face the Facts

Game; 30 min; CBS 3/13/61 to 9/29/62

Object: For players to bet points and predict the outcome of a redramatized criminal case.

Host: Red Rowe

Producer: Irving Mansfield

Face the Music

Variety; 15 min; CBS 5/3/48 to 12/10/48

Four singers perform current, popular songs.

Singers: Johnny Desmond, Shaye Cogan, Sandra Deel, Carole Coleman

Music: The Tony Mottola Trio

Producer: Ace Ochs

Face the Music

Game; 30 min; Syn. 1/80

Object: For players to identify persons, places, or things from song titles. Highest scorers play the bonus wherein they win $10,000 if they identify a celebrity within six musical clues.

Host: Ron Ely

Vocalist: Lisa Donovan

Model: Jane Nelson

Orchestra: Tommy Oliver

Producer: David Levy, Roy Horl

Face to Face

Game; 30 min; NBC 6/9/46 to 1/26/47

Object: For players to identify celebrities from verbal clues. Also featured is a segment where an artist attempts to draw a person from verbal clues.

Host: Eddie Dunn

Artist: Bill Dunn

The Facts

Comedy Pilot; 35 min; CBS 12/10/82

Sketches that spoof various aspects of society.

Host: Richard Lewis

Regulars: Richard Belzer, Lois Bromfield, Rebecca Reynolds, John Paragon, Nick Ullett, Rod Burton, Betty Ciarrocchi, Phil Harmon, Paul Provenza

Music: Garth Hudson

Producer: Richard Goldstein

The Facts of Life

Comedy; 30 min; NBC 8/24/79 (Premiere)

Events in the lives of four girls (Blair, Jo, Tootie, and Natalie) as they grow from adolescence to young women. Early episodes are set at the Eastland School for Girls in Peekskill, New York; later, when Blair and Jo attend Langley College, former teacher Edna Garrett opens Edna's Edibles, a gourmet food store. When this is destroyed by fire, Edna and the girls open Over Our Heads, a variety store. In 1986 (9/27) when Edna marries Robert Gaynes (Robert Mandan), her sister, Beverly Ann, replaces her as a substitute mother to the girls.

Edna Garrett	Charlotte Rae
Blair Warner	Lisa Whelchel
Jo Polniaszek	Nancy McKeon
Dorothy "Tootie"	
Ramsey	Kim Fields
Natalie Greene	Mindy Cohn
Beverly Ann	Cloris Leachman
Cindy Webster	Julie Ann Haddock
Nancy Olsen	Felice Schachter
Sue Anne Weaver	Julie Piekarski
Molly Parker	Molly Ringwald
Steven Bradley	John Lawlor
Mr. Harris	Ken Mars
Emily Mahoney	Jenny O'Hara
Kelly Affenato	Pamela Segall
Boots St. Clair	Jami Gertz
Monica Warner	Pam Huntington
	Marj Dusay
Charlie Polniaszek	Alex Rocco
Rose Polniaszek	Claire Malis
Andy	MacKenzie Astin
George Burnett	George Clooney
Charles Parker	Roger Perry
Geri Warner	Geri Jewell
Howard	Hugh Gillian
Steve	Greg Bradford
Eddie Brennan	Clark Brandon

Theme Vocal ("The Facts of Life"): Charlotte Rae (1st season); Gloria Loring

Producer: Jack Elinson, Jerry Mayer, John Maxwell Anderson, Linda Marsh, Margie Peters

The Faculty

Comedy Pilot; 30 min; ABC 6/20/86

Life at Harrigan High School as seen through the eyes of six educators.

Valerie Arnold	Blair Brown
Dr. Julius Pepper	Richard Lawson
Edna McCauley	Allyn Ann McLerie
Leon Pakulski	Max Wright
Finney Morgan	Jason Bernard
Jonathan Covington	Albert Macklin
George Dent	Richard McKenzie
Tina Jackson	Megan Follows

Producer: Bernie Brillstein, Jay Tarses

Faerie Tale Theatre

Anthology; 50 min; SHO 9/11/82 (Premiere)

Modern adaptations of classic children's fairy tales. Stories include "Aladdin and His Wonderful Lamp" (with Valerie Bertinelli, Robert Carradine, James Earl Jones, Leonard Nimoy), "The Dancing Princesses" (Lesley Ann Warren, Peter Weller), "Goldilox and the Three Bears" (Tatum O'Neal, Hoyt Axton, John Lithgow), "Hansel and Gretel" (Joan Collins, Bridgette Anderson, Ricky Schroder), and "The Little Mermaid" (Pam Dawber, Karen Black, Treat Williams).

Hostess-Producer: Shelley Duvall.

Fair Exchange

Comedy; CBS; 60 min (9/21/62 to 12/28/62) 30 min (3/28/63 to 9/19/63)

The story of two families, one in New York (the Walkers) and one in England (the Finches), who exchange teenage daughters for one year. Episodes relate the experiences of Patty, the American, as she attends London's Royal Academy of Dramatic Arts, and Heather, British, as she acquaints herself with the American way of life.

Eddie Walker	Eddie Foy Jr.
Dorothy Walker	Audrey Christie
Patty Walker	Lynn Loring
Larry Walker	Flip Mark
Tommy Finch	Victor Maddern
Sybil Finch	Diana Chesney
Heather Finch	Judy Carne
Neville Finch	Dennis Waterman

Producer: Cy Howard

Fairmeadows, U.S.A.

Drama; 30 min; NBC 11/4/51 to 4/27/52

Life in a small American town (Fairmeadows) as seen through the eyes of John Olcott, a general store owner. Also known as "House in the Garden."

John Olcott	Howard St. John
	Lauren Gilbert
John's wife	Ruth Mattheson
John's daughter	Hazel Dawn Jr.
	Monica Lovett
Evvie Olcott	Mimi Strongin

Producer: Ezra McIntosh

Faith Baldwin's Theatre of Romance

Anthology; 30 min; ABC 1/20/51 to 10/20/51

Dramatizations based on the problems faced by people in their everyday lives.

Hostess: Faith Baldwin

Producer: Jack Barry, Dan Enright

The Falcon

Adventure; 30 min; Syn. 1955

The exploits of Michael Waring, a former private detective turned troubleshooter for the U.S. Army. (The title refers to Waring's underground name.)

Michael Waring	Charles McGraw
General Rawlings	Robert Carson

Producer: Buster Collier

Falcon Crest

Drama; 60 min; CBS 12/4/81 (Premiere)

The lives of the Channings, a powerful family who own the Falcon Crest Vineyards in California's Napa Valley.

Angela Channing	Jane Wyman
Chase Gioberti	Clu Gulager*
	Robert Foxworth
Maggie Gioberti	Samantha Eggar*
	Susan Sullivan
Victoria Gioberti	Jamie Rose
Cole Gioberti	William R. Moses
Julia Cumson	Abby Dalton
Emma Channing	Margaret Ladd
Lance Cumson	Lorenzo Lamas
Melissa Agretti	Ana Alicia
Philip Erikson	Mel Ferrer
Gus Noyes	Nick Ramus
Chao-Li	Chao-Li Chin
Alicia Noyes	Silvana Gallardo
Mario Noyes	Mario Marcelino
Jacqueline Perrault	Lana Turner
Douglas Channing	Stephen Elliott
Carlo Agretti	Carlos Romero
Richard Channing	David Selby
Pamela Lynch	Sarah Douglas
Diana Hunter	Shannon Tweed
Linda Caproni	Mary Kate McGeehan
Francesca Gioberti	Gina Lollobrigida
Joel McCarthy	Parker Stevenson
Kit Marlowe	Kim Novack
Jennifer Roberts	Morgan Fairchild
Dr. Michael Ranson	Cliff Robertson
Corene Powers	Victoria Racimo
Vince Caproni	Harry Basch
Appollonia	Apollonia Kotero
Jeff Wainwright	Edward Albert
Paul Hartford	Andrew Duggan
Anna Rossini	Celeste Holm
Peter Stavros	Cesare Romero
Casandra Wilder	Anne Archer
Greg Reardon	Simon MacCorkindale
Dina Wells	Robin Greer

"Falcon Crest" Theme: Bill Conti

Producer: Earl Hamner, Michael Filerman, Anne Marcus

*Roles in the never-televised pilot, "The Vintage Years."

The Fall and Rise of Reginald Perrin

Comedy; 30 min; Syn. 1978

The dreary day-to-day life of Reginald Perrin, an executive with Sunshine Desserts in England.

Reginald Perrin	Leonard Rossiter
Elizabeth Perrin	Pauline Yates
Joan Greengross	Sue Nicholls
C.J.	John Barron
Linda	Sally-Jane Spencer
Mark Perrin	David Warwick
Doc Morrisey	John Horsley
C.J.'s wife	Dorothy Frere
Tony Webster	Trevor Adams

The Fall Guy

Adventure; 60 min; ABC 11/4/81 to 5/2/86

The exploits of Colt Seavers, a stuntman (Fall Guy Stunt Association) who is also a bounty hunter for the L.A. Criminal Courts System.

Colt Seavers	Lee Majors
Jody Banks	Heather Thomas
Howie Munson	Douglas Barr
Samantha Jack*	Jo Ann Pflug
Terri Michaels*	Markie Post
Pearl Sperling*	Nedra Volz
Edmond Trench*	Robert Donner

Theme Vocal ("The Unknown Stuntman"): Lee Majors

Producer: Glen A. Larson, Lee Majors

*Owners of a bail bond agency who use Colt's services.

Fame

Drama; 60 min; NBC 1/7/82 to 8/4/83
Syn. 10/83 (Premiere)

The dreams, ambitions, and frustrations of the students who attend New York's High School for the Performing Arts.

Lydia Grant	Debbie Allen
Prof. Benjamin	
Shorofsky	Albert Hague
Elizabeth Sherwood	Carol Mayo Jenkins
David Reardon	Morgan Stevens
Quinton Morloch	Ken Swofford
Bob Dyrenforth	Graham Jarvis
Peggy Persky	Randee Heller
Gertrude Berg	Ann Nelson
Julie Miller	Lori Singer
Coco Hernandez	Erica Gimpel
Doris Schwartz	Valerie Landsburg
Bruno Martelli	Lee Curreri
Danny Amatello	Carlo Imperato
Leroy Johnson	Gene Anthony Ray
Holly Laird	Cynthia Gibb
Cleo Hewitt	Janet Jackson
Nicole Chapman	Nia Peeples
Jesse Valesquez	Jesse Borrego
Kate Riley	Page Hannah
Reggie Higgins	Carrie Hamilton
Dusty Taylor	Loretta Chandler
Jillian	Elisa Heinsohn
Ian Waire	Michael Cerveris
Chris	Billy Hufsey
Lou Mackie (owner of Lou's Lane's; the hangout)	Dick Miller
Paul (teacher)	Eric Pierpont

Theme Vocal ("Fame"): Erica Gimpel

Producer: William Blinn, Gerald I. Isenberg, Mel Swope

Fame, Fortune and Romance

Human Interest; 60 min; ABC 6/16/86 to 5/29/87

The lives of successful people and how they overcame impossible odds to achieve their goals.

Host: Robin Leach

Reporters: Patrice Chanel, Matt Lauer

Narrator: Bill St. James

Producer: Robin Leach, Al Masini

Family

Drama; 60 min; ABC 3/9/76 to 6/25/80

Incidents in the day-to-day lives of the Lawrences, a family of six living at 1230 Holland Street in Pasadena, California.

Doug Lawrence	James Broderick
Kate Lawrence	Sada Thompson
Nancy Maitland	Elayne Heilveil
	Meredith Baxter Birney
Lititia "Buddy" Lawrence	Kristy McNichol
Willie Lawrence	Gary Frank
Annie Cooper Lawrence	Quinn Cummings
Jeff Maitland	John Rubinstein
Salina Magee	Season Hubley
Timmy Maitland	Michael Shackelford David Shackelford
Audrey Pfeiffer	Louise Foley
Elaine Hogan	Priscilla Morrill
Fred Hogan	William Putch
Robin Trask	Helen Hunt
Mary Beth/Debbie	Dana Plato
T.J. Latimer	Willie Aames
James Lawrence	David Wayne Henry Fonda
Rachel Peters	Devon Ericson
Mrs. Canfield	Mary Grace Canfield

Producer: Aaron Spelling, Leonard Goldberg, Mike Nichols

Family Affair

Comedy; 30 min; CBS 9/12/66 to 9/9/71

When his brother and sister-in-law are killed in a car crash, bachelor Bill Davis decides to raise their children. Stories relate Bill's efforts to provide love and security to three lonely children (Cissy, Buffy and Jody).

Bill Davis	Brian Keith
Giles French	Sebastian Cabot
Cissy Davis	Kathy Garver
Jody Davis	Johnny Whitaker
Buffy Davis	Anissa Jones
Miss Faversham	Heather Angel
Nigel French	John Williams
Gregg Bartlett	Gregg Fedderson
Emily Turner	Nancy Walker
Scotty	Karl Lucas

Producer: Don Fedderson

Family Business

Comedy Pilot; 30 min; ABC 5/5/83

The misadventures of Lucille Garabaldi, owner of the Garabaldi Construction Company, and her two inept sons, Sal and Freddy. Aired on "Too Close for Comfort."

Lucille Garabaldi	Lainie Kazan
Sal Garabaldi	George Deloy
Freddy Garabaldi	Jimmy Baio
Donna Sullivan	Hillary Bailey

Producer: Arne Sultan, Earl Barrett

Family Feud

Game; 30 min; ABC 7/12/76 to 12/20/85

Two five-member families compete. A question, based on a survey of one hundred people, is stated. One family must supply the answers (three to ten) from the survey. Failure allows the other family the chance to win the round by supplying a correct response. Highest scoring families are the winners.

Host: Richard Dawson

Announcer: Gene Wood

Producer: Mark Goodson, Bill Todman

Family Genius

Comedy; 30 min; DuMont 9/9/49 to 9/30/49

A short-lived series, of which very little is known, about Tommy Howard, a child prodigy.

Tommy Howard	Jack Diamond
Tommy's mother	Phyllis Lowe
Tommy's father	Arthur Edwards

Producer: James L. Caddigan, Elwood Hoffman

The Family Holvak

Drama; 60 min; NBC 9/7/75 to 10/27/75

The efforts of Tom Holvak, a minister in Bensfield, Tennessee, in 1933, to feed his family and maintain the faith of his congregation.

Tom Holvak	Glenn Ford
Elizabeth Holvak	Julie Harris
Ramey Holvak	Lance Kerwin
Julie Mae Holvak	Elizabeth Cheshire
Deputy Jim Shanks	William McKinney
Chester Purdle	Ted Gehring
Ida	Cynthia Hayward

Theme Vocal ("Look How Far We've Come"): Denny Brooks

Producer: Roland Kibbee, Dean Hargrove

Family Honor

Experimental; 30 min; NBC 6/16/39

An original TV comedy about two brothers who live together but seldom agree on anything. With Paul Ballantine and William Shea as the brothers, and Helen Scully as the girlfriend. Produced by Edward Sobol.

Family in Blue

Crime Drama Pilot; 60 min; CBS 6/10/82

The lives of the Malones, a family of law enforcers: Marty, a former police captain turned private eye; Matt, his son, a sergeant; Julie, his daughter, a lab technician; Dabney, his cousin, a lab technician; and his brother, Chester, a police chief.

Marty Malone	Efrem Zimbalist Jr.
Matt Malone	Dirk Benedict
Julie Malone	Nancy Dolman
Chester Malone	Dick O'Neill
Dabney Malone	Michael Corneilson
Bernice Malone	Doris Singleton
Tina Royce	Cindy Pickett
Barney Hathaway	Edward Winter

Producer: Frank Glicksman

The Family Martinez

Comedy Pilot; 30 min; CBS 8/2/86

The story of Hector Martinez, a former gang member turned trial lawyer.

Hector Martinez	Robert Beltran
Anita Martinez	Anne Betancourt
Rainbow Martinez	Karla Montana
Romeo Ortega	Daniel Faraldo
Rachel McCann	Denise Crosby
Sister Mary Luke	Diana Bellamy
Judge Yamamoto	James Shigeta

Producer: Tommy Chong, Howard Brown

Family Ties

Comedy; 30 min; NBC 9/22/82 (Premiere)

Events in the lives of the Keatons: parents Elyse and Steven, and their children Alex, Mallory, Jennifer, and Andrew

Elyse Keaton	Meredith Baxter Birney
Steven Keaton	Michael Gross
Alex P. Keaton	Michael J. Fox
Mallory Keaton	Justine Bateman
Jennifer Keaton	Tina Yothers
Andrew Keaton	Garrett Merriman
	Andy Merriman
	Brian Bonsall
Irwin "Skippy" Handelman	Marc Price
Ellen Reed	Tracy Pollan
Nick Moore	Scott Valentine
Rebecca Ryan	Melinda Culea
Arlene Handelman	Tanya Fenmore
Karen Nicholson	Geena Davis
Jeff	John Dukakis

Theme Vocal ("Without Us"): Mindy Sterling, Dennis Tufano (first 10 episodes); Johnny Mathis, Deniece Williams

Producer: Gary David Goldberg

Family Tree

Drama; 60 min; NBC 1/22/83 to 2/26/83

The story of Annie Benjamin and Kevin Nichols, divorced parents who marry and attempt to begin a new life together. See also "The Six of Us."

Annie Benjamin	Anne Archer
Kevin Nichols	Frank Converse
Tess Benjamin	Melora Hardin
Jake Nichols	James Spader
Sam Benjamin	Martin Hewitt
Toby Benjamin	Jonathan Hall Kovacs
Elizabeth Nichols	Joanna Cassidy
Molly Nichols-Tyler	Ann Dusenberry
Elyse Kennedy	Cassie Yates

Producer: Nigel Mackeand, Deanne Bearkley

The Famous Adventures of Mr. Magoo

Cartoon; 30 min; NBC 9/19/64 to 8/21/65

Adaptations of legendary tales and figures of past history with the near-sighted Quincy Magoo as host and star.

Quincy Magoo	Jim Backus

Additional voices: Marvin Miller, Howard Morris, Julie Bennett, Paul Frees, Shepard Menkin

Producer: Henry Saperstein

Famous Jury Trials

Drama; 30 min; DuMont 10/12/49 to 3/12/52

Dramatizations of actual murder cases are reenacted through flashbacks.

Prosecutor	Jim Bender
Defense Attorney	Truman Smith

Famous Lives

Interview Pilot; 60 min; NBC 4/4/83

Revealing interviews with famous celebrities.

Host: Wayne Rogers

Guests: Stefanie Powers, Tom Selleck, Jack Klugman, Magic Johnson

Producer: Gary David Goldberg

Fan Club

Magazine; 30 min; Syn. 9/87

The program, aimed at teenagers, features interviews with celebrities and segments wherein fans can talk to and meet their favorite stars via a contest and video letters.

Host: Mitch Gaylord

Producer: Ron Ziskin, Clay Harrison

Fanfare

A CBS Summer series (7/7/59 to 9/8/59) of repeat dramas from other anthology programs.

Fanfare

Variety; 60 min; CBS 6/19/65 to 9/11/65

Music and songs with host Al Hirt, the Donald McKayle Dancers and the orchestra of Mort Lindsey.

Fang Face

Cartoon; 30 min; ABC 9/9/78 to 9/8/79

The misadventures of Sherman "Fang" Fangsworth, a teenager who changes into a werewolf under a full moon and reverts to normal at sunup.

Fang	Jerry Dexter
Kim	Susan Blu
Biff	Frank Welker
Puggsy	Bart Braverman

Producer: Joe Ruby, Ken Spears

The Fantastic Four

Cartoon; 30 min; ABC 9/9/67 to 3/15/70

When their space ship is caught in a strange radioactive field, four scientists acquire amazing powers. Reed Richards acquires the ability to stretch; his wife, Sue, can become invisible at will; Ben Grimm becomes "The Thing," and Johnny Storm becomes "The Human Torch." Stories depict their battle against evil.

Reed Richards	Gerald Mohr
Sue Richards	Jo Ann Pflug
Ben Grimm	Paul Frees
Johnny Storm	Jack Flounders

Producer: William Hanna, Joseph Barbera

The Fantastic Four

Cartoon; 30 min; NBC 9/9/78 to 9/1/79

While testing a rocket, three people are bombarded by strange cosmic rays that alter their DNA structures. Scientist Reed Richards becomes the plastic-skinned Mr. Fantastic; his wife, Sue, becomes The Invisible Girl; and Ben Grimm, their assistant, becomes the powerful Thing. Stories depict their battle against evil.

Reed Richards	Mike Road
Sue Richards	Ginny Tyler
Ben Grimm	Ted Cassidy
Herbie the Robot	Frank Welker

Producer: David DePatie, Friz Freleng

The Fantastic Journey

Adventure; 60 min; NBC 2/3/77 to 6/17/77

While on a research expedition, a scientific party is engulfed by a mysterious cloud and transported to a forbidding island. There, they learn from Varian, a man from the 23rd century, that they have passed through a time warp and are in a land where the past, future and present co-exist. Episodes relate their attempts to find their way back to their time and world.

Varian	Jared Martin
Jonathan Willaway	Roddy McDowall
Dr. Fred Walters	Carl Franklin
Liana (alien)	Katie Saylor
Dr. Paul Jordan	Scott Thomas
Scott Jordan	Ike Eisenmann
Dr. Eve Costigan	Susan Howard
Dr. Jill Sands	Karen Sommerville

Producer: Bruce Lansbury, Leonard Katzman

Fantastic Voyage

Cartoon; 30 min; ABC 9/14/68 to 9/5/70

The story of four people who, through the Combined Miniature Defense Force, are reduced to microscopic size. Episodes relate their efforts to battle the unseen enemies of the free world.

Jonathan Kidd	Ted Knight
Erica Stone	Jane Webb
Cosby Birdwell	Ted Knight
The Guru	Marvin Miller

Producer: Norm Prescott, Lou Scheimer

Fantasy

Human Interest; 60 min; NBC 9/13/82 to 10/28/83

The wants of pre-selected people are granted in a daily series that makes dreams come true.

Host: Peter Marshall, Leslie Uggams

Co-Host: Jill Whelan, Glenn Scarpelli

Remote Segment Hosts: Meredith MacRae, Randy Hamilton

Announcer: Bill Armstrong

Producer: Merrill Heatter

Fantasy Island

Anthology; 60 min; ABC 1/28/78 to 7/21/84

Stories of people who have paid an unspecified amount for a three day stay on Fantasy Island, a mysterious tropical resort run by Mr. Roarke, to have their dreams become a reality.

Mr. Roarke	Ricardo Montalban
Tattoo (assistant)	Herve Villechaize
Lawrence (assistant)	Christopher Hewett
Julie (assistant)	Wendy Schaal
Cindy (assistant)	Kimberly Beck
The Devil	Roddy McDowall
Princess Nyah (mermaid)	Michelle Phillips

Producer: Aaron Spelling, Leonard Goldberg

Far Out Space Nuts

Comedy; 30 min; CBS 9/6/75 to 9/4/77

While loading food aboard a NASA rocket, crewmen Barney and Junior accidentially launch the ship and are propelled into outer space. Stories relate their adventures on distant planets as they attempt to return to Earth.

Barney	Chuck McCann
Junior	Bob Denver
Honk	Patty Maloney
Lantana	Eve Bruce

Producer: Sid and Marty Krofft

Faraday and Company

Crime Drama; 90 min; NBC 9/26/73 to 1/9/74

After escaping from a Caribbean prison (interned for 28 years on false charges), Frank Faraday returns to Los Angeles and resumes his role as a detective with his now grown son, Steve. Stories relate Frank's investigations and the 1940s-style methods he uses to apprehend the 1970s breed of criminal.

Frank Faraday	Dan Dailey
Steve Faraday	James Naughton
Louise "Lou" Carson	Geraldine Brooks
Holly Barrett	Sharon Gless
Capt. Brinkley	Andrew Duggan

Producer: Leonard B. Stern

Faraway Hill

Serial; 30 min; DuMont 10/2/46 to 12/18/46

Network TV's first serial. The story of a woman (Karen) who seeks to escape the memories of her life with her husband after his death.

Karen St. John	Flora Campbell
Karen's love interest	Mel Brandt
Karen's uncle	Frederick Scott
Karen's aunt	Ann Stell

Producer-Director: David P. Lewis

The Farmer's Daughter

Comedy; 30 min; ABC 9/20/63 to 9/2/66

Hoping to acquire a government teaching job, a Minnesota farm girl (Katy) travels to Washington, D.C., to seek the help of her congressman (Glen). When an application delay puts Katy in a bind (where to stay), Glen offers to let her reside with his family. Katy quickly wins over the widowed Glen's children and accepts Glen's offer to become governess to Steve and Danny. Stories relate Katy's attempts to adjust to city and political life.

Katy Holstrom	Inger Stevens
Glen Morley	William Windom
Steve Morley	Mickey Sholdar
Danny Morley	Rory O'Brien
Agatha Morley	Cathleen Nesbitt
Chester Cooper	Philip Coolidge
Charles Ames	David Lewis
Margaret	Nancy Rennick
	Barbara Bostock
Lars Holstrom	Walter Sande
Mama Holstrom	Alice Frost

Producer: Harry Ackerman

Fashion Coming and Becoming

Experimental; 30 min; DuMont 1945

Fashion advice for women with hostess Betty Furness.

Fashion Magic

A CBS (11/10/50 to 6/15/51) series of beauty tips with hosts Ilka Chase and Arlene Francis.

The Fashion Story

Variety; 30 min; ABC 11/4/48 to 3/1/49

Fashion previews coupled with a skit about Lucky Marshall, a young model struggling to break into show business as a singer.

Lucky Marshall	Marilyn Day
Lucky's boss	Dennis Bohan

Regulars: Elaine Joyce, Carl Reiner, Doris Lane, Pamela O'Neill, Patsy Davis, Don Saxon

Music: Roger Stearns

Fashions on Parade

Women; 30 min; DuMont 2/5/48 to 4/24/49
ABC 4/27/49 to 6/29/49

Adelaide Hawley as the host of a program that features fashion previews, guests, and interviews with designers. Produced by Leon Roth and Charles Caplin.

Fast Draw

Game; 30 min; Syn. 9/68

One member of a two-member team is given a secret phrase. The other team member must guess its identity through charades drawn by his partner.

Host: Johnny Gilbert

Announcer: Fred Scott

Fast Food

Comedy Pilot; 30 min; ABC 8/9/85

The misadventures of Phil Jenkins, the long-suffering manager of Space Burger, a gimmicky hamburger joint that adjoins a college campus.

Phil Jenkins	Avery Schreiber
Crackers	Keanu Reeves
Alixe	Roberta Weiff
Gary	Michael Riley
Father	Geoffrey Bowes
Repair man	Derek McGrath

Producer: Al Rogers

Fast Times

Comedy; 30 min; CBS 3/5/86 to 4/23/86

The comic adventures of a group of students at California's Ridgemont High School. Based on the film, "Fast Times at Ridgemont High."

Linda Barrett	Claudia Wells
Stacy Hamilton	Courtney Thorne-Smith
Jeff Spicoli	Dean Cameron
Mike Damone	Patrick Dempsey
Barbara DeVillvus	Moon Zappa
Brad Hamilton	James Nardini
Arnold Hand	Ray Walston
Hector Vargas	Vincent Schiavelli
Leslie Melon	Kit McDonough
Mark Ratner	Wally Ward
Gillis	Bill Calvert
Doris	Twink Kaplan

Theme Vocal ("Fast Times"): Oingo Boingo

Producer: Allen Rucker, Amy Heckerling

Fat Albert and the Cosby Kids

Cartoon; 30 min; CBS 9/9/72 to 9/8/84

Bill Cosby's recollections of his Northern Philadelphia friends. Also known as "The New Fat Albert Show."

Bill Cosby/Fat
  Albert/
Mush Mouth/Dumb
  Donald   Bill Cosby
Russell/Bucky   Jan Crawford
Weird Harold   Bill Cosby
                 Gerald Edwards

Producer: Bill Cosby, Norm Prescott, Lou Scheimer, Arthur H. Nadel

Father Brown

Mystery; 60 min; PBS 11/2/82 to 11/23/82

The exploits of Father John Brown, a Catholic parish priest who dabbles as an amateur detective. Based on the G.K. Chesterton stories.

Father John Brown   Kenneth More
Det. H. Flambeau   Dennis Burgess

Producer: Ian Fordyce

Father Dear Father

Comedy; 30 min; Syn. 1977

The misadventures of Patrick Glover, a British thriller writer, as he attempts to cope with his ex-wife, Barbara, his beautiful daughters, Anna and Karen, and his housekeeper, Matilda.

Patrick Glover   Patrick Cargill
Anna Glover   Natasha Pyne
Karen Glover   Ann Holloway
Matilda Harris
  (Nanny)   Noel Dyson
Barbara Mossman   Ursula Howells
Bill Mossman   Tony Britton
                 Patrick Holt
Georgie Thompson Sally Bazley
               Dawn Addams
Mrs. Glover   Joyce Carey
Philip Glover   Donald Sinden
Timothy Tanner   Jeremy Child

Producer: William Stewart

Father Knows Best

Comedy; 30 min; CBS 10/3/54 to 3/27/55
                NBC 8/31/55 to 9/17/58
                CBS 9/22/58 to 9/17/62

The dreams, ambitions and frustrations of the Andersons: Jim, manager of the General In-surance Company, his wife, Margaret, and their children Betty, Bud and Kathy.

Jim Anderson   Robert Young
Margaret Anderson   Jane Wyatt
Betty Anderson   Elinor Donahue
Bud Anderson   Billy Gray
Kathy Anderson   Lauren Chapin
Ed Davis   Robert Foulk
Myrtle Davis   Vivi Jannis
Miss Thomas   Sarah Selby
Claude Messner   Jimmy Bates
Kippy Watkins   Paul Wallace
Joyce Kendall   Roberta Shore
Joe Phillips   Peter Heisser
Ralph Little   Robert Chapman
Patty Davis   Tina Thompson
                 Reba Waters
Dottie Snow   Yvonne Lime
Burgess Vale/Grover
  Adams   Richard Eyer

Producer: Eugene B. Rodney, Robert Young

Father Knows Best (Pilot)

Comedy Pilot; 30 min; NBC 5/27/54

The prototype episode, titled "Keep It in the Family" for "Father Knows Best" (about an American family of five: parents Tom and Grace, and their children, Peggy, Jeff, and Patty). Broadcast on "Ford Theatre." Written by Paul West and Roswell Rogers and directed by William Russell.

Tom   Robert Young
Grace   Ellen Drew
Peggy   Sally Fraser
Jeff   Gordon Gebert
Patty   Tina Thompson

Producer: Eugene B. Rodney

The Father Knows Best Reunions

Comedy; 90 min; NBC 5/15/77 and 12/18/77

On May 15, 1977, NBC presented the first reunion episode of the "Father Knows Best" series called "The Father Knows Best Reunion." In the story, the original cast is reunited to celebrate Jim and Margaret's 35th wedding anniversary. In the second special, "Home for Christmas," the original Anderson family gathers to celebrate the holidays. (Betty, the eldest daughter, is a widow with two girls, Ellen and Jenny; Bud, the middle child, is married to Jean and the father of a son [Robby]; and Kathy, the youngest child, is engaged to Dr. Jason Harper.)

Jim Anderson	Robert Young
Margaret Anderson	Jane Wyatt
Betty Anderson	Elinor Donahue
Bud Anderson	Billy Gray
Kathy Anderson	Lauren Chapin
Jean Anderson	Susan Adams
Ellen	Kyle Richards
Jenny	Cari Anne Warder
Robby Anderson	Christopher Gardner
Dr. Jason Harper	Hal England

Father Murphy

Drama; 60 min; NBC 11/3/81 to 12/28/82

The story of John Michael Murphy, an 1870s frontiersman who pretends to be a priest in an attempt to care for the orphaned children of the Gold Hill School.

John Murphy	Merlin Olsen
Moses Gage	Moses Gunn
Mae Woodward	Katherine Cannon
Will Adams	Timothy Gibbs
Lizette Winkler	Lisa Trusel
Ephram Winkler	Scott Mellini
Howard Rodman	Charles Tyner
Evelyn Tuttle	Ivy Bethune
Paul Garrett	Burr DeBenning
Caleb	Charles Cooper
Father Joseph Parker	Richard Bergman
Matt Gilbert	Byron Thames
David Gilbert	Kirk Brennan
Jenny	Tracey Gold
Beatrice	Tina Yothers
Eli	Chez Lester

Producer: Michael Landon, Kent McCray

Father O Father

Comedy Pilot; 30 min; ABC 8/22/77

The clash between Father Flicker, the conservative pastor of Sts. Peter and Paul Church in Boston, and Father Morgan, his liberal assistant.

Father Flicker	Iggie Wolfington
Father Morgan	Dennis Dugan
Helen Harper	Barbara Sharma
Mrs. Taylor	Kathleen Freeman
Handyman Hocker	Spo-Dee-Odee

Producer: Jerry Weintraub

Father of the Bride

Comedy; 30 min; CBS 9/29/61 to 9/14/62

The struggles of newlyweds Kay and Buckley Dunston; and the trials and tribulations of Kay's father, Stanley, who is having a hard time adjusting to the fact that his little girl has married.

Stanley Banks	Leon Ames
Ellie Banks	Ruth Warrick
Kay Banks	Myrna Fahey
Buckley Dunston	Burt Metcalfe
Tommy Banks	Rickie Sorensen
Delilah	Ruby Dandridge
Herbert Dunston	Ransom Sherman
Doris Dunston	Lurene Tuttle

Producer: Robert Maxwell

Father on Trial

Comedy Pilot; 30 min; NBC 9/3/72

The romantic misadventures of Mike Bryan, a widowed judge with five children, and Billie Roman, a younger woman who is attempting to date him despite the differences in their age.

Mike Bryan	Darren McGavin
Billie Roman	Barbara Feldon
Maggie	Joan Tompkins
Stevie Bryan	Moosie Drier
Mike Bryan Jr.	Kieran Mullaney
Mike's daughter	Michelle Tobin
Mike's daughter	Cheri Mepham
Mike's son	Dermott Downs

Producer-Writer-Director: Melville Shavelson

Fathers and Sons

Comedy Pilot; 30 min; NBC 6/16/85

The humorous and sometimes heartwarming relationship between a group of boys and their fathers. Changed somewhat for the series (next title).

Buddy Landau	Merlin Olsen
Ellen, Buddy's wife	Kelly Sanders
Lanny, Buddy's son	Jason Late
Sean Flynn, Lanny's friend	Andre Gower
Michael, Sean's father	Rick Nelson
Matt Bolen, Lanny's friend	Ian Fried
Richard, Matt's father	Nicholas Guest
Brandon Russo, Lanny's friend	Hakeem Abdul-Samad

Producer: Michael Zinberg, Nick Arnold

Fathers and Sons

Comedy; 30 min; NBC 4/6/86 to 5/4/86

The story of Buddy Landau, a dedicated coach at the Charles Lindberg Elementary School. (In the pilot, above title, Buddy had been a construction worker.)

Buddy Landau	Merlin Olsen
Ellen, his wife	Kelly Sanders
Lanny, his son	Jason Late
Sean Flynn, Lanny's friend	Andre Gower
Matt Bolen, Lanny's friend	Ian Fried
Brandon Russo, Lanny's friend	Hakeem Abdul-Samad
Tony Salvadore, Buddy's assistant	Bert Rosario
Richard, Matt's father	Nicholas Guest
Audrey, Sean's mother	Susan Walden
Mr. Belnap, a teacher	Sal Viscuso

Producer: Michael Zinberg

Father's Day

Comedy Pilot; 30 min; ABC 7/25/86

Incidents in the life of Robert Morgan, an harrassed IRS auditor.

Robert Morgan	Robert Klein
Mary Ellen Morgan	Frances Lee McCain
Daisy Morgan	Royana Black
Jonathan Morgan	Josh Blake

Producer: Merrill Grant, Mort Lackman

Fawlty Towers

Comedy; 30 min; Syn. 1977

The chaotic misadventures of Basil Fawlty, the rude and totally incompetent innkeeper of Fawlty Towers, a hotel at 16 Elwood Avenue in Devonish, England.

Basil Fawlty	John Cleese
Sybil Fawlty	Prunella Scales
Polly Sherman	Connie Booth
Manuel	Andrew Sachs
Terry	Brian Hall
Major Gowen	Ballard Berkeley
Miss Tibbs	Gilly Flower
Miss Gatsby	Renee Roberts

Producer: John Davies

Fay

Comedy; 30 min; NBC 9/4/75 to 10/23/75

The romantic misadventures of Fay Stuart, a middle-aged divorcee living in San Francisco.

Fay Stuart	Lee Grant
Jack Stuart	Joe Silver
Linda Baines	Margaret Willock
Dr. Elliott Baines	Stewart Moss
Lillian	Audra Lindley
Danny Messina	Bill Gerber
Al Cassidy	Norman Alden
Letty Gilmore	Lillian Lehman

Producer: Paul Junger Witt

Faye and Skitch

Variety; 15 min; NBC 10/26/53 to 10/22/54

Music, songs and interviews with Hosts Faye Emerson and Skitch Henderson. Producer: Johnny Stearns.

Faye Emerson's Wonderful Town

Interview; 30 min; CBS 6/16/51 to 4/19/52

The program, broadcast from a different locale each week, features interviews with outstanding citizens.

Hostess: Faye Emerson

Vocalists: The Don Large Chorus

Music: Skitch Henderson

Producer: Gil Fates

The FBI

Crime Drama; 60 min; ABC 9/19/65 to 9/1/74

Dramatizations based on the files of the Federal Bureau of Investigation.

Insp. Lewis Erskine	Efrem Zimbalist Jr.
Arthur Ward	Philip Abbott
Jim Rhodes	Stephen Brooks
Barbara Erskine	Lynn Loring
Tom Colby	Tom Reynolds
Chris Daniels	Shelly Novack
Chet Randolph	Anthony Eisley
Narrator	Marvin Miller

Producer: Quinn Martin

F.D.R.

Documentary; 30 min; ABC 1/8/65 to 9/10/65

The life and administration of President Franklin D. Roosevelt with his writings read by Charlton Heston. Hosted by Arthur Kennedy.

Fearless Fosdick

Children; 30 min; NBC 6/1/52 to 9/8/52

The comic escapades of Fearless Fosdick, a police detective created by Al Capp. Characters are marionettes.

Voice/Puppeteer: Hope and Mory Bunin

The Feather and Father Gang

Crime Drama; 60 min; ABC 3/7/77 to 8/6/77

The cases of Toni "Feather" Danton, an attorney with Huffaker, Danton and Binkwell, and her father, Harry, an ex-con who incorporates his knowledge of the confidence game to help his daughter solve crimes.

Toni Danton	Stefanie Powers
Harry Danton	Harold Gould
Lou	Lewis Charles
Margo	Joan Shawlee
Enzo	Frank Delfino
Michael	Monte Landis
Murphy	Dick O'Neill
J.C. Hadley	Edward Winter
"Huff" Huffaker	William H. Bassett
Binkwell	Allen Williams

Theme Song "The Feather and Father Theme" by George Romanis

Producer: Larry White

Feather Your Nest

Game; 30 min; NBC 10/4/54 to 7/27/56

Players first select items from a merchandise showcase then have to find a feather that is hidden somewhere in the article. Each feather contains a question that, if correctly answered, awards him that article.

Host: Bud Collyer

Assistant: Lou Prentiss, Janice Carter, Jean Williams

Producer: Jack Selden

Featherstone's Nest

Comedy Pilot; 30 min; CBS 8/1/79

The story of pediatrician Charlie Featherstone and his attempts to run a house and cope with two daughters while his wife is away at law school.

Charlie Featherstone	Ken Berry
Kelly Featherstone	Susan Swift
Courtney Featherstone	Dana Hill
Bella Beacham	Virginia Capers
Everett Buhl	Phil Leeds
Dr. John DeMott	Fred Morsell
Sue Sue	Rhonda Foxx

Producer: Danny Thomas, Ronald Jacobs

Federal Agent

Crime Drama Pilot; 30 min; DuMont 7/20/49

A proposed series of dramatizations based on the files of Edward E. Conroy, a chief of the

FBI in N.Y.C. Aired on "Program Playhouse."

Narrator	Edward E. Conroy
Gangster	Joe DeSantis
Sheriff	Arnold Robinson

Producer: Chick Vincent, James L. Caddigan

Federal Men

See "Treasury Men in Action."

Feel the Heat

Crime Drama Pilot; 60 min; ABC 8/5/83

The exploits of Andy Thorn, an ex-cop turned private detective (in Key Blanco, Florida) and Honor Campbell, a state attorney (in Bouldon County), as they team to solve crimes.

Andy Thorn	Nick Mancuso
Honor Campbell	Lisa Eichhorn
Capt. Barney Hill	Robert Hooks
Sally Long	Paula Kelly
Det. Frank Dawson	Philip Clark

Producer: Edward K. Milkis, Ronald Cohen

Felix the Cat

Cartoon; 4 min; Syn 1960

Cliff-hanger type episodes about the adventures of Felix, a cat who possesses a magic black bag.

Jack Mercer as the voice of: Felix, The Professor, Rockbottom and Poindexter

The Felony Squad

Crime Drama; 30 min; ABC 9/12/66 to 1/31/69

The exploits of Sam Stone and Jim Briggs, plainclothes detectives with the L.A.P.D.

Det. Sam Stone	Howard Duff
Det. Jim Briggs	Dennis Cole
Sgt. Dan Briggs	Ben Alexander
Capt. Ed Franks	Barney Phillips
Capt. Nye	Frank Maxwell

Producer: Walter Grauman

The Feminine Touch

Variety; 15 min; ABC 6/18/51 to 8/17/51

Music and songs with host John Conte and vocalist Marguerite Hamilton. Music by the Tony Mottola Trio.

Fernwood 2-Night

Satire; 30 min; Syn. 9/77

A satirization of the TV talk show as seen through the intentionally appalling interviews of Barth Gimble, the host of "Fernwood 2-Night" on fictional Channel 6 in Fernwood, Ohio. See also "America 2-Night."

Barth Gimble	Martin Mull
Jerry Hubbard	Fred Willard
Happy Kayne	Frank DeVol

Producer: Louis J. Horvitz, Alan Thicke

The Fess Parker Show

Comedy Pilot; 30 min; CBS 3/28/74

The story of a widower (Fess) and his attempts to raise three mischievous daughters (Susie, Beth and Holly).

Fess Hamilton	Fess Parker
Susie Hamilton	Cynthia Eilbacher
Beth Hamilton	Dawn Lyn
Holly Hamilton	Michelle Stacy
Esther Crowe	Florence Lake
Julie Weston	Linda Dano

Producer: Don Fedderson

Festival of Stars

An NBC series (6/30/56 to 9/8/56 and 7/2/57 to 9/17/57) of repeat dramas from "The Loretta Young Theater."

Fibber McGee and Molly

Comedy; 30 min; NBC 9/15/59 to 1/26/60

The trials and tribulations of Fibber and Molly McGee, a married couple who are beset with problems due to Fibber, an amateur inventor and expert liar. Set in the town of Wistful Vista.

Fibber McGee	Bob Sweeney
Molly McGee	Cathy Lewis
Mayor Charles LaTrivia	Hal Peary
Roy Norris	Paul Smith
Hazel Norris	Elisabeth Fraser
Dr. John Gamble	Addison Richards
Teeny	Barbara Beaird
Mrs. LaTrivia	Dorothy Neumann

Producer: William Asher

15 With Faye

Variety; 15 min; CBS 10/4/49 to 4/12/52

A daily series of music and interviews with hostess Faye Emerson, regulars Mary Bennett and Kenneth Banghart, and the music of Skitch Henderson.

The 54th Street Revue

Variety; 60 min; CBS 5/5/49 to 3/25/50

A music and comedy revue, featuring new talent discoveries, from a studio on 54th Street in New York.

Host: Al Bernie, Billy Vine, Jack Sterling, Joey Faye

Regulars: Carl Reiner, Patricia Bright, Marilyn Day, Cliff Edwards, Bambi Linn, Russell Arms, Joe Silver, Annabell Lyons

Music: Albert Selden, Harry Sosnik, Bill Scudder

50 Grand Slam

Game; 30 min; NBC 10/4/76 to 12/31/76

Players attempt to win $50,000 by competing in eight stages of question and answer rounds. An incorrect answer can cost a player all that he has earned and it is his decision at what cash amount to quit.

Host: Tom Kennedy

Announcer: John Harlan

Producer: Ralph Edwards

Fight Back: With David Horowitz

Advice; 30 min; Syn. 9/80

The program is designed to make viewers aware of new products and inform them of problems in shopping and purchasing goods.

Host: David Horowitz

Theme Vocal ("Fight Back"): Steve Donn

Producer: Lloyd Thaxton

The Fighting Nightingales

Comedy Pilot; 30 min; CBS 1/16/78

Incidents in the lives of combat-weary nurses stationed in Korea during the war.

Maj. Kate Steele	Adrienne Barbeau
Col. H. Jonas Boyette	Ken Mars
Lt. Angie Finelli	Livia Genise
Lt. Hope Phillips	Stephanie Faracy
Pvt. Tyrone Vallone	Randy Stumpf
Sgt. George Baker	George Whiteman

Producer: Barry Sand, Alan Uger

The Files of Jeffrey Jones

Crime Drama; 30 min; Syn. 1955

The exploits of Jeffrey Jones, a New York-based confidential private investigator.

Jeffrey Jones	Don Haggerty
Michele "Mike" Malone	Gloria Henry

Producer: Lindsley Parsons

Filthy Rich

Comedy; 30 min; CBS 8/9/82 to 6/14/83

The last will and testament of Big Guy Beck stipulates that the wealthy, snobbish Beck family must share a Memphis, Tennessee, mansion with their poor relations, the Weschesters. Stories relate the efforts of both families to live together to inherit Big Guy's vast estate.

Big Guy Beck	Slim Pickens
	Forrest Tucker
Kathleen Beck	Delta Burke
Carlotta Beck	Dixie Carter
Marshall Beck	Michael Lombard
Stanley Beck	Charles Frank
Wild Bill Weschester	Jerry Hardin
Bootsie Weschester	Ann Wedgeworth
Winona "Mother B"	
Beck	Nedra Volz

Theme Vocal ("Filthy Rich"): Bucky Jones, Ronnie McDowall

Producer: Linda Bloodworth

Finder of Lost Loves

Drama; 60 min; ABC 9/22/84 to 8/24/85

When his wife dies and Cary Maxwell finds that he cannot replace her love, he begins Maxwell Ltd., an organization that helps people who deeply love each other, but have drifted apart, find their love again.

Cary Maxwell	Anthony Franciosa
Daisy Lloyd	Deborah Adair
Rita Hargrove	Anne Jeffreys
Brian Fletcher	Richard Kanter
Lyman	Larry Flash Jenkins

Producer: Aaron Spelling, Douglas S. Cramer

A Fine Romance

Comedy Pilot; 30 min; CBS 7/20/83

The story of two opposites—Laura Prescott, a linguist, and Mike Selway, a landscape artist—who meet, fall in love, and begin an unlikely relationship.

Laura Prescott	Julie Kavner
Mike Selway	Leo Burmester
Helen	Kristen Meadows
Phil	Kevin Conroy
Jean	Amy Wright
Harry	Jeffrey Jones

Producer: Don Taffner

Fireball Fun for All

Variety; 60 min; NBC 6/28/49 to 10/27/49

Burlesque-style music, songs, and comedy sketches.

Host: John "Ole" Olsen, Harold "Chick" Johnson

Regulars: Patricia Donahue, Marty May, June Johnson, Bill Hayes, J.C. Olsen, The Lynn Duddy Singers

Orchestra: Al Goodman, Charles Sanford

Producer: Ezra Stone

Fireball XL-5

Marionettes; 30 min; NBC 10/5/63 to 9/25/65

The futuristic exploits of Steve Zodiak, a Galaxy Patrol Ranger and pilot of Fireball XL-5, as he protects the planets of a united solar system.

Voices: Paul Maxwell, Sylvia Anderson, David Graham, John Bluthal

Producer: Gerry Anderson

Firehouse

Drama; 30 min; ABC 1/17/74 to 8/1/74

The work of the men of Engine Company Number 23 of the L.A. County Fire Department.

Capt. Spike Ryerson	James Drury
Fireman Hank	
Myers	Richard Jaeckel
Fireman Sonny	
Capito	Michael Delano
Fireman Cal Dakin	Bill Overton
Fireman Scotty	
Smith	Scott Smith
Fireman Billy	
Dalzell	Brad David

Producer: Aaron Spelling, Leonard Goldberg

Fireside Theatre

Anthology; 30 min; NBC 4/5/49 to 8/23/55

Filmed dramas that feature both well known and obscure performers. Stars include Amanda Blake, Yul Brynner, Wally Cox, Irene Vernon, Hugh O'Brian, Jim Davis, Gloria Marshall, George Reeves, Marjorie Lord, Keye Luke, Alan Hale Jr., Claude Akins, Ernest Borgnine, Angela Lansbury,

Maureen O'Sullivan, Barbara Billingsley and Betty Lynn.

Producer: Frank Wisbar

The Firm

Crime Drama Pilot; 60 min; NBC 8/23/83

The cases of Martin Barry and Grace Harmon, a New York-based father and daughter legal team.

Martin Barry	Wilford Brimley
Grace Harmon	Anne Twomey
Francine	Carolyn Byrd
Dick Albright	Paul Dooley
Jane Albright	Lori Putnam
Peter Blau	Kevin Conway
Sgt. Albioni	Tony Turco
Sgt. Johnson	Ann Maria Horsford

Producer: Herbert Brodkin

First and Ten

Comedy; 30 min; HBO 9/3/85 to 1/21/86

When she catches her husband having an affair (with another man), Diane Barrow sues for divorce and receives as part of the settlement, the California Bulls, a professional football team. Episodes focus on Diane's efforts to run the team. Contains nudity, strong language, and adult situations. See also "First and Ten: The Championships" and "Training Camp: The Bulls Are Back."

Diane Barrow	Delta Burke
Coach Ernie Dinardo	Reid Shelton
Rona	Ruta Lee
Bob Dorsey	Geoffrey Scott
Roger Barrow	Robert Logan*
	Clayton Landley
Mace Petty	Marshall Teague
Carl Witherspoon	Sam Scarber
Brice Smith	Jeff East
Betty Ann Smith	Cathy Silvers
Sal Arcola	Michael Gazzo
Ray "Mad Dog" Smears	Tony Longo
Bubba Kincaid	Prince Hughes
Jethro Snell	Marcus Allen
Otis	Cliff Fraser
Fran Tarkenton	Himself

Producer: Peter Locke, Donald Kushner

*Role in the pilot (12/11/84).

First and Ten: The Championships

Comedy; 30 min; HBO 12/30/86 to 1/20/87

A continuation from "Training Camp: The Bulls Are Back," which follows the California Bulls as they head toward the championships.

Diane Barrow	Delta Burke
Coach Ernie Dinardo	Reid Shelton
T.D. Parker	O.J. Simpson
Tom Yinessa	Jason Beghe
Mad Dog	Tony Longo
Jamie Waldrom	Jeff Kaate
Bubba Kincaid	Prince Hughes
Fred Grier	Stan Kamber
Jethro	Marcus Allen
Rhonda	Gloria Gifford

Producer: Donald Kushner, Peter Locke

The First Hundred Years

Drama; 15 min; CBS 12/4/50 to 6/27/52

Incidents in the lives of Chris and Connie Thayer, a young newlywed couple.

Chris Thayer	Jimmy Lydon
Connie Thayer	Anne Sargent
	Olive Stacey
Connie's father	Robert Armstrong
Connie's mother	Nana Bryant
Chris's father	Don Tobin
Chris's mother	Valerie Cassort

Producer: Hoyt Allen

The First Hundred Years

Comedy Pilot; 30 min; CBS 5/27/62

The story of an engineering student (Ben) who must work nights in a supermarket to support his family.

Ben Duncan	Roger Perry
Connie Duncan	Joyce Bulifant
Richard Martin	Nick Adams
Dina Martin	Barbara Bostock

Producer: Everett Freeman, John Forsythe

First Person Singular

Anthology; 30 min; DuMont 7/3/53 to 9/11/53

Dramas that incorporate the subjective camera. The TV camera becomes the eyes of the main character; and an unseen voice sets the emotional tone. See also "The Plainclothesman."

First Time, Second Time

Comedy Pilot; 30 min; CBS 10/25/80

The story of a think-tank executive (Doug) whose personal and professional worlds merge to cause unusual problems.

Doug Fitzpatrick	Ronny Cox
Karen Fitzpatrick	Julie Cobb
David Fitzpatrick	David Hollander
Joan Armstrong	Mary Frann
Jhampur Nehrudi	Sumant

Producer: Bob Comfort, Rick Kellard

Fish

Comedy; 30 min; ABC 2/5/77 to 6/8/78

The story of Phil Fish, a retired detective, and his wife, Bernice, and their efforts to care for five streetwise delinquents that have been assigned to them. A spin-off from "Barney Miller."

Phil Fish	Abe Vigoda
Bernice Fish	Florence Stanley
Jilly	Denise Miller
Diane	Sarah Natoli
Mike	Lenny Bari
Victor	John Cassisi
Loomis	Todd Bridges
Charlie Harrison	Barry Gordon
Manuel	David Yanez

Producer: Danny Arnold

Fisherman's Wharf

Comedy Pilot; 30 min; NBC 2/1/81

The bickering relationship* between the Barberas and the Funuccis, two Italian-American families.

Vince Barbera	Tom Quinn
Nina Barbera	Elaine Giftos
Johnny Barbera	Lenny Bari
Michael Barbera	Glenn Scarpelli
Tony Funucci	Bruce Gordon
Tom Funucci	Louis Gordon
Pa Funucci	Joe Vitalie
Muldoon	Rex Everhart
Laverne	Lola Mason

Producer: Roger Schulman, John Baskin

*Began in Sicily in 1910 when Grandpa Funucci accused Grandpa Barbera of breaking his toe line.

Fit for a King

Comedy Pilot; 30 min; NBC 6/11/82

The problems that befall the King of Braeland (a mythical European kingdom), his wife, and their children.

King Alfred	Dick Van Patten
Queen Mary Ella	Katherine Helmond
Princess Nicole	Talia Balsam
Prince Conrad	Adam Redfield
Price Maximillian	Todd Waring
Duchess Edwina	Maxine Stuart
Lord Dupree	Leonard Frey
Victor	Gregory Brown
Sandra Bacon	Audrey Landers

Producer: Eugenie Ross-Leming, Brad Buckner

Fitz and Bones

Crime Drama; 60 min; NBC 10/24/81 to 11/14/81

The story-gathering assignments of Ryan Fitzpatrick, on-the-air reporter for San Francisco's KSFB-TV "Newsline 3," and his cameraman, Bones Howard.

Ryan Fitzpatrick	Dick Smothers
Bones Howard	Tom Smothers
Terri Seymour	Diana Muldaur
Lt. Rosie Cochran	Lynnette Mettey
Robert Whitemore	Mike Kellin
Lawrence Brody	Roger C. Carmel
Sgt. Charlie Wright	Tom Stern
Judy Fong	Momo Yashima
Mel Bishop	Doug Hale

Producer: James D. Parriott, Lou Shaw

The Fitzpatricks

Drama; 60 min; CBS 9/5/77 to 1/10/78

Events in the lives of the Fitzpatricks, an Irish-Catholic family of six living in Detroit, Michigan.

Mike Fitzpatrick	Bert Kramer
Maggie Fitzpatrick	Mariclare Costello
Maureen Fitzpatrick	Michele Tobin
Jack Fitzpatrick	James McNichol
Max Fitzpatrick	Sean Marshall
Sean Fitzpatrick	Clark Brandon
Kerry Gerardi	Helen Hunt

Producer: Philip Mandelker

Five Fingers

Mystery; 60 min; NBC 10/3/59 to 1/6/60

The exploits of Victor Sebastian and Simone Genet, U.S. counterintelligence agents based in Europe.

Victor Sebastian	David Hedison
Simone Genet	Luciana Paluzzi
Mr. Robertson	Paul Burke

Producer: Martin Manulis

Flamingo Road

Drama; 60 min; NBC 1/6/81 to 7/13/82

Events in the lives of the Weldons, a wealthy Florida family whose lives are corrupted by power and greed.

Titus Semple	Howard Duff
Claude Weldon	Kevin McCarthy
Eudora Weldon	Barbara Rush
Constance Weldon	Morgan Fairchild
Lute Mae Saunders	Stella Stevens
Lane Ballou	Cristina Raines
Fielding Carlysle	Mark Harmon
Sam Curtis	John Beck
Skip Semple	Woody Brown
Elmo Tyson	Peter Donat
Jasper	Glenn Richards
Michael Tyrone	David Selby
Sande Swanson	Cynthia Sikes
Vanessa Curtis	Trisha Noble
	Andra Akers
Christine Kovacs	Denise Galik
Alice Kovacs	Marcia Rodd
Slade	Michael Baseleon
Harrison Brand	Charles Cioffi

Producer: Michael Filerman, Rita Lakin, Lee Rich

Flannery and Quilt

Comedy Pilot; 30 min; NBC 2/1/76

The misadventures of Luke Flannery and Samuel Quilt, argumentative senior citizens who live together but disagree on everything.

Luke Flannery	Red Buttons
Samuel Quilt	Harold Gould
Rose Caselli	Pat Finley
Kevin Caselli	Howard Storm
Adam Flannery	Michael Lembeck

Producer-Director: Carl Reiner

Flash Gordon

Adventure; 30 min; Syn. 1953

The futuristic exploits (2203 A.D.) of Flash Gordon, Dale Arden and Alexis Zarkov, members of the Galactic Bureau of Investigation, as they strive to maintain peace in outer space. Filmed in West Berlin.

Flash Gordon	Steve Holland
Dale Arden	Irene Champlin
Dr. Alexis Zarkov	Joseph Nash
Cmdr. Paul Richards	Henry Beckman

Producer: Wenzel Luedecke

Flash Gordon

Cartoon; 30 min; NBC 9/8/79 to 12/1/79

The exploits of Flash Gordon as he and Dale Arden and Dr. Zarkov struggle to protect the universe from the evil Ming the Merciless, ruler of the planet Mongo.

Flash Gordon	Robert Ridgely
Dale Arden	Diane Pershing
Dr. Hans Zarkov	Alan Oppenheimer
Ming	Alan Oppenheimer
Princess Aura	Melendy Britt
Thun	Allan Melvin
Prince Barin	Robert Ridgely
Queen Fria	Diane Pershing
Vulcan	Allan Melvin

Producer: Norm Prescott, Lou Scheimer

Flatbush

Comedy; 30 min; CBS 2/26/79 to 3/12/79

The misadventures of the Fungos, a close-knit Brooklyn, New York street gang.

Presto Prestopolos	Joseph Cali
Socks Palermo	Adrian Zmed
Turtle Romero	Vincent Bufano
Joey Dee	Randy Stumpf
Figgy Figueroa	Sandy Helberg
Mrs. Fortunato	Helen Verbit
Mr. Esposito	Anthony Ponzini

Producer: Philip Capice, Gary Adelson

Flatbush/Avenue J

Comedy Pilot; 30 min; ABC 8/24/76

The struggles of newlyweds Stanley and Frannie Rosello as they begin their new lives together on Avenue J in Flatbush, Brooklyn, N.Y.

Stanley Rosello	Paul Sylvan
Frannie Rosello	Brooke Adams
Annie Yukaminelli	Jamie Donnelly
Wimpy Morzallo	Paul Jabara

Producer: Martin Davidson

Flatfoots

Comedy Pilot; 30 min; NBC 7/3/82

The misadventures of Frank Shackelford and Gabe Fortunato, two bumbling L.A.P.D. officers.

Off. Frank Shackelford	John Reilly
Off. Gabe Fortunato	Todd Susman
Sgt. Lindsey Andrews	Jason Bernard
Off. April Mikulanitz	April Clough
Off. Dave Heinrich	Gary Epp
Off. George Pesky	Raymond Singer
Sunny	Tracie Savage

Producer: A.C. Lyles, Lowell Ganz, Arthur Silver

Flight to Rhythm

Variety; 15 min; DuMont 3/10/49 to 9/22/49

Music and songs with hostess Delora Bueno and the music of Miguelito Valdez.

The Flim-Flam Man

Comedy Pilot; 30 min; NBC 9/1/69

The story of Mordecai Jones, a Robin Hood-like con man who cheats only those who deserve to be flim-flammed.

Mordecai Jones	Forrest Tucker
Curley Treadway	Don Scardino
Mr. Packard	James Gregory
Mrs. Packard	Elena Verdugo
Bonnie Lee	Lada Edmonds Jr.
Weehunt	Dub Taylor

The Flintstone Kids

Cartoon; 60 min; ABC 9/13/86 (Premiere)

The prehistoric adventures of Fred, Barney, Wilma, and Betty as children growing up in Bedrock. See also "The Flintstones."

Voices: Charlie Adler, Bever-Leigh Banfield, Jon Bauman, Michael Bell, Mel Blanc, Susan Blu, Hamilton Camp, Henry Corden, Julie Dees, Rick Dees, Pat Farley, June Foray, Arte Johnson, Ken Mars, Howard Morris, George O'Hanlon, Avery Schreiber, Ronnie Schell, Marilyn Schreffler, John Stephenson, Lennie Weinrib, Frank Welker

Producer: William Hanna, Joseph Barbera

The Flintstones

Cartoon; 30 min; ABC 9/30/60 to 9/2/66

Events in the lives of Fred and Wilma Flintstone and their friends Barney and Betty Rubble, prehistoric families who live in Bedrock in the year 1,000,040 B.C.

Fred Flintstone	Alan Reed
Wilma Flintstone	Jean VanderPyl
Barney Rubble	Mel Blanc
Betty Rubble	Bea Benadaret
	Gerry Johnson
Dino	Don Messick
Pebbles Flintstone	Jean VanderPyl
Bamm Bamm Rubble	Don Messick
George Slate	John Stephenson

Producer: William Hanna, Joseph Barbera

The Flintstones

Cartoon; 30 min; NBC 10/4/81 to 10/18/81

Continued events in the lives of the Flintstone and Rubble families.

Fred Flintstone	Henry Corden
Wilma Flintstone	Jean VanderPyl
Pebbles Flintstone	Jean VanderPyl
Barney Rubble	Mel Blanc
Betty Rubble	Gay Autterson
Bamm Bamm Rubble	Don Messick
Dino	Mel Blanc

The Flintstones Comedy Hour

Cartoon; 60 min; CBS 9/9/72 to 1/26/74

Events in the lives of the Flintstone and Rubble families.

Fred Flintstone	Alan Reed
Wilma Flintstone	Jean VanderPyl
Pebbles Flintstone	Mickey Stevens
Barney Rubble	Mel Blanc
Betty Rubble	Gay Hartwig
Bamm Bamm Rubble	Jay North
George Slate	John Stephenson
Penny	Mitzi McCall
Moonrock	Lennie Weinrib
Schleprock	Don Messick

Flintstones Family Adventures

Cartoon; 60 min; NBC 11/22/80 to 9/5/81

Segments: "The Flintstones" (the lives of Fred, Wilma, Barney, and Betty); "Pebbles, Dino and Bamm Bamm" (the antics of Pebbles and Bamm Bamm as they attend Bedrock High School); "The Bedrock Cops" (Fred and Barney as police officers); "Dino and the Cave Mouse" (Dino's efforts to catch the mouse that lives in Fred's home); "The Frankenstones" (a family of movie-like monsters); "Captain Caveman" (Wilma and Betty as reporters aided by the crime-fighting Captain Caveman).

Fred Flintstone	Henry Corden
Wilma Flintstone	Jean VanderPyl
Pebbles Flintstone	Russi Taylor
Barney Rubble	Mel Blanc
Betty Rubble	Gay Autterson
Bamm Bamm Rubble	Michael Sheehan
Dino	Mel Blanc
Sgt. Boulder	Lennie Weinrib
Cavemouse	Russi Taylor
Frank Frankenstone	Charles Nelson Reilly
Oblivia Frankenstone	Pat Parris
Hidea Frankenstone	Ruta Lee
Stubby Frankenstone	Jim MacGeorge
Freaky	Paul Reubens
Atrocia	Zelda Rubinstein
Rockjaw	Frank Welker
Lou Granite	Ken Mars
Captain Caveman	Mel Blanc

The Flintstones Funnies

Cartoon; 30 min; NBC 9/11/81 to 9/8/84

The misadventures of the Flintstone and Rubble families and their new neighbors, the Frankenstones, a family who resemble "The Addams Family."

Fred Flintstone	Henry Corden
Wilma Flintstone	Jean VanderPyl
Pebbles Flintstone	Russi Taylor
Barney Rubble	Mel Blanc
Betty Rubble	Gay Autterson
Bamm Bamm Rubble	Michael Sheehan
Frank Frankenstone	Charles Nelson Reilly
Oblivia Frankenstone	Pat Parris
Hidea Frankenstone	Ruta Lee
Atrocia Frankenstone	Zelda Rubinstein
Freaky	Paul Reubens
Rockjaw	Frank Welker

Producer: William Hanna, Joseph Barbera

The Flip Wilson Show

Variety; 60 min; NBC 9/17/70 to 6/27/74

Music and comedy with host Flip Wilson, regulars Maguerite DeLain, Ka Ron Brown, Jaki Morrison, Bhety Waldron, Mary Vivian and Edward Little, and the orchestra of George Wyle. Produced by Bob Henry.

Flipper

Adventure; 30 min; NBC 9/19/64 to 5/14/67

The story of Porter Ricks, park ranger at Florida's Coral Key Park, his sons Sandy and Bud, and their pet dolphin, Flipper, as the struggle to protect the marine preserve from evil-doers.

Porter Ricks	Brian Kelly
Sandy Ricks	Luke Halpin
Bud Ricks	Tommy Nordon
Ulla Norstrand	Ulla Stromstedt
Hap Gorman	Andy Devine
Flipper	Susie

Producer: Ivan Tors

Theme Vocal (last season; "Flipper"): Frankie Randall

Flo

Comedy; 30 min; CBS 3/24/80 to 7/21/81

A spin-off from "Alice" which relates Flo's attempts to run "Flo's Golden Rose," a bar in her hometown of Cowtown, Texas.

Flo Castleberry	Polly Holliday
Earl Tucker	Geoffrey Lewis
Miriam Willoughby	Joyce Bulifant
Fran Castleberry	Lucy Lee Flippen
Velma Castleberry	Sudie Bond
Lee Kincaid	Stephen Keep
Randy Stumphill	Leo Burmester
Farley Waters	Jim B. Baker
Wendell Tubbs	Terry Wills

Theme Vocal ("Flo's Golden Rose"): Hoyt Axton

Producer: Jim Mulligan

Flo's Place

Comedy Pilot; 30 min; NBC 8/9/76

The misadventures of the staff and clientele of Flo's Place, a small dockside hotel and restaurant.

Flo	Della Reese
Louis	Eric Laneuville
Beito	Art Metrano
Eddie	Johnny Silver
Abner	Danny Wells
Hoffman	Bernie Kopell

Producer: Stanley Ralph Ross

Floor Show

Variety; 30 min; NBC 1/1/49 to 10/1/49
                           CBS 5/13/50 to 6/24/50

Performances by jazz musicians with hosts Eddie Condon and Carl Reiner, regulars Wild Bill Davidson, Sidney Bechet, Joe Bushkin, Billy Butterfield, and Peewee Russell, and the music of Eddie Condon's All Stars.

The Florian ZaBach Show

Variety; 15 min; CBS 3/10/51 to 6/9/51

Music and songs with violinist Florian ZaBach and singer Leila Hyer.

The Florian ZaBach Show

Variety; 30 min; Syn. 1954

Music and songs with host Florian ZaBach, regulars Mary Ellen Terry and Ronnie Deauville, and the orchestra of Harry Zimmerman.

The Flying Doctor

Adventure; 30 min; Syn. 1959

The exploits of Greg Graham, an American doctor in Australia, who uses a plane to help those far removed from society.

Dr. Greg Graham	Richard Denning
Mary (his nurse)	Jill Adams
Dr. Harrison	Peter Madden
Charley (Greg's pilot)	Alan White

Producer: David MacDonald

Flying High

Comedy-Drama; 60 min; CBS 9/29/78 to 1/23/79

Events in the lives of Pam, Marcy and Lisa, three beautiful stewardess for Sun West Airlines.

Pam Bellagio	Kathryn Witt
Lisa Benton	Connie Sellecca
Marcy Bower	Patricia Klous
Capt. Doug March	Howard Platt
Raymond Strickland	Ken Olfson

Theme Music ("Flying High"): David Shire

Producer: Mark Carliner

The Flying Nun

Comedy; 30 min; ABC 9/7/67 to 9/18/70

Desiring to help the less fortunate, Elsie Ethrington decides to join a convent. Ordained as Sister Bertrille, she is assigned to the Convent San Tanco in San Juan, Puerto Rico. Stories relate her efforts to help the people of her poor community. (The title refers to Sister Bertrille's ability to fly when the strong winds strike her nun's uniform.)

Sister Bertrille	Sally Field
Mother Plaseato	Madeleine Sherwood
Sister Jacqueline	Marge Redmond
Sister Ana	Linda Dangcil
Sister Sixto	Shelley Morrison
Sister Teresa	Naomi Stevens
	Cynthia Hull
Carlos Ramirez	Alejandro Rey
Capt. Gaspar Fomento	Vito Scotti
Salazar	Michael Pataki
Chief Galindo	Don Diamond
	Rodolfo Hoyos
Father Lundigan	Paul Lynde

Producer: Harry Ackerman

FM TV

Magazine; 2 hrs; Syn. 8/82

A look at the recording industry with interviews and performances by rock stars. Narrated by Frankie Crocker.

Fog

Comedy Pilot; 30 min; CBS 5/23/81

When the radar fails and the ship, Queen of the Seas, rams into two submarines, Jack Drummond is demoted and assigned to skipper the SS Sagina, a 40-year-old freighter. The unsold series was to relate Jack's efforts redeem himself with the maritime board.

Jack Drummond	Dick O'Neill
Ned Dancer	Robert Ayres
Mr. Peabody	Scoey Mitchlll
Doc Curtis	George Pentecost
Kenneth Toomey	Steven Peterman
Mr. Carrion	G.W. Bailey
Fortunato	Demetre Phillips

Producer: Lawrence J. Cohen, Fred Freeman

Foley Square

Comedy; 30 min; CBS 12/11/85 to 4/8/86

The story of Alexandra "Alex" Harrigan, a beautiful Assistant D.A. with the N.Y.C. Criminal Courts Building.

Alex Harrigan	Margaret Colin
Jesse Steinberg	Hector Elizondo
Peter Newman	Michael Lembeck
Molly Dobbs	Cathy Silvers
Denise Willums	Vernee Watson
Carter DeVries	Sanford Jensen
Angel Gomez	Israel Juarbe
Zito	Robert Costanzo
Spiro Papadopolis	Richard C. Sarafian

Producer: Saul Turteltaub, Bernie Orenstein

Follow the Leader

Game; 30 min; CBS 7/7/53 to 8/4/53

Two three-minute sketches are enacted by the hostess. Selected studio audience members must reeanct the same situations. Prizes are awarded to the best performers.

Hostess: Vera Vague

Follow the Sun

Adventure; 60 min; ABC 9/17/61 to 9/9/62

The assignments of Ben Gregory and Paul Templin, free-lance magazine writers based in Honolulu, Hawaii.

Ben Gregory	Barry Coe
Paul Templin	Brett Halsey
Eric Jason	Gary Lockwood
Katherine Ann	
Richards	Gigi Perreau
Lt. Frank Roper	Jay Sanin

Producer: Anthony Wilson

Follow Your Heart

Serial; 15 min; NBC 8/3/53 to 1/8/54

The story of June Fielding and her efforts to break set traditions within her wealthy family.

June Fielding	Sallie Brophy
Mrs. Fielding	Nancy Sheridan
Peter David	Grant Richards

Fonz and The Happy Days Gang

Cartoon; 30 min; ABC 11/8/80 to 9/18/82

When Cup Cake, a 25th century girl lands in Milwaukee in 1957, she befriends the "Happy Days" characters Fonzie, Richie and Ralph and invites them aboard her time machine. During a demonstration, they become lost in time. Stories relate Cup Cake's efforts to find the way back to 1957 Milwaukee.

Fonzie	Henry Winkler
Richie	Ron Howard
Ralph	Donny Most
Cup Cake	Didi Conn
Mr. Cool	Frank Welker
Announcer	Wolfman Jack

Producer: William Hanna, Joseph Barbera

Foodini the Great

Children; 15 min; ABC 8/25/51 to 12/29/51

The puppet misadventures of an inept, villainous magician (Foodini) and his assistant Pinhead. A spin-off from "Lucky Pup."

Hostess: Ellen Parker, Doris Brown, Lou Prentis

Voices/Puppeteers: Hope and Mory Bunin

Foofur

Cartoon; 30 min; NBC 9/14/86 (Premiere)

Following the death of his master, a lovable hound dog (Foofur) inherits an old mansion. Stories relate the mishaps that occur when Foofur opens the house to friends and relatives.

Voices: Jared Barclay, Michael Bell, Susan Blu, William Callaway, Hamilton Camp, Pat Carroll, Victoria Carroll, Peter Cullen, Jennifer Darling, David Doyle, June Foray, Melanie Gaffin, Dick Gautier, Jonathan Harris, Ken Mars, Allan Melvin, Lynne Moody, Susan Silo, Susan Tolsky, Frank Welker

Producer: William Hanna, Joseph Barbera

Foot in the Door

Comedy; 30 min; CBS 3/28/83 to 5/2/83

The story of Jonah Foot, a recent widow who, after forty years of marriage, decides to move in with his newlywed son, Jim and his wife Harriet. Stories relate their misadventures.

Jonah Foot	Harold Gould
Jim Foot	Kenneth Gilman
Harriet Foot	Diana Canova
Mrs. Griffin	Marian Mercer

Producer: Jay Folb, Irma Kalish

Footlights Theatre

A CBS Summer series (7/4/52 to 9/26/52 and 7/3/53 to 9/25/53) of original dramas and adaptations from novels.

For Better or Worse

Anthology; 30 min; CBS 6/2/59 to 6/24/60

Dramas based on actual marital court cases.

Host-Narrator: Dr. James A. Peterson

Announcer: Jim Bannon

Producer: John Guedel, Hal Cooper

For Love and Honor

Drama; 60 min; NBC 9/23/83 to 12/27/83

The lives of the men and women of the peacetime Army's 88th Airborne, a crack military unit stationed at Fort Geller in Texas.

Sgt. Eugene Allard	Cliff Potts
Capt. Carolyn Engel	Shelley Smith
Cpl. Grace Pavlik	Rachel Ticotin
Capt. Steve Wiecek	Gary Grubbs
Sgt. James "China"	
Bell	Yaphet Kotto
Phyllis Wiecek	Shanna Reed
Pvt. Rusty Berger	David Caruso
Pvt. Chris Dolan	Pete Kowanko
Pvt. Georgio Lucas	Eddie Velez
Pvt. Duke Johnson	Keenan Ivory
	Wayans
Pvt. Utah Wilson	Tony Becker
Mary Lee	Kelly Preston
Sharon	Amy Steele

Producer: David Gerber

For Love or Money

Game; 30 min; CBS 6/30/58 to 1/30/59

Object: For players to win their choice of prizes by answering a series of questions associated with it.

Host: Bill Nimmo

Producer: Walt Framer

For Members Only

Comedy Pilot; 30 min; CBS 7/11/83

The antics of the caddys at Crestview, a posh country club.

Austin Ruggles	Robert Mandan
Richie Newman	Joe Davis
Gilbert Kovacs	Stephen Furst
Ginger Blakely	Kristine DeBell
Eddie Holmes	Kevin Hooks
Alicia McKnight	Gretchen Wyler
Sherman Ralston	Earl Boen
Monica Mitchell	Jami Gertz

Producer: Saul Ilson

For the Love of Mike

Comedy Pilot; 30 min; CBS 7/10/62

When Mike Stevens, an Ohio intern receives the opportunity to complete his internship at New York's Hudson General Hospital, he and his wife, Betty, a professional singer, move to Manhattan. The unsold series was to relate Betty's efforts to supplement Mike's salary of $98 a month by acquiring engagements as a singer.

Betty Stevens	Shirley Jones
Mike Stevens	Burt Metcalfe
Fran Broxton	Faye DeWitt
Ed Broxton	Jack Weston
Emil Sinclair	Gale Gordon

Producer: Harry Ackerman

For the People

Drama; 60 min; CBS 1/31/65 to 5/9/65

The exploits of David Koster, an assistant district attorney for the city of New York.

David Koster	William Shatner
Phyllis Koster	Jessica Walter
D.A. Anthony	
Celese	Howard DaSilva
Det. Frank Malloy	Lonny Chapman

Producer: Herbert Brodkin

For Your Pleasure

Variety; 15 min; NBC 4/15/48 to 9/10/49

A casual program of music and songs with hostess Kyle MacDonnell, and the music of Norman Paris and Earl Shelton.

Force Seven

Crime Drama Pilot; 60 min; NBC 5/23/82

The exploits of Force Seven, a secret undercover martial arts unit of the L.A.P.D. Aired on "CHIPS."

Lt. John LeGarre	Fred Dryer
Cindy Miwa David	Donna Kei Benz
Sly Angelitti	Tony Longo
Rick Nicholls	Tom Reilly

Producer: Cy Chermak

Ford Festival

Variety; 60 min; NBC 4/5/51 to 6/26/52

Music, sketches and songs with host James Melton, regulars Vera Vague, Billy Barty and the Wiere Brothers, and the orchestra of David Broekman

Ford Star Revue

Variety; 60 min; NBC 7/6/50 to 3/29/51

Music, songs and comedy with host Jack Haley, regulars Mindy Carson and the Mellolarks, and the orchestra of Carl Hoff and David Broekman

Ford Television Theatre

Anthology; 30 min; NBC 10/2/52 to 9/27/56
                ABC 10/3/56 to 6/26/57

A series of quality dramatic presentations under the sponsorship of the Ford Motor Company. Produced by Fletcher Markle, Garth Montgomery, Joseph Hoffman, Winston O'Keefe.

Ford Theatre Hour

Anthology; 60 min; NBC 10/17/48 to 6/29/51

A series of dramatic presentations sponsored by the Ford Motor Company. Produced by Marc Daniels and Jules Bricken.

Foreign Intrigue: Cross Current

Adventure; 30 min; Syn. 1954-55

The exploits of Christopher Storm, a Vienna hotel owner who helps people in trouble with the international underworld.

Christopher Storm   Gerald Mohr

Producer: Sheldon Reynolds

Foreign Intrigue: Dateline Europe

Adventure; 30 min; Syn. 1951-53

The assignments of Robert Cannon and Helen Davis, foreign correspondents for "Consolidated News"; and Steve Powers, a correspondent for the "Amalgamated News Service."

Robert Cannon	Jerome Thor
Helen Davis	Sydna Scott
Steve Powers	Robert Arden
Betty Cartier	Doreen Denning

Producer: Sheldon Reynolds

Foreign Intrigue: Overseas Adventures

Adventure; 30 min; Syn. 1953-54

The exploits of Michael Powers and Patricia Bennett, foreign correspondents for the "Associated News."

Michael Powers	James Daly
Patricia Bennett	Ann Preville
Their Aide	Nikole Milinaire

Producer: Sheldon Reynolds

Foreign Legionnaire

See "Captain Gallant of the Foreign Legion."

Forest Ranger

Adventure Pilot; 30 min; Unaired (Produced in 1956)

A never-televised pilot about the work of forest rangers. Based on actual files from the U.S. Forestry Service.

Will Roberts	Dick Foran
Dave Erickson	Adam Kennedy
Frank Jennings	John Dehner
Ann Loring	Susan Cummings
Harry Clark	Allen Jenkins
Chet Wiley	Charles Smith
Ted Borton	Dabbs Greer

Producer: Hal Roach Jr.

Forest Rangers

Adventure; 30 min; Syn. 1965

A Canadian-produced series about the adventures of the Junior Ranger Club as they assist the forest rangers of the Canadian North Woods.

Ranger Keeley	Graydon Gould
Joe Two Rivers	Michael Zenon
Sgt. Scott	Gordon Pinsent
Uncle Raoul	Rolland Bedard
Chub*	Ralph Endersby
Denise*	Barbara Pierce
Kathy*	Susan Conway
Steve*	Don Mason
Ted*	George Allen
Mike*	Peter Hagon
	Peter Tully

*Members of the Junior Ranger Club.

Forever Fernwood

Serial; 30 min; Syn. 10/77

The series, a revision of "Mary Hartman," without Louise Lasser, depicts incidents in the hectic lives of the citizens of mythical Fernwood, Ohio.

Tom Hartman	Greg Mullavey
Heather Hartman	Claudia Lamb
Loretta Haggers	Mary Kay Place
Charlie Haggers	Graham Jarvis
Martha Schumway	Dody Goodman
George Schumway	Tab Hunter
	Philip Bruns
Cathy Schumway	Debralee Scott
Merle Jeeter	Dabney Coleman
Wanda Jeeter	Marian Mercer
Raymond Larkin	Victor Kilian
Eleanor Major	Shelley Fabares
Penny Major	Judith Kahan
Jerry Hubbard	Fred Willard
Mickey Jo Jeeter	Tony Palmer
Annabelle Kearns	Renee Taylor
Mel Beach	Shelly Berman
Dr. Popesco	Severn Darden
Eva	Nancy Malone
Elke Sommer	Herself
Mac Slattery	Dennis Burkley
Rev. Brim	Orson Bean
Sal DiVito	Joe Penny
Jeffrey DiVito	Randall Carver
Nat Dearden	Lou Frizzell
Bob Truss	Ben Piazza
Piersall	Ronnie Schell

Producer: Norman Lear, Eugenie Ross-Leming, Brad Buckner

The Form of Things Unknown

See "The Unknown."

Fortune Dane

Crime Drama; 60 min; ABC 2/15/86 to 3/22/86

When Fortune Dane, a celebrated Twin Rivers police detective, comes to the attention of Amanda Harding, the mayor of Bay City, California, she hires him as her special investigator. Stories depict Dane's case investigations.

Fortune Dane	Carl Weathers
Mayor Amanda Harding	Penny Fuller
Kathy "Speed" Davenport	Daphne Ashbrook
Perfect Tommy	Joe Dallesandro
Chief Bukowski	Morgan Upton
April Saunders	Eva Gholson

Producer: Barney Rosenzweig, Carl Weathers, Ronald M. Cohen

The Fortune Hunter

Experimental; 55 min; NBC 10/27/39

A TV adaptation of the stage play about a city lady who accepts a job in a country drug store as a soda jerk.

The Lady	Gloria Blondell
Her Boyfriend	Lowell Gilmore
Store Owner	Percy Kilbride

Producer: Edward Sobol

Foul Play

Comedy-Adventure; 60 min; ABC 1/26/81 to 8/30/81

The story of Gloria Munday, host of "Gloria's World" (on KSF-TV, Channel 8, San Francisco) and Tucker Pendleton, a klutzy police detective, lovers who team to solve crimes.

Gloria Munday	Deborah Raffin
Tucker Pendleton	Barry Bostwick
Ben Bernard	Greg Rice
Beau Bernard	John Rice
Capt. Vito Lombardi	Richard Romanus
Stella Rinko	Mary Jo Catlett
Tom Sweeney	Richard Narita

Producer: Thomas L. Miller, Edward K. Milkis, Robert L. Boyett

Foul Ups, Bleeps and Blunders

Comedy; 30 min; ABC 1/10/84 to 10/16/84

A series of outtakes from TV shows, movies, and commercials.

Host: Don Rickles, Steve Lawrence

Regular: Noel Edmonds

Announcer: Dick Tufeld

Producer: Barry Parnell, Bob Booker

Four Eyes

Crime Drama Pilot; 60 min; NBC 3/6/84

The exploits of Tracy and Jean, two beautiful Southern California private detectives. Aired on "Riptide."

Tracy	Stepfanie Kramer
Jean	D.D. Howard
Joan Ramsdale	Joan Freeman
Roger Ramsdale	Michael Baseleon
Ellie	Mary Beth Evans
Myron	Danny Wells

Producer: Stephen J. Cannell, Frank Lupo

Four in Love

Comedy Pilot; 30 min; ABC 7/19/85

The misadventures of Linda Armstrong, a beautiful model turned art director for "Style" magazine.

Linda Armstrong	Judy Landers
Dick	Geoffrey Bowes
Jason	Derek McGrath
Pam	Mary Long
Lenore	Mary Ann McDonald
Jerry	Brian George
Quinn	Eric Keenleyside

Producer: Al Rogers, Miles Dale

Four-in-One

Drama; 60 min; NBC 9/16/70 to 9/8/71

The title for four rotating series. See: "McCloud," "Night Gallery," "The Psychiatrist," and "San Francisco International Airport."

The Four Just Men

Adventure; 30 min; Syn. 9/57

Four World War II friends, summoned to the bedside of their dying former commander, agree to carry on his crusade and battle injustice. Stories relate the rotational exploits of Tim, a journalist; Ben, a private detective; Ricco, a hotel owner; and Jeff, an attorney.

Tim Collier	Dan Dailey
Ben Manfred	Jack Hawkins
Ricco Poccari	Vittorio De Sica
Jeff Ryder	Richard Conte

Producer: Jack Wrather, Hannah Fisher

The Four of Us

Comedy Pilot; 30 min; ABC 7/18/77

The story of a young mother (Julie) and her attempts to begin a new life for herself and her children after the sudden death of her husband.

Julie Matthews	Barbara Feldon
Chrissie Matthews	Vicky Dawson
Caroline Matthews	Kathy Jo Kelly
Andy Matthews	William McMillian
Marie	K Callan
Walter	Lawrence Keith
Estelle Robinson	Marcia Jean Kurtz
Annie Ray	Heather MacRae

Producer: Herbert Brodkin

The Four Seasons

Comedy; 30 min; CBS 1/29/84 to 6/17/84

The story of Danny Zimmer, a frustrated N.Y. dentist who decides to move to California and seek a better life.

Danny Zimmer	Jack Weston
Claudia Zimmer	Marcia Rodd
Boris Elliott	Allan Arbus
Lorraine Elliott	Barbara Babcock
Ted Bolen	Tony Roberts
Pat Devon	Joanna Kerns
Beth Burroughs	Elizabeth Alda
Lisa Callahan	Beatrice Alda

Producer: Alan Alda, Martin Bregman

The 416th

Comedy Pilot; 30 min; CBS 8/25/79

The story, set during the Vietnam War, relates the antics of the men attached to the U.S. Army's 416th Medical Department and Supply Distribution Team.

Col. Davis	Raymond St. Jacques
Lt. Jackson MacCalvey	John Larroquette
Pvt. Rick Michaels	Richard Lewis
Pvt. Billy Henderson	Donald Petrie
Pvt. Myron Kowalski	Bo Kaprall
Iris Michaels	Joan Hotchkis
Phyllis	Louise Hooven
Heather	Susan Lanier

Producer: Rick Bernstein

Four Star Playhouse

Anthology; 60 min; CBS 9/25/52 to 9/27/56

A series of dramatic presentations from the studios of Four Star Television.

Regular Performers: Dick Powell, Charles Boyer, David Niven, Ida Lupino

Producer: Don Sharpe, Roy Kellin, Charles Boyer, Dick Powell, David Niven, William Frye

Fractured Flickers

Comedy; 30 min; Syn. 1963

Hans Conried as the host of a Jay Ward produced series of silent films with added zany dialogue.

Fractured Phrases

Game; 30 min; NBC 9/27/65 to 12/31/65

Object: For players to identify slogans, titles, or songs that are phonetically written and flashed on a screen.

Host: Art James

Fraggle Rock

Children; 30 min; HBO 1/10/83 (Premiere)

The activities of the residents of Fraggle Rock: the small, fun-loving Fraggles; the diminutive Doozers; and the gargantuan Gorgs, who enjoy munching on Fraggles. Characters are the Muppet creations of Jim Henson.

Doc	Gerald Parkes

Muppet Voices: Jerry Nelson, David Goelz, Steve Whitmore, Kathryn Mullen, Richard Hunt, Patricia Leeper, Robert Mills, Cheryl Wagner, Terry Angus

Producer: Jim Henson

The Frances Langford-Don Ameche Show

Variety; 60 min; ABC 9/10/51 to 3/14/52

Music, songs and comedy sketches coupled with audience participation segments. The recurring comedy skit, "The Couple Next Door" (about the trials and tribulations of marriage) became the series "Heaven for Betsy" (which see).

Hosts: Frances Langford, Don Ameche

Skit Cast: Jack Lemmon, Cynthia Stone, Neil Hamilton

Orchestra: Tony Romano

Producer: Ward Byron

Frances Langford Presents

Variety Pilot; 60 min; NBC 3/15/59

Performances by top-name entertainers.

Hostess: Frances Langford

Guests: Bob Hope, Julie London, Hugh O'Brian, Edgar Bergen, George Sanders, Jerry Colonna

Orchestra: David Rose

Producer: Charles Wick

Frank Merriwell

Comedy Pilot; 30 min CBS 7/25/66

The adventures of Frank Merriwell, the pride of Yale University at the turn of the century.

Frank Merriwell	Jeff Cooper
Elsie Stanhope	Tisha Sterling
Binkie Stubbs	Bruce Hyde
Brandon Drood	Beau Bridges
Bart Farge	Murvyn Vye
Dayton Skagg	Harry Dean Stanton

Producer: Leslie Stevens

The Frank Sinatra Show

Variety; 30 min; CBS 10/7/50 to 4/1/52

Music and songs with host Frank Sinatra, regulars Roberta Lee, Erin O'Brien, Ben Blue, Sidney Fields, Pat Gaye, and Joey Walsh, and the orchestra of Axel Stordahl. Produced by Max Gordon.

The Frank Sinatra Show

Variety; 30 min; ABC 10/18/57 to 6/27/58

A mixture of music and songs with anthology-like dramas.

Host: Frank Sinatra

Orchestra: Nelson Riddle

Producer: Paul Dudley

Frank's Place

Comedy-Drama; 30 min; CBS 9/14/87 (Premiere)

Following the death of his father, Boston college professor Frank Parrish inherits the Chez Louisiane, a Creole restaurant in New Orleans. Stories relate Frank's efforts to run the restaurant-bar.

Frank Parrish	Tim Reid
Hanna Griffin	Daphne Maxwell Reid
Anna May Thomas	Frances E. Williams
Sol "Bubba" Weisberger	Robert Harper
Big Arthur Kendall	Tony Burton
Tiger	Charles Lampkin
Miss Marie	Francesca P. Roberts
Rev. Tyrone Deal	Lincoln Kilpatrick
Cool Charles	William Thomas Jr.
Bertha	Virginia Capers
Shorty	Don Yesso
Pokie La Carre	Raymond Oliver

Producer: Hugh Wilson, Tim Reid

Frankenstein Jr. and the Impossibles

Cartoon; 30 min; CBS 9/10/66 to 9/7/68

The exploits of Frankenstein Jr., a 30-foot robot, and the Impossibles (Coil Man, Fluid Man, Multi Man) as they battle evil.

Frankenstein Jr.	Ted Cassidy
Coil Man	Hal Smith
Fluid Man	Paul Frees
Multi Man	Don Messick

Producer: William Hanna, Joseph Barbera

Frankie and Annette: The Second Time Around

Comedy Pilot; 60 min; NBC 11/18/78

The story reunites Annette Funicello and Frankie Avalon, the stars of a series of 1960s "Beach Party" films. The series was to relate incidents in the lives of Dee Dee, now a sorority housemother, and Frankie, a singer; friends who pick up their lives together after 12 years of separation.

Dee Dee	Annette Funicello
Frankie	Frankie Avalon
Dean Burroughs	Don Porter
Tiki	Helaine Lembeck
Sharkey	Herb Edelman
Bradley	Doug Rowe

Producer: Dick Clark

Frankie Carle Time

Variety; 60 min; CBS 8/7/56 to 10/29/56

Music and songs with pianist Frankie Carle and regulars the Mellolarks, the Lynn Duddy Singers, and the James Starbuck and Edith Barstow Dancers. Music by Perry Botkin, Russ Case and Jimmy Carroll.

The Frankie Laine Show

Variety; 30 min; Syn. 1954

Music and songs with host Frankie Laine and singer Connie Haines and the orchestra of Harry Zimmerman.

Frankie Laine Time

Variety; 15 min; CBS 7/10/55 to 9/7/55; 8/1/56 to 9/19/56

Music and songs with host Frankie Laine, regulars Connie Haines, the James Starbuck Dancers, and the Lynn Duddy Singers, and the orchestras of Hank Sylvern and Jimmy Carroll.

Fraud Squad

Comedy Pilot; 30 min; ABC 5/17/85

The adventures of an all-female group of police officers assigned to the Bunco Division of the L.A.P.D.

Deputy Kelly Myerson	Ann Dusenberry
Deputy Bonnie	Nana Visitor
Deputy Joyce Betterman	Audrie J. Neenan
Deputy Carmen	Beverly Todd
Deputy Buster Belkan	Lu Leonard
Deputy Dershwick	Christie Claridge
Lt. Charles Reiner	Ted Ross

Producer: Buddy Bregman

Fred and Barney

Cartoon; 60 min; NBC 9/22/79 to 11/15/80

Segments: "Fred and Barney" (prehistoric antics with Fred and Wilma Flintstone and Barney and Betty Rubble); "The Shmoo" (adventures of the Shmoo, a creature able to change its form, and its friends Nita, Mickey and Billie Joe); and "The Thing" (the story of Benjy Grimm, a student who can change himself into The Thing, an orange hulk he uses to battle crime).

Fred Flintstone	Henry Corden
Wilma Flintstone	Jean VanderPyl
Barney Rubble	Mel Blanc
Betty Rubble	Gay Autterson
Pebbles Flintstone	Jean VanderPyl
Bamm Bamm Rubble	Don Messick
The Shmoo	Frank Welker
Nita	Dolores Cantu-Primo
Billie Joe	Chuck McCann
Mickey	Bill Idelson
Benjy	Wayne Morton
The Thing	Joe Baker
Betty	Marilyn Schreffler
Spike	Art Metrano

Producer: William Hanna, Joseph Barbera

Fred Flintstone and Friends

A syndicated (1977) cartoon series hosted by Fred Flintstone (voiced by Henry Corden) that features repeat segments of "The Flintstones Comedy Hour," "Goober and the Ghost Chasers," "Jeannie," "Partridge Family: 2200 A.D.," "Pebbles and Bamm Bamm," and "Yogi's Gang."

The Fred Waring Show

Variety: CBS 4/17/49 to 5/30/54 (60 min)
7/22/57 to 8/30/57 (30 min)

A twice-weekly program of music and songs.

Host: Fred Waring

Regulars: Suzanne Lovell, Hugh Brannum, Joan Woodward, Jane Wilson, Joanne Wheatley, Joe Marine, Gordon Goodman, Sylvia Textor, Virginia Gearhart, Livingston Gearhart, Bob Sands, Nadine Gae, Frances Wyatt, The Pennsylvanians

Announcer: Red Barber

Orchestra: Fred Waring

Free Country

Comedy; 30 min; ABC 6/24/78 to 7/22/78

Events in the lives of Joseph and Anna Bresner, Lithuanian immigrants struggling to make a new life for themselves in New York City.

Joseph Bresner	Rob Reiner
Anna Bresner	Judith Kahan
Ida Gewertzman	Renne Lippin
Sidney Gewertzman	Fred McCarren
Leo Gold	Larry Gelman
Louie Peschi	Joe Pantoliano
Willie Bresner	Larry Hankin

Producer: Rob Reiner, Phil Mishkin

Freebie and the Bean

Crime Drama; 60 min; CBS 12/6/80 to 1/24/81

The exploits of Tim "Freebie" Walker and Dan "The Bean" Delgado, police sergeants who work for the San Francisco District Attorney's office.

Tim Walker	Tom Mason
Dan Delgado	Hector Elizondo
D.A. Walter Cruskshank	William Daniels
Rodney Axel	Mel Stewart

Producer: Philip Saltzman

Freedom Rings

Game; 30 min; CBS 3/3/53 to 8/27/53

Object: For a female player to suggest a solution for a household crisis that is enacted on stage.

Host: John Beal

Regulars: Alice Ghostley, Joy Hilton, Malcolm Broderick, Ted Tillis, Chuck Taylor

Announcer: Vince Williams

Orchestra: Ben Ludlow

Freeman

Comedy Pilot; 30 min; ABC 6/19/76

The story of a ghost (Freeman) who refuses to vacate his colonial home; and the efforts of the new occupants (the Wainwrights) to cope with an unexpected family member.

Freeman	Stu Gilliam
Dwight Wainwright	Linden Chiles
Helen Wainwright	Beverly Sanders
Timmy Wainwright	Jimmy Baio
Madam Arkadinia	Melinda Dillon

Producer: Bernie Kukoff, Jeff Harris

The Freewheelers

Comedy Pilot; 30 min; CBS 7/4/64

The misadventures of Lincoln Wheeler, a traveling author and newspaper columnist.

Lincoln Wheeler	Tommy Noonan
Monica Wheeler	Patricia Barry
Coco Sorel	Jacques Bergerac

Producer: Stanley Rubin

Friday the 13th: The Series

Thriller; 60 min; Syn. 10/87

Following the mysterious death of their uncle Lewis, estranged cousins Micki and Ryan inherit his antique shop. With neither Micki or Ryan wanting to keep the store, they sell off the inventory. Later, when they meet an old friend of their uncle's (Jack) and learn that the antiques are hexed, they make a vow to get them back before tragedy befalls the items' owners. Stories relate their efforts to retrieve the cursed antiques. Adapted from the series of theatrical films.

Michele "Micki" Foster	Robey
Ryan Dallion	John D. Le May
Jack Marshak	Chris Wiggins
Uncle Lewis	R. G. Armstrong

Producer: Frank Mancuso Jr., Barbara Sachs

Fridays

Comedy; 100 min; ABC 4/11/80 to 10/22/82

A humorous look at the foibles of modern-day society.

Regulars: Mark Blankfield, Maryedith Burrell, Melanie Chartoff, Larry David, Darrow Igus, Brandis Kemp, Kenny Loggins, Bruce Mahler, Michael Richards, John Roarke

Announcer: Jack Burns

Producer: Bill Lee, John Moffitt

Friends

Comedy Pilot; 30 min; CBS 8/19/78

The story of two once-popular rock singers (Teddy and Scott) who forsake the "road" to become staff songwriters for a Hollywood record company.

Teddy Serrano	Michael Tucci
Scott Rollins	Darrell Fetty
Susan Rollins	Susan Buckner
Kevin Rollins	Stephen Mond
J.B. Henderson	Brian Cutler
Leslie Frankel	Dori Brenner

Producer: Lorenzo Music, Steve Pritzker

Friends

Comedy-Drama; 60 min; ABC 3/25/79 to 4/22/79

A look at growing pains as seen through the eyes and experiences of three 11-year-olds (Nancy, Pete and Randy) who live in Westerby, California.

Nancy Wilks	Jill Whelan
Pete Richards	Charles Aiken
Randy Summerfield	Jarrod Johnson
Frank Richards	Andy Romano
Pamela Richards	Karen Morrow
Cynthia Richards	Alicia Fleer
Jane Summerfield	Janet MacLachlan
Warren Summerfield	Roger Robinson
Charlie Wilks	Dennis Redfield

Producer: Aaron Spelling, Douglas S. Cramer

Friends and Lovers

Comedy Pilot; 30 min; CBS 5/16/74

The pilot for "Paul Sand in Friends and Lovers." The story of Robert Dreyfuss, a bachelor violinist with the Boston Symphony Orchestra.

Robert Dreyfuss	Paul Sand
Maggie	Lynne Lipton
Charlie Dreyfuss	Michael Pataki
Janice Dreyfuss	Penny Marshall
Sally	Kathleen Miller

Producer: Allan Burns, James L. Brooks

From a Bird's Eye View

Comedy; 30 min; NBC 3/19/71 to 8/16/71

The misadventures of Millie Grover and Maggie Ralston, stewardesses for the London-based International Airlines.

Millie Grover	Millicent Martin
Maggie Ralston	Pat Finley
Clyde Beachamp	Peter Jones
Bert Grover	Robert Cawdron
Miss Fosdyke	Noel Hood

Producer: Ralph Levy

From Here to Eternity

Drama; 60 min; NBC 3/10/80 to 8/16/80

The personal lives of the civilians and military personnel (G Company, 24th Infantry) following the attack on Pearl Harbor in Hawaii on December 8, 1941.

Karen Holmes	Natalie Wood*
	Barbara Hershey
Sgt. Milt Warden	William Devane
Maj. Dana Holmes	Roy Thinnes
Lorene Rogers	Kim Basinger
Gert Kipfer	Salome Jens
Jeff Pruitt	Don Johnson
Emily Austin	Lacey Neuhaus
Lt. David Ross	David Spielberg
Lt. Ken Barrett	John Gavin
Pvt. Ignacio	
Carmona	Rocky Echevarria
Sgt. Cheney	Will Sampson
Lt. George	
Bennington	Colby Chester
Lt. Rosemary Clark	Joan Goodfellow
Col. Harry	
Thompson	John Crawford
Curt Von Norland	Richard Erdman
Dr. Anne Brewster	Claire Malis
Sgt. James Holden	Peter Boyle*
General Slater	Andy Griffith*
Pvt. Robert Pruitt	Steve Railsbach*
Pvt. Stack	Andrew Robinson*

Producer: Harve Bennett, Harris Katleman

*Miniseries role (NBC; 6 hrs; 2/14/79 to 2/28/79).

The Front Page

Comedy-Drama; 30 min; CBS 9/29/49 to 1/26/50

The comic escapades of Hildy Johnson, a reporter for a small town newspaper (the Center City "Examiner").

Hildy Johnson	Mark Roberts
Walter Burns	John Daly
Peggy Grant	Jan Shaw
Mrs. Grant	Leona Powers
Mayor	Cliff Hall

Producer: Donald Davis

Front Page Detective

Crime Drama; 30 min; DuMont 7/6/51 to 11/13/53
Syn. 1953

The exploits of David Chase, a New York newspaper columnist and amateur sleuth.

Based on stories from "Front Page Detective" magazine.

David Chase	Edmund Lowe
Lt. Rodney	Frank Jenks
David's girlfriend	Paula Drew

Producer: Jerry Fairbanks

Front Page Story

A syndicated (1959) series of dramas based on front page newspaper stories. Hosted by Paul Stewart.

Front Row Center

Variety; 60 min; DuMont 3/25/49 to 4/2/50

A musical revue with guests from the Broadway stage.

Host: Frank Fontaine

Regulars: Phil Leeds, Monica Moore, Joan Fields, Marian Bruce, Cass Franklin, Bibi Osterwald, Danny Shore

Producer: Milton Douglas

Front Row Center

Anthology; 30 min; CBS 6/1/55 to 4/21/56

A live series of original dramas and adaptations from Broadway plays and works by noted authors.

Producer: Fletcher Markle

Frontier

Anthology; 30 min; NBC 9/25/55 to 9/9/56

Western dramas that depict the problems facing the pioneers who journed west during the 1800s.

Host-Narrator: Walter Coy

Producer: Worthington Miner, Carroll Chase

Frontier Adventures

A syndicated (1970) series of repeat dramas from "Death Valley Days."

Frontier Circus

Adventure; 60 min; CBS 10/5/61 to 9/20/62

The saga of the traveling one ring Thompson and Travis Combined Circus as it journeys across the frontier of the 1880s.

Col. Casey Thompson	Chill Wills
Ben Travis	John Derek
Tony Gentry	Richard Jaeckel

Producer: Richard Irving

Frontier Doctor

Western; 30 min; Syn. 1958

The role of the doctor during the early settlement days of the 20th-century, as seen through the eyes of Bill Baxter, a doctor in Rising Springs, Arizona.

Dr. Bill Baxter	Rex Allen

Producer: Edward J. White

Frontier Judge

Western; 30 min; Syn. 1956

A relatively unknown series about John Cooper, a circuit riding judge of the Old West.

John Cooper	Leon Ames

Frontier Justice

A CBS series of "Zane Grey Theatre" repeats with hosts Lew Ayres (7/58 to 9/58), Melvyn Douglas (7/59 to 9/59), and Ralph Bellamy (8/61 to 9/61).

F Troop

Comedy; 30 min; ABC 9/14/65 to 9/7/67

The series, set at Fort Courage (Kansas) in 1866, relates the misadventures of Captain Wilton Parmenter, as he struggles to maintain the peace and cope with a troop of misfit soldiers.

Capt. Wilton Parmenter	Ken Berry
Sgt. Morgan O'Rourke	Forrest Tucker
Cpl. Randolph Agarn	Larry Storch
"Wrangler" Jane Thrift	Melody Patterson
Chief Wild Eagle	Frank DeKova
Pvt. Hannibal Dobbs	James Hampton
Pvt. Duffy	Bob Steele
Pvt. Vanderbilt	Joe Brooks
Pvt. Hoffenmueller	John Mitchum
Crazy Cat	Don Diamond
Pvt. Dudleson	Ivan Bell
Major Duncan	James Gregory
Pvt. Wrongo Starr	Henry Gibson

Producer: William T. Orr, Hy Averback

FTV

Comedy; 30 min; Syn. 9/85

Spoofs of music videos coupled with performances by rock stars.

Host: Don Felder

Regulars: Bridget Michele, Stephen Bishop, Vic Dunlop, Pam Mattheson, Lynne Wood, Khandi Alexander, John Paragon

Producer: Chris Bearde

The Fugitive

Drama; 60 min; ABC 9/17/63 to 8/29/67

One night, while driving home, Indiana doctor Richard Kimble spies a one-armed man running from his home. Upon entering his home, Richard finds his wife, Helen, dead. Unable to prove his innocence, Richard is arrested, tried, and convicted of murder (for which he is sentenced to death).
Enroute to the death house, Richard escapes the bounds of police lieutenant Philip Gerard. Stories relate Kimble's desperate efforts to find the mysterious one-armed man and clear his name.

Richard Kimble	David Janssen
Lt. Philip Gerard	Barry Morse
Fred Johnson (the one-armed man)	Bill Raisch
Helen Kimble	Diane Brewster
Donna Kimble-Taft	Jacqueline Scott
Leonard Taft	Richard Anderson James B. Sikking
Dr. John Kimble	Robert Keith
Ray Kimble	Andrew Prine
David (Donna's son)	Billy Mumy
Billy (Donna's son)	Clint Howard
Marie Gerard	Barbara Rush
Police Captain	Paul Birch
Philip "Flip" Gerard Jr.	Kurt Russell

Narrator: William Conrad

"The Fugitive Theme" by Pete Rugolo

Producer: Quinn Martin

Full Circle

Drama; 30 min; CBS 6/27/60 to 3/10/61

The story of Gary Donovan, a footloose wanderer who remains in one place only long enough to earn the money he needs to continue his travels.

Gary Donovan	Robert Fortier

Producer: Norman Morgan

Full House

Comedy Pilot; 30 min; NBC 8/2/76

The misadventures that befall three generations of one family living in the same house.

Frank Campbell	Ken Mars
Pauline Campbell	Aneta Corsaut
Eloise Campbell	Nora Marlowe
Henry Campbell	Liam Dunn
Susan Campbell	Doney Oatman
Jamie Campbell	Poindexter Yothers
Phil Campbell	Cameron Clarke

Producer: Charles Fries

Full House

Comedy-Drama Pilot; 60 min; CBS 9/20/83

The story of a disorganized and almost broke playwright (Ivan) as he struggles to raise five children.

Ivan Travalian	Dennis Dugan
Debbie Travalian	Ari Meyers
Bonnie Travalian	Shelby Balik
Igor Travalian	Eric Gurry
Spike Travalian	Scott Nemes
Geraldo Esposito	Danny Ponce
Arthur Krantz	Ken Mars
Bobbie Hall	Mirian Flynn

Producer: Marc Merson

Full House

Comedy; 30 min; ABC 9/22/87 (Premiere)

Shortly after the death of his wife, Danny Tanner, the father of three daughters (D.J., age 10; Stephanie, age 5; and infant Michele) invites his brother-in-law, Jesse, and best friend, Tony, to live with him and help him raise the girls. Stories relate the guys efforts to care for and raise three young girls.

Danny Tanner	Bob Saget
D.J. (Donna Jo) Tanner	Candace Cameron
Stephanie Tanner	Jodie Sweetin
Jesse Cochran	John Stamos
Joey Gladstone	David Coulier
Irene (Jesse's mother)	Rhoda Gemignani
Mindy (Joey's mother)	Beverly Sanders
Clair (Danny's mother)	Alice Hirson

Producer: Jeff Franklin, Thomas L. Miller, Robert L. Boyett

Full Speed Anywhere

Comedy Pilot; 30 min; CBS 9/13/60

The story of a Navy yeoman (Stubby) assigned to shore duty who longs for action on the high seas.

Stubby Fox	Stubby Kaye
Ensign Jones	Conrad Janis
Doc Clemens	George Dunn
Slim Jackson	Glenn Turnbull
Lew	Jose Gonzalez-Gonzalez

Producer: Charles Isaacs

The Fun Factory

Variety; 30 min; NBC 6/14/76 to 10/1/76

Music, songs and various game contests wherein studio audience members compete for prizes.

Host: Bobby Van

Regulars: Jane Nelson, Betty Thomas, Deborah Harmon, Doug Steckler

Announcer: Jim Thompson

Music: Stan Worth

Fun for the Money

Game; 30 min; ABC 6/17/49 to 12/9/49

Object: For players to identify, within four clues, a merchandise item that is hidden behind "The Magic Curtain."

Host: Jack Lescoulie, Johnny Olsen

Producer: James Saphier, Mildred Fenton

The Funky Phantom

Cartoon; 30 min; ABC 9/11/71 to 9/1/72

During the Revolutionary War, Jonathan "Musty" Muddlemore hides in a grandfather clock to escape from British soldiers. The clock door locks and traps him. Three hundred years later, three teenagers (April, Skip, and Augie) open the clock door. The spirit of Musty emerges and befriends them. Stories relate their adventures as they team to battle evil-doers.

Musty	Daws Butler
April	Kristina Holland
Skip	Mickey Dolenz
Augie	Tommy Cook

Producer: William Hanna, Joseph Barbera

Funny Boners

Game; 30 min; NBC 11/20/54 to 7/9/55

Children compete in question-and-answer rounds with players performing penalty stunts for wrong answers.

Host: Jimmy Weldon

Funny Face

Comedy; 30 min; CBS 9/18/71 to 12/11/71

Events in the life of Sandy Stockton, a pretty student teacher (at U.C.L.A.) and a part-time actress with the Prescott Advertising Agency. See also "The Sandy Duncan Show."

Sandy Stockton	Sandy Duncan
Alice MacRaven	Valorie Armstrong
Pat Harwell	Henry Beckman
Kate Harwell	Kathleen Freeman
Maggie Prescott	Nita Talbot

Producer: Jerry Davis

The Funny Manns

A syndicated (1961) children's comedy in which Cliff Norton hosts in disguises such as Milk Mann, Police Mann, and Rich Mann, edited theatrical comedy shorts.

The Funny Side

Variety; 60 min; NBC 9/14/71 to 12/28/71

The funny side of everyday life as seen through the eyes of five couples.

Host	Gene Kelly
Blue collar husband	Warren Berlinger
Blue collar wife	Pat Finley
Sophisticated husband	Dick Clair
Sophisticated wife	Jenna McMahon
Young husband	Michael Lembeck
Young wife	Joyce Ames*
	Cindy Williams
Black husband	John Amos
Black wife	Teresa Graves
Elderly husband	Burt Mustin
Elderly wife	Queenie Smith

Orchestra: Jack Elliott, Allyn Ferguson

Producer: Bill Persky, Sam Denoff

*Pilot episode (9/12/71).

The Funny World of Fred & Bunni

Variety Pilot; 60 min; CBS 8/30/78

Skits and musical numbers with a live (Fred) and animated host (Bunni).

Host: Fred Travalena

Guests: Sandy Duncan, Vicki Lawrence, Pat Harrington

Orchestra: Jack Elliott, Allyn Ferguson

Producer: Joseph Barbera

Funny You Should Ask

Game; 30 min; ABC 10/28/68 to 9/5/69

Before air time, five celebrities are asked specific questions. On stage, the same questions are read to three players, but the answers are given in mixed order. To earn merchandise prizes, players must match the celebrity with what he or she said.

Host: Lloyd Thaxton

Producer: Stan Dreben

The Funtastic World of Hanna-Barbera

The overall syndicated title (9/85) for three half-hour cartoons. See "The Paw Paws," "Goltar and the Golden Lance," and "Yogi's Treasure Quest."

The Furst Family of Washington

Comedy Pilot; 30 min; ABC 9/11/73

The misadventures of Oscar Furst, the owner of a Washington, D.C., barber shop that doubles as a men's community center. Served as the basis for "That's My Mama."

Oscar Furst	Godfrey Cambridge
Eloise "Mama" Furst	Thelma Merritt
Earl Jefferson	Theodore Wilson
King Osborne	Eddy C. Dyer
Low Lead	Dewayne Jessie
Junior	Eric Laneuville

Producer: Norman Campbell

The Further Adventures of Ellery Queen

Crime Drama; 60 min; NBC 9/26/58 to 9/4/59

The exploits of Ellery Queen, a sophisticated gentleman detective and writer living in New York. See also "The Adventures of Ellery Queen" and "Ellery Queen."

Ellery Queen	George Nader
	Lee Philips
Insp. Richard Queen	Les Tremayne

Producer: Albert McCleery

The Further Adventures of Spin and Marty

Comedy; 30 min; ABC 11/5/57 to 12/12/57

A "Mickey Mouse Club" sequel to "Spin and Marty" which continues to depict events in the lives of Triple R Ranch campers Spin and Marty as they vie for the affections of Annette, a pretty Circle H camper. See also "The New Adventures of Spin and Marty."

Spin Evans	Tim Considine
Marty Markham	David Stollery
Annette	Annette Funicello
Darlene	Darlene Gillespie
Jim Logan	Roy Barcroft
Bill Burnett	Harry Carey Jr.
Ollie	Dennis Moore
Moochie O'Hara	Kevin Corcoran
Ambitious	B.G. Norman
Joe	Sammy Ogg
Speckle	Tim Hartnagel

Producer: Walt Disney

The Further Adventures of Wally Brown

Comedy Pilot; 30 min; NBC 8/21/80

The antics of Wally Brown, a track star for Stephen Foster High School.

Wally Brown	Clinton Derricks-Carroll
Douglas Burdett	Peter Scolari
Warren Burdett	Ron Masak
Arlene Burdett	Sally Hightower
Coach Fleischman	Marvin Braverman
Bernstein	Gilbert Gotfried

Producer: Mark Rothman, Lowell Ganz

Fury

Drama; 30 min; NBC 10/15/55 to 9/3/66

When an innocent boy (Joey) is wrongly accused of breaking a window, rancher Jim Newton clears his name and begins adoption procedures when he learns that Joey is an orphan. Stories relate Joey's adventures in and around the Broken Wheel Ranch with his black Stallion, Fury. Also known as "Brave Stallion."

Jim Newton	Peter Graves
Joey Newton	Bobby Diamond
Pete	William Fawcett
Helen Watkins	Ann Robinson
Pee Wee Jenkins	Jimmy Baird
Packey Lambert	Roger Mobley
Harriet Newton	Nan Leslie
Sheriff Davis	James Seay
Deputy Sheriff	Guy Teague
Fury	Gypsy

Producer: Leon Fromkess

Future Cop

Crime Drama; 60 min; ABC 3/5/77 to 8/6/77

In an attempt to battle crime, Dr. Tingley invents an almost human robot, named John Haven, that she programs to be the perfect cop. Stories relate Haven's exploits as he is teamed with Cleaver and Bundy, two Los Angeles police officers.

Joe Cleaver	Ernest Borgnine
Bill Bundy	John Amos
John "Kid" Haven	Michael Shannon
Captain Skaggs	Herbert Nelson
Dr. Tingley	Irene Tsu

Producer: Anthony Wilson

The Fuzz Brothers

Comedy Pilot; 60 min; ABC 3/5/73

The story of Luther Prince and Francis Buchanan, Los Angeles police officers who are plagued by life's endless mishaps.

Det. Francis Buchanan	Lou Gossett
Det. Luther Prince	Felton Perry
Capt. Philip Lean	Jeff Corey
Herbert Flowers	Don Porter
Ben	Mitchell Ryan

Producer: John D.F. Black

Fuzzbucket

Comedy Pilot; 60 min; ABC 5/18/86

When Michael, a young boy with an over-active imagination, feeds a special food mixture to an invisible friend he calls Fuzzbucket, a furry creature materializes and appears only to Michael. The unsold series was to relate Michael's misadventures with Fuzzbucket.

Michael Gerber	Chris Hebert
Fuzzbucket	Phil Fondacaro
Joseph Gerber	Joe Regalbuto
Carol Gerber	Wendy Phillips
Stevie Gerber	Robyn Lively
Fuzzbucket's Voice	Hal Smith
Principal	John Vernon
Tina	Deena Maria Consiglio

Producer: John Landis

The Gabby Hayes Show

Children; 30 min; NBC 12/11/50 to 1/1/54
ABC 5/12/56 to 7/14/56

Stories of the American West (set at the Double Bar M Ranch).

Host-Story Teller: George "Gabby" Hayes

Regulars: Lee Graham, Clifford Sales, Robert F. Simon, Michael Strong, Malcolm Keer, Irving Winter

Producer: E. Roger Muir, Martin Stone, Joe Clair

Gabe and Walker

Drama Pilot; 60 min; ABC 7/20/81

The story of Gabe and Walker, the owners of a contemporary but financially troubled horse ranch in California.

Marion Walker	Frank Converse
Gabe Peterson	Charles Martin Smith
Cassie	Katherine Cannon
Kevin	Jason Harvey
Sexy girl	Lisa Loring
Sweet Billy	Hugh Gillin
Iris O'Reilly	Claire Mills

Producer: Henry Winkler, Allan Manings

Gabrielle

Music and songs with French singer Gabrielle. ABC 7/13/48 to 8/12/48.

Galactica 1980

Adventure; 60 min; ABC 1/27/80 to 5/4/80

A spin-off from "Battlestar Galactica." After many years in space, the starship Galactica reaches Earth. Stories relate the efforts of the Galacticans to establish a colony on Earth as seen through the experiences of scouts Troy and Dillon and Jamie, the Earth girl who befriends and assists them.

Commander Adama	Lorne Greene
Capt. Troy	Kent McCord
Lt. Dillon	Barry Van Dyke
Jamie Douglas	Robyn Douglass
Col. Boomer	Herb Jefferson Jr.
Dr. Zee	Robbie Rist
	Patrick Stuart
Col. Sydell (Air Force agent seeking Troy and Dillon)	Allan Miller
Mr. Brooks	Fred Holliday
Anne	Sharon Acker
Miss Carlysle	Pamela Susan Shoop
Xavier (renegade Galactican)	Richard Lynch
Dr. Donald Mortinson	Robert Reed

Galactican children: Georgi Irene, Lindsay Kennedy, Michael Brick, Jeff Cotler, Mark Everett, Nicholas Davis, Tracy Justrich, Eric Larson, Eric Taslitz, Jerry Supiran, Michele Larson

Producer: Glen A. Larson

The Galaxy Goofups

Cartoon; 30 min; NBC 11/14/78 to 3/3/79

The antics of Yogi Bear and Huckleberry Hound as members of a futuristic, celestial police force.

Yogi Bear	Daws Butler
Huckleberry Hound	Daws Butler
The General	John Stephenson
Scare Bear	Joe Besser
Quackup	Mel Blanc

Producer: William Hanna, Joseph Barbera

Galaxy High School

Cartoon; 30 min; CBS 9/13/86 (Premiere)

The adventures of a group of students, from every planet in the universe, as they attend Galaxy High School.

Aimee Brighttower	Susan Blu
Biddy McBrain	Pat Carroll
Gilda Gossip	Nancy Cartwright
Earl Ecchh	Gary Christopher
Ollie Oilslick	Gino Conforti
Wendy Garbo	Jennifer Darling
Coach Frogface	Pat Fraley
Aimee's Locker	Henry Gibson
The Creep	Danny Mann
Rotten Roland	Neilson Ross
Prof. MacGreed	Howard Morris

Producer: Barry Glasser

"Galaxy High School" theme vocal by Don Felder

The Gale Storm Show

Comedy; 30 min; CBS 9/29/56 to 4/11/59
                          ABC 10/1/59 to 3/24/60

The adventures of Susanna Pomeroy, the beautiful social director of the luxury liner "SS Ocean Queen." Also titled "Oh! Susanna."

Susanna Pomeroy	Gale Storm
Esmerelda "Nugey" Nugent	ZaSu Pitts
Capt. Simon Huxley	Roy Roberts
Dr. Eugene Reynolds	Rolfe Sedan
Cedric	James Fairfax
Purser	Joe Cranston

Producer: Hal Roach Jr., Alex Gottlieb, Lou Derman

The Galen Drake Show

Variety; 30 min; ABC 1/12/57 to 5/11/57

Music and songs geared to children with host Galen Drake and regulars Rita Ellis, Stuart Foster, and The Three Beaus and a Peep.

The Gallant Men

Drama; 60 min; ABC 10/5/62 to 9/14/63

The W.W. II story of Conley Wright, a combat correspondent assigned to the 36th Infantry of the American 5th Army, as he reports the experiences of men desperately seeking to end the war and return home.

Conley Wright	Robert McQueeney
Capt. James Benedict	William Reynolds
Pvt. Roger Gibson	Roger Davis
Sgt. John McKenna	Richard X. Slattery
Pvt. Peter D'Angelo	Eddie Fontaine
Pvt. Sam Hanson	Robert Gothie
Pvt. Ernie Lucavich	Roland LaStarza
Lt. Frank Kimbro	Robert Ridgely

Producer: Richard Bluel

The Gallery of Madame Liu Tsong

Drama; 30 min; DuMont 8/27/51 to 11/21/51

Originally (five episodes) the experiences of a beautiful Chinese art gallery proprietress (Liu Tsong) as she ventures forth in searth of art objects. The revised format (last six episodes) found Liu Tsong as a Chinese exporter battling evil-doers.

Madame Liu Tsong	Anna May Wong

The Galloping Gourmet

Cooking; 30 min; Syn. 1969

An entertaining approach to gourmet cooking with Graham Kerr, an international culinary expert known as the Galloping Gourmet.

Host: Graham Kerr

Assistants: Patricia Burgess, Wilhelmina Meerakker

Producer: Treena Kerr

Gambit

Game; 30 min; CBS 9/4/72 to 12/10/76

A deck of 52 playing cards is opened and one card is exposed. The first team to correctly answer a question that is read, can either keep or pass the card to their opponents. Questions continue with the first team to score 21 points (or as close to it without going over) receiving $100.

Host: Wink Martindale

Card Dealer: Elaine Stewart

Announcer: Kenny Williams

Producer: Merrill Heatter, Bob Quigley

Gamble on Love

Game; 30 min; DuMont 7/16/54 to 8/20/54

Three married couples compete in a question and answer session with the highest scoring couple receiving a chance to win a mink coat by answering "The Cupid Question."

Hosts: Denise Darcell, Ernie Kovacs

Producer: Robert K. Adams

The Game Game

Game; 30 min; Syn. 1969

A psychological question that contains five parts is read. For each part, five answers are revealed. Players (one contestant and three celebrity guests) score points according to their selection of answers. The contestant scores $25 for each celebrity's score he beats.

Host: Jim McKrell

Announcer: Johnny Jacobs

Producer: Chuck Barris

Games People Play

Human Interest; 60 min; NBC 8/21/80 to 12/25/80

A review of sporting games in which average people compete.

Host: Bryant Gumbel

Co-Host: Cyndy Garvey, Donna de Varona, Johnny Bench, Mike Adamle

Announcer: Gary Owens

Producer: Don Ohlmeyer, Howard Katz

Gangbusters

Anthology; 30 min; NBC 3/10/52 to 12/25/52

Dramas, based on the files of local and federal law enforcement authorities, that depict police apprehension methods. Syndicated as "Captured."

Host-Narrator: Phillips H. Lord

Host-Narrator: (under "Captured"): Chester Morris

Producer: Richard Bare, Phillips H. Lord

The Gangster Chronicles

Crime Drama; 60 min; NBC 2/12/81 to 5/8/81

The rise of organized crime as seen through the experiences of Charlie "Lucky" Luciano, Benny "Bugsy" Siegel, and Michael Lasker, three friends who grew up in poverty and who would later help forge "The Secret American Empire," now known as organized crime.

Charlie Luciano	Michael Nouri
Benny Siegel	Joe Penny
Michael Lasker	Brian Benben
Ruth Lasker	Madeline Stowe
Joy Osler	Chad Redding
Stella Siegel	Kathleen Lloyd
Chris Brennan	Markie Post
Joe Masseria	Richard Castellano
Al Capone	Louis Giambalvo
Dutch Schultz	Jonathan Banks
Mr. Goodman	Allan Arbus
Salvatore Maranzano	Joseph Mascolo
Vito Genovese	Robert Davi
Albert Anastasia	Robert Burke
Tommy Lucchese	Jon Polito
Vincent "Mad Dog" Coll	David Wilson
Thomas Dewey	Kenneth Tigar
Legs Diamond	Robert F. Lyons
Gina Genovese	Theresa Saldana
Charlie (as a boy)	Tony Raymond
Charlie (teenager)	Paul Regina
Michael (as a boy)	Tony Latorre
Michael (teenager)	John Friedrich
Benny (as a boy)	Cyril O'Reilly
Benny (teenager)	Mitchell Schorr

Narrator (episodes 1–7): E.G. Marshall

Narrator (episodes 8–10): Danny Dark

"The Gangster Chronicles" theme by Billy Goldenberg

Producer: Jack Laird, Matthew Rapf, Jack McAdams

The Garlund Touch

See "Mister Garlund"

Garrison's Gorillas

Adventure; 60 min; ABC 9/5/67 to 9/10/68

U.S. Army lieutenant Craig Garrison and four convicts (culled from various federal pens) attempt to demoralize German troops in Europe during W.W. II.

Lt. Craig Garrison	Ron Harper
Casino (thief)	Rudy Solari
Actor (con artist)	Cesare Danova
Goniff (pickpocket)	Christopher Cary
Chief (knife expert)	Brendon Boone

Producer: Selig J. Seligman

Garroway

A syndicated (1969) live series of discussions with host Dave Garroway. Produced by Rick Rosner and Stu Billet.

Garroway at Large

Variety; 30 min; NBC 4/16/49 to 6/24/51

An informal program of music, song, and chatter.

Host: Dave Garroway

Regulars: Connie Russell, Jack Haskell, Betty Shetland, Betty Chappel, Carolyn Gilbert, Cliff Norton, Aura Vainio, The Songsmiths

Announcer: Jack Haskell

Music: Joseph Gallachio

Producer: Ted Mills

The Garry Moore Show

Variety; 60 min; CBS 9/30/58 to 6/16/64

A relaxed, informal program of music, songs, and comedy.

Host: Garry Moore

Regulars: Durward Kirby, Carol Burnett, Dorothy Loudon, Denise Lor, Ken Carson, Marion Lorne, Ron Martin

Announcer: Durward Kirby

Music: Irwin Kostal, Howard Smith

Producer: Bob Banner

The Garry Moore Show

Variety; Various (30, 45 and 60 min); CBS 6/26/50 to 6/27/58

Music, song, chatter, and comedy.

Host: Garry Moore

Regulars: Durward Kirby, Denise Lor, Hattie Colbert, Ken Carson

Announcer: Durward Kirby

Music: Hank Jones, Howard Smith

Producer: Herb Sanford

The Garry Moore Show

Variety; 60 min; CBS 9/11/66 to 1/29/67

Music, songs, and comedy.

Host: Garry Moore

Regulars: Durward Kirby, Carol Corbett, Pete Barbutti, John Byner, Ron Carey, Eddie Lawrence, Dick Davey, Patsy Elliott

Announcer: Durward Kirby

Music: Bernard Green

Producer: Sylvester "Pat" Weaver, Bob Banner, Joe Hamilton

The Gary Coleman Show

Cartoon; 30 min; NBC 9/18/82 to 9/10/83

The story of Andy LeBeau, a mischievous apprentice angel who is sent to Earth to perform good deeds.

Andy LeBeau	Gary Coleman
Angelica	Jennifer Darling
Hornswoggle	Sidney Miller
Tina	LaShana Dendy
Spence	Calvin Mason
Bart	Jerry Houser
Chris	Lauren Anders
Lydia	Julie McWhirter

Producer: William Hanna, Joseph Barbera

Gavilan

Adventure; 60 min; NBC 10/26/82 to 3/18/83

The exploits of Robert Gavilan, an ex-CIA agent turned consultant for the Malibu, California-based DeWitt Institute, an oceanographic research organization.

Robert Gavilan	Robert Urich
Milo Bentley	Patrick Macnee
Marion Jawoiski	Kate Reid
Girl Gavilan Meets on the Beach	Jennifer Wallace

Producer: Leonard Goldberg

"Gavilan's Theme" by Steve Dorf

The Gay Coed

Variety Pilot; 25 min; DuMont 11/1/47

A musical comedy that depicts the life of a college coed during America's reckless and carefree 1920s.

Coed	Sandra Barkin
Her boyfriend	Gary McHugh
Football star	Bernard Barrow
His girlfriend	Evelyn Bennet
Student	Chuck Tranum
	Melvin Nodell

Gay 90s Revue

Variety; 30 min; ABC 8/11/49 to 11/14/49

The program, set in a gaslight nightclub, recalls the music, songs, and comedy of early vaudeville (1890s).

Hosts: Joe Howard, Gus Van

Regulars: J. Pat O'Malley, Lulu Bates, Loraine Fontaine, Romona Lang, The Townsmen Quartet

Orchestra: Ray Bloch

The Gayelord Hauser Show

A daily women's program of beauty tips and advice with host Gayelord Hauser. Produced by Sherman Dryer. ABC 10/31/51 to 4/25/52.

The G.E. College Bowl

Game; 30 min; CBS 1/4/59 to 6/16/63
NBC 9/23/63 to 6/14/70

Two four-member college teams compete in a series of question and answer rounds with the highest scoring team receiving a scholarship grant.

Hosts: Allen Ludden, Robert Earle

Producer: Jack Cleary

G.E. Guest House

Interview; 60 min; CBS 7/1/51 to 8/26/51

Weekly discussions on the various aspects of the entertainment industry. Sponsored by General Electric.

Hosts: Durward Kirby, Oscar Levant

Producer: Frank Telford

G.E. Summer Originals

Anthology; 30 min; ABC 7/3/56 to 9/4/56

A summer series of original dramatic presentations sponsored by General Electric.

G.E. Theatre

Anthology; 30 & 60 min; CBS 2/1/53 to 9/16/62

A long-running series of quality dramas under the sponsorship of the General Electric Corporation.

Host: Ronald Reagan

Opening Theme ("Emblem"): Elmer Bernstein

Closing Theme ("Progress"): Elmer Bernstein

Producer: Stanley Rubin, William Frye, Mort Abrhams, Bob Moser, Joe Connelly, Arthur Ripley, Gilbert Ralston, Harry Tugend

G.E. True

Anthology; 30 min; CBS 9/30/62 to 9/22/63

Dramatizations based on stories that have appeared in "True Magazine." Sponsored by General Electric and syndicated as "True."

Host-Narrator: Jack Webb

Producer: Jack Webb, Michael Meshekoff

The Gemini Man

Adventure; 60 min; NBC 9/23/76 to 10/28/76

While recovering a space capsule from the ocean, International Security Technics agent Sam Casey is caught in a radioactive explosion and rendered invisible when his DNA structure is affected. By wearing a special DNA stabilizer, he is able to control his invisibility for short periods of time. Stories relate Sam's investigations on behalf of the U.S. government research organization.

Sam Casey	Ben Murphy
Dr. Abby Lawrence	Katherine Crawford
Leonard Driscoll	Richard Dysart*
	William Sylvester

Producer: Harve Bennett

*Role in the 2-hour pilot (5/10/76).

The Gene Autry Show

Western; 30 min; Syn. 1951

The exploits of Gene Autry and his assistant Pat Buttram, roving defenders of range justice.

Gene Autry	Himself
Pat Buttram	Himself
Gail (occasional aide)	Gail Davis

Producer: Armand Schaefer, Louis Gray

Gene Autry's Melody Ranch

Variety; 30 min; Syn. 1966

Performances by country and western entertainers.

Host-Producer: Gene Autry

The General Foods Summer Playhouse

Pilot Films; 30 min; CBS 6/28/65 to 9/6/65

See: "Adventures of a Model," "Hello Dere," "Kibbe Hates Fitch," "Mr. Belvedere" (1965), "Sally and Sam," "Starr, First Baseman," "Take Him—He's All Yours," and "Young in Heart."

The Generation Gap

Game; 30 min; ABC 2/7/69 to 5/23/69

Two teams, the younger vs. the older, compete in a series of questions designed to test the younger's knowledge of the past, and the older's knowledge of the present.

Host: Dennis Wholey, Jack Barry

Announcer: Fred Foy

Music: Norman Paris

Producer: Dan Melnick

Gentle Ben

Adventure; 30 min; CBS 9/10/67 to 8/31/69

While in a game preserve, a young boy (Mark) watches as a hunter kills a mother bear and takes its cub. Later, when Mark befriends the cub (whom he names Ben) and learns that it is going to be killed, he persuades his father, Tom (a Florida game warden) to purchase the bear. Stories relate the adventures shared by a boy and his pet bear.

Tom Wedloe	Dennis Weaver
Ellen Wedlow	Vera Miles*
	Beth Brickell
Mark Wedloe	Clint Howard
Henry Boomhauer	Rance Howard
Willie	Angelo Rutherford
Miss Salsbury	Eleanor LaForge

Producer: Andy White, Ivan Tors, George Sherman

*Mark's mother in the theatrical pilot film.

Gentry's People

Drama Pilot; 30 min; NBC 7/7/59

The story of Gentry, a warm-hearted Los Angeles reporter-columnist. Aired as "Good Deed" on "The David Niven Theatre."

Gentry	Keefe Brasselle	Clara Bagley	Irene Hervey
Frank Simms	James Best	Joe Bagley	Michael Waylen
Hazel	Virginia Gregg	Joey Bagley Jr.	Garry Marshall
Sgt. Nelson	Jay C. Flippen	Harry Morton Sr.	Russell Hicks
Frank's mother	Jeanette Nolan		

Producer: Vincent M. Fennelly

Announcer: Bill Goodwin, Harry Von Zell

Music: Mahlon Merrick

Producer: Al Simon, Fred DeCordova, Ralph Levy, Rod Amateau

George and Mildred

Comedy; 30 min; Syn. 8/84

The British series on which "The Ropers" is based. The comic adventures of George and Mildred Roper as they sell their apartment house (see "Man About the House") and begin new lives in an exclusive British neighborhood.

George Roper	Brian Murphy
Mildred Roper	Yootha Joyce
Jeffrey Fourmile	Norman Eashley
Anne Fourmile	Sheila Fern
Tristam Fourmile	Nicholas Bond-Owen
Tarquin Fourmile	Simon Lloyd

The George Burns and Gracie Allen Show

Comedy; 30 min; CBS 9/12/50 to 9/22/58

Events in the day-to-day lives of comedian George Burns and his scatterbrained wife, Gracie, a woman who possesses the ability to complicate situations that are seemingly uncomplicatable.

George Burns	Himself
Gracie Allen	Herself
Ronnie Burns	Himself
Harry Von Zell	Himself
Blanche Morton	Bea Benaderet
Harry Morton	Hal March
	John Brown
	Bob Sweeney
	Fred Clark
	Larry Keating
Ralph Grainger	Robert Ellis
Bonnie Sue McAfee	Judi Meredith
Imogene Reynolds	Carol Lee
Mr. Beasley	Rolfe Sedan
Chester Vanderlip	Grandon Rhodes
Lucille Vanderlip	Sarah Selby
Emily Vanderlip	Millie Daws

George Burns Comedy Week

Anthology; 30 min; CBS 9/18/85 to 12/25/85

A weekly series of original comedy presentations with one episode, "The Couch," serving as the pilot for "Leo and Liz in Beverly Hills."

Host: George Burns

Theme music by: Charles Fox

Producer: Steve Martin, Carl Gottlieb

The George Burns Show

Comedy; 30 min; NBC 10/21/58 to 4/14/59

The life of George Burns, a comedian turned theatrical producer. (Gracie, George's wife, had retired from show business in 1958).

George Burns	Himself
Ronnie (his son)	Ronnie Burns
Harry Von Zell	Himself
Blanche Morton	Bea Benaderet
Harry Morton	Larry Keating
Lily	Barbara Stuart
Julie Meredith	Herself
Miss Tenkins	Lisa Davis

Announcer: Harry Von Zell

Producer: Rod Amateau

The George Gobel Show

Variety; 60 min; NBC 10/2/54 to 6/29/57

A relaxed program of music and comedy.

Host: George Gobel

Regulars: Jeff Donnell, Peggy King

Orchestra: John Scott Trotter

Producer: Bud Yorkin, Edward Sobol

The George Gobel Show

Variety; 60 min; NBC 9/4/57 to 3/10/59

Music, songs, and comedy (alternates with "The Eddie Fisher Show").

Host: George Gobel

Regulars: Eddie Fisher, Phyllis Avery, Peggy King, The Johnny Mann Singers

Orchestra: John Scott Trotter

Producer: Fred DeCordova, Al Lewis

The George Hamilton IV Show

Variety; 30 min; ABC 4/13/59 to 5/29/59

Performances by country and western artists.

Host: George Hamilton IV

Regulars: Roy Clark, Clint Miller, Joe Davis, Jan Crockett, Mary Klick, Elton Britt, Smitty Irvin, The Country Lads

Music: Alex Houston and the Texas Wildcats

George Jessel's Show Business

Variety; 60 min; ABC 9/13/53 to 4/11/54

Testimonial dinners that honor personalities of the entertainment world.

Host: George Jessel

Producer: Mannie Manheim

George of the Jungle

Cartoon; 30 min; ABC 9/9/67 to 9/6/70

Segments: "George of the Jungle" (about a tree-crashing prone, simple-minded klutz who aides people in distress); "Super Chicken" (the exploits of Henry Cabot Henhouse III, a scientist who invents super sauce, a liquid that makes him a daring crime fighter); "Tom Slick" (about a simple-minded racing car driver).

Voices: Bill Scott, June Foray, Paul Frees, William Conrad, Walter Tetley, Barbara Baldwin, Skip Craig

Producer: Jay Ward

The George Ross Show

Experimental; 15 min; NBC 9/5/39

Interviews with Broadway personalities. One of the first TV programs to be sponsored (by Geller's Shoes) and use a spokesperson.

Host: George Ross

Spokeswoman: Mildred Murray, Mildred Gale

Announcer: Gilbert Martin

Guests: Mary Dowell, Tony Soma

Producer: Edward Sobol

The George Sanders Mystery Theatre

Anthology; 30 min; NBC 6/22/57 to 9/14/57

A summer series of mystery dramas with host George Sanders. Directors include Fletcher Markle, Gerd Oswald, James Neilson, Oscar Rudolph, and John Meredyth Lucas.

George Schlatter's Comedy Club

Comedy; 30 min; Syn. 9/87

A weekly series that features performances by stand-up comedians and specialty acts.

Host: George Schlatter

Comics: Jenny Jones, George Miller, Bob Nelson, Don King, Margaret Smith, Kevin Meaney, Robert Gruenberg, Bob Zany

Producer: George Schlatter, Maria Schlatter, Don Hoyer

Georgia Gibbs Million Record Show

Variety; 30 min; NBC 7/1/57 to 9/2/57

Renditions of songs that have sold over a million copies with hostess Georgia Gibbs and the orchestra of Eddie Safronski.

Gerald McBoing-Boing

Cartoon; 30 min; CBS 12/16/56 to 3/10/57
5/30/58 to 10/3/58

The adventures of Gerald McCloy, a young boy who speaks in sound effects ("Boing! Boing!") rather than words.

Commentator................Bill Goodwin
Voices......................Marvin Miller

Producer: Stephen Bosustow, Robert Cannon

Geraldo

Discussion; 60 min; Syn. 9/87

A daily discussion series with appropriate guests on topical issues. Hosted by Geraldo Rivera and produced by Bonny Kaplan.

The Get Along Gang

Cartoon; 30 min; CBS 9/15/84 to 9/6/86

The adventures of the Get Along Gang (Montgomery Moose, Zipper Cat, Dotty Dog, Bing Beaver, Woolma Lamb, and Portia Porcupine) as they battle the evils of Catchum Crocodile and Leland Lizard.

Voices: Bettina Bush, Timothy Gibbs, Georgi Irene, Nicky Katt, Robbie Lee, Sherry Lynn, Sparky Marcus, Chuck McCann, Don Messick, Frank Welker

Producer: Jean Chalopin, Andy Heyward

Get Christie Love!

Crime Drama; 60 min; ABC 9/11/74 to 7/18/75

The exploits of Christie Love, an undercover police woman with the L.A.P.D.

Christie Love	Teresa Graves
Lt. Casey Reardon	Harry Guardino*
Lt. Matthew Reardon	Charles Cioffi
Capt. Arthur P. Ryan	Jack Kelly
Lt. Steve Belmont	Dennis Rucker
Lt. Joe Caruso	Andy Romano
Off. Pete Gallagher	Michael Pataki
Det. Valencia	Scott Peters

Producer: David L. Wolper, Glen A. Larson

*90 min pilot role (1/22/74).

Get it Together

Variety; 30 min; ABC 1/3/70 to 9/5/70

Performances by rock personalities with hosts Sam Riddle and Cass Elliot. Produced by Dick Clark.

Get Smart

Comedy; 30 min; NBC 9/18/65 to 9/13/69
CBS 9/26/69 to 9/11/70

The battle against KAOS, an organization of evil, as seen through the exploits of two CONTROL agents: Maxwell Smart, alias Agent 86, a bumbling klutz, and Agent 99, his beautiful, level-headed partner.

Maxwell Smart	Don Adams
Agent 99	Barbara Feldon
CONTROL Chief Thaddeus	Edward Platt
KAOS Head Siegfried	Bernie Kopell
KAOS Agent Starker	King Moody
CONTROL Agent Larrabee	Robert Karvelas
CONTROL Robot Hymie	Dick Gautier
CONTROL Agent 13	Dave Ketchum
CONTROL Agent 44	Victor French
Dr. Steele*	Ellen Weston
Professor Windish*	Robert Cornthwaite
Professor Carlson*	Stacy Keach
Dr. Bascomb*	George Ives
99's Mother	Jane Dulo
Det. Harry Hoo	Joey Forman
Adm. Harold Harmon Hargrade (former CONTROL chief)	William Schallert

Producer: Leonard B. Stern, Jess Oppenheimer, Jay Sandrich, Burt Nodella, Arnie Rosen, James Komack

Creator: Mel Brooks, Buck Henry

*CONTROL agents.

Get the Message

Game; 30 min; ABC 3/30/64 to 12/25/64

Object: For players to identify names, places or slogans through word-association clues. $100 is awarded to the first player to score three identifications.

Host: Frank Buxton, Robert Q. Lewis

Producer: Mark Goodson, Bill Todman

Getting Ready

Children; 30 min; Syn. 1978

A program of music, songs, puppet antics, and arts and crafts for children.

Hostess: Renee Sweeney

Producer: Irene Berner

Getting There

Comedy Pilot; 30 min; CBS 2/12/80

The story of husband-and-wife partners (Harry and Rose's West-East Auto Delivery Firm) who seldom agree on how to run the company.

Harry Miller	George S. Irving
Rose Miller	Brett Somers
Mary	Cathryn Damon
Jim	Norman Fell

Producer: Lila Garrett

Getting Together

Comedy; 30 min; ABC 9/18/71 to 1/8/72

The story of two unknown songwriters (Bobby and Lionel) and their attempts to make a name for themselves in the music business. See also "A Knight in Shining Armor" for the pilot information.

Bobby Conway	Bobby Sherman
Lionel Poindexter	Wes Stern
Jenny Conway	Susan Neher
Rita Simon	Pat Carroll
Rudy Colcheck	Jack Burns

Theme Vocal ("Getting Together") by Bobby Sherman

Producer: Bob Claver, Paul Junger Witt

Ghost

Game; 30 min; NBC 7/27/52 to 9/21/52
                                 6/21/53 to 9/13/53

Object: For players to identify words by suggesting individual letters. Each correct suggestion places the letter in its appropriate position (a wrong suggestion or giving the last letter of the word defeats a player). Players with the most correct identifications are the winners. Also titled "Super Ghost" (second date listing).

Host: Dr. Bergen Evans

Panelists: Shirley Stern, Gail Compton, Hope Ryder, Robert Pallock

The Ghost and Mrs. Muir

Comedy; 30 min; NBC 9/21/68 to 9/6/69
                                 ABC 9/18/69 to 9/18/70

Following the death of her husband, Carolyn Muir, a free-lance magazine writer, moves to Schooner Bay, New England, and into a cottage that is haunted by the spirit of its 19th-century owner (Captain Daniel Gregg). Stories relate Carolyn's efforts to make Gull Cottage her home despite the protests of the captain, who refuses to leave.

Carolyn Muir	Hope Lange
Daniel Gregg	Edward Mulhare
Candy Muir	Kellie Flanagan
Jonathan Muir	Harlan Carraher
Martha Grant	Reta Shaw
Claymour Gregg	Charles Nelson Reilly
Ed Peevey	Guy Raymond
Noorie Coolidge	Dabbs Greer

Producer: David Gerber, Gene Reynolds, Howard Leeds, Stanley Rubin

Ghost Breaker

Drama Pilot; 60 min; NBC 9/8/67

The exploits of Barnaby Cross, a university professor who dables in the occult.

Barnaby Cross	Kerwin Matthews
Cassandra	Diana Van Der Vlis
Lt. P.J. Hartunian	Norman Fell
Tim Selfridge	Richard Anderson
Waldo Kent	Larry Blyden
Florence Blackstone	Anne Jeffreys
Oscar Jensen	Michael Constantine
Ivy Rumson	Margaret Hamilton

Producer: Norman Felton

The Ghost Busters

Comedy; 30 min; CBS 9/6/75 to 9/4/76

The escapades of Kong and Spencer, operatives of Ghost Busters, Inc., and Tracy, a gorilla, as they attempt to dematerialize ghosts.

Kong	Forrest Tucker
Eddie Spencer	Larry Storch
Tracy	Bob Burns

Producer: Norman Abbott

Ghost Busters

Cartoon; 30 min; Syn. 9/86

The exploits of Jake Kong, Eddie Spenser, and Tracy the Gorilla as they battle the evil ghosts of Prime Evil, the most diabolical spirit in the universe.

Voices: Susan Blu, Pat Fraley, Peter Cullen, Alan Oppenheimer, Linda Gary, Erika Scheimer, Erik Gunden

Producer: Lou Scheimer

Ghost of a Chance

Comedy Pilot; 30 min; ABC 7/7/80

The marital misadventures of Jenny and Wayne Clifford, newlyweds whose lives are complicated by the ghost of Jenny's first husband (Tom Chance), who has come back to haunt them and voice his objections to her remarriage.

Jenny Clifford	Shelley Long
Wayne Clifford	Barry Van Dyke
Tom Chance	Steven Keats
Frances	Gretchen Wyler
Leslie	Rosalyn Kind

Producer: Austin and Irma Kalish

Ghost Story

Anthology; 60 min; NBC 9/15/72 to 12/29/72

Suspense dramas that depict the plight of people who are suddenly confronted with the supernatural. See also "Circle of Fear."

Host (Winston Essex)	Sebastian Cabot

"Ghost Story" theme by Billy Goldenberg

Producer: William Castle, Joel Rogosin

G.I. Joe

Cartoon; 30 min; Syn. 9/83

The exploits of G.I. Joe, military code for The American Special Mission Force, a team of daring government agents who battle diabolical villains.

Voices: Liz Aubrey, Michael Bell, Peter Cullen, Buster Jones, Rob Paulsen, Marla Scott, John Stephenson, B.J. Ward, Frank Welker

Producer: Joe Bacal, David DePatie, Tom Griffin

The G.I.'s

Comedy Pilot; 30 min; CBS 7/29/80

The World War II adventures of a squad of American servicemen who serve as "mop-up" troops during the Italian campaign.

Cpl. Peter Buchanan	Kenneth Gilman
Sgt. John Vitella	Jonathan Banks
Pvt. T.J. Witherspoon	Gregg Berger
Pvt. Leroy Lumpkin	Michael Binder
Pvt. Harry Freedman	Lorry Goldman
Pvt. Joseph Battaglia	Chuck Vennera

Producer: Bernard Rothman, Jack Wohl

The Giant Step

Game; 30 min; NBC 11/7/56 to 5/29/57

Object: For a child (7 to 17 years of age) to select a category and answer questions of increasing difficulty. Players who manage to answer all the questions associated with their subjects win a college education.

Host: Bert Parks

Announcer: Mike Fitzmorris

Gibbsville

Drama; 60 min; NBC 11/11/76 to 12/30/76

Events in the lives of the citizens of Gibbsville, Pennsylvania, a mining town of the 1940s, as seen through the eyes of Ray Whitehead, a reporter for "The Gibbsville Courier." Based on stories by John O'Hara.

Ray Whitehead	Gig Young
Jim Malloy	John Savage
Dr. Michael Malloy	Biff McGuire
Mrs. Malloy	Peggy McCay
Editor Pell	Bert Remsen
Lefty Lintzie	Frank Campanella

Producer: David Gerber

Gideon's Way

Crime Drama; 60 min; Syn. 1966

The exploits of Commander George Gideon, the chief inspector of the Criminal Investigation Division of England's New Scotland Yard. Also known as "Gideon, C.I.D."

| George Gideon | John Gregson |

Gidget

Comedy; 30 min; ABC 9/15/65 to 9/1/66

The story of a Santa Monica, California, teen-age girl (Frances "Gidget" Lawrence) and her adventures at home, in school, and at the beach, where she is actively involved in the world of surfing. See also "The New Gidget."

Frances Lawrence	Sally Field
Russell Lawrence	Don Porter
Anne Cooper	Betty Conner
John Cooper	Peter Deuel
Jeff "Moondoggie" Matthews	Steven Miles
Larue	Lynette Winter
Eleanor "Treasure" Chest	Beverly Adams
Pokey	Heather North
Janie Carmichael	Bonnie Franklin
Peter "Siddo" Stone	Michael Nader
Shirely Marshall	Beverly Washburn
Sally	Bridget Hanley
Betty	Barbara Hershey
Ken	Tim Rooney
Ellen	Pamela McMyler
Randy	Rickie Sorensen
Beautiful blonde roles	Joy Harmon

Theme Vocal ("Gidget"): Johnny Tillotson

Producer: Harry Ackerman, Bob Claver, William Sackheim

Gidget Gets Married

Comedy Pilot; 90 min; ABC 1/4/72

A second attempt (see "Gidget Grows Up") to revive the "Gidget" series. Incidents in the life of Frances "Gidget" Lawrence, now a housewife and married to her surfer sweetheart, Jeff "Moondoggie" Stevens.

Frances Stevens	Monie Ellis
Jeff Stevens	Michael Burns
Russell Lawrence	Macdonald Carey
Otis Ramsey	Don Ameche
Claire Ramsey	Joan Bennett
Louis B. Latimer	Paul Lynde
Medley Blaine	Elinor Donahue

Producer: Harry Ackerman, E. W. Swackhamer

Music: Mike Post and Pete Carpenter

Gidget Grows Up

Comedy Pilot; 90 min; ABC 12/30/69

The first attempt to revise the "Gidget" series. The story relates Frances "Gidget" Lawrence's adventures, now as a young woman, as she leaves Santa Monica and heads for New York City to begin a career as a United Nations tour guide.

Frances Lawrence	Karen Valentine
Jeff Griffin	Paul Petersen
Louis B. Latimer	Paul Lynde
Russell Lawrence	Bob Cummings
Alex MacLaughlin	Edward Mulhare
Bibi Crosby	Nina Foch
Arnold	Michael Lembeck
Diana	Susan Batson

Producer: Jerome Courtland

Music: Shorty Rogers

Gidget's Summer Reunion

Comedy Pilot; 2 hrs; Syn. 6/85

The pilot film for "The New Gidget," which relates incidents in the life of Frances "Gidget" Lawrence who is now twenty-seven, married to Jeff "Moondoggie" Griffin, the owner of her own business, "Gidget Travel," and the guardian of her niece, Kim, a beautiful teenager with a knack for finding trouble.

Frances Griffin	Caryn Richman
Jeff Griffin	Dean Butler
Kim	Allison Barron
Russ Hoover	William Schallert
Larue Powell	Anne Lockhart
Anne Bedford	Mary Frann
The Great Kahuna	Don Stroud
Mickey	Vincent Van Patten
Ron Levering	Ben Murphy

Producer: Harry Ackerman, Ralph Riskin

Theme Vocal ("Everybody's Down at the Beach") by Jan and Dean and the Bel Air Bandits

Gigantor

Cartoon; 30 min; Syn. 1966

A Japanese produced series about an indestructible robot (Gigantor) and his 12-year-old master (Jimmy Sparks) and their battle against interplanetary evil. Music by Lou Singer.

Gigglesnort Hotel

Children; 30 min; Syn. 1979

Various aspects of the world are related to children via the people (puppets) who inhabit the Gigglesnort Hotel.

B.J. (manager)	Bill Jackson

Voices: Ian Harris, Nancy Wettler

Producer: Bill Jackson

The Gil Lamb Show

Comedy Pilot; 30 min; DuMont 9/20/50

Comedy vignettes that are designed to showcase the comedy talents of comedian Gil Lamb. With Martha Tilson and the orchestra of Buzz Adlam. Aired on "Premiere Theatre."

Gilligan's Island

Comedy; 30 min; CBS 9/26/64 to 9/3/67

The series, set on an uncharted South Pacific island, relates the adventures of the seven members of the shipwrecked SS Minnow, a sightseeing boat that was destroyed in a trop-ical storm at sea, as they struggle for survival and seek a way off the island. Three NBC TV movies, based on the series, were also produced: "Rescue from Gilligan's Island" (10/14/78) wherein the castaways are rescued; "The Castaways on Gilligan's Island" (5/3/79) in which millionaire Thurston Howell III turns the island into a tropical resort; and "The Harlem Globetrotters on Gilligan's Island" (5/15/81), wherein an evil billionaire seeks a rare mineral found on the island. With the exception of Ginger, the cast has remained the same. See also "Gilligan's Planet" and "The New Adventures of Gilligan."

Jonas Grumby (Skipper)	Alan Hale Jr.
Gilligan (First Mate)	Bob Denver
Ginger Grant	Tina Louise
Thurston Howell III	Jim Backus
Lovey Howell	Natalie Schafer
Mary Ann Summers	Dawn Wells
Prof. Roy Hinkley	Russell Johnson
Ginger (1st & 2nd films)	Judith Baldwin
Ginger (3rd film)	Constance Forslund

Producer: Sherwood Schwartz.

Theme Vocal ("The Ballad of Gilligan's Isle"): The Wellingtons

Gilligan's Planet

Cartoon; 30 min; CBS 9/18/82 to 9/10/83

A spin-off from "Gilligan's Island." In an attempt to escape from the island, the Professor constructs a rocket that, during its flight, becomes damaged and maroons the castaways on an unknown planet. Stories relate their efforts to repair their rocket and return to Earth.

Gilligan	Bob Denver
Skipper	Alan Hale Jr.
Ginger and Mary Ann	Dawn Wells
Thurston Howell III	Jim Backus
Lovey Howell	Natalie Schafer
The Professor	Russell Johnson

Producer: Norm Prescott, Lou Scheimer

Gimme a Break

Comedy; 30 min; NBC 10/29/81 (Premiere)

While singing in a Glenlawn, California night club, Nell Harper meets Margaret Kennedy, an old friend who is now married to a policeman (Carl) and the mother of three daughters (Katie, Julie, and Samantha). Five weeks later, as Nell is about to leave, Margaret tells her a secret that she has kept from her family: that she is dying. When Margaret asks Nell to raise her girls (knowing that Carl could never manage alone) she agrees to do one last favor for her dearest friend. Stories, set years later, relate Nell's attempts to care for a tough police chief and his three pretty, but troublesome teenage daughters.

Following the death of the chief, and with the girls going their separate ways, the format changed to relate Nell's adventures in New York City and the guardian of two orphaned boys, Joey and Matthew Donovan.

Nell Harper	Nell Carter
Carl Kanisky	Dolph Sweet
Katie Kanisky	Kari Michaelsen
Julie Kanisky	Lauri Hendler
Samantha Kanisky	Lara Jill Miller
Off. Ralph Simpson	Howard Morton
Stanley Kanisky	John Hoyt
Mildred Kanisky	Lili Valenty
	Elvia Allman
	Elizabeth Kerr
	Jane Dulo
Ed Kanisky	Ed Schrum
Joey Donovan	Joey Lawrence
Matthew Donovan	Matthew Lawrence
Addy Wilson	Telma Hopkins
Angie McDaniel	Alvernette Jimenez
Margaret Kanisky	Sharon Spelman
Maggie O'Brien	Rosie O'Donnell
B.J. O'Brien	Blake Clark
Marty	Paul Sand

Theme Vocal ("Gimme a Break"): Nell Carter

Producer: Mort Lachman, Rod Parker, Hal Cooper

The Ginger Rogers Show

Comedy Pilot; 30 min; CBS 7/22/63

Events in the lives of twin sisters Margaret and Elisabeth Harcourt, an artist and a fashion designer, who help each other out in times of need.

Margaret/Elisabeth	Ginger Rogers
Eli Harcourt	Charlie Ruggles
Mario Cellini	Cesare Danova
Gardner McKay	Himself

Producer: Roy Huggins

Girl About Town

Variety; 20 min; NBC 4/15/48 to 9/10/49

A live series of music and songs with film inserts of singer Kyle MacDonnell visiting various New York night clubs. Also known as "The Kyle MacDonnell Show."

Hostess: Kyle MacDonnell

Regulars: Johnny Downs, Earl Wrightson

Music: The Norman Paris Trio

Producer: Fred Coe, Craig Allen

The Girl from U.N.C.L.E.

Adventure; 60 min; NBC 9/13/66 to 9/5/67

A spin-off from "The Man from U.N.C.L.E." The exploits of April Dancer and Mark Slate, agents for the United Network Command for Law Enforcement, as they battle the evils of the criminal organization, THRUSH. See also "The Moonglow Affair."

April Dancer	Stefanie Powers
Mark Slate	Noel Harrison
Alexander Waverly	Leo G. Carroll
Randy Kovacs	Randy Kirby

Producer: Norman Felton

The Girl in My Life

Testimonial; 30 min; ABC 7/9/73 to 12/20/74

A girl, who has performed an unselfish deed, is united with the recipient of the act and awarded merchandise prizes.

Host: Fred Holliday

Announcer: John Harlan

Producer: Bill Carruthers

Girl of My Dreams

Drama; 30 min; Syn. 1/87

When a plane crash claims the life of Lenore Mattson, a beautiful con artist who robbed from the rich and poor alike, she is given the opportunity to atone for her past sins by performing good deeds. Granted a special status, she is given the ability to enter a person's dreams and become a part of the dreamer's problems. The program relates how Lenore's intrusion in fate helps or hinders that person's life when, during the next day, his or her dream becomes a reality.

Lenore Mattson	Dina Caroleo
The High One	Josh Randall
Lusty Lucy	Ann Marie Conato

Producer: Dina Caroleo, Skip Turner

Theme Vocal ("She's the Girl of My Dreams"): Dina Caroleo

Girl on the Run

Crime Drama Pilot; 90 min; ABC 10/10/58

The second of two pilot films for "77 Sunset Strip" (see also "Anything for Money"). The exploits of Stuart Bailey, a veteran of the Office of Strategic Services, turned two-fisted private detective. Originally intended as a theatrical film.

Stuart Bailey	Efrem Zimbalist Jr.
Kathy Allen/Kathy Shay	Erin O'Brien
James McCullough	Sheppard Strudwick
Ken Smiley	Edd Byrnes
Francis Brannigan	Barton MacLane
Lt. Harper	Ray Teal

Producer: William T. Orr, Roy Huggins

Girl Talk

Talk; 30 min; Syn. 1963–70

Guests, mainly women, discuss their thoughts, fears, joys, and sorrows.

Hosts: Virginia Graham (1963–69), Gloria DeHaven (1969), Betsy Palmer (1969–70)

Producer: Monty Morgan

The Girl with Something Extra

Comedy; 30 min; NBC 9/14/73 to 5/24/74

Events in the lives of the Burtons: John, an attorney with Metcalfe, Klein, and Associates, and his wife, Sally, a beautiful girl who possesses ESP and can perceive his every thought.

Sally Burton	Sally Field
John Burton	John Davidson
Jerry Burton	Jack Sheldon
Anne	Zohra Lambert
Owen Metcalfe	Henry Jones
Angela	Stephanie Edwards
Stewart Klein	William Windom

Producer: Bob Claver, Mel Swope

The Girls

Comedy; 30 min; CBS 1/1/50 to 3/25/50

The comic escapades of Cornelia, a hopeful actress, and her friend, Emily, a would-be writer, as they seek fame and fortune in Manhattan. Originally titled "Young and Gay."

Cornelia Otis Skinner	Bethel Leslie
	Gloria Stroock
Emily Kimbrough	Mary Malone

Producer: Carol Irwin

A Girl's Life

Comedy Pilot; 30 min; NBC 8/4/83

The romantic misadventures of Gay Brooks, a beautiful single girl looking for Mr. Right. Heightened by Gay's speaking directly to the audience.

Gay Brooks	Karen Valentine
Evelyn	Joan Hackett
Johnny Paloney	Fred Dryer
Gay (as a girl)	Nea Bryant
David Rudolph	Chris Allport
Gay's father	Lyman Ward

Producer: Michael Zinberg, Susan Seeger

The Gisele MacKenzie Show

Variety; 30 min; NBC 9/28/57 to 3/29/58

A weekly program of music and songs.

Hostess: Gisele MacKenzie

Vocalists: The Double Daters

Announcer: Jack Narz, Tom Kennedy

Orchestra: Axel Stordahl

Producer: Jack Benny, Charles Isaacs

Give and Take

Game; 30 min; CBS 3/20/52 to 6/12/52

Object: For players to answer general knowledge questions in return for merchandise prizes.

Host: Bill Cullen, John Reed King

Producer: Jack Carney

Give-n-Take

Game; 30 min; CBS 9/8/75 to 12/10/76

Four female players are seated around an electronic spinning arrow. When a player correctly answers a question, she presses a button that slowly stops the arrow. The player selected by the arrow has the option of either keeping or passing a prize. The object is for players, who are unaware of actual selling prices, to build a merchandise showcase that does not exceed $5,000. The player who comes closest to that amount wins her prizes.

Host: Jim Lange

Models: Jane Nelson, Judy Rich

Announcer: Johnny Jacobs

Producer: Bill Carruthers

Gladys Knight and the Pips

Variety; 60 min; NBC 7/10/75 to 7/31/75

Music and songs with Gladys Knight and the Pips and the orchestra of George Wyle. Produced by Bob Henry.

Glamour-Go-Round

Women; 15 min; CBS 2/4/50 to 5/3/50

A program of beauty tips and advice.

Hostess: Ilka Chase

Announcer: Durward Kirby

Music: Billy Nalle

Glamour Girl

Women; 30 min; NBC 7/6/53 to 1/8/54

A woman, selected from the audience, becomes the subject for wardrobe advice, beauty treatments, and other tips that are designed to make the average woman a glamour girl.

Host: Harry Babbitt, Jack McCoy

Producer: Jack McCoy

The Glen Campbell Goodtime Hour

Variety; 60 min; CBS 6/23/68 to 6/13/72

A country-western accented program of music and comedy.

Host: Glen Campbell

Regulars: Jerry Reed, Eddie Mayehoff, R.G. Brown, John Hartford, Pat Paulsen, Mel Tillis, The Mike Curb Congregation

Announcer: Roger Carroll

Orchestra: Marty Paich

Producer: Jack Shea, Rich Eustis

The Glen Campbell Music Show

Variety; 30 min; Syn. 9/82

A weekly program of music and songs with host Glen Campbell and the orchestra of T.J. Kuensler. Produced by Pierre Cossette.

Glencannon

Adventure; 30 min; Syn. 1958

The exploits of Colin Glencannon, skipper of the freighter, Inchcliffe Castle, as he roams the Caribbean. See also "Mr. Glencannon Takes All."

Colin Glencannon	Thomas Mitchell
Bos'n Hughes	Patrick Allen
Colin's shipmates	Barry Keegan
	Charles Carson

Producer: Donald Hyde

Glenn Miller Time

Variety; 60 min; CBS 7/10/61 to 9/11/61

A recreation of the sound of the Big Band Era, in particular the Glenn Miller Orchestra.

Host: Ray McKinley, Johnny Desmond

Singers: Patty Clark, The Castle Sisters

Orchestra: Glenn Miller

Producer: William O. Harbach

Glitter

Drama; 60 min; ABC 9/20/84 to 10/4/84
                          12/11/84 to 12/25/84
                          12/13/85 to 12/27/85

Incidents in the lives of celebrities as seen through the eyes of reporters for "Glitter," "the hottest celebrity magazine on the newsstands."

Mark Hughes	Van Johnson
	Arthur Hill
Kate Simpson	Morgan Brittany
Sam Dillon	David Birney
Jennifer Douglas	Dianne Kay
Angela Timini	Tracy Nelson
Terry Randolph	Melinda Culea
Pete Bozak	Christopher Mayer
Clive Richlin	Arte Johnson
Shelley Sealy	Barbara Sharma
Chip Craddock	Timothy Patrick Murphy
Julie Tipton	Kristen Meadows
Marion	Barbara McNair
Earl Tobin	Dorian Harewood

Producer: Aaron Spelling, Lynn Loring

Gloria

Comedy; 30 min; CBS 9/26/82 to 9/21/83

A spin-off from "All in the Family" although the pilot aired as "Gloria Comes Home" on "Archie Bunker's Place" (2/28/82). Following her separation from her husband, Gloria returns to her father's home in Queens. Shortly after, she acquires a job in Fox Ridge (Duchess County, N.Y.) as the assistant to Willard Adams, an aging veterinarian. Stories relate Gloria's experiences and her attempts to raise her son, Joey.

Gloria Bunker Stivic	Sally Struthers
Joey Stivic	Christian Jacobs
Dr. Willard Adams	Burgess Meredith
Dr. Maggie Lawrence	Jo DeWinter
Clark Uhley	Lou Richards

Theme music: "Gloria's Theme" by Tony Greco

Producer: Steve Marshall, Dan Guntzelman

The Gloria DeHaven Show

Variety; 15 min; ABC 10/9/53 to 1/25/54

Music and songs with actress-singer Gloria DeHaven, musician Bobby Hackett and the music of the Tony Mottola Trio.

The Gloria Swanson Hour

Women's Pilot; 55 min; DuMont 6/23/48

A program of fashion trends, glamour, cooking, and other points of interest to women.

Hostess: Gloria Swanson

Assistant: Pat Murray

Producer: Dick Rose

The Gloria Swanson Show

See "Crown Theatre with Gloria Swanson."

G.L.O.W.

Variety; 60 min; Syn. 1/87

A glitzy variety program in which a bevy of beautiful women put on well coordinated wrestling matches coupled with songs, blackouts, and sketches. The title refers to "The Gorgeous Ladies of Wrestling." Taped at the Rivera Hotel in Las Vegas.

Host: David McLane

Producer: David McLane, Edwin Pearlstein, David Amiri, Barbara Hayes

Glynis

Comedy; 30 min; CBS 9/25/63 to 12/18/63

The misadventures of Glynis Granville, a beautiful mystery-story author and amateur sleuth, as she attempts to solve crimes to acquire story material. See also "Hide and Seek."

Glynis Granville	Glynis Johns
Keith Granville	Keith Andes
Chick Rogers	George Mathews

Music: George Duning

Producer: Jess Oppenheimer, Edward H. Feldman

Go

Game; 30 min; NBC 10/3/83 to 1/20/84

Two teams compete with the object being to guess the identity of words within the least amount of time.

Host: Kevin O'Connell

Announcer: Johnny Gilbert

Producer: Bob Stewart

The Go Go Gophers

Cartoon; 30 min; CBS 9/14/68 to 9/6/69

The efforts of Ruffled Feathers and Running Board, two gophers who resemble Indians, to safeguard their domain from Kit Coyote, an Army colonel determined to rid the west of gophers.

Ruffled Feathers	Sandy Becker
Running Board	George S. Irving
Kit Coyote	Kenny Delmar

Go Lucky

Game; 30 min; CBS 7/15/51 to 9/2/51

Object: For contestants to identify common phrases from skits that are performed by a group of players.

Host: Jan Murray

Producer: Herb Morris

The Godzilla Power Hour

Cartoon; 60 min; NBC 9/9/78 to 9/5/81

Segments: "Godzilla" (about scientist Carl Rogers and Godzilla, the 30-story-tall creature he controls, as they battle evil); and "Jana of the Jungle" (about a young girl, rescued from a shipwreck by Montaro, who grows up to defend her African home from evil-doers).

Godzilla	Ted Cassidy
Carl Rogers	Jeff David
Quinn	Brenda Thompson
Pete	Al Eisenmann
Brock	Hilly Hicks
Godzuki	Don Messick
Jana	B.J. Ward
Montaro	Ted Cassidy
Dr. Ben Cooper	Michael Bell
Natives	Ross Martin

Producer: William Hanna, Joseph Barbera

Going Bananas

Comedy; 30 min; NBC 9/15/84 to 12/8/84

The story of Roxanna Banana, an orangutan endowed with super powers*, as she and her adopted brother and sister, James and Louise, battle injustice.

James Cole	Tim Topper
Louise Cole	Emily Moultrie
Gran	Marie Denn
Hubert Gritz	Bill Saluga
Hank Gritz	James Avery
Roxanna Banana	J.R.

*Zapped by a ray from a UFO after she escaped from a zoo.

Going My Way

Comedy-Drama; 60 min; ABC 10/3/62 to 9/11/63

The clash between Father Charles O'Malley, a young Catholic priest with progressive ideas, and Father Fitzgibbon, the stubborn, conservative pastor of New York's St. Dominic's Parish. Based on the feature film.

Father Charles O'Malley	Gene Kelly
Father Fitzgibbon	Leo G. Carroll
Tom Colwell	Dick York
Mrs. Featherstone	Nydia Westman

Producer: Joe Connelly, Bob Mosher

Going Places

Comedy Pilot; 30 min; NBC 3/19/73

The story of Wes Tucker, a small-town writer struggling to make a living in New York City.

Wes Tucker	Todd Susman
Gloria	Jill Clayburgh
Mr. Shaw	Norman Fell
Steve	Jed Allan
Ellen	Judith DeHart

Producer: Arnold Margolin, Jim Parker

The Goldbergs

Comedy; 30 min; CBS 1/17/49 to 6/18/51
NBC 2/4/52 to 7/14/52
NBC 7/3/53 to 9/25/53
DuMont 4/13/54 to 10/19/54

Events in the lives of the Goldbergs, a poor Jewish family living in the Bronx, New York. See the following title also.

Molly Goldberg	Gertrude Berg
Jake Goldberg	Philip Loeb
	Harold J. Stone
	Robert H. Harris
Rosalie Goldberg	Arlene McQuade
Sammy Goldberg	Larry Robinson
	Tom Taylor
David Romaine	Eli Mintz
Mrs. Bloom	Olga Fabian

Producer: Worthington Miner, William Berke

The Goldbergs

Comedy; 30 min; Syn. 9/55

A revised version of the previous title, which continues to depict events in the lives of the Goldbergs as they move from the Bronx to Haverville, a small, mythical town. Also titled "Molly."

Molly Goldberg	Gertrude Berg
Jake Goldberg	Robert H. Harris
Rosalie Goldberg	Arlene McQuade
Sammy Goldberg	Tom Taylor
David Romaine	Eli Mintz
Dora Barnett	Betty Bendyke

Producer: William Berke, Cherney Berg

The Golddiggers

Variety; 30 min; Syn. 9/71

A weekly series of music and songs featuring the Golddiggers; Susan Lund, Jackie Chidsey, Michelle and Tanya Della Fave, Jimmie Cannon, Loyita Chapel, Lee Crawford, Liz Kelley, Francie Mendenhall, Nancy Reichart, Janice Whitby, Lucy Codham, Barbara Sanders, Karen Cavanaugh, and Rebecca Jones.

Regulars: Larry Storch, Alice Ghostley, Charles Nelson Reilly, Jackie Vernon, Lonnie Shorr, Barbara Heller, Jennifer Burnier

Producer: Greg Garrison

Orchestra: Van Alexander

The Golddiggers in London

Variety; 60 min; NBC 7/16/70 to 9/10/70

A summer series of music and songs with the Golddiggers: Pauline Anthony, Wanda Bailey, Jackie Chidsey, Paula Cinko, Rosetta Cox, Michelle and Tanya Della Fave, Tara Leigh, Susan Lund, and Jimmie Cannon.

Host: Charles Nelson Reilly

Regulars: Marty Feldman, Julie Chagrin, Tommy Tune

Producer: Greg Garrison

Orchestra: Jack Parnell

The Golden Girls

Comedy; 30 min; NBC 9/14/85 (Premiere)

Events in the lives of Dorothy, Rose, and Blanche, three women sharing their golden years together in a Miami Beach home owned by Blanche.

Dorothy Zbornak	Bea Arthur
Blanche Devereaux	Rue McClanahan
Rose Nyland	Betty White
Sophia Petrillo, Dorothy's mother	Estelle Getty
Stan, Dorothy's ex husband	Herb Edelman
Kate, Dorothy's daughter	Lisa Jane Persky

Dennis, Kate's husband	Dennis Drake
Virginia, Blanche's sister	Sheree North
"Big Daddy" Hollingsworth, Blanche's father	Murray Hamilton
Gloria, Dorothy's sister	Doris Belack
Kristen, Rose's daughter	Christine Belford
Lucy, Blanche's niece	Hallie Todd
Lilly, Rose's sister	Polly Holliday
Bridget, Rose's daughter	Marilyn Jones
Michael, Dorothy's son	Scott Jacoby
Angela, Sophie's sister	Nancy Walker

Producer: Paul Junger Witt, Tony Thomas

The Golden Griffon

Adventure, 30 min; Syn. 1954

The series, set in 12th-century England, relates the adventures of the Golden Griffon, a mysterious figure who battles injustice.

Golden Griffon	William Andrews
His aide	Mischa Auer

Theme Vocal ("The Ballad of the Golden Griffon"): Otto Henning

Music: Kai Rosenberg

Producer: Richard H. Gordon, Jr., Erik Witte

The Golden Years of Television

Anthology; 60 min; Syn. 1984

The overall title for a collection of TV series episodes from the 1950s. Produced by Michael Avery and featuring such series as "Biff Baker, USA," "Topper," "Tales of Tomorrow," "Andy's Gang," "Sky King," "Racket Squad," "Space Patrol," "The Falcon," "Boston Blackie," "Brave Eagle," "26 Men," and "My Friend Irma."

Goldie and the Bears

Crime Drama Pilot; 60 min; ABC 5/26/85

Following the death of Red Hawkins, coach of the Chicago Bears football team, three team members (Mac, Rhino and Walker) team with Red's daughter, Goldie, the owner of Hawkins Investigations. The unsold series was to relate their case investigations.

Goldie Hawkins	Stephanie Faracy
Mac MacKenna	Terry "Hulk" Hogan
Thomas "Rhino" Rhiner	Ben Davidson
Walker Johnson	Julius J. Carry III
Paul Ellison	William Prince
Caroline Morse	Dorothy Fielding
Judy	Annie O'Neill

Producer: Dean Hargrove

Goldie Gold and Action Jack

Cartoon; 30 min; ABC 9/12/81 to 9/18/82

The adventures of Goldie Gold, the world's richest teenage girl, and her friend, Jack Travis, a reporter for her paper, "The Gold Street Journal," as they seek story material.

Goldie Gold	Nellie Bellflower
Jack Travis	Booker Bradshaw

Producer: Ken Ruby, Joe Spears

Goltar and the Golden Lance

Cartoon; 30 min; Syn. 9/86

Following a raid on a village by the tyrant Tormak, a young warrior (Goltar) who is seeking Tormak for killing his parents, finds a lone survivor, the Princess Golita. When Goltar learns that Tormak has stolen the sacred shield to Golita's kingdom (Dindlar), he and Golita join forces to find him. Stories relate their adventures as they seek Tormak.

Voices: Bob Arbogast, Corey Burton, Henry Corden, Peter Cullen, Jennifer Darling, George DiCenzo, Walker Edmiston, Linda Gary, Dick Gautier, Helen Hunt, Chuck McCann, Allan Melvin, Brock Peters, Bob Ridgely, William Schallert, Frank Welker, Ted Zeigler

Producer: William Hanna, Joseph Barbera

Gomer Pyle, U.S.M.C.

Comedy; 30 min; CBS 9/25/64 to 9/19/69

The life of Gomer Pyle, a naive private with the Second Platoon, B Company of Camp Henderson, a marine base in Los Angeles. A spin-off from "The Andy Griffith Show."

Gomer Pyle	Jim Nabors
Sgt. Vince Carter	Frank Sutton
Pvt. Duke Slattery	Ronnie Schell
Pvt. Frankie Lombardi	Ted Bessell
Bunny Olsen	Barbara Stuart
Sgt. Charles Hacker	Allan Melvin
Cpl. Charles Boyle	Roy Stuart
Lou Anne Poovie	Elizabeth MacRae
Col. Edward Grey	Forrest Compton
Pvt. Hummer	William Christopher

Producer: Sheldon Leonard, Aaron Ruben, Ronald Jacobs

The Gong Show

Variety; 30 min; NBC 6/14/76 to 7/21/78

Three celebrity judges rate the performances of undiscovered talent. The highest rated act receives a cash prize.

Host: Chuck Barris

Assistant: Siv Aberg

Announcer: Johnny Jacobs

Producer: Chuck Barris, Chris Bearde, Gene Banks

Note: John Barbour was the original host of the first five episodes that never aired.

Goober and the Ghost Chasers

Cartoon; 30 min; ABC 9/8/73 to 8/31/75

The adventures of Ted, Tina, Gillie, and Goober, a cowardly dog, as they seek story material for "Ghost Chasers" magazine. Also featured are "The Partridge Family" kids (Laurie, Danny, Chris, and Tracy) as their occasional assistants.

Goober	Paul Winchell
Ted	Jerry Dexter
Tina	Jo Ann Harris
Gillie	Ronnie Schell
Laurie	Susan Dey
Tracy	Suzanne Crough
Danny	Danny Bonaduce
Chris	Brian Forster

Producer: William Hanna, Joseph Barbera

Goober and the Truckers' Paradise

Comedy Pilot; 30 min; CBS 5/17/78

The misadventures of Goober Pyle, "The Andy Griffith Show" garage mechanic, as he moves to a small Atlanta town to open a truck-stop cafe with his sister, Pearl.

Goober Pyle	George Lindsey
Pearl Pyle	Leigh French
Charlene (the waitress)	Sandie Newton
Becky Pyle (Goober's niece)	Aubrey Landers
Toni Pyle (Goober's sister)	Lindsay Bloom

Producer: Rich Eustis

Theme Vocal ("Goober and the Truckers' Paradise"): Ray Stevens

Good Company

Celebrity interviews with host attorney F. Lee Bailey. Produced by David Susskind. ABC 9/7/67 to 12/21/67.

The Good Guys

Comedy; 30 min; CBS 9/25/68 to 1/23/70

Seeking to better their lives, life-long friends Bert and Rufus pool their resources and purchase a diner in Los Angeles. Episodes relate their efforts to run "Bert's Place."

Rufus Butterworth	Bob Denver
Bert Gramus	Herb Edelman
Claudia Gramus	Joyce Van Patten
Big Tom	Alan Hale Jr.
Gertie	Toni Gilman
Hal	George Furth
Andy	Ron Masak
D.W. Watson	Liam Dunn
Arlene	Joan Delaney

Producer: Jerry Davis, Leonard B. Stern

Good Heavens

Anthology; 30 min; ABC 2/29/76 to 6/24/76

Varying comedy stories in which a celestial messenger (Mr. Angel) is sent to Earth to fulfill the fantasies of deserving people.

| Mr. Angel | Jose Ferrer* |
| | Carl Reiner |

Producer: Carl Reiner, Mel Swope, Austin & Irma Kalish

"Good Heavens" Theme by Patrick Williams

*Role in the never televised pilot, "Everything Money Can't Buy."

The Good Life

Comedy; 30 min; NBC 9/18/71 to 1/8/72

Seeking to escape life's endless problems, marrieds Albert and Jane Miller pose as a butler and cook and acquire a position with the wealthy Charles Dutton. Stories relate their efforts to enjoy "The Good Life."

Albert Miller	Larry Hagman
Jane Miller	Donna Mills
Charles Dutton	David Wayne
Grace Dutton	Kate Reid*
	Hermione Baddeley
Nick Dutton	Danny Goldman

Producer: Lee Rich, Claudio Guzman

*Role in the pilot (NBC, 8/23/71).

Good Morning, Miss Bliss

Comedy Pilot; 30 min; NBC 7/11/87

The story of Carrie Bliss, a beautiful and caring 6th grade school teacher. In the pilot episode, star Hayley Mills' first attempt at an American series, Carrie tries to help a troubled student.

Carrie Bliss	Hayley Mills
Tina Paladrino	Maria O'Brien
Charlie Davis	Charles Siebert
Lonnie Maple	Julie Ronnie
Gerald Belding	Oliver Clark
Janet Hillyard	Sharon Jo Martin
Wendy	Samantha Mills
Bradley	Gabriel Damon

Producer: Peter Engel, Sam Bobrick

Good Morning World

Comedy; 30 min; CBS 9/5/67 to 9/17/68

The home and working lives of disc jockeys Dave Lewis and Larry Clark, hosts of the Los Angeles-based "Lewis and Clark" morning radio show.

Dave Lewis	Joby Baker
Larry Clark	Ronnie Schell
Linda Lewis	Julie Parrish
Roland B. Hutton Jr.	Billy DeWolfe
Sandy Kramer	Goldie Hawn
Vinnie	Burt Taylor
Big Jack Jackson	Gene Klavin

Producer: Sheldon Leonard, Carl Reiner, Bill Persky, Sam Denoff

Good Neighbors

Comedy; 30 min; Syn. 1980

Events in the lives of Barbara and Tom Good, a British couple who abandon their corporate rat race to live off the land and be totally self sufficient.

Barbara Good	Felicity Kendal
Tom Good	Richard Briers
Margot Ledbetter	Penelope Keith
Jeremy Ledbetter	Paul Eddington

Producer: John Howard Davies

Good Ol' Boys

Comedy Pilot; 30 min; NBC 6/7/79

The story of Traveler and Cooter, two hopeful country music stars making time as vending machine maintenance men.

Traveler	Jerry Reed
Cooter	Lance Caudell
Isaac	Mel Stewart
Mary	Linda Thompson
Forklift	Dennis Harrison

Producer: Perry Lafferty

Theme Vocal ("Good Ol' Boys"): Jerry Reed

The Good Old Days

Comedy Pilot; 30 min; CBS 7/11/66

The story, set in prehistoric times, of a young caveman (Rok), and his efforts to find a life of peace and quiet away from his nagging parents.

Rok	Dwayne Hickman
Mommy	Kathleen Freeman
Daddy	Ned Glass
Pantha	Chris Noel
Cavegirl	Beverly Adams
Kid	Dean Moray
Soc	Jacques Aubuchon
Ugh	Dodo Denney
Brute	Charles Horvath
Slag	Bruce Yarnell
Kook	Joe Bova

Producer: Hal Goodman, Larry Klein

Good Penny

Comedy Pilot; 30 min; NBC 9/1/77

The misadventures of an emotionally disturbed young woman (Penny) who joins an outlandish therapy group.

Penny	Renee Taylor
Al	Scott Brady
Pauline	Gloria LeRoy
Jerry	Carmine Caridi
Dr. Frosman	Roger Bowen
Herb	Bobby Alto
Receptionist	Lila Teigh

Producer: Joseph Bologna (also the writer with Renee Taylor)

Good Time Harry

Comedy; 30 min; NBC 7/19/80 to 9/13/80

The story of Harry Jenkins, a sportswriter for the "San Francisco Journal" and an accomplished womanizer who often confuses sport and play.

Harry Jenkins	Ted Bessell
Jimmy Hughes	Eugene Roche
Carol Younger	Marcia Strassman
Billie Howard	Jesse Welles
Sally	Ruth Manning
Lenny	Richard Karron
Stan	Barry Gordon
Martin Springer	Steven Peterman
Debbie Howard	Kyle Richards
Carmine Howard	Dan Hedaya

Theme Vocal ("Wild About Harry"): Norman Brooks

Producer: Steve Gordon

Good Times

Comedy; 30 min; CBS 2/8/74 to 8/1/79

A spin-off from "Maude," which follows the struggles of the Evanses, a poor black family living in a Chicago Project (at 763 North Gilbert, Apt. 17-C of the Cabrini Housing Project).

James Evans	John Amos
Florida Evans	Esther Rolle
James "J.J." Evans Jr.	Jimmie Walker
Thelma Evans	BernNadette Stanis
Michael Evans	Ralph Carter
Willona Woods	Ja'net DuBois
Penny Gordon	Janet Jackson
Nathan Bookman	Johnny Brown
Violet Bookman	Marilyn Coleman
Keith Anderson	Ben Powers
Cal Dickson	Moses Gunn

Producer: Norman Lear, Allan Manings, Austin and Irma Kalish

Goodbye, Charlie

Comedy Pilot; 30 min; ABC 6/4/85

While hang gliding, Charlie Sorrell, a womanizing ad agency vice president, drowns when he crashes into a river. Shortly after, a beautiful woman appears at the door of George Erskine, Charlie's co-worker. Soon it is realized that the woman is Charlie, who has been reincarnated as a member of the opposite sex. The would-be series was to relate Charlie's efforts to adjust from male to female.

Charlie Sorrell	Suzanne Somers
George Erskine	John Davidson
Vickie	Kathleen Wilhoite
Ray Lemmon	Ray Buktenica
Troy Benjamin	Brant Van Hoffman

Theme ("Goodbye, Charlie") by Al Kasha, Joel Hirschorn

Producer: Patricia Nardo

Goodbye Doesn't Mean Forever

Comedy Pilot; 30 min; NBC 5/28/82

A proposed series based on "The Goodbye Girl." The relationship between Paula McFadden, a beautiful single mother and aspiring dancer, and Elliott Garfield, a struggling actor with whom she shares an apartment.

Paula McFadden	Karen Valentine
Elliott Garfield	Michael Lembeck
Lucy McFadden	Lili Haydn

Theme Vocal ("Goodbye Doesn't Mean Forever"): David Gates

Producer: Allan Katz

The Goodies

Comedy; 30 min; Syn. 1976

The chaotic misadventures of the Goodies (Graeme, Tim, and Bill), three British men who will do anything to succeed in the business world.

Graeme	Graeme Garden
Tim	Tim Brooke-Taylor
Bill	Bill Oddie

Regulars: Patricia Hayes, Michael Aspel, Milton Reid, Julie Desmond

Producer: John Davis

Goodnight, Beantown

Comedy; 30 min; CBS 4/3/83 to 1/15/84

The rocky home and working lives of Matt Cassidy and Jennifer Barnes, co-anchors of Boston's WYN, Channel 11, "Evening News" program, and neighbors in the same apartment building.

Matt Cassidy	Bill Bixby
Jennifer Barnes	Mariette Hartley
Susan Barnes	Tracey Gold
Dick Novak	George Coe
Albert Aldleson	G.W Bailey
Valerie	Stephanie Faracy
Frank Fletcher	Jim Staahl
Sam Holliday	Peter Levin

Producer: A.J. Crothers, Bill Bixby, Charles B. Fitzsimons

Goodtime Girls

Comedy; 30 min; ABC 1/22/80 to 8/29/80

The experiences of Camille, Betty, Edith, and Loretta, four working girls sharing a Washington, D.C., apartment and enduring the 1942 homefront hardships of World War II—including rationing and the man shortage.

Camille Rittenhouse	Francine Tacker
Betty Crandall	Lorna Patterson
Edith Beatlemeyer	Annie Potts
Loretta Smoot	Georgia Engel
Frankie Molardo	Adrian Zmed
Irma Coolidge	Marcia Lewis
George Coolidge	Merwin Goldsmith
Benny Lohman	Peter Scolari

Theme Vocal ("Back in the 40s"): The Charles Fox Singers

Producer: Thomas L. Miller, Edward K. Milkis, Robert L. Boyett

The Goodyear Revue

Variety; 30 min; ABC 11/6/49 to 3/20/52

Music, songs, and light comedy. Sponsored by Goodyear.

Host: Earl Wrightson

Regulars: Maureen Cannon, The Ray Porter Chorus

Orchestra: Glenn Osser

Producer: William H. Brown Jr., Richard Eckler

Goodyear Theatre

See "The Alcoa/Goodyear Theatre."

The Gook Family

Comedy Pilot; 30 min; NBC 7/25/49

The outrageous antics of the Gooks (Vic, Sade, and Rush), a not-so-typical American family. Based on the radio series "Vic and Sade."

Vic Gook	Frank Dane
Sade Gook	Bernadine Flynn
Rush Gook	Dick Conan
Mr. Starbright	Norman Gottschalk
Mrs. Starbright	Eleanor Eagle
Mrs. Call	Hope Summers
Mr. Kneesuffer	Cliff Soubier

Producer-Director: Norman Felton

The Gordon MacRae Show

Variety; 15 min; NBC 3/5/56 to 8/27/56

Music and songs with host Gordon MacRae, the Cheerleaders (singers) and the orchestra of Van Alexander.

Gossip

Comedy Pilot; 30 min; NBC 6/10/79

The antics of the editorial staff of the "National Gossip," a Hollywood-based scandal sheet.

Goldie	Judy Landers
Milton	Jeff Altman
April James	Sarah Daly
Mac	Charles Levin
Leech	Raymond Singer
Ed Stone	Thomas Hill
Luanda Neester	Fern Fitzgerald

Producer: Roger Gimbel, Mort Lachman

Gossip

Comedy Pilot; 30 min; NBC 7/10/79

A second pilot about the antics of the "National Gossip," a Hollywood-based scandal sheet.

Mr. Dempster	John Hillerman
Mrs. Gallup	Dena Dietrich
Jeb	Charles Levin
Mittie	Mary Catherine Wright
Flash	Jeff Altman
Tip	Robbie Rist

Producer: Roger Gimbel, Tony Converse

The Gourmet

A syndicated (1969) series of cooking instruction with David Wade. Announcer: Jack Harrison.

The Gourmet Club

A syndicated (1958) cooking program hosted by Dione Lucas and featuring guest celebrities preparing gourmet meals.

The Governor and J.J.

Comedy; 30 min; CBS 9/23/69 to 1/6/71

Incidents in the lives of William Drinkwater, governor of an unidentified Midwestern state, and his beautiful 23-year-old daughter, J.J. (Jennifer Jo), the curator of a children's zoo.

William Drinkwater	Dan Dailey
J.J. Drinkwater	Julie Sommars
George Callison	James Callahan
Maggie McCloud	Neva Patterson
Sara	Nora Marlowe
Orrin Hacker	Edward Platt

Producer: Leonard B. Stern, Arne Sultan

Grady

Comedy; 30 min; NBC 12/4/75 to 3/4/76

A spin-off from "Sanford and Son" wherein Grady Wilson begins a new life with his daughter, Ellie, her husband Hal, and their children Laurie and Haywood.

Grady Wilson	Whitman Mayo
Ellie Marshall	Carol Cole
Hal Marshall	Joe Morton
Laurie Marshall	Rosanne Katon
Haywood Marshall	Haywood Nelson
Mr. Pratt (landlord)	Jack Fletcher
Rose (neighbor)	Alix Elias

Producer: Saul Turteltaub, Bernie Orenstein

The Grady Nutt Show

Comedy Pilot; 30 min; NBC 7/24/81

The misadventures of Grady Williams, an ordained minister (of the Rockwell Community Church) and his family (his wife, Ellie, and daughter Becky).

Grady Williams	Grady Nutt
Ellie Williams	Elinor Donahue
Becky Williams	Debby Lynn
Randy	Michael Dudikoff
Joe	Raleigh Bond
Jeremy	Ed Marshall
Liz	Peggy Pope
Mona Thompson	Candice Azzara

Producer: John Aylesworth

Graffiti Rock

A syndicated (6/84) pilot for a proposed series of music videos with host Michael Shannon. Produced by Stephen Memishiar and Gail Baker.

The Grand Jury

Crime Drama; 30 min; Syn. 1958

The cases of Harry Driscoll and John Kennedy, investigators for the Los Angeles Grand Jury. Based on official files.

Harry Driscoll	Lyle Bettger
John Kennedy	Harold J. Stone
Thomas Grant	Douglas Dumbrille
Bill Thompson	Richard Travis

Producer: Mort Briskin

The Grand Ole Opry

Variety; 60 min; ABC 10/15/55 to 9/15/56

Country and western music with host Red Foley and regulars Les Paul and Mary Ford, Chet Atkins, Minnie Pearl, Ernest Tubb, Jimmy Dickens, Cal Smith, The Lovin' Brothers, The Grand Ole Opry Dancers.

The Grand Tour

Human Interest Pilot; 60 min; Syn. 12/85

Tours of interesting places around the world with a focus on the people and their customs.

Host: Dick Cavett, Jenilee Harrison

Narrator: Jenilee Harrison, Karen Kasaba

Producer: Philip A Brady

Grandpa Goes to Washington

Comedy-Drama; 60 min; NBC 9/20/78 to 1/16/79

The political adventures of Joe Kelley, a former political science professor who is now a U.S. Senator, as he tries to practice what he taught—honest government.

Joe Kelley	Jack Albertson
Kevin Kelley	Larry Linville
Rose Kelley	Sue Ane Langdon
Cathleen Kelley	Michele Tobin
Kevin Kelley Jr.	Sparky Marcus
Madge	Madge Sinclair
Tony DuVall	Tom Mason
President	Richard Eastman

Producer: Leonora Thuna, Robert Stambler

Grandpa Max

Comedy Pilot; 30 min; CBS 3/28/75

The bickering relationship between "Grandpa" Max Sherman, a crusty, caustic widower, and his son, Paul, who treats his young-at-heart father like an old man.

Max Sherman	Larry Best
Paul Sherman	Michael Lerner
Liz Sherman	Suzanne Astor
Michael Sherman	Brad Savage
Louis Yates	Shimen Ruskin
Mr. Unger	Dick Van Patten
Betty	Susan Alpern

Producer: Aaron Ruben, John Rich

The Gray Ghost

Adventure; 30 min; Syn. 1957

The exploits of John Mosby, a Civil War major known as "The Gray Ghost," as he conducts cunning raids against the Union Army in hopes of fostering a Confederate victory.

John Mosby	Tod Andrews
Lt. St. Clair	Phil Cambridge

Producer: Lindsley Parsons

Great Adventure

Anthology; 60 min; CBS 9/27/63 to 9/18/64

Dramatizations based on the people and events that helped to shape America.

Narrator (episodes 1–13): Van Heflin

Narrator (episodes 14–26): Russell Johnson

Producer: John Houseman

Music: Richard Rodgers

Great Bible Adventures

Anthology Pilot; 60 min; ABC 9/11/66

A proposed series based on stories from the Bible. The pilot episode, "Seven Rich Years ... And Seven Lean," tells of the Hebrew Joseph's rise out of bondage to his reign as the pharaoh's minister.

Joseph	Hugh O'Brian
Pharaoh	Joseph Wiseman
Aton	Eduardo Cinnelli
Potiphar	Torin Thatcher
Asenath	Katharine Ross
Baker	Sorrell Booke

Great Day

Comedy Pilot; 30 min; ABC 5/23/77

The misadventures of a group of skid-row derelicts living at an inner-city mission in Los Angeles.

Peavey	Al Molinaro
Doc	Dub Taylor
Boomer	Guy Marks
Jabbo	Spo-De-Odee
Moose	Joseph Elic
Billy	Billy Barty
Pop	Pat Cranshaw
Molly	Alice Nunn
Mrs. Graham	Audrey Christie

Producer: Aaron Ruben

Great Day

Comedy Pilot; 30 min; CBS 11/19/83

The story of Howard Simpson, a family man and homeowner who is plagued by life's seemingly endless problems.

Howard Simpson	Tim Conway
Jennifer Simpson	Joanna Gleason
Carla Simpson	Jill Schoelen
Ricky Simpson	Corky Pigeon
Ralph Maxwell	Gordon Jump

Producer: Fred Silverman, Edward H. Feldman

Great Ghost Tales

Anthology; 30 min; NBC 7/6/61 to 9/21/61

A series of twelve mystery and suspense stories that feature such stars as Lee Grant, Arthur Hill, Lois Nettleton, Kevin McCarthy, Joanne Linville, Vincent Gardenia, Salome Jens, Richard Thomas, and James Broderick.

Host: Frank Gallop

The Great Gildersleeve

Comedy; 30 min; Syn. 1954

The home and working life of Throckmorton P. Gildersleeve, the water commissioner of Summerfield, and the bachelor uncle to his orphaned niece and nephew, Marjorie and Leroy.

Throckmorton Gildersleeve	Willard Waterman
Marjorie Forrestor	Stephanie Griffin
Leroy Forrestor	Roland Keith
Leila Ransom	Shirley Mitchell
Lois	Doris Singleton
Birdie Lee Coggins	Lillian Randolph
Mayor Terwilliger	Willis Bochey
Peavey	Forrest Lewis
Judge Hooker	Earle Ross
Bessie	Barbara Stuart

Producer: Frank Pittman, Matthew Rapf

The Great Grape Ape Show

Cartoon; 30 min; ABC 9/11/77 to 9/3/78

The adventures of a 40-foot purple gorilla (Grape Ape) and his friend Beegle Beagle, a fast-talking dog.

Grape Ape	Bob Holt
Beegle Beagle	Marty Ingels

Producer: William Hanna, Joseph Barbera

The Great Merlini

Crime Drama Pilot; 30 min; Syn. 1951

The exploits of the Great Merlini, a master illusionist and escape artist who helps the police solve baffling crimes.

The Great Merlini	Jerome Thor
Julie Boyd	Barbara Cook
Insp. Gavigan	Robert Noe
Cornell	E.G. Marshall
Willoughby	Mike Myers
Hat Check Girl	Linda Lombard

Producer: Felix Greenfield, Robert Whitman

The Great Movie Cowboys

A syndicated (1977) series of rarely-broadcast western films of the 1930s and 40s. Hosted by Roy Rogers.

The Great Mysteries of Hollywood

Anthology Pilot; 30 min; Syn. 3/81

A proposed series that was to explore various Hollywood mysteries (e.g., in the pilot, "Did America Kill John Wayne?", explores the possibility that Wayne, Susan Hayward, Agnes Moorehead, and Dick Powell were exposed to atomic radiation while filming "The Conquerer" in Nevada in 1955).

Host: Chuck Conners

Guests: June Allyson, Bob Hope, Lee Van Cleef

Producer: Norman Baer

The Great Space Coaster

Variety; 30 min; Syn. 1/81

Music, songs and sketches that relate various aspects of the world to children.

Francine	Emily Bindiger
Danny	Chris Gifford
Roy	Ray Stephens
Goriddle Gorilla	Kevin J. Clash
Baxter	Frances Kane
Knock Knock	John Lovelady
Gary Gnu/Mr. T	Jim Martin
Edison/Speed Reader	Ken Myles

Producer: Tom Griffin, Dave Bacall, John Claster

The Greatest American Hero

Fantasy; 60 min; ABC 3/18/81 to 2/3/83

While on a field trip, Whitney High School teacher Ralph Hinkley, and Bill Maxwell, an FBI agent stranded in the same area, are chosen by aliens to save Earth from destroying itself. Ralph is presented with a special costume that endows him with amazing powers; Bill is selected to aid him with information about endangering situations. Complications set in when Ralph loses the suit's instruction manual and has to wing it on being "The Greatest American Hero." Stories relate Ralph's efforts to crush evil like no man has ever done before.

Ralph Hinkley	William Katt
Bill Maxwell	Robert Culp
Pam Davidson	Connie Sellecca
Kevin Hinkley	Brandon Williams
Alicia Hinkley	Simone Griffeth
Rhonda Harris	Faye Grant
Tony Villacona	Michael Pare
Paco Rodriquez	Don Cervantes
Agent Carlyle	William Bogert
Palmer Bradshaw	William Frankfather
Ray Buck	Robby Weaver
Alice Davidson	June Lockhart

Theme Vocal ("Believe It Or Not"): Joey Scarbury

Producer: Stephen J. Cannell, Juanita Bartlett

Greatest Headlines of the Century

A three-minute syndicated (1970) series of mini documentaries that briefly recall events of the world. Narrated by Tom Hudson and Produced by Sherman Grinberg.

Greatest Heroes of the Bible

Anthology; Various (60 min; 2 hrs); NBC
11/19/78 to 11/22/78
5/8/79 to 5/22/79
7/26/81 to 8/15/81

Dramatizations based on stories from the Old Testament.

Narrator: Victor Jory

Announcer: Brad Crandall

Music: Bob Summers

Producer: Charles E. Sellier Jr., James L. Conway

The Greatest Man on Earth

Game; 30 min; ABC 12/3/52 to 2/9/53

Five male contestants compete in various stunt and question-and-answer contests with the best performer being named "The Greatest Man on Earth."

Host: Ted Brown

Hostess: Vera Vague

Assistant: Pat Conway

Producer: Walt Framer, Stanley Colbert

The Greatest Show on Earth

Drama; 60 min; ABC 9/17/63 to 9/8/64

The problems faced by the performers of the Ringling Brothers & Barnum and Bailey Circus.

Johnny Slate	Jack Palance
Otto King	Stu Erwin
Louisa Johansen*	Tuesday Weld
Inge Johansen*	Ruth Roman
Ringmaster	William Woodson
Circus Fat Lady	Barbara Pepper

Theme Song ("March of the Clowns") by Richard Rodgers

Producer: Stanley Colbert

*Intended series regulars—a trapeze artist (Louisa) and her mother—during shooting of the pilot.

Green Acres

Comedy; 30 min; CBS 9/15/65 to 9/7/71

Oliver Douglas, a New York attorney who yearns to be a farmer, purchases the 160-acre Haney Farm in Hooterville. Stories relate Oliver's attempts, reluctantly assisted by his glamorous wife, Lisa, to successfully re-establish the run-down Haney Farm.

Oliver Douglas	Eddie Albert
Lisa Douglas	Eva Gabor
Eb Dawson	Tom Lester
Eustace Haney	Pat Buttram
Hank Kimball	Alvy Moore
Fred Ziffel	Hank Patterson
Doris Ziffel	Fran Ryan
	Barbara Pepper
Sam Drucker	Frank Cady
Newt Kiley	Kay E. Kuter
Alf Monroe	Sid Melton
Ralph Monroe	Mary Grace Canfield
Joe Carson	Edgar Buchanan
Eunice Douglas	Eleanor Audley
Darleen Wheeler	Judy McConnell
Matt Wheeler	Robert Foulk
Brian Williams	Rick Lenz
Lori Baker	Victoria Meyerink
Grandpappy Miller	Victor Baldwin
Sarah	Merle Earle

Theme Vocal ("Green Acres"): Eddie Albert, Eva Gabor

Producer: Paul Henning, Jay Sommers

The Green Hornet

Adventure; 30 min; ABC 9/9/66 to 7/14/67

The exploits of Britt Reid, publisher of the "Daily Sentinel" and secretly the Green Hornet, a daring crime fighter who struggles to protect the rights and lives of decent citizens.

Britt Reid	Van Williams
Kato	Bruce Lee
Lenore "Casey" Case	Wende Wagner
Frank Scanlon	Walter Brooke
Mike Axford	Lloyd Gough
Frank's secretary	Sheila Leighton
TV Newscaster	Gary Owens

Theme Song Performer ("Flight of the Bumble Bee"): The Billy May Orchestra

Trumpet Solo: Al Hirt

Producer: William Dozier

Griff

Crime Drama; 60 min; ABC 9/29/73 to 1/4/74

The exploits of Wade "Griff" Griffin, a former police captain turned private detective.

Wade Griffin	Lorne Greene
Mike Murdoch	Ben Murphy
Grace Newcombe	Patricia Stich
Capt. Barney Marcus	Vic Tayback
Dr. Rayburn	Jared Martin

Music: Mike Post and Pete Carpenter

Producer: David Victor, Steven Bochco

Grindl

Comedy; 30 min; NBC 9/15/63 to 9/13/64

The antics of Grindl, a fumbling maid with Foster's Temporary Employment Service.

Grindl	Imogene Coca
Anson Foster	James Millhollin

Music: Frank DeVol

Producer: Harry Ackerman, Winston O'Keefe

Growing Pains

Comedy; 30 min; ABC 9/24/85 (Premiere)

When Maggie Seavers, a housewife and mother, seeks to resume her career (reporter for the Long Island Daily Herald), Jason, her husband, quits his job at Long Island General Hospital and moves his psychiatric practice to his home. Stories relate Jason's attempts to run a home, care for his kids, and conduct a practice.

Jason Seavers	Alan Thicke
Maggie Seavers	Joanna Kerns
Carol Seavers	Elizabeth Ward*
	Tracey Gold
Mike Seavers	Kirk Cameron
Ben Seavers	Jeremy Miller

Theme Vocal ("As Long As We've Got Each Other"): B.J. Thomas and Jennifer Warnes

*Carol in the never telecast pilot.

Growing Paynes

Comedy; 30 min; DuMont 10/20/48 to 1/12/49 (local N.Y.) 1/19/49 to 8/3/49 (network)

A live series about the day-to-day lives of the Payne family: George, an insurance salesman, Laraine, his wife, and their son, John.

George Payne	John Harvey*
	Ed Holmes
Laraine Payne	Judy Parrish*
	Elaine Stritch
John Payne	David Anderson
Birdie (their maid)	Ann Sullivan

Producer-Director: Pat Fay

*Stars of the local version.

Gruen Guild Playhouse

Anthology; 30 min; ABC 9/27/51 to 12/20/51 DuMont 3/27/52 to 9/23/52

Varying presentations, including comedy, drama, and fantasy. Stars include Bonita Granville, Shirley Jones, Raymond Burr, Marjorie Reynolds, Dane Clark, Bruce Cabot, Buddy Ebsen, Vincent Price, Cesar Romero, Craig Stevens, and Patrick O'Neal. Sponsored by Gruen watches.

Producer: Leon Fromkess

Guess Again

Game; 30 min; CBS 6/14/51 to 6/21/51

Object: For contestants to answer questions based on a skit that is performed on stage.

Host: Mike Wallace

Regulars: Joey Faye, Bobbi Martin, Mandy Kaye

Producer: Al Span

Guess What?

Game; 30 min; DuMont 7/8/52 to 8/26/52

Object: For panelists to identify a famous person, place, or object from quotations or statements that are read to them by the host.

Host: Richard Kollmar

Panelists: Cliff Norton, Audrey Christie, Lisa Fenaday, Virginia Peine, Quenton Reynolds, Mark Hanna

Producer: Larry White, Manny Rosenberg

Guess What Happened?

Game; 30 min; NBC 8/7/52 to 8/21/52

A person, who is, or was involved in a news story, is the guest. Through indirect questions, panelists must guess the situation in which their guest was or is involved.

Host: John Cameron Swayze, Ben Grauer

Panelists: Maureen Stapleton, Neva Patterson, Frank Gallop, Jack Norton, Roger Price, H. Allen Smith

Guess What I Did Today?

Comedy Pilot; 30 min; NBC 9/10/68

The misadventures of Warren Springer, a paint company chemist and amateur inventor who spends his free time brewing up weird concoctions.

Warren Springer	Fred Gwynne
Bonnie Springer	Bridget Hanley
Sally Springer	Pamelyn Ferdin
Phoebe	Reta Shaw

Guess Who's Coming to Dinner?

Comedy Pilot; 30 min; ABC 5/28/75

A story of an interracial marriage and its comical problems as seen through the eyes of Joanna Drayton, a white girl who marries a black (John).

Joanna Prentiss	Leslie Charleson
John Prentiss	Bill Overton
Christine Drayton	Eleanor Parker
Matt Drayton	Richard Dysart
Ralph Prentiss	Lee Weaver
Sarah Prentiss	Madge Sinclair

Producer-Director: Stanley Kramer

A Guest in Your House

Variety; 15 min; NBC 3/5/51 to 3/30/51

Music, poetry, and conversation with host Edgar Guest and his assistant Rachel Stevenson. Music by Paul Arnold.

Guest Shot

A syndicated (1962) series of celebrity interviews with hosts Army Archerd, Earl Wilson, Hank Grank, Vernon Scott, and Dan Jenkins.

Guestward Ho

Comedy; 30 min; ABC 9/20/60 to 9/21/61

Dissatisfied with the congestion of city living, ad executive Bill Hooten purchases Guestward Ho, a dude ranch in New Mexico. Stories relate his efforts to make a success of the ranch.

Bill Hooten	Mark Miller
Babs Hooten	Joanne Dru
Brook Hooten	Flip Mark
Chief Hawkeye	J. Carrol Naish
Pink Cloud	Jolene Brand
Lonesome	Earl Hodgins
Rocky	Tony Montenaro

Producer: Jerry Thorpe

Guestward Ho

Comedy Pilot; 30 min; Unaired (produced for CBS in 1959).

The original cast concept for the above series. Based on the book by Barbara Hooten and produced by Desilu.

Bill Hooten	Leif Erickson
Barbara Hooten	Vivian Vance

Also: Bella Bruck

Producer-Director: Ralph Levy

Guide Right

Variety; 30 min; DuMont 2/25/52 to 10/30/53

An enlistment program (for the Korean War) that showcases both civilian and military talent.

Host: Don Russell

Orchestra: Elliot Lawrence

Guilty or Innocent

Game; 30 min; Syn. 10/84

Object: For twelve players, acting as jurors, to determine the guilt or innocence of a defendant in an actual, redramatized trial.

Host: Melvin Belli

Jury Moderator: John Shearin

Producer: Sherman Rubinstein

Guilty or Not Guilty

Drama Pilot; 60 min; NBC 3/9/66

The exploits of Gregg Collier, a New York City Assistant D.A. Aired on "The Bob Hope Chrysler Theatre."

Gregg Collier	Leslie Nielsen
Judy Collier	Diana Hyland
Andrew Dixon	Robert Ryan
Ben Stafford	Leif Erickson
Catherine Collier	Pippa Scott
Frank Reeser	Robert Duvall

Producer: Gordon Oliver, Jack Laird

The Guinness Game

Game; 30 min; Syn. 9/79

Object: For players to bet money on whether or not an ordinary person can either establish or break a "Guinness Book" record.

Host: Don Galloway

Assistant: Donny Evans, Toby Hoffman

Announcer: Charlie O'Donnell, Tony McClay

Producer: Marvin Minoff

Gulf Playhouse

Anthology; 30 min; NBC 10/3/52 to 12/24/52

A live drama series, produced by Frank Telford, and sponsored by the Gulf Oil Corporation.

Gumby

Children; 30 min; NBC 3/23/57 to 11/16/57

The animated (clay) adventures of a boy (Gumby) and his horse, Pokey. Currently syndicated in five minute segments as "The Gumby Show."

Host: Bob Nicholson, Pinky Lee

Producer: Bob Clokey

Gun Shy

Comedy; 30 min; CBS 3/15/83 to 4/12/83

The series, set in Quake City, California (circa 1869) tells the story of Russell Donovan, a gambling dandy, as he struggles to raise Clovis and Celia, two orphans he won in a poker game, and shape up two bumbling outlaws (Theodore and Amos) who constantly plague his life. Based on the film, "The Apple Dumpling Gang." See also "Tales of the Apple Dumpling Gang."

Russell Donovan	Barry Van Dyke
Celia	Bridgette Anderson
Clovis	Keith Mitchell
Theodore	Tim Thomerson
Amos	Geoffrey Lewis
Homer McCoy	Henry Jones
Nettie McCoy	Janis Paige
Colonel Mound	Pat McCormick

Producer: William Robert Yates

Note: Adam Rich played Clovis in two nevertelevised episodes.

Gung Ho

Comedy; 30 min; ABC 12/5/86 to 2/6/87

Shortly after the Hadleyville Auto Plant in Pittsburgh closes down, Assan Motors of Japan reopens it and assigns a Japanese foreman (Kazuhiro) to work alongside his American counterpart (Hunt). Stories relate the efforts of both the Japanese and American workers to co-exist while at the same time retaining their traditional work habits.

"Kaz" Kazuhiro	Gedde Watanabe
Hunt Stevenson	Scott Bakula
Buster	Stephen Lee
Mr. Saito	Sab Shimono
Googie	Clint Howard
Ito	Rodney Kageyama
Yukiko	Emily K. Kuroda
Kenji	Scott Atari
Willie	Willie Walton
Umeki	Patti Yasutake
Randi	Heidi Banks

Producer: John Rappaport, George Sunga

The Guns of Will Sonnett

Western; 30 min; ABC 9/8/67 to 9/15/69

The travels of ex-cavalry scout Will Sonnett and his 20-year-old grandson, Jeff, as they roam the west of the 1880s seeking to find James Sonnett, Jeff's father, a killer who deserted his family in the 1860s. In the series last episode, Will and Jeff find James and convince him to give up his life of running. Hoping to start new lives, the Sonnet's settle in the town of Sampson. There, Will becomes the sheriff and Jeff and James his deputies. Had the series been renewed, it would have focused on the Sonnett's efforts to maintain law and order in Sampson.

Will Sonnett	Walter Brennan
Jeff Sonnett	Dack Rambo
James Sonnett	Jason Evers

Producer: Danny Thomas, Aaron Spelling

Gunslinger

Western; 30 min; CBS 2/9/61 to 9/5/61

The exploits of Cord, a U.S. Cavalry undercover agent (stationed at Fort Scott in Los Flores, New Mexico) who poses as a gunslinger in an attempt to apprehend criminals wanted by the Army.

Cord	Tony Young
Capt. Zachary Wingate	Preston Foster
Amber Hollister	Midge Ware
Pico McGuire	Charles Gray
Bill Urchin	Dee Pollock
Murdock	John Pickard

Theme Vocal ("Gunslinger") by Frankie Laine

Producer: Charles Marquis Warren

Gunsmoke

Western; 30 and 60 min; CBS 9/10/55 to 9/1/75

The exploits of Matt Dillon, Marshal of Dodge City, Kansas, during the 1860s.

Marshal Matt Dillon	James Arness
Kitty Russell	Amanda Blake
"Doc" Galen Adams	Milburn Stone
Deputy Chester Goode	Dennis Weaver
Deputy Festus Hagen	Ken Curtis
Newly O'Brien	Buck Taylor
Quint Asper	Burt Reynolds
Sam	Glenn Strange
	Robert Brubaker
Nathan Burke	Ted Jordan
Hank Patterson	Hank Patterson
Thad Greenwood	Roger Ewing
Mr. Jones	Dabbs Greer
Barney	Charles Seel
Ma Smalley	Sarah Selby
Mr. Bodkin	Roy Roberts
Howie	Howard Culver
Percy Crump	John Harper
Lathrop	Woody Chambliss
Louis Pheeters	James Nusser
Ed O'Conner	Tod Brown
Dr. John Chapman	Pat Hingle
Miss Hannah	Fran Ryan

Producer: Charles Warren, John Mantley, Philip Leacock

Guy Lombardo and His Royal Canadians

Variety; 30 min; Syn. 1954

A weekly program of music and songs with orchestra leader Guy Lombardo and regulars Carmen, Lebert, and Victor Lombardo, Kenny Gardner, Toni Arden, and Bill Flannigan

Guy Lombardo's Diamond Jubilee

Variety; 30 min; CBS 3/20/56 to 6/19/56

Music and songs with host Guy Lombardo and regulars Victor, Carmen, and Lebert Lombardo (his brothers). Produced by Herbert Sussan.

The Guy Mitchell Show

Variety Pilot; 60 min; CBS 3/6/57

A proposed weekly series of music and songs.

Host: Guy Mitchell

Regulars: Polly Bergen, Jack E. Leonard, The Four Lads, The Spellbinders

Orchestra: Bert Farber

Announcer: Tony Marvin

Producer: Lee Cooley

The Guy Mitchell Show

Variety; 30 min; NBC 10/7/57 to 1/13/58

A weekly series of music and songs.

Host: Guy Mitchell

Regulars: Dolores Hawkins, The Guy Mitchell Singers, The Ted Cappy Dancers

Orchestra: Van Alexander

Producer: Phil Cohan

Gypsy

A daily syndicated (1966) series of interviews with people from all walks of life with hostess Gypsy Rose Lee.

The Gypsy Rose Lee Show

Variety; 90 min; Syn. 1958

Music, talk, and celebrity interviews with hostess Gypsy Rose Lee and her regulars Stan Freeman, Earl Wrightson, and Mary Ellen Terry.

The Gypsy Warriors

Adventure Pilot; 60 min; CBS 5/12/78

The W.W. II exploits of Shelly Alhern and Ted Brinkerhoff, U.S. Army captains who pose as gypsies (with Ganault, his daughter, Lela, and his son Androck) and tackle dangerous assignments behind enemy lines.

Shelly Alhern	James Whitmore Jr.
Ted Brinkerhoff	Tom Selleck
Ganault	Joseph Ruskin
Lela	Lina Raymond
Androck	Michael Lane
Bruno Schlagel	Albert Paulsen
Schulman	Kenneth Tigar
Lady Britt	Kathryn Leigh Scott

Producer: Stephn J. Cannell, Alex Beaton

Hagen

Crime Drama, 60 min; CBS 3/1/80 to 2/24/80

The exploits of Paul Hagen, an investigator for the San Francisco-based law firm of Carl Palmer and Associates, who uses his knowledge as an Idaho trapper to apprehend criminals.

Paul Hagen	Chad Everett
Carl Palmer	Arthur Hill
Mrs. Chavez	Carmen Zapata
Jody	Aldine King

Theme Song ("Hagen") by George Romanis

Producer: Frank Glicksman

Haggis Baggis

Game; 30 min; NBC 6/20/58 to 9/29/58 (evening run)
6/30/58 to 6/19/59
(daytime run)

Contestants first pick a category and then answer questions that are related to it. For each correct response, a portion of a concealed photograph is revealed. The first player to identify the photo wins the round. The player with the highest score receives his choice of either the Haggis (luxury) or the Baggis (utility) prizes.

Host (Afternoon): Fred Robbins, Bert Parks

Host (Evening): Jack Linkletter, Dennis James

Assistant: Lillian Naud

Producer: Gilbert Cates

Hail the Champ

Game; 30 min; ABC 12/22/51 to 5/20/53

Six children compete in various athletic contests with the best performer receiving merchandise prizes.

Host: Herb Allen, Howard Roberts

Assistant: Angel Casey, Jim Andelin

Producer: Herb Allen

Hail to the Chief

Comedy; 30 min; ABC 4/9/85 to 5/21/85

A political satire that focuses on the hectic home and working life of Julia Mansfield, the first woman President of the U.S.

Julia Mansfield	Patty Duke	Rocky Nelson	Joe Pesci
Oliver Mansfield	Ted Bessell	Annie O'Hara	Victoria Jackson
Lucy Mansfield	Quinn Cummings	Chester Long	Fred Williamson
Doug Mansfield	Ricky Paull Goldin	Lt. Clarence	
Willie Mansfield	Taliesin Jaffe	Hummel	Gary Grubbs
Lenore	Maxine Stuart	Kurt	Bubba Smith
Helmut Luger	Herschel Bernardi	Beau	Dick Butkus
LaRue Hawks	Glynn Turman	Dean Martin	Himself
Gen. Hannibal			
Stryker	John Vernon		
Randy	Joel Brooks		
Raoul	Chick Vennera		
Ivan Zolotov	Dick Shawn		
Madame Zolotov	Susan Kellerman		
Rev. Billy Joe			
Bickerstaff	Richard Paul		
Darlene Lubin	Alexa Hamilton		
Sam Cotton	Murray Hamilton		
Irving Metzman	George Wyner		

Announcer: Raechel Donahue

Producer: Paul Junger Witt, Tony Thomas

Hal Roach Presents

A syndicated (1978) series of half-hour programs produced by the Hal Roach Studios in the 1950s. Episodes from "My Little Margie," "Love That Jill," and "Screen Director's Playhouse" comprise the series.

The Half-Hour Comedy Hour

Comedy; 30 min; ABC 7/5/83 to 8/9/83

Fast-paced comedy sketches that spoof TV, movies, and real life.

Regulars: Victoria Jackson, John Moschitta Jr., Vic Dunlop, Jan Hooks, Rod Hall, Diane Stilwell, John Paragon, Peter Isacksen

Music: Eddie Karam

Producer: Dick Clark, Chris Bearde

Half Nelson

Crime Drama; 60 min; NBC 3/24/85 to 5/10/85

The exploits of Rocky Nelson, a diminutive private detective with the Beverly Hills Patrol, an organization started by celebrities who want their lives safe and private.

Opening Theme Vocal ("L.A. You Belong to Me"): Randy Newman

Closing Theme Vocal ("L.A. Is My Home"): Dean Martin

Producer: Glen A. Larson, Lou Shaw

Half-Pint Party

Children; 15 min; ABC 2/12/51 to 5/10/52

Music and songs for children with Host Al Gannaway.

Half the George Kirby Comedy Hour

Variety; 30 min; Syn. 9/72

A weekly series of music, songs, and comedy sketches.

Host: George Kirby

Regulars: Connie Martin, Jack Duffy, Julie Amato, Steve Martin, Joey Hollingsworth, The Walter Painter Dancers

Orchestra: Hank Marr

Producer: Burt Rosen, David Winters, Bernard Rothman, Jack Wohl

The Halls of Ivy

Comedy; 30 min; CBS 10/19/54 to 10/13/55

The incidents that befall the faculty and students of the mythical Ivy College in Ivy, U.S.A.

Dr. William	
Todhunter Hall	Ronald Colman
Vicky Hall	Benita Hume
Alice	Mary Wickes
Clarence Wellman	Herb Butterfield
Mrs. Wellman	Sarah Selby
Prof. Warren	Arthur Q. Bryan

Producer: William Frye

The Hamptons

Drama; 60 min; ABC 7/27/83 to 8/24/83

The lives, loves, and ambitions of the Chadways and Mortimers, two wealthy families who live on the Hamptons in Long Island, N.Y.

Adrienne Mortimer	Bibi Besch
Tracy Mortimer	Holly Roberts
Jay Mortimer	John Reilly
Peter Chadway	Michael Goodwin
Brian Chadway	Craig Sheffer
Miranda Chadway	Martha Byrne
Cheryl Ashcroft	Kate Dezina
Penny Drake	Jada Rowland
Lee Chadway	Leigh Taylor-Young
Ed Morrissey	Michael Higgins
Ada	Fran Carlon
Nick Atwater	Daniel Pilon
David Landau	Phil Chasnoff

Theme Song ("The Hamptons") by Billy Goldenberg

Producer: Gloria Monty

Handle with Care

Anthology; 30 min; ABC 10/7/54 to 12/30/54

Dramas based on the problems encountered by the U.S. Postal Service in its handling of the mails. Originally titled "The Mail Story."

Producer: Robert L. Shayon

Handle with Care

Comedy Pilot; 30 min; CBS 5/9/77

The experiences of Liz Baker and Jackie Morse, Army nurses assigned to an all-female M*A*S*H unit during the Korean War. Originally titled "Nurses."

Liz Baker	Marlyn Mason
Jackie Morse	Didi Conn
Maj. Charlotte Hinkley	Mary Jo Catlett
Nurse Shirley Nichols	Betsy Slade
Nurse Turk	Jeannie Wilson
Col. Marvin Richardson	Brian Dennehy
Cpl. Carp	Robert Lussier
Cpl. Tillingham	Ted Wass

Producer: Nancy Malone

Hands of Destiny

See "Hands of Murder."

Hands of Murder

Anthology; 30 min; DuMont 9/30/49 to 4/7/50 (as "Hands of Murder") 4/14/50 to 6/30/50 (as "Hands of Destiny") 9/8/50 to 5/18/51 (as "Hands of Mystery") 5/25/51 to 12/25/51 (as "Hands of Destiny")

Dramatizations that depict the plight of people caught in a web of supernatural intrigue. Also titled "Hands of Destiny" and "Hands of Mystery."

Producer: James L. Caddigan

Hands of Mystery

See "Hands of Murder."

Handsome Harry's

Comedy Pilot; 60 min; NBC 4/25/86

The misadventures of Harry Marquette, the owner of a barber shop (Handsome Harry's) in St. Louis, Missouri.

Harry Marquette	Scoey Mitchlll
Harvey "Speedy" Sims	Art Evans
Pearline Simms	Ketty Lester
Edna Miller	Michelle Davison
Louis Horwitz	Cliff Norton
Elmo Sweet	Don Bexley
Tank	Rockne Tarkington
Dooey	Al Fann
Roosevelt	Tyrone G. Jones

Theme Vocal ("Handsome Harry's") by Harry Middlebrooks

Producer: Scoey Mitchlll, Josef Vinson

Hanging In

Comedy; 30 min; CBS 8/8/79 to 8/29/79

The experiences of Louis Harper, a former football hero who becomes the president of Braddock University.
Originally intended to star Bea Arthur. When she rejected the idea, it was titled "Onward

and Upward'' and John Amos was chosen as the star. A format dispute caused Amos to quit and Lou Gossett was brought on to replace him in what was now called "Mr. Dooley." When Gossett rejected the role, Cleavon Little taped several episodes as "Mr. Dugan." Due to an unfavorable portrayal of blacks, the series never actually aired.

Louis Harper	Bill Macy
Maggie Gallagher	Barbara Rhoades
Sam Dickey	Dennis Burkley
Pinky Nolan	Neda Volz
Rita Zepperette	Darian Mathias

Producer: Sy Rosen

Hangin' In

Comedy; 30 min; Syn. 6/86

A Canadian series about Kate Brown, a social worker who runs the College Street Youth Services, an inner-city youth counseling center.

Kate Brown	Lally Cadeau
Mike DeFalco	David Eisner
Doris Webster	Ruth Springford
Rosanna Fellachi	Gina Wilkinson
Mrs. Brown	Kate Reid
Lou Fellachi	Henry Ramey

Producer: Jack Humphrey, James Partington

Hank

Comedy; 30 min; NBC 9/17/65 to 9/2/66

The story of an enterprising young businessman (Hank) who operates several campus concessions and attends classes at Western State University in an attempt to achieve a long-awaited dream—his college education.*

Hank Dearborn	Dick Kallman
Tina Dearborn	Katie Sweet
Doris Royal	Inelda DeMartin**
	Linda Foster
Dr. Lewis Royal	Howard St. John
Franny	Kelly Jean Peters
Ralph	Don Washbrook
Loretta	Margaret Blye
Arlene Atwater	Lisa Gaye
Prof. McKillup	Lloyd Corrigan

Coach Weiss	Dabbs Greer
Miss Mittlemen	Dorothy Neumann
Mrs. Weiss	Sheila Bromley

Producer: William T. Orr, Hugh Benson

*Denied the chance when his parents were killed in a car accident and he had to quit high school and care for his sister, Tina.

**Hank's girlfriend in the pilot episode.

The Hank McCune Show

Comedy; 30 min; NBC 9/9/50 to 10/9/50

The story of Hank McCune, a kind-hearted bumbler who seeks, but inevitably fails to achieve success.

Hank McCune	Himself
Lester	Hanley Stafford

Also: Sara Berner, Arthur Q. Bryan, Larry Keating

Announcer: Dick Farrell, Hank McCune, Edward Brends

The Hanna-Barbera Happiness Hour

Variety; 60 min; NBC 4/13/78 to 5/4/78

Music and songs with life-size puppets Honey and Sis.

Honey's voice	Udana Power
Sis's voice	Wendy McKenzie

Orchestra: Billy Barnes

Producer: Joseph Barbera, Ken and Mitzi Welch

Hanna-Barbera's World of Super Adventure

The syndicated (9/80) title for repeats of "Birdman," "The Herculoids," "Shazzan!" and "Space Ghost."

Hannibal Cobb

Mystery; 3½ min; Syn. 1959

A short program which challenges viewers to find the one clue that can solve a mystery before the intrepid Inspector Hannibal Cobb does.

Hannibal Cobb   James Craig

Producer: Howard Daniels

The Happeners

Drama Pilot; 60 min; Syn. 3/67

The story of a trio of folk-rockers seeking to make a name for themselves. Originally made for (and rejected by) ABC.

Trio Members   Chris Ducey
                                Suzannah Jordan
                                Craig Smith
Proprietor   Lou Jacobi
Engineer   Lou Gossett

Producer: Herbert Brodkin

Happening '68

Variety; 30 min; ABC 1/6/68 to 9/20/69

Music, comedy, fashion shows and other information geared to teenagers with host Mark Lindsey and regulars Freddie Welles, Keith Allison, and Paul Revere and the Raiders. Produced by Dick Clark.

Happily Ever After

Comedy Pilot; 30 min; NBC 8/25/61

The struggles of Bill and Laurie Stewart, newlyweds who are forced to move in with Laurie's parents after a financial setback leaves them with no place to live.

Bill Stewart   John Armstrong
Laurie Stewart   Olive Sturgess
Ruth Garrison   Catherine McLeod
Gordon Garrison   Walter Coy
Patti Garrison   Cheryl Holdridge
Donald Quinn   Steve Terrell
Doris Browning   Mary Ellen Terry
Judge Chambers   Ned Weaver
Lawyer   Olan Soule
Manager   Michael Ross

Music: Irvin Talbot

Producer: Jerry Stagg, Devery Freeman

Happy Birthday

Children; 30 min; DuMont 5/15/47 to 6/23/49

Preselected children's birthdays are celebrated with parties, games, and prizes.

Host: Ted Brown, Bill Slater, Aunt Grace

Producer: George Scheck

Happy

Comedy; 30 min; NBC 6/6/60 to 9/2/60
                              1/13/61 to 9/8/61

The story of Sally and Chris Day, the owners of the Desert Palm Hotel in Palm Springs, California. As they struggle to operate the hotel, their infant son, Christopher Hapgood "Happy" Day, observes and, through voice-over dubbing, comments on their activities.

Sally Day   Yvonne Lime
Chris Day   Ronnie Burns
Happy Day   David & Steven
                                Born
Charley Dooley   Lloyd Corrigan
Clara Mason   Doris Packer

Producer: E.J. Rosenberg

Happy Days

Variety; 60 min; CBS 6/25/70 to 9/10/70

The music, song, dance and comedy of the 1930s.

Host: Louis Nye

Regulars: Chuck McCann, Laara Lacey, Julie McWhirter, Bob Elliott and Ray Goulding, Alan Copeland, Jim MacGeorge, Jimmy Dexter, The Wisa D'Orso Dancers, Clive Clerk

Orchestra: Jack Elliott, Allyn Ferguson

Producer: Jack Burns, George Yanok

Happy Days

Comedy; 30 min; ABC 1/15/74 to 7/19/84

A nostalgic backward glance into the Eisenhower era as seen through the experiences of Richie Cunningham, a teenage high school student growing up in Milwaukee, Wisconsin, in the late 1950s.

Howard Cunningham	Tom Bosley Harold Gould*
Marion Cunningham	Marion Ross
Richie Cunningham	Ron Howard
Joanie Cunningham	Erin Moran Susan Neher*
Chuck Cunningham	Ric Carrott Gavan O'Herlihy Randolph Roberts
Warren "Potsie" Weber	Anson Williams
Arthur "Fonzie" Fonzarelli	Henry Winkler
Ralph Malph	Donny Most
Charles "Chachi" Arcola	Scott Baio
Louisa Arcola	Ellen Travolta
Lori Beth Allen	Lynda Goodfriend
Ashley Pfister	Linda Purl
Heather Pfister	Heather O'Rourke
Arnold Takahashi	Pat Morita
Al Delvecchio	Al Molinaro
Jenny Piccalo	Cathy Silvers
K.C. Cunningham	Crystal Bernard
Arlene	Tannis G. Montgomery
Gloria	Linda Purl
Marsha Simms	Beatrice Colen
Bill "Sticks" Downey	John Anthony Bailey
Pinky Tuscadero	Roz Kelly
Lola (a Pinkette)	Kelly Sanders
Tina (a Pinkette)	Doris Hess
Leather Tuscadero	Suzy Quatro
Kat Mandu	Deborah Pratt
Spike	Danny Butch
Laverne DeFazio	Penny Marshall
Shirley Feeney	Cindy Williams
Officer Kirk	Ed Peck
Father Delvecchio	Al Molinaro
Eugene "The Wimp" Belvin	Denis Mandell
Danny	Danny Ponce
Roger Phillips	Ted McGinley
Leopold "Flip" Phillips	Billy Warlock
Richie Cunningham Jr.	Bo Sharron
Mork	Robin Williams

Producer: Garry K. Marshall, Thomas L. Miller, Edward K. Milkis, Jerry Paris, William Bickley

*Role in the pilot, "Love and the Happy Days" (which see). Spin-off series: "Joanie Loves Chachi," "Laverne and Shirley," "Mork and Mindy," "Fonz and the Happy Days Gang," and "Laverne and Shirley with the Fonz."

The Happy Time

Drama Pilot; 30 min; Syn. 4/59

The story, set in Ottawa, Canada, during the 1920s, relates incidents in the life of Bibi Bonnard, a mischievous adolescent.

Bibi Bonnard	Miko Oscard
Jacques Bonnard	Claude Dauphin
Mignonette Chappuis	June Vincent
Uncle Desmonde	Mischa Auer

Producer: James A. Schulke

Harbor Command

Crime Drama; 30 min; Syn. 1957

The exploits of Ralph Baxter, a chief of the U.S. Harbor Command.

Capt. Ralph Baxter	Wendell Corey

Producer: Herbert L. Strock

Harbourmaster

Adventure; 30 min; CBS 9/26/57 to 12/26/57 (as "Harbourmaster") 1/5/58 to 6/29/58 (as "Adventures at Scott Island")

The story of David Scott, captain of the "Blue Chip II" and owner of a boat repair service on Scott Island in Cape Ann, Mass.

Capt. David Scott	Barry Sullivan
Jeff Kittredge	Paul Burke
Anna Morrison	Nina Wilcox
Danny Morrison	Evan Elliot
Cap'n Dan	Michael Keene
Prof. Wheeler	Murray Matheson

Producer: Jon Epstein, Leon Benson, Eddie Davis, Felix Feist

Hard Copy

Crime Drama; 60 min; CBS 1/25/87 to 2/22/87

The series, set in the press room of the California Metro Police Department, relates the experiences of reporters Andy Omart (of the "Morning Express") and Blake Calisher (of the "City Wire Service"), as they work with the police to solve crimes and acquire stories.

Andy Omart	Michael Murphy
Blake Calisher	Wendy Crewson
Lt. Guyla Cook	Fionnula Flanagan
David DeValle	Dean Devlin
William Boot	Charles Cooper

Producer: William Sackheim, Daniel Pyne, Lynn Morgan

Hard Knocks

Comedy; 30 min; SHOWTIME 4/20/87 (Premiere)

The escapades of Gower and Nick, mismatched private eyes who wreak havoc in New York City's worst neighborhoods as they attempt to get their man.

Gower Rhodes	Bill Maher
Nick Bronco	Tommy Hinkley

Producer: Gary Nardino, Chris Thompson

Hardcase

Crime Drama Pilot; 60 min; NBC 12/6/81

The exploits of Grover Harding Case, a tough lieutenant with the New Orleans Police Department.

Lt. Grover Case	Beau Kayzer
Off. Jane "Stretch" Ryan	Debra Feuer
Capt. Paul Morgan	G.W. Bailey
Cliff Mulburgher	Stephen Elliott
Laura Tinkerbell	Andra Akers
Rita	Joanna Martin
Stripper	Shawn McKay
Mink	Jeremy Summers
Perk Dawson	Mickey Rourke

Producer: Frank Konigsberg

Hardcastle and McCormick

Crime Drama; 60 min; ABC 9/18/83 to 7/23/86

Seeking a way to bring to justice the criminals who are freed on legal technicalities, retired judge Milton C. Hardcastle offers two-time loser Mark McCormick a choice: either work with him or do time. Stories relate their efforts to bring to justice the criminals the judge believes were wrongly set free.

Milton Hardcastle	Brian Keith
Mark McCormick	Daniel Hugh-Kelly
Sara	Mary Jackson
Lt. Delaney	John Hancock
Lt. Bill Giles	Ed Bernard
Lt. Frank Harper	Joe Santos
Sonny Daye	Steve Lawrence

Theme Vocalists: David Morgan (1st season theme, "Drive") and Joey Scarbury ("Back to Back")

Producer: Stephen J. Cannell, Patrick Harsburgh, Jo Swerling Jr.

Hardesty House

Crime Drama Pilot; 60 min; ABC 7/5/86

While in law school, six students vow to one day open their own practice. Ten years later, they pool their resources and purchase a rundown California beach house they name Hardesty House (after a professor). The would-be series was to relate their exploits as they use any method possible to clear their clients.

Charlotte Montgomery	Susan Anton
Jack Kenan	Robert Ginty
Judy Werner	Melanie Chartoff
Ray Gonzales	Paul Rodriquez
Max Eaton III	Harley Venton
Robbie Hudson	Randy Brooks
Sara Werner	Brigette Desper
Jamie Werner	Tiffany Desper
April	Cec Verrell
Mr. Donovan	Kenneth Kimmons
William Johnson	Arnold Johnson

Music: Fred Karlin

Producer: Robert Ginty, Gerald I. Isenberg

The Hardy Boys

Mystery Pilot; 60 min; NBC 9/8/67

The crime solving exploits of amateur detectives Joe and Frank Hardy. The pilot relates their efforts to help their detective father (Fenton) locate a stolen jade collection.

Joe Hardy	Tim Matthieson
	(Tim Matheson)
Frank Hardy	Rick Gates
Fenton Hardy	Richard Anderson
Gertrude Hardy	Portia Nelson
Susie	Teri Garr
Milly	Trudy Ames
Tony Prito	Jan-Michael Vincent
Chet Morton	Stephen John
Dr. Montrose	Edward Andrews
George Ti-Ming	James Shigeta
Jim Foy	Brian Fong

Producer: Richard Murphy

The Hardy Boys

Cartoon; 30 min; ABC 9/6/69 to 9/4/71

The global adventures of the Hardy Boys, a rock and roll group, as they stumble upon and attempt to solve mysteries.

Frank Hardy	Byron Kane
Joe Hardy	Dallas McKennon
Wanda Kay	Jane Webb

Producer: Norm Prescott, Lou Scheimer

The Hardy Boys and the Mystery of Ghost Farm

Mystery; 30 min; ABC 9/30/57 to 10/15/57

A "Mickey Mouse Club" serial about the adventures of amateur sleuths Joe and Frank Hardy and their efforts to solve the mystery of a farm that is haunted by a ghost.

Joe Hardy	Tim Considine
Frank Hardy	Tommy Kirk
Fenton Hardy	Russ Conway
Viola Morton	Carole Ann
	Campbell
Gertrude Hardy	Sarah Selby

Producer: Walt Disney, Bill Walsh

The Hardy Boys and the Mystery of the Applegate Treasure

Mystery; 30 min; ABC 1/7/57 to 2/1/57

The efforts of amateur detectives Joe and Frank Hardy to solve the baffling theft of pirate treasure from the estate of Silas Applegate. A "Mickey Mouse Club" serial.

Joe Hardy	Tim Considine
Frank Hardy	Tommy Kirk
Viola Morton	Carole Ann
	Campbell
Fenton Hardy	Russ Conway
Gertrude Hardy	Sarah Selby
Silas Applegate	Florenz Ames
Jackley	Robert Foulk

Producer: Walt Disney, Bill Walsh

The Hardy Boys Mysteries

Crime Drama; 60 min; ABC 1/30/77 to 8/26/79

The investigations of juvenile detectives Frank and Joe Hardy, the sons of world-famous private detective Fenton Hardy. Originally broadcast as "The Hardy Boys/Nancy Drew Mysteries."

Frank Hardy	Parker Stevenson
Joe Hardy	Shaun Cassidy
Fenton Hardy	Edmund Gilbert
Gertrude Hardy	Edith Atwater
Cally Shaw	Lisa Eilbacher
Harry Hammond	Jack Kelly

Producer: Glen A. Larson, Michael Sloan

The Harlem Globetrotters

Cartoon; 30 min; CBS 9/12/70 to 5/13/73

The antics of basketball wizards the Harlem Globetrotters as they help good defeat evil.

Meadowlark Lemon	Scatman Crothers
Curly Neal	Stu Gilliam
Gip	Richard Elkins
Bobby Joe	Eddie Anderson
Geese	Johnny Williams
Pablo	Robert DoQui

Producer: William Hanna, Joseph Barbera

The Harlem Globetrotters Popcorn Machine

Variety; 25 min; CBS 9/7/74 to 8/30/75

Musical numbers and comedy sketches, hosted by the Harlem Globetrotters, that are designed to relate social messages to children.

Regulars: Avery Schreiber, Rodney Allen Rippy.

Music: Jack Elliott, Allyn Ferguson

Producer: Frank Peppiatt, John Aylesworth

Harold Lloyd's World of Comedy

Comedy; 30 min; Syn. 1977

Edited for television silent theatrical shorts featuring the comedy antics of Harold Lloyd. The 1920s films contain music, sound effects and narration.

Star: Harold Lloyd

Narrator: Henry Corden

Theme Vocal: The Jimmy Joyce Singers

Film Music: The Don Peake Orchestra

Music Composers: Neil Hefti, Jack Lloyd

Producer: Eleanor Graves

Harper Valley

Comedy; 30 min; NBC 10/29/81 to 8/14/82

A revised version of "Harper Valley, PTA" which drops the PTA aspect to relate the adventures of Stella Johnson as the executive assistant to Otis Harper, the intoxicated mayor of Harper Valley, Ohio.

Stella Johnson	Barbara Eden
Dee Johnson	Jenn Thompson
Winslow Homer "Uncle Buster" Smith	Mills Watson
Cassie Bowman	Fannie Flagg
Otis Harper	George Gobel

Flora Simpson Reilly	Anne Francine
Wanda Reilly Taylor	Bridget Hanley
Bobby Taylor	Rod McCary
Scarlett Taylor	Suzi Dean
Tom Meechum	Christopher Stone

Theme Vocal ("Harper Valley U.S.A."): Carol Chase

Producer: Jerry Davis, Bill Dial, Greg and Sam Strangis

Harper Valley, PTA

Comedy; 30 min; NBC 1/16/81 to 8/28/81

Seeking to start a new life after her husband's death, Stella Johnson, a beautiful, outspoken mother, moves to Harper Valley, Ohio, a hotbed of hypocrisy. Because of her flamboyant style, Stella encounters the objections of the PTA, a group of prudes who believe she is a bad influence. Stories relate Stella's efforts to begin a new life despite the PTA's efforts to find a way to get her to leave town. Based on the feature film.

Stella Johnson	Barbara Eden
Dee Johnson	Jenn Thompson
Cassie Bowman	Fannie Flagg
Mayor Otis Harper	George Gobel
Flora Simpson Reilly	Anne Francine
Wanda Reilly Taylor	Bridget Hanley
Bobby Taylor	Rod McCary
Scarlett Taylor	Suzi Dean
Vivian Washburn	Mari Gorman
Willa Mae Jones	Edie McClurg
Cliff Willoughby	Robert Gray
Norman Clayton	Gary Allen
Doug Peterson	Fred Holliday

Theme Vocal ("Harper Valley, PTA"): Jeannie C. Riley

Producer: Sherwood Schwartz, Gordon Mitchell, Jerry Ross

Harper Valley, U.S.A.

Variety Pilot; 30 min; NBC 8/11/69

Music, songs, and comedy skits set against the background of the mythical Harper Valley, U.S.A.

Host: Jerry Reed

Guests: Jeannie C. Riley, Mel Tillis, Tom T. Hall

Producer: Don Van Atta

Harrigan and Son

Comedy; 30 min; ABC 10/14/60 to 9/29/61

The story of a father and son legal team and their efforts to defend clients as each believes is correct (the senior Harrigan feels the human angle is necessary; the younger Harrigan believes in doing it by the book).

James Harrigan Sr.	Pat O'Brien
James Harrigan Jr.	Roger Perry
Gypsy	Georgine Darcy
Miss Claridge	Helen Kleeb

Producer: Cy Howard

Harris Against the World

Comedy; 30 min; NBC 10/5/64 to 1/4/65

The trials and tribulations of Alan Harris, a movie studio plant superintendent, as he struggles to survive the barrage of everyday problems. Aired as a segment of "90 Bristol Court."

Alan Harris	Jack Klugman
Kate Harris	Patricia Barry
Dee Dee Harris	Claire Wilcox
Billy Harris	David Macklin
Helen Miller	Faye DeWitt
Norm Miller	Sheldon Allman
Cliff Murdock	Guy Raymond

Producer: Joe Connelly, Devery Freeman

Harris and Company

Drama; 60 min; NBC 3/15/79 to 4/5/79

A realistic approach to the problems facing a black family as seen through the eyes of Mike Harris, a widowed mechanic and the father of five children.

Mike Harris	Bernie Casey
Juanita "J.P." Harris	Lia Jackson
Liz Harris	Renee Brown
David Harris	David Hubbard
Tommy Harris	Eddie Singleton
Richard Allen Harris	Dian Turner
Charlie Adams	Stu Gilliam
Harry Foreman	James Luisi
Angie Adams	C. Tilley Banks
Louise Foreman	Lois Walden

Producer: Stanley G. Robertson

Harry

Comedy; 30 min; ABC 3/4/87 to 3/25/87

The story of Harry Porschak, an unorthodox, heart-of-gold scam artist who runs the purchasing department of a New York Community General Hospital.

Harry Porschak	Alan Arkin
Nurse Ira Duckett	Holland Taylor
Lawrence Pendleton	Thom Bray
Bobby Katz	Matt Craven
Dr. Sandy Clifton	Barbara Dana
Wyatt Lockhart	Kurt Knudson
Richard Breskin	Richard Lewis

Producer: Barry Levinson, Alan Arkin, Mark Johnson

Harry

Crime Drama Pilot; 60 min; CBS 5/13/87

The adventures of Harriet "Harry" Quayle, a beautiful Australian private detective now operating in New York City. In the pilot, broadcast on "The New Mike Hammer," Harry enlists Mike's help in tracking down a mysterious and elusive novelist.

Harriet Quayle	Mary Frann
Laura (The Face)	Donna Denton
Mike Hammer	Stacy Keach
Milo	Philip Richard Allen
Carl	Marco St. John
Mildred	Mimi Maynard

Producer: Jay Bernstein

Harry and Maggie

Comedy Pilot; 30 min; CBS 4/25/75

The bickering relationship between Harry Kellogg, a grumpy Iowa widower, and Maggie Sturdivant, his aggressive sister-in-law who lives with him and takes charge of his life.

Harry Kellogg	Don Knotts
Maggie Sturdivant	Eve Arden
Clovis Kellogg	Kathy Davis
Arlo Wilson	Tom Poston
Thelma	Lucille Benson
Max	Eddie Quillan

Producer: James Parker, Arnold Margolin

Harry and the Kids

Comedy Pilot; 30 min; ABC 7/5/85

The story of Harry Stover, a middle-aged fisherman, and his attempts to raise three toublesome orphans (Elizabeth, Philip, and Jason) in Key West, Florida.

Harry Stover	Max Gail
Elizabeth	Lisa Coristine
Jason	Danny Kohn
Philip	Keram Malichki-Sanchez
Mavis	Patricia Idelette
Mr. Winegar	Geoffrey Bowes
Otis	Derek McGrath

Producer: Al Rogers

Harry O

Crime Drama; 60 min; ABC 9/12/74 to 8/12/76

While responding to a burglary-in-progress, L.A. police officer Harry Orwell is shot in the back and disabled when the bullet lodges in his spine. Stories relate Orwell's case investigations when he retires from the force and becomes a private detective.

Harry Orwell	David Janssen
Lt. Manny Quinn	Henry Darrow
Lt. K.C. Trench	Anthony Zerbe
Det. Don Roberts	Paul Tully

Sue Ingham	Farrah Fawcett
Betsy	Katherine Baumann
Linzy	Loni Anderson
Dr. Fong	Keye Luke
Lester Hodges	Les Lannom
Lt. Arvin Grainger	Mel Stewart*
Manny's Niece	
Marilyn	Kathleen Lloyd

Producer: Jerry Thorpe, Buck Houghton, Alex Beaton

*Proposed regular from the pilot film (ABC, 3/11/73).

Harry's Battles

Comedy Pilot; 30 min; ABC 6/8/81

The endless frustrations of Harry Fitzsimons, an average guy who constantly battles the bureaucratic errors that seem to plague his life.

Harry Fitzsimons	Dick Van Dyke
Mary Carol Fitzsimons	Connie Stevens
Herb	Danny Wells
Diane	Marley Sims
Dr. Harwood	Joseph Regalbuto
Nurse Hewitt	Brooke Alderson
Patient	Florence Halop

Producer: Martin Stager

Harry's Business

Comedy Pilot; 30 min; NBC 7/21/61

The story of a young woman (Ellen) and her attempts to begin a new life for herself in San Francisco.

Ellen Burton	Elena Verdugo
Harry Burns	Ray Walston
Brad	Michael Burns
Fred	Bill Mulliken

Harry's Girls

Comedy; 30 min; NBC 9/13/63 to 1/3/64

The romantic misadventures of Lois, Rusty, and Terry, three beautiful entertainers who comprise Harry's Girls, a vaudeville-like song-and-dance act that is touring Europe. Based on the film "Les Girls." See the following title also.

Harry Burns	Larry Blyden
Lois	Dawn Nickerson
Rusty	Susan Silo
Terry	Diahn Williams

Producer: Billy Friedberg

Harry's Girls

Comedy; 30 min; Unaired (Produced in 1960)

An unaired series, based on the film "Les Girls," which relates the misadventures of Harry's Girls, an American song and dance team touring Europe.

Harry Burns	Larry Blyden
Rusty	Ellen McRae (Ellen Burstyn)
Lois	Kris Garner
Teri	Marsha Rivers

"Harry's Girls" Theme: Ray Noble

Producer: Ralph Levy, Richard Fisher

Hart to Hart

Crime Drama; 60 min; ABC 9/22/79 to 7/3/84

The adventures of Jonathan Hart, the wealthy head of Hart Industries, and his beautiful wife, Jennifer, a writer, as they help people in trouble.

Jonathan Hart	Robert Wagner
Jennifer Hart	Stefanie Powers
Max	Lionel Stander
Deanne	Mimi Maynard
Stanley Frieson	Lee Wilkof
Marcus Wheeler	Eugene Roche* Alex Dreier
Lt. Moss	Michael Lerner
Lt. Wilbur Gillis	Richard B. Shull
Lt. Herschel Gray	Wynn Irwin
Steven Edwards	Ray Milland
Lt. Draper	Lyman Ward

Theme Song ("Hart to Hart"): Roger Nichols

Producer: Aaron Spelling, Leonard Goldberg

*Pilot episode role (ABC, 8/25/79).

The Hartmans

Comedy; 30 min; NBC 1949

Comical events in the lives of Paul and Grace Hartman, a married couple who live in the small town of Forrest Heights.

Paul Hartman	Himself
Grace Hartman	Herself
Their nephew	Bob Shawley
Grace's sister	Valerie Cossart
Grace's brother	Loring Smith
Neighbor	Gage Clark

Producer: Harry Herrmann

The Harvey Korman Show

Comedy Pilot; 30 min; ABC 5/19/77

The misadventures of Francis A. Kavanaugh, a flamboyant "old school" actor who runs an offbeat acting class from his home. See the following title also.

Francis Kavanaugh	Harvey Korman
Maggie Kavanaugh	Susan Lawrence
Jake Winkleman	Milton Selzer
Stuart Stafford	Barry Van Dyke
Carmine Despiccio	Dino Natali
Honey Bushkin	Penelope Windust
Howie Hoff	Bart Braverman
Chris	Donna Ponterotto

Producer: Hal Dresner, Don Van Atta

The Harvey Korman Show

Comedy; 30 min; ABC 3/4/78 to 8/4/78

The story of Harvey Kavanaugh, an aging actor with a small career, as he attempts to find work in a world that he feels is passing him by.

Harvey Kavanaugh	Harvey Korman
Maggie Kavanaugh	Christine Lahti
Jake Winkleman	Milton Selzer
Stuart Stafford	Barry Van Dyke
Bernie	Harry Gold

Music: Peter Matz

Producer: Hal Dresner, Don Van Atta

The Hathaways

Comedy; 30 min; ABC 10/6/61 to 8/31/62

The trials and tribulations of the Hathaways: Walter, a Los Angeles real estate salesman, and his wife, Elinor, the owner and manager of Enoch, Charlie, and Candy, three theatrical chimpanzees.

Walter Hathaway	Jack Weston
Elinor Hathaway	Peggy Cass
Jerry Roper	Harvey Lembeck
Amanda Allison	Mary Grace Canfield
Enoch, Charlie, Candy	The Marquis Chimps

Producer: Ezra Stone

Have a Heart

Game; 30 min; DuMont 5/3/55 to 6/14/55

Four players, divided into two teams of two, compete in a question-and-answer session with the highest scoring team donating its winnings to their favorite hometown charities.

Host: John Reed King

Have Gun—Will Travel

Western; 30 min; CBS 9/14/57 to 9/21/63

When an unnamed ex-army officer loses at cards and finds himself in debt to a land baron, he agrees to repay the debt by killing Smoke, an outlaw who has been plaguing the land baron. Following a confrontation in which the man kills Smoke, he decides to adopt his guise—a black outfit and the symbol of the Paladin—and hire his guns and experience to those who are unable to protect themselves. Stories, set in San Francisco during the 1870s, relate the exploits of a man called Paladin as he attempts to help people in trouble.

Paladin	Richard Boone
Hey Boy	Kam Tong
Hey Girl	Lisa Lu
Mr. McGunnis (Hotel Carlton Manager)	Olan Soule
Smoke/Young Paladin	Richard Boone*
Land Baron	William Conrad*

Theme Vocal ("The Ballad of Paladin"): Johnny Western

Producer: Frank Pierson, Don Ingalls, Robert Sparks, Julian Claman

*From the "Genesis" episode which relates how Paladin came to be.

Having Babies

Drama Pilot; 2 hrs; ABC 10/28/77

Personal dramas about the joys and traumas of childbirth that fostered the "Julie Farr, M.D." series (which see). A sequel "Having Babies" film aired on 3/3/78.

Dr. Julie Farr	Susan Sullivan
Trish Canfield	Paula Prentiss
Aaron Canfield	Tony Bill
Sally McGee	Carol Lynley
Martha Cooper	Lee Meriwether
Lou Plotkin	Wayne Rogers
Paula Plotkin	Cassie Yates
Teenage Girl	Rosanna Arquette

Producer: Gerald W. Abrams

Hawaii Calls

A syndicated (1966) series of Hawaiian music, song, and dance with host Webley Edwards

Hawaii Five-O

Crime Drama; 60 min; CBS 9/26/68 to 4/5/80

The work of Steve Garrett, a plainclothes detective with Five-O, a special investigative branch of the Hawaiian Police Department.

Det. Steve McGarrett	Jack Lord
Det. Danny Williams	James MacArthur
Det. Chin Ho Kelly	Kam Fong
Det. Kono	Zulu
Det. Ben Kokua	Al Harrington
Det. Lori Wilson	Sharon Farrell
Det. James "Kimo" Carew	William Smith
Off. Moe "Truck" Kealoha	Moe Keale
Doc Bergman	Al Eben
Governor	Richard Denning
Che Fong (Coroner)	Harry Endo

Attorney Gen. John Manicote	Morgan White
Wo Fat (Steve's nemesis)	Khigh Dhiegh
Tony Alika (mobster)	Ross Martin
Det. Duke Mikila	Herman Wedemeyer
Edna (secretary)	Barbara Luna
Jenny Sherman (Steve's secretary)	Peggy Ryan
	Patricia Barne
Dr. Judith Patrick	Linda Ryan
Jonathan Kaye (Naval Intelligence)	Bill Edwards

Producer: Philip Leacock, Bob Sweeney, Gene Levitt, B.W. Sandefur, Stanley Kallis, Leonard Katzman, Leonard B. Kaufman

Hawaiian Eye

Mystery; 60 min; ABC 10/7/59 to 9/10/63

The exploits of Tom Lopaka, Tracy Steele, and Gregg MacKenzie, the owners of the Honolulu-based Hawaiian Eye Investigations, and their assistant, Cricket Blake (singer at the Hawaiian Village Hotel), as they team to solve crimes.

Cricket Blake	Connie Stevens
Tracy Steele	Anthony Eisley
Tom Lopaka	Robert Conrad
Gregg MacKenzie	Grant Williams
Kim	Poncie Ponce
Philip Barton	Troy Donahue
Quon	Mel Prestidge
Sunny Dae	Tina Cole

Producer: William T. Orr, Stanley Niss, Charles Hoffman, Ed Jurist

Hawaiian Heat

Crime Drama; 60 min; ABC 9/14/84 to 12/21/84

With little chance for promotion and fed up with Chicago, Metro Police Officers Mac Riley and Andy Sendowski decide to reconstruct their lives and head for Hawaii. Shortly after, when they help the police solve a complex case, they are offered jobs as detectives. Stories relate their undercover assignments with the Criminal Investigation Unit of the Hawaiian Police Department.

Det. Mac Riley	Robert Ginty
Det. Andy Sendowski	Jeff McCracken
Irene Gorley	Tracy Scoggins
Maj. Taro Oshira	Mako
Det. Harker	Branscombe Richmond
Dr. Robin Barnett	Diane Civita
Tina (Irene's roommate)	Tina Marie Machado
Leila (Irene's roommate)	Leila Hee Olson
Julie (Irene's roommate)	Julie Marie Olson
Earl the Pearl (Snitch)	James Grant Benton
Florence (Andy's Mother)	Shelley Winters

Theme Song ("Goodbye Blues") by Tom Scott and Candy Patterson

Producer: James D. Parriott

Hawk

Crime Drama; 60 min; ABC 9/15/66 to 12/29/66

The story of John Hawk, a detective for the Manhattan D.A.'s special investigation squad, an elite team that is designed to corrupt the inner workings of the underworld.

Det. John Hawk	Burt Reynolds
Det. Dan Carter	Wayne Grice
Sam Crown	John Marley
Murray Slacken	Bruce Glover
Ed Gorten	Leon Janney

Producer: Hubbell Robinson, Paul Bogart

Hawkeye and the Last of the Mohicans

Adventure; 30 min; Syn. 1957

The founding and growth of America during the 1750s as seen through the adventures of Nat Cutler, a fur trader and pioneer who is known as Hawkeye, and his blood brother Chingachgook, the last of the Mohican tribe, as they assist pioneers and battle the constant Huron uprisings as scouts for the U.S. Cavalry.

Hawkeye	John Hart
Chingachgook	Lon Chaney Jr.

Producer: Sigmund Neufeld

Hawkins

Crime Drama; 90 min; CBS 10/2/73 to 9/3/74

The story of Billy Jim Hawkins, a shrewd criminal attorney working out of West Virginia.

Billy Jim Hawkins	James Stewart
R.J. Hawkins	Strother Martin
D.A. Harrelson	David Huddleston

Producer: Norman Felton, David Karp

Hawkins Falls, Population 6200

Drama; 15 min; NBC 6/17/50 to 10/12/50

Personality sketches of small town American life as seen through the eyes of Clate Weathers, the editor of the local newspaper.

Clate Weathers	Frank Dane
Laif Flaigle	Win Strackle
Mrs. Catherwood	Hope Summers
Judge	Philip Lord
Lorna Cary	Bernadene Flynn
Dr. Floyd Cary	Michael Golda
Millie Flaigle	Roz Twohey
Betty Sawtel	Helen Bernie
Spec Bassett	Russ Reed
Elmira Cleebe	Elmira Rossler

Producer: Ben Park

Hay Fever

Experimental; 80 min; NBC 7/28/39

A satire based on the impoliteness of hosts toward their guests as seen through the lives of a family of four and the four guests who arrive at their home for a dinner party.

Mother	Judith Bliss
Father	Montgomery Clift
Daughter	Virginia Campbell
Son	Dennis Hoey
Maid	Florence Edney

Dinner guests: Nancy Sheridan, Barbara Leeds, Lowell Gilmore, Carl Harbord

Producer: Edward Sobol

Hayes and Henderson

See "Oldsmobile Music Theatre."

Hayloft Hoedown

Variety; 30 min; ABC 7/10/48 to 9/18/48

Country and western music with host Elmer Newman and regulars Jesse Rogers, Jack Day, Wesley Tuttle, The Murray Sisters, and The Hoedown Ranch Square Dancers. Music by The Sleepy Hollow Gang.

Hazard's People

Crime Drama Pilot; 60 min; CBS 4/9/76

The story of John Hazard, a renowned criminal attorney whose style and flair, as well as his inherent sense of larceny, sets him apart from his peers. In the pilot, Hazard and his associates (Michael, Trish, and Ernest) defend a doctor accused of murdering his mistress.

John Hazard	John Houseman
Michael Crowder	John Elerick
Trish Corelli	Jesse Welles
Ernest Clay	Roger Hill
Sylvia Freed	Doreen Lang
D.A. Robert Powell	Stefan Gierasch
Dr. Carl DeLacy	Michael Tolan
Mrs. DeLacy	Hope Lange

Producer: Jo Swerling Jr., Roy Huggins

Hazel

Comedy; 30 min; NBC 9/28/61 to 9/6/65
CBS 9/10/65 to 9/5/66

The adventures of Hazel, a meddlesome maid, as she cares for the Baxters: George, an attorney with Butterworth, Hatch, and Noell, his wife Dorothy, and their son Harold. In 1965, when George is transferred to the Middle East, Hazel becomes the maid to Steve, George's brother (a real estate salesman), his wife, Barbara, and their daughter, Susie.

Hazel Burke	Shirley Booth	Richard Hollister	Richard Benjamin
George Baxter	Don DeFore	Paula Hollister	Paula Prentiss
Dorothy Baxter	Whitney Blake	Oscar North	Jack Cassidy
Harold Baxter	Bobby Buntrock	Andrew Humble	Hamilton Camp
Steve Baxter	Ray Fulmore	Harry Zarakardos	Ken Mars
Barbara Baxter	Lynn Borden	Norman Nugent	Harold Gould
Susie Baxter	Julia Benjamin	Murray Mouse	Alan Oppenheimer
Rosie Hamicker	Maudie Prickett		
Deirdre Thompson	Cathy Lewis		
Harry Thompson	Robert P. Lieb		
Nancy Thompson	Davey Davison		
Harvey Griffin	Howard Smith		
Miss Scott	Molly Dodd		
Clara	Alice Backus		
Gus Jenkins	Patrick McVey		
Harriet Johnson	Norma Varden		
Herbert Johnson	Donald Foster		
Mona Williams	Mala Powers		
Fred Williams	Charles Bateman		
Jeff Williams	Pat Cardi		
Millie Ballard	Ann Jillian		
Bill Fox	Lawrence Haddon		

Producer: Harry Ackerman, James Fonda

The Hazel Bishop Show

Variety; 30 min; NBC 7/12/51 to 12/5/51

Music and songs with bandleader Freddy Martin and regulars Merv Griffin, Judy Lynn, and Murray Arnold. Sponsored by Hazel Bishop Cosmetics and also known as "The Freddy Martin Show." Produced by Perry Lafferty.

The Hazel Scott Show

Variety; 15 min; DuMont 7/3/50 to 9/29/50

Music and songs with pianist Hazel Scott. Produced by Barry Shear and featuring the announcing of Gloria Lucas.

He and She

Comedy; 30 min; CBS 9/6/67 to 9/18/68

Events in the hectic lives of the Hollisters: Richard, a cartoonist and creator the comic strip-turned TV series, "Jetman," and his beautiful wife, Paula, a scatterbrained traveler's-company aide.

Theme Song ("He and She"): Jerry Fielding

Producer: Arne Sultan, Arnie Rosen

He Said, She Said

Game; 30 min; Syn. 1969

Four celebrity couples compete. In round one, the wives are isolated backstage and the husbands are asked to give personal responses associated with a series of topics. The wives, who are brought on stage, must identify what their husbands said when a topic and one response is revealed. Round two is played in reverse and the team with the most points wins.

Host: Joe Garagiola

Announcer: Johnny Olsen

Producer: Howard Felsher, Ira Skutch

He's the Mayor

Comedy; 30 min; ABC 1/10/86 to 3/21/86

When Carl Burke, a 25-year-old college graduate decides to run for mayor and initiates a program of improving the quality of life, he is unexpectedly elected. Stories relate his attempts to solve the problems that befall an unidentified city.

Carl Burke	Kevin Hooks
Alvin Burke	Al Fann
Paula Hendricks	Mari Gorman
Kelly Enright	Margot Rose
Harlan Nash	David Graf
Wardell Halsley	Wesley Thomas
Chief Walter Padgett	Pat Corley
Ivan Bronsky	Stanley Brock

Theme Vocal ("He's the Mayor"): Thelma Houston, Wesley Thompson

Producer: Alessandro Veith, Terry Hart

Head of the Class

Game Pilot; 30 min; NBC 6/24/60

Object: For players to reach the finish line of a large game board by answering questions based on comedy sketches or musical numbers.

Host: Gene Rayburn

Regulars: Marilyn Lovell, The Noteworthies

Orchestra: Elliot Lawrence

Head of the Class

Comedy; 30 min; ABC 9/17/86 (Premiere)

The misadventures of Charlie Moore, a good-natured teacher, as he attempts to cope with a group of brilliant students in an Honors Program at Manhattan High School in N.Y.C. (later called Fillmore High School).

Charlie Moore	Howard Hesseman
Bernadette Meara	
(assist. principal)	Jeanetta Arnette
Principal Samuels	William G. Schilling
Students:	
Darlene	Robin Givens
Simone	Khrystyne Haje
Alan	Tony O'Dell
Janice Lazarotto	Tannis Vallely
Eric	Brian Robbins
Arvid Engan	Dan Frischman
Jawaharlal	Jory Husain
Maria Tomlinson	Leslie Bega
Dennis Blunden	Dan Schneider

Producer: Michael Elias, Rich Eustis

Head of the Family

Comedy Pilot; 30 min; CBS 7/19/60

The pilot for "The Dick Van Dyke Show." The misadventures of Rob Petrie, head writer for the fictitious "Alan Sturdy Show."

Rob Petrie	Carl Reiner
Laura Petrie	Barbara Britton
Richie Petrie	Gary Morgan
Buddy Sorrell	Morty Gunty
Sally Rogers	Sylvia Miles
Alan Sturdy	Jack Wakefield

Producer: Marty Poll, Stuart Rosenberg

Headline Chasers

Game; 30 min; Syn. 9/85

Object: For players to answer questions based on headline stories.

Host: Wink Martindale

Announcer: Johnny Gilbert

Producer: Wink Martindale, John Tobyansen

Headline Story

See "Big Town."

Headliners with David Frost

Interview; 60 min; NBC 5/31/78 to 7/5/78

Interviews with prominent people with host David Frost and reporters Liz Smith and Kelly Garrett. Produced by David Frost and John Gilroy.

Headmaster

Comedy-Drama; 30 min; CBS 9/18/70 to 1/1/71

A tender portrait of student-teacher relationships as seen through the eyes of Andy Thompson, the headmaster of Concord, a small California school.

Andy Thompson	Andy Griffith
Margaret Thompson	Claudette Nevins
Jerry Brownell	Jerry Van Dyke
Mr. Purdy	Parker Fennelly
Judy	Lani O'Grady

Theme Vocal ("He's Only a Man"): Linda Ronstadt

Producer: Richard O. Linke, Aaron Ruben

Heart Beat

Drama Pilot; 60 min; NBC 8/14/85

Drama and music videos are combined to relate the adventures of Erica, Monica, and Carla, three beautiful dancers struggling to make it as professionals in New York City.

Erica	Karen Kopins
Monica	Whitney Kershaw
,Carla	Christine Langer
Kevin	Michael Sabatino
Antonia	Bernice Massi
Frank	Bradford Bancroft
Susan	Karen McArn
Nick	Stephen Shellen

Theme Vocal ("Heart Beat"): Bobby Carlisle, Brenda Russell

Producer: Gary Adelson, James H. Brown

Heart of the City

See "Big Town."

Heart of the City

Crime Drama; 60 min; ABC 9/21/86 to 1/10/87

The story of Wes Kennedy, an L.A.P.D. detective struggling to cope with his wife's recent death, his job, and his two teenage children, Robin and Kevin.

Wes Kennedy	Robert Desiderio
Robin Kennedy	Christina Applegate
Kevin Kennedy	Jonathan Ward
Cmdr. Ed Van Duzer	Dick Anthony Williams
Sgt. Halui	Branscombe Richmond
Det. Arno	Kario Salem
Susan (Wes's wife; flashbacks)	Irene Ferris
Kathy Priester (Wes's friend)	Kay Lenz
Det. Stanley	Robert A. Browne
Det. Neal Rickers	Tony Longo

Music: Patrick Williams

Producer: Michael Zinberg, E. Arthur Kean

Hearts Island

Comedy Pilot; 30 min; NBC 8/31/85

The story, set in Shreveport, Louisiana, in 1952, relates the misadventures of Johnnie Baylor, a resourceful widow struggling to make ends meet and provide for her family.

Johnnie Baylor	Dorothy Lyman
Tammy Jean Baylor	Sydney Penny
Buster Baylor	Christopher Burton
Clay Tanner	Gary Sandy
Mattie	Clarice Taylor
Sarge	Court Miller
Patsy	Donna Bullock

Theme Vocal ("Everything We Need Is Here"): Rosemary June

Producer: David W. Duclon, Rick Hawkins, Liz Sage

Hearts of Steele

Comedy Pilot; 30 min; ABC 6/13/86

When her partner backs out of a deal to turn her bar into a restaurant, a group of laid-off steel workers pool their resources and join with Annie to open a restaurant in Pennsylvania. The unsold series was to relate the group's efforts to run the restaurant.

Annie (owner)	Annie Potts
Michelle (chef)	Tracy Nelson
Eddie (waiter)	Matt Craven
Tom (waiter)	Gregory Salata
Jake (waiter)	Kevin Scannell
Granville (waiter)	Harold Sylvester

Producer: Paul Junger Witt, Tony Thomas

The Heathcliff and Dingbat Show

Cartoon; 30 min; ABC 10/4/80 to 9/5/81

Segments: "Heathcliff" (about a mischievous cat who enjoys annoying others), and "Dingbat and the Creeps" (the misadventures of Dingbat, a vampire dog, Bone Head, a skeleton, and Nobody, a pumpkin, as they attempt to help people in trouble).

Voices: Mel Blanc, Julie McWhirter, Marilyn Schreffler, Michael Bell, Melendy Britt, Henry Corden, Joan Van Ark, Joe Baker, Alan Oppenheimer, Shep Menkin

Producer: Joe Ruby, Ken Spears

The Heathcliff and Marmaduke Show

Cartoon; 30 min; ABC 9/12/81 to 9/18/82

Segments: "Heathcliff" (the antics of a mischievous alley cat), and "Marmaduke" (about a lovable but mischievous Great Dane).

Heathcliff	Mel Blanc
Sonia	Marilyn Schreffler
Spike	Mel Blanc
Marmaduke	Don Messick
Marmaduke's owner	Paul Winchell
Barbie	Marilyn Schreffler

Producer: Joe Ruby, Ken Spears

Theme Vocal: Scatman Crothers

Heave Ho Harrigan

Comedy Pilot; 30 min; NBC 9/22/61

The antics of a Navy Flagman (Heave Ho Harrigan) stationed on an aircraft carrier.

Heave Ho Harrigan	Myron McCormick
Capt. Towers	Allyn Joslyn
Ensign Smithers	Darryl Hickman
Miss Willoughby	Della Sharman
Interpreter	Lawrence Dobkin
State Department Official	David White
Poliaiokoff	Ben Aster
Russian	Nestor Paiva
First Sailor	Michael Mahoney
Second Sailor	Peter Haymen

Producer-Creator-Writer: Norman Retchin

Heaven for Betsy

Comedy; 30 min; CBS 9/30/52 to 12/25/52

The struggles that make up a marriage as seen through the experiences of Peter Bell, an assistant New York store toy buyer, and his wife, Betsy, a secretary turned homemaker. Originally presented on "The Frances Langford–Don Ameche Show."

Peter Bell	Jack Lemmon
Betsy Bell	Cynthia Stone

Heaven Help Us

Comedy Pilot; 30 min; CBS 8/14/67

The story of Dick Cameron, a magazine editor whose late wife (Marge) returns to earth to find him a new mate.

Dick Cameron	Barry Nelson
Marge Cameron	Joanna Moore
Mildred	Mary Grace Canfield
Mr. Walker	Bert Freed
Ruth	Sue Randall
Mr. Collins	Skip Ward
Linda	Sandra Warner

Producer: Stan Shpetner

Heaven on Earth

Comedy Pilot; 30 min; NBC 6/28/79

When Roxy and Karen, two beautiful showgirls, are killed in a car crash caused by bungling celestial powers, they are immediately returned to their earthly status. The would-be series was to relate their efforts to repay the kindness by performing good deeds.

Roxy	Carol Wayne
Karen	Donna Ponterotto
Sebastian Parnell	William Daniels

Producer: Peter Meyerson

Heaven on Earth

Comedy Pilot; 60 min; NBC 4/12/81

In an attempt to give three fledgling angels a chance to earn their wings, the Almighty offers them the opportunity to do so by performing good deeds among the living. The unsold series was to relate the efforts of Katie, Jerry, and Luis to make up for their past misgivings by helping deserving individuals.

Almighty's Representative	Jack Gilford
Katie Fredericks	Ilene Graff
Jerry Davidson	Douglas Sheehan
Luis Padia	Ron Contreras
Amy Henderson	Nora Morgan
Harvey Mitgard	Rod McCary
Model	Patch MacKenzie
Lenny Caldwell	Christopher J. Brown

Producer: George Eckstein

Heavens to Betsy

Comedy; 30 min; NBC 1949

The comic struggles of Betsy and Mary, young hopefuls seeking Broadway careers.

Betsy	Elizabeth Cote
Mary	Mary Best
Landlord	Nick Dennis
Cabbie	Russell Nype

Producer-Director: Fred Coe

Hec Ramsey

Western; Various (90 min; 2 hrs); NBC 10/8/72 to 8/25/74

The exploits of Deputy Hector "Hec" Ramsey, an ex-gunfighter turned law enforcer (of New Prospect, Oklahoma in 1901), as he uses scientific methods to solve crimes.

Hec Ramsey	Richard Boone
Sheriff Oliver Stamp	Rick Lenz
Amos Coogan	Harry Morgan
Norma Muldoon	Sharon Acker
Andy Muldoon	Brian Dewey

Narrator: Harry Morgan

Producer: Douglas Benton, Harold Jack Bloom

The Heckle and Jeckle Show

Cartoon; 30 min; Syn. 1955

The antics of two talking magpies (Heckle and Jeckle). Also aired on CBS and NBC from 10/24/56 to 9/4/71.

Heckle & Jeckle	Paul Frees

Producer: Bill Weiss

Heck's Angels

Comedy Pilot; 30 min; CBS 8/31/76

The misadventures of Colonel Gregory Heck and his Aero Squadron 35, a group of inferior aviators who battle the Huns in France during W.W. I.

Col. Gregory Heck	William Windom
Lt. David Webb	Joe Barrett
Lt. Billy Bowling	Chris Allport
Lt. George McIntosh	Jillian Kesner
Odette	Susan Silo
Pierre Ritz	Henry Polic II
Lt. Eddy Almont	Chip Zien
Ludwig von Stratter	Abraham Soboloff

Theme Song ("Heck's Angels March") performed by Jack Elliott and Allyn Ferguson

Producer: Frank Peppiatt, John Aylesworth

The Hector Heathcote Show

Cartoon; 30 min; NBC 10/5/63 to 9/25/65

The story of a scientist (Hector) who uses his time machine to investigate the major events that have shaped the world.

Hector Heathcote	John Myers

Producer: Bill Weiss

Hee Haw

Variety; 60 min; CBS 6/15/69 to 7/13/71
Syn. 9/71

Country and western music, songs, and comedy skits and blackouts.

Host: Roy Clark, Buck Owens

Regulars: Barbi Benton, Slim Pickens, Misty Rowe, Kathie Lee Johnson, Gunilla Hutton, Cathy Baker, Grady Nutt, Don Harron, Jeannine Riley, John Henry Faulk, Buck Trent, Archie Campbell, Grandpa Jones, Sheb Wooley, Gordie Tapp, Susan Raye, George Lindsey, Alvin "Junior" Samples, Lulu Roman, Minnie Pearl, Claude Phelps, Jimmy Riddle, Don Rich, Ann Randall, Lisa Todd, Jennifer Bishop, Linda Johnson, Zella Lehr, The Hagers, The Buckaroos, The Inspiration, The Nashville Addition

Music: George Richey, Charlie McCoy

Producer: Frank Peppiatt, John Aylesworth

The Hee Haw Honeys

Comedy Pilot; 30 min; Syn. 6/78

The story of three bit regulars from "Hee Haw" (Chrissy, Lee Ann, and Toby) as they seek stardom as the singing "Hee Haw Honeys."

Chrissy	Kathie Lee Johnson
Toby	Catherine Hickland
Lee Anne	Muffy Durham
Kenny (manager)	Kenny Price

Music: Charlie McCoy

Producer: Sam Louvello

The Hee Haw Honeys

Comedy; 30 min; Syn. 9/78

The story of the Honey family, the owners of a country music nightclub in Nashville.

Kenny Honey	Kenny Price
Lulu Honey	Lulu Roman
Kathie Lee Honey	Kathie Lee Johnson
Misty Honey	Misty Rowe
Willy Billy Honey	Gailard Sartain

Music: Charlie McCoy

Producer: Sam Louvello

Heinz Studio '57

See "Studio '57."

The Helen O'Connell Show

Variety; 15 min; NBC 5/29/57 to 9/6/57

A twice-weekly program of music and songs with singer Helen O'Connell. Orchestrations by David Rose.

The Helen Reddy Show

Variety; 60 min; NBC 6/28/73 to 8/16/73

Music and songs with singer Helen Reddy, The Jaime Rogers Dancers, and the orchestra of Nelson Riddle. Produced by Flip Wilson.

Hell Town

Crime Drama; 60 min; NBC 9/11/85 to 1/1/86

The exploits of Father Noah "Hardstep" Rivers, an ex-con turned Catholic priest (and pastor of St. Dominic's parish and orphanage), as he becomes "the guardian angel of the streets," seeking to protect the people of Hell Town, a tough East Los Angeles neighborhood.

Father Noah Rivers	Robert Blake
"One Ball"	
Tremayne	Whitman Mayo
Mother Maggie	Natalie Core
Sister Indigo	Vonetta McGee
Sister Angel Cakes	
(Anastasia)	Isabel Grandin
Sister Daisy	Rhonda Dotson
Poko Loco	Eddie Quillan
Lawyer Sam	Jeff Corey
Crazy Horse	Zitto Kazann
Brandywine	Tracy Morgan
Matthew the Cop	Guy Stockwell

Theme Vocal ("Hell Town"): Sammy Davis Jr.

Producer: Lyman P. Docker, Robert Hargrove, Ronald Austin

The Hellcats

Adventure Pilot; 60 min; ABC 11/24/67

The adventures of Lee, Buggs, and Rippy, three intrepid, trouble-prone student fliers.

Lee Ragdon	George Hamilton
Buggs Middle	John Craig
Rippy Sloane	Warren Berlinger
Melinda	Barbara Eden
El Primero	Nehemiah Persoff

Hello Dere

Comedy Pilot; 30 min; CBS 8/9/65

The antics of Marty and Steve, a pair of bumbling TV reporters.

Marty Allen	Himself
Steve Rossi	Himself
Vincent J. Vincent	Roland Winters
Miss Malone	Nina Shipman
Tanya	Lisa Pera

Producer: Al Broadax, Ed Jurist

Hello, Larry

Comedy; 30 min; NBC 1/26/79 to 4/26/81

The story of Larry Alder, host of "Hello, Larry" (later "The Larry Alder Show"), a KLOW phone-in radio program in Portland, Oregon, and the divorced father of two pretty teenage daughters (Ruthie and Diane).

Larry Alder	McLean Stevenson
Ruthie Alder	Kim Richards
Diane Alder	Donna Wilkes
	Krista Errickson
Morgan Winslow	Joanna Gleason
Earl	George Memmoli
Leona Wilson	Ruth Brown
Meadowlark Lemon	Himself
Henry Alder	Fred Stuthman
Marion Alder	Shelley Fabares
Tommy Roscini	John Femia
Marie Roscini	Rita Taggart
Lionel Barton I	Parley Baer
Lionel Barton II	David Landesberg
Wendell	Will Hunt

Producer: Dick Bensfield, Perry Grant, George Tibbles

Note: Character names for the three leads was originally Adler, which changed shortly after the premiere.

Hellzapoppin

Variety Pilot; 60 min; ABC 3/1/72

A proposed series of vaudeville and burlesque-like music, comedy and song.

Hosts: Jack Cassidy, Ronnie Schell

Guests: Ruth Buzzi, Peter Lupus, Lyle Waggoner, Lynn Redgrave, Rex Reed, The Jackson Five

Orchestra: Nick Perito

Producer: Alexander H. Cohen, Carolyn Raskin

Help! It's the Hair Bear Bunch

Cartoon; 30 min; CBS 9/11/71 to 9/2/72

The antics of three bears (Hair, Square and Bubi) as they struggle to improve living conditions at the Wonderland Zoo.

Hair Bear	Daws Butler
Bubi Bear	Paul Winchell
Square Bear	Bill Calloway
Mr. Peevley	John Stephenson
Botch	Joe E. Ross

Producer: William Hanna, Joseph Barbera

He-Man and the Masters of the Universe

Cartoon; 30 min; Syn. 9/83

When Adam, Prince of Eternia and defender of the secrets of the Castle Greyskull, holds aloft a magic sword and speaks the words "By the power of Greyskull," he is transformed into He-Man, the mightiest being in the universe. Stories relate his efforts to defend the castle from Skelitor, an evil being bent on learning its secrets to control the universe.

He-Man	George DiCenzo

Additional voices: Linda Gary, Alan Oppenheimer, John Erwin, Eric Gunden

Producer: Lou Scheimer, Arthur H. Nadel

Hennessey

Comedy; 30 min; CBS 9/28/59 to 9/17/62

The story of Lt. Charles J. "Chick" Hennessey, a doctor assigned to the San Diego Naval Base in California.

Lt. Charles Hennessey	Jackie Cooper
Nurse Martha Hale	Abby Dalton
William Hale	Harry Holcombe
Harvey Spencer Blair III	James Komack
Chief Max Bronsky	Henry Kulky
Lt. Dan Wagner	Herb Ellis
Capt. Schaefer	Roscoe Karns
Commander Wilker	Steve Roberts
Dr. King	Robert Gist
Chief Branman	Ted Fish
Seaman Pulaski	Frank Gorshin
Seaman Shatz	Arte Johnson

Theme Song ("Hennessey") by Sonny Burke

Producer: Jackie Cooper, Don McGuire

Henny and Rocky

Variety; 15 min; ABC 6/1/55 to 8/31/55

A filler series of music and comedy presented after the ABC network fights.

Host: Henny Youngman, Rocky Graziano

Vocalist: Marion Colby

Music: The Bobby Hackett Jazz Combo

Henry Fonda Presents the Star and the Story

Anthology; 30 min; Syn. 1/55

A 39 episode series of dramas based on stories selected by a guest star. Also known as "Star and Story."

Host: Henry Fonda

Henry Morgan's Great Talent Hunt

Variety; 30 min; NBC 1/26/51 to 6/1/51

Performances by unusual talent acts.

Host: Henry Morgan

Regulars: Arnold Stang, Art Carney, Kaye Ballard, Pert Kelton, Dorothy Claire

Producer: Mike Levin

Herb Shriner Time

Variety; 30 min; ABC 10/11/51 to 4/3/52

Music and comedy with the homespun philosophy of comedian Herb Shriner.

Host: Herb Shriner

Regulars: Lenka Peterson, Peggy Allenby, Biff McGuire, Joseph Sweeney, Eda Heineman, Paul Hurber

Orchestra: Milton DeLugg, Bernard Green

Producer: Mel Ferber, Jack Mosman, Ashmead Scott

Herbie, The Love Bug

Comedy, 60 min; CBS 3/17/82 to 4/14/82

The adventures of Jim Douglas, head of the Famous Driving School and owner of Herbie, a magical Volkswagen that has a mind and personality of its own. Stories also focus on Jim's courtship of a pretty widow (Susan) and the efforts of Susan's ex-fiance (Rodney) to win his former love back.

Jim Douglas	Dean Jones
Susan McLane	Patricia Harty
Julie McLane	Claudia Wells
Martin McLane	Nicky Katt
Robbie McLane	Douglas Emerson
Rodney Bigelow	Larry Linville
Bo Phillips	Richard Paul
Mrs. Bigelow	Natalie Cole

Theme Vocal ("Herbie, My Best Friend"): Dean Jones

Producer: William Robert Yates, Kevin Corcoran

Hercule Poirot

Crime Drama Pilot; 30 min; CBS 4/1/62

The exploits of Hercule Poirot, a Belgian detective who uses sheer wit to solve crimes. Aired on "G.E. Theatre."

Hercule Poirot	Martin Gabel
Mrs. Davenham	Nina Foch
Chief McMannus	Philip Ober
Detective Floyd	James Callahan
Billy Kellett	John Harding

Hercules

Adventure Pilot; 60 min; ABC 9/12/65

The exploits of Hercules, the mythical Greek hero possessed of superhuman strength.

Hercules	Gordon Scott
Diogenes	Paul Stevens
Ulysses	Mart Hulswit
Diana	Diana Hyland
Petra	Steve Garrett
Leander	Giorgio Ardisson

Narrator: Everett Sloane

Producer: Joseph E. Levine

The Herculoids

Cartoon; 30 min; CBS 9/9/67 to 9/6/69

The story of the Herculoids, animals who struggle to protect their king, Zandor, and their utopian planet from evil.

Zandor/Zok/Igoo	Mike Road
Tarra	Virginia Gregg
Dorno	Teddy Eccles
Gloop/Gleep	Don Messick

Producer: William Hanna, Joseph Barbera

Hereafter

Comedy Pilot; 30 min; NBC 11/27/75

The story of three forgotten singers who make a pact with the devil's youngest son in return for a year at the top of the music world. See also "A Year at the Top."

Cliff	Greg Evigan
Nathan	Josh Mostel
Rick	Don Scardino
Lionel	Paul Shaffer
Lillian	Vivian Blaine
Frank	Robert Donley
Lou	Phil Leeds
Joe	John J. Fox
Rick	Antonio Fargas
Assistant	Kay Dingle

Producer: Woody Kling

Here Come the Brides

Adventure; 60 min; ABC 9/25/68 to 9/18/70

The adventures of three brothers (Jason, Joshua, and Jeremy) who run a logging camp in Seattle Washington, in the 1870s. The title refers to the one hundred marriageable women Jason transported from Mass. to satisfy his woman-starved loggers.

Jason Bolt	Robert Brown
Joshua Bolt	David Soul
Jeremy Bolt	Bobby Sherman
Lottie Hatfield	Joan Blondell
Candy Pruitt	Bridget Hanley
Aaron Stemple	Mark Lenard
Francis Clancey	Henry Beckman
Molly Pruitt	Patti Cohoon
Chris Pruitt	Eric Chase
Biddie Cloon	Susan Tolsky
Essie Gillis	Mitzi Hoag
Corky Sam McGee	Bo Svenson
	Robert Biheller
Rev. Gaddings	William Schallert
Uncle Duncan Bolt	Denver Pyle
Ben Perkins	Hoke Howell

Theme Vocal ("Seattle"): The New Establishment

Producer: Bob Claver, Paul Junger Witt

Here Come the Double Deckers

Comedy; 30 min; ABC 9/12/70 to 9/3/72

The adventures of seven children who attempt to solve problems without help from the adult world. The title refers to their club house, a double decker bus that is parked in a London junkyard.

Scooper	Peter Firth
Spring	Brinsley Forde
Billie	Gillian Bailey
Tiger	Debbie Russ
Sticks	Bruce Clark
Doughnut	Douglas Simmonds
Brains	Michael Anderson

Here Come the Stars

Variety; 60 min; Syn. 1968

Testimonial dinners that honor special guests.

Host: George Jessel

Producer: William Hanna, Joseph Barbera

Here Comes Melinda

Comedy Pilot; 30 min; Unaired; Produced in 1960

The comical adventures of Melinda Gray, a baby sitter for the Westwood Baby Sitters Service in California.

Melinda Gray	Spring Byington
Paula Trowbridge	Alice Backes
Ann Gray	Toby Michaels
Judy Saunders	Roberta Shore
Phyllis Saunders	Maxine Stuart
Martin Saunders	John Zaremba
Grandpa Cooper	Charlie Ruggles
Johnny Douglas	Jimmy Hawkins
Mr. Winigrad	Hal Smith

Producer: Harry Ackerman, Charles B. Fitzsimons

Here Comes the Grump

Cartoon; 30 min; NBC 9/6/69 to 9/4/71

As a magic fantasy land is put under the Curse of Gloom by the evil Grump, a young boy (Terry) is magically transported to the kingdom. There, Terry meets Princess Dawn and learns that in the Cave of the Whispering Orchids, the Grump has hidden the Crystal Key, which can lift the curse. Stories relate Terry and Dawn's efforts to find the key; and the Grump's attempts to foil their search.

Princess Dawn	Stefanianna Christopher
Terry Baxter	Jay North
The Grump	Rip Taylor

Producer: Friz Freleng, David DePatie

Here We Go Again

Comedy; 30 min; ABC 1/20/73 to 6/23/73

The struggles of newlyweds Richard and Susan Evans to find serenity in a neighborhood where Richard's ex-wife (Judy) and Susan's ex-husband (Jerry) live and constantly intrude on their privacy.

Richard Evans	Larry Hagman
Susan Evans	Diane Baker
Judy Evans	Nita Talbot
Jerry Standish	Dick Gautier
Jan Standish	Kim Richards
Cindy Standish	Leslie Graves
Jeff Evans	Chris Beaumont

Theme Vocal ("Here We Go Again"): Carol Sagar, Peter Allen

Producer: Charles Fries, Stan Schwimmer

Here's Barbara

A syndicated (1969) interview series with hostess Barbara Coleman.

Here's Boomer

Anthology; 30 min; NBC 3/14/80 to 8/14/82

The story of Boomer, an unowned, roving shaggy dog who aids people in distress. See also "A Christmas for Boomer."

Star	Boomer
Voice of Boomer's thoughts	Tom Moore

Theme Song ("Here's Boomer): Zoey Wilson, Edward Leonetti

Producer: Daniel Wilson, A.C. Lyles, Fran Sears

Here's Edie

Variety; 30 min; ABC 9/26/63 to 3/19/64

Music and songs with hostess Edie Adams and the orchestra of Peter Matz. Produced by David Oppenheimer, Barry Shear. Also known as "The Edie Adams Show."

Here's Hollywood

Interview; 30 min; NBC 9/26/60 to 12/28/62

Intimate aspects of celebrities' lives are revealed through in-depth interviews.

Hosts: Joanne Jordan, Dean Miller

Producer: Jess and Pier Oppenheimer

Here's Lucy

Comedy; 30 min; CBS 9/23/68 to 9/2/74

The antics of Lucille Carter, the overzealous secretary to Harrison Otis Carter, her brother-in-law and owner of the Unique Employment Agency ("Unusual Jobs for Unusual People").

Lucille Carter	Lucille Ball
Harrison Carter	Gale Gordon
Kim Carter	Lucie Arnaz
Craig Carter	Desi Arnaz Jr.
Mary Jane Lewis	Mary Jane Croft

Music: Marl Young

Producer: Gary Morton, Cleo Smith

Here's Richard

Variety; 30 min; Syn. 10/82

Celebrity interviews, skits, and nutritional information.

Host: Richard Simmons

Theme Song ("Here's Richard"): Wendy Fraser, Stacy Widelitz

Producer: Woody Fraser

Note: The 30 minute pilot, which featured Judy Landers and Erma Bombeck, aired in April of 1982.

Here's the Show

Variety; 30 min; NBC 7/9/55 to 9/24/55

A weekly series of music and comedy.

Host: Jonathan Winters, Ransom Sherman

Regulars: Kay O'Grady, Stephanie Antie, Tommy Knox, The Double Daters, The Ted Carpenter Singers

Orchestra: John Scott Trotter

Hernandez, Houston P.D.

Crime Drama Pilot; 60 min; NBC 1/16/73

The exploits of Juan Hernandez, a detective with the Houston, Texas, Police Department.

Det. Juan Hernandez	Henry Darrow
Sgt. Lukas Desmond	Desmond Dhooge
Jackman	Dana Elcar
Roper	Ronny Cox
Penner	G. D. Spradlin

Producer: David Levinson

Herndon and Me

Comedy Pilot; 30 min; ABC 8/26/83

The misadventures of Herndon P. Pool, a clumsy computer genius who is employed by the Judicto Computer Company in San Jose, California.

Dr. Herndon P. Pool	Michael Richards
Jeff Shackelson (his friend; title)	Ted McGinley
Hillary Swanson	Randi Brooks
Miss Helter	Anne Ramsey
Connie Kokorium	Robin Riker
Larua	Marla Pennington
Stanley	Tony Longo
Paula	Sharon Thomas

Producer: Garry K. Marshall, Ronny Hallin, Lowell Ganz

The Hero

Comedy; 30 min; NBC 9/8/66 to 1/5/67

The home and working life of Sam Garrett, a klutz who portrays a fearless law enforcer on the TV series, "Jed Clayton, U.S. Marshal."

Sam Garrett	Richard Mulligan
Ruth Garrett	Mariette Hartley
Paul Garrett	Bobby Horan
Fred Gilman	Victor French
Adele Gilman	Maureen Arthur
Burton Gilman	Joey Baio
"Jed Clayton" director	Norman Palmer
"Jed Clayton" bartender	Jack Perkins
	John Harmon
Marilyn (Sam's niece)	Laurel Goodwin

"The Hero" Theme by: Jack Marshall

Producer: Leonard B. Stern, Jay Sandrich

Hey, Jeannie

Comedy; 30 min; CBS 9/5/56 to 5/4/57

The story of Jeannie MacLennan, a young lass newly arrived in New York from Scotland, as she struggles to adjust to the American way of life.

Jeannie MacLennan	Jeannie Carson
Al Murray	Allen Jenkins
Liz Murray	Jane Dulo

Producer: Charles Isaacs

Hey, Landlord

Comedy; 30 min; NBC 9/11/66 to 5/14/67

The story of two bachelors (Woody and Chuck), an aspiring writer and actor, as they struggle to operate a ten-room apartment house in New York City.

Woody Banner	Will Hutchins
Chuck Hookstratten	Sandy Baron
Jack Ellenhorn	Michael Constantine
Timmie Morgan	Pamela Rodgers
Kyoko Mitsui	Miko Mayama
Mrs. Henderson	Ann Morgan Guilbert
Mrs. Teckler	Kathryn Minner
Bonnie Banner	Sally Field
Lloyd Banner	Tom Tully
Marcy Banner	Ann Doran
Leon Hookstratten	Joseph Leon
Fanny Hookstratten	Naomi Stevens
Woody's Uncle Dwight	Jack Albertson

"Hey Landlord" Theme by Quincy Jones

Producer: Lee Rich, Garry K. Marshall, Jerry Belson

Hey Mulligan

Comedy; 30 min; NBC 8/28/54 to 6/4/55

The story of Mickey Mulligan, a page at the mythical International Broadcasting Company, as he tackles various part-time jobs in an attempt to discover his goal in life. Also known as "The Mickey Rooney Show."

Mickey Mulligan	Mickey Rooney
Patricia Hardy	Carla Balenda
Joe Mulligan	Regis Toomey
Nell Mulligan	Claire Carleton
Mr. Brown	John Hubbard
Freddie	Joey Forman
Mickey's Drama Teacher	Alan Mowbray

Music: Van Alexander

Producer: Mickey Rooney, Maurice Duke

Note: The station at which Mickey works, I.B.C., is based on screening episodes.

Hey Teacher

Comedy Pilot; 30 min; CBS 6/15/64

The story of Joe Hannon, the only male teacher in an elementary school dominated by females.

Joe Hannon	Dwayne Hickman
Mrs. Foley	Reta Shaw
Lester Tinney	Wallace Ford

Producer: Bob Sweeney

Hi Mom

Information; 60 min; NBC 9/15/57 to 3/20/59

Advice and information geared to young mothers.

Host: Shari Lewis, Johnny Andrews

Regulars: Paul and Mary Ritts, Jane Palmer, Josephine McCarthy

Hickey Vs. Anybody

Comedy Pilot; 30 min; NBC 9/19/76

The story of Julius V. Hickey, a lawyer who will tackle any case.

Julius V. Hickey	Jack Weston
Phyllis	Liberty Williams
Netty	Beverly Sanders
Willie	Malcolm Atterbury
Dr. McCaffery	Jack Gilford
Mrs. Nelson	Jessamine Miller

Producer: Marc Merson

Director-Writer: Alan Alda

Hickory Hideout

Children; 30 min; Syn. 9/85

The series, set at the Hickory Hideout (located in a forest) relates various aspects of the world to children via sketches and the antics of Nutso and Shirl, two squirrel puppets.

Cassie	Cassandra Wolfe
Wayne	Wayne Turney
Pam	Camille Harvey
Tsai	Chi-Tsai Tang
Buzz Buzzsaw	David O. Frazier
Puppeteers	Nancy Sander
	Linda Wells

Producer: Robert T. Noll

Hidden Treasure

Game; 60 min; Syn. 1957

Object: For players to piece together clues in musical numbers to distinguish between similar words (e.g., "padded" or "added").

Host: Robert Q. Lewis

Vocalists: Russell Arms, Judy Johnson, Eve DeLuca, Richard Hayes

Orchestra: Ray Bloch

Trumpet Soloist: Bobby Hackett

Producer: William T. Clemons

Hide and Seek

Comedy Pilot; 30 min; CBS 8/5/63

The pilot for "Glynis." The story of Glynis Granville, a scatterbrained wife who, with her ineffable sense of logic, helps her attorney husband, John, solve crimes.

Glynis Granville	Glynis Johns
John Granville	Keith Andes
Detective	Michael Constantine
Mrs. Green	Phyllis Love
Mrs. Gombert	Mary Gregory

Producer: Jess Oppenheimer, Jack Ballard

The High Chaparral

Western; 60 min; NBC 9/10/67 to 9/10/71

The saga of the Cannon family as they struggle to maintain the High Chaparral Ranch in Tucson, Arizona, during the 1870s.

John Cannon	Leif Erickson
Buck Cannon	Cameron Mitchell
Victoria Cannon	Linda Cristal
Billy Blue Cannon	Mark Slade
Don Sebastain de Montoya	Frank Silvera
Manolito de Montoya	Henry Darrow
Sam Butler	Don Collier
Ira	Jerry Summers
Soldado	James Almonza
Ted Reno	Ted Markland
Pedro	Roberto Contreras
Wind	Ruby Ramos
Joe	Bob Hoy
Vaquero	Rodolfo Acosta

Producer: David Dortort, William F. Claxton

High Feather

Comedy; 30 min; PBS 1980

The misadventures of a group of children attening the High Feather Camp for the Summer.

Leslie	Jacqueline Allen
Stan	Brian Goldberg
Leo	Virgil Hayes
Tom	Richard Levey
Suzanne	Cindy O'Neal
Cathy	Emily Wagner
Ann Campbell	Taisha Washington
Domingo	Tino Zaldivar
Kim	Robert Y. R. Chung
Mrs. Riggs (counselor)	Barbara Brown
Mario (chef)	Ernesto Gonzalez
Mrs. Rodriquez (nurse)	Romona Brito

Producer: Judy Seeger

High Finance

Game; 30 min; CBS 7/7/56 to 12/15/56

Contestants, selected from various cities, are quizzed on items that appear in their local papers. Players can either keep their winnings or risk it on additional questions, attempting to win the $35,000 grand prize.

Host: Dennis James

Announcer: Jay Simms, Jack Gregson

Producer: Peter Arnell

High Five

Comedy Pilot; 30 min; NBC 7/22/82

The misadventures of the staff of KBHX, Channel 55, an all-black TV station in Watts, Los Angeles.

Al Cook	Harrison Page
Wilson Porter	Franklyn Seales
Stacey	Cindy Herron
Calvin T. Washburn	Ted Ross
Velma Williams	Clarice Taylor
Jamol	Clinton Derricks-Carroll
Truman Murdock	Roscoe Lee Browne

Producer: O. J. Simpson, John Baskin, Roger Schulman

High Low

Game; 30 min; NBC 7/4/57 to 9/19/57

Object: For a player to challenge a panel of three experts by answering one or more parts of questions that contain several segments. The player has to match the panelist who has the most answers (High) or the fewest (Low). $1500 is awarded if the player matches the High; $1000 if he matches the Low.

Host: Jack Barry

Panelists: Burl Ives, Patricia Medina, Walter Slezak

Producer: Jack Barry, Dan Enright

High Performance

Adventure; 60 min; ABC 3/2/83 to 3/23/83

The exploits of Kate, Blue and Shane, the top operatives for High Performance, an elite protection agency that tackles hazardous assignments for a price ($5,000 a day).

Kate Flannery	Lisa Hartman
Blue Stratton	Jack Scalia
Shane Adams	Rick Edwards
Brennan Flannery	Mitchell Ryan
O. T. Fletcher	Jason Bernard

Producer: Paul R. Picard

High Rollers

Game; 30 min; NBC 7/1/74 to 6/11/76
            Syn. 9/75
            NBC 4/22/78 to 6/10/80

The first player to correctly answer a question receives the option of either keeping or passing the roll of two dice. When the dice are rolled, players have to match the numbers that appear by selecting numbers from a large board. Numbers contain a prize and once selected they become inactive. A player is disqualified when a rolled number cannot be duplicated on the board. Winners receive the prizes they have accumulated.

Host: Alex Trebek

Dice Roller: Ruta Lee, Elaine Stewart

Substitute Dice Roller: Linda Kay Henning, Suzanne Somers, Dawn Wells, Nanette Fabray, Leslie Uggams

Announcer: Kenny Williams

Producer: Merrill Heatter, Bob Quigley

High School Hollywood

See "Hollywood High" (two titles that aired back-to-back on July 21, 1977) for information.

High School, U.S.A.

Comedy Pilot; 2 hrs; NBC 10/16/83

The first of two pilots (see following title) about the antics of the students and faculty of the mythical Excelsior Union High School in Indiana.

Mr. Plaza	Dwayne Hickman
Miss D'Angelo	Angela Cartwright
Pete Kinney	Tony Dow
Dr. Fritz Hauptmann	Steve Franken
Miss Lori Lee	Dawn Wells
Mr. Krinsky	David Nelson
Mr. Sirota	Barry Livingston
Beth Franklin	Nancy McKeon
Cara Ames	Dana Plato
Peggy	Cathy Silvers
Nadene	Lauri Hendler
Jay Jay Manners	Michael J. Fox
Beau Middleton	Anthony Edwards
Ann Marie Conklin	Crystal Bernard
Otto Lipton	Todd Bridges
Chuckie Dipple	Michael Zorek
Leo Bandini	Tom Villard
Milton Feld	Bob Denver
Janet Franklin	Elinor Donahue
Baxter Franklin	Ken Osmond

Producer: Philip Mandelker, Leonard Hill

High School, U.S.A.

Comedy Pilot; 60 min; NBC 5/26/84

A second pilot (see prior title) about the students and faculty of Exclesior Union High School in Indiana.

Pete Kinney	Rick Nelson
Roman Ing	Henry Gibson
Mrs. Crosley	Harriet Nelson
Cindy Franklin	Melody Anderson
Mr. Sirota	Jerry Mathers
Biology Teacher	Ken Osmond
Teacher	Burt Ward
Coach	Paul Petersen
Superintendant McCarthy	Dick York
Mrs. McCarthy	Barbara Billingsley
Jay Jay Manners	Ben Marley
Chuckie	Michael Zorek
Anne Marie Conklin	Crystal Bernard
Bo Middleton	Crispin Glover
Leo Bandini	Jonathan Gries
Beth Franklin	Anne-Marie Johnson
Peggy	Tegan West
Nadene	Joann Willett
Stripper	Julie Newmar

Producer: Leonard Hill

Highcliffe Manor

Comedy; 30 min; NBC 4/12/79 to 5/3/79

A gothic farce about the eccentric residents of the Blacke Foundation, a scientific institute located in Highcliffe Manor on a desolate island.

Helen Blacke	Shelley Fabares
Frances Cascan	Eugenie Ross-Leming
Wendy Sparks	Audrey Landers
Rebecca	Jenny O'Hara
Bram Shelley	Christian Marlowe
Dr. Felix Morger	Gerald Gordon
Rev. Ian Glenville	Stephen McHattie
Smythe	Ernie Hudson
Cheng	Harold Sakata
Dr. Sanchez	Luis Avalos
Dr. Knootz	Marty Zagon

Narrator: Peter Lawford

Theme Song ("Highcliffe Manor"): Frank DeVol

Producer: Eugenie Ross-Leming, Brad Buckner

Higher and Higher, Attorneys-at-Law

Comedy-Mystery Pilot; 60 min; CBS 9/9/68

The adventures of Liz and John Higher, a wife-and-husband law team.

Liz Higher	Sally Kellerman
John Higher	John McMartin
Arthur Greene	Dustin Hoffman
Doug Payson	Robert Forster
Frank St. John	Alan Alda
Colin St. John	Barry Morse
David Arnold	Billy Dee Williams
Astrid	Gunilla Hutton
McElheny	Eugene Roche

Producer: Jacqueline Babbin

The Highway Honeys

Comedy Pilot; 60 min; NBC 1/13/83

The misadventures of Carol Lee and Datona Shepherd, a sister-and-brother team of clean-living tow truckers (for the Good Shepherds Towing Service in Sierra Madre, Texas).

Carol Lee Shepherd	Mary Davis Duncan
Datona Shepherd	Will Bledsoe
Cannonball Shepherd	Don Collier
Sheriff Wilbur Mossburgh	Glen Ash
Draggin' Lady*	Kirstie Alley
Deputy Conchita Valdez	Tina Gail Hernandez
Wolfe Crawley*	Matt Clark
Amigo*	Miguel Rodriquez
Tattoo Calhoune*	Keenan Waynns
Pig Long*	Michael Crabtree

Narrator: Don Collier

Producer: Rod Amateau

*Operators of the corrupt Apocalypse Towing Service.

Highway Patrol

Crime Drama; 30 min; Syn. 1956

The exploits of Dan Matthews, chief of the Highway Patrol.

Dan Matthews	Broderick Crawford
Sgt. Williams	William Boyett

Narrator: Art Gilmore

"Highway Patrol" Theme: Richard Llewellyn

Producer: Jack Herzberg, Vernon E. Clark

Highway to Heaven

Drama; 60 min; NBC 9/19/84 (Premiere)

The story of Jonathan Smith, an earth-bound angel whose mission is to help people overcome their difficulties through kindness and understanding.

Jonathan Smith	Michael Landon
Mark Gordon (his human assistant)	Victor French

Theme Music by Henry Mancini

Producer: Michael Landon, Kent McCray

The Highwayman

Adventure Pilot; 30 min; NBC 8/17/58

The adventures of James McDonald, an apparent fop who is actually a highwayman in the England of the 1750s.

James McDonald	Louis Hayward
Luke	Richard O'Sullivan
Lady Sylvia	Adrienne Corri
Jerry Bridger	Sam Kydd

Producer: Sidney Cole

The Hilarious House of Frightenstein

Children; 30 min; Syn. 9/75

Music, songs, and comedy that revolve around Count Frightenstein, his servant Igor, and their misguided attempts to bring to life Bruce, an "out of order" Frankenstein-type of monster.

Host	Vincent Price
Count Frightenstein	Billy Van
Igor	Rais Fishka

Regulars: Prof. Julius Sumner Miller, Guy Big, Joe Torby

Producer-Writer-Director-Creator: Riff Markowitz

Hill Street Blues

Crime Drama; 60 min; NBC 1/15/81 to 5/19/87

The series, set at the Hill Street Police Station in the worst neighborhood of an unidentified city, relates the experiences of the men and women who place their lives on the line each day to protect the innocent.

Capt. Frank Furillo	Daniel J. Travanti
Joyce Davenport	Veronica Hamel
Sgt. Philip Esterhaus	Michael Conrad
Det. Mick Belker	Bruce Weitz
Off. Andy Renko	Charles Haid
Off. Bobby Hill	Michael Warren
Det. Ray Calletano	Rene Enriquez
Det. John LaRue	Keil Martin
Sgt. Lucy Bates	Betty Thomas
Sgt. Howard Hunter	James B. Sikking
Off. Neil Washington	Tauren Blacque
Fay Furillo	Barbara Bosson
Grace Gardner	Barbara Babcock
Off. Joe Coffey	Ed Marinaro
Chief Daniels	Jon Cypher
Mayor Ozzie Cleveland	J. A. Preston
Irwin Bernstein	George Wyner
Off. Leo Schnitz	Robert Hirschfeld
Off. Clara Tilsky	Jane Kaczmarek
Off. Robin Tataglia	Lisa Sutton

Nydorf (coroner)	Pat Corley
Det. Sal Benedetto	Dennis Franz
Alan Wachtel	Jeffrey Tambor
Det. Harry Garabaldi	Ken Olin
Sgt. Stanislaus Jablonski	Robert Prosky
Det. Patricia Mayo	Mimi Kuyzk
Off. Terry Flaherty	Robert Clohessy
Sgt. Tina Russo	Megan Gallagher
Off. Marty Nichols	Lynne Moody
Off. Norman Buntz	Dennis Franz
Sid the Snitch	Peter Jurasik
Sgt. Henry Goldblume	Joe Spano
Daryl Ann Renko	Debbie Richter
Jesus Martinez	Trinidad Silva
Capt. Jerry Fuchs	Vincent Lucchesi
Myrna Schnitz	Jane Alden
Det. Ralph Macafee	Dan Hedaya
Deputy Chief Mahoney	Ron Parady
Off. Crawford	Franklyn Seales
D. A. Jenkins	Essex Smith

Theme Song ("Hill Street Blues"): Mike Post

Producer: Steven Bochco, Michael Kozall, Gregory Hoblitt, Anthony Yerkovitch

Hippodrome

Variety; 60 min; CBS 7/5/66 to 9/6/66

A showcase for European circus acts. Music by Peter Knight and Produced by Joseph Cates. Guests host.

Hiram Holliday

See "The Adventures of Hiram Holliday."

The His and Her of It

A syndicated (1969) discussion series with husband and wife hosts Geoff and Suzanne Edwards.

His and Hers

Comedy Pilot; 30 min; CBS 5/15/84

Events in the lives of the newlywed McCabes: Jimmy, a former playboy struggling to adjust to marriage, and Barbara, his beautiful and sometimes understanding wife.

Jimmy McCabe	Richard Kline
Barbara McCabe	Shelley Fabares
Kelly McCabe	Dana Kimmell
Stacy McCabe	Shannen Doherty
Sharon	Leslie Easterbrook
Larry	Richard Forongy
Inga	Pamela Newman

Theme Vocal ("His and Hers"): David Shiels

Producer: Frank Konigsberg, Arnold Kane

His Honor, Homer Bell

Comedy; 30 min; Syn. 2/55

Events in the life of Homer Bell, the understanding and respected Justice of the Peace in Spring City.

Homer Bell	Gene Lockhart
Cassandra "Casey"	
Bell	Mary Lee Dearing
Maude	Jane Moutrie

Producer: Hy Brown

His Model Wife

Comedy Pilot; 30 min; CBS 9/4/62

The misadventures of a beautiful model (Jean), her husband, John, a magazine publisher, and their children, Benjy and Chris.

Jean Lauren	Jeanne Crain
John Lauren	John Vivyan
Chris Lauren	Lorrie Thomas
Benjy Lauren	Jimmy Gaines
Miss Bickle	Alice Frost
Cappy Norton	Jack Mullavey

Producer: Norman Tokar, Tony Owen

Hit Man

Game; 30 min; NBC 1/3/83 to 4/1/83

Questions, based on a previously read story, are asked of three contestants. For each correct response a player gives, an animated Hit Man fills one of six blank spaces assigned to each player. The first player to score six correct answers wins $300.

Host: Peter Tomarken

Announcer: Rod Roddy

Producer: Jay Wolpert

Hitched

Drama Pilot; 90 min; NBC 3/31/73

The story of young newlyweds (Roselle and Clare) struggling to begin a new life in the old west of the 1880s.

Roselle Bridgeman	Sally Field
Clare Bridgeman	Tim Matheson

Producer: Richard Alan Simmons

The Hitchhiker

Anthology; 30 min; HBO 11/23/83 (Premiere)

The adventures of a mysterious hitchhiker and the effects his presence has on those he encounters: evil people who are led to experience the terrors of the unknown. Contains nudity, sexual situations, and adult language.

The Hitchhiker	Nicholas Campbell
	Page Fletcher

"The Hitchhiker" theme by Michel Rubini

Producer: Richard Rothstein, Lewis Chesler, Riff Markowitz

The Hitchhiker's Guide to the Galaxy

Satire; 30 min; PBS 11/4/82 to 12/16/82

Seconds before the Earth is destroyed by a Vogon construction fleet (to make way for a hyperspace bypass), Ford Perfect, an alien from the planet Betelguese and a researcher for "The Hitchhiker's Guide," rescues Englishman Arthur Dent from the impending doom. Soon, they are marooned in space and stories follow their adventures as they become hitchhikers in space.

Ford Perfect	David Dixon
Arthur Dent	Simon Jones
Voice of the Book	Peter Jones
Trillian	Saundra Dickinson
Marvin	David Lerner
Voice of Eddie	David Tate
Voice of Marvin	Stephen Moore
Zaphod Beeblebrox	Stephen Moore
Voice of Deep	
Thought	Valentine Dyall

Theme Music: Bernie Leadon

Producer: Alan J. W. Bell

Hizzoner

Comedy; 30 min; NBC 5/10/79 to 6/24/79

The life and times of Michael Cooper, the kindly mayor of an unidentified Midwestern city.

Michael Cooper	David Huddleston
Ginny Linden	Diana Muldaur
Annie Cooper	Kathy Cronkite
Nails Doyle	Mickey Deems
Melanie	Gina Hecht
Timmons	Don Galloway
James Cooper	Will Selzer

Theme Vocal ("Hizzoner"): David Huddleston

Producer: David Huddleston, Sheldon Keller

Hobbies in Action

A syndicated (1958) series that spotlights people and their hobbies. Hosted by Steve Booth.

Hobby Lobby

Variety; 30 min; ABC 9/30/59 to 3/23/60

A showcase for people and their hobbies. Celebrities appear to lobby their hobbies.

Charley Weaver (host)	Cliff Arquette

Announcer: Tom Reddy

Music: John Gart

Producer: Art Stark

Hogan's Heroes

Comedy; 30 min; CBS 9/17/65 to 7/4/71

The antics of the American, French, and English inmates of Stalag 13, a W.W. II German prisoner-of-war camp, as they attempt to aid the Allies and obtain enemy information for their superiors.

Col. Robert Hogan	Bob Crane
Col. Wilhelm Klink	Werner Klemperer
Sgt. Hans Schultz	John Banner
Helga	Cynthia Lynn
Hilda	Sigrid Valdis
Col. Crittendon	Bernard Fox
Maj. Hockstedder	Howard Caine
Marya	Nita Talbot
Gen. Alfred Burkhalter	Leon Askin
Gertrude Linkmier	Kathleen Freeman
Cpl. Lewis LeBeau	Robert Clary
Cpl. Peter Newkirk	Richard Dawson
Sgt. Andrew Carter	Larry Hovis
Cpl. Richard Baker	Kenneth Washington
Cpl. James Kinchloe	Ivan Dixon

Producer: Edward H. Feldman

Hold 'er Newt

Children; 15 min; ABC 9/11/50 to 10/13/50

The marionette antics of Newton Figg, the proprietor of a general store in Figg Center.

Newton Figg	Don Tennant

Producer: Don Tennant, Les Weinrott

Hold it Please

Game; 30 min; CBS 5/8/49 to 5/22/49

A telephone call is placed at random to a viewer. If the viewer correctly answers a question, he wins a prize and the opportunity to win valuable merchandise by identifying a celebrity portrait that is shown on a spinning wheel.

Host: Gil Fates

Regulars: Cloris Leachman, Mort Marshall, Evelyn Ward, Bill McGraw

Producer: Frances Buss

Hold that Camera

Game; 30 min; DuMont 8/27/50 to 12/15/50

Four players compete: two home viewers and two studio contestants. The viewer, whose voice is amplified over the telephone, directs his partner through a series of shenanigans; the other team competes in the same manner.

The team who took the least amount of time to perform win merchandise prizes.

Hosts: Jimmy Blaine, Kyle MacDonnell

Producer: West Hooker, Ted Kneeland

Hold that Note

Game; 30 min; NBC 1/22/57 to 4/2/57

Object: For players to identify song titles as fast as possible and in as few notes as possible

Host: Bert Parks

Announcer: Johnny Olsen

Holiday Hotel

Variety; 30 min; ABC 3/23/50 to 6/28/51

Entertainment acts set against the background of the Pelican Room of the Holiday Hotel on New York's Park Avenue.

Host: Edward Everett Horton

Regulars: Betty Brewer, Dorothy Greener, Don Sadler, The Don Craig Chorus, The June Graham Dancers

Orchestra: Bernard Green

Producer: Monte Proser

Holiday Lodge

Comedy; 30 min; CBS 6/2/61 to 10/8/61

The antics of Johnny and Frank, the social directors at the plush Holiday Lodge in New York State.

Johnny Miller	Johnny Wayne
Frank Boone	Frank Shuster
J. W. Harrington	Justice Watson
Dorothy Johnson	Maureen Arthur
Woodrow	Charles Smith

Producer: Cecil Baker

Holloway's Daughters

Comedy-Drama Pilot; 60 min; NBC 5/1/66

The investigations of Nick Holloway, owner of the Holloway Detective Agency, his son, George, and his two beautiful grand-daughters, amateur sleuths Fleming and Casey. Aired on "The Bob Hope Chrysler Theatre."

Nick Holloway	Robert Young
George Holloway	David Wayne
Martha Holloway	Marion Moses
Fleming Holloway	Brooke Bundy
Casey Holloway	Barbara Hershey
Miss Purdy	Ellen Corby

Director: Ida Lupino

Hollywood a Go Go

A syndicated (1965) variety series that features performances by rock stars. Hosted and produced by Sam Riddle.

Hollywood and the Stars

Documentary; 30 min; NBC 9/30/63 to 9/28/64

The behind-the-scenes story of Hollywood—its stars and its films.

Host-Narrator: Joseph Cotten

Music: Elmer Bernstein, Jack Tillar

Producer: David L. Wolper, Jack Haley Jr.

Hollywood Backstage

A syndicated (1965) series that reports on the Hollywood people, parties, and premieres. Hosted by John Willis.

Hollywood Beat

Crime Drama; 60 min; ABC 9/21/85 to 11/30/85

The exploits of Nick McCarren and Jack Rado, L.A.P.D. undercover cops who use elaborate disguises to apprehend criminals.

Nick McCarren	Jack Scalia
Jack Rado	Jay Acavone
Lita Delaware	Ann Turkel
Capt. Wes Biddle	Edward Winter
Capt. Milton Treadwell	Lane Smith
George Grinsky	John Matuszak
Lady Di	Barbara Cason
Norman (alias Capt. Crusader)	Robert Englund
Billy Night Eyes	Michael Horse

Theme Vocal ("Hollywood Beat"): Natalie Cole

Producer: Aaron Spelling, Douglas S. Cramer

Hollywood Close-Up

Magazine; 30 min; Syn. 9/85

Information about the world of Hollywood—
its stars and its films.

Hosts: Cynthia Allison, Steve Edwards

Announcer: Robert Ridgely

Producer: Craig Haffner, Mack Anderson,
Donna Lusitana

The Hollywood Connection

Game; 30 min; Syn. 1977

Six celebrities appear and are divided into
two three-member teams. A question is read
that involves one team in a hypothetical situation. One contestant (two compete) has to
predict how each member of the team re-
sponded to the question. The player with the
most correct predictions wins merchandise
prizes.

Host: Jim Lange

Announcer: Jay Stewart

Producer: Jack Barry, Dan Enright

Hollywood High

Comedy Pilot; 30 min; NBC 7/21/77

The story of Phoebe and Dawn, students at
Hollywood High School. The pilot relates
their efforts to break their dates with the class
undesirables.

Phoebe	Annie Potts
Dawn	Kim Lankford
Wheeler	Chris Pina
Bill	Rory Stevens
Icky	John Megna
Dr. Bad	Sam Kwasman

Producer: Gerald I. Isenberg

Hollywood High

Comedy Pilot; 30 min; NBC 7/21/77

A second pilot (see prior title) about students
at Hollywood High School. In the second
story, journalism student Paula Lindell attempts to cope with an uncomfortable situation when she and a male student (Eugene)
are forced to spend the night in a motel room.

Paula Lindell	Annie Potts
Eugene Langley	Darren O'Connor
Allison	Roberta Wallach
Judith	Beverly Saunders
Janet	Janet Wood
Stu	John Cuerrasio

Producer: Gerald I. Isenberg, Gerald W.
Abrams

Hollywood Historama

A five minute syndicated (1962) series that
profiles celebrities via newsreel footage,
home movies and footage shot especially for
the program. Directed by Joseph Juliano.

Hollywood Junior Circus

Variety; 30 min; NBC 3/25/51 to 7/1/51
ABC 9/8/51 to 1/19/52

Circus variety acts under the sponsorship of
Hollywood Candy.

Ringmaster	Art Jacobson
	Paul Barnes
Zero	Max Bronstein
Clown	Carl Marx

Regulars: Marie Louise, George Cesar, Bill
Hughes

Orchestra: Brad Case

Producer: Bill Hyer

Hollywood off Beat

Crime Drama; 30 min; Syn. 1952
DuMont 11/7/52 to
1/30/53
CBS 6/16/53 to 8/11/53

The exploits of Steve Randall, an unjustly dis-
barred attorney turned private detective, who
seeks those responsible for framing him and
regain his right to practice law. Also known as
"Steve Randall."

| Steve Randall | Melvyn Douglas |

Producer: Lester Lewis, Marlon Parsonnet

Hollywood Opening Night

Anthology; 30 min; CBS 7/20/51 to 3/28/52
NBC 10/6/52 to 3/23/53

A series of filmed (CBS) and live (NBC) comedies and dramas from the West Coast (actually the first anthology series to originate from Hollywood).

Producer: William Corrigan

Hollywood Reporter

Magazine Pilot; 30 min; Syn. 12/85

A proposed daily series of show business gossip.

Host: Peter Tomarken

Reporters: Meredith MacRae, David Krief

Producer: Earl Greenberg, Arthur Kassel

Hollywood Starr

Crime Drama Pilot; 60 min; ABC 2/23/85

The exploits of Dani Starr, a beautiful detective with the L.A.P.D. Hollywood Station, Vice Squad Division. Aired on "T. J. Hooker."

Det. Dani Starr	Sharon Stone
Chrissy Wild	Mary-Margaret Humes
Frankie Gable	Jonathan Goldsmith
Alan Hartman	Stewart Moss
Jake Moreno	Eric Server
Vic Kolt	Madison Arnold
Andrea Kolt	JoAnn Millette

Theme Vocal ("Hollywood Starr"): Paulette McWilliams

Producer: Aaron Spelling, Leonard Goldberg

The Hollywood Palace

Variety; 60 min; ABC 1/4/64 to 2/7/70

Entertainment acts from the Hollywood Palace Theatre in California. Weekly guests host.

Card Holder	Raquel Welch

Regulars: The Ray Charles Singers, The Buddy Schwab Dancers

Announcer: Dick Tufeld

Orchestra: Mitchell Ayres

Producer: Nick Vanoff, William O. Harbach

Hollywood Screen Test

Anthology; 30 min; ABC 8/15/48 to 5/18/53

Dramatic stories in which young hopefuls appear with established stars.

Host: Bert Lytell, Neil Hamilton, Hurd Hatfield, Betty Furness

Co-Host: Martha Wayne, Robert Quarry

Announcer: Ted Campbell

Producer: Lester Lewis

The Hollywood Squares

Game; 30 min; NBC 10/17/66 to 6/20/80

Nine celebrity guests appear and are situated in a large tic-tac-toe board. A celebrity, chosen by a player (two compete), is asked a question. The player agrees or disagrees with the celebrity's answer. A correct guess wins the player the square. The first player to score three squares in a row wins the game and $200. See also "The Match Game-Hollywood Squares Hour" and "The New Hollywood Squares."

Host: Peter Marshall

Announcer: Kenny Williams

Regulars: Wally Cox, Paul Lynde, Cliff Arquette, Rose Marie, Karen Valentine, George Gobel

Producer: Merrill Heatter, Bob Quigley

Hollywood Talent Scouts

Variety; 60 min; CBS 7/3/62 to 9/11/62
7/2/63 to 9/17/63
6/22/65 to 9/7/65
9/20/65 to 9/5/66

Performances by the undiscovered professional talent of celebrity guests. The 1963 version, created by Irving Mansfield and Jacqueline Sussan, is also known as "Irving Mansfield's Talent Scouts."

Host (1962)	Jim Backus
Host (1963)	Merv Griffin
Host (1965–66)	Art Linkletter

Orchestra (1962, 63): Harry Sosnik

Orchestra (1965–66): Herman Zimmerman

Producer: Irvin S. Atkins, Irving Mansfield, Perry Cross

Hollywood Teen

A syndicated (9/78) program of interviews and celebrity performances with host James McNichol. Produced by Sam Riddle.

Hollywood Theatre Time

Anthology; 30 min; NBC 10/8/50 to 10/6/51

An early dramatic series from Hollywood and produced by George M. Cahan and Thomas Sarnoff.

Hollywood's Talking

Game; 30 min; CBS 3/26/73 to 6/23/73

A video tape, showing celebrities expressing their views on a specific topic, is played. Players have to determine exactly what is being talked about in return for cash prizes.

Host: Geoff Edwards

Announcer: Johnny Jacobs

Producer: Richard Kline, Kenneth Johnson

Holmes and Yoyo

Comedy; 30 min; ABC 9/25/76 to 12/11/76
                              8/1/77 (one episode)

The exploits of Alexander Holmes, a dim-witted Los Angeles police officer, and his partner, Gregory "Yoyo" Yoyonovich, a not-yet perfected computer robot designed to combat crime.

Sgt. Alexander Holmes	Richard B. Shull
Sgt. Gregory Yoyonovich	John Schuck
Capt. Harry Sedford	Bruce Kirby
Off. Maxine Moon	Andrea Howard
Chief Dwight Buchanan	Ben Hammer
Mimi Buchanan	Fritzi Burr
Police Commissioner	G. Wood

Producer: Leonard B. Stern, Arne Sultan

Home

Women; 60 min; NBC 3/1/54 to 8/9/57

A daily program of information for women that is presented in a series of segments that correspond to a magazine.

Hostess: Arlene Francis

Substitute Hostess: June Lockhart

Activities Editor: Arlene Francis

Beauty Editor: Eve Hunter

Decorating Editor: Sydney Smith

Food Editor: Poppy Cannon

Repairs Editor: Will Peiglebeck.

Special Projects Editor: Estelle Parsons

Variety Editor: Johnny Johnston

Music Editors: The Norman Paris Trio

Announcer: Hugh Downs

Producer: Richard Linkroum

Home

Drama Pilot; 60 min; ABC 3/6/87

Events in the day-to-day lives of the Costigans, a family of five living in Chicago and struggling to salvage its values.

Will Costigan	Max Gail
Maggie Costigan	Anne Twomey
Susan Costigan	Tracy Nelson
Kelly Costigan	Michael Sharrett
Brian Costigan	Jody Lambert
Katherine Edison	Barbara Baxley
	Kevin McCarthy
Scott Diamond	Kristoffer Tabori
Valerie Kane	Robin Wright

Producer: Leonard Goldberg, Deborah Aal

Home Cookin'

Comedy Pilot; 30 min; ABC 7/11/75

The story of Adelle and Ernie, a married couple who run a truck stop diner.

Ernie	Wynn Irwin
Adelle	Fannie Flagg
Dinette	Nancy Fox
Jammer	Burton Gilliam
Bevo	Frank McRay
Trooper	Walker Edmiston
Shorty	Bill McLean

Producer: Lawrence Gordon, Don Van Atta

The Home Front

Drama Pilot; 60 min; CBS 10/9/80

The story, set in Shelter Cove, Mass., during W.W. II, relates events in the lives of John Travis, a shipyard owner, and his wife, Enid, and the problems they and their friends and family face during wartime.

John Travis	Craig Stevens
Enid Travis	Jean Simmons
Kate Travis	Martina Deignan
Chris Travis	Dane Witherspoon
Cynthia Travis	Maylo McCaslin
Jack Travis	Nicholas Hammond
Helen Maddox	Chris DeLisle
Leona Spinelli	Eunice Christopher
Angela Spinelli	Delta Burke
Rocco Spinelli	Joe Penny

"The Home Front" Theme: Pete Rugolo

Producer: Charles Fries, Rita Lakin

Home Room

Comedy Pilot; 30 min; ABC 8/10/81

The misadventures of Karen and Craig Chase, students at Hancock High School.

Karen Chase	Ally Sheedy
Craig Chase	Michael Spound
Annette Savinski	Irene Arranga
Elvis Clone	Lee Lucan
Billy Coe	Donald Fullilove
Rona Carp	Eddie Deezen
"Crazy" Willie	Antony Alda
Scott Thomas	Nicholas Pryor
Mr. Melish	Severn Darden
Steve	Andrew Levant
Tina	Faye Grant

Theme Vocal ("High School"): Brett Tuggle

Producer: Dale McRaven

Homemaker's Exchange

A women's program of cooking, household tips, and shopping advice with Louise Leslie. Producer: Ken Redford. CBS 10/10/49 to 1/25/52.

Hometown

Comedy-Drama; 60 min; CBS 8/22/85 to 10/15/85

The series, set in the college town of Whitley, explores the lives and relationships of a group of friends who met in college in the 1960s and are now part of the 1980s establishment. Based on the film "The Big Chill."

Mary Newell-Abbott	Jane Kaczmarek
Ben Abbott	Franc Luz
Barbara Donnelly	Margaret Whitton
Christopher Springer	Andrew Rubin
Peter Kincaid	John Bedford-Lloyd
Jane Parnell	Christine Estabrook
Joey Nathan	Daniel Stern
Jennifer Abbott	Erin Leigh Peck
Tess Abbott	Donna Vivino

Theme Vocal ("My Hometown"): Tony Berg

Producer: Ira Marvin, Joseph Kane, Dinah Kirgo, Julie Kirgo, Gene Reynolds, Dick Berg

Hondo

Western; 60 min; ABC 9/8/67 to 12/29/67

The exploits of Hondo Lane, a U.S. Army troubleshooter, as he attempts to resolve the conflict between settlers and Apache Indians over the prospect of land (Arizona, 1860s).

Hondo Lane	Ralph Taeger
Buffalo Baker	Noah Beery Jr.
Angie Dow	Kathie Brown
Johnny Dow	Buddy Foster
Apache Chief Vittoro	Michael Pate
Capt. Richards	Gary Clarke

Music: Richard Markowitz

Producer: Andrew J. Fenady

Honest Al's a-ok Used Car and Trailer Rental Tigers

Comedy Pilot; 30 min; Syn. 1/78

The story of "Honest" Al, a used car salesman who undertakes sponsorship of the Tigers, a youth league football team.

"Honest" Al	Herb Edelman
Franklin	Danny Bonaduce
Ethel	Zoey Wilson
Moody	Kyra Stempel
Doc	Marc Jason
Chicago	J. R. Miller

Producer: Daniel Wilson, Fran Sears

Honestly, Celeste!

Comedy; 30 min; CBS 10/10/54 to 12/5/54

The story of Celeste Anders, a Minnesota college teacher, as she struggles to acquire journalism experience as a reporter for the "New York Express."

Celeste Anders	Celeste Holm
Mr. Wallace	Geoffrey Lumb
Bob Wallace	Scott McKay
Marty Gordon	Mike Kellin
Mary	Mary Finney
Obit editor	Henry Jones

Music: Jerry Fielding

Producer: Joseph Scibetta

Honey West

Crime Drama; 30 min; ABC 9/17/65 to 9/2/66

The investigations of Honey West, the beautiful owner of H. West and Company, a private detective organization.

Honey West	Anne Francis
Sam Bolt (partner)	John Ericson
Honey's Aunt Meg	Irene Hervey

Producer: Jules Levy, Arthur Gardner, Arnold Laven

Honeymoon Hotel

See "Isabel Sanford's Honeymoon Hotel."

The Honeymoon Race

Game; 30 min; ABC 7/20/67 to 4/1/68

Three newlywed couples, situated in Florida's Hollywood Shopping Mall, compete in a scavenger hunt by seeking clues hidden in various items. The items that are found become their prizes.

Host: Bill Malone

Honeymoon Suite

Comedy Pilot; 90 min; ABC 7/26/72 (1st pilot)
                       1/30/73   (2nd pilot)

Vignettes that depict brief incidents in the lives of couples who check into Room 300 of the Honeymoon Suite of the Beverly Hills Hotel.

Maggie (maid)	Rose Marie
Charlie (bellboy)	Morey Amsterdam
	Henry Gibson
Duncan (manager)	Richard Deacon

Producer: Douglas S. Cramer, Wilford Lloyd Baumes

The Honeymooners

Comedy; 30 min; CBS 10/1/55 to 9/22/56

The misadventures of two neighboring Brooklyn, N.Y. families: Ralph and Alice Kramden, and Ed and Trixie Norton. Ralph is a bus driver on the Madison Avenue Line with the Gotham Bus Company; Ed is a sewer worker with the Department of Sanitation. Stories tenderly detail their struggles to better their lives.

Ralph Kramden	Jackie Gleason
Alice Kramden	Audrey Meadows
Ed Norton	Art Carney
Trixie Norton	Joyce Randolph

Various roles: Frank Marth, George O. Petrie

Theme Song ("You're My Greatest Love"): Jackie Gleason, Bill Templeton

Producer: Jack Philbin, Jack Hurdle

The Honeymooners

Comedy; 60 min; Syn. 1977

An update of the prior title, which continues to depict events in the lives of Ralph and Alice Kramden and their friends Ed and Trixie Norton. Originally broadcast as segments of "The Jackie Gleason Show."

Ralph Kramden	Jackie Gleason
Alice Kramden	Sheila MacRae
Ed Norton	Art Carney
Trixie Norton	Jane Kean

Announcer: Johnny Olsen

Orchestra: Sammy Spear

Producer: Jack Philbin

The Honeymooners: The Lost Episodes

Comedy; 30 min; SHO 9/85 to 9/86
                           Syn. 9/86

The series is comprised of 66 half-hour programs culled from "The Honeymooners" sketches that were broadcast live on "The Jackie Gleason Show" from 1952 through 1957. The early Pert Kelton (as Alice) segments are not included. The original comic adventures of Ralph and Alice Kramden and their friends Ed and Trixie Norton.

Ralph Kramden	Jackie Gleason
Alice Kramden	Audrey Meadows
Ed Norton	Art Carney
Trixie Norton	Joyce Randolph

Orchestra: Ray Bloch

Producer: Jack Philbin, Jack Hurdle

Hong Kong

Adventure; 60 min; ABC 9/21/60 to 9/27/61

The adventures of Glenn Evans, a foreign correspondent for "World Wide News," whose beat is the mystery, glamour, and intrigue of exotic Hong Kong.

Glenn Evans	Rod Taylor
Chief Insp. Neil W. Campbell	Lloyd Bochner
Mr. Ling (Neil's assistant)	Gerald Jann
Tully (owner of Tully's Bar)	Jack Kruschen
Ching Mei (waitress at Golden Dragon Cafe)	Mai Tai Sing
Ahting (Glenn's houseboy)	Harold Fong

Producer: Herbert Hirschman

Hong Kong Phooey

Cartoon; 30 min; ABC 9/7/74 to 9/4/76

The story of a meek police station janitor (Henry) who can transform himself into the disaster-prone Hong Kong Phooey, "America's secret weapon against crime." Stories relate his battle against crime.

Henry	Scatman Crothers
Sgt. Flint	Joe E. Ross
Rosemary	Kathi Gori
Spot	Don Messick

Producer: William Hanna, Joseph Barbera

The Hoofer

Comedy Pilot; 30 min; CBS 8/15/66

The struggles of Donald and Freddy, an unsuccessful comedy team, as they attempt to make a name for themselves in vaudeville (1920s).

Donald Dugan	Donald O'Connor
Freddy Brady	Soupy Sales
Brainsley Gordon	Jerome Cowan
Finnegan	Jackie Coogan
Wake	Cliff Norton
Wanda	Jolene Brand
Nurse	Carole Cook

Producer: Jack Donohue

Hooperman

Comedy-Drama; 30 min; ABC 9/23/87 (Premiere)

Events in the chaotic day-to-day life of Harry Hooperman, an inspector with the San Francisco P.D. who is also the landlord of a rundown apartment building at 633 Columbus Avenue, and the owner of a vicious little dog named Bijoux.

Insp. Harry Hooperman	John Ritter
Capt. Celeste Stern	Barbara Bosson
Betty Bushkin	Alix Elias
Det. Boris "Bobo" Pritzger	Clarence Felder
Off. Maureen DeMott	Sydney Walsh
Det. Clarence McNeil	Felton Perry
Off. Rick Silardi	Joseph Gian
Susan Smith	Debrah Farentino
Lou Stern	Dan Lauria

Producer: Steve Bochco, Terry Louise Fisher

Hooray for Hollywood

Comedy Pilot; 30 min; CBS 6/22/64

The misadventures of Jerome P. Baggley, a 1920s movie mogul and owner of World Goliath Studios.

Jerome P. Baggley	Herschel Bernardi
Vanda Renee	Joyce Jameson
Miss Zikle	Joan Blondell
Albert Leviathan	John Litel
Ruby	Ruby Keeler

Producer: Warren Lewis, Barry Shear

Hooray for Love

Comedy Pilot; 30 min; CBS 9/9/63

The comic struggles of newlyweds Schuyler "Sky" Young and his wife, Abby.

Sky Young	Darryl Hickman
Abby Young	Yvonne Craig
Clara Boone	Beverly Willis
Gillie Boone	Don Edmonds
Otis Platt	Alvy Moore
Samantha Soo	Cherylene Lee

Producer: Bob Fisher

Hootenanny

Variety; 60 min; ABC 4/6/63 to 9/21/63

Performances by folk artists.

Host: Jack Linkletter

Regular: Glenn Yarbrough

Music: The Chad Mitchell Trio

Producer: Richard Lewine

Hopalong Cassidy

Western; 30 min; Syn. 1948

The exploits of Hopalong Cassidy, a rancher (owner of the Bar 20 Ranch) and a daring defender of range justice.

Hopalong Cassidy	William Boyd
Red Connors	Edgar Buchanan

Producer: William Boyd, Toby Anguist

Hoppity Hopper

See "The Adventures of Hoppity Hopper from Foggy Bogg."

The Horace Heidt Show

Variety; 30 min; CBS 10/2/50 to 9/24/51

Performances by undiscovered talent with orchestra leader Horace Heidt. Produced by Glenn Miller and Ralph Branton.

Hornblower

Adventure Pilot; 60 min; ABC 2/28/63

The adventures of Horatio Hornblower, captain of the "HMS Firedrake," a British warship. The pilot, broadcast on "Alcoa Premiere" and set in 1803 England, relates Horatio's efforts to find his missing sister ship.

Horatio Hornblower	David Buck
Lt. Bush	Terence Longdon
Nathaniel Sweet	Peter Arne
Lt. Carlon	Sean Kelly
Brown	Nigel Green
Bowser	Jeremy Bulloch

Producer: Julian Plowden, Collier Young

Hot

Music; 30 min; Syn. 6/84

A daily countdown of the top music videos.

Host: Michael Binder*, Claud Mann

Announcer: Tom Pino

Theme Song ("HOT"): Chris Christian

Producer: Bob Banner, Stephen Pouliot

*Pilot film host (1/84). The title refers to "The Hits of Today."

Hot City Disco

Music; 30 min; Syn. 1978

Performances by disco artists with hosts Shadoe Stevens and Davy Jones. Produced by Marc Merson and Ed Warren and featuring the Jeff Kutect Dancers.

Hot Dog

Children; 30 min; NBC 9/12/70 to 9/4/71

Woody Allen, Jonathan Winters, and Jo Anne Worley as the hosts of a series that explores various aspects of the adult world. Produced by Lee Mendelson and featuring the music of The Youngbloods.

Hot Hero Sandwich

Children; 60 min; NBC 11/10/79 to 4/5/80

A potpourri of celebrity interviews, music, and comedy.

Regulars: Vicky Dawson, Paul O'Keefe, Matt McCoy, Denny Dillon, Nan-Lynn Nelson, Andy Breckman, Andrew Duncan, Frankie Faison, Saundra McClain, Adam Ross, Claudette Sutherland

Theme Song ("Hot Hero Sandwich"): Bruce Hart, Stephen Lawrence

Producer: Carole Hart, Bruce Hart

Hot l Baltimore

Comedy; 30 min; ABC 1/24/75 to 6/13/75

Life in the seedy Hotel Baltimore (the E in the neon sign has burned out) as seen through the activities of eleven people who share the decaying Maryland residence.

Bill Lewis	James Cromwell
Clifford Ainsley	Richard Masur
Suzy Marta Rocket	Jeannie Linero
April Green	Conchata Ferrell
Winthrop Morse	Stan Gottlieb
Charles Bingham	Al Freeman Jr.
Jackie	Robin Wilson
Millie	Gloria LeRoy
Esmee Belotti	Charlotte Rae
George	Lee Bergere
Gordon	Henry Calvert

"Hot 1 Baltimore" theme: Marvin Hamlisch

Producer: Rod Parker, Norman Lear

Hot Off the Wire

See "The Jim Backus Show—Hot Off the Wire."

Hot Potato

Game; 30 min; NBC 1/23/84 to 6/29/84

Two three-member teams compete in a series of question-and-answer rounds wherein the first team to score seven points receives the opportunity to win $5,000 by answering a series of questions that begin at $300 and increase with difficulty to $5,000.

Host: Bill Cullen

Announcer: Charlie O'Donnell

Producer: Jack Barry, Dan Enright

Hot Pursuit

Adventure; 60 min; NBC 9/22/84 to 12/28/84

In an attempt to stop her husband (Victor) from manufacturing a car she feels will be a disaster, Estelle Modrian has Victor killed and frames Kate Wyler, the car's designer, for the crime. Following a trial in which Kate is convicted of murder, Jim, Kate's husband, spots the real killer, a dead ringer for Kate. When she escapes and Jim is unable to convince authorities that Kate was set up, he ambushes the car that is carrying Kate to prison and the two escape. Stories relate Kate and Jim's efforts to clear Kate by finding the real killer.

Kate Wyler	Teri Keane
Jim Wyler	Eric Pierpoint
Estelle Modrian	Dina Merrill
Alex Shaw	Mike Preston
Victor Modrian	Bradford Dillman
Kate's double	Teri Keane

Producer: Kenneth Johnson, Harry and Renee Longstreet

Hot Seat

Game; 30 min; ABC 7/12/76 to 10/22/76

One member of a husband-and-wife team is placed in a sound proof booth that contains a chair designed to measure emotional responses. The stage player is asked to predict how his mate will respond to a specific question. If he is correct (when the machine registers the mate's response) they score points. Two couples compete and the highest scorers are the winners.

Host: Jim Peck

Announcer: Kenny Williams

Producer: Merrill Heatter, Bob Quigley

Hot Shots

Crime Drama; 70 min; CBS 9/23/86 to 12/16/86

The story-gathering assignments of Amanda Reed and Jason West, reporters for "Crime World" magazine.

Amanda Reed	Dorothy Parke
Jason West	Booth Savage
Nicholas Broderick (editor)	Paul Burke
Receptionist	Mung Ling

Producer: Sonny Grosso, Larry Jacobson

Hot W.A.C.S.

Comedy Pilot; 30 min; ABC 6/1/81

The misadventures of a group of U.S. Army W.A.C.S. stationed at Ford Ord in Monterey, California.

Pvt. Pamela Jordan	Ellen Regan
Pvt. Kitty Trumpp	Dana Vance
Pvt. Leslie Bates	Damita Jo Freeman
Maj. Janet Morehead	Julie Payne
Pvt. Charlene Kellogg	Susan Duvall
Pvt. Heather Cassidy	Rebecca Holden
Maj. Philip Seabrook	Richard Jaeckel
Sgt. O'Neal	David-James Carroll
Col. Loveday	Herbert Voland

Producer: Milt Josefsberg, Joel Zwick

Hot Wheels

Cartoon; 30 min; ABC 9/6/69 to 9/4/71

The experiences of a group of responsible young teenage drivers and members of the Hot Wheels racing club in Metro City.

Jack Wheeler	Bob Arbogast
Janet Martin	Melinda Casey
Mickey Barnes	Albert Brooks
Ardeth Pratt	Susan Davis
Tank Mallory	Casey Kasem
Mother O'Hara	Nora Marlowe
Dexter Carter	Casey Kasem
Mike Wheeler	Michael Rye
Kip	Albert Brooks
Doc Warren	Bob Arbogast

Theme Vocal ("Hot Wheels"): Mike Curb and the Curbstones

Producer: Ken Snyder

Hotel

Drama; 60 min; ABC 9/21/83 (Premiere)

Vignettes that depict brief incidents in the lives of the guests of the fashionable St. Gregory Hotel in San Francisco. Based on the novel by Arthur Hailey.

Laura Trent	Bette Davis*
Victoria Cabot	Anne Baxter
Peter McDermott	James Brolin
Christine Francis	Connie Sellecca
Mark Danning	Shea Farrell
Julie Gillette	Shari Belafonte-Harper
Billy Griffin	Nathan Cook
Megan Kendall	Heidi Bohay
Dave Kendall	Michael Spound
Khi	Michael Yama
Janet McDermott	Cathy Lee Crosby
Charles Cabot	Efrem Zimbalist Jr.
Jessica Cabot	Dina Merrill
Jake Cabot	Ralph Bellamy
Elizabeth Bradshaw	Michelle Phillips
Drew Hayward	John Bennett Perry
Cheryl Dolan	Valerie Landsburg
Ryan Thomas	Susan Walters
Eric Lloyd	Ty Miller

Theme Song ("Hotel"): Henry Mancini

Producer: Aaron Spelling, Douglas S. Cramer

*The hotel owner in the pilot.

Hotel Broadway

Variety; 30 min; DuMont 1/20/49 to 3/17/49

Music, songs, and comedy.

Hostess: Jerri Blanchard

Regulars: Avon Long, Dancers Rose and Rana, The Striders

Music: The Harry Ranch Sextet

Producer: Harvey Marlowe

Hotel Cosmopolitan

Drama; 15 min; CBS 8/19/57 to 4/11/58

Dramas based on incidents in the lives of the people who frequent the Hotel Cosmopolitan as seen through the eyes of TV actor Donald Woods.

Donald Woods   Himself
House Detective Henderson Forsythe

Producer: Roy Windsor

Hotel De Paree

Western; 30 min; CBS 10/2/59 to 9/23/60

The exploits of The Sundance Kid, an ex-gunfighter turned law enforcer and owner of Georgetown, Colorado's, Hotel De Paree, one of the West's (1870s) most colorful gathering places.

Sundance   Earl Holliman
Annette Devereaux Jeanette Nolan
Monique Devereaux Judi Meredith
Aaron Donager   Strother Martin

Producer: William Self, Stanley Rubin

The Houndcats

Cartoon; 30 min; NBC 9/9/72 to 9/1/73

A "Mission: Impossible" spoof in which a group of dog and cat agents battle crime.

Studs   Daws Butler
Muscle Mutt   Aldo Ray
Rhubarb   Arte Johnson
Puddy Puss   Joe Besser
Ding Dog   Stu Gilliam

Producer: Friz Freleng, David DePatie

Hour Glass

Variety; 60 min; NBC 5/9/46 to 3/6/47

One of the first hour-long variety programs with hosts Helen Parrish and Eddie Mayehoff and featuring performances by well-known celebrities. Produced by Howard Reilly and directed by Edward Sobol.

The Hour Glass

A long running anthology series about the plight of people caught in sudden, unexpected situations. ABC 12/3/52 to 9/27/56.

Hour Magazine

Magazine; 60 min; Syn. 9/80

A daily series of celebrity interviews and discussions on topics that affect people in their everyday lives.

Host: Gary Collins

Regulars: Pat Mitchell, Bonnie Strauss, Sandi Newton

Producer: Martin Berman

Hour of Stars

A syndicated (1958) series of dramas that originally aired on "The 20th Century-Fox Hour."

House Calls

Comedy; 30 min; CBS 12/17/79 to 9/13/82

The antics of the staff of the fictional Kensington General Hospital in Los Angeles. Based on the feature film.

Dr. Charley Nichols   Alex Rocco*
Dr. Charley
 Michaels   Wayne Rogers
Ann Anderson   Lynn Redgrave
Jane Jeffreys   Sharon Gless
Dr. Amos
 Weatherby   David Wayne
Dr. Norman
 Solomon   Ray Buktenica
Nurse Bradley   Aneta Corsaut
Dr. Floyd
 Beiderbeck   Roger Bowen
Mrs. Phipps   Deedy Peters
Conrad Peckler   Mark L. Taylor
Dr. Sinberg   Dick Martin
Admissions Nurse Sharon DeBord
Nurse Nancy
 McMillan   Beth Jacobs

Producer: Jerry Davis, Kathy & Bill Greer

*Role in the never aired pilot.

The House on High Street

Drama; 30 min; NBC 9/28/59 to 2/5/60

The cases of John Collier, a Los Angeles defense counselor. Stories are based on files from the Domestic Relations Court.

John Collier   Philip Abbott
Judge James Gehrig   Himself
Dr. Harris B. Peck   Himself

Houston Knights

Crime Drama; 60 min; CBS 3/11/87 to 4/29/87

The exploits of Joey LaFiamma and LeVon Lundy, sergeants with the Houston, Texas, Police Department, and Joanne Beaumont, a lieutenant with the Major Crimes Unit of the H.P.D.

Sgt. Joey LaFiamma	Michael Pare
Sgt. LeVon Lundy	Michael Beck
Lt. Joanne Beaumont	Robyn Douglass
Lt. Sherina McLaren*	Leigh Taylor-Young
Chicken (bar owner)	John Hancock
Capt. Scully	James Hampton
Det. Lipscombe	Bill McKinney
Det. McCandless	James Crittenden
Joey's Uncle Mikey	Richard Bright

Producer: Jay Bernstein, Clyde Phillips

*First episode only; replaced by Robyn Douglass.

How Do You Rate?

Game; 30 min; CBS 3/31/58 to 6/28/58

Players compete in a series of tests designed to test their intelligence and reasoning power. Prizes are awarded to the players who are best at completing their tasks.

Host: Tom Reddy

Announcer: Jack Clark

Producer: Steve Carlin

How the West Was Won

Western; Various (60 min; 2 hrs);
ABC 2/6/77 to 2/14/77
  2/12/78 to 5/21/78
  1/15/79 to 4/23/79

The saga of the Macahans, a Virginia homesteading family, as they attempt to establish a new life on the Great Plains during the mid-1860s.

Zeb Macahan	James Arness
Kate Macahan	Eva Marie Saint
Luke Macahan	Bruce Boxleitner
Laura Macahan	Kathryn Holcomb
Jessie Macahan	Vicki Schreck
Josh Macahan	William Kirby Cullen
Molly Macahan	Fionuala Flanagan
Timothy Macahan	Richard Kiley
Jim Anderson	Don Murray
Martin Grey	Anthony Zerbe
Cully Madigan	Jack Elam
Hilary Grant	Elyssa Davalos
Orville Grant	Lloyd Bridges
Captain Harrison	William Shatner
Doreen	Kay Lenz
Tap Henry	Slim Pickens
Beth	Vera Miles
Coulee John	Cameron Mitchell
Bishop Benjamin	John Dehner
Elam Hanks	Royal Dano
Henry Coe	Morgan Woodward
Colonel Flint	Richard Basehart
Satangkai	Ricardo Montalban
Lee Stonecipher	Brian Keith
Gen. Sheridan	Ramon Bieri
Jeremiah Taylor	John Reilly
Hal Burton	Mel Ferrer
Curt Grayson	Tim Matheson
Frank Grayson	Jared Martin
Francis Britten	Eric Braeden
Marshal Russell	Michael Conrad
Capt. Harrison	William Shatner

Narrator: William Conrad

Producer: John Mantley, John G. Stephens, Jeffrey Hayden

How To

Discussion; 30 min; CBS 7/10/51 to 9/11/51

The host and three panelists attempt to solve the problems of their guests.

Host: Roger Price

Panelists: Anita Martel, Leonard Stern, Stanley Adams

Announcer: Bob Lemond

Producer: Richard Linkroum, Larry Berns

How to Marry a Millionaire

Comedy; 30 min; Syn. 1958

The story of three beautiful New York career girls (Loco, Mike, and Greta; a model and two secretaries) as they seek to secure a dream: marrying a millionaire.

Loco Jones	Barbara Eden
Michele "Mike" Page	Merry Anders
Greta Lindquist	Lori Nelson
Gwen Laurel (replaced Greta)	Lisa Gaye
Jack Connors (Loco's press agent)	George O'Hanlon
Girls Landlord	Stacy Keach Sr.
	Willard Waterman
Jesse (elevator operator)	Jimmy Cross

Music: Alec Compinsky

Producer: Nat Perrin

How to Succeed in Business Without Really Trying

Comedy Pilot; 30 min; ABC 6/27/75

The story of J. Piermont "Ponty" Finch, a young lad who is determined to make it in the business world—even if it means starting at the bottom.

Piermont Finch	Alan Bursky
Rosemary	Susan Blanchard
Mr. Bratt	Larry Haines
Frump	Jim Jansen
Smitty	Marcella Lowery
J. B. Biggey	Max Showalter
Miss Jones	Polly Rowles
Twimble	Sam Smith

Producer-Writer: Abe Burrows

How's Business?

Comedy Pilot; 30 min; NBC 12/28/59

A second pilot (see also "Another Day, Another Dollar"), about the adventures of Augie Adams, a toy company salesman.

Augie Adams	Jack Carson
Joyce Adams	Jean Gillespie
Robbie Adams	Flip Mark
Miss King	Norma Connolly
Scotty	Scott Marlowe
Seymour	Timmy Cletro
Ronnie	Ronnie Dapo

Producer: William Sackheim

How's Your Mother-in-Law?

Game; 30 min; ABC 10/2/67 to 3/1/68

Object: For three guest celebrities to judge (through question-and answer rounds) which of three contestants are the best mothers-in-law.

Host: Wink Martindale

Producer: Chuck Barris, Mike Metzger, Gene Law

The Howard Miller Show

See "Club 60."

Howdy

Variety Pilot; 30 min; NBC 8/1/69

Music and comedy set against the background of mythical Mildew, Arkansas.

Host: Ferlin Husky

Regulars: Chanin Hale, Lyle Talbot, Sidney Blackmer, Bob Hastings, William Sylvester

Orchestra: Alan Copeland

Producer: Jay Sommers

Howdy Doody

Children; 30 & 60 min; NBC 12/27/47 to 9/24/60

On December 27, 1941, in Doodyville, Texas, twin boys, named Howdy and Double, are born to the wife of a ranch hand named Doody. Six years later the boys learn that their rich Uncle Doody has bequeathed them a parcel of land in New York City. When NBC offered to purchase the land for a TV studio, Mr. Doody arranged it so that Howdy, who yearned to run a circus, could have his dream come true. Buffalo Bob Smith was appointed as Howdy's guardian and the series, set in Doodyville, related the efforts of a circus troupe to perform against numerous obsticles, in particular Phineas T. Bluster, an old man who is opposed to people having fun.

Buffalo Bob Smith	Bob Smith
Clarabelle Hornblow	Bob Keeshan
	Henry McLaughlin
	Bob Nicholson
	Lew Anderson
Story Princess	Arlene Dalton
Chief Thunderthud	Bill Lecornec
Tim Tremble	Don Knotts
Princess Summerfall	
Winterspring	Judy Tyler
	Linda Marsh
Bison Bill (Bob's	
temporary	
replacement)	Ted Brown
Ugly Sam	Dayton Allen
Gabby Hayes	George Hayes
Howdy Doody	Bob Smith
Howdy (1954)	Allen Swift
Phineas T. Bluster	Dayton Allen
Double Doody	Bob Smith
Dilly Dally	Bill Lecornec
Flubadub	Dayton Allen
Lecturer	Lowell Thomas Jr.

Producer: Martin Stone, E. Roger Muir, Simon Rady

The Hoyt Axton Show

Drama Pilot; 60 min; NBC 9/28/81

The story of Del Parsons, a constantly-on-the-road singer-musician, who is forced by the death of his wife to settle down and raise his estranged children (Jenny, Norma, and Dean).

Del Parsons	Hoyt Axton
Jenny Parsons	Tonja Walker
Norma Sue Parsons	Tonya Crowe
Dean Parsons	John Shepherd
Carol Dean	Joy Garrett
Mrs. Carucci	Sally Kemp
Walker Lee	Reid Smith

Theme Vocal ("Honeysuckle Rose"): Hoyt Axton

Producer: Joy Byrne, Paul Picard

Director: Richard Crenna

H. R. Pufnstuf

Adventure; 30 min; NBC 9/6/69 to 9/4/71

While playing, Jimmy and his talking gold flute, Freddie, board a boat that beckons to them. Later, the evil Miss Witchiepoo, who is seeking Freddie, casts a spell and the boat vanishes. Jimmy and Freddie are rescued by H. R. Pufnstuf, the mayor of Living Island. Stories relate H. R.'s efforts to help Jimmy battle Miss Witchiepoo and find the way back to his world.

Jimmy	Jack Wild
Miss Witchiepoo	Billie Hayes

Also (portraying life-size puppets): Joan Gerber, Felix Silla, Jerry Landon, Angelo Rosetti, Hommy Stewart, Buddy Douglas

Producer: Sid and Marty Krofft

The Huckleberry Hound Show

Cartoon; 30 min; Syn. 1958

Segments: "Huckleberry Hound" (about a dog who tackles various jobs); "Pixie and Dixie" (two mice who plague Mr. Jinks the cat); "Hokey Wolf" (adventures of a conniving wolf); and "Yogi Bear" (a bear's efforts to acquire picnickers' lunch baskets in Jellystone Park).

Huckleberry Hound/	
Mr. Jinks/Dixie/	
Hokey Wolf/Yogi	
Bear	Daws Butler
Pixie/Boo Boo Bear/	
Ranger Smith	Don Messick

Producer: William Hanna, Joseph Barbera

The Hudson Brothers Razzle Dazzle Comedy Show

Variety; 30 min; CBS 9/7/74 to 4/17/77

Music, songs, and comedy sketches that are designed to convey value-related messages to children.

Hosts: Bill, Brett, and Mark Hudson

Regulars: Peter Cullen, Ted Zeigler, Billy Van, Murray Langston, Scott Fisher, Freeman King

Orchestra: Jimmy Dale

Producer: Allan Blye, Chris Bearde

The Hudson Brothers Show

Variety; 30 min; CBS 7/31/74 to 8/28/74

A Summer series of music and comedy.

Hosts: Bill, Brett, and Mark Hudson

Regulars: Stephanie Edwards, Katee Mc-Clure, Gary Owens, Ronny Graham, Rod Hull, The Jaime Rogers Dancers

Orchestra: Jack Eskew

Producer: Allan Blye, Chris Bearde

Hulk Hogan's Rock 'n' Wrestling

Children; 60 min; CBS 9/14/85 to 6/13/87

The program features wrestler Terry "Hulk" Hogan in live action comedic wrestling segments and in animated adventures outside the ring as he battles evil.

Hulk Hogan	Himself
Announcer	Gene Oakland

Voices: Charles Allen, Lewis Arquette, Jodi Carlisle, George DiCenzo, Neilson Ross, Pat Fraley, Ernest Harada

Producer: Jean Chalopin, Andy Heyward, Tetsuo Katayama

Hullabaloo

Variety; 30 & 60 min; NBC 1/12/65 to 8/29/68

Performances by the top names in rock and roll music. Guests host.

Regulars: Lada Edmonds Jr., Sheila Forbes, The David Winters and Hullabaloo Dancers

Orchestra: Peter Matz

Producer: Gary Smith

Human Adventure

Experimental; 60 min; NBC 8/15/39

A program of science fact and fiction with dramatizations to illustrate specific principals.

Host: Frank Gallop

Guests: Kenny Delmar, John Gibson, Vicki Vola, Ruth York, Ted DeCorsia, Dwight Weist

Producer: Edward Sobol

The Human Comedy

Comedy Pilot; 30 min; CBS 9/19/64

The story of Homer Macauley, a 13-year-old boy who is determined to become the man of the house after his father's death.

Homer Macauley	Timmy Rooney
Alice Macauley	Phyllis Avery
Ulysses Macauley	Jimmy Homer
Grogan	Arthur O'Connell
Mrs. Windler	Minerva Urecal

Producer: Rudy E. Abel

The Human Jungle

Drama; 60 min; Syn. 1964

The work of Roger Corder, a London-based psychiatrist.

Dr. Roger Corder	Herbert Lom
Dr. Davis	Michael Johnson

The Hunter

Adventure; 30 min; CBS 7/3/52 to 9/24/52
Syn. 1952–54

The exploits of Bart Adams, a mysterious U.S. government undercover agent, known as "The Hunter," who uses unorthodox methods to corrupt the forces of Communism in the Western world.

Bart Adams	Barry Nelson
	Keith Larsen
Liz (his friend in Prague)	Anna Minot
Janet Wood (reporter)	Lisa Howard
Rita (his friend in Copenhagen)	Barbara Bolton
Ruby Ellis (Bart's old flame)	Susanna TaFel

Music: Frank Lewin

Producer: Edward J. Montagne

Hunter

Adventure; 60 min; Syn. 1968

The exploits of John Hunter, an operative for COSMIC (the Office of Security and Military Intelligence), a British government organization that battles the sinister elements of

CUCW (the Council for the Unification of the Communist World). Produced in Australia.

John Hunter	Tony Ward
Eve Halliday	Glyn Fernande
Blake	Nigel Lovell
Gil Martin	Rod Millinar
Smith	Ronald Morse
Kragg	Gerard Kennedy

Producer: Henry Crawford

Hunter

Adventure; 60 min; CBS 2/18/77 to 5/27/77

The exploits of James Hunter and Marty Shaw, U.S. government special intelligence agents who cover the world of contemporary espionage.

James Hunter	James Franciscus
Marty Shaw	Linda Evans
Harold Baker	Ralph Bellamy
Mr. Meeker	Broderick Crawford*

Theme Song ("Hunter"): Richard Shores

Producer: Lee Rich, Philip Capice

*Hunter and Shaw's superior in the pilot (CBS, 9/14/76).

Hunter

Crime Drama; 60 min; NBC 9/18/84 (Premiere)

The exploits of Rick Hunter, a mobster's son turned honest cop, and Dee Dee McCall, a beautiful maverick cop nicknamed "The Brass Cupcake"—undercover officers and partners with Division 122 of the L.A.P.D.

Det. Rick Hunter	Fred Dryer
Det. Dee Dee McCall	Stepfanie Kramer
Capt. Lester Cain	Michael Cavanaugh
	Arthur Rosenberg
Sgt. Bernie Terwilliger	James Whitmore Jr.
Off. Dabney Smith	Gary Crosby
Lt. Ambrose Finn	John Shearin
Captain (unnamed)	John Amos
Capt. Charles Devane	Bruce Davison
Sporty (snitch)	Garrett Morris

Producer: Stephen J. Cannell, Jo Swerling Jr.

Hunter's Moon

Adventure Pilot; 60 min; CBS 12/1/79

The story, set in Wyoming during the range wars between cattlemen and sheepherders at the turn of the century, follows the trail of Fayette Randall, a mysterious figure working for justice.

Fayette Randall	Cliff DeYoung
Isham Hart	Robert DoQui
The Captain	Alex Cord
George Randall	Leif Erickson
Hobble	Dan O'Herlihy
Nels Johansen	John Ericson
Marshal	John Quade
Peter Randall	Morgan Stevens

"Hunter's Moon" theme by Harry Sukman

Producer: David Dortort

Hurdy Gurdy

Variety; 30 min; Syn. 1967

The music, song, and dance of the Gay 90s era.

Host: Pete Lofthouse

Regulars: Barbara Kelly, The Sportsmen, The Hurdy Gurdy Girls

Music: The Second Story Men

Husbands and Wives

Comedy Pilot; 60 min; CBS 7/18/77

The pilot for "Husbands, Wives and Lovers," which see for storyline information.

Murray Zuckerman	Alex Rocco
Paula Zuckerman	Cynthia Harris
Harry Bell	Ed Barth
Joy Bell	Suzanne Zenor
Lennie Bell	Mark Lonow
Rita Bell	Randee Heller
Ron Cutler	Ron Rifkin
Helene Cutler	Linda Miller
Dixon Fielding	Charles Siebert
Courtney Fielding	Claudette Nevins

Music: Jack Elliott, Allyn Ferguson

Producer: Edgar Rosenberg, Hal Dresner

Husbands, Wives and Lovers

Comedy; 60 min; CBS 3/10/78 to 6/30/78

The hassles, foibles, and frivolities of five San Fernando Valley couples, each with diverse backgrounds. See the prior title also.

Murray Zuckerman	Alex Rocco
Paula Zuckerman	Cynthia Harris
Harry Bellini	Ed Barth
Joy Bellini	Lynne Stewart
Lennie Bellini	Mark Lonow
Rita DeLatorre	Randee Heller
Ron Willis	Ron Rifkin
Helene Willis	Jesse Welles
Dixon Fielding	Charles Siebert
Courtney Fielding	Claudette Nevins

Theme Song ("Husbands, Wives and Lovers"): Mitzi Welch, Ken Welch

Producer: Edgar Rosenberg, Hal Dresner

I am the Greatest: The Adventures of Muhammad Ali

Cartoon; 30 min; NBC 9/10/77 to 9/2/78

The exploits of boxing champ Muhammad Ali as he helps good defeat evil.

Muhammad Ali	Himself

Producer: Fred Calvert

I and Claudie

Comedy Pilot; 30 min; CBS 7/2/64

The adventures of Clint and Claudie, buddies who devise unique schemes to make a living.

Clint Hightower	Jerry Lanning
Claudie Hughes	Ross Martin
Nancy Gifford	Barbara Stuart
Jo Anne Smith	Jennifer Billingsley

Producer: Warren Lewis, Frank O'Conner

I Cover Times Square

Crime Drama; 30 min; ABC 10/5/50 to 1/11/51

The investigations of Johnny Warren, a crusading Broadway newspaper columnist whose beat is the out-of-town newsstand on Seventh Avenue in Times Square.

Johnny Warren	Harold Huber

Producer: Harold Huber, Saul Levitt

I Do, I Don't

Comedy Pilot; 30 min; ABC 9/2/83

The story of Shelley Hewitt, a woman married for the second time, who finds her life plagued by the constant attempts of her first husband (Ivan) to win her back.

Shelley Hewitt	Linda Purl
Earl Hewitt	Bo Svenson
Lisa Hewitt	Martha Byrne
Zach Hewitt	Scott Schutzman
Ivan	Charles Rocket
Taffee McDermott	Robin Eisenmann
Sheriff McDermott	Sandy Ward

Producer: Chris Thompson, Tom Werner, Marcy Carsey

I Dream of Jeannie

Comedy; 30 min; NBC 9/18/65 to 9/8/70

In ancient Bagdad, a young girl is transformed into a genie, placed in a bottle, and sentenced to a life of loneliness on a deserted island when she refuses to marry a powerful genie (the Blue Djin). Two thousand years later, a NASA test rocket malfunctions and crash lands on a deserted island in the South Pacific. Its pilot, astronaut Tony Nelson, finds a strange green bottle and opens it. A pink smoke emerges and materializes into a beautiful girl dressed as a Harem dancer. With the genie's help, Tony is rescued and becomes her master. Stories, set in Cocoa Beach, Florida, relate a master's efforts to control the antics of a fun-loving genie (whom he calls Jeannie). See also "Jeannie."

Jeannie	Barbara Eden
Capt. (later Maj.) Anthony Nelson	Larry Hagman
Capt. (later Maj.) Roger Healey	Bill Daily
Dr. Alfred Bellows	Hayden Rorke
Amanda Bellows	Emmaline Henry
Gen. Martin Peterson	Barton MacLane
Gen. Winfield Schaefer	Vinton Hayworth
The Blue Djin	Michael Ansara
Hadji	Abraham Sofaer
Jeannie's Sister	Barbara Eden

Theme Narration: Paul Frees

Producer: Sidney Sheldon, Claudio Guzman

I Gave at the Office

Comedy Pilot; 30 min; NBC 8/15/84

The comic adventures of the indecisive staff of the Denver-based Brinker Advertising Agency.

Larry Brinker	Michael Lerner
Michael Boatwright	Matt DeGanon
K. C. Conklin	Kathleen York
Julie	Candy Clark
Janet Holloway	Janet Carroll
Jimbo	Max Wright
Yvonne	Jill Jacobson

Producer: Sam Strangis, Larry Konner

I Had Three Wives

Crime Drama; 60 min; CBS 8/14/85 to 9/11/85

The story of Jackson Beaudine, a private detective with three beautiful assistants—his ex-wives (Liz, Samantha, and Mary) who lend a hand when a case requires their help.

Jackson Beaudine	Victor Garber
Liz Bailey	Shanna Reed
Samantha Collins	Teri Copley
Mary Parker	Maggie Cooper
Andrew	David Faustino
Johnny Shane	Walter Olkewicz
Lt. Gomez	Luis Avalos

Producer: Nick Thiel, Carla Singer, Marc Merson, Peter Lefcourt

I Led Three Lives

Drama; 30 min; Syn. 1953

The story of Herbert Philbrick, a man who led three lives: private citizen, undercover agent, and FBI counterspy. Stories relate his life as a counterspy and efforts to inform the U.S. government of the Red Military movement.

Herbert Philbrick	Richard Carlson
Eva Philbrick	Virginia Stefan
Constance Philbrick	Patricia Morrow
Agent Steve Daniels	John Beradino
Agent Joe Carney	Charles Maxwell

I Love Her Anyway!

Comedy Pilot; 30 min; ABC 8/3/81

The story of a level-headed husband (Jerry) and his attempts to cope with and solve the situations that occur through the actions of Laurie, his pretty but scatterbrained wife.

Jerry Martin	Dean Jones
Laurie Martin	Diane Stilwell
Fred Martin	Charles Levin
Mona Martin	Jane Daly
Willie Winslow	Peter Boyden
Dr. Peterson	Howard Witt

Producer: Jerome Zeitman, Irving Fein

I Love Lucy

Comedy; 30 min; CBS 10/15/51 to 6/24/57

Events in the lives of the Ricardo family: Ricky, an orchestra leader at the Tropicana Club (later the Ricky Ricardo Babalu Club), and his scatterbrained wife, Lucy, who longs for a career in show business. See also "The Lucille Ball-Desi Arnaz Show."

Ricky Ricardo	Desi Arnaz
Lucy Ricardo	Lucille Ball
Fred Mertz	William Frawley
Ethel Mertz	Vivian Vance
Little Ricky Ricardo	James John Gouzer
	Richard Lee
	Simmons
	The Mayer Twins
	Richard Keith
Jerry (Ricky's agent)	Jerry Houser
Mrs. Trumbull	Elizabeth Patterson
Mrs. Magilicuddy	Catherine Card
Betty Ramsey	Mary Jane Croft
Ralph Ramsey	Frank Nelson
Tropicana Club Maitre d'	William Hamill

Announcer: Johnny Jacobs

Music Conductor: Wilbur Hatch

Producer: Desi Arnaz, Jess Oppenheimer

I Love My Doctor

Comedy Pilot; 30 min; CBS 8/14/62

The story of a doctor (Jim Barkley) as he attempts to begin a new practice in a suburban community (having just relocated from the city).

Dr. Jim Barkley	Don Porter
Connie Barkley	Phyllis Avery
Liz Barkley	Terry Burnham
Albert Barkley	Ricky Kelman

Producer: Everett Freeman

I Married a Dog

Comedy Pilot; 30 min; NBC 8/4/61

An unsold series in which a man (Peter) and a woman (Joyce) marry only to find their life hindered by Jonah, Joyce's extremely jealous French poodle.

Peter Chance	Hal March
Joyce Chance	Marcia Henderson
Madge Kellogg	Mary Carver
Fred Bender	Dave Willock
Granek	Oscar Beregi
Justice of the Peace	Jack Albertson
Receptionist	Melinda Markey
Bartender	Clark Gordon

Producer: Richard M. Powell, Philip Rapp

I Married Dora

Comedy; 30 min; ABC 9/22/87 to 1/8/88

When Dora Calderon, an illegal alien and the housekeeper to widower Peter Farrell and his two children, faces deportation, Peter gallantly proposes to her. Their marriage of convenience allows Dora to remain in the U.S. Stories relate the misadventures that occur as Peter and Dora pretend to be happily married (as the need arises) yet maintain a plutonic relationship.

Peter Farrell	Daniel Hugh Kelly
Dora Calderon	Elizabeth Pena
Kate Farrell	Juliette Lewis
Will Farrell	Jason Horst
Hughes Whitney Lennox	Henry Jones
Marisol Calderon	Evelyn Guerrero
Janice Desmond	Alley Mills
Dolf Mennenger	Sanford Jensen
Lucille Farrell	Peggy McCay

Producer: Michael Leeson

I Married Joan

Comedy; 30 min; NBC 10/15/52 to 4/6/55

The misadventures of Bradley Stevens, a Los Angeles domestic relations court judge whose life is constantly plagued by the antics of his well-meaning but scatterbrained wife Joan.

Joan Stevens	Joan Davis
Bradley Stevens	Jim Backus
Janet Tobin	Sheila Bromley
Kerwin Tobin	Dan Tobin
Charlie	Hal Smith
Mabel	Geraldine Carr
Mildred Webster	Sandra Gould
Beverly Grossman	Beverly Wills
Minerva Parker	Hope Emerson
Florry Stevens	Norma Varden
Joan's Aunt Vera	Elvia Allman

Theme Vocal ("I Married Joan"): The Robert Wagner Singers

Producer: P. J. Wolfson, Dick Mack

I Remember Caviar

Comedy Pilot; 30 min; NBC 5/11/59

The story of a once wealthy family (the Randalls) who must learn to live with poverty when their wealth is lost through bad investments. See also "All in the Family" (1960 version).

Maggie Randall	Patricia Crowley
Caroline Randall	Lurene Tuttle
Eric Randall	Elliott Reid
Lester	Jack Mulhall

Producer: Winston O'Keefe

I Remember Mama

Comedy-Drama; 30 min; CBS 7/1/49 to 3/17/57

Incidents in the lives of the Hansons, a Norwegian family living busily in a large American city (San Francisco in 1910) as seen through the eyes of Katrin, the eldest daughter, an aspiring writer who records their daily activities in her diary. Also known as "Mama."

Marta "Mama" Hanson	Peggy Wood
Lars "Papa" Hanson	Judson Laire
Katrin Hanson	Rosemary Rice
	Iris Mann
Dagmar Hanson	Robin Morgan
	Toni Campbell
Nels Hanson	Dick Van Patten
Jenny (Marta's sister)	Ruth Gates
Trina (Marta's sister)	Alice Frost
Marta's Uncle Gunnar	Carl Frank
Igeborg (Marta's niece)	Patricia McCormack
T. R. Ryan	Kevin Coughlin
Nel's friend	Paul Newman
	James Dean
	Jack Lemmon

Music: Billy Nalle

Producer: Carol Irwin, Ralph Nelson, Don Richardson

I Spy

Anthology; 30 min; Syn. 1956

Tales of intrigue and espionage that span time from the sixteenth to the twentieth centuries.

Anton the Spy Master	Raymond Massey

Producer: William Berke

I Spy

Adventure; 60 min; NBC 9/15/65 to 9/9/68

The exploits of U.S. government undercover agents Kelly Robinson (posing as a tennis champion) and Alexander Scott, his partner (who poses as his trainer).

Kelly Robinson	Robert Culp
Alexander Scott	Bill Cosby

Theme Song ("I Spy"): Earle Hagen

Producer: Sheldon Leonard

I Was a Bloodhound

Comedy Pilot; 30 min; CBS 2/15/59

The story of Barney Colby, a private detective with an uncanny sense of smell—a gift he uses to solve crimes.

Barney Colby	Ernie Kovacs
Eunice Colby	Yvonne White
Jennie	Shirley Mitchell
Singh	Larry Dobkin
Prince Purannajab	Bart Bradley

Producer: Harry Tugend

The Ian Tyson Show

A syndicated (1970) variety series, hosted by Ian and Sylvia Tyson, that features U.S. and Canadian folk and country and western artists.

Ichabod and Me

Comedy; 30 min; CBS 9/26/61 to 9/18/62

Dissatisfied with city life, a widower (Bob Major) quits his job and moves to Phippsboro, a small New England community. There, he purchases the local paper (the "Bulletin") and becomes its new editor (replacing Ichabod Adams, now the traffic commissioner, and his consultant). Stories relate incidents in the lives of the people of a small town as seen through the eyes of a newspaper publisher.

Bob Major	Robert Sterling
Ichabod Adams	George Chandler
Abby Adams	Christine White
Benjie Major	Jimmy Mathers
Aunt Lavinia	Reta Shaw
Cleever	Philip Coolidge
Olaf	Burt Mustin
Martin	Gene Raymond
Jonathan	Jimmy Hawkins
Colby	Forrest Lewis
Bob's Uncle Lippy	Jesse White

Producer: Irving Paley, Joe Connelly, Bob Mosher

The Ice Palace

Variety; 60 min; CBS 5/23/71 to 7/25/71

Entertainment acts set against the background of a mythical ice palace.

Guest Hosts: Vikki Carr, Dean Jones, Leslie Uggams, Jack Jones, Johnny Mathis, John Davidson, and Peggy, Janet, Dianne and Kathy Lennon

Regulars: Linda Carbonetto, Don Knight, Tim Wood, Billy Chappell, Roy Powers, Sandy Parker, The Bob Turk Ice Dancers

Orchestra: Alan Copeland

Producer: Peter Engel

I'd Like to See

Documentary; 15 min; NBC 3/15/48 to 8/7/48

Highlights of past historic events are shown through film clips.

Host-Narrator: Ray Morgan

Producer: Bernard E. Karlen

I'd Rather be Calm

Comedy Pilot; 30 min; CBS 8/24/82

The lives, loves, and relationships of a group of singles who gather in a swinging singles restaurant-bar in Cleveland, Ohio.

Katherine Lange	Susan Spilker
Julie Williams	Melissa Steinberg
Sissy Shaefer	Trisha Hilka
Leslie Weinstein	Fran Drescher
Wally Weinstein	Charles Levin
Michael Riley	Buddy Powell
Jack Minkus II (bar owner)	Paul Stolarsky
Seymour (waiter)	Justin Lord

Theme ("I'd Rather Be Calm"): Carol Connors, Mark Snow

Producer: Gail Parent, Ann Elder

The Ida Lupino Theatre

Anthology; 30 min; Syn. 1956

A series of dramatic productions, produced especially for syndication, with hostess and frequent star, actress Ida Lupino.

If I Love You, Am I Trapped Forever?

Comedy Pilot; 30 min; CBS 3/22/74

The story of Alan Bennett, a non-conformist high school student touting the joys of unrequited love.

Alan Bennett	Teddy Eccles
Leah Pennington	Tannis G. Montgomery
Alice Bennett	Elinor Donahue
Sophie Pennington	Denise Nickerson
Grandfater Bennett	Liam Dunn
Lucius Luther	Joe DiReda
Doomed	Rod Berger
Gwen Graney	Vicky Huxtable

Producer: Gene Reynolds, Larry Gelbart

If You Knew Tomorrow

Drama Pilot; 30 min; NBC 10/7/58

The story of Ned Carver, a newscaster whose teletype machine reports news that will happen, and his efforts to help the people whose lives are affected by his knowledge of the future.

Ned Carver	Bruce Gordon
Julie Brewster	Judith Ames
Stanley Brewer	Dan Barton

Producer: Vincent M. Fennelly

The Igor Cassini Show

A DuMont series (10/25/53 to 2/28/54) of celebrity interviews with columnist Igor Cassini.

I'll Bet

Game; 30 min; NBC 3/29/65 to 9/24/65

Object: For a celebrity panel to guess, through a series of indirect question-and-answer rounds with the host, the identity of an object submitted by a home viewer.

Host: Mike Wallace

Panelists: Hans Conried, Vanessa Brown, Robin Chandler, Audrey Meadows, Albert Mooreland

Producer: Peter Arnell

I'll Never Forget What's Her Name

Comedy Pilot; 30 min; ABC 3/29/76

The story of Rosa Dolores, a New York girl who dreams of becoming a star in Hollywood. Aired on "On the Rocks."

Rosa Dolores	Rita Moreno
Lillian	Yvonne Wilder
Howie Weston	Hamilton Camp

Music: Jerry Fielding

Producer: John Rich

The Ilona Massey Show

Variety; 30 min; DuMont 11/1/54 to 1/3/55

Music and songs, set against the background of a Continental supper club, with hostess Ilona Massey and the music of the Irving Fields Trio.

I'm a Big Girl Now

Comedy; 30 min; ABC 10/31/80 to 8/7/81

The story of Diana Cassidy, a young divorcee and mother (of Rebecca), as she struggles to begin a new life (employed by the Kramer Research & Testing Company in Washington, D.C.) and contend with a father (Ben) who still treats her like a child. For unexplained reasons, the format changed (last three episodes) to depict Diana's adventures as a columnist for the "Arlington Dispatch."

Diana Cassidy	Diana Canova
Benjamin Douglas	Danny Thomas
Rebecca Cassidy	Rori King
Edie McKendrick	Sheree North
Walter Douglas	Michael Durrell
Karen Hawks	Deborah Baltzell
Neal Stryker	Martin Short
Polly Douglas	Joan Welles
Preston Kramer	Richard McKenzie

Theme Vocal ("I'm a Big Girl Now"): Diana Canova

Producer: Paul Junger Witt, Tony Thomas

I'm Dickens . . . He's Fenster

Comedy; 30 min; ABC 9/28/62 to 9/13/63

The misadventures of two carpenters: Harry Dickens, who is married (to Kate), and Arch Fenster, his friend, a swinging young bachelor.

Harry Dickens	John Astin
Arch Fenster	Marty Ingels
Kate Dickens	Emmaline Henry
Mr. Bannister	Frank DeVol
Mel Warshaw	Dave Ketchum
Mulligan	Henry Beckman

Theme Song ("The Dickens and Fenster March"): Irving Szathmary

Producer: Leonard B. Stern

I'm Telling

Game; 30 min; NBC 9/12/87 (Premiere)

Three two-member teams compete, each composed of an actual brother and sister. In round one, the brothers are isolated backstage and the sisters are asked three questions regarding their relationship. The brothers are brought on stage and asked the same questions. Each time the brother gives the same response as his sister, they score points. Round two reverses round one and the team with the highest score is the winner.

Host: Laurie Faso

Announcer: Dean Goss

Producer: Haim Saban, Andy Heyward

I'm the Law

Crime Drama; 30 min; Syn. 1953

The exploits of George Kirby, a tough, plainclothes N.Y.P.D. police detective. Also known as "The George Raft Casebook."

Lt. George Kirby   George Raft

Producer: Pat Costello

The Immortal

Adventure; 60 min; ABC 9/24/70 to 9/8/71

When Jordan Braddock, a dying billionaire is injured, he is given a transfusion of Type O blood donated by Ben Richards, an employee of Braddock Industries. When Braddock miraculously recovers, it is learned that Richards possesses a rare blood type that makes him immune to old age and disease. Stories relate Braddock's efforts to insure a second lifetime (through transfusions) by capturing an elusive Ben Richards (who fled upon learning of Braddock's plan to imprison him).

Ben Richards	Christopher George
Jordan Braddock	Barry Sullivan
Fletcher	Don Knight
Sylvia Cartwright	Carol Lynley
Janet Braddock	Jessica Walter
Jason Richards	Michael Strong
Dr. Matthew Pearce	Ralph Bellamy

Producer: Anthony Wilson, Lou Morheim

The Imogene Coca Show

Variety; 60 min; NBC 10/2/54 to 6/25/55

A weekly series of music and comedy.

Hostess: Imogene Coca

Regulars: Billy DeWolfe, Hal March, Ruth Donnelly, Bibi Osterwald, David Burns

Orchestra: George Bassman

Producer: Ernest D. Glucksman, Marc Daniels, Don Appel

The Imperial Grand Band

Comedy Pilot; 60 min; ABC 2/22/75

The story of Sue Barton, a young woman who inherits the Imperial Grand, a Canadian hotel badly in need of repair. The unsold series was to relate her attempts to repair the hotel and make it profitable once again. The title refers to Sue's brother's band.

Sue Barton	Libby Stevens
Dick Barton	Jaro Dick
Skip Jenkins	Shimmy Plener
Marvin Baxter	Martin Short
Albert Flynn	Jack Creley
Margaret Flynn	Kay Hawtrey

Producer: Dick Clark, Seymour Berns

In Common

Game; 30 min; CBS 3/9/54 to 5/8/54

Object: For three people, who have never met, but possess something in common, to question each other and discover the common denominator.

Host: Ralph Story

In the Kelvinator Kitchen

Women; 15 min; NBC 5/21/47 to 6/30/48

Alma Kitchell as the host of a program of cooking instruction sponsored by Kelvinator Kitchen Appliances.

In Search of. . .

Documentary; 30 min; Syn. 9/76

The program explores and offers possible solutions to the various mysteries that surround us in everyday life.

Host-Narrator: Leonard Nimoy

Producer: Alan Landsburg, Robert Lang, Alex Pomansanoff

In Security

Comedy Pilot; 30 min; CBS 7/7/82

The experiences of Annie Leighton, a security officer in the Philadelphia-based Mayfield Department Store.

Annie Leighton	Annie Potts
Doris Gleen	Cara Williams
Eldon Radford	John Randolph
Garrett Lloyd	James Murtaugh
Jennie Lloyd	Kari Ann Patterson
Rudy DeMayo	James Keane
Henry	Peter Jurasik
Shoplifter	Margaret Wheeler
Mr. Bowman	John Dennis
Man in Crowd	Greg Lewis
Cookware Lady	Esther McCarroll
Draperies Man	Robert Lussier

Music: Patrick Williams

Producer: Bob Ellison

In the Beginning

Comedy; 30 min; CBS 9/20/78 to 11/1/78

The clash between Father Dan Cleary, a conservative priest, and Sister Agnes, a streetwise nun, as they join forces, but seldom agree on how to run a mission to help the people of their poor community.

Father Dan Cleary	McLean Stevenson
Sister Agnes	Priscilla Lopez
Sister Lillian	Priscilla Morrill
Monsignor Frank	
Barlow	Jack Dodson
Willie*	Olivia Barash
Jerome*	Bobby Ellerbee
Tony*	Cosie Costa
Bad Lincoln*	Michael Anthony
Frank*	Fred Lehne

Producer: Mort Lachman, Rita Dillon

*Kids who hang out at the mission.

In the Dead of Night

Thriller Pilot; 60 min; ABC 8/30/69

A gothic suspense chiller about a ghost hunter (Jonathan Fletcher). The pilot relates Fletcher's efforts to exorcise the spirits from an estate owned by Angela Martin.

Jonathan Fletcher	Kerwin Matthews
Sajeed Rau	Cal Bellini
Angela Martin	Marj Dusay
Seth Blakely	Thayer David
Commodore Blaise	Louis Edmonds

Music: Robert Cobert

Producer-Director: Dan Curtis

In the Morgan Manner

Variety; 30 min; ABC 3/1/50 to 7/30/50

Music and songs with Russ Morgan and his orchestra.

In Town Today

Interview Pilot; 20 min; NBC 8/22/46

A proposed series of live celebrity interviews.

Host: Ben Grauer

Producer: Garry Simpson

In Trouble

Comedy Pilot; 30 min; ABC 8/24/81

The misadventures of three prankish high school girls (Ivy, Annie, and Janey). In the pilot, the girls take jobs in a strip joint to help pay for Janey's new contact lenses

Ivy Miller	Lisa Freeman
Annie Monahan	Nancy Cartwright
Janey Zerneck	Deena Freeman
Irma DeGroot	Doris Roberts
Mr. Damrush	Tim Thomerson
Abenauer	Charles Bloom
Elaine	Cathy Cutler
Mr. Zerneck	Peter Michael Getz
Lou	Martin Azarow

Theme Vocal ("In Trouble"): Leslie Bricusse

Producer: Bernie Kukoff, Jeff Harris

The Ina Ray Hutton Show

Variety; 30 min; NBC 7/4/56 to 9/5/56

Performances by female guests (a no male allowed policy) coupled by a bevy of beautiful regulars.

Hostess: Ina Ray Hutton

Regulars: Helen Smith, Helen Wooley, Evie Howeth, Dee Dee Ball, Margaret Rinker, Janice Davis, Peggy Fairbanks, Helen Hammond, Mickey Anderson, Zoe Ann Willy, Judy Van Buer

Announcer: Diane Brewster

Music: The All-Girl Ina Ray Hutton Orchestra

Producer: Jerry Bowen

Inch High, Private Eye

Cartoon; 30 min; NBC 9/8/73 to 8/31/74

The exploits of Inch High, the world's smallest man and a detective with the Finkerton Organization.

Inch High	Lennie Weinrib
Laurie	Kathi Gori
Bravehart	Don Messick
Mr. Finkerton	John Stephenson
Mrs. Finkerton	Jean VanderPyl

Producer: William Hanna, Joseph Barbera

The Incredible Hulk

Adventure; 60 min; CBS 3/10/78 to 5/19/82

During an experiment to discover how certain people can tap hidden resources of strength, Dr. David Banner is exposed to an extreme overdose of Gamma radiation. The overdose causes a change in his DNA chemistry: whenever he becomes enraged, David's mild nature is transformed into a green creature of incredible strength. Upon relaxing, the metamorphis is reversed and Banner again becomes himself. The series relates David's adventures as he travels across the country* seeking a means by which to reverse the process.

Dr. David Banner	Bill Bixby
The Hulk	Lou Ferrigno
Jack McGee	Jack Colvin
The Demi Hulk (Hulk to human stage)	Ric Drasin

Producer: Kenneth Johnson, Nicholas Corea, James D. Parriott

*The creature is pursued by "National Register" reporter Jack McGee who mistakingly believes the Hulk killed both David and his assistant, Elaina (Susan Sullivan). He has vowed to bring the creature to justice.

Incredible Kids and Company

Variety Pilot; 30 min; Syn. 8/81

The program encourages children to pursue their talents by showcasing talented youngsters.

Hosts: Mickey Dougherty, Bobby Day

Producer: Donald Merl

Indemnity

Drama Pilot; 30 min; NBC 8/10/58

The exploits of Paul Scott, an insurance company investigator.

Paul Scott	Richard Kiley
Lt. Mike Kappell	Chuck Webster
George Thompson	George Chandler
Girl	Ruta Lee
Thief	Michael Healey

Producer: Joe Graham, Sam Grad

The Indian

Western Pilot; 30 min; ABC 2/17/59

The pilot for "Law of the Plainsman." The story of Sam Buckhart, an Apache Indian who is also a U.S. Marshal. Aired on "The Rifleman."

Sam Buckhart	Michael Ansara
Lucas McCain	Chuck Connors
Mark McCain	Johnny Crawford
Gorman	Herbert Rudley
Slade	Lewis Charles
Old Chief	Frank DeKova
Apache	Eddie Little Sky

Producer: Jules Levy, Arthur Gardner

Information Please

Game; 30 min; CBS 6/29/52 to 9/21/52

Object: For "The Brain Panel" to answer questions submitted by home viewers.

Host: Clifton Fadiman

Panelists: Oscar Levant, Franklin P. Adams, John Kiernan

The Inhumanoids

Cartoon; 30 min; Syn. 12/86

In a future era, a deadly breed of creatures called the Inhumanoids arise and threaten to destroy all living creatures. Stories relate the efforts of Earth Core, a specialized unit of humans, to defeat their deadly enemies.

Voices: Michael Bell, William Callaway, Fred Collins, Brad Crandall, Dick Gautier, Ed Gilbert, Chris Latta, Neilson Ross, Stanley Ralph Ross, Richard Sanders, Susan Silo, John Stephenson

Producer: Joe Bacall, Margaret Loesch, Tom Griffin

The Inner Sanctum

Anthology; 30 min; Syn. 1/54

Mysteries that relate the plight of people who are suddenly confronted with perilous situations. Based on the radio series.

Narrator (as the unseen Raymond)	Paul McGrath

Innocent Jones

Comedy Pilot; 30 min; NBC 8/11/61

The adventures of Innocent Jones, a footloose, free-lance magazine reporter.

Innocent Jones   Chris Warfield
Prudence Brown   Merry Anders
Insp. Javent   Henry Corden

Inside America

Magazine; 60 min; ABC 4/4/82 to 4/25/82

Informative features that explore various aspects of American life.

Host: Dick Clark

Correspondents: Shawn Weatherly, Rex Reed, Anson Williams, Lynn Shawn

Producer: Al Schwartz, Dick Clark

Inside Detective

See "Rocky King, Detective."

Inside O.U.T.

Comedy Pilot; 30 min; NBC 3/22/71

The exploits of Ron Hart, chief operative of O.U.T. (the Office of Unusual Tactics), a semi-official government agency that tackles the cases that nobody else wants.

Ron Hart   Bill Daily
Pat Boulion   Farrah Fawcett
Edgar Winston   Alan Oppenheimer
Chuck Dandy   Mike Henry
Finance Director   Edward Andrews
Bendix Man   Val Bisoglio
Chicken Man   Paul Smith

Music: Jerry Fielding

Producer: Harry Ackerman, Fred Freeman

Inside U.S.A. with Chevrolet

Variety; 30 min; CBS 9/29/49 to 3/16/50

Music and songs under the sponsorship of Chevrolet.

Host: Peter Lind Hayes, Mary Healy

Regulars: Marion Colby, Sheila Bond

Orchestra: Jay Blackton

Producer: Arthur Schwartz

The Insiders

Crime Drama; 60 min; ABC 9/25/85 to 1/8/86

The exploits of Nick Fox, an investigative reporter for "Newspoint" magazine, and his partner, James Mackey, an ex-con gone straight, men who acquire their stories by becoming a part of them.

Nick Fox   Nicholas Campbell
James Mackey   Stoney Jackson
Alice West (editor)   Gail Strickland
Melissa (her
  secretary)   Kelly Ann Conn
Nick's Cousin
  Roxanne   Jeannie Elias
Louise Browning
  (Alice's mother)   Jane Greer

Producer: Calvin Clements Jr., Leonard Hill, Lou Shaw, Bobby Roth

Inspector Fabian of Scotland Yard

Crime Drama; 30 min; Syn. 1955

The exploits of Robert Fabian, Superintendant of Detectives at London's New Scotland Yard.

Insp. Robert Fabian   Bruce Seton

Inspector Gadget

Cartoon; 30 min; Syn. 9/83

The exploits of Inspector Gadget, a dim-witted and bumbling bionic crime fighter (half human, half contraption) for the Metro City Police Force.

Inspector Gadget   Don Adams
Penny   Mona Marshall
Brain   Frank Welker
Chief Quimbly   Jesse White
Dr. Claw   Frank Welker

Producer: Jean Chalopin, Andy Heyward

Inspector Perez

Crime Drama Pilot; 60 min; NBC 1/8/83

The exploits of Antonio Perez, an inspector with the Homicide Division of the L.A.P.D. The pilot relates Perez's efforts to solve the mysterious murders of several beautiful Chinese women.

Insp. Antonio Perez	Jose Perez
Capt. R. C. Hodges	Dana Elcar
Sgt. Richards	Michael Corneilson
Mama Perez	Betty Carvalho
Danny McMahon	Cyril O'Reilly
Lisa Soong	Irene Yah Ling Sun
Benson Liu	James Hong
Mrs. Liu	Beulah Quo
Jane Langley	Annie Bloom
Patricia Liu	Lydia Lei
Master Fong	Chao Li-Chi

Producer: Joe Byrne, Robert Dozier

Instant Family

Comedy Pilot; 30 min; NBC 7/28/77

In an attempt to cut expenses, two single fathers (Clifford and Frank) pool their resources and rent an apartment. The unsold series was to relate the efforts of both families to live together.

Clifford Beane	William Daniels
Kevin Beane	Jeff Harlan
Ernie Beane	Robbie Rist
Alexander Beane	Sparky Marcus
Frank Boyle	Lou Criscuolo
Lisa Boyle	Wendy Fredericks

Producer: Lila Garrett, Mort Lachman

The International Animation Festival

Cartoon; 30 min; PBS 4/7/75 to 6/30/75

Jean Marsh as the host of a series of award winning cartoons from around the world. Produced by Zev Putterman.

International Detective

Crime Drama; 30 min; Syn. 1959

The exploits of Ken Franklin, the chief investigator for the William J. Burns Detective Agency, an agency that handles international cases.

Ken Franklin	Arthur Fleming

"International Detective" Theme Song: Sidney Shaw, Leroy Holmes

Producer: Eddie Sutherland

International Showtime

Variety; 60 min; NBC 9/15/61 to 9/10/65

Highlights of various European circuses.

Host: Don Ameche

Producer: Joseph Cates, Phil Levin, Larry White, Pat Pleven

The Interns

Drama; 60 min; CBS 9/18/70 to 9/10/71

The personal and professional lives of a group of interns at New North Hospital in Los Angeles.

Dr. Pete Goldstone	Broderick Crawford
Dr. Pooch Hardin	Christopher Stone
Dr. Lydia Thorpe	Sandra Smith
Dr. Sam March	Mike Farrell
Dr. Greg Pettit	Stephen Brooks
Dr. Cal Barrin	Hal Frederick
Bobbie Marsh	Elaine Giftos

Producer: Bob Claver, Charles Larson

Interpol Calling

Crime Drama; 30 min; Syn. 2/60

The exploits of Paul Duval, a chief inspector for Interpol (the International Police Organization).

Insp. Paul Duval	Charles Korvin
Police Inspector	Edwin Richfield

Producer: J. Arthur Rank, Jack Wrather

Intertect

Crime Drama Pilot; 60 min; ABC 3/11/73

The exploits of John McKennon, the chief investigator and founder of Intertect, an international investigative organization.

John McKennon	Stuart Whitman
Amanda Hollister	Pamela Franklin
Curt Lowens	David Soul
Sylvia Doyle	Sherry Alberoni
Barrett	Bernard Fox
Emhardt	Eric Braeden

Producer: Quinn Martin, Philip Saltzman

Into the Unknown

Human Interest Pilot; 60 min; Syn. 8/86

A proposed series that explores and attempts to explain paranormal phenomena (e.g., UFO's, faith healing).

Host: Kevin Sanders

Narrator: Rod McKuen

Producer: John Ernst, William Carpenter, John Fuller

The Invaders

Adventure; 60 min; ABC 1/10/67 to 9/17/68

While driving on a deserted country road, architect David Vincent witnesses the landing of an alien craft. When the aliens, who appear in human form and plan to take over the Earth, fail in their initial attempt to kill David, he becomes their mortal enemy. Stories relate David's attempts to thwart alien objectives and convince a disbelieving world "that the nightmare has already begun."

David Vincent	Roy Thinnes
Edgar Scoville	Kent Smith

Producer: Quinn Martin, Alan A. Armer

The Investigator

Crime Drama; 30 min; NBC 6/3/58 to 9/2/58

The story of Jeff Prior, a New York-based private detective.

Jeff Prior	Lonny Chapman
Lloyd Prior	Howard St. John

The Investigators

Crime Drama; 60 min; CBS 9/21/61 to 12/28/61

The investigations of Steve Banks and Russ Andrews, highly paid and highly skilled New York-based private insurance detectives.

Steve Banks	James Philbrook
Russ Andrews	James Franciscus
Maggie Peters	Mary Murphy
Bill Davis	Al Austin
Polly Walters	June Kenny

Producer: Richard Irving, Michael Garrison

The Invisible Man

Adventure; 30 min; CBS 11/4/58 to 9/22/60

While experimenting with the problems of optical density, scientist Peter Brady is exposed to a leaking conductor and rendered invisible when the gasses mix with the oxygen. Stories relate Brady's attempts, lacking the knowledge to again become visible, to use his great advantage to help the British government by tackling hazardous assignments.

Peter Brady	Anonymous*
Diane Wilson	Lisa Daniely
Sally Wilson	Deborah Watling
Sir Charles	Ernest Clark
	Ewen MacDuff

Producer: Ralph Smart

*Though seen and heard, the actor portraying the role has not been revealed.

The Invisible Man

Adventure; 60 min; NBC 9/8/75 to 1/9/76

While working on a formula to transfer matter, KLAE scientist Daniel Weston injects himself with a serum that renders him invisible. When Weston discovers that his serum is to be used for military purposes, he destroys the formula—and his only means to again become visible. By wearing a special mask and hands developed by a friend (Nick), Daniel appears as he did before the experiment. Stories relate Daniel's exploits as an investigator for the KLAE Corporation, a research center that tackles government contracts.

Daniel Weston	David McCallum
Kate Weston	Melinda Fee
Walter Carlson	Jackie Cooper*
	Craig Stevens
Nick Maggio	Henry Darrow

Producer: Harve Bennett, Leslie Stevens.

*Pilot film role (5/6/75).

The Invisible Woman

Comedy Pilot; 2 hrs; NBC 2/13/83

While visiting her scientist uncle (Dudley), "Daily Express" reporter Sandy Martinson touches a spilled chemical solution that renders her invisible. By wearing a wig, makeup and contact lenses, Sandy appears as before, but is unable to become fully visible due to Dudley's inability to reduplicate the formula. The unsold series was to relate Sandy's investigations, using her invisibility to solve crimes, and Dudley's efforts to make Sandy visible again.

Sandy Martinson	Alexa Hamilton
Dudley Plunkett	Bob Denver
Neil Gilmore	David Doyle
Lt. Dan Williams	Jacques Tate
Spike Mitchell	Ron Palillo
Carlisle Edwards	Harvey Korman
Orville	Richard Sanders

Theme Song ("She Must Be Around Here Someplace"): David Frank

Producer: Sherwood Schwartz, Lloyd J. Schwartz

The Ireene Wicker Show

Children's Pilot; 15 min; ABC 8/15/46

A proposed program of story telling for children. See also: "Ireene Wicker Sings" and "The Singing Lady."

Hostess: Ireene Wicker

Producer: Harvey Marlowe

Ireene Wicker Sings

Experimental; 15 min; NBC 7/28/39

A fifteen minute songfest in which Ireene Wicker, a popular star of radio, performs the top hits of the day in her first TV appearance.

Hostess: Ireene Wicker

Producer-Director: Edward Sobol

Ireene Wicker Story Time

See "The Singing Lady."

Irene

Comedy Pilot; 30 min; NBC 8/19/81

The story of Irene Cannon, a hopeful actress and singer from Omaha who comes to New York to seek her fame and fortune.

Irene Cannon	Irene Cara
Dede Thomas	Dee Dee Rescher
Lois Swenson	Julia Duffy
Lloyd Cannon	Theodore Wilson
Dotty Bushmill	Kaye Ballard
Michael	Michael Winslow

Theme Vocal: Irene Cara

Producer: James S. Henerson, James G. Hirsch

Iron Horse

Western; 60 min; ABC 9/12/66 to 1/6/68

During a high stakes card game, rugged gentleman cowboy Ben Calhoun wins the near-bankrupt Buffalo Pass, Scalplock, and Defiance Railroad. Stories, set in Wyoming during the 1870s, relate Ben's efforts to make the line a profitable operation.

Ben Calhoun	Dale Robertson
Dave Tarrant	Gary Collins
Barnabas Rogers	Bob Random
Julie Parsons	Ellen McRae (Ellen Burstyn)
Nils Torvold	Roger Torrey

Producer: Matthew Rapf

The Iron Mask

Adventure; 30 min; Syn. 1958

The exploits of the Iron Mask, a mysterious, escaped political prisoner who helps defend people against the soldiers of King Louis XIV (17th century France).

Phillippe (The Iron Mask)	?*
Louise	Lynne Roberts
Chief of Police	Carl Esmond
Constance	Dorothy Patrick

Producer: Ralph Smart

*The identity of the actor portraying the lead has not been revealed.

Ironside

Crime Drama; 60 min; NBC 9/14/67 to 1/16/75

While vacationing, Robert T. Ironside, a San Francisco Chief of Detectives, is shot by an assassin and crippled when the bullet shatters his spinal column. Stories relate Ironside's investigations, made a special consultant to the S.F.P.D. and assigned a special squad, as he continues his battle against crime.

Robert Ironside	Raymond Burr
Sgt. Eve Whitfield	Barbara Anderson
Sgt. Ed Brown	Don Galloway
Sgt. Fran Belding	Elizabeth Baur
Marc Sanger	Don Mitchell
Diana Sanger	Jane Pringle
Commissioner Randall	Gene Lyons

Producer: Joel Rogosin, Cy Chermak, Frank Price

Is There a Doctor in the House?

Comedy Pilot; 30 min; NBC 3/22/71

The story of a young female doctor named Michael and her attempts to win over the people of a small town (Wendell Falls, New England) when she becomes the assistant to the town's conservative doctor (Newley).

Dr. Timothy Newley	William Windom
Dr. Michael Griffin	Rosemary Forsyth
Emma	Margaret Hamilton
Lisa Hancock	Kim O'Brian
Mrs. Hancock	Jill Foster
Peggy Tyler	Cynthia Hull
Josh Miller	Ray Young
Charlie Larkin	William Hanser
Amos Sweeny	Ian Wolfe
Joe Tyler	Jordan Rhodes

Producer: Harry Ackerman, E. W. Swackhamer

Isabel Sanford's Honeymoon Hotel

Comedy Pilot; 30 min; Syn. 1/87

A five-part pilot for a proposed series about Isabel Scott, the owner of Isabel's Honeymoon Hotel, a debt-ridden inn staffed by an assortment of less-than-believable characters.

Isabel Scott	Isabel Sanford
Carlton (manager)	John Lawlor
Martha (assistant manager)	Rhonda Bates
Mel (bartender)	Earl Boen
Jolie (Isabel's niece)	Renee Jones
Agnes (chambermaid)	Lana Schwab
K. C. Scott (Isabel's ex-husband)	Ernie Banks

Announcer: Casey Kasem

Producer: Gordon Farr, Fred Silverman

Isis

Adventure; 30 min; CBS 9/6/75 to 9/2/78

While on a scientific expedition in Egypt, Andrea Thomas, a beautiful California high school science teacher, finds a magic amulet that grants her the powers of the Goddess Isis (control over the elements of earth, sea, and sky). Stories relate Andrea's battle against injustice as the mysterious Isis. Also titled "The Secrets of Isis."

Andrea Thomas/Isis	JoAnna Cameron
Rick Mason	Brian Cutler
Cindy Lee	Joanna Pang
Renee Carroll	Ronalda Douglas
Dr. Barnes	Albert Reed

Producer: Norm Prescott, Lou Scheimer, Dick Rosenbloom

The Islanders

Adventure; 60 min; ABC 10/2/60 to 3/26/61

The exploits of Sandy Wade and Zack Malloy, the pilots of the Islander, a two-man, one plane airline based on the Spice Islands in the West Indies.

Zack Malloy	James Philbrook
Sandy Wade	William Reynolds
Wilhelmina "Steamboat Willie" Vandeveer	Diane Brewster
Naja	Daria Massey
Skipwreck Callahan	Roy Wright

Producer: Richard L. Bare

It Could Be You

Game; 30 min; NBC 7/2/58 to 3/12/59 (evening run)
6/4/56 to 12/29/61 (day-time run)

Object: For married couples to reenact personal situations that were brought on as the result of a popular song.

Host: Bill Gwinn

It Happens in Spain

Crime Drama; 30 min; Syn. 1958

The story of Joe Jones, a private detective working in Spain, who helps distressed American tourists.

Joe Jones	Scott McKay
Tina	Elena Barra

It Pays to be Ignorant

Game; 30 min; CBS 6/6/49 to 9/19/49
NBC 7/5/51 to 9/27/51

A contestant picks a question from the Dunce Cap and reads it aloud (e.g., "What was the color of the horse in Black Beauty?"). While three panelists attempt to evade the correct answer by providing comic responses, the contestant must try to get a word in and extract the correct response. Prizes are awarded for participating.

Host: Tom Howard

Panelists: Harry McNaughton, George Shelton, Lulu McConnell

Singers: The Townsmen Quartet

Announcer: Dick Stark

Organist: Ray Morgan

Producer: Tom Howard

It Pays to be Married

Quiz; 30 min; NBC 7/4/55 to 10/28/55

Married couples are first interviewed then compete in a series of question-and-answer rounds in return for prizes.

Host: Bill Goodwin

Announcer: Jay Stewart

Producer: Stefan Hatos

It Takes a Thief

Adventure; 60 min; ABC 1/9/68 to 9/14/70

Alexander Mundy, a sophisticated and cunning thief, is granted a pardon when he agrees to become a spy for the U.S. government. Stories relate Mundy's exploits as he uses the wizardry of his craft to accomplish his assignments.

Alexander Mundy	Robert Wagner
SIA Chief Noah Bain	Malachi Throne
Alister Mundy	Fred Astaire
Chief Wally Powers	Edward Binns
SIA Agent Dover	John Russell
Charlotte "Chuck" Brown	Susan Saint James

Producer: Frank Price, Gordon Oliver, Jack Arnold

It Takes Two

Game; 30 min; NBC 3/31/69 to 8/1/70

Object: For a selected studio audience member to guess which of three celebrity couples, previously asked a question that has to be answered with a number, has come closest to the correct answer.

Host: Vince Scully

Announcer: John Harlan

Producer: Bill Yageman

It Takes Two

Comedy; 30 min; ABC 10/14/82 to 9/1/83

Events in the lives of the Quinns: Molly, the Assistant D.A., Sam, her husband, chief of surgery at the Rush-Thornton Medical Center, their children Lisa and Andy, and Molly's senile mother, Anna.

Molly Quinn	Patty Duke
Dr. Sam Quinn	Richard Crenna
Lisa Quinn	Helen Hunt
Andy Quinn	Anthony Edwards
Anna	Billie Bird
Dr. Walter Chenkins	Richard MacKenzie
Judge Caroline Phillips	Della Reese
Jeffrey Maxies	Charles Levin
Jeremy Fenton	Jerry Houser

Theme Vocal ("Where Love Spends the Night"): Crystal Gayle, Paul Williams

Producer: Paul Junger Witt, Tony Thomas

It Takes Two

Comedy Pilot; 30 min; ABC 8/2/85

The misadventures of Kate Weston, an attractive but neurotic psychiatrist.

Kate Weston	Beth Howland
Elliott Weston	Geoffrey Bowes
Melvin	Derek McGrath
Melba	Lynne Griffin
Emily	Mary Ann McDonald

Producer: Al Rogers

It was a Very Good Year

Documentary; 30 min; ABC 5/10/71 to 8/30/71

The events of various years (from 1918 through 1968) are recalled through film clips.

Host: Mel Torme

Producer: Alan Landsburg

It's a Business

Variety; 30 min; DuMont 3/19/52 to 5/27/52

The series, set against the background of the New York-based Broadway Music Publishing Company in the 1900's, relates the struggles of song pluggers in an era when the performer visited the publisher to find material.

Song Plugger	Bob Haymes
	Leo DeLyon
Secretary	Dorothy Loudon

Producer: Paul Rosen

It's a Gift

Game; 30 min; CBS 1/29/46 to 7/6/46

One of the very first TV game shows that features contestants answering questions in return for prizes.

Host: John Reed King

Producer-Director: Frances Buss

It's a Great Life

Comedy; 30 min; NBC 9/7/54 to 6/3/56

The misadventures of Denny David and Steve Connors, two ex-GI's struggling to better their position in life. Also titled, for syndication purposes, "The Bachelors."

Denny David	Michael O'Shea
Steve Connors	William Bishop
Earl Morgan	James Dunn
Amy Morgan	Frances Bavier
Katy Morgan	Barbara Bales

Producer: Dick Chevillat, Ray Singer

It's a Great Life

Magazine; 30 min; Syn. 10/85

A program of celebrity interviews, visits to exotic locales, and life-styles segments.

Hosts: Robert and Rosemarie Stack

Producer: Earl D. Greenburg, Bill Walker, Marsha Lewis

It's a Hit

Game; 30 min; ABC 6/1/57 to 9/21/57

Object: For children, aged seven to fourteen, to answer questions based on subjects they are studying in school.

Host: Happy Felton

Regulars: George Able, Jack Norwine, Al Chotin

Producer: Happy Felton, Ted Westcott

It's a Living

Comedy; 30 min; ABC 10/30/80 to 8/4/81

The story of five beautiful waitresses (Lois, Jan, Cassie, Vickie, and Dot) at the Above the

Top restaurant in Los Angeles as they tackle life and customers head on. See also the following title and "Making a Living."

Lois Adams	Susan Sullivan
Jan Hoffmeyer	Barrie Youngfellow
Cassie Cranston	Ann Jillian
Dot Higgins	Gail Edwards
Vickie Allen	Wendy Schaal
Nancy Beebee	Marian Mercer
Sonny Mann	Paul Kreppel
Mario	Bert Remsen
Ellen Hoffmeyer	Lili Haydn
Amy Adams	Tricia Cast

Theme Vocal ("It's a Living"): Leslie Bricusse

Producer: Paul Junger Witt, Tony Thomas

It's a Living

Comedy; 30 min; Syn; 9/85

A revised version of the previous title which continues to relate the adventures of Jan, Cassie, Dot, and Amy, four beautiful waitresses in Above the Top, a posh L.A. restaurant.

Jan Hoffmeyer	Barrie Youngfellow
Cassie Cranston	Ann Jillian
Dorothy "Dot" Higgins	Gail Edwards
Amy Tompkins	Crystal Bernard
Ginger (replaced Cassie)	Sheryl Lee Ralph
Nancy Beebee	Marian Mercer
Sonny Mann	Paul Kreppel
Howard Miller	Richard Stahl
Richie Gray	Richard Kline
Jan's Daughter Ellen	Virginia Keehne
Howard's Daughter Lori	Sue Ball
Nancy's Sister Gloria	Linda G. Miller

Theme Vocal ("It's a Living"): Leslie Bricusse

Producer: Tony Thomas, Paul Junger Witt

It's a Man's World

Comedy-Drama; 60 min; NBC 9/17/62 to 1/28/63

The comical adventures of Wes, Tom Tom, and Vern, three carefree young men who re-side on the "Elephant," a houseboat that is docked in Cordella, an Ohio River town.

Wes Macauley	Glenn Corbett
Tom Tom DeWitt	Ted Bessell
Vern Hodges	Randy Boone
Howie Macauley	Michael Burns
Alma Jean Dobson	Jeannie Cashell
Iona Dobson	Kate Murtagh
Virgil Dobson	Scott White
Nora Fitzgerald	Ann Schuyler
Irene Hoff	Jan Norris
Houghton Scott	Harry Harvey Jr.
Molly	Dawn Wells
Lois	Joyce Bulifant
Jeri	Diane Sayer
Jeff	James Bonnet
Helen	Sally Mills
Mrs. Meredith	Mary Adams
Sue	Cathy Birch

Music: Jack Marshall

Producer: Peter Tewksbury

It's a Small World

Comedy Pilot; 30 min; Syn. 4/57

The pilot for "Leave It to Beaver." The story of Wally and the Beaver, two young brothers, and their experiences growing up in a small American town. The pilot relates the boys efforts to collect 1,000 milk bottle caps to win a bicycle. Aired on "Studio '57."

Beaver	Jerry Mathers
Wally	Paul Sullivan
June	Barbara Billingsley
Ward	Max Showalter*
Ward's boss	Richard Deacon

Producer: Richard Lewis

*Played the role under the name Casey Adams.

It's About Time

Game; 30 min; ABC 3/4/54 to 5/2/54

Object: For players to identify incidents from the past from various clues (e.g., verbal, scrambled headlines, dramatic vignettes).

Host: Dr. Bergen Evans

Panelists: Ruth Duskin, Sherl Stern, Robert Pollack

It's About Time

Comedy; 30 min; CBS 9/11/66 to 9/3/67

While testing a NASA rocket, astronauts Mac and Hector are propelled back in time to the prehistoric era. Stories relate their adventures as they attempt to repair their ship and return to the present. Five months later, when they find the copper they need to make repairs, a cave family they had befriended sneak aboard the ship. With their unknown passengers, Mac and Hector manage to again break the time barrier and land in present-day Los Angeles. Episodes relate Mac and Hector's efforts to conceal the cave family from NASA officials; and a cave family's struggles to understand a modern world.

Capt. Mac MacKenzie	Frank Aletter
Lt. Hector Wyland	Jack Mullaney
Gronk (cave father)	Joe E. Ross
Shad (his wife)	Imogene Coca
Mlor (their daughter)	Mary Grace
Breer (their son)	Pat Cardi
Cave Boss	Cliff Norton
Mrs. Boss	Kathleen Freeman
Boss's aide (Clon)	Mike Mazurki
Gen. Morley	Frank Wilcox
Mr. Tyler	Alan DeWitt
Dr. Hamilton	Jan Arvan

Producer: Sherwood Schwartz, George Cahan

It's Always Jan

Comedy; 30 min; CBS 9/10/55 to 6/30/56

The home and working lives of three New York career girls: Janis, a nightclub entertainer; Valerie, a shapely blonde model; and Patricia, a secretary with a heart of gold.

Janis Stewart	Janis Paige
Valerie Malone	Merry Anders
Patricia Murphy	Patricia Bright
Josie (Jan's daughter)	Jeri Lou James
Stanley Schrieber	Arch Johnson
Harry Cooper	Sid Melton

Producer: Arthur Stander, Paul Jacobs

It's Always Sunday

Comedy Pilot; 30 min; NBC 1/11/56

The story of a soft-touch minister (Charles) whose kind reputation constantly causes trouble. Aired on "Screen Director's Playhouse."

Rev. Charles Parker	Dennis O'Keefe
Mary Parker	Fay Wray
Nancy Parker	Eileen Janssen
George	Sheldon Leonard
Eddie	Chick Chandler
Sue Stradler	Diane Jergens

Writer-Director: Allan Dwan

It's Anybody's Guess

Game; 30 min; NBC 6/13/77 to 9/30/77

An answer to a question that is read appears on a screen that is visible to the two players who compete. Each player must predict whether or not a panel of five studio audience members can answer the question. Correct predictions score points, and the highest point scorer is the winner.

Host: Monty Hall

Announcer: Jay Stewart

Producer: Stefan Hatos, Monty Hall, Stu Billet

It's Garry Shandling's Show

Comedy; 30 min; SHO 9/10/86 to 10/15/86

Events in the life of Garry Shandling, a comedian whose life is plagued by an assortment of odd-ball characters.

Garry Shandling	Himself
Nancy	Molly Cheek
Pete Schumaker	Michael Tucci
Grant Schumaker	Scott Nemes
Louis	Geoffrey Blake
Jackie Schumaker	Bernadette Birkett
Leonard Smith	Paul Willson

Producer: Bernie Brillstein, Bard Grey, Vic Kaplan, Alan Zweibel

It's Happening

Variety; 30 min; ABC 7/15/68 to 10/25/68

Mark Lindsay as the host of a program featuring guest rock stars, amateur band contests and other entertainment geared to teenagers. With Allison Keith and Freddie Welles. Produced by Dick Clark.

It's Magic

Children; 30 min; CBS 7/31/55 to 9/4/55

Performances by guest magicians with host Paul Tripp and the music of Hank Sylvern.

It's News to Me

Game; 30 min; CBS 7/2/51 to 8/27/54

A celebirty panel is given a prop or picture that is associated with a news event. Each panelist relates a story, but only one is telling the truth. Players have to determine which panelist is telling the truth.

Host: John Daly, Walter Cronkite, Quincy Howe

Panelists: Anna Lee, Nina Foch, Quentin Reynolds, Constance Bennett, John Henry Faulk

Producer: Mark Goodson, Bill Todman

It's Not Easy

Comedy; 30 min; ABC 9/29/83 to 10/27/83

The story of a divorced couple, Jack and Sharon (who has recently remarried to Neal) and their attempts to live their own lives while sharing custody of their children, Carol and Johnny.

Jack Long	Ken Howard
Sharon Townsend	Carlene Watkins
Neal Townsend	Bert Convy
Carol Long	Rachel Jacobs
Johnny Long	Evan Cohen
Ruth Long (Jack's mother)	Jayne Meadows
Matthew (Neal's son)	Billy Jacoby
Sherry (Jack's friend)	Christine Belford

Producer: Frank Konigsberg, Patricia Nardo

It's Only Human

Human Interest Pilot; 60 min; NBC 11/13/81

Taped interviews with people who speak their minds on subjects that concern them.

Host: Allen Funt

Guests: Barbara Eden, Reggie Jackson

Producer: Allen Funt

It's Polka Time

Variety; 60 min; ABC 7/13/56 to 9/24/57

A weekly series of polka music, songs, and dances.

Host: Bruno Zielinski

Regulars: Carolyn DeZurik, The Polka Chips, The Konal Siodmy Dancers

Music: Stan Wolowic's Band

Producer: Dan Schuffman

It's Rock and Roll

Game Pilot; 30 min; Syn. 1/83

Object: For players to answer questions based on the thirty year history of rock and roll music. Encompasses rare film clips and live performances.

Host: Mike Egan

Music: The Residents

Producer: Edward Finoh, Arnie Rosenberg

It's Rod Hull and Emu

Children; 15 min; Syn. 1973

The antics of Emu, the large puppet bird of Rod Hull, as he tells of his adventures traveling from Australia to England (where the program is taped).

It's Showtime at the Apollo

Variety; 60 min; Syn. 9/87

A weekly variety series that features performances by popular entertainers, highlights of the famed Apollo Theater's past, and highlights of the theater's Amateur Night. Taped at New York's Apollo Theater.

Guests host. Produced by Bob Barnes and Percy E. Sutton. Music by Joey Carbone.

It's Time for Ernie

Comedy; 15 min; NBC 5/14/51 to 6/29/51

Satirical comedy skits featuring the genius of Ernie Kovacs.

Host: Ernie Kovacs

Regulars: Edie Adams, Hugh Price

Producer: Ned Cramer

It's Your Bet

Game; 30 min; Syn. 1969

Two celebrity couples play for studio audience members. A small wall is placed between each player. One partner is asked a question over a telephone and bets points on whether or not his mate can answer the question. The partner is asked the question aloud and points are scored accordingly. The team with the highest score wins a merchandise prize for its audience member.

Host: Hal March, Tom Kennedy, Dick Gautier, Lyle Waggoner

Announcer: John Harlan

It's Your Move

Game; 30 min; Syn. 1967

Two teams first bid on the amount of time they feel they need to guess a charade, then, while one member performs the charade, the other must guess it within the specified time limit. Points are scored for each correctly performed charade. The highest point scorers receive merchandise prizes.

Host: Jim Perry

Producer: Art Baer, Ben Joelson

It's Your Move

Comedy; 30 min; NBC 9/26/84 to 3/16/85

The comic adventures of Matt Burton, a 14-year-old wheeler dealer. Focal point of the series is Matt's attempts to breakup his beautiful widowed mother's (Eileen) romance with Norman, a struggling writer he feels is not good enough for her.

Matt Burton	Jason Bateman
Eileen Burton	Caren Kaye
Julie Burton	Tricia Cast
Norman Lamb	David Garrison
Eli	Adam Sadowsky
Lou Donatelli	Ernie Sabella
Dwight Ellis	Garrett Morris

Theme Song ("It's Your Move"): Rik Howard, Bob Wirth

Producer: Ron Leavitt, Michael Moye

Ivan the Terrible

Comedy; 30 min; CBS 8/21/76 to 9/18/76

The trials and tribulations of Ivan Petrovsky, head waiter at the Hotel Metropole in Moscow, Russia, and the head of a family of nine living in a three-and-a-half room apartment.

Ivan Petrovsky	Lou Jacobi
Olga Petrovsky	Maria Karnilova
Sonia Petrovsky	Caroline Kava
Sascha Petrovsky	Matthew Barry
Sventlana Petrovsky	Nan Tucker
Vladimir	Phil Leeds
Tationa	Despo
Raoul Sanchez	Manuel Martinez
Federov	Christopher Hewell
Mr. Yoshanka	Joseph Leon

Producer: Alan King, Rupert Hitzig

Ivanhoe

Adventure; 30 min; Syn. 1957

The exploits of Ivanhoe, a young Saxon knight, as he battles the forces of injustice in England during the 1190s.

Ivanhoe	Roger Moore
The Monk	Robert Brown
King Richard	Bruce Seton
Sir Maverick	Paul Whitsun
Bart	John Pike

Producer: Herbert Smith, Bernard Coote, Seymour Friedman

I've Got a Secret

Game; 30 min; CBS 6/26/52 to 9/3/67

Object: For a celebrity panel to guess the secret of a guest contestant.

Host: Garry Moore, Steve Allen

Panelists: Henry Morgan, Betsy Palmer, Faye Emerson, Jayne Meadows, Bill Cullen, Orson Bean, Laraine Day. Eddie Bracken, Walter Kirenan, Louise Albritton, Steve Allen, Laura Hobson

Announcer: John Cannon, Johnny Olsen

Producer: Gilbert Cates, Roger Peterson, Chester Feldman

I've Got a Secret

Game; 30 min; Syn. 1972

A revised version of the previous title, which see.

Host: Steve Allen

Panelists: Jayne Meadows, Nanette Fabray, Pat Carroll, Gene Rayburn, Richard Dawson, Anita Gillette, Henry Morgan

Announcer: Johnny Olsen

Producer: Mark Goodson, Bill Todman

I've Got a Secret

Game; 30 min; CBS 6/15/76 to 7/6/76

Four celebrity panelists attempt to identify a guest's secret through indirect question-and-answer rounds.

Host: Bill Cullen

Panelists: Elaine Joyce, Henry Morgan, Phyllis George, Richard Dawson, Pat Collins

Announcer: Johnny Olsen

Producer: Mark Goodson, Bill Todman

I've Got News For You

See "Up to Paar."

Ivy League

Comedy Pilot; 30 min; CBS 3/13/59

The story of Bull Mitchell, an ex-Marine sergeant newly enrolled in college, as he struggles to adjust to a nonmilitary life.

Bull Mitchell	William Bendix
Timmy Mitchell	Tim Hovey
Mamie Parker	Florence MacMichael
Dean	Bartlett Robinson

Students: Mary Tyler Moore, Arte Johnson, Doug McClure

Teachers: Sheila Bromley, Kathleen Warren

J.J. Starbuck

Crime Drama; 60 min; NBC 9/26/87 (Premiere)

The exploits of J.J. (Jerome Jeremiah) Starbuck, an eccentric Texas billionaire who meddles into other people's business in the name of justice.

J.J. Starbuck	Dale Robertson
Jill Starbuck	Shawn Weatherly
Charlie	David Huddleston
	Jimmy Dean

Producer: Stephen J. Cannell, Babs Greyhosky

Jabberjaw

Cartoon; 30 min; ABC 9/11/76 to 9/3/78

The series, set in a futuristic undersea world, relates the adventures of the Neptunes, a rock group composed of Biff, Shelley, Bubbles, Clam Head and Jabberjaw (a white shark who plays drums) as they battle evildoers.

Jabberjaw	Frank Welker
Bubbles	Julie McWhirter
Shelley	Pat Parris
Biff	Tommy Cook
Clam Head	Barry Gordon

Producer: William Hanna, Joseph Barbera

Jabberwocky

Variety; 30 min; Syn. 1974

Music, songs, and sketches geared to children.

Cast: Joanna Spoko, Peter Johnson, Carl Thomas, Bob Porsky, Bob Fromy, Joseph Williams

Music: David Lucas

Producer: Gail Frank

Jack and Mike

Drama; 60 min; ABC 9/16/86 to 5/28/87

Incidents in the lives of two people: Jackie Shea, a beautiful columnist ("Our Kind of Town") for the Chicago "Mirror," and her husband, Mike Brennan, a hip restauranteur.

Jackie Shea	Shelley Hack
Mike Brennan	Tom Mason
Charlotte Branigan	Carol Rossen
Nora Adler	Jacqueline Brookes
Carol Greene	Holly Fulger
Anthony Kubecek	Kevin Dunn
Belinda	Noelle Bou-sliman
Rick Scotti	Vincent Baggetta
Mike's Sister	
Kathleen	Carol Potter

"Jack and Mike" theme song: Johnny Mandel

Producer: David Gerber, Jack Bender, Liz Coe

The Jack Benny Program

Comedy; 30 min; CBS 10/29/50 to 9/15/64
            NBC 9/25/64 to 9/10/65

The home and working life of comedian Jack Benny, an actor whose life is constantly plagued by the antics of his television family.

Jack Benny	Himself
Mary Livingston	Herself
Rochester	Eddie Anderson
Don Wilson	Himself
Dennis Day	Himself
Lois Wilson	Lois Corbett
Harlow Wilson	Dale White
Prof. LeBlanc	Mel Blanc
Fred (Jack's director)	Fred DeCordova
Joe (Jack's agent)	Russ Conway
Sam (Jack's writer)	Herb Vigran
Miss Gordon (Jack's	
secretary)	Maudie Prickett
Si (Mexican foil)	Mel Blanc
Mr. Kitzel (Jewish	
foil)	Artie Auerbach
The "Yes" Man	Frank Nelson

Various Roles: Iris Adrian, Barbara Nichols, Joan Benny (Jack's daughter), Ruth Brady, Benny Rubin, Beverly Hills

Announcer: Don Wilson

Orchestra: Mahlon Merrick

Producer: Irving Fein, Fred DeCordova, Ralph Levy

The Jack Carson Show

Variety; 60 min; NBC 10/22/54 to 3/11/55

Music, songs, and comedy sketches.

Host: Jack Carson

Regulars: Connie Towers, Don Ameche, Kitty Kallen, Donald Richards, Peggy Ryan, Ray McDonald

Announcer: Ed Peck, Bud Heistand

Orchestra: Harry Sosnik, Vic Schoen

Jack Carter and Company

Variety; 30 min; ABC 3/12/49 to 4/21/49

A weekly series of music, songs, and comedy.

Host: Jack Carter

Regulars: Jack Albertson, Elaine Stritch, Bill Callahan, Sonny King, Paul Castle

Orchestra: Harry Sosnik

Producer: Kenny Lyons, Ernest D. Glucksman

The Jack Carter Show

Variety; 60 min; NBC 2/25/50 to 6/2/51

Music and comedy with host Jack Carter and regulars Don Richards and Bill Callahan. Music by Lou Breese and Harry Sosnik and produced by Danny Dare.

The Jack Cole Dancers

Experimental; 30 min; NBC 6/16/39

A thirty minute program of music and dance with Jack Cole and his dance troupe. Produced by Edward Sobol.

The Jack Paar Show

Variety; 30 min; CBS 11/13/53 to 5/24/56

Music, talk, and light comedy.

Host: Jack Paar

Regulars: Edie Adams, Martha Wright, Richard Hayes, Betty Clooney, Johnny Desmond, Jose Melis, Jack Haskell

Orchestra: Ivan Ditmars, Pupi Campo, Jose Melis

The Jack Paar Show

Variety; 60 min; NBC 9/21/62 to 9/10/65

Celebrity interviews with host Jack Paar. Music by Jose Melis and produced by Paul Orr.

Jack Paar Tonight

Variety; 90 min; ABC 1/8/73 to 11/16/73

A nightly program of music, interviews, and chatter.

Host: Jack Paar

Co-Host: Peggy Cass

Orchestra: Charles Randolph Grean

Producer: Bob Carman

Jack the Ripper

Mystery; 60 min; Syn. 1974

A modern-day attempt, through the investigations of Detecives Barlow and Watt, to discover the identity of Jack the Ripper, a mysterious killer of women who terrorized London from August 31 to November 9, 1888.

Detective Barlow	Alan Stratford-Johns
Detective Watt	Frank Windsor

Host: Sebastian Cabot

Jackie and Darlene

Comedy Pilot; 30 min; ABC 7/8/78

The misadventures of two West Valley Precinct police officers: Jackie Clifton, a street cop, and her roommate Darlene, a radio dispatcher.

Jackie Clifton	Sarina Grant
Darlene Shilton	Anna L. Pagan
Sgt. Guthrie	Lou Frizzell
Simpson	Jeff Hollis
Garcia	Richard Beauchamp

Producer: Aaron Ruben

Jackie Gleason and His American Scene Magazine

Variety; 60 min; CBS 9/29/62 to 6/4/66

Music, songs, and skits culled from the mythical "American Scene Magazine."

Host: Jackie Gleason

Regulars: Frank Fontaine, Sidney Fields, Phil Bruns, Alice Ghostley, Sue Ane Langdon, Jan Crockett, Patricia Wilson, Rip Taylor, Barney Martin, Stan Ross, Frank Marth, Stormy Berg, The June Taylor Dancers, Pat Dahl, The Glea Girls

"It Pays to Be Ignorant" Cast: Jayne Mansfield, Prof. Irwin Corey, Frank Fontaine

Announcer: Johhny Olsen

Orchestra: Sammy Spear

Producer: Frank Bunetta

The Jackie Gleason Show

Variety; CBS 9/20/52 to 6/18/55 (60 min)
9/29/56 to 6/22/57 (60 min)
10/3/58 to 1/2/61 (30 min)

A weekly series of music and comedy. "The Honeymooners" skits performed on the series (1952–57) have been reedited and syndicated as "The Honeymooners: The Lost Episodes."

Host: Jackie Gleason

Regulars: Art Carney, Audrey Meadows, Joyce Randolph, George O. Petrie, Frank Marth, Buddy Hackett, The Glea Girls, The June Taylor Dancers

Announcer: Jack Lescoulie

Orchestra: Ray Bloch

Producer: Jack Philbin, Jack Hurdle

The Jackie Gleason Show

Variety; 60 min; CBS 9/17/66 to 9/12/70

A weekly program of music, song, and comedy that features a rebirth of "The Honeymooners" with Jackie Gleason (Ralph), Art Carney (Ed), Sheila MacRae (Alice), and Jane Kean (Trixie). The hour segments were re-edited and syndicated as "The Honeymooners" in 1977.

Host: Jackie Gleason

Regulars: Lanita Kent, Jami Henderson, Andrea Duda, Carlos Bas, The Glea Girls, The June Taylor Dancers

Announcer: Johnny Olsen

Orchestra: Sammy Spear

Producer: Jack Philbin, Frank Bunetta

Jackpot

Game; 30 min; NBC 1/7/74 to 9/26/75

Object: For players to solve riddles in return for cash prizes.

Host: Geoff Edwards

Announcer: Don Pardo

Producer: Bob Stewart

Jackson and Jill

Comedy; 30 min; Syn. 1949

A virtually unknown domestic comedy about Jackson and Jill Jones, young marrieds who live in a one room apartment at 167 Oak Street in Manhattan.

Jackson Jones	Todd Karns
Jill Jones	Helen Chapman

Producer: Jerry Fairbanks

The Jackson Five

Cartoon; 30 min; ABC 9/11/71 to 9/1/73

The misadventures of the Jackson Five, a Motown rock group.

Voices (as themselves): Michael, Randy, Jackie, Tito, and Marlon Jackson

Producer: Arthur Rankin Jr., Jules Bass

The Jacksons

Variety; 30 min; CBS 6/16/76 to 7/7/76
                                    1/26/77 to 3/9/77

A weekly series of music and songs featuring the Jackson brothers (Michael, Marlon, Randy, Jackie, and Tito) and their sisters (Maureen, Latoya, and Janet).

Regulars: Marty Cohen, Jim Samuels

Orchestra: Rick Wilkins

Producer: Joe Jackson, Richard Arons

The Jacqueline Susann Show

Women; 30 min; DuMont 5/7/51 to 6/18/51

Fashion previews, guests, and celebrity interviews. Also known as "Jacqueline Susann's Open Door."

Hostess: Jacqueline Sussan

Announcer: Cy Newman, John McNight

Producer: Dick Randall, Cy Newman

Jacques Fray's Music Room

Variety; 30 min; ABC 2/29/49 to 10/9/49

Music by Jacques Fray and performances by aspiring talent.

Host: Jacques Fray

Regulars: Bess Myerson, Jeri Nagle, Bob Calder, Joan Francis, Dancers Fussell and Aura

Orchestra: Charles Stark

Jake and the Fatman

Crime Drama; 60 min; CBS 9/26/87 (Premiere)

The exploits of J.L. "Fatman" McCabe, a tough, cagey D.A. (of an unnamed Southern California city) and Jake Styles, his smooth and fashionable investigator; two dedicated men who blend their talents to solve crimes.

J.L. McCabe	William Conrad
Jake Styles	Joe Penny
Det. Katy Grant	Rebecca Rush
Gertrude	Lu Leonard
Derek	Alan Campbell

Producer: Robert Hamilton, Joel Steiger

Jake's Way

Crime Drama Pilot; 60 min; CBS 6/28/80

The exploits of Jake Rudd, sheriff of Fox County, a rural town near San Antonio, Texas.

Jake Rudd	Robert Fuller
Sam Hargis	Slim Pickens
Daniel Doggett	Steve McNaughton
Steve Cantwell	Ben Lemon
Christina O'Toole	Lisa LeMole
Mace Kaylor	Andrew Duggan
Luanna Kaylor	Kristen Griffith

Producer: Richard Lewis

Jambo

Anthology; 30 min; NBC 9/6/69 to 9/4/71

A weekly program of wildlife stories aimed at children. Filmed on location in Africa (the title means "Hello").

Host: Marshall Thompson

Producer: Ivan Tors

Jamboree

Variety; 60 min; DuMont 6/5/50 to 8/9/50

Music and light comedy with hostess Gloria Van, regulars Paula Raye, Jane Broekman, Jimmy McPartland, Danny O'Neill, Bud Tygett, and the music of Julian Stockdale.

James at 15

Drama; 60 min; NBC 10/27/77 to 7/27/78

The problems faced by today's teenagers as seen through the experiences of James Hunter, a student at Bunker Hill High School in Boston. Also titled (episodes 11 through 21) "James at 16."

James Hunter	Lance Kerwin
Paul Hunter	Linden Chiles
Joan Hunter	Lynn Carlin
Sandy Hunter	Kim Richards
Kathy Hunter	Deirdre Berthrong
Marlene Mahoney	Susan Myers
Ludwig "Sly" Hazeltine	David Hubbard

Theme Vocal ("James"): Lee Montgomery

Producer: Martin Manulis, Joseph Hardy

The James Boys

Comedy Pilot; 30 min; NBC 6/25/82

The relationship between Willie James, a divorced construction worker (for Heinwell Construction) and his young son, Sam—people who struggle to share each other's interests.

Willie James	Brian Kerwin
Sam James	Eric Coplan
Kate Allgood	Kelly Harmon
Emily Allgood	Viveka Davis
Jake	Edward Edwards
Mindy	Liberty Godshall

Music: Patrick Williams

Producer: Michael Zinberg, Susan Seeger

Jamie

Comedy; 30 min; ABC 10/5/53 to 10/4/54

Events in the life of Jamieson John Francis McHummer (Jamie) a young orphan who comes to live with relatives after the death of his parents.

Jamie McHummer	Brandon DeWilde
Grandpa McHummer	Ernest Truex
Liz McHummer	Eva Marie Saint*
	Kathleen Nolan
Laurie McHummer	Polly Rowles
Annie Moakum	Alice Pearce
Aunt Ella	Kathleen Comegys

Producer: Herbert Brodkin (pilot), Julian Claman (series)

*Pilot film role (4/26/53).

The Jan Murray Show

Variety; 15 min; NBC 2/11/55 to 5/6/55

Music and comedy with host Jan Murray, regulars Tina Louise, Fletcher Peck, the Novelettes, and the music of Milton DeLugg.

Jane Eyre

Experimental; 95 min; NBC 10/12/39

The story of Jane Eyre, the governess to Adele, the young ward of Edward Rochester, the owner of Thornfield Hall in England. Based on the novel by Charlotte Bronte.

Jane Eyre	Flora Campbell
Edward Rochester	Dennis Hoey
Adele	Effie Shannon
Grace Poole	Daisy Belmore
Mrs. Fairfax	Ruth Mattheson
Mason	Philip Tonge

Producer: Edward Sobol

Jane Froman's U.S.A. Canteen

Variety; 15 min; CBS 10/18/52 to 6/23/55

Performances by the men and women of the U.S. Armed services. Also known as "The Jane Froman Show."

Hostess: Jane Froman

Regulars: The Peter Birch Dancers

Announcer: Allyn Edwards

Orchestra: Alfredo Antonini

Producer: Byron Paul

The Jane Pickens Show

Variety; 15 min; ABC 1/31/54 to 9/5/54

Music and songs with hostess Jane Pickens and regulars the Vikings. Music by Milton DeLugg.

Jane Wyman Presents the Fireside Theatre

Anthology; 30 min; NBC 8/30/55 to 5/22/58

A continuation of "Fireside Theatre" under a new title. Filmed dramas that encompass both well-known and lesser-known performers.

Hostess: Jane Wyman

Producer: Frank Wisbar, William Asher, Peter Barry, Jules Bricken, Albert McCleery

The Jane Wyman Theatre

Anthology; 30 min; CBS 8/28/56 to 6/25/57

Tense, highly dramatic productions.

Hostess: Jane Wyman

Announcer: Joel Crager

Producer: Eva Wolas, William Rousseau

Janet Dean, Registered Nurse

Drama; 30 min; Syn. 1954

The experiences of Janet Dean, a private duty nurse working in New York City.

Janet Dean	Ella Raines

Producer: Joan Harrison

Jason King

Crime Drama; 60 min; Syn. 1971

A spin-off from "Department S." The exploits of Jason King, the author of Mark Cain mystery novels, who lends his expertise to help the British government solve crimes.

Jason King	Peter Wyngarde

Producer: Monty Berman

Jason of Star Command

Science Fiction; 30 min; CBS 9/15/79 to 8/29/81

The exploits of Jason, a pilot with the futuristic police station, Star Command, as he battles Dragos, the most evil being in the universe.

Jason	Craig Littler
Cmdr. Carnarvin	James Doohan
Cmdr. Stone	John Russell
Cadet Nicole	Susan O'Hanlon
Prof. E. J. Parsafoot	Charlie Dell
Cadet Samantha	Tamara Dobson
Dragos	Sid Haig

Producer: Norm Prescott, Lou Scheimer

The Jaye P. Morgan Show

Variety; 15 min; ABC 6/13/56 to 8/24/56

A lively program of music and songs.

Hostess: Jaye P. Morgan

Regulars: Dick, Charlie and Duke Morgan

Orchestra: Joel Herron

The Jean Carroll Show

Comedy; 30 min; ABC 11/4/53 to 1/6/54

Incidents in the life of an average American housewife as interpreted by commedienne Jean Carroll. Also known as "Take It from Me."

Housewife	Jean Carroll
Husband	Alan Carney
Daughter	Lynn Loring
Neighbor	Alice Pearce

Music: Bernard Green

Producer: Alan Dinehart

Jeannie

Cartoon; 30 min; CBS 9/8/73 to 8/30/75

While surfing, a Center City high school student (Corey) is overcome by a wave and washed ashore. There, he finds a bottle in the sand and opens it. A beautiful young genie, named Jeannie, and her inept genie friend, Babu, emerge and become his slaves. Stories relate Corey's efforts to now live a normal life; and Jeannie's efforts to adjust to life in the 1970s.

Jeannie	Julie McWhirter
Corey Anders	Marc Hammil
Henry Glopp	Bob Hastings
Babu	Joe Besser

Producer: William Hanna, Joseph Barbera

Jefferson Drum

Western; 30 min; NBC 4/25/58 to 4/23/59

The series, set in the lawless gold-mining town of Jubilee during the 1850s, tells of Jefferson Drum, an embittered newspaper editor struggling to establish peace through the power of the press. Also known as "The Pen and the Quill."

Jefferson Drum	Jeff Richards
Joey Drum	Eugene Martin
Lucius Coin	Cyril Delevanti
Big Ed	Robert J. Stevenson
Hickey	Hal Smith

Producer: Matthew Rapf, Mark Goodson, Bill Todman

The Jeffersons

Comedy; 30 min; CBS 1/17/75 to 7/23/85

Events in the lives of the Jeffersons: George, the snobbish and wealthy owner of several dry cleaners; his tolerant, long-suffering wife, Louise, and their son, Lionel. A spin-off from "All in the Family." See also "Checking In."

George Jefferson	Sherman Hemsley
Louise Jefferson	Isabel Sanford
Lionel Jefferson	Mike Evans
	Damon Evans
Tom Willis	Franklin Cover
Helen Willis	Roxie Roker
Jenny Willis	Berlinda Tolbert
Harry Bentley	Paul Benedict
Florence Johnston	Marla Gibbs
Olivia Jefferson	Zara Cully
Ralph Hart	Ned Wertimer
Jessica Jefferson	Ebonie Smith
Sammy Kelsey	Frank DeVol

Theme Song ("Movin' On Up"): Jeff Barry, Ja'net BuBois

Producer: George Sunga, Jay Moriarity, Mike Mulligan, Don Nicoll, Michael Ross, Bernie West

Jeff's Collie

Drama; 30 min; CBS 9/12/54 to 12/1/57

Following the death of a neighbor, young Jeff Miller inherits Lassie, a beautiful collie. Stories, set on the Miller farm in Calverton, relate Jeff and Lassie's adventures. Jon Provost (Timmy) became a regular on 9/8/57 (when Lassie found the runaway) and remained with the Millers until 12/1/57 (when he was adopted by the Martins (see "Timmy and Lassie"). Originally broadcast as "Lassie."

Jeff Miller	Tommy Rettig
Ellen Miller	Jan Clayton
George Miller (Gramps)	George Cleveland
Sylvester "Porky" Brockway	Donald Keeler
Matt Brockway	Paul Maxey
Sheriff Clay Horton	Richard Garland
Dr. Peter Wilson/Dr. Frank Weaver (vet)	Arthur Space
Jenny	Florence Lake
Timmy	Jon Provost

Producer: Jack Wrather, Sheldon Leonard

Jem

Cartoon; 30 min; Syn. 5/86

In an effort to help his daughter, Jerrica, run the Starlight Orphanage for Girls, Professor Benton creates Center G, a sophisticated holographic device that transforms Jerrica into Jem, a beautiful singer who is the leader of the Holograms, a stunning all-female rock group. Stories relate Jerrica's adventures as she uses the power of her holographic image to help others and battle the evils of Pizazz, the leader of the Misfits, who deviously plots to dethrone Jem and become the number one rock star.

Voices: Charlie Adler, Pat Albrecht, Marlene Aragon, Ellen Bernfield, Bobbi Block, Catherine Blore, Susan Blu, Anne Bryant, Kim Carlson, T. K. Carter, Cathy Cavadini, Diva Gray, Ford Kinder, Ullanda McCullough, Cindy McGee, Samantha Newark, Noelle North, Britta Philps, Neilson Ross, Florence Warner

Theme Song ("Jem: Truly Outrageous"): Ford Kinder, Anne Bryant

Producer: Joe Bacal, Margaret Loesch, Tom Griffin

Jennifer Slept Here

Comedy; 30 min; NBC 10/21/83 to 9/5/84

Five years after the death of Jennifer Farrell, a beautiful movie actress, the Elliots move from New York to California and into her Beverly Hills home. Shortly after, Jennifer's spirit appears to and befriends Joey, the son of George and Susan Elliot. Stories relate Joey's misadventures as Jennifer, who appears only to him, decides to "guide" his life.

Jennifer Farrell	Ann Jillian
Joey Elliot	John P. Navin Jr.
Susan Elliot	Georgia Engel
George Elliot	Brandon Maggart
Marilyn (Joey's sister)	Mya Akerling
Marc (Joey's friend)	Glenn Scarpelli
Alice (Jennifer's mother)	Debbie Reynolds

Theme Vocal ("Jennifer Slept Here"): Joey Scarbury

Producer: Larry Rosen, Larry Tucker

Jeopardy

Game; 30 min; NBC 4/30/64 to 1/3/75

Three players compete in a rapid-fire question-and-answer session wherein they must supply the correct questions for the answers that are given. The player with the highest score wins.

Host: Art Fleming

Announcer: Don Pardo, John Harlan

Producer: Robert H. Rubin, Lynette Williams

Jeopardy

Game; 30 min; Syn. 9/84

A revised version of the previous title, which see for format.

Host: Alex Trebek

Announcer: Johnny Gilbert

Producer: Alex Trebek, Kevin McCarthy

Jeremiah of Jacob's Neck

Comedy Pilot; 30 min; CBS 8/13/76

The story of a modern-day family (parents Tom and Anne, and their children, Tracy and Clay) who move to the town of Jacob's Neck, New England, and into a beach house that is haunted by the ghost of its 18th-century owner (Jeremiah). The unsold series was to relate the efforts of both parties to adjust to each other.

Jeremiah Starbuck	Keenan Wynn
Tom Rankin	Ron Masak
Anne Rankin	Arlene Golonka
Tracy Rankin	Quinn Cummings
Clay Rankin	Brandon Cruz
Wilbur Smith	Elliott Street
Dick Baker	Pitt Herbert
Leonard	Amzie Strickland
Max	Les Lannom

Producer: Edgar J. Scherick, Art Stolnitz

Jericho

Adventure; 60 min; CBS 9/15/66 to 1/19/67

The W.W. II exploits of three Allied Agents as they attempt to infiltrate enemy lines and sabotage and discredit the Germans. (Jericho is the code name under which they operate). Also known as "Code Name: Jericho."

Franklin Sheppard	Don Francks
Nicholas Gage	John Leyton
Jean-Gaston Andre	Marino Mase

Producer: Norman Felton, Stanley Niss, David Victor

Jerry

Comedy Pilot; 30 min; CBS 5/16/74

The story of Jerry Edwards, a 30-year-old bachelor who yearns for an exciting romance.

Jerry Edwards	Robert Walden
Nina Pope	Linda Lavin
Winston Barlow	Norman Alden
Frank Fuller	Bob Hastings
Gloria Fuller	Beatrice Colen
Morree Wu	Keone Young

Music: Marvin Hamlich

Producer: Edward H. Feldman

The Jerry Colonna Show

Variety; 30 min; ABC 5/28/51 to 11/17/51

A weekly program of music, songs, and comedy.

Host: Jerry Colonna

Regulars: Barbara Ruick, Frankie Laine, Isabel Randolph, Arthur Duncan, Louis Colonna, Gordon Polk

Announcer: Del Sharbutt

Music: The Cookie Fairchild Band

The Jerry Lester Show

Variety; 60 min; ABC 9/28/53 to 5/14/54

Sketches, music, and songs.

Host: Jerry Lester

Regulars: Nancy Walker, Bobby Sherwood, Betty George, Kathy Collin, Eddie Russell, Leon Belasco, Lorenzo Fuller

Orchestra: Buddy Weed

Producer: Vernon P. Becker

Jerry Lester's Blind Date

Game Pilot; 31 min; Unaired (produced in 1951)

NBC's original, unaired pilot for "Blind Date," which see for format.

Host: Jerry Lester

Orchestra: Harry Sosnik

Producer: Richard Lewis

The Jerry Lewis Show

Variety; 2 hrs; ABC 9/21/63 to 12/22/63

Guest performances, interviews, and entertainment acts.

Host: Jerry Lewis

Announcer: Del Moore

Orchestra: Lou Brown

Producer: Ernest D. Glucksman

The Jerry Lewis Show

Variety; 60 min; NBC 9/12/67 to 5/26/69

A weekly program of music, song, and comedy.

Host: Jerry Lewis

Regulars: Debbie Macomber, Bob Harvey, The Osmond Brothers, The George Wyle Singers, The Nick Castle Dancers

Orchestra: Lou Brown

Producer: Bob Finkel, Bill Foster

The Jerry Lewis Show

Interview Pilot; 60 min; Syn. 6/11/84 to 6/15/84

A five episode pilot for a proposed series of celebrity interviews.

Host: Jerry Lewis

Announcer: Charlie Callas

Orchestra: Lou Brown

Producer: Bill Richmond, Joe Stable

Jerry Mahoney's Club House

Children; 30 min; NBC 11/20/54 to 2/25/56

A Saturday morning program of comedy and games for children with ventriloquist Paul Winchell and the antics of his dummy friends, Jerry Mahoney and Knucklehead Smiff.

Host: Paul Winchell

Regulars: Hilda Vaughn, Dorothy Claire, Jimmy Blaine, Sid Raymond

Orchestra: John Gart

Producer: Paul Winchell

The Jerry Reed When You're Hot, You're Hot Hour

Variety; 60 min; CBS 6/20/72 to 7/25/72

A country-western accented program of music, songs, and comedy.

Host: Jerry Reed

Regulars: Spencer Quinn, Carl Wilson, Merie Earle, John Twomey, Norman Alexander, The Lou Regas Dancers

Announcer: Bill Thompson

Orchestra: George Wyle

Producer: Al Rogers, Rich Eustis

Jerry Visits

A syndicated (1971) interview series in which celebrities open their homes and reveal aspects of their public and private lives. Hosted by Jerry Dunphy (also the producer).

Jessica Novak

Drama; 60 min; CBS 11/5/81 to 12/3/81

The news gathering assignments of Jessica Novak, an on-the-air reporter for "Closeup News" on KLA-TV, Channel 6 in Los Angeles.

Jessica Novak	Helen Shaver
Max Kenyon	David Spielberg
Phil Bonelli	Andrew Rubin
Audrey Styler	Nina Wilcox
Ricky Duran	Eric Kilpatrick
Jackson Gage	Michael D. Roberts
Vince Halloran	Kenneth Gilman
Katie Robins	Lara Parker
Richie	Scott Thompson
KLA Dispatcher	Frank Taylor

Producer: Marc Merson, Jerry Ludwig

Jessie

Crime Drama; 60 min; ABC 9/18/84 to 11/13/84

The story of Jessie Hayden, a beautiful police psychiatrist with the Behavioral Science Department of the Metro Division of the San Francisco Police Department.

Jessie Hayden	Lindsay Wagner
Molly Hayden	Celeste Holm
Lt. Alex Ascoli	Tony LoBianco
Sgt. Mac McClellan	William Lucking
Off. Floyd Comstock	Peter Isacksen
Ellie	Renee Jones
Phil	James David Hinton

Producer: Eric Bercovici, David Gerber

Jet Fighter

Adventure Pilot; 30 min; ABC 6/28/53

The adventures of Chuck Powers, a Captain with the U.S. Air Force.

Capt. Chuck Powers	John Granger
Sgt. Gunner Maddigan	Tige Andrews
Col. Warner	Ben Hammer

Narrator: Jackson Beck

Producer: Herbert Brodkin

Jet Jackson, Flying Commando

See "Captain Midnight."

The Jetsons

Cartoon; 30 min; ABC 9/23/62 to 9/8/63

The 21st-century adventures of the Jetsons: George, an employee of Spacely Space Sprockets; his wife, Jane; and their children Judy and Elroy. See also "The New Jetsons."

George Jetson	George O'Hanlon
Jane Jetson	Penny Singleton
Judy Jetson	Janet Waldo
Elroy Jetson	Daws Butler
Astro	Don Messick
Rosie	Jean VanderPyl
Cosmo G. Spacely	Mel Blanc
Henry Orbit	Howard Morris

Producer: William Hanna, Joseph Barbera

Jigsaw

Crime Drama; 60 min; ABC 10/12/72 to 8/11/73

The exploits of Frank Dain, a lieutenant with the Sacramento State Bureau of Missing Persons, who possesses a genius for solving clueless mysteries. Aired on "The Men."

Lt. Frank Dain	James Wainwright

Producer: Stanley Kallis, Harry Tatelman

Jigsaw John

Crime Drama; 60 min; NBC 2/2/76 to 9/13/76

The exploits of John St. John, an L.A.P.D. homicide detective nicknamed "Jigsaw John" for his uncanny ability to solve complex crimes.

John St. John	Jack Warden
Maggie Hearn	Pippa Scott
Det. Sam Donner	Alan Feinstein

Producer: Ronald Austin, James David Buchanan

Jim and Judy in Teleland

Cartoon; 5 min; Syn. 1953

Various adventures in the lives of two youngsters.

Jim	Merrill Jolls
Judy	Honey McKenzie

The Jim Backus Show—Hot Off the Wire

Comedy; 30 min; Syn. 1960.

The misadventures of John Michael O'Toole, the editor-reporter of the "Headline Press Service," a newspaper fraught with problems.

John O'Toole	Jim Backus
Dora Miles	Nita Talbot
Sidney	Bobs Watson

Producer: Ray Singer, Dick Chevillat

Jim Bowie

See "The Adventures of Jim Bowie."

Jim Henson's Muppet Babies

Cartoon; 30 min; CBS 9/15/84 (Premiere)

The adventures and fantasies of the Muppets as babies.

Kermit	Frank Welker
Piggie	Laurie O'Brien
Fozzie	Greg Berg
Rowlf	Katie Lee
Skeeter	Howie Mandel
Beaker	Frank Welker
Gonzo	Russi Taylor
Animal	Howie Mandel
Scooter	Greg Berg
Nanny (nursemaid)	Barbara Billingsley

Producer: Jim Henson, Ron Richardson

The Jim Nabors Hour

Variety; 60 min; CBS 9/25/69 to 5/20/71

Music, songs, and comedy sketches.

Host: Jim Nabors

Regulars: Ronnie Schell, Frank Sutton, Karen Morrow, The Nabors Kids, The Tony Mordente Dancers

Orchestra: Paul Weston

Producer: E. Duke Vincent, Bruce Johnson

The Jim Nabors Show

Variety; 60 min; Syn. 9/78

A daily series of music, songs, and interviews.

Host: Jim Nabors

Regulars: Susan Ford, Ronnie Schell

Orchestra: Fred Werner

Producer: Carolyn Raskin

The Jim Stafford Show

Variety; 60 min; ABC 7/30/75 to 9/3/75

A Summer series of music and comedy.

Host: Jim Stafford

Regulars: Debbie Allen, Valerie Curtin, Richard Stahl, Lyndi Wood, Gallagher, Jeannie Sheffield, The Carl Jablonski Dancers

Orchestra: Eddie Karam

Producer: Al Rogers, Rich Eustis

The Jimmie Rodgers Show

Variety; 30 min; NBC 3/31/59 to 9/8/59

A weekly series of music and songs.

Host: Jimmie Rodgers

Regulars: Connie Francis, The Kirby Stone Four, The Clay Warnick Singers

Orchestra: Byron Morrow

Producer: Bob Claver

The Jimmie Rodgers Show

Variety; 60 min; CBS 6/16/69 to 9/1/69

A Summer series of music and comedy.

Host: Jimmie Rodgers

Regulars: Vicki Lawrence, Lyle Waggoner, Nancy Austin, Don Crichton, Bill Fanning, The Burgundy Street Singers

Announcer: Lyle Waggoner

Orchestra: Harry Zimmerman, Frank Comstock

Producer: Joe Hamilton

The Jimmy Dean Show

Variety; Various (30, 45, & 60 min); CBS 4/8/57 to 8/30/58

A country accented program of music, songs, and light comedy.

Host: Jimmy Dean

Regulars: Jo Davis, Jeri Miyazaki, Herbie Jones, Mary Klick, Jan Crockett, The Double Daters, The Country Lads, The Noteworthies, Alec Houston's Wildcats

Orchestra: Joel Herron

The Jimmy Dean Show

Variety; 60 min; ABC 9/19/63 to 4/1/66

Music, songs, and comedy set against a country-western atmosphere.

Host: Jimmy Dean

Regulars: Molly Bee, The Grass Roots Band, The Doerr-Hutchinson Dancers, The Chuck Cassey Singers, Rowlf (hound dog muppet)

Orchestra: Peter Matz, Al Pellegrini, Don Sebesky

Producer: Bob Banner

Jimmy Durante Presents the Lennon Sisters Hour

Variety; 60 min; ABC 9/26/69 to 7/4/70

An entertaining series that features the lovely Lennon Sisters and comedian Jimmy Durante in music, songs, and comedy.

Host: Jimmy Durante

Hostesses: Dianne, Peggy, Janet, Kathy Lennon

Regulars: Bernie Kukoff, Edna O'Dell

Announcer: Charlie O'Donnell

Orchestra: George Wyle

Producer: Bernie Kukoff, Jeff Harris

The Jimmy Durante Show

Variety; 30 min; CBS 6/29/57 to 9/21/57

The misadventures of comedian Jimmy Durante as he attempts to run a night club (The Club Durant) fraught with problems.

Host: Jimmy Durante

Regulars: Eddie Jackson, Doris Singleton, Jules Buffano, The Durante Girls, Jack Roth

Orchestra: Roy Bargy

Producer: William Harmon

The Jimmy Durante Show

Comedy Pilot; 30 min; CBS 7/18/64

The story of a famous comedian (Jimmy Banister) and his efforts to convince his son, Eddie, who has no interest in show business, to follow in his footsteps.

Jimmy Banister — Jimmy Durante
Rosie Banister — Audrey Christie
Eddie Banister — Eddie Hodges
Mr. Dureen — John McIntire
Chet Hanson — Ralph Bell
Frank Peterson — Daryl Richard

Producer: Hy Averback

Jimmy Hughes, Rookie Cop

Crime Drama; 30 min; DuMont 5/8/53 to 7/3/53

When he returns home from the service (Korea) and learns that his father, a New York cop, has been killed in the line of duty, Jimmy Hughes joins the force in an attempt to find the killers. Later, when Jimmy learns to serve for reasons other than revenge, he is given his father's badge. Stories relate the exploits of a rookie cop.

Off. Jimmy Hughes — Billy Redfield
— Conrad Janis
Insp. Ferguson — Rusty Lane
Jimmy's sister — Wendy Drew

Producer: Bary Shear

The Jimmy Stewart Show

Comedy; 30 min; NBC 9/19/71 to 9/3/72

The trials and tribulations of James K. Howard, an anthropology professor at Josiah Kessel College in Easy, Valley, California.

James Howard — Jimmy Stewart
Martha Howard — Julie Adams
P. J. Howard — Jonathan Daly
Wendy Howard — Ellen Geer
Teddy Howard — Dennis Larson
Jake Howard — Kirby Furlong
Luther Quince — John McGiver

Producer: Hal Kanter

The Jo Stafford Show

Variety; 15 min; CBS 2/2/54 to 6/28/55

Music, songs, and celebrity interviews.

Hostess: Jo Stafford

Vocalists: The Starlighters

Orchestra: Paul Weston

Producer: Paul Harris, Bernie Gold

The Joan Edwards Show

Variety; 15 min; DuMont 7/4/50 to 10/24/50

A twice-weekly program of music and songs with singer-pianist Joan Edwards. Produced by Martin Goodman.

Joan of Arkansas

Comedy Pilot; 30 min; Unaired; Produced for NBC in 1958

A proposed series that was to follow the antics of Joan Jones, a dental technician from Hot Springs, Arkansas, when she is chosen by the Saraback Computer to become the first human in Space.

Joan Jones — Joan Davis
Dr. John Dolan — John Emery
Prof. Henry Newkirk — Wilton Graff
Dr. Curtis Short — Bob Brubaker
Nurse Kelly — Jolene Brand
Mrs. Putnam — Lee Patrick
Mr. Kepler — Olan Soule

Producer: Philip Rapp, Robert Stillman

Joanie Loves Chachi

Comedy; 30 min; ABC 3/23/83 to 9/13/83

A spin-off from "Happy Days." Shortly after Al Delvecchio and Louisa Arcola marry and move to Chicago, Chachi, Louisa's son, joins a motley music group (Mario, Bingo, and Annette) which he feels he can improve by hiring a pretty lead singer. Through an arrangement with her father, Joanie Cunningham (Chachi's girlfriend) is permitted to move to Chicago and join the band. Stories relate Joanie and Chachi's efforts to make a name for themselves in the music world.

Joanie Cunningham — Erin Moran
Chachi Arcola — Scott Baio
Louisa Delvecchio — Ellen Travolta
Al Delvecchio — Al Molinaro
Louisa's Uncle Rico — Art Metrano
Mario — Derrel Maury
Bingo — Robert Peirce
Annette — Winifred Freeman

Theme Vocal ("You Look at Me"): Erin Moran, Scott Baio

Producer: Garry K. Marshall, Lowell Ganz, Ronny Hallin, Thomas L. Miller

Joanna

Comedy Pilot; 30 min; ABC 4/30/85

When Joanna Weston, a Los Angeles girl, moves to N.Y. to live with her boyfriend and finds that he has run off with another woman, she decides to stay. She later acquires a job as the executive director of the Rosebud Trucking Company. The unsold series was to relate Joanna's efforts to run the company.

Joanna Weston	Cindy Williams
Michael Braxton	Reni Santoni
Elvis Valentine	Ron Karabatsos
Mrs. Benson	Florence Halop
Little Joe	Larry Hankin
Paulie	John DelRagno
Sigourney Schultz	Julie Payne
Petey Flowers	Danny Mora
Dean	Larry Joshua
Napoleon Flipper	W. H. Macy

Producer: Greg Antonacci, Gary Nardino, Stu Silver

Joanne Carson's V.I.P.'s

A syndicated (1972) series of celebrity interviews with Joanne Carson. Announcer: Hugh Douger.

Joe and Mabel

Comedy; 30 min; CBS 9/10/55 to 9/17/55
                       6/26/56 to 9/25/56

The story of two young lovers: Joe Sparton, a N.Y. cab driver who feels he is not ready for marriage, and Mabel Spooner, a manicurist who yearns to become his wife.

Joe Sparton	Larry Blyden
Mabel Spooner	Nita Talbot
Mrs. Spooner	Luella Gear
Sherman Spooner	Michael Mann
Mike	Norman Fell

Producer: Alex Gottlieb

Joe and Sons

Comedy; 30 min; CBS 9/9/75 to 1/13/76

The story of a widowed New Jersey sheet metal worker (Joe) and his attempts to raise his two teenage sons (Mark and Nick).

Joe Vitalie	Richard Castellano
Mark Vitalie	Barry Miller
Nick Vitalie	Mitch Brown
	Jimmy Baio
Estelle	Maureen Arthur
	Bobbi Jordan
Josephine Molonaire	Florence Stanley
Mo Molonaire	Sorrell Booke
Gus Duzik	Jerry Stiller

Producer: Douglas S. Cramer, Bernie Kukoff, Jeff Harris

Joe and Valerie

Comedy; 30 min; NBC 4/24/78 to 5/10/78

The romantic misadventurs of Joe Pizo, an apprentice plumber, and Valerie Sweetzer, a cosmetics salesgirl. See the following title also.

Joe Pizo	Paul Regina
Valerie Sweetzer	Char Fontane
Frank Berganski	Bill Beyers
Thelma Medina	Donna Ponterotto
Stella Sweetzer	Pat Benson
Paulie Barone	David Elliott

Theme Vocal: Char Fontane, Randy Winburn

Producer: Linda Hope, Bernie Kahn

Joe and Valerie

Comedy; 30 min; NBC 1/5/79 to 1/19/79

An updated version of the previous title which focuses on the courtship and marriage of Joe, a plumber, to Valerie, a clothing salesgirl.

Joe Pizo	Paul Regina
Valerie Sweetzer	Char Fontane
Stella Sweetzer	Arlene Golonka
Rita	Donna Ponterotto
Vince Pizo	Robert Costanzo
Frank Berganski	Lloyd Alann
Paulie Barone	David Elliott
Ed Sweetzer	Jack Riley

Theme Vocal: Patti Brooks, Jean Raposo

Producer: Linda Hope, Hal Dresner

Joe Bash

Comedy; 30 min; ABC 3/28/86 to 5/10/86

The comical adventures of Joe Bash and Willie Smith, officers with New York's 33rd Precinct, who patrol a ghetto section of the city at night.

Off. Joe Bash	Peter Boyle
Off. Willie Smith	Andrew Rubin
Sgt. Carmine DiSalvo	Val Bisoglio
Lt. Pendleton	Michael Cavanaugh

Producer: Danny Arnold, Chris Hayward

The Joe DiMaggio Show

Children; 15 min; Syn. 1950

Baseball star Joe DiMaggio chats with youngsters, answers their questions, and interviews guest stars. Assisted by Jack Barry with the announcing of Ted Brown.

Joe Forrester

Crime Drama; 60 min; NBC 9/9/75 to 8/30/76

A realistic depiction of police work in action as seen through the experiences of Joe Forrester, a veteran cop who rejects a desk job to walk his old beat.

Off. Joe Forrester	Lloyd Bridges
Sgt. Bernie Vincent	Eddie Egan
Georgia Cameron	Patricia Crowley
Jolene Jackson	Dwan Smith
Det. Marshall	Michael Warren
Sgt. Storm	Lynn Redding
Assistant D.A. Johnson	Andra Akers
Polygraph Operator	Dale Tarter
Det. Will Carson	Taylor Lacher

Producer: David Gerber

The Joe Namath Show

Interview; 30 min; Syn. 1969

Interviews with sports personalities and show business celebrities.

Host: Joe Namath

Co-Host: Dick Schaap

Announcer: Louisa Moritz

Producer: Larry Spangler

The Joe Palooka Story

Comedy; 30 min; Syn. 1954

The fictitious story of Joe Palooka, a naive heavyweight boxer. Based on the Ham Fisher character.

Joe Palooka	Joe Kirkwood Jr.
Ann Howe	Cathy Downs
Knobby Walsh	Louis Van Rooten
Humphrey Pennyworth	Maxie Rosenbloom

Producer: William Berke

The Joe Pyne Show

A syndicated (1966) discussion series with Joe Pyne. Produced by Marv Gray.

Joe's World

Comedy; 30 min; NBC 12/28/79 to 7/26/80

Events in the day-to-day lives of the Wabash family: Joe, a painter; his wife, Katie; and their children Maggie, Steve, Jimmy, Linda, and Rick.

Joe Wabash	Ramon Bieri
Katie Wabash	K Callan
Maggie Wabash	Melissa Sherman
Steve Wabash	Christopher Knight
Jimmy Wabash	Michael Sharrett
Linda Wabash	Missy Francis
Rick Wabash	Ari Zeltzer
Judy Wilson*	Misty Rowe
Brad Hopkins*	Russ Banham
Andy*	Frank Coppola
Tessie (bar owner)	Joan Shawlee

Producer: Mel Tolkin, Larry Rhine, Jack Elinson

*Member of Joe's crew.

Joey and Dad

Variety; 60 min; CBS 7/6/75 to 7/27/75

A weekly program of music, song, and light comedy with Joey Heatherton and her father, Ray.

Hosts: Joey Heatherton, Ray Heatherton

Regulars: Henny Youngman, Pat Paulsen, Bob Einstein, Dorothy Meyers, Pat Proft

Announcer: Peter Cullen, David Black

Orchestra: Lex DeAzevedo

Producer: Allan Blye, Bob Einstein

The Joey Bishop Show

Comedy; 30 min; NBC 9/20/61 to 6/20/62

The story of Joey Barnes, a public relations man with the firm of Wellington, Willoughby, and Jones. See also "Everything Happens to Me."

Joey Barnes	Joey Bishop
Stella Barnes	Marlo Thomas
Mrs. Barnes	Madge Blake
Larry Barnes	Warren Berlinger
Betty	Virginia Vincent
Frank	Joe Flynn
J. P. Willoughby	John Briggs
Peggy	Jackie Russell
Barbara Simpson	Nancy Hadley

Producer: Danny Thomas

The Joey Bishop Show

Comedy; 30 min; NBC 9/15/62 to 9/20/64
                        CBS 9/27/64 to 9/7/65

A revised version of the previous title, which relates the home and working life of comedian Joey Barnes.

Joey Barnes	Joey Bishop
Ellie Barnes	Abby Dalton
Freddie	Guy Marks
Larry	Corbett Monica
Jillson	Joe Besser
Joey Barnes Jr.	Matthew David Smith
Dr. Sam Nolan	Joey Forman
Hilda	Mary Treen

Producer: Danny Thomas

The Joey Bishop Show

Variety; 90 min; ABC 4/17/67 to 12/20/69

A nightly series of celebrity interviews.

Host: Joey Bishop

Announcer: Regis Philbin

Orchestra: Johnny Mann

Producer: Paul Orr

Joey Faye's Frolics

Comedy Pilot; 30 min; CBS 4/5/50 to 4/12/50

A two episode comedy that spotlights the talents of comedian Joey Faye.

Host: Joey Faye

Regulars: Audrey Christie, Mandy Kaye, Joe Silver, Danny Dayton

The John Byner Comedy Hour

Variety; 60 min; CBS 8/1/72 to 8/29/72

A weekly program of music and comedy.

Host: John Byner

Regulars: Patty Deutsch, R. G. Brown, Linda Sublette, Gary Miller, Dennis Flannigan, The Lori Regas Dancers

Announcer: Bill Thompson

Orchestra: Ray Charles

Producer: Rich Eustis, Al Rogers

John Conte's Little Show

Variety; 15 min; NBC 6/27/50 to 11/22/51
                        ABC 4/3/53 to 6/19/53

A series of music and songs that is also known as "The Little Show" and "Van Camp's Little Show" (under sponsorship of Stokley-Van Camp Foods).

Host: John Conte

Regulars: Maguerite Hamilton, The Three Beaus and a Peep, The Jesse Bradley Trio

Music: The Tony Mottola Trio

Producer: Robert Smith

The John Davidson Show

Variety; 60 min; ABC 5/30/69 to 9/12/69

A British-produced series of music and songs.

Host: John Davidson

Regulars: Rich Little, Mireille Mathieu, Amy McDonald

Orchestra: Jack Parnell

Producer: Colin Clews

The John Davidson Show

Variety; 60 min; NBC 5/24/76 to 6/14/76

A weekly hour of music and songs.

Host: John Davidson

Announcer: Pete Barbutti

Orchestra: Lenny Stack

Producer: Dick Clark

The John Davidson Show

Variety; 60 min; Syn. 9/80

A daily series of music and interviews.

Host: John Davidson

Announcer: Jerry Bishop

Orchestra: John Toben

Producer: Frank R. Miller, Frank Brill

The John Forsythe Show

Comedy; 30 min; NBC 9/13/65 to 8/29/66

Following the death of a relative, U.S. Air Force major John Foster inherits the Foster School for Girls in California. Episodes relate his attempts to run the school. Several months later, the format changed to depict John's adventures as a secret agent when the government recalls him for active duty.

Maj. John Foster	John Forsythe
Sgt. Ed Robbins	Guy Marks
Margaret Culver	Elsa Lanchester
Miss Wilson	Ann B. Davis
Joanna	Peggy Lipton
Marcia	Page Forsythe
Kathy	Darleen Carr
Pamela	Pamelyn Ferdin
Janice	Sara Ballantine
Susan	Tracy Strafford
Norma Jean	Brooke Forsythe
Connie	Celia Kaye
Jeannie Hayes	Lisa Gaye

Producer: Peter Kortner, Dick Wesson

The John Gary Show

Variety; 60 min; CBS 6/22/66 to 9/7/66

A weekly series of music and songs.

Host: John Gary

Regulars: The Jimmy Joyce Singers, The Jack Regas Dancers

Orchestra: Mitchell Ayres

Producer: Ernest Chambers, Saul Ilson

The John Gary Show

A syndicated (1968) series of music and songs with host John Gary and the orchestra of Sammy Spear.

Johnny Blue

Mystery Pilot; 60 min; CBS 9/4/83

The exploits of Johnny Blue, a New Orleans restaurant owner ("Mr. Blues") and a detective who helps the police solve baffling crimes.

Johnny Blue	Gil Gerard
Chief Mitch Mitchell	Eugene Roche
Chef Saffron	George Kee Cheung
Kathy Weatherby	Rebecca Holden
Joanne Kruger	Delta Burke
Jenny	Patricia Klous

Producer: Robert Carrington

The Johnny Carson Show

Variety; 30 min; CBS 6/30/55 to 3/29/56 (evening run) 5/28/56 to 9/28/56 (daytime run)

A program of music, interviews, songs, and comedy skits.

Host: Johnny Carson

Regulars: Barbara Ruick, Jill Corey, Virginia Gibson, Glenn Turnbull, Laurie Carroll, Peter Hanley, Hank Simms

Orchestra: Lud Gluskin, Cal Gooden

Producer: Nat Perrin

The Johnny Cash Show

Variety; 60 min; ABC 6/7/69 to 5/21/71

A country-western accented program of music, songs, and comedy.

Host: Johnny Cash

Regulars: June Carter, Carl Perkins, The Carter Family, The Statler Brothers, The Tennessee Three

Announcer: Mike Lawrence

Orchestra: Bill Walker

Producer: Joseph Cates

Johnny Come Lately

Comedy Pilot; 30 min; CBS 8/8/60

The story of Johnny Martin, a TV newscaster who will go to any lengths to get a story.

Johnny Martin	Jack Carson
Angela Talbot	Marie Windsor
Holly	Tracy Morgan
Eddie	Dick Reeves
Andy	Alvy Moore

Producer: Milt Josefsberg

The Johnny Dugan Show

Variety; 30 min; NBC 5/19/52 to 9/5/52

A Hollywood-based program of music and songs with Johnny Dugan and regulars Barbara Logan and Arch Presby.

Johnny Garage

Comedy Pilot; 30 min; CBS 4/13/83

The misadventures of Johnny Antonizzio, the owner of a financially troubled garage in Queens, New York.

Johnny Antonizzio	Ron Carey
Frankie Parker	Val Bisoglio
Mike	Timothy Van Patten
Harriet Garfield	Glynn Carlin

Producer: Larry Jacobson, Sonny Grosso

Johnny Guitar

Drama Pilot; 30 min; CBS 7/31/59

The story of a singing cowboy (Johnny Guitar) who helps people in trouble. Aired as "Ballad to Die By" on "Stripe Playhouse."

Johnny Guitar	William Joyce
Anna Carrick	Fay Spain
Harry Shay	Reg Parton

Producer: Robert Carney

The Johnny Johnston Show

Variety; 45 min; CBS 1/22/51 to 2/9/51

A daily songfest with host Johnny Johnston and singer Rosemary Clooney.

Johnny Jupiter

Fantasy; 30 min; DuMont 3/21/53 to 6/13/53
                                 ABC 9/5/53 to 5/29/54

While fiddling with a TV set, amateur inventor Ernest P. Duckweather, a clerk in the Frisbee General Store, contacts the people of another planet. Stories relate Ernest's adventures as he speaks with the people (puppets) of Jupiter. In the revised format (ABC), Ernest, a janitor in a TV station, sneaks into the control room one day, and while playing producer, contacts the people of Jupiter. Episodes revolve around Ernest's adventures with his alien friend, Johnny Jupiter.

Ernest P. Duckweather	Wright King
Mr. Frisbee	Vaughn Taylor
Ernest's boss (ABC)	Cliff Hall
Ernest's girlfriend	Patricia Peardon
Johnny Jupiter/B-12/ Reject the Robot	Gilbert Mack

Producer: Jerome Coopersmith

Johnny Mann's Stand Up and Cheer

Variety; 30 min; Syn. 1971

The program presents America in a musical revue.

Host: Johnny Mann

Regulars: Cathy Cahill, Thurl Ravenscroft, the Johnny Mann Singers

Orchestra: Johnny Mann

Producer: Pierre Cossette, Burt Sugarman, Dean Whitmore

Johnny Midnight

Crime Drama; 30 min; Syn. 1960

The exploits of Johnny Midnight, a New York actor turned private detective.

Johnny Midnight   Edmond O'Brien
Sgt. Sam Olivera   Arthur Batanides
Lt. Geller   Barney Phillips
Aki   Yuki Shimoda

Theme Song ("The Lullaby of Broadway"):
   Joe Bushkin

Producer: Jack Chertok

Johnny Nighthawk

Adventure Pilot; 30 min; CBS 9/1/59

The exploits of Johnny Nighthawk, the adventurous owner of a one-plane airline. Aired as "Forced Landing" on "Geritol Adventure Showcase."

Johnny Nighthawk   Scott Brady
Matt Brent   Richard Erdman
Lorna Kendiss   Maggie Mahoney
Mac Ustich   Joe DeSantis

Producer: Harold Greene

Johnny Olsen's Rumpus Room

Variety; 30 min; DuMont 1/17/49 to 7/4/52

Music, comedy, and songs coupled with audience participation segments for prizes.

Host: Johnny Olsen

Regulars: Kay Armen, Gene Kirby, Hal McIntyre

Music: Buddy Weed, Hank D'Amico

Producer: John Gibbs

Johnny Ringo

Western; 30 min; CBS 10/1/59 to 9/29/60

The story of Johnny Ringo, an ex-gunfighter turned sheriff as he attempts to maintain law and order in Velardi, Arizona, during the 1870s. See also "The Loner" (1959 version).

Johnny Ringo   Don Durant
Deputy Cully "Kid"
   Adonas   Mark Goddard
Cason Thomas   Terence DeMarney
Laura Thomas   Karen Sharpe

Theme Vocal ("Johnny Ringo"): Don Durant

Producer: Aaron Spelling

Johnny Risk

Adventure Pilot; 30 min; NBC 6/16/58

The adventures of Johnny Risk, a gambling boat entrepreneur in Alaska in 1896.

Johnny Risk   Michael Landon

Also: Lew Ayres, DeForest Kelley, Alan Hale Jr., Bonnie Holding

Producer: Vincent M. Fennelly

Johnny Sokko and His Flying Robot

Science Fiction; 30 min; Syn. 1968

When a prehistoric creature, brought to Earth by aliens, attacks a Japanese ship, two people, Jerry Mono (a Unicorn Defense Organization Agent) and a young boy, Johnny Sokko, escape to the safety of a nearby island. While exploring, they discover it to be the aliens base and learn that a giant robot is being readied to destroy the Earth. In an attempt to thwart their objectives, Jerry and Johnny attack the aliens guarding the robot. During the scuffle, Johnny finds the robot's voice command control and speaks to it. He becomes the robot's master. With the help of Giant Robot, Jerry and Johnny escape and return to Tokyo. Stories relate Unicorn's battle against alien invaders.

Johnny Sokko   Mitsundbu Kaneko
Jerry Mono   Akjo Ito

Producer: Salvatore Billitera

Johnny Staccato

Crime Drama; 30 min; NBC 9/10/59 to 3/24/60

The exploits of Johnny Staccato, a jazz musician turned private detective working out of New York City.

Johnny Staccato   John Cassavetes
Waldo   Eduardo Ciannelli

Music: Elmer Bernstein

Producer: William Frye

Jokebook

Cartoon; 30 min; NBC 4/23/82 to 5/7/82

Short cartoon segments that are tied together by a variety of characters (e.g., Eve and Adam, Treeman, The Nerd).

Voices: Henry Corden, Joyce Jameson, Frank Welker, Lennie Weinrib, Marilyn Schreffler, Janet Waldo, Sidney Miller, Ronnie Schell

Producer: William Hanna, Joseph Barbera

Joker! Joker!! Joker!!!

Game; 30 min; Syn. 1/80

A children's version of "The Joker's Wild" (which see for format).

Host: Jack Barry

Announcer: Jay Stewart

Producer: Jack Barry, Dan Enright

The Joker's Wild

Game; 30 min; CBS 9/4/72 to 10/31/75
                    Syn. 9/76

One of two players pulls a lever that spins five category topics. The machine pinpoints three topics, one of which the player chooses to answer. Each correct answer scores money and the first player to reach $500 wins. (The spinning wheels also contain jokers, which when appearing with a category, allow players to double or triple the available money.)

Host: Jack Barry, Jim Peck, Bill Cullen

Announcer: Johnny Jacobs, Jay Stewart, Charlie O'Donnell

Producer: Jack Barry, Dan Enright

The Jonathan Winters Show

Comedy; 15 min; NBC 10/2/56 to 6/25/57

An interlude series of comedy skits with Jonathan Winters, the Platters (vocalists) and the Eddie Safronski Orchestra.

The Jonathan Winters Show

Variety; 60 min; CBS 12/27/67 to 5/1/69

A lively program of music and comedy.

Host: Jonathan Winters

Regulars: Abby Dalton, Paul Lynde, Alice Ghostley, Cliff Arquette, Dick Curtis, Pamela Rodgers, Debi Storm, Georgene

Barnes, Jerry Renneau, The Establishment, The Wisa D'Orso Dancers, The Andre Tayer Dancers

Announcer: Bern Bennett

Orchestra: Paul Weston

Producer: Frank Peppiatt, Sheldon Keller

The Jones Boys

Comedy Pilot; 30 min; CBS 8/21/67

The misadventures of Oliver Jones, owner of the Jones Maintenance Company, and the leader of a group of boisterous employees.

Oliver Jones	Mickey Shaughnessy
Mary Jones	Jeanne Arnold
Betty Kelly	Barbara Stuart
Moose	Bob Dishy
Nick Matero	Dick Gautier
Dixie	Norman Grabowski
Susan	Joi Lansing
Mr. Simpson	Cliff Norton
Mrs. Simpson	Barbara Morrison
Miss Tyler	Suzie Kaye

Producer: Arne Sultan, Marvin Worth

Jonny Quest

See "The Adventures of Jonny Quest."

Joseph Schildkraut Presents

Anthology; 30 min; DuMont 10/28/53 to 1/21/54

A series of filmed dramas with host Joseph Schildkraut. Produced by Ray Benson.

Josephine Little

Adventure Pilot; 30 min; NBC 11/14/60 (1st pilot)
                    1/30/61 (2nd pilot)
                    3/20/61 (3rd pilot)

The exploits of Josephine Little, the beautiful owner of an import-export business in Hong Kong. Broadcast as three episodes of "The Barbara Stanwyck Theatre:" "The Miraculous Journey of Tadpole Chan,'' "Dragon By the Tail,'' and "Adventures in Happiness.''

Josephine Little   Barbara Stanwyck

Producer: Louis F. Edelman

Josie and the Pussycats

Cartoon; 30 min; CBS 9/12/70 to 9/2/72

The global adventures of Josie and the Pussycats, an all-girl rock group.

Josie (speaking)	Janet Waldo
Josie (singing)	Cathy Douglas
Melody (speaking)	Jackie Joseph
Melody (singing)	Cheryl Ladd
Valerie (speaking)	Barbara Pariot
Valerie (singing)	Patricia Holloway
Alexandra	Sherry Alberoni
Alan	Jerry Dexter
Alexander	Casey Kasem
Sebastian	Don Messick

Producer: William Hanna, Joseph Barbera

Josie and the Pussycats in Outer Space

Cartoon; 30 min; CBS 9/9/72 to 1/26/74

While posing for pictures in a NASA space ship, Alexandra, a member of the rock group Josie and the Pussycats, accidentally launches the craft and sends the group into outer space. Stories relate their adventures as they seek a way to return to Earth. For cast information, see the prior title.

Joshua's World

Drama Pilot; 60 min; CBS 8/21/80

The story of Joshua Torrance, a doctor in the small town of Strawee, Arkansas, during the 1930s.

Joshua Torrance	Richard Crenna
Thorpe Torrance	Tonya Crowe
James Torrance	Randy Gray
Donie	Mary Alice
Caroline Morgan	Carol Vogel
Dawn Starr	Alexandra Pauley
Josie	LaShana Dendy
Nathaniel	Carl Franklin

Producer: Lee Rich, Earl Hamner, Michael Filerman

Journey to the Center of the Earth

Cartoon; 30 min; ABC 9/9/67 to 9/6/69

When Oliver Lindenbrook uncovers the long lost trail of a lone explorer (Arnie Saccnuson) who made a descent to the earth's center but died with its secret, he organizes an expedition to follow the trail. Unknown to him, a descendant (Count Saccnuson) follows them, seeking to claim the earth's core for his own sinister purposes. Hoping to kill Oliver and his team (Alex, Cindy, and Lars) the Count orders his servant, Torg, to set off a dynamite charge. The explosion seals the entrance and traps them all. Stories relate their efforts to find the secret of the way back to the earth's surface.

Oliver Lindenbrook/ Count Saccnuson	Ted Knight
Cindy Lindenbrook	Jane Webb
Alex Hewitt/Lars/ Torg	Pat Harrington Jr.

Producer: Lou Scheimer, Norm Prescott

Journey to the Unknown

Anthology; 60 min; ABC 9/26/68 to 1/30/69

A British-produced series of mystery and suspense stories of people caught between the worlds of nightmare and reality.

Music: Harry Robinson

"Journey To The Unknown'' Theme: Norman Kaye, David Lindup

Producer: Joan Harrison

Joyce and Barbara: For Adults Only

A syndicated (1970) discussion series with hosts Joyce Susskind and Barbara Howar. Produced by David Susskind.

The Joyce Davidson Show

A syndicated (1975) celebrity interview series with Joyce Davidson. Produced by Sandra Faire.

The Joyce Jillson Show

Astrology coupled with celebrity interviews in a 1978 syndicated program hosted by Joyce Jillson. Produced by Steve Syatt. Announcer: Charlie Tuna.

The Joyce Matthews Show

Joyce Mathews as hostess of a CBS (5/18/50 to 6/29/50) celebrity interview series.

Jubilee U.S.A.

Variety; 60 min; ABC 1/22/55 to 9/24/60

Performances by country and western artists. Also known as "Ozark Jubilee."

Host: Red Foley

Regulars: Wanda Jackson, Suzi Arden, Norma Jean, Chuck Bowers, Smiley Burnette, Shug Fisher, Slim Wilson, Bobby Lord, Bill Wimberly

Producer: Si Sherman, Carl Fox

The Jud Strunk Show

Variety Pilot; 60 min; ABC 8/17/72

An unsold series of music and comedy with Jud Strunk, a comic singer from Maine.

Host: Jud Strunk

Guests: Andy Griffith, Tina Cole, Louis Nye, Jack Burns, The Lovin' Spoonful

Producer: Frank Peppiatt, John Aylesworth

Judd, for the Defense

Drama; 60 min; ABC 9/8/67 to 9/19/69

The story of Clinton Judd, a freewheeling defense lawyer based in Texas.

Clinton Judd	Carl Betz
Ben Caldwell	Stephen Young

Producer: Paul Monash, Harold Gast, Charles Russell

The Judge

Drama Pilot; 60 min; NBC 2/5/63

The story of Daniel Zachary, a newly appointed Supreme Court Judge. Aired on "The Dick Powell Show."

Daniel Zachary	Richard Basehart
Justice Caleb Cooke	Otto Kruger
Karen Holmes	Mary Murphy
Matthew Connors	Edward Binns

Producer: Bernard L. Kowalski, Bruce Geller

The Judge

Drama; 30 min; Syn. 9/86

Courtroom dramas based on actual cases involving family disputes.

Judge Robert J. Franklin	Robert F. Shield

Producer: Barry Cahn, Larry Gottlieb, Judy Cole, Gregg Ross, Sandi Spidell

Judge for Yourself

Variety; 30 min; NBC 8/18/53 to 5/11/54

Undiscovered talent is judged by three studio audience members and three guest judges. In a later format, a panel rated the merit of new songs performed by a company of singers.

Host: Fred Allen, Dennis James

Vocalists: Kitty Kallen, Bob Carroll, Judy Johnson, The Skylarks

Announcer: Dennis James

Orchestra: Milton DeLugg

Producer: Mark Goodson, Bill Todman

Judge Roy Bean

Western; 30 min; Syn. 12/55

When Roy Bean, a storekeeper in Langtry, Texas (1870s) becomes fed up with the lawlessness, he establishes himself as a judge and introduces a system of law and order. Stories relate his attempts to maintain the law in "America's most lawless region."

Judge Roy Bean	Edgar Buchanan
Letty Bean	Jackie Loughery
Deputy Jeff Taggard	Jack Beutel
Steve (Texas Ranger)	Russell Hayden

Producer: Russell Hayden

Judgement Day

Drama Pilot; 60 min; NBC 12/6/81

An unusual story that is set in a celestial courtroom where Mr. Heavener and Mr. Heller battle for the soul of an individual who is currently in limbo. Flashbacks are used to recall the defendant's life (in the pilot, Harriet Egan) with the Judge determining whether the soul should be sent to Heaven or Hell.

The Judge	Barry Sullivan
Mr. Heavener	Victor Buono
Mr. Heller	Roddy McDowall
Harriet Egan	Carol Lynley
Vicki Connors	Beverly Garland
Charles Egan	Robert Webber
Joseph Pierson	Hari Rhodes
Burton Randolph	John Larch

Producer: Ed Friendly

The Judy Garland Show

Variety; 60 min; CBS 9/29/63 to 3/29/64

A lively series of music, songs, and light comedy with Judy Garland and her celebrity friends (as guests).

Hostess: Judy Garland

Regular: Jerry Van Dyke

Orchestra: Mort Lindsey

Special Musical Material: Mel Torme

Producer: Gary Smith, Norman Jewison, Bill Hobin, George Schlatter

The Judy Lynn Show

A syndicated (1969) program of country and western music with hostess Judy Lynn.

Judy Splinters

Children; 15 min; NBC 6/13/49 to 6/30/50

The antics of Judy Splinters, the female dummy of ventriloquist Shirley Dinsdale.

Hostess: Shirley Dinsdale

Producer: Norman Felton, E. Roger Muir

Juke Box

See "Britt Ekland's Juke Box" and "Twiggy's Juke Box."

Julia

Comedy; 30 min; NBC 9/17/68 to 5/25/71

The story of Julia Baker, a nurse with the Los Angeles-based Inner Aero-Space Health Center, as she struggles to readjust to life and raise her young son (Corey) following the death of her husband.

Julia Baker	Diahann Carroll
Dr. Morton Chegley	Lloyd Nolan
Corey Baker	Marc Copage
Earl J. Waggedorn	Michael Link
Marie Waggedorn	Betty Beaird
Len Waggedorn	Hank Brandt
Hannah Yarby	Lurene Tuttle
Carol Deering	Alison Mills
Sol Cooper	Ned Glass
Ted Neumann	Don Marshall
Paul Carter	Chuck Wood
Steve Bruce	Fred Williamson
Melba Chegley	Mary Wickes
Julia's Uncle Lou	Eugene Jackson
Mrs. Bennett	Jeff Donnell

Producer: Hal Kanter

The Julie Andrews Hour

Variety; 60 min; ABC 9/13/72 to 4/28/73

A weekly program of music, songs, and comedy.

Hostess: Julie Andrews

Regulars: Rich Little, Alice Ghostley, The Tony Charmoli Dancers, The Dick Williams Singers

Announcer: Dick Tufeld

Orchestra: Nelson Riddle

Producer: Nick Vanoff, William O. Harbach

Julie Farr, M.D.

Drama; 60 min; ABC 3/7/78 to 6/26/79

The story of Julie Farr, an obstetrician at City Memorial Hospital in Los Angeles. The series, originally titled "Having Babies," dealt with the joys and traumas of childbirth.

Dr. Julie Farr	Susan Sullivan
Dr. Blake Simmons	Mitchell Ryan
Kelly Williams	Beverly Todd
Rod Danvers	Dennis Howard
Nurse	Deborah Green

Theme Vocal ("There Will Be Love"): Marilyn McCoo

Producer: B. W. Sandefur, Gerald I. Isenberg, Gerald W. Abrams

The Julius LaRosa Show

Variety; 15 min; NBC 6/27/55 to 9/23/55

A weekly series of music and songs.

Host: Julius LaRosa

Regulars: Connie Desmond, Irene Carroll, Bix Brent

Orchestra: Russ Case

Producer: Byron Paul

The Julius LaRosa Show

Variety; 60 min; NBC 7/14/56 to 8/4/56

A series of music and songs.

Host: Julius LaRosa

Regulars: George DeWitt, The Mariners, The Spellbinders, The Evans Dancers

Orchestra: Mitchell Ayres

Jump

Variety Pilot; 30 min; NBC 5/31/84

Seven dancers combine interpretations of rock numbers with recollections from their personal lives.

Dancers: Peggy Holmes, Vincent Paterson, Lynda Baines Johnson, Chelsea Field, Kenneth Jezek, Kim Smith

Choreographer: Kenny Ortega

Producer: Bernie Brillstien, Sandy Wernick

Jump!

Variety Pilot; 30 min; NBC 1/16/85

A revised version of the previous title which, set in the Jump studios, spotlights eight dancers as they perform video-style vignettes that sketch the moods of the songs they perform.

Dancers: Peggy Holmes, Bard Jeffries, Chelsea Field, Kenneth Jezek, Lynda Baines Johnson, Kim Smith, Peter Tramm, Wanja McIntire

Music: Gary Scott

Producer: Bernie Brillstein, Sandy Warnick

The June Allyson Show

Anthology; 30 min; CBS 9/21/59 to 6/12/61

Varying dramatic presentations, including episodes written especially for June Allyson.

Hostess: June Allyson

Producer: Dick Powell

The June Havoc Show

A syndicated (1964) interview series with actress June Havoc.

Jungle Boy

See "The Adventures of a Jungle Boy."

Jungle Jim

Adventure; 30 min; Syn. 1955

The series, set in Africa, relates the adventures of a guide known as Jungle Jim. Based on characters created by Alex Raymond.

Jungle Jim	Johnny Weissmuller
Skipper	Martin Houston
Kaseem	Norman Fredric
Tamba (Jim's chimp)	Peggy

Producer: Harold Greene

Junior Almost Anything Goes

Game; 30 min; ABC 9/11/76 to 9/4/77

A children's version of "Almost Anything Goes," which features three four-member teams competing in outrageous outdoor games for prizes.

Host: Soupy Sales

Commentator: Eddie Alexander

Producer: Bob Banner, Beryl Vertue

Junior High Jinks

Children; 30 min; CBS 3/2/52 to 5/25/52

The antics of Willie the Worm, the puppet of ventriloquist and host Warren Wright, coupled with edited comedy shorts of the 1920s and 30s.

Junior Rodeo

A children's program of music and game contests with host Bob Atcher. ABC 11/15/52 to 12/13/52.

Just Friends

See "Stockard Channing in Just Friends."

Just Married

Comedy Pilot; 30 min; ABC 5/10/85

An unsold series about young newlyweds (Linda and Michael) and their struggles to survive the first year of marriage on a limited income.

Linda Altobello	Gail Edwards
Michael Altobello	Paul Reiser
Jake Shaughnessey	Barton Heyman
Doreen Banasack	Kathleen Wilhoite
Buddy Banasack	Matt Craven
Bob	Tony Longo

Music: George Aliceson Tipton

Producer: Paul Junger Witt, Tony Thomas

Just Men

Game; 30 min; NBC 1/3/83 to 4/1/83

Object: For a female contestant (two compete) to predict with a yes or no answer, how seven male celebrities will respond to questions that are asked of them.

Host: Betty White

Producer: Rick Rosner

Just Our Luck

Comedy; 30 min; ABC 9/20/83 to 1/3/84

While jogging, TV weatherman (later reporter for KPOX, Ch. 6 in Venice, Calif.) Keith Barrow bumps into a souvenir stand and cracks an odd-looking green bottle (which he is forced to buy). Later, Keith's pet cat knocks over the bottle and breaks it. A black genie, named Shabu, emerges from the rubble and becomes Keith's slave. Stories relate Shabu's adventures, having spent 196 years in the bottle, as he struggles to please his new master.

Shabu	T. K. Carter
Keith Barrow	Richard Gilliland
Megan Huxley	Ellen Maxted
Nelson Marriot	Rod McCary
Professor Bob	Hamilton Camp
Chuck	Richard Schaal
Jim Dexter	Leonard Simon
Bag Lady (in open)	Connie Sawyer

Producer: Ronald Frazer

Justice

Drama Pilot; 30 min; ABC 4/12/53

The pilot for the series of the same title. The story, based on a Legal Aid Society file, tells of an impoverished wife who seeks help when she learns that her husband is being blackmailed.

Judge	John Lehine
Wife	Lee Grant
Husband	Paul Douglas

Producer: Herbert Brodkin

Justice

Drama; 30 min; NBC 4/8/54 to 3/25/56

The investigations of Richard Adams and Jason Tyler, attorneys for the Legal Aid Society in New York.

Richard Adams	Dane Clark
	William Prince
Jason Tyler	Gary Merrill

Narrator: Westbrook Van Voorhis

Producer: David Susskind, Gordon Duff

Justice of the Peace

Drama Pilot; 30 min; NBC 6/30/59

The story of Mark Johnston, a small town Justice of the Peace. Aired as "The Vengeance" on "The David Niven Theatre."

Mark Johnston	Dan Duryea
Ellen Johnston	Dorothy Green
Escapee	Adam Williams

Producer: Vincent M. Fennelly

Juvenile Jury

Children; 30 min; NBC 4/3/47 to 10/3/53
CBS 10/11/53 to 9/14/54
NBC 1/2/55 to 3/27/55
Syn. 1971

A panel of five bright children answer questions submitted by home viewers or presented by studio audience members.

Host: Jack Barry

Producer: Jack Barry, Dan Enright, Kenneth Johnson

K-9 and Company

Adventure; 60 min; Syn. 8/85

A spin-off from "Dr. Who." Shortly after Sarah Jane Smith, the beautiful companion to the Tom Baker "Dr. Who," part company, she returns to work as a journalist. Sometime later, when she visits her aunt, she learns that a large crate has been waiting for her. Upon opening it, she discovers its contents to be the mechanical dog, K-9—a gift from the Doctor. Stories relate their experiences as they team to solve crimes.

Sarah Jane Smith	Elisabeth Sladen
Voice of K-9	John Leeson
Sarah's Aunt	
Lavinia	Mary Wimbush

Theme Song ("K-9 and Company") by Fiachra Trench and Ian Levine

Producer: John Nathan Turner

The Kaiser Aluminum Hour

Anthology; 60 min; NBC 7/3/56 to 6/18/57

Dramatic stories that feature such stars as Natalie Wood, Eli Wallach, Andrew Duggan, Nanette Fabray, Jacqueline Scott, Kim Hunter, June Lockhart, Paul Newman, Claude Rains, Roddy McDowall, Forrest Tucker, Jan Sterling, and Albert Salmi. Broadcast on an alternating basis with "The Armstrong Circle Theatre," "The U.S. Steel Hour," "The 20th Century-Fox Hour," and "Playwrights '56."

The Kallikaks

Comedy; 30 min; NBC 8/3/77 to 8/31/77

The story of a poor appalachia family who migrate west (to Nowhere, California) to seek a better life (as the owners of a rundown gas station).

Jasper Kallikak Sr.	David Huddleston
Venus Kallikak	Edie McClurg
Bobbi Lou Kallikak	Bonnie Ebsen
Jasper Kallikak Jr.	Patrick J. Petersen
Oscar Heinz	Peter Palmer

Theme Vocal ("Beat the System"): Roy Clark

Producer: Stanley Ralph Ross, George Yanok

Kangaroos in the Kitchen

Comedy Pilot; 30 min; NBC 7/25/82

The misadventures of Ginny Provost, an animal talent scout whose Greenwich Village (N.Y.) apartment is overrun with animals.

Ginny Provost	Lauralee Bruce
Richard Provost	Sam Freed
Lila	Peggy Pope
Kenneth Beckley	Meeno Peluce
Mrs. Burgess	Nancy Andrews
Judge	Fred Stuthman

Music: Earle Hagen

Producer: David Gerber

Karen

Comedy; 30 min; NBC 10/5/64 to 1/4/65 (segment of "90 Bristol Court")
1/11/65 to 8/30/65 (as "Karen")

Events in the life of Karen Scott, a beautiful high school girl with an uncontrollable penchant for mischief.

Karen Scott	Debbie Watson
Steve Scott	Richard Denning
Barbara Scott	Mary LaRoche
Mimi Scott	Gina Gillespie
Mrs. Rowe	Grace Albertson
Candy	Trudi Ames
Janis	Bernadette Winters
Spider	Murray MacLeod
David	Richard Dreyfuss
Karen's grandmother	Josephine Hutchinson
Cliff Murdock	Guy Raymond

Theme Vocal ("Karen"): The Beach Boys

Producer: Joe Connelly, Bob Mosher

Karen

Comedy; 30 min; ABC 1/30/75 to 6/19/75

The story of Karen Angelo, an idealistic staff worker for Open America, a Capitol Hill citizens' lobby in Washington, D.C.

Karen Angelo	Karen Valentine
Dale W. Bush	Denver Pyle
	Charles Lane
Dena Madison	Dena Dietrich
Cissy Peterson	Aldine King
Adam Cooperman	Will Selzer
Jerry Siegel	Oliver Clark
Cheryl Siegel	Alix Elias
Sen. Bob Hartford	Edward Winter
Captain Pike	Liam Dunn
Ernie	Joseph Stone

Producer: Gene Reynolds, Larry Gelbart

The Karen Valentine Show

Comedy Pilot; 30 min; ABC 5/21/73

The story of Karen Scott, a beautiful Girl Friday to Buddy Loudon, a zany public relations dynamo who handles clients nobody else wants.

Karen Scott	Karen Valentine
Buddy Loudon	Charles Nelson Reilly
Eddie	Kenneth Mars
Chic	Henry Gibson
Sam	Louis Zorich
Regis Philbin	Himself

Producer: William P. D'Angelo

Karen's Song

Comedy; 30 min; FOX 7/18/87 to 9/12/87

An honest approach to the problems of an older woman-younger man relationship as seen through the experiences of Karen Matthews, a 40-year-old publishing executive, and Steve Foreman, a 28-year-old food caterer.

Karen Matthews	Patty Duke
Steve Foreman	Louis Smith
Claire Steiner	Lainie Kazan
Laura Matthews	Teri Hatcher
Michael Brand	Charles Levin

Producer: Margie Peters, Linda Marsh

Kate and Allie

Comedy; 30 min; CBS 3/19/84 (Premiere)

Kate and Allie, divorced mothers and friends since high school, decide to save on expenses by sharing a Greenwich Village apartment. Stories relate events in the lives of the two families as they attempt to live together.

Kate McArdle	Susan Saint James
Allie Lowell	Jane Curtin
Jennie Lowell	Allison Smith
Emma McArdle	Ari Meyers
Chip Lowell	Frederick Koehler
Charles Lowell (Allie's ex-husband)	Paul Hecht
Ted Bartelo	Gregory Salanta
Allie's mother	Rosemary Murphy
Max (Kate's ex-husband)	John Herd

Theme Vocal ("Along Comes a Friend"): John Leffler

Producer: Mort Lachman, Merrill Grant

Kate Loves a Mystery

Mystery; 60 min; NBC 10/18/79 to 12/6/79

Following her divorce from famed TV detective Lt. Columbo, Kate resumes her maiden name (Callahan) and acquires a job as a reporter for the "Valley Advocate" in San Fernando. Stories relate her investigations. See also "Mrs. Columbo."

Kate Callahan   Kate Mulgrew
Jenny Callahan   Lili Haydn
Josh Alden   Henry Jones
Sgt. Mike Varrick   Don Stroud
Stuart   Robert Hardy
Mrs. Barish   Ceil Cabot

Producer: Bill Driskill, James McAdams

Kate McShane

Crime Drama; 60 min; CBS 9/10/75 to 11/12/75

The cases of Kate McShane, an uninhibited and unorthodox lawyer working in Los Angeles.

Kate McShane   Anne Merara
Pat McShane   Sean McClory
Ed McShane   Charles Haid
Julie   Rachel Malkin

Producer: E. Jack Neumann

The Kate Smith Evening Hour

Variety; 60 min; NBC 9/19/51 to 6/11/52

A prime-time version of the following title that features music and songs with Kate Smith.

Hostess: Kate Smith

Regulars: Ted Collins, Susan Douglas, Paul Lukas, Ann Thomas, The Jack Allison Singers, The John Butler Dancers, The Stuart Morgan Dancers

Announcer: Bob Warren

Orchestra: Harry Sosnik

Producer: Ted Collins, Greg Garrison, Barry Wood

The Kate Smith Hour

Variety; 60 min; NBC 9/25/50 to 6/18/54

An afternoon program of music, songs, and comedy. Featured segments: "Ethel and Albert" (with Peg Lynch, Alan Bunce), "The World of Mr. Sweeney" (Charlie Ruggles, Glenn Walker), "House in the Garden" (Vignettes about small town life), and "The Talent Showcase."

Hostess: Kate Smith

Regulars: Peggy Ryan, Jeff Clark, Nelson Ray, Ray MacDonald, Fran Barber, Billy Mills, Robert Maxwell, Diane Carol, Ruth Mattheson, Barry Wood, Dorothy Day, Lauren Gilbert, Arlene Dalton, The McGuire Sisters, The John Butler Dancers, The Jack Allison Singers

Announcer: Andre Baruch

Orchestra: Jack Miller

Producer: Ted Collins, Barry Wood

The Kate Smith Show

Variety; 30 min; CBS 1/25/60 to 7/18/60

A weekly series of music, songs, and light comedy.

Hostess: Kate Smith

Regulars: The Harry Simeone Chorale

Orchestra: Neal Hefti, Bill Stegmeyer

Producer: Ted Collins, Jack Philbin

Kay Kyser's Kollege of Musical Knowledge

Variety-Quiz; 30 min; NBC 12/1/49 to 9/12/54

Musical numbers are interspersed with a quiz segment wherein players must identify song titles from a few bars that are played by the orchestra.

Host: Kay Kyser, Tennessee Ernie Ford

Regulars: Mike Douglas, Liza Palmer, Sue Bennett, Ken Spaulding, Donna Brown, Maureen Cassidy, Spring Mitchell, Diana Sinclair, The Honeydreamers

Announcer: Jack Narz, Verne Smith

Orchestra: Carl Hoff, Kay Kyser, Frank DeVol

Producer: Perry Lafferty

Kay O'Brien

Drama; 60 min; CBS 9/25/86 to 11/13/86

The victories and defeats of Kay "Kayo" O'Brien, an attractive second year surgical resident at Manhattan General Hospital in New York City. Filmed in Canada. Originally titled "Kay O'Brien, Surgeon."

Dr. Kay O'Brien	Patricia Kalember
Dr. Robert Moffitt	Lane Smith
Nurse Rosa	
Villanueva	Priscilla Lopez
Dr. Mark Doyle	Brian Benben
Dr. Cliff Margolis	Tony Soper
Dr. Michael Kwan	Keone Young
Dr. Josef Wallach	Jan Rubes
Jack O'Brien (Kay's	
father)	John McMartin
Lucille O'Brien	
(Kay's mother)	Scotty Block
Lee Villanueva	
(Rosa's husband)	Walter Boone
Allison (Rosa's	
daughter)	Lisa Jakub
Danny (Rosa's son)	Stuart Stone

"Kay O'Brien" Theme Song: Mark Snow

Producer: William Asher, Diana Gould, Brad Markowitz

The Kay Starr Show

A syndicated (1957) series of music and songs with Kay Starr and the orchestra of Pete King.

Kaz

Crime Drama; 60 min; CBS 9/10/78 to 8/19/79

While serving a six-year sentence for auto theft, Martin "Kaz" Kazinski studies to become a lawyer. Following his release, and passing the bar exam, he acquires a position with the Los Angeles firm of Bennett, Reinhart, and Calcourt. Stories relate his investigations.

Martin Kazinski	Ron Leibman
Samuel Bennett	Patrick O'Neal
Mary Parnell	Gloria LeRoy
Malloy	Dick O'Neill
Katie McKenna	Linda Carlson
Irv	Floyd Levine
Illsa Fogel	Edith Atwater
D.A. Frank Revko	George Wyner

Producer: Lee Rich, Marc Merson

The Keane Brothers Show

Variety; 30 min; CBS 8/12/77 to 9/2/77

A weekly program of music and songs.

Hosts: John and Tom Keane

Regulars: Jimmy Caesar, The Anita Mann Dancers

Orchestra: Alan Copeland

Producer: Pierre Cossette

The Keefe Brasselle Show

Variety; 60 min; CBS 6/2/63 to 9/17/63

A weekly program of music, songs, and light comedy.

Host: Keefe Brasselle

Regulars: Ann B. Davis, Rocky Graziano, Noelle Adam, The Style Sisters, The Buddy Foster Dancers

Orchestra: Charles Sanford

Producer: Keefe Brasselle, Greg Garrison

Keep it in the Family

Game; 30 min; ABC 10/12/57 to 2/8/58

Two five-member families compete in a game wherein each member, beginning with the youngest, must answer general-knowledge questions.

Host: Keefe Brasselle

Announcer: Johnny Olsen

Keep on Crusin'

Variety; 60 min; CBS 1/9/87 (Premiere)

A weekly series that showcases music and comedy acts from Los Angeles.

Host: Stephen Bishop

Co-Host: SinBad

Music: Stephen Bishop

Producer: Dick Clark, Barry Adelman, Larry Kline

Keep on Truckin'

Comedy; 60 min; ABC 7/12/75 to 8/2/75

A potpourri of broad comedy skits and free-wheeling spoofs and blackouts.

Regulars: Didi Conn, Fred Travalena, Rhonda Bates, Wayland Flowers, Richard Lee Sung, Jeannie Burnier, Katherine Baumann, Charles Fleischer, Franklyn Ajaye, Gailard Sartain, Larry Ragland

Orchestra: Marvin Laird

Producer: Frank Peppiatt, John Aylesworth

Keep Talking

Game; 30 min; CBS 7/15/58 to 9/2/59
            ABC 10/19/59 to 5/3/60

Two two-member celebrity teams compete. One member is given a secret phrase that he must work into an ad-libbed story. His teammate must identify the phrase within a specific time limit. Celebrities prizes are awarded to home and studio audience members.

Host: Monty Hall, Carl Reiner, Merv Griffin

Panelists: Joey Bishop, Ilka Chase, Elaine May, Audrey Meadows, Morey Amsterdam, Orson Bean, Paul Winchell, Pat Carroll, Peggy Cass, Danny Dayton

Producer: Lester Gottlieb

Keep the Faith

Comedy Pilot; 30 min; CBS 4/14/72

The various misadventures of two rabbis (Miller and Mossman).

Rabbi Miller	Bert Convy
Rabbi Mossman	Howard DaSilva
Hosentha	Henry Corden
Sophie	Nancy Walker
Judy	Linda March
Pink	Milton Selzer

Director: Jackie Cooper

Keeper of the Wild

Drama Pilot; 30 min; Syn. 1/77

The experiences of Jim, Holly, and Paul, the owners of an animal preserve in Africa.

Jim Donaldson	Denny Miller
Holly James	Pamela Susan Shoop
Paul Limkula	James Reynolds

Producer: Leonard B. Kaufman

Keeping an Eye on Denise

Comedy Pilot; 30 min; CBS 6/19/73

The story of a happy-go-lucky single who is suddenly saddled with the care of an uninhibited teenage daughter he never knew he had from a Korean War romance.

Father	Jackie Cooper
Denise (daughter)	Lynne Frederick
Friend	Richard Dawson

Producer: Harry Ackerman, Hy Averback

Keeping Up with the Joneses

Comedy Pilot; 30 min; NBC 4/24/72

The story of two couples, one white (Ernie and Pat) and one black (Walt and Liz) who share the same New York brownstone and the same surname—Jones.

Ernie Jones	Warren Berlinger
Pat Jones	Pat Finley
Walt Jones	John Amos
Liz Jones	Teresa Graves

Producer: Douglas S. Cramer, Gordon Farr, Arnold Kane

Kelly Monteith

Comedy; 30 min; TEC 7/82 to 3/83

A British produced series of comedy skits about life with American comedian Kelly Monteith.

Host: Kelly Monteith

Regulars: Gabrielle Drake, Nicholas McArdle, Louise Mansi, Michael Stainton

Music: Ronnie Hazelhurst

Producer: James Moir

The Kelly Monteith Show

Variety; 30 min; CBS 6/16/76 to 7/7/76

A weekly series of music and comedy sketches.

Host: Kelly Monteith

Regulars: Nellie Bellflower, Henry Corden

Orchestra: Dick DeBenedictis

Producer: Robert Tamplin

Kelly's Kids

Comedy Pilot; 30 min; ABC 1/4/74

Events in the lives of Ken and Kathy Kelly, a childless couple who adopt three children of different ethnic backgrounds: Matt (white), Steve (Oriental), and Dwayne (black). Aired on "The Brady Bunch." Revised twelve years later as "Together We Stand" (which see).

Ken Kelly	Ken Berry
Kathy Kelly	Brooke Bundy
Matt	Todd Lookinland
Steve	Carey Wong
Dwayne	William Attmore
Mrs. Payne	Molly Dodd
Miss Phillips	Jackie Joseph

Producer: Sherwood Schwartz

The Ken Berry Wow Show

Variety; 60 min; ABC 7/15/72 to 8/12/72

The music, song, and comedy of the 1930s through the 1960s.

Host: Ken Berry

Regulars: Cheryl Ladd, Billy Van, Steve Martin, Teri Garr, Carl Gottlieb, Barbara Joyce, Don Ray, The New Seekers, The Jaime Rogers Dancers

Orchestra: Jimmy Dale

Producer: Allan Blye, Chris Bearde

The Ken Murray Show

Variety; 60 min; CBS 1/7/50 to 6/21/53

Novelty acts, music, songs, dramatic vignettes, and blackouts.

Host: Ken Murray

Regulars: Darla Jean Hood, Joe Besser, Laurie Anders, Betty Lou Walters, Art Lund, Pat Conway, Jack Marshall, Johnny Johnston, Anita Gordon, Herbert Marshall, Lillian Farmer, The Ken Murray Dancers, The Glamour Lovelies

Announcer: Nelson Case

Orchestra: David Broekman, Jane Bergmeler

Producer: Ken Murray, Ben Brady, Howard Reilly, Frank Salem

The Kenny Everett Video Show

Variety; 30 min; Syn. 9/81

An imaginative series that incorporates many visual and audio effects to present music and comedy skits. Produced in England.

Host: Kenny Everett

Regulars: Kay Bush, Katie Boyle, Arlene Phillips, Hot Gossip (sexy female singers and dancers)

Producer: David Mallet

Kentucky Jones

Drama; 30 min; NBC 9/19/64 to 9/11/65

Shortly after the death of his wife, ranch owner Kenneth "Kentucky" Jones, attempts but fails to stop the adoption of a Chinese orphan he and his wife had planned to raise. Stories relate Kentucky's efforts, assisted by his partner, Seldom Jackson, to raise ten-year-old Dwight Eisenhower "Ike" Wong.

Kentucky Jones	Dennis Weaver
Seldom Jackson	Harry Morgan
Ike Wong	Ricky Der
Annie Ng	Cherylene Lee
Thomas Wong	Keye Luke
Miss Thorncroft	Nancy Rennick
Mr. Ng	Arthur Wong

Music: Vic Mizzy

Producer: Buzz Kulik

Key Club Playhouse

An ABC series (5/31/57 to 10/11/57) of episodes that originally aired on "Ford Theatre."

Key Tortuga

Adventure Pilot; 60 min; CBS 9/11/81

The exploits of John Tyree, captain of the Hemingston, the boat he uses as the owner of a fishing charter and salvage service in Key Tortuga, Florida.

John Tyree	Scott Thomas
Laura Tyree	Janet Julian
Matt Tyree	Brett Cullen
Cyclone Williams	Paul Winfield

Producer: Arthur Fellows, Terry Keegan

Khan!

Crime Drama; 60 min; CBS 2/7/75 to 2/28/75

The exploits of Khan, a Chinese private detective working out of San Francisco's Chinatown. "Khan!" is the only known series in which the star refused billing.

Det. Khan	Khigh Dhiegh
Anna Khan	Irene Yah-Ling Sun
Kim Khan	Evan Kim
Lt. Gubbins	Vic Tayback
Kibbee	Michael Bell
Fitch	Chuck McCann
Kate	Lynnette Mettey
Peg	Bonnie Boland
Capt. Fox	Alan Oppenheimer
Walter	George Furth
Nun	Reva Rose
Cop	Noam Pitlik
Grogan	Bob Hastings
Monica	Valorie Armstrong
Henshaw	Johnny Haymer
Fireman	Keith Walker

Producer: Laurence Heath, Joseph Henry

Music: Frank DeVol

Producer-Writer: Fred Freeman, Larry Cohen

Director: Robert Scheerer

Kibbee Hates Fitch

Comedy Pilot; 30 min; CBS 8/2/65

The story of two New York City firemen (Kibbee and Fitch) and the misadventures that occur when Kibbee is promoted to captain of Hook and Ladder Company No. 23. The program has the screen title of "The Neighbors"; "Kibbee Hates Fitch" is the TV Guide and press release title. See the following title also.

Russell Kibbee	Don Rickles
Arthur Fitch	Lou Jacobi
Marcia Fitch	Pert Kelton
Selena Kibbee	Nancy Andrews
Kevin Kibbee	William Ade
Nancy Fitch	Karleen Wiese
Captain O'Brien	Ralph Dunne
Callahan	Herb Edelman
Walsh	Bob Kaliban

Producer-Director: Stanley Prager

Writer-Creator: Neil Simon

Kibbee Hates Fitch, Fitch Hates Kibbee

Comedy Pilot; 30 min; Unaired (Produced in 1974)

A remake of the above United Artists title (this one produced by Paramount) about two sisters (Kate and Peg) who marry two bickering firemen (Kibbee and Fitch) and who happen to live the same duplex.

Kicks

A syndicated (1979) series of performances by disco stars. Hosted by Jeff Kutash and produced by Kip Walton.

The Kid-a-Littles

Comedy; 30 min; Syn. 9/84

The series, set in the offices of a newspaper called "The Daily Typo," relates learning experiences to children via the puppet characters who work for editor Clipper (the only live character).

Editor Clipper   John Wheeler

Puppeteers/Voices: Wayne Katz, Tony Pope, Alice Tweedle, Alan Tuterman

Producer: Gary Blohm

Kid Gloves

Children; 30 min; CBS 2/24/51 to 8/4/51

Two children compete in a series of three thirty-second boxing bouts that follow the rules of the professionals.

Commentator: Bill Sears

Referee: Frank Goodman

Ring Announcer: Barry Cassel

Producer: Alan Bergman

Kid Power

Cartoon; 30 min; ABC 9/16/72 to 9/1/74

The story of a group of children (Rainbow Club members) as they share thoughts on teamwork and responsibility.

Wellington	Charles Kennedy Jr.
Oliver	Jay Silverheels Jr.
Nipper	John Gardiner
Jerry	Allan Melvin
Connie	Carey Wong
Sybil	Michele Johnson
Diz	Jeff Thomas
Ralph	Gary Shapiro
Albert	Greg Thomas

Producer: Arthur Rankin Jr., Jules Bass

The Kid Super Power Hour with Shazam

Cartoon; 60 min; NBC 9/12/81 to 9/11/82

Segments; "Hero High" (the exploits and antics of the students at Hero High, a school for super heroes); "Shazam!" (the adventures of Billy Batson, alias Shazam, Mary Freeman, alias Mary Marvel, and Freddy Freeman, alias Captain Marvel).

Capt. California	Christopher Hensel
Glorious Gal	Becky Perle
Dirty Trixie	Maylo McCaslin
Misty Magic	Jere Fields
Rex Ruthless	John Berwick
Weatherman	John Greenleaf
Punk Rock	John Venocour
Mr. Sampson	Alan Oppenheimer
Miss Grim	Erica Scheimer
Mary Freeman	Erica Scheimer
Billy Batson	Burr Middleton
Freddy Freeman	Barry Gordon

Producer: Lou Scheimer, Norm Prescott

Kid Talk

Children; 30 min; Syn. 1972

Two guest celebrites discuss topical issues with four children.

Host: Bill Adler

Panelists: Mona Tera, Andy Yamamoto, Nellie Henderson, Alan Winston

Announcer: Johnny Olsen

Producer: Bill Adler

Kidd Video

Cartoon; 30 min; NBC 9/15/84 (Premiere)

While rehearsing, the rock group Kidd Video is transported to an animated flip side of reality by the evil wizard Master Blaster. Stories relate their adventures as they seek the way back to reality.

Kidd Video	Bryan Scott
Carla	Gabrielle Bennett
Whiz	Robbie Rist
Ash	Steve Alterman
Glitter	Cathy Cavadini
Master Blaster	Peter Renady
Fat Cat	Marshall Efron
Cool Kitty	Robert Towers

Producer: Andy Heyward, Jean Chalopin

Kideo TV

Cartoon; 90 min; Syn. 4/86

The title for three half-hour cartoons (which see): "The Popples," "Rainbow Brite," and "Ulysses 31."

Kids and Company

Variety; 30 min; DuMont 9/1/51 to 6/1/52

Performances by aspiring child talent.

Host: Johnny Olsen

Assistant: Ham Fisher

Organist: Al Greiner

Kids are People Too

Children; 90 & 60 min; ABC 9/10/78 to 12/19/82

Various entertainment (cartoons, skits, interviews) that is geared to show children that they are people too.

Host: Bob McAllister, Michael Young, Randy Hamilton

Regulars: Ellie Dylan, Joy Behar

Producer: Lawrence Einhorn, Marilyn Olin

Kids' Biz

Magazine Pilot; 30 min; Syn. 11/86

A program of music, fashion, advice, exercise, and other information and entertainment for children.

Hostess: Stacy Scott

Regular: Suzy Stone

Producer: Stacy Scott, Jim Duffy

The Kids from C.A.P.E.R.

Comedy; 30 min; NBC 9/11/76 to 9/3/77

The escapades of four teenage boys (P.T., Bugs, Doomsday, and Doc) who comprise the Civilian Authority for the Protection of Everybody, Regardless) a special crime-fighting unit of Northeast Southwestern's 927th Police Precinct.

P.T.	Steve Bonino
Bugs	Cosie Costa
Doomsday	Biff Warren
Doc	John Lansing
Reporter Clintsinger	Robert Lussier

Producer: Alan Landsburg, Don Kirshner, Stanley Z. Cherry

Kids Incorporated

Comedy; 30 min; Syn. 9/85

The adventures of five talented children who comprise a rock group called Kids Incorporated.

Gloria	Martika Marrero
Stacy	Stacy Ferguson
Renee	Renee Sands
Ryan	Ryan Lambert
Kid	Rashaan Patterson
Riley (club owner)	Moosie Drier

Producer: Earl Glick

The Kidsong TV Show

Children; 30 min; Syn. 9/87

When a group of children discover an abandoned TV studio, they make it their clubhouse. Soon they learn how to operate the equipment and set up their own station—Kidsongs. Borrowing its format from "Your Hit Parade," the series presents songs for children sung by children (the Kidsong Kids).

Hosts: Tristen Potter, Chris Lytton

The Kidsong Kids: Todd Alyn Durboraw, David Chan, Julie Ann Gourson, Hillary Hollingsworth, Tiffany Johnson, Nicole Mandich, Robby Rosellen, Scott Trent

Producer: Bruce Gowers, Carol Rosenstein

Kiernan's Kaleidoscope

A syndicated (1949) children's series, hosted by John Kiernan, that explores scientific principals.

Kimba, the White Lion

Cartoon; 30 min; Syn. 1966

A Japanese-produced series about Kimba, a rare African white lion, and his efforts to protect his homeland from evil.

Kimba	Billie Lou Watt

"Kimba, the White Lion" theme song: Florence Kaye, Bernie Baum, Bill Grant

Kincaid

Drama Pilot; 60 min; ABC 4/22/63

The story of Andy Kincaid, a sergeant with the juvenile division of a large metropolitan police department. Aired on "Stoney Burke."

Sgt. Andy Kincaid	Dick Clark
Dianne Banner	Sarah Marshall
Frankie Sommers	David Macklin
Lip	David Winters

Producer: Bob Barbash

The King Family Show

Variety; ABC 1/23/65 to 1/8/66 (30 min)
3/12/69 to 9/10/69 (60 min)

A weekly program of music and song featuring the thirty-six member King Family.

Featured: Tina Cole, The King Cousins, The King Sisters

Orchestra: Alvino Rey

Producer: Yvonne King Birch, Louise King Rey, Del Jack, Nick Vanoff

Director: Tony Charmoli

King Features Trilogy

Cartoon; 30 min; Syn. 8/63

Segments: "Barney Google" (a hillbilly hustler and his friend, Snuffy); "Beetle Bailey" (antics of a private at Camp Swampy); "Krazy Kat" (a love-sick cat plagued by Ignatz Mouse).

Barney Google	Allan Melvin
Snuffy Smith	Howard Morris
Beetle Bailey	Howard Morris
Sgt. Snorkel	Allan Melvin
Krazy Kat	Penny Phillips
Ignatz Mouse	Paul Frees

Producer: Paul Brodax

The King Kong Show

Cartoon; 30 min; ABC 9/10/66 to 8/31/69

While exploring Mondo Island, Bobby Bond, the son of a professor, befriends the legendary King Kong. Stories relate Professor Bond's efforts, assisted by Bobby and Kong, to battle the evils of a power-mad scientist named Dr. Who.

Producer: Arthur Rankin Jr

King Leonardo and His Short Subjects

Cartoon; 30 min; NBC 10/15/60 to 9/28/63

Segments: "King Leonardo" (adventures of the ruler of Bongoland and his assistant, Odie Colognie, as they battle the evil Itchy Brother and Biggy Rat); "The Hunter" (a beagle detective's efforts to apprehend the cunning Fox) "Tutor the Turtle" (a turtle becomes whatever he wishes through the magic of Mr. Wizard, the lizard).

King Leonardo	Jackson Beck
Odie Colognie	Allen Swift
Biggy Rat	Jackson Beck
Itchy Brother	Allen Swift
The Hunter	Kenny Delmar
The Fox	Ben Stone
Tutor	Allen Swift
Mr. Wizard	Frank Milano

Producer: Treadwell Covington, Peter Piech

King of Diamonds

Adventure; 30 min; Syn. 9/61

The exploits of John King, a rugged investigator for the diamond industry.

John King	Broderick Crawford
Casey O'Brien	Ray Hamilton

Producer: John Robinson

King of Kensington

Comedy; 30 min; Syn. 1977

Events in the life of Larry King, the owner of King's Variety Store in Kensington (Toronto, Canada). Produced in Canada in 1975.

Larry King	Al Waxman
Cathy King	Fiona Reid
Gladys King	Helene Winston
Nestor Best	Ardon Bess
Duke Zaro	Bob Vinci
Max	John J. Dee
Rosa Zaro	Vivian Reis

Theme Vocal ("King of Kensington"): Bob Francis

Producer: Perry Rosemond

King of the Road

Comedy Pilot; 30 min; CBS 5/10/78

Following his retirement, singer Cotton Grimes buys a motel in Muscle Shoals, Alabama. The unsold series was to relate his adventures running the motel.

Cotton Grimes	Roger Miller
Maureen Kenney	Lee Crawford
Sam Braffman	Larry Haines
Mildred Braffman	Marian Mercer
Billy Dee Huff	R. G. Brown
Rick	Ric Carrott
John Davidson	Himself
Jenny Kleegle	Jenny Neumann
Karen Kleegle	Karen Specht
Beth Kleegle	Beth Specht

Producer: Norman Lear, Jerry Weintraub

King's Crossing

Drama; 60 min; ABC 1/16/82 to 2/27/82

The lives of the Hollisters, a close-knit family who move from Chicago to King's Crossing, a small California village, to rebuild their shattered lives.

Paul Hollister	Bradford Dillman
Nan Hollister	Mary Frann
Carey Hollister	Marilyn Jones
Lauren Hollister	Linda Hamilton
Louisa Beauchamp	Beatrice Straight
Billy McCall	Daniel Zippi
Jillian	Doran Clark
Willa	Jean LeBouvier
	Dorothy Meyer
Jonathan Hardari	Michael Zaslow
Carol Hardari	Stephanie Braxton
Sam Garrett	Mitchell Ryan
Robert Garrett	Brian Patrick Clarke

"King's Crossing" Theme Song: Jerrold Immel

Producer: Lee Rich, Michael Filerman

King's Crossroads

The program features first televised showings of theatrical shorts. Hosted and narrated by Carl King and broadcast on ABC (10/10/51 to 10/10/52).

King's Party Line

Variety; 30 min; CBS 7/13/46 to 12/28/46

An early program of music and audience participation segments for prizes.

Host: Carl King

Producer-Director: Frances Buss

King's Row

Drama; 60 min; ABC 9/13/55 to 1/17/56

The story of Parris Mitchell, a psychiatrist in the town of King's Row at the turn of the century. Aired on "Warner Brothers Presents."

Dr. Parris Mitchell	Jack Kelly
Randy Monaghan	Nan Leslie
Elsie Sandor	Peggy Webber
Drake McHugh	Robert Horton
Dr. Alex Tower	Victor Jory
Dr. Gordon	Robert Burton

Host: Gig Young

Producer: Roy Huggins

Kingpins

Comedy Pilot; 30 min; CBS 9/18/87

The misadventures of Hank Whittaker, the harrassed owner of a bowling alley (Kingpins) in Akron, Ohio.

Hank Whittaker	Dorian Harewood
Lindsay Whittaker	Marie-Alise
	Recasner
Sonny Whittaker	Ji-Tu Cumbuka
Darla Easterwood	Diana Bellamy
Deter Philbin	David Alan Grier
Vince Haines	Bill Henderson
Vern Puckett	Jason Bernard
Spud Bunsen	Leonard Garner
Milt Simmons	Tommy Hicks

Producer: Barton Dean

Kingston: Confidential

Crime Drama; 60 min; NBC 3/23/77 to 8/10/77

The story of R. B. Kingston, editor-in-chief of the Frazier News Group, an organization of newspapers and TV stations in California.

R. B. Kingston	Raymond Burr
Beth Kelly	Pamela Hensley
Jessica Frazier	Lenka Peterson*
	Nancy Olson
Lt. Vokeman	Milt Kogan

Producer: David Victor

*Pilot role (2 hrs, 9/15/76)

Kissyfur

Cartoon; 30 min; NBC 12/15/85 (Premiere)

Dissatisfied with life in the circus, a young cub (Kissyfur) and his father (Gus) leave the big top and begin life elsewhere. Stories relate their adventures as they attempt to enjoy their new lives in a swampland kingdom.

Voices: Neilson Ross, Russi Taylor, Lennie Weinrib, Frank Welker, Edmund Gilbert, Terence McGovern, R. J. Williams

Producer: Andy Heyward, Jean Chalopin

The Kitty Wells/Johnny Wright Family Show

A syndicated (1969) program of country and western music with hosts Kitty Wells and

Johnny Wright, and regulars Carol Sue Wright, Bill Phillips, Bobby Wright, and Rudy Wright.

Klein Time

Comedy; 30 min; CBS 8/2/77

A proposed series of comedy sketches.

Host: Robert Klein

Regulars: Michael Keaton, Gailard Sartain, Hilary Bean

Guests: Madeline Khan, Peter Boyle

Producer: Bud Austin

Klondike

Adventure; 30 min; NBC 10/10/60 to 2/13/61

The series, set in Alaska in the late 1890s, relates the struggles of Kathy O'Hara as she attempts to maintain an honest hotel; and the adventures of Mike Halliday as he searches for gold in the Northland.

Kathy O'Hara	Marie Blanchard
Mike Halliday	Ralph Taeger
Jeff Durain	James Coburn
Goldie	Joi Lansing
Kathy's Uncle Jonah	J. Pat O'Malley
Joe Teel	L. Q. Jones

"Klondike" theme song: Vic Mizzy

Producer: William Conrad

A Knight in Shining Armour

Comedy Pilot; 30 min; ABC 3/19/71

The pilot for "Getting Together." The story of a composer (Bobby) and a tone-deaf lyricist (Lionel) as they attempt to make a name for themselves in the music world. Aired on "The Partridge Family."

Bobby Conway	Bobby Sherman
Lionel Poindexter	Wes Stern

Producer: Paul Junger Witt

Knight Rider

Adventure; 60 min; NBC 9/26/82 to 8/8/86

When Police officer Michael Long is shot, he is saved by Wilton Knight, a dying billionaire who arranges life-saving surgery, including a new face and identity—that of Michael Knight. Michael is then given a special Trans-Am car (the Knight Industries 2000, nicknamed KITT) and a mission: apprehend criminals that are above the reach of the law. Stories relate Michael's exploits as he performs missions for the Foundation for Law and Government.

Michael Knight	David Hasselhoff
Devon Miles	Edward Mulhare
Voice of KITT	William Daniels
Bonnie Barstow	Patricia McPherson
April Curtis	Rebecca Holden
Garthe Knight (Wilton's evil son)	David Hasselhoff
Voice of KARR*	Peter Cullen
Reginald Corneilius III	Peter Parros
Stevie Mason	Catherine Hickland
Jennifer Knight (Wilton's daughter)	Kate McGeehan
Wilton Knight	Richard Basehart

Producer: Glen A. Larson, Robert Cinader, Robert Foster

*Knight Automated Roving Robot, the evil prototype for KITT.

Knight's Gambit

Drama Pilot; 60 min; NBC 3/26/64

The story of Anthony Knight, a reporter who uses unorthodox methods to acquire stories.

Anthony Knight	Roger Smith
Dorian Smith	Eleanor Parker
Blaine Davis	Chester Morris
Douglas Henderson	Murray Mateson
Tout	Vito Scotti
Bijou	Erika Peters

Music: Johnny Williams

Producer: Robert Blees

Knockout

Game; 30 min; NBC 10/3/77 to 4/21/78

Three contestants compete in a game wherein they must spell the word "knockout" by identifying the one out-of-place item in four items that are shown. Each correct identification awards the player one letter of the word. The first player to spell the word wins merchandise prizes.

Host: Arte Johnson

Announcer: Jay Stewart

Producer: Ralph Edwards

Knots Landing

Drama; 60 min; CBS 12/27/79 (Premiere)

A spin-off from "Dallas," which set in fictional Knots Landing, California, follows the lives of Valene and Gary Ewing, the out-cast members of the oil-rich Ewing family of Dallas.

Valene Ewing	Joan Van Ark
Gary Ewing	Ted Shackelford
Karen Fairgate	Michele Lee
Sid Fairgate	Don Murray
Ginger Ward	Kim Lankford
Kenny Ward	James Houghton
Laura Avery	Constance McCashin
Richard Avery	John Pleshette
Abby Cunningham	Donna Mills
Lilimae Clements	Julie Harris
Diana Fairgate	Claudia Lonow
Mack McKenzie	Kevin Dobson
Greg Sumner	William Devane
Ruth Sumner	Ava Gardner
Mary Sumner	Danielle Brisebois
Ciji Dunn/Cathy Geary	Lisa Hartman
Jillian Meredith	Teri Austin
Joe Cooper	Stephen Macht
Annie Fairgate	Karen Allen
Michael Fairgate	Pat Peterson
Olivia Cunningham	Tonya Crowe
Jason Avery	Justin Dana
	Danny Gellis
	Danny Ponce
Susan Philby	Claudette Nevins
Brian Cunningham	Bobby Jacoby
Jeff Cunningham	Barry Jenner
Ben Gibson	Douglas Sheehan
Det. Janet Raines	Joanna Pettet
Tony Finese (alias Chip Roberts)	Michael Sabatino
Paul Galveston	Howard Duff
Annette Cunningham	Carol Bruce
Sylvia Lean	Ruth Roman
Peter Hollister	Hunt Block
Eric Fairgate	Steve Shaw
Paige	Nicollette Sheridan
Anne Winston	Michelle Phillips

"Knots Landing" Theme: Jerrold Immel

Producer: Lee Rich, Michael Filerman, David Jacobs

Kobb's Corner

Variety; 30 min; CBS 10/6/48 to 6/15/49

Music, songs, and comedy set at the Shufflebottom General Store, a southern establishment that sponsors a variety get-together on Wednesday evenings.

Maw Shufflebottom	Hope Emerson
Josie Belle Shufflebottom	Jo Hurt

Regulars: Jimmy Allen, Stan Fritz, Marty Gold, Joan Nobles, Eddie Grosso, Howard McElroy, Charlie Koenig, The Korn Kobblers

Producer: Barry Wood

Kodak Request Performance

An NBC series (4/13/55 to 9/28/55) of repeat anthology dramas sponsored by Kodak.

Kodiak

Crime Drama; 30 min; ABC 9/13/74 to 10/11/74

The exploits of Cal McKay, a member of the Alaska State Police Patrol.

Cal McKay	Clint Walker
Abraham Imhook	Abner Biberman
Mandy	Maggie Blye

Producer: Stan Shpetner

Kojak

Crime Drama; 60 min; CBS 10/24/73 to 4/1/78

The exploits of Lt. Theo Kojak, a plainclothes detective with New York's Manhattan South Precinct.

Lt. Theo Kojak	Telly Savalas
Chief Frank McNeil	Dan Frazer
Lt. Bobby Crocker	Kevin Dobson
Det. Stavros	George Savalas
Det. Rizzo	Vince Conti
Det. Saperstein	Mark Russell
Det. Agajanian	Darrell Zivering
Det. Prince	Borah Silver
Marie Stella (restaurant owner)	Carole Cooke
Irene Van Patten (Theo's love interest)	Diane Baker

Producer: Matthew Rapf, James McAdams, Jack Laird

Komedy Tonite

Variety Pilot; 60 min; NBC 5/9/78

A proposed series of music and comedy starring black performers.

Regulars: Cleavon Little, Paula Kelly, Marion Ramsey, Shon Vaughn, Charles Valentino

Orchestra: H. B. Barnum

Producer: Lawrence Kasha

The Kopycats

Variety; 60 min; ABC 6/21/72 to 8/10/72

The program features skits involving impersonations of show-business personalities.

Kopycats: Rich Little, Marilyn Michaels, Frank Gorshin, Charlie Callis, George Kirby, Joe Baker, Fred Travalena

Featured: The Norman Maen Dancers

Orchestra: Jack Parnell

Producer: Gary Smith, Dwight Hemion

Korg: 70,000 B.C.

Adventure; 30 min; ABC 9/7/74 to 8/31/75

The series, set in 70,000 B.C., and based on assumptions, relates the struggles of a Neanderthal family.

Korg	Jim Malinda
Bok	Bill Ewing
Mara	Naomi Pollack
Tane	Christopher Man
Tor	Charles Morted
Ree	Janelle Pransky

Producer: William Hanna, Joseph Barbera

Kosta and His Family

Comedy Pilot; 60 min; NBC 12/31/73

The misadventures of Herb Kosta, an unemployed aerospace technician too qualified for the jobs he might find, and his slightly wacky family.

Herb Kosta	Herb Edelman
Isabel Kosta	Barbara Barrie
Gina Kosta	Ellen Sherman
Jimmy Kosta	Jack David Walker
Al Kosta	Albert Anderson

Producer: Leonard B. Stern

Kovacs on the Corner

Comedy; 60 min; NBC 1/7/51 to 3/28/52

Sketches and blackouts that satirize everyday life.

Host: Ernie Kovacs

Regulars: Edie Adams, Peter Boyle

Music: The Dave Appel Trio

Producer: Ned Cramer, Joe Behar

The Kowboys

Comedy Pilot; 30 min; NBC 7/13/70

A musical comedy about the exploits of four flower children (Matthew, Smitty, Zak, and Sweetwater) who roam throughout the Old West.

Matthew	Boomer Castleman
Smitty	Joy Bang
Zak	Michael Martin Murphy
Sweetwater	Jamie Carr
Mayor	Edward Andrews
Clem	Frank Welker

Producer: Ernest Pintoff

The Kraft Music Hall

Variety; 60 min; NBC 10/8/58 to 6/6/62

A weekly program of music and songs sponsored by Kraft Foods.

Hosts: Milton Berle, Perry Como, Dave King

Regulars: Ken Carpenter, The Bill Foster Dancers, The Jerry Packer Singers

Announcer: Ed Herlihy

Orchestra: Billy May, Mitchell Ayres

Producer: Nick Vanoff, Ray Charles

The Kraft Music Hall

Variety; 60 min; NBC 9/13/67 to 5/12/71

Music and comedy programs tailored to the talents of weekly guest hosts. Sponsored by Kraft Foods.

Regulars: The Peter Gennero and Michael Bennett Dancers

Announcer: Ed Herlihy

Orchestra: Peter Matz

Producer: Gary Smith, Dwight Hemion

The Kraft Music Hall Presents Dave King

Variety; 60 min; NBC 5/26/59 to 9/23/59

A hour of music and song with Dave King, the British version of Perry Como.

Host: Dave King

Regulars: The Jerry Packer Singers, The Bill Foster Dancers

Announcer: Ed Herlihy

Orchestra: Vic Schoen

The Kraft Music Hall Presents Sandler and Young

Variety; 60 min; NBC 5/14/69 to 6/13/69

Music and comedy featuring comedians Sandler and Young. Taped in London and sponsored by Kraft Foods.

Host: Tony Sandler, Ralph Young

Regulars: Judy Carne, The Paddy Stone Dancers

Announcer: Paul Griffith

Orchestra: Jack Parnell

The Kraft Mystery Theatre

Anthology; 60 min; NBC 6/14/61 to 9/27/61
                              6/13/62 to 9/26/62
                              6/19/63 to 9/11/63

A series of mystery and suspense dramas originally intended for British TV as well as repeats of dramas that aired on other filmed anthology programs. Sponsored by Kraft Foods.

Host: Frank Gallop

Announcer: Ed Herlihy

The Kraft Summer Music Hall

Variety; 60 min; NBC 6/6/66 to 8/29/66

A Summer series of music, songs, and light comedy.

Host: John Davidson

Regulars: George Carlin, Richard Pryor, The King Cousins, Jackie and Gayle, The Lively Set

Announcer: Ed Herlihy

Orchestra: Jimmie Haskell

Producer: Ken Welch

The Kraft Suspense Theatre

Anthology; 60 min; NBC 10/10/63 to 9/9/65

A weekly series of mystery and suspense presentations. Sponsored by Kraft Foods and featuring such stars as Sally Kellerman, Tippi Hedren, Pat O'Brien, Eddie Albert, Lee Marvin, Norman Fell, Sharon Farrell, Gig Young, Katharine Ross, Anne Francis, Gloria Swanson, Telly Savalas, Jack Klugman, Nancy Malone, Beverly Garland, Brian Keith, and Ted Knight.

"Theme from the Kraft Suspense Theatre" by Johnny Williams

The Kraft Television Theatre

Anthology; 60 min; NBC 5/7/47 to 10/1/58
                              ABC 10/15/53 to 1/6/55

Dramas and comedies featuring Broadway veterans, well-known, and lesser-known actors. Sponsored by Kraft Foods, "Theatre" was the first 60 minute anthology series to be broadcast to the Midwest by coaxial cable (1949).

Announcer: Ed Herlihy, Charles Stark

Producer: Stanley Quinn, Maury Holland, David Susskind, Dick Dunlap, Harry Herrmann, Alex March, Fielder Cook, Robert Herridge

The Krofft Komedy Hour

Variety Pilot; 60 min; ABC 7/29/78

A proposed series of comedy sketches.

Host: Patty Harrison, Robin Tyler

Regulars: Bart Braverman, Sheryl Lee Ralph, Deborah Malone, Gino Conforti, Kaptain Kool and the Kongs

Producer: Sid and Marty Krofft

The Krofft Supershow

Children; 60 min; ABC 9/11/76 to 9/3/77

The overall title for three series: "Dr. Shrinker," "Electra Woman and Dyna Girl," and "Wonderbug." See individual titles. Music by the hosts, Kaptain Kool and the Kongs.

Kaptain Kool	Michael Lembeck
Superchick	Debra Clinger
Nashville	Louise Duart
Turkey	Micky McMeel

Producer: Sid and Marty Krofft

The Krofft Supershow II

Children; 60 min; ABC 9/10/77 to 9/2/78

The overall title for three series: "Big Foot and Wild Boy," "Magic Mongo," and "Wonderbug." Music by the hosts, Kaptain Kool and the Kongs (see prior cast listing). Produced by Sid and Marty Krofft.

The Krypton Factor

Game; 30 min; ABC 8/7/81 to 9/4/81

Four players compete in various mental and physical contests. The one player who scores highest receives $500 in gold. The title refers to the ultimate test of mental and physical ability.

Host: Dick Clark

Announcer: Dick Tufeld

Gymnastics Coach: Dick Wolfe

Music: Roy Prendergast

Producer: Alan Landsburg, Merrill Grant, Woody Fraser

Kuda Bux, Hindu Mystic

Variety; 15 min; CBS 3/2/50 to 6/17/50

Feats of magic, illusions, and mind reading.

Host: Kuda Bux

Assistant: Janet Tyler

Announcer: Rex Marshall

Producer: Roger Bowman

Kudzu

Comedy Pilot; 30 min; CBS 8/18/83

The misadventures of Odell "Kudzu" DuBose, a small town (Bypass, North Carolina) teenager who hopes to one day become a writer.

Kudzu DuBose	Tony Becker
Mavis DuBose	Linda Kaye Henning
Dub Dennible	James Hampton
Betty Jane	Mallie Jackson
Maurice	Larry B. Scott
Veranda	Teri Landrum
Preacher Dan	John Campbell

Producer: Thomas W. Moore, Rod Daniel

Kukla, Fran and Ollie

Children; 15 & 30 min; NBC 11/12/49 to 6/13/54 ABC 9/6/54 to 8/30/57

The antics of the Kuklapolitans, a group of puppets created by Burr Tillstrom (including Ollie, Kukla, Beulah Witch, Madam Ooglepuss, Colonel Crockie, Cecil Bill, Dolores Dragon, and Mercedes Rabbit). Aired locally in Chicago from 1947–49.

Hostess: Fran Allison

Puppeteer/Voices: Burr Tillstrom

Regulars: Carolyn Gilbert, Caesar Giovannini

Announcer: Hugh Downs

Producer: Burr Tillstrom, Beulah Zachary

Kung Fu

Drama; 60 min; ABC 10/14/72 to 6/27/75

The exploits of Kwai Chang Caine, a Shaolin priest, as he wanders across the American frontier of the 1870s seeking an unknown brother. Stories also relate Caine's strict training to become a priest; his efforts to help people in trouble; and his attempts to live free despite bounty hunters who are seeking him (wanted by the Chinese Legation for killing a royal nephew during a rukus that took the life of his favorite teacher, Master Po).

Kwai Chang Caine	David Carradine
Danny Caine (brother)	Tim McIntire
Margit McLean (cousin)	Season Hubley
Master Po	Keye Luke
Master Kan	Philip Ahn
Master Teh	John Leoning
Caine (age 6)	Stephen Manley
Caine (older)	Radamas Pera

"Kung Fu" Theme: Jim Helms

Producer: Jerry Thorpe

The Kwicky Koala Show

Cartoon; 30 min; CBS 9/21/81 to 9/11/82

Segments; "Kwicky Koala" (an Australian Koala bear plagued by the get-rich-quick-schemes of Wilfred Wolfe); "Dirty Dog" (A down-on-his luck dog and his equally ragged pal, Ratso); "Crazy Claws" (a quick-witted wild cat's efforts to outwit Rawhide, a hunter who seeks his hide); and "The Bungle Brothers" (antics of George and Joey, two trouble-prone brothers).

Kwicky Koala	Robert Allen Ogle
Wilfred Wolfe	John Stephenson
Dirty Dog	Frank Welker
Ratso	Marshall Efron
Crazy Claws	Jim MacGeorge
Rawhide	Robert Allen Ogle
Joey	Allan Melvin
George	Michael Bell

Producer: William Hanna, Joseph Barbera

The Kyle MacDonnell Show

See "Girl About Town."

L.A. Law

Crime Drama; 60 min; NBC 10/3/86 (Premiere)

The lives and loves of a group of ambitious lawyers with the Los Angeles firm of McKenzie, Brackman, Chavey, and Kuzak.

Michael Kuzak	Harry Hamlin
D.A. Grace Van Owen	Susan Dey
Arnold Becker	Corbin Bernsen
Ann Kelsey	Jill Eikenberry
Douglas Brackman Jr.	Alan Rachins
Abby Perkins	Michele Greene
Judge Alice Patakowski	Juanin Clay
Victor Sifuentes	Jimmy Smits
Roxanne Melman	Susan Ruttan
Leland McKenzie	Richard Dysart
Stewart Markowitz	Michael Tucker
Iris Hubbard	Cynthia Harris
Sheila Brackman	Joanna Frank

Music: Mike Post

Producer: Steven Bochco, Gregory Hoblitt

Ladies Be Seated

Game; 30 min; ABC 4/22/49 to 6/17/49

Female members of the studio audience compete in various games for merchandise prizes.

Host: Tom Moore

Assistant: Phil Patton

Announcer: George Ansbro

Music: The Buddy Weed Trio

Producer: William Berns, Tom Moore, Greg Garrison, Phil Patton

Ladies Before Gentlemen

Discussion-Game; 30 min; DuMont 2/28/51 to 5/2/51

A female guest must defend the woman's point of view on a topical issue (against a panel of men) to maintain her position on a pedestal. If she fails, the argument is scored in favor of the men.

Host: Ken Roberts

Panelists: Fred Robbins, Harvey Stone, Robert Sylvester, John Kullers, Harvey Stone

Premiere Guest: Cara Williams

Producer: Henry Misrock

Ladies' Choice

Variety; 30 min; NBC 6/8/53 to 9/25/53

Performances by undiscovered talent that are presented by female talent scouts; guests selected by various women's clubs; and a quiz segment that asks players to identify an unrecognizable photo through a single hint or jingle.

Host: Johnny Dugan

Ladies in Blue

Crime Drama Pilot; 60 min; ABC 3/19/80

The exploits of Casey Hunt and Britt Blackwell, two beautiful police women with the San Francisco P.D. Aired on "Vegas."

Off. Casey Hunt	Michelle Phillips
Off. Britt Blackwell	Tanya Roberts
Capt. Turner	Peter Haskell
Casey's mother	Natalie Schafer
Sam	Peter Mark Richman
Dottie	Peggy Cass
Derek	Andrew Robinson

Producer: Aaron Spelling, Douglas S. Cramer

Ladies' Man

Comedy; 30 min; CBS 10/27/80 to 2/21/81

The story of Alan Thackery, a bachelor father and the token male writer on "Women's Life," a New York-based magazine whose staff is totally female.

Alan Thackery	Lawrence Pressman
Elaine Holstein	Louise Sorel
Amy Thackery	Natasha Ryan
Betty Brill	Karen Morrow
Andrea Gibbons	Betty Kennedy
Gretchen	Simone Griffeth
Susan	Allison Argo
Reggie	Herb Edelman
Sheila Thackery	Julie Cobb

Producer: Herbert B. Leonard, Michael Loman, Lee Miller

Lady Blue

Crime Drama; 60 min; ABC 9/26/85 to 1/25/86

The violent exploits of Katy Mahoney, a beautiful detective with the Chicago Metro Police Department (Violent Crimes Division), a female "Dirty Harry" who can "read a crime in progress like most guys read the sports page."

Det. Katy Mahoney	Jamie Rose
Lt. Terry McNichols	Danny Aiello
Off. Cassidy	Bruce A. Young
Det. Gino Gianelli	Ron Dean
Rose Gianelli	Diane Dorsey
Willow (Terry' niece)	Nan Woods
Harvey (Katy's contact)	Ricardo Gutierrez

Theme Vocal ("Lady Blue") by Arnetia Walker

Producer: David Gerber

The Lady Died at Midnight

Anthology Pilot; 60 min; NBC 2/23/58

The pilot for "Pursuit." The story of a convicted murderer who vows revenge on the people who were responsible for his capture.

Capt. McCaffrey	Paul Douglas
Wayne Pilgrim	Earl Holliman
Paul Gorman	Gary Merrill
Porter	Larry Dobkin
Hanson	Eddie Firestone

Producer: Norman Felton

Lady Lovelylocks and the Pixietails

Cartoon; 30 min; Syn. 4/87

The series, set in the enchanted land of Lovelylocks, relates the adventures of its beautiful Princess, Lovelylocks, as she struggles to save her kingdom from Ravenwaves, an evil duchess who seeks to control it. The title refers to Lovelylocks' magical animal helpers (Pixie, Sparkle, Beauty, and Shine).

Lady Lovelylocks	Jeannie Elias
Ravenwaves	Louise Vallance

Other Voices: Brian George, Danny Mann, Tony St. Vincent

Producer: Andy Heyward

Lady Luck

Comedy Pilot; 30 min; NBC 2/12/73

The story of a beautiful, mysterious woman who magically appears to assist people who are in need of a little Lady Luck.

Lady Luck (Laura)	Valerie Perrine
Roger	Paul Sand
Penny	Sallie Shockley
Clay	Bert Convy
Walter	J. D. Cannon
Fran	Carole Cook

Producer: James Komack

The Lady Next Door

Madge Tucker as the host of an NBC (3/9/49 to 9/14/49) program of stories for children.

The Lambs Gambol

Variety; 30 min; NBC 2/27/49 to 5/22/49

Performances by members of the all-male Lambs Club, a fraternal order of show business people.

Host: Bert Lytell

Music: Johnny McManus

Producer: Herb Leder

Lancelot Link, Secret Chimp

Comedy; ABC, 9/12/70 to 9/4/71 (60 min)
                  9/11/71 to 9/2/72 (30 min)

The exploits of Lancelot Link, a fumbling spy for the Agency to Prevent Evil (A.P.E.), as he battles the evils of C.H.U.M.P. (Criminal Headquarters for Underground Master Plan). Characters are chimpanzees with voice-over dubbing.

Producer: Allan Sandler, Stan Burns, Mike Marmer

Lancer

Western; 60 min; CBS 9/24/68 to 9/8/70

Stories, set on the Lancer Ranch in California's San Joaquin Valley, relate the efforts of three men (Murdoch Lancer and his sons Scott and Johnny) to maintain the 100,000-acre timberland ranch during the lawless 1870s.

Murdoch Lancer	Andrew Duggan
Scott Lancer	Wayne Maunder
Johnny Madrid Lancer	James Stacy
Teresa O'Brien	Elizabeth Baur
Jelly Hoskins	Paul Brinegar

"Lancer" Theme: Jerome Moross

Producer: Sam Wanamaker, Alan A. Armer

Land of Hope

Drama Pilot; 60 min; CBS 5/13/76

The struggles of four immigrant families living on New York's Lower East Side during the early 1900s.

Reva Barsky	Marian Winters
Isaac Barsky	Phil Fisher
Devvie Barsky	Roberta Wallach
Herschel Barsky	Richard Liberman
Benji Barsky	Joseph Miller
Gerda Gottschalk	Ariane Munker
Gustav Gottschalk	Roy Poole
Ernst Gottschalk	Donald Warfield
Rose Dwyer	Robin Rose
Kevin Dwyer	Colin Duffy
Lea Gianni	Maria Tucci
Angelo Gianni	John Dunn

Producer: Herbert Brodkin

Land of the Giants

Adventure; 60 min; ABC 9/22/68 to 9/6/70

A plane (the Spinthrift) enroute to London, passes through an atmospheric disturbance that badly damages it. The craft crash lands in a dense forest in a world of human giants. As the crew and passengers become known, they are sought as fugitives and a reward is offered for their capture. Stories relate their struggle for survival and attempts to return to their own world.

Steve Burton	Gary Conway
Dan Erickson	Don Marshall
Betty Hamilton	Heather Young
Valerie Scott	Deanna Lund
Alexander Fitzhugh	Kurt Kasznar
Mark Wilson	Don Matheson
Barry Lockridge	Stefan Arngrim
SIB Insp. Kobic	Kevin Hagen

Producer: Irwin Allen, Bruce Fowler

Land of the Lost

Adventure; 30 min; NBC 9/4/74 to 9/3/77

While exploring the Colorado River on a raft, forest ranger Rick Marshall and his children (Holly and Will) are caught in a time vortex and transported to a forbidding world called the Land of the Lost. Stories relate their struggle for survival and attempts to find their way back to their world.

Rick Marshall	Spencer Milligan
Holly Marshall	Kathy Coleman
Will Marshall	Wesley Eure
Jack Marshall	
(replaced Rick)	Ron Harper
Sleestak Leader	
Enik	Walker Edmiston
Chaka (monkey-boy)	Philip Paley
Sa (monkey-girl)	Sharon Baird
Ta (Palcus leader)	Scott Fullerton
Malak	Richard Kiel
Sleestak	Jon Locke

Producer: Sid and Marty Krofft

Landon, Landon & Landon

Comical Mystery Pilot; 60 min; CBS 6/14/80

Shortly after he is murdered during a case investigation, private detective Ben Landon returns to earth (as a ghost) to be the father he never was to his grown children, Holly and Nick, now the owners of the Hollywood-based Landon, Landon & Landon Investigations. The unsold series was to relate Holly and Nick's investigations as they use the ghost of their father to help solve crimes.

Ben Landon	William Windom
Holly Landon	Nancy Dolman
Nick Landon	Daren Kelly
Judith Saperstein	Millie Slavin
Insp. Ulysses	
Barnes	Richard O'Brien
George Rumford	Norman Bartold
Billie	Sudie Bond
White Suite	Paul Tuerpe

Producer: Don Reo, Bruce Kalish

Lanigan's Rabbi

Crime Drama; 90 min; NBC 1/30/77 to 7/3/77

The work of Cameron, California Police Chief Paul Lanigan and his sometimes assistant, David Small, rabbi of the Temple Beth Halell Synagogue. Aired on "The NBC Sunday Mystery Movie."

Chief Paul Lanigan	Art Carney
Rabbi David Small	Stuart Margolin*
	Bruce Solomon
Kate Lanigan	Janis Paige
Miriam Small	Janet Margolin
Lt. Osgood	Robert Doyle
Bobbi Whittaker	Barbara Carney
Hannah Price	Reva Rose

Producer: Leonard B. Stern, Don Mankiewicz, David J. O'Connell

*Pilot film role (6/17/76).

The Lanny Ross Show

Variety; 30 min; NBC 4/1/48 to 8/4/49

Music and songs with singer Lanny Ross, regulars Martha Logan and Sandra Gahle, and the orchestra of Harry Simeone.

The Laraine Day Show

See "Daydreaming with Laraine."

Laramie

Western; 60 min; NBC 9/15/59 to 9/17/63

Events in the shaping of Laramie, Wyoming, during the 1880s as seen through the eyes of

Slim Sherman and Jess Harper, ranchers who operate a swing station (ranch and stage depot) for the Great Overland Mail Stage Lines.

Slim Sherman	John Smith
Jess Harper	Robert Fuller
Jonesy	Hoagy Carmichael
Andy Sherman	Robert Crawford Jr.
Mike Williams	Dennis Holmes
Daisy Cooper	Spring Byington
Sheriff Douglas	Roy Barcroft
Sheriff Mort Cory	Stuart Randall

"Laramie" Theme Song: Cyril Mockridge

Producer: Don Williams, Richard Lewis, Robert Pirosh

Laredo

Western; 60 min; NBC 9/16/65 to 9/8/67

The antics of three bickering Texas Rangers (Reese, Chad, and Joe) who are based in Laredo during the 1860s.

Reese Bennett	Neville Brand
Chad Cooper	Peter Brown
Joe Riley	William Smith
Capt. Edward Parmalee	Philip Carey
Ranger Cotton Buckmeister	Claude Akins

"Laredo" Theme Song by Russell Garcia

Producer: Frederick Shorr

The Larry Kane Show

A syndicated (1971) variety series, hosted by Larry Kane, and featuring interviews with rock personalities.

The Larry Storch Show

Variety; 60 min; CBS 7/11/53 to 9/12/53

A weekly series of music, songs, and comedy.

Host: Larry Storch

Regulars: Georgann Johnson, Milton Frome, Russell Hicks, Ethel Owen, Tomi Romer, Mildred Hughes, The June Taylor Dancers and Singers

Announcer: Jack Lescoulie

Orchestra: Sammy Spear, Ray Bloch

Las Vegas Beat

Crime Drama Pilot; 60 min; Unaired; Produced in 1964

The exploits of Bill Ballin, a highly respected private detective who works closely with the police in an attempt to solve crimes.

Bill Ballin	Peter Graves
Gopher	Jamie Farr
R. G. Joseph	William Bryant
Lt. Bernard McFeety	Dick Bakalyan
Cynthia Rain	Diana Millay
Helen Leopold	Maggie Mahoney
Fredericks	Lawrence Dobkin

Producer: Andrew J. Fenady

Las Vegas Gambit

Game; 30 min; NBC 10/27/80 to 11/27/81

A revised version of "Gambit," wherein two couples answer general knowledge questions and attempt to score Blackjack by either keeping or passing playing cards. The couple who come closest to twenty-one win the round. A three match game is played and the winning couple receives $200 per match. Taped in Las Vegas.

Host: Wink Martindale

Card Dealer: Beverly Malden, Lee Manning

Announcer: Kenny Williams

Producer: Robert Noah, Merrill Heatter, Bob Quigley

The Las Vegas Show

Variety; 2 hrs; United Network 5/1/67 to 5/31/67

Variety acts from various Las Vegas night clubs. "The Las Vegas Show" was the only series to be produced by a proposed fourth network. After financial problems, the network folded.

Host: Bill Dana

Regulars: Ann Elder, Jo Anne Worley, Pete Barbutti, Cully Richards, Danny Meehan

Music: Jack Sheldon

Producer: David Sontag, Howard Leeds, Jerry Goldsmith

Lash of the West

A syndicated (1951) children's series in which western film star Lash LaRue demonstrated his cowboy skills. Also aired on ABC (1/4/53 to 4/26/53).

Lassie

Drama; 30 min; 9/64 to 9/68

A continuation from where "Timmy and Lassie" leaves off. The need for farmers overseas prompts the Martins to sell the farm and move to Australia. Unable to take Lassie because of quarantine laws, Timmy leaves her with his friend Cully. Later, when Cully recovers from a heart attack, but is no longer able to care for Lassie, he gives her to forest ranger Corey Stuart. Stories relate Lassie's adventures as she assists Cory.

Ranger Cory Stuart	Robert Bray
Ranger Scott Turner	Jed Allan
Ranger Kirby Newman	John Archer

Producer: Jack Wrather, Bonita Granville

Lassie

Drama; 30 min; CBS 9/68 to 9/71

A continuation of the prior title wherein Lassie, no longer bound to a human master, roams and assists both human and animals in trouble.

Lassie	Lassie

Producer: Jack Wrather, Bonita Granville Wrather

Lassie

Drama; 30 min; Syn. 1972

A revised version of the prior title. Though still somewhat of a wanderer, Lassie finds a temporary home at the California ranch of Keith Holden. Stories relate her adventures in and around the ranch.

Keith Holden	Larry Pennell
Dale Mitchell	Larry Wilcox
Ron Holden	Skip Burton
Mike Holden	Joshua Albee
Lucy Baker	Pamelyn Ferdin
Sue Lambert	Sherry Boucher

Producer: Jack Wrather

Lassie: The New Beginning

Drama Pilot; 60 min; ABC 9/17/78 (Part 1)
9/24/78 (Part 2)

The adventures of Lassie and her new masters: Samantha and Chip Stratton, orphans who live with their Uncle Stuart, the editor of the Lake Pines, California, "Journal."

Stuart Stratton	John Reilly
Sally Stratton	Sally Boyden
Chip Stratton	Shane Sinutko
Kathy McKendrick	Lee Bryant
Dr. Amos Rheams	David Wayne
Sheriff J. D. Marsh	Gene Evans
Buzz McKendrick	Jeff Harlan
Ada Stratton	Jeanette Nolan

Producer: Tom McDermott, William Beaudine Jr.

Lassie's Rescue Rangers

Cartoon; 30 min; ABC 9/8/73 to 8/30/75

The exploits of the collie Lassie as the leader of the Rescue Force, the animal assistants of the Turner family rescue team.

Ben Turner	Ted Knight
Laura Turner	Jane Webb
Jackie Turner	Lane Scheimer
Susan Turner	Erica Scheimer
Ranger Jean Fox	Ted Knight

Producer: Norm Prescott, Lou Scheimer

Lassiter

Crime Drama Pilot; 60 min; CBS 7/6/68

The exploits of Pete Lassiter, an investigative reporter for "Contrast" magazine.

Pete Lassiter	Burt Reynolds
Joanie Mears	Sharon Farrell
Stan Marchek	Cameron Mitchell
Russ Faine	Gerald S. O'Loughlin
Jerry Burns	Larry Haddon
Charlie Leaf	Nicholas Colasanto

Producer: Richard Alan Simmons

The Last Chance Cafe

Comedy-Drama Pilot; 30 min; ABC 2/28/86

An unsold series about a mysterious old man (Virgil) who runs The Last Chance Cafe, a diner where customers are given the opportunity to "see" crucial moments from their pasts—with themselves as they were many years ago.

Virgil	Henry Jones
Melissa	Anne Lockhart
Bill	Richard Hatch
Young Melissa	Heidi Helmer
Young Bill	Tim Ryan
Willy	Charles Stratton

Producer: Gordon Farr, Arnold Kane, David Yarnell

The Last Electric Knight

The pilot for "Sidekicks" (which see).

The Last of the Private Eyes

Comedy Pilot; 60 min; NBC 4/30/63

The exploits of J. F. Kelly, a bumbling private detective who solves crimes quite by accident.

J. F. Kelly	Bob Cummings
Susan Lane	Linda Christian
Elsie	Jeanne Crain
Lt. Duff Peterson	Macdonald Carey
Donald Joe	Arnold Stang
LaVern	Janis Paige
George Lane	William Bendix

Producer: Aaron Spelling

The Last Precinct

Comical Crime Drama; 60 min; NBC 4/11/86 to 5/30/86

When faced with the problem of what to do with a group of odd-ball police officers, the commissioner of an unidentified city assigns them to Precinct 56, a former morgue turned station house. Stories relate the outrageous antics of the Last Precinct officers as they attempt to uphold the peace.

Capt. Rob Wright	Adam West
Off. Melanie "Mel" Brubaker	Randi Brooks
Sgt. Price Pascall	Jonathan Perpich
Off. William "Raid" Rader	Rick Ducommun
Sgt. Tremayne "Night Train" Lane	Ernie Hudson
Sheriff Ronald J. Hobbs	Wings Hauser
Deputy Justin Dial	Geoffrey Elliott
Sgt. Martha Haggerty	Yana Narvana
Off. Butch Briscoe	Keenan Wynn
Off. Sundance	Hank Rolike
Off. Rina Starland	Lucy Lee Flippen
Chief Arnold Bludhorn	James Cromwell
Off. Shivamanbhai Pouncawilla ("Alphabet")	Vijay Amritraj
"Dead Eye" Al Demarta	Carl Strano
Solly (Al's aide)	Robert Miranda
Stacy (waitress at "Honey Bunns")	Nicolette Sheridan
The King (an officer)	Pete Willcox

Music: Mike Post and Pete Carpenter

Producer: Frank Lupo, Stephen J. Cannell

The Last Resort

Comedy; 30 min; CBS 9/19/79 to 3/17/80

The story of four college students (Michael, Gail, Duane, and Zack) who turn a gentell mountain hotel into a madhouse while working there as waiters during their summer vacation.

Michael Lerner	Larry Breeding
Gail Collins	Stephanie Faracy
Duane Kaminski	Zane Lasky
Zack Comstock	Walter Olkewicz
Jeffrey Barron	
(waiter)	Ray Underwood
Kevin (cook)	John Fujioka
Murray (maitre d')	Robert Costanzo
Mrs. Trilling (hotel	
guest)	Dorothy Konrad

Music: Patrick Williams

Producer: Gary David Goldberg

The Last Word

Comedy Pilot; 30 min; NBC 5/10/86

The misadventures of Nicky and Tyler, the assistant managers of The Last Word, a restaurant for the young at heart.

Stefan Popalardo	Reuven Bar-Yotam
Nicky Popalardo	Harry Basil
Tyler McVey	Brian Becker
Sherry	Melody Hamilton
Gloria	Shari Ballard

Producer: Mort Lachman, Arthur Julian

Late Bloomer

Comedy Pilot; 30 min; CBS 1/19/87

Hoping to find more meaning to life, Julia Peterson, a beautiful actress, relinquishes her career and enrolls in New York's Washington Square College, where she hopes to become a psychologist. The unsold series was to relate Julia's adventures at school (where she also teaches drama) and at home (where she teaches cooking). Aired on "Kate and Allie" where it was originally scheduled to run in May of 1986.

Julia Peterson	Lindsay Wagner
Ann (her mother)	Barbara Barrie
Henry (her father)	Roger Bowen
Millie (her friend)	Mercedes Reuhl
Keith (her ex-	
husband)	Sam Freed
Sandy (a student)	Kelly Wolfe

Producer: Bill Persky, Bob Randall

The Late Fall, Early Summer Bert Convy Show

Variety; 60 min; CBS 8/25/76 to 9/15/76

A weekly hour of music and comedy.

Host: Bert Convy

Regulars: Sallie Janes, Donna Ponterotto, Henry Polic II, Lennie Schultz, Susie Guest, Shirley Kirkes, Judy Pierce, Darcell Wynne

Announcer: Donna Ponterotto

Orchestra: Perry Botkin Jr.

Producer: Sam Denoff

Late Night with David Letterman

Variety: 60 min; NBC 2/1/82 (Premiere)

A late night series of celebrity (and non-celebrity) interviews and offbeat, satirical sketches.

Host: David Letterman

Featured: Larry "Bud" Melman

Announcer: Bill Wendell

Orchestra: Paul Shaffer

Producer: Jack Rollins, Barry Sand

The Late Show Starring Joan Rivers

Talk-Variety; 60 min; FOX 10/9/86 to 5/15/87
5/22/87 ("The Late Show" Premiere)

A live, nightly program of talk, music, and interviews. The premiere program of the Fox Broadcasting Company, a fourth broadcast network. After eight months on the air, Joan Rivers was relieved of her duties as host. On May 22, 1987, the program became "The Late Show" and featured daily guest hosts in an attempt to boost its less-than desirable ratings.

Hostess: Joan Rivers

Announcer: Clint Holmes

Music: Mark Hudson and the Party Boys Plus the Tramp

Producer: Edgar Rosenberg, Bill Sammeth

Laugh-in

See "Rowan and Martin's Laugh-In."

Laugh-In

Variety; 60 min; NBC 9/5/77 to 2/8/78

A cast of virtual unknowns (at the time) perform skits that satirize everyday life.

Cast: Nancy Bleiwess, Ed Bluestone, Kim Braden, Claire Faulkonbridge, Antoinette Attell, Wayland Flowers, June Gable, Jim Giovanni, Ben Powers, Bill Rafferty, Michael Sklar, Lennie Schultz, April Tatro, Robin Williams

Orchestra: Tommy Oliver

Producer: George Schlatter

Laugh Line

Game; 30 min; NBC 4/6/59 to 6/11/59

Object: For celebrities to supply comic captions for cartoons that are presented in tableau form.

Host: Dick Van Dyke

Panelists: Elaine May, Orson Bean, Mike Nichols, Dorothy Loudon

Laugh Trax

Variety; 60 min; Syn. 9/82

Comedy skits coupled with performances by rock stars. See also "Rock Comedy."

Host: Jim Staahl

Regulars: Gail Matthius, Lucy Webb, Frank Welker, Howie Mandel, Jim Fisher

"Laugh Trax" Theme Music: Bob Summers

Producer: Toby Martin

Laughs for Sale

Comedy; 30 min; ABC 10/20/63 to 12/22/63

Guest comics perform material that is submitted by fledging comedy writers. The material is then evaluated and offered for sale. Interested parties can purchase material by contacting the producers.

Host: Hal March

Producer: Arne Sultan

Laurel and Hardy Laughtoons

Comedy; 30 min; Syn. 1979

Edited versions of silent Stan Laurel and Oliver Hardy theatrical shorts of the 1920s.

Producer: Hal Dennis, Richard Feiner

Music: George Korngold

The Laurel and Hardy Show

Comedy; 90 min; Syn. 9/86

A collection of Stan Laurel and Oliver Hardy theatrical shorts and feature films of the 1930s and 40s. Incorporates new prints made directly from the original negatives.

Producer: Rob Word, Mike Dimich

Laverne and Shirley

Comedy; 30 min; ABC 1/27/76 to 5/10/83

The original format (1976–80) relates the adventures of Laverne DeFazio, a realist, and Shirley Feeney, a romantic; two working girls (bottle cappers at the Shotz Brewery in Milwaukee) and roommates (Apt. A at 730 Hamton Street). Following their dismissal from the brewery, Laverne and Shirley move to Burbank, California where their antics as clerks in the Bardwell Department Store are depicted (from 1980–82). When a contract dispute forced Cindy Williams to leave the show, her character (Shirley) is seen marrying Dr. Walter Meany and departing to join her Army husband overseas. The remainder of the series (1982–83) relates Laverne's misadventures as a single girl looking for romance, and working for the Ajax Aerospace Company.

Laverne DeFazio	Penny Marshall
Shirley Feeney	Cindy Williams
Andrew "Squiggy" Squigman	David L. Lander
Lenny Kosnoski	Michael McKean
Carmine Raguso	Eddie Mekka
Frank DeFazio	Phil Foster
Edna Babbish	Betty Garrett
Rosie Greenbaum	Carol Ita White
Norman Hughes	Bo Kaprall

Mrs. Havenhurst	Helen Page Camp
Rhonda Lee	Leslie Easterbrook
Sonny St. Jacques	Ed Marinaro
Harvey Hilderbrand	Norman Bartold
Sgt. Alvinia T. Plout	Vicki Lawrence
Sal Melina	Paul Sylvan
Bill Ajax	Raleigh Bond
G. "Bullets" Klein	Robert Hogan
Helmut Squigman	Wynn Irwin
Squendelyn Squigman (Squiggy's sister)	David L. Lander

Theme Vocal ("Making Our Dreams Come True"): Cyndi Grecco

Producer: Thomas L. Miller, Edward K. Milkis, Garry K. Marshall

Laverne & Shirley & Company

The syndicated (1981) title for off-network re-runs of "Laverne and Shirley" while the series remains in first run on ABC.

Laverne and Shirley in the Army

Cartoon; 30 min; ABC 10/10/81 to 9/18/82

The antics of Laverne and Shirley as privates with the U.S. Army.

Pvt. Laverne DeFazio	Penny Marshall
Pvt. Shirley Feeney	Cindy Williams
Sgt. Squeely	Ron Palillo
Sgt. Turnbuckle	Ken Mars

Producer: William Hanna, Joseph Barbera.

Laverne and Shirley with the Fonz

Cartoon; 30 min; ABC 9/25/82 to 9/3/83

The misadventures of Army recruits Laverne and Shirley and motor pool private Arthur "The Fonz" Fonzarelli, all of whom are supervised by Sgt. Squeely, the Army's only talking pig.

Pvt. Laverne DeFazio	Julie McWhirter
Pvt. Shirley Feeney	Lynne Stewart
The Fonz	Henry Winkler
Sgt. Squeely	Ron Palillo
Mr. Cool (Fonzie's dog)	Frank Welker

Producer: William Hanna, Joseph Barbera.

The Law and Harry McGraw

Crime Drama; 60 min; CBS 9/27/87 (Premiere)

The exploits of Harry McGraw, a seedy and abrasive private detective working out of Boston. Based on the character that appeared on "Murder, She Wrote."

Harry McGraw	Jerry Orbach
Ellie Maginnis	Barbara Babcock
E.J.	Juli Donald
Tyler Chase	Peter Haskell
Steve	Shea Farrell
Sgt. Howard Sternhagen	Earl Boen

Producer: Peter S. Fischer, Robert F. O'Neil

The Law and Mr. Jones

Drama; 30 min; ABC 10/7/60 to 9/22/61

The story of Abraham Lincoln Jones, a tough but honest criminal attorney working in New York City.

Abraham Jones	James Whitmore
Marsha Spear	Janet DeGore
C. E. Carruthers	Conlan Carter
Thomas Jones	Russ Brown

Theme Adaptation ("When the Saints Go Marching In"): Hans Salter

Producer: Sy Gomberg

The Law Enforcers

Crime Drama; 60 min; NBC 9/28/69 to 9/6/70

The relationship between Deputy Police Chief Sam Danforth and D.A. William Washburn as they attempt to maintain the order in an unnamed city beset by urban crises. Aired on "The Bold Ones."

Sam Danforth	Leslie Nielsen
William Washburn	Hari Rhodes

Producer: Jack Laird

Law of the Plainsman

Western; 30 min; NBC 10/1/59 to 9/22/60

During a battle between the cavalry and the Apache, a 14-year-old brave befriends a wounded captain. Soon the captain and the brave (whom the captain calls Sam Buckhart)

become blood brothers. Two years later, when the captain is killed in an ambush, Sam inherits a vast wealth that enables him to attend Harvard University, as once did the captain. With a desire to help his people, Sam becomes a U.S. Marshal. Stories, set in New Mexico during the 1880s, relate Sam's efforts to apprehend outlaws and establish the long-sought road to peace between the Apache and White Man. See also "The Indian."

Sam Buckhart	Michael Ansara
Billy Lordan	Robert Harland
Tess Logan	Gina Gillespie
Martha Cominter	Nora Marlowe
Marshal Andrew Morrison	Dayton Loomis

Theme Song ("The Plainsman Theme"): Leonard Rosenman

Producer: Jules Levy, Arthur Gardner, Arnold Laven

The Lawless Years

Crime Drama; 30 min; NBC 4/16/59 to 9/3/59

The exploits of Barney Ruditsky, a plainclothes police detective in New York City during the 1920s.

Det. Barney Ruditsky	James Gregory
Max (his partner)	Robert Karnes

Producer: Jack Chertok

Lawman

Western: 30 min; ABC 10/5/58 to 10/9/62

The story of Marshal Dan Troop and his efforts to maintain law and order in Laramie, Wyoming, during the 1870s.

Marshal Dan Troop	John Russell
Deputy Johnny McKay	Peter Brown
Lilly Merrill (saloon owner)	Peggie Castle
Jake (bartender)	Dan Sheridan
Dru Lemp (cafe owner)	Bek Nelson
Julie Tate (editor)	Barbara Lang

Producer: William T. Orr, Charles Trapnell

The Lawrence Welk Show

Variety; 60 min; ABC 7/2/55 to 9/3/71

A long-running series of music, songs, and dances.

Host: Lawrence Welk

Champagne Lady: Alice Lon, Norma Zimmer

Regulars: Dianne, Kathy, Peggy, and Janet Lennon, Joe Feeney, Dick Dale, Bobby Burgess, Mary Lou Metzger, Gail Farrell, Sandi Jensen, Barbara Boylan, Pete Fountain, Bob Ralston, Jerry Burke, Myron Floren, Jo Ann Castle, Natalie Nevins, Cissy King, Archie Duncan, Clay Hart, Lynn Anderson, Andrea Willis, Paula Stewart, Tanya Falan, Ralna English, Guy Hovis, Peanuts Hucko, Rocky Rockwell, Aladdin, Clay Hart, Tom Netherland, Henry Cuesta, Bob Lido, The Symanski Sisters

Announcer: Bob Orrin

Music Director: George Cates

Producer: Sam Lutz, James Hobson, Edward Sobol

The Lawrence Welk Show

Variety; 60 min; Syn. 9/71 to 4/83

A syndicated version of the above title.

Host: Lawrence Welk

Regulars: Bobby Burgess, Ava Barber, Henry Cuesta, Dick Dale, Ken Delo, Gail Farrell, Arthur Duncan, Myron Floren, Sandi Griffiths, Charlotte Harris, Clay Hart, Larry Hooper, Guy Hovis, Ralna Netherton, Bob Ralston, Norma Zimmer, Tanya Welk, The Symanski Sisters, Joe Feeney, The Otwell Twins

Announcer: Bob Orrin

Music Director: George Cates

Producer: James Hobson

Lawrence Welk's Top Tunes and New Talent

Variety; 60 min; ABC 7/2/55 to 5/27/59

Performances by undiscovered talent. Also titled "The Plymouth Show Starring Lawrence Welk."

Host: Lawrence Welk

Regulars: Alice Lon, Myron Floren, Buddy Merrill, The Lennon Sisters, Bob Brunner, Brenda Kay, Marjorie Meinert, Bob Lido, Larry Hooper

Music Director: George Cates

Producer: Sam Lutz, Edward Sobol

The Lawyers

Crime Drama; 60 min; NBC 9/21/69 to 9/10/72

The cases of Walter Nichols, a Los Angeles attorney, and his proteges Brian Darrell and his brother, Neil. Aired on "The Bold Ones."

Walter Nichols	Burl Ives
Brian Darrell	Joseph Campanella
Neil Darrell	James Farentino
Lt. Paul Hewitt	John Milford
Walter's secretary	Marcelle Fortier
D. A. Braddock	George Murdock
D. A. Dekker	Charles Brewer
Deputy D. A. Jeff Skinner	Todd Martin
Judge Howe	Walter Brooke

Producer: Roy Huggins, Jo Swerling Jr.

The Lazarus Syndrome

Drama; 60 min; ABC 9/11/79 to 10/9/79

The story of MacArthur St. Clair, a no-nonsense cardiologist at Webster Memorial Hospital. The title refers to a situation where a patient believes a doctor is a miracle worker.

Dr. MacArthur St. Clair	Louis Gossett Jr.
Gloria St. Clair	Sheila Frazier
Joe Hamill	Ronald Hunter
Stacy	Peggy McCay
Virginia Hamill	Peggy Walker
Admissions Nurse	Christina Alvila

Producer: Jerry Thorpe, William Blinn

Lazer Tag Academy

Cartoon; 30 min; NBC 9/13/86 (Premiere)

While escaping from police, Draxon Dreer, an evil criminal in the year 2010, crashes his ship into the ocean. A gas escapes and places him in a state of suspended animation. One thousand years later, Draxon is found and revived. While learning about the future, Dreer steals a time machine device and returns to the past to change the course of history. When it is learned that Draxon has returned to 1987 to stop Beth Jerren from developing time travel technology, Jamie Jarren, a member of the Lazer Tag Academy (future government), and a descendant of Beth's, is sent back in time to stop Draxon. Stories relate Jerren's efforts to stop Draxon before he changes the course of history.

Voices: Booker Bradshaw, Pat Farley, Noelle Harling, Billy Jacoby, Christina MacGregor, Tress MacNeille, Sid McCoy, Frank Welker, R. J. Williams, Susan Blu

Producer: Joe Ruby, Ken Spears

Leave it to Beaver

Comedy; 30 min; CBS 10/11/57 to 9/26/58
ABC 10/3/58 to 9/12/63

Events in the lives of the Cleavers, a family of four living in Mayfield: Ward, the father; June, his wife; and their mischievous children, Wally and Theodore (nicknamed "Beaver"). See also: "It's a Small World," "The New Leave It to Beaver," and "Still the Beaver."

Ward Cleaver	Hugh Beaumont
June Cleaver	Barbara Billingsley
Wally Cleaver	Tony Dow
Beaver Cleaver	Jerry Mathers
Eddie Haskell	Ken Osmond
Clarence "Lumpy" Rutherford	Frank Bank
Julie Foster	Cheryl Holdridge
Larry Mondello	Rusty Stevens
Gilbert Bates	Stephen Talbot
Hubert "Whitey" Witney	Stanley Fafara
Fred Rutherford	Richard Deacon
Gwen Rutherford	Helen Parrish
	Majel Barrett
	Margaret Stewart
Violet Rutherford	Wendy Winkleman
	Veronica Cartwright
Alice Landers	Sue Randall
Cornelia Rayburn	Doris Packer
Judy Hessler	Jeri Weil
Gus	Burt Mustin
Mrs. Mondello	Madge Blake

Harrison "Tuey"	
Brown	Stanley Fafara
Richard Rockover	Richard Correll
Chester Anderson	Buddy Hart
Ward's Uncle Billy	Edgar Buchanan
George Haskell	Karl Swenson
	George O. Petrie
Agnes Haskell	Ann Doran
	Ann Barton
Benjy Bellamy	Joey Scott
Mary Ellen Rogers	Pamela Beaird
Penny Woods	Karen Sue Trent
Benjy's mother	Sara Anderson
	Ann Doran
Mrs. Canfield	Diane Brewster

Producer: Harry Ackerman, Joe Connelly, Bob Mosher

Leave it to Larry

Comedy; 30 min; CBS 10/14/52 to 12/23/52

The home and working life of Larry Tucker, a fumbling but good-natured clerk who works in a shoe store owned by his father-in-law (Mr. Koppel).

Larry Tucker	Eddie Albert
Amy Tucker	Betty Kean
	Katherine Bard
Harriet Tucker	Lydia Schaeffer
Steve Tucker	Glenn Walkin
Mr. Koppel	Ed Begley

Producer: Leo Solomon

Leave it to the Girls

Discussion; 30 min; NBC 4/27/49 to 12/30/51
ABC 10/3/53 to 3/27/54

Three female panelists and one male guest discuss topical issues.

Hostess: Maggi McNellis

Host: Eddie Dunn

Panelists: Robin Chandler, Faye Emerson, Eloise McElhone, Peggy Ann Garner, Eva Gabor, Binnie Barnes

Producer: Martha Roundtree

Leave it to the Women

Discussion; 30 min; Syn. 1981

A panel of women discuss various topical issues.

Hostess: Stephanie Edwards

Announcer: Johnny Jacobs

Producer: Chuck Barris, Woody Fraser, Susan Walker

The Left Over Revue

Variety; 60 min; NBC 9/17/51 to 11/9/51

Music, songs, and comedy that replaced the cancelled "Broadway Open House" for a short time.

Host: Wayne Howell

Vocalist: Verna Massey

Music: Milton DeLugg

Leg Work

Crime Drama; 60 min; CBS 10/3/87 to 11/7/87

Dissatisfied with her job as an assistant D.A. in New York, Claire McCarron quits to become her own boss as the owner of a private detective company (McCarron Investigations). Stories relate Claire's investigations and attempts to make her business a success. (The title refers to Claire's legs, which do a lot of walking, but which are also displayed via mini skirts.)

Claire McCarron	Margaret Colin
Lt. Fred McCarron	Patrick James Clarke
Willie Pipal	Frances
	McDormand
Jeff	Robert Dorfman

Producer: Frank Abatemarco

The Legend of Custer

Adventure; 60 min; ABC 9/6/67 to 12/27/67

Found guilty of dereliction of duty, U.S. Cavalry General George Armstrong Custer is reduced in rank (to Lt. Col.) and sent to Fort Hays in Kansas and made commander of the Seventh Labor Batallion. Refusing to treat his Company C as a work detail, Custer fashions them into the Fighting Seventh. Stories, set in the late 1860s, relate Custer's exploits in Indian affairs; and his personal conflict with Sioux Indian Chief Crazy Horse.

Col. George Custer	Wayne Maunder
Scout Joe Miller	Slim Pickens
Sgt. James Bustard	Peter Palmer
Capt. Myles Koegh	Grant Woods
Gen. Alfred Terry	Robert F. Simon
Chief Crazy Horse	Michael Dante

Producer: David Weisbar, Frank Glicksman

The Legend of Jesse James

Western; 30 min; ABC 9/13/65 to 9/5/66

In an attempt to force the James family off their land, railroad officials kill the mother of Frank and Jesse. Stories, set in Saint Joseph, Missouri, during the 1860s, relate Frank and Jesse's adventures as they turn outlaw to strike back against the Great Western Railroad and return stolen property to its rightful owners.

Jesse James	Chris Jones
Frank James	Allen Case
Marshal Sam	
Corbett	Robert J. Wilke
Cole Younger	John Milford
Bob Younger	Bob McIntire
Mrs. James	Ann Doran

Producer: Don Siegel

Legends of the Screen

Documentary Pilot; 60 min; Syn. 1/83

The program recalls screen legends via film clips and interviews with the stars themselves.

Hostess: Nancy Collins

Guests: Rhonda Fleming, Ginger Rogers, Myrna Loy, Dorothy Lamour

Music: Bobby Sherman

Producer: Ward Sylvester

Legends of the West: Truth and Tall Tales

Anthology Pilot; 60 min; ABC 3/22/81

A proposed series that attempts to separate western fact from fiction through dramatizations and film clips from various western feature films.

Host: Don Meredith	
Co-Host: Matthew Laborteaux	
Sheriff: Jack Elam	
Music: Dennis McCarthy	
Producer: Martin Starger	

Legmen

Crime Drama; 60 min; NBC 1/20/84 to 4/6/84 9/1/84 (1 episode)

The adventures of Jack Gage and David Taylor, two students working their way through college as the legmen for Oscar Amismedi, the owner of the Los Angeles-based Tri-Star Bail Bonds Agency (later owned by Tom Bannon).

Jack Gage	Bruce Greenwood
David Taylor	J. T. Terlesky
Oscar Amismedi	Don Calfa
Chico	Anthony Munoz
Lt. Tedisco	Robert DoQui
Tom Bannon	Claude Akins
Mrs. Yehudi	Connie Sawyer

Producer: Andrew Mirisch, Richard Chapman, Bill Dial

Legs

Comedy Pilot; 60 min; NBC 5/19/78

The misadventures of a company of entertainers who are struggling to make ends meet by working in a not-so-posh Las Vegas hotel. Became the basis for "Who's Watching the Kids?"

Stacy Turner	Caren Kaye
Angie Bates	Lynda Goodfriend
Melissa Turner	Tammy Lauren
Frankie Bates	Scott Baio
Cochise	Shirley Kirkes
Bridget	Elaine Bolton
Memphis Blake	Lorrie Mahaffey
Dixie	Sayra Hammel
Major Putnam	David Ketchum
Norma Kay	Marcia Lewis
Rimshot	Dawson Mays

Producer: Garry K. Marshall, Tony Mordente, Marty Nadler

394 The Lennon Sisters Show

The Lennon Sisters Show

Variety Pilot; 60 min; ABC 5/6/69

The pilot for "Jimmy Durante Presents the Lennon Sisters Hour." A well-coordinated program that highlights the talents of the lovely Lennon Sisters.

Host: Jimmy Durante

Hostesses: Peggy, Dianne, Janet, and Kathy Lennon

Guest: Bobby Goldsboro

Orchestra: Nelson Riddle

Producer: Harold Cohen, Bernie Kukoff, Jeff Harris

Leo and Liz in Beverly Hills

Comedy; 30 min; CBS 4/25/86 to 6/6/86

When his bra manufacturing company suddenly begins to show a profit, Leo and Liz Greene leave New Jersey and relocate to the glamour of Beverly Hills. Stories relate their misadventures as they attempt to become part of the rich and famous. See also "The Couch."

Liz Greene	Valerie Perrine
Leo Greene	Harvey Korman
Mitzi Greene	Sue Ball
Lucille Trumbley	Julie Payne
Leonard	Michael J. Pollard
Diane Fedderson	Deborah Harmon
Jerry Fedderson	Ken Kimmons
Gardner Winthrop	Reid Shelton
Abigail Winthrop	Gloria Henry
Bunky Fedderson	Peter Aykroyd
Gwen	Kelli Maroney

Producer: Steve Martin, Paul Perlove

The Les Crane Show

Discussion; 90 min; ABC 11/9/64 to 11/12/65

The program, also known as "ABC's Night Life," features discussions on topical issues.

Host: Les Crane

Regulars: Nipsey Russell, Jimmy Cannon, William B. Williams

Music: Don Trenner, Cy Coleman, Elliot Lawrence

The Les Paul and Mary Ford Show

A syndicated five minute series with Les Paul and Mary Ford that consists of a quick opening, two songs, one commercial, and a short closing. Produced in 1954.

The Leslie Uggams Show

Variety; 60 min; CBS 9/28/69 to 12/21/69

A weekly series of music, songs, and comedy.

Hostess: Leslie Uggams

Regulars: Johnny Brown, Lillian Hayman, Alison Mills, Lincoln Kilpatrick, The Howard Roberts Singers, The Donald McKayle Dancers

Announcer: Roger Carroll

Orchestra: Nelson Riddle

Producer: Saul Ilson, Ernest Chambers, Steve Binder

Let's Dance

Variety; 60 min; ABC 9/18/54 to 10/16/54

A live musical hour featuring ballroom dancing. Broadcast from both New York and Chicago.

New York Host: Ralph Mooney

New York Hostess: Martha Wright

Dancers (N.Y.): Bud Robinson, Cece Robinson

Singer (N.Y.): Julius LaRosa

Chicago Host: Art Mooney

Chicago Hostess: Fran Allison

Singer (Chicago): June Valli

Orchestra (N.Y.): Ralph Flanagan

Orchestra (Chicago): Art Mooney

Let's Go Go

A syndicated variety series, hosted and produced by Sam Riddle, that features performances by rock stars.

Let's Join Joanie

Comedy Pilot; 30 min; CBS 1/12/51

Events in the life of Joan Davis, a misadventure-prone salesgirl for Hats By Anatole.

Joan Davis .... Herself
Mr. Anatole .... Joe Flynn

Music: Lyn Murray

Producer: Dick Linkroun, Frank Galen, Dick Mack

Let's Make a Deal

Game; 30 min; NBC 12/30/64 to 12/27/68
ABC 12/30/68 to 7/9/76

A player, selected from forty studio audience members, seeks to trade something he possesses for a chance at something better, usually what is behind a curtain on stage. A first deal usually assures the player a decent prize; a second or third deal tests greed as valuable prizes and large amounts of cash are at stake (a wrong decision nets a player a "zonk" prize).

Host: Monty Hall

Assistant/Announcer: Jay Stewart

Model: Carol Merrill

Producer: Stefan Hatos

Let's Make a Deal

Game; 30 min; Syn. 9/80

A syndicated version of the previous title.

Host: Monty Hall

Producer: Stefan Hatos, Monty Hall, Ian MacLennan

Let's Make a Deal

Game; 30 min; Syn. 9/84

A revised version of the prior titles and also known as "The All-New Let's Make a Deal."

Host: Monty Hall

Producer: Stefan Hatos, Alan Gilbert, Bob Synes

Let's Play Post Office

Game; 30 min; NBC 9/27/65 to 7/1/66

A line of a fictitious letter, which could have been written by a famous person, is revealed. The first of three competing players who associates the content with the author scores one point. The highest point scorer receives merchandise prizes.

Host: Don Morrow

Let's Take a Trip

Children; 30 min; CBS 3/17/55 to 2/23/58

The program attempts to help children learn about their world via visits to places of interest.

Host: Sonny Fox

Assistants: Ginger McManus, Brian Flanegan

A Letter to Loretta

Anthology; 30 min; NBC 9/20/53 to 6/27/54

Responsive dramas based on problems expressed in fan letters to actress Loretta Young. Became "The Loretta Young Theatre" the following year.

Hostess/Star: Loretta Young

Featured: Beverly Washburn, John Newland

Announcer: Bob Wilson

Music: Harry Lubin

Producer: Matthew Rapf, Tom Lewis

Director (all 36 episodes): Robert Florey

Letters to Laugh-In

Comedy Game; 30 min; NBC 9/29/69 to 3/3/70

Four joke tellers relate jokes submitted to "Laugh-In" by home viewers. The joke that scores highest (rated from 0 to 100) at the end of the week wins its sender merchandise prizes. The writer of the lowest scoring joke wins "Seven action-packed days in beautiful downtown Burbank."

Host: Gary Owens

Producer: Alan Newman

Lewis and Clark

Comedy; 30 min; NBC 10/29/81 to 7/30/82

Tired of the daily grind of city living, Stewart Lewis uproots his family and moves to Luckenbach, Texas, where he purchases a saloon called the Nassau County Cafe. Stories relate his efforts to run the saloon; and his family's attempts to adjust to a life they do not particularly care about.

Stewart Lewis	Gabriel Kaplan
Alicia Lewis	Ilene Graff
Kelly Lewis	Amy Linker
Keith Lewis	David Hollander
Roscoe Clark (Stewart's partner; hence the title)	Guich Koock
Wendy (waitress)	Wendy Holcombe
John (bartender)	Michael McManus
Silas Jones	Clifton James
Lester	Aaron Fletcher
Josie	Dana Laurita

Theme Vocal ("The Lewis and Clark Theme"): Bob Duncan

Producer: Tom Tenowich, Ed Scharlach, George Shapiro

The Liar's Club

Game; 30 min; Syn. 1969

Four celebrity guests describe in detail the purpose of a real, but unusual item. The two players who compete must determine which one celebrity is telling the truth. The player with the highest score wins $100.

Host: Rod Serling

Resident Liar: Betty White

Announcer: Jim Isaics

The Liar's Club

Game; 30 min; Syn. 9/76

A revised version of the previous title, which see for format.

Host: Bill Armstrong, Allen Ludden

Resident Liars: Larry Hovis, Buddy Hackett, Joey Bishop, Dick Gautier, Betty White, Dody Goodman

Announcer: Joe Sider, Bill Beary

Producer: Ralph Andrews, Larry Hovis

The Liberace Show

Variety; 15 min; NBC 7/1/52 to 8/28/52

A program of music with pianist Wladziu Valentino Liberace.

Host: Liberace

Music Director: George Liberace

Producer: Joe Landis

The Liberace Show

Variety; 30 min; Syn. 1953

Music with pianist Liberace.

Host: Liberace

Music Director: George Liberace

Music Arranger: George Robinson

Producer: Louis D. Sander, Robert Sander

The Liberace Show

Variety; 30 min; ABC 10/13/58 to 4/10/59

A program of music with pianist Liberace.

Host: Liberace

Regulars: Erin O'Brien, Marilyn Lovell, Dick Roman

Announcer: Steve Dunne

Orchestra: Gordon Robinson

The Liberace Show

Variety; 60 min; CBS 7/15/69 to 9/16/69

A British-produced series with pianist Liberace.

Host: Liberace

Regulars: Georgia Moon, Richard Wattis, The Irving Davies Dancers

Orchestra: Jack Parnell

Producer: Robert Tamplin, Bernard Rothman, Colin Clews

The Lid's Off

A syndicated (1969) series of interviews with people from all walks of life. Hosted by Art Linkletter and produced by John Guedel.

Lidsville

Comedy; 30 min; ABC 9/11/71 to 9/1/73

Following a magician's performance, a young boy (Mark) sneaks upon stage and picks up his magic hat. When the hat begins to grow and Mark is no longer able to hold it, he places it on the floor. While attempting to look inside, Mark falls in and reappears in Lidsville, the land of living hats. When captured as a spy and imprisoned by the evil Whoo Doo (leader of the evil hats), Mark meets Weenie, a genie who helps him escape to the village of the good hats. Stories relate Mark's efforts to find his way back to his world and avoid capture by Whoo Doo, who seeks to recapture his escaped prisoner.

Mark   Butch Patrick
Whoo Doo   Charles Nelson
                        Reilly
Weenie   Billie Hayes

Hats: Sharon Baird, Joy Campbell, Angelo Rosetti, Van Snowden, Jerry Manning, Felix Silla, Hommy Stewart

Voices: Joan Gerber, Lennie Weinrib, Walker Edmiston

Theme Song ("Lidsville"): Les Szarvas

Producer: Sid and Marty Krofft

Lie Detector

Reality; 30 min; Syn. 1/83

The program offers people the opportunity to substantiate any claims by means of a polygraph (lie detector) test. Most notable of the guests was Linda Lovelace who proved on the air that she had been forced into pornography.

Host: F. Lee Bailey

Polygraph Examiner: Ed Gelb

Producer: Ralph Andrews, Robert Gunnette, Tom Cole

The Lieutenant

Drama; 60 min; NBC 9/14/63 to 9/25/64

The personal and professional lives of Raymond Rambridge, William Rice, and Samwell Panosian, officers stationed at the Camp Pendleton Marine Base in Oceanside, California.

Lt. William Rice   Gary Lockwood
Capt. Raymond
   Rambridge   Robert Vaughn
Lt. Samwell
   Panosian   Steve Franken
Lilly   Carmen Phillips
Lt. Harris   Don Penny
Various Roles   Chris Noel

"The Lieutenant" Theme Song: Jeff Alexander

Producer: Gene Roddenberry, Norman Felton

The Life and Legend of Wyatt Earp

Western; 30 min; ABC 9/6/55 to 9/26/61

The series, set first in Dodge City, Kansas, then in Tombstone, Arizona, during the 1870s, tells the story (based loosely on fact) of Wyatt Earp, a U.S. Marshal and his efforts to maintain law and order.

Marshal Wyatt Earp   Hugh O'Brian
Deputy Morgan
   Earp   Dirk London
Deputy Virgil Earp   John Anderson
                             Ross Elliott
Shotgun Gibbs   Morgan Woodward
Doc John Holliday   Myron Healey
                             Douglas V. Fowley
Kate Holliday   Carole Stone
Nellie Cashman   Randy Stuart
Ned Buntline   Lloyd Corrigan
Mayor Kelly
   (Dodge)   Ralph Sanford
                             Paul Brinegar
Mayor John Clum
   (Tombstone)   Stacy Harris
Sheriff John Behan   Lash LaRue
                             Steve Brodie
Old Man Clanton   Trevor Bardette
Emma Clanton   Carol Thurston
Phin Clanton   Steve Rowland
Bat Masterson   Alan Dinehart
Dr. Goodfellow   Damian O'Flynn
Abbie Crandall   Gloria Talbot

Judge Spicer   James Seay
Johnny Ringo   Britt Lamond
Ben Thompson   Denver Pyle
Dora Hard   Margaret Hayes
Marshal Murdock   Don Haggerty
Curly Bill Brocius   William Phipps

Theme Vocal ("The Legend of Wyatt Earp"):
The Ken Darby Singers

Producer: Robert Sisk, Louis F. Edelman,
Roy Roland

The Life and Times of Eddie Roberts

Drama; 30 min; Syn. 1/7/80 to 3/28/80

Events in the dreary day-to-day life of Eddie
Roberts, an anthropology professor at Cranpool College in Anaheim, California.

Eddie Roberts   Renny Temple
Dolores Roberts   Udana Power
Chrissy Roberts   Allison Balson
Harold Knitzer   Allen Case
Dr. Zindell   Anne O'Donnell
Cynthia Lombocker   Wendy Schaal
Vivian Blankett   Loyita Chapel
Tony Cranpool   Stephen Parr
Prof. Boggs   Jon Lormer
Chiquita Zamora   Maria O'Brien
Gertrude McQuillan   Victoria Carroll
                            Lenore Nemetz
Lydia Knitzer   Joan Hotchkis
William Billy   Billy Barty
Sen. Lombocker   William Wintersole

Producer: Anne Marcus, Ellis Marcus, Marc
Daniels

The Life and Times of Grizzly Adams

Adventure; 60 min; NBC 2/9/77 to 7/26/78
                        12/19/78 (1 episode)

When he is falsely accused of killing a man,
James Adams flees to the wilderness and later
becomes known as mountain man Grizzly
Adams. Stories concern his adventures in the
wilderness of the 1850s.

James Adams   Dan Haggerty
Mad Jack   Denver Pyle
Nakuma   Don Shanks
Robbie Cartman   John Bishop

Narrator: Denver Pyle

Theme Vocal: Thom Pace

Producer: Charles E. Sellier Jr.

Life Begins at 80

Senior citizens discuss issues either submitted by home viewers or presented by guests.
Hosted by Jack Barry (also the producer with
Dan Enright and Fred W. Friendly) and
broadcast on ABC, DuMont, and NBC at
various times from 1/1/50 to 2/25/56.

The Life of Riley

Comedy Pilot; 25 min; NBC 4/13/48

The misadventures of Chester A. Riley, a
good-natured, but henpecked riveter who is
plagued by life's endless problems. Based on
the radio series. See also the following two
titles.

Chester A. Riley   Herb Vigran
Peg Riley   Alice Drake
Jim Gillis   Lou Krugman
Honeybee Gillis   Jo Gilbert

Producer: Andy Potter

The Life of Riley

Comedy; 30 min; DuMont 10/4/49 to 3/28/50

The story of Chester A. Riley, a good-natured
bumbler employed as a riveter with Stevenson
Aircraft and Associates in Los Angeles.

Chester A. Riley   Jackie Gleason
Peg Riley   Rosemary DeCamp
Barbara "Babs"
  Riley   Gloria Winters
Chester Riley Jr.   Lanny Rees
Jim Gillis   Sid Tomack
Olive "Honeybee"
  Gillis   Maxine Semon
Egbert Gillis   George McDonald
Dibgy "Digger"
  O'Dell   John Brown
Waldo Binny   Bob Jellison
Carl Stevenson   Bill Green
                            Emory Parnell
Millie   Mary Treen
Simon
  Vanderhopper   Jimmy Lydon

Producer: Irving Brecher

The Life of Riley

Comedy; 30 min; NBC 1/2/53 to 8/22/58

The misadventures of Chester A. Riley, a riveter for Cunningham Aircraft in Los Angeles.

Chester A. Riley	William Bendix
Peg Riley	Marjorie Reynolds
Barbara "Babs" Riley	Lugene Sanders
Chester Riley Jr.	Wesley Morgan
Jim Gillis	Tom D'Andrea
Olive "Honeybee" Gillis	Veda Ann Borg
	Marie Brown
	Gloria Blondell
Egbert Gillis	Gregory Marshall
Don Marshall	Martin Milner
Babs and Don's baby	Melodie Chaney
Waldo Binny	Sterling Holloway
Otto Schmidlap	Henry Kulky
Calvin Dudley	George O'Hanlon
Belle Dudley	Florence Sundstrom
Annie Riley	Larraine Bendix
Cissy Riley	Mary Jane Croft
Pa Riley	James Gleason
	James Gavin
Ma Riley	Sarah Pudden
Mr. Cunningham	Douglas Dumbrille
Hank Hawkins	Emory Parnell
Lorna Hawkins	Isabel Withers
Moose Larkin	Denny Miller
Arnold Willis	Joe Conley
Alvin Winkley	Arthur Shields
Peg's Uncle Bixby	Jack Kirkwood
Mrs. Hayes	Reta Shaw
Roger Ganaway	Steve Pendleton
Constance Ganaway	Pamela Britton
	Sheila Bromley
Honeybee's mother	Bea Benaderet

Producer: Tom McKnight

The Life of Vernon Hathaway

Comedy Pilot; 30 min; NBC 11/9/55

The story of Vernon Hathaway, a meek watch repairman who daydreams himself into exciting adventures. Aired on "Screen Director's Playhouse."

Vernon Hathaway	Alan Young
Irma	Cloris Leachman
Red Beecham	Douglas Dumbrille
Howard Baines	Raymond Bailey

Director: Norman Z. McLeod

Life with Buster Keaton

A syndicated (1952) comedy series composed of Buster Keaton theatrical shorts of the 1930s and 40s and of vignettes in which Buster plays a man struggling to cope with life's endless problems.

Life with Elizabeth

Comedy; 30 min; Syn. 1953

Events in the lives of the newlywed Whites (Elizabeth and Alvin) as they struggle to survive the difficult first years of marriage.

Elizabeth White	Betty White
Alvin White	Del Moore
Chloe Skinner	Jack Narz
Richard Munch	Dick Garton
Mac MacDonald	Roy Lennert

Producer: George Tibbles, Don Fedderson

Life with Father

Comedy; 30 min; CBS 11/22/53 to 7/5/55

Events in the day-to-day lives of the Days, a middle-class American family of turn-of-the-century New York, who are plagued by the stubbornness of a father who refuses to accept the progress of a rapidly changing world. Based on the feature film.

Clarence Day Sr.	Leon Ames
Vinnie Day (wife)	Lurene Tuttle
Clarency Day Jr.	Ralph Reed
	Steve Terrell
Whitney Day	Ronald Keith
	B. G. Norman
	Fred Ridgeway
John Day	Freddie Leiston
	Malcolm Cassell
Harlan Day	Harvey Grant
Nora (their maid)	Marion Ross

Announcer: Bob Lemond

Producer: Ben Feiner, Fletcher Markle

Life with Linkletter

Variety; 30 min; ABC 10/6/50 to 4/25/52

A casual program of music, interviews, and audience participation contests for prizes.

Host: Art Linkletter

Announcer: Jack Slattery

Music: The Muzzy Marcellino Trio

Producer: John Guedel

Life with Lucy

Comedy; 30 min; ABC 9/21/86 to 11/15/86

Following her husband's death, Lucy Baker moves in with her daughter (Margo) and her family (husband Ted, and kids Becky, and Kevin) and joins Curtis, her husband's partner, as his new partner in the M&B Hardware Store. Stories relate Lucy's endless misadventures.

Lucy Baker	Lucille Ball
Curtis McGibbon	Gale Gordon
Margo McGibbon	Ann Dusenberry
Ted McGibbon	Larry Anderson
Becky McGibbon	Jenny Lewis
Kevin McGibbon	Philip J. Amelio
Leonard Stoner	Donovan Scott

Theme Vocal ("Life with Lucy"): Eydie Gorme

Producer: Aaron Spelling, Gary Morton, Douglas S. Cramer

Life with Luigi

Comedy; 30 min; CBS 9/22/52 to 12/22/52
4/9/53 to 6/4/53

The simple pleasures and trying times of Luigi Basco, an immigrant who runs an antique shop in Chicago, as he struggles to adjust to the American way of life. Titled "The New Life with Luigi" in 1953.

Luigi Basco	J. Carrol Naish
Pasquale	Vito Scotti
	Alan Reed
	Thomas Gomez
Rosa	Jody Gilbert
	Muriel Landers
Miss Spaulding	Mary Shipp
Schultz	Sig Rumin
Horwitz	Joe Forte
Olson	Ken Peters

Producer: Mac Benoff, Cy Howard, Calvin Kuhl, Norman Tokar

Life with Snarky Parker

Children; 15 min; CBS 1/9/50 to 9/29/50

A marionette series about Deputy Sheriff Snarky Parker and his efforts to maintain the law in the town of Hot Rock.

Voices/Puppeteers: Bil and Cora Baird

Producer-Director: Yul Brynner

Life with the Erwins

See "Trouble with Father."

Life with Virginia

Comedy Pilot; 30 min; CBS 9/18/62

The story of Virginia Carol, a pretty teenage girl with a penchant for trying to solve other people's problems.

Virginia Carol	Candy Moore
Agnes Carol	Maggie Hayes
Harold Carol	Karl Swenson
Joan Carol	Roberta Shore
Maggie	Margaret Hamilton

Producer: Lewis Rackmil

Lifestyles of the Rich and Famous

Human Interest; 60 min; Syn. 4/84

The private lives of famous celebrities and people of great wealth.

Host-Narrator: Robin Leach

Additional Narration: David Perry

Music: David Dutcher

Theme Song ("Come Fly With Me Now"): Bill Conti, Norman Gimbel

Producer: Robin Leach, Jim Cross

Note: Also appeared in a first-run, half-hour version on ABC from 4/7/86 to 9/6/86.

Lights, Camera, Action!

An NBC variety series (7/4/50 to 8/20/50) of performances by undiscovered talent. Hosted by Walter Woolf King.

Light's Out

Anthology; 30 min; NBC 7/12/49 to 9/29/52

A live series of mystery and suspense tales that had a four week experimental run on NBC in 1946 (8/11 to 9/1) making it the first known attempt to bring a weekly anthology series to television. Based on the radio program.

Host: Jack LaRue, Frank Gallop

Producer: Herbert Swope Jr., Fred Coe, Ernest Walling

Light's Out

Anthology Pilot; 60 min; NBC 1/15/72

A proposed series of suspense stories. The pilot, titled "When Widows Weep," tells of a doll maker whose creations trigger a series of bizarre deaths.

Sabina	Joan Hackett
Howard	Laurence Luckinbill
Karen	Louisa Horton
State Trooper	Michael McGuire
Helen	Kathryn Walker

Producer: Herbert Brodkin

Like Magic

Variety Pilot; 30 min; CBS 6/13/81

An unsold series idea that was to spotlight guest magicians.

Host: Chris Kirby

Guests: Melissa Gilbert, Ricky Jay

Producer: Armand Grant

Li'l Abner

Comedy Pilot; 30 min; NBC 9/5/67

Incidents in the lives of the citizens of Dog Patch, U.S.A., a comic strip community created by Al Capp. The story finds a senator arriving to investigate the magical charm of Daisy Mae, the most beautiful resident of Dog Patch.

Li'l Abner	Sammy Jackson
Daisy Mae	Jeannine Riley
Mammy Yokum	Judy Canova
Pappy Yokum	Jerry Lester
Senator Cod	Robert Reed

Producer: Howard Leeds

Li'l Abner

Comedy Pilot; 60 min; NBC 4/26/71

A second pilot about the residents of mythical Dog Patch, U.S.A. In the story, the residents wage a war against pollution.

Li'l Abner	Ray Young
Daisy Mae	Nancee Parkinson
Mammy Yokum	Billie Hayes
Pappy Yokum	Billy Bletcher
Marryin' Sam	Dale Malone
Nightmare Alice	Bobo Lewis

Producer: Allan Blye, Chris Bearde

The Lilli Palmer Show

A CBS interview series (1/4/51 to 6/28/51) with actress Lilli Palmer. Produced by Charles Kebbe.

The Lili Palmer Theatre

Anthology; 30 min; Syn. 9/56

Dramatic productions, produced especially for syndication, that feature virtually unknown performers (including Wendy Hiller, Andre Morrell, Brian Wilde, Derrick De-Marney, Mona Washburn, Brenda Hogan, Ada Reeve, David Tomlinson, and Mary Clare).

Hostess: Lilli Palmer

Producer: Charles Kebbe

Lily

Comedy Pilot; 30 min; NBC 6/12/74

Events in the life of a pretty single girl (Lily) with marriage-minded parents and a marriage-shy boyfriend.

Lily	Brenda Vaccaro
Jonathan	Mike Farrell
Lily's mother	Eileen Heckart
Ruthie	Beverly Sanders
Ernie	Michael Lombard
Elaine	Yvonne Wilder
Father Menotti	Frank Campanella

Producer: Bob Finkel, Jackie Cooper

Lily

Comical Adventure Pilot; 60 min; CBS 6/14/86

The exploits of Lily Miniver, the assistant curator of the Jeffersonian Museum in Washington, D.C.

Lily Miniver	Shelley Duvall
John Farnsworth	Donald Moffat
Claudia	Beverly Hope Atkinson
Wesley	Peter Jurasik
David Rand	Tom Conti
Ziaukus	Spiros Focas
Mrs. Hudson	Ruth DeSusa
Museum Employee	Stephen Davies
Woman	Paddi Edwards

Producer: Shelley Duvall, Andy Borowitz, Joel Rogosin

Lime Street

Adventure; 60 min; ABC 9/21/85 to 11/2/85

The global exploits of James Greyson Culver, an American-based investigator (in Middleburgh, Virginia) for Lime Street, a London-based insurance company. The series is dedicated to Samantha Smith*.

James Culver	Robert Wagner
Edward Wingate	John Standing
Henry Wade Culver	Lew Ayres
Elizabeth Culver	Samantha Smith
Margaret Ann Culver	Maia Brewton
Celia (James's secretary)	Julie Fulton
Evelyn (Eliz. and Margaret's nanny)	Anne Haney
Sir Geoffrey Rimbatten (head of Lime Street)	Patrick Macnee

"Lime Street" Theme by Lee Holdridge.

Producer: Robert Wagner, Harry Thomason, Linda Bloodworth-Thomason

*Samantha, who was 13, died tragically in a plane crash in August 1985 after filming 4 episodes.

The Line

Comedy Pilot; 30 min; NBC 7/29/87

The misadventures of Karen Cooper, a pretty but naive young woman who works on an assembly line in an airplane factory.

Karen Cooper	Dinah Manoff
Jo	Lori Petty
Denise Powell	Alfre Woodard
Anna Mae	C.C.H. Pounder
Lucy	Park Overall
Ken Morris	Andrew Rubin
Benyo	Brian George

Producer: Paul Junger Witt, Tony Thomas

The Line-Up

Crime Drama; CBS 10/1/54 to 9/23/59 (30 min)
9/30/59 to 1/20/60 (60 min)

The exploits of a group of detectives attached to the San Francisco Police Department. Syndicated as "San Francisco Beat."

Lt. Ben Guthrie	Warner Anderson
Insp. Matt Grebb	Tom Tully
Off. Sandy McCallister	Jan Brooks
	Rachel Ames
Off. Pete Larkin	Bob Palmer
	Skip Ward
Insp. Dan Delaney	William Leslie
Insp. Charlie Summers	Tod Burton
Insp. Fred Asher	Marshall Reed
Various Roles	Ruta Lee

Theme Song ("San Francisco Blues"): Jerry Goldsmith

Producer: Cecil Baker, Jaime Del Valle, Robert Sparks

Announcer: Art Gilmore

The Linkletter Show

See "Art Linkletter's House Party."

Linus the Lionhearted

Cartoon; 30 min; CBS 9/26/64 to 9/3/66

The adventures of Linus, the gentle ruler of animals in Africa.

Linus	Sheldon Leonard
Danny Kangaroo	Carl Reiner
Mockingbird	Ed Graham
Giant	Jonathan Winters
Sugar Bear	Sterling Holloway

Producer: Ed Graham

Lippy the Lion

Cartoon; 5 min; Syn. 1962

The antics of a trouble-prone lion (Lippy) and his friend Hardy Har Har.

Lippy the Lion	Daws Butler
Hardy Har Har	Mel Blanc

Producer: William Hanna, Joseph Barbera.

The Lisa Hartman Show

Variety Pilot; 60 min; ABC 6/30/79

A lively hour of music, songs, and comedy sketches.

Hostess: Lisa Hartman

Guests: Karen Turner, Andy Kaufman, Bill Kirchenbauer, Ruci Martin

Theme Vocal ("Hot Stuff"): Lisa Hartman

Orchestra: Johnny Harris

Producer: George Schlatter, Rod Warren, David Winters

Little House on the Prairie

Drama; 60 min; NBC 9/11/74 to 9/21/82

The series, set in Walnut Grove in Plumb Creek, Minnesota, during the 1870s, follows events in the lives of the pioneering Ingalls family. Their experiences as homesteaders is viewed through the sentimental eyes of Laura Ingalls, the second-born daughter.

Charles Ingalls	Michael Landon
Caroline Ingalls	Karen Grassle
Laura Ingalls	Melissa Gilbert
Mary Ingalls	Melissa Sue Anderson
Carrie Ingalls	Lindsay Greenbush
	Sidney Greenbush
Grace Ingalls	Wendi Turnbaugh
	Brenda Turnbaugh
Albert	Matthew Laborteaux
Cassandra	Missy Francis
James	Jason Bateman
Adam Kendall	Linwood Boomer
Nels Oleson	Richard Bull
Harriet Oleson	Katherine MacGregor
Nellie Oleson	Alison Arngrim
Willie Oleson	Jonathan Gilbert
Lars Hanson	Karl Swenson
Isaiah Edwards	Victor French
Grace Edwards	Bonnie Bartlett
John Edwards	Radamas Pera
Aliscia Edwards	Kyle Richards
Jonathan Garvey	Merlin Olsen
Alice Garvey	Hersha Parady
Andy Garvey	Patrick Laborteaux
Grace Beadle	Charlotte Stewart
Eliza Jane Wilder	Lucy Lee Flippen
Almanzo Wilder	Dean Butler
Rev. Robert Alden	Dabbs Greer
Ebenezer Sprague	Ted Gehring
Percival Dalton	Steve Tracy
Dr. Baker	Kevin Hagen
Mr. Toms	Fredric Downs
Hester Sue	Ketty Lester
Nancy Oleson	Allison Balson

Producer: Michael Landon, Ed Friendly

Little House: A New Beginning

Drama; 60 min; NBC 9/27/82 to 3/21/83

A spin-off from "Little House on the Prairie." When Charles Ingalls is unable to make a living in Plumb Creek, he sells his "Little House" to John and Sarah Carter, a young couple with two children, and moves to Iowa (where he becomes a purchasing agent). Laura, Charles's second-born daughter, and her husband, Almanzo, remain behind to continue the lumber mill previously operated by her father. Stories relate incidents in the lives of the people of Plumb Creek.

Laura Ingalls Wilder	Melissa Gilbert
Almanzo Wilder	Dean Butler
John Carter	Stan Ivar
Sarah Carter	Pamela Roylance
Jeb Carter	Lindsay Kennedy
Jason Carter	David Friedman
Isaiah Edwards	Victor French
Jenny Wilder	Shannen Doherty
Etta Plum	Leslie Landon
Nels Oleson	Richard Bull
Harriet Oleson	Katherine MacGregor
Nancy Oleson	Allison Balson
Hester Sue	Ketty Lester
Bill Anderson	Sam Edwards
Rev. Robert Alden	Dabbs Greer
Dr. Baker	Kevin Hagen

Producer: Michael Landon, Kent McCray

Little Leatherneck

Comedy Pilot; 30 min; ABC 7/29/66

When young Cindy Fenton becomes fascinated by her father (Mike), a Marine drill sergeant, she decides to follow in his footsteps—and become a Marine. The unsold series was to relate her adventures as unofficial Marine.

Cindy Fenton	Donna Butterworth
Sgt. Mike Fenton	Scott Brady
Delores	Sue Ane Langdon
Miss Reymond	Jean Innes
Mess Sergeant	Ned Glass

Theme Vocal ("Little Leatherneck"): Donna Butterworth

Little Lulu

Comedy Pilot; 30 min; ABC 11/4/78

The misadventures of Little Lulu, a precocious pre-teenage girl.

Little Lulu	Lauri Hendler
Gloria	Annrae Walterhouse
Annie	Lulu Baxter
Iggie	Robbie Rist
Tubby	Kevin King Cooper
Willy	Eddie Singleton

Producer: Robert Chenault, Ann Elder, Cindy Leonetti

The Little People

Comedy; 30 min; NBC 9/15/72 to 9/7/73 (as "The Little People") 9/21/73 to 8/30/74 (as "The Brian Keith Show")

The story of a father (Sean) and daughter (Anne) team of pediatricians based in Kahala, Hawaii.

Dr. Sean Jamison	Brian Keith
Dr. Anne Jamison	Shelley Fabares
Nurse Puni	Victoria Young
Ronnie Collins	Michael Gray
Alfred Landis	Stephen Hague
Moe O'Shaughnessy	Moe Keale
Stewart	Sean Tyler Hill
Dr. Spencer Chaffey	Roger Bowen
Millar Gruber	Nancy Kulp

Producer: Jerry Thorpe, Garry K. Marshall

The Little Prince

Cartoon; 30 min; Syn. 9/84

The adventures of The Little Prince, ruler of the planet B6-12, as he and his friend, Swiftee the Space Bird, travel to various planets in an attempt to learn about life on other worlds.

The Little Prince	Kathy Leigh
	Julie McWhirter
Swiftee	Hal Smith

Producer: Jameson Brewer

The Little Rascals

Cartoon; 30 min; ABC 9/25/82 to 9/1/84

A TV adaptation of the popular theatrical shorts of the 1920s, 30s, and 40s, about a group of very mischievous children.

Spanky	Scott Menville
Alfalfa	Julie McWhirter
Darla	Patty Maloney
Buckwheat	Shavar Ross
Porky	Julie McWhirter
Butch	B. J. Ward
Woim	Julie McWhirter
Waldo	B. J. Ward
Pete the dog	Peter Cullen

Producer: William Hanna, Joseph Barbera.

The Little Revue

Variety; 30 min; ABC 9/4/49 to 4/28/50

A live program of music and song from Chicago.

Host:·Bill Sherry

Regulars: Gloria Van, Nancy Evans, Dick Larkin, Billy Johnson, Dick France

Orchestra: Rex Maupin

Little Shots

Comedy Pilot; 30 min; NBC 6/25/83

The adventures of the Little Shots, a group of pre-teen neighborhood children.

Pete*	Joey Lawrence
Spitter*	Robbie Kiger
Griddy*	Keri Houlihan
Linda*	Mya Akerling
Ralph*	Jeff Cohen
Wiener*	Kevin Burlat
Iris*	Erin Nicole Brown
Smokey Joe	Vincent Schiavelli
Samantha	Soleil Moon Frye
Nancy	Kelly Grogan

"The Little Shots" Theme Song: James P. Dunne

Producer: Anson Williams, Ron Howard, Bruce Johnson

*The Little Shots.

The Little Show

See "John Conte's Little Show."

Little Vic

Drama; 30 min; Syn. 2/77

The story of a 14-year-old boy (Gillie) who yearns to become a jockey. (Little Vic is the horse he trains and later rides in the Santa Anita Derby.)

Gillie Walker	Joey Green
Clara Scott	Carol Ann Seflinger
Julie Sayer	Doney Oatman
Richie Miller	David Levy
Mr. Hammer	Del Hinkley
Mr. Lawson	Charles Stewart
George Gordon	Med Flory
Dr. Freeman	J. Jay Saunders
Fred Amble	Myron Natwick

Producer: Daniel Wilson, Linda Marmelstein

Little Women

Drama; 30 min; Syn. 1971

A British series based on the novel by Louisa May Alcott. The story, set in 1860s New England, follows the joys and sorrows of the four close-knit March sisters (Jo, Meg, Amy, and Beth).

Josephine "Jo" March	Angela Down
Margaret "Meg" March	Jo Rowbottom
Amy March	Janina Faye
Beth March	Sarah Craze
Margaret "Marmee" March	Stephanie Bidmead
Jonathan March	Patrick Troughton
Aunt Kathryn March	Jean Anderson
Theodore "Laurie" Lawrence	Stephen Turner
Prof. Friedrich Bhaer	Frederick Jaeger
Hannah	Pat Nye
James Lawrence	John Welsh

Producer: John McRae

Little Women

Drama; 60 min; NBC 2/8/79 to 3/8/79

The series, set in Concord, Massachusetts, during the late 1860s, follows the dreams, ambitions, and frustrations of the March sisters

(Jo, Meg, Amy, and Beth). As seen through the sentimental eyes of Jo, an aspiring writer, stories of Victorian manners and mores unfold.

Josephine "Jo"	
March	Susan Dey*
	Jessica Harper
Margaret "Meg"	
March	Meredith Baxter
	Birney*
	Susan Walden
Amy March	Ann Dusenberry
Beth March	Eve Plumb
Margaret "Marmee"	
March	Dorothy McGuire
Rev. Jonathan March	William Schallert
Aunt Kathryn	
March	Greer Garson*
	Mildred Natwick
Melissa Jane	
Driscoll	Eve Plumb
Prof. Friedrich	
Bhaer	William Shatner*
	David Ackroyd
Theodore "Laurie"	
Lawrence	Richard Gilliland
James Lawrence	Robert Young
John Brooke	Cliff Potts
Hannah	Virginia Gregg
Amanda	Maggie Malooly

Music: Elmer Bernstein

Producer: David Victor, Richard Collins

*TV Movie roles (NBC, 10/2 and 10/3/78).

The Littles

Cartoon; 30 min; ABC 9/10/83 (Premiere)

One day, while investigating a noise, Henry Bigg discovers that a race of little people live in the walls of his house. Befriending Tom and Lucy Little, Henry learns that they are being sought by the evil Dr. Hunter, who is seeking to prove that the Littles really do exist. Stories Henry's adventures with the Littles and his efforts to keep them a secret from Dr. Hunter.

Voices: Bettina Bush, Jimmy Keegan, Pat Parris, Alvy Moore, Robert David Hall, Laurel Page, Ken Sansom, Mona Marshall, Candy Craig, John Stephenson

Producer: Jean Chalopin, Andy Heyward

The Littlest Hobo

Adventure; 30 min; Syn. 1964

The adventures of London, a masterless German Shepherd dog who helps people in distress. Produced by Darrell McGowan and Stuart McGowan.

The Littlest Hobo

Anthology; 30 min; Syn. 9/80

The adventures of London, an unowned, roving German Shepherd who helps people in distress.

Theme Vocal ("Maybe Tomorrow"): Terry Bush

Producer: Ed Richardson, Seymour Berns

Live Like a Millionaire

Game; 30 min; CBS 1/5/51 to 3/14/52
ABC 10/25/52 to 2/7/53

Undiscovered professional talent competes, seeking possible discovery and the top prize of one week's tax on a million dollars.

Host: John Nelson, Jack McCoy

Assistant: Michael O'Halloran, Connie Clawson

Announcer: Jack McCoy

Producer: Ivan Ditmars, John Reddy, John Nelson, John Masterson

The Lively Ones

Variety; 60 min; NBC 7/26/62 to 9/13/62
7/25/63 to 9/12/63

Music, songs and dances set against offbeat electronic backgrounds.

Host: Vic Damone

Regulars: Joan Staley, Shirley Yelm, Gloria Neil, Quinn O'Hara, The Earl Brown Dancers

Orchestra: Jerry Fielding

Producer: Barry Shear

Living Easy

A syndicated (1973) women's program of fashion, decorating, interviews, and advice. Hosted by Dr. Joyce Brothers. Music by Bernard Green with Mike Darrow as the announcer.

The Living End

Comedy Pilot; 30 min; CBS 3/17/72

The misadventures of Doug Newman, a veteran defensive end for the Chicago Cherokees football team. See also "Two's Company."

Doug Newman	Lou Gossett
Nancy Newman	Diana Sands
Coach Bullets	Dick O'Neill
Richie Rosen	Paul Cavonis
Mickey	John Calvin
Henry	Roger Mosley
Stan	Don Sherman

Producer: Saul Ilson, Ernest Chambers

Living in Paradise

Comedy Pilot; 30 min; NBC 2/1/81

The misadventures of Vincent Slattery, a carefree, retired bachelor living in Paradise Park.

Vincent Slattery	Eddie Albert
Winnie Coogan	Georgann Johnson
Jason Slattery	Jerry Houser
Hazel Adamson	Debralee Scott
Mel Adamson	Alan Oppenheimer
Donna	Patti Townsend

Theme Vocal ("That's the Way I Am"): Eddie Albert

Producer: Bob Schiller, Bob Weiskopf

The Lloyd Bridges Show

Anthology; 30 min; CBS 9/11/62 to 9/3/63

Dramatic presentations that recount the stories of free-lance journalist Adam Sheppard. The pilot episode, "The Death of the Temple Bay," aired on "The June Allyson Show" on April 3, 1961 (at the time, the intended series title was "The Adventures of Adam Fable").

Adam Sheppard   Lloyd Bridges

Producer: Aaron Spelling, Everett Chambers

Lloyd Bridges Water World

A syndicated (1972) travel series in which Lloyd Bridges visits various tropical islands and gives tips on boating safety. Produced by Norman Jacobson. Music by Marty Gould.

The Lloyd Thaxton Show

A syndicated (1964) music series, hosted by Lloyd Thaxton, and featuring performances by rock stars. Regulars are Lynne Marta and Michael Storm.

Lobo

Crime Drama; 60 min; NBC 12/30/80 to 8/25/81

When the governor of Atlanta discovers that Orly County, Georgia, is virtually crime-free due to what he believes is the honest work of the larcenous Sheriff Lobo, he hires Lobo and his deputies to help curb the rising crime rate. Stories relate Lobo's attempts to do for Atlanta what they did in Orly. A spin-off from "The Misadventures of Sheriff Lobo."

Sheriff Elroy P. Lobo	Claude Akins
Deputy Perkins	Mills Watson
Deputy Birdwell Hawkins	Brian Kerwin
Chief John E. Carson	Nicholas Coster
Off. Brandy Ames	Tara Buckman
Off. Peaches McLain	Amy Botwinick
Sgt. Hildy Jones	Nell Carter
Governor	William Schallert
	Mark Roberts
George (lab technician)	Dudley Knight

Producer: Glen A. Larson, Jo Swerling Jr., Frank Lupo, Bill Dial

Local 306

Comedy Pilot; 30 min; NBC 8/23/76

The misadventures of Harvey Gordon, the newly appointed chief steward of Plumber's Local 306, as he attempts to adjust to his new position.

Harvey Gordon	Eugene Roche
Rose Gordon	Miriam-Byrd Nethery
Helene Gordon	Susan Sennett
Hutchings	Milton Parsons
Rocco	Roy Stewart
Fillmore	Hilly Hicks
Darlene	Barrie Youngfellow
Daniel	Raymond Singer

Producer: Mark Carliner, Stanley Ralph Ross

Lock Up

Crime Drama; 30 min; Syn. 1959

The story of Herbert L. Maris, a Philadelphia-based lawyer who defends unjustly accused people.

Herbert L. Maris	Macdonald Carey
Weston (his legman)	John Doucette

Producer: Henry Kessler

Logan's Run

Adventure; 60 min; CBS 9/16/77 to 1/16/78

Following a holocaust in the year 2319, the surviving segment of civilization establishes itself in the City of Domes. Because of restrictions, it is ruled that no one is permitted to live past the age of thirty. Those who defy this tradition and believe there is a place of freedom called "Sanctuary," are labeled Runners and become the prey of the Sandmen, who pursue and destroy them. Stories follow the adventures of two Runners (Logan and Jessica) as they seek freedom; and the efforts of a Sandman (Francis) to capture them.

Logan	Gregory Harrison
Jessica	Heather Menzies
Francis	Randolph Powell
Rem	Donald Moffat
Morgan	Morgan Woodward
Jonathan	Wright King
Martin	E. J. Andre
Benjamin	Stan Stratton

Producer: Ivan Goff, Ben Roberts

Lollipop Louie

Comedy-Drama Pilot; 60 min; ABC 1/10/63

The story of Louie Mastraeani, a happy-go-lucky dreamer who earns his living as a fisherman in California.

Louie Mastraeani	Aldo Ray
Emma	Barbara Turner
Tony	Paul Comi
Uncle Peter	Ralph Manza

Producer: Fred Finkelhoff

London and Davis in New York

Crime Drama Pilot; 60 min; CBS 9/9/84

The exploits of a world famous photojournalism team who are also lovers: Claudia London (photographer) and John Greyson Davis (journalist). In the pilot, they come to N.Y. to seek "The Bachelor Killer."

Claudia London	Season Hubley
John Davis	Richard Crenna
Paul Fisk	Roddy McDowall
Brandon Wesphal	James Carroll Jordan
Frances Meyers	Vernee Watson
Sam Gains	Gerald S. O'Loughlin
Adrienne Crowe	Karen Austin
Tony Tannen	Macon McCalman

Theme Song ("The Love Theme from London and Davis"): Chuck Magione

Producer: Harry Thomason, Linda Bloodworth

The London Palladium

Variety; 60 min; NBC 5/26/66 to 8/12/66

Entertainment acts from England's London Palladium Music Hall.

Guest Hosts: Lorne Greene, Kate Smith, Jonathan Winters, Hugh O'Brian, Roger Moore

Regulars: The Mike Sammes Singers, The Paddy Stone Dancers

Orchestra: Jack Parnell

Producer: Bill Ward

The Lone Ranger

Western; 30 min; ABC 9/15/49 to 9/4/65

While trailing the Butch Cavendish Gang, six Texas Rangers are ambushed and left for dead at Bryant's Gap canyon. Tonto, a Potawatomie Indian, discovers a lone survivor, John Reid, brother of the slain captain. While nursing Reid back to health, Tonto digs six graves, the sixth marked with the name John Reid, to conceal the fact that one ranger had lived to avenge the others. At Tonto's suggestion, Reid fashions a mask from the black cloth of his brother's vest and later tracks down and apprehends the Cavendish Gang.

Stories, set in Texas during the 19th-century, follow the trail of the Lone Ranger and Tonto as they strive to maintain law and order.

The Lone Ranger	Clayton Moore
	John Hart
Tonto	Jay Silverheels
Dan Reid (John's	
nephew)	Chuck Courtney
Jim Blaine (miner)	Ralph Littlefield
George Wilson	
(banker)	Lyle Talbot
Father Paul	David Leonard
Butch Cavendish	Glenn Strange
Outlaw Roles	Ben Weldon

Announcer: Fred Foy

Producer: Sherman Harris, Geroge W. Trendle, Jack Chertok, Paul Landers, Harry H. Poppe

The Lone Ranger

Cartoon; 30 min; CBS 9/10/66 to 9/6/69

The further adventures of The Lone Ranger and his Indian friend, Tonto, as they strive to maintain the peace.

The Lone Ranger	Michael Rye
Tonto	Shepard Menkin

Producer: Arthur Jacobs, Herbert Klein

Lone Star

Crime Drama Pilot; 60 min; NBC 7/31/83

The story of two modern-day Texas Rangers (brothers Ben and George) battling crime and corruption in the Lone Star State.

Ben McCollum	Lewis Smith
George McCollum	Alan Autry
Deputy Cissy Wells	Terri Garber
Luther McCollum	John McIntire
Capt. Sam Mellon	Sandy McPeak
Jake Farrell	Chuck Connors
Amanda Talbot	Nancy Stafford
Maggie Holloway	Amanda Wyss

Producer: Lawrence and Charles Gordon

The Lone Wolf

Adventure; 30 min; Syn. 4/54

The exploits of Michael Lanyard, a private detective who is known as The Lone Wolf, as he crusades against the global forces of tyranny and injustice. Also known as "Streets of Danger."

Michael Lanyard	Louis Hayward

Producer: Jack Gross, Philip Krasne

The Loner

Western Pilot; 30 min; CBS 3/5/59

The pilot for "Johnny Ringo." Seeking to go straight and find a place to settle down, ex-gunfighter Johnny Ringo becomes the sheriff of an Arizona town. In the pilot he attempts to help a derelict citizen. Aired on "Zane Grey Theatre."

Johnny Ringo	Don Durant
Cason Thomas	Thomas Mitchell
Laura Thomas	Marilyn Erskine
Evans	Scott Forbes

Producer: Hal Hudson

The Loner

Western; 30 min; CBS 9/18/65 to 4/30/66

The story of William Colton, a disillusioned Civil War officer who, one month after Appomattox, resigns his Union commission and heads West to search for the meaning of life.

William Colton	Lloyd Bridges

Producer: William Dozier, Andy White, Bruce Lansbury

Creator: Rod Serling

The Long Hot Summer

Drama; 60 min; ABC 9/19/65 to 7/3/66

Shortly after he returns to his home in Frenchman's Bend, Mississippi, drifter Ben Quick befriends the beautiful Clara Varner, the daughter of the town banker (Will). When Will, who dislikes Ben, discovers that his spoiled daughter has fallen for Ben, he forbids her to see him. An angry Clara defies Will and sets her goal to acquire Ben's love. Stories relate the conflicts that exist between Ben and Will as Ben struggles to rebuild his farm and prove himself worthy of Clara.

Will Varner	Edmond O'Brien
	Dan O'Herlihy
Ben Quick	Roy Thinnes
Clara Varner	Nancy Malone
Eula Varner	Lana Wood
Jody Varner	Paul Geary
Minnie Littlejohn	Ruth Roman
Duane Galloway	John Kerr
Lucas Taney	Warren Kemmerling
Harve Anders	Paul Bryar
John Johnson	Zalman King
Amy	Anne Helm
Mitch Taney	Brian Cutler
Shad Taney	Michael Zaslow
Agnes	Josie Lloyd
Dr. Clark	Jason Wingreen

Producer: Frank Glicksman

Long John Silver

See "The Adventures of Long John Silver."

Longstreet

Crime Drama; 60 min; ABC 9/16/71 to 8/10/72

A bomb blast, meant to kill insurance investigator Michael Longstreet instead claims the life of his wife, Ingrid. Michael, left blinded, enrolls in a special clinic and later, with the help of his seeing eye dog (Pax) apprehends the culprits. Stories relate Michael's exploits as a blind investigator for the Great Pacific Casualty Insurance Company in New Orleans.

Michael Longstreet	James Franciscus
Nikki Bell	Martine Beswick*
	Marlyn Mason
Duke Paige	Bradford Dillman*
	Peter Mark Richman
Li Tsung	Bruce Lee
Mrs. Kingston	Ann Doran
Ingrid Longstreet	Judy Jones

Producer: Stirling Silliphant, Joel Rogosin

*Pilot film role (ABC 2/23/71).

Look at Us

Magazine; 30 min; Syn. 9/81

Reports on current issues and a lifestyles segment on the achievements of famous people.

Host: Richard Crenna

Producer: George Schlatter, Bob Wynn

Look Ma, I'm Acting

See "Say It with Acting."

Look Out World

Comedy Pilot; 30 min; NBC 7/27/77

The adventures of four young men working at a Santa Monica, California, car wash. Based on the film "Car Wash."

Cannonball	Michael Huddleston
Benny	Justin Lord
Delfi	Bart Braverman
Beau	Steve Doubet
Gus	Arnold Soboloff
Darcy	Maureen Arthur
Byron	Damon Raskin
Byron's mother	Susan Bay

Producer: Perry Lafferty

Look What They've Done to My Song

Comedy Pilot; 30 min; Syn. 7/80

Spoofs of popular melodies via sketches based on the songs.

Host: Norman Fell

Regulars: Karen Rushmore, Damita Jo Freeman, Gale Garnet, Howard Iskowitz, Marsha Myers, Sherry Worth, Ty Whitney

Orchestra: Bob Rosario

Producer: Ernest Chambers

The Lorenzo and Henrietta Music Show

Variety; 60 min; Syn. 9/76

Music, interviews, songs, and sketches.

Hosts: Lorenzo and Henrietta Music

Regulars: Samantha Harper, Dave Willock, Bob Gibson, Murphy Dunne, Erick Darling, Sandy Helberg

Announcer: Dave Willock

Orchestra: Jack Eskew

Producer: Lorenzo Music, Lewis Arquette

The Loretta Young Show

Comedy-Drama; 30 min; CBS 9/24/62 to 3/18/63

Serial-like episodes that relate the meeting, courtship, and marriage of Christine Massey, a widowed children's story book writer (and mother of seven children) living in Ellendale, Connecticut, and Paul Belzer, a bachelor magazine editor who falls in love with her when she comes to submit an article for publication. Also known as "The New Loretta Young Show."

Christine Massey	Loretta Young
Paul Belzer	James Philbrook
Vickie Massey	Beverly Washburn
Maria Massey	Tracy Stratford
Marnie Massey	Celia Kaye
Judy Massey	Sandy Descher
Dack Massey	Dack Rambo
Dirk Massey	Dirk Rambo
Binkie Massey	Carol Sydes
Mrs. Teasdale	Hope Summers
Teedee Dooley	Kelly Harmon
Bascombe Beebee	Leif Erickson
Rain Beebee	Regina Gleason

Producer: John London, Ruth Roberts

The Loretta Young Theatre

Anthology; 30 min; NBC 8/29/54 to 9/10/61

Quality dramatic productions with film star Loretta Young as the host and frequent star. See also "A Letter to Loretta."

Hostess: Loretta Young

Regulars: Beverly Washburn, John Newland

Substitute Hostess (1955): Dinah Shore, Merle Oberon, Barbara Stanwyck

Music: Harry Lubin

Producer: John London, Ruth Roberts, Bert Granet, Tom Lewis

The Losers

Western Pilot; 60 min; NBC 1/15/63

The Old West adventures of Dave Blassingame and Burgandy Smith, drifters who help people in trouble. Aired on "The Dick Powell Theatre."

Dave Blassingame	Lee Marvin
Burgandy Smith	Keenan Wynn
Melissa	Rosemary Clooney
Old Isaiah	Russ Brown
Bland Johnny	Adam Lazzard

Host: Robert Mitchum

Producer: Dick Powell, Aaron Spelling

Lost in Space

Adventure; 60 min; CBS 9/15/65 to 9/11/68

In 1997, as the planet Earth becomes critically overpopulated, the Robinson family is selected to begin the conquest of space. As the "Jupiter II" is readied for its journey to the star Alpha Centauri (which scientists believe can be colonized), Dr. Zachary Smith, an enemy agent, begins to sabotage the ship. As the Robinsons enter the freezing chambers (where they are to spend the five-and-a-half year voyage in suspended animation) all hatches are sealed and Smith is trapped inside the ship.

Shortly after its launch, the "Jupiter II" is damaged in a meteor shower. Unable to save the ship, Smith releases the pilot (West) and the Robinsons. Although thrown off course and technically lost in space, the Robinsons agree to continue with the original goal. Stories relate Smith's endless attempts to thwart their efforts and return the ship to Earth.

John Robinson	Guy Williams	Andrew Bass	James Stacy
Maureen Robinson	June Lockhart	Arleigh Marley	Ben Cooper
Penny Robinson	Angela Cartwright	Milovan Drumm	Bo Svenson
Judy Robinson	Marta Kristen	Albert Sanchez	Tige Andrews
Will Robinson	Billy Mumy	Mika	Danielle DeMetz
Donald West	Mark Goddard	Niklaus	Fritz Weaver
Zachary Smith	Jonathan Harris	Egasto	Roger C. Carmel
Environmental Robot	Bob May		

Producer: Leo Davis, Herbert B. Leonard

Robot's Voice	Dick Tufeld
Athena (Green Alien Lady)	Vittina Marcus
Verda (android)	Dee Hartford
Space Beauty Nancy Pi Squared	Dee Hartford
Mr. Zumdish (Celestial Dept. Store keeper)	Fritz Field
Farnum the Great	Leonard J. Stone
Jeremiah Smith	Henry Jones
Computer Voices	Sue England
Alien Roles	Dawson Palmer

"Lost in Space" Theme by Johnny Williams

Producer: Irwin Allen

The Lost Saucer

Comedy; 30 min; ABC 9/6/75 to 9/4/76

While exploring the universe, androids Fi and Fum (from the planet ZR-3) penetrate a time warp and land on Earth. Anxious to make friends, they invite earthlings Alice and Jerry aboard their saucer-like ship. When curious people begin to gather, Fum becomes scared and hurridly launches the ship. The craft is sent back into space, where it becomes lost in time. Stories relate Fi and Fum's efforts to return their passengers to Earth.

Fi	Ruth Buzzi
Fum	Jim Nabors
Alice	Alice Playten
Jerry	Jarrod Johnson
The Dorse	Larry Larson

Producer: Si Rose, Sid and Marty Krofft

Lost Treasure

Adventure Pilot; 60 min; CBS 6/28/71

The exploits of a trio of treasure hunters (Andrew, Arleigh, and Milovan).

Lotsa Luck

Comedy; 30 min; NBC 9/10/73 to 5/24/74

The trials and tribulations of Stanley Belmont, a clerk in the lost and found department of the N.Y.C. Bus Lines.

Stanley Belmont	Dom DeLuise
Iris Belmont	Kathleen Freeman
Olive Swann	Beverly Sanders
Arthur Swann	Wynn Irwin
Bummy Fitzer	Jack Knight

Producer: Bill Persky, Sam Denoff

Lottery

Anthology; 60 min; ABC 9/3/83 to 3/29/84

Incidents in the lives of people who have won great wealth in a lottery. Each week the lives of three people are depicted as seen through Patrick Flaherty, the man who dispenses the money for the Intersweep Lottery, and Eric Rush, the IRS agent who accompanies Patrick—to collect the government's share.

Patrick Flaherty	Ben Murphy
Eric Rush	Marshall Colt

Theme Vocal ("Turn of the Cards"): Alan Graham

Producer: Rick Rosner, Robert Janes

Lou Grant

Drama; 60 min; CBS 9/20/77 to 9/13/82

A behind-the-scenes look at the newspaper world as seen through the experiences of Lou Grant, city editor of the Los Angeles "Tribune."

Lou Grant	Edward Asner
Billie Newman	Linda Kelsey
Joe Rossi	Robert Walden
Charlie Hume	Mason Adams
Margaret Pynchon	Nancy Marchand
Dennis "Animal" Price	Daryl Anderson
Art Donovan	Jack Bannon
Carla Mardigan	Rebecca Balding
Adam Wilson	Allen Williams
Marion Hume	Peggy McCay
Heidi	Cassandra Foster
Foreign Editor	Lawrence Haddon
National Editor	Sidney Clute
	Emilio Delgado
Photo Editor	Billy Beck
Financial Editor	Gary Pagett
Greg Serantino	Vincent Baggetta
Ted McLovey	Cliff Potts

Producer: Allan Burns, James L. Brooks, Gene Reynolds

Love, American Style

Anthology; 30 & 60 min; ABC 9/22/69 to 1/11/74

Comedy vignettes that tackle the ups and down of love. Segments are interspersed with blackouts. See also "New Love American Style."

Blackout Regulars: Phyllis Davis, Bernie Kopell, James Hampton, Stuart Margolin, Clifton Davis, Jed Allan, Tracy Reed, Buzz Cooper, Marty Grover, Bill Calloway, Lynne Marta, Barbara Minkus, Jacki De-Mar, Richard Williams

Theme Vocal ("Love American Style"): The Charles Fox Singers

Producer: Ray Allen, Harvey Bullock, Jim Parker, Arnold Margolin

Love and Learn

Comedy Pilot; 30 min; NBC 8/1/79

The story of a beautiful showgirl (Holly) who marries a college English professor (Jason) and their efforts to live a normal life despite their differences in occupations.

Holly Brewster	Candy Clark
Jason Brewster	Lawrence Pressman
Mark Brewster	James Van Patten
Harvey	Earl Boen
Natalie	Natalie Core
Denise Pfeiffer	Kelly Bishop

Producer: George Burditt, Paul Wayne

Love and Marriage

Comedy; 30 min; NBC 9/21/59 to 1/25/60

A behind-the-scenes look at a music publishing company as seen through the experiences of Bill Harris, the owner of the near-bankrupt Harris Music Publishing Company.

Bill Harris	William Demarest
Pat Baker	Jeanne Bal
Steve Baker	Murray Hamilton
Susan Baker	Susan Reilly
Jenny Baker	Jeannie Lynn
Stubby Wilson	Stubby Kaye
Sophie	Kay Armen

Producer: P. J. Wolfson

Love and the Happy Days

Comedy Pilot; 30 min; ABC 2/25/72

The pilot film for "Happy Days," which aired on "Love, American Style." A nostalgic backward look at life in the 1950s as seen through the eyes of Richie Cunningham, a high school student who, in the story, desperately seeks a way to impress a beautiful girl named Arlene.

Richie Cunningham	Ron Howard
Howard Cunningham	Harold Gould
Marion Cunningham	Marion Ross
Joanie Cunningham	Susan Neher
Potsie Weber	Anson Williams
Chuck Cunningham	Ric Carrott
Arlene	Tannis G. Montgomery
Uncle Harold	Jackie Coogan
Aunt Bessie	Peggy Rea

Producer: Garry Marshall

Love at First Sight

Comedy Pilot; 30 min; CBS 10/13/80

The problems of a not-so-typical marriage as seen through the experiences of Karen Alexander, a housewife, and her husband, Jonathan, a blind jingles writer for the Fame Advertising Agency in N.Y. In the first pilot (see next title) Jonathan prepares to meet Karen's parents for the first time.

Karen Alexander	Susan Bigelow
Jonathan Alexander	Philip Levien
Francis Fame	Pat Cooper
Genevieve Lamont	Deborah Baltzell
Denise	Angela Aames
Mr. Bellamy	Robert Rockwell
Mrs. Bellamy	Peggy McCay

Music: Jose Feliciano

Producer: Nick Arnold, Peter Locke

Love at First Sight

Comedy Pilot; 30 min; CBS 3/29/82

A second pilot (see prior title) about a housewife (Karen) and her husband (Jonathan), a blind jingles writer. In the second story, Karen and Jonathan contemplate buying a gun after their apartment is robbed.

Karen Alexander	Susan Bigelow
Jonathan Alexander	Philip Levien
Mr. Sawyer	Macon McCalman
Stan	Reni Santoni

Music: Jose Feliciano

Producer: Nick Arnold, Peter Locke

The Love Boat

Comedy-Drama; 60 min; ABC 9/29/77 to 9/5/86

The series, set on the luxury liner "Pacific Princess" (later "Royal Princess") relates incidents in the lives of the passengers who board "The Love Boat" (its nickname) seeking romance.

Capt. Merrill Stubing	Gavin MacLeod
Capt. Tom Allenford*	Ted Hamilton
Capt. Tom Madison**	Quinn Redeker
Julie McCoy (cruise director)	Lauren Tewes
Judy McCoy (replaced Julie)	Patricia Klous
Jeri Landers (cruise director)*	Teri O'Mara
Sandy Summers (cruise director)**	Diane Stilwell
Dr. Adam Bricker	Bernie Kopell
Dr. Adam O'Neil*	Dick Van Patten
Purser Burl 'Gopher' Smith	Fred Grandy
Gopher*	Sandy Helberg
Isaac Washington (bartender)	Ted Lange
Isaac*	Theodore Wilson
Vicki Stubing (Merrill's daughter)	Jill Whelan
Emily Haywood (married Merrill)	Marion Ross
Ashley "Ace" Covington	Ted McGinley
April Lopez	Charo
The Love Boat Mermaids:	
Susie	Deborah Bartlett
Maria	Tori Brenno
Jane	Nancy Lynn Hammond
Amy	Teri Hatcher
Patti	Deborah Johnson
Sheila	Macarena
Starlight	Andrea Moen
Mary Beth	Beth Myatt

Theme Vocal ("The Love Boat"): Jack Jones, Dionne Warwick (last season)

Producer: Aaron Spelling, Douglas S. Cramer, Gordon Farr

*"The Love Boat I" TV Movie role (9/17/76)

**"The Love Boat II" TV Movie role (1/21/77)

The Love Connection

Game; 30 min; Syn. 6/83

Prior to the game, a single person views three videotaped interviews with a single person of the opposite sex. On stage, the subject is interviewed and the audience is shown excerpts from those video tapes. The audience then selects the person they feel would be right for the subject. At a latter date, the subjects return and state the results of a date arranged for them by the program.

Host: Chuck Woolery

Announcer: Rod Roddy, Gene Wood

Producer: Eric Leiber, Karen Therman

The Love Experts

Advice; 30 min; Syn. 9/78

A panel of four celebrities offers advice to real people on the problems of living and loving in today's world.

Host: Bill Cullen

Regular: Geoff Edwards

Announcer: Jack Clark

Producer: Bob Stewart, Anne Marie Schmitt

Love, Long Distance

Comedy Pilot; 30 min; CBS 7/30/85

Leslie Cummings is an assistant anthropologist who works in New York, but lives in Philadelphia; David Cummings, her husband, is an architect who works and lives in Philadelphia. The would-be series was to relate their efforts to live a commuter marriage.

Leslie Cummings	Tricia Pursley
David Cummings	Jack Rose
Sybil Sylver	Cristine Rose
Stan Cummings	Mike Starr
Dr. Arthur Ruskin	Austin Pendleton

Theme Vocal ("Love, Long Distance"): John Leffler

Producer: Jerry Davis, Sherry Coben

Love, Natalie

Comedy Pilot; 30 min; NBC 7/11/80

A satirization of family life as seen through the eyes of Natalie Miller, wife, mother, and overall problem solver. The title is derived from Natalie's closing in her letter to her mother, which she reads during the opening theme.

Natalie Miller	Judith Kahan
Peter Miller	Christopher Allport
Nora Miller	Kimberly Woodward
Franklin Miller	Corey Feldman
Ruth Newman	Jean DeBaer
Mel Orlorfsky	Kenneth Tigar

Producer: Judith Kahan, Patricia Rickey

Love Nest

Comedy Pilot; 30 min; CBS 3/14/75

The story of Ned and Jenny, widowed senior citizens who live together in a Florida trailer court.

Ned Cooper	Charles Lane
Jenny Ludlow	Florida Friebus
Mort Cooper	Dana Elcar
Dorothy Ludlow	Dee Carroll
Dickie Ewing	Burt Mustin
Mary Francis	Alice Nunn

Producer: Saul Ilson, Ernest Chambers

Love on a Rooftop

Comedy; 30 min; ABC 9/6/66 to 1/6/67

Dave Lewis, an apprentice architect, and Julie Hammond, the spoiled daughter of a wealthy car salesman, marry and establish housekeeping in a rooftop apartment at 1400 MacDoogal Street in San Francisco. Stories relate their struggles to survive the difficult first years of marriage.

Julie Willis	Judy Carne
Dave Willis	Peter Deuel
Stan Parker	Rich Little
Carol Parker	Barbara Bostock
Fred Hammond	Herbert Voland
Phyllis Hammond	Edith Atwater
Jim Lucas	Sandy Kenyon
Bert Bennington	Charles Lane
Mrs. Bennington	Hope Summers

Producer: Harry Ackerman, E. W. Swackhamer

The Love Report

Magazine; 30 min; ABC 6/18/84 to 7/27/84

A live program of up-to-the-minute information on love relationships.

Hosts: Tawny Schneider, Chuck Henry

Regulars: Dr. Joyce Brothers, Betty White, Dr. Theresa Crenshaw, Dr. Ruth Westheimer, Dr. Meryle Gellman, Ellie Dylan, Johnny Mountain

Producer: Fred Silverman, E. V. DiMissa Jr.

Love, Sidney

Comedy; 30 min; NBC 10/28/81 to 8/29/83

Sidney Shorr, a lonely commercial artist, meets Laurie Morgan, an aspiring actress who is sweet, a bit kooky, and full of life. When Sidney discovers that Gloria has no place to live, and that his life has suddenly taken on a new meaning, he invites her to live with him. Laurie accepts when she discovers that Sidney is gay*. Several months later, when Laurie becomes pregnant by a man who deserts her (Jimmy), Sidney becomes a father figure to the child that is born (Patti). The series, set seven years later, relates events in the lives of Sidney, Laurie (now an actress on the TV serial "As Thus We Are") and her daughter, Patti.

Sidney Shorr	Tony Randall
Laurie Morgan	Lorna Patterson**
	Swoosie Kurtz
Patti Morgan	Kaleena Kiff
Jason Stoller	Chip Zien
Jimmy	David Huffman**
	Graham Beckel
Mort Harris	Alan North
Mrs. Gaffney	Barbara Bryne
Dan Morgan	Hansford Rowe
Eve Morgan	Lenka Peterson
Nancy	Lynne Thigpen

Theme Vocal ("Friends Forever"): Tony Randall, Swoosie Kurtz, Kaleena Kiff; later by Gladys Knight, Bubba Knight

Producer: George Eckstein, Rod Parker, Hal Cooper

*Objections forced NBC to alter the character to a point where it could have been either straight or gay.

**TV Movie roles ("Sidney Shorr," NBC 2/1/80).

Love Songs

Music; 30 min; Syn. 9/85

A daily series of music videos coupled with personal ads for singles seeking a mate.

Narration Host: Dick Summer

Producer: Stuart Shapiro

Love Story

Anthology; 30 min; DuMont 4/20/54 to 6/29/54

A series of live dramas that emphasize the goodness in nature and the kindness in man. Performers include Patricia Breslin, Leslie Nielsen, Audra Lindley, Peggy McCay, Murray Matheson, James Gregory, Beatrice Straight, Basil Rathbone, and Lee Bowman.

Producer: David Lowe

Love Story

Game; 30 min; CBS 10/31/55 to 3/30/56

Married couples are first interviewed and then compete in a question-and-answer session wherein the highest scoring couple receives an expense-paid two week honeymoon in Paris.

Host: Jack Smith

Assistant: Patricia Meikle

Love Story

Anthology; 60 min; NBC 10/3/73 to 1/2/74

Adult and contemporary variations on the theme of love. Performers include Kay Lenz, Jan Smithers, Janet Leigh, Victoria Principal, Susan Oliver, Lynnette Mettey, Jodie Foster, Larry Hagman, Don Murray, Frank Langella, Samantha Eggar, Kim Darby, Valerie Perrine, Anne Baxter, James Farentino, and Diane Baker.

Theme Song ("Love Story") by Francis Lai

Producer: George Schaefer

Love that Bob

Comedy; 30 min; NBC 1/2/55 to 9/25/55
CBS 10/5/55 to 9/19/57
NBC 9/22/57 to 9/15/59

The romantic misadventures of Bob Collins, a suave and sophisticated bachelor-photographer living in Hollywood. Originally titled "The Bob Cummings Show."

Bob Collins	Bob Cummings
Margaret MacDonald	Rosemary DeCamp
Chuck MacDonald	Dwayne Hickman
Charmaine "Schultzy" Schultz	Ann B. Davis
Harvey Helm	King Donovan
Ruth Helm	Mary Lawrence
Tommy Helm	Charles Herbert
Shirley Swanson	Joi Lansing
Paul Fonda	Lyle Talbot
Francine Williams	Diane Jergens
Joe DePew	Robert Ellis
Pamela Livingston	Nancy Kulp
Frank Crenshaw	Dick Wesson
Mary Beth Hall	Gloria Marshall
Tammy Johnson	Tammy Marihugh
Ingrid	Ingrid Goude
Collette DuBois	Lisa Gaye
Josh Collins	Bob Cummings
Bertha Krause	Kathleen Freeman
Fanny Neemeyer	Marjorie Bennett

Announcer: Bill Baldwin

Producer: Al Simon, Paul Henning

Love that Jill

Comedy; 30 min; ABC 1/20/58 to 4/28/58

The romantic rivalry between two model agency owners, Jill Johnson (Model Girls, Inc.) and Jack Gibson (The House That Jacques Built), and their individual attempts to become number one.

Jill Johnson	Anne Jeffreys
Jack Gibson	Robert Sterling
Richard (Jill's secretary)	Jimmy Lydon
Pearl (Jack's secretary)	Betty Lynn
Ginger (Jill's model)	Barbara Nichols
Peaches (Jill's model)	Kay Elhardt
Monte (Jack's friend)	Henry Kulky

Producer: Hal Roach Jr., Alex Gottlieb

Love Thy Neighbor

Comedy; 30 min; ABC 6/15/73 to 9/19/73

Events in the lives of two couples, one white, the other black, who live side by side on North Robin Hood Road in San Fernando's Sherwood Forest Estates: Charlie (white), a shop steward at Turner Electronics, and his wife, Peggy; and Ferguson (black), the efficiency expert at Turner, and his wife, Jackie.

Charlie Wilson	Ron Masak
Peggy Wilson	Joyce Bulifant
Ferguson Bruce	Harrison Page
Jackie Bruce	Janet MacLachlan
Murray	Milt Kamen
Louie	Louis Guss

Theme Vocal ("Love Thy Neighbor"): Solomon Burke

Producer: Ted Bergman, Norman Rush, Arthur Julian

The Lovebirds

Comedy Pilot; 30 min; CBS 7/18/79

The misadventures of marrieds Janine and Al Burley.

Janine Burley	Lorna Patterson
Al Burley	Louis Welch
Patricia Wexelblatt	Ellen Regan
Fred Wexelblatt	Eugene Levy

Theme Vocal ("The Lovebirds"): Bobby Van

Producer: Mark Rothman, Lowell Ganz

Lovers and Other Strangers

Comedy Pilot; 30 min; ABC 7/22/83

Events in the day-to-day lives of the Delvecchios, a not-so-typical American family.

Frank Delvecchio	Harry Guardino
Bea Delvecchio	Carol Teitel
Susan Delvecchio	Randi Oakes
Mike Delvecchio	Brian Benben
Mary Claire Delvecchio	Claudia Wells
Jerry Delvecchio	Alan Hayes
Pauline	Helen Verbit
Bruno Delvecchio	R. J. Williams
Marie Delvecchio	Keri Houlihan

Producer: David Susskind, Renee Taylor, Joseph Bologna

Loves Me, Loves Me Not

Comedy; 30 min; CBS 3/20/77 to 4/27/77

The romantic escapades of Jane Benson, a beautiful grammar school teacher, and Dick Phillips, a klutzy newspaper reporter, as they struggle to make it through the travails of a latter 1970s romance.

Jane Benson	Susan Dey
Dick Phillips	Kenneth Gilman
Sue (Jane's friend)	Udana Power
	Phyllis Glick
Tom (Dick's friend)	Art Metrano

"Loves Me, Loves Me Not" Theme Song: Charles Fox, Norman Gimbel

Producer: Paul Junger Witt, Tony Thomas, Susan Harris

Low Man on the Totem Pole

Comedy Pilot; 30 min; CBS 8/1/64

Humorous events in the life of H. Allen Smith, a kind-hearted newspaper columnist.

H. Allen Smith	Dan Dailey
Nelle Smith	Diana Lynn
Mr. Trumbull	John McGiver
Pepe	Pedro Gonzalez-Gonzalez
Manager	Cliff Norton

Producer: Andrew Gerard

Lucan

Adventure; 60 min; ABC 9/12/77 to 12/4/78

While stalking game in Minnesota during the Summer of 1967, a group of hunters find a 10-year-old boy who eats, sleeps, and hunts like a wolf. When the authorities are unable to discover who the boy is, he is sent to a research center and taught the ways of modern man. Originally, the series was to relate the boy's adventures (named Lucan by scientists) when he is set free ten years later to search for his natural parents. Later, instead of being set free, the revised storyline finds Lucan escaping from the authorities who tried to keep him captive (fearing he would revert back to wolf) to search for his parents. Stories relate Lucan's efforts, which are hindered by Prentiss, a police lieutenant who is relentlessly pursuing him.

Lucan	Kevin Brophy
Dr. Don Hoagland	John Randolph
Lt. Prentiss	Don Gordon
Lucan (age 10)	Todd Olsen

Producer: Barry Lowen, David Greene, Harold Gast

Lucas Tanner

Drama; 60 min; NBC 9/11/74 to 8/20/75

A realistic portrayal of student-teacher relationships as seen through the eyes of Lucas Tanner, an English teacher at Harry S. Truman Memorial High School in Webster Groves, Missouri.

Lucas Tanner	David Hartman
Margaret Blumenthal	Rosemary Murphy
John Hamilton	John Randolph
Glendon Farrell	Robbie Rist
Jaytee Druman	Alan Abelew
Cindy Damin	Trish Soodik
Terry	Kimberly Beck
Wally	Michael Dwight-Smith
Grace Baden	June Dayton

Producer: David Victor, Charles S. Dubin, Jay Benson

The Lucie-Desi Comedy Hour

See "The Lucille Ball-Desi Arnaz Show" for information.

The Lucie Arnaz Show

Comedy; 30 min; CBS 4/2/85 to 6/11/85

Events in the life of Dr. Jane Lewis, a psychologist, advice columnist, and radio call-in program host ("The Love and Lucas Show" on New York's WPLE) who expertly solves the problems of others, but can't seem to work out her own. Based on the British series "Agony."

Dr. Jane Lucas	Lucie Arnaz
Jim Gordon (station manager)	Tony Roberts
Loretta (Jane's secretary)	Karen Jablons-Alexander
Jill (Jane's sister)	Lee Bryant
Larry Love (Jane's co-anchor)	Todd Waring
Peggy Gordon (Jim's wife)	Gwyn Gillis
Sarah (Jill's daughter)	Melissa Hart
Billy (Jill's son)	Sandy Schwartz
Mr. Beverlee (Jane's neighbor)	Douglas Seale

Producer: Sam Denoff, Susan Seeger, Kathy Speer

The Lucille Ball-Desi Arnaz Show

Comedy; 60 min; CBS 10/6/58 to 4/1/60

A continuation of "I Love Lucy," wherein Lucy and Ricky, and their friends Fred and Ethel, travel to various places and become involved with a different guest star in each episode. Aired as segments of "The Desilu Playhouse."

Lucy Ricardo	Lucille Ball
Ricky Ricardo	Desi Arnaz
Fred Mertz	William Frawley
Ethel Mertz	Vivian Vance
Little Ricky Ricardo	Richard Keith

Music: Wilbur Hatch

Producer: Desi Arnaz, Bert Granet

Lucky Letters

Game; 30 min; NBC 6/1/50 to 7/5/50

Object: For players to unscramble words from clues given through music, visual aids or verse.

Host: Frankie Masters

Regulars: Phyllis Myles and the West Twins

Lucky Partners

Game; 30 min; NBC 6/30/58 to 8/22/58

Two stage players and each member of the audience is given a piece of paper with the word LUCKY on it. Players, using their own dollar bills, copy the last five digits under LUCKY. The first two audience members who match the stage players' numbers join them and compete for prizes via a question-and-answer session.

Host: Carl Cordell

Lucky Pup

Children; 15 min; CBS 8/23/48 to 6/23/51

When a dog (Lucky Pup) is left a five million dollar inheritance, he comes to the attention of Foodini, an evil magician who has high hopes for the money. Stories relate Foodini's fumbling attempts to acquire Lucky Pup's money. Characters are the puppet creations of Hope and Morey Bunin.

Hostess: Doris Brown

Voices/Puppeteers: Hope and Morey Bunin

Producer: Hope and Morey Bunin, Lloyd Gross, Clarence Schummel

The Lucy Monroe Show

Experimental; 30 min; NBC 7/28/39

A program of music and songs with singer Lucy Monroe. Produced and directed by Edward Sobol.

The Lucy Show

Comedy; 30 min; CBS 10/1/62 to 9/16/68

Original format (1961–65): The story of a widowed mother (Lucy) and her divorced friend (Vivian) and their hairbrained attempts to acquire money. The revised format (1965–68) moves the locale from Connecticut to San Francisco, where Lucy's adventures as a secretary to Westland Bank vice president Theodore J. Mooney are depicted.

Lucy Carmichael	Lucille Ball
Chris Carmichael	Candy Moore
Jerry Carmichael	Jimmy Garrett
Vivian Bagley	Vivian Vance
Sherman Bagley	Ralph Hart
Theodore J. Mooney	Gale Gordon
Mr. Barnsdahl	Charles Lane
Harry Connors	Dick Martin
Mary Jane Lewis	Mary Jane Croft
Harrison Cheever	Roy Roberts
Lucy's sister Marge	Janet Waldo
Ted Mooney Jr.	Michael J. Pollard
Bob Mooney	Eddie Applegate
Audrey Simmons	Mary Jane Croft

Producer: Desi Arnaz, Lucille Ball, Gary Morton, Elliott Lewis

Luke and the Tenderfoot

Comedy Pilot; 30 min; CBS 8/6/65 (Part 1) 8/13/65 (Part 2)

The adventures of Luke Herkimer, a crooked wagon peddler, and Pete Queen, his partner, a young tenderfoot, as they peddle their wares throughout the Old West.

Luke Herkimer	Edgar Buchanan
Pete Queen	Carleton Carpenter
John Hardin	Charles Bronson
John's sidekick	Richard Jaeckel
Tough	Michael Landon

Producer: Steve Fisher

Lum and Abner

Comedy Pilot; 30 min; CBS 11/2/49

The misadventures of Lum Edwards and Abner Peabody, the owner-operators of the Jot'em Down General Store in Pine Ridge, Arkansas. Based on the radio series.

Lum Edwards	Chester Lauck
Abner Peabody	Norris Goff

Announcer: Wendell Niles

The Lux Video Theatre

Anthology; 30 & 60 min. CBS 10/2/50 to 6/24/54
NBC 8/26/54 to 9/12/57
NBC 10/3/58 to 9/18/59

Quality dramas sponsored by Lux Soap Products. In 1958, the series switched from 60 to 30 minutes and became "The Lux Playhouse."

Host: James Mason, Otto Kruger, Gordon MacRae, Ken Carpenter

Luxury Liner

Drama Pilot; 60 min; NBC 2/12/63

Dramatic events in the lives of people who book passage on luxury liner as seen through the eyes of its captain (Victor Kihlgren).

Capt. Victor Kihlgren	Rory Calhoun
Selena Royce	Jan Sterling
Dr. Lyman Savage	Carroll O'Connor
Digo	Michael Davis
Jan Veltman	Ludwig Donath
Sam Barrett	Ed Kemmer
La Guerne	Oscar Beregi
Mr. Marion	Danny Scholl

Host: James Stewart

Producer: Dick Powell, Aaron Spelling

Ma and Pa

Comedy Pilot; 30 min; CBS 3/7/74

The misadventures of a young-at-heart elderly couple living in Chicago.

Ma	Mary Wickes
Pa	Arthur Space
Dorothy (daughter)	Dorothy Loudon
Celia (daughter)	Marian Hailey
Emily (daughter)	Barbara Sharma

Producer: Jeff Harris

The Mac Davis Show

Variety; 60 min; NBC 7/11/74 to 8/29/74 12/19/74 to 5/22/75

A weekly Summer series of music and songs.

Host: Mac Davis

Regulars: Kay Dingle, Bo Kaprall, The Tony Mordente Dancers

Orchestra: Mike Post

Producer: Sandy Gallin, Arnie Rosen, Bob Ellison

The Mac Davis Show

Variety; 60 min; NBC 3/18/76 to 6/17/76

A weekly hour of music and songs.

Host: Mac Davis

Regulars: Robert Shields and Lorene Yarnell, Ron Silver, The Strutts

Orchestra: Tom Bahler, Mike Post

Producer: Gary Smith, Dwight Hemion

McClain's Law

Crime Drama; 60 min; NBC 11/20/81 to 8/24/82

When his friend (Sid) is killed and the police investigation dissatisfies him, retired police detective Jim McClain rejoins the force to solve the crime as it should be done—"by the gut." Stories relate the investigations of a 52-year-old veteran cop (McClain) and his by-the-books young partner (Harry), detectives with the San Pedro Police Department.

Det. Jim McClain	James Arness
Det. Harry Gates	Marshall Colt
Lt. Ed DeNisco	George DiCenzo
Det. Jerry Cross	Carl Franklin
Vangie Cruise	Conchata Ferrell
Grace Bannon	Cheryl Anderson
Marie DeNisco	Brooke Bundy
Susan Cross	Tanya Boyd
Sid Lammon (first episode)	Gerald S. O'Loughlin

Theme Music ("McClain's Law"): James Di-Pasquale

McCloud

Crime Drama; Various (60, 90 & 120 min); NBC 9/16/70 to 8/28/77

Hoping to study big city crime detection methods, Sam McCloud, a deputy marshal from Taos, New Mexico, is sent to Manhattan's 27th Precinct to observe New York's finest in action. Stories relate Sam's attempts to become actively involved in the cases he is assigned to observe.

Sam McCloud	Dennis Weaver
Chief Peter B. Clifford	J. D. Cannon
Sgt. Joe Broadhurst	Terry Carter
Chris Coughlin	Diana Muldaur
Sgt. Maggie Clinger	Sharon Gless
	Nancy Fox
Det. Grover	Ken Lynch

Producer: Leslie Stevens, Glen A. Larson

Note: Aired on both "Four-in-One" and "The NBC Sunday Mystery Movie."

McCoy

Crime Drama; 2 hrs; NBC 9/5/75 to 9/12/76

The exploits of McCoy, an engaging private detective who incorporates his unique skills as a con artist to solve crimes. Aired on "The NBC Sunday Mystery Movie."

McCoy	Tony Curtis
Gideon Gibbs	Roscoe Lee Brown
Lucy	Lucille Meredith

Producer: Roland Kibbee

McDuff, the Talking Dog

Comedy; 30 min; NBC 9/11/76 to 11/20/76

Shortly after he begins a veterinary service in the town of Peach Blossom, Calvin Campbell acquires something he didn't expect—McDuff, the ghost of a sheep dog who appears and speaks only to him. Stories relate Calvin's misadventures as he attempts to cope with McDuff's antics.

Calvin Campbell	Walter Willson
Kimmy Campbell	Michelle Stacy
Amos Ferguson	Gordon Jump
Squeaky	Johnnie Collins III
Mrs. Osgood	Monty Margetts
McDuff's Voice	Jack Lester

Producer: William P. D'Angelo, Ray Allen, Harvey Bullock

McGarry and Me

Comedy Pilot; 30 min; CBS 7/5/60

The story of a kind-hearted policeman (Dan) and his wife (Kitty).

Off. Dan McGarry	Michael O'Shea
Kitty McGarry	Virginia Mayo
Captain	Les Tremayne
Officer	Richard Gaines

Producer: Hal Roach Jr., Stanley Shapiro

McGhee

Comedy Pilot; 30 min; CBS 6/28/65

Following the death of a distant relative, Willie McGhee, an impoverished artist, inherits Cleveland, California, a town of 209 people. The unsold series was to relate Walter's efforts to get his town back on its feet after he dscovers it is bankrupt.

Willie McGhee	Jeremy Slate
Ann Dorsey	Karen Steele
Sheriff George	George Chandler
Cousin Hilda	Connie Sawyer

Producer: Don McGuire

The McGonigle

Comedy Pilot; 30 min; NBC 7/28/61

The misadventures of Mac McGonigle and Scuttlebutt Baines, two well-meaning but trouble-prone sailors stationed aboard the USS Okinawa.

Mac McGonigle	Mickey Shaughnessy
Scuttlebutt Baines	Tom D'Andrea
Capt. Amboy	Frank Gerstle
CPO Commissar Jones	Wally Cassell
Bottleneck	Paul Picerni
Hammerhead	Norman Grabowski
Nina Dale	Diane Jergens
Artie Dale	Mark Damon

Producer: Dick Chevillat, Ray Singer

MacGruder and Loud

Crime Drama; 60 min; ABC 1/20/85 to 9/3/85

The exploits of Malcolm MacGruder and Jenny Loud, L.S.P.D. patrol car officers who are secretly married (in defiance of departmental orders). Episodes relate their efforts to perform as a team and keep their marriage a secret.

Off. Malcolm MacGruder	John Getz
Off. Jenny Loud	Kathryn Harrold
Sgt. Bob Myhrum	Frank McCarthy
Sgt. Jim Egi	Arlen Dean Snyder
Det. Don Debbin	Ted Ross
Sgt. Hanson	Lee de Broux
Sgt. Geller	Rick Rossovich
Mary Margaret Myhrum	Susan Tyrrell

Producer: Aaron Spelling, Douglas S. Cramer

MacGyver

Adventure; 60 min; ABC 9/29/85 (Premiere)

The exploits of MacGyver, a survival expert, scientific genius, and former special forces agent who tackles seemingly impossible missions for the government. (During the second season, MacGyver works for a think tank organization called The Phoenix Corporation.)

MacGyver	Richard Dean Anderson
Peter Thornton (Mac's superior)	Dana Elcar
Debra Easton (Mac's former fiance)	Marilyn Jones
Harry Jackson (Mac's grandfather)	John Anderson
Connie Thornton (Peter's ex-wife)	Penelope Windust
Michael Thornton (Peter's son)	Scott Coffey
Penny Parker (Mac's scatterbrained friend)	Teri Hatcher

Producer: Henry Winkler, John Rich, Jerry Ludwig

McHale's Navy

Comedy; 30 min; ABC 9/11/62 to 8/30/66

The original format (1962–65), set on the South Pacific island of Taratupa during W.W. II, follows the relationship between Quinton McHale, commander of Squadron 19 and PT Boat 73, and Wallace B. Binghampton, the commanding officer, who feels his life is plagued by the antics of McHale and his motley crew. The revised format (1965–66), set in Voltafiore, Italy, continues to depict the bickering relationship between McHale and Binghampton when they are transferred to the European theatre of war. See also "Seven Against the Sea" and "Broadside."

Lt. Quinton McHale	Ernest Borgnine
Capt. Wallace Binghampton	Joe Flynn
Ensign Charles Pulver	Tim Conway
Seaman Lester Gruber	Carl Ballantine
Seaman Harrison "Tinker" Bell	Billy Sands
Seaman Willy Moss	John Wright
Seaman Happy Haines	Gavin MacLeod
Seaman Virgil Edwards	Edson Stroll
Quarter Master Christopher	Gary Vinson
Lt. Elroy Carpenter	Bob Hastings
Nurse Molly Turner	Jane Dulo
Adm. Bruce Rogers	Roy Roberts
Fuji Kobiaji (McHale's POW)	Yoshio Yoda
Chief Tali Urulu	Jacques Aubuchon
Adm. Benson	Bill Quinn
Mario Lugatto	Jay Novello
Dino Baroni	Dick Wilson
Mama Rose Giovanni	Peggy Mondo
Lt. Gloria Winters	Cindy Robbins
Col. Harrigan	Henry Beckman

Producer: Edward J. Montagne, Si Rose.

Mack and Myer for Hire

Comedy; 15 min; Syn. 1963

A 200-episode series about the antics of two bumbling craftsman struggling to succeed in the business world.

Mack	Mickey Deems
Myer	Joey Faye

Producer: Sandy Howard

McKeever and the Colonel

Comedy; 30 min; NBC 9/23/62 to 6/16/63

The series, set at the Westfield Military Academy for Boys, relates the antics of cadet Gary McKeever, and the efforts of Harvey Black-

well, the school's commander, to discipline him. See the following title also.

Col. Harvey Blackwell	Allyn Joslyn
Cadet Gary McKeever	Scott Lane
Sgt. Barnes	Jackie Coogan
Miss Warner	Elisabeth Fraser
Cadet Tubby Anderson	Keith Taylor
Cadet Monk	Johnny Eimen
Major McKeever	Peter Hanson
Harvey's niece Andrea	Susan Gordon
Sgt. Barnes' father	Charlie Ruggles
Blackwell's mother	Ellen Corby
Tubby's father	Benny Baker
Tubby's mother	Doris Singleton

Producer: Tom McKnight, Bill Harmon

McKeever and the Colonel

Comedy Pilot; 43 min; Unaired (Produced in 1962).

The original pilot for the above series. Basically the same format, but with a slightly different regular cast (Jackie Coogan and Elisabeth Fraser were not cast and Gary McKeever was seen with his brother, Don).

Col. Harvey Blackwell	Allyn Joslyn
Gary McKeever	Scott Lane
Don McKeever	David Kent
Cadet Monk	Johnny Eimen
Cadet Tubby	Keith Taylor
Snuffy	Donald Losby
Benson	Frank Albertson
Bacon	Don Beddoe
White	Nelson Olmstead
Earnshaw	Steve Mines
Mansfield	Hugh Sanders
Doc Jeffries	Charles Lane

Producer: Billy Friedberg

The MacKenzies of Paradise Cove

Drama; 60 min; ABC 3/27/79 to 5/18/79

Following the tragic death of their parents in a sailing accident, the five MacKenzie children (Bridget, Kevin, Celia, Michael, and Timothy) convince Cuda Weber, a fisherman who runs the "Viking" charter boat service, to become their substitute "uncle" so authorities will not split them up for adoption. Stories, set in Honolulu, Hawaii, relate the adventures of the MacKenzies as they struggle to remain a family.

Cuda Weber	Clu Gulager
Bridget MacKenzie	Lory Walsh
Kevin MacKenzie	Sean Roche*
	Shawn Stevens
Celia MacKenzie	Randi Kiger
Michael MacKenzie	Sean Marshall
Timothy MacKenzie	Keith Mitchell
"Big" Ben Kalikini	Moe Keale
"Little" Ben	
Kalikini	Sean Tyler Hall
Richie Kalikini	Scott Kingston
Ben's wife	Leinaala Heine
Barney	Harry Chang

Producer: Jerry Thorpe, William Blinn

*TV Movie role ("Stickin' Together," ABC 4/14/78).

MacKenzie's Raiders

Adventure; 30 min; Syn. 9/58

In an attempt to end the reign of terror begun by marauding Mexican renegades in Texas during the 1870s, the U.S. Fourth Cavalry assigns Colonel Ranald S. MacKenzie to head a special detail of undercover agents. Stories relate MacKenzie's efforts to establish a system of law and order.

Col. Ranald S. MacKenzie	Richard Carlson

Raiders: Louis Jean Heydt, Morris Ankrum, Brett King, Jim Bridges, Kenneth Alton

Narrator: Art Gilmore

Producer: Elliott Lewis

McLaren's Riders

Adventure Pilot; 60 min; CBS 5/17/77

Seeking to help small town police departments, the federal government establishes the McLaren Project, an agency that assists understaffed law enforcement agencies. The unsold series was to relate the exploits of Sam Downing and T. Wood, McLaren Project agents.

Sam Downing	George DiCenzo
T. Wood	Ted Neeley
Bill Willett	Harry Morgan
Kate Britain	Hilary Thompson
Wanda	Joan Goodfellow
Lamarr	James Best
Bobby Britain	Brad Davis

Producer: Herbert F. Solow

The McLean Stevenson Show

Comedy; 30 min; NBC 12/1/76 to 3/9/77

The misadventures of Mac Ferguson, a hardware store owner (in Evanston, Illinois) as he struggles to cope with life at home and at work.

Mac Ferguson	McLean Stevenson
Peggy Ferguson	Barbara Stuart
Janet	Ayn Ruyman
Chris Ferguson	Steve Nevil
Muriel	Madge West
David	David Hollander
Jason	Jason Whitney

Music: Paul Williams

Producer: Monty Hall, Arnold Margolin, Don Van Atta

McMillan

Crime Drama; 90 min; NBC 12/5/76 to 8/21/77

A spin-off from "McMillan and Wife" (see next title) without co-star Susan Saint James (whose character was killed off in a plane crash). Stories relate the investigations of Stewart McMillan, the Police Commissioner of San Francisco.

Stewart McMillan	Rock Hudson
Agatha Thorton	Martha Raye
Lt. Charles Enright	Charles Schuck
Sgt. DiMaggio	Richard Gilliland
Maggie	Gloria Stroock
Chief Paulsen	Bill Quinn

Producer: Leonard B. Stern

McMillan and Wife

Crime Drama; Various (90 min; 2hrs); NBC 9/29/71 to 9/12/76

The exploits of Stewart "Mac" McMillan, the San Fransicso Police Commissioner, and his beautiful wife, Sally, a girl with an uncanny knack for finding trouble.

Stewart McMillan	Rock Hudson
Sally McMillan	Susan Saint James
Sgt. Charles Enright	John Schuck
Mildred	Nancy Walker
Maggie	Gloria Stroock
Chief Paulsen	Bill Quinn
Mac's mother	
(Beatrice)	Mildred Natwick

Producer: Leonard B. Stern

McNab's Lab

Comedy Pilot; 30 min; ABC 7/22/66

The misadventures of Andrew McNab, a small-town druggist and amateur inventor.

Andrew McNab	Cliff Arquette
Ellen McNab	Sherry Alberoni
Timmy McNab	David Bailey
Harvey Baxter	Paul Smith
Coach	Elisha Cook
Steve Wilson	Jan Crawford
Martha	Dee Carroll
Henry	Gary Owens

Producer: George Burns

McNamara's Band

Comedy Pilot; 30 min; ABC 5/14/77

The adventures of a group of bumbling undercover agents who are sent to occupied Norway during W.W. II. In the first story (see next title) the band attempts to save a U.S. fleet.

Johnny McNamara*	John Byner
Zoltan*	Sid Haig
Gaffney*	Bruce Kirby Sr.
Milgrim*	Joseph Sicari
Aggie*	Steve Doubet
Hedy	Denise Galik
Schnell	Henry Polic II
Dr. Fuchtenstein	Joe Mell
Gen. Grosshtecker	Ben Wright

Producer: Bernie Kukoff, Jeff Harris

*McNamara's Band

McNamara's Band

Comedy Pilot; 30 min; ABC 12/5/77

In an attempt to infiltrate enemy lines, the U.S. Government recruits a motley gang of roughnecks and con men as secret agents during W.W. II. In the second pilot (see prior title) Johnny McNamara and his "dirty one-third of a dozen" attempt to keep a brilliant German general away from his command.

Johnny McNamara*	John Byner
Zoltan*	Sid Haig
Gaffney*	Bruce Kirby Sr.
Frankie*	Joe Pantoliano
Aggie*	Steve Doubet
Wilhelm Zimhoff	Albert Paulsen
Helga Zimhoff	Laurette Spang
Schlesser	Ron Soble
Hildegard	Kate Murtaugh

Producer: Bernie Kukoff, Jeff Harris

*McNamara's Band.

McNaughton's Daughter

Crime Drama; 60 min; NBC 3/24/76 to 4/7/76

The story of Laurel McNaughton, a trial lawyer and the deputy district attorney of Los Angeles.

Laurel McNaughton	Susan Clark
Lou Farragut	James Callahan
Charles Quintero	Ricardo Montalban
Ed Hughes	John Elerick

Producer: David Victor, Harold Gast

Macreedy's Woman

Drama Pilot; 30 min; NBC 9/23/58

Following the death of her husband, Brandy Macreedy, a singing hostess, becomes the owner of the San Francisco supper club he once owned. The unsold series was to relate Brandy's efforts to run the club, and help the people in trouble she encounters. Aired on "Colgate Theatre."

Brandy Macreedy	Jane Russell
Nicky Weston	Don Durant
Aristotle	Sean McClory

Producer: David Heilweil

Madame's Place

Comedy; 30 min; Syn. 9/82

The misadventures of Madame (the puppet of Wayland Flowers), a legendary film star who hosts "Madame's Place," a TV talk show from her lavish Hollywood mansion.

Madame	Wayland Flowers
Sara Joy Pitts	Judy Landers
Bernadette Van Gilder	Susan Tolsky
Walter Pinkerton	Johnny Haymer
Barney Wolff	Ty Henderson
Buzzy St. James	Corey Feldman
Larry Lunch	John Moschitta Jr.
Salaria	Edie McClurg
Lynn LaVecque	Barbara Cason
R. Ray Randall	R. Chandler Garrison
Eric Honest ("Mr. Honest")	Don Sparks
Rollin Espinoza	Hector Elias
Carla St. James	E.J. Peaker
Max St. James	John Reilly
Madame's Place Pianist	George Wyle

Theme Vocal ("Here at Madame's Place"): Denise DeCaro

Producer: Brad Lachman, Bob Sand, Don Van Atta

Made in America

Game; 30 min; CBS 4/5/64 to 5/3/64

Object: For a celebrity panel to guess how their guests, actual millionaires, acquired their wealth.

Host: Bob Maxwell

Panelists: Jan Sterling, Don Murray, Walter Slezak

Producer: Steve Carlin, Mark Goodson, Bill Todman

The Madhouse Brigade

Comedy; 30 min; Syn. 9/78

A series of comedy skits that satirize politics and culture.

Regulars: Karen Rushmore, Joe Piscopo, Frank Nastagi, J.J. Lewis, Nola Fairbanks, Rocket Ryan, Alexander Marshall, Dan Resin, Carlos Carrasco

Music: Tony Monte

Producer: Jim Larkin

Madigan

Crime Drama; 90 min; NBC 9/20/72 to 8/22/73

The exploits of Dan Madigan, an embittered plainclothes detective with the Manhattan 10th Precinct in New York. Aired on "The NBC Wednesday Mystery Movie."

Sgt. Dan Madigan   Richard Widmark

Producer: Roland Kibbee

Maggie

Comedy Pilot; 30 min; CBS 8/29/60

The misadventures of Maggie Bradley, the pretty but mischievous daughter of a famous acting couple (Mark and Annie).

Maggie Bradley	Margaret O'Brien
Mark Bradley	Leon Ames
Annie Bradley	Fay Baker
Miss Caldwell	Jesslyn Fax

Producer: Bill Manoff

Maggie

Comedy; 30 min; ABC 10/24/81 to 5/21/82

Events in the hectic day-to-day lives of the Westons, a Dayton, Ohio, family of five: Maggie, the mother; Len, her husband, the vice principal at Fillmore High School; and their children, Mark, Bruce, and the never-seen L. J.

Maggie Weston	Miriam Flynn
Len Weston	James Hampton
Mark Weston	Billy Jacoby
Bruce Weston	Christian Jacobs
Loretta Davenport	Doris Roberts
Buffy Croft	Judith-Marie Bergan
Chris	Margie Impert
Tiffany Dietrich	Rachel Jacobs

Hostess: Erma Bombeck

Theme Music ("Maggie's Theme"): Patrick Williams

Producer: Erma Bombeck, Tom Whedon, Bill Davenport

Maggie

Crime Drama Pilot; 60 min; CBS 6/19/86

Following the death of her husband, Maggie Webb, a beautiful widow left with numerous debts and back tax problems, finds help from her wealthy sister-in-law, Diane, who hires her for her London public relations firm. The unsold series was to relate Maggie's adventures as she attempts to pay her creditors, the tax man, and begin a new life.

Maggie Webb	Stefanie Powers
Diane Webb	Ava Gardner
Harry "Pidge" Pidgeon	Herb Edelman
Jeremy Ashton-Davis	Jeremy Lloyd
Jimmy Farnsworth	Barry Corbin
Alyce Farnsworth	Deborah Foreman
Denholm Sinclair	Ian Ogilvey
Charlotte Farnsworth	Alley Mills
Charlie McClain	Marshall Colt
Eulene Booker	Betsy Blair

Producer: William Hill, Michael S. McClean

Maggie Brown

Comedy Pilot; 30 min; CBS 9/23/63

The story of Maggie Brown, the owner of Maggie Brown's, a Pacific Island club for American sailors.

Maggie Brown	Ethel Merman
Jeannie Brown	Susan Watson
McChesney	Walter Burke
John Farragut	Roy Roberts
Joe Beckett	Mark Goddard
Marv	Marvin Kaplan

Producer: Jerry Thorpe

Maggie Malone

Drama Pilot; 30 min; NBC 6/9/59

The story of Maggie Malone, a singer who is also part owner (with Pete) of a successful nightclub. Aired on "The David Niven Theatre."

Maggie Malone	Julie London
Pete	Steve Brodie
Frank Dennison	Stacy Harris
Andy Cullen	Regis Toomey
Thug	John Wilder

Producer: Vincent M. Fennelly

Maggi's Private Wire

Women; 15 min; NBC 4/12/49 to 7/2/49
                ABC 7/31/52 to 12/11/52

A program of celebrity interviews, human interest accounts, fashion previews, and gossip. Also titled "The Maggi McNellis Show" (1952).

Hostess: Maggi McNellis

The Magic Clown

Children; 15 min; NBC 9/11/49 to 6/27/54

Games, songs, and magic geared to children and set against a circus background.

Magic Clown	Zovella
	Richard DuBois

Producer: Al Garry, Nat Eisenberg

The Magic Cottage

Children; 30 min; DuMont 7/18/49 to 2/9/51

Stories, fairy tales, art instruction, and games geared to children.

Hostess: Pat Meikle

Assistant: Robert Wilkinson

Producer: Hal Cooper

The Magic Garden

Children; 30 min; Syn. 1974

The series, set in the Magic Garden, a forest-like area where the make-believe becomes real, presents songs, stories, and music geared to children.

Carole	Carole Demas
Paula	Paula Janis
Voice of Sherlock & Flap	Cary Antebi

Producer: Irv Jarvis, Joseph L. Hall, Virginia Martin

The Magic Lady

Children; 15 min; Syn. 1951

Fairy tales, guests, songs, and feats of magic geared to children.

Magic Lady	Geraldine Larsen
Boko (her helper)	Jerry Maren

The Magic Land of Allakazam

Children; 30 min; CBS 10/1/60 to 9/22/62
ABC 9/29/62 to 12/12/64

Magic, cartoons, and various entertainment set against the background of the magic kingdom of Allakazam.

Mark Wilson	Himself
Nana Darnell	Herself
Mike Wilson	Himself
Rebo the Clown	Bev Bergerson
The King	Bob Towner
Perriwinkle	Chuck Barnes

Producer: Mark Wilson

Magic Midway

Variety; 30 min; NBC 9/22/62 to 3/16/63

Performances by entertainers from the circus world.

Host: Claude Kirchner

Regulars: Bonnie Lee, Bill "Boom Boom" Bailey, Phil "Coo Coo" Kiley, Douglas "Mr. Pocus" Anderson

Producer: Jack Miller

Magic Mongo

Comedy; 15 min; ABC 9/10/77 to 9/2/78

While walking on the beach, Donald Connelly finds a strange bottle. Upon opening it, a genie, named Magic Mongo, emerges and becomes his slave. Stories relate Donald's misadventures as he attempts to control a mischievous genie. Aired on "The Krofft Supershow."

Magic Mongo	Lennie Weinrib
Donald	Paul Hinckley
Laraine	Helaine Lembeck
Christy	Robin Dearden
Ace	Bart Braverman
Duncey	Larry Larsen
Huli	Sab Shimono

Producer: Sid and Marty Krofft

The Magic of Mark Wilson

Variety; 30 min; Syn. 9/77

The series, produced by Herb Waterson, spotlights the talents of magician Mark Wilson. Assistants: Nina Darnell and Greg Wilson.

The Magic Ranch

Children; 30 min; ABC 9/30/61 to 12/17/61

Don Alan as the host of a program that features performances by guest magicians. Produced by George Anderson.

The Magic Slate

Anthology; 30 min; NBC 6/2/50 to 6/24/51

Dramatizations, geared to children, that feature adaptations of classic and contemporary stories.

Host: Norman Grant

Regulars: Valerie McElory, Bob Borlek, Homer Yates, Don Peggins

Producer: Norman Grant

The Magician

Adventure; 60 min; NBC 10/2/73 to 5/20/74

Ten years after he is imprisoned on a trumped up espionage charge, Anthony Blake and his cellmate escape from a South American prison. The dying cellmate, grateful for the few months of freedom Blake has given him, rewards him with a vast wealth. Stories relate Blake's exploits as he uses his wizardry as a magician to help people who are seeking escape but who are unable to turn to the police for help.

Anthony Blake	Bill Bixby
Max Pomeroy (his contact)	Keene Curtis
Jerry Anderson (his pilot)	Jim Watkins
Dennis Pomeroy (Max's son)	Tod Crespi
Dominick (Magic Castle Club owner)	Joseph Sirola

"The Magician" Theme: Patrick Williams

Producer: Laurence Heath

Note: In the TV Movie (3/17/73) Bill Bixby is referred to as Anthony Dorian.

The Magilla Gorilla Show

Cartoon; 30 min; Syn. 1964

Segments: "Magilla Gorilla" (about a mischievous, fun-loving gorilla); "Ricochet Rabbit" (Sheriff Ricochet Rabbit's efforts to uphold the law in Hootin' Holler); "Punkin Puss and Mush Mouse" (antics of a hillbilly cat and mouse).

Magilla Gorilla	Allan Melvin
Mr. Peebles	Howard Morris
Ogee	Jean VanderPyl
Ricochet Rabbit	Don Messick
Deputy Droop-a-Long	Mel Blanc
Punkin Puss	Allan Melvin
Mush Mouth	Howard Morris

Producer: William Hanna, Joseph Barbera

Magnavox Theatre

Anthology; 60 min; CBS 9/15/50 to 12/8/50

A short-lived series of comedies and dramas produced by Garth Montgomery and sponsored by the Magnavox Corporation.

The Magnificent Marble Machine

Game; 30 min; NBC 7/7/75 to 6/11/76

The highest scoring player during a question-and-answer session receives the opportunity to play a large pinball machine. The player receives one minute at play and attempts to hit bumpers to earn cash prizes.

Host: Art James

Announcer: Johnny Gilbert

Producer: Merrill Heatter, Bob Quigley

Magnum, P.I.

Crime Drama; 60 min; CBS 12/11/80 (Premiere)

For reasons that are not explained, Naval Intelligence Agent Thomas Magnum leaves the service to become a private detective. Later, in Hawaii, he becomes the security force for Robin Masters, a never-seen, successful pulp writer. Stories relate Magnum's case investigations.

Thomas Magnum	Tom Selleck
Jonathan Higgins	John Hillerman
T. C. Calvin	Roger E. Mosley
Rick Wright	Larry Manetti
Lt. Poole	Jean Bruce Scott
Assistant D. A. Carol Baldwin	Kathleen Lloyd
Doc Ibold	Glenn Cannon
Luther Gillis	Eugene Roche
Madelyn Jones	Margie Impert
Voice of Robin Masters	Orson Welles
Robin Masters (from back)	Bruce Atkinson
Francis "Ice Pick" Hofstedter	Elisha Cook
Lt. Tanaka	Kwan Hi Lim

"Magnum, P.I." Theme Song: Mike Post, Pete Carpenter

Producer: Donald P. Bellisario, Glen A. Larson, Joel Rogosin, John G. Stephens, Douglas Benton

Mahalia Jackson Sings

A syndicated (1961) five-minute filler program that features songs by Mahalia Jackson.

The Mail Story

See "Handle with Care."

Maintenance Ms.

A syndicated (1975) filler program of household tips and advice for women by a woman (Jane Norman).

Maisie

Comedy Pilot; 30 min; CBS 9/12/60

The misadventures of Maisie Ravier, a beautiful showgirl who works the small night club circuit.

Maisie Ravier	Janis Paige
Andy Clary	Lin McCarthy
Sgt. Blankenhorn	Joe Sawyer
Mrs. Clary	Olive Carey
Mayor	James Maloney

Producer: Richard Maibaum

Major Adams, Trailmaster

The syndicated title for "Wagon Train," which see.

Major Dell Conway of the Flying Tigers

Adventure; 30 min; DuMont 4/14/51 to 3/2/52

The exploits of Dell Conway, chief pilot of the Los Angeles-based Flying Tigers Airline, as he investigates cases on behalf of G-2, an American Military Intelligence organization.

Dell Conway	Eric Fleming
	Ed Peck
	Art Fleming*
Caribou (his assistant)	Luis Van Rooten
	Bern Hoffman

*Screen credit under the title "The Flying Tigers"

Majority Rules

Game; 30 min; ABC 9/2/49 to 7/30/50

Object: For a panel of three players to answer a question based on a majority decision (two players must agree on any given answer).

Host: Ed Prentiss

Make a Face

Game; 30 min; ABC 10/2/61 to 12/22/62

Object: For players to assemble and identify celebrities whose pictures are cut into pieces and placed on revolving wheels. The player with the most idenfications receives merchandise prizes.

Host: Bob Clayton

Hostess: Rita Mueller

Producer: Art Baer, Herbert Gottlieb

Make a Wish

Children; 30 min; ABC 9/12/71 to 9/3/77

Through animation, films, sketches and songs, the differences between fantasy and the real world are explained to children.

Host: Tom Chapin

Orchestra: Bernard Green

Producer: Lester Cooper, Tom Bywaters

Make Me Laugh

Game; 30 min; ABC 3/20/58 to 6/12/58

Object: For a contestant to remain straight-faced while three guest comics attempt to make him laugh. Players receive one dollar per second until they laugh.

Host: Robert Q. Lewis

Hostess: Renny Peterson

Producer: Sylvester "Pat" Weaver, Mort Green, George Foster, Johnny Stearns

Make Me Laugh

Game; 30 min; Syn. 9/79

A contestant is placed in front of a panel of three guest comics who, in turn, attempt to make him laugh. For each second that the contestant remains straight-faced, he receives one dollar (to a limit of $360).

Host: Bobby Van

Announcer: Bill Peary

Producer: George Foster

Make Mine Music

Variety; 30 min; CBS 12/31/48 to 5/19/49

Carole Coleman as the host of a program of music and songs with regulars Bill Skipper, Larry Douglas, and the music of the Tony Mottola Trio. Produced by Alex Leftwich.

Make More Room for Daddy

Comedy Pilot; 60 min; NBC 11/6/67

An attempt to revive the "Make Room for Daddy" series, which picks up the lives of the Williams family three years later, focusing on parents Danny and Kathy, and their children Linda (now in college) and Rusty (in the Army and about to be married to Susan).

Danny Williams	Danny Thomas
Kathy Williams	Marjorie Lord
Linda Williams	Angela Cartwright
Rusty Williams	Rusty Hamer
Susan McAdams	Jana Taylor
Charlie Halper	Sid Melton
Louise	Amanda Randolph
Col. McAdams	Edward Andrews

Producer: Danny Thomas

Make Room for Daddy

Comedy; 30 min; ABC 9/29/53 to 7/17/57 (as "Make Room for Daddy") CBS 10/7/57 to 9/14/64 (as "The Danny Thomas Show")

Events in the life of Danny Williams, a night club comedian at the Copa Club in New York, whose career often leaves him little time to spend with his family (wife, Margaret; later Kathy, and their children Teresa, Rusty, and Linda). See also "Make More Room for Daddy" and "Make Room for Granddaddy."

Danny Williams	Danny Thomas
Margaret Williams	Jean Hagen
Kathy Williams	Marjorie Lord
Teresa "Terry" Williams	Sherry Jackson
	Penny Parker
Russell "Rusty" Williams	Rusty Hamer
Linda Williams	Angela Cartwright
Patty Williams*	Lelani Sorenson
Louise	Louise Beavers
	Amanda Randolph
Charlie Halper	Sid Melton
Bunny Halper	Pat Carroll
Jesse Leeds	Jesse White
Phil Arnold	Horace McMahon
Elizabeth O'Neal	Mary Wickes
Benny	Ben Lessy
Patty (Benny's wife)	Patricia Moore
Chips Collins	Harvey Lembeck
Frank	Frank Jenks
Danny's Uncle Tonoose	Hans Conried
Pat Hannegan	Pat Harrington Jr.
Harry	Harry Ruby
Gina Minelli	Annette Funicello
Piccola Pupa	Herself
Buck	Richard Tyler
Jose Jiminez	Bill Dana
Mr. Daly	William Demarest
Mr. Heckendorn	Gale Gordon
Alfie	Bernard Fox
Peggy Conroy	Eileen Janssen

Music: Herbert Spencer, Earle Hagen

Producer: Louis F. Edelman, Charles Stewart, Sheldon Leonard, Jack Elinson, Ronald Jacobs

*Kathy's original daughter in 1957.

Make Room for Granddaddy

Comedy; 30 min; ABC 9/23/70 to 9/2/71

Continued events in the lives of the Williams family: Danny, a night club comedian; Kathy, his lovely wife; Linda, their daughter; Rusty, their son; Terry, their married daughter; and Michael, Danny's grandson (Terry's son). The 60-minute pilot aired on CBS on 9/14/69.

Danny Williams	Danny Thomas
Kathy Williams	Marjorie Lord
Linda Williams	Angela Cartwright
Rusty Williams	Rusty Hamer
Terry Johnson	Sherry Jackson
Susan Williams	Jana Taylor
Michael Johnson	Michael Hughes
Uncle Tonoose	Hans Conried
Charlie Halper	Sid Melton
Rosey Robbins	Rosey Grier
Henry	Stanley Myron Handleman
Bunny Halper (pilot only)	Pat Carroll

Producer: Danny Thomas, Richard Crenna

Make the Connection

Game; 30 min; NBC 7/7/55 to 9/29/55

Through a series of question-and-answer rounds with two contestants, a celebrity panel of four have to determine when, where, and how their paths crossed with the laymen players.

Host: Gene Rayburn, Jim McKay

Panelists: Gloria DeHaven, Eddie Bracken, Gene Klaven, Betty White

Producer: Mark Goodson, Bill Todman

Make Your Own Kind of Music

Variety; 60 min; NBC 7/20/71 to 9/7/71

A summer series of music and comedy skits.

Hosts: Karen and Richard Carpenter

Regulars: Tom Patchett, Jay Tarses, Al Hirt, Mark Lindsay, The New Doodletown Pipers

Orchestra: Jack Elliott, Allyn Ferguson

Producer: Arnold Kane, Gordon Farr

Makin' It

Comedy; 30 min; ABC 2/1/79 to 3/16/79

The misadventures of Billy Manucci, an easy-going young man who lives at home—and in the shadow of a swinging older brother—while working his way through college to become a teacher.

Billy Manucci	David Naughton
Joseph Manucci	Lou Antonio
Dorothy Manucci	Ellen Travolta
Tina Manucci	Denise Miller
Tony Manucci	Greg Antonacci
Corky Crandall	Rebecca Balding
Al "Kingfish"	
Sorrentino	Ralph Seymour
Bernard Fusco	Gary Prendergast
Ivy Papastegios	Jennifer Perito
Suzanne	Wendy Hoffman
Felice	Diane Robin
Roxanne	Leslie Winston

Theme Vocal ("Makin' It"): David Naughton

Producer: Thomas L. Miller, Edward K. Milkis, Lowell Ganz, Mark Rothman

Making a Living

Comedy; 30 min; ABC 10/24/81 to 9/10/82

A spin-off from "It's a Living," which continues to depict events in the lives of four

beautiful waitresses (Cassie, Jan, Maggie, and Dot) at the posh Los Angeles Above the Top Restaurant.

Katie Lou "Cassie"	
Cranston	Ann Jillian
Jan Hoffmeyer	Barrie Youngfellow
Maggie McBirney	Louise Lasser
Dot Higgins	Gail Edwards
Nancy Beebee	Marian Mercer
Sonny Mann	Paul Kreppel
Dennis Humner	Earl Boen

Theme Vocal ("Making a Living"): Leslie Bricusse

Producer: Paul Junger Witt, Tony Thomas

Making It

Comedy Pilot; 30 min; NBC 8/30/76

The misadventures of four students (Steve, Pete, Jay, and Greg) as they struggle to survive the difficult years of law school.

Steve	Ed Begley Jr.
Pete	Ben Masters
Jay	Alvin Kupperman
Greg	Evan Kim
Prof. Harry Ebberly	Renny Roker
Cloris	Jeanne Arnold
Janice	Sandy Faison

Producer: Lee Rich, Lawrence Marks

Making the Grade

Comedy; 30 min; CBS 4/5/82 to 5/10/82

The problems that befall the faculty of the problem-plagued Franklin High School in St. Louis, Missouri.

Harry Barnes	James Naughton
Jack Felspar	Graham Jarvis
Sara Canover	Alley Mills
Dave Wasserman	Philip Charles
	MacKenzie
Anton Zemeckis	Zane Lasky
Jeffrey Kelton	Steven Peterman
Cynthia Wasserman	
(Dave's wife)	Ellen Regan
Mindy (student)	Annabell Price
Walt (student)	Dan Frischman
Arnold (student)	Christopher Blande

Producer: Gary David Goldberg, Lloyd Garver.

Malibu Run

Adventure; 30 min; CBS 3/1/61 to 9/27/61

A revamped version of "The Aquanauts" that relates the exploits of Mike Madison and Larry Lahr, diving instructors and part time private detectives based in Malibu Beach, California.

Mike Madison	Ron Ely
Larry Lahr	Jeremy Slate
Capt. Chaplan	Charles Thompson

Producer: Ivan Tors

Malibu U.

Variety; 30 min; ABC 7/21/67 to 9/1/67

The series, set at the mythical Malibu University on California's Malibu Beach, presents performances by the top names in rock music.

Host (The Dean): Ricky Nelson

Regulars: Erin Gray, Robbie Porter, The Bob Banas Dancers, The Malibuties

Theme Vocal ("Malibu U"): Harpers Bizzare

Producer: Al Burton

Mama

See "I Remember Mama."

Mama Malone

Comedy; 30 min; CBS 3/7/84 to 7/21/84

The series, set in the Brooklyn home of "Mama" Ranata Malone, where the TV show, "Cooking with Mama Malone" is taped, relates Ranata's efforts to conduct a live show despite constant interruptions from friends and family.

Ranata Malone	Lila Kaye
Connie (her daughter)	Randee Heller
Frankie (Connie's son)	Evan Richards
Dino Forresti (Ranata's brother)	Don Amendolia
Austin (director)	Raymond Singer
Padre Guardiano	Ralph Manza
Father Jose Silva	Richard Yniquez
Stanley (TV announcer)	Sam Anderson
Jackie (script girl)	Joey Jupiter
Harry (floor director)	Mitchell Group
Ken (assistant director)	Pendleton Brown
Rosa (Ranata's niece)	Candice Azzara
Neta Cavelli (Ranata's friend)	Alice Ghostley

Theme Song ("Mama Malone"): John Kander, Fred Ebb

Producer: Richard Lewis, Paul Bogart

Mama Rosa

A virtually unknown serial about an Italian-American family. The series, broadcast live on ABC (4/23/50 to 6/15/50) in California and seen on kinescope elsewhere, was the first series to originate on the West Coast (where it began as a local show on KFI-TV in 1948). Additional information is not known.

Mama's Boy

Comedy; 30 min; NBC 9/19/87 (Premiere)

When Molly McCaskey loses her money and is forced to leave Florida, she moves to New York and into the apartment of her bachelor son, Jake, a writer (of the Column "McCaskey") for the "Manhattan Examiner." Stories relate Jake's efforts to cope with the situations that arise as his mother begins to dominate his life.

Jake McCaskey	Bruce Weitz
Molly McCaskey	Nancy Walker
Victoria	Susan Blakely
Lucky	James Cromwell
Mickey	Dan Hedaya
Agnes	Grace Zabriskie
Ginger	Maggie Roswell

Producer: David Pollock, Elias Davis, Paul Junger Witt, Tony Thomas

Mama's Family

Comedy; 30 min; NBC 1/22/83 to 9/15/84

Events in the hectic day-to-day lives of the Harpers, a not-so-typical American family living in Raytown, U.S.A. Based on sketches performed on "The Carol Burnett Show." See following title also.

Thelma "Mama" Harper	Vicki Lawrence
Vinton Harper	Ken Berry
Naomi Oates-Harper	Dorothy Lyman
Fran Crawley	Rue McClanahan
Sonia Harper	Karin Argoud
Buzz Harper	Eric Brown
Ellen Jackson	Betty White
Eunice Higgins	Carol Burnett
Ed Higgins	Harvey Korman
Alistair Quince (the host)	Harvey Korman
Leonard (Naomi's ex-husband)	Jerry Reed

Theme Song ("Bless My Happy Home"): Peter Matz

Producer: Joe Hamilton, Ed Simmons, Dick Clair, Jenna McMahon

Mama's Family

Comedy; 30 min; Syn. 9/86

A revised version of the previous title, which continues to depict events in the lives of the Harper family of Raytown, U.S.A.

Thelma "Mama" Harper	Vicki Lawrence
Naomi Harper	Dorothy Lyman
Vinton Harper	Ken Berry
Bubba Higgins	Allan Kayser
Iola Bolen	Beverly Archer
Mama's Aunt Effie	Dorothy Van
Thelma's Sister Ellen	Betty White

Producer: Joe Hamilton, Robert Wright

Man About the House

Comedy; 30 min; Syn. 6/83

The British series on which "Three's Company" is based. The misadventures of Jo and Chrissy, two girls who share a flat in England, and the problems that ensue when their landlords raise the rent and they sublet a room to Robin Tripp, a male cookery student. See also "Robin's Nest" and "George and Mildred."

Robin Tripp	Richard O'Sullivan
Jo	Sally Thomsett
Chrissy Plummer	Paula Wilcox
George Roper	Brian Murphy
Mildred Roper	Yootha Joyce
Larry Simmons	Doug Fisher
Norman Tripp	Norman Eshley

Producer: Peter Frazer-Jones

Man About Town

Comedy Pilot; 30 min; ABC 7/11/86

The misadventures of Leon Feddick, a New York bachelor with few dates, few friends, and very little excitement in his life.

Leon Feddick	Daniel Stern
Terry Bishop	Jayne Modean
Sandy	Karlene Crockett
Vic LeMeara	Tom Henschel
Dean Feddick	Sam Whipple
Mike the Mailman	George Wyner
Ellen Nance	Toni Kalem

Producer: Richard Rosenstock, Roy Teicher

The Man Against Crime

Crime Drama; 30 min; CBS 10/7/49 to 10/2/53
DuMont 10/11/53 to 4/4/54
NBC 7/1/56 to 8/26/56

The exploits of Mike Barnett, a two-fisted private detective based in New York City. Also known as "Follow That Man."

Mike Barnett	Ralph Bellamy
	Frank Lovejoy
Pat Barnett	Robert Preston
Bellamy's stand-in	Art Fleming

Producer: Edward J. Montagne, Paul Nickell

The Man Against Crime

Crime Drama Pilot; 30 min; NBC 9/21/58

The story of a young lawyer (Dan Garrett) and his relentless battle against injustice. Aired on "Decision."

Dan Garrett	Darren McGavin
Sam Mitschner	David Opatoshu
Robbie Mitschner	Stanley Peck
Spotsy	Terry Greene
Voorhes	Joe Sullivan

Producer: Richard L. Bare

The Man and the Challenge

Adventure; 30 min; NBC 9/12/59 to 9/3/60

The story of a U.S. government research scientist (Glenn Barton) and his efforts to test the limits of human endurance.

Glenn Barton	George Nader
Lynn Allen	
(assistant)	Jayne Meadows

Producer: Ivan Tors

The Man and the City

Drama; 60 min; ABC 9/15/71 to 1/5/72

The life of Thomas Jefferson Alcala, the mayor of an unnamed New Mexican city, who strays from the offices of city hall to mix with the people and help solve their problems.

Thomas Alcala	Anthony Quinn
Andy Hays	Mike Farrell
Marian Crane	Mala Powers
Josefina	Carmen Zapata

Producer: David Victor, Stanley Rubin

The Man Behind the Badge

Anthology; 30 min; CBS 10/11/53 to 10/1/55

Dramas based on the official law enforcement records of the men and women who risk their lives to protect people.

Host-Narrator: Charles Bickford, Norman Rose

Announcer: Joel Aldred

Producer: Jerome Robinson, Bernard Prockter

A Man Called Ragan

Western Pilot; 60 min; ABC 4/23/62

The pilot for "The Dakotas." The exploits of Frank Ragan, a U.S. Marshal stationed in the lawless Dakotas of the 1860s. Aired on "Cheyenne."

Marshal Frank	
Ragan	Larry Ward
Deputy J.D. Smith	Jack Elam
Deputy Del Stark	Chad Everett
Ben Stark	Arch Johnson

A Man Called Shenandoah

Western; 30 min; ABC 9/13/65 to 9/5/66

For unknown reasons, a man is shot and left for dead on the prairie. He is found by two bounty hunters and brought to a town where he is nursed back to health by a saloon girl (Kate). Later, he finds that he is without a memory and unaware of who or what he was. Stories, set in the 1860s, follows the trail of an amnesiac, "A Man Called Shenandoah," as he seeks his identity and a home.

Shenandoah	Robert Horton
Kate	Beverly Garland

Theme Vocal ("Shenandoah"): Robert Horton

Producer: Fred Freiberger

A Man Called Sloane

Adventure; 60 min; NBC 9/22/79 to 9/12/80

The exploits of Thomas Remington Sloane III, Priority One Agent for UNIT, a select counterespionage team, as he battles the evils of KARTEL, an enemy organization that seeks to destroy the world.

Thomas Sloane	Robert Conrad
	Robert Logan*
Torgue (assistant)	Ji-Tu Cumbuka
Mr. Director	Dan O'Herlihy
Kelly O'Neal (agent)	Karen Purcell
Effie (EFI Computer Voice)	Michele Carey
Sara (Sloane's girlfriend)	Diane Stilwell

Announcer: Michele Carey

Theme Song ("A Man Called Sloane"): Patrick Williams

Producer: Philip Saltzman, Quinn Martin

*Role in the TV Movie "Death Ray 2000" (NBC 3/5/81).

A Man Called Strait

See "Man of the World" for information.

The Man Called X

Adventure; 30 min; Syn. 1956

The exploits of Ken Thurston, a U.S. intelligence agent who operates under the code name X.

| Ken Thurston | Barry Sullivan |

Producer: Eddie Davis

The Man from Atlantis

Adventure; 60 min; NBC 9/22/77 to 7/25/78

When a storm deep within the Pacific Ocean unearths the sole survivor of the kingdom of Atlantis, he is brought to the Oceanic Research Foundation in California. When the Atlantian becomes ill, Elizabeth Merrill, a doctor who names him Mark Harris, saves his life by returning him to the ocean. Mark, although set free, decides to remain with the foundation to gain his own knowledge about us. Stories relate Mark's work on behalf of the foundation.

Mark Harris	Patrick Duffy
Dr. Elizabeth Merrill	Belinda J. Montgomery
Dr. Simon Miller	Kenneth Tigar
Ginny Mendoza	Annette Cardona
C. W. Crawford	Alan Fudge
Mr. Schubert	Victor Buono
Brent	Robert Lussier
Jane	Jean Marie Hon
Jimmy	J. Victor Lopez
Jumo	Anson Downs

Producer: Herbert F. Solow, Herman Miller, Robert Lewin

The Man from Blackhawk

Western; 30 min; ABC 10/9/59 to 9/23/60

The exploits of Sam Logan, a special investigator for the Blackhawk Insurance Company during the lawless 1870s.

| Sam Logan | Robert Rockwell |

Producer: Herb Meadow

The Man from Cochise

The syndicated title for 78 episodes of "Sheriff of Cochise" and 78 episodes of "U.S. Marshal." See individual titles.

The Man from Denver

Western Pilot; 30 min; CBS 4/30/59

The story of Ward Pendleton, an examiner for a chain of banks, as he travels throughout the Old West. Aired as "Checkmate" on "Zane Grey Theatre."

Ward Pendleton	Mark Miller
Sara Martin	Marsha Hunt
Joel Begley	James Whitmore
Sheriff	Jim Roarke

Producer: Hal Hudson

The Man from Everywhere

Comical Western Pilot; 30 min; CBS 4/13/61

The story of Branch Taylor, a happy-go-lucky drifter of the Old West who will tackle any job. Aired on "Zane Grey Theatre."

Branch Taylor	Burt Reynolds
Jenny Aldrich	Ruta Lee
Tom Bowdry	Cesar Romero
Jed Morgan	King Calder
Moose	Peter Whitney

Producer: Hal Hudson

The Man from Galveston

Western Pilot; 54 min; Unaired (Produced in 1963)

The pilot for "Temple Houston." The story of a circuit-riding frontier lawyer (Timothy Higgins). In the story, produced for TV, but released theatrically, Higgins defends a woman accused of murder.

Timothy Higgins	Jeffrey Hunter
Homer Black	Preston Foster
Rita Dillard	Joanna Moore
Boyd Palmer	James Coburn
Texas Rose	Grace Lee Whitney
Hyde	Edward Andrews
Stonewall Gray	Martin West
Cole Marteen	Ed Nelson
Sheriff	Karl Swenson

Producer: Jack Webb, Michael Meshekoff

The Man from Interpol

Crime Drama; 30 min; NBC 1/23/60 to 10/22/60

The exploits of Tony Smith, a New Scotland Yard inspector who has been assigned to active duty with Interpol (the International Police Force).

Tony Smith	Richard Wyler
Superintendant Mercer	John Longden

Producer: Edward J. and Harry Lee Danziger.

The Man from U.N.C.L.E.

Adventure; 60 min; NBC 9/22/64 to 1/15/68

The exploits of Napoleon Solo and Illya Kuryakin, agents for U.N.C.L.E. (the United Network Command for Law Enforcement), as they battle T.H.R.U.S.H., an enemy organization bent on world domination. See also "The Girl from U.N.C.L.E."

Napoleon Solo	Robert Vaughn
Illya Kuryakin	David McCallum
Alexander Waverly	Leo G. Carroll
Lisa Rogers	Barbara Moore
Del Floria	Mario Siletti
U.N.C.L.E. Girl (Heather)	May Heatherly
U.N.C.L.E. Girl	Julie Ann Johnson
	Sharon Hillyer

"The Man from U.N.C.L.E." Theme Song: Lalo Schifrin

Producer: Norman Felton, Sam H. Rolfe, Anthony Spinner, Boris Ingster

Man in a Suitcase

Adventure; 60 min; ABC 5/3/68 to 9/20/68

The series, set in London, relates the adventures of John McGill, a former American intelligence agent turned private detective.

John McGill	Richard Bradford

Producer: Sidney Cole

Man in the Middle

Comedy Pilot; 30 min; CBS 4/14/72

The story of a conservative family man (Norman) who is caught between a left-wing daughter (Debbie), a right-wing mother (Belle) and a middle-aged business partner (Harvey) on a youth trip.

Norman	Van Johnson
Harriet (his wife)	Nancy Malone
Debbie	Heather Menzies
Belle	Ruth McDevitt
Harvey	Allan Melvin
Kirk	Michael Brandon

Producer: Harvey Bullock, Ray Allen

Man of the Comstock

Western Pilot; 30 min; NBC 11/3/53

The story of an attorney (Bill Stewart) as he attempts to maintain the peace in the Comstock mining area of Colorado during the Civil War. Aired on "Fireside Theatre."

Bill Stewart	Bruce Bennett
Joseph Goodman	Morris Ankrum
Annie Foote	Andrea King
John McKay	Jonathan Hale
Sam Brown	Glenn Strange
Mrs. Kirkland	Ruth Clifford
El Dorado Johnny	Robert Griffin
Governor Nye	Emmett Vogan

Producer: Frank Wisbar

Man of the West

See "Frontier Doctor."

Man of the World

Drama; 60 min; Syn. 1962

A not widely syndicated series about Michael Strait, an international photojournalist who helps people in trouble.

| Michael Strait | Craig Stevens |

Producer: Ralph Smart

Man to Woman

A five minute syndicated (1971) insert series (for magazine programs) wherein host (and producer) Jack Douglas speaks his mind to today's women.

The Man Who Never Was

Adventure; 30 min; ABC 9/7/66 to 1/4/67

While being pursued by East German police, American espionage agent Peter Murphy finds shelter on an estate owned by Mark Wainwright a millionaire who is his exact double. When the police mistake Mark for Peter and kill him, Peter finds the perfect cover by stepping into the shoes and likeness of the man with his face. Stories relate Peter's efforts, assisted by Mark's beautiful wife, Eva*, to carry out hazardous missions for the U.S. government.

Peter Murphy	Robert Lansing
Eva Wainwright	Dana Wynter
Roger Berry	Alex Devion
Jack Forbes	Murray Hamilton
Grant	Paul Stewart

Producer: Robert L. Jacks, John Newland.

*When Eva learns what has happened, she agrees to keep Peter's secret, provided that he help her regain control of her family corporation from Roger Berry, Mark's scheming brother.

Man with a Camera

Crime Drama; 30 min; ABC 10/10/58 to 1/29/60

The story of Mike Kovac, a New York-based free-lance photo-journalist who acquires material by assisting the police and solving crimes against insurance companies.

| Mike Kovac | Charles Bronson |
| Lt. Donovan | James Flavin |

Producer: Warren Lewis, Don Sharpe, A. E. Houghton

Man Without a Gun

Western; 30 min; ABC 10/10/58 to 1/29/60

The series, set in Yellowstone, Dakota, during the 1870s, relates the efforts of newspaper editor Adam MacLean ("The Yellowstone Sentinel") to establish peace through the power of the press. See next title also.

| Adam MacLean | Rex Reason |
| Marshal Frank Tallman | Mort Mills |

Producer: Peter Packer, Alan A. Armer, Mel Epstein

Man Without a Gun

Western Pilot; 30 min; Unaired (Produced in April, 1957)

The original pilot for the above series, with Robert Rockwell as Adam MacLean. Produced by Peter Packer and directed by Christian I. Nyby.

The Mancini Generation

Variety; 30 min; Syn. 9/72

A weekly program of music and songs with orchestra leader Henry Mancini and the forty-piece Mancini orchestra. Additional orchestrations by Alan Copeland. Produced by Burt Sugarman and Stan Harris.

Mandrake the Magician

Adventure; 30 min; Syn. 1954

In a mysterious Tibetan Valley where the ancient secrets of Egypt and the magic of China have been preserved over the centuries, a young boy is taught the secrets by Theron, the Master of Magic. Upon his release from the College of Magic, he teams with his servant, Lothar, and together set out to battle evil. Stories relate their attempts to help people in trouble.

Mandrake	Coe Norton
Lothar	Woody Strode

Manhattan Honeymoon

Game; 30 min; ABC 2/22/54 to 4/30/54

Three engaged or married couples compete in a series of question-and-answer rounds with the highest scoring players winning an expenses-paid honeymoon in New York.

Hostess: Neva Patterson

Manhattan Showcase

Variety; 15 min; CBS 2/28/49 to 6/16/49

Performances by undiscovered professional talent.

Host: Johnny Downs

Co-Hostess: Helen Gallagher

Regulars: Norma Shepherd, Loren Walsh

Music: The Tony Mottola Trio

Producer: Barry Wood

The Manhattan Transfer

Variety; 60 min; CBS 8/10/75 to 8/31/75

A nostalgic series that recalls the music, songs, and dances of the 1930s and 40s.

The Manhattan Transfer: Laurel Masse, Janis Siegel, Alan Paul, Tim Hauser

Regulars: Laraine Newman, Fayette Hauser, Leland Palmer, Archie Hahn

Orchestra: Ira Newborn

Producer: Bernard Rothman, Jack Wohl

Manhunt

Crime Drama; 30 min; Syn. 1959

The story of a San Diego police lieutenant (Howard Finucane) and a police reporter (Ben Andrews) who team to solve crimes.

Howard Finucane	Victor Jory
Ben Andrews	Patrick McVey

Producer: Jerry Briskin

Manhunter

Crime Drama; 60 min; CBS 9/11/74 to 4/10/75

The series, set in Idaho during the public enemy days of the Depression (1934), relates the work of Dave Barrett, a W.W. I ex-marine turned bounty hunter, who tracks down criminals to claim the rewards.

Dave Barrett	Ken Howard
Lizabeth Barrett	Shirley O'Hara*
	Hilary Thompson
James Barrett	Ford Rainey
Mary Barrett	Claudia Bryar
Sheriff Paul Tate	Robert Hogan

Producer: Quinn Martin, Sam. H. Rolfe

*TV Movie role ("Manhunter," CBS 2/26/74).

Manimal

Adventure; 60 min; NBC 9/30/83 to 12/31/83

When he becomes of age, Jonathan Chase is taught a rare gift by his father: the ability to transform himself into any animal; secrets of transmutation he learned in an unknown Tibetin Valley. Stories, set at a time when Jonathan is a behaviorial sciences professor at New York University, relate his attempts to help the police solve baffling crimes as the mysterious Manimal.

Jonathan Chase	Simon MacCorkindale
Det. Brooke McKenzie	Melody Anderson
Tyrone C. Earll	Glynn Turman Michael D. Roberts
Lt. Nick Rivera	Reni Santoni
Jonathan's father	Don Knight

Narrator: William Conrad

"Manimal" Theme Song: Paul Chihara

Producer: Glen A. Larson, Paul Mason

Mannix

Crime Drama; 60 min; CBS 9/9/67 to 8/27/75

Originally, the exploits of Joe Mannix, an investigator for Intertect, a Los Angeles-based private detective organization. After one year, the format changed to relate Joe's exploits as a private detective working independently from his home at 17 Paseo Verde in Los Angeles.

Joe Mannix	Mike Connors
Lou Wickersham	Joseph Campanella
Peggy Fair	Gail Fisher
Lt. Arthur Malcolm	Ward Wood
Lt. Adam Tobias	Robert Reed
Lt. Daniel Ives	Jack Ging
Toby Fair	Mark Stewart

Producer: Ivan Goff, Ben Roberts

Creator: Richard Levinson, William Link

Mantrap

Discussion; 30 min; Syn. 1971

Three female panelists and one male guest discuss topics of current interest.

Host: Al Hamel

Panelists: Phyllis Kirk, Meredith MacRae, Jaye P. Morgan, Carol Wayne, Selma Diamond

Producer: Al Hamel, Bill Lee

Many Happy Returns

Comedy; 30 min; CBS 9/21/64 to 4/12/65

The misadventures of Walter Burnley, the harrassed manager of the complaint department of Krockmeyer's Department Store.

Walter Burnley	John McGiver
Joan Randall	Elinor Donahue
Bob Randall	Mark Goddard
Laurie Randall	Andrea Sacino
Lynn Hall	Elena Verdugo
Joe Foley	Mickey Manners
	Richard Collier
Wilma Fritter	Jesslyn Fax
J. L. Fox	Jerome Cowan
Owen Sharp	Russell Collins

Producer: Parke Levy

The Many Loves of Arthur

Comedy Pilot; 60 min; NBC 5/23/78

The story of a zoo veterinarian (Arthur) who relates better to animals than to people.

Arthur Murdock	Richard Masur
Gail Corbett	Caroline McWilliams
Karen	Constance McCashin
Nancy	Lee Bryant
Jake	Robert Ridgely
Michelle	Linda Lukens
Dr. Chase	David Dukes

Producer: Philip Barry

The Many Loves of Dobie Gillis

See "Dobie Gillis."

Maple Town

Cartoon; 30 min; Syn. 4/87

Stories, set in a magical land called Maple Town, follow the adventures of Patty Rabbit and her family and friends.

Hostess (Mrs. Maple): Janice Adams

Voices: Jeff Iwai, Wayne Kerr, Bibi Linet, Heidi Lenard, Lou Pitt, John Zahler, Alice Smith

Producer: Haim Saban

Mapp and Lucia

Satire; 60 min; Syn. 5/86

A satiric view of English life during the 1920s as seen through the experiences of Elizabeth Mapp, owner of a home (Tilling on the Sea in Sussex) and her tenant, Emmeline Lucas, who is known to one and all as Lucia. Based on the novel by E. F. Benson.

Elizabeth Mapp	Prunella Scales
Emmeline Lucas	Geraldine McEwan
Georgie	Nigel Hawthorne
Daisy	Carol Macready
Quaint Irene	Cecily Hobbs
Major Benjy	Denis Lill
Diva	Mary MacLeod

Producer: Michael Dunlop

Marblehead Manor

Comedy; 30 min; Syn. 9/87

Events in the lives of Hilary and Randolph Stonehill, millionaires who own a mansion (Marblehead Manor) staffed by a group of eccentric misfits.

Hilary Stonehill	Linda Thorson
Randolph Stonehill	Bob Fraser
Albert Dudley	Paxton Whitehead
Jerry Stockton	Phil Morris
Lupe	Dyana Ortelli
Dwayne Stockton	Rodney Scott Hudson
Elvis	Humberto Ortiz
Rick	Michael Richards
Heather Bevington	Kristi Somers
Randolph's Aunt Charlotte	Natalie Core

Producer: Bob Fraser, Rob Dames, Gary Nardino

March of Time Through the Years

Documentary; 30 min; ABC 2/23/51 to 8/27/51
                                          10/8/52 to 12/10/52
Screenings of old March of Time theatrical newsreels.

Host: John Daly

Narrator: Westbrook Van Voorhis

Producer: Arthur Tourtellot, Dick Krolik, Fred Feldkamp

Marcus Welby, M.D.

Drama; 60 min; ABC 9/23/69 to 5/11/76

Following a heart attack that makes him realize he must lighten his work load, the elder Dr. Marcus Welby hires a young assistant named Steven Kiley. Stories, set in Santa Monica, relate the experiences of two caring doctors in private practice and as part-time physicians at Lang Memorial Hospital.

Dr. Marcus Welby	Robert Young
Dr. Steven Kiley	James Brolin
Nurse Consuelo Lopez	Elena Verdugo
Nurse Kathleen Faverty	Sharon Gless
Janet Blake	Pamela Hensley
Sandy Porter	Anne Schedeen
Myra Sherwood	Anne Baxter

"Marcus Welby" Theme Song: Leonard Rosenman

Producer: David Victor, David J. O'Connell

The Marge and Gower Champion Show

Comedy; 30 min; CBS 3/31/57 to 6/9/57

Feeling that the demands of show business are hindering their personal lives, professional dancers Marge and Gower decide to establish a life apart from their business world. Stories relate their efforts to enjoy their new life, despite a hectic schedule.

Marge Champion	Herself
Gower Champion	Himself
Marge's father	Jack Whiting
Cozy	Buddy Rich
Amanda	Peg LaCentra
Miss Weatherly	Barbara Perry

Producer: Joe Connelly, Bob Mosher, Paul Harrison

Marge and Jeff

Comedy; 15 min; DuMont 9/21/53 to 9/24/54

Events in the lives of Marge and Jeff Green, newlyweds struggling to survive the difficult first years of marriage.

Marge Green	Herself
Jeff Green	Himself

Producer: Ernest Walling

Margie

Comedy; 30 min; ABC 10/12/61 to 8/31/62

The series, set in the small New England town of Madison during the 1920s, follows the life of Margie Clayton, a pretty high school girl with a penchant for mischief.

Margie Clayton	Cynthia Pepper	Marie Owens	Marie Osmond
Harvey Clayton	Dave Willock	Carla Coburn	Ellen Travolta
Nora Clayton	Wesley Tackitt	K.C. Jones	Telma Hopkins
Cornell Clayton	Johnny Bangert	Sandra	Zan Charisse
Phoebe Clayton	Hollis Irving	Pancho	Tony Ramierz
Maybell Jackson	Penny Parker	Edgar Merton	Bruce Kirby Sr.
Heywood Botts	Tommy Ivo	Det. Driscoll	Stephen Shortridge
Johnny Green	Richard Gering	Sgt. Dryer	Cliff Pellow
Mrs. Jackson	Maxine Stuart		
Mr. Jackson	Herb Ellis		

Theme Vocal: Marie Osmond

Producer: Hal Goodman, Larry Klein

Producer: Norman Paul, Joseph Bonaduce

Marie

Mariah

Variety; 60 min; NBC 12/12/80 to 9/26/81

Drama; 60 min; ABC 4/1/87 to 5/13/87

The series, set in Mariah, a small country town, focuses on the lives of the people on both sides of the walls of Mariah State, a large, antiquated maximum security prison which houses 2500 men and women inmates. Originally titled "Mariah State."

A comedy-accented series that spotlights the many talents of singer-actress Marie Osmond.

Hostess: Marie Osmond

Regulars: Nancy Steen, Shirley Mitchell, Melissa Multray, Greg Norberg, Scott Mullaney, Debbie Ing, Jim Hudson, The Lester Wilson Dancers

Ned Sheffield	John Getz
Dr. Deena Hertz	Tovah Feldshuh
Rev. Howard Bouchard	William Allan Young
James Malone	Philip Baker Hall
Leda Cervantes	Wanda DeJesus
Brandis LaSalle	Kathleen Layman
Maggie Malone	Susan Brown
Linda Grancato	Renee Lippin
Father Timothy Quinlan	Chris Wiggins
Guard	John Rutter

Announcer: Eric Chase

Orchestra: Bob Rozario, D'Vaughn Pershing

Producer: Alan Osmond, Jay Osmond, Jerry McPhie

Marie and George

Experimental; 30 min; NBC 6/16/39

Songs in French by singer Marie Eve and impersonations of famous people by George Lloyd. Produced by Edward Sobol.

Producer: Gerald I. Isenberg, Gabe Katcka, Michael Rhodes

The Marilyn McCoo and Billy Davis Jr. Show

Variety; 30 min; CBS 6/15/77 to 7/20/77

Marie

Comedy Pilot; 30 min; ABC 12/1/79

A Summer series of music and songs.

Hosts: Marilyn McCoo, Billy Davis Jr.

Hoping for a career in show business, a beautiful Nebraska girl (Marie) packs her belongings and heads for New York City. The unsold series was to relate her misadventures as she encounters setback after setback.

Regulars: Jay Leno, Tim Reid, Lewis Arquette

Orchestra: John Myles

Producer: Ann Elder, Ed Scharlach

Marine Boy

Cartoon; 30 min; Syn. 10/66

The adventures of Marine Boy, an agent for the Ocean Patrol, a 21st-century organization that battles evil. Produced in Japan.

Marine Boy/Neptina	Corinne Orr
Dr. Mariner	Jack Curtis
Piper	Jack Grimes
Bulton	Peter Fernandez

Producer: Stanley Jaffe

Mark Saber

Crime Drama; 30 min; ABC 10/5/51 to 6/30/54

The exploits of Mark Saber, a plainclothes detective with the Homicide division of the N.Y.P.D. Originally titled "Mystery Theatre" then "Inspector Mark Saber." Syndicated titles: "Homicide Squad" and "The Vise." See also "Saber of London."

Mark Saber	Tom Conway
Sgt. Tim Maloney	James Burke

Producer: Edward J. and Harry Lee Danziger.

Mark Twain's Tom Sawyer and Huckleberry Finn

Adventure; 30 min; Syn. 1967

A French-produced series about the adventures of Tom Sawyer and his friend, Huckleberry Finn. Based on the Mark Twain stories.

Tom Sawyer	Roland Demongeot
Huck Finn	Marc Dinapoli

Markham

Drama Pilot; 60 min; NBC 6/23/58

The pilot for the series. The exploits of Roy Markham, a tough private detective. Aired as "Eye for Eye" on "Suspicion."

Roy Markham	Ray Milland
Lorene	Kathleen Crowley
Ben Forbes	Macdonald Carey
Guthrie	Andrew Duggan

Producer: Richard Lewis

Markham

Crime Drama; 30 min; CBS 5/2/59 to 9/15/60

The story of Roy Markham, a Los Angeles-based criminal attorney. See the prior title also.

Roy Markham	Ray Milland
John Riggs	Simon Scott

Producer: Joseph Sistrom, Warren Duff

Marlo and the Magic Movie Machine

Children; 30 min; CBS 4/3/77 to 6/8/81

While employed by the L. Dullo Computer Company, Marlo Higgins secretly develops the Magic Movie Machine, a computer that can talk, tell jokes, and show a variety of films. Acting as a disc jockey, Marlo and his computer present entertainment geared to children.

Marlo Higgins	Laurie Faso
Computer voice	Mert Hoplin

Producer: Stanford H. Fisher

The Marriage

Comedy-Drama; 30 min; NBC 7/1/54 to 8/19/54

Incidents in the lives of the close-knit Marriott family: Ben, an attorney; his wife, Liz; and their children Emily and Peter.

Ben Marriott	Hume Cronyn
Liz Marriott	Jessica Tandy
Emily Marriott	Susan Strasberg
Peter Marriott	Malcolm Brodrick
Bobby Logan	William Redfield

Producer: Hume Cronyn

The Marriage Broker

Comedy-Drama Pilot; 60 min; CBS 6/12/57

When her husband is stolen by another woman, Mae Swasey begins a matrimonial bureau to pair off lonely hearts. The unsold series was to relate her attempts to arrange marriages for people whom she believes should be together. Aired as "The Model and the Marriage Broker" on "The 20th Century-Fox Hour."

Mae Swasey	Glenda Farrell	Al Bundy	Ed O'Neill
Matt Hornbeck	William Bishop	Peggy Bundy	Katey Sagal
Christina Bradley	Kipp Hamilton	Kelly Bundy	
Mike Feeney	Harry Morgan	(daughter)	Christina Applegate
Shirley Larkin	Helen Walker	Bud Bundy (son)	David Faustino
Emmie Swasey	Lee Patrick	Steve Rhoades	
Captain Sam	Lloyd Corrigan	(neighbor)	David Garrison
Minerva Comstock	Ellen Corby	Marcy Rhoades	
		(Steve's wife)	Amanda Bearse
		Luke Ventura (Al's	
		co-worker)	Ritch Shydner

Producer: Peter Packer

Producer: Katherine Green, Richard Gurman, Ron Leavitt, Michael Moye

Married: The First Year

Drama; 60 min; CBS 2/28/79 to 3/21/79

The courtship and marriage of teenagers Billy and Joanna and their struggles to survive the difficult first year of marriage.

Billy Baker	Leigh McCloskey
Joanna Huffman-	
Baker	Cindy Grover
Barbara Huffman	Claudette Nevins
Mike Huffman	Joshua Bryant
Cheryl Huffman	Constance
	McCashin
Jennifer Huffman	Tracy Justrich
Cathy Baker	K Callan
Bert Baker	Stanley Grover
Millie Baker	Jennifer McAllister
Emily Gorey	Christine Belford
Sharon Kelly	Stepfanie Kramer
Cookie Levin	Gigi Vorgan
Tom Liberatore	Gary Epp
Elizabeth Gorey	Martha Scott
Calvin Gorey	Pitt Herbert

Theme Vocal: Charles Cochran

Producer: Lee Rich, Philip Capice, David Jacobs

Married . . . With Children

Comedy; 30 min; FOX 4/5/87 (Premiere)

Events in the day-to-day lives of the Bundys, an argumentative but happily married couple with two children: Al, a Chicago shoe salesman (for Gary's Shoe Accessory) and his wife, Peggy.

Marshal Dillon

See "Gunsmoke."

The Marshal of Gunsight Pass

Western; 30 min; ABC 3/12/50 to 9/30/50

A low-budgeted western about a Marshal, his comical deputy, and their efforts to maintain law and order in the town of Gunsight Pass. Based on the radio series.

Marshal	Russell Hayden
	Eddie Dean
Deputy	Roscoe Ates
Ruth	Jane Adrian

Producer: Philip Booth

The Martha Raye Show

Variety; 60 min; NBC 3/20/54 to 5/29/56

Music and songs coupled with slapstick comedy sketches.

Hostess: Martha Raye

Regulars: Rocky Graziano, The Martha Raye Dancers

Orchestra: Carl Hoff

Producer: Norman Lear, Ed Simons, Karl Hoffberg

The Martha Wright Show

Variety; 15 min; ABC 4/18/54 to 12/5/54

A program of music and songs. Sponsored by Packard automobiles and also known as "The Packard Showroom."

Hostess: Martha Wright

Featured: The Norman Paris Chorus

Orchestra: Bobby Hackett

Producer: Matt Harlib

Martin Kane, Private Eye

Crime Drama; 30 min; NBC 9/11/49 to 8/20/53

The story of Martin Kane, a New York-based private detective who achieves his results through determination and force of character. See also the "The New Adventures of Martin Kane."

Martin Kane	William Gargan
	Lloyd Nolan
	Lee Tracy
Capt. Burke	Frank M. Thomas
Sgt. Ross	Nicholas Saunders
Happy McMann (runs the El Doredo Tobacco Shop)	Walter Kinsella
Don (replaced Happy)	Don Morrow
Capt. Willis	Horace McMahon
Lt. Grey	King Calder
Lt. Bender	Fred Hillebrand

Announcer: Fred Uttal

Producer: Edward C. Kahan, Eddie Sutherland

The Marty Feldman Comedy Machine

Comedy; 30 min; ABC 4/12/72 to 8/23/72

A blend of contemporary humor with the Max Sennett era of slapstick comedy.

Host: Marty Feldman

Regulars: Barbara Feldon, Orson Welles, Spike Milligan, Fred Smoot, Lennie Schultz, Thelma Houston, Fred Roman

Producer: Greg Garrison

The Marty Robbins Spotlite

Variety; 30 min; Syn. 9/77

The program pays tribute to country and western music by spotlighting a guest and his music.

Host: Marty Robbins

Orchestra: Tom Tappan

Producer: Bill Graham, Reg Dunlap, Ralph Emery

Mary

Variety; 60 min; CBS 9/24/78 to 10/8/78

A comedy-accented series that spotlights the talents of Mary Tyler Moore as a comedienne, singer, and dancer.

Hostess: Mary Tyler Moore

Regulars: Swoosie Kurtz, Judith Kahan, Dick Shawn, James Hampton, Michael Keaton, David Letterman, David Barr, Jack O'Leary

Orchestra: Alf Clausen

Producer: Tom Patchett, Jay Tarses

Mary

Comedy; 30 min; CBS 12/11/85 to 4/8/86

When "Women's Digest," the fashion magazine for which she writes folds, Mary Brennan, an attractive divorcee, hires on as a consumer helpline columnist for the "Chicago Eagle," a second-rate scandal sheet. Stories relate her experiences as she attempts to cope with a job she feels is beneath her dignity (but the only available job in her home town).

Mary Brennan	Mary Tyler Moore
Frank DeMarco	James Farentino
Ed LaSalle	John Astin
Susan Parks	Carlene Watkins
Josephine "Jo" Tucker	Katey Sagal
Tully	David Byrd
Lester Mintz	James Tolkan
Mr. Yummy	Robert Pastorelli
Harry	Harold Sylvester
Charles Tucker	Dennis Patrick
Norma Tucker	Doris Belack

Producer: Ken Levine, David Isaacs

The Mary Hartline Show

Children; 30 min; ABC 2/12/51 to 6/15/51

Mary Hartline, "Queen of the Super Circus," in her own program of music, songs, and games for children. Music by Chet Robel.

Mary Hartman, Mary Hartman

Serial; 30 min; Syn. 1/6/76 to 7/3/77

A satirization of life as seen through the endless frustrations of Mary Hartman, a pretty, middle-aged housewife and mother living in the Woodland Heights section of mythical Fernwood, Ohio. See also: "Forever Fernwood."

Mary Hartman	Louise Lasser
Tom Hartman	Greg Mullavey
Heather Hartman	Claudia Lamb
Cathy Schumway	Debralee Scott
George Schumway	Philip Bruns
Martha Schumway	Dody Goodman
Loretta Haggers	Mary Kay Place
Charlie Haggers	Graham Jarvis
Raymond Larkin	Victor Kilian
Sgt. Dennis Foley	Bruce Solomon
Mae Olinsky	Salome Jens
Mona McKenzie	Sallie Janes
Muriel Haggers	L.C. Downey
Clete Meizenheimer	Michael Lembeck
Betty McCullough	Vivian Blaine
Howard McCullough	Beeson Carroll
Ed McCullough	Lawrence Haddon
Jimmy Jo Jeeter	Sparky Marcus
Merle Jeeter	Dabney Coleman
Wanda Jeeter	Marian Mercer
Patty Gimble	Susan Browning
Garth Gimble	Martin Mull
Garth Gimble Jr.	Eric Shea
Lila	Marjorie Battles
Roberta Walashak	Samantha Harper
Steve Fletcher	Ed Begley Jr.
Mac Slattery	Dennis Burkley
Voice in opening theme	Dody Goodman

Music: Earle Hagen

Producer: Norman Lear, Viva Knight, Eugenie Ross-Leming

Mary Kay and Johnny

Comedy; 30 min; DuMont 11/18/47 to 8/24/48
NBC 10/10/48 to 2/13/49
CBS 2/23/49 to 6/1/49
NBC 6/13/49 to 3/11/50

The marital misadventures of Mary Kay and Johnny, TV's first domestic couple. Based on their own experiences.

Mary Kay	Mary Kay Stearns
Johnny	Johnny Stearns
Christopher	Christopher Stearns
Mary Kay's mother	Nydia Westman
Howie	Howard Thomas

Announcer: Jim Stevenson

Producer: Ernest Walling

The Mary Margaret McBride Show

Interview; 30 min; NBC 9/21/48 to 12/14/48

A program of celebrity interviews with hostess Mary Margaret McBride.

Announcer: Vincent Connolly

Producer: Stella Karn, George Foley

The Mary Tyler Moore Comedy Hour

Variety; 60 min; CBS 4/4/79 to 6/6/79

A show within a show that focuses on the home and working life of Mary McKinnon, a TV performer whose program, "The Mary McKinnon Show," provides a vehicle for guests to perform, and whose off-camera life provides the backdrop for the comedy play and interactions of Mary's staff and friends.

Mary McKinnon	Mary Tyler Moore
Harry Sinclair	Michael Lombard
Iris Chapman	Joyce Van Patten
Ken Christy	Michael Keaton
Artie Miller	Ron Rifkin
Crystal	Doris Roberts
	Dody Goodman
Mort Zimmick	Bobby Ramsen

Orchestra: Alf Clausen

Producer: Perry Lafferty

The Mary Tyler Moore Show

Comedy; 30 min; CBS 9/19/70 to 9/3/77

Following a breakup with her fiance (Bill), Mary Richards leaves New York and decides to begin a new life in Minneapolis. There, after securing an apartment from her friend, Phyllis, Mary applies for and receives the job of assistant producer on WJM-TV, Channel

12's "Six O'Clock News Program." Stories relate Mary's comic adventures both at home and at work. See also "Phyllis" and "Rhoda."

Mary Richards	Mary Tyler Moore
Lou Grant	Edward Asner
Murray Slaughter	Gavin MacLeod
Ted Baxter	Ted Knight
Rhoda Morganstern	Valerie Harper
Phyllis Lindstrom	Cloris Leachman
Bess Lindstrom	Lisa Gerritsen
Gordie Howard	John Amos
Ida Morganstern	Nancy Walker
Martin Morganstern	Harold Gould
Debbie Morganstern	Liberty Williams
Georgette Franklin	Georgia Engel
Sue Anne Nivens	Betty White
Dotty Richards	Nanette Fabray
Walter Richards	Bill Quinn
Marie Slaughter	Joyce Bulifant
Bonnie Slaughter	Sherry Hursey
	Tammi Bula
Laurie Slaughter	Helen Hunt
Edie Grant	Priscilla Morrill
Charlene McGuire	Sheree North
Janey Grant	Nora Heflin
Andy Rivers	John Gabriel
David Baxter	Robbie Rist
Joe Warner	Ted Bessell
Chuckles the Clown	Mark Gordon
	Richard Schaal
Philly	Dick Balduzzi
Flo Meredith	Eileen Heckart
Paula Kovacs	Penny Marshall
Bill	Angus Duncan
WJM-TV Announcer	Lee Vines

Theme Vocal ("Love Is All Around"): Sonny Curtis

Music: Patrick Williams

Producer: James L. Brooks, Allan Burns, Stan Daniels, Ed Weinberger

M*A*S*H

Comedy-Drama; 30 min; CBS 9/17/72 to 9/19/83

A semi-comical view of the Korean War as seen through the lives and experiences of the men and women of the 4077th M*A*S*H, a U.S. Mobile Army Surgical Hospital that is assigned to the war zone. See also "After-MASH."

Capt. Benjamin "Hawkeye" Pierce	Alan Alda
Capt. "Trapper John" McIntire	Wayne Rogers
Lt. Col. Henry Blake	McLean Stevenson
Maj. Margaret "Hot Lips" Houlihan	Loretta Swit
Col. Sherman Potter	Harry Morgan
Capt. B.J. Hunnicutt	Mike Farrell
Maj. Frank Burns	Larry Linville
Maj. Charles Winchester III	David Ogden Stiers
Cpl. Walter "Radar" O'Reilly	Gary Burghoff
Father Francis Mulcahy	George Morgan / William Christopher
Cpl. Maxwell Klinger	Jamie Farr
Supply Sgt. Zale	Johnny Haymer
Pvt. Luther Rizzo	G. W. Bailey
Lt. Ginger Ballis	Odessa Cleveland
Lt. Leslie Scorch	Linda Meiklejohn
Lt. Jones	Barbara Brownell
Nurse Louise Anderson	Kelly Jean Peters
Nurse Maggie Cutler	Marcia Strassman
Lt. Nancy Griffin	Lynnette Mettey
Nurse Bigelow	Enid Kent
Nurse Abel	Judy Farrell
Nurse Baker	Jean Powell / Lynne Stewart / Linda Kelsey / Jan Jorden
Nurse Mary Jo Walsh	Mary Jo Catlett
Nurse Joanne Kelly	Kellye Nakahara
Igor the Cook	Joseph Perry / Jeff Maxwell
Colonel Flagg	Edward Winter
Maj. Sidney Freedman	Allan Arbus
Gen. Hamilton Hammond	G. Wood
Ugly John	Patrick Adiarte
Nurse Lacey	Rita Wilson
Nurse Shari	Shari Saba
P.A. System Voice	Sal Viscuso
Newscaster-Interviewer	Clete Roberts
Daniel Pierce	Robert Alda

Theme Song ("Suicide Is Painless"): Johnny Mandel

Producer: Larry Gelbart, Gene Reynolds, Burt Metcalfe, John Rappaport

The Mask

Mystery; 60 min; ABC 1/10/54 to 5/16/54

The story of Walter and Peter Guilfoyle, brothers and attorneys working out of New York. TV's first hour-long mystery series.

Walter Guilfoyle	Gary Merrill
Peter Guilfoyle	William Prince

Producer: Leonard Valenta, Robert Stevens, Hallstead Wells

Mask

Cartoon; 30 min; Syn. 5/85

The exploits of MASK (Mobile Armed Strike Kommand), the code name for a top secret U.S. government fleet of sophisticated espionage vehicles manned by seven highly trained agents designed to corrupt the forces of evil throughout the world.

Voices: Doug Stone, Mark Halloran, Brendan McKane, Graeme McKenna, Sharon Noble, Brennan Thicke

Producer: Jean Chalopin, Andy Heyward, Tetsuo Katayama

Masland at Home

Earl Wrightson as the host of a program of music and songs under the sponsorship of Masland carpets. Music by the Norman Paris Trio and produced by Franklin Heller.

Mason

Comedy Pilot; 30 min; ABC 7/4/77

The story of a precocious boy named Mason Bennett.

Mason Bennett	Mason Reese
Howard Bennett	Barry Nelson
Peggy Bennett	Barbara Stuart
Joyce Bennett	Lee Lawson
Linc	Keith Charles
Bernice	Lee Meredith

Producer: Ira Barmak

Masquerade

Anthology; 30 min; PBS 10/5/71 to 12/28/71

A cast of regulars perform improvisational adaptations of classic fairy tales.

Cast: Avery Schreiber, Barbara Sharma, Alice Playten, Barbara Minkus, Seth Allen, Bill Hinnant, Jacque Lynn Colton, Louise Lasser, J. J. Barry, Phil Bruns, Sudie Bond, Abraham Soboloff, Barbara Tracy

Masquerade

Adventure; 60 min; ABC 12/15/83 to 4/20/84

When the government decides that it requires the skills of special people who are not associated with the government, it establishes Operation Masquerade, a special division of the NIA (National Intelligence Agency) that recruits people for special missions. Stories relate the exploits of the people chosen for Operation Masquerade.

Mr. Lavender (NIA head)	Rod Taylor
Agent Casey Collins	Kirstie Alley
Agent Danny Doyle	Greg Evigan

Theme Vocal ("Masquerade"): Crystal Gayle

Producer: Glen A. Larson, Renee Valente

Masquerade Party

Game; 30 min;	NBC 7/14/52 to 8/25/52
	CBS 6/22/53 to 9/14/53
	CBS 6/21/54 to 9/27/54
	ABC 9/29/54 to 12/29/56
	NBC 3/6/57 to 9/4/57
	CBS 8/4/58 to 9/15/58
	NBC 10/2/58 to 9/24/59
	NBC 1/29/60 to 9/23/60

Object: For five celebrity panelists to guess the identity of elaborately disguised guest personalities

Host (1952): Bud Collyer.
     (1953): Douglas Edwards.
     (1954–56): Peter Donald.
     (1957): Eddie Bracken.
     (1958): Robert Q. Lewis.
     (1958–60): Bert Parks.

Panelists: Audrey Meadows, Bobby Sherwood, Phil Silvers, Ilka Chase, Adele Jergens, Peter Donald, Madge Evans, Buff Cobb, John Young, Johnny Johnston, Betsy Palmer, Jonathan Winters, Jinx Falkenberg, Pat Carroll, Faye Emerson, Gloria DeHaven, Sam Levenson, Lee Bowman

Announcer: Don Morrow, William T. Lazar

Producer: Herb Wolf, Lloyd Gross

Masquerade Party

Game; 30 min; Syn. 9/74

Three celebrity panelists attempt to identify an elaborately disguised guest from a series of indirect question-and-answer rounds.

Host: Richard Dawson

Panelists: Lee Meriwether, Bill Bixby, Nipsey Russell

Announcer: Jay Stewart

Producer: Stefan Hatos, Monty Hall

The Master

Adventure; 60 min; NBC 1/20/84 to 8/31/84

When he receives a letter from a daughter (Terry) he never knew he had, John P. McCallister leaves Japan (where he had become a Ninja Master) to search for her in America. However, because John has broken the Ninja code by leaving Japan, he is sentenced to die and is followed by Okasa, a Ninja who has been ordered to kill him.

With only the letter's postmark as a guide, John travels to Ellerston, where he befriends Max, a young drifter who helps him out of a scrape. When Max learns of John's quest, he offers to help him; in return, John promises to teach him the Ninja art. Stories relate John's search for Terry, and his efforts to avoid Okasa.

John McCallister	Lee Van Cleef
Max Keller	Timothy Van Patten
Okasa	Sho Kosugi
Cat Hellman (Max's friend)	Tara Buckman
Patrick Keller (Max's father)	Doug McClure

Narrator: Timothy Van Patten

"The Master" Theme Music by: Bill Conti

Producer: Michael Sloan

Masterpiece Playhouse

Anthology; 60 min; NBC 7/23/50 9/3/50

A live series of adaptations of well-known literary works. Stars include Boris Karloff, Diana Douglas, Jessica Tandy, Walter Abel, William Windom, Rita Colton, Constance Ford, Mary Boland, Torin Thatcher, Alfred Rider, Olive Deering, and Tod Andrews.

Masters of Magic

Variety; 15 min; CBS 2/16/49 to 5/11/49

A live series of performances by guest magicians. Hosted by Andre Baruch and produced by Sherman H. Dryer.

The Match Game

Game; 30 min; NBC 12/31/62 to 9/20/69

A question that contains a blank is read to two three-member teams. Each player writes down the word he feels will best complete the thought. If two players on the same team match, they each score $25; if their celebrity captain matches them, they score $50. The first team to score $100 is the winner.

Host: Gene Rayburn

Announcer: Johnny Olsen

Producer: Mark Goodson, Bill Todman

The Match Game

Game; 30 min; CBS 6/25/73 to 4/20/79

An incomplete sentence, which contains a blank, is read to six celebrities (who fill in the blank with a word that best completes the thought). A player is asked to verbally give a response. He scores one point for each celebrity he matches. The highest point scorer receives $250.

Host: Gene Rayburn

Regulars: Richard Dawson, Charles Nelson Reilly, Brett Somers

Announcer: Johnny Olsen

Producer: Mark Goodson, Bill Todman

The Match Game-Hollywood Squares Hour

Game; 60 min; NBC 10/31/81 to 7/21/84

Two former game shows comprised in a one-hour format. For formats, see the prior "Match Game" title and "The Hollywood Squares."

Match Game Host: Gene Rayburn

Hollywood Squares Host: Jon Bauman

Announcer: Gene Wood

Producer: Mark Goodson, Robert Sherman

Matches 'N' Mates

A syndicated (1967) game wherein married couples have to match hidden answers with concealed questions. Hosted by Art James and produced by E. Roger Muir and Nick Nicholson.

Matinee at the Bijou

Anthology; 90 min; PBS 9/80 to 9/86

A collection of rare or never before telecast theatrical cartoons, serials, shorts, and feature films of the 1930s.

Host: W. Scott Devenney

Usherettes: Rebecca Delorme, Karen Davis, Kathleen Blackerby, Barbara Seuss, Jennifer McPhee

Theatre-Goers; Linda Van Dusen, Steve Starr, Mark Zewe, Carol Childress, John Zewe

Theme Vocal ("At the Bijou"): Rudy Vallee

Producer: Colin Dougherty, John Gailbraith

Matinee in New York

Variety; 60 min; NBC 6/9/52 to 9/5/52

Music, celebrity interviews, and game contests.

Host: Bill Cullen, Bill Goodwin

Interviewer: Ted Collins

Announcer: Andre Baruch

Orchestra: Jack Miller, John Lesko

Producer: Ted Collins

Matinee Theatre

Anthology; 60 min; NBC 10/31/55 to 6/27/58

A daily series of dramatic productions from Hollywood.

Host: John Conte

Producer: Albert McCleery, Darrell Ross, Ethel Frank, Winston O'Keefe

Matlock

Drama; 60 min; NBC 9/23/86 (Premiere)

The exploits of Ben and Charlene Matlock, a father and daughter team of Atlanta-based attorneys who specialize in sensational cases.

Ben Matlock	Andy Griffith
Charlene Matlock	Lori Lethin
	Linda Purl
Tyler Hudson	Kene Holliday
Sarah	Betty Lynn
Lt. Frank Daniels	James McEachin
D. A. Burgess	Michael Durrell
Julie March	Julie Sommars
Cassie Phillips	Kari Lizer
Michelle Thomas	Nancy Stafford

Producer: Fred Silverman, Dean Hargrove

The Matt Dennis Show

Variety; 15 min; NBC 6/27/55 to 8/29/55

A musical interlude series with pianist Matt Dennis.

Host: Matt Dennis

Musicians: Trigger Albert, Mundell Lowell, Jimmy Campbell

Off-Camera Introductions: Frank Sinatra

Producer: Gordon Auchincloss

Matt Helm

Crime Drama; 60 min; ABC 9/20/75 to 11/3/75

The exploits of Matt Helm, a former government intelligence agent turned Los Angeles private detective.

Matt Helm	Anthony Franciosa
Claire Kronski	Laraine Stephens
Lt. Hanrahan	Gene Evans
Ethel	Jeff Donnell

Producer: Frank Pierce, Charles B. Fitzsimons

Matt Houston

Crime Drama; 60 min; ABC 9/26/82 to 3/29/85

The story of Matt Houston, millionaire, cattle rancher, oil baron, playboy, and compassionate private detective who helps people in deep trouble.

Matlock "Matt" Houston	Lee Horsley
C. J. Parsons	Pamela Hensley
Roy Houston	Buddy Ebsen
Lt. Vince Novelli	John Aprea
Lt. Michael Hoyt	Lincoln Kilpatrick
Mama Novelli	Penny Santon
Murray Chase	George Wyner
Chris	Cis Rundle
Too Mean	Rockne Tarkington
Charlie Eagle	Cal Bellini
Slim	D. D. Howard
Lamar Pettybone	Paul Brinegar
Bo	Dennis Fimple

"Matt Houston" Theme by Dominic Frontiere

Producer: Aaron Spelling, Douglas S. Cramer, Lawrence Gordon

Matt Lincoln

Drama; 60 min; ABC 9/24/70 to 1/14/71

The story of Matt Lincoln, a Los Angeles-based psychiatrist who practices preventive psychiatry and struggles to help people in the early stages of emotional distress.

Matt Lincoln	Vince Edwards
Tag*	Chelsea Brown
Ann*	June Harding
Jimmy*	Felton Perry
Kevin*	Michael Larrain
Matt Lincoln Sr.	Dean Jagger

Producer: Frank Pierce

*Matt's young assistants. In the TV Movie, "Dial Hot Line," (ABC, 3/8/70), Vince Edwards portrays David Leopold.

Matty's Funday Funnies

Cartoon; 30 min; ABC 10/11/59 to 12/31/61
1/6/62 to 9/22/62

The title for a series of Harvey theatrical cartoons, including "Casper, the Friendly Ghost," "Baby Huey," "Little Audrey," and "Buzzy the Crow." The series, sponsored by Mattel Toys, is hosted by the animated Matty and Sisterbelle. Titled, in 1962, "Matty's Funnies with Beany and Cecil."

Maude

Comedy; 30 min; CBS 9/12/72 to 8/29/78

Events in the life of Maude Findlay, an outspoken liberal, as she struggles to solve the incidents that creep in, disrupt and threaten to destroy her attempts to achieve a lasting relationship with Walter, her fourth husband. A spin-off from "All in the Family." See also "Good Times."

Maude Findlay	Beatrice Arthur
Walter Findlay	Bill Macy
Carol Trener	Marcia Rodd*
	Adrienne Barbeau
Philip Trener	Brian Morris
	Kraig Metzinger
Dr. Arthur Harmon	Conrad Bain
Vivian Harmon	Rue McClanahan
Florida Evans	Esther Rolle
Henry Evans	John Amos
Nell Naugatuck	Hermione Baddeley
Victoria Butterfield	Marlene Warfield
Dr. Hubie Binder	Larry Gelman

Theme Vocal ("And Then There's Maude"): Donny Hathaway

Producer: Norman Lear, Rod Parker

*Role on "All in the Family"

Maureen

Comedy Pilot; 30 min; CBS 8/24/76

The story of a middle-aged department store lingerie saleswoman (Maureen) with a heart of gold.

Maureen	Joyce Van Patten
Ruth	Sylvia Sidney
Mr. Frederick	Alan Oppenheimer
Alice	Karen Morrow
Damon	Jack Bannon
Trudy	Leigh French
Jackie	Timothy Blake

Producer: Mark Carliner, Martin Cohan

Maurice Woodruff Predicts

A syndicated (1969) program of predictions by master mentalist Maurice Woodruff. Hosted by Robert Q. Lewis and Vidal Sassoon.

Maverick

Western; 60 min; ABC 9/22/57 to 7/8/62

The series, set in the West of the 1860s, relates the adventures of Bret and Bart Maverick, two untrustworthy gentlemen gamblers seeking rich prey—and more often than not, helping people in trouble. See also "Bret Maverick" and "Young Maverick."

Bret Maverick	James Garner
Bart Maverick	Jack Kelly
Beau Maverick	Roger Moore
Brent Maverick	Robert Colbert
Samantha Crawford	Diane Brewster
Dandy Jim Buckley	Efrem Zimablist Jr.
Beauregard "Pappy" Maverick	James Garner
Gentleman Jack Darby	Richard Long

Producer: William T. Orr, Roy Huggins, Howie Horwitz

Max

Comedy Pilot; 30 min; NBC 4/28/83

When Max Greene, a deli owner, catches a young girl shoplifting and later finds that she is an orphan, he decides to take her (Danny) under his wing. The unsold series was to relate Max's efforts to raise the girl. Aired on "Gimme a Break."

Max Greene	Don Rickles
Danny	LaShana Dendy
Shopper	Barbara Hamilton

Producer: Mort Lachman

Max and Me

Comedy Pilot; 30 min; ABC 7/12/85

The story of Max Brenner, a middle-aged man seeking a rejuvenated lifestyle by moving back to the city (Manhattan) with his wife and his memories of their children who have since moved out of their suburban coop.

Max Brenner	Pat Harrington Jr.
Anne Brenner	Dawn Greenall
Ogden Dust	Brian George
Leo Winter	Derek McGrath
Ginger	Mary Ann McDonald
Sheldon Nelson	Geoffrey Bowes
Suzy	Mary Long

Producer: Al Rogers

Max Headroom

Adventure; 60 min; ABC 3/31/87 to 5/5/87

In a future era when TV cannot be turned off and ratings are all that matter, Network 23 develops "Blipverts," a process that compresses thirty second commercials into three seconds to prevent channel switching. The process, however, kills overweight and inactive people. When Network 23 reporter Edison Carter discovers what is happening, he attempts to expose it. Before he can do so, the "Blipverts" creator arranges an almost fatal accident that robs Edison of his memory and creates Max Headroom*, his computer alter ego. When an attempt is made to erase Max, he escapes into the network's computer system. With Max's help, Edison exposes the lethal "Blipverts." Stories relate Edison's exploits as he and Max struggle to keep the "Blank" generation informed. Relies heavily on computer animation. Originally titled "Max Headroom: 20 minutes Into the Future."

Edison Carter/Max Headroom	Matt Frewer
Theora Jones	Amanda Pays
Ben Cheviot	George Coe
Murray	Jeffrey Tambor
Bryce Lynch	Chris Young
Blank Reg	Morgan Sheppard
Dominique	Concetta Tomei
Mel	Scott Kraft
Rik	J. W. Smith
Shawn Jones (Theora's brother)	Peter Cohi

Producer: Philip DeGuere, Peter Wagg

*Before his car accident, Edison last saw a road sign that read "Max. Headroom." Thus the name Max Headroom.

The Max Headroom Show

Talk; 30 min; Cinemax 10/85 Premiere

An unusual talk show wherein guests are interviewed by a computerized image (Max Headroom) that appears on a TV screen. (Actually, an actor, heavily made up in rubber makeup and enhanced by computer animation, creates the Max Headroom image).

Max Headroom	Matt Frewer

Producer: Peter Wagg

Max Liebman Presents

Anthology; 90 min; NBC 9/12/54 to 6/4/55
10/1/55 to 6/9/56

A monthly series of lavish variety specials (22 episodes in all).

Regulars: Bambi Linn, Rod Alexander, The Bil and Cora Baird Puppets

Orchestra: Charles Sanford

Producer: Max Liebman, Bill Hobin

Maximum Security

Drama; 30 min; HBO 3/9/85 to 4/23/85

A gritty, realistic look at prison life as seen through the eyes of Frank Murphy, a long-term inmate (convicted of a crime of passion) at the Riverdale Correctional Facility.

Frank Murphy	Geoffrey Lewis
Harry Kanschneider	Robert Desiderio
Dr. Allison Brody	Jean Smart
Benny	Trinidad Silva
Papa Jack	Stan Shaw
Warden Robert McShane	Stephen Elliott
Patty Mucelli	Murphy Cross
Bonnie Murphy	Caroline McWilliams
Puck	Ponchita Gomez
Leslie Bandercar	Kerry Sherman

Producer: Tony Ganz, Ron Howard

Maya

Adventure; 60 min; NBC 9/16/67 to 2/11/68

When Terry Bowen, the son of a famous American hunter (Hugh) arrives in India to join his father, he learns that he is missing and believed to be dead. Believing that no animal could kill his father, Terry begins a search to find him. Enroute, he meets Raji, an orphaned Indian boy, and his pet elephant, Maya, whom he seeks to return to her land of birth and freedom. Stories relate the adventures of two 14-year-old boys as they join forces to help each other: Terry to find his father; Raji to set Maya free.

Terry Bowen	Jay North
Raji	Sajid Kahn

Narrator: Marvin Miller

Producer: Frank King, Maurice King

Mayberry R.F.D.

Comedy; 30 min; CBS 9/23/68 to 9/6/71

The simple pleasures and trying times of Sam Jones, a full-time farmer and part-time city councilman in Mayberry, North Carolina. A spin-off from "The Andy Griffith Show."

Sam Jones	Ken Berry
Mike Jones	Buddy Foster
Millie Swanson	Arlene Golonka
Goober Pyle	George Lindsey
Bee Taylor	Frances Bavier
Howard Sprague	Jack Dodson
Emmet Clark	Paul Hartman
Martha Clark	Mary Lansing
Aunt Alice	Alice Ghostley
Ralph	Richard Steele
Arnold	Sheldon Collins

Producer: Andy Griffith, Richard O. Linke

Mayor of Hollywood

Variety; 30 min; NBC 7/29/52 to 9/18/52

Tours of Hollywood and celebrity interviews as Walter O'Keefe attempts to win voters for his fictional quest to become the Mayor of Hollywood.

Walter O'Keefe	Himself
Lou	Lou Crosby
Bill	Bill Baldwin
Jeanne	Jeanne Dyer
Lina	Lina Romay

Orchestra: Irvine Orton

Producer: Homer Canfield

Mayor of the Town

Comedy; 30 min; Syn. 1954

Events in the life of Thomas Russell, mayor of a small American town (Springdale).

Thomas Russell	Thomas Mitchell
Minnie	Jean Byron
Butch Russell	David Saber
Marilly	Kathleen Freeman
Joe Ainsley	Tudor Owen

Me and Benjy

Comedy Pilot; 30 min; NBC 7/27/70

The misadventures of two small-town American boys (Homer and Benjy).

Homer Baker	Tony Frazer
Ruth Baker	Audrey Dalton
Fred Baker	John Lupton
Winifred Baker	Cindy Cassell
Benjy Smith	Kevin Herron
Beverly Smith	Tracy Reed
Joe Smith	Bernie Hamilton
Vivian Smith	Kim Hamilton

Me and Ducky

Comedy Pilot; 30 min; NBC 6/21/79

Incidents in the lives of Carol Munday and Cidra "Ducky" Hopnagel, two very pretty teenage girls attending San Francisco High School.

Carol Munday	Linda Cook
Cidra Hopnagel	Jayne Modean
Dawn Duval	Dawn Dunlap
Babs Hulet	Valerie Landsburg
Toby Wells	Susan Duvall
Rims	Gary Imoff
Carol's mother	Kathleen Doyle
Carol's father	James Karen

Producer: Lee Rich, Marc Merson

Me and Maxx

Comedy; 30 min; NBC 3/22/80 to 9/12/80

After caring for Maxx, a very pretty young girl, for eleven years, her mother decides that it is time for her estranged husband, Norman, to care for her. With no choice but to take Maxx in when she arrives on his doorstep with her suitcases, Norman begins to rearrange his life to accommodate her. Stories focus on the relationship between Maxx and Norman as each struggles to please the other.

Norman Davis	Joe Santos
Maxx Davis	Melissa Michaelsen
Barbara	Jenny Sullivan
Mitch Russell	Jim Weston
Gary	Denny Evans

Theme Vocal ("Is It Because of Love?"): Lenore O'Malley

Producer: James Komack, Don Van Atta, George Tricker, Neil Rosen

Me and Mom

Crime Drama; 60 min; ABC 4/5/85 to 5/17/85

The story of Kate Morgan, a beautiful criminologist; Zena Hunnicutt, her wealthy, glamorous mother; and Lou Garfield, a tough ex-cop—all partners in the Los Angeles-based Morgan, Garfield, and Hunnicutt Detective Agency. Stories relate the unorthodox methods they use to apprehend criminals.

Kate Morgan	Lisa Eilbacher
Zena Hunnicutt	Holland Taylor
Lou Garfield	James Earl Jones
Lt. Mike Rojas	Henry Darrow

Theme Vocal ("Me and Mom"): Amy Holland

Producer: Dean Hargrove, Hal Sitowitz

Me and Mrs. C.

Comedy Pilot; 30 min; NBC 3/18/84

Rather than spend her golden years with her son, an independent widow (Ethel) takes in a young black girl (Geri) to help with expenses. The pilot (for the series, next title) relates Ethel's attempts to find Geri, an ex-con, a job.

Ethel Connelly	Doris Roberts
Geri Monroe	Deborah Malone
Ethan Connelly	Terrence McGovern
Kathleen Connelly	Mary Armstrong

Theme Vocal ("Me and Mrs. C."): Deborah Malone

Producer: Scoey Mitchlll

Me and Mrs. C.

Comedy; 30 min; NBC 6/21/86 to 7/26/86

A series based on the prior title which relates the efforts of an independent widow (Ethel) and her tenant, a young ex-con named Geri, to live together and make ends meet.

Ethel Conklin	Peg Murray
Geri Kilgore	Misha McK
Ethan Conklin	Gary Bayer
Kathleen Conklin	Ellen Regan
Reverend Kilgore	Scoey Mitchlll
Jamie Conklin	Jeremy Brown

Theme vocal ("Side by Side"): LaVonne Rucker

Producer: Scoey Mitchlll, George Sunga

Me and the Chimp

Comedy; 30 min; CBS 1/13/72 to 5/18/72

After escaping from an Air Force testing lab, a chimpanzee takes refuge in a drain pipe in a playground. There, he is found by Kitty and Scott Reynolds, the children of a dentist (Mike), who take him home and adopt him. Stories relate a reluctant Mike's efforts to adjust to his children's new found pet, Buttons (named after his habit of pressing buttons).

Mike Reynolds	Ted Bessell
Liz Reynolds	Anita Gillette
Kitty Reynolds	Kami Cotler
Scott Reynolds	Scott Kolden
Buttons	Jackie

Producer: Garry K. Marshall, Alan Rafkin

Meatballs and Spaghetti

Cartoon; 30 min; CBS 9/18/82 to 9/10/83

The adventures of a rock and roll group called Meatballs and Spaghetti.

Voices: Jack Angel, Wally Burr, Sally Julian, Peter Cullen, Ron Masak, Ronnie Schell, Marilyn Schreffler, Hal Smith, Frank Welker, Paul Winchell

Producer: Fred Silverman, David DePatie

Medallion Theatre

See "Chrysler Medallion Theatre."

Medic

Anthology; 30 min; NBC 9/13/54 to 11/19/56

Dramas that present authentic and sophisticated approaches to medical problems and practices.

Dr. Konrad Styner (Host)	Richard Boone

Theme Song ("Blue Star"): Victor Young, Edward Heyman

Producer: Frank LaTourette, Worthington Miner

Medical Center

Drama; 60 min; CBS 9/24/69 to 9/6/76

The dramatic story of Paul Lochner, the administrative surgeon of University Medical Center in Los Angeles, and Joe Gannon, a professor of surgery.

Dr. Paul Lochner	James Daly
Dr. Joe Gannon	Chad Everett
	Richard Bradford*
Jenny Lochner	Tyne Daly
Nurse Chambers	Jayne Meadows
Dr. Bartlett	Corinne Comacho
Nurse Wilcox	Audrey Totter
Nurse Holmby	Barbara Baldavin
Nurse Courtland	Chris Huston
Nurse Higby	Catherine Farrar
Nurse Crawford	Virginia Hawkins
Lt. Samuels	Martin E. Brooks
Sgt. Boyce	Jonathan Lippe
Dr. Corelli	Robert Walden
Dr. Barnes	Fred Holliday

"Medical Center" Theme Music: Lalo Schifrin

Producer: Frank Glicksman, Al C. Ward

*Role in TV Movie "U.M.C" (CBS, 4/17/69)

Medical Story

Anthology; 60 min; NBC 9/4/75 to 1/8/76

Dramas that stress an open, human approach to the problems of medicine as seen through the eyes of the doctor, rather than the patient.

Producer: David Gerber, Abby Mann

Meet Betty Furness

Women; 15 min; CBS 1/2/53 to 7/3/53

Interviews, fashion, guests, and other topics of interest to women.

Hostess: Betty Furness

Regulars: Don Cherry, Hank Ford, Bill Stern, David Ross

Music: The Buddy Weed Trio

Producer: Lester Lewis

Meet Corliss Archer

Comedy; 30 min; CBS 7/12/51 to 8/10/51
1/26/52 to 3/29/52

The comic adventures of Corliss Archer, a very pretty teenage girl with a penchant for finding trouble. Based on the radio series. See also the following two titles.

Corliss Archer	Lugene Sanders
Harry Archer	Fred Shields
Janet Archer	Frieda Inescort
	Irene Tedrow
Dexter Franklin	Bobby Ellis

Announcer: John Heistand

Music: Felix Mills

Producer: Tom McAvity, Helen Mack

Meet Corliss Archer

Comedy; 30 min; Syn. 1954

A filmed version of the above live title, which see for storyline.

Corliss Archer	Ann Baker
Harry Archer	John Eldridge
Janet Archer	Mary Bain
Dexter Franklin	Bobby Ellis

Narrator: Hy Averback

Meet Corliss Archer

Comedy Pilot; 60 min; NBC 8/5/56

A color pilot about a pretty but mischievous girl named Corliss Archer. See the prior two titles also.

Corliss Archer	Robin Morgan
Harry Archer	Jerome Cowan
Janet Archer	Polly Rowles
Dexter Franklin	Warren Berlinger
Lenny Archer	John Connell
Mildred Pringle	Marian Randall
Mr. Pringle	Howard St. John
Mrs. Franklin	Florida Friebus

Producer: Philip Barry

Meet Julie

Cartoon Pilot; 60 min; Syn. 12/87

While experimenting with new security devices, engineer David McCallister develops a special doll he names Julie and gives it to his daughter, Carol, as a companion. The doll, magically brought to life one night by unknown forces, becomes Carol's guardian. The proposed series was to relate Carol and Julie's adventures.

Julie   Nicole Lyn
Carol   Karen Burthwright

Other Voices: Blarne Fariman, Dan Hennessey, Peggy Mahon, Greg Morton

Producer: Andy Heyward

Meet McGraw

Crime Drama Pilot; 30 min; CBS 2/25/54

The pilot for the series. The exploits of McGraw, a hood with a price on his head, who hires out his services (as a detective) to help people who cannot turn to the police for help.

McGraw   Frank Lovejoy
Woman   Audrey Totter
Husband   Paul Picerni

Producer: George Haight

Meet McGraw

Crime Drama; 30 min; NBC 7/2/57 to 6/24/58

The story of McGraw, a roving private detective "who wanders from state to state minding other peoples' business."

McGraw   Frank Lovejoy

Producer: Don Sharpe, Warren Lewis

Meet Me in St. Louis

Comedy Pilot; 30 min; ABC 9/2/66

A would-be series, set in St. Louis in 1903, about a beautiful young debutante (Esther) and her adventures as she struggles to adjust to a new life style (having just moved from New York to Missouri).

Esther Smith   Shelley Fabares
Anne Smith   Celeste Holm
Glenn Smith   Larry Merrill
Faye Morse   Judy Lang
Katie   Rita Shaw
Mr. Smith   Wesley Addy
Agnes   Suzanne Cupito
                               (Morgan Brittany)
Tootie   Tammy Locke
John Truitt   Michael Blodgett

Meet Millie

Comedy; 30 min; CBS 10/25/52 to 3/6/56

The story of a New York secretary (Millie) who is secretly in love with her boss's son (Johnny) and her mother's efforts to spark a romance between the two.

Millie Bronson   Elena Verdugo
Johnny Boone Jr.   Ross Ford
Mrs. Bronson   Florence Halop
J. R. Boone Sr.   Earl Ross
Alfred Prinzmetal   Marvin Kaplan
Mrs. Boone   Isabel Randolph
Mr. Weems   Harry Cheshire

Announcer: Bob Lemond

Producer: Frank Galen

Meet Mr. McNutley

Comedy; 30 min; CBS 9/17/53 to 7/15/54

The trials and tribulations of Ray McNutley, a drama professor at the all-girl Lynnhaven College. See also "The Ray Milland Show."

Ray McNutley   Ray Milland
Peggy McNutley   Phyllis Avery
Pete Thompson   Gordon Jones
Ruth Thompson   Jacqueline DeWit
Josephine Bradley   Minerva Urecal

Announcer: Del Sharbutt

Producer: Joe Connelly, Bob Mosher

Meet the Girls

Comedy Pilot; 30 min; CBS 8/30/60

The story of three New York career girls: Maybelle ("The Shape," a model); Lacey ("The Face," an ad executive); and Josephine ("The Brain," a department store buyer) as they search for fame, fortune, and rich husbands.

Maybelle Perkins   Mamie Van Doren
Lacey Sinclair   Gale Robbins
Josephine Dunning   Virginia Field
Ken Evans   John Bryant
Darlene   Darlene Fields
Cindy   Cynthia Leighton

Producer: Harry Sauber

Meet the Governor

Comedy Pilot; 30 min; NBC 10/5/55

The story of a midwestern lawyer (Clem) who possesses a dream to become governor of the state. Aired on "Screen Director's Playhouse."

Clem Waters	Herb Shriner
June Waters	Barbara Hale
Sonny Waters	Bobby Clark
Mrs. Larkin	Rita Lynn
Mr. Dirkes	Paul Harvey
Hurley	Arthur Q. Bryan

Writer-Director: Leo McCarey

Meet Your Cover Girl

Interview; 30 min; CBS 10/24/50 to 11/1/51

A daytime series in which fashion models discuss various aspects of their careers.

Hostess: Robin Chandler

Producer: Stanley Poss

Meet Your Match

Game; 30 min; NBC 8/25/52 to 9/1/52

Two players compete in a question-and-answer session wherein correct responses score a player $25, but an incorrect answer defeats a player and pits the champion against a new challenger.

Host: Jan Murray

Meeting at Apalachin

Crime Drama Pilot; 60 min; CBS 1/22/60

The story of a dedicated police detective (Ed Croswell) with the Chicago P.D. In the pilot episode, broadcast on "Desilu Playhouse," Ed attempts to expose a gang of underworld bosses. Based on a true incident.

Sgt. Ed Croswell	Frank Behrens
Lt. Horlick	Joe Sullivan
Gino Rospond	Cameron Mitchell
Midge Rospond	Cara Williams
Sal Raimondi	Luther Adler
Tommy	Nicholas Georgiade
Joan	Edith Claire

Producer: Bert Granet

Mel and Susan Together

Variety; 30 min; ABC 4/22/78 to 5/13/78

A weekly program of music and songs.

Hosts: Mel Tillis, Susan Anton

Orchestra: Bob Rozario

Producer: Jerry McPhie, Toby Martin

The Mel Torme Show

Variety; 30 min; CBS 9/17/51 to 8/21/52

A daytime program of music and song.

Host: Mel Torme

Regulars: Kaye Ballard, Peggy King, Ellen Martin, Jean Dustine

Music: The Red Norvo Trio, The Terry Gibbs Quintet

Producer: Bob Bach

Melba

Comedy; 30 min; CBS 1/28/86 to 8/2/86

The series, set in New York City, follows the life and romantic misadventures of Melba Patterson, a divorced mother and the director of the Manhattan Visitors Center, and her best friend and sister* Susan Slater, a carefree single seeking to find a husband and begin a family.

Melba Patterson	Melba Moore
Susan Slater	Gracie Harrison
Tracy Patterson	Jamila Perry
Rose	Barbara Meek
Jack	Lou Jacobi
Gil	Evan Mirand
Virginia Atwater	Ellen Tobie

Theme Vocal ("We're Sisters"): Melba Moore

Producer: Saul Ilson, Ernest Chambers, Kim Weiskopf, Michael Baser

*Raised by Rose, Melba's mother, after her mother's death.

The Melba Moore-Clifton Davis Show

Variety; 60 min; CBS 6/7/72 to 7/5/72

A program of music and songs set against the background of a Manhattan brownstone.

Host: Melba Moore, Clifton Davis

Regulars: Liz Torres, Ron Carey, Timmy Rogers, Richard Libertini

Announcer: Johnny Olsen

Orchestra: Charles H. Coleman

Producer: Stan Harris

Melba Moore's Collection of Love Songs

Music; 30 min; Syn. 9/85

A weekly showcase of music videos with the narration hosting of Melba Moore. Producer: Melba Moore, Jerald Silverhardt, Beau Higgins.

Melody, Harmony, Rhythm

Variety; 15 min; NBC 12/13/49 to 2/16/50

Lynne Barrett as the host of a twice weekly program of music and songs with regulars Carol Reed and Charlie Dobson. Music by the Tony DeSimone Trio.

Melody Street

Variety; 30 min; DuMont; 9/23/53 to 2/5/54

The program features a cast lip-synching popular songs (which are played against dramatic scenes).

Host: Elliot Lawrence, Tony Mottola

Regulars: Roberta McDonald, Lynn Gibbs, Jo Bowen

Music: The Tony Mottola Trio

Producer: Roger Gerry

Melody Tour

Variety; 30 min; ABC 7/8/54 to 9/30/54

Tours of the world via music.

Host: Stan Freeman

Regulars: Jonathan Lucas, Nancy Kenyon, Nellie Fisher, Norman Scott, Robert Rounseville, Jane Remes, Peter Gladke

Orchestra: Harry Sosnik

The Melting Pot

A syndicated series (1978) hosted by Orson Bean and featuring guest celebrities preparing their favorite meals. Produced by Fred Rheinstein.

Memories with Lawrence Welk

A syndicated series of selected repeats of "The Lawrence Welk Show" with Lawrence Welk serving as the host to each particular episode. See both "Lawrence Welk" shows for additional information.

The Memory Game

Game; 30 min; NBC 2/15/71 to 7/30/71

Five women players are each given a packet of five questions to study for twenty seconds. At the end of the time, the questions are taken back and players are asked a series of questions based on what they had memorized. Correct answers score points and the player with the highest score is the winner.

Host: Joe Garagiola

Announcer: Johnny Olsen

Producer: John Tobyansen

The Men

Adventure; 60 min; ABC 9/21/72 to 9/1/73

The overall title for three series (which see): "Assignment: Vienna," "The Delphi Bureau," and "Jigsaw."

Men at Law

Crime Drama; 60 min; CBS 2/3/71 to 9/1/71

A revised version of "The Storefront Lawyers." The cases of a group of lawyers attached to the Neighborhood Legal Services Offices in Century City (Los Angeles).

David Hansen	Robert Foxworth
Deborah Sullivan	Sheila Larken
Gabriel Kay	David Arkin
Devlin McNeil	Gerald S. O'Loughlin
Kathy	Nancy Jeris

Producer: Leonard Freeman, Robert Stivers

The Men from Shiloh

Western; 90 min; NBC 9/16/70 to 9/8/71

The story of four men (Alan MacKenzie, the owner of the Shiloh Ranch in Medicine Bow; The Virginian, the foreman; and ranch hands Trampas and Tate) and their attempts to maintain the peace in Wyoming during the 1890s. A spin-off from "The Virginian."

The Virginian	James Drury
Col. Alan MacKenzie	Stewart Granger
Trampas	Doug McClure
Roy Tate	Lee Majors

Producer: Herbert Hirschman, Leslie Stevens

Men into Space

Adventure; 30 min; CBS 9/30/59 to 9/7/60

The U.S. government's attempts to further its space program as seen through the eyes of Air Force Colonel Edward McCauley.

Edward McCauley	William Lundigan
Mary McCauley	Angie Dickinson
	Joyce Taylor
Peter McCauley	Charles Herbert
Lt. Johnny Baker	Corey Allen
Capt. Harvey Sparkman	Kem Dibbs
Gen. Norgath	Tyler McBey

Theme Song ("Men Into Space"): David Rose

Producer: Lewis Rachmill

Men of Annapolis

Anthology; 30 min; Syn. 1957

Dramas based on incidents in the training of men attending Annapolis, the U.S. Naval Academy. The midshipmen of Annapolis appear in all stories.

Narrator: Art Gilmore

Producer: William Castle

Menasha the Magnificent

Comedy; 30 min; NBC 7/30/50 to 9/11/50

The story of a hapless manager (Menasha) of a decrepit restaurant that is owned by a domineering woman (Mrs. Davis).

Menasha	Menasha Skulnik
Mrs. Davis	Jean Cleveland

Producer: Martin Goodman

The Merv Griffin Show

Variety; 55 min; NBC 10/1/62 to 3/29/63

Music coupled with celebrity interviews.

Host: Merv Griffin

Producer: Bob Shanks

The Merv Griffin Show

Variety; 90 min; Syn. 1965

A daily series of music and celebrity interviews.

Host: Merv Griffin

Announcer-Assistant: Arthur Treacher

Orchestra: Mort Lindsey

Producer: Walter Kempley, Bob Shanks

The Merv Griffin Show

Variety; 90 min; CBS 8/18/69 to 2/11/72

A late-night program of celebrity interviews.

Host: Merv Griffin

Announcer-Assistant: Arthur Treacher

Orchestra: Mort Lindsey

Producer: Bob Shanks

The Merv Griffin Show

Variety; 60 min; Syn. 9/72 to 9/86

A daily, entertaining program of celebrity interviews.

Host: Merv Griffin

Featured: Jack Sheldon (band member), Mrs. Dorothy Miller (studio audience member)

Orchestra: Mort Lindsay

Producer: Murray Schwartz, Bob Murphy

Messing Prize Party

Game; 30 min; CBS 12/6/48 to 6/17/49

Couples perform stunts in return for prizes. Sponsored by Messing Bakeries.

Host: Bill Slater

Producer: Ken Redford

The M-G-M Parade

Variety; 30 min; ABC 9/14/55 to 5/2/56

A behind-the-scenes look at filmmaking with guests, interviews, and tours of sound stages in Metro-Goldwyn-Mayer's first TV series.

Hosts: George Murphy, Walter Pidgeon, Pete Smith

Miami Undercover

Crime Drama; 30 min; Syn. 1961

In an attempt to curtail the rising crime rate in Florida, the Miami Hotel Owners Association hires Jeff Thompson, a private detective who poses as a man-about-town, as their troubleshooter. Stories relate Jeff's efforts to keep Miami crime free.

Jeff Thompson	Lee Bowman
Rocky (partner)	Rocky Graziano

Producer: Aubrey Schenk, Howard W. Koch

Miami Vice

Crime Drama; 60 min; NBC 9/16/84 (Premiere)

The exploits of Sonny Crockett and Ricardo Tubbs, undercover police detectives with the Miami Police Department's Vice Squad.

Det. Sonny Crockett	Don Johnson
Det. Ricardo Tubbs	Philip Michael Thomas
Caroline Crockett	Belinda J. Montgomery
Lt. Lou Rodriquez	Gregory Sierra
Det. Gina Navarro	Saundra Santiago
Det. Trudy Joplin	Olivia Brown
Det. Stanley Switek	Michael Talbott
Det. Larry Zito	John Diehl
Lt. Martin Castillo	Edward James Olmos
Noogie Lamont	Martin Ferrero
Izzy Moreno	John Hernandez
Darlene	Ellen Greene

Music: Jan Hammer

Producer: Michael Mann, Anthony Yerkovitch

Michael Nesmith in Television Parts

Variety; 30 min; NBC 6/14/85 to 7/5/85

A series of music and comedy videos produced by ex-Monkee Michael Nesmith.

Host: Michael Nesmith

Regulars: Billy Beck, Richard Brunelle, Tina Caspary, Michael Castellano, Randy Doney, Nancy Gregory, John Hobbs, Alan McRae, Dani Minnick, Donna Rupert, Jeff Scott, Nick Shields, Linda Stayer, Kevin Thompson, The Whispers

Producer: Michael Nesmith, Ken Kragen

Music: Joseph Chemay, John Hobbs

Michael Shayne, Detective

Crime Drama Pilot; 30 min; NBC 9/28/58

The story of Michael Shayne, a two-fisted private detective. The pilot for the series, which was broadcast as "Man on a Raft" on "Decision."

Michael Shayne	Mark Stevens
Lucy (his secretary)	Merry Anders
Tim Rourke (reporter)	Robert Brubaker
Ann Conway	Diane Brewster
Turner	Steve Mitchell
Sara Redford	Mary Adams

Producer: Mark Stevens

Michael Shayne, Private Detective

Crime Drama; 60 min; NBC 9/30/60 to 9/22/61

The exploits of Michael Shayne, a two-fisted private detective working out of Miami Beach, Florida. See also "Michael Shayne, Detective."

Michael Shayne	Richard Denning
Lucy Hamilton	Patricia Donahue
	Margie Regan
Tim Rourke	Jerry Paris
Chief Will Gentry	Herbert Rudley
Dick Hamilton	Gary Clarke

"Theme from Michael Shayne" by Leith Stevens

Producer: Joseph Hoffman

The Michele Lee Show

Comedy Pilot; 30 min; CBS 4/5/74

The story of Michele Burton, a pretty newsstand clerk at the Wilshire Hotel in Beverly Hills.

Michele Burton	Michele Lee
Gladys Gooch	Joyce Bulifant
Mr. Zelensky	Herbie Faye
Dr. Steven Mayhill	Stephen Collins
Customer	Sidney Clute

Theme Vocal: Michele Lee

Producer: Chuck Fries, Fred Coe

Mickey

Comedy; 30 min; ABC 9/16/64 to 1/13/65

Shortly after he retires, Mickey Grady inherits the Newport Arms, a hotel fraught with problems, in Newport Beach, California. Stories relate the efforts of Mickey and his family (wife Nora, and children Timmy and Buddy) to make a success of the hotel.

Mickey Grady	Mickey Rooney
Nora Grady	Emmaline Henry
Timmy Grady	Timmy Rooney
Buddy Grady	Brian Nash
Sammy Ling	Sammee Tong
Mr. Swidler	Alan Reed

Producer: Selig J. Seligman, Bob Fisher, Arthur Marx

Mickey and the Contessa

Comedy Pilot; 30 min; CBS 8/12/63

When Mickey Brennan, a former football all-star retires and acquires a job as a basketball coach, he hires, sight unseen, a housekeeper for his two children, Sissy and Mike. Several days later, Czigoina, a beautiful but impoverished Hungarian Contessa, arrives and presents herself as his housekeeper. The unsold series was to relate the Contessa's efforts to run the Brennan household.

Mickey Brennan	Mickey Shaughnessy
Contessa Czigoina	Eva Gabor
Sissy Brennan	Ann Marshall
Mike Brennan	Bill St. John
Arney Tanner	John Fielder
Butch Gorkey	Michael Green

Producer: Cy Howard

The Mickey Mouse Club

Children; 30 min; ABC 10/3/55 to 9/25/59

A classic series of music, songs, cartoons, and adventure serials with a group of talented children (the Mouseketeers) and the warm hosting of Jimmie Dodd. For information on the major serials, see the following titles: "Adventures in Dairyland," "Annette," "Corky and White Shadow," "The Hardy Boys and the Mystery of the Applegate Treasure," "The Hardy Boys and the Mystery of Ghost Farm," "Spin and Marty," "The Further Adventures of Spin and Marty," and "The New Adventures of Spin and Marty."

Host: Jimmie Dodd

Co-Host: Roy Williams

Assistant: Bob Amsberry

Voice of Jiminy Cricket: Cliff Edwards

Voice of Mickey Mouse: Jim MacDonald

Mouseketeers: Annette Funicello, Darlene Gillespie, Carl "Cubby," O'Brien, Bobby Burgess, Karen Pendleton, Tommy Cole, Cheryl Holdridge, Lynn Ready, Doreen Tracy, Linda Hughes, Lonny Burr, Bonni Lynn Fields, Sharon Baird, Ronnie Young, Jay Jay Solari, Margene Storey, Nancy Abbate, Billie Jean Beanblossom, Mary Espinosa, Bonnie Lou Kern, Mary Lou Sartori, Bronson Scott, Dennis Day, Dickie

Dodd, Michael Smith, Ronald Steiner, Mark Sutherland, Don Underhill, Sherry Allen, Paul Petersen, Judy Harriett, John Lee Johnson, Eileen Diamond, Charley Laney, Mickey Rooney Jr., Tim Rooney, Johnny Crawford, Larry Larson, Don Grady

Producer: Walt Disney, Bill Walsh, Dick Darley

The Mickey Rooney Show

See "Hey Mulligan."

Mickey Rooney's Small World

Discussion; 30 min; Syn. 1975

Eight children, aged four to eight and who vary from program to program, discuss various matters with celebrity guests.

Host: Mickey Rooney

Producer: Mickey Rooney

Mickey Spillane's Mike Hammer

Crime Drama; 30 min; Syn. 1958

The exploits of Mike Hammer, a rugged private detective based in New York City. Also known as "Mike Hammer, Detective." See also the following title.

Mike Hammer	Darren McGavin
Capt. Pat Chambers	Bart Burns

Narrator: Darren McGavin

Theme Song ("Riff Blues"): Dave Kahn, Melvyn Lenard

Producer: Richard Irving

Mickey Spillane's Mike Hammer

Crime Drama; 60 min; CBS 1/26/84 to 1/12/85

The exploits of Mike Hammer, a rugged private detective working out of New York City. Based on the character created by Mickey Spillane. See also "The New Mike Hammer."

Mike Hammer	Stacy Keach
	Kevin Dobson*
Velda	Lindsay Bloom
	Cindy Pickett*
Capt. Pat Chambers	Don Stroud
	Charles Hallahan*
Lawrence Barrington	Kent Williams
Ozzie the Answer	Danny Goldman
Moochie the Pimp	Ben Powers
The Face**	Donna Denton

Theme Song ("Harlem Nocturne"): Earle Hagen

Producer: Jay Bernstein, Robert Singer

*TV Movie roles ("Mickey Spillane's Margin for Murder," 10/15/81)

**A beautiful girl in various roles.

Mickie Finn's

Variety; 30 min; NBC 4/21/66 to 9/1/66

The music, songs, and dances of the Gay 90s to the 1960s.

Hosts: Mickie Finn, Fred Finn

Regulars: Spider Marillo, Bobby Jensen, Story Gormley, Owen Leinhard, Don Van Paulta, The Mickie Finn Waitresses

Music: The Mickie Finn Band

Producer: Bob Finkel, Dean Whitmore

Midnight Mystery

Mystery Pilot; 60 min; NBC 6/5/57

A proposed, but unsold NBC anthology series. In the pilot, "Rain in the Morning," a terrified housewife attempts to escape from a lunatic who traps her in her home. Aired on "Matinee Theatre."

Jane Wilson	Peggy McCay
Larry	Robert Morse
Mr. Wallace	Theodore Newton
Frank Wilson	Robert Karnes
Bess Carlson	Barbara Drew
Harper	Tom Greenway

Producer: Albert McCleery

The Midnight Special

Music; 90 min; NBC 2/2/73 to 5/1/81

Performances by rock, pop, soul, and country and western entertainers. Syndicated in 1982 as the 60-minute "Best of the Midnight Special."

Hostess: Helen Reddy (for a short period)

Regular: Carol Wayne

Announcer: Wolfman Jack, Mike Carruthers

Producer: Burt Sugarman, Stan Harris, Dick Ebersol

Midwestern Hayride

Variety; Various (30 & 60 min); Syn. 1947 to 1967
ABC 6/29/57 to 9/22/58

Performances by country and western entertainers.

Host: Paul Dixon, Dean Richards, Willie Thall, Bill Thall

Regulars: Phyllis Brown, Helen Scott, Bonnie Lou, Paul Arnold, Billy Scott, Mary Jane Johnson, Phyllis Holmes, Bill Holmes, Freddy Langdon, Tommy Watson, Martha Hendricks, Barney Sefton, Ernie Lee, Judy Perkins, Kenny Roberts, The Trail Blazers, The Girls of the Golden West, The Midwesterners, The Lucky Pennies

Announcer: Hal Woodard

Producer: James B. Hill, John Morris

The Mighty Hercules

Cartoon; 5 min; Syn. 1960

The exploits of Hercules, the legendary hero of mythology, as he protects the Learien Valley from the villainous wizard Deadalus.

Hercules	Jerry Bascombe
Helena	Helene Nickerson
Newton/Tweet/ Deadalus	Jimmy Tapp

Theme Vocal ("Mighty Hercules"): Johnny Nash

Producer: Joseph Orilio, Roger Carlin

The Mighty Mouse Playhouse

Cartoon; 30 min; CBS 12/10/55 to 9/2/67

While experimenting, a mouse scientist develops a potion called "Atomic Energy," that when taken transforms him into the courageous and powerful Mighty Mouse. Stories relate his battle to help good defeat evil.

Mighty Mouse	Tom Morrison

Narrator: Tom Morrison

Producer: Bill Weiss

Mighty O

Comedy Pilot; 30 min; CBS 8/21/62

The antics of two Chief Petty Officers (Joe and Barney) who are assigned to the Coast Guard cargo vessel "Ortega," affectionately nicknamed "Mighty O."

Joe Slattery	Craig Stevens
Barney Blaney	Alan Hale Jr.
Chief Muldoon	Richard Jaeckel
Mary	Lola Albright

The Mighty Orbots

Cartoon; 30 min; ABC 9/8/84 to 8/31/85

When the evil Shadow, the ruler of the planet Umbra, threatens to destroy the Earth, Rob Simmons, a 23rd-century scientist with the Galactic Patrol, constructs an army of robots (Bort, Tur, Beau, Crunch and Ono) to battle Shadow. Stories relate the Galactic Patrol's battle against Shadow.

Voices: Sherry Alberoni, Julie Bennett, Jennifer Darling, Barry Gordon, Jim MacGeorge, Robert Ridgely, Don Messick, Bill Martin

Producer: Fred Silverman

Mike and Buff

Interview; 45 min; CBS 8/2/51 to 2/27/53

Celebrity interviews with Mike Wallace and his wife Buff Cobb. Produced by Jess Kimmel.

Mike and the Mermaid

Comedy Pilot; 60 min; ABC 1/5/68

While fishing in a river, a young boy (Mike) catches a legendary creature of the sea—a mermaid. The unsold series was to relate Mike's adventures when he befriends and attempts to keep the mermaid's existence a secret.

Mermaid	Jeri Lynn Fraser
Mike Malone	Kevin Brodie
Nellie Malone	Rachel Ames
Jim Malone	Med Flory

The Mike Douglas Show

Variety; 90 min; Syn. 1966–1981

A daily series of celebrity interviews.

Host: Mike Douglas

Announcer: Jay Stewart

Music: Ellie Frankel, Joe Harnell, Frank Hunter, Joe Massimino

Producer: Jack Reilly, Woody Fraser, E. V. DiMissa Jr.

Mike Hammer

See "Mickey Spillane's Mike Hammer."

The Mike Wallace Profiles

Biography (Pilot); 30 min; CBS 11/17/81

Profiles of famous people via interviews, newsreel footage, and film clips.

Host: Mike Wallace

Music: Bob Israel

Producer: Harry Moses

Milestones of the Century

A three-and-one-half minute insert series, narrated by Ed Herlihy, that uses Pathe newsreel film footage to cover one event for each day of the year. Syndicated in 1960.

The Milky Way

Experimental; 60 min; NBC 10/20/39

The story of Burleigh Sullivan, a milk delivery boy who becomes a world champion boxer. The first TV program to use rear projection.

Burleigh Sullivan	James Corner

Also: June Blossom, Ross Hertz, Claudia Morgan, Lowell Gilmore, Fred Stewart

Producer: Edward Sobol

The Millionaire

Drama; 30 min; CBS 1/19/55 to 9/28/60

When a doctor orders multi-billionaire John Beresford Tipton to find a means of relaxation, he decides to give a tax free gift of one million dollars to specially selected people; people who are unaware of him, and who must sign a document never to reveal the source of their sudden wealth. Stories relate the results of Tipton's gift on the lives of its recipients as seen through the eyes of Michael Anthony, Tipton's executive secretary, who delivers the checks and records the results.

Michael Anthony	Marvin Miller
Voice of John Beresford Tipton	Paul Frees
Andrew V. McMahon (bank vice president)	Roy Gordon

Announcer: Ed Herlihy

Producer: Fred Henry, Don Fedderson

The Milton Berle Show

Variety; 60 min; NBC 9/29/53 to 6/14/55

A program of music, songs, and slapstick comedy.

Host: Milton Berle

Regulars: Connie Russell, Arnold Stang, Nancy Walker, Fred Clark, Charlie Applegate, The Herb Rose Dancers

Announcer: Jack Lescoulie

Orchestra: Allen Roth

Producer: Milton Berle, Ford Henry

The Milton Berle Show

Variety; 60 min; NBC 9/27/55 to 6/5/56

A program of music and comedy that varies according to the talents of its guests.

Host: Milton Berle

Orchestra: Victor Young

Producer: Milton Berle, Irving Gray

The Milton Berle Show

Variety; 60 min; ABC 9/9/66 to 1/6/67

Milton's variety series comeback after a ten year absence; music, songs, and slapstick comedy.

Host: Milton Berle

Regulars: Bobby Rydell, Donna Loren, Irving Benson, The Louis DaPron Dancers, The Berle Girls

Announcer: Dick Tufeld

Orchestra: Mitchell Ayres

Producer: William O. Harbach, Nick Vanoff

The Milton the Monster Cartoon Show

Cartoon; 30 min; ABC 10/9/65 to 9/2/67

Segments: "Milton the Monster" (a lovable Frankenstein-type of monster); "Fearless Fly" (a mild-mannered insect who becomes a daring crime fighter); "Flukey Luke" (a cowboy who doubles as a private eye); "Muggy Doo" (antics of a fast-talking con artist); and "Penny Penguin" (antics of a mischievous child).

Milton	Bob McFadden
Prof. Weirdo/ Fearless Fly/ Flukey Luke	Dayton Allen
Florrie/Penny Penguin	Beverly Arnold
Muggy Doo	Larry Best

Producer: Hal Seeger

Mimi

Comedy Pilot; 30 min; CBS 8/29/64

The antics of a dietician (Mimi) and a therapist (Phil) at the Garden of Eden Health Spa.

Mimi	Mimi Hines
Phil	Phil Ford
Peavey	Dan Tobin
Quibideaux	Thomas Gomez
Miss Birch	Lee Patrick
Giselle	Lili Garner
Council	Lloyd Kino

Producer-Writer-Director: Philip Rapp

Mindreaders

Game; 30 min; NBC 8/12/79 to 1/11/80

A question that requires a yes or no answer is read to one of the two teams that compete. One member of that team (turns rotate) must predict how each of his teammates answered the question. Each correct guess scores the team $50.

Host: Dick Martin

Announcer: Johnny Olsen

Producer: Mark Goodson, Bill Todman

Mindy Carson Sings

Variety; 30 min; NBC 1949

A program of music and songs.

Hostess: Mindy Carson

Regulars: Danny Horton, Florian ZaBach

Announcer: Don Pardo

Orchestra: Earl Sheldon, Norman Cloutier

The Misadventures of Sheriff Lobo

Comical Crime Drama; 60 min; NBC 9/18/79 to 9/2/80

The exploits of Elroy P. Lobo, the slightly dishonest sheriff of Orly County, Georgia, who dispenses his own brand of justice—for profit. A spin-off from "B. J. and the Bear." See also "Lobo."

Sheriff Elroy P. Lobo	Claude Akins
Deputy Perkins	Mills Watson
Deputy Birdwell Hawkins	Brian Kerwin
Sarah Cumberland	Leann Hunley
Rose Perkins	Cydney Crampton
Margaret Ellen Mercer	Janet Lyn Curtis
Oscar Gorley	J. D. Cannon
Mayor Hawkins	William Schallert
Hotel waitress	Pamela Myers
Hotel bartender	Dick Winslow
Elroy's mother	Rosemary DeCamp

Theme Vocal ("The Ballad of Sheriff Lobo"): Frankie Laine

Producer: Glen A. Larson, William P. D'Angelo.

The Mischief Makers

Comedy; 12 ½ min; Syn. 1960

The TV title for a series of selected "Our Gang" comedy shorts of the 1920s. Music (by Jack Saunders) and sound effects have been added to the silent films produced by Hal Roach.

The Misfits of Science

Fantasy; 60 min; NBC 10/4/85 to 2/21/86

The exploits of Billy Hayes, a research scientist; Elvin "El" Lincoln, who possesses the ability to reduce his eighty-eight inch height to the size of a Ken doll; Johnny Bukowski, a former rock star who was "fried" by twenty thousand volts of electricity and is now capable of storing power and discharging lightning bolts; and Gloria Dinallo, a pretty 17-year-old girl who possesses amazing telekenetic powers—four rejects who form the Misfits of Science, extraordinary people who use their powers to help people who happen to be different—and in trouble.

Dr. Billy Hayes	Dean Paul Martin
Dr. Elvin Lincoln	Kevin Peter Hall
Johnny Bukowski	Mark Thomas Miller
Gloria Dinallo	Courteney Cox
Dick Stetmeyer (their superior at H.I.T.*)	Max Wright
Jane Miller (Gloria's probation officer)	Jennifer Holmes
Miss Nance (secretary at H.I.T.)	Diane Civita

Producer: James D. Parriott, Alan J. Levi

*The Human Investigative Team; later Humandine, the research company for which the Misfits work.

The Miss and the Missiles

Comedy Pilot; 30 min; CBS 7/25/64

The romantic misadventures of Connie Marlowe, a magazine writer, and Bill Adams, an Air Force test pilot.

Connie Marlowe	Gisele MacKenzie
Bill Adams	John Forsythe
Buzz Marlowe	Gordon Gerbert
Emma	Kathleen Freeman
John P. MacBain	John McGiver
Spider	Michael J. Pollard

Producer: Jack Chertok

Miss Bishop

Comedy Pilot; 30 min; NBC 9/1/61

An unsold idea based on the 1941 film, "Cheers for Miss Bishop," about a dedicated school teacher in a small midwestern college.

Miss Bishop	Jan Clayton
Pupil	Tom Helmore
Girl mechanic	Julie Payne

Miss Pepperdine

Comedy Pilot; 30 min; Unaired (Produced for CBS in 1959)

Hoping to become a model, Marie Pepperdine, a beautiful mailroom clerk for the Pontifore and Company Dresses, finds her chances becoming a reality when she is promoted to a receptionist. The unsold series was to relate Marie's efforts to achieve a dream.

Marie Pepperdine	Marie Wilson
Simon Pontifore (her boss)	Jack Durant
Lily Baldwin (her friend)	Hildy Parks
Bentley Pontifore (Simon's nephew)	Paul Percini
Herbie (shipping clerk)	Paul Smith
Hazel (Marie's neighbor)	Mary Beth Hughes
Gus (Hazel's husband)	Harry Clark

Producer: Everett Freeman

Miss Stewart, Sir

Comedy Pilot; 30 min; CBS 3/31/72

The story of Kate Stewart, a boys' school housemother.

Kate Stewart	Joanna Pettet
Principal Prentiss	Murray Matheson
Buzz	Gary Vinson
Joe	Michael Witney
Hannah	Norah Marlowe
George	Don Clarke
Mike	Lee Hollingshead

Producer: Peter Tewksbury

Miss Susan

Serial; 15 min; NBC 3/12/51 to 12/28/51

The dramatic story of a handicapped criminal attorney working out of Ohio.

Susan Peters	Herself
Her Nurse	Katherine Grill
Her Housekeeper	Natalie Priest

Producer: Ted Ashley, Kenneth Buckridge

Miss Winslow and Son

Comedy; 30 min; CBS 3/28/79 to 5/2/79

Several months after the birth of her son (Edmund), Susan Winslow, a pretty single mother, acquires a job as a commercial artist with the Callahan Agency. Stories relate Susan's attempts to make a life for herself and her baby. Based on the British series "Miss Jones and Son."

Susan Winslow	Darleen Carr
Harold Neistader	Roscoe Lee Browne
Warren Winslow	Elliott Reid
Evelyn Winslow	Sarah Marshall
Joseph Callahan	William Bogert
Edmund Winslow	Benjamin Margolis
Rosa Vallone	Ellen Sherman
Angelo Vallone	Joe Rassulo

Music: Pete Rugolo

Producer: Mimi Seawell, Don Van Atta

Missing Links

Game; 30 min; NBC 9/9/63 to 3/27/64
ABC 3/30/64 to 12/25/64

A story that contains a number of specific blanks is read. A player chooses one of three celebrity guests and bets points on the celebrity's ability to fill in the blanks. Each correct bet scores the player points and the highest scorer is the winner.

Host: Ed McMahon, Dick Clark

Mission: Impossible

Adventure; 60 min; CBS 9/17/66 to 9/8/73

The cases of the I.M.F. (Impossible Missions Force), a top secret U.S. government organization that handles dangerous and highly sensitive international assignments.

Dan Briggs	Steven Hill
Jim Phelps	Peter Graves
Cinnamon Carter	Barbara Bain
Rollin Hand	Martin Landau
Barney Collier	Greg Morris
Willy Armitage	Peter Lupus
Paris	Leonard Nimoy
Dana	Lesley Ann Warren
Casey	Lynda Day George
Mimi Davis	Barbara Anderson
Dr. Doug Lang	Sam Elliott
Recorded Voice that gives Jim his assignment	Bob Johnson
Tracy*	Lee Meriwether
Lisa*	Michele Carey
Beth*	Sally Ann Howes
Monique*	Julie Gregg
Nora*	Antoinette Bower
Valerie*	Jessica Walter
Various Villainous Roles	Sid Haig

"Mission Impossible" Theme: Lalo Schifrin

Producer: Bruce Geller, Stanley Kallis, Lee H. Katzin, Bruce Lansbury, Laurence Heath, Joseph Gantman

*Agents used in the interim between Barbara Bain and Lesley Ann Warren.

Mission Magic

Cartoon; 30 min; ABC 9/8/73 to 8/31/74

The story of Miss Tickle, a beautiful school teacher with amazing magical powers that she uses to help good defeat evil.

Miss Tickle	Erica Scheimer
Rick Springfield	Himself
Carol*	Lola Fisher
Vinnie*	Lane Scheimer
Kim*	Lola Fisher
Harvey*	Howard Morris
Franklin*	Lane Scheimer
Socks*	Howard Morris

Producer: Lou Scheimer, Norm Prescott

*Students of Miss Tickle

The Mississippi

Drama; 60 min; CBS 3/25/83 to 3/6/84

Fed up with the rat race of the big city, attorney Ben Walker heads for Mississippi, where, as the owner of the tug boat "Mississippi," he finds the life he had been searching for. Stories relate Ben's attempts to enjoy his new life, while still practicing law and helping the people who live by the river.

Ben Walker	Ralph Waite
Stella McMullen	Linda Miller
Lafayette Tate	Stan Shaw
Rachel Walker	Laurie Prange

Theme Song ("Theme from the Mississippi"): Lee Holdridge

Producer: George Eckstein

The Missus Goes a Shopping

Game; 30 min; CBS 11/19/47 to 1/12/49

The series, broadcast live from various Manhattan supermarkets, features women shoppers competing in various contests for prizes. CBS TV's first daytime series.

Host: John Reed King, Bud Collyer

Assistant: Jimmy Brown

Producer: Ralph Levy

Mitchell and Woods

Crime Drama Pilot; 60 min; NBC 12/18/81

The exploits of Paula Woods and Melanie Mitchell, two beautiful plainclothes detectives with the Ocean City, California P.D.

Det. Paula Woods	Jayne Kennedy
Det. Melanie Mitchell	Cindy Morgan
Lt. Richards	Paul Gale
Chickie Anderson	Pamela Susan Shoop
Eleanor Martin	Ann Coleman
Wilder	John David Carson
Lawrence	Michael Maguire

Producer: Cy Chermak

Mixed Doubles

Comedy; 30 min; NBC 8/5/49 to 10/29/49

The trials and tribulations of the Abbotts and Colemans, two newlywed couples who live side by side in a New York apartment building.

Bill Abbott	Billy Idelson
Ada Abbott	Ada Friedan
Eddy Coleman	Eddie Firestone
Elaine Coleman	Rhoda Williams
	Bonnie Baken

Producer: Carleton E. Morse

Mixed Nuts

Comedy Pilot; 30 min; ABC 5/12/77

The comic adventures of a group of patients assigned to the Rosewood State Psychiatric Center.

Dr. Sarah Allgood	Zohra Lambert
Dr. Folder	Emory Bass
Bugs (inmate)	Dan Barrows
Logan (inmate)	Richard Karron
Moe (inmate)	Morey Amsterdam
Gato (inmate)	James Victor
Jamie (inmate)	Ed Begley Jr.
Nurse Cassidy	Conchata Ferrell

Producer: Jerry Belson, Mark Carliner

The M & M Candy Carnival

Variety; 30 min; CBS 1/6/52 to 6/28/53

Undiscovered talent performs (against a carnival backdrop) with the hope of winning a $25 savings bond and a week's booking at the Hamid Steel Pier in Atlantic City. Sponsored by M & M Candies.

Host: Gene Crane

Ringmaster: Barry Cossell

Clown: Don Lenox, Bill Bailey

Judge: George Hammond

Music: Gene Grane

Producer: Charles Vanda

Mo and Jo

Comedy Pilot; 30 min; CBS 3/7/74

The story of a middle-aged couple (Mo and Jo) who worry that life is passing them by.

Maureen "Mo" Lambert	Louise Lasser
Jo Lambert	Michael Tolan
Julian Lambert	Andrea McCardle
Edward Lambert	Matthew Anton
Iris Lambert	Judith Kahan
Sandy	Nina Wilcox
Ralph	Adam Arkin

Producer: Marc Merson

Mobile Medics

Drama Pilot; 30 min; CBS 5/10/77

The exploits of four doctors who operate a mobile medical unit, a mini-lab and operating room they use to help people who require immediate attention.

Dr. Liz Rheiner	Ellen Weston
Dr. Robb Spencer	Jack Stauffer
Dr. Pete Vasquez	Jaime Tirelli
Dr. Craig Bryant	Ben Masters
Cheryl	Julie Cobb
Foreman	Robert DoQui
Nurse	Maggie Malooly
Fire Captain	John Pickard

Producer: Bruce Lansbury

Mobile One

Drama; 60 min; ABC 9/12/75 to 12/29/75

Hoping to acquire a job as a reporter for KONE-TV, Channel 1 in Southern California, Pete Campbell, a seasoned news reporter, but a former alcoholoic, is given the opportunity to prove himself by Maggie Spencer, the station assignment editor. Stories relate Pete's exploits as he gathers story material (assisted by his cameraman, Doug).

Pete Campbell	Jackie Cooper
Doug McKnight	Mark Wheeler
Maggie Spencer	Julie Gregg
Lt. Baker	Warren Stevens
Bruce Daniels	Gary Crosby

Music: Nelson Riddle

Producer: Jack Webb

Moby Dick and the Mighty Mightor

Cartoon; 30 min; CBS 9/9/67 to 9/6/69

Segments: "Moby Dick" (exploits of the legendary white whale as he struggles to protect his human foundlings, Tom and Tub); and "The Mighty Mightor" (about Tor, who battles evil as the Mighty Mightor).

Tom	Bobby Resnick
Tub	Barry Balkin
Scooby	Don Messick
Mightor	Paul Stewart
Tor	Bobby Diamond
Sheera	Patsy Garrett
Pondo	John Stephenson
Li'l Rock	Norma McMillan

Producer: William Hanna, Joseph Barbera

The Mod Squad

Crime Drama; 60 min; ABC 9/24/68 to 8/23/73

Following the arrest of three young adults, L.A.P.D. Captain Adam Greer recruits them (Pete, Julie, and Linc) to form the Mod Squad, a special detail of undercover agents designed to infiltrate organizations that are impenetrable by police. Stories focus on their case investigations and Pete, Julie, and Linc's attempts to work out their own identities.

Pete Cochrane	Michael Cole
Julie Barnes	Peggy Lipton
Linc Hayes	Clarence Williams III
Capt. Adam Greer	Tige Andrews
Barney Metcalf	Simon Scott

Producer: Aaron Spelling, Danny Thomas

Modern Romances

Anthology; 15 min; NBC 10/4/54 to 9/19/58

Serialized dramas based on modern romance stories.

Host-Narrator: Martha Scott, Mel Brandt

Producer: Wilbur Stark, Jerry Layton

Modesty Blaise

Adventure Pilot; 60 min; ABC 9/12/82

The exploits of Modesty Blaise, a beautiful and mysterious woman who performs hazardous assignments for the SIB (Special Intelligence Bureau). Based on the British comic book character created by Peter O'Donnell.

Modesty Blaise	Ann Turkel
Willie Garvin	Lewis Van Bergen
Wang	Sab Shimono
Gerald Tarent	Keene Curtis
Jack	Douglas Dirkson
Emma Woodhouse	Sarah Rush
Debbie DeFarge	Carolyn Seymour
Leo Bazin	Charles Cioffi

Producer: Barney Rosenzweig

The Mohawk Showroom

Variety; 15 min; NBC 5/12/49 to 12/9/49

A musical interlude series under the sponsorship of Mohawk Carpets.

Hosts: Roberta Quinlan, Morton Downey

Regulars: Carmen Mastren, The Chieftains

Announcer: Bob Stanton

Orchestra: Harry Clark

Producer: E. Roger Muir, George R. Nelson

Moll Flanders

Drama; 60 min; PBS 1980

The adventures of Moll Flanders, a 17th-century woman who was married five times, was twelve years a prostitute, and twelve years a thief. Contains nudity and sexual situations.

Moll Flanders	Julia Foster
Meg	Karin MacCarthy
Thomas	Patrick Newell
Robin	Paul Lavers
Humphrey Oliver	Ian Ogilvy
Catherine	Lynne Jones
Jenny	Sheila Reid
William Stubbs	Barry Jackson
Mrs. Oliver	Madge Ryan

Producer: Cedric Messina

The Molly Picon Show

An early ABC variety series (3/1/49 to 4/12/49) with stage and movie star Molly Picon.

Moment of Decision

An ABC series (7/3/57 to 9/25/57) of repeat dramas from "Ford Theatre."

Moment of Fear

Dramatizations that depict the plight of people who are suddenly confronted with perilous situations. The eight episodes broadcast on NBC in 1960 (7/1/60 to 9/9/60) were first run, while the 1964 (5/19 to 9/15) and 1965 (5/25 to 8/10) consisted of repeats from other anthology series.

Mona

Comedy Pilot; 30 min; ABC 5/12/87

Following his retirement from the military, Corneilius Rockwell invites his sister, Mona, to a reunion in Manhattan. There, he talks Mona into using her savings to purchase a hotel (the seedy Nottingham) that he feels he can turn into a money-making venture. The would-be series was to relate Mona's efforts to protect her investment by helping Corneilius run the hotel. Aired on "Who's the Boss?"

Mona Robinson	Katherine Helmond
Corneilius Rockwell	James B. Sikking
Don West	Joe Regalbuto
Packard Vance	Paul Sand
Kitty	Susan Walters
Eddie	Robert Petkoff
Tessie	Billie Bird
Mr. Radcliff	David Hedison
Mrs. Padnick	Lin Shaye
Mr. Padnick	Don Sparks
Mona (as a girl)	Candace Cameron
Corneilius (as a boy)	Gabreil Damon

Producer: Blake Hunter, Martin Cohan

Mona McCluskey

Comedy; 30 min; NBC 9/16/65 to 4/14/66

Following her marriage to U.S. Air Force Sgt. Mike McCluskey, Mona Carroll, a beautiful film actress who earns $5000 a week agrees to live on his salary of $500 a month. Stories relate Mona's comic adventures as she struggles to do what she promised, yet secretly supplement their income to enjoy a more comfortable life. The series was originally scheduled as "Presenting Mona McCluskey" and a pilot, written, produced, and directed by Don McGuire, was filmed.

Mona McCluskey	Juliet Prowse
Mike McCluskey	Denny Miller
Mr. Caldwell	Bartlett Robinson
Sgt. Stan Gruzewsky	Robert Strauss
Alice	Elena Verdugo
Gen. Crone	Herbert Rudley
Mona's Aunt	
Margaret	Madge Blake
Mona's Aunt Agatha	Dorothy Neumann

Theme Song Adaptation ("Yes Sir, That's My Baby"): Sonny Burke

Producer: George Burns

Monchhichis

Cartoon; 30 min; CBS 9/10/83 to 9/1/84

The series, set in Monchhia, a city in the clouds above very tall trees, relates the efforts of the monkey-like Monchhichis to preserve their peaceful existence by battling the Grumplins, evil creatures who seek to enslave them.

Voices: Jack Angel, Julie Bennett, Susan Blu, Victoria Carroll, Bill Callaway, Nancy Cartwright, Peter Cullen, Walker Edmiston, Joan Gerber, Patty Maloney, Julie McWhirter, Gregg Marx, Scott Menville, Laurel Page, Robert Ridgely, Shavar Ross, Frank Welker, William Windom, Ted Zeigler

Producer: William Hanna, Joseph Barbera

Monday Theatre

Pilot Films; 30 min; NBC 7/6/70 to 8/3/70

See the following titles: "The Boys," "The Kowboys," "Me and Benjy," "Run Jack Run," and "Southern Fried."

The Money Maze

Game; 30 min; ABC 12/23/74 to 7/4/75

Two married couples compete in a series of question-and-answer rounds. The first team to score eight points plays the Money Maze. One player stands before a large maze that contains five boxes (each worth one figure of $10,000). His partner stands above the maze and must direct his player through the maze. The object is for the maze player to touch as many boxes as possible and return to the starting point within a sixty second time limit. Money is awarded based on the number of boxes hit and their total.

Host: Nick Clooney

Announcer: Alan Caulfield

Producer: Don Lipp

The Monk

Crime Drama Pilot; 90 min; ABC 10/21/69

The exploits of Gus Monk, a two-fisted private detective who wanders from state to state seeking work. The pilot relates Monk's efforts to clear himself of a false murder charge. Developed by Blake Edwards.

Gus Monk	George Maharis
Janice Barnes	Janet Leigh
Tinker	Jack Albertson
Wideman	Rick Jason
Danny	Carl Betz
Ed Heritage	Raymond St. Jacques

Leo Barnes	William Smithers	Clayt Monroe	Michael Anderson Jr.
Hip Guy	Jack Soo		
Lisa Daniels	Linda Marsh	Kathleen Monroe	Barbara Hershey
Mrs. Medford	Mary Wickes	Amy Monroe	Tammy Locke
Herbie	Joe Besser	Jefferson Monroe	Keith Schultz
Stranger	George Burrafato	Fennimore Monroe	Kevin Schultz
Sgt. Mawson	George Saurel	Jim (renegade Indian)	Ron Soble
Charlie	John Hancock		
Doorman	Bob Nash	Major Mapoy (land baron)	Liam Sullivan

Producer: Danny Thomas, Aaron Spelling

Ruel Jaxon (Mapoy's aide)	James Westmoreland
Sleeve (Mapoy's aide)	Ben Johnson
John Bradford (Mapoy's aide)	Buck Taylor
Albert Monroe	Russ Conway
Mary Monroe	Marilyn Moe
Barney Wales (rancher)	Robert Middleton
Dalton Wales (son)	James Brolin
Billy Dan Wales (son)	Tom O'Kelly
Lorna Wales (daughter)	Lisa Jak

The Monkees

Comedy; 30 min; NBC 9/12/66 to 8/19/68

Slapstick situations are played within non-realistic frameworks to relate the antics of the Monkees (Davy, Mike, Peter, and Mickey) a zany rock and roll group.

Davy Jones	Himself
Mike Nesmith	Himself
Peter Tork	Himself
Mickey Dolenz	Himself
Mr. Babbitt (landlord)	Henry Corden
Mrs. Purdy (neighbor)	Jesslyn Fax
Davy's grandfather	Ben Wright
Mike's Aunt Kate	Jacqueline DeWitt

Producer: Ralph Riskin, Ward Sylvester

"The Monroes" Theme Music: David Rose

Producer: Frederick Brogger, Al C. Ward

The Monster Squad

Comedy; 30 min; NBC 9/11/76 to 9/2/77

While working the night watch at Fred's Wax Museum, Walt, a criminology student, activates a crime computer he has invented and, through its oscillating vibrations, brings to life Frankenstein, Dracula, and the Wolfman. Hoping to make up for their past misgivings, they join Walt and attempt to solve crimes.

Walt	Fred Grandy
Count Dracula	Henry Polic II
Bruce W. Wolf	Buck Kartalian
Frank N. Stein	Michael Lane
Off. McMac Mac	Paul Smith

Producer: William P. D'Angelo, Harvey Bullock, Ray Allen

The Monroes

Western; 60 min; ABC 9/7/66 to 8/30/67

Shortly after the Monroes, a pioneering family arrives in Wyoming in 1875, the mother and father (Albert and Mary) are killed while attempting to cross a treacherous river. The orphaned children (Clayt, Kathleen, Amy, Jefferson and Fennimore) agree to continue with their parents quest and find a lone valley their father had laid claim to ten years earlier. After a long trek, and with only a handmade map to guide them, the children find the valley. Stories relate the Monroe children's efforts to establish their parents dream—a homeland.

The Monte Carlo Show

Variety; 60 min; Syn. 9/80

The series, taped in Monte Carlo, presents American and European variety acts.

Host: Patrick Wayne

Regulars: Les Girls, Andre Cahoune

Orchestra: Dennis McCarthy

Producer: Marty Pasetta, Michael Seligman

The Montefuscos

Comedy; 30 min; NBC 9/4/75 to 10/23/75

The trials and tribulations of three generations of the Montefuscos, a large Italian-American family living in New Canaan, Connecticut.

Tony Montefusco	Joseph Sirola
Rose Montefusco	Naomi Stevens
Frankie Montefusco	Ron Carey
Theresa Montefusco	Phoebe Dorin
Joseph Montefusco	John Aprea
Nunzio Montefusco	Sal Viscuso
Angelina Cooney	Linda Dano
Jim Cooney	Bill Cort
Carmine Montefusco	Jeffrey Palladini
Gina Montefusco	Dominique Pinassi
Jerome Montefusco	Robby Paris
Anthony Cooney	Damon Raskin

Producer: Bill Persky, Sam Denoff

Montgomery's Summer Stock

Anthology; 60 min; NBC 7/14/52 to 8/25/52
                                   7/6/53 to 8/24/53
                                   6/28/54 to 9/13/54
                                   7/4/55 to 9/5/55
                                   7/2/56 to 9/3/56

Original dramatic productions that aired as the Summer replacement for "Robert Montgomery Presents."

Regulars: Elizabeth Montgomery, Vaughn Taylor, Judy Parrish, Jan Miner, John Newland, Margaret Hayes, Anne Seymour, Cliff Robertson, Charles Drake, Augusta Dabney, House Jameson, Dorothy Blackburn, Eric Sinclair, Mary K. Wells, Tom Middleton

Producer: Robert Montgomery

Monty Nash

Adventure; 30 min; Syn. 9/71

An adaptation of the Richard Jessup spy yarns about Monty Nash, a U.S. Government special investigator who handles top-secret White House affairs.

Monty Nash   Harry Guardino

Theme Music ("Monty Nash"): Michael Lloyd

Producer: Everett Chambers, Richard M. Rosenbloom

Monty Python's Flying Circus

Comedy; 30 min; PBS Syndication 10/74

An absolutely meaningless title for a program of tasteless, uneven, and insane material that is ingeniously interwoven into an enjoyable half-hour series.

Cast: John Cleese, Graham Chapman, Eric Idle, Terry Jones, Michael Palin

Regulars: Carol Cleveland, Rita Davis, Donna Reading, Ian Davidson, Sandra Richards, Dick Vosburg, The Fred Tomalson Singers

Producer: Ian MacNaughton, John Davies

The Moonglow Affair

Adventure Pilot; 60 min; NBC 2/25/66

The pilot for "The Girl from U.N.C.L.E." which relates the adventures of agents April Dancer and Mark Slate as they attempt to find a means to stop a radiation projector from rendering U.N.C.L.E. agents helpless. Aired on "The Man from U.N.C.L.E."

April Dancer	Mary Ann Mobley
Mark Slate	Norman Fell
Alexander Waverly	Leo G. Carroll
Napoleon Solo	Robert Vaughn
Illya Kuryakin	David McCallum
Arthur Caresso	Kevin McCarthy
Jean Caresso	Mary Carver

Producer: Norman Felton

Moonlighting

Satirical Crime Drama; 60 min; ABC 3/5/85 (Premiere)

When her business manager embezzles her funds, leaving Madeline "Maddie" Hayes, a beautiful model who was once "The Blue

Moon Shampoo Girl,'' penniless, she decides to recoup her losses by selling a business she owns (City of Angels Investigations). Her mind is changed, however, when the agency manager, David Addison, persuades her to save the company by becoming her partner in the renamed Blue Moon Detective Agency. Stories relate Maddie and David's continual bickering over cases and procedure as they strive to make the agency a success.

Maddie Hayes	Cybill Shepherd
David Addison	Bruce Willis
Agnes Dipesto	Allyce Beasley
Virginia Hayes	Eva Marie Saint
Richie Addison	Charles Rocket
Alexander Hayes	Robert Webber
David Addison Sr.	Paul Sorvino
Herbert Viola	Curtis Armstrong

Theme Vocal ("Moonlighting"): Al Jarreau

Producer: Glenn Gordon Caron, Jay Daniel, Artie Mandelberg

The Moonman Connection

A syndicated (1979) disco version of "American Bandstand" with hosts Moonman-Bacote and Alfie Williams. Produced by Willie Bacote.

More Real People

The syndicated title for "Real People."

The Morecambe and Wise Show

Comedy; 30 min; Syn. 9/80

A British-produced series of burlesque-type comedy.

Hosts: Eric Morecambe, Ernie Wise

Regulars: Ann Hamilton, Kenny Ball, Peter Hansen

Music: Peter Knight

Producer: Madelyn Goldberg, Peter Hansen

The Morey Amsterdam Show

Variety; 30 min; CBS 12/17/48 to 3/7/49
DuMont 4/21/49 to 10/12/50

Music, songs, and comedy set against the background of the Silver Swan Cafe.

Host	Morey Amsterdam
Newton (waiter)	Art Carney
Rosemary (singer)	Rosemary Clooney
Jacqueline (cigaret girl)	Jacqueline Sussan

Regulars: Vic Damone, Francey Lane, Mary Raye

Announcer: Don Russell

Orchestra: Ray McKinley, Johnny Guarnieri

Producer: Irving Mansfield, Barry Wood, Morey Amsterdam

Mork and Mindy

Comedy; 30 min; ABC 9/14/78 to 8/5/82

While driving home, Mindy McConnell meets Mork, an alien from the planet Ork who has been sent to Earth to study its life form. When Mindy learns of Mork's mission, she agrees to help him, and begins by allowing him to live with her (at her apartment at 1619 Pine Street in Boulder, Colorado). Stories relate Mork's attempts to learn about—and adjust to—life on Earth. See the following title also.

Mork	Robin Williams
Mindy McConnell	Pam Dawber
Fred McConnell	Conrad Janis
Cora Hudson	Elizabeth Kerr
Frank Bickley	Tom Poston
Remo DiVinci	Jay Thomas
Jeanie DiVinci	Gina Hecht
Nelson Flavor	Jim Staahl
Exidor	Robert Donner
Orson	Ralph James
Susan Taylor	Morgan Fairchild
Ambrosia Malspar	Georgia Engel
Cathy McConnell	Shelley Fabares
Glinda Comstock	Crissy Wilzak
Eugene	Jeffrey Jacquet
Miles Sternhagen	Foster Brooks
Daniel Pierson	Charles Bloom
Jack Loomis	Pat Cranshaw
Judy	Jillian Kessler
The Orkin Elder	Vidal Peterson
Mearth*	Jonathan Winters
Mrs. Flower	Priscilla Morrill
Lola	Amy Tenowich
Stephanie	Stephanie Kona
Billy	Corey Feldman

Producer: Garry K. Marshall, Tony Marshall

*The son of Mork and Mindy (who married on 10/5/81).

Mork and Mindy

Cartoon; 30 min; ABC 9/25/82 to 9/3/83

On orders from Orson, his superior on Ork, Mork and his Earthling friend, Mindy, enroll in Mt. Mount High School in an attempt to supply Orson with information about life on primitive Earth. The extension series relates Mork's adventures as he attempts to become a typical American high school kid.

Mork	Robin Williams
Mindy McConnell	Pam Dawber
Fred McConnell	Conrad Janis
Principal Carruthers	Stanley Jones
Orson	Ralph James
Eugene	Shavar Ross
Hamilton	Mark L. Taylor
Doing (Mork's pet)	Frank Welker

Producer: William Hanna, Joseph Barbera

Morning Court

A daily ABC series (10/10/60 to 5/12/61) of reenactments of actual courtroom cases. William Gwinn and Georgiana Hardy portray the judges.

The Morning Show

A daily syndicated (1969) program of music, talk and celebrity interviews with host Ed Nelson and regulars Rona Barrett, Dr. Julius Sumner Miller, and Mr. Blackwell.

Morning Star/Evening Star

Drama; 60 min; CBS 3/26/86 to 5/6/86

When a fire destroys the Morning Star children's orphanage, Debbie Flynn, manager of the Evening Star retirement home, arranges for the homeless orphans to remain with her senior citizens. Stories relate the heartwarming adventures shared by members of both generations.

Debbie Flynn	Sherry Hursey
Bob Lane (her	
assistant)	Darrell Larson
Binnie Byrd Baylor*	Sylvia Sidney
Bill MacGregor*	Jeff Corey

Kathy Kelly*	Elizabeth Wilson
Excell Dennis*	Scatman Crothers
Gordon Blair*	Mason Adams
Martha Cameron*	Kate Reid
Alice Blair*	Teresa Wright
Nora Blake*	Ketty Lester
Lisa Thurston**	Tammy Lauren
Sarah Bishop**	Missy Francis
Alan Bishop**	Fred A. Savage
Eugenia Waters**	Ebonie Smith
Doug Roberts**	Leaf Phoenix
Martin Palmer**	David Goldsmith
Kevin Murphy**	Chris Peters

Producer: Earl Hamner, Fred Silverman

*Senior citizens.

**Youngsters.

Moscow Bureau

Comedy Pilot; 30 min; ABC 6/6/86

The story, set in the U.S.S.R., relates the experiences of Christine Nichols, an American magazine reporter (for "News Today") assigned to the Moscow Bureau.

Chris Nichols	Caroline McWilliams
Herb Medlock	William Windom
Sasha Zhukov	Elya Basin
Connie Uecker	Nancy Lane
Tim Carmichael	Dennis Drake
Nigel Blake	Barrie Ingham

Producer: Paul Junger Witt, Tony Thomas

The Most Deadly Game

Crime Drama; 60 min; ABC 10/10/70 to 1/16/71

The exploits of a master criminologist (Ethan) and his proteges (Vanessa and Jonathan) as they attempt to solve crimes of the most deadly nature—murder. Originally titled "Zig Zag" and intended to star Inger Stevens.

Ethan Arcane	Ralph Bellamy
Vanessa Smith	Yvette Mimieux
Jonathan Croft	George Maharis

Producer: Aaron Spelling, Joan Harrison, Morton Fine, David Friedkin

Most Wanted

Crime Drama; 60 min; ABC 10/16/76 to 4/4/77

The exploits of the Most Wanted Unit, an elite law enforcement division of the L.A.P.D. that is designed to apprehend criminals on the most wanted list.

Capt. Lincoln Evers	Robert Stack
Sgt. Charlie Nelson	Shelly Novack
Off. Kate Manners	Jo Ann Harris
Mayor Dan Stoddard	Harry Rhodes
Off. Lee Herrick	Leslie Charleson*
Off. Tom Roybo	Tom Selleck*

Producer: Quinn Martin

*"Most Wanted" TV Movie roles (ABC 3/21/76).

Mother and Me, M.D.

Comedy Pilot; 30 min; NBC 6/14/79

The story of Barrie Tucker, a young female doctor, as she begins her internship in a New York hospital where her mother, Lil, works as the head nurse.

Barrie Tucker	Leah Ayres
Lil Brenner	Rue McClanahan
Evan Murray	Jack Riley
Dr. Mace Oatfield	Ken Gilman
Dr. Sam Kanin	Howard Witt

Producer: Michael Zinberg

Mother, Juggs, and Speed

Comedy Pilot; 30 min; ABC 8/17/78

The story of Mother, a hard-drinking driver; Juggs, a beautiful and very well endowed doctor; and Speed, an embittered ex-cop; three paramedics who work for Harry Fishbine, the greedy owner of the near-bankrupt F&B Private Ambulance Company. Based on the feature film.

Mother	Ray Vitte
Juggs	Joanne Nail
Speed	Joe Penny
Harry Fishbine	Harvey Lembeck
Mrs. Fishbine	Barbara Minkus
Whiplash Moran	Shay Duffin
Murdock	Rod McCary

Producer: John Rich

Mothers Day

Game: 30 min; ABC 10/13/58 to 1/2/59

Three mothers compete in various games based on the operation of a household. The most successful player is crowned "Mother for a Day" and awarded prizes.

Host: Dick Van Dyke

Co-Hostess: Dotty Mack, Betty Anders

Producer: Carl Jampel

The Mothers-in-Law

Comedy; 30 min; NBC 9/10/67 to 9/7/69

When Susie Hubbard and Jerry Buell, neighbors and sweethearts since childhood, decide to marry, it has a common effect on their mothers: both Eve (Susie's mother) and Kaye (Jerry's mother) become meddlesome in-laws. Stories relate Susie and Jerry's struggles as newlyweds and their efforts to cope with their mothers constant intervention into their lives.

Eve Hubbard	Eve Arden
Kaye Buell	Kaye Ballard
Herb Hubbard	Herbert Rudley
Roger Buell	Roger C. Carmel
	Richard Deacon
Susie Hubbard-Buell	Kay Cole*
	Deborah Walley
Jerry Hubbard	Jerry Fogel
Dr. Butler	Herbert Voland
Raphael del Gado	Desi Arnaz

Music: Wilbur Hatch

Producer: Desi Arnaz, Elliott Lewis

*Susie in the never-telecast, CBS pilot version of the series.

Motor Mouse

Cartoon; 30 min; ABC 9/12/70 to 9/4/71

A spin-off from "The Cattanooga Cats." The endless efforts of Auto Cat to beat Motor Mouse in a car race.

Auto Cat	Marty Ingels
Motor Mouse	Dick Curtis

Producer: William Hanna, Joseph Barbera

The Motorola Television Hour

Anthology; 60 min; CBS 11/3/53 to 5/18/54

A series of live dramas from New York. Sponsored by the Motorola Corporation. Produced by Herbert Brodkin.

Motown Revue

Music; 60 min; NBC 8/9/85 to 9/13/85

A five-part series that salutes Detroit performers and the hit songs of the 60s, 70s, and 80s.

Host: Smokey Robinson

Regulars: Arsenio Hall, Leo O'Brien, The Hitsville Gang Dancers

Music: Bruce Miller

Producer: Robert Illes, James Stein, Steve Binder

The Mouse Factory

Children; 30 min; Syn. 9/72

Guest celebrities, assisted by the use of clips from various Disney films, attempt to explain aspects of the world to children.

Included Guests: Annette Funicello, Jo Anne Worley, Jonathan Winters, John Astin, Pat Buttram, Pat Paulsen, Joe Flynn, Johnny Brown, Wally Cox

Producer: Ward Kimball

The Movie Game

Game; 30 min; Syn. 1969

Object: For players to answer questions based on films and film stars.

Host: Sonny Fox, Larry Blyden

Assistant: Army Archerd

Announcer: Johnny Gilbert

Movie Museum

A syndicated (1954) series that features screenings of theatrical comedy shorts of the 1920s, 30s, and 40s. Produced by Paul Killiam, who also serves as the curator of the Movie Museum.

Movieland Quiz

Game; 30 min; ABC 8/19/48 to 10/26/48

Object: For players to identify stars and titles of old films from selected scenes.

Host: Arthur Q. Bryan, Ralph Dumke

Co-Hostess: Patricia Bright

Producer: Lester Lewis

Movin' On

Adventure Pilot; 65 min; NBC 7/24/72

Possessing a common goal to see America, a stock car racer (Clint) and a cycle racer (Johnny) pool their resources and begin their quest. The unsold series was to relate their experiences.

Clint Daniels	Patrick Wayne
Johnny Lake	Geoffrey Deuel
Cory	Kate Jackson
Jeff	David Soul
Mrs. Lake	Meg Wyllie
Clint's father	Walter Barnes

Producer: Douglas S. Cramer, Jerome Courtland

Movin' On

Drama; 60 min; NBC 9/12/74 to 9/14/76

The adventures of two gypsy truck drivers: Sonny Pruitt, a tough, uneducated veteran; and his partner, Will Chandler, a rebellious, college-educated youth who is seeking to discover how the other half lives.

Sonny Pruitt	Claude Akins
Will Chandler	Frank Converse
Benjy (trucker)	Rosey Grier
Moose (trucker)	Art Metrano
Myrna (Sonny's girlfriend)	Janis Hansen
Betty (Will's girlfriend)	Ann Coleman

Theme Vocal ("Movin' On"): Merle Haggard

Producer: Barry Whitz, Philip D'Antoni, Ernie Frankel

Mr. Adams and Eve

Comedy; 30 min; CBS 1/4/57 to 9/23/58

The home and working lives of Howard Adams and Eve Drake, a happily married show business couple.

Howard Adams	Howard Duff
Eve Adams	Ida Lupino
J.B. Hafter (producer)	Alan Reed
Steve (agent)	Hayden Rorke
Elsie Carstairs (housekeeper)	Olive Carey
Walter (Elsie's nephew)	Patrick Wayne
Director	Larry Dobkin
Slate Boy	Alan Wood
Assistant Director	Paul Grant

Producer: Collier Young, Howard Duff, William Webb, Fred DeCordova

Mr. & Mrs. & Mr.

Comedy Pilot; 30 min; CBS 9/1/80

A year after her husband (Jimmy) was reported killed in a plane crash in the Caribbean, a widow (Jenny) marries a sportswriter (Jeff). Shortly after, Jimmy, who was found by an Indian fisherman and nursed back to health, appears at Jenny's home. The unsold series was to focus on the problems that exist as Jenny, now with two husband's who both claim she is his wife, desperately seeks a way to resolve the situation and live a normal, happily married life—with one husband.

Jenny Collins	Rebecca Balding
Jimmy York	Kale Browne
Jeff Zelinka	Patrick Collins
Susan Masters (Jenny's friend)	Eda Zahl

Theme Vocal ("Mr. & Mrs. & Mr."): Joanie Sommers

Producer: Hal Cooper, Rod Parker

Mr. and Mrs. Carroll

Variety; 15 min; DuMont 10/18/50 to 4/13/51

Music, songs, and chatter with Jimmy and Rita Carroll.

Mr. and Mrs. Cop

Crime Drama Pilot; 30 min; CBS 5/3/74

A would-be series about a newlywed couple's adjustment to marriage, made more difficult by their jobs as police officers.

Off. Paul Roscommon	Anthony Costello
Off. Nancy Roscommon	Marianne McAndrew
Lt. Ocala	Richard Angarola
Sgt. Baum	William Campbell
Off. Irv Pyle	Redmond Gleeson
Albanel	Max Gail
Chester	Howard Platt
Al Johnson	Tom Falk

Music: Peter Matz

Producer: Leonard B. Kaufman

Mr. and Mrs. Dracula

Comedy Pilot; 30 min; ABC 9/5/80

After 618 years of marriage, vampire Vladimir Dracula, his wife, Sonia, and their children Minna and Sonny, decide to leave Transylvania and relocate to the Bronx (N.Y.) when angry villagers force them from their castle. The unsold series was to relate a vampire family's adventures in a new homeland.

Vladimir Dracula	Dick Shawn
Sonia Dracula	Carol Lawrence
Minna Dracula	Gail Mayron
Sonny Dracula	Anthony Battaglia
Voice of Gregor the Bat	Johnny Haymer
Cousin Anton	Barry Gordon
Mario	Rick Aviles

Producer: Robert Klane

Mr. and Mrs. Mystery

Crime Drama; 15 min; Syn. 1949

The exploits of a New York criminologist (John Gay) and his unofficial assistant, his wife, Barbara.

John Gay	Himself
Barbara Gay	Herself

Mr. and Mrs. North

Crime Drama Pilot; 30 min; NBC 7/4/49

The story of Jerry North, a private detective turned publisher, and his wife, Barbara, and their attempts to solve crimes. See the following title also.

Jerry North	Joseph Allen
Pamela North	Mary Lou Taylor

Producer: John W. Loveton

Mr. and Mrs. North

Crime Drama; 30 min; CBS 10/3/52 to 9/25/53
                        NBC   1/26/54   to
                        7/20/54

An adaptation of the Frances and Richard Lockridge stories about Jerry North, a private detective turned publisher, and his wife, Barbara, a level-headed woman with a knack for stumbling upon crimes.

Jerry North	Richard Denning
Pamela North	Barbara Britton
Lt. Bill Weingard	Francis DeSales

Producer: John W. Loveton, Bernard L. Schubert

Mr. and Mrs. Ryan

Comedy-Drama Pilot; 60 min; ABC 4/12/86

Shortly after she is rescued from kidnappers, Ashley Hamilton, a Beverly Hills socialite, marries the man who saved her life, L.A. police lieutenant Michael Ryan. The unsold series was to focus on Ashely's misadventures as she attempts to help Michael solve crimes.

Ashley Hamilton- Ryan	Sharon Stone
Lt. Michael Ryan	Robert Desiderio
Stockwell	Joseph Maher
Margo Slater	Christine Belford
Kolvak	Nicholas Worth
Beckerman	Frederick Coffin
Sloan	Walter Dalton

Producer: Aaron Spelling, Douglas S. Cramer, E. Duke Vincent

Mr. and Ms.

Crime Drama Pilot: 90 min; ABC 12/16/75

The exploits of David and Mandy Robbins, a husband-and-wife private detective team. In the first pilot (see next title), titled "The Magic Studio Mystery," David and Mandy seek the killer of a young woman found dead in a magician's trick iron maiden.

David Robbins	John Rubinstein
Mandy Robbins	Lee Kroeger
Lt. Ben Robbins	Milton Selzer
Sally	Angela Cartwright
Barbara	Udana Power
Bob	Rod Browning
Herb	Darrell Fetty

Producer: Dick Clark

Mr. and Ms.

Crime Drama Pilot; 90 min; ABC 12/23/75

The second of two pilots about David and Mandy Robbins, a husband-and-wife private detective team. In the second story (see prior title), titled "The Bandstand Murders," David and Mandy investigate the death of a British rock star.

David Robbins	John Rubinstein
Mandy Robbins	Lee Kroeger
Lt. Ben Robbins	Milton Selzer
Dick Clark	Himself
Dottie	Lezlie Dalton
Betty	Vicky Huxtable
Harry	Casey Kasem
Byron	Marc Alaimo

Producer: Dick Clark

Mr. Arsenic

Anthology; 30 min; ABC 5/8/52 to 6/26/52

Dramas based on actual criminal cases.

Host: Burton Turkus

Producer: Jerry Layton

Mr. Belvedere

Comedy Pilot; 30 min; CBS 7/12/65

The story of Lynn Belvedere, man-about-town and master of various arts, crafts, and professions, who involves himself in other people's lives.

Lynn Belvedere	Victor Borge
Lily Van Cleve	Debbie Paine
Mr. Van Cleve	Leland Howard
Mrs. Van Cleve	Louise Troy
Harry	Harry Bellaver
Miss Briggs	Pamela Truman
Mooney	Martin Brill

Producer: Richard Sale

Mr. Belvedere

Comedy; 30 min; ABC 3/15/85 (Premiere)

Humorous events in the lives of the Owens, a chaotic but otherwise typical American family that is presided over by Lynn Belvedere, an upper crust British butler known for his culinary expertise and ability to handle any family—even the Owens.

Lynn Belvedere	Christopher Hewett
Marsha Owens	Ilene Graff
George Owens	George Uecker
Heather Owens	Tracy Wells
Kevin Owens	Rob Stone
Wesley Owens	Brice Beckham
Jennifer Simpson	Tricia Cast
Angela	Michele Matheson

Producer: Frank Dungan, Jeff Stein, Tony Sheehan

Mr. Bevis

Fantasy Pilot; 30 min; CBS 6/3/60

The story of James Bevis, an eccentric young man who is loved by everyone and watched over by J. Hardy Hempstead, his guardian angel. Broadcast as a segment of "The Twilight Zone," although it was originally written as the pilot for a series.

James Bevis	Orson Bean
J. Hardy Hempstead	Henry Jones
Mr. Peckinpaugh	Charles Lane
Policeman	William Schallert
Bartender	Horace McMahon
Landlady	Dorothy Neuman
Young lady	Colleen O'Sullivan

Producer: Buck Houghton.

Mr. Bill's Real Life Adventures

Comedy Pilot; 30 min; SHO 9/11/86

The adventures of the inches-tall Mr. Bill, a down-trodden clay figure living in his own world and falling prey to countless pit falls. Based on "Saturday Night Live" sketches.

Mr. Bill	Peter Scolari
Mr. Sluggo	Mike McManus

Producer: Shelley Duvall

Mr. Black

Anthology; 30 min; ABC 9/19/49 to 11/7/49

Mystery and suspense productions in which the "bad guys" get their just deserts.

Mr. Black (Host)	Anthony Christopher

Producer: Tony Rizzo

Mr. Boogedy

Comedy Pilot; 60 min; ABC 4/20/86

In the 1600s, a small group of pilgrims settle in a section of New England they name Lucifer Falls. William Hanover, an outcast member who delights in scaring children (thus named Mr. Boogedy) falls in love with Marion, a widow who refuses his marriage proposal. Hoping to acquire Marion's love, Hanover sells his soul to the Devil in return for a magic cape. The cape, however, fails to grant Hanover's desire and instead destroys him and his house in an explosion. Hanover, now disfigured, remains on his property, destined to haunt it forever.

More than 300 years later (1986), Carlton Davis, a novelty salesman for Gag City, and his family move into a house that was constructed on the original Hanover land. They encounter the wrath of the spirit of Mr. Boogedy. The unsold series was to relate the Davises efforts enjoy their home and find a way to rid their lives of the practical joke-playing Mr. Boogedy.

Carlton Davis	Richard Masur
Eloise Davis	Mimi Kennedy
Jennifer Davis	Kristy Swanson
Ahri Davis	Benjamin Gregory
Corwin Davis	David Faustino
Mr. Boogedy	Howard Witt
Neil Witherspoon	John Astin
Widow Marion	Kelly Lang

Producer: Ed Lahti, Steven North

Mr. Broadway

Drama; 60 min; CBS 9/26/64 to 12/26/64

Events in the life of Michael Bell, a sophisticated Broadway press agent and the owner of a public relations firm (Michael Bell & Associates) in New York City.

Michael Bell	Craig Stevens
Hank McClure	Horace McMahon
Toki	Lani Miyazaki

Producer: David Susskind, Dan Melnick

Mr. Chips

Instruction; 30 min; Syn. 1975

Home repairs and advice with Bill Brown ("Mr. Chips, the Do-It-Yourselfer") and host Don Megowan. Produced by Don Forsythe and Lou Albert.

Mr. Citizen

Anthology; 30 min; ABC 4/20/55 to 7/13/55

Dramas that detail the unselfish acts of ordinary people. The person whose story is selected receives the "Mr. Citizen" award.

Host: Allyn Edwards

Awards Presenter: Clifford Chase

Music: John Gart

Mr. Deeds Goes to Town

Comedy; 30 min; ABC 9/26/69 to 1/16/70

Following the death of his Uncle Alonzo, Longfellow Deeds, a simple country gentleman, inherits the multi-million dollar Deeds Enterprises in New York City. Stories relate Longfellow's efforts to run his corporation as he feels it should—to help people, not take advantage of them.

Longfellow Deeds	Monte Markham
Tony Lawrence	Pat Harrington Jr.
Henry Masterson	Herbert Voland
George	Ivor Barry

Producer: Harry Ackerman, E.W. Swackhamer

Mr. District Attorney

Crime Drama; 30 min; Syn. 1951

Case dramatizations based on the files of the District Attorney's office as seen through the investigations of Paul Garrett, alias Mr. District Attorney, the "champion of the people, defender of truth, and guardian of our fundamental rights to life, liberty, and the pursuit of happiness."

Paul Garrett	Jay Jostyn
	David Brian
Edith Miller	Vicki Vola
	Jackie Loughery
Harrington	Len Doyle

Announcer: Fred Uttal

Producer: Edward Byron

Mr. Dugan

Comedy; 30 min; CBS Unaired (Produced in 1979)

An unaired series (but scheduled to run in March of 1979) about Matthew Dugan, a fledging black congressman. When pre-screening outrages by black officials found the program to be offensive, Norman Lear withdrew the three taped episodes and re-worked the idea as "Hanging In" (which see).

Matthew Dugan	Cleavon Little
Maggie Gallagher	Barbara Rhoades
Sam Dickey	Dennis Burkley
Pinkie Nolan	Nedra Volz
Aretha Balducci	Sarina Grant

Producer: Norman Lear

Mr. Ed

Comedy; 30 min; Syn. 1960 to 1961
CBS 10/1/61 to 9/4/66

Shortly after moving into their new Los Angeles home, newlyweds Wilbur and Carol Post find an unexpected resident in the barn—a horse (named Mr. Ed) left by the previous owner. Later, Wilbur discovers that Mr. Ed possesses the ability to speak; and because Wilbur is the only human he likes well enough to talk to, he will talk only to him. Stories relate Wilbur's misadventures as the owner of a talking horse. See the following title also.

Wilbur Post	Alan Young
Carol Post	Connie Hines
Mr. Ed's Voice	Allan "Rocky" Lane
Roger Addison	Larry Keating
Kay Addison	Edna Skinner
Gordon Kirkwood	Leon Ames
Winnie Kirkwood	Florence MacMichael
Paul Fenton	Jack Albertson
Mr. Carlisle	Barry Kelly
Dr. Baker	Richard Deacon

Producer: Al Simon, Arthur Lubin

Mr. Ed (The Wonderful World of Wilbur Pope)

Comedy Pilot; 30 min; Unaired (Produced in 1960)

The original pilot for "Mr. Ed" that relates how Wilbur and Carlotta Pope acquire a talking horse (see above title).

Wilbur Pope	Scott McKay
Carlotta Pope	Sandra White
Mr. Ed's Voice	Allan "Rocky" Lane
Florence Reese	Peggy Converse
John Reese	Ray Walker

Producer: Arthur Lubin, William Burns

Mr. Garlund

Drama; 60 min; CBS 10/7/60 to 1/13/61

An apparently orphaned boy is taken in and raised by a Chinese gentleman named Po Chang. The boy, named Frank Garlund and whose ancestry remains a mystery, becomes, by age thirty, a financial wizard; a youthful tycoon who is also a key figure in worldwide business affairs. In flashback sequences, events in the lives of the people who had come in contact with Garlund in his struggle to reach the top are dramatized. Also titled "The Garlund Touch."

Frank Garlund	Charles Quinlivan
Po Chang	Philip Ahn
Kam Chang	Kam Tong

Producer: Bernard Girard

Mr. Glencannon Takes All

Adventure Pilot; 30 min; ABC 4/19/53

The exploits of Colin Glencannon, the skipper of the freighter "Inchcliff Castle." Based on the stories by Guy Gilpatric. See also "Glencannon."

Colin Glencannon	Robert Newton

Also: Melville Cooper, Myron McCormick

Producer: Herbert Brodkin

Mr. I. Magination

Children; 30 min; CBS 4/24/49 to 6/28/52

The series, set in the magical kingdom of Imagination Town, relates music, stories and dramatizations of past historical events.

Mr. I. Magination	Paul Tripp

Regulars: Ruth Enders, Ted Tiller, Donald Devlin, David McKay, Johnny Stewart, Robin Morgan, Richard Boone, Clifford Sales

Organist: David Roberts

Orchestra: Ray Carter

Producer: Worthington Miner, Norman Pincus, Irving Pincus

Mr. Lucky

Adventure; 30 min; CBS 10/24/59 to 9/10/60

The story of Mr. Lucky, a gambler and owner of the Fortuna, a fancy supper club and gambling yacht docked in Los Angeles. After fifteen episodes, the format changed to depict Lucky's adventures as the owner of a floating night club when he coverts the Fortuna.

Mr. Lucky	John Vivyan
Andamo	Ross Martin
Maggie Shank Rutherford	Pippa Scott
Lt. Rovacs	Tom Brown
Fortuna Maitre d'	Joe Scott
Police Captain	Paul Genge

Theme Song ("Mr. Lucky"): Henry Mancini

Producer: Gordon Oliver, Jack Arnold

Mr. Magoo

Cartoon; 5 min; Syn. 1963

The misadventures of the near-sighted Quincy Magoo

Quincy Magoo	Jim Backus
Charlie and Prezley	Jerry Hansen
Uncle Waldo	Daws Butler

Producer: John Hubley, Henry Saperstein, Glen Heisch

Mr. Mayor

Children; 60 min; CBS 9/20/64 to 9/18/65

Various aspects of the adult world are explained to children via the activities of a kindhearted mayor.

Mr. Mayor	Bob Keeshan
Miss Melissa/Aunt Maude	Jane Connell
Dudley and Herman	Bill McCutcheon
Rollo and Russell	Cosmo Allegretti

Producer: Dave Connell, Al Hyslop

Mr. Merlin

Comedy; 30 min; CBS 10/7/81 to 8/18/82

After a 1600 year absence, Merlin Silvestra (alias Merlin the Magician) reappears in modern-day San Francisco as Max Merlin, the owner of a garage. Because he has fallen behind in his performance of good deeds, Merlin is ordered to find an apprentice and teach him the art of sorcery. When an awkward, girl-crazy teenager (Zach) responds to his help wanted ad, Merlin chooses him as his apprentice*. Stories relate their efforts to help people in distress.

Max Merlin	Barnard Hughes
Alexandra	Elaine Joyce
Zach Rogers	Clark Brandon
Leo Samuels	Jonathan Prince
Laurie	Mickie MacKenzie
Elizabeth Rogers	Betty Garrett

Producer: Larry Rosen, Larry Tucker

*When Zach pulls a crowbar out of a block of cement (like King Arthur and his Excalibar Sword) it is destined that he become the sorcerer's apprentice.

Mr. Mom

Comedy Pilot; 30 min; ABC 11/30/84

When Jack Butler, an automotive engineer is laid off from work, his wife, Caroline finds a job as an advertising executive. The unsold series was to relate Jack's misadventures as he assumes the household duties, including raising three children (Curtis, Kenny, and Megan).

Jack Butler	Barry Van Dyke
Caroline Butler	Rebecca York
Curtis Butler	Brendon Blincoe
Kenny Butler	Sean deVeritch
Megan Butler	Heidi Zeigler
Joan Hampton (neighbor)	Phyllis Davis

Theme Vocal: Gary Portnoy, Judy Hart Angelo

Producer: Frank Dugan, Jeff Stein, Patricia Rickey

Mr. Moon's Magic Circus

Variety; 30 min; Syn. 9/82

The series is set at Mr. Moon's Magic Circus where the antics of the performers is presented.

Mr. Moon	John Sarantos
Cosmos	Mark Ganzel
Tanzy	Marilyn Magness
Barnaby	Hank Adams
Fatima	Marcia Lewis
Stan	Chuck Quinlon

Producer: Sandra Turbow, Herb Silvers

Mr. Novak

Drama; 60 min; NBC 9/24/63 to 8/31/65

Incidents in the lives of the students and teachers of the Los Angeles-based Jefferson High School as seen through the eyes of John Novak, an English instructor.

John Novak	James Franciscus
Principal Albert Vane	Dean Jagger
Vice Principal Jean Pagano	Jeanne Bal
Principal Martin Woodbridge	Burgess Meredith
Ruth Wilkinson (girl's vice principal)	Phyllis Avery
Rosemary Dorsey (secretary)	Marjorie Corley
Paul Webb*	David Sheiner

Mr. Peeples*	Stephen Roberts
Marilyn Scott*	Marian Collier
Peter Butler*	Vince Howard
Mr. Parkson*	Peter Hanson
Mrs. Vreeland*	Anne Seymour
Ann Floyd*	Kathleen Ellis
Mr. Galo*	Donald Barry
Jerry Allen*	Steve Franken
Jim Hendrix*	Larry Thor
Julie Dean**	Kim Darby
George**	Tony Dow
Gail Andrews**	Marta Kristen
Cathy Williams**	Noreen Corcoran
Alfreida 'Chalky' White**	Heather Angel
Shirley Whittier**	Brooke Bundy
Pat Knowland**	Beau Bridges
Sue Johnson**	Brenda Scott
Gloria**	Patricia Morrow
Dani Cooper**	Shelley Fabares
Holly Metcalfe**	Joey Heatherton

Theme Song ("Theme from Mr. Novak"): Lyn Murray

Producer: E. Jack Neuman, Joseph Calvelli, William Froug, John T. Dugan

*Teachers.
**Students.

Mr. O'Malley

Comedy Pilot; 30 min; CBS 12/20/59

When a six-year-old boy (Barnaby) wishes upon a star for a fairy godmother who can make his dreams come true, he is answered by O'Malley, a cigar-smoking, jovial, pink-winged fairy godfather. The unsold series was to relate O'Malley's adventures as the fairy godfather to a young boy.

Mr. O'Malley	Bert Lahr
Barnaby Baxter	Ron Howard
Alice Baxter	June Dayton
George Baxter	William Redfield
Leprechaun Voice	Mel Blanc
Janie	Debbie Megowan
Dr. Harvey	Don Beddoe

Producer: Stanley Rubin

Mr. Peepers

Comedy; 30 min; NBC 7/3/52 to 6/12/55

The simple pleasures and trying times of Robinson J. Peepers, a timid and mild-mannered Biology instructor at Jefferson Junior High School in Jefferson City.

Robinson J. Peepers	Wally Cox
Harvey Weskitt	Tony Randall
Royala Dean	Norma Crane
Nancy Remington	Patricia Benoit
Marge Weskitt	Georgann Johnson
Principal Gabriel Gurney	Joseph Foley
Principal Bascomb (later)	Gage Clark
Mrs. Gurney	Marion Lorne
Mr. Remington	Ernest Truex
Mrs. Remington	Sylvia Field
Agnes Peepers	Jenny Egan
Robinson's mother	Ruth McDevitt

Producer: Fred Coe, Hal Keith

Mr. President

Comedy; 30 min; FOX 5/3/87 (Premiere)

The story of a former Wisconsin governor (Sam Tresch) who runs for and is elected President of the U.S. Stories focus on the efforts of America's newest First Family to adjust to a life that is more public than private. Created by Johnny Carson and Gene Reynolds.

Sam Tresch	George C. Scott
Meg Tresch (his wife)	Carlin Glynn
Cynthia Tresch (daughter)	Maddie Corman
Nick Tresch (son)	Andre Gower
Jennifer (married daughter)	Susan Wheeler Duff
Fred (Jennifer's husband)	Daniel McDonald
Charley Ross (Sam's aide)	Conrad Bain

Producer: Gene Reynolds

Mr. Roberts

Comedy-Drama; 30 min; NBC 9/17/65 to 9/2/66

The series is set in the South Pacific during World War II. The story of Douglas Roberts, cargo officer of the "Reluctant," A U.S. Navy ship nicknamed "The Bucket," as he seeks a transfer to a fighting vessel. Through Robert's continual attempts to convince his captain that he is worthy of the transfer, a rarely seen sentimental picture of the war is presented.

Lt. Douglas Roberts	Roger Smith
Capt. John Morton	Richard X. Slattery
Ensign Frank Pulver	Steve Harmon
Doc (the physician)	George Ives
Seaman D'Angelo	Richard Sinatra
Seaman Mannion	Ronald Starr
Seaman Reber	Roy Reese
Adm. Weatherby	Barry Kelly

Producer: James Komack

Mr. Smith

Comedy; 30 min; NBC 9/23/83 to 12/16/83

When two orangutans are found wandering on the road, the humane society captures one of them (Cha Cha) and sends it to a government research center in Washington, D.C. Shortly after, Cha Cha escapes from his cage and drinks a chemical solution that is designed to increase human intelligence. Suddenly, Cha Cha is able to talk and is found to possess an IQ of 256. He is named Mr. Smith and made a government consultant. Stories relate Mr. Smith's adventures as he attempts to become human.

Raymond Holyoke (Mr. Smith's secretary)	Leonard Frey
Tommy Atwood (Cha Cha's owner)	Tim Dunigan
Ellie Atwood (Tommy's sister)	Laura Jacoby
Dr. Judy Tyson	Terri Garber
Dr. Tracy Randolph	Lauren Chase
Dr. Kline	Stuart Margolin
Mr. Smith's Voice	Ed Weinberger
Mr. Smith	C.J.

Music: Patrick Williams

Producer: Ed Weinberger, Stan Daniels

Mr. Smith Goes to Washington

Comedy; 30 min; ABC 9/29/62 to 3/30/63

Following the death of a senator, a country politician named Eugene Smith is elected to replace in. Stories relate Smith's efforts to adjust to the norms of Capitol life in Washington, D.C. Based on the feature film.

Eugene Smith	Fess Parker
Patricia Smith	Sandra Warner
Uncle Cooter Smith	Red Foley
Miss Kelly	Rita Lynn
Arnie	Stan Irwin

Theme Song ("Mr. Smith Goes to Washington"): Hal Stanley, Irving Taylor

Producer: Hal Stanley

Mr. Success

Comedy Pilot; 30 min; NBC 6/23/84

The misadventures of Vernon Silt, the hapless manager of the complaint department of Dorfman's Department Store.

Vernon Silt	James Coco
Helen Silt	Miriam Flynn
Libby Silt	Viveka Davis
Andy Silt	Pat Cochran
Lonnie Barst	Murphy Dunne
Louise	Patsy Pease
Marie	Ivana Moore
Lara	Jennifer Savadge

Theme Vocal ("Mr. Success"): James Coco

Producer: Ian Praiser, Howard Gewirtz

Mr. Sunshine

Comedy; 30 min; ABC 3/28/86 to 9/10/86

The story of Paul Stark, an acerbic English professor at Kenyon College, who uses dry wit and fast thinking to deal with life after an accident cost him his sight.

Prof. Paul Stark	Jeffrey Tambor
June Swinford	Barbara Babcock
Grace D'Angelo	Nan Martin
Janice Hall	Cecila Hart
Gary Franz	Brian Benben
Leon Walters	Leonard Frey
Warren Leftwich	David Knell
Jane Patrick	Molly Hagan
Dean Woodman	Werner Klemperer
Woodman's secretary	Annie Gager
Chris Stark	John P. Navin Jr.
Ellen Stark	Patricia McCormack

Producer: John Rich, Henry Winkler

Mr. T

Cartoon; 30 min; NBC 9/17/83 to 9/6/86

The adventures of Mr. T as the coach of a U.S. gymnastics team (Kim, Robin, Spike, Jeff, Woody, and Toby) that battles evil at various meets around the world. Programs are designed to teach children to believe in themselves.

Mr. T	Mr. T (Lawrence Tero)

Voices: Amy Linker, Philip LaMar, Siu Ming, Shawn Lieber, Ted Field III, Takayo Fischer

Producer: Joe Ruby, Ken Spears

Mr. T. and Tina

Comedy; 30 min; ABC 9/26/76 to 10/30/76

Following his move from Tokyo to Chicago to establish an American branch of Moyati Industries, Taro Takahashi hires Tina Kelly, a pretty, but dizzy American girl to care for his motherless children, Sachi and Aki. Stories relate Tina's misadventures as she cares for Sachi and Aki.

Taro Takahashi	Pat Morita
Tina Kelly	Susan Blanchard
Sachi Takahashi	June Angela
Aki Takahashi	Gene Profanata
Uncle Mitsu	Jerry Hatsuo Fujikawa
Michi	Pat Suzuki
Miss Llewellyn	Miriam Byrd-Nethery
Harvard	Ted Lange

Theme Music ("Chicago"): George Aliceson Tipton

Producer: James Komack, Madelyn Davis, Bob Carroll Jr.

Mr. Terrific

Comedy; 30 min; CBS 1/9/67 to 8/28/67

While experimenting with methods to cure the common cold, a government scientist discovers a power pill that produces incredible strength in animals, but makes the strongest of men quite ill. Faced with a problem, Barton J. Reed, the Bureau of Special Projects subchief, begins a search to find a human who can harness the pill's power. Stanley Beemish, co-owner of Hal and Stanley's Gas Station, is found to be the man the government is seeking. Seconds after taking the pill, Stanley is transformed into Mr. Terrific, an invincible crime fighter. Stories relate Stanley's exploits as a midadventure-prone super hero. See the following title also.

Stanley Beemish	Stephen Strimpell
Hal Walters	Dick Gautier
Barton J. Reed	John McGiver
Henley Trent	Paul Smith
Dr. Reynolds	Ned Glass
Hal's mother	Ellen Corby

"Mr. Terrific" Theme Song: Gerald Fried

Producer: David J. O'Connell

Mr. Terrific

Comedy Pilot; 30 min; Unaired (Produced in 1966)

The original pilot for the "Mr. Terrific" series. The pilot features Stanley as a clerk in a shoe store owned by Mr. Finney and becoming Mr. Terrific to work for the Office of Special Assignments. Gloria was seen as Stanley's girlfriend, and the Hal Walters role (Stanley's partner) was not a part of the show.

Stanley Beemish	Alan Young
The Chief	Edward Andrews
Gloria Dickinson	Sheila Wells
Mr. Finney	Jesse White
Tony Lawrence	Richard Merrifield

Producer: Edward J. Montagne

Mr. Tutt

Drama Pilot: 30 min; NBC 9/10/58

An adaptation of the Arthur Twain stories about the respected judge (Mr. Tutt) of a small-town in New York State. Aired as "Strange Counsel" on "Colgate Theatre."

Mr. Tutt	Walter Brennan
Olive	Olive Blakeney
Charlie	Harry Harvey Jr.
Judy Gregory	Vera Miles
Aunt Sarah	Geraldine Carr
Mrs. Phillips	Barbara Fuller
Nate Phillips	George Weise

Producer: Winston O'Keefe

Mr. Wizard

Educational; 30 min; NBC 3/5/51 to 9/6/65
9/11/71 to 9/2/72

The basis of various scientific principals are explained to children.

Host (Mr. Wizard): Don Herbert

Producer (1st series): James Pewolar

Producer (2nd series): Del Jack

Mrs. Columbo

Crime Drama; 60 min; NBC 2/26/79 to 9/6/79

The life of Kate Columbo, the pretty wife of TV's famed Lt. Columbo, as a journalist for the "Weekly Advertiser" in San Fernando, California. See also "Kate Loves a Mystery."

Kate Columbo	Kate Mulgrew
Jenny Columbo	Lili Haydn
Josh Alden	Henry Jones

Producer: James McAdams, David Levinson

Mrs. G. Goes to College

Comedy; 30 min; CBS 10/4/61 to 4/5/62

Seeking to fulfill a dream and acquire a college education, Sarah Green, a middle-aged widow, enrolls in an unidentified Southern California University. Stories relate Sarah's adventures as a college student.

Sarah Green	Gertrude Berg
Prof. Crayton	Sir Cedric Hardwicke
Maxfield	Mary Wickes
Joe Caldwell	Skip Ward
Susan	Marion Ross
Jerry	Leo Penn
George Howell	Paul Smith
Carol	Karyn Kupcinet

Producer: Hy Averback

M Squad

Crime Drama; 30 min; NBC 9/20/57 to 1/29/60

The exploits of Frank Ballinger, a special plainclothes detective with M Squad, a special division of the Chicago P.D. that investigates cases that surpass the requirements of systematic law-enforcement procedure.

Lt. Frank Ballinger	Lee Marvin
Capt. Grey	Paul Newlan

"M Squad" Theme Song: Count Basie

Producer: Richard Lewis, John Larkin

Ms. Fixer Upper

A syndicated (1980) insert series of one-and-a-half to three-and-a-half minute spots of home repair advice for women by a woman (Kay Arnold).

MTV Top 20 Video Countdown

Music; 60 min; Syn. 6/86

The program features a rundown of the week's (preceeding the broadcast) most popular music videos coupled with interviews with music stars and musicians. Surveys are based on the MTV (Music Television) cable channel.

Host: Marc Goodman

Producer: Julian Goldberg, Rene Garcia, John Norris

Muggsy

Drama; 30 min; NBC 9/11/76 to 4/9/77

Life in an unidentified inner city as seen through the eyes of Margaret "Muggsy" Malloy, a 13-year-old orphan, and her half-brother, Nick Malloy, a cab driver.

Margaret Malloy	Sarah MacDonnell
Nick Malloy	Ben Masters
Gus Gardician	Paul Michael
Clytemnestra	Star-Shemah
T.P.	Danny Cooper

Theme Vocal ("Keepin' It Together"): Blood, Sweat & Tears

Producer: George A. Heinemann

Mulligan's Stew

Drama; 60 min; NBC 10/25/77 to 12/13/77

Following the death of his sister and her husband in a plane crash, Mike Mulligan and his wife, Jane, take in his sister's children (Stevie, Adam, Polly, and Kimmy). Stories relate the efforts of the adopted children and Mike and Jane's natural children (Mark, Melinda, and

Jimmy) to accept and understand each other's differences.

Mike Mulligan	Lawrence Pressman
Jane Mulligan	Elinor Donahue
Mark Mulligan	Johnny Whitaker*
	Johnny Duran
Melinda Mulligan	Julie Anne Haddock
Jimmy Mulligan	K.C. Martel
Stevie Freeman	Suzanne Crough
Polly Freeman	Lory Kochheim
Kimmy Freeman	Sunshine Lee
Adam Freeman	Christopher Ciampa

Producer: Joanna Lee

*Role in the TV Movie (6/20/77).

The Munsters

Comedy; 30 min; CBS 9/24/64 to 9/8/66

Events in the lives of the Munsters, a family who resemble movie monsters: Herman (Frankenstein-like), a funeral director for Gateman, Goodbury, and Graves; Lily, his wife (vampire); Eddie, their son (werewolf); Count Dracula, Lily's father; and Marilyn, their poor, unfortunate niece, a beautiful young woman who is the black sheep of the family. See the following title also.

Herman Munster	Fred Gwynne
Lily Munster	Yvonne DeCarlo
Grandpa (Count	
Dracula)	Al Lewis
Marilyn Munster	Beverley Owen
	Pat Priest
	Debbie Watson*
	Jo McDonnell**
Eddie Munster	Butch Patrick
	K.C. Martel**
Mr. Gateman	John Carradine
Dr. Edward Dudley	Paul Lynde
	Dom DeLuise
Nurse Fairchild	Alice Backes
Lily's Uncle Gilbert	Richard Hale
Clyde Thorton	Chet Stratton

Theme Song ("At the Munsters"): Jack Marshall

Producer: Joe Connelly, Bob Mosher

*Role in the 1966 feature, "Munster, Go Home."
**Role in the TV Movie, "The Munsters' Revenge" (2/27/81).

The Munsters

Comedy Pilot; 30 min; Unaired (Produced in 1964).

The original color pilot for the above black and white series. The pilot episode, titled "My Fair Munster," was reshot and used as a part of the series with the new cast listed above.

Herman Munster	Fred Gwynne
Phoebe Munster	Joan Marshall
Grandpa	Al Lewis
Marilyn Munster	Beverley Owen
Eddie Munster	Happy Derman

Producer: Joe Connelly

Director: Norman Abbott

Writer: Norm Liebman, Ed Haas

The Muppet Show

Variety; 30 min; Syn. 1976 to 1981

Comedy skits that feature guest stars performing with the Muppets—the fanciful puppet creations of Jim Henson.

Kermit/Rowlf	Jim Henson
Miss Piggy/Fozzie	
Bear/Sam the	
Eagle	Frank Oz
Gonzo/Zoot/Bunsen/	
Beauregard	Dave Goelz
Sweetums/Scooter/	
Janis	Richard Hunt
Pops/Floyd	Jerry Nelson

"The Muppets Theme" Music: Sam Pottle

Orchestra: Jack Parnell

Producer: Jim Henson, David Lazer

Murder Ink

Mystery Pilot; 60 min; CBS 9/6/83

The adventures of Laura Ireland, an avid mystery fan and owner of a New York bookstore called Murder Ink, who helps her husband, a police detective, solve baffling crimes.

Laura Ireland   Tovah Feldshuh
Sgt. Lou Ireland   Daniel Hugh-Kelly
Sgt. Martin
  Wilkinson   Ron McLarty
Claire   Marcia Jean Kurtz
Hilly   Anna Maria
                                      Horsford
Ellen Gray   Ellen Barkin
Ray Stahlmeyer   Harris Laskaway
Pink Musso   Brent Collins

Producer: Charles Fries, Alan Sacks

Murder, She Wrote

Crime Drama; 60 min; CBS 9/30/84 (Premiere)

When a manuscript, written by Jessica Fletcher, a widow who lives in Cabot Cove, Maine, is submitted to Covington House Publishers in New York by her nephew (Grady), she suddenly finds herself in the limelight when the mystery becomes a best seller. Stories relate Jessica's efforts to solve baffling crimes.

Jessica Fletcher   Angela Lansbury
Sheriff Amos Tupper   Tom Bosley
Dr. Seth Hazlitt   William Windom
Ethan Cragg
  (Jessica's friend)   Claude Akins
Grady Fletcher*   Michael Horton
Carol Donovan*   Anne Kerry
Pamela Crane*   Belinda J.
                                  Montgomery
Nita Cochrane*   Alice Krige
Calhoun Fletcher*   Peter Bonerz
Jessica's Aunt
  Mildred   Penny Singleton
Jessica's Cousin
  Emma   Angela Lansbury
Carol Fletcher*   Courteney Cox
Neil Fletcher*   Jackie Cooper
Vickie Brand*   Genie Francis

Producer: Peter S. Fischer, Richard Levinson, William Link

*Featured relatives in Jessica's large family.

The Murdocks and the McClays

Comedy Pilot; 30 min; ABC 9/2/70

A hillbilly-accented comedy about a feud that exists between two families (the Murdocks and the McClays).

Angus McClay   Dub Taylor
Julianna McClay   Kathy Davis
Calvin Murdock   Noah Beery Jr.
Calvin Murdock Jr.   John David Carson
Grandpa Murdock   William Fawcett
Grandma Murdock   Nydia Westman
Sheriff Bates   James Westerfield
Turkey   George C. Fisher

Producer: Jerry Belson, Garry K. Marshall, Jerry Davis

Music Bingo

Game; 30 min; ABC 5/29/58 to 9/11/58
                 NBC 12/5/58 to 1/1/60

Object: For players to complete a Bingo board by identifying song titles from brief selections that are played by an orchestra.

Host: Johnny Gilbert

Orchestra: Harry Salter

Producer: Johnny Stearns

Music Central

Variety Pilot; 60 min; Syn. 8/81

A program of live performances by rock stars coupled with interviews and film clips of concerts.

Host: Dan Daniel

Guests: Olivia Newton-John, Deborah Harry, Pat Benatar, Paul Simon, Roberta Flack, Kim Carnes, George Benson

Producer: Jackie Barnett

Music City U.S.A.

A syndicated (1968) program of country and western music with hosts Jerry Naylor and Teddy Bart.

Music '55

Variety; 30 min; CBS 7/12/55 to 9/13/55

The program, presented as an intimate party, explores the various fields of music.

Host: Stan Kenton

Announcer: Stu Metz

Orchestra: Johnny Richards

Producer: Richard Lewine, Bob Bach

Music for a Spring Night

Variety; 60 min; ABC 3/30/60 to 5/4/60

A springtime series of music and songs.

Host: Glenn Osser

Featured: The Glenn Osser Singers and the Glenn Osser Orchestra

Producer: Frederick Heider

Music for a Summer Night

Variety; 60 min; ABC 6/3/59 to 9/21/59

A Summer series of music and songs with host Glenn Osser and his orchestra and chorus. Produced by Frederick Heider.

Music from the Meadowbrook

Variety; 60 min; ABC 5/23/53 to 9/26/53

Jimmy Blaine and Bill Williams host a program that features performances by orchestras from Frank Dailey's Meadowbrook in Cedar Grove, N.J.

Music Hall America

Variety; 60 min; Syn. 9/76

Performances by country and western entertainers.

Regulars: Sadi Burnett, Dean Rutherford, The Even Dozen

Orchestra: Bill Walker

Producer: Roy Smith

Music in Velvet

Variety; 30 min; ABC 1/16/49 to 10/28/51

A Chicago-based program of music and songs.

Host: Johnny Hill

Regulars: Don Lindley and the Velveteers

Orchestra: Rex Maupin

Producer: Ed Skotch

Music on Ice

Variety; 60 min; NBC 5/8/60 to 9/11/60

Music and songs set against the background of an ice show.

Host: Johnny Desmond, Jill Corey

Regulars: Jacqueline DuBief, The Dancing Blades, The Skip Jacks

Orchestra: Robert Boucher

Producer: George Charles

The Music Machine

Contest; 30 min; Syn. 4/87

Three aspiring entertainers compete in a challenge round by performing an original music video. A panel of three celebrity guests judge and score the video based on vocal ability and showmanship. The current winner and the week's prior winner compete against each other in the championship round. At the end of the season, a grand champion is chosen and receives an array of prizes.

Host: Curtis Gadson

Producer: Laurie Oberman, Curtis Gadson, Danny DiCarlo

The Music Maker

Drama Pilot; 30 min; NBC 1/24/63

An unsold series that was to focus on the experiences of Andy Ballard, a jazz musician. Aired as "Five, Six, Pick Up Sticks" on "Alcoa Premiere."

Andy Ballard	John Forsythe
Babe Simms	Mickey Rooney
Willy Simms	Barbara Nichols
Lorraine Gardner	Geraldine Brooks

Producer: Dick Berg

The Music Mart

Comedy Pilot; 30 min; NBC 2/8/80

Following their retirement from show business, Wally and Carol, a song and dance team, open a music store called Coogan's Music Mart. The unsold series was to relate their misadventures as they attempt to run a business.

Wally Coogan	Donald O'Connor
Carol Coogan	Gloria DeHaven
Scotty Coogan	Scotty Plummer
Lola	Mickie MacKenzie
Al Coody	Sidney Miller
Sister Hitchcock	Lucille Ball

Producer: Lucille Ball, Hal Kanter

The Music Scene

Variety; 45 min; ABC 9/22/69 to 1/12/70

Performances by the top artists in music. Broadcast back-to-back with "The New People" to form a 90-minute block.

Host: David Steinberg

Regulars: Lily Tomlin, Pat Williams, Paul Reid Roman, Larry Hankin

Orchestra: Patrick Williams

Producer: Ken Fritz, Stan Harris

The Music Shop

Variety; 30 min; NBC 1/11/59 to 3/8/59

Performances by the recording industry's top artists.

Host: Buddy Bregman

Orchestra: Buddy Bregman

Producer: Maurice Duke

The Music Show

Variety; 60 min; DuMont 5/19/53 to 10/17/54

An unsponsored, solid hour of music and songs from Chicago.

Host: Robert Trendler

Regulars: Mike Douglas, Jackie Van, Eleanor Warner, Henri Noel, Dolores Peterson

Orchestra: Robert Trendler

Producer: J. E. Faraghan

Music World

A syndicated (6/80) program of performances by country and western artists. Produced by Steven Rutt and Billy J. Rippy.

Musical Chairs

Game; 30 min; NBC 7/9/55 to 9/17/55

A vocal group presents a musically oriented question to three celebrity panelists. The first panelist who is able to give the correct answer by impersonating the original recording artist receives one point. The panelist with the highest scores wins a cash prize for a home viewer.

Host: Bill Leyden

Vocalists: The Cheerleaders

Panelists: Johnny Mercer, Mel Blanc, Bobby Troup

Orchestra: Bobby Troup

Musical Chairs

Game; 30 min; CBS 6/16/75 to 10/31/75

A song is stopped one line before its conclusion and three possible last lines are shown. Four players press a button and lock in their guess as to the correct last line. The correct line is revealed and a player scores money if he is correct.

Host: Adam Wade

Announcer: Pat Hernan

Orchestra: Derek Smith

Producer: Bill Chastain

Musical Comedy Time

Anthology; 30 min; NBC 10/2/50 to 3/19/51

Guests recreate great moments from hit Broadway musicals. Guests include Gloria DeHaven, Martha Raye, John Conte, John Riatt, Jackie Gleason, Nancy Walker, Billy Gilbert, Jack Gilford, Melville Cooper, Anne Jeffreys, Bert Lahr and John Conte.

Producer: Richard Berger, Bernard L. Schubert

Musical Merry-Go-Round

Variety; 20 min; NBC 7/25/47 to 3/11/49

Jack Kilty as the host of a live and recorded music program of performances by relatively unknown entertainers. Regulars are Eve Young, Penny Gerard, and Fred DeWilde.

My Boy Googie

Comedy Pilot; 30 min; CBS 7/24/67

The misadventures of Googie Wallace, a problem eight-year-old boy.

Bill Wallace (father)	Jerry Van Dyke
Kate Wallace (mother)	Jeanne Ranier
Googie Wallace	Teddy Eccles
Fannie Wallace (daughter)	Pamela Dapo
Mrs. Audobon	Alice Pearce

Producer: Herbert W. Browar

My Buddy

Comedy Pilot; 30 min; NBC 7/3/79

Following the death of a good friend, Woodrow "Buddy" Johnson, an average guy and owner of Buddy's Bar in San Francisco, suddenly becomes rich when he inherits the multi-million dollar Worth Enterprises. The unsold series was to relate Buddy's misadventures as he enters high society.

Buddy Johnson	Redd Foxx
Catherine Worth	Pamela Mason
Slappy	Slappy White
Butler	Basil Hoffman
Buddy's friend	Irwin C. Watson

Producer: Redd Foxx, Norman Hopps

My Darling Judge

Comedy Pilot; 30 min; CBS 4/23/61

The misadventures of Cyrus Dunn, a Beverly Hills judge.

Cyrus Dunn	Fred Clark
Betsy Dunn	Audrey Totter
Charlotte Dunn	Melinda Plowman
Leila Dunn	Anne Whitefield
Willie	Willie Tsang

Producer: Sidney Lanfield

My Favorite Husband

Comedy; 30 min; CBS 9/12/53 to 12/27/55

The trials and tribulations of the Coopers: George, a young bank executive, and Liz, his attractive but scatterbrained wife.

Liz Cooper	Joan Caulfield
	Vanessa Brown
George Cooper	Barry Nelson
Gilmore Cobb	Bob Sweeney
Myrna Cobb	Alexandra Talton

Announcer: Dick Joy

Producer: Edmund Hartmann, Norman Tokar

My Favorite Martian

Comedy; 30 min; CBS 9/23/63 to 9/4/66

While enroute to the office, "Los Angeles Sun" newspaper reporter Tim O'Hara witnesses the crash of a U.F.O. Investigating, he befriends its pilot, a professor of anthropology from Mars. Tim takes the marooned alien back to his apartment, where the Martian adopts the guise of Tim's Uncle Martin. Stories relate Martin's efforts to keep his true identity a secret while at the same time find the scarce items he needs to repair his craft and return home. See also "My Favorite Martians."

Martin O'Hara	Ray Walston
Tim O'Hara	Bill Bixby
Lorelei Brown	Pamela Britton
Det. Bill Brennan	Alan Hewitt
Annabell Brown	Ina Victor
Angela Brown	Ann Marshall
Harry Burns	J. Pat O'Malley
Police Captain	Roy Engle
Mr. Phelps	J. Edward McKinley
Lorelei's Niece Paula	Marlo Thomas
Tim's Cousin Harvey	Paul Smith
Lorelei's Brother Alvin	Gavin MacLeod

Producer: Jack Chertok

My Favorite Martians

Cartoon; 30 min; CBS 9/8/73 to 8/30/75

When a damaged spacecraft lands on Earth, its occupants (Uncle Martin, his nephew Andy, and their dog Oakie Doakie) are befriended by Tim O'Hara, a newspaper reporter, and his niece Katy. Tim shelters the

Martians at his home, but arouses the suspicions of a security officer (Bill) who seeks to uncover their secret. Stories relate Martin's efforts to adjust to Earth and find the materials he needs to repair his ship. A spin-off from "My Favorite Martian."

Uncle Martin	Jonathan Harris
Tim O'Hara	Lane Scheimer
Katy O'Hara	Jane Webb
Bill Brennan	Lane Scheimer
Lorelei Brown	Jane Webb
Andy and Brad	Edward Morris

Producer: Norm Prescott, Lou Scheimer

My Friend Flicka

Adventure; 30 min; CBS 2/10/56 to 9/23/59
ABC 9/30/59 to 12/31/63

In an attempt to teach his son, Ken, some responsibility, Rob McLaughlin, the owner of the Goose Bar Ranch in Coulee Springs, Wyoming (early 1900s) gives Ken, Flicka (Swedish for Little Girl), a recently captured black stallion. Stories relate the adventures shared by a boy and his horse.

Rob McLaughlin	Gene Evans
Nell McLaughlin	Anita Louise
Ken McLaughlin	Johnny Washbrook
Gus Broeberg	Frank Ferguson
Hildy Broeberg	Pamela Beaird
Sheriff Walt Downey	Hugh Sanders
	Sydney Mason
Sgt. Tim O'Gara	Tudor Owen
U.S. Marshal	Craig Duncan

Producer: Alan A. Armer, Peter Packer, Sam White

My Friend Irma

Comedy; 30 min; CBS 1/8/52 to 6/26/54

The misadventures of Irma Peterson, a beautiful but dumb blonde secretary (to attorney Milton J. Clyde), and her roommate Jane Stacey, a level-headed girl who is constantly plagued by Irma's scatterbrained antics. Stories focus primarily on their romantic heartaches: Irma and her impoverished boyfriend, Al (later, Joe), and Jane and her millionaire employer, Richard, an investment broker. One year later, when Jane is transferred to Panama, Irma acquires a new roommate, Kay

Foster, a reporter for the New York "Chronicle" (who is in love with the paper's city editor, Brad Jackson). Stories continue to relate Irma's antics.

Irma Peterson	Marie Wilson
Jane Stacey	Cathy Lewis
Kay Foster	Mary Shipp
Richard Rhinelander III	Brooks West
Al	Sid Tomack
Joe Vance	Hal March
Brad Jackson	Gerald Mohr
Milton J. Clyde	Donald MacBride
Mrs. O'Reilly	Gloria Gordon
Prof. Kropotkin	Sig Arno
Bobby Peterson	Richard Eyer
Richard's mother	Margaret DuMont
Mr. Corday	John Carradine

Producer: Cy Howard, Richard Whorf

My Friend Tony

Crime Drama; 60 min; NBC 1/5/69 to 8/31/69

The exploits of John Woodruff, a private detective and criminologist professor at U.C.L.A., and his Italian partner, Tony Novello, whom he befriended as a boy while in service during World War II.

John Woodruff	James Whitmore
Tony Novello	Enzo Ceruscio

Producer: Sheldon Leonard

My Hero

Comedy; 30 min; NBC 11/8/52 to 9/12/53

The trials and tribulations of Robert S. Beanblossom, a carefree and easygoing salesman for the Los Angeles-based Thackery Realty Company. Also known as "The Robert Cummings Show."

Robert S. Beanblossom	Bob Cummings
Julie Marshall	Julie Bishop
Willis Thackery	John Litel

Producer: Mort Green

My Little Margie

Comedy; 30 min; CBS 6/16/52 to 9/8/52
CBS 6/1/53 to 7/10/53
NBC 9/9/53 to 8/24/55

Events in the lives of Vernon Albright, an investment counselor for Honeywell & Todd, and his beautiful, unpredictable 21-year-old daughter, Margie.

Margie Albright	Gale Storm
Vern Albright	Charles Farrell
Freddie Wilson	Don Hayden
Roberta Townsend	Hillary Brooke
George Honeywell	Clarence Kolb
Clarissa Odettes	Gertrude Hoffman
Charlie	Willie Best
Mr. Todd	George Meader
Mrs. Todd	Lizz Sisler
Betty Fuller	Charmine Harker
Freddie's mother	Lela Bliss
Freddie's father	Harry Hayden

Producer: Hal Roach Jr.

My Little Pony 'n' Friends

Cartoon; 30 min; Syn. 9/86

Segments: "My Little Pony" (the serial-like adventures of Megan, a beautiful young girl, and her friends, the multi-colored Ponies, as she struggles to protect Dream Valley from evil); "Potato Head Kids" (the misadventures of the Potato Head family); "Glo and Friends" (about tiny creatures who battle the evil Mooligans).

Megan	Ginny McSwain

Voices: Susan Blu, Charlie Adler, Nancy Cartwright, Peter Cullen, Linda Gary, Scott Grimes, Keri Houlihan, Katie Leigh, Sherry Lynn, Ken Mars, Sarah Partridge, Ken Mars, Frank Welker, Russi Taylor

Producer: Joe Bacal, Margaret Loesch, Tom Griffin

My Living Doll

Comedy; 30 min; CBS 9/27/64 to 9/8/65

When he completes U.S. Space Project AF 709, a beautifully constructed female robot (controlled by the birthmarks on her back), Dr. Carl Miller assigns her to psychiatrist Bob McDonald to mold her character. Stories relate Bob's misadventures as he takes control of the robot (whom he names Rhoda Miller and introduces as Carl's niece) and attempts to mold her character. Originally titled "Living Doll."

Rhoda Miller	Julie Newmar
Bob McDonald	Bob Cummings
Irene Adams	Doris Dowling
Dr. Peter Robinson	Jack Mullaney
Dr. Carl Miller	Henry Beckman
Dr. Russell Cooper	Herbert Rudley

"My Living Doll" Theme: George Greeley

Producer: Jack Chertok, Harry H. Poppe

My Lucky Penny

Comedy Pilot; 30 min; CBS 8/8/66

The story of Jenny Penny, a dental student's wife, who works as a secretary to a never-seen, eccentric boss who communicates with her via tape recordings.

Jenny Penny	Brenda Vaccaro
Ted Penny	Richard Benjamin
Freddy Rockefeller	Joel Gray
Sybil Rockefeller	Luana Anders
Commodore	Larry Storch

Producer: Arne Sultan, Marvin Worth

My Mother the Car

Comedy; 30 min; NBC 9/14/65 to 9/6/66

While looking for a car, lawyer Dave Crabtree becomes fascinated with a decrepit 1928 Porter. When he hears a female's voice coming from the car's radio, he discovers that it is his mother, who has been reincarnated as a car. Dave, who purchases the car and has it customized in a body shop, returns home to find that his family is opposed to the car. Stories relate Dave's attempts to defend his mother against a family who want a station wagon, and from the devious attempts of antique car collector Bernard Manzini to add the Porter to his collection.

Dave Crabtree	Jerry Van Dyke
Barbara Crabtree	Maggie Pierce
Cindy Crabtree	Cynthia Eilbacher
Randy Crabtree	Randy Whipple
Bernard Manzini	Avery Schreiber
Voice of Mother	Ann Sothern
Suzy	Peggy Miller
Fred	Chuck Grodin

Theme Vocal ("My Mother the Car"): Paul Hampton

Producer: Rod Amateau

My Partner the Ghost

Crime Drama; 60 min; Syn. 1973

While investigating a case, British private detective Marty Hopkirk is killed. Later, he returns as a ghost to help his former partner, Jeff Randall, solve his murder, but violates an ancient adage* and is cursed to remain on Earth for 100 years. Stories follow Jeff's exploits as he and his partner attempt to solve crimes.

Marty Hopkirk	Kenneth Cope
Jeff Randall	Mike Pratt
Jean Hopkirk	Annette Andre
Insp. Large	Ivor Dean

Producer: Monty Berman

*"Before the sun shall rise on you, each ghost unto his grave must go. Cursed be the ghost who dares to stay and face the awful light of day."

My Sister Eileen

Comedy; 30 min; CBS 10/5/60 to 4/12/61

The adventures of Ruth and Eileen Sherwood, two Ohio sisters who come to New York to further their careers: Ruth as a writer, and Eileen as an actress. See also "You Should Meet My Sister."

Eileen Sherwood	Shirley Boone
Ruth Sherwood	Elaine Stritch
Mr. Appopolous	Leon Belasco
Marty	Stubby Kaye
Robert Beaumont	Raymond Bailey
Chick Adams	Jack Weston
Bertha Bronsky	Rose Marie
The Wreck	Hal Baylor
Wreck's wife	Treva Frazee
Susie	Tammy Marihugh
Aunt Harriet	Agnes Moorehead

Producer: Harry Ackerman

My Sister Hank

Comedy Pilot; 30 min; CBS 3/31/72

The misadventures of Hank Bennett, a pretty teenage tomboy.

Hank Bennett	Jodie Foster
Eunice Bennett	Pippa Scott
Willis Bennett	Jack Ging
Grandpa Bennett	Edgar Bergen
Dianne Bennett	Suzanne Hillard
Arthur	Todd Bass

Producer: Norman Tokar

My Sister Sam

Comedy; 30 min; CBS 10/6/86 (Premiere)

Yearning to live with her older sister, Samantha, in San Francisco, Patti Russell runs away from the aunt (Elsie) she had been living with in Oregon. After locating Samantha, a photographer who runs the Russell Scouts Studio, Patti finds a new home when Sam agrees to let her live with her. Stories relate Sam's efforts to care for her 16-year-old sister and make a success of her business.

Samantha Russell	Pam Dawber
Patti Russell	Rebecca Schaeffer
Dixie Roundazzo	Jenny O'Hara
J.D. Lucas	Joel Brooks
Jack Kincaide	David Naughton
Aunt Elsie	Nan Martin

Theme Vocal ("Room Enough for Two"): Kim Carnes

My Son Jeep

Comedy; 30 min; ABC 7/4/53 to 9/22/53

The series, set in Grove Falls, relates the antics of Jeep Allison, the mischievous son of a doctor.

Dr. Allison	Jeffrey Lynn
Jeep Allison	Martin Houston
Peggy Allison	Betty Lou Keim
Barbara Miller	Anne Sargeant
Mrs. Birby	Leona Powers

My Son the Doctor

Comedy Pilot; 30 min; CBS 8/22/66

The story of Peter Piper, a doctor whose total dedication to work often leaves him little time to spend with his wife, Barbara.

Dr. Peter Piper	Jefferson Davis
Barbara Piper	Julie Gregg
Dr. Jeffrey Barry	Dick Patterson
Jenny Piper	Kay Medford
Miss Primrose	Patsy Kelly
Doris	Lee Meriwether
Phil	Cliff Norton
Gilmore	Dave Willock

Producer: Jack Donohue

My Three Sons

Comedy: 30 min; ABC 9/29/60 to 9/9/65
CBS 9/16/65 to 8/24/72

Events in the lives of the Douglas family: Steve, a widowed aeronautical engineer (who later marries Barbara Harper), and his children Mike (marries Sally Ann Morrison), Robbie (marries Katie Miller), Chip (marries Polly Thompson), and his adopted son, Ernie.

Steve Douglas	Fred MacMurray
Mike Douglas	Tim Considine
Robbie Douglas	Don Grady
Richard "Chip" Douglas	Stanley Livingston
Ernie Douglas	Barry Livingston
Michael Francis "Bub" O'Casey	William Frawley
Charles O'Casey	William Demarest
Sally Ann Morrison	Meredith MacRae
Barbara Harper	Beverly Garland
Katie Miller	Tina Cole
Polly Thompson (a.k.a. Polly Williams)	Ronne Troup
Dodie Harper	Dawn Lyn
Steve Douglas Jr.	Joseph Todd
Charley Douglas	Michael Todd
Robbie Douglas II	Daniel Todd
Bob Walters	Russ Conway
	John Gallaudet
Sylvia Walters	Irene Hervey
Priscilla	Jodie Foster
Tom Williams	Norman Alden
Margaret Williams	Doris Singleton

"My Three Sons" Theme by Frank DeVol

Producer: Don Fedderson, Edmund Hartmann, Fred Henry, George Tibbles

My Town

Comedy Pilot; 60 min; ABC 5/25/86

In an attempt to attract new business to Wheelerville, Ohio, banker Lucas Wheeler, hits on the idea to promote the town as a place where people can get a fresh start in life. The unsold series was to relate people's attempts to start new lives as seen through the eyes of Amber Wheeler, a pretty orphan who lives with her grandfather (Lucas).

Lucas Wheeler	Glenn Ford
Amber Wheeler	Meredith Salenger
Tug Wheeler	Parker Jacobs
Mrs. McDaniel	Mary Jackson
Laura Adams	Kate Mulgrew
Cynthia Fisher	Laraine Newman
Hal Fisher	James Widdoes
Billy Fisher	Matt Norero

Narrator: Meredith Salenger

Producer: Gil Grant, John Garbett

My True Story

Anthology; 30 min; ABC 5/5/50 to 9/22/50

Dramatic adaptations of stories that appear in "My True Story" magazine.

Announcer: Herbert Duncan

Producer: Charles Powers

My Two Dads

Comedy; 30 min; NBC 9/20/87 (Premiere)

At the reading of the will for Marcy Bradford, two of her former lovers, Joey Harris and Michael Taylor, are reunited and appointed guardian of Marcy's 12-year-old daughter, Nicole, when it cannot be determined who is the actual father. Stories relate the efforts of two bachelors to raise a very pretty young girl.

Joey Harris	Greg Evigan
Michael Taylor	Paul Reiser
Nicole Bradford	Staci Keanan
Judge Margaret Wilbur	Florence Stanley
Ed Klawicki	Dick Butkus

Producer: Michael Jacobs, Danielle Alexander

My Wife Next Door

Comedy Pilot; 30 min; NBC 12/31/75

The story of Suzy and George Bassett, a newly separated young couple awaiting a divorce settlement who become sparring partners again when they accidentally rent neighboring apartments.

Suzy Bassett	Julie Sommars
George Bassett	James Farentino
Suzy's mother	Martha Scott
Ronnie	Jordan Crittenden

Producer: Bill Persky, Sam Denoff

My Wife Next Door

Comedy Pilot; 30 min; CBS 9/11/80

While awaiting a divorce settlement, Lisa Pallick, a TV commercials producer, and Paul Gilmore, her soon-to-be ex-husband, a big league ballplayer, accidentally rent adjoining apartments in the same San Francisco building. The unsold series was to relate their misadventures as they again become sparring partners.

Lisa Pallick	Lee Purcell
Paul Gilmore	Granville Van Dusen
Jan Pallick	Desiree Boschetti
Vinnie Messina	Michael DeLano
Lionel	Frank Dent
Artie	Phil Rubinstein

Producer: Martin Starger

My Wives Jane

Comedy Pilot; 30 min; CBS 8/1/71

The misadventures of Jane Franklin, an actress, married to a doctor, who also portrays a doctor's wife on a TV serial.

Jane Franklin	Janet Leigh
Dr. Nat Franklin	Barry Nelson
Vic Semple	John Dehner
Dirk Bennett	McLean Stevenson
Molly	Mia Bendixsen
Magda	Nora Marlowe

Producer: Edward H. Feldman

My World . . . and Welcome To It

Comedy; 30 min; NBC 9/15/69 to 9/7/70

The real life and dream world of John Monroe, a cartoonist for "Manhattanite" magazine. Animation is coupled with live action to depict John's imagined world; a world where his problems seem to disappear and he is a king. Based on the drawings and stories of James Thurber. See also "The Secret World of John Monroe."

John Monroe	William Windom
Ellen Monroe	Joan Hotchkis
Lydia Monroe	Lisa Gerritsen
Hamilton Greeley	Harold J. Stone
Phil Jensen	Henry Morgan
Ruth Jensen	Olive Dunbar

Producer: Sheldon Leonard, Danny Arnold

Mysteries of Chinatown

Crime Drama; 30 min; ABC 12/4/49 to 10/23/50

The exploits of Dr. Yat Fu, an amateur crime sleuth who is also the owner of a curio shop in San Francisco's Chinatown.

Dr. Yat Fu	Marvin Miller
Ah Toy	Gloria Saunders
Lt. Cummings	Edmund MacDonald
	Richard Crane
	William Eythe
Lt. Hargrove (earlier role)	William Eythe

Producer: Bob Finkel, Ray Buffum

Mystery and Mrs.

Crime Drama Pilot; 30 min; DuMont 9/27/50

The exploits of a husband and wife private detective team.

Wife	Gale Storm
Husband	Don DeFore
Villain	Robert Shayne

Also: Eve Whitney, Goerge Pelham

Producer: Walter Grauman, Walter Wolfe King, Al Aimer

Mystery Chef

Cooking; 30 min; NBC 3/1/49 to 6/29/49

Step-by-step cooking instruction in one of NBC's first daytime shows. Hosted by John McPherson (who was not identified when the program first began, hence the title).

Mystery File

See "Q.E.D."

Mystery Is My Business

See "Ellery Queen."

Naked City

Crime Drama; 30 min; ABC 9/30/58 to 9/29/59

The gruelling day-to-day activities of Dan Muldoon and Jim Halloran, plainclothes police detectives with the Manhattan 65th Precinct in New York City.

Det. Lt. Dan Muldoon	John McIntire
Det. Jim Halloran	James Franciscus
Janet Halloran	Suzanne Stors
Lt. Mike Parker	Horace MacMahon

Theme Song ("This Is the Naked City"): George Duning, Ned Washington

Producer: Bert Leonard

Naked City

Crime Drama; 60 min; ABC 10/12/60 to 9/11/63

A revised version of the previous title, which continues to depict the day-to-day assignments of detectives attached to the Manhattan 65th Police Precinct in New York.

Det. Adam Flint	Paul Burke
Sgt. Frank Arcaro	Harry Bellaver
Lt. Mike Parker	Horace MacMahon
Libby Kingston	Nancy Malone
Lt. Vincent Busti	Edward Asner
Evie Busti	Marco Lungreen
Off. Sam Gode	Sam Gray
Commissioner Bucky	Matt Crawley
Police lab technician	William Cottrell

Theme Songs: "The Naked City Theme" by Billy May, and "The New Naked City Theme" by Nelson Riddle

Producer: Herbert B. Leonard, Charles Russell

Nakia

Crime Drama; 60 min; ABC 9/21/74 to 12/28/74

The story of Nakia Parker, a Navaho Indian deputy sheriff in Davis County, New Mexico.

Nakia Parker	Robert Forster
Sheriff Sam Jericho	Arthur Kennedy
Deputy Irene James	Gloria DeHaven
Deputy Hubbel Martin	Joe Kapp*
	Taylor Lacher
Ben Redearth	Victor Jory
Half Cub	John Tenorio Jr.

Producer: Charles Larson, Ernest Losso, George Sunga

*TV Movie role (4/17/74).

The Name of the Game

Crime Drama; 90 min; NBC 9/20/68 to 9/10/72

The exploits of three men: Glenn Howard, the publisher of "Crime" magazine, a man who built the then-fictional "People" magazine into the multimillion-dollar Howard Publications; Dan Farrell, the senior editor; and Jeff Dillon, editor of the People segment of "Crime." Their individual attempts to uncover story material are depicted on a rotational basis.

Glenn Howard	Gene Barry
Dan Farrell	Robert Stack
Jeff Dillon	Tony Franciosa
Peggy Maxwell	Susan Saint James
Joe Sample	Ben Murphy
Andy Hill	Cliff Potter
Ross Craig	Mark Miller

Theme Song ("Name of the Game"): Dave Grusin

Producer: Richard Irving, Richard Levinson, William Link, Leslie Stevens

Name That Tune

Game; 30 min; NBC 7/6/53 to 6/14/54
            CBS 9/2/54 to 10/19/59

Players attempt to win prizes by identifying song titles from a few bars of music.

Host: Red Benson, Bill Cullen, George DeWitt

Vocalist: Vicki Mills

Announcer: Johnny Olsen, Wayne Howell

Orchestra: Harry Salter, Ted Rapf

Producer: Al Singer

Name That Tune

Game; 30 min; NBC 7/29/74 to 1/3/75
                             1/3/77 to 6/10/77

The basic format calls for players to identify song titles after hearing a few notes played by an orchestra.

Host: Dennis James

Announcer: John Harlan

Orchestra: Bob Alberti, Tommy Oliver

Producer: Ralph Edwards

Name That Tune

Game; 30 min; Syn 9/74

Players must identify song titles from very brief musical clues. See also "The $100,000 Name That Tune."

Host: Tom Kennedy

Announcer: John Harlan

Orchestra: Bob Alberti

Producer: Ralph Edwards

The Name's the Same

Game; 30 min; ABC 12/12/51 to 10/7/55

Object: For a celebrity panel to identify the birth names of guests who have the same names as famous personalities. Players receive money based on the number of indirect questions used by the panel.

Host: Robert Q. Lewis, Dennis James, Bob Elliott, Ray Goulding

Panelists: Bess Myerson, Gene Rayburn, Arnold Stang, Abe Burrows, Meredith Wilson, Audrey Meadows, Joan Alexander, Laraine Day, Walter Slezak, Roger Price

Announcer: John Reed King, Lee Vines

Producer: Mark Goodson, Bill Todman

The Namedroppers

Game; 30 min; NBC 10/2/69 to 3/27/70

A contestant appears on stage and briefly tells how he is related to one of three celebrity guests. Each celebrity then tells a story concerning his relationship with the player. The object is for two studio audience contestants to determine which celebrity is telling the truth.

Host: Al Lohman, Roger Barkley

Announcer: Kenny Williams

Producer: Art Alisi

Nancy

Comedy; 30 min; NBC 9/17/70 to 1/7/71

The series, set in Center City, Iowa, relates the courtship and marriage of Nancy Smith, daughter of the U.S. President, to Adam Hudson, a veterinarian, and their attempts to live a life that is more public than private.

Nancy Smith	Renne Jarrett
Adam Hudson	John Fink
Abby Townsend	Celeste Holm
Everett Hudson	Robert F. Simon
Willie Wilson	Eddie Applegate
Tom	Frank Aletter
Agent Turner	William H. Bassett
Agent Rodriquez	Ernesto Macias

Producer: Sidney Sheldon, Jerome Courtland

The Nancy Drew Mysteries

Crime Drama; 60 min; ABC 2/6/77 to 7/30/78

The adventures of Nancy Drew, the beautiful teenage daughter of criminal attorney Carson Drew, as she helps her father solve baffling crimes. Originally broadcast as "The Hardy Boys/Nancy Drew Mysteries."

Nancy Drew	Pamela Sue Martin
	Janet Louise Johnson
Carson Drew	William Schallert
George Fyne	Jean Rasey
	Susan Buckner
Ned Nickerson	George O'Hanlon Jr.
	Rick Springfield
Bess	Ruth Cox
Sheriff Kane	Robert Karnes

Producer: Glen A. Larson, B.W. Sandefur

The Nancy Dussault Show

Comedy Pilot; 30 min; CBS 5/8/73

The adventures of Nancy Clancy, a Broadway understudy who becomes a star when her leading lady becomes ill.

Nancy Clancy	Nancy Dussault
Bill Clancy	Lawrence Pressman
Claire	Karen Morrow
David Froelich	John Byner

Producer: Byron Paul

Writer: Carl Reiner

Director: Dick Van Dyke

The Nancy Walker Show

Comedy; 30 min; ABC 9/30/76 to 12/23/76
                                    7/11/77 (1 episode)

The story of Nancy Kitteridge, a Hollywood theatrical agent whose troubles stem not only from her difficulty in handling clients, but with her inability to cope with her family.

Nancy Kitteridge	Nancy Walker
Kenneth Kitteridge	William Daniels
Lorraine	Beverly Archer
Glen	James Cromwell
Terry Folson	Ken Olfson

Theme Vocal ("Nancy's Blues"): Nancy Walker

Producer: Norman Lear, Rod Parker

Nanny and the Professor

Comedy; 30 min; ABC 1/21/70 to 12/27/72

The story of Phoebe Figalilly, the enchanting housekeeper of Professor Harold Everett (a math teacher at Clinton College), who is neither a witch or a magician, but possesses the ability to spread love and joy.

Phoebe Figalilly (Nanny)	Juliet Mills
Harold Everett	Richard Long
Hal Everett	David Doremus
Prudence Everett	Kim Richards
Bentley (Butch) Everett	Trent Lehman
Francine Fowler	Eileen Baral
Florence Fowler	Patsy Garrett
Nanny's Aunt Henrietta	Elsa Lanchester
College Dean	Harry Hickox

Producer: David Gerber, Wes McAffe, Charles B. Fitzsimons

The Nash Airflyte Theatre

Anthology; 30 min; CBS 9/21/50 to 3/15/51

A series of dramatic productions under the sponsorship of Nash Products. Hosted by William Gaxton and produced by Marc Daniels.

Nashville 99

Crime Drama; 60 min; CBS 4/1/77 to 4/22/77

The exploits of Stonewall "Stoney" Huff, and Trace Mayne, detectives attached to the Nashville Metropolitan Police Department in Tennessee. (The title refers of Stoney's badge number.)

Det. Lt. Stoney Huff	Claude Akins
Det. Trace Mayne	Jerry Reed
Birdie Huff	Lucille Benson
Deputy R.B.	Charley Pride

Theme Vocal ("Nashville 99"): Jerry Reed

Producer: Ernie Frankel

The Nashville Palace

Variety; 60 min; NBC 10/24/81 to 8/7/82

Performances by country and western entertainers. Featured skit: "The Coots," about a wacky family living in Looney Corners, Tenn.

Pa Coot	Hamilton Camp
Ma Coot	Donna Siegel
Amelia Coot	Terri Gardner
Thomas Alva Coot	Harry Murphy
Granny Coot	Wendy Suits

Host/Announcer: Slim Pickens

Music: Charlie McCoy and His Palace Pickers

Producer: John Aylesworth, Sam Lovullo

Nashville Now

See "The Ian Tyson Show."

The Nat King Cole Show

Variety; 30 min; NBC 11/5/56 to 12/17/57

A charming half-hour of music with singer Nat King Cole, the first black singer to host a major network series.

Host: Nat King Cole

Regulars: The Randy Van Horne Singers, The Boataneers

Orchestra: Gordon Jenkins, Nelson Riddle

Producer: Bob Henry

National Lampoon's Hot Flashes

Comedy; 30 min; Syn. 6/84

A limited run series that takes an off-the-wall look at the antics of "National Lampoon's Hot Flashes," an evening news show, as they prepare for broadcast.

Kimberly Clark	Lois Robbins
John B. Goode	Mark King
Barry Gold	Kevin Pollak
Walter Conkrite	Franklyn Ajaye
Samantha	Wendy Goldman
Ali	Blake Clarke
Juan Jones	Jeff Marder
Chuck Fodder	Rodger Bumpass

Producer: Matty Simmons, Julian Weber

National Lampoon's Two Reelers

Comedy Pilot; 30 min; NBC 8/28/81

The misadventures of Stephen and Rodger, students who decide to leave school and travel around the world. The unsold series was to relate their misadventures as they become involved in the problems of others.

Stephen	Stephen Furst
Rodger	Rodger Bumpass
Waitress	Penny Peyser
Villain	Pierrino Mascarino
General	Victor Brandt
Postman	Owen Bush

Producer: Matty Simmons, Caryn Snyder

The National Snoop

Satire Pilot; 30 min; NBC 8/18/83

The unsold pilot for a satirical TV news-magazine series that, set at the newsroom of the "National Snoop," presents unusual news and human interest stories.

Co-Anchors: Catherine Bergstrom, Phil Hartman, Lennie Weinrib

Regulars: Dr. Joyce Brothers, Sheila Frazier, Don Calfa, K.C. Winkler, Bob Yerkes, Rose Lau, Allan Katz, Greg Lewis, Terrence McGovern

Producer: Allan Katz

National Velvet

Drama; 30 min; NBC 9/18/60 to 9/10/62

The story of a young girl (Velvet Brown) and her attempts to train her horse, King, for competition in the Grand National Steeplechase. The series, based on the Elizabeth Taylor movie, also focuses on Velvet's adventures in and around her family's Midwestern dairy farm.

Velvet Brown	Lori Martin
Herbert Brown	Arthur Space
Martha Brown	Ann Doran
Edwina Brown	Carole Wells
Donald Brown	Joey Scott
Mi Taylor	James McCallion
Homer Ede	Tim Graham
Aggie Ede	Nora Marlowe
Teddy	Carl Crow
Velvet's Grandfather	Edgar Buchanan
John	Ricky Kelman

Theme Song ("National Velvet"): Robert Armbruster

Producer: Robert Maxwell

The Natural Look

Comedy Pilot; 30 min; NBC 7/6/77

The story of Reedy Harrison, a cosmetics executive for Contessa Toiletries.

Reedy Harrison	Barbara Feldon
Dr. Bud Harrison	Bill Bixby
Countess	Brenda Forbes
Edna	Sandy Sprung
Jane	Caren Kaye
Arthur	Michael MacRae

Producer: Lillian Gallo, Leonora Thuna

Navy Log

Anthology: 30 min; CBS 9/20/55 to 9/25/56
ABC 10/17/56 to 9/25/58

Dramas that relate incidents in the lives of the men in service of the U.S. Navy. Produced by Leslie Harris and Sam Gallu.

NBC Action Playhouse

Anthology; 60 min; NBC 6/24/71 to 9/7/71
5/23/72 to 9/5/72

Peter Marshall as the host of a Summer series of repeat dramas from "The Bob Hope Chrysler Theatre."

NBC Adventure Theatre

Anthology; 60 min; NBC 6/24/71 to 9/4/71
6/15/72 to 8/31/72

Repeat episodes of "The Bob Hope Chrysler Theatre" with hosts Art Fleming (1971) and Ed McMahon (1972).

NBC Bandstand

See "Bandstand."

NBC Comedy Hour

Variety; 60 min; NBC 1/8/56 to 6/10/56

Music, songs, comedy skits, and perform-ances by new talent discoveries.

Hostess: Gale Storm

Regulars: Jonathan Winters, Hy Averback

Announcer: Hy Averback

NBC Comedy Theatre

Anthology; 60 min; NBC 7/7/71 to 8/30/71
7/8/72 to 9/4/72

Jack Kelly as the host to comedy episodes originally broadcast on "The Bob Hope Chrysler Theatre."

NBC Comics

See "The Telecomics."

The NBC Follies

Variety; 60 min; NBC 9/13/73 to 12/27/73

A revue based on the music and comedy of vaudeville.

Host: Sammy Davis Jr.

Regulars: Mickey Rooney, The Carl Jablonski Dancers

Orchestra: Harper McKay

Producer: Sy Marsh, Bob Wynn

NBC Playhouse

Anthology; 30 min; NBC 6/28/60 to 9/6/60

Jeanne Bal as the host of a Summer series of dramas that were originally broadcast on other anthology series.

NBC Repertory Theatre

A live NBC (4/17/49 to 7/10/49) drama series featuring a new cast and story each week.

NBC Saturday Prom

Variety Pilot; 30 min; NBC 10/15/60

A proposed series that was to spotlight the top names in music.

Host: Merv Griffin

Guests: Conway Twitty, Anita Bryant, Johnny and the Americans

Orchestra: Si Zentner

Producer: Ed Pierce

The NBC Sunday Mystery Movie

Crime Drama; Various (90 min & 2 hrs); NBC 9/15/71 to 9/4/77

The title for nine rotating series: "Amy Prentiss," "Columbo," "Hec Ramsey," "Lanigan's Rabbi," "McCloud," "McCoy," "McMillan," "McMillan and Wife," and "Quincy, M.E." See individual titles.

Neat and Tidy

Comedy Adventure Pilot; 2 hrs; Syn. 12/86

Seeking to find her mother, who is presumed killed in a car crash, Valentena Tidelio, a mobster's daughter, runs away from her father's jailer, music school headmistress Bruno Van Kleef. Fearing that he killed his partner, auto mechanic Nick Pratt, flees, thinking the police are seeking him. By chance Valentena, who pretends to be Tena Tidy, and Nick, who assumes the name Nick Neat, meet and team to help each other out. The proposed series was to relate their adventures as they seek Tena's mother (Loretta) and attempt to escape from their relentless pursuer—Headmistress Bruno.

Tena Tidy	Jill Whitlow
Nick Neat	Skyler Cole
Bruno Van Kleef	Elke Sommer
Loretta Kimbell	Stella Stevens
Flo	Edie Adams
Hackum	John Astin
Sheriff	Larry Storch

Producer: Dennis Abbe, Patrick Hayes, Peter Millhouse

Needles and Pins

Comedy; 30 min; NBC 9/21/73 to 12/28/73

Life in the aggravating world of the garment industry as seen through the experiences of Wendy Nelson, a struggling young apprentice fashion designer with Lorelei Fashions in New York City.

Wendy Nelson	Deirdre Lenihan
Nathan Davidson	Norman Fell
Harry Karp	Louis Nye
Charlie Miller	Bernie Kopell
Sonia Baker	Sandra Deel
Max	Larry Gelman
Myron Russo	Alex Henteloff
Julius Singer	Milton Selzer
Elliott	Joshua Shelley

Producer: David Gerber, Hy Averback

The Neighbors

Game; 30 min; ABC 12/29/75 to 4/9/76

Of the five actual female neighbors who appear, two are selected as the players; the remaining three serve as the panel. Players must determine if a statement by her neighbor refers to her or her opponent. Each correct guess scores the player money and the highest scoring player is the winner.

Host: Regis Philbin

Models: Jane Nelson, Sylvia Neils

Announcer: Joe Sinan

Producer: Bill Carruthers, Joel Stein

Nero Wolfe

Mystery; 60 min; NBC 1/16/81 to 8/25/81

The story of Nero Wolfe, gourmet, horticulturist, and master criminologist who helps the police solve baffling crimes. Based on the characters created by Rex Stout.

Nero Wolfe	William Conrad
Archie Goodwin	Lee Horsley
Saul Panzer	George Wyner
Fritz Brenner	George Voskovec
Theodore Hortsmann	Robert Coote
Insp. Cramer	Allan Miller

Producer: Ivan Goff, Ben Roberts

Never Again

Comedy Pilot; 30 min; ABC 11/30/84

Incidents in the lives of Abby, Larry, and Mitchell, three singles who share adjoining apartments.

Abby Cartwright	Jamie Rose
Larry Newman	Judge Reinhold
Mitchell Franklin	Allen Garfield
Denise	Margot Rose
Dawn Stevenson	Loyita Chapel

Producer: Sandy Veith, Wendy Riche, Paula Lavenback

Never Say Never

Comedy Pilot; 30 min; CBS 7/11/79

The story of Harry Walters, a widowed 54-year-old plumbing supply company businessman who falls in love with Dr. Sarah Keaton, a poised and beautiful 32-year-old pediatrician. The unsold series was to relate their romantic misadventures.

Harry Walters	George Kennedy
Dr. Sarah Keaton	Anne Schedeen
Florence	Irene Tedrow
Paul Walters	Bruce Kimmel
Ronnie	Rick Podell
Sarah's nurse	Maidie Norman

Producer: Leonard Rosenberg

The New Adventures of Batman

Cartoon; 25 min; CBS 2/12/77 to 9/2/78

The exploits of Batman and Robin as they battle crime in Gotham City. See also "Batman."

Batman	Adam West
Robin	Burt Ward
Batgirl	Melendy Britt
Batmite	Lennie Weinrib

Producer: Norm Prescott, Lou Scheimer

The New Adventures of Beans Baxter

Comedy; 30 min; FOX 7/11/87 (Premiere)

The comical exploits of Beans Baxter, a 17-year-old high school student in Washington, D.C., who is also a spy currier for the Network, a secret U.S. government agency that battles the evils of U.G.L.I. (Underground Government Liberation Intergroup), an enemy organization.

Beans Baxter	Jonathan Ward
Mom (his mother)	Elinor Donahue
Cake Lase	Karen Mistal
Woodshop	Stuart Fratkin
Scooter	Scott Bremner

Producer: Savage Steve Holland, Tony Eaton

The New Adventures of Charlie Chan

Mystery; 30 min; Syn. 1957

The exploits of Charlie Chan, the courteous, shrewd, and philosophical Chinese Detective. Based on characters created by Earl Derr Biggers.

Charlie Chan	J. Carrol Naish
Barry Chan	James Hong
Insp. Duff	Rupert Davies
Insp. Carl Marlowe	Hugh Williams

Producer: Leon Fromkess

The New Adventures of Gilligan

Cartoon; 30 min; ABC 9/7/74 to 9/4/77

A spin-off from "Gilligan's Island," which continues to depict the misadventures that befall the shipwrecked survivors of the S.S. Minnow as they struggle for survival and seek a way off the island.

The Skipper	Alan Hale Jr.
Gilligan	Bob Denver
Ginger Grant	Jane Webb
Thurston Howell III	Jim Backus
Lovey Howell	Natalie Schafer
The Professor	Russell Johnson
Mary Ann	Jane Edwards

Producer: Norm Prescott, Lou Scheimer

The New Adventures of Huckleberry Finn

Adventure; 30 min; NBC 9/15/68 to 9/7/69

Pursued by the vengeful Injun Joe, Huckleberry Finn, Becky Thatcher, and Tom Sawyer run into a cave where they are engulfed by a raging river and transported to a strange fantasy land that is inhabited by cartoon characters. Stories relate their adventures as they seek to find their way back to Hannibal, Missouri in 1845. Based on the Mark Twain stories.

Huckleberry Finn	Michael Shea
Becky Thatcher	Lu Ann Haslam
Tom Sawyer	Kevin Schultz
Injun Joe	Ted Cassidy
Aunt Polly	Anne Bellamy
Mrs. Thatcher	Dorothy Tennant

Character Voices: Peggy Webber, Paul Frees, Marvin Miller, Vic Perrin, Julie Bennett

Producer: William Hanna, Joseph Barbera

The New Adventures of Martin Kane

Crime Drama; 30 min; NBC 8/27/53 to 6/17/54

A revised version of "Martin Kane," which, set in Europe, relates Kane's exploits as he assists various international police depart-ments. Also known as "Assignment Danger."

Martin Kane	Mark Stevens
	William Gargan
Inspector	Brian Reece

Producer: Frank Burns, Harry Alan Towers

The New Adventures of Mighty Mouse and Heckle and Jeckle

Cartoon; 55 min; CBS 9/8/79 to 9/12/82

Segments: "Mighty Mouse" (newly animated adventures of the heroic mouse as he battles evil; see also "The Mighty Mouse Play-house"); and "Heckle and Jeckle" (the mis-chievous talking magpies in newly animated adventures; see also "Heckle and Jeckle").

Mighty Mouse	Alan Oppenheimer
Pearl Pureheart	Diane Pershing
Oilcan Harry	Alan Oppenheimer
Heckle and Jeckle	Frank Welker

Producer: Norm Prescott, Lou Scheimer

The New Adventures of Pinocchio

Children; 5 min; Syn. 1961

Marionette adventures of Pinocchio, the wooden boy who comes to life to please a lonely old man (Gepetto). Produced by Arthur Rankin Jr. and Jules Bass.

The New Adventures of Spin and Marty

Comedy; 30 min; ABC 9/30/58 to 11/6/58

A "Mickey Mouse Club" serial that relates further events in the lives of Triple R Camp-ers Spin and Marty (and their efforts to stage a variety show to pay for damages done by Marty's jalopy). See also "Spin and Marty" and "The Further Adventures of Spin and Marty."

Spin Evans	Tim Considine
Marty Markham	David Stollery
Jim Logan	Roy Barcroft
Bill Burnett	Harry Carey Jr.
Ollie	Dennis Moore
Annette	Annette Funicello
Darlene	Darlene Gillespie
Moochie O'Hara	Kevin Corcoran
Speckle	Tim Hartnagel
George	Joe Wong
Joe	Sammy Ogg
Ambitious	B. G. Norman

Producer: Walt Disney, Bill Walsh

The New Adventures of Superman

Cartoon; 30 min; CBS 9/10/66 to 9/2/67

The crime-fighting exploits of Clark Kent, alias Superman; and the adventures of Clark as a teenager in a "Superboy" segment.

Clark/Superman	Bud Collyer
Lois Lane	Joan Alexander
Superboy	Bob Hastings
Perry White	Ted Knight

Producer: Allen Ducovny, Norm Prescott, Lou Scheimer

The New Adventures of Wonder Woman

See "Wonder Woman" (Series 2) for informa-tion.

The New Andy Griffith Show

Comedy; 30 min; CBS 1/8/72 to 6/4/72

The story of Andy Sawyer, a former sheriff and justice of the peace turned mayor of Greenwood, North Carolina.

Andy Sawyer	Andy Griffith
Lee Sawyer	Lee Meriwether
Lori Sawyer	Lori Ann Rutherford
T. J. Sawyer	Marty McCall
Nora	Ann Morgan Guilbert
Buff MacKnight	Glen Ash
Mrs. Gossage	Ruth McDevitt

Music: Earle Hagen

Producer: Richard O. Linke, Aaron Ruben

The New Avengers

Adventure; 70 min; CBS 9/15/78 to 3/23/79

An updated version of "The Avengers," which depicts the exploits of John Steed, a debonaire British government agent, and his new partners, Purdy and Mike Gambit, as they battle sinister villains.

John Steed	Patrick Macnee
Purdy	Joanna Lumley
Mike Gambit	Gareth Hunt

Producer: Albert Fennell, Brian Clemens

The New Bill Cosby Show

Variety; 60 min; CBS 9/11/72 to 5/17/73

Sketches, coupled with songs and dances, that depict the world as seen through the eyes of comedian Bill Cosby.

Host: Bill Cosby

Regulars: Susan Tolsky, Lola Falana, Foster Brooks, Erin Fleming, Oscar DeGrury, The Donald McKayle Dancers

Announcer: Lola Falana

Orchestra: Quincy Jones, Bobby Bryant

Producer: George Schlatter

The New Breed

Crime Drama; 60 min; ABC 10/3/61 to 9/15/62

The exploits of the Metropolitan Squad, an elite team of Los Angeles Police Department detectives assigned to disrupt the workings of organized crime.

Lt. Price Adams	Leslie Nielsen
Sgt. Vince Cavelli	John Beradino
Capt. Keith Gregory	John Clark
Off. Pete Garcia	Greg Roman

Producer: Quinn Martin

The New Card Sharks

Game; 30 min; CBS 1/6/86 (Premiere)

A revised version of "Card Sharks," which see for format.

Host: Bob Eubanks

Card Dealers: Susanna Williams, Lacey Pemberton

Announcer: Gene Wood

Producer: Mark Goodson, Chester Feldman

The New Christy Minstrels Show

Variety; 30 min; NBC 8/6/64 to 9/3/64

A weekly program of music and song featuring the New Christy Minstrels singing group.

New Christy Minstrels: Ann White, Paul Potash, Barry Kane, Karen Gunderson, Barry McGuire, Clarence Treat, Larry Romos

Regulars: The Chuck Cassey Singers, The Doerr-Hutchinson Dancers

Orchestra: Peter Matz

Producer: Gary Smith, Dwight Hemion

New Comedy Showcase

Pilot Films; 30 min; CBS 8/1/60 to 9/19/60

See the following titles: "Johnny Come Lately," "Maggie," "Maisie," "Slezak and Son," "They Went Thataway," "You're Only Young Once," and "You're Only Young Twice."

The New Ernie Kovacs Show

Comedy; 30 min; ABC 9/61 to 1/62

Sketches and blackouts that satirize life. See also "The Ernie Kovacs Show," "It's Time for Ernie," "Kovacs on the Corner," and "Kovacs Unlimited."

Host: Ernie Kovacs

Regulars: Jolene Brand, Maggi Brown, Joe Mikalos, Bobby Laugher, Francis McHale, Bob Warren

Orchestra: Harry Geller

Producer: Ernie Kovacs, Milt Hoffman

The New Dating Game

Game; 30 min; Syn. 9/86

A revised version of "The Dating Game," which see for format, and which also features a rarity in TV—a beautiful female host.

Hostess: Elaine Joyce

Announcer: Bob Hilton

Producer: Chuck Barris

The New Dick Van Dyke Show

Comedy; 30 min; CBS 9/18/71 to 9/3/73

The trials and tribulations of Dick Preston, host of "The Dick Preston Show," a 90-minute talk-variety program on KXIU-TV, Channel 2, in Phoenix.

Dick Preston	Dick Van Dyke
Jenny Preston	Hope Lange
Bernie Davis	Marty Brill
Carol Davis	Nancy Dussault
Michele "Mike" Preston	Fannie Flagg
Annie Preston	Angela Powell
Lucas Preston	Michael Shea
Ted Atwater	David Doyle

Producer: Carl Reiner, Bernie Orenstein, Saul Turteltaub

The New Dick Van Dyke Show

Comedy; 30 min; CBS 9/10/73 to 9/3/74

A revised version of the previous title which, set in Tarzana, California, relates the home and working life of Dick Preston, an actor who portrays Dr. Brad Fairmont on the TV serial "Those Who Care."

Dick Preston	Dick Van Dyke
Jenny Preston	Hope Lange
Annie Preston	Angela Powell
Max Mathias	Dick Van Patten
Alex Montez	Henry Darrow
Dennis Whitehead	Barry Gordon
Richard Richardson	Richard Dawson
Connie Richardson	Chita Rivera
Margot Brighton	Barbara Rush

Producer: Byron Paul, Bernie Orenstein, Saul Turteltaub

The New Fred and Barney Show

Cartoon; 30 min; NBC 2/3/79 to 9/15/79

Continued events in the lives of Fred and Wilma Flintstone, and their neighbors Barney and Betty Rubble.

Fred Flintstone	Henry Corden
Wilma Flintstone	Jean VanderPyl
Barney Rubble	Mel Blanc
Betty Rubble	Janet Waldo
Pebbles Flintstone	Jean VanderPyl
Bamm Bamm Rubble	Don Messick

Producer: William Hanna, Joseph Barbera

The New Gidget

Comedy; 30 min; Syn. 9/76

A revised version of the "Gidget" series which finds Gidget married (to Jeff "Moondoggie" Griffin), the owner of her own business (the Gidget Travel Agency), and the guardian of her beautiful teenage niece, Danni, while her parents are in Europe. Stories focuses on both Danni's antics as a typical high school girl, and Gidget's misadventures as she attempts to cope with life. See also "Gidget's Summer Reunion."

Frances "Gidget" Griffin	Caryn Richman
Jeff Griffin	Dean Butler
Danni Collins	Sydney Penny
Russ Lawrence	William Schallert
Larue Wilson	Jill Jacobson
Gail	Lili Haydn
Karen	Krista Errickson
Julie	Eve LaRue
Tracy	Suzanne Townsend
The Great Kahuna	Don Stroud
Wilton Parmenter	Richard Paul

Story Teller: Caryn Richman

Producer: Harry Ackerman, Ralph Riskin, Carole J. Coates, Larry Molin

New Girl in His Life

Comedy Pilot; 30 min; CBS 5/26/57

The pilot for "Bachelor Father." The story of a confirmed bachelor (Bentley Gregg) whose carefree lifestyle is suddenly changed when he becomes the guardian of his teenage niece (Kelly) following the death of her parents in a car accident. In the story, broadcast on "G.E. Theatre," Bentley attempts to help Kelly pick out a formal gown. Proposed series title at the time: "Uncle Bentley."

Bentley Gregg	John Forsythe
Kelly Gregg	Noreen Corcoran
Peter Tong	Sammee Tong
Vicky	J. D. Thompson
Rita	Barbara Darrow
Nancy	Patricia Morrow

Producer: Richard Lewis

The New Healers

Drama Pilot; 60 min; ABC 3/27/72

The story of two ex-Vietnam medics (Calvin and Jimmy) and a former nurse (Michelle) who join forces to help an aging doctor (Simmons) care for the people of Hope, a rural California community.

Michelle Johnson	Kate Jackson
Calvin Briggs	Robert Foxworth
Jimmy Martin	Jonathan Lippe
Dr. Simmons	Burgess Meredith
Dr. Victor Briggs	Leif Erickson
Mr. Farrigan	William Windom
Terri	Susan Moffatt
Mrs. Spencer	Barbara Baldavin

Producer: Stirling Silliphant

The New Hollywood Squares

Game; 30 min; Syn. 9/86

A revised version of "The Hollywood Squares," which see for format. See also "The Match Game-Hollywood Squares Hour."

Host: John Davidson

Announcer: Shadoe Stevens

Producer: Rick Rosner, Scott Sternberg

The New Howdy Doody Show

Children; 30 min; Syn. 9/76

An update of the 1947–60 series about the adventures of the puppet Howdy Doody. The new version relates songs, stories, and sketches geared to children.

Buffalo Bob Smith	Bob Smith
Clarabell Hornblow	Lew Anderson
Happy Harmony	Marilyn Patch
Fletcher the Sketcher	Milt Neil
Corneilius Cobb	Nick Nicholson
Nicholson Muir	Bill LeCornec
Jackie	Jackie Davis
Howdy's Voice	Bob Smith
Phineas T. Bluster's Voice	Dayton Allen

Producer: Nick Nicholson, E. Roger Muir

The New Jetsons

Cartoon; 30 min; Syn. 9/85

Newly animated adventures in the lives of the Jetsons: George, his wife, Jane, and their children Judy and Elroy, a 21st century family fraught with problems.

Voices: Mel Blanc, Susan Blu, Earl Boen, Foster Brooks, Daws Butler, Ruth Buzzi, Victoria Carroll, Didi Conn, Henry Corden, Peter Cullen, Julie Dees, Jerry Dexter, Selma Diamond, June Foray, Joan Gardner, Ken Mars, Howard Morris, Don Messick, Tim Rooney, Penny Singleton, Avery Schreiber, Fred Travalena, Paul Winchell, William Windom

Producer: William Hanna, Joseph Barbera

The New Land

Drama; 60 min; ABC 9/14/74 to 10/19/74

The life and struggles of the Larsens, Scandinavian immigrants, as they attempt to build a new life for themselves in Minnesota in 1858.

Christian Larsen	Scott Thomas
Ann Larsen	Bonnie Bedelia
Annaliase Larsen	Debbie Lytton
Tuliff Larsen	Todd Lookinland
Bo Larsen	Kurt Russell
Lars Lundstrom	Donald Moffat
Molly Lundstrom	Gwen Arner
Rhodie Lundstrom	Stephanie Steele
Mr. Murdock	Lou Frizzell

Producer: William Blinn, Philip Leacock

The New Leave It to Beaver

Comedy; 30 min; TBS 9/86 (Premiere)

A continuation of the "Still the Beaver" series which depicts further events in the lives of the Cleaver family: June, a widow, and her two children: Wally, a lawyer with a wife (Mary Ellen) and a daughter (Kelly), and Theodore "Beaver" a divorced father of two mischievous boys (Kip and Ollie). See also "It's a Small World," "Leave It to Beaver," and "Still the Beaver."

June Cleaver	Barbara Billingsley
Wally Cleaver	Tony Dow
Beaver Cleaver	Jerry Mathers
Mary Ellen Cleaver	Janice Kent
Kelly Cleaver	Kaleena Kiff
Kip Cleaver	Kipp Marcus
Ollie Cleaver	John Snee
Eddie Haskell	Ken Osmond
Freddie Haskell	Eric Osmond
Clarence "Lumpy" Rutherford	Frank Bank
J. J. Rutherford	Keri Houlihan

Producer: Brian Levant, Cindy Begel, Lesa Kite

The New Loretta Young Show

See "The Loretta Young Show."

The New Lorenzo Music Show

Comedy Pilot; 30 min; ABC 8/10/76

The story of Lorenzo Music, a nervous, anxiety-ridden writer who hosts a talk-variety show on TV.

Lorenzo Music	Himself
Henrietta Music	Herself

Guests: David Ogden Stiers, Jack Eagle, Lewis Arquette, Roz Kelly

Producer: Lorenzo Music, Carl Gottlieb

A New Kind of Family

Comedy; 30 min; ABC 9/16/79 to 1/5/80

The story of two families, the Flanagans and the Stones (later the Ashtons) and the problems that arise when they both agree to share a house at 1836 Loma Linda Drive in Los Angeles.

Kit Flanagan	Eileen Brennan
Hilary Flanagan	Lauri Hendler
Tony Flanagan	Rob Lowe
Andy Flanagan	David Hollander
Abby Stone	Gwynne Gilford
Jill Stone	Connie Hearn
Jessica Ashton	Telma Hopkins
JoJo Ashton	Janet Jackson
Harold Zimmerman	Chuck McCann
Michael Jansen	Robert Hogan
Carl Ashton	Scoey Mitchlll

Producer: Margie Gordon, Jane Eisner

The New Love American Style

Anthology; 30 min; ABC 12/23/85 to 8/15/86

A daily series of comedy vignettes that tackle the ups and downs of love, marriage, and divorce. Segments are interspersed with blackouts. A revised version of "Love, American Style."

Regulars: Marcia Wallace, Damita Jo Freeman, Norm Crosby, Amy Yasbeck, Barry Pearl, Arsenio Hall

Theme Vocal ("Love American Style"): Lou Rawls

Producer: Gordon Farr, Arnold Kane

The New Mickey Mouse Club

Children; 30 min; Syn. 1/77

An update of "The Mickey Mouse Club," which features twelve new Mouseketeers in songs and dances, and an array of Disney cartoons.

Mouseketeers: Lisa Whelchel, Kelly Parsons, Julie Piekarski, Mindy Feldman, Nita DiGiampaolo, Curtis Wong, Shawnte Northcutte, Allison Fonte, Todd Turquand, Angel Florez, Scott Craig

Voice of Mickey Mouse: Wayne Allwine

Voice of Jiminy Crickett: Cliff Edwards

Producer: Ron Miller

The New Mike Hammer

Crime Drama; 60 min; CBS 9/27/86 (Premiere)

A continuation of "Mickey Spillane's Mike Hammer" that depicts the further exploits of Mike Hammer, the hard-boiled New York detective created by Mickey Spillane.

Mike Hammer	Stacy Keach
Velda	Lindsay Bloom
Capt. Pat Chambers	Don Stroud
Lawrence Barrington	Kent Williams
Ozzie the Answer	Danny Goldman
The Face	Donna Denton

Theme Song ("Harlem Nocturne"): Earle Hagen

Producer: Jay Bernstein, Howard Berk, Ray Danton

The New Monkees

Comedy; 30 min; Syn. 9/87

An updated version of the cult series "The Monkees," which relates the adventures of the New Monkees (Marty, Dino, Larry, and Jared), four musicians who live in a very large and bizarre mansion. Each episode features two music videos and a new adventure.

Marty	Marty Ross
Dino	Dino Kovacs
Larry	Larry Saltis
Jared	Jared Chandler
Manfred (butler)	Gordon Oas-Heim
Helen (computer voice)	Liz Godfrey
Rita (waitress)	Bess Motta

Producer: Bob Bain, Victor Fresco

The New Newlywed Game

Game Pilot; 30 min; ABC 2/13/84 to 2/17/84

Four recent newlywed couples compete. In round one, the wives are isolated offstage while the husbands are asked four questions regarding their marriage. The wives, who are brought on stage, are asked the same questions and must predict what their husbands said. Points are scored for each correct match. Round two reverses the first round and the couple with the highest score is the winner.

Host: Jim Lange

Producer: Chuck Barris, Walt Case

The New Newlywed Game

Game; 30 min; Syn. 9/85

A syndicated version of the above unsold pilot (which see for format).

Host: Bob Eubanks

Announcer: Bob Hilton

Producer: Chuck Barris

The New Odd Couple

Comedy; 30 min; ABC 10/29/82 to 6/9/83

A revised version of "The Odd Couple," which continues to depict events in the lives of two mismatched roommates (black, in this instance): Felix Unger, a perfectionist photographer; and Oscar Madison, a sloppy sportswriter. Most episodes are recast versions of prior "Odd Couple" scripts.

Felix Unger	Ron Glass
Oscar Madison	Demond Wilson
Mira	Liz Torres
Cecily Pigeon	Sheila Anderson
Gwen Pigeon	Ronalda Douglas
Off. Murray Greschner	John Schuck
Frances Unger	Telma Hopkins
Roy	Bart Braverman
Vinnie	Marvin Braverman
Speed	Christopher Joy

Producer: Garry K. Marshall

The New Operation Petticoat

Comedy; 30 min; ABC 9/25/78 to 8/3/79

A revised version of "Operation Petticoat." When most of her crew transfers, the pink submarine "Sea Tiger" is restaffed and assigned to duty as a seagoing ambulance. Stories relate the crew's misadventures in the South Pacific during World War II.

Capt. Sam Haller	Robert Hogan
Lt. Michael Bender	Randolph Mantooth
Lt. Dolores Crandall	Melinda Naud
Lt. Katherine	
O'Hara	Jo Ann Pflug
Lt. Betty Wheeler	Hilary Thompson
Chief Stanley	
Dobritch	Warren Berlinger
Yeoman Alvin	
Hunkle	Richard Brestoff
Lt. Travis Kern	Sam Chew Jr.
Seaman Broom	Jim Varney
Seaman Horner	Don Sparks
Seamon Doplos	Fred Kareman
Chief Manhiannini	Martin Azarow
Seaman Kostos	Peter Mamakos

Producer: Jeff Harris, Bernie Kukoff

The New $100,000 Name That Tune

Game; 30 min; Syn. 9/84

A revised version of "The $100,000 Name That Tune," wherein two players attempt to identify song titles from brief musical clues. The highest scoring player receives the opportunity to win $100,000 by guessing a song from only one note.

Host: Jim Lange

Announcer: John Harlan

Orchestra: Tommy Oliver

Producer: Nelson Davis

The New, Original Wonder Woman

See "Wonder Woman" (Series 1).

The New People

Drama; 45 min; ABC 9/22/69 to 1/12/70

While enroute to Manila, a small plane is caught in a fierce storm and damaged. The plane crash lands on Bormano, a remote Pacific island once chosen as a hydrogen bomb test site, but abandoned due to fear of contamination by trade winds. Of the fifty passengers on board, forty American college students in a cultural exchange program survive. Stories relate their struggles to establish a society that is untouched by the destruction of modern man. In the first episode, written by John Phillips and directed by George Mc-

Cowan, an adult survivor of the crash (Mr. Hanachek, played by Richard Kiley) helps "The New People" establish themselves on the island (Hannachek later dies of the injures he suffered in the crash).

Susan Bradley	Tiffany Bolling
Robert E. Lee	Zooey Hall
Eugene "Bones"	
Washington	David Moses
George Potter	Peter Ratray
Errol "Bull" Wilson	Lee Jay Lambert
Dexter	Kevin Michaels
Wendy	Donna Baccala
Ginny	Jill Jaress
Gloria	Nancy DeCarol
Brenda	Brenda Sykes
Jack	Clive Clerk
Stanley	Dennis Olivieri
	Kevin O'Neal
Dan Stoner	Carl Reindel

Theme Vocal ("The New People"): The First Edition

Producer: Aaron Spelling, Danny Thomas

Creator: Rod Serling

The New Perry Mason

Crime Drama; 60 min; CBS 9/16/73 to 1/27/74

The cases of Perry Mason, a brilliant criminal attorney working out of Los Angeles. See also "Perry Mason."

Perry Mason	Monte Markham
Della Street	Sharon Acker
Hamilton Burger	Harry Guardino
Paul Drake	Albert Stratton
Lt. Arthur Tragg	Dane Clark
Gertie Lade	Brett Somers

Producer: Cornwell Jackson, Ernie Frankel, Art Seid

The New Phil Silvers Show

Comedy; 30 min; CBS 9/28/63 to 6/27/64

The story of Harry Grafton, a maintenance superintendent for Osborne Industries, who manipulates his men and his company for the benefit of himself.

Harry Grafton	Phil Silvers	Shmoo	Frank Welker
Audrey (his sister)	Elena Verdugo	Nita	Dolores Cantu-Prima
Susan (Audrey's daughter)	Sandy Descher	Billy Joe	Chuck McCann
Andy (Audrey's son)	Ronnie Dapo	Mickey	Bill Idelson
Mr. Brink (Harry's boss)	Stafford Repp		

Producer: William Hanna, Joseph Barbera

Louise (Brink's secretary)	Elaine Gardner
Waluska (worker)	Herbie Faye
Lester (worker)	Jim Shane
Roxy (worker)	Pat Renella
Scarpitta (worker)	Norman Grabowski
	Henry Scott

Producer: Nat Hiken, Rod Amateau

The New Price Is Right

Game; 30 min; CBS 9/4/72 to 10/31/75

A revised version of "The Price Is Right," which requires players to guess the suggested retail price of specific merchandise items.

Host: Bob Barker

Assistants: Nancy Myers, Pamela Parker, Anitra Ford, Holly Hallstrom, Janice Pennington, Dian Parkinson

Announcer: Johnny Olsen

Producer: Frank Wayne

The New Steve Allen Show

Variety; 60 min; ABC 9/27/61 to 12/27/61

A weekly program of music and comedy.

Host: Steve Allen

Regulars: Tom and Dick Smothers, Louis Nye, Pat Harrington Jr., Bill Dana, Joey Forman, Tim Conway

Producer: Bill Harbach

The New Shmoo

Cartoon; 30 min; NBC 9/22/79 to 12/1/79

The adventures of the Shmoo, an Al Capp comic strip character, as it and its three human friends, Nita, Mickey and Billy Joe, investigate psychic phenomena.

The New Show

Variety; 30 min; NBC 1/6/84 to 3/23/84
8/18/84 (1 episode)

Topical comedy sketches coupled with music by top name guest stars.

Regulars: Dave Thomas, John Candy, Buck Henry, Valri Bromfield, Maggie Jacobson, Tom Davis, J. D. Smith, Laura Monahan

Announcer: Jeff Bergman

Orchestra: Howard Shore

Producer: Lorne Michaels

The New Soupy Sales Show

Variety; 30 min; Syn. 1979

A series of music, songs, and outlandish comedy sketches.

Host: Soupy Sales

Regulars: Clyde Adler, Marty Brill

Producer: Sheldon Brodsky, Perry Cross

The New Stu Erwin Show

See "Trouble with Father."

The New Super Friends Hour

Cartoon; 55 min; ABC 9/10/77 to 9/2/78

A spin-off from "The Super Friends," which continues to depict their battle against evil.

Superman	Danny Dark
Wonder Woman	Shannon Farnon
Batman	Olan Soule
Robin	Casey Kasem
Aquaman	Norman Alden
Zan	Michael Bell
Jayna	Liberty Williams
Narrator	William Woodson
	Bob Lloyd

Producer: William Hanna, Joseph Barbera

The New Treasure Hunt

Game; 30 min; Syn. 9/73

Three players each stand before a jack-in-the-box. The player whose box contains a Treasure Hunt card chooses one of thirty boxes that are displayed on stage. The contents, or a cash bribe not to take the box, becomes the player's prize. See also "Treasure Hunt."

Host: Geoff Edwards

Assistant: Jane Nelson, Siv Aberg

Check Guard: Emil Autre

Announcer: Johnny Jacobs

Producer: Chuck Barris, Mike Metzger

The New Truth or Consequences

Game; 30 min; Syn. 9/77

Contestants who are unable to answer a nonsense riddle must pay the consequences and perform stunts. Prizes are awarded based on a player's performance. See also "Truth or Consequences."

Host: Bob Hilton

Announcer: John Harlan

Producer: Jon Ross, Ralph Edwards, Bruce Belland

The New Truth or Consequences

Game; 30 min; Syn. 9/87

A revised version of the prior title, which see for format.

Host: Larry Anderson

Regulars: Hillary Safire, Murray Langston

Producer: Ralph Edwards, Stu Billet

The New Temperatures Rising Show

Comedy; 30 min; ABC 9/25/73 to 8/30/74

A satirization of medical series as seen through the antics of the staff of Capitol General Hospital in Washington, D.C. A spin-off from "Temperatures Rising."

Dr. Paul Mercy	Paul Lynde
Dr. Jerry Noland	Cleavon Little
Nurse Wendy Winchester	Jennifer Darling
Nurse Tillis	Barbara Cason
Dr. Charles Claver	John Dehner
Dr. Lloyd Axton	Jeff Morrow
Edwina Mercy	Alice Ghostley
Agatha Mercy	Sudie Bond
Nurse Kelly	Barbara Rucker
	Sharleen Cotwright
Orderly Haskell	Jerry Houser
Orderly Jackson	Ken Smedberg
Nurse Hamlin	Sandy Freeman
Nurse Reed	Mary Batten

Producer: Bruce Johnson, E. Duke Vincent

The New Three Stooges

Cartoon; 10 min; Syn. 1966

Animated adventures that follow the antics of the Three Stooges (Moe, Larry, and Curly). Adapted from the series of theatrical shorts made in the thirties and forties.

Moe	Moe Howard
Larry	Larry Fine
Curly	Curly Joe Howard
	Joe DeRita

Producer: Dick Brown

The New $25,000 Pyramid

Game; 30 min; CBS 9/20/82 (Premiere)

One team (two compete) chooses one category from six that are displayed on a large pyramid. Within a thirty second time limit, one member must relay the category's subjects to his partner via one word clues. Each team plays three categories and the highest scoring player receives the opportunity to win $25,000 by attempting to guess six subjects within sixty seconds. The program was originally syndicated in January as "The $50,000 Pyramid" before becoming a daily CBS series in September of 1982.

Host: Dick Clark

Announcer: Alan Calder, Jack Clark, Charlie O'Donnell

Producer: Bob Stewart, Anne Marie Schmitt

The New Voice

Comedy-Drama; 30 min; PBS 1981

The lives of a group of students who write for the "New Voice," the newspaper of Boston's Lincoln High School.

Lorraine George	Lorraine Gauli
Millie	Millie Santiago
Ken	Ken Mochizuki
Claudio	Claudio Martinez
Larry	Larry B. Scott
Kiko	Kiko Mckee Redwing
Mr. Morfi	Shawn Elliott
Mrs. Carrington	Carmen DeLavallad

Producer: Frank Marrero

New York Confidential

Crime Drama; 30 min; Syn. 1958

The exploits of Lee Cochran, a tough newspaper reporter-columnist working out of New York City.

Lee Cochran	Lee Tracy

Producer: Leon Fromkess

The New Zoo Revue

Children; 30 min; Syn. 1972

The series, set in a zoo, describes various aspects of the world to children via sketches, songs, and stories.

Emmy Jo (host)	Emily Peden
Doug (host)	Doug Momary
Charlie (owl)	Sharon Baird
Charlie's Voice	Bill Callaway Bob Holt
Freddie (frog)	Yanco Inone
Freddie's Voice	Joni Robbins
Henrietta (hippo)	Thomas Cari Larry Thomas
Henrietta's Voice	Hazel Shermit
Mr. Dingle	Chuck Woolery
Miss Goodbody	Fran Ryan

Producer: Gordon Wiles, Thomas A. Hill

Newhart

Comedy; 30 min; CBS 10/25/82 (Premiere)

The story of Dick Loudon, a history buff and "how to" book author who moves from New York City to Vermont to run a 200-year-old inn (The Stratford Inn). Stories relate his and his wife, Joanna's efforts to run the inn.

Dick Loudon	Bob Newhart
Joanna Loudon	Mary Frann
Leslie Vanderkellen	Jennifer Holmes
Stephanie Vanderkellen	Julia Duffy
George Utley	Tom Poston
Kirk Devane	Steven Kampmann
Cindy Parker	Rebecca York
Larry	William Sanderson
Darryl One	Tony Papenfuss
Darryl Two	John Volstedt
Michael Harris	Peter Scolari
Arthur Vanderkellen	Richard Roat Jose Ferrer
Mary Vanderkellen	Priscilla Pointer
Jim Dixon	Thomas Hills
Chester Wanamaker	William Lanteau
Shirley Dixon	Lois de Banzie
Beverly Dutton	Linda Carlson
Constable Shifflett	Todd Susman
Harley Estin	Jeff Doucette

"Newhart" Theme Song: Earle Hagen

Producer: Barry Kemp, Sheldon Bull

The Newlywed Game

Game; 30 min; ABC 7/11/66 to 12/20/74

Four husband-and-wife teams compete. The object calls for the wives to predict how their husbands answered certain questions, and vice versa. Highest scoring teams are the winner. See also "The All New Newlywed Game" and "The New Newlywed Game."

Host: Bob Eubanks

Announcer: Johnny Jacobs

Producer: Chuck Barris

Newman's Drugstore

Comedy Pilot; 30 min; NBC 8/30/76

The story, set in Brooklyn, N.Y., during the Depression, tells of a druggist (Charles Newman) who is overly generous with his hard-luck customers—a generosity that threatens to sink his business.

Charles Newman	Herschel Bernardi
Woody Newman	Michael LeClair
Shirley Tinker	June Gable
Leon Rossoff	Allan Rich
Murray Tinker	Robert Lussier
Dora Goldman	Fritzi Burr
Marcy Goldman	Dominique Pinassi

Producer: Robert Lovenheim, Mitchell Brower

The News Is the News

Comedy; 30 min; NBC 6/15/83 to 7/13/83

A satirization of television newsmagazine series. Also known as "TN-2."

Newscaster: Simon Jones, Charlotte Moore, Lynne Thigpen, Michael Davis, Trey Wilson

London Correspondent: Michael Palin

Announcer: Karen Dale

Music: Bob Mounsey

Producer: Herb Sargent

Newsstand Theatre

A short-lived ABC anthology (1/16/52 to 2/6/52) of dramatizations based on short stories. Produced by Wilbur Stark.

The Next Step Beyond

Anthology; 30 min; Syn. 9/78

True stories of psychic happenings. An update of "One Step Beyond."

Host-Narrator: John Newland

Theme Song ("The Next Step Beyond"): Mark Snow

Producer: Collier Young, Alan Jay Factor

Nichols

Western; 60 min; NBC 9/16/71 to 8/8/72

After an absence of eighteen years, Nichols (no first name) returns to his home town (Nichols) and discovers that it has been homesteaded from his mother by the evil Scully brothers. While attempting to drown his sorrows, Nichols is inolved in a barroom brawl and arrested. When he is unable to pay for the damages, Ma Ketchum, the self-appointed law, makes him the sheriff (so he can repay the debt through his salary). Stories, set in Nichols, Arizona, in 1914, relate the less-than-honorable exploits of Nichols as he attempts to maintain the law.

Nichols	James Garner
Jim Nichols*	James Garner
Deputy Mitchell	Stuart Margolin
Sara "Ma" Ketchum	Neva Patterson
Ruth (barmaid)	Margot Kidder
Ketchum (Ma's son)	John Beck
Salter (bar owner)	John Harding
Johnson (con artist)	Paul Hampton
Bertha (saloonkeeper)	Alice Ghostley
Judge Thatcher	Richard Bull
Gabe (store owner)	M. Emmett Walsh
Scully One	John Quade
Scully Two	Jesse Wayne

Producer: Meta Rosenberg

*In the last episode, Nichols is killed while attempting to stop a barroom brawl. His twin brother, Jim was introduced in an attempt to present a more forceful lead. The series, however, was not renewed.

Nichols and Dymes

Comical Adventure Pilot; 60 min; NBC 10/7/81

The exploits of Buck Nichols and Willy Dymes, two unconventional federal undercover agents.

Buck Nichols	Rocky Bauer
Willy Dymes	Robin Strand
Chief Whitney	George McDaniel
Sgt. Wilkins	Bill Cross
Laura Jean	Teddi Siddall
Aunt Lydia	Kate Murtaugh

Producer: Bob Comfort, Rick Kellard

Nick and Nora

Mystery Pilot; 90 min; ABC 3/4/75

A potential series based on "The Thin Man" characters created by Dashiell Hammett, about Nick and Nora Charles, a husband-and-wife private detective team. See also "The Thin Man."

Nick Charles	Craig Stevens
Nora Charles	Jo Ann Pflug
Sgt. Steinmetz	Jack Kruschen
Mickey Garrity	Denny Miller
Capt. Kingsley	Charles Lampkin
Madeline	Judith Brown
Mrs. Thurston	Carmel Myers

Producer: Seymour Berns

Nick and the Dobermans

Crime Drama Pilot; 60 min; NBC 4/25/80

The story of Nick Macazie, a private detective who receives assistance from three smart Doberman pinschers.

Nick Macazie	Michael Nouri
Lt. Elbone	Robert Davi
Barbara Gateon	Judith Chapman
Roger Vincent	John Cunningham
Speed Queen	Vivian Bonnell

Producer: Harve Bennett, Harris Katleman

Night Club

Experimental; 30 min; NBC 6/9/39

A program of music and song set against the background of a New York nightclub.

Performers: Jean and Frank Huber, Ella Logan, Bob Nellor, Charlie Carrer, Joe Jackson Jr., Buck & Bubbles

Producer-Director: Edward Sobol

Night Court

Drama; 30 min; Syn. 1965

Dramatizations based on the files of New York and Los Angeles Night Court hearings.

Judge	Jay Jostyn
Public Defender	Sandy Spillman
	Barney Biro

Night Court

Comedy; 30 min; NBC 1/4/84 (Premiere)

The antics of Harold T. Stone, an oddball judge in a Manhattan night court.

Judge Harold T. Stone	Harry Anderson
Lana Wagner	Karen Austin
Dan Fielding	John Larroquette
Sheila Gardner	Gail Strickland
Bull Shannon	Richard Moll
Selma Hacker	Selma Diamond
Liz Williams	Paula Kelly
Charli Tracy	D. D. Howard
Mac Robinson	Charles Robinson
Billie Young	Ellen Foley
Christine Sullivan	Markie Post
Florence Kleiner	Florence Halop
Quan Le Duc	Denice Kumagai
Leon	Bumper Robinson
Christine Lund	Margot Rose
Roz Russell	Marsha Warfield
Al Craven	Terry Kiser

Producer: Reinhold Weege

Night Editor

Anthology; 15 min; DuMont 3/18/54 to 9/8/54

The work of newspapermen as seen through the eyes of Hal Burdick, the night editor of a newspaper.

Host-Narrator: Hal Burdick

Producer: Irving Mansfield, Ward Byron

Night Gallery

Anthology; NBC 9/15/71 to 9/6/72 (60 min)
9/17/72 to 8/12/73 (30 min)

Stories of the occult and supernatural. Originally broadcast as a segment of "Four-In-One."

Host (Guide Through a Bizarre Night Gallery): Rod Serling

"Night Gallery" Theme Song: Gil Melle

Producer: Jack Laird

Night Heat

Crime Drama; 70 min; CBS 1/31/85 (Premiere)

The series, set in Toronto, Canada, focuses on the rewards, frustrations, and comradeship of detectives working the night shift as seen through th eyes of Tom Kirkwood, a reporter whose column "Night Heat" (for "The Eagle") depicts the gritty realism of urban crime.

Tom Kirkwood	Allan Royal
Det. Kevin O'Brien	Scott Hylands
Det. Frank Giambone	Jeff Wincott
Det. Florence Toland	Wynda Mason Green
Dorothy Fredericks	Wendy Crewson
Lt. Bob Hogan	Sean McCann
Nicole	Susan Hogan
Dr. Freddie Carson	Stephen Mendel
Det. Colby Burns	Eugene Clark
Off. Elaine Jeffers	Debra Grover
Off. Stephanie Brody	Louise Vallance
Helen Hogan	Maxine Miller
Whitey Low	Tony Rosato

"Night Heat" theme vocal: B. J. Cook

Producer: Sonny Grosso, Larry Jacobson

The Night Stalker

Mystery; 60 min; ABC 9/13/74 to 8/30/75

The exploits of Carl Kolchak, a reporter for the Chicago-based Independent News Service, as he strives to solve bizarre, supernatural-based crimes.

Carl Kolchak	Darren McGavin
Tony Vincenzo	Simon Oakland
Ron Updyke	Jack Grinnage
Monique Marmelstein	Carol Ann Susi
Emily Cowles	Ruth McDevitt
Gordon "The Ghoul" Spangler	John Fielder

Narrator: Darren McGavin

Producer: Cy Chermak, Paul Playdon

The Nightengales

Crime Drama Pilot; 60 min; NBC 5/19/79

The exploits of Jenny Palermo and Cotton Gardner, two beautiful Los Angeles undercover police women, called "The Nightengales," who work the Hollywood beat at night.

Off. Jenny Palermo	Marcia Strassman
Off. Cotton Gardner	Colette Blonigan
Big Duane	James Spinks
Sgt. Donovan	Richard Hatch
Fingernail Dolly	Sheree North
Ice	Dennis Redfield
James	Ji-Tu Cumbuka
"Humphrey Bogart"	Jerry Lacy

Producer: Lawrence Gordon, Jay Benson

Nightmare

A syndicated (1958) series of dramas that depict the plight of people who are suddenly involved in perilous situations.

Nightside

Drama Pilot; 60 min; ABC 4/15/73

The story of Carmine Kelly, a press agent who covers the midnight action in New York City.

Carmine Kelly	John Cassavetes
Smitty	Alexis Smith
Aram Bessoyggian	Mike Kellin
Vantura Davis	June Havoc
Jabbo	Joe Santos
Grudin	Joseph Wiseman
Shane	Seth Allen

Producer: Herbert B. Leonard

Creator: Pete Hamill

90 Bristol Court

Comedy; 90 min; NBC 10/5/64 to 1/4/65

The title for three comedies set against the background of 90 Bristol Court, a fictitious apartment-motel in Southern California. For information, see the following titles: "Harris Against the World," "Karen" (1964 version), and "Tom, Dick, and Mary."

9 to 5

Comedy; 30 min; ABC 3/25/82 to 4/15/82
9/28/82 to 10/27/83

The comical problems faced by secretaries in a large Cleveland, Ohio-based corporation run by a sexist boss. (During the first season, it is Consolidated Industries; it became American Household Products for the remainder of the series.) Based on the Dolly Parton feature film. See also the following title.

Violet Newstead	Rita Moreno
Doralee Rhoades	Rachel Dennison
Judy Burnley	Valerie Curtin
Linda Bowman	Leah Ayres
Franklin Hart Jr.	Jeffrey Tambor
	Peter Bonerz
Roz Keith	Jean Marsh
Harry Pearlman	Herb Edelman
Mike Anderson	George Deloy
Dag Larson	James Komack
Lois Hart	Gail Strickland
Mr. O'Malley	Peter Hobbs
Betty	Peggy Pope
Roberta	Suzanne Stone
Denise	Mary Farrell
Claire	Ann Weldon
Tommy Newstead	Tony LaTorre
O'Neal	Jane Fonda

Theme Vocal ("Nine to 5"): Phoebe Snow (1st season); Dolly Parton

Producer: Jane Fonda, Bruce Gilbert, James Komack

9 to 5

Comedy; 30 min; Syn. 9/86

A revised version of the prior title which continues to depict events in the lives of a group of secretaries for Berkley Foods International, a world-wide corporation based in New York City.

Marsha McMurray	Sally Struthers
Judy Burnley	Valerie Curtin
Doralee Brooks	Rachel Dennison
Sharman Cunningham	Dorian Lopinto
William "Bud" Coleman	Edward Winter
Russ Merman	Peter Evans
Morgan	Art Evans

Theme Vocal ("Nine to Five"): Dolly Parton

Producer: Michael Kagan, Ava Nelson

No Complaints!

Comedy Pilot; 30 min; NBC 7/24/85

After a 12-year absence, former college roommates and best friends Valerie Anastas (a housewife with two children), and Joanna Newman (a vice president with the Burken, Wain & Burken ad agency) resume their friendship when they again meet. The unsold series was to relate the misadventures of two best friends.

Valerie Anastas	Diana Canova
Joanna Newman	Anne Twomey
Jack Wain	Harold Gould
Nick Anastas	James Sutorius
Melanie Anastas	Emily Moultrie
Michael Burken	Brad O'Hare
Raymond Anastas	Matt Dill
Millie	Martha McFarland
Claire	Donna Ponterotto

"No Complaints" Theme by Judy Hart Angelo and Gary Portnoy

Producer: Margie Peters, Linda Marsh, Asaad Kelada

No Holds Barred

Comedy; 70 min; CBS 9/12/80 to 10/3/80

A look at the crackpot side of contemporary American life via film and videotaped segments.

Host: Kelly Monteith

Music: Tony Romeo

Producer: Herbert Banska

No—Honestly

Comedy; 30 min; PBS 7/9/75 to 9/3/75

The series, set in England, follows the courtship and early married life of the Danbys: Charles, an actor, and his scatterbrained wife Clara, author of "Otto the Otter" stories for children.

Charles Danby	John Addison
Clara Danby	Pauline Collins
Lord Burrell	James Berwick
Lady Burrell	Fanny Rowe
Royal	Kenneth Benda

Producer: Humphrey Barclay

No Place Like Home

Comedy Pilot; 30 min; CBS 9/6/85

When Marsha and Diana, girlhood friends come to the conclusion that the only way they can afford their lifelong dream of owning a home is to buy one together, they convince their mates of the decision. The unsold series was to relate the misadventures of Marsha (and her husband, Paul) and Diana (and her live-in boyfriend, Murray) as they attempt to share a house.

Diana	Susan Hess
Marsha Brayfield	Molly Cheek
Paul Brayfield	Rick Lohman
Murray McCoy	Jack Blessing
Roxy	Erica Yohn
Rick	Archie Hahn
Benny	Jeff Silverman

Music: Joe Raposo

Producer: Don Taffner, Jeff Harris

No Soap, Radio

Comedy; 30 min; ABC 4/15/82 to 5/13/82

The series, set at the floundering Hotel Pelican in Atlantic City, N.J., focuses on the antics of the staff and its residents.

Roger (proprietor)	Steve Guttenberg
Sharon (desk clerk)	Brianne Leary
	Hillary Bailey
Mr. Plitzky (resident)	Bill Dana
Morris (bellboy)	Jerry Marin
Mrs. Belmont (resident)	Fran Ryan
Al Tuttle (detective)	Stuart Pankin
Marian (resident)	Edie McClurg
Gunther (resident)	Johnny Haymer
Victoria (resident)	Victoria Carroll

Various Roles: Joe Baker, Gary Owens, Jack Kruschen, Bob Hastings, Renny Peterson, Sidney Miller, Roselyn Royce

Producer: Mort Lachman, Bill Richmond

No Time for Sergeants

Comedy; 30 min; ABC 9/19/64 to 9/6/65

The story of Will Stockdale, a naive Georgia farm boy who is drafted into the Air Force, and his attempts to adjust to military life. Based on the feature film.

Will Stockdale	Sammy Jackson
Sgt. Orville King	Harry Hickox
Capt. Paul Martin	Paul Smith
Pvt. Ben Whitledge	Kevin O'Neil
Millie Anderson	Laurie Sibbald
Grandpa Anderson	Andy Clyde
Pvt. Irving Blanchard	Greg Benedict
Pvt. Jack Langdon	Michael McDonald
Pvt. Neddick	Joe E. Tata
Col. Farnsworth	Hayden Rorke
Tilda Jay Stockdale	Stacey Maxwell
Pa Stockdale	Frank Ferguson

Producer: William T. Orr, George Burns

No Warning

Anthology; 30 min; NBC 4/6/58 to 9/7/58

A revised version of "Panic" that relates the plight of people whose lives are suddenly placed in peril by an unexpected crisis.

Narrator: Westbrook Van Voorhis

Producer: Al Simon

Noah's Ark

Drama; 30 min; NBC 9/18/56 to 2/26/57

The work of Sam Rinehart and Noah McCann, two dedicated veterinarians.

Dr. Noah McCann	Paul Burke
Dr. Sam Rinehart	Vic Rodman
Nurse Liz Clark	May Wynn
Agnes Marshall	Natalie Masters
Davy Marshall	Paul Engle
Glenn White	Russell Whitney

Theme Vocal ("Noah"): The Hi-Los

Producer-Director: Jack Webb

Nobody's Perfect

Comedy; 30 min; ABC 6/26/80 to 8/28/80

The exploits of Roger Hart, a brilliant Scotland Yard inspector attached to the San Francisco Police Department's 22nd Precinct, who suffers from one imperfection: he is calamity prone.

Insp. Roger Hart — Ron Moody
Off. Jennifer
Dempsey — Cassie Yates
Lt. Vince
DeGennaro — Michael Durrell
Careful Eddie — Danny Wells
Det. Jacobi — Victor Brandt
Det. Grauer — Tom Williams
Det. Ramsey — Renny Roker
Dreyfus — Greg Monaghan
Police Woman — Melody Rogers

Producer: Norman Barasch, Arne Sultan, Chris Hayward

The Noel Edmonds Show

Comedy Pilot; 60 min; 6/21/86 to 6/27/86

A five-part pilot for a potential late-night potpourri of music, comedy, unusual variety acts, and celebrity interviews.

Host: Noel Edmonds.

Orchestra: Kevin Kiner

Producer: Bob Booker, Barbara Booker, Troy Miller

The Noonday Show

Variety; 25 min; NBC 12/15/75 to 12/19/75

A short-lived, daily program of news, music, and comedy.

Host: David Steinberg

Regulars: Stan Cann, Jane Dulo, Gailard Sartaine, Bill Saluga, Carol Androsky

Orchestra: David Foster

Producer: Marty Pasetta

N.O.P.D.

Crime Drama; 30 min; Syn. 1956

The exploits of Detectives Beaujac and Conroy, law enforcers with the New Orleans Police Department.

Det. Beaujac — Stacy Harris
Det. Conroy — Lou Sirgo

Producer: Frank Phares

Norby

Comedy; 30 min; NBC 1/5/55 to 4/6/55

Incidents in the lives of the Norbys: Pearson, vice president of the First National Bank of Pearl River (N.Y.), his wife, Helen, and their children, Diane and Hank.

Pearson Norby — David Wayne
Helen Norby — Joan Lorring
Diane Norby — Susan Holloran
Hank Norby — Evan Elliott
Bobo (neighbor) — Jack Weston
Maureen (Bobo's wife) — Maxine Stuart
Wahleen Johnson (operator) — Janice Mars
Bank President — Paul Ford
Maude Endles (president, later) — Carol Veazie
Mr. Rudge (efficiency expert) — Ralph Dunn

Producer: David Swift

Norma Rae

Drama Pilot; 60 min; NBC 11/21/81

The experiences of Norma Rae Webster, a textile mill worker in the town of Oakalona. Based on the 1979 Sally Field feature film.

Norma Rae Webster — Cassie Yates
Willie Webster — Nancy Jarnagin
Craig Webster — Keith Mitchell
Vernon Witchard — Barry Corbin
Alma Woodruff — Jane Atkins
Frank Osborne — Jordan Clarke
William Poole — Ernest Hardin Jr.
Reuben — Gary Frank
Emery — Mickey Jones

Producer: Tamara Asseyer, Nigel Mackeand

Norman Corwin Presents

A syndicated (1971) series of dramatic stories hosted by Norman Corwin. Produced by Arthur Joel Katz.

Northwest Passage

Adventure; 30 min; NBC 9/14/58 to 9/7/59

The series, set during the French and Indian Wars (1754–59) relates the adventures of Major Robert Rogers, an explorer and Indian fighter, as he organizes a group of men (his Rogers Rangers) to search for the fabled Northwest Passage, a waterway that links the East and West.

Maj. Robert Rogers	Keith Larsen
Sgt. Hunk Marriner	Buddy Ebsen
Ensign Langdon Towne	Don Burnett
Gen. Amherst	Philip Tonge
Natula	Lisa Davis
Black Wolf	Larry Chance
Rivas	Pat Hogan
Jonas	Jim Hayward

Producer: Adrian Samish

Not for Hire

Crime Drama; 30 min; Syn. 1959

The exploits of Steve Dekker, a sergeant with the U.S. Army's Criminal Investigation Division, as he attempts to solve crimes associated with the military. Also known as "Sgt. Steve Dekker."

Sgt. Steve Dekker	Ralph Meeker
WAC Sonia Zametoo	Lizabeth Rush
Cpl. Zimmerman	Ken Drake

Producer: John Florea

Not for Publication

Drama; 30 min; DuMont 4/27/51 to 8/27/51

Stories of human interest (later facts behind the headline making stories) as seen through the eyes of Collins, a reporter for the New York "Ledger." Also known as "Reporter Collins."

Collins	William Adler
	Jerome Cowan

Producer: Charles J. Parson, Barry Shear

Not in Front of the Kids

Comedy Pilot; 30 min; ABC 6/16/84

Events in the lives of Ben and Millie Rosen, a middle-aged couple who are temporarily caring for their grandchildren, Amy and Jimmy, while their parents are away.

Ben Rosen	Don Ameche
Millie Rosen	Katherine Helmond
Amy	Amanda Herman
Jimmy	Jason Naylor
Iris Bunch	Bette Ford
Airport official	Liz Torres

Producer: Mort Lachman, Sy Rosen

Not Necessarily the News

Satire; 30 min; HBO 1/3/83 (Premiere)

The series combines actual news footage (slightly edited for laughs) with sketches and blackouts that satirize television news programs. Based on the British series "Not the Nine O'Clock News" (see the following title). The pilot aired 9/14/82.

Regulars: Annie Bloom, Stuart Pankin, Lucy Webb, Danny Breen, Rich Hall, Audrie Neenan, Sam McMurray, Tommy Koenig

Announcer: Bill Martin

Producer: John Moffitt, Pat Lee

Not the Nine O'Clock News

Satire; 30 min; Syn. 6/81

A series of topical sketches that spoof TV news programs. A British series that became the basis for "Not Necessarily the News."

Regulars: Rowan Atkinson, Pamela Stephenson, Mel Smith, Griff Rhys Jones

Producer: Sean Hardie, John Lloyd

Not Until Today

Comedy Pilot; 30 min; NBC 6/27/79

Events in the life of Jason Swan, a police chief.

Jason Swan	Darren McGavin
Jake Warren	Michael Horton
Mae	Lynn Carlin
Francis Dacey	Dick Sargent
Sally	Alexandra Stoddard

Producer: Michael Zinberg, David Lloyd

Nothing But the Best

Variety; 30 min; NBC 7/7/53 to 9/13/53

Eddie Albert as the host of a program of celebrity interviews and performances by guests. Music by Skitch Henderson.

Nothing But the Truth

Game; 30 min; CBS 12/18/56 to 12/25/56

Three contestants appear and each claims to be the same person. Through a series of indirect question-and-answer rounds, a celebrity panel has to determine which contestant is telling the truth. Became "To Tell the Truth" three weeks later.

Host (12/18): John Cameron Swayze

Host (12/25): Clayton "Bud" Collyer

Panelists: Polly Bergen, Dick Van Dyke, Mike Wallace

Producer: Mark Goodson, Bill Todman

Nothing in Common

Comedy; 30 min; NBC 4/2/87 to 5/14/87

The relationship between David Basner, the head of a struggling ad agency in Chicago (David Basner and Associates) and his recently divorced father, Max, a toy salesman who constantly interferes in his life. Based on the 1986 feature film and developed for TV by Garry Marshall.

David Basner	Todd Warring
Max Basner	Bill Macy
Jacqueline North	Wendy Kilbourne
Victoria Upton-Smythe	Elizabeth Bennett
Norma Starr	Mona Lyden
Roland Reed	Paul Tinder
Mark Glick	Bill Applebaum
Myron Nipper	Patrick Richwood
Joey D.	Billy Wirth

Producer: Garry Marshall, Alexandra Rose

Nothing Is Easy

Comedy; 30 min; CBS 2/8/87 to 4/24/87

A revised version of "Together We Stand." Following the death of her husband in a car accident, Lori Randall secures a job and enrolls in school to become a court stenographer. Stories relate Lori's efforts to contend with a job, raise four mischievous children, and complete her studies.

Lori Randall	Dee Wallace
Amy Randall (her daughter)	Katie O'Neill
Jack Randall (son)	Scott Grimes
Sam (son)	Ke Huy Quan
Sally (daughter)	Natasha Bobo
Marion (neighbor)	Julia Migenes

Producer: Sherwood Schwartz, Paul Haggis, John H. Ward

Now Is Tomorrow

Anthology Pilot; 30 min; Unaired; Produced in 1961

An unsold series about people who are placed in situations that could change the course of mankind. The pilot tells of an air force captain who is given the power (and authority) to destroy the world should the need arise.

Host: Charles Bickford	
Capt. David Blair	Robert Culp
Col. Hilyard	Simon Scott
Capt. Stein	Sidney Pollack
Capt. Ward	Warren Vanders

Producer: Alvin Cooperman

Now We're Cookin'

Comedy Pilot; 30 min; CBS 4/19/83

The misadventures of Cookie, Rolly, and Tony, three ex-cons working in a diner and struggling to go straight.

Cookie Porter	Lyman Ward
Rollin "Rolly" Hutton	Cleavon Little
Tony Tarzola	Paul Carafotes
Marge (diner owner)	Carol Cooke
Janine Rogers (parole officer)	Lynne Moody
Vern	Gary Allen
Ernie	Joe Mantegna
Roxanne La Tucci	Toni Kalem

Producer: Joel Schumacher, Noam Pitlik, Leonard Ripps

Now You See It

Game; 30 min; CBS 4/1/74 to 6/13/75

A board is displayed that contains four vertical lines of run-on letters. The four vertical lines, numbered 1 to 4, are the "line," and the fourteen letters each line contains (numbered 1 to 14) are the "position." One member (of a two member team) sits with his back to the board. A question is read and the teammate must locate the answer by calling a "line." If he is correct, his partner faces the board and has to call the "position" of the answer. Points are scored by the total of the "line" and "position." Two teams compete and the highest scorers are the winners.

Host: Jack Narz

Announcer: Johnny Olsen, Gene Wood

Producer: Frank Wayne, Mark Goodson, Bill Todman

Number Please

Game; 30 min; ABC 1/31/61 to 12/29/61

A line of twenty spaces is placed before each player. After a clue is given, the host calls a number, which players then remove from their line. A letter is revealed and players must identify the concealed phrase. The game continues in this manner until the phrase is identified.

Host: Bud Collyer

Number 13 Demon Street

Thriller; 30 min; Syn. 1962

When a 17-year-old girl (Santanya) kills herself over a lover's quarrel, she is sent to Hell. Because suicide is a special case, Santanya is offered the opportunity to escape Hell if she becomes a messenger for the Devil. Her assignment: Deliver a special invitation called a "Passport" which contains the evil necessary to make people candidates for Hell. Produced in Sweden.

The Devil	Lon Chaney Jr.
Santanya	Karen Kadler

Producer: Curt Siodmak, Gustaf Unger, Leo Guild

Number 96

Comedy; 60 min; NBC 12/10/80 to 1/2/81

The outrageous sexual activities of a group of people who reside at Number 96 Pacific Way,

a Los Angeles apartment building. Based on the Australian series.

Lou Sugarman	Eddie Barth
Rita Sugarman	Ellen Travolta
Max Quintzel	Greg Mullavey
Marion Quintzel	Randee Heller
Mark Keaton	Howard McGillin
Jill Keaton	Sherry Hursey
Sharon St. Clair	Hilary Thompson
Ginny Ramirez	Maria O'Brien
Anthea Bryan	Rosine Widdowson-Reynolds
Horace Batterson	Barney Martin
Sandy Galloway	Jill Choder
Maureen Galloway	Betsy Palmer
Nathan Sugarman	Todd Susman
Chick Walden	John Reilly
Lisa Brendon	Christine Jones
Roger Busky	James Murtaugh
Robert Leon	William Brian Curran
Dorothy	Sharon Spelman
Hildy	Elaine Giftos
Lyle Bixler	Charles Bloom

Producer: Bob Ellison, Allan Manings

Nurse

Drama; 60 min; CBS 4/2/81 to 5/7/81
11/11/81 to 5/21/82

The dramatic story of Mary Benjamin, a middle-aged widow who attempts to begin a new life by resuming her career as a head nurse at New York's Grant Memorial Hospital.

Mary Benjamin	Michael Learned
Dr. Kenneth Rose (later Adam Rose)	Robert Reed
Chip Benjamin	Christopher Marcantel
Joseph Calvo	Dennis Boutsikaris
Nurse Toni Gillette	Hattie Winston
Nurse Penny Brooks	Bonnie Hellman
Nurse Betty LaSada	Hortensia Colorado

Producer: Robert Halmi

The Nurses

Drama; 60 min; CBS 9/27/62 to 9/17/64
9/22/64 to 9/7/65

The personal and professional lives of Liz Thorpe and Gail Lucas, dedicated nurses at

New York's Alden General Hospital. On September 22, 1964, the series became "The Doctors and the Nurses" and focused also on the experiences of doctors Alex Tazinski and Ted Steffen.

Nurse Liz Thorpe	Shirl Conway
Nurse Gail Lucas	Zina Bethune
Dr. Ted Steffen	Joseph Campanella
Dr. Alex Tazinski	Michael Tolan
Nurse Ayres	Hilda Simms
Dr. Lowry	Stephen Brooks
Dr. Kiley	Edward Binns
Dr. Henden	John Beal
Dr. Felix Reisner	Fred Stewart

Producer: Herbert Brodkin, Arthur Lewis, Robert Costello

Nuts and Bolts

Comedy Pilot; 30 min; ABC 8/24/81

The story of Miles Fenton, a widowed computer engineer, who uses his homemade robots to help him raise his two children (Lucy and Alex).

Miles Fenton	Rich Little
Lucy Fenton	Tammy Lauren
Alex Fenton	Justin Dana
Martha Fenton	Eve Arden
Karen Prescott	Jo Ann Pflug
Robot Primo	Mitchell Young Evans
Robot Victor	Tommy McLoughlin
Primo's Voice	Douglas V. Fowley
Victor's Voice	Garnett Smith
Warren Berlinger	William Daniels

Producer: David Gerber

N.Y.P.D.

Crime Drama; 30 min; ABC 9/5/67 to 9/16/69

The exploits of Johnny Corso, Mike Haines, and Jeff Ward, plainclothes detectives with the 27th precinct of the New York Police Department.

Det. Mike Haines	Jack Warden
Det. Johnny Corso	Frank Converse
Det. Jeff Ward	Robert Hooks

Producer: Dan Melnick, Bob Markell

The Oath

Anthology Pilot; 60 min; ABC 8/24/76 (first pilot) 8/26/76 (second pilot)

A proposed series of medical dramas. In the first pilot, "33 Hours in the Life of God," a cold, impersonal cardiologist (Dr. Abbott) begins to realize that his total dedication to work is affecting his health and marriage. The second pilot, "The Sad and Lonely Sundays," tells of an aging doctor (Sorenson) who enters medical school to catch up on forty years of medical progress.

Dr. Simon Abbott	Hal Holbrook
Alison Abbott	Carol Rossen
Dr. Paul Jaffe	Hume Cronyn
Nurse Levitt	Louise Latham
Paula Handy	Doris Roberts
Dr. George Sorenson	Jack Albertson
Lucas Wembley	Will Geer
Dr. Sweeny	Sam Jaffe
Sandy	Dori Brenner
Hester	Doreen Lang

Producer: Aaron Spelling, Leonard Goldberg

The Object Is

Game; 30 min; ABC 12/30/63 to 3/27/64

Object: For players to identify personalities from object clues.

Host: Dick Clark

Occasional Wife

Comedy; 30 min; NBC 9/13/66 to 8/29/67

In an attempt to acquire an executive position with the Brahm's Baby Food Company that is only available to a married man, Peter Christopher, a swinging young bachelor, solves his problem by proposing to a beautiful hat check girl (Greta) and asking her to be his wife . . . occasionally. Greta agrees when Peter offers to pay for her rent and art lessons. Stories relate the problems that ensue as two unmarried people, who live in the same N.Y. apartment building, attempt to affect a normal, happy marriage.

Peter Christopher	Michael Callan
Greta Patterson	Patricia Harty
Max Brahms	Jack Collins
Peter's mother	Sara Seeger
Man in the Middle	Bryan O'Bryne
Lydia Brahms	Joan Tompkins
Wally Frick	Jack Riley
Vera Frick	Susan Silo
Bernie	Stuart Margolin
Amanda	Eileen Baral
Greta's mother	Pert Kelton
Greta's father	Paul Hartman
Marilyn	Chris Noel

Narrator: Vince Scully

Producer: Harry Ackerman

O'Connor's Ocean

Adventure Pilot; 60 min; NBC 12/13/60

The exploits of Torin O'Connor, a yachtsman and lawyer for a marine law firm.

Torin O'Connor	John Payne
Victoria Arden	Irene Hervey
Ben Matthews	Edward Andrews
Jason Chambers	Charles Cooper

Producer: John Payne

Ocean Quest

Adventure; 60 min; NBC 8/18/85 to 9/15/85

A rather unusual network series about a beautiful girl's experiences as she explores the oceans of the world. The series follows the girl, former Miss Universe Shawn Weatherly, as she is chosen for the quest and devotes one year of her life to help document the mysteries of the ocean. Shawn's amazing experiences, as she teams with underwater photographer Al Giddings, are presented in documentary style.

Shawn Weatherly	Herself
Al Giddings	Himself

Narrator: Ray Willes

Producer: Peter Guber, Jon Peters, Al Giddings

Octavius and Me

Comedy Pilot; 30 min; CBS 7/17/62

The story of Octavius and Hattie Todd, a retired couple who spend their time traveling from trailer court to trailer court.

Octavius Todd	Dub Taylor
Hattie Todd	Loie Bridge
Blanche Hannigan	Grace Albertson
George Hannigan	George O'Hanlon
Bess Drake	Kay Elhardt
John Drake	James Douglas

Producer: Don Taylor

The Odd Couple

Comedy; 30 min; ABC 9/24/70 to 7/4/75

The misadventures of two divorced men struggling to share a Manhattan apartment: Oscar Madison, an irresponsible slob who writes a sports column for the "New York Herald," and Felix Unger, a commercial photographer who is a perfectionist. See also "The New Odd Couple." Based on characters created by Neil Simon.

Oscar Madison	Jack Klugman
Felix Unger	Tony Randall
Myrna Turner	Penny Marshall
Off. Murray Grechner	Al Molinaro
Miriam Welby	Elinor Donahue
Dr. Nancy Cunningham	Joan Hotchkis
Gloria Unger	Janis Hansen
Blanche Madison	Brett Somers
Cecily Pigeon	Monica Evans
Gwen Pigeon	Carole Shelley
Edna Unger	Pamelyn Ferdin
	Doney Oatman
Leonard Unger	Leif Garrett
	Willie Aames
Speed	Garry Walberg
Vinnie	Larry Gelman
Roy	Ryan MacDonald
Mimi Grechner	Alice Ghostley
Oscar's mother	Elvia Allman
	Fran Ryan
Howard Cosell	Himself

Producer: Garry K. Marshall, Jerry Belson, Harvey Miller, Sheldon Keller

The Oddball Couple

Cartoon; 30 min; ABC 9/6/75 to 9/3/77

A take-off on "The Odd Couple," which relates the antics of two trouble-prone magazine writers: Fleabag, a canine slob; and Spiffy, a perfectionist cat.

Fleabag	Paul Winchell
Spiffy	Frank Nelson
Goldie Hound	Joan Gerber

Producer: David DePatie, Friz Freleng

Odyssey

Anthology; 30 min; CBS 1/6/57 to 6/16/57

Charles Collingwood as the host and narrator of stories based on events that shaped the world. Produced by Charles Romini and Ted Sack.

Of All Things

Variety; 30 min; CBS 7/23/56 to 8/31/56

A Summer series of music and songs.

Hostess: Faye Emerson

Regulars: Jack Haskell, Ilene Woods

Announcer: Del Sharbutt

Orchestra: Billy Clifton

Producer: Byron Paul

Of This Time, Of That Place

Drama Pilot; 60 min; ABC 3/6/62

The pilot for "Channing." The story of Joseph Howe, an English professor at Channing University. Broadcast on "The Alcoa Hour."

Joseph Howe	Jason Evers
Dean Baker	Henry Jones
Mary Howe	Nancy Hadley
Marsha	Stephanie Hill
Tertan	Burt Brinckerhoff
Blackburn	Paul Carr
Miss Marks	Alice Frost
Hilda	Barbara Jean Hunter

Host: Fred Astaire

Off Campus

Comedy Pilot; 30 min; CBS 6/8/77

A comic look at life in a coed rooming house as seen through the eyes of a group of college students preparing for graduation and adulthood.

Janet	Marilu Henner
Steve	Josh Mostel
Bonnie	Ann Risley
Josh	Chip Zien
Stanley	Paul Reigert
Weineke	Joe Bova
Alexis	Alexa Kenin

Producer: Gilbert Cates

Off the Rack

Comedy; 30 min; ABC 3/15/85 to 9/6/85

When his business partner dies, Sam Waltman, the gruff owner of the near-bankrupt H&W Garment Company, suddenly finds himself with a new partner when Kate Halloran, his late partner's wife, decides to take an active interest in the firm. Stories relate the misadventures that occur as the incompatible Sam and Kate attempt to run a business together.

Sam Waltman	Edward Asner
Kate Halloran	Eileen Brennan
Shannon Halloran	Claudia Wells
Timothy Halloran	R. J. Williams*
	Cory Yothers
Brenda Patagorski	Pamela Brull
Cletus Maxwell	Dennis Haysbert
Skip Wagner	Sandy Simpson
Maria	Anita Hamilton
Rosa Perez	Marcia Del Mar

Producer: Dan Guntzelman, Marc Merson, Steve Marshall

*Pilot film role (12/7/84).

Off the Record

Comedy; 30 min; DuMont 10/19/48 to 10/26/48

The misadventures of a millionaire Park Avenue (N.Y.) radio disc jockey and his Man

Friday. One of the first situation comedies, and one of the first to be cancelled shortly after its premiere (a dispute between the star and producer). The live series was originally scheduled to premiere on October 12, 1948, but was delayed one week due to the illness of its announcer.

Disc Jockey   Zero Mostel
Man Friday   Joey Faye

Announcer: Ken Roberts

Producer: Martin Gosch

Off the Wall

Comedy Pilot; 30 min; NBC 5/7/77

A comic look at life as seen through a group of students at Hopkins Hall, a coed dorm on the grounds of Ohio Western College.

Matt Bozeman   Todd Susman
Jeannie   Dana House
Flash   Harry Gold
Lennie   Cindy Helberg
Tammy   Sally Hightower
Gordon   Sean Roche
Arthur   Frank Helberg
Melvin   Sandy Helberg
George   Frank O'Brien
Mother   Hal Williams

Producer: Frank Burton, George Tricker, Neil Rosen

Off the Wall

Comedy; 30 min; Syn. 9/86

Sketches, performed by a repetory company, that poke fun at TV, commercials, politics, life, and fairy tales.

Regulars: Joe Baker, Louise Duart, Susan Elliot, Pat Fraley, Shelley Herman, Terry Kiser, John Roarke, Cynthia Stevenson

Producer: Peter Alex, Jackie Kahane, Martin Roth

Off to See the Wizard

Anthology; 60 min; ABC 9/8/67 to 9/20/68

A combination of pilot adventure films and reedited theatrical films hosted by animated "Wizard of Oz" characters. For pilot film information, see: "Alexander the Great," "The Hellcats," "Mike and the Mermaid," and

"Tarzan the Ape Man." Produced by Chuck Jones and Abe Levitow.

Off We Go

Comedy Pilot; 30 min; CBS 9/5/66

Anxious to participate in the war effort (during W.W. II), a brilliant 16-year-old boy (Rod Ryan) who looks older than he is, enlists with the U.S. Army Air Corps. Quicky he rises to the rank of colonel and is placed in charge of a small air base in England. The unsold series was to relate Ryan's experiences as he and his squad attempt to carry out their assignments.

Col. Rod Ryan   Michael Burns
Lt. Casey Slade   Dick Foran
Capt. Julian Imbro   Dick Curtis
Lt. Sue Chamberlain   Nancy Kovack
Debbie Towbridge   Ann Jillian
Lt. Jefferson Dale   Alan Sues
Maj. Stivers   Monroe Arnold
Josie Ryan   Elisabeth Fraser
Carl Ryan   Dave Willock
Lt. Stanley   Berkeley Harris

Producer: Robert Blees

Official Detective

Anthology; 30 min; Syn. 1957

Everett Sloane as the host and narrator of dramas based on stories appearing in "Official Detective" magazine. Produced by Mort Briskin.

Oh, Baby!

A five-minute program in which Jack Barry talks to infants who respond via voice-over dubbing. Produced by Jack Barry and Dan Enright and syndicated in 1952.

Oh, Boy!

Variety; 30 min; ABC 7/16/59 to 9/3/59

Performances by country and western entertainers.

Host: Tony Hall

Regulars: Brenda Lee, Lorie Mann, Dickie Pride, Cherry Warner, Mike Preston, Chris Andrews, Neville Taylor, Tony Sheridan

Oh, Kay!

Variety; 30 min; ABC 2/24/51 to 8/18/51

A live program of music and songs from Chicago.

Hostess: Kay Westfall

Regulars: Mary Ellen White, Jim Dimitri

Orchestra: David LeWinter

Producer: Dan Schuffman

Oh Madeline

Comedy; 30 min; ABC 9/27/83 to 3/13/84

The problems of a modern marriage as seen through the antics of Madeline Wayne, a housewife, and her husband, Charlie, a romance novelist who writes under the pen name Crystal Love.

Madeline Wayne	Madeline Kahn
Charlie Wayne	James Sloyan
Annie McIntyre	Francine Tacker
Robert Leone	Louis Giambalvo
Doris Leone	Jesse Wells

Producer: Marcy Carsey, Tom Werner

Oh, Nurse!

Comedy Pilot; 30 min; CBS 3/17/72

An unsold series about the comic frustrations of a group of student nurses.

Kathi (nurse)	Susan Foster
LuAnne (nurse)	Heather Young
Maria (nurse)	Lori Saunders
Nurse Conklin	Pat Carroll
Gail (nurse)	Judy Pace
Jimmy (intern)	Stephen Young
Steve (intern)	Norman Grabowski

Producer: David Gerber, Charles B. Fitzsimons

Oh! Susanna

See "The Gale Storm Show."

Oh, Those Bells

Comedy; 30 min; CBS 3/8/62 to 5/31/62

The misadventures of Harry, Herbert, and Sylvester Bell, three financially insecure brothers who are the custodians of the Hollywood Prop Shop (also known as Cinema Rents).

Herbert Bell	Herbert Wiere
Harry Bell	Harry Wiere
Sylvester Bell	Sylvester Wiere
Henry Slocum	Harry Morgan
Kitty Matthews	Carol Byron
Mrs. Stanfield	Reta Shaw

Theme Song ("Oh Those Bells"): Tutti Camarata

Producer: Ben Brady, Tom McKnight

Ohara

Crime Drama; 60 min; ABC 1/17/87 (Premiere)

The story of Lieutenant Ohara, a compassionate, twenty-year (Asian) cop with the L.A.P.D. who relys on mental acuity to solve crimes, but will resort to the martial arts when necessary.

Lt. Ohara	Pat Morita
Det. Cricket Sideris	Catherine Keener
Capt. Lloyd Hamilton	Kevin Conroy
Det. Jesse Guerrera	Richard Yniquez
Sgt. Phil O'Brien	Jack Wallace
Gussie Lemmone (diner owner)	Madge Sinclair

Producer: Brian Grazer, Hal Sitowitz, Skip Ward

O'Hara, United States Treasury

Crime Drama; 60 min; CBS 9/17/71 to 9/8/72

The exploits of James O'Hara, a Treasury Department agent, as he investigates crimes perpetrated against Internal Revenue, Customs, and Secret Service.

James O'Hara	David Janssen
Insp. Ed Miller	Paul Picerni
Ben Hazzard	Stacy Harris

Producer: Jack Webb, Leonard B. Kaufman

The O. Henry Playhouse

Anthology; 30 min; Syn. 1/57

Dramas based on the stories of William Sidney Porter who, while in prison, wrote under the pen name of O. Henry.

Host-Narrator: Thomas Mitchell

Producer: Donald Hyde

O.K. Crackerby

Comedy; 30 min; ABC 9/16/65 to 1/6/66

Anxious for his children, Cynthia and Hobart, to become a part of the genteel society circle, a rugged Oklahomian and the world's richest man (O.K. Crackerby) moves to the plush and splendor of Palm Springs, California. There, he hires St. John Quincy to tutor his children in the ways of society. O.K.'s battle of wits against snobbery is the focal point of the program.

O.K. Crackerby	Burl Ives
Cynthia Crackerby	Brooke Adams
Hobart Crackerby	Joel Davison
St. John Quincy	Hal Buckley
Susan Wentworth	Laraine Stephens
Slim	Dick Foran
O.K.'s Nephew	
Davey	Jonathan Daly
O.K.'s chauffeur	John Indrisano

Producer: Rod Amateau, Norman Henry

Creator: Cleveland Amory, Abe Burrows

Okay Mother

Testimonial; 30 min; DuMont 11/1/48 to 7/6/51

Dennis James as the host of a program that salutes mothers of celebrities or mothers who have become famous on their own.

Old Friends

Comedy Pilot; 30 min; ABC 7/12/84

After his wife deserts him, Jerry Forbes, a successful New York lawyer, relinquishes his job and returns to his hometown of Columbus, Ohio, to begin a new life. The unsold series was to relate Jerry's attempts to establish his new life style.

Jerry Forbes	Christopher Lloyd
Laura King	Jennifer Salt
Phil Forbes	John Randolph
Susan King	Deborah Goodrich
Charlie	Stanley Kamel
George Neal	Steve Ryan
Mark Forbes	Grant Forsberg

Producer: Elliot Shoenman, Tom Cherones

The Old Nickerbocker Music Hall

Mystery-Game Pilot; 30 min; CBS 10/9/48

The program begins with a dramatization (in the pilot, "The Times Square Story") during which a crime is committed. Patrons of the Old Nickerbocker Music Hall, a Gay Nineties Revue in New York (where the live broadcast originates) receive the opportunity to win prizes by attempting to identify the culprit. One of the first TV programs to experiment with live, remote pickups.

Performer: Darren McGavin, Jack Lemmon, Sally Gracie, Madeleine Lee, Maureen Stapleton, Farrell Pelley, Henry Lascoe

Producer: Paul E. Moss

The Oldest Rookie

Crime Drama; 60 min; CBS 9/16/87 to 1/6/88

When his friend is killed in the line of duty, Ike Porter, a 25-year veteran, resigns from his job (Deputy Chief of Public Relations for the L.A.P.D.) to become a street cop. After a brief stint as a rookie, Ike calls in an old favor (from the mayor) and is promoted to detective. Stories relate Ike's experiences as he and his partner, Tony, attempt to solve crimes.

Det. Ike Porter	Paul Sorvino
Det. Tony Jones	D. W. Moffett
Lt. Marc Zaga	Raymond J. Barry
Det. Garry Lane	Marshall Bell
Chief Black	Patrick Cronin
Sandy Porter	Mira Sorvino
Nina Zaga	Leah Ayres

Producer: Gil Grant, Richard Chapman

The Oldsmobile Music Theatre

Anthology; 30 min; NBC 3/26/59 to 5/7/59

The program, also known as "Hayes & Henderson," interweaves songs of the past and present into dramatic stories.

Hosts: Florence Henderson, Bill Hayes

Music: The Herbie Mann Quartet

Producer: David Susskind, Jacqueline Babbin

O'Malley

Crime Drama Pilot; 60 min; NBC 1/8/83

The story of Mike O'Malley, a 1940s style private detective working in a 1980s New York City.

Mike O'Malley	Mickey Rooney
Amanda O'Malley	Anne Francis
Guy Fleming	Peter Coffield
Denny	Sarah Abrell
Bernie	Martin Rosenblatt
Mrs. Douglas	Paula Trueman
Paul	Tom Waites
Donna	Robin Mary Paris
Public Defender	Mark Linn-Baker
Secretary	Cherry Jones

Producer: Frank Cardea, George Schenck

The Omega Factor

Mystery; 60 min; Syn. 7/81

The story of Tom Crane, a newspaper journalist who is secretly a member of Department 7, a British government organization that uses people possessed of special occult powers to investigate crimes. (The title refers to the ultimate potential that is possible from the human mind.) Produced in England.

Tom Crane	James Hazeldine
Dr. Anne Reynolds	Louise Jameson
Andrew Scott-	
Erskine	Brian Derby
Dr. Roy Martindale	John Carlisle
Julia Crane	Joanna Tope
Michael Crane	Nicholas Coppin
Edward Drexel	Cyril Luckham
Spirit Voices	Sheila Duffy
Spirit	Monica Brady

Producer: George Gallaccio

Omni: The New Frontier

Magazine; 30 min; Syn. 9/81

The series, based on articles in "Omni" magazine, explores the scientific wonders that will shape the future.

Host-Narrator: Peter Ustinov

Producer: Bob Guccione, Kathy Keeton, Vivian Moss, John Savage

Omnibus

Anthology; 60 min; CBS 11/9/52 to 4/1/56
ABC 10/7/56 to 3/31/57
NBC 10/20/57 to 4/16/61

Dramatic presentations, discussions, and demonstrations concerning music, dance, history, theatre, opera, ballet, and literature.

Host: Alistair Cooke

Producer: William Spier, Robert Saudek

On Broadway Tonight

Variety; 60 min; CBS 7/8/64 to 9/16/64
1/1/65 to 3/12/65

Performances by undiscovered professional talent.

Host: Rudy Vallee

Orchestra: Harry Sosnik

Producer: Irving Mansfield

On Our Own

Comedy; 30 min; CBS 10/9/77 to 8/27/78

The misadventures of two women in the creative department of the Bedford Advertising Agency in New York: Julia Peters, a copyrighter, and Maria Bonino, an art director.

Julia Peters	Bess Armstrong
Maria Bonino	Lynnie Greene
Toni McBain	Gretchen Wyler
April Baxter	Dixie Carter
Phil Goldstein	Michael Tucci
Eddie Barnes	John Christopher Jones
Craig Boatwright	Dan Resin
Mrs. Oblenski	Sasha von Scherler
Corkey Boatwright	Mary Denham
J. M. Bedford	Bob Randall

Producer: David Susskind, Sam Denoff

On Our Way

Drama Pilot; 60 min; CBS 6/29/85

The story of Kate and Sam Walsh, a retired couple who purchase a motor home and decide to explore America.

Kate Walsh .... Janet Leigh
Sam Walsh .... Harry Guardino
Tom Beckwith .... G. W. Bailey
Matthew .... Scott Paulin
Farley Barnes .... Andrew Prine
Melinda .... Gail Strickland
Bea .... Brenda Lilly

Producer: Frank Von Zernick, William Beaudine Jr.

On Parade

Variety; 30 min; NBC 7/17/64 to 9/18/64

A series of musical programs, produced by the CBC and first shown in Canada.

Program Hosts: Rosemary Clooney (7/17), Tony Bennett (7/24), Henry Mancini (7/31), Phil Ford and Mimi Hines (8/7), Juliet Prowse (8/14), Diahann Carroll (8/21), Julius LaRosa (8/28), Jane Morgan (9/4), The Limelighters (9/11), and Steve Lawrence and Eydie Gorme (9/18)

Orchestra: Nelson Riddle

On Stage America

Variety; 2 hrs. Syn. 4/84

A combination magazine and variety series that presents in-depth celebrity profiles and performances.

Hostess: Randi Oakes, Susie Bono

Host: Steve Edwards, Todd Christianson

Regulars: Minnie Pearl, John Barbour

Orchestra: Dennis McCarthy

Producer: Nick Vanoff, Gary Smith, Dwight Hemion

On the Corner

Variety; 30 min; ABC 4/18/48 to 5/16/48

The program presents talent acts culled from the Vaudeville section of "Variety."

Host: Henry Morgan

Regulars: Virginia Austin, George Guest, Roy Davis, The Clark Sisters

Producer: Charles Holden

On the Go

Variety; 30 min; CBS 4/27/59 to 7/8/60

Guests, interviews, and visits to various Los Angeles areas.

Host: Jack Linkletter

Announcer: Johnny Jacobs

Producer: Irvin S. Atkins, William Kayden

On the Rocks

Comedy; 30 min; ABC 9/11/75 to 5/17/76

Life in the Alamesa State Minimum Security Prison as seen through the eyes of convict Hector Fuentes, a streetwise petty thief. Based on the British series "Porridge."

Hector Fuentes .... Jose Perez
Lester DeMott .... Hal Williams
Cleaver .... Rick Hurst
Nick Palik .... Bobby Sandler
Mr. Gibson .... Mel Stewart
Mr. Sullivan .... Tom Poston
Gabby .... Pat Cranshaw
Warden Wilbur
  Poindexter .... Logan Ramsey
Dorothy Burgess ..... Cynthia Harris

Producer: John Rich

On Top All Over the World

Magazine Pilot; 2 hrs. Syn. 4/85

A fascinating survey of the entertainment industry world wide (the best in TV, movies, and music).

Hosts: Morgan Brittany, Stephen J. Cannell

Guests: Olivia Newton-John, Morgan Fairchild, Linda Blair, Roger Moore, Raquel Welch, Ben Gazzara, Joan Collins, Victoria Principal, David Hasselhoff, Bonnie Franklin, Elizabeth Taylor, Edward Asner

Announcer-Narrator: Steve O'Brien

Producer: Robin Leach, Al Masini

On Trial

Anthology; 30 min; CBS 9/14/56 to 9/13/57

The series, also known as "The Joseph Cotten Show," dramatizes actual court cases.

The pilot, titled "On Trial," aired on NBC on 9/23/55.

Host-Narrator: Joseph Cotten

On Trial

A syndicated (1978) anthology pilot of dramatizations based on actual courtroom cases. Produced by Alan P. Sloane and Robert H. Justman.

On Your Account

Game; 30 min; CBS 7/5/54 to 3/30/56

Subjects appear on stage and relate their troubles. A panel then questions them to determine the seriousness of their individual situations. Each question that is asked deposits five dollars in a bank. The person who is deemed the most desperate receives the money.

Host: Eddie Albert, Win Elliot, Dennis James

Announcer: Bill Rogers

Producer: Bob Quigley

On Your Mark

Game; 30 min; CBS 9/23/61 to 12/30/61

Children, with the same career goal, compete in a series of question-and-answer rounds based on that goal. The highest scoring player receives prizes.

Host: Sonny Fox

On Your Way

Game; 30 min; DuMont 9/9/53 to 1/20/54
ABC 1/23/54 to 4/17/54

Selected studio audience members compete in a series of question-and-answer rounds with the highest scoring player receiving an all-expenses paid trip to his place of desire.

Host: Bud Collyer, John Reed King, Kathy Godfrey

Producer: Larry White

Once a Hero

Fantasy; 60 min; ABC 9/19/87 to 10/3/87

While saving the life of Pleasantville citizens Rachel Kirk and her sister, Tippy Young, comic book hero Captain Justice (a.k.a. The Crimson Crusader) begins to fade. Captain Justice realizes that people in the "real" world are becoming disinterested in him and he will soon cease to exist. In an attempt to make people remember him, the Captain crosses the Forbidden Zone into the real world with a plan to battle crime. In Los Angeles, he establishes himself as Brad Steele, meets his creator (Abner) and learns that his publisher (Pizazz Comics) is planning to drop the strip. Shortly after, rulers of the comic book world send Gumshoe through the Forbidden Zone to protect the Captain (now without his amazing powers) and eventually bring him back. Stories relate the Captain's efforts to restore his lost honor by righting wrongs.

Captain Justice	Jeff Lester
Gumshoe	Robert Forster
Emma Greely	Caitlin Clarke
Abner Bevis	Milo O'Shea
Woody Greely	Josh Blake
Rachel Kirk	Dianne Kay
Tippy Young	Dana Short
Max Mayhem	Harris Laskawy
Lobsterman	Trevor Henley
Victor Lazarus	Richard Lynch

Producer: Dusty Kay

Once Upon a Fence

Children; 30 min; NBC 4/13/52 to 7/20/52

Stories coupled with music with Katherine Heger (as the Story Princess) and Dave Kargler as her assistant.

Once Upon a Tune

Anthology; 60 min; DuMont 3/6/51 to 5/15/51

A rather ambitious series for its time which presents a complete musical each week, usually an adaptation of a Broadway show.

Regulars: Sondra Lee, Phil Hanna, Reginald Beane, Bernice Parks, Ed Holmes

Music: Reginald Beane

Producer: Bob Loew

One Big Family

Comedy; 30 min; Syn. 9/86

Following the death of his parents in a car accident, a Seattle, Washington, police officer (Don) and his recent bride (Jan) become the legal guardians of his brothers and sisters (Mary Ann, Kate, Brian, and Roger). Stories relate the misadventures that occur as Don and Jan, assisted by Don's Uncle Jake, attempt to care for the children.

Jake Hatton	Danny Thomas
Don Hatton	Anthony Starke
Jan Hatton	Kim Gillingham
Mary Ann Hatton	Anastasia Fielding
Kate Hatton	Allison McMillan
Brian Hatton	Michael DeLuise
Roger Hatton	Gabriel Damon
Phil (Jake's friend)	Barney Martin

Producer: Paul Junger Witt, Tony Thomas, David Pollack, Elias Davis

One Big Family (a.k.a. Morning Maggie)

Comedy Pilot; Unaired; Produced in 1987

The story of the McAllisters, the owners of a small radio station (WINT) in Schenectady, N.Y., during the 1940s.

Maggie McAllister	Ellen Greene
Mack McAllister	John Vickery
Dorothy McAllister	Marita Geraghty
Bradley McAllister	Matthew Perry
Aunt Esther	Eileen Heckart

Producer: Nelle Nugent

One Day at a Time

Comedy; 30 min; CBS 12/6/75 to 9/2/84

Incidents in the lives of Ann Romano, a pretty divorcee, and her two teenage daughters, Barbara and Julie Cooper (who retain their father's name). When the series first began, Ann acquired a job as an account executive for the Connors and Davenport Advertising Firm. Later, she joined with Nick Handris to form Romano and Handris. When the agency folded, Ann teamed with her beautiful rival, Francine Webster, to form their own ad agency.

Ann Romano	Bonnie Franklin
Barbara Cooper	Valerie Bertinelli
Julie Cooper	Mackenzie Phillips
Dwayne Schneider	Pat Harrington Jr.
Francine Webster	Shelley Fabares
Kathryn Romano	Nanette Fabray
David Kane	Richard Masur
Ginny Wroblinki	Mary Louise Weller
Ed Cooper	Joseph Campanella
Max Horvath	Michael Lembeck
Claude Connors	John Hillerman
Jerry Davenport	Charles Siebert
Bob Morton	John Putch
Cliff Randall	Scott Colomby
Vickie Cooper	Fawne Harriman
Nick Handris	Ron Rifkin
Alex Handris	Glenn Scarpelli
Felicia Handris	Elinor Donahue
Beerbelly	Chuck McCann
Mark Royer	Boyd Gaines
Sam Royer	Howard Hesseman
Beerbelly's wife (Selma)	Beverly Sanders
Mr. Erskine	Howard Morton
Marge Royer	Claudette Nevins
Annie Horvath	J. C. & R. C. Dilley
	Paige & Lauren Maloney
Mr. Gonagin	Jack Riley

Producer: Norman Lear, Mort Lachman, Norman Paul, Jack Elinson, Alan Rafkin, Dick Bensfield, Perry Grant, Allan Manings, Bud Wiser

One Happy Family

Comedy; 30 min; NBC 1/13/61 to 9/8/61

The misadventures that occur as three generations of one family try to live together as one happy family.

Penny Cooper	Judy Warner
Dick Cooper	Dick Sargent
Barney Hogan	Chick Chandler
Mildred Hogan	Elisabeth Fraser
Charley Hackett	Jack Kirkwood
Lovey Hackett	Cheerio Meredith

Producer: Mark Goodson, Bill Todman

100 Centre Street

Comedy Pilot; 30 min; ABC 8/31/84

The misadventures of the judges attached to the Hall of Justice, located at 100 Centre Street in Manhattan.

Judge Charles Felt	Len Carriou
Judge Nell Hartigan	Dee Wallace
Judge Earl Doucette	J. A. Preston
Judge Ramon Robledo	Henry Darrow
Pam Verderamo	Lela Ivey
Louis Keck	James Canning
Leo Kelly	Ernie Hudson
Harry Pike	Ernie Sabella
Fran Felt	Christine Belford
Andre Bussey	Wright Dorsey

Producer: Norman Steinberg

One Hundred Grand

Game; 30 min; ABC 9/15/63 to 9/29/63

A player, possessing knowledge in at least one specific field, answers questions posed by five professional authorities. Each correct response earns large cash prizes, but an incorrect answer defeats a player and costs him everything he has won to that point. Players are permitted to continue or quit at any time. $100,000 is awarded if a player survives several rounds and is able to answer the final five questions: those submitted by a home viewer.

Host: Jack Clark

Producer: John B. Green

The $100,000 Big Surprise

Game; 30 min; CBS 9/18/56 to 4/2/57

A player selects either the "easy" or "difficult" question category and is quizzed with cash prizes being awarded for each correct response. An incorrect answer defeats a player, who vies for $100,000 by answering increasingly difficult questions in his chosen category.

Host: Jack Barry, Mike Wallace

Assistants: Sue Oakland, Mary Gardiner

Producer: Steve Carlin

The $100,000 Name That Tune

Game; 30 min; Syn. 9/76

Two players compete in a game wherein they must identify song titles from a few bars of music. The highest scoring player receives a chance to win $100,000 by identifying a song from one note. See also "The New $100,000 Name That Tune" and "Name That Tune."

Host: Tom Kennedy

Assistant: Jeri Fiala

Vocalists: Monica Buris, Steve March

Orchestra: Tommy Oliver, Stan Worth

$100,000 Pianist: Joe Harnell

Producer: Ralph Edwards

The $100,000 Pyramid

Game; 30 min; Syn. 9/85

One team (two compete) selects one subject from six that are displayed on a board. Within a thirty second time limit, one player must relate the seven associated objects to his partner in one word clues. Each team plays three rounds. The highest scoring team receives the opportunity to play the pyramid (receive up to $25,000 by guessing seven subjects within sixty seconds). The three players who took the least amount of time at the pyramid return at a later date to compete for $100,000.

Host: Dick Clark

Announcer: Johnny Gilbert

Producer: Bob Stewart, Anne Marie Schmitt

The $128,000 Question

Game; 30 min; Syn. 9/76

A player, who possesses knowledge in a specific field is asked a series of questions ranging from $64 to $64,000. Players, who can lose everything if an incorrect answer is given, can continue and quit after any question. Once a player earns $64,000, he returns at a later date for another $64,000.

Host: Mike Darrow, Alex Trebek

Models: Cindy Reynolds, Lauri Locks, Pattie Lee, Sylvia Garant

Announcer: Alan Calter, Sandy Hoyt

Producer: Steve Carlin

One in a Million

Game; 30 min; ABC 4/3/67 to 6/16/67

Object: For players to discover (through probe rounds) the secrets that are shared by a panel of four guest celebrities.

Host: Danny O'Neil

Producer: Stu Billett

One in a Million

Comedy; 30 min; ABC 1/8/80 to 6/23/80

Following the death of a wealthy friend, cab driver Shirley Simmons inherits controlling interest in the $200 million Grayson Enterprises. Stories relate Shirley's efforts to run the company.

Shirley Simmons	Shirley Hemphill
Roland Cushing	Keene Curtis
Nancy Boyer	Dorothy Fielding
Barton Stone	Richard Paul
Raymond Simmons	Mel Stewart
Edna Simmons	Ann Weldon
Max Kalamo	Carl Ballantine
Grace Cushing	Louise Sorel
Duke	Ralph Wilcox

Producer: Saul Turteltaub, Bernie Orenstein

One Man Show

Comedy; 30 min; Syn. 1969

Performances by guest comedians, including Bob Elliott and Ray Goulding, Groucho Marx, Steve Allen, Rip Torn, and Morey Amsterdam. Produced by Richard Lewine and Ted Fetter.

One Man's Experience

Drama; 15 min; DuMont 10/6/52 to 4/10/53

Human interest accounts that depict the joys and sorrows of men. Produced by Lawrence Menkin.

One Man's Family

Drama; 15 & 30 min; NBC 11/4/49 to 4/1/55

Events in the day-to-day lives of the Barbours, a seven-member family living in the swank Sea Cliff section of Bay City in San Francisco. Based on the radio series.

Henry Barbour	Bert Lytell
	Theodore Van Eltz
Frances "Fanny" Barbour	Marjorie Gateson
	Mary Adams
Hazel Barbour	Lillian Schaff
	Linda Reighton
Claudia Barbour	Nancy Franklin
	Eva Marie Saint
	Anne Whitfield
Jack Barbour	Robert Wigginton
	Martin Dean
	Arthur Cassell
Clifford Barbour	Frankie Thomas Jr.
	Billy Idelson
	James Lee
Paul Barbour	Paul Thorson
Beth Holly	Mercedes McCambridge
	Susan Shaw
John Roberts	Michael Higgins
	Jack Edwards
Billy Herbert	Les Tremayne
	Walter Brooke
Teddy Barbour	Medaline Bugard
Athena Lorde	Judith Richardson

Announcer: Bob Sheppard

Music: Paul Watson

Producer: Carleton E. Morse, Richard Clemmer

The $1,000,000 Chance of a Lifetime

Game; 30 min; Syn. 1/86

Two teams compete, each composed of two members. One member of each team stands before a line of blank spaces. Letters to the formation of a clue word appear, one at a time. The first player to identify the word receives money and the chance to identify the mystery puzzle by selecting two letters that appear in the unknown name, place, or object. The first player to identify the puzzle wins money. Players rotate turns and the highest scoring team plays the bonus round. To win $1,000,000 the team first selects one category from three that are shown, then has to guess six related subjects (from letters that appear) within sixty seconds. Successful players win $5,000 and the chance to compete again.

$10,000 is awarded if the team wins the next day's game and is successful in the bonus round. The $1,000,000 is awarded if the team can win both a third game and bonus round.

Host: Jim Lange

Assistant: Karen Thomas

Announcer: Johnny Gilbert

Producer: Bob Synes, Jay Feldman, Scott Stone

One Minute Please

Game; 30 min; DuMont 7/6/54 to 2/17/55

A topic is stated and each member (of a three-member team) must incorporate it in a conversation for one minute without repetition, hesitation, or straying from the point. The wordiest talkers win prizes for studio audience members.

Host: John K. M. McCaffery, Allyn Edwards

Panelists: Ernie Kovacs, Beatrice Straight, Hermione Gingold, Alice Pearce, Jimmy Cannon, Marc Connelly

One More Try

Comedy Pilot; 30 min; CBS 3/31/82

The story of Dede March and Adam Margolin, a couple who decide to marry despite the fact that each has been previously divorced.

Dede March	Lucie Arnaz
Adam Margolin	Laurence Luckinbill
Jenny Marlowe	Judy Gibson
Paul Margolin	Randall Batinkoff
Daniel Margolin	Benjamin Bernouy
Mr. Liebowitz	Maurice Shrong
Dwayne	Jeff Brooks

Theme Vocal ("One More Try"): Lucie Arnaz

Producer: Jerry Davis

One Night Band

Drama Pilot; 60 min; CBS 5/28/83

The adventures of a struggling country and western group called One Night Band (Michael, Vikki, Tony, and Zack).

Vikki Royelle	Stepfanie Kramer
Michael Harrison	Brad Maule
Tony Glazer	George Deloy
Zack Radford	George Cassel
Betty	Monica Parker
Claire	Marji Martin
Shelley	Patrika Darbo
Helen	Deborah Lampel
Carlysle	Eric Helland

Producer: Bob Comfort, Rick Kellard

One of the Boys

Comedy; 30 min; NBC 1/23/82 to 8/20/82

Following his retirement, 66-year-old Oliver Nugent moves in with his grandson (Adam) and his roommate (Jonathan), both students at Sheffield University in New Jersey. Stories relate the trio's adventures as they struggle to live together.

Oliver Nugent	Mickey Rooney
Adam Shields	Dana Carvey
Jonathan Burns	Nathan Lane
Bernard Solomon	Scatman Crothers
Mrs. Green	Francine Beers
Linda Burns	Lauren White
Debbie	Elizabeth Berridge
Ann Burns	Valerie French
Violet Shields	Rosemary Prinz
George Shields	Peter Michael Goetz

Producer: Saul Turteltaub, Bernie Orenstein

One Step Beyond

Anthology; 30 min; Syn. 1962

Dramas based on true events that are strange, frightening, and unexplainable in terms of normal human experience. Originally broadcast as "Aloca Presents" on ABC from 1/26/59 to 10/3/61. See also "The Next Step Beyond."

Host: John Newland

"One Step Beyond" Theme: Harry Lubin

Producer: Larry Marcus, Collier Young

One, Two, Three—Go!

Children; 30 min; NBC 10/8/61 to 5/27/62

Filmed and taped explorations to places of interest to children.

Host: Jack Lescoulie

Assistant: Richard Thomas

Producer: Jack Kuney

One Woman's Experience

Drama; 15 min; DuMont 10/6/52 to 4/3/53

Human interest accounts that depict the joys and sorrows of women. Produced by Lawrence Menkin.

The Onedin Line

Drama; 60 min; Syn. 1976

The series, set in 1860s Liverpool, England, relates the adventures of tradesman James Onedin, captain of the "Charlotte Rhodes," as he struggles to maintain a cargo transporting business.

James Onedin	Peter Gilmore
Anne Onedin	Anne Stallybrass
Robert Onedin	Brian Rawlinson
	James Garbutt
Elizabeth Frazer	Jessica Benton
Joshua Webster	James Hayter
Sarah Onedin	Mary Webster
Albert Frazer	Philip Bond
Emma Fogarty	Jane Seymour
Jack Frazer	John Phillips

Producer: Peter Graham Scott

The O'Neills

Drama; 30 min; DuMont 9/6/49 to 1/10/50

The story of Peggy O'Neill, a widowed fashion designer, and her struggles to raise her children, Janice and Eddie. Based on the radio series.

Peggy O'Neill	Vera Allen
Janice O'Neill	Janice Gilbert
Eddie O'Neill	Michael Lawson
Bill O'Neill	Ian Martin
Mrs. Bailey	Jane West
Mrs. Levy	Celia Bubkin
Mr. Levy	Ben Fishbein

Producer: Ed Wolf

Only in America with Greg Jackson

A syndicated (1986) series of in-depth celebrity interviews with host Greg Jackson. Produced by Dolores Danska and Randy Robinson.

Open All Hours

Comedy; 30 min; TEC 7/82 to 12/82

The misadventures of Arkwright, a stubborn survivor of the supermarket age who owns a corner shop and competes by staying open all hours. Became the basis for "Open All Night."

Arkwright	Ronnie Barker
Granville	David Jason
Gladys Emmanuel	Lynda Brown
Mavis	Maggie Ollernshaw

Producer: Sydney Lotterby

Open All Night

Comedy; 30 min; ABC 11/28/81 to 3/5/82

Events in the life of Gordon Feester, the owner of an Englewood, California "364 Store," a 24-hour-a-day grocery store fraught with problems, as he attempts to cope with life at home and at work. Based on the British series "Open All Hours."

Gordon Feester	George Dzundza
Gretchen Feester	Susan Tyrrell
Terry Hofmeyster	Sam Whipple
Officer Steve	Jay Tarses
Officer Edie	Bever-Leigh Banfield
Robin	Bubba Smith
Larry Bud Hofmeyster	James Gallery
Wayne Feester	Art Kassul
Connie Feester	Mary Jackson

Producer: Bernie Brillstein, Tom Patchett, Jay Tarses

Opening Night

Arlene Dahl as the host for an NBC Summer series (6/14/58 to 9/8/58) of repeats from "Ford Theatre."

Opera Cameos

Giovanni Martinelli as the host of a DuMont series (11/8/53 to 1/9/55) that presents condensed versions of popular operas.

Opera vs. Jazz

Music; 30 min; ABC 5/25/53 to 9/21/53

A musical symposium in which two guests discuss and perform operatic arias and standard tunes.

Hostess: Nancy Kenyon

Regulars: Jan Peerce, Don Cornell, Robert Merrill, Alan Dale, The Strawhatters

Orchestra: Johnny Reo

Producer: Frederick Heider

Operating Room

Comedy Pilot; 30 min; NBC 10/4/79

The antics of the doctors attached to Memorial Hospital in Los Angeles.

Dr. Jim Lawrence	David Spielberg
Dr. Charles Webner	Oliver Clark
Dr. Robert Robinson	James Sutorius
Jean Lawrence	Barbara Babcock
Girl	Trish Barnstable
Girl	Cyb Barnstable

Music: Mike Post, Pete Carpenter

Producer: Mark Tinker

Operation: Entertainment

Variety; 60 min; ABC 1/5/68 to 4/26/68
9/27/68 to 1/31/69

U.S.O.-type performances that are geared to American servicemen.

Host: Jim Lange

Regulars: The Operation Entertainment Girls

Orchestra: Terry Gibbs

Announcer: Johnny Jacobs

Producer: Chuck Barris, Bill Carruthers

Operation Greasepaint

Comedy Pilot; 30 min; CBS 8/12/68

The World War II adventures of a ragtag entertainment unit assigned to tour the Normandy Combat Zone.

Spivak	Avery Schreiber
Minihane	Jack Burns
Bower	Fred Willard
Brown	Johnny Haymer
Keller	Robert Fitch

Producer: Bud Yorkin

Operation: Neptune

Adventure; 30 min; NBC 6/8/53 to 8/16/53

The exploits of Bill Hollister, the commander of a U.S. Navy submarine, who is known as Captain Neptune for his extensive undersea work. The serialized story, set in the undersea kingdom of Nadiria, relates Hollister's efforts to stop the evil Kabeda from a power-mad plan to control the world by killing the surface population. Broadcast live and also known as "Captain Neptune."

Bill Hollister	Tod Griffin
Dink Melvin	Humphrey Davis
Admiral Bigelow	Rusty Lane
Dick Saunders	Richard Holland
Thirza	Margaret Stewart
Kabeda	Harold Conklin
Mersennus	Del Berti

Operation Petticoat

Comedy; 30 min; ABC 9/17/77 to 8/25/78

The World War II adventures of the crew of the USS Sea Tiger, a shocking pink* submarine, as it roams the South Pacific. Based on the feature film. See also "The New Operation Petticoat."

Capt. Matthew
  Sherman .... John Astin
Lt. Nick Holden ...... Richard Gilliland
Lt. Dolores Crandall ..... Melinda Naud
Maj. Edna Hayward ..... Yvonne Wilder
Lt. Barbara Duran ... Jamie Lee Curtis
Lt. Ruth Colfax ...... Dorrie Thompson
Lt. Claire Reid .... Bond Gideon
Yeoman Alvin
  Hunkle .... Richard Brestoff
Ensign Stovall .... Christopher J.
                         Brown
Seaman Dooley .... Kraig Cassity
Chief Herbert
  Molumphrey .... Wayne Long
Seaman Gossett ...... Michael Mazes
Chief Tostin .... Jack Murdock
Seaman Horwich ...... Peter Schuck
Lt. Watson .... Raymond Singer
Seaman Broom .... Jim Varney
Seaman Williams ..... Richard Marion
Seaman Ramone
  Gallardo .... Jesse Dizon
Cpl. Maurice
  Milgrim .... James Ray

Producer: Leonard B. Stern, Si Rose

*Only a pink undercoat was possible before an enemy plane destroyed their supply of gray paint.

Operation: Runaway

Drama; 60 min; NBC 4/27/78 to 8/31/78

The story of David McKay, a former vice squad officer now in private practice as a psychiatrist who specializes in tracking down runaways. See also "The Runaways."

Dr. David McKay .... Robert Reed
Karen Wingate .... Kate Machon
Mark Johnson .... Michael Biehn
Susan Donovan .... Ruth Cox

Producer: William Robert Yates, Mark
  Rodgers

The Oprah Winfrey Show

A syndicated (9/86) daily discussion series with hostess Oprah Winfrey. Produced by Mary K. Clinton, Ellen Pakieten, and Diann Hudson.

The Orchid Award

Variety; 15 min; ABC 5/24/53 to 1/24/54

A program of show business achievement awards in which selected individuals are presented with an orchid and then perform their material.

Host: Bert Lytell, Ronald Reagan, Donald
  Woods

Announcer: John Heistand

Orchestra: Paul Weston

Producer: Allen Dingwell, Harold Romm

The Oregon Trail

Western; 60 min; NBC 9/21/77 to 11/30/77

The series, set in the 1840s, follows the journey of a group of pioneers traveling by wagon train from Illinois to Oregon to begin new lives.

Evan Thorpe .... Rod Taylor
Andrew Thorpe ..... Andrew Stevens
Rachel Thorpe ... Gina Maria Smika
William Thorpe .... Tony Becker
Margaret Devlin ...... Darleen Carr
Luther Sprague ..... Charles Napier
Mr. Cutler .... Ken Swofford

Theme Vocal ("The Oregon Trail"): Danny
  Darst

Producer: Michael Gleason, Richard Collins

The Orient Express

A syndicated (1953) series of dramas set on the Orient Express, a famous European passenger train. Produced by Robert Spafford.

The Orphan and the Dude

Comedy Pilot; 30 min; ABC 7/18/75

The adventures of Oliver Smith, a mild-mannered garage mechanic; Curtis, his feisty roommate; and Leonard, Curtis's adopted son.

Oliver Smith	Oliver Clark
Curtis Brown	Art Evans
Leonard Brown	Todd Bridges
Sam Brodsky	Ed Barth
Amber	Lynne Holmes
Dan	David Moody
Fast Eddie	Frank MacRae

Producer: Arnold Margolin, James Parker

Orson Welles' Great Mysteries

Orson Welles as the host of a British-produced series of mystery stories produced especially for syndication (1973). Produced by Alan P. Sloane.

The Osmond Family Show

Variety; 60 min; ABC 1/28/79 to 5/27/79

Basically, a revised version of "Donny and Marie," wherein various members of the Osmond family perform.

Host: Marie and Donny Osmond

Regulars: Johnny Dark, The Osmond Family, The Ice Angels

Announcer: Wayne Osmond

Orchestra: Bob Rozario

Producer: Alan Osmond, Phil Hahn

The Osmonds

Cartoon; 30 min; ABC 9/9/72 to 9/1/74

The global adventures of the Osmond Brothers pop group as they attempt to promote understanding between nations as goodwill ambassadors (for the U.S. Music Committee).

Voices: The Osmond Brothers (Alan, Jay, Donny, Merrill, Wayne, and Jimmy) as themselves, and Paul Frees as Fugi the dog

Producer: Arthur Rankin Jr., Jules Bass

O.S.S.

Adventure; 30 min; ABC 9/26/57 to 3/14/58

The World War II exploits of Frank Hawthorne, an agent for the Office of Strategic Services (O.S.S.).

Capt. Frank Hawthorne	Ron Rondell
Sgt. O'Brien	Robert Gallico
O.S.S. Chief	Lionel Murton

Producer: Col. William Eliscu, Jules Buck

Otherworld

Fantasy; 60 min; CBS 1/26/85 to 3/16/85

While sightseeing in Egypt, the Sterling family are engulfed by a space time warp that transports them to a world that resembles ours, but has its own history and evolution. Immediately, they encounter Kommander Kroll, a paramilitary policeman who becomes suspicious of them and believes them to be terrorists. As the Sterlings attempt to blend in, they discover that the Masters of Inmar have the power to return them to their world. Stories relate the Sterlings efforts to find the Masters and escape from Kroll, who is seeking to capture them.

Hal Sterling	Sam Groom
June Sterling	Gretchen Corbett
Gina Sterling	Jonna Lee
Trace Sterling	Tony O'Dell
Smith Sterling	Brandon Crane
	Chris Hebert
Kommander Kroll	Jonathan Banks
Nova the Android	Amanda Wyss

"Otherworld" Theme Song: Sylvester Leavy

Producer: Roderick Taylor, Alex Beaton

Our Daughters (Our Five Daughters)

Drama; 30 min; NBC 1/26/62 to 9/28/62

Dramatic incidents in the lives of the Lee family: Parents Helen and Jim, and their daughters, Ann, Marjorie, Barbara, Mary and Jane.

Helen Lee	Esther Ralston
Jim Lee	Michael Keene
Barbara Lee	Patricia Allison
Mary Lee	Wynne Miller
Jane Lee	Nuella Dierking
Marjorie Lee	Iris Joyce
Ann Lee	Jacqueline Courtney
Don Weldon	Ben Hayes

Our Family Honor

Drama; 60 min; ABC 9/17/85 to 1/3/86

Serialized stories about two families on opposite sides of the law: The McKays, of the New York Police Department; and the Danzigs, of Organized Crime.

Vincent Danzig (syndicate boss)	Eli Wallach
August Danzig (his son)	Michael Madsen
Jerry Cole (his son)	Michael Woods
Patrick McKay (police commissioner)	Kenneth McMillan
Off. Liz McKay (his daughter)	Daphne Ashbrook
Det. Frank McKay (his son)	Tom Mason
Katherine McKay (Patrick's wife)	Georgann Johnson
Marianne Danzig (Vincent's wife)	Barbara Stuart
Rita Danzig (August's wife)	Sheree J. Wilson
Roxanne McKay (Frank's wife)	Juanin Clay
Mark Danzig (August's son)	Scott Sherk
Off. Ed Santini	Ray Liotta
George Bennett (Vincent's aide)	Ron Karabatsos
Police Chief Jonas Jones	Dick Anthony Williams

Producer: Lawrence Gordon, Charles Gordon, Leonard Katzman

Our House

Comedy-Drama; 60 min; NBC 9/11/86 (Premiere)

Following the death of her husband, Jessie Witherspoon finds a helping hand when her father-in-law, Gus, a widower set in his ways, offers to let her and her children (Kris, Molly, and David) live with him. Stories tenderly relate incidents in the day-to-day lives of the Witherspoons.

Gus Witherspoon	Wilford Brimley
Jessie Witherspoon	Deidre Hall
Kris Witherspoon	Shannen Doherty
Molly Witherspoon	Keri Houlihan
David Witherspoon	Chad Allen
Joe Kaplan (Gus's friend)	Gerald S. O'Loughlin
Bertha (Molly's friend)	Nicole Dubuc
Carrie (Kris's friend)	Angela Skinner
Lefkowitz (Gus's friend)	Larry Gelman
Mr. Cathcart (Jessie's boss)	John McCook
Sheila (Jessie's sister)	Laurie Burton

"Our House" Theme Song: Billy Goldenberg

Producer: William Blinn, Jerry Thorpe

Our Man Flint

Adventure Pilot; 90 min; ABC 3/17/76

The exploits of Derek Flint, a U.S. government undercover agent.

Derek Flint	Ray Danton
Sandra	Sharon Acker
Benita	Gaye Rowan
Lahoud	Donnelly Rhodes
Girl	Susan Sullivan
Runzler	Lawrence Dane

Producer: Stanley Colbert, R. H. Anderson

Our Man Higgins

Comedy; 30 min; ABC 10/3/62 to 9/11/63

When the MacRoberts, a middle-class American family inherit an expensive silver service from a British relative, they receive also Higgins, a high-tone English butler whom they must retain to keep the silver service. Stories relate the attempts of both Higgins and the MacRoberts to adjust to each other.

Higgins	Stanley Holloway
Duncan MacRoberts	Frank Maxwell
Alice MacRoberts	Audrey Totter
Joanne MacRoberts	Regina Groves
Tommy MacRoberts	Ricky Kelman
Dinghy MacRoberts	K. C. Butts

Producer: Paul Harrison

Our Miss Brooks

Comedy; 30 min; CBS 10/3/52 to 9/21/56

The trials and tribulations of Connie Brooks, an English teacher at Madison High School, and later (1955–56) a teacher at Mrs. Nestor's Private Elementary School.

Connie Brooks	Eve Arden
Osgood Conklin	Gale Gordon
Philip Boynton	Robert Rockwell
Walter Denton	Richard Crenna
Harriet Conklin	Gloria McMillan
Margaret Davis	Jane Morgan
Stretch Snodgrass	Leonard Smith
Gene Talbot	Gene Barry
Clint Albright	William Ching
Benny Romero	Ricky Vera
Mrs. Nestor	Nana Bryant
	Isabel Randolph
Martha Conklin	Virginia Gordon
	Paula Winslow
Winston "Bones"	
Snodgrass	Eddie Ryder
Angela Nestor	Jesslyn Fax
Mr. Romero	Hy Averback
Superintendent	
Stone	Joseph Kearns
Oliver Munsey	Bob Sweeney

Producer: Larry Berns

Our Place

Variety; 60 min; CBS 7/2/67 to 9/3/67

A weekly program of music, songs, and comedy.

Hosts: Jack Burns and Avery Schreiber

Regulars: The Doodletown Pipers

Orchestra: George Wilkins

Producer: Bill Angelos, Buz Kohan

Our Planet Tonight

Satire Pilot; 60 min; NBC 4/22/87

A satirical spoof of newsmagazine series that reports on outrageous "news" stories (e.g., seeing eye cats, Japanese leisure wear, a talking dog). Uses the old "Ben Casey" theme as its theme song.

Hosts: John Houseman, Morgan Fairchild.

Correspondents: Jim Staahl, Jay Leno, Rich Hall, Mitch Laurance, Martha Quinn, Father Guido Sarducci (Don Novello)

Producer: David Zucker, Jerry Zucker

Our Time

Variety; 30 min; NBC 7/27/85 to 9/7/85

The program recalls the music, TV shows, movies, and world events of the 1960s in a comical way.

Hostess: Karen Valentine

Regular: Harry Anderson

Announcer: M. G. Kelly

Orchestra: Lenny Stack

Producer: John J. McMahon, Barry Adelman, Tom Tenowich

Our World

Documentary; 60 min; ABC 9/25/86 (Premiere)

Linda Ellerbee and Ray Gandolf as the hosts of a program that recalls specific years via clips, music, objects, and witnesses. Produced by Susan Lester, Ellen Rossen, and Peter Simmons.

Out of Our Minds

Comedy Pilot; 30 min; Syn. 12/84

A series of comedy sketches based on odd but documented facts.

Host: David Steinberg, Sherry Miller

Regulars: Maggie Butterfield, Eugene Clark, Ben Gordon, Don Lake, Kathy Laksy, Debra McGrath, Max Smith, Nerene Virgin, Roy Wordsworth

Producer: Paul Palmer, Steve Smith

Out of the Blue

Comedy Pilot; 30 min; CBS 8/12/68

Hoping to make a study of the Earth, four aliens from the planet Kurzon, secretly land on Earth and visit the home of Josh Enders, a physics professor living in Hollywood. When Josh learns of their plan, he agrees to help them. The unsold series was to relate the adventures of four aliens (Dr. Aphrodite, Claude, Ethel, and Solly) as they attempt to study life on Earth.

Dr. Aphrodite	Shirley Jones
Josh Enders	John McMartin
Claude	Carl Ballantine
Ethel	Marvin Kaplan
Solly	Barry Dennen
Girl	Phyllis Davis
Captain	John Hubbard
Woman	Nydia Westman
Murphy	Richard Erdman

Producer-Writer: Sol Saks

Out of the Blue

Comedy; 30 min; ABC 9/9/79 to 10/21/79
12/6/79 (1 episode)

When the five Richards children are suddenly orphaned by the death of their parents in a plane accident, an angel (Random) is sent to earth to watch over them (posing as a high school science teacher and revealing his identity only to the children). Stories relate Random's efforts to care for the children without interfering in human destiny.

Angel Random	James Brogan
Boss Angel	Eileen Heckart
Chris Richards	Clark Brandon
Laura Richards	Olivia Barash
Stacey Richards	Tammy Lauren
Jason Richards	Jason Keller
Shane Richards	Shane Keller
Marion MacNelmor	
(their aunt)	Dixie Carter
Gladys	
(housekeeper)	Hannah Dean

Producer: Austin & Irma Kalish

Out of the Inkwell

Cartoon; 5 min; Syn. 1961

The antics of Koko the Clown, his girlfriend Kokete, his dog, Kokonut, and their antagonist Mean Moe. A TV version of the silent theatrical cartoons made between 1915 and 1929.

Koko/Kokete/Mean	
Moe	Larry Storch

Producer: Hal Seeger

Creator: Max Fleischer

Out of This World

Comedy; 30 min; Syn. 9/87

While on an earthly assignment, an alien astronaut from the planet Antereus (Troy), meets and falls in love with a beautiful human (Donna). The two blend life forms and nine months later, as Troy returns home, a baby girl (Evie) is born to Donna. The series, set thirteen years later in Marlowe, California, relates incidents in the life of Evie, a beautiful teenage girl who is part alien, as she struggles to cope with her unearthly powers.

Donna Garland	Donna Pescow
Evie Garland	Maureen Flannigan
Kyle Applegate	Doug McClure
Beano Froelich	Joe Alaskey
Lindsay Selkirk	Christina Nigra
Voice of Troy	Burt Reynolds

Producer: Bob Booker, John Boni, Barbara Booker

Out There

Anthology; 30 min; CBS 10/28/51 to 1/13/52

A live series of science fiction dramas culled from a variety of sources, including original stories and pulp magazines. One of the first series to integrate filmed special effects in a live story. Produced by Donald Davis and John Haggodd.

The Outcasts

Western; 60 min; ABC 9/23/68 to 9/15/69

Bound to an alliance of survival, two outcasts, Earl Corey, an uprooted Virginian aristocrat, and Jemal David, an ex-slave freed by the Proclamation, team and become bounty hunters. Stories, set in the post-Civil War West, relate their exploits as they seek bounty and help people in trouble.

Earl Corey	Don Murray
Jemal David	Otis Young

Producer: Hugh Benson, E. W. Swackhamer

The Outer Limits

Anthology; 60 min; ABC 9/16/63 to 1/16/65

Science fiction dramas that explore the mysteries of the mind, universe, and humanity.

Control Voice: Vic Perrin

"The Outer Limits" Theme Song: Dominic Frontiere

Producer: Joseph Stefano, Leslie Stevens

The Outlaws

Western; 60 min; NBC 9/29/60 to 9/13/62

The series, set in the town of Stillwater, Oklahoma, during the 1890s, relates the events surrounding the apprehension of outlaws as seen, during the first season, through the eyes of the outlaw being sought; and during the second season, through the eyes of Marshal Frank Caine.

Marshal Frank Caine	Barton MacLane
Deputy Heck Martin	Jack Gaynor
Deputy Will Foreman	Don Collier
Deputy Chalk Breeson	Bruce Yarnell
Constance Masters	Judy Lewis
Slim	Slim Pickens

Producer: Frank Telford

Outlaws

Adventure; 60 min; CBS 12/28/86 to 4/4/87

Four bank-robbing outlaws (Harlan, Wolf, Billy, and Isaiah), pursued by a sheriff (Grail) in 1899 Houston, Texas, are struck by a mysterious bolt of lightning and transported to 1986 Houston. Soon, the five men reconcile their differences and learn to survive in their new world. With their stolen gold coins (now worth a fortune) they purchase a ranch and soon afterward meet Maggie Randall, their neighbor and law enforcer, who helps them establish the Double Eagle Ranch Detective Agency. Stories relate their exploits as they dispense their own brand of justice to modern-day outlaws.

John Grail	Rod Taylor
Harlan Pike	William Lucking
Isaiah "Ice" McAdams	Richard Roundtree
Wolfson "Wolf" Lucas	Charles Napier
Billy Pike	Patrick Houer
Maggie Randall	Christina (Christine) Belford

Producer: Nicholas Corea, Stephen Caldwell

Outpost

Western Pilot; 60 min; NBC 3/22/62

The exploits of three bickering cavalry scouts (Ben, Frank, and Myles). Aired as "Charge!" on "The Outlaws."

Sgt. Ben Thompson	Claude Akins
Sgt. Frank Burling	Jay Lanin
Sgt. Myles Ree	Chris King
Chief White Tongue	Frank DeKova
Foreman	Don Collier
Breeson	Bruce Yarnell

Producer: Frank Telford

The Outside Man

Crime Drama Pilot; 60 min; CBS 4/8/77

The exploits of Richie Martinelli, a streetwise federal agent who goes undercover to apprehend criminals (thus making him the "outside man" in dangerous situations).

Richie Martinelli	Ron Leibman
Shaker Thompson	Woody Strode
Rosalie	Janet Margolin
Stalio	Nicholas Colasanto
Sal	Al Ruscio
Leo	Pepper Martin
Armand	Robert Donner

Producer: Paul Magistretti

The Outsider

Crime Drama; 60 min; NBC 9/18/68 to 9/10/69

The exploits of David Ross, an embittered ex-cop turned private detective working out of Los Angeles.

David Ross	Darren McGavin

Producer: Roy Huggins, Gene Levitt

Over and Out

Comedy Pilot; 30 min; NBC 8/11/76

The antics of five female communications officers stranded on an all-male Army base in the South Pacific during World War II.

Capt. Betty Jack Daniels	Michele Lee
Sgt. Cookie Dobson	Susan Lanier
Lt. Paula Rabinowitz	Pat Finley
Sgt. "Lizard" Gossamer	Alice Playten
Sgt. Alice Pierson	Mary Jo Catlett
Capt. Paddy Patterson	Ken Berry
Sgt. Travis Shelby	Stewart Moss
Lt. Sam Launius	Dean Santoro

Music: Peter Matz

Producer: Bob Claver

Overland Trail

Western; 30 min; Syn. 1960

The experiences of Fred Thomas and Frank Flippen, a former Civil War engineer and his young assistant, as they attempt to maintain and establish a route for the Overland Stage Lines from Missouri and California and back during the late 1860s.

Fred Thomas	William Bendix
Frank Flippen	Doug McClure

Producer: Nat Holt, Samuel A. Peeples

Owen Marshall: Counselor at Law

Crime Drama; 60 min; ABC 9/16/71 to 8/24/74

The cases of Owen Marshall, a Santa Barbara-based criminal attorney.

Owen Marshall	Arthur Hill
Melissa Marshall	Christine Matchett
Frieda Krause	Joan Darling
Jess Brandon	Lee Majors
Danny Paterno	Reni Santoni
Ted Warrick	David Soul
D. A. Grant	Russell Johnson
Assistant D. A. Charlie Giannetta	Pat Harrington Jr.
Sgt. Roy Kessler	Henry Beckman
Judge	Lindsay Workman
	Bill Quinn
	John Zaremba

Producer: David Victor, Jon Epstein

Ozmoe

Children; 15 min; ABC 3/6/51 to 4/12/51

The antics of a group of electronically operated marionettes: Ozmoe, a monkey; Roderick Dhon't, the leprechaun; Horatio, the caterpillar; Misty Waters, a mermaid; Sam the Clam; and Throckmorton, the sea serpent.

Voices: Bradley Bolke, Jack Urbant, Elinor Russell, Alan Stapleton, Jack Kindler

Producer: Henry Banks

Ozzie and Harriet

See "The Adventures of Ozzie and Harriet."

Ozzie's Girls

Comedy; 30 min; Syn. 9/73

When their sons, Dave and Ricky, move away from home, Ozzie and Harriet Nelson, rent their room to Susan and Brenda, two beautiful college students. Stories relate incidents in the lives of a retired couple (Ozzie and Harriet) and their young boarders (Susan and Brenda). In the pilot film, which aired on NBC on September 10, 1972, the "Brenda" character had been called "Jennifer."

Ozzie Nelson	Himself
Harriet Nelson	Herself
Susan Hamilton	Susan Sennett
Brenda MacKenzie	Brenda Sykes
Lenore Morrison	Lenore Stevens
Alice Morrison	Joie Guerico
Prof. McCutcheon	David Doyle
Gaye	Gaye Nelson
Mike	Mike Wagner
Tom	Tom Harmon
Mailman	Jim Begg

Producer: Al Simon, Ozzie Nelson

Pac-Man

Cartoon; 30 min; ABC 9/25/83 to 9/1/84

The exploits of video arcade game characters Pac-Man, his wife, Pepper, and their child, Baby Pac, as they battle Mezmaron, an evil being who seeks the location of the Power Forest (which supplies Pac-Man with his power) so he can become ruler of Pac Land.

Pac-Man	Marty Ingels
Pepper	Barbara Minkus
Baby Pac	Russi Taylor
Chomp Chomp	Frank Welker
Sour Puss	Peter Cullen
Mezmaron	Alan Laurie
Sue Monster	Susan Silo
Inky Monster	Barry Gordon
Blinky & Pinky	
Monster	Chuck McCann
Clyde Monster	Neil Ross

Producer: William Hanna, Joseph Barbera

The Packard Showroom

See "The Martha Wright Show."

Paddington Bear

Cartoon; 30 min; Syn. 6/81

When his Aunt Lucy (a bear) retires to the home for retired bears in Peru, her nephew stows away on a ship bound for England. In Paddington Station, he is found and adopted by a couple who name him after the station. Stories relate Paddington's experiences as he learns various aspects of life.

Host: Joel Grey

Paddington's Voice: Michael Horden

Producer: Pepper Weiss

Paddy the Pelican

Children; 15 min; ABC 9/11/50 to 10/13/50

The adventures of Paddy, a pelican puppet whose escapades unfold through comic strip drawings.

Paddy's Voice	Helen York
Pam (Paddy's	
assistant)	Mary Frances
	Desmond
Additional Voices	Ray Suber

Artist: Sam Singer

Producer: Sam Singer

Painting with Elke Sommer

Instruction; 30 min; Syn. 3/85

Painting instruction with actress Elke Sommer, whose talent extends to beautiful art work. Produced by Joan Owens and Carroll Ellerbee.

The Palace

Variety; 60 min; Syn. 9/79

Celebrity guests perform against the background of the Hamilton Palace in Toronto, Canada.

Host: Jack Jones

Orchestra: Tommy Banks

Producer: R. David Close, J. Arnold Gordon

Pall Mall Playhouse

An ABC Summer series (7/20/55 to 9/9/55) of repeat dramas from other anthology programs. Sponsored by Pall Mall cigarettes.

Palmerstown, U.S.A.

Drama; 60 min; CBS 3/20/80 to 5/1/80
3/17/81 to 6/9/81

The series, set in Palmerstown, Tennessee, in 1935, presents a view of life in a small town where whites and blacks co-exist for economic survival, as seen through the eyes of two boys: David Hall (white) and Booker T. Freeman (black), friends who struggle to remain friends in a world that does not approve of their friendship. Also titled "Palmerstown."

W. D. Hall	Beeson Carroll
Coralee Hall	Janis St. John
David Hall	Brian G. Wilson
Willie Joe Hall	Michael J. Fox
Luther Freeman	Bill Duke
Bessie Freeman	Jonelle Allen
Booker T. Freeman	Jermain H. Johnson
Diana Freeman	Star-Shemah Bobatoon
Sheriff	Kenneth White
Auntie Calpurnia	Claudia McNeil
Mrs. Miller	Sarina C. Grant
Mailman Jackson	Morgan Freeman
Banker Hodges	John Carter
Widder Brown	Iris Kern
Reverend Teasdale	Davis Roberts
Deacon Shaw	Fred Pinkard
Deacon Lewis	Stack Pierce
Willy	Michael Greene

Producer: Norman Lear, Alex Haley, Ronald Rubin

Palms Precinct

Crime Drama Pilot; 60 min; NBC 1/8/82

The exploits of Alexandra Brewster and Carmine Monaco, detectives with the Palms City, California Police Department.

Insp. Alexandra Brewster	Sharon Gless
Insp. Carmine Monaco	Steve Ryan
Capt. Edward Hammersman	James Gallery
Jeanine Monaco	Tricia O'Neil
Albert Brunswick	Jack Kelly
Patti Halliwell	Lonora May
Barry Wittenberg	Mark Thomas
Dean Kelsey	Bruce Fisher

Music: Mike Post, Pete Carpenter

Producer: David Chase, J. Rickley Dumm

Pals

Comedy Pilot; 30 min; NBC 7/31/81

The misadventures of two brothers-in-law: the stolid Harry Miller, and the impetuous Frank Greene (married to Beverly, the sister of Harry's wife, Shirley).

Frank Greene	Tony LoBianco
Harry Miller	Jeffrey Tambor
Shirley Miller	Linda Carlson
Beverly Greene	Margaret Willock

Producer: Larry Rosen, Larry Tucker

Panic!

Anthology; 30 min; NBC 3/5/57 to 9/17/57

Suspense dramas that depict the plight of people suddenly confronted with unexpected and perilous situations. See also "No Warning."

Host-Narrator: Westbrook Van Voorhis

Producer: Al Simon

Panhandle Pete and Jennifer

Children; 15 min; NBC 9/18/50 to 6/28/51

The series, which is set in Chickamoochie Country and incorporates a cartoon story format, illustrates yarns told by Johnny Coons, Jennifer Holt and her life-size dummy, Panhandle Pete.

Jennifer Holt	Herself
Johnny Coons	Himself

Cartoonist: Bill Newton

Producer: Stefan Hatos

Pantomine Quiz

Game; 30 min; CBS 10/4/49 to 8/20/51
                    NBC 1/2/52 to 3/26/52
                    CBS 7/4/52 to 3/26/52
                    DuMont 10/20/53 to 4/13/54
                    CBS 7/9/54 to 8/27/54
                    ABC 1/22/55 to 3/6/55
                    ABC 4/8/59 to 9/21/59

One member of a four member team is given a charade that he must perform to his teammates. The amount of time it takes for the team to identify the charade is calculated. The opposing team competes in the same manner and eight charades are played (allowing each player a chance to perform). The team with the lowest overall performance time is the winner. See also "Stump the Stars."

Host: Mike Stokey

Regulars: Angela Lansbury, Hans Conried, Jackie Coogan, Carol Burnett, Vincent Price, Dorothy Hart, Rocky Graziano, Beverly Tyler, Robert Clary, Milt Kamen, Howard Morris, Denise Darcell, Stubby Kaye, Tom Poston, Coleen Gray, Robert Stack, Sandra Spence, Dave Willock, Fred Clark, George O'Brien, Frank DeVol, Virginia Field

Announcer: Ken Niles, Art Fleming, Ed Reimers

Producer: Mike Stokey

Papa Cellini

Comedy; 30 min; ABC 9/28/52 to 11/16/52

Events in the lives of the Cellinis, an Italian-American family living in New York City.

Papa Cellini	Tito Virolo
Mama Cellini	Carlo DeAngelo
Nita Cellini	Carol Sinclair
Antonio Cellini	Aristide Sigismondi

Papa G.I.

Comedy Pilot; 30 min; CBS 6/29/64

While performing in Korea, U.S. Army entertainer Mike Parker crosses the path of Kim Chi and Quang Duc, a homeless sister and brother who attach themselves to him. When Mike discovers that they are orphans, he takes them under his wing and makes them a part of his act. The unsold series was to relate Mike's efforts to care for his new found family.

Sgt. Mike Parker	Dan Dailey
Kim Chi	Cherylene Lee
Quang Duc	Douglas Moe
Soldiers	Noam Pitlik
	Billy Halop

Producer: Edward H. Feldman

Papa Said No

Comedy Pilot; 30 min; CBS 4/4/58

The misadventures of Suzanne Stacey, a beautiful, marriage-minded young woman in search of the ideal husband. Aired on "Schlitz Playhouse of Stars."

Suzanne Stacey	Yvonne Craig
John Stacey	Patric Knowles
Gabrielle Stacey	Jeanne Manet
Calvin Penny	Scott Brady

Producer: Frank P. Rosenberg

The Paper Chase

Drama; 60 min; CBS 9/9/78 to 7/17/79

The joys and frustrations of first-year law students at a prestigious, but unidentified northeastern university. The program focuses in particular on the relationship between James Hart, an earnest Minnesota farm boy, and Professor Charles Kingsfield Jr., a brilliant contract law instructor who, feared for his classroom tyranny, either makes or breaks students. Based on the novel by John Jay Osborn Jr.

Prof. Charles Kingsfield Jr.	John Houseman
James T. Hart	James Stephens
Elizabeth Logan	Francine Tacker
Franklin Ford	Tom Fitzsimmons
Willis Bell	James Keane
Thomas Anderson	Robert Ginty
Jonathan Brooks	Jonathan Segal
Asheley Brooks	Deka Beaudine
Laura Nottingham	Betty Harford
Linda O'Connor	Katherine Dunfee
Gregarian	Stanley DeSantis
Ernie	Charles Hallahan
Carol	Carole Goldman
Dean Rutherford	Jack Manning

Theme Vocal ("The First Years"): Seals and Crofts

Producer: Robert J. Thompson

The Paper Chase: The Second Year

Drama; 53 min; SHO 4/15/83 to 11/15/83
5/22/84 to 8/14/84

A continuation of the previous title, which relates events in the life of James Hart, now a second-year law student (who attends Prof. Kingsfield's contract law seminars) and who works as a researcher-writer for the school newspaper ("The Law Review").

Prof. Charles	
Kingsfield Jr.	John Houseman
James T. Hart	James Stephens
Franklin Ford	Tom Fitzsimmons
Willis Bell	James Keane
Connie Lehman	Jane Kaczmarek
Gerald Golden	Michael Tucci
Laura Nottingham	Betty Harford
Rita Harriman	Clare Kirkconnell
Laura	Andra Millian
Vivian	Penny Johnson
Morrison	Michael Shannon
Zeiss	Worthham Krimmer

Producer: Lynn Roth

The Paper Chase: The Third Year

Drama; 53 min; SHO 5/11/85 to 8/3/85

A continuation of the prior title. The final year experiences of law student James T. Hart, now president of "The Law Review."

Prof. Charles	
Kingsfield Jr.	John Houseman
James T. Hart	James Stephens
Franklin Ford	Tom Fitzsimmons
Willis Bell	James Keane
Laura Nottingham	Betty Harford
Rita Harriman	Clare Kirkconnell
Laura	Andra Millian
Tom Ford	Peter Nelson
Rose Samuels	Lainie Kazan
Prof. Martha Tyler	Diana Douglas

Producer: Lynn Roth

The Paper Chase: The Graduation Year

Drama; 53 min; SHO 6/24/86 to 7/15/86

A five-episode conclusion of "The Paper Chase" series with the regulars from the prior versions (Hart, Ford, and Bell) graduating and beginning their law careers.

Prof. Charles	
Kingsfield Jr.	John Houseman
James T. Hart	James Stephens
Franklin Ford	Tom Fitzsimmons
Willis Bell	James Keane
Laura Nottingham	Betty Harford
Prof. Martha Tyler	Diana Douglas
Rita Harriman	Clare Kirkconnell
Laura	Andra Millian
Rose Samuels	Lainie Kazan
Gerald Golden	Michael Tucci
Tom Ford	Peter Nelson
Vivian	Penny Johnson

Producer: Lynn Roth

Paper Dolls

Drama; 60 min; ABC 9/23/84 to 12/25/84

The experiences of Taryn Blake and Laurie Casswell, two beautiful fashion models; Julia Blake and Dinah Casswell, their domineering mothers; and Racine and Grant Harper, two powerful people actively involved in the world of high fashion.

Taryn Blake	Daryl Hannah*
	Nicolette Sheridan
Laurie Casswell	Alexandra Paul*
	Terry Farrell
Julia Blake	Joan Hackett*
	Brenda Vaccaro
Dinah Casswell	Jennifer Warren
Racine	Joan Collins*
	Morgan Fairchild
Grant Harper	Lloyd Bridges
Colette Ferrier	Lauren Hutton
Wesley Harper	Dack Rambo
Marjorie Harper	Nancy Olson
Blair Harper-Fenton	Mimi Rogers
Michael Casswell	Craig T. Nelson*
	John Bennett Perry
David Fenton	Richard Beymer
Sara Frank	Anne Schedeen
Sandy Paris	Jonathan Frakes
Christopher York	Don Bowen
John Waite	Himself
Grayson Carr	Larry Linville

Producer: Leonard Goldberg, Michele Rappaport

*TV Movie Role (5/24/83).

Paper Moon

Comedy; 30 min; ABC 9/12/74 to 1/2/75

The series, set in the Midwest during the 1930s, relates the adventures of Moses "Moze" Prey, a con artist and fast-talking salesman for the Dixie Bible Company, and his 11-year-old daughter, Addie, as they struggle to survive the Depression through imaginative schemes. Based on the feature film.

Moses Pray	Christopher Connelly
Addie Pray	Jodie Foster

Producer: Anthony Wilson

The Parent Game

Game; 30 min; Syn. 1972

Three married couples compete in a game that compares their ideas about raising children with those of a child psychologist. A question, that has four possible answers, is revealed. Couples choose the answer they believe is correct. The correct answer is revealed and points are awarded accordingly. The highest scorers win a specially selected prize.

Host: Clark Race

Announcer: Johnny Jacobs

Producer: Chuck Barris

Paris

Crime Drama; 60 min; CBS 9/29/79 to 1/15/80

The story of Woodrow "Woody" Paris, a college criminology professor who is also captain of the Metro Squad division of the Los Angeles Police Department.

Capt. Woodrow Paris	James Earl Jones
Barbara Paris	Lee Chamberlain
Chief Jerome Bench	Hank Garrett
Sgt. Stacey Erickson	Cecilia Hart
Sgt. Charlie Bogart	Jake Mitchell
Sgt. Ernie Villas	Frank Ramirez
Sgt. Willie Miller	Michael Warren

Producer: Steven Bochco

Paris Cavalcade of Fashion

A fifteen minute NBC program (11/11/48 to 1/20/49) of films that feature the latest Paris fashions. Narrated by Faye Emerson and Julie Gibson.

Paris Precinct

Crime Drama; 30 min; ABC 4/3/55 to 12/18/55

The series, also known as "World Crime Hunt," relates the investigations of Surete (Paris) Inspectors Bolbec and Beaumont.

Insp. Bolbec	Claude Dauphin
Insp. Beaumont	Louis Jourdan

Producer: Andre Hakim

Paris 7000

Adventure; 60 min; ABC 1/22/70 to 6/4/70

The exploits of Jack Brennan, an American troubleshooter based in Paris who helps distressed U.S. citizens. (The title refers to the U.S. Consulate's phone number).

Jack Brennan	George Hamilton
Jules Maurois	Jacques Aubuchon
Robert Stevens	Gene Raymond

"Paris 7000" Theme Song: Michel Colombier

Producer: Richard Caffey, John Wilder, Michael Gleason

Park Place

Comedy; 30 min; CBS 4/9/81 to 4/30/81

The misadventures of a group of eager young attorneys attached to the Legal Assistance Bureau, a legal-aid clinic on Park Place in New York City.

David Ross	Harold Gould
Joel "Jo" Keene	Mary Elaine Monti
Jeff O'Neal	David Clennon
Howard Beech	Don Calfa
Ernie Rice	Cal Gibson
Aaron MacRae	Lionel Smith
Brad Lincoln	James Widdoes
Frances Heine	Alice Drummond

Producer: Reinhold Weege

The Partners

Comedy; 30 min; NBC 9/18/71 to 1/8/72

The exploits of Lennie Crooke (inept) and George Robinson (level-headed), police sergeants with the 33rd Precinct in Los Angeles.

Sgt. Lennie Crooke	Don Adams
Sgt. George Robinson	Rupert Crosse
Capt. Aaron Andrews	John Doucette
Sgt. Nelson Higgenbottom	Dick Van Patten
Freddie Butler	Robert Karvelas

"The Partners" Theme Song: Lalo Schifrin

Producer: Don Adams, Arne Sultan

Partners in Crime

Crime Drama; 60 min; NBC 9/22/84 to 12/29/84

When private detective Raymond Caulfield is murdered, his unusual will bequeathes that his two beautiful ex-wives, Carole (a photographer) and Sydney (an aspiring musician) inherit his business, the Caulfield Detective Agency, and his mansion. When Carole and Sydney meet for the first time—at the funeral—they become "Partners in Crime" by solving Ray's murder. Stories, set in San Francisco, relate the light-hearted adventures of Carole and Sydney, television's most beautiful private detectives.

Carole Stanwyck	Lynda Carter
Sydney Kovak	Loni Anderson
Lt. Ed Vronsky	Leo Rossi
Jeanine	Eileen Heckart
Harvey Shain	Walter Olkewicz
Duke Kovak	Cameron Mitchell

"Partners in Crime" Theme Song: Ken Heller, Nathan Sassover

Producer: Bill Driskill, Larry Brody, Everett Chambers

Partners in Crime

Comedy-Mystery; 60 min; PBS Syn. 10/85

When Tuppence and Tommy Beresford, a wealthy British couple discover that a detective agency is up for sale, they purchase it with the hope of finding the same type of adventure they find as avid readers of detective novels. Stories, set in London, relate their lighthearted exploits as the owner-operators of Blunt's International Detective Agency. Based on characters created by Agatha Christie.

Tuppence Beresford	Francesca Annis
Tommy Beresford	James Warwick
Albert	Reece Dinsdale
Insp. Marriott	Arthur Cox

Producer: Jack Williams

The Partridge Family

Comedy; 30 min; ABC 9/25/70 to 9/7/74

The comic adventures of the Partridges, an ordinary family who become a famous pop group when the sale of a demonstration tape leads to a recording contract and fame. See the following title also.

Shirley Partridge	Shirley Jones
Keith Partridge	David Cassidy
Laurie Partridge	Susan Dey
Danny Partridge	Danny Bonaduce
Tracy Partridge	Suzanne Crough
Chris Partridge	Jeremy Gelbwaks
	Brian Forster
Reuben Kincaide	Dave Madden
Walter Renfrew	Ray Bolger
	Jackie Coogan
Amanda Renfrew	Rosemary DeCamp
Doris Stevens	Nita Talbot
Donna Stevens	Ronne Troup
Ricky Stevens	Ricky Segal
Richard Lawrence	Bert Convy
Julie Lawrence	Jodie Foster
Gloria Hickey	Patti Cohoon
Bonnie Kleinschmitt	Elaine Giftos
Punky Lazaar	Gary Dubin
Snake	Rob Reiner
	Stuart Margolin

Various Roles: Gordon Jump, Mitzi Hoag, Vic Tayback, Bruce Kimmell, Yvonne Wilder (waitress roles)

Producer: Bob Claver, Mel Swope, William S. Bickley, Michael Warren

Partridge Family: 2200 A.D.

Cartoon; 30 min; CBS 9/7/74 to 3/9/75

The misadventures of a futuristic Partridge family as they tour various planets with their musical act.

Shirley Partridge	Sherry Alberoni
Laurie Partridge	Susan Dey
Danny Partridge	Danny Bonaduce
Tracy Partridge	Suzanne Crough
Chris Partridge	Brian Forster
Keith Partridge	Chuck McLennan
Reuben Kincaid	Dave Madden
Marion	Julie McWhirter
Beannie	Allan Melvin

Producer: William Hanna, Joseph Barbera

Party Line

Game; 30 min; NBC 6/8/47 to 8/31/47

An early quiz program, hosted by Bert Parks, wherein a viewer is telephoned and asked to answer a question in return for money.

Party Time at Club Roma

Variety; 30 min; NBC 10/14/50 to 1/6/51

The program, sponsored by Roma Wines, features audience participation, game contests, quizzes, and performances by young talent.

Host: Ben Alexander

Producer: Ben Alexander

Pass the Buck

Game; 30 min; NBC 4/3/78 to 6/30/78

A category is revealed (e.g., types of fruit). Each of the four competing players must name an item that relates to the subject. Each correct answer scores money; an incorrect answer defeats a player and a new topic is used. The one player who remains wins what money has been accumulated.

Host: Bill Cullen

Announcer: Bob Clayton

Producer: Bob Stewart, Sande Stewart

Passport to Danger

Adventure; 30 min; Syn. 1954

The exploits of Steve McQuinn, a U.S. diplomatic courier, and the unwitting decoy of the Hungarian Secret Police.

Steve McQuinn	Cesar Romero

Producer: Hal Roach Jr.

Password

Game; 30 min; CBS 10/2/61 to 9/15/67

Two two-member teams compete. One member of each team receives a password (e.g., "bottle") and must relay its meaning to his partner via one-word clues. Teams score points based on the number of clues used to identify the word. The highest scoring team is the winner.

Host: Allen Ludden

Announcer: John Harlan, Jack Clark

Producer: Frank Wayne, Bob Stewart

Password

Game; 30 min; ABC 4/5/71 to 6/27/75

A revised version of the prior title, which see for format.

Host: Allen Ludden

Announcer: John Harlan

Producer: Frank Wayne, Howard Felscher

Password Plus

Game; 30 min; NBC 1/8/79 to 3/26/82

One player on each two-member teams receives a password. Through one word clues, he must relate its meaning to his partner. When the password is guessed, it is placed on a board and becomes one of four clues to the identity of a person, place, or object (which scores a player an extra $100 if he guesses it). The first player to win a two-out-of-three match competition is the champion.

Host: Allen Ludden, Bill Cullen, Tom Kennedy

Announcer: Gene Wood, Bob Hilton, Rich Jeffries

Producer: Howard Felscher, Robert Sherman

Pat Boone in Hollywood

Variety; 90 min; Syn. 1969

Music, songs, and celebrity interviews.

Host: Pat Boone

Announcer: Jay Stewart

Orchestra: Paul Smith

Producer: Bernie Kukoff, Jeff Harris

The Pat Boone Show

Variety; 30 min; NBC 10/17/66 to 3/31/67

A daily program of music, songs, and interviews.

Host: Pat Boone

Orchestra: Paul Smith

Producer: Armand Grant

The Pat Boone Show

Variety; 30 min; ABC 10/3/57 to 6/25/59

A weekly program of music and songs. Also known as "The Pat Boone Chevy Show."

Host: Pat Boone

Regulars: Louise O'Brien, The McGuire Sisters, The Artie Malvin Chorus

Orchestra: Mort Lindsey

Pat Paulsen's Half a Comedy Hour

Comedy; 30 min; ABC 1/22/70 to 3/9/70

Sketches and blackouts that satirize the contemporary scene.

Host: Pat Paulsen

Regulars: Jean Byron, Sherry Miles, Bob Einstein, Vanetta Rogers, Peppe Brown, Pedro Regas

Announcer: Billy Sands

Orchestra: Denny Vaughn

Producer: Bill Carruthers

The Patrice Munsel Show

Variety; 30 min; ABC 10/18/57 to 6/13/58

A live series that showcases the versatile talents of Metropolitan Opera soprano Patrice Munsel.

Hostess: Patrice Munsel

Regulars: The Martins Quartet

Orchestra: Charles Sanford

Producer: Clark Jones, Robert Schuler

The Patricia Bowan Show

Variety; 15 min; CBS 8/11/51 to 11/3/51

A live variety series that showcases the dancing abilities of ballerina Patricia Bowan.

Hostess: Patricia Bowan

Regulars: Maureen Cannon, Paul Shelly, The Pastels

Music: The Norman Paris Trio

Patrick Stone

Comedy Pilot; 30 min; CBS 7/16/65

The exploits of Patrick Stone, a not-too-bright private detective.

Patrick Stone	Jeff Davis
Janine D'Arcy	Joanna Barnes
Bill Tanner	Keenan Wynn

Producer-Director: Sheldon Leonard

Patrol Car

See "Inspector Fabian of Scotland Yard."

The Patti Page Show

Variety; 15 min; Syn. 1955

A program of music and songs.

Hostess: Patti Page

Regulars: The Page Five Singers

Orchestra: Jack Rael

Producer: Joseph Stanley

The Patti Page Show

Variety; 30 min; NBC 6/16/56 to 7/16/56

A Summer series of music and songs.

Hostess: Patti Page

Regulars: The Spellbinders, The Frank Lewis Dancers

Orchestra: Carl Hoff

The Patti Page Show

Variety; 15 min; CBS 2/9/57 to 6/11/58

A program of music and songs.

Hostess: Patti Page

Regulars: The Matt Maddox Dancers

Orchestra: Vic Schoen

The Patti Page Show

Variety; 30 min; ABC 9/24/58 to 3/16/59

A weekly program of music and songs.

Hostess: Patti Page

Regulars: Rocky Cole, The Jerry Packer Singers, The Matt Maddox Dancers

Orchestra: Vic Schoen

Producer: Ted Mills

Pattie Pool and Family

Comedy Pilot; 30 min; NBC 1/18/88

A proposed spin-off from "Valerie's Family" that focuses on the antics of Pattie Pool, the slightly wacky housewife, and her husband, Peter.

Pattie Poole	Edie McClurg
Peter Poole	Willard Scott
Mother Poole	Kathleen Freeman

Producer: Chip Keys, Doug Keys, Judy Pioli

The Patty Duke Show

Comedy; 30 min; ABC 9/18/63 to 8/31/66

When widowed foreign correspondent Kenneth Lane realizes that his job may interfere with his daughter, Cathy's, education, he arranges for her to live with relatives in Brooklyn, N.Y.—a situation that causes an unexpected turn of events when Cathy and her cousin, Patty, meet for the first time and find they are identical look-a-likes. Stories relate events in the lives of two pretty high school girls who sometimes switch identities to help the other out in times of need.

Patty and Cathy Lane	Patty Duke
Martin Lane	William Schallert
Natalie Lane	Jean Byron
Ross Lane	Paul O'Keefe
Richard Harrison	Eddie Applegate
Sue Ellen Turner	Kitty Sullivan
Ted Brownley	Skip Hinnant
Gloria	Kelly Wood
J. R. Castle	John McGiver
William Smithers	Ralph Bell
Sammy	Sammy Smith
T. J. Blodgett	Alan Bruce
	Robert Carson
Kenneth Lane	William Schallert
Louie	Bobby Diamond
Monica Robinson	Laura Barton
	Kathy Garver
Mrs. MacDonald	Margaret Hamilton
Alfred	Jeff Siggins
Betsy (Patty's Southern cousin)	Patty Duke
Patty Duke's double	Rita McLaughlin

Producer: William Asher, Robert Costello

The Paul Arnold Show

A 15-minute interlude series of music and songs with Paul Arnold. Broadcast on CBS from 10/24/49 to 6/23/50.

Paul Bernard—Psychiatrist

Drama; 30 min; Syn. 1972

The program dramatizes sessions between psychiatrist Dr. Paul Bernard and his patients. Produced in Canada.

Dr. Paul Bernard   Chris Wiggins

Music: Milani Kymlicka

The Paul Dixon Show

Variety; 60 min; ABC 8/8/51 to 9/4/52
                    DuMont 9/29/52 to 4/8/55

A weekly program of music and songs.

Host: Paul Dixon

Regulars: Dotty Mack, Wanda Lewis, Lennie Gorrian

Producer: Dick Perry, Jack Taylor

The Paul Dixon Show

A syndicated (1974) program of music and conversation geared to women with host Paul Dixon, regulars Bonnie Lou and Coleen Sharp, and the music of Bruce Brownfield. Produced by Jack Taylor.

The Paul Hartman Show

See "Pride of the Family."

The Paul Hogan Show

Comedy; 30 min; Syn. 6/81

An Australian-produced series of adult-oriented comedy sketches.

Host: Paul Hogan

Regulars: Delvene Delaney, Roger Stevens, John Blackman, Karen Pini, Sue McIntosh, Andrew Harwood

Producer: John Cornell, Paul Hogan

The Paul Lynde Show

Comedy; 30 min; ABC 9/13/72 to 9/8/73

The misadventures of attorney Paul Simms as he struggles to cope with life, his job, and his family (his wife, Martha; his daughters, Sally and Barbara, and Barbara's annoying husband, Howie).

Paul Simms	Paul Lynde
Martha Simms	Elizabeth Allen
Barbara Dickerson	Jane Actman
Sally Simms	Pamelyn Ferdin
Howie Dickerson	John Calvin
J. J. McNish	Herbert Voland
Barney Dickerson	Jerry Stiller
Grace Dickerson	Anne Meara
Alice	Allison McKay
Jimmy Fowler	Anson Williams
Jimmy Lyons	Stuart Getz

Producer: Harry Ackerman, William Asher

Paul Sand in Friends and Lovers

Comedy; 30 min; CBS 9/14/74 to 1/4/75

The life, fantasies, and romantic misadventures of Robert Dreyfuss, a young bachelor and bass violinist with the Boston Symphony Orchestra. See also "Friends and Lovers."

Robert Dreyfuss	Paul Sand
Charlie Dreyfuss	Michael Pataki
Janis Dreyfuss	Penny Marshall
Fred Myerback	Steve Landesberg
Jack Reardon	Dick Wesson
Mason Woodruff	Craig Richard Nelson
Ben Dreyfuss	Jack Gilford
Marge Dreyfuss	Jan Miner
Estelle Milner	Dena Dietrich
Doris Myerback	Karen Morrow
Susan	Sharon Spelman

Music: Patrick Williams

Producer: James L. Brooks, Allan Burns

Paul Whiteman's Saturday Night Revue

Variety; 30 min; ABC 11/6/49 to 3/30/52

Music and songs with bandleader Paul Whiteman.

Host: Paul Whiteman

Regulars: Earl Wrightson, Lina Romay, Eric Viola, Joe Young, Maureen Cannon

Producer: Tony Stanford, Ward Byron, Richard Eckler

Paul Whiteman's Teen Club

Variety; 60 min; ABC 4/2/49 to 3/28/54

A program of music and song that also features performances by undiscovered teenage talent. Winners, who are chosen by a celebrity guest, receive professional coaching and the opportunity to appear at a later date.

Host: Paul Whiteman

Co-Host: Margo Whiteman, Nancy Lewis

Regulars: Maureen Cannon, June Keegan, Andrea McLaughlin, The Ray Porter Singers

Orchestra: Paul Whiteman

Producer: Skip Dawes, Jack Steck, Paul Whiteman

The Paul Williams Show

Comedy Pilot; 30 min; NBC 6/27/79

The story of Paul Hamilton, an aspiring TV personality who portrays Marvin the Martian on a kid show for KFAP-TV in Denver, Colorado.

Paul Hamilton	Paul Williams
Denny Morton	Rick Podell
Deborah	Dana Hill
Victoria Woodbridge	Amanda McBroom
Barbara	Sandra Kerns

Music: Paul Williams

Producer: Peter Engel

The Paul Winchell and Jerry Mahoney Show

Variety; 30 min; NBC 9/18/50 to 6/9/56

A potpourri of music, songs, comedy, and quizzes with Paul Winchell and his dummy friends Jerry Mahoney and Knucklehead Smiff. The quiz segment, "What's My Name?" calls for players to identify a famous person via clues provided by Paul and his dummies.

Host: Paul Winchell

Regulars: Dorothy Claire, Mary Ellen Terry, Ken Spaulding, Margaret Hamilton, Patricia Bright, Jimmy Blaine, Sid Raymond, Hilda Vaughn

Orchestra: Milton DeLugg, John Gart

Producer: Sherman Marks, Hudson Faussett, Will Covan

The Paul Winchell Show

Variety Pilot; 30 min; CBS 5/10/56

An unsold series of music and comedy with ventriloquist Paul Winchell and his dummy friends Jerry Mahoney and Knucklehead Smiff.

Host: Paul Winchell

Guests: Jaye P. Morgan, Bobby Van

Announcer: Tony Marvin

Orchestra: Hank Sylvern

Producer: Lester Gottlieb, Jerome Shaw

The Paul Winchell Show

Children; 30 min; ABC 9/29/57 to 4/3/60
12/25/60 to 4/16/61

A program of music and comedy featuring the antics of Jerry Mahoney and Knucklehead Smiff, the dummies of ventriloquist Paul Winchell.

Paula Stone's Toy Shop

Children; 60 min; Syn. 1955

A program of music, comedy, and song set against the background of a toy store.

Hostess: Paula Stone

Freddie Fun: Tim Herbert

Producer-Writer-Director: Paula Stone

The Paw Paws

Cartoon; 30 min; Syn. 9/85

The adventures of the Paw Paws, a group of magical bears who help good defeat evil. Stories relate in particular the good Princess Paw Paw's efforts to prevent the evil Dark Paw from taking over her kingdom.

Voices: Susan Blu, Ruth Buzzi, Scatman Crothers, Jerry Dexter, Pat Fraley, Billie Hayes, Mitzi McCall, Howard Morris, Robert Ridgely, Neil Ross, Marilyn Schreffler, Frank Welker

Producer: William Hanna, Joseph Barbera

Pay Cards

Game; 30 min; Syn. 1968

Twenty cards are displayed face down on an electronic board. Each of the three players who compete select five cards. The player with the best poker hand wins cash ($10 for a pair; $30 for three of a kind; $100 for four of a kind).

Host: Art James

Announcer: Fred Collins

Producer: E. Roger Muir, Nick Nicholson

P.D.Q.

Game; 30 min; Syn. 1965

One member of each two-member team is placed in a soundproof booth. The outside player of one team stands before a phrase that is spelled out in large plastic letters. The booth player must identify the phrase from key letters that his partner places on the wall. The opposing team competes in the same manner. The team who use the fewest overall letters is the winner.

Host: Dennis James

Announcer: Kenny Williams

Producer: Merrill Heatter, Bob Quigley

The Pearl Bailey Show

Variety; 60 min; ABC 1/23/71 to 5/5/71

A weekly program of music and song.

Hostess: Pearl Bailey

Regulars: The Robert Sidney Dancers, The Allan Davies Dancers

Orchestra: Louis Bellson

Announcer: Roger Carroll

Producer: Bob Finkel

Pebbles and Bamm Bamm

Cartoon; 30 min; CBS 9/11/71 to 9/2/72

The adventures of Pebbles, the teenage daughter of Fred and Wilma Flintstone, and Bamm Bamm, the adopted son of Betty and Barney Rubble. A spin-off from "The Flintstones."

Pebbles Flintstone	Sally Struthers
Bamm Bamm Rubble	Jay North
Moonrock	Lennie Weinrib
Fabian	Carl Esser
Penny	Mitzi McCall
Cindy & Wiggy	Gay Hartwig

Producer: William Hanna, Joseph Barbera

Peck's Bad Girl

Comedy; 30 min; CBS 5/5/59 to 8/4/59

The misadventures of Torey Peck, a mischievous 12-year-old girl who prefers to remain a tomboy rather than face the world as a young lady.

Torey Peck	Patricia McCormack
Steve Peck	Wendell Corey
Jennifer Peck	Marsha Hunt
Roger Peck	Roy Ferrell
Francesca	Reba Waters

Producer: Norman Felton

The Pee Wee King Show

Variety; 30 min; ABC 5/23/55 to 9/5/55

Performances by country and western entertainers with band leader Pee Wee King and regulars Ellen Long, Chuck Wiggins, Bonnie Sloane, Redd Stuart, The Golden West Cowboys, The Cleveland Jamboree.

Pee Wee King's Flying Ranch

Variety; 30 min; Syn. 10/54

Performances by country and western entertainers.

Host: Pee Wee King

Regulars: Ellen Long, Redd Stewart

Music: The Teddy Raymond Quartet

Producer: Peter Katz

Pee Wee's Playhouse

Children; 30 min; CBS 9/13/86 (Premiere)

A live on film (and expensive) Saturday-morning series that features Pee Wee Herman in zany skits set against a dazzling, magical playhouse.

Pee Wee Herman	Paul Reubens
Captain Carl	Phil Hartman
Opal	Natasha Lyonne
King of Cartoons	Gilbert Lewis
Dixie	Joann Carlo
Cowboy Curtis	Larry Fishburn
Miss Yvonne	Lynn Stewart
Randy/Dirty Dog	Wayne White
Jambi	John Paragon
Conky Knucklehead	Gregory Harrison
Housewife	Alison Mork

Producer: Paul Reubens, Stephen Oakes, Peter Rosenthal

Pen 'n' Inc.

Comedy Pilot; 30 min; CBS 8/15/81

Events in the life of Alan Ozley, an artist for a small town newspaper (the Essex, Connecticut "Register") who hopes to one day become the political cartoonist.

Alan Ozley	Matt McCoy
Debbie Winston	Brianne Leary
T. W. Winston	Peter Hobbs
Gretchen	
Vanderwyck	Andra Akers
Raymond Babbitt	Charles Thomas
	Murphy
Dexter Budd	Doug Cox
Ralph	Fred Willard

Producer: Robert Wolterstorff, Paul M. Belous

The Pendulum

The syndicated (1956) title for 65 episodes of "The Vise." Hosted by John Bentley and produced by Bob Breckner.

Pennies from Heaven

Fantasy; 75 min; Syn. 1979

The series, set in England during the 1930s, combines dramatic action with period songs to chronicle the travels of Arthur Parker, a sheet-music salesman who fantasizes about the songs he sells.

Arthur Parker	Bob Hoskins
Janet Parker	Gemma Craven
Eileen	Cheryl Campbell
Accordian Man	Kenneth Colley

Producer: Kenith Trodd

Penny to a Million

Game; 30 min; ABC 5/11/55 to 10/19/55

Two five-member teams compete in a question-and-answer session wherein eight of the ten players are defeated by incorrect responses. The two remaining players compete in a spelling bee wherein they receive one penny doubled to a possible million ($10,000) for each word they spell correctly.

Host: Bill Goodwin

Producer: Herb Wolf

Pentagon Confidential

See "Pentagon U.S.A."

Pentagon U.S.A.

Drama; 30 min; CBS 8/6/53 to 10/1/53

Factual dramas based on the files of the U.S. Army, Criminal Investigation Division. The program premiered as "Pentagon Confidential," but changed to the above title on its second telecast.

Division Colonel	Addison Richards
Police Detective	Gene Lyons
Army Investigator	Edward Binns
	Larry Fletcher

Producer: William Dozier, Alex March

Penthouse Party

Variety; 15 min; ABC 9/15/50 to 6/8/51

A program of music, songs, and celebrity interviews.

Hostess: Betty Furness

Vocalist: Don Cherry

Music: The Buddy Weed Trio

Producer: Lester Lewis

Penthouse Sonata

Variety; 30 min; ABC 6/19/49 to 6/26/49

A program of music and song with hostess June Browne and the music of the Fine Arts Quartet. Produced by Ed Skotch.

People

Interview Pilot; 30 min; ABC 12/15/57

Interviews with people "The Man" (host) meets while walking on the street.

The Man: Ben Alexander

Producer: Frank LaTourette

People

Variety; 30 min; CBS 9/17/78 to 11/6/78

An adaptation of "People" magazine to TV: celebrity profiles and interviews.

Hostess: Phyllis George

Producer: David Susskind, Clay Cole

People are Funny

Comedy; 30 min; NBC 9/9/54 to 4/2/61

Pre-selected people are asked to perform specific stunts in return for prizes. 150 (of the 246 produced episodes) are syndicated.

Host: Art Linkletter

Announcer: Jack McGeehan

Producer: John Guedel

People are Funny

Comedy; 30 min; NBC 3/24/84 to 6/9/84

A revised version of the prior title which challenges ordinary people to perform outrageous tasks for laughs.

Host: Flip Wilson

Announcer: Dick Tufeld

Music: Milton DeLugg

Producer: Don Ohlmeyer, Perry Rosemond

People do the Craziest Things

Comedy; 60 min; ABC 9/20/84 to 10/4/84

The program looks at the comical side of human nature as it spotlights the reactions of ordinary people in unusual situations. The pilot aired on 4/8/84.

Host: Bert Convy

Producer: Alan Landsburg, Woody Fraser

People Like Us

Drama Pilot; 60 min; NBC 4/19/76

The story of a contemporary American family (the Allmans) and their struggles to retain their close ties amid economic instability and a changing moral climate.

Davy Allman	Eugene Roche
Irene Allman	Katherine Helmond
Sharon Allman	Eileen McDonough
Lennie Allman	Grant Goodeve
Anna Allman	Irene Tedrow

Producer: Lee Rich, Gene Reynolds

People to People

Interview Pilot; 30 min; ABC 1/9/84 to 1/13/84

An unsold five-part pilot for a daily series of celebrity interviews.

Hostess: Rona Barrett

Producer: Alan Landsburg, Woody Fraser, Merrill Grant

People Will Talk

Game; 30 min; NBC 7/1/63 to 12/27/63

A yes-or-no question is read to fifteen studio audience members (who each lock in their answer). Each of the two contestants who compete chooses a player and has to predict how that person answered the question. Each correct prediction scores one point. The highest point scorer receives merchandise prizes.

Host: Dennis James

Producer: Merrill Heatter, Bob Quigley

The People's Choice

Comedy; 30 min; CBS 10/6/55 to 8/25/58

The series, set in New City, California, depicts events in the life of Socrates "Sock" Miller, a Bureau of Fish and Wildlife ornithologist studying to become a lawyer.

Socrates "Sock" Miller	Jackie Cooper
Amanda "Mandy" Peoples	Patricia Breslin
Mayor John Peoples	Paul Maxey
Augusta "Gus" Miller	Margaret Irving
Hexley "Hex" Rollo	Dick Wesson
Pierre	Leonid Kinskey
Voice of Cleo (the basset hound who comments on happenings)	Mary Jane Croft

Producer: Irving Brecher, Jackie Cooper, E. J. Rosenberg, Bob Finkel

The People's Court

Human Interest; 30 min; Syn. 9/81

The program features real people fighting real legal battles before a real judge in a California Municipal Court.

Judge	Joseph A. Wapner
Bailiff	Rusty Burrell
Reporter	Doug Llewellyn
Legal Advisor	Harvey Levin

Producer: Ralph Edwards, Stu Billett

The People's Court of Small Claims

A syndicated (1958) series that reenacts actual small claims court hearings. Orrin B. Evans appears as the judge.

Pepsi-Cola Playhouse

Anthology; 30 min; ABC 10/2/53 to 7/10/55

A series of live and filmed dramas, hosted by Arlene Dahl, Anita Colby, and Polly Bergen, under the sponsorship of Pepsi-Cola soda.

The Perfect Match

Game; 30 min; Syn. 1967

Before air time, a computer matches three men with three women. Through a series of question-and-answer probe rounds, each man must determine which girl the computer has matched him with and vice versa. Players who match each other receive $50; players who paired themselves as did the computer, have a perfect match and each receive $200.

Host: Dick Enberg

The Perfect Match

Game; 30 min; Syn. 1/86

Prior to the broadcast, three husband and wife couples are separated and asked a series of questions. On stage, the husbands must determine their wives responses to specific questions (and vice versa). Each correct match scores a couple money and the highest scorers are the winners.

Host: Bob Goen

Announcer: Johnny Gilbert

Producer: Bob Synes, Scott Stone, Jay Feldman

Perfect Strangers

Comedy; 30 min; ABC 3/26/86 (Premiere)

Seeking to live the American Dream, Balki, a Mediterranean sheep herder from the island of Bevous, journeys to the U.S. In Chicago, Balki finds his distant cousin, Larry, and convinces him to let him share his apartment. Stories relate Balki's misadventures as he struggles to adjust to the American way of life.

Balki Batokomous	Bronson Pinchot
Larry Appleton	Louie Anderson*
	Mark Linn-Baker
Donald "Twinkie" Twinkacetti	Ernie Sabella
Edwina Twinkacetti	Belita Moreno
Marie Twinkacetti	Erica Gayle
Susan Campbell	Lise Cutler
Jennifer	Melanie Wilson
Mary Anne	Rebeca Arthur

Theme Vocal ("Nothing's Gonna Stop Me Now"): David Pomerantz

Producer: Thomas Miller, Robert Boyett, Dale McRaven

*Role in the never telecast pilot film.

The Perils of Penelope Pitstop

Cartoon; 30 min; CBS 9/13/69 to 9/4/71

When Sylvester Sneekly becomes the legal guardian of Penelope Pitstop, a vulnerable young race car driver, he secretly dons the guise of the Hooded Claw and plans to kill her to acquire her wealth. Stories relate Penelope's adventures as she and her protectors, the Ant Hill Mob, struggle to foil the Hooded Claw's sinister efforts.

Penelope Pitstop	Janet Waldo
Hooded Claw	Paul Lynde
Claude/Softy	Paul Winchell
Zippy/Pockets/Dum Dum/Snoozy	Don Messick

Narrator: Gary Owens

Producer: William Hanna, Joseph Barbera

The Perkins Family

Drama; 30 min; PBS Syn. 10/86

Incidents in the daily lives of the Perkins, an American family of five. All roles are played by children and stories are ad-libbed.

Elaine Perkins	Betsy Bleil
Jonathan Perkins	Stapp Beaton
Tracy Perkins	Chandra Wilson
Chris Perkins	Veronica Rosas
Alex Perkins	Wiley Wiggins

Producer: Dighton E. Spooner, John Binkley

Perry Como Presents the Julius LaRosa Show

Variety; 60 min; NBC 6/15/57 to 9/7/57

The 1957 Summer replacement for "The Perry Como Show"; a program of music and songs with singer Julius LaRosa, regulars Steve Ashton, Lou Cosler, the Louis DaPron Dancers, the Artie Malvin Chorus, and the orchestra of Mitchell Ayres.

The Perry Como Show

Variety; 15 min; CBS 10/2/50 to 6/24/55

A program of music and songs.

Host: Perry Como

Regulars: Geri, Margie, and Bea Fontaine, The Ray Charles Singers

Announcer: Frank Gallop, Durward Kirby, Dick Stark

Orchestra: Mitchell Ayres

Producer: Lee Cooley

The Perry Como Show

Variety; 60 min; NBC 9/17/55 to 6/6/59

A relaxed hour of music and songs.

Host: Perry Como

Regulars: Geri, Margie, and Bea Fontaine, Mindy Carson, Don Adams, Joey Heatherton, Kaye Ballard, Milt Kamen, Sandy Stewart, The Ray Charles Singers, The Louis DaPron Dancers

Announcer: Ed Herlihy, Frank Gallop

Orchestra: Mitchell Ayres

Producer: Lee Cooley

Perry Mason

Crime Drama; 60 min; CBS 9/21/57 to 9/4/66

The cases of Perry Mason, a brilliant criminal attorney working out of Los Angeles. Based on the character created by Erle Stanley Gardner. The "Perry Mason" concept, with Raymond Burr as Mason, Barbara Hale as Della Street, and William Katt as Paul Drake Jr., was revived by NBC for three TV movies (to date): "Perry Mason Returns" (12/1/85), "Perry Mason: The Case of the Notorious Nun" (5/25/86), and "Perry Mason: The Case of the Shooting Star" (11/9/86). See also "The New Perry Mason."

Perry Mason	Raymond Burr
Della Street	Barbara Hale
Paul Drake	William Hopper
Lt. Arthur Tragg	Ray Collins
Hamilton Burger	William Talman
Lt. Steve Drumm	Richard Anderson
Gertie Lade	Connie Cezon
Margo	Paula Courtland
David Gideon	Karl Heid
Lt. Andy Anderson	Wesley Lau
Sgt. Brice	Lee Miller

Producer: Gail Patrick Jackson, Arthur Marks

Perry Presents

Variety; 60 min; NBC 6/13/59 to 9/5/59

A program of music and songs that replaced "The Perry Como Show" during the Summer of 1959.

Hosts: Jaye P. Morgan, Teresa Brewer, Tony Bennett

Regulars: Hans Conried, The Four Lads, The Modernaires, The Louis DaPron Dancers, The Mel Pahl Chorus

Announcer: Ed Herlihy

Orchestra: Mitchell Ayres, Jimmy Lytell

Producer: Perry Como

Person to Person

Interview; 30 min; CBS 10/2/53 to 7/2/59
                                6/23/61 to 9/16/61

The host, seated in a studio, interviews prominent people from their homes via remote pickup.

Host (1953–59): Edward R. Murrow

Host (1961): Charles Collingwood

Announcer: Bob Dixon

Producer: John Aaron, Jesse Zousmer, Charles Hill, Edward R. Murrow

Personal and Confidential

Magazine Pilot; 60 min; NBC 7/1/83 to 7/5/83

An unsold five-part pilot for a daily series of celebrity interviews, gossip, beauty tips, and health advice.

Hosts: Christine Belford, Steve Edwards, Cathy Cronkite, Ruth Batchelor

Producer: Woody Fraser, Alan Landsburg, Kay Hoffman

Personality

Game; 30 min; NBC 7/3/67 to 9/26/69

Object: For three guest celebrities to determine how well they know each other, as well as themselves. Three rounds are played that tests each celebrity's knowledge of himself and his colleagues. Each correct answer scores $25 for the home viewer each celebrity represents.

Host: Larry Blyden

Announcer: Jack Clark

Producer: Bob Stewart

Personality Puzzle

Game; 30 min; ABC 3/19/53 to 6/25/53

Object: For players to guess the identities of celebrity guests via an examination of the tools of the guest's trade and a series of question-and-answer rounds. The player (four compete) with the most correct answers wins merchandise prizes.

Host: John Conte, Robert Alda

Regular: Lisa Ferraday

Producer: Alan Pottasch

The Persuaders!

Adventure; 60 min; ABC 9/18/71 to 6/14/72

Unable to pursue his cause of investigating criminal cases that he feels were unjustly

tried alone, a retired judge (Fulton) tricks two playboys (British Lord Brett Sinclair and self-made American millionaire Danny Wilde) into helping him. Stories relate the exploits of two reluctant troubleshooters as they seek the facts behind cases the judge feels warrant further investigation.

Brett Sinclair	Roger Moore
Danny Wilde	Tony Curtis
Judge Fulton	Laurence Naismith
Chivers (Brett's butler)	George Merritt

Producer: Robert S. Baker

The Pet Set

A syndicated (1971) series of pet care and advice with hostess Betty White and regulars Ralph Helfer and Dare Miller.

Pete and Gladys

Comedy; 30 min; CBS 9/19/60 to 9/10/62

Events in the hectic lives of the Porters: Pete, a salesman for the Springer, Slocum, and Klever Insurance Company in Los Angeles, and his beautiful but scatterbrained wife, Gladys. A spin-off from "December Bride."

Gladys Porter	Cara Williams
Peter Porter	Harry Morgan
Hilda Crocker	Verna Felton
Paul Porter	Gale Gordon
Bruce	Bill Hinnant
Henry Hooper	Ernest Truex
Cyrus J. Slocum	Barry Kelly
Mrs. Slocum	Helen Kleeb
Mr. Higgins	Willard Waterman
Peggy Briggs	Mina Kolb
Ernie Briggs	Joe Mantell
Howie	Alvy Moore
Alice	Barbara Stuart
George Colton	Peter Leeds
Janet Colton	Shirley Mitchell
Newton Norwood	Cliff Norton

Producer: Parke Levy, Devery Freeman

Pete Kelly's Blues

Drama; 30 min; NBC 4/5/59 to 9/4/59

Events in the lawless era of prohibition and gangsterism as seen through the eyes of Pete

Kelly, a cornet player and leader of "The Big Seven," a jazz band that plays steadily at 17 Cherry Street (in Kansas City), a brownstone-turned-funeral parlor-turned speakeasy. Based on the feature film.

Pete Kelly	William Reynolds
Savanah Brown	Connee Boswell
George Lupo	Phil Gordon
Off. Johnny Cassino	Anthony Eisley

Band Members: Johnny Silver, Thann Wyenn, Fred Beems, Ricky Allen, Dick Cathcart

Theme Vocal ("Pete Kelly's Blues"): Connee Boswell

Music for the Club Scenes: The Matty Matlock Combo

Offscreen Cornet Player for Pete: Dick Cathcart

Producer: Jack Webb

Pete 'N' Tillie

Comedy Pilot; 30 min; CBS 3/28/74

The comic adventures of Pete and Tillie, a newlywed couple who, after many years of living alone, must now adjust to marriage.

Tillie Schaefer	Cloris Leachman
Pete Schaefer	Carmine Caridi
Norma Jean	
Ryerson	Mabel Albertson
Alan Kipeck	Dick Balduzzi

Producer: Carl Kleinschmitt

The Peter and Mary Show

Comedy; 30 min; NBC 11/23/50 to 3/29/51

A live comedy about the experiences of Peter and Mary, a husband and wife show business couple who entertain celebrities in their New Rochelle (N.Y.) home.

Peter	Peter Lind Hayes
Mary	Mary Healy
Claude (their friend)	Claude Stroud
Miss Wickes	
(housekeeper)	Mary Wickes

Orchestra: Bert Farber

Producer: Allen Ducovny

Peter Gunn

Crime Drama; 30 min; NBC 9/2/58 to 9/27/60
ABC 10/3/60 to 9/21/61

The exploits of Peter Gunn, a Los Angeles-based private detective.

Peter Gunn	Craig Stevens
Edie Hart	Lola Albright
Lt. Jacoby	Herschel Bernardi
Mother	Hope Emerson
	Minerva Urecal
Sgt. Lee Davis	Morris Erby
Lt. Vasquez	Peter Mamakos
Babby (pool hustler)	Billy Barty
Leslie (Maitre d' at	
Edie's club)	James Lanphier
Wilbur (coffee house	
owner)	Herb Ellis

"Peter Gunn" Theme Music: Henry Mancini

Producer: Gordon Oliver, Blake Edwards

Peter Hunter, Private Eye

Crime Drama Pilot; 30 min; Syn. 1948

The earliest known syndicated pilot. The exploits of Peter Hunter, a tough private detective working out of New York City.

Peter Hunter	Frank Albertson

Producer: Stuart Ludlam

The Peter Lind Hayes Show

Variety; 60 min; ABC 10/13/58 to 4/10/59

A weekly program of music and songs with singers Peter Lind Hayes and his wife Mary Healy, and regulars Don Cherry, John Bubbles, the Four Voices, and the Malagon Sisters. Orchestrations by Bert Farber and produced by Frank Musiello.

Peter Loves Mary

Comedy; 30 min; NBC 10/12/60 to 5/31/61

Events in the lives of Peter and Mary Lindsey, a show business couple who are struggling to divide their time between a career on Broadway and a home life in Oakdale, Connecticut, with their two children (Leslie and Steve).

Peter Lindsey	Peter Lind Hayes
Mary Lindsey	Mary Healy
Leslie Lindsey	Merry Martin
Steve Lindsey	Gil Smith
Wilma (housekeeper)	Bea Benaderet
Happy Richman (agent)	Alan Reed
Charlie (Wilma's beau)	Arch Johnson

Producer: Al Simon, William Friedberg

The Peter Marshall Variety Show

A syndicated (1976) ninety-minute variety program with host Peter Marshall, regulars Rod Gist, Danny Evans, and the Chapter Five, and the orchestra of Alan Copeland. Produced by David Salzman and Rocco Urbisci.

The Peter Potamus Show

Cartoon; 30 min; Syn. 1964

Segments: "Peter Potamus" (global adventures of a purple hippo and So So the monkey); "Yippie, Yappie, and Yahooey" (three mischievous dogs attempting to guard their king); and "Breezly and Sneezly" (Breezly the polar bear and Sneezly the seal's efforts to find warmth at Camp Frostbite in the North Pole).

Peter Potamus	Daws Butler
So So	Don Messick
Yippie/The King	Hal Smith
Yappie/Yahooey	Daws Butler
Breezly	Howard Morris
Sneezly	Mel Blanc
Army Colonel	John Stephenson

Producer: William Hanna, Joseph Barbera

Peter Potter's Juke Box Jury

Discussion; 30 min; ABC 9/13/53 to 3/28/54

Hollywood personalities judge and discuss the merits of new or prereleased recordings. Hosted and produced by Peter Potter.

Petrocelli

Crime Drama; 60 min; NBC 9/11/74 to 3/2/76

The story of Tony Petrocelli, a Harvard-educated attorney working out of San Remo, a southwestern cattle town.

Tony Petrocelli	Barry Newman
Maggie Petrocelli	Susan Howard
Pete Toley	Albert Salmi
Frank Kaiser	Michael Bell
Lt. John Clifford	David Huddleston

Producer: Thomas L. Miller, Edward K. Milkis

Petticoat Girl

Satirical Adventure Pilot; 30 min; Unaired; Produced in 1981

The story, which places live actors in comic book-like sets, relates the adventures of a beautiful girl named Jane; a girl who is constantly in peril, constantly losing her dress— and constantly overcoming insurmountable odds clad only in sexy lingerie. A rather risque program for American television that is based on the British series "Jane" (which stars Glynis Barber).

Jane	Carol Lee
Her Evil Pursuer	Cal Penny

Producer: Sid Walsh

Theme Vocal ("In Peril Again"): Carol Lee

Petticoat Junction

Comedy; 30 min; CBS 9/24/63 to 9/12/70

The original format relates incidents in the lives of Kate Bradley, a widow and owner of the Shady Rest Hotel in Hooterville, and her three beautiful daughters, Billie Jo, Bobbie Jo, and Betty Jo. A later format, after the death of Bea Benaderet (Kate), switched to focus on the antics of Joe Carson, the new manager of the Shady Rest.

Kate Bradley	Bea Benaderet	Ada Jacks	Evelyn Scott
Joe Carson	Edgar Buchanan	Stephen Cord	James Douglas
Billie Jo Bradley	Jeannine Riley	Martin Peyton	George Macready
	Gunilla Hutton	Hannah Cord	Ruth Warwick
	Meredith MacRae	Matthew Swain	Warner Anderson
Bobbie Jo Bradley	Pat Woodell	Laura Brooks	Patricia Breslin
	Lori Saunders	Dr. Harry Miles	Percy Rodrigues
Betty Jo Bradley	Linda Kaye Henning	Marsha Russell	Barbara Rush
Charley Pratt	Smiley Burnett	Alma Miles	Ruby Dee
Floyd Smoot	Rufe Davis	Lew Miles	Glynn Turman
Sam Drucker	Frank Cady	Stella Chernak	Lee Grant
Steve Elliott	Mike Minor	Adrienne Van	
Homer Bedloe	Charles Lane	Leyden	Gena Rowlands
Norman Curtis	Roy Roberts	Rachel	Leigh Taylor-Young
Dr. Janet Craig	June Lockhart	Gus Chernak	Bruce Gordon
Dr. Barton Stuart	Regis Toomey	Joe Chernak	Don Quinn
Wendell Gibbs	Byron Foulger	Vincent Markham	Leslie Nielsen
Henrietta Plout	Lynette Winter	Russ Gehring	David Canary
Kathy Jo Elliott	Elaine & Danielle	Anna Howard	Susan Oliver
	Hubbel	Susan Winter	Diana Hyland
Herby Bates	Don Washbrook	Claire Morton	Mariette Hartley
Fred Ziffel	Hank Patterson	David Schuster	William Smithers
Ben Miller	Tom Fadden	Doris Schuster	Gail Kobe
Newt Kiley	Kay E. Kuter		
Cousin Mae	Shirley Mitchell		
Cousin Helen	Rosemary DeCamp		
Selma Plout	Virginia Sale		
	Elvia Allman		
Orville Miggs	Jimmy Hawkins		
Grandpa Miller	Walter Baldwin		

"Peyton Place" Theme: Franz Waxman

Producer: Paul Monash, Everett Chambers

Producer: Charles Stewart, Al Simon, Paul Henning, Dick Wesson

The Phil Donahue Show

Discussion; 60 min; Syn. 11/67

A long-running program of penetrating discussions on the contemporary issues that affect people in their daily lives.

Host: Phil Donahue

Producer: Don Mischer, Patricia McMillen, Sheri Singer, Darlene Hayes

Peyton Place

Serial; 30 min; ABC 9/15/64 to 6/2/69

Dramatic incidents in the lives of the people of Peyton Place, a small New England town. Based on the novel by Grace Metalious.

Constance MacKenzie	Dorothy Malone
	Lola Albright
Elliott Carson	Tim O'Connor
Dr. Michael Rossi	Ed Nelson
Alison MacKenzie	Mia Farrow
Rodney Harrington	Ryan O'Neal
Eli Carson	Frank Ferguson
Norman Harrington	Christopher Connelly
Betty Harrington	Barbara Parkins
Rita Jacks Harrington	Patricia Morrow
Leslie Harrington	Paul Langton

The Phil Silvers Show

Comedy; 30 min; CBS 9/20/55 to 9/18/59

The life of Master Sergeant Ernest Bilko, a master con artist in charge of the motor pool (at the Camp Freemont Army Base in Roseville, Kansas). Totally dedicated to acquiring money, he ingeniously schemes to bamboozle the system and manipulate the U.S. Army for his personal benefit. (Later episodes are set in Grove City, California.) Originally titled "You'll Never Get Rich."

Sgt. Ernest Bilko	Phil Silvers
Col. John T. Hall	Paul Ford
Sgt. Joan Hogan	Elisabeth Frazer
Pvt. Duane Doberman	Maurice Gosfield
Cpl. Henshaw	Allan Melvin
Pvt. Dino Paparelli	Billy Sands
Pvt. Sam Fender	Herbie Faye
Pvt. Fielding Zimmerman	Mickey Freeman
Cpl. Rocco Barbella	Harvey Lembeck
Sgt. Rubert Ritzik	Joe E. Ross
Sgt. Francis Grover	Jimmy Little
Pvt. Mullin	Jack Healy
Pvt. Lester Mendelsohn	Gerald Hiken
Pvt. Greg Chickeriny	Bruce Kirby
Sgt. Stanley Sowicki	Harry Clark
Pvt. Dillingham	Walter Cartier
Pvt. P. J. Palmer	P. J. Sidney
Sgt. Andy Pendleton	Ned Glass
Pvt. Gomez	Bernie Fein
Pvt. Fleishman	Maurice Brenner
Pvt. Gander	Tige Andrews
Nell Hall	Hope Sansberry
Emma Ritzik	Beatrice Pons
Capt. Barker	Nicholas Saunders
Maj. Spangler	Heywin Broome Jr.
"Stacked" Suzy	Julie Newmar
WAC Helen	Kay Lighter
Edna	Skippy Colby
Various M. P. Roles	George Kennedy

Producer: Edward J. Montagne, Aaron Ruben

The Philco Television Playhouse

Anthology; 60 min; NBC 10/3/48 to 2/12/56

A series of quality dramas that first aired under its own title (and under sponsorship of the Equity-Philco Company), from October 3, 1948 to October 7, 1951. On October 21, 1951, it began alternating with "The Goodyear Theatre" (until August 21, 1955). On September 4, 1955, both "Philco" and "Goodyear" theatres began alternating with "The Alcoa Hour" (which premiered on October 16, 1955). By February 12, 1956, "The Philco Television Playhouse" had its last showing, being displaced by both "Alcoa" and "Goodyear."

Host (1948–49): Bert Lytell

Producer: Fred Coe, Gordon Duff, Garry Simpson

Philip and Barbara

Comedy Pilot; 30 min; NBC 8/31/76

The comic adventures of Philip and Barbara Logan, a married couple who are employed as TV script writers.

Barbara Logan	Patty Duke Astin
Philip Logan	John Astin
Edna	Rosemary DeCamp
George	Leonard Frey
Shirley	Ann Prentiss
Secretary	Patti Jerome
Roger	Alex Henteloff

Producer: Leonard B. Stern

Philip Marlowe

Crime Drama; 30 min; ABC 10/6/59 to 3/29/60

The exploits of Philip Marlowe, a rugged private detective who wanders from state to state to track down criminals and solve crimes. Based on characters created by Raymond Chandler.

Philip Marlowe	Philip Carey

Producer: Glen Wang

Philip Marlowe, Private Eye

Mystery; 60 min; HBO 4/16/83 to 5/14/83
4/27/86 to 6/8/86

The exploits of Philip Marlowe, a tough private detective working out of Los Angeles during the 1930s.

Philip Marlowe	Powers Boothe
Annie Riordan*	Kathryn Leigh Scott
Lt. Violets Magee*	William Kearns

Producer: David Wickes (1983 version)

Producer: Gabriel Katzka, Jon Slan (1986)

*In 1983 version only.

Philip Morris Playhouse

Anthology; 30 min; CBS 10/8/53 to 3/4/54

A series of live dramas sponsored by Philip Morris Cigarettes.

Host: Charles Martin, Kent Smith

Announcer: Joe King

Producer: Charles Martin

The Phoenix

Fantasy; 60 min; ABC 3/26/82 to 4/16/82

During an archaeological expedition in Peru, a sarcophagus that bears the seal of the Phoenix (ancient symbol of rebirth) is discovered. In Los Angeles, the sarcophagus is opened and an ancient astronaut named Bennu is awakened before his time. Possessing extraordinary powers, which he derives from the sun, and unsure of his assignment, Bennu escapes from his captors and begins a search to find Mira, his partner from the planet El DeBrande. Mira, it is learned, knows Bennu's mission, which is to effect the Earth's future. Stories relate Bennu's search for Mira, and his attempts to escape from Preminger, a man who believes Bennu is an extraterrestrial and seeks to capture him.

Bennu of the Golden Light	Judson Scott
Preminger	Richard Lynch
Mira	Sheila Frazier
Dr. Ward Frazier	E. G. Marshall

Producer: Mark Carliner

Photocrime

Crime Drama; 30 min; ABC 9/21/49 to 12/14/49

The exploits of Hannibal Cobb, an inspector with the New York City Police Department.

Insp. Hannibal Cobb	Chuck Webster

Photon

Science Fiction; 30 min; Syn. 9/86

Before the beginning of time, there existed Photon, the source of all power in the universe. For unknown reasons, Photon exploded and divided itself into two separate universes—one good, the other evil, with both seeking to control the power of the Photon.

In an attempt to help good defeat evil (in particular the Warlord of Arr), a group of aliens (Tivia, Lord Beathan, Uncle Pike, Leon, and Percival) ban together to fight the warlord. Seeking additional help, the aliens recruit Christopher Jarvis (alias Bhodi Li), an exceptional Earthling who agrees to help them.

Stories relate the Photon warriors efforts to defeat the warlord and protect the cosmos from his evil attempts to rule it.

Bhodi Li	Christopher Lockwood
Tivia	Loretta Haywood
Lord Beathan	Graham Ravey
Percival	Eros Rivers
Leon	Alciyoshi Ono
Uncle Pike	Kazuhisa Kahamaru
Destructaar	Yoshito Nagatsuka
Mandaar	David Anthony

Producer: Jean Chalopin, Andy Heyward, Tetsuo Katayama

Phyl and Mikhy

Comedy; 30 min; CBS 5/26/80 to 6/30/80

When Phyllis "Phyl" Wilson, a pretty track star for Pacific Western University, and Mikhail "Mikhy" Orlov, a Russian track star who has defected meet, they fall in love, marry, and set up housekeeping in the home of Max Wilson, Phyl's father. Stories relate Phyl and Mikhy's efforts to make their marriage work; and Mikhy's attempts to adjust to the American way of life.

Phyllis Orlov	Murphy Cross
Mikhy Orlov	Rick Lohman
Max Wilson	Larry Haines
Vladimir Gimenko	Michael Pataki
Edgar "Truck" Morley	Jack Dodson
Gwyn Bates	Rae Allen
Connie	Deborah Pratt
TV Announcer	Sammy Jones

Producer: Rod Parker, Hal Cooper

Phyllis

Comedy; 30 min; CBS 9/8/75 to 8/30/77

A spin-off from "The Mary Tyler Moore Show." The first format relates the misadventures of Phyllis Lindstrom as assistant to Julie

Erskine, the owner of Erskine's Commercial Photography Studio in San Francisco. The second format found Phyllis as the administrative assistant to Dan Valenti, an executive for the San Francisco Board of Supervision.

Phyllis Lindstrom	Cloris Leachman
Bess Lindstrom	Lisa Gerritsen
Julie Erskine	Barbara Colby
	Liz Torres
Leo Heatherton	Richard Schaal
Audrey Dexter	Jane Rose
Jonathan Dexter	Henry Jones
Sally Dexter	Judith Lowry
Dan Valenti	Carmine Caridi
Leonard Marsh	John Lawlor
Harriet Hastings	Garn Stephens
Mark Valenti	Craig Wasson
Van Horn	Jack Elam

Producer: Ed Weinberger, Stan Daniels

The Phyllis Diller Show

See "The Beautiful Phyllis Diller Show" and "The Pruitts of Southampton."

Piccadilly Palace

Variety; 60 min; ABC 5/20/67 to 9/2/67

A program of music, songs, and comedy from London's Piccadilly Palace.

Hostess: Millicent Martin

Regulars: Eric Morecombe, Ernie Wise, The Michael Sammes Singers, The Paddy Stone Dancers

Orchestra: Jack Parnell

Producer: Colin Crews, Philip Casson

Pick and Pat

Variety; 60 min; ABC 1/20/49 to 3/17/49

A weekly series that features performances by minstrel acts (a TV first, but also short lived).

Hosts: Pick and Pat

Regulars: Jack Carter, Mary Small

Producer: Ed Wolf

Picture This

Game; 30 min; CBS 6/25/63 to 9/17/63

One member of each two member team is given a secret phrase. This player directs his partner by telling him what clues to draw to identify it. The "artist" who is first to identify the phrase wins the round.

Host: Jerry Van Dyke

Producer: Ben Joelson, Art Baer

Pine Lake Lodge

Comedy Pilot; 30 min; Syn. 6/61

The pilot film for an unsold series called "The Bill Bendix Show." The story of Bill Parker, the owner-operator of Pine Lake Lodge, a mountain vacation resort. Aired as a segment of "Mr. Ed."

Bill Parker	William Bendix
Martha (assistant)	Nancy Kulp
Ann (Bill's niece)	Coleen Gray
Cindy (Ann's daughter)	Marlene DeLamater
Milo Simmons (handyman)	John Quaylen

Producer: Al Simon, Arthur Lubin

Pink Lady

Variety; 60 min; NBC 3/1/80 to 4/4/80

Music, comedy, and songs from Pink Lady, Japan's top-rated singers, and Jeff Altman, an American comic. Originally titled "Pink Lady—and Jeff."

Host: Jeff Altman

Hostesses: Pink Lady (Mie and Kei)

Regulars: Sid Caesar, Jim Varney, Sherry Eiken, Anna Mathias, The Peacock Dancers

Orchestra: Matthew McCauley

Producer: Alvin J. Tenzer, Sid and Marty Krofft

The Pink Panther

Cartoon; Various (30, 60 & 90 min); NBC 9/6/69 to 9/1/79

The adventures of the non-talking Pink Panther, a nonconformist animal that evolved from "The Pink Panther Theme" by Henry Mancini. The program, also titled "The Pink Panther Laugh & Half Hour and a Half Show," also features the antics of "Inspector Clouseau," "The Ant and the Aardvark," "Texas Toads," and "Mister Jaw."

Host: Lennie Schultz

Voices: John Byner, Paul Frees, Dave Barry, Rich Little, Marvin Miller, Athena Ford, June Foray, Mel Blanc, Arte Johnson, Joan Gerber, Pat Harrington, Paul Winchell, Larry Storch

Producer: David DePatie, Friz Freleng

Pink Panther and Sons

Cartoon; 30 min; NBC 9/15/84 to 9/6/86

The misadventures of Pinky and Panky, the mischievous offspring of the Pink Panther (from the Henry Mancini song, "The Pink Panther Theme").

Voices: Hamilton Camp, Marshall Efron, Sherry Linn, Don Messick, Frank Welker, William Windom, Sherry Linn, Jeannie Elias, Neil Ross

Producer: William Hanna, Joseph Barbera

Pinky and Company

Experimental; 30 min; NBC 7/28/39

A half-hour comedy venture in which vaudeville comic Pinky Lee and two unidentified assistants perform various comedy sketches. Produced and directed by Edward Sobol.

The Pinky Lee Show

Comedy; 30 min; NBC 4/19/50 to 11/9/50

The burlesque-style humor of comedian Pinky Lee as seen through the antics of a fumbling stagehand who is called upon to fill in for indisposed performers.

Pinky	Pinky Lee
Stage Manager	William Bakewell

The Pinky Lee Show

Variety; 30 min; NBC 1/4/50 to 5/11/56 (daily) 3/5/55 to 6/9/56 (Saturday)

A program of music, songs, circus variety acts, and burlesque-like comedy routines.

Host: Pinky Lee

Lily Chrysanthemum: Betty Jane Howarth

Regulars: Roberta Shore, Mel Knootz, Jimmy Brown

Announcer: Ken Mayer

Music: The Charlie Couch Trio

Producer: Lee Warren, Larry White

Pioneer Spirit

Comedy Pilot; 30 min; NBC 7/21/69

Dissatisfied with city life, Jeff Wilson, a route map maker for the L.A. Auto Club, convinces his wife, Cherry (and friends Harvey and Carl) to move to Nome, Alaska, where they can get 1600 acres of land free if they homestead it. The unsold series was to relate their adventures as homesteaders.

Jeff Wilson	Rich Little
Cherry Wilson	Marcia Rodd
Harvey	Roy Clark
Ada (Harvey's wife)	Donna Jean Young
Carl	Craig Huebing
Jenny (Carl's wife)	Francine York

Theme Vocal ("Pioneer Spirit"): Roy Clark

Producer: Jay Sommers

The Pioneers

The syndicated (1964) title for selected repeat episodes of "Death Valley Days." Hosted by Will Rogers Jr.

Pip the Piper

Children; 30 min; ABC 1/1/61 to 5/28/61 NBC 6/24/61 to 9/22/62

The fantasy-like adventures of Pip the Piper and his friends Miss Merrynote and Mr. Leader.

Pip the Piper — Jack Spear
Miss Merrynote — Phyllis Spear
Mr. Leader — Lucien Kaminsky

Producer: Jack Miller

Piper's Pets

Comedy Pilot; 30 min; NBC 5/31/79

The misadventures of Donald Piper, a nervous veterinarian, and his not-too-bright assistant, Lester.

Dr. Donald Piper — Don Knotts
Lester — Peter Isacksen
Maggie — Maggie Roswell
Thelma — Jacque Lynn Colton

Producer: Aaron Ruben

Pippi Longstocking

Comedy-Adventure Pilot; 30 min; ABC
11/2/85 (Part 1)
11/9/85 (Part 2)

The outrageous fantasy-like adventures of Pippi Longstocking, a fiesty red-haired little girl who lives without adults (in Villa Villekula) spins tall tales, and enjoys exciting adventures.

Pippalotta "Pippi"
  Longstocking — Carrie Heim
Annika — Alyson Court
Tommy — Eric Hebert
Capt. Efrem
  Longstocking — David Walden
Mrs. Prysselius — Rita Tushingham
Mrs. Settegren — Linda Goranson
Mrs. Granberg — Pam Hyatt
Miss Grum — Judy Sinclair

Producer: Joanne Curley

Based on the books by Astrid Lindgren

Pippi Longstocking

Fantasy; 60 min; ABC 1/8/61

The first TV adaptation of the above title. The story of a young girl (Susan) whose dreams of a magical girl are seen as Pippilotta Delicatessa Windowshade Mackrelmint Efriam Longstocking, a brilliant girl whose father is a cannibal king and who lives in a strange house with a horse and a monkey. Adapted by Walter Crewson from the Astrid Lindgren story. Aired on "The Shirley Temple Theatre."

Pippi/Susan — Gina Gillespie
Mrs. Scholfield — Barbara Eiler
Papa Efriam — Willard Waterman
Miss Lindquist — Renie Raino

Music: Walter Scharf

The Pirates of Flounder Bay

Comedy Pilot; 30 min; ABC 8/26/66

The story, set in the 1800s, relates the efforts of Barnaby Kidd, the kindhearted, trouble-prone grandson of the infamous pirate, Captain Kidd, to achieve fame.

Capt. Barnaby Kidd — William Cort
Governor — Basil Rathbone
Capt. Jack Slash — Keenan Wynn
Mayor Abner
  Bunker — Harold Peary
Molly Bunker — Bridget Hanley
Sidney — Jack Soo
Taggert — Charles Dierkop
Flint — Burt Mustin
Wimple — Jim Connell
Chips — Peter Bonerz
Lookout — Jim Begg

Pistols 'n' Petticoats

Comedy; 30 min; CBS 9/17/66 to 8/26/67

The series, set in Wretched, Colorado, in 1871, relates the saga of the gun-toting Hanks family and their efforts to maintain law and order in a restless territory.

Henrietta "Hank" Hanks	Ann Sheridan
Lucy Hanks	Carole Wells
Andrew Hanks	Douglas V. Fowley
Grandma Hanks	Ruth McDevitt
Harold Sikes	Gary Vinson
Bernard Courtney	Robert Lowery
Mark Hangman	Morgan Woodward
Jed Timmins	Stanley Adams
Eagle Shadow	Lon Chaney Jr.
Great Bear	Jay Silverheels
Mrs. Tinsley	Eleanor Audley
Cyrus Breech	Leo Gordon
Town Drunk	Gil Lamb
W. C. Fields type who hangs out in the saloon	Bill Oberlin

Producer: Joe Connelly, Irving Paley

Pistols 'n' Petticoats

Comedy Pilot; 30 min; Unaired (Produced for CBS in 1966)

The original, unaired pilot for the above series. The story (untitled) but remade as the series episode "Quit Shootin' Folks, Grandma," relates the Hanks efforts to put down an Indian uprising.

Henrietta Hanks	Ann Sheridan
Lucy Hanks	Chris Noel
Andrew Hanks	Douglas Fowley
Grandma Hanks	Ruth McDevitt
Sheriff Eric	Joel D. McCrae
Eagle Shadow	Lon Chaney Jr.

Producer: Joe Connelly

Pitching Horseshoes

See "Billy Rose's Playbill."

Pitfall

Game; 30 min; Syn. 9/81

The host reads a question to which four answers appear on a board. Each of the four players who compete selects one answer. Players who choose the correct response receive one point. The highest scorer plays the bonus round wherein he must cross a bridge of eight squares by answering eight questions within 100 seconds. A wrong answer stops a player on a square until he gives a correct response. $100 is awarded per correct response.

Host: Alex Trebek

Announcer: John Barton

Producer: Bill Armstrong

Pixanne

Children; 30 min; Syn. 1978

The series, set in a magic forest, follows the adventures of a pretty fairy (Pixanne) as she relates songs, stories, and educational information to children.

Pixanne	Jane Norman

Regulars: The Addis Williams Puppets

Producer: Jane Norman, Alan J. Shalleck

Place the Face

Game; 30 min; CBS 7/2/53 to 8/26/54
NBC 9/25/54 to 9/13/55

Specially selected contestants are placed opposite someone from their past. Through a series of indirect clues that are provided by the host, the player's have to associate each other's faces.

Host: Jack Smith, Jack Paar, Bill Cullen

Producer: Joe Landis, Edwin Barclay

Places Please

Variety; 15 min; CBS 7/5/48 to 2/25/49

Barry Wood as the host (and producer) of a series that spotlights new talent discoveries and performers from Broadway and nightclubs.

The Plainclothesman

Crime Drama; 30 min; DuMont 10/12/49 to 9/12/54

The subjective camera is used to detail the investigations of a never-seen lieutenant with the N.Y.P.D. By use of the subjective camera, which enacts emotion and becomes the eyes of the lieutenant, the viewer hears the actor's voice and experiences situations as if he were actually present.

The Lieutenant Ken Lynch
Sgt. Brady Jack Orrinson

Producer: John L. Clark

The Plant Family

Comedy Pilot; 30 min; CBS 9/2/78

Events in the lives of the Plant family, residents of a run-down house in a borderline neighborhood in southern California.

Lyla Plant	Joyce Van Patten
Augie Plant	Norman Alden
Ava	Kay Heberle
Art	Larry Hankin
Geneva	Jo Marie Payton
Leo Harrell	Jesse White
Homer Jay	DeWayne Hessie

Producer: Bud Austin, Robert D. Wood

Planet of the Apes

Adventure; 60 min; CBS 9/13/74 to 12/27/74

An air force space capsule, launched in 1988, penetrates a radioactive turbulence area and passes through a time barrier that propels it to the year 3085 and into a world ruled by intellectual apes. When the astronauts (Alan and Pete) are captured and imprisoned, Galen, an intellectual ape, befriends them and helps them to escape. Stories relate Alan and Pete's efforts, assisted by Galen, to return to the Earth of the 1980s. Adapted from the feature film series.

Galen	Roddy McDowall
Alan Virdon	Ron Harper
Pete Burke	James Naughton
Ape Leader Zaius	Booth Colman
Urko	Mark Lenard

Music: Lalo Schifrin

Producer: Herbert Hirschman

Planet Patrol

Marionette Adventure; 30 min; Syn. 1963

The exploits of Larry Dart, an agent for the Galasphere Patrol, the interplanetary police force of the future, as he attempts to maintain peace in space. Produced by Hal Seeger.

The Plasticman Comedy/Adventure Show

Cartoon; Various (2 hrs; 90 & 30 min); ABC 9/22/79 to 9/5/81

Segments: "Plasticman" (the exploits of Plasticman, an agent for the National Bureau of Investigation); "Mightyman and Yukk" (adventures of the world's smallest superhero and the world's ugliest dog); "Rickety Rocket" (exploits of a space-age group of detectives: Cosgrove, Venus, Splashdown, and Sunstroke); "Fangface" (antics of Sherman Fangsworth, a teenager who changes into a werewolf under the moon and reverts to normal at sunup). Syndicated in a thirty minute format as "Plasticman."

Plasticman	Michael Bell
Penny	Melendy Britt
Hoola Hoola	Joe Baker
Mightyman	Peter Cullen
Yukk	Frank Welker
Rickety Rocket	Al Fann
Cosgrove	Bobby Ellerbee
Venus	Dee Timberlake
Splashdown	Johnny Brown
Sunstroke	John Anthony Bailey
Sherman	Jerry Dexter
Kim	Susan Blu
Puggsy	Bart Braverman
Biff	Frank Welker

Producer: Ken Ruby, Joe Spears

Play the Game

Experimental; 30 min; NBC 1941
     DuMont 9/24/46 to 12/17/46

An early attempt to bring the popular game of charades to TV via "Play the Game." The program was originally an experimental NBC project and later picked up by DuMont for 13 episodes.

Host: Dr. Henry Zorbaugh

Producer: Edward Sobol

Play the Percentages

Game; 30 min; Syn. 9/80

A question, based on a survey of 300 people is read. One member, of each two member team, has to predict the number of people surveyed who were able to answer it. The answer is revealed and the correct player wins the percentage value in points. The first team to score three hundred points receives that amount in cash.

Host: Geoff Edwards

Announcer: Jay Stewart

Producer: Ron Greenberg, Dan Enright, Jack Barry

Play Your Hunch

Game; 30 min; CBS 6/30/58 to 9/5/58
                   NBC 1/5/59 to 5/8/59
                   NBC 12/7/59 to 9/26/63

Three sets that pertain to one subject are displayed. Each of the three couples that compete have to determine the factor that distinguishes one from the others. The first couple to score three identifications is the winner.

Host: Richard Hayes, Gene Rayburn, Merv Griffin, Robert Q. Lewis

Assistant: Liz Gardner

Producer: Ira Skutch, Bob Rowe

Playboy after Dark

Variety; 60 min; Syn. 1969

A program of music and conversation with "Playboy" magazine publisher Hugh Hefner.

Host: Hugh Hefner

Bunny Hostess: Barbi Benton

Regulars: The Playboy Bunnies, The Checkmates

Music: Tommy Oliver

Producer: Rupert Hitzig

Playboy's Penthouse

Variety; 60 & 90 min. Versions; Syn. 1959

The series, set in the Chicago penthouse of "Playboy" magazine publisher Hugh Hefner, features guests, conversation, and entertainment. Available to stations in either a 60 or 90 minute format.

Host: Hugh Hefner

Regulars: The Playboy Bunnies

Music: The Marty Rubertson Trio

Playhouse '54

The alternate title for "Pepsi Cola Playhouse."

Playhouse 90

Anthology; 90 min; CBS 10/4/56 to 5/18/60

A series of quality dramatic stories featuring top name stars. Produced by Martin Manulis, John Houseman, Russell Stoneman, Fred Coe, Arthur Penn, Hubbell Robinson.

Playhouse of Mystery

A CBS series (9/3/57 to 9/24/57) of repeat episodes of "The Schlitz Playhouse of Stars."

Playhouse of Stars

Irene Dunne as the host of a short-lived CBS seies of dramatic presentations (5/30/52 to 9/10/52).

Playwrights '56

Anthology; 30 min; NBC 10/4/55 to 6/19/56

A series of quality dramas that was broadcast on an alternating basis with "The Armstrong Circle Theatre," "The U.S. Steel Hour," and "The 20th Century-Fox Hour." Produced by Fred Coe.

Please Don't Eat the Daisies

Comedy; 30 min; NBC 9/14/65 to 9/2/67

Events in the lives of the Nash family: Jim, an English professor at Ridgemont College; his wife, Joan, a free-lance writer who uses the pen name Joan Holliday; and their children, Kyle, Joel, Trevor and Tracy. Based on the book by Jean Kerr.

Joan Nash	Patricia Crowley
Jim Nash	Mark Miller
Kyle Nash	Kim Tyler
Joel Nash	Brian Nash
Trevor Nash	Jeff Fithian
Tracy Nash	Joe Fithian
Marge Thornton	Shirley Mitchell
Herb Thornton	King Donovan
Ed Hewey	Dub Taylor
Gerald Carter	Bill Quinn
Ethel Carter	Jean VanderPyl
Martha O'Reilly	Ellen Corby
Joan's Father	J. Pat O'Malley

Producer: Paul West

Please Stand By

Comedy; 30 min; Syn. 9/78

The comic adventures of Frank Lambert as he struggles to run TV station KRDA, Channel 4, from his garage in DeQueen, New Mexico.

Frank Lambert	Richard Schaal
Carol Lambert	Elinor Donahue
Susan Lambert	Darian Mathias
David Lambert	Stephen M. Schwartz
Rocky Lambert	Bryan Scott
Vickie Janes	Marcie Barkin
Dennis "Crash" Lopez	Danny Mora
Sam	Gary Oakes

Theme Vocal ("Please Stand By"): Stephen M. Schwartz

Producer: Bob Banner, William S. Bickley, Michael Warren

Poetry and Music

Variety Pilot; 30 min; DuMont 11/1/46

A proposed series of music and songs with hostess Vera Massey. Produced by Bob Henry.

Pole Position

Cartoon; 30 min; CBS 9/15/84 to 9/6/86

When a mysterious accident claims the lives of their parents, the Darret children (Dan, Tess, and Daisy) follow in their footsteps and become agents for Pole Position, a secret organization that battles crime and corruption. Stories relate their exploits.

Voices: Lisa Lindgren, Kaleena Kiff, Marilyn Schreffler, Darryl Hickman, Neil Ross, Paul Kirby

Producer: Jean Chalopin, Andy Heyward

Police Squad!

Satire; 30 min; ABC 4/4/82 to 4/25/82
7/22/82 to 8/5/82

A spoof of TV police dramas as seen through the investigations of Frank Drebin, a detective lieutenant in battle against the criminal elements that befoul a big city. The comedy stems from sight gags as Drebin, a member of the crack Police Squad (in an unidentified city) strives to solve crimes—despite the bizarre circumstances that seem to follow him like a shadow.

Lt. Frank Drebin	Leslie Nielsen
Capt. Ed Hocken	Alan North
Ted Olson	Ed Williams
Officer Norberg	Peter Lupus
Johnny (shoeshine boy)	William Duell

Producer: Jerry Zuker, Jim Abrahams, David Zuker

Police Station

Crime Drama; 30 min; Syn. 1959

The day-to-day operations of a police station (Precinct 11) of a big city. Dramatizes real cases that follow the crime from the arrest to the conviction.

Sgt. White	Baynes Barron
Sgt. Stan Albertson	Henry Beckman
Det. Pat Green	Roy Wright
Det. Chuck Mitchell	Larry Kerr

Producer: Richard Dickson

Police Story

Anthology; 30 min; CBS 4/4/52 to 8/1/52

Dramas based on the files of various police departments. The series, narrated by Norman Rose and produced by Jerome Robinson, is broadcast live from New York City.

Police Story

Crime Drama Pilot; 30 min; NBC 9/8/67

The exploits of James Paige, the captain of a large metropolitan police department.

Capt. James Paige	Steve Ihnat
Lt. Roy Haggerty	Rafer Johnson
Lab Chief	DeForest Kelley
Sgt. Lily Monroe	Grace Lee Whitney
Questor	Gary Clarke
Garrison	Malachi Throne
Dorian	Ann Atmore

Producer-Writer: Gene Roddenberry

Police Story

Anthology; 60 min; NBC 10/2/73 to 4/28/80

Dramatizations, based on official law enforcement files, depicting the day-to-day struggles of police officers.

Creator: Joseph Wambaugh

Producer: Stanley Kallis, David Gerber, Liam O'Brien, Christopher Morgan, Hugh Benson, Mel Swope, Larry Brody

Police Surgeon

Crime Drama; 30 min; Syn. 1972

The exploits of Simon Locke, a doctor with the Canadian Medical Emergency Unit of the Metropolitan Police Department. A spin-off from "Dr. Simon Locke."

Dr. Simon Locke	Sam Groom
Lt. Dan Palmer	Len Birman
Lt. Jack Gordon	Larry D. Mann
Tony	Marc Hebet
Radio Dispatcher	Nerene Virgin

Producer: Wilton Schiller

Police Woman

Crime Drama; 60 min; NBC 9/13/74 to 8/30/78

When Lee Anne "Pepper" Anderson, a beautiful high fashion model, feels that her life is becoming a drag, she applies for a position with the Los Angeles Police Department (at first assigned to Vice, then to the Criminal Conspiracy Division). Stories relate Pepper's exploits as an undercover police woman. See the following title also.

Sgt. Pepper Anderson	Angie Dickinson
Sgt. William Crowley	Earl Holliman
Investigator Pete Royster	Charles Dierkop
Investigator Joe Styles	Ed Bernard
Lt. Paul March	Val Bisoglio
Capt. Parks	John Crawford
Cheryl Anderson (Pepper's sister)	Nicole Kallis
Harriet Styles (Joe's wife)	Kandi Keith
Linda Summers (Pepper's snitch)	Paula Kelly
Jackie Crowley (Bill's ex-wife)	Bibi Besch

Producer: David Gerber, Douglas Benton, Edward DeBlasio

Note: Pepper's first name is also known to be Suzanne.

Police Woman: The Gamble

Crime Drama Pilot; 60 min; NBC 3/26/74

The exploits of Lisa Beaumont, a beautiful vice squad detective with the L.A.P.D. In the pilot, broadcast on "Police Story," Lisa poses as prostitute to expose the leader of a gambling syndicate. The pilot for "Police Woman."

Det. Lisa Beaumont	Angie Dickinson
Sgt. William Crowley	Bert Convy
Det. Royster	Charles Dierkop
Det. Styles	Ed Bernard
Carl Vitalie	Joseph Campanella
Lloyd Day	Peter Brown
Harold	Cesare Danova
Willy	Theodore Wilson

Producer: David Gerber, Stanley Kallis

The Polly Bergen Show

Variety; 30 min; NBC 9/21/57 to 5/31/58

A weekly series of music and songs.

Hostess: Polly Bergen

Regulars: Bill Bergen, The Peter Gennero Dancers

Orchestra: Luther Henderson Jr.

Producer: Bill Colleran

Pony Express

Western; 30 min; Syn. 1960

The exploits of Brett Clark, a troubleshooter for the Central Overland Express Company, better known as the Pony Express, during the 1860s.

Brett Clark	Grant Sullivan
Tom Clyde	Bill Cord
Donovan	Don Dorell

Producer: Robert Stillman, Tom McKnight

Poor Richard

Comedy Pilot; 30 min; CBS 1/21/84

When Richard Manning III, a wealthy playboy loses his money, and Rudy Hopper, an Iowa Country bumpkin who became a millionaire by inventing a pig feed supplement, buys his Beverly Hills mansion, Richard convinces Rudy to hire him on as his butler. The unsold series was to relate Richard's misadventures as he seeks to one day buy back his mansion and retain the appearance of a wealthy playboy until that day comes.

Richard Manning III	George Hamilton
Rudy Hopper	Geoffrey Lewis
Terry Robinson	Alley Mills
Vicki Hollingsworth	Cynthia Sikes
Randi	Nancy Stafford
Jimmy	John Hunsaker
Jonathan Kingsley	Glynn Turman

Producer: Jerry Weintraub

P.O.P.

Comedy Pilot; 30 min; NBC 8/29/84

The story of P. Oliver Pendergast, a lovable con artist who suddenly moves back into the lives of his former wife (Rosalyn) and their two grown sons (Johnny and Russell) after a twenty year absence.

P. Oliver Pendergast	Charles Durning
Rosalyn Gordon	Beatrice Arthur
Johnny Gordon	Todd Graff
Russell Pendergast	James Lashly
Maggie Newton	Fran Drescher
Dana McNeil	Jane Anderson
Frank Wilkey	Antonio Fargas
Marc Alderman	Anthony Holland
Betty Jo	Marianne Muellerleile

Producer: Norman Lear

Pop! Goes the Country

Variety; 30 min; Syn. 9/74

Performances by country and western entertainers.

Host: Ralph Emery

Theme Vocal ("Pop! Goes the Country"): The Statler Brothers

Producer: Bill Graham, Reg Dunlap

The Pop 'n' Rocker Game

Game; 30 min; Syn. 9/83

In round one, a music-oriented question is read that is accompanied by a visual clue. The first player (of three who compete) to give the correct answer scores $50. The second half of the program consists of a rapid-fire question and answer session wherein $50 is scored for each correct answer.

Host: Jon Bauman

Music: Bruce Gray

Producer: Ron Greenberg, David Yarnell

The Popcorn Kid

Comedy; 30 min; CBS 3/23/87 to 4/24/87

The antics of Scott, Lynne Holly, Gwen, and Willie, four teenage ushers who operate the popcorn concession of the Majestic Theatre, a movie palace in Kansas City.

Scott Creasman	Bruce Norris	Abraham Rodriquez	Hector Elizondo
Lynne Holly		Luis Rodriquez	Dennis Vasquez
Brickhouse	Faith Ford	Abraham Rodriquez	
Gwen Stutlemeyer	Penelope Ann Miller	Jr.	Anthony Perez
Willie Dawson	Jeffrey Joseph	Lupe	Liz Torres*
Marlon Bond	John Christopher		Edith Diaz
	Jones	Angelo Maggio	Lou Criscuolo
Yvonne Brickhouse	Deborah May	Mr. Diaz	Frank Lugo
Beryl Creasman	James Staley		

Producer: Barry Kemp, Emily Marshall

Producer: Herbert B. Leonard, Arne Sultan

*Pilot film role (5/2/75).

Popeye the Sailor

Cartoon; 6 min; Syn. 1956

A series of theatrical cartoons, produced from 1933 to 1954, which relates the adventures of Popeye, a sailor who derives great strength from spinach, and which he uses to help good defeat evil.

Popeye	Det Poppen
	Floyd Buckley
	Jack Mercer
Bluto	Jackson Beck
Olive Oyl	Olive LaMoy
	Mae Questel
Wimpy	Charles Lawrence

Producer: Dave Fleischer

Popeye the Sailor

Cartoon; 6 min; Syn. 1962

A made-for-television version of the theatrical series (see prior title) about the exploits of Popeye the Sailor.

Popeye	Jack Mercer
Olive Oyl	Mae Questel
Brutus	Jackson Beck
Sea Hag/Swee'pea	Mae Questel

Producer: Al Brodax, Jack Kinney, Larry Harmon

Popi

Comedy; 30 min; CBS 1/20/76 to 8/24/76

The story of Abraham Rodriquez, a hardworking Puerto Rican father, and his efforts to raise his two mischievous and motherless sons (Luis and Abraham Jr.). Based on the feature film.

Popples

Cartoon; 30 min; Syn. 4/86

While exploring the treasures of their attic, a young sister and brother (Bonnie and Billy) discover an old box of toys and a group of friendly creatures who inhabit it called Popples. Stories relate the misadventures that occur as Bonnie and Billy strive to keep secret the existence of the very mischievous Popples.

Voices: Len Carlson, Diane Fabian, Dan Hennessey, Hadley Kaye, Jazmin Lausanna, Barbara Redpath, Linda Sorenson, Louise Vallance, Noam Zylberman

Producer: Jean Chalopin, Andy Heyward

Porky Pig and Friends

Cartoon; 30 min; ABC 9/9/64 to 9/2/67

A packaged series of Warner Brothers theatrical cartoons, produced from 1948 to 1965, that relate the antics of Porky Pig, Daffy Duck, Bugs Bunny, Sylvester and Tweety, and Foghorn Leghorn. Voices by Mel Blanc and produced by Hal Geer.

The Porter Wagoner Show

Variety; 30 min; Syn. 1960

Performances by country and western artists.

Host: Porter Wagoner

Regulars: Dolly Parton, Barbara Lee, Spec Rose, Bruce Osborne

Announcer: Don Housner

Music: The Wagon Masters

Portia Faces Life

Drama; 15 min; CBS 4/5/54 to 7/1/55

The story of Portia Manning, an attorney and mother, as she struggles to divide her time between the office and home.

Portia Manning	Fran Carlon
	Frances Reid
Walter Manning	Karl Swenson
	Donald Woods
Shirley Manning	Ginger McManus
	Renne Jarrett
Dick Manning	Charles Taylor
Karl Manning	Patrick O'Neal

Producer: Beverly Smith

Portrait of a Legend

Tribute; 30 min; Syn. 6/81

A weekly series of tributes to great legends of music. Film clips and interviews are used to recall a subject's career.

Host: James Darren

Producer: Syd Vinnedge, Tony Scotti, Casey Kasem

Pottsville

Comedy Pilot; 60 min; CBS 2/27/80

The story of Bulldog O'Halloran, an harassed labor leader and the president of Local 605 of the National Factory Workers Union in a small manufacturing town (Pottsville).

Bulldog O'Halloran	Forrest Tucker
Grace O'Halloran	Jan Miner
Tinker O'Halloran	George O'Hanlon Jr.
Bill Gentry	Richard Brestoff
Holden Farraday	John Lawlor
Gardy Farraday	Nina Foch
Ted Farraday	Jimmy Samuels
Snell	Hamilton Camp
Randy	Jane Daly
Pippa	Heidi Gold
Helen	Edie McClurg
Sundance Ewbanks	Rory Calhoun
Frank	James Cromwell

Producer: Rod Parker, Hal Cooper

Pound Puppies

Cartoon; 30 min; ABC 9/13/86 (Premiere)

The story of a group of puppies, living in a pound and awaiting adoption, who explore the outside world via a secret tunnel.

Voices: Adrienne Alexander, Chad Allen, Ruth Buzzi, Pat Carroll, Nancy Cartwright, Danny Cooksey, Peter Cullen, Ami Foster, Joan Gardner, Linda Gary, June Lockhart, Chuck McCann, Ronnie Schell, B. J. Ward, Frank Welker

Producer: William Hanna, Joseph Barbera

The Powder Room

Comedy Pilot; 30 min; NBC 8/26/71

A proposed series of vignettes that explores life as seen through the eyes of women.

Host: Dean Martin

Guests: Joey Heatherton, Jack Cassidy, Elaine Stritch, Jeanine Burnier

Producer: Greg Garrison, Rod Parker

The Powers of Matthew Star

Science Fiction; 60 min; NBC 9/17/82 to 9/11/83

When the planet Quadris is invaded by aliens, its young prince, Ehawk, is sent to Earth to develop his powers. Ehawk assumes the role of a high school student (Matthew Star) and his guardian, Dehay, becomes Walt Shepherd, a science teacher at Crestridge High School. Stories relate Star's efforts to develop his powers and battle the enemies of Quadris who have come to Earth to destroy him. In the original pilot film (4/5/83) the title character is called David Star, and his guardian, Max, is played by Gerald S. O'Loughlin.

Matthew Star	Peter Barton
Walt Shepherd	Louis Gossett Jr.
Pam Elliott	Amy Steele
Gen. Fred Tucker	John Crawford
Mr. Wymore	James Karen
Mr. Curtis	Barry Van Dyke
Principal Heller	Michael Fairman
Queen Nadra (Matt's mother)	Tricia O'Neil

"The Powers of Matthew Star" Theme Song: Michel Rubini, Denny Jaeger

Producer: Harve Bennett, Bruce Lansbury

Powers Play

Adventure Pilot; 60 min; CBS 8/30/86

Following the death of the father she never knew, Rowena Powers inherits BPI (Ben Powers International), a powerful world-wide conglomerate based in Arizona. The unsold series was to relate Rowena's adventures as she struggles to protect her interest in the company.

Rowena Powers	Sheree J. Wilson
Lucas Cord	David Birney
Rowena's Grandfather (Harry)	Noah Beery Jr.
Major Heckinkamp	Kurtwood Smith
Paul Boudea	Thaao Penghlis
Jennifer	Alex Greene

Producer: John Furia Jr., James David Buchanan, Noreen Stone

The Practice

Comedy; 30 min; NBC 1/30/76 to 1/20/77

The story of Dr. Jules Bedford, a gruff but lovable doctor who practices on New York's Lower East Side.

Dr. Jules Bedford	Danny Thomas
Dr. David Bedford	David Spielberg
Jenny Bedford	Shelley Fabares
Molly Gibbons	Dena Dietrich
Helen	Didi Conn
Paul Bedford	Allen Price
Tony Bedford	Damon Raskin
Dr. Roland Caine	John Byner
Nate	Sam Laws
Dr. Byron Fisk	Barry Gordon
Lenny	Mike Evans
Harry Bedford	Jan Murray

Producer: Danny Thomas, Paul Junger Witt, Tony Thomas

Premiere

Pilot Films; 60 min; CBS 7/1/68 to 9/9/68

See the following titles: "Call to Danger," "Crisis," "Higher and Higher, Attorneys at Law," "Lassiter," "Operation Greasepaint," "Out of the Blue," "The Search," and "A Walk in the Night."

Presenting Susan Anton

Variety; 60 min; NBC 4/26/79 to 5/17/79

A variety hour that spotlights the music and comedy talents of Susan Anton.

Hostess: Susan Anton

Regulars: Barbara Brownell, Jack Fletcher, Terry McGovern, Jimmy Martinez, Marcie Vosburgh, Dick Wilson, Donovan Scott, Jack Knight, The Walter Painter Dancers

Announcer: Jack Fletcher

Orchestra: Ian Bernard, Larry White

Producer: Jack Stein, Ernest Chambers

Press Your Luck

Game; 30 min; CBS 9/19/83 to 9/26/86

Players answer questions in return for spins on a large electronic game board. The board is divided into twenty squares, each of which revolves rapidly. Squares contain cash, merchandise, and Whammies. The object is for a player to accumulate as much cash and merchandise as possible within his allotted spins without hitting a Whammie (which erases a player's earnings).

Host: Peter Tomarken

Announcer: Rod Roddy

Producer: Bill Carruthers

Preview Theatre

Pilot Films; 30 min; NBC 7/14/61 to 9/22/61

See the following titles: "Five's a Family," "Happily Ever After," "Harry's Business," "Heave Ho Harrigan," "I Married a Dog," "Innocent Jones," "Miss Bishop," and "Shore Leave."

Preview Tonight

Pilot Films; 60 min; ABC 8/14/66 to 9/11/66

See the following titles: "The Cliff Dwellers," "Great Bible Adventures," "Pursue and Destroy," "Roaring Camp," and "Somewhere in Italy . . . Company B."

The Price Is Right

Game; 30 min; NBC 11/26/56 to 9/6/63
ABC 9/9/63 to 9/3/65

The object calls for players to guess the manufacturer's suggested retail price for various merchandise items.

Host: Bill Cullen, Jack Clark

Assistants: Beverly Bentley, Toni Wallace, June Ferguson

Producer: Beth Ferro, Bob Stewart

The Price Is Right

Game; 30 min; Syn. 1972

A syndictaed version of the game that challenges players to guess the suggested retail price of merchandise items.

Host: Dennis James, Bob Barker

Assistants: Anitra Ford, Holly Hallstrom, Janice Pennington, Dian Parkinson

Announcer: Johnny Olsen

Producer: Frank Wayne, Mark Goodson, Bill Todman

The Price Is Right

Game; 60 min; CBS 11/3/75 (Premiere)

Object: For players to guess the suggested retail selling price of merchandise items.

Host: Bob Barker

Models: Anitra Ford, Janice Pennington, Dian Parkinson, Nancy Myers, Pamela Parker, Holly Hallstrom

Announcer: Johnny Olsen, Rod Roddy, Bob Wilkens

Producer: Frank Wayne, Barbara Hunter, Philip Wayne

The Price Is Right Special

Game; 60 min; CBS 8/14/86 to 9/18/86

A six week prime time version of the popular daytime series (prior title) that challenges players to guess the suggested retail price of merchandise items.

Host: Bob Barker

Models: Dian Parkinson, Holly Hallstrom

Announcer: Rod Roddy

Producer: Frank Wayne, Philip Wayne

Pride of the Family

Comedy; 30 min; ABC 10/9/53 to 9/24/54

Events in the lives of the Morrison family: Albie, the advertising head of a small town newspaper; his wife, Catherine; and their children, Ann and Albie Jr. Also known as "The Paul Hartman Show."

Albie Morrison	Paul Hartman
Catherine Morrison	Fay Wray
Ann Morrison	Natalie Wood
Albie Morrison Jr.	Bobby Hyatt

Producer: Bob Finkel

The Primary English Class

Comedy Pilot; 30 min; ABC 8/15/77

The story of Sandy Lambert, an English teacher in a California night school for foreign-born adults new to the U.S.

Sandy Lambert	Valerie Curtin
Hal	Murphy Dunne
Yosef Ari	Harvey Jason
Lupe	Maria O'Brien
Sergio	Joe Bennett
Wilhelm Ritterman	Bob Holt
Yoko	Suesie Elene
Chuma	Freeman King

Producer: Joe Hamilton

The Prime of Miss Jean Brodie

Drama; 60 min; PBS 5/7/79 to 6/11/79

The experiences of Jean Brodie, a vain and eccentric teacher at the Marcia Blaine School for Girls in Scotland during the 1930s. Produced by Scottish TV (based on the Muriel Spark novel).

Jean Brodie	Geraldine McEwan
Mrs. MacDonald	Madeleine Christie
Miss Gaunt	Georgine Anderson
Sandy	Lynsey Baxter
Jenny Gray	Amanda Kirby
Rose Stanley	Tracy Childs
Mary	Jean McKinley
Ted Lloyd	John Castle

Hostess: Julie Harris

Producer: Beryl Vertue, Richard Bates, Lisa Seguin

Prime Times

Variety Pilot; 60 min; NBC 4/4/83

The program spoofs TV—its past, present, and imagined future via intercutting clips from old series with new sketches.

Host: Leslie Nielsen

Regulars: Hamilton Camp, Julie Payne, Deborah Pratt, Jan Hooks, Lewis Arquette, Thom Bray

Theme Music ("Prime Times"): Michael Gore, Dean Pitchford

Producer: Andrew Solt, Malcolm Leo

Primus

Adventure; 30 min; Syn. 1971

The exploits of oceanographer Carter Primus, a global underwater troubleshooter working out of Nassau.

Carter Primus	Robert Brown
Toni Hyden	Eva Renzi
Charlie Kingman	Will Kuluva

Producer: Ivan Tors, Andy White

Prince Planet

Cartoon; 30 min; Syn. 9/66

The exploits of Prince Planet, a youngster from the Universal Peace Corps of the planet Radion, as he uses his unique powers to maintain peace in the universe. Produced by Mitsuteru Tokoyama.

The Prisoner

Adventure; 60 min; CBS 6/1/68 to 9/21/68

When secret agent John Drake* resigns his position with the British government, the Ministry feels he is too vital to let go free and kidnap him. Drake is given a number (6) and made a prisoner of a self-contained community known as the Village, a fantasy-like area boarded by mountains and ocean from which there is no escape. Stories relate Drake's desperate attempts to discover who his captors are (and the reason for his imprisonment) and efforts to escape from the Village.

Number 6	Patrick McGoohan
Silent Butler	Angelo Muscat
Number 2	Colin Gordon
	Clifford Evans
	Mary Morris
	John Sharpe
	Peter Wyngarde
	Guy Doleman
	Leo McKern
Village President	Kenneth Griffith

"The Prisoner" Theme: Ron Grainer

Producer: Patrick McGoohan, David Tomblin

*Assumed to be John Drake as "The Prisoner" is a continuation from the last episode of "Secret Agent."

Prisoner: Cell Block H

Drama; 30 min; Syn. 1/80

An adult-oriented drama that details life in the Wentworth Detention Center, a woman's prison in Melbourne, Australia.

Prisoners:

Karen Travers	Peita Toppano
Lynnette Warner	Kerry Armstrong
Frieda "Frankie" Doyle	Carol Burns
Bea Smith	Val Lehman
Marilyn Anne Mason	Margaret Laurence
Doreen Anderson	Colette Mann
Jeannie "Mum" Brooks	Mary Ward
Lizzie Birdsworth	Sheila Florance
Chrissy Latham	Amanda Muggleton
Anne Yates	Kristy Child
Noelene Burke	Jude Kuring
Barbara Davidson	Sally Cahill
Sharon Gilmour	Margot Knight

Prison Personnel:

Erica Davidson	Patsy King
Meg Jackson	Elspeth Ballantyne
Vera Bennett	Fiona Spence
Greg Miller	Bill Quinn
Jean Vernon	Christine Amor
Jim Fletcher	Gerald Maguire
Jock Stewart	Tommy Dysart

Additional Regulars:

Judith Ann (Mum's granddaughter)	Kim Deacon
Gary Doyle (Frankie's brother)	Greg Stroud
Steve Wilson (lawyer)	Jim Smillie
Leila Fletcher (Jim's wife)	Penny Ramsey
Col Burke (Noelene's brother)	Brian Granrott
Alex Frazier (reporter)	Geoff Collins
Kevin Burns (Doreen's friend)	Ian Gilmour
Judy Bryant (Sharon's lover)	Betty Bobbitt
Andrew Reynolds (factory owner)	Johnny Lee

Theme Vocal ("On the Inside"): Lynne Hamilton

Producer: Reg Watson, Godfrey Philipp

Private Benjamin

Comedy; 30 min; CBS 4/6/81 to 9/5/83

Bored with her lifestyle, Judy Benjamin, the spoiled daughter of a wealthy family, decides to join the Army to find more excitement. She soon finds herself totally out of place when she discovers that the system does not exactly fulfill her needs. Judy's misadventures, as she tries to get the Army to do things her way—and the Army's efforts to turn her into a real soldier—provide the program's essential conflict. The series, based on the Goldie Hawn film, is first set at Fort Trams, then at Fort Bradley in Hobart, California.

Pvt. Judy Benjamin	Lorna Patterson
Capt. Doreen Lewis	Eileen Brennan
Sgt. Lucien C. Ross	Hal Williams
Col. Lawrence Fielding	Robert Mandan
Pvt. Maria Gianelli	Lisa Raggio
Pvt. Rayleen White	Joyce Little
Pvt. Carol Winter	Ann Ryerson
Pvt. Barbara Ann Glass	Joan Roberts
Pvt. Lu Anne Hubble	Lucy Webb
Pvt. Harriet Dorsey	Francesca Roberts
Pvt. Jackie Sims	Damita Jo Freeman
Pvt. Stacy Kouchalakas	Wendie Jo Sperber
Maj. Amanda Allen	Polly Holliday
Lt. Billy Dean	Joel Brooks
Harriet Benjamin (Judy's mother)	Barbara Barrie K Callan
Ted Benjamin (Judy's father)	William Daniels
Pvt. Sherry Stern (Judy's cousin)	Stephanie Faracy
Benjamin Benjamin (Judy's grandfather)	Arthur Peterson

Theme Music ("Judy's Song"): Madelyn Davis, Bob Carroll Jr.

Producer: Don Reo, Madelyn Davis, Bob Carroll Jr., Nick Arnold

Private Eye

Crime Drama; 60 min; NBC 9/13/87 (Premiere)

The exploits of Jack Cleary, a tough private detective working in Los Angeles during the 1950s (1956).

Jack Cleary	Michael Woods
Johnny Betts	Josh Brolin
Det. Charlie Fontana	Bill Sadler
Dottie	Lisa Jane Persky

Producer: Anthony Yerkovich, Scott Brazil

Private Secretary

Comedy; 30 min; CBS 2/1/53 to 9/10/57

The misadventures of Susie Camille McNamara, a former stage actress turned private secretary to Peter Sands, a theatrical agent and owner of the International Artists agency in New York City. Syndicated as "Susie."

Susie McNamara	Ann Sothern
Peter Sands	Don Porter
Violet "Vi" Praskins	Ann Tyrrell
Sylvia Platt	Joan Banks
Mickey "Cagey" Calhoune	Jesse White
Buddy Rice	George E. Stone

Producer: Jack Chertok

Prize Performance

Variety; 30 min; CBS 7/5/50 to 8/2/50

Performances by undiscovered professional talent with host Cedric Adams, and regulars Arlene Francis and Peter Donald. Produced by Byron Paul.

Professional Father

Comedy; 30 min; CBS 1/8/55 to 7/2/55

Events in the lives of the Wilson family: Thomas, a child psychologist; his wife, Helen; and their children, Kit and Twig.

Thomas Wilson	Steve Dunne
Helen Wilson	Barbara Billingsley
Kathryn "Kit" Wilson	Beverly Washburn
Thomas "Twig" Wilson	Ted Marc
Nana (housekeeper)	Ann O'Neal
Fred (neighbor)	Joseph Kearns
Madge (Fred's wife)	Phyllis Coates
Mr. Boggs (handyman)	Arthur Q. Bryan

Producer: Harry Kronman

Profiles in Courage

Anthology; 60 min; NBC 11/8/64 to 5/9/65

Dramas based on events in past American history. Stories stress the valor of political figures who risked their careers to tackle unpopular causes. Based on the book by John F. Kennedy.

Producer: Robert Saudek, Gordon Oliver, Michael Ritchie

Program Playhouse

Pilot Films; 30 min; DuMont 6/22/49 to 9/14/49

A series of half-hour pilot films (then called test films) for DuMont. See the following titles: "Federal Agent," "Murder and Mrs.," "The Timid Soul," and "Trouble, Inc."

Project UFO

Drama; 60 min; NBC 2/19/78 to 1/4/79
                                         7/5/79 to 8/30/79

Dramatizations of UFO incidents as seen through the investigations of U.S.A.F. Major Jake Gatlin and his assistant, Harry Fitz. Based on Project Blue Book, the government's record of UFO investigations.

Maj. Jake Gatlin	William Jordan
Sgt. Harry Fitz	Caskey Swaim
Capt. Ben Ryan	Edward Winter
Libby (secretary)	Aldine King

Narrator: Jack Webb

Producer: Jack Webb, Gene Levitt

Projection Room

Ruth Gilbert as the host of a short-lived ABC series of live mystery presentations (3/19/52 to 3/26/52).

Pros and Cons

Crime Drama Pilot; 60 min; ABC 1/26/86

The exploits of the Fraud and Bunco Squad, a special division of the Los Angeles County Sheriff's office that investigates the bilking schemes of confidence men. See also "Fraud Squad."

Lt. Bernie Rollins	Bernie Casey
Patty Finley*	Carol Potter
Audrey*	Wendy Cutler
Christie*	Jennifer Runyon
Val*	Sheryl Lee Ralph
Dolly*	Lu Leonard
Det. Morry Stein	James Sloyan

Producer: Allen Epstein, Jim Green, Buddy Bregman

*Team members.

The Protectors

Adventure; 30 min; Syn. 9/72

The exploits of Harry Rule (American), Contessa Caroline di Contini (British), and Paul Buchet (French), three private detectives who are members of the Protectors, an organization of the world's finest investigators united in the battle against crime in Europe.

Harry Rule	Robert Vaughn
Caroline di Contini	Nyree Dawn Porter
Paul Buchet	Tony Anholt
Suki	Yasuko Nagazumi
Chino	Anthony Chinn

Theme Vocal ("Avenues and Alleyways"): Tony Christie

Producer: Sherwood Price, Gerry Anderson, Reg Hill

Prudence and the Chief

Comedy Pilot; 30 min; ABC 8/26/70

On behalf of the United Council of Churches, Prudence MacKenzie, a widowed teacher and missionary, is chosen to establish a school on a Cheyenne Indian reservation. The unsold series was to relate Prudence's efforts to establish a school and teach Indian children in the west of the 1870s.

Prudence MacKenzie	Sally Ann Howes
Chief Snow Eagle	Rick Jason
Letitia MacKenzie	Kathryn Givney
Gavin MacKenzie	Teddy Quinn
Fergus MacKenzie	Johnny Lee
Major O'Toole	Rhodes Reason
Lt. Burns	Mac Krell

Producer: David Gerber

Prudential Family Playhouse

A live CBS series (10/10/50 to 3/27/51) of dramatic productions sponsored by Prudential Life Insurance. Produced by Donald Davis.

The Pruitts of Southampton

Comedy; 30 min; ABC 9/6/66 to 1/6/67
1/13/67 to 9/1/67 (as "The Phyllis Diller Show").

When an Internal Revenue audit discovers that she owes ten million dollars in back taxes, society matron Phyllis Pruitt is forced to sell her valuables and drastically reduce her living style. The series, set on Southampton (Long Island, N.Y.) relates Phyllis's efforts to pay her back taxes, yet maintain an appearance of wealth and social status. In mid season, the format changed to depict Phyllis's adventures as a landlady when she turns her home into a boarding house to pay off her debt.

Phyllis Pruitt	Phyllis Diller
Stephanie Pruitt	Pamela Freeman
Ned Pruitt	Reginald Gardner
Sturgis	Grady Sutton
Regina Wentworth	Gypsy Rose Lee
Suzy Wentworth	Lisa Loring
IRS Agent Baldwin	Richard Deacon
General Cannon	John McGiver
Norman Krump	Marty Ingels
Vernon Bradley	Billy DeWolfe
Phyllis's Cousin Rudy	John Astin
Phyllis's Brother Harvey	Paul Lynde

Theme Vocal ("The Pruitts of Southampton"): Phyllis Diller

Producer: David Levy, Everett Freeman

Pryor's Place

Children; 30 min; CBS 9/22/84 to 6/15/85

The series, set in a neighborhood called Pryor's Place, relates lessons about life to children via sketches.

Host: Richard Pryor.

Little Richie	Akili Prince
Miss Stern	Marla Gibbs
Wally	Cliffy Magee
Meatrack	Keland Love
Solly	Milt Kogan
Rita	Kim Fields

Theme Vocal ("Pryor's Place"): Ray Parker Jr.

Producer: Alvin J. Tenzer, Carl Kleinschmitt, Sid & Marty Krofft

The Psychiatrist

Drama; 60 min; NBC 2/3/71 to 9/1/71

The story of James Whitman, a young Los Angeles psychiatrist who practices the new but controversial techniques of therapy.

Dr. James Whitman	Roy Thinnes
Dr. Bernard Altman	Luther Adler

Producer: Norman Felton

Public Defender

Drama; 30 min; CBS 3/11/54 to 6/23/55

The exploits of Bart Matthews, a public defender of indigent people.

Bart Matthews   Reed Hadley

Producer: Hal Roach Jr., Carroll Chase

The Public Life of Cliff Norton

Comedy; 5 min; NBC 1/17/52 to 2/29/52

Capsule skits that depict one man's approaches and solutions to everyday problems.

Host/Demonstrator: Cliff Norton

Producer: Roy Windsor

Public Prosecutor

Mystery-Game; Syn. 1947–48 (20 min)
                    DuMont 9/6/51 to 2/28/52 (30 min)

The original concept (1947) featured short mystery programs designed to be used in twenty minute spots. In 1951, when DuMont acquired the program, it became a mystery game series in which a panel of three detective-fiction experts would view a fifteen minute mystery that was stopped prior to the denouncement. Each was asked to identify the culprit. The film was played to reveal the answer. Also known as "Crawford Mystery Theatre."

Prosecuting Attorney	John Howard
His Assistant	Anne Gwynne
Police Lieutenant	Walter Sande
Host (DuMont)	Warren Hull

Producer: Jerry Fairbanks

Publicity Girl

A not widely seen syndicated comedy (1956) in which Jan Sterling plays a publicity girl for a public relations firm in Southern California.

Pud's Prize Party

Variety; 30 min; ABC 6/21/52 to 12/13/52

Todd Russell as the host of a program wherein nonprofessional children compete against each other for merchandise prizes and the title "The Most Talented Child of the Week."

Pulitzer Prize Playhouse

Anthology; 60 min; ABC 10/6/50 to 6/4/52

Adaptations of Pulitzer Prize-winning stories. Hosted by Elmer Davis and produced by Edgar Peterson and Lawrence Carra.

Pulse of the City

A DuMont anthology series (9/15/53 to 3/9/54) of dramas set against the background of New York City.

Pumpboys and Dinettes on Television

Variety Pilot; 60 min; NBC 8/15/83

The story, set along Highway 57 in Frog Level, North Carolina, relates the musical adventures of four pumpboys (Jim, L.M., Jackson, and Eddie) who work the L&M Gas Station, and two sisters, Rhetta and Prudie, who operate the Double Cupp Diner. Adapted from the Broadway show.

Jim	Jim Wann
L.M.	Mark Hardwick
Jackson	John Foley
Eddie	John Schimmel
Rhetta Cupp	Cass Morgan
Prudie Cupp	Debra Monk
Uncle Bob	Dub Taylor
Tanya Tucker	Herself
Mona	Teresa Ganzel
Dominique	Brandis Kemp

Orchestra: George Wyle

Producer: Allan Baumrucker, Ernest Chambers

Punky Brewster

Comedy; 30 min; NBC 9/16/84 to 9/7/86

When her husband walks out on her, a mother and her daughter pack their belongings and head for Chicago. While in a shopping mall, the mother abandons her 7-year-old daughter, Penelope "Punky" Brewster. With no place to go, the girl takes to the streets and finds shelter in an empty apartment of a building managed by Henry Warnimont, a photographer. When she is found and Henry learns of her plight, he decides to care for her. Stories relate Henry's misadventures as an adorable young girl strives to bring some cheer into his dull life. See the following title also.

Punky Brewster	Soleil Moon Frye
Henry Warnimont	George Gaynes
Betty Johnson	Susie Garrett
Cherie Johnson	Cherie Johnson
Margaux Kramer	Ami Foster
Allen Anderson	Casey Ellison
Michael Fulton	T. K. Carter
Randi Mitchell	Talia Balsam
Eddie Malvin	Eddie Deezen
Lisa	Robyn Lively

Theme Vocal ("Everytime You Turn Around"): Gary Portnoy

Producer: David Duclon, Gary Menteer, Rick Hawkins, Liz Sage

Note: The real Punky Brewster, Peyton B. Rutledge, appeared on the episode of 11/10/85 ("The Search"). Peyton, known in her childhood as "Punky Brewster," is the daughter of the headmaster of a school attended by NBC president Brandon Tartikoff. It was Tartikoff who remembered the name and suggested it for the title character.

Punky Brewster

Cartoon; 30 min; NBC 9/14/85 (Premiere)

An animated version based on the live series (above title). Continued events in the life of Punky Brewster, a mischievous little girl who is the adopted daughter of a gruff photographer (Henry).

Punky Brewster	Soleil Moon Frye
Henry Warnimont	George Gaynes
Margaux Kramer	Ami Foster
Allen Anderson	Casey Ellison
Cherie	Cherie Johnson

Producer: Joe Ruby, Ken Spears

Purex Special for Women

Anthology; 60 min; NBC 10/14/60 to 8/29/61

Sympathetic dramas based on the problems faced by women. Following the story, a brief discussion is conduced with a doctor. Sponsored by Purex and also known as "Special for Women."

Hostess: Pauline Fredericks

Producer: Irving Gitlin, George Lefferts

Pursue and Destroy

Drama Pilot; 60 min; ABC 8/14/66

The experiences of the officers and crew of a U.S. Naval submarine during World War II.

Lt. Cmdr. Russ Enright	Van Williams
Lt. Barney Redesko	Paul Comi
Lt. James Ford	David Thorpe
Chief Alex Jacobs	Ward Wood
Chip Malloy	Dee Pollack
Iris Milbanke	Dame Judith Anderson
Vivien Scott	Jessica Walter
Adm. Rockland	Henry Wilcoxon
Lonnie Cole	Thad Williams

Producer: Thomas J McDermott, Don Taylor

Pursuit

Anthology; 60 min; CBS 10/22/58 to 1/14/59

Dramatizations that depict the plight of people being pursued by others. Produced by Norman Felton, Charles Russell, and Peter Kortner.

The Pursuit of Happiness

Comedy; 30 min; ABC 10/30/87 to 1/8/88
The misadventures of David Hanley, an assistant professor to Roland G. Duncan, a senior history instructor at the John Marshall University in Philadelphia.

Roland Duncan	Brian Keith
David Hanley	Paul Provenza
Sara Duncan	Judie Aronson
Margaret Callahan	Wendel Meldrum
Vernon Morris	Wesley Thompson
Ms. Lopez	Wanda DeJesus
Prof. Gruber	Mary Farrell
Prof. Stevens	John Petlock

Producer: Michael J. Weithorn

Puttin' on the Hits

Contest; 30 min; Syn. 9/84

The program spotlights ordinary people as they mimic their favorite performers. Each act is judged, and the highest rated act is the winner.

Host: Allen Fawcett

Theme Music ("Puttin on the Hits"): David Russo

Producer: Dick Clark, Chris Bearde

Puttin' on the Kids

Contest; 30 min; Syn. 9/86

A juvenile version of "Puttin' on the Hits" wherein children (aged 6 to 12) pantomime recordings of famous songs. Acts, scored on originality, lip-sync, and performance are rated one to one hundred with the highest scorer receiving a $500 savings bond.

Host: Michael Young

Producer: Dick Clark, Chris Bearde, R. A. Clark, Kimber Rickenbaugh

Q.E.D.

Game; 30 min; ABC 4/3/51 to 10/9/51

Object: For a celebrity panel to solve mystery stories that are submitted by home viewers. The host relays the facts and each panelist receives one guess. The viewer receives a prize if the mystery remains unsolved. Also known as "Mystery File."

Host: Fred Uttal, Doug Browning

Panelists: Nina Foch, Hy Brown

Q.E.D.

Adventure; 60 min; CBS 3/23/82 to 4/27/82

Constantly mocked as a fool for his ingenious inventions, Quentin E. Deverill, an American science professor at Harvard, resigns in mid-semester to pursue his own private research. The series, set in London in 1912, follows Deverill's exploits as an amateur sleuth and slightly eccentric inventor.

Quentin E. Deverill	Sam Waterson
Betsy Stevens	Sarah Berger
Charlie Andrews	A. C. Weary
Phipps	George Innes
Jenny Martin	Carolyn Langrishe
Dr. Stephen Kilkiss	Julian Glover

Producer: John Hawkesworth

Q.T. Hush

Cartoon; 3½ min; Syn. 9/60

The exploits of Q.T. Hush, a fumbling private detective, and his assistants Shamus (dog) and Quincy (his shadow, which is able to operate independently of him). Produced by M. Alexander.

Quadrangle

Variety; 15 min; CBS 3/14/49 to 4/22/49

A twice-weekly program of music and songs. Also known as "Campus Corner."

Hostess: Beverly Fite

Regulars: Claire Granville, Frank Stevens, Burt Taylor, Dean Campbell, Bob Burkhardt, Ray Kirschner

Producer: Ralph Levy

Quark

Comedy; 30 min; NBC 2/24/78 to 4/14/78

The voyages of an interplanetary garbage scow whose mission, on behalf of the United Galaxy Sanitation Patrol, is to clean up the Milky Way.

Capt. Adam Quark	Richard Benjamin
Betty I	Trish Barnstable
Betty II	Cyb Barnstable
Gene/Jean	Tim Thomerson
Ficus Panderato	Richard Kelton
Andy	Bobby Porter
Otto Palindrome	Conrad Janis
The Head	Alan Caillou

Producer: David Gerber, Mace Neufeld, Bruce Johnson

The Queen and I

Comedy; 30 min; CBS 1/16/69 to 5/1/69

The story of master schemer Duffy, the first mate of the "Amsterdam Queen," a decrepit ocean liner (docked in New York Harbor), and his attempts to save his floating paradise of money making schemes from the scrap yards.

Charles Duffy	Larry Storch
Oliver Nelson	Billy DeWolfe
Capt. Washburn	Liam Dunn
Commodore Dodds	Reginald Owen
Wilma Winslow	Barbara Stuart
Crewman Ozzie	Dave Willock
Crewman Max Kowalski	Dave Morrick
Crewman Becker	Carl Ballantine
Crewman Barney	Pat Morita

Producer: Edward H. Feldman

Queen for a Day

Contest; 30 min; NBC 1/3/56 to 9/20/60
ABC 9/28/60 to 1/2/64

Four women appear and bear their souls, stating their single most needed object. Through electronic voting, the audience selects the one woman they feel is the neediest. The woman is crowned "Queen for a Day" and receives, in addition to what she sought, merchandise prizes.

Host: Jack Bailey

Co-Host: Jeanne Cagney

Announcer: Gene Baker

Producer: Elbert Walker

Queen for a Day

Contest; 30 min; Syn. 1970

Dick Curtis and Nancy Myers as the host of a revised version of the prior title; plays in the same manner.

The Quest

Western; 60 min; NBC 9/22/76 to 12/22/76

A wagon train, traveling across the prairie is attacked by Cheyenne Indians. Young Morgan Baudine and his sister Patricia are captured and taken by separate tribes. Eight years later, Morgan "Two Persons" Baudine is freed by the Army. Learning that his sister is still living with the Cheyenne, Morgan begins a search to find her. By chance, he meets Quentin, his long-lost brother, who has also begun a search for Patricia. Stories relate their efforts as they travel the rugged west of the latter 1800s.

Morgan Baudine	Kurt Russell
Quentin Baudine	Tim Matheson

Producer: David Gerber

The Quest

Adventure; 60 min; ABC 10/22/82 to 11/19/82

When it is realized that Charles Phillipe, the aging king of Glendora, a small European monarchy, is the last of his line, a search is begun to find an heir. Four Americans (Dan, Carrie, Art, and Cody), who are found to be descendants of the royal family, are summoned to the mythical Glendora. Because the British possession will revert back to French rule without a king (or queen), a quest is held to find the one who is most noble to rule. Stories relate the American's individual efforts to prove their worthiness, and their joint effort to defeat Louie Dardinay, an exiled Glendora Count who seeks to regain his title by letting Glendora revert back to the French.

Dan Underwood — Perry King
Caroline "Carrie"
  Welby — Karen Austin
Art Henley — Noah Beery Jr.
Cody Johnson — Ray Vitte
Charles Phillipe — Ralph Michael
Louie Dardinay — Michael Billington
Sir Edward Vallier — John Rhys Davies

Theme Vocal ("Kings and Queens"): Lisa Lee

Producer: Juanita Bartlett, Stephen J. Cannell, Jo Swerling Jr.

Quick and Quiet

Comedy Pilot; 30 min; CBS 8/18/81

When T.C. (Thaddeus Clark) Cooper, a private detective who runs an agency called Quick and Quiet, is killed, he returns as a ghost to help his son, a ne'er-do-well who has taken over the agency, become a productive citizen. The unsold series was to relate T.C.'s ghostly efforts to help Elliott run the agency.

T. C. Cooper — William Windom
Elliott Cooper — Rich Lohman
Camille — Millie Slavin
Margo Hilliard — Lynda Day George
Walter Hilliard — Henry Jones
Leonard Plumb — Warren Berlinger
Bambi Wilson — Lois Areno
Trixie Hilliard — Joan Roberts

Music: Jack Elliott

Producer: Ed Self, Bill Brademan

Quick as a Flash

Game; 30 min; ABC 3/12/53 to 2/25/54

A film that describes a person, place or thing is played. The first player (two two-member teams compete) who flashes his light signal receives a chance to identify the subject. A correct guess scores points; an incorrect answer defeats the team and the opponents view the entire film and receive one free guess. The highest scoring team wins merchandise prizes.

Host: Bobby Sherwood, Bud Collyer

Regulars: Jimmy Nelson, Faye Emerson

Producer: Charles Moss, Dick Lewis

The Quick Draw McGraw Show

Cartoon; 30 min; Syn. 1959

Segments: "Quick Draw McGraw" (about a dim-witted horse and his efforts to maintain law and order); "Snooper and Blabber" (a cat and mouse crime-fighting team); "Augie Doggie and Doggie Daddy" (a father's efforts to control his potentially juvenile delinquent son).

Quick Draw
  McGraw/Baba
  Looey/Snooper/
  Blabber/Augie
  Doggie — Daws Butler
Doggie Daddy — Doug Young

Producer: William Hanna, Joseph Barbera

Quick on the Draw

Game; 30 min; DuMont 1/8/52 to 12/9/52

Object: For contestants to identify phrases that are suggested by a series of cartoon drawings. Originally broadcast locally in New York from 1950–52.

Hostess (local version): Eloise McElhone

Hostess (network): Robin Chandler

Artist: Bob Dunn

Quincy, M.E.

Crime Drama; (Various 2 hrs; 60 min); NBC 10/3/76 to 9/5/83

The exploits of R. Quincy, a medical examiner for the Los Angeles Coroner's office, who prefers to probe as a detective rather than just work in a lab.

Dr. R. Quincy	Jack Klugman
Lee Potter	Lynnette Mettey
Dr. Emily Hanover	Anita Gillette
Dr. Robert Astin	John S. Ragin
Dr. Sam Fugiyama	Robert Ito
Lt. Frank Monihan	Garry Walberg
Danny Travo	Val Bisoglio
Sgt. Brill	Joseph S. Roman
Robin	Karen Philipp
Dr. Alice Ting	Amie Eccles
Marc	Marc Scott Taylor
Diane	Diane Markoff
Johnny	Johnny Nolan
Dr. Janet Carlisle	Diana Muldaur
Eddie	Eddie Garrett
Helen Quincy (Quincy's wife; flashbacks)	Anita Gillette
Girl in open (in bikini)	Lynnette Mettey

"Quincy" Theme Song: Glen A. Larson

Producer: Glen A. Larson, Jud Kinberg, Richard Irving, Donald P. Bellisario, Robert A. Cinader, Hannah L. Shearer, David Moessinger, Sam Egan

The Quiz Kids

Game; 30 min; NBC 7/6/49 to 11/2/51
NBC 7/7/52 to 8/18/52
CBS 1/17/53 to 11/8/53
CBS 1/12/56 to 9/27/56

Five exceptionally bright children attempt to answer very difficult questions. Based on the radio series.

Host: Joe Kelly, Clifton Fadiman

Producer: Louis Cowan, John LeWellen, Larry Woolf

The Quiz Kids

Game; 30 min; Syn. 1980

The basic format has a panel of five bright children answering difficult questions in return for scholarship dollars.

Host: Jim McKrell

Announcer: Michael Adams

Producer: Geoffrey Cowan, Seymour Berns

Quizzing the News

Game; 30 min; ABC 11/8/48 to 3/5/49

Object: For panelists to identify news events through a series of three cartoon drawings.

Host: Alan Prescott

Panelists: Mary Hunter, Arthur Q. Bryan, Milton Caniff, Ray Joseph, Albee Treider

Producer: Robert Brenner

The Raccoons

Cartoon; 30 min; Syn. 10/86

The adventures of Bert, Ralph, and Melissa Raccoon as they attempt to protect the Evergreen Forest from the greedy lumber baron Cyril Sneer.

Cyril Sneer/Snag	Michael Magee
Bert	Len Carlson
Cedric Sneer	Marvin Goldhar
Schaeffer	Carl Banas
Ralph	Bobby Dermer
Sophia/Melissa/Bron	Sharon Lewis
Dan the Forest Ranger	Murray Cruchley
Sam Sneer	Les Lyle

Narrator: Geoffrey Winter

Producer: Sheldon S. Wiseman

Racket Squad

Crime Drama; 30 min; Syn. 1950
CBS 6/7/51 to 9/28/53

Dramas that expose the confidence game and its organizers as seen through the investigations of Captain John Braddock of the San Francisco Racket Squad.

Capt. John Braddock	Reed Hadley

Narrator: Reed Hadley

Theme Song ("Parade of the Chessmen"): Joseph Mullendore

Producer: Hal Roach Jr., Carroll Chase

Radio Picture Show

Music Pilot; 60 min; Syn. 1/80

A proposed video radio program wherein the top names in music perform their hits.

Host: Tommy Goodwin

Announcer: Rhonda Cramer

Producer: John S. Brown, Kenny Green, Brian Smart

Rafferty

Drama; 60 min; CBS 9/5/77 to 11/28/77

The story of Sid Rafferty, a former Army doctor turned diagnostician both in private practice and as a part-time doctor at City General Hospital in Los Angeles.

Dr. Sid Rafferty	Patrick McGoohan
Dr. Daniel Gentry	John Getz
Nurse Vera Wales	Millie Slavin
Nurse Beryl Keynes	Joan Pringle
Nurse Koscinski	Eddie Benton

"Rafferty's Theme" Song by Leonard Rosenman

Producer: Jerry Thorpe, Norman S. Powell

The Rag Business

Comedy Pilot; 30 min; ABC 7/8/78

The antics of a group of dressmakers in the Los Angeles garment industry.

Mr. Fisher	Dick O'Neill
Connie	Conchata Ferrell
Jackie	Sarina Grant
Susan	Susan Lawrence
Coco	Jeannie Linero
Darlene	Anna L. Pagan
Alma	Sudie Bond
Rita	Peggy Pope

Producer: Aaron Ruben

Rags to Riches

Drama; 60 min; NBC 3/9/87 (Premiere)

In an attempt to refine his flamboyant, girl-chasing playboy image and impress clients, Nick Foley, the son of a brick layer who made millions with Foley's Frozen Foods, adopts six orphan girls (the residents of Room 204 of the Margaret Keating Home for Orphan Girls). Stories, set in Los Angeles in 1961 and featuring musical numbers, relate Nick's efforts to care for five* tough, street-wise and irresistible girls who have vowed to remain a family.

Nick Foley	Joseph Bologna
Diane (orphan)	Bridget Michele
Mickey (orphan)	Heidi Zeigler
Rose (orphan)	Kimiko Gelman
Marva (orphan)	Tisha Campbell
Patti (orphan)	Blanca DeGarr
Nina (orphan)	Heather McAdam
Clapper (Nick's butler)	Douglas Seale
Gloria Lang (Patti's mother)	Gina Hecht
Frankie (Nick's brother)	Joe Cortese
Billy (Nick's godson)	Richard Grieco

Producer: Len Hill, Bernie Kukoff, Stephen Cragg

*Nina was dropped after the first episode.

Rainbow Brite

Cartoon; 30 min; Syn. 4/86

Rainbow Brite, a young alien girl, is sent to a world of gloom and misery with orders to transform it into a land of beauty. As she begins her quest, she meets and befriends Twink, a resident, who tells her that his world is ruled by The Evil One, a being who enjoys misery. Stories relate Rainbow's efforts to defeat The Evil One and protect Rainbow Land from darkness and gloom.

Rainbow Brite	Bettina Bush
Twink	Pat Fraley
Starbright	Robbie Lee
The Evil One	Peter Cullen

Producer: Andy Heyward, Jean Chalopin

The Rainbow Girl

Comedy Pilot; 30 min; NBC 6/4/82

The story of Annie Jordan, a beautiful singer who appears as "The Rainbow Girl" on "The Miles Starling Family Dance Party," a local TV show on Channel 66 in New York City. Originally titled "The Ann Jillian Show."

Annie Jordan	Ann Jillian
Natalie Jordan	Candice Azzara
Irena Jordan	Rae Allen
Miles Starling	Cesar Romero
Armando	Michael Tucci
Sam	Robert Alan Browne
George	Dick Dean
Bert Connolly	Dallas Alinder
Ted Black	John McCook

Theme Vocal ("The Rainbow Girl"): Ann Jillian

Producer: Ernest Chambers

Ramar of the Jungle

Adventure; 30 min; Syn. 1952

Stories, some of which are set in Africa, others in India, relate the experiences of Dr. Thomas Reynolds, a research scientist who is known as Ramar (White Witch Doctor) by the natives.

Dr. Thomas Reynolds	Jon Hall
Prof. Howrad Ogden	Ray Montgomery

Producer: Rudolph Flothow, Leon Fromkess, Jon Hall, Harry Rothschild

Rambo

Cartoon; 30 min; Syn. 4/86

The series, based on the Sylvester Stallone character in the "First Blood" films, relates the exploits of Rambo, a fearless soldier of fortune who leads an undercover strike force against the evil General Warhawk and his sinister organization of evil (SAVAGE).

Rambo	Neil Ross
General Warhawk	Michael Ansara

Additional Voices: Alan Oppenheimer, Lennie Weinrib, Petter Cullen, Mona Marshall, Frank Welker, Robert Ito, Michael Bell, Russi Taylor

Producer: Joe Ruby, Ken Spears

Ranch Party

A syndicated (1957) program of country and western music with host Tex Ritter and regulars Tex Williams, Bonnie Guitar, Smiley Burnette, Johnny Cash, Bobby Helms, and Ray Price.

The Range Rider

Western; 30 min; Syn. 1951

The exploits of the Range Rider, and Dick West, his sidekick, daring defenders of justice during the early pioneering years of California.

Range Rider	Jock Mahoney
Dick West	Dick Jones

Producer: Armand Schaefer

Rango

Comedy; 30 min; ABC 1/13/67 to 6/25/67

The series, set at the Deep Wells Texas Ranger Station in Gopher Gulch, Texas, during the 1870s, relates the exploits of Rango, a fumbling Ranger who struggles to apprehend outlaws and glorify the dignity of the Texas Rangers.

Ranger Rango	Tim Conway
Pink Cloud	Guy Marks
Captain Horton	Norman Alden

Theme Vocal ("Rango"): Frankie Laine

Producer: Danny Thomas, Aaron Spelling

The Ransom Sherman Show

Variety; 30 min; NBC 7/3/50 to 8/25/50

A program of music and comedy with comedian Ransom Sherman, regulars Nancy Wright and Johnny Bradford, and the music of the Art Van Damme Quintet.

The Rat Patrol

Adventure; 30 min; ABC 9/12/66 to 9/16/68

The World War II exploits of the Rat Patrol, a squadron of four desert allies assigned to harass and demoralize Rommel's Afrika Korps.

Sgt. Sam Troy	Christopher George
Sgt. Jack Moffitt	Gary Raymond
Pvt. Tully Pettigrew	Justin Tarr
Pvt. Mark Hitchcock	Larry Casey
Hans Dietrich (German nemesis)	Hans Gudegast (Eric Braeden)

"The Rat Patrol Theme" by Dominic Frontiere

Producer: Tom Gries

Rawhide

Western; 60 min; CBS 1/1/59 to 1/5/66

Events in the lives of the men who risk their lives to drive cattle from Texas (San Antonio) to Kansas (Sedalia) during the rugged and lawless 1860s.

Gil Favor (trail boss)	Eric Fleming
Rowdy Yates (ramrod)	Clint Eastwood
Pete Nolan (scout)	Sheb Wooley
Wishbone (cook)	Paul Brinegar
Mushy Mushgrove (drover)	James Murdock
Clay Forrester (drover)	Charles Gray
Jim Quince (drover)	Steve Raines
Hey Soos (drover)	Robert Cabal
Joe Scarlett (drover)	Rocky Shahan
Simon Blake (drover)	Raymond St. Jacques
Ian Cabot (drover)	David Watson
Jed Colby (drover)	John Ireland
Pee Jay (drover)	L. Q. Jones
Yo Yo (drover)	Paul Comi
Teddy (drover)	John Erwin

Theme Vocal ("Rawhide"): Frankie Laine

Producer: Charles Warren, Bernard L. Kowalski, Bruce Geller, Endre Bohem, Vincent M. Fennelly

The Ray Anthony Show

Variety; 60 min; Syn. 1956
ABC 10/12/56 to 5/3/57

Music and songs with bandleader Ray Anthony and regulars Don Durant, Med Flory, Frank Leahy, the Brookends, the Four Freshmen, and the Belvadeers.

The Ray Anthony Show

Variety; 60 min; Syn. 1962

A program of music and songs.

Host: Ray Anthony

Regulars: Vikki Carr, Kellie Greene, Lisa Marne, The Bookends

Orchestra: Ray Anthony

Producer: Lawrence Riport

The Ray Bolger Show

See "Where's Raymond."

The Ray Bradbury Theatre

Anthology Pilot; 90 min; HBO 2/22/86

A proposed series of dramatizations based on stories by Ray Bradbury. The pilot presents three stories: "The Town Where No One Got Off" (with Jeff Goldblum as a man stalked by a stranger seeking to kill him); "The Screaming Woman" (Drew Barrymore as a girl who believes she hears a woman screaming from beneath the ground); and "Banshee" (with Peter O'Toole as an eccentric film director who believes he is haunted by a Banshee—the spirit of a woman who roams the night when someone is about to die).

Host: Ray Bradbury

Producer: Michael MacMillan, John Roth, Larry Wilcox, Ray Bradbury

The Ray Knight Revue

Variety; 30 min; ABC 5/15/49 to 8/25/49

Music and songs with bandleader Ray Knight.

Host: Ray Knight

Regulars: Phyllis Gehrig, Joan Fields, Jonathan Lucas, Don Weismuller, Harry Archer, Ernie Burtis, Tony Craig, Kaye Conner

Orchestra: Ray Knight

Producer: Michael Cramoy

The Ray Milland Show

Comedy; 30 min; CBS 9/16/54 to 9/30/55

The trials and tribulations of Ray McNutley, a drama professor at Comstock University, a coeducational college. A spin-off from "Meet Mr. McNutley."

Ray McNutley	Ray Milland
Peggy McNutley	Phyllis Avery
Dean Dodsworth	Lloyd Corrigan

Announcer: Del Sharbutt

Producer: Harry Tugend

The Ray Perkins Revue

Experimental; 30 min; NBC 6/22/39

Ray Perkins as the host of a program of music and songs with guests Fifi D'Orsay, Martha Graham, Paul and Eva Reyes, and the Rhumba Band. Produced by Edward Sobol.

The R.C.A. Show

Experimental; 2 hrs; NBC 11/25/48

An early test of a two-hour variety special with host Wendell Niles and guests Eddy Arnold, Betty Keane, Jane Pickens, Bill Robinson, Eve Young, and Helen Ryan. Music by Cleveland Aires and Walbert Brown.

The R.C.A. Show

Comedy-Variety; 30 min; NBC 11/23/51 to 8/2/54

The title for four programs starring two performers (Ezio Pinza and Dennis Day). From 11/23/51 to 4/4/52, Ezio portrayed a bachelor who, along with his guests, would entertain from his apartment. On 4/11/52, the format became that of an anthology wherein Ezio appeared in dramas with musical overtones. At first, the Dennis Day segment related the comic struggles of a singer (Dennis) who is nagged by his mother to leave "The Jack Benny Show" and find a better job. The revised format focused on the adventures of Dennis Day as a young bachelor struggling to make a name for himself in Hollywood. Sponsored by R.C.A.

Ezio Pinza	Himself
Dennis Day	Himself
Dennis's mother	Verna Felton
Kathy (Day's girlfriend, 1952)	Kathy Phillips
Lois (girlfriend, 1952–53)	Lois Butler
Peggy (girlfriend, 1953)	Barbara Ruick
Marian (girlfriend, 1954)	Carol Richard
Charley Weaver (janitor)	Cliff Arquette
Susan (Lois's sister)	Jeri Lou James
Hal (Day's friend)	Hal March
Lavinia (Charlie's girlfriend)	Ida Moore

Dancers: Tom and Jean Mahoney

Orchestra: Charles "Bud" Dante

Producer: Paul Henning, Joseph Stanley

Reach for the Stars

Game; 30 min; NBC 1/31/67 to 3/31/67

Bill Mazer as the host of a game wherein players perform stunts in return for prizes.

Ready and Willing

Comedy Pilot; 30 min; CBS 4/22/74

The comical exploits of two bumbling police detectives (Ready and Willing) and Pamela Stevens, a beautiful but dizzy criminologist who assists them.

Sgt. Joe Ready	Joe Flynn
Sgt. Herbert Willing	Jack Weston
Pamela Stevens	Melodie Johnson
Lt. Perkins	John Zaremba
Julia Prescott	Susan Saint James
Wilma O'Brien	Lola Albright
Mrs. Jonas	Kathleen Freeman

Producer: Jack Laird

Real George

Comedy Pilot; 30 min; NBC 7/24/56

The story of a trouble-prone salesman (George) who works for a boss (Tutwiler) who believes he is still a Marine drill sergeant.

George Gidley	George O'Hanlon
Janet	Gloria Henry
Mr. Tutwiler	Ray Collins

The Real Ghostbusters

Cartoon; 30 min; ABC 9/13/86 (Premiere)

The further exploits of Pete, Ray, Winston, and Egon, the Ghostbusters (of the 1984 movie) as they continue to battle unearthly phenomena.

Voices: Arsenio Hall, Maurice LaMarche, Lorenzo Music, Laura Summer, Frank Welker

Producer: Michael Gross, Joe Medjuck, Jean Chalopin, Andy Heyward

Real Kids

Human Interest Pilot; 60 min; NBC 3/1/81

A juvenile version of "Real People" that spotlights the usual and unusual abilities of children.

Hosts: Elizabeth Hoy, Peter Billingsley, Karissa Noel, Shawn Carson, Dale Pullman

Producer: George Schlatter, Sarah Purcell, Bob Wynn

Real Life Stories

Human Interest Pilot; 30 min; CBS 4/13/81 to 4/17/81

A five-episode pilot for a proposed daily series of dramas that examine crises that occur in real life families.

Hosts: Barbara Feldon, Tom Cottle

Producer: Kay Hoffman, Sandra Harmon

The Real McCoys

Comedy; 30 min; ABC 10/3/57 to 9/20/62
                            CBS 9/24/62 to 9/22/63

Events in the lives of the McCoys, a poor farm family newly relocated from Virginia to the San Fernando Valley: Grandpa Amos, a widower and head of the clan; Luke, his grandson; Kate, Luke's wife; and Hassie and Little Luke, Luke's sister and brother.

Amos McCoy	Walter Brennan
Luke McCoy	Richard Crenna
Kate McCoy	Kathleen Nolan
Hassie McCoy	Lydia Reed
Little Luke McCoy	Michael Winkleman
Pepino Garcia	Tony Martinez
George MacMichael	Andy Clyde
Flora MacMichael	Madge Blake
Mac Maginnis	Willard Waterman
Lela Maginnis	Shirley Mitchell
Louise Howard	Janet DeGore
Gregg Howard	Butch Patrick
Frank	John Qualen
Winifred Jordan	Joan Blondell
Rightly Ralph McCoy	Jack Oakie
Mrs. Jensen	Connie Gilchrist
Helga	Eva Norde
Hank Johnson	Lloyd Corrigan

Producer: Irving Pincus, Danny Thomas, Danny Arnold, Norman Pincus

The Real McKay

Variety; 15 min; CBS 4/6/51 to 6/7/51

Music and songs with host Jim McKay, regulars Peggy Ann Ellis and Mac Perrin, and the orchestra of Milt Green. Produced by Jim McKay.

Real People

Human Interest; 60 min; NBC 4/18/79 to 7/4/84

A magazine series that spotlights real but eccentric and unusual people.

Hosts: Sarah Purcell, Skip Stephenson, Fred Willard, Mark Russell, Bill Rafferty, Byron Allen, Peter Billingsley, Jimmy Breslin

Announcer: Jack Herrold

Producer: George Schlatter, Robert Long, Gary Necessary, Bob Wynn, John Barbour

The Real Tom Kennedy Show

Variety; 90 min; Syn. 1970

A program of music, comedy, and celebrity interviews.

Hosts: Tom Kennedy

Regulars: Kelly Garrett, John McCormick, Foster Brooks

Orchestra: Dave Pell

Producer: Roger E. Ailes

Really Weird Tales

Anthology; 30 min; HBO 10/4/86 to 10/25/86

Joe Flaherty as the host of a series of comical tales of people confronted by strange situations. Produced by Michael McMillan and Joe Flaherty. The theme vocal, "Weird Tales," by Fred Mollin.

Rear Guard

Comedy Pilot; 30 min; ABC 8/10/76

The World War II antics of an American Civil Defense volunteer group. Based on the British series, "Dad's Army."

Raskin	Lou Jacobi
Rosatti	Cliff Norton
Wayne	Eddie Foy Jr.
Crawford	John McCook
Muldoon	Arthur Peterson
Col. Walsh	James McCallion
Henderson	Dennis Kort
German Captain	Conrad Janis

Producer: Herman Rush, Arthur Julian

The Rebel

Western; 30 min; ABC 10/4/59 to 9/24/61

The exploits of Johnny Yuma, an embittered, leather-tough young Confederate who journeys west after the war to seek self-identity.

Johnny Yuma   Nick Adams

Theme Vocal ("The Rebel—Johnny Yuma"): Johnny Cash

Producer: Andrew J. Fenady

Note: While Johnny Cash is known to be the theme vocalist, it is virtually unknown that Elvis Presley recorded the theme song for the pilot (which, apparently the producers did not like, and they went with the Cash version).

Rebound

A filmed anthology of dramas broadcast first on ABC (2/8/52 to 5/30/52) then on DuMont (12/5/52 to 1/16/53). Produced by Basil Grillo.

The Rebus Game

Game; 30 min; ABC 3/29/65 to 9/24/65

One member of each two member team is given a secret phrase. This player must draw clues to its identity on a large board. The teammate who is first to identify the phrase scores one point. The team with the highest score wins.

Host: Jack Linkletter

Reckoning

A CBS series of repeat dramas from "Climax," "Pursuit," and "Studio One." Aired 7/11/59 to 9/26/59; 6/8/60 to 8/31/60; 6/26/63 to 9/18/63.

The Recovery Room

Comedy Pilot; 30 min; CBS 7/16/85

Hoping to escape the pressures of the medical profession, Kaye Brenner, an OR Nurse, and Steve Griffin, a first year resident, pool their resources and buy a bar/restaurant (which they name Kaye and Steve's Recovery Room) that caters to the doctors and nurses of the nearby Knickerbocker Hospital in Manhattan. The unsold series was to relate their attempts to make a success of their new business.

Kaye Brenner	Kelly Bishop
Steve Griffin	Mark Linn-Baker
Dr. Nina Farrell	J. Smith Cameron
Dr. Milt Sherman	Adam LeFevre
Jerry Himmel	Charles Kimbrough
Dr. Russell	Christopher Rich
Nurse Gail	Lynne Thigpen
Nurse Jill	Yeardly Smith
Mrs. Sriffin	Eileen Heckart

Producer: John Lollos, Steve Haft, Robert Ellison

The Red Buttons Show

Variety; Various (30 & 60 min);
    CBS 10/14/52 to 6/14/54
    NBC 10/1/54 to 5/27/55

The original format (CBS) features music, songs, and various comedy sketches. The revised NBC format relates the antics of Red Buttons as a trouble-prone TV comedian.

Red Buttons	Himself
Red's wife (CBS)	Dorothy Joliffe
Red's wife (NBC)	Phyllis Kirk
Network Vice Pres. (NBC)	Paul Lynde

Regulars: Beverly Dennis, Jean Carson, Jimmy Little, Sara Seeger, Ralph Stanley, Howard Smith, Johnny Birch, Allan Walker, Joe Silver, Betty Ann Grove, The Ho Ho Kids

Announcer: Harry Kramer, Nelson Case

Orchestra: Elliot Lawrence

Producer: Joe Kimmel, Ben Brady, Don Appel, Leo Morgan

Red Ryder

Western; 30 min; Syn. 1956

The exploits of Red Ryder and his Indian friend, Little Beaver, as they struggle to maintain law and order throughout the West of a century ago.

Red Ryder	Rocky Lane
Little Beaver	Louis Letteri
The Dutchess	Elizabeth Slifer

The Red Skelton Show

Variety; Various (30 and 60 min);
    NBC 9/30/51 to 6/12/53
    CBS 9/22/53 to 6/15/70

A weekly program of music, songs, and comedy sketches.

Host: Red Skelton

Regulars: Chanin Hale, Stanley Adams, Dorothy Lowe, Mike Wagner, Peggy Rea, Kathryn Card, Lester Matthews, Beverly Powers, Adam Kaufman, Ida Moe McKenzie, Lloyd Kino, Jan Davis, Helen Fuani, Billy Barty, Bob Duggan, Stuart

Lee, Linda Sue Risk, The Tom Hansen Dancers, The Alan Copeland Singers

Announcer: Art Gilmore

Orchestra: David Rose

Producer: Nat Perrin, Cecil Barker, Freeman Keyes, Ben Brady, Gerald Garner, Bill Hobin, Seymour Berns

The Red Skelton Show

Variety; 30 min; NBC 9/14/70 to 8/29/71

A revised version of the previous title; an additional series of music and comedy with comedian Red Skelton.

Host: Red Skelton

Regulars: Emmaline Henry, Chanin Hale, Jan Arvan, Brad Logan, Peggy Rea, Jackson Bostwick, The Burgundy Street Singers

Announcer: Art Gilmore

Orchestra: David Rose

Producer: Guy Della Cioppa, Gerald Gardner, Dee Caruso

The Redd Foxx Comedy Hour

Variety; 60 min; ABC 9/15/77 to 1/26/78

A series of comedy sketches that spotlights the comedic talents of Redd Foxx.

Host: Redd Foxx

Regulars: Deborah Pratt, Howard Smith, Slappy White, Murray Langston, Damita Jo Freeman, Bill Saluga, LaWanda Page, Walt Hanna, Dick Owens, Andrew Johnson

Announcer: Roger Carroll

Orchestra: Gerald Wilson

Producer: Allan Blye, Bob Einstein

The Redd Foxx Show

Comedy; 30 min; ABC 1/18/86 to 3/19/86

Original format: The efforts of Al Hughes, the cantankerous and widowed owner of a coffee shop and newsstand (Al's Grill) to care for Toni Rutledge, a very pretty 15-year-old girl and potential jailbird he takes under his wing when he learns that she was about to do time in the less-than-perfect juvenile detention system. The revised format follows Al's efforts to cope with a foster son (Brian), a money-hungry ex-wife (Felicia), and a beautiful new waitress (Jessica, who replaced Diana from the prior format).

Al Hughes	Redd Foxx
Diana Olms	Rosana DeSoto
Toni Rutledge	Pamela Segall
Rachel Adams	Lynne Moody
Sgt. Dwight Stryker	Barry Van Dyke
Felicia Clemmons	Beverly Todd
Jessica Houston	Vanessa Williams
Brian Lightfoot	SinBad
Darcie Dix	Ursaline Bryant
Jim-Jam Jarvis	Nathaniel Taylor
	Theodore Wilson
Duds	Iron Jaw Wilson

The Street Corner Singing Do-Wop Moving Company: Ron Jason, Phil Perry, Theo Forrest, Oren Waters

Theme Vocal ("Heart of the City"): Kool and the Gang

Producer: Rick Kellard, Stuart Sheslow, George Sunga

Redigo

Drama; 60 min; NBC 9/24/63 to 12/31/63

A spin-off from "Empire," which depicts Redigo's efforts to maintain his own vast cattle ranch in Mesa, New Mexico.

Jim Redigo	Richard Egan
Gerry (Gold Hotel manager)	Elena Verdugo
Linda Franks (ranch cook)	Mina Martinez
Mike (ranch hand)	Roger Davis
Frank (ranch hand)	Rudy Solari

Producer: Andy White, Howie Horwitz

The Reel Game

Game; 30 min; ABC 1/18/71 to 9/3/71

Three players compete in a game wherein they must wager on their ability to answer questions based on film clips. Correct answers add money; incorrect responses deduct the bet amount. The player with the highest cash score is the winner.

Host: Jack Barry

Announcer: Jack Clark

Producer: Kenneth Johnson

Reggie

Comedy; 30 min; ABC 8/2/83 to 9/1/83

The story of Reggie Potter, a 47-year-old executive of Fun Time Ice Cream Desserts, who confronts middle-age through Walter Mitty-like fantasies. Based on the British series, "The Fall and Rise of Reginald Perrin."

Reggie Potter	Richard Mulligan
Elizabeth Potter	Barbara Barrie
Linda Potter Lockett	Dianne Kay
Mark Potter	Timothy Busfield
Tom Lockett	Timothy Stack
Joan Reynolds	Jean Smart
C. J. Wilcox	Chip Zien

Theme Vocal ("The Real Me"): Richard Mulligan

Producer: Barbara Corday, Bernie Kukoff, Dinah Kirgo, Julie Kirgo

The Regis Philbin Show

A syndicated (1964) music and interview series with host Regis Philbin and the music of the Terry Gibbs Sextet.

The Regis Philbin Show

Variety; 30 min; NBC 11/30/81 to 4/9/82

Celebrity interviews, cooking, fashion, astrology, and other topics of interest.

Host: Regis Philbin

Hostess: Mary Hart

Producer: Fred Tatashore, E. V. DiMissa Jr.

Rehearsal Call

Variety; 15 min; ABC 3/20/49 to 4/24/49

Dee Parker as the host of a program of music, songs, and behind-the-scenes previews of TV programs. Music by the Leonard Stanley Trio and produced by Stanley Pival.

The Reluctant Dragon and Mr. Toad

Cartoon; 30 min; ABC 9/12/70 to 9/3/72

Segments: "The Reluctant Dragon" (the efforts of Sir Malcolm to protect Tobias, a 400-year-old dragon cursed to breathing fire, from a little girl who delights in teasing him); "Mr. Toad" (adventures of a carefree gadabout frog).

Voices: Paul Soles, Donna Miller, Carl Banas

Producer: Arthur Rankin Jr., Jules Bass

The Reluctant Spy

Anthology Pilot; 60 min; ABC 10/12/62

The pilot episode for an unsold and untitled series of dramas dealing with international intrigue. In the pilot, broadcast on "77 Sunset Strip," detective Stuart Bailey investigates a woman's claim that her husband was killed by foreign agents.

Stuart Bailey	Efrem Zimbalist Jr.
Lucy Norton	Randy Stuart
Hank Rush	Simon Scott
Foreka	Chana Eden
Valentin	Oscar Beregi

Producer: Fenton Earnshaw

Remington Steele

Crime Drama; 60 min; NBC 10/1/82 to 8/2/86

When Laura Holt, a beautiful young private detective begins her own business (Laura Holt Investigations), she soon discovers that no one is willing to hire a female detective. In an attempt to attract clients, Laura creates a mythical boss named Remington Steele, renames her company (Remington Steele Investigations), and suddenly business is booming. Shortly after, a mysterious man—the man with Remington's face—appears and cons Laura into making him her partner, the mysterious Remington Steele. The charming series combines humor and mystery as it details Laura and Remington's case investigations.

Laura Holt	Stephanie Zimbalist
Remington Steele	Pierce Brosnan
Murphy Michaels	James Read
Bernice Foxx	Janet DeMay
Mildred Krebs	Doris Roberts
Major Decoine*	Guy Boyd
Minor Decoine (his daughter)	Quinn Cummings
Daniel Chalmers (Steele's former cohort in crime)	Efrem Zimbalist Jr.
George E. Mulch (the "idea man")	Michael Constantine
Abigail (Laura's mother)	Beverly Garland
Frances (Laura's sister)	Maryedith Burrell
Fred (Laura's chauffeur)	Blake Clarke
Detective Jarvis	Gary Frank
Norman Keyes (insurance detective)	James Tolkan
Eva Wilson (agency plant lady)	Jennifer Tilly

Theme Song ("Remington's Theme"): Henry Mancini

Producer: Michael Gleason, Glenn Gordon Caron, Karen Arthur

*Decoine holds Laura and Steele responsible for the death of his wife. And now, with his daughter, he plans to even up the score.

Rendezvous

Drama; 30 min; ABC 2/13/52 to 3/5/52

The adventures of a mysterious woman, supposedly engaged in underground activities during World War II, and now the owner of the Chez Nikki Night Club in Paris, who helps people in trouble.

Woman	Ilona Massey
Newspaperman	David McKay

Music: Edward Vito

Rendezvous

The syndicated (1958) title for selected repeats of episodes from "Rheingold Theater." Hosted by Charles Drake and produced by Edwin Knopf.

Rendezvous with Adventure

Adventure; 30 min; Syn. 1963

Lee Green as the host of films that relate the hazardous expeditions of various explorers.

Rendezvous with Music

Variety; 30 min; NBC 7/11/50 to 8/8/50

A weekly program of music and songs.

Hostess: Carol Reed

Regulars: Rosemary Bangham, Mary Jane Boone, Andy McCann, Tommy Johnson, Teddy Katz, Don Gallagher

Music: The Tony DeSimone Trio

Renegade

Adventure Pilot; 60 min; NBC 12/27/60

The story, set in 1861, relates the adventures of Rory O'Neill and Burtram Smythe, two footlose, roguish adventurers who help people in trouble.

Rory O'Neill	Steve Cochran
Burtram Smythe	Richard Ney
Felicia Post	Constance Towers
H.P. Daggett	Jack Warden
Capt. Flood	Dayton Loomis
Mr. Wilson	Robert Brubaker

Producer: John Lee Mahin, Mark Rackin

The Renegades

Crime Drama; 60 min; ABC 3/4/83 to 4/8/83

In an attempt to get into places and do things professional cops can't, an L.A.P.D. lieutenant (Frank Marciano) recruits seven young gang leaders to form the Renegades, a special police squad of undercover agents. Stories, which update "The Mod Squad," relate the exploits of Bandit (Ace Gang), Tracy (Satin Doll Gang), Eagle (Chiefs Gang), Dancer (Bomber Gang), Dragon (Shanghai Shieks Gang), Gaucho (Wild Cats Gang), and J.T. (Romans Gang).

Bandit	Patrick Swayze
Tracy	Tracy Scoggins
	Cheryl Paris*
Eagle	Randy Brooks
Dancer	Robert Thaler
	Philip Casnoff*
Dragon	Brian Tochi
	Peter Kwong*
Gaucho	Fautso Bara
	Angel Granados Jr.*
J.T.	Paul Mones
Lt. Frank Marciano	James Luisi
Capt. Joseph Scanlon	Kurtwood Smith
Julie Robinson (corrections officer)	Kathryn Leigh Scott

Producer: Charles Gordon, Lawrence Gordon, Nicholas Corea

*TV Movie roles (8/11/82).

Renfrew of the Royal Mounted

Adventure; 30 min; Syn. 1953

The exploits of Douglas Renfrew, a Royal Canadian Mounted Policeman.

Douglas Renfrew	James Newell
Carol Girard	Louise Stanley
Constable Kelly	Dave O'Brien

Report to Murphy

Comedy; 30 min; CBS 4/5/82 to 5/31/82

The misadventures of Eddie Murphy, an idealistic parole officer with the Department of Correction and Rehabilitation, who believes in a psychological approach to dealing with his charges.

Eddie Murphy	Michael Keaton
Blanche Nesbitt	Olivia Cole
JoAnn Baker	Margot Rose
Charlie Dawson	Donnelly Rhodes
Lucy Webb	Donna Ponterotto
"Big" Walter Lewis	Ken Foree
Norm	Jack O'Leary
Vinnie	Jonathan Banks

Producer: Roger Gimbel, Harry Colomby

The Reporter

Drama; 60 min; CBS 9/25/64 to 12/25/64

The exploits of Danny Taylor, a reporter-columnist for the New York "Globe."

Danny Taylor	Harry Guardino
Lou Sheldon	Gary Merrill
Artie Burns	George O'Hanlon
Ike Dawson	Remo Pisani

Theme Song ("The Reporter"): Kenyon Hopkins

Producer: Keefe Brasselle, John Simon

Reporter Collins

See "Not for Publication."

Rescue 8

Drama; 30 min; Syn. 1958

The experiences of Wes Cameron and Skip Johnson, paramedics with the Rescue 8 Division of the L.A. County Fire Department.

Wes Cameron	Jim Davis
Skip Johnson	Lang Jeffries
Patty Johnson	Nancy Rennick
Susan Johnson	Mary K. Cleary
Chief	Tom McKee

Producer: Herbert B. Leonard

The Restless Gun

Western; 30 min; NBC 9/23/57 to 9/14/59
ABC 10/12/59 to 9/30/60

The exploits of Vint Bonner, a wandering ex-gunfighter (known as "The Six Gun") who helps people in trouble. See the following title also.

Vint Bonner	John Payne

Producer: John Payne, David Dortort

The Restless Gun

Western Pilot; 30 min; CBS 3/29/57

The pilot for the above series which, set in the 1800s, tells the story of an ex-gunfighter (Britt Ponset) who helps people in need. In the pilot, broadcast on "Schlitz Playhouse of Stars," Britt attempts to save an old friend from a ruthless killer.

Britt Ponset	John Payne
Dan Maler	William Hopper
Red Dawson	Andrew Duggan
Mary	Joyce Smight
Sandy	Michael Landon

Producer: Felix Jackson

The Return of Captain Nemo

Adventure; 60 min; CBS 3/8/78 to 3/22/78

While searching for Atlantis, the submarine Nautilus wedges itself under a coral reef. Unable to free the sub, its captain, Nemo, suspends himself in a crystalline chamber. One hundred years later (1978), during U.S. Navy war games, divers Franklin and Porter discover the Nautilus (set free by the game depth charges). Upon boarding the sub, they meet Nemo and learn his fate. Nemo is put in contact with Hamilton Miller, a Naval intelligence head, who agrees to repair Nemo's sub if he will perform certain missions for the government. Stories relate Nemo's adventures as he aids the government while seeking the lost Kingdom of Atlantis.

Captain Nemo	Jose Ferrer
Cmdr. Tom Franklin	Tom Hallick
Lt. Jim Porter	Burr DeBenning
Kate Melton	Lynda Day George
Prof. Waldo Cunningham	Burgess Meredith
Hamilton Miller	Warren Stevens

Producer: Irwin Allen

Return of the Saint

Adventure; 60 min; CBS 12/21/79 to 8/15/80

An updated version of "The Saint," which continues to depict the adventures of Simon Templar, a dashing, free-lance troubleshooter who helps people in distress.

Simon Templar	Ian Ogilvy

"The New Saint Theme" by Brian Dae

Producer: Robert S. Baker, Anthony Spinner

Creator: Leslie Charteris

Return to the Planet of the Apes

Cartoon; 30 min; NBC 9/6/75 to 9/4/76

While manning the NASA spacecraft Venture, three astronauts (Bill, Judy, and Jeff) penetrate a time vortex and are projected to Earth in the year 3979; a world that is ruled by intellectual apes. Stories relate the astronauts' adventures as they seek a way to return to the Earth of 1975.

Bill Hudson	Tom Williams
	Richard Blackburn
Judy Franklin	Claudette Nevins
Jeff Carter	Austin Stoker
Dr. Cornelius	Edwin Mills
Dr. Zira	Phillippa Harris
General Urko	Henry Corden

Producer: David DePatie, Friz Freleng

Revenge of the Gray Gang

Comedy-Drama Pilot; 60 min; NBC 10/20/81

The story of five retired senior citizens (Milo, Reuben, Daisy, Joe, and Walter) who ban together to battle crime.

Milo Hoots	Noah Beery Jr.
Reuben	Scatman Crothers
Daisy Duffy	Maxine Stuart
Joe Malcheski	Mike Mazurki
Walter Smith	Richard Whiting
Off. Francis Hoots	Pat McNamara
Theodore Koestler	Tony LaTorre
Millie Koestler	Peggy Pope
Jimmy Steinbrenner	Adrian Zmed
Charlene	Susan Niven

Theme Vocal ("Still Goin' Strong"): Scatman Crothers

Producer: David Gerber, Gary Nelson

Revlon Mirror Theatre

Anthology; 30 min; NBC 6/23/53 to 9/1/53
CBS 9/19/53 to 12/5/53

Live dramas, broadcast from New York, and sponsored by Revlon Cosmetics.

Hostess: Robin Chandler

The Revlon Revue

Variety; 60 min; CBS 1/28/60 to 6/16/60

A weekly series of variety programs tailored to the talents of its hosts, including Connie Francis, Mickey Rooney, Peggy Lee, Joey Forman, Jackie Cooper, Maurice Chevalier, and Dick Shawn. Sponsored by Revlon Cosmetics.

Commercial Spokespeople: Barbara Britton, Ralph Storey

Producer: Abe Burrows, Perry Lafferty

Rex Reed's Movie Guide

A syndicated (1980) series of film reviews coupled with celebrity interviews. Hosted by Rex Reed and produced by Mort Zimmerman.

Rheingold Theatre

Anthology; 30 min; Syn. 1955

Dramatic productions sponsored by Rheingold Beer and hosted by Henry Fonda and Douglas Fairbanks Jr.

Rhoda

Comedy; 30 min; CBS 9/9/74 to 12/9/78

A spin-off from "The Mary Tyler Moore Show." The original format relates events in the lives of Rhoda, a window dresser (owner of Windows By Rhoda) and her husband, Joe, the owner of the New York Wrecking Company. The revised format (two years after Rhoda and Joe's divorce), follows the romantic misadventures of Rhoda, now single, and a designer with the Doyle Costume Company.

Rhoda Morganstern	Valerie Harper
Brenda Morganstern	Julie Kavner
Joe Gerard	David Groh
Ida Morganstern	Nancy Walker
Martin Morganstern	Harold Gould
Carlton the	
Doorman (Voice)	Lorenzo Music
Mae	Cara Williams
Alice Barth	Candice Azzara
Justin Culp	Scoey Mitchlll
Sally Gallagher	Anne Meara
Nick Lobo	Richard Masur
Lenny Fielder	Wes Stern
Gary Levy	Ron Silver
Donny Gerard	Todd Turquand
	Shane Sinutko
Marian Gerard	Joan Van Ark
Jack Doyle	Kenneth McMillan
Benny Goodwin	Ray Buktenica
Tina Molinari	Nancy Lane

Johnny Venture	Michael DeLano
Myrna Morganstein	Barabra Sharma
Carlton's Mother	Ruth Gordon
Paul Gerard	Robert Alda
Ruth Gerard	Paula Victor
Mr. Pennick	Will MacKenzie

"Rhoda's Theme" Song by Billy Goldenberg

Producer: Charlotte Brown, James L. Brooks, Allan Burns

Rhyme and Reason

Game; 30 min; ABC 7/7/75 to 7/9/76

Two players write down a word that rhymes with the last word of a phrase that is read to them. One player chooses one celebrity (from six) who must make up a word to complete the phrase. If the celebrity uses the same word as the player, he scores two points; if the celebrity matches the opponent, the opponent scores one point. Three points are played per round and the first player to win two games receives $500.

Host: Bob Eubanks

Regulars: Nipsey Russell, Jaye P. Morgan, Conny Van Dyke, Charlie Brill, Pat Harrington Jr., Frank Gorshin, Jaime Farr

Announcer: Johnny Jacobs

Producer: Stephen Friedman, Walt Case

The Rich Little Show

Variety; 60 min; ABC 2/2/76 to 5/18/76

A weekly hour of music and comedy.

Host: Rich Little

Regulars: Julie McWhirter, Charlotte Rea, Joe Baker, R. G. Brown, Mel Bishop

Orchestra: Robert E. Hughes

Producer: Jerry Goldstein, Rich Eustis, Al Rogers

Rich Man, Poor Man

Drama; 60 min; ABC 9/21/76 to 3/8/77

The series, adapted from the 12 hour miniseries of the same title (2/1/76 to 3/22/76) continues to depict events in the life of Rudy

Jordache, now as a U.S. Senator. The miniseries, based on the Irwin Shaw novel, was a depiction of the changes in America from World War II through the mid-1960s, as seen through the experiences of the Jordache brothers: Rudy, the straight one who moves up the establishment ladder; and Tom, the troublemaker.

Rudy Jordache	Peter Strauss
Kate Jordache	Kay Lenz
Maggie Porter	Susan Sullivan
Ramona Scott	Penny Peyser
Wesley Jordache	Gregg Henry
Billy Abbott	James Carroll Jordan
Bill Falconetti	William Smith
Diane Porter	Kimberly Beck
Mr. Scott	John Anderson
Charles Estep	Peter Haskell
Claire Estep	Laraine Stephens
Rod Dwyer	Herb Jefferson Jr.
Marsh Goodwin	Van Johnson
Marie Falconetti	Dimitra Arliss
Phil Greenberg	Sorrell Booke
Annie Adams	Cassie Yates
Arthur Raymond	Peter Donat
Senator Paxton	Barry Sullivan
Ernest Dettmer	Nehemiah Persoff
Vickie St. John	Colleen Camp
Jake Logan	Richard X. Slattery
Tom Jordache	Nick Nolte*
Julie Prescott	Susan Blakely*
Axel Jordache	Edward Asner*
Mary Jordache	Dorothy McGuire*
Wesley Jordache	Willie Aames*
	Michael Morgan*
Duncan Calderwood	Ray Milland*
Virginia Calderwood	Kim Darby*
Teddy Boylan	Robert Reed*
Linda Quales	Lynda Day George*
Willie Abbott	Bill Bixby*

Producer: Michael Gleason, Jon Epstein

*Principal miniseries roles only.

The Richard Boone Show

Anthology; 60 min; NBC 9/24/63 to 9/15/64

Dramatic presentations featuring a regular cast of performers.

Host-Star: Richard Boone

Cast: Harry Morgan, Laura Devon, Robert Blake, Warren Stevens, Bethel Leslie, June Harding, Guy Stockwell, Lloyd Bochner,

Ford Rainey, and Suzanne Cupito (Morgan Brittany)

Theme Song: "How Soon" by Henry Mancini and Al Stillman

Producer: Mark Goodson, Bill Todman, Buck Houghton

Richard Diamond, Private Detective

Crime Drama; 30 min; CBS 7/1/57 to 9/23/57
CBS 12/25/59 to 1/25/60
NBC 2/15/59 to 1/25/60

The exploits of Richard Diamond, a private detective operating out of New York and later Hollywood. In the New York-based episodes, Diamond operates without police help and lets his life rest in the hands of a woman named Sam, a beautiful, sexy-voiced telephone operator who possesses the ability to sense danger and summon help. Sam, who operates from a small room in Manhattan, is never fully seen. She is situated in a dimly lit atmosphere that is designed to display her shapely figure. Also known as "Call Mr. D."

Richard Diamond	David Janssen
Sam	Mary Tyler Moore
	Roxanne Brooks
Karen Wells	Barbara Bain
Lt. McGough	Regis Toomey
Lt. Pete Kile	Russ Conway
Sgt. Alden	Richard Devon

"Richard Diamond" Theme Song by Pete Rugolo

The Richard Pryor Show

Variety; 60 min; NBC 9/13/77 to 10/20/77

Various comedy sketches that spotlight the comedic talents of Richard Pryor.

Host: Richard Pryor

Regulars: Paula Kelly, Charles Fleischer, Jeff Corey, Sam Laws, Jimmy Martinez, Juanita Moore, The Chuck Davis Dancers

Orchestra: Johnny Pate

Producer: Burt Sugarman, Rocco Urbisci

The Richard Simmons Show

Health; 30 min; Syn. 9/81

Richard Simmons as the host of an entertaining program of health advice, nutritional guidance, exercises, skits, and cooking. Produced by Woody and Nora Fraser. See also "Here's Richard."

Richard Simmons Slim Cooking

Health; 30 min; Syn. 9/87

Richard Simmons as the host of a program of dieting tips and low-calorie meal preparations. Produced by Bill Hillier and Ken Marangell.

Richie Brockelman, Private Eye

Crime Drama; 60 min; NBC 3/17/78 to 4/14/78

The exploits of Richie Brockelman, a 23-year-old who, despite scrapes with the law, is determined to become a private detective. A spin-off from "The Rockford Files."

Richie Brockelman	Dennis Dugan
Sharon Peterson	Barbara Bosson
Sgt. Ted	
Coopersmith	Robert Hogan
Richie's Mother	Helen Page Camp
Richie's Father	Norman Fell*
	John Randolph

Music: Mike Post, Pete Carpenter

Producer: Stephen J. Cannell, Steven Bochco

*TV Movie role (10/27/76).

The Richie Rich Show

Cartoon; 30 min; ABC 11/8/80 to 9/18/82

The adventures of Richie Rich, the world's wealthiest youngster.

Richie Rich	Sparky Marcus
George Rich	Stanley Jones
Richie's Mother	Joan Gerber
Dollar	Frank Welker
Gloria	Nancy Cartwright
Reggie Van Dough	Dick Beals
Freckles	Christian Hoff

Producer: William Hanna, Joseph Barbera

Riding for the Pony Express

Western Pilot; 60 min; CBS 9/3/80

The Old West adventures of Jed Beechum and Albie Foreman, riders for the Pony Express.

Jed Beechum	John Hammond
Albie Foreman	Harry Crosby
Irving G. Peacock	Victor French
Billy Bloss	Glenn Withrow
Willie Gomes	Richard Lineback
Nancy Durfee	Susan Myers

Producer: Terry Becker

Riding High

Comedy Pilot; 30 min; NBC 8/25/77

The story, set in Hollywood during the early 1930s, relates the misadventures of Lewis Tater, a fledging screenwriter, who takes a job as a stuntman with Tumbleweed Productions to make ends meet.

Lewis Tater	Charles Frank
Wendy Trout	Wendy Phillips
Howard Pike	Lonny Chapman
Bert Kessler	Allan Miller
Sid	Don Calfa
Lyle Montana	Allen Case
Wally	Bill Hart
Bear	Pat Cranshaw

Producer: Marc Merson

The Rifleman

Western; 30 min; ABC 9/30/58 to 7/1/63

The story of Lucas McCain, "The Rifleman" (the fastest man with a .44-40 hair-trigger rifle) and his young son Mark, ranchers struggling to maintain a small cattle spread in North Fork, New Mexico, during the late 1880s. See also "The Sharpshooter."

Lucas McCain	Chuck Connors
Mark McCain	Johnny Crawford
Marshal Micah Torrence	Paul Fix

Hattie Denton	Hope Summers
Millie Scott	Joan Taylor
Eddie Holstead	John Harmon
Lou Mallory	Patricia Blair
Nils Svenson	Joe Higgins
Sweeney	Bill Quinn
Dr. Jay Burrage	Edgar Buchanan
	Jack Kruschen
	Ralph Moody
Angus	Eddie Quillan
John Hamilton	Harlan Wade
Aggie Hamilton	Sarah Selby
Nancy Moore (original hotel owner; replaced by Eddie, then Lou)	Abby Dalton
Millie's niece Sally	Cheryl Holdridge
Eddie's Daughter Lillian	Gloria DeHaven

"The Rifleman Theme" by Herschel Burke Gilbert

Producer: Jules Levy, Arthur Gardner, Arnold Laven

Riker

Crime Drama; 60 min; CBS 3/14/81 to 4/11/81

The exploits of Frank Riker, a special undercover investigator for Bryce Landis, the Deputy District Attorney of San Francisco.

Frank Riker	Josh Taylor
Bryce Landis	Michael Shannon

Producer: Christopher Morgan, David Gerber

Rimfire

Western Pilot; 60 min; ABC 2/19/68

A proposed spin-off from "The Big Valley" which relates the exploits of Dave Barrett, sheriff of the ruthless gold mining town of Rimfire. In the pilot, Dave helps Jarrod Barkley protect a young Chinese couple from a ruthless businessman who is seeking their mine.

Dave Barrett	Van Williams
Daniel Barrett	John Daniels
Sidney Glover	Robert Middleton
Wong Lo	Mako
Ling	Lisa Lu
Judge Power	Alexander Lockwood
Jarrod Barkley	Richard Long

Producer: Jules Levy, Arthur Gardner, Arnold Laven

Rin Tin Tin

See "The Adventures of Rin Tin Tin."

Ripcord

Adventure; 30 min; Syn. 1961

The exploits of Jim Buckley and Ted McKeever, instructors for Ripcord, a sky-diving school.

Jim Buckley	Ken Curtis
Ted McKeever	Larry Pennell

Producer: Ivan Tors, Maurice Unger, Leon Benson

Ripley's Believe It or Not

Human Interest; 60 min; ABC 9/26/82 to 9/2/86

An exploration of the unique and bizarre throughout the world. Based on the 1918 syndicated newspaper column by Robert L. Ripley. See also "Believe It Or Not."

Host: Jack Palance

Co-Hostess: Holly Palance, Marie Osmond, Catherine Shirriff

Theme Music: Henry Mancini

Producer: Jack Haley Jr., Mel Stuart, Marshall Flaum

Riptide

Adventure; 30 min; Syn. 1965

The series, set in Bermuda, relates the adventures of Moss Andrews, captain of the charter boat service, Riptide, Inc.

Moss Andrews	Ty Hardin
His Secretary	Jacki Hickmont

Riptide

Adventure; 60 min; NBC 1/3/83 to 4/18/86
8/22/86 (1 episode)

The exploits of Nick Ryder and Cody Allen, struggling gumshoes who operate the Pier 56 Detective Agency (later, The Riptide Agency), in King Harbor (California), and Murray "The Boz" Bozinski, a bumbling electronics genius and former Army buddy they take on as a partner to salvage their floundering business.

Nick Ryder	Joe Penny
Cody Allen	Perry King
Murray Bozinski	Thom Bray
Mama Jo	Anne Francis
Lt. Ted Quinlan	Jack Ging
Lt. Joanna Parisi	June Chadwick
Straightaway	Gianni Russo
Mama Max	Marsha Warfield
Kirk Dooley	Ken Olandt
Melba (Boz's sister)	Geena Davis
Angelo (oceanographer)	Cesar Romero
Giovanna (Angelo's daughter)	Ava Lazar
Myron Bell (con artist)	Danny Wells
Tammy*	Marla Heasley
	Robin Evans
Debbie*	Ingrid Anderson
Kimba*	Karen Kopins
Bambi*	K. C. Winkler

Music: Mike Post, Pete Carpenter

Producer: Stephen J. Cannell, Frank Lupo, Jo Swerling Jr., Babs Greyhosky

*Members of Mama Jo's cruise ship, the "Contessa."

Rise and Shine

Comedy Pilot; 30 min; CBS 8/25/81

The misadventures of a group of students at Buckminster's Coed Boarding School.

Andy Cooper   Christopher Barnes
Richard Moore   Joey Green
Chris Dobbs   Jonah Pesner
Patsy D'Allisandro   Claudia Wells
Carla Franklin   DeaCarla Kilpatrick
Joel Beidermeyer   Scott Schutzman
Principal Moffett   Jayne Meadows
Coach Tillman   Art Metrano
Librarian Hope
  Kelly   Jeannie Fitzsimmons

Producer: Bill Persky, Sam Denoff

Risko

Crime Drama Pilot; 60 min; CBS 5/9/76

The story of Joe Risko, a street-wise ex-con who works as a legman for a lawyer (Allen Burnett).

Joe Risko   Gabriel Dell
Allen Burnett   Joel Fabiani
Sharon   Joyce DeWitt
Marie   Karen Machon
Pollack   Peter Haskell
Max   Norman Fell
Maggie   Hilary Thompson
Jenny   Barbara Sharma
Susan Grainger   Laraine Stephens

Producer: Larry White

Rita

Comedy Pilot; 30 min; CBS 8/13/86

The misadventures of Rita Barnes, a businesswoman who operates Rita's Toys from her Manhattan apartment.

Rita Barnes   Rita Moreno
Max Barnes
  (husband)   Barry Primus
Mandy Barnes
  (daughter)   April Lerman
Adrian Barnes
  (daughter)   Mollie Hall
Nicky Barnes (son)   Jeremy Scheim
Mrs. G
  (housekeeper) Ruth Jaroslow

Theme Vocal ("Theme from Rita"): Rita Moreno

Producer: Patricia Nardo, Gabriel Katzka

The Rita Moreno Show

Comedy Pilot; 30 min; CBS 5/2/78

The story of Marie Constanza, the owner of a hotel fraught with problems.

Marie Constanza   Rita Moreno
Leo   Victor Buono
Mr. Gladstone   Louis Nye
Carol Constanza   Kathy Bendett
Miss Forbush   Kit McDonough
Doris   Shirley Mitchell

Music: Peter Matz

Producer: Mark Rothman, Lowell Ganz

Rituals

Drama; 30 min; Syn. 9/84

The series, set in Winfield (Washington, D.C.) focuses on the lives of the students and faculty of an exclusive women's college.

Taylor Chapin   Jo Ann Pflug
                          Tina Louise
Carter Robertson   Monte Markham
Cheryl Lane   Sharon Farrell
Christina Robertson   Christine Jones
Noel Gallagher   Karen Kelly
Tracy   Julie Sommars
Marissa   Patti Davis
Diandra Santiago   Gina Gallego
Tom Gallagher   Kevin Blair
Logan Williams   George Lazenby
Eddie Gallagher   Greg Mullavey
Patrick Chapin   Dennis Patrick
Brady Chapin   Marc Poppel
Lacey Jarrett   Philece Sampler
Mike Gallagher   Kin Shriner
Dakota Lane   Claire Yarlett
Sara Gallagher   Lorrine Vozoff
Maddie Washington   Ketty Lester
Michele Davenport   Kelly Bennett
Katharine Vance   Patti Gilbert

Producer: Frank Koningsberg, Jorn Winther

Rivak, The Barbarian

Adventure Pilot; 60 min; NBC 10/4/60

The story, set in 3rd-century, B.C., relates the adventures of Rivak, a Celtic prince, during the Punic Wars between Carthage and Rome. Based on the novel by F. Van Wyck Mason and filmed on location in Italy. The pilot, which cost NBC $750,000 was for a projected series called "The Barbarians."

Rivak	Jack Palance
Princess Tiratha	Milly Vitale
Creoda	Melody O'Brien

Also: Richard Wyler, Guy Rolfe, Austin Willis

Producer: John Lee Mahin, Martin Rackin

Riverboat

Adventure; 60 min; NBC 9/1/59 to 1/16/61

The series, set along the Mississippi and Missouri rivers during the 1840s, relates the adventures of Grey Holden, captain of the riverboat "Enterprise," as he attempts to acquire freight and passengers and make the boat (which he won in a poker game) profitable.

Capt. Grey Holden	Darren McGavin
Ben Frazer	Burt Reynolds
Bill Blake	Noah Beery Jr.
Capt. Brad Turner	Dan Duryea
Jimmy "Chip" Kessler	Michael McGreevy
Joshua	Dick Wessell
Pickalong	John Mitchum
Terry Blake	Bart Patton

"The Riverboat Theme" by Elmer Bernstein

Producer: Jules Bricken, Richard H. Bartlett, Richard Lewis

Road of Life

Drama; 15 min; CBS 12/13/54 to 6/24/55

The dramatic story of Dr. Jim Brent and his wife, Jocelyn. Based on the radio series.

Jim Brent	Don McLaughlin
Jocelyn Brent	Virginia Dwyer
Malcolm Overton	Harry Holcombe
Sybil Overton	Barbara Becker
Conrad Overton	Charles Dingle
Aunt Reggie	Dorothy Sands

Narrator: Nelson Case

Producer: John Egan

The Road Runner Show

Cartoon; 30 min; ABC 9/11/71 to 9/2/72

The endless attempts of a hungry coyote (Wile E. Coyote) to catch himself a decent meal—a foxy Road Runner. Comprised of both theatrical and made-for-TV cartoons.

Voices: Mel Blanc

Producer: Leon Schlesinger

The Road to Reality

Drama; 30 min; ABC 10/17/60 to 3/31/61

The program dramatizes what happens at a group therapy session as seen through the eyes of Dr. Lewis and six patients who discuss their emotional problems.

Dr. Lewis	John Beal
Rosalind	Robin Howard
Vic	Robert Drew
Margaret	Eugenia Rawls
Joan	Judith Braun
Lee	James Dimitri
Chris	Kay Doubleday

Producer: Julia Bercovici

The Road West

Western; 60 min; NBC 9/12/66 to 9/4/67

The adventures of the homesteading Pride family as they struggle to begin new lives in Lawrence County, Kansas, during the 1860s.

Ben Pride	Barry Sullivan
Elizabeth Pride	Kathryn Hays
Tim Pride	Andrew Prine
Midge Pride	Brenda Lee
Chance Reynolds	Glenn Corbett
Chris "Kip" Pride	Kelly Corcoran
Thomas Jefferson Pride	Charles Seel

Producer: James McAdams

Roald Dahl's Tales of the Unexpected

See "Tales of the Unexpected."

Roar of the Rails

Drama; 15 min; CBS 10/26/48 to 12/12/49

The series dramatizes events in railroading history as told via narration over scenes of model railroads in action. Sponsored by A.C.

Gilbert Electric Trains. See also "Tales of the Red Caboose."

Hostess: Mimi Stangin

Narrator: Rusty Slocum

Producer: Raymond E. Nelson

Roaring Camp

Western Pilot; 60 min; ABC 9/4/66

The story of Cain, a gunslinger who joins a U.S. Marshal to help maintain the law in Roaring Camp, a California mining camp struck by gold fever.

Cain	Jim McMullan
Marshal Walker	Richard Bradford
Rachel	Katherine Justice
Angus	Ian Hendry
Mary	Bibi Osterwald
Brady	Mike Wagner

The Roaring 20s

Crime Drama; 60 min; ABC 10/15/60 to 9/2/62

The series, set in New York City during the 1920s, relates the exploits of Pat Garrison and Scott Norris, reporter-columnists for the "Record," and their sometimes assistant, Pinky Pinkham, a beautiful singer at the Charleston Club.

Pinky Pinkham	Dorothy Provine
Pat Garrison	Donald May
Scott Norris	Rex Reason
Chris Higbee	Gary Vinson
Jim Duke Williams	John Dehner
City Editor	
McDonald	Emile Meyer
Dixie	Carolyn Komant
Chauncey Kowalski	Wally Brown
Lt. Joe Switolski	Mike Road

Producer: William T. Orr, Tom McKnight, Barry Ingster, Jim Davis, Jerome Schermer

Dorothy's Musical Backing: Pinky and Her Playboys

Dorothy's Chorus Girls: And the Girls

The Robert Herridge Theatre

Anthology; 30 min; Syn. 1960

Dramas, hosted by Robert Herridge, that are based on stories by noted authors. Produced by Robert Herridge.

Robert Montgomery Presents

Anthology; 60 min; NBC 1/30/50 to 6/24/57

A series of quality dramatic productions sponsored by Lucky Strike Cigarettes and also known as "Robert Montgomery Presents Your Lucky Strike Theatre."

Host-Narrator: Robert Montgomery

Producer: Robert Montgomery, Samuel Chotzinoff

Robert Montgomery's Summer Stock

See "Montgomery's Summer Stock."

Robert Q's Matinee

Variety; 30 min; CBS 7/16/50 to 5/22/56

A program of music and songs.

Host: Robert Q. Lewis

Regulars: Jaye P. Morgan, Rosemary Clooney, Merv Griffin, Earl Wrightson, Jill Corey, Lois Hunt, Jan Ardan, Nat Cantor, Pat Lytell

Orchestra: Ray Bloch, George Wright

Producer: Lester Gottlieb, Rai Purdy

The Roberta Quinlan Show

Variety; 15 min; NBC 5/3/49 to 11/23/51

Singer Roberta Quinlan as host of a program of music and songs. Music by The Harry Clark Trio, The Tony Mottola Trio, and The Elliot Lawrence Orchestra. Announcing by Bob Stanton.

The Robbins Nest

Variety; 15 min; ABC 9/29/50 to 12/22/50

Comedy sketches that satirize various aspects of life.

Host: Fred Robbins

Regulars: Nat Cantor, Frank Gregory

Announcer: Cynthia Carlin

Producer: Theodore B. Sills

Robin's Nest

Comedy; 30 min; Syn. 8/83

The British series (a spin-off from "Man About the House") on which "Three's a Crowd" is based. When Robin Tripp becomes a qualified chef, he and his girlfriend, Victoria, move into an apartment above a defunct restaurant. Soon afterward, Robin rents the restaurant and turns it into a bistro called Robin's Nest. Stories relate Robin's efforts to make a success of his new business.

Robin Tripp	Richard O'Sullivan
Victoria Nicholls	Tessa Wyatt
James Nicholls (Victoria's father)	Tony Britton
Albert Riddle (Robin's dishwasher)	David Kelly
Marian Nicholls (James's ex-wife)	Honor Blackman

Producer: Peter Frazer-Jones

Robinson Crusoe

Adventure; 30 min; Syn. 1964

An adaptation of the Daniel Defoe novel about a shipwrecked young Englishman's attempts to survive on a deserted island from which there is no escape.

Robinson Crusoe	Robert Hoffman

Robotech

Cartoon; 30 min; Syn. 1985

The futuristic battle between Earth and the creatures of the planet Zantari as seen through the experiences of Rick Hunter, a member of the Earth organization, Veratech, and his assistant, Linay. (The title refers to the sophisticated robot technology used in the wars.)

Rick Hunter	Greg Snow
Linay	Reba West

Producer: Ahmel Agrama

Robotman

Cartoon Pilot; 30 min; Syn. 4/85

The adventures of Robotman, Stellar, and Oops, robots who need to be recharged regularly with human love, as they leave their mechanical world to help humans in trouble.

Voices: Gregg Berg, Karen Hartman, Adam Karl, Katie Leigh, Phil Proctor, Frank Welker

Producer: Jean Chalopin, Andy Heyward

A Rock and a Hard Place

Comedy Pilot; 30 min; NBC 3/8/81

The misadventures of Hunter Crockett, a dissatisfied Texas assembly line worker who retires to seek an easy life and easy money through imaginative money-making schemes.

Hunter Crockett	Jay Kerr
Sherri Crockett	Celia Weston
R. J. Taggart	Guich Koock
Bubba	Walt Hunter
Donna Jo	Joan Roberts
Len Hooker	Michael McManus
Larry	Ken Kimmons

Producer: Don Reo, Judith Allison

Rock Candy

Comedy; 30 min; Syn. 1/87

The story of Nickie and Shari Waverly, two beautiful sisters who are the lead singers for the rock group Rock Candy and the Jawbreakers.

Nickie Waverly	Audrey Landers
Shari Waverly	Judy Landers
Walter Waverly	Dick Van Patten
Violet	Marcia Wallace
Howard Brandon	Lyle Waggoner
Louis Kingsland	David L. Lander

Producer: Jerry Harrison, Ruth Landers

Rock Comedy

Variety Pilot; 60 min; Syn. 5/82

Sketches and blackouts coupled with performances by the top names in music. The pilot for "Laugh Trax."

Host: Jim Staahl

Regulars: Gail Matthius, Howie Mandell, Frank Welker, Lynne Stewart, Sean Morey

Guests: Linda Blair, Rita Coolidge, Billy Preston

Producer: Toby Martin, Carolyn Raskin

The Rock Follies

Drama; 60 min; PBS 3/5/77 to 3/10/77

A musical drama that follows the progress of "The Little Ladies," a three-girl British rock group, as they struggle to succeed in the music world. Produced in England.

Anna Wynd	Charlotte Cornwell
Nancy Cunard de Longchamps	Rula Lenska
Devonia Rhoades	Julia Covington
Derek Huggin (manager)	Emlyn Price

Producer: Andrew Brown

Rock-N-America

Variety; 60 min; Syn. 4/84

A weekly program of comedy sketches coupled with performances by rock personalities.

Hosts: Rick Ducommun, Frazer Smith, Russ Parr

Regulars: Jamie Alcroft, Russ Parr

Theme Music ("She Controls Me"): Strange Advance

Producer: Mark Levinson, Bob Hart, Bob Cambridge, Tony Quin

The Rock 'N' Roll Evening News

Magazine; 60 min; Syn. 9/86

Interviews, gossip, and behind-the-scenes reports regarding the world of music.

Host: Steve Kmetko

Field Reporters: Adrienne Meltzer, Eleanor Mondale, Marjorie Wallace, Andy Friendly

Producer: Andy Friendly

The Rock 'N' Roll Show

Magazine Pilot; 30 min; Syn. 7/82

A backstage look at the world of rock music via interviews and concert film footage.

Hosts: Carol Miller, Mark Goodman

Producer: Dennis Somach, Dave Nelson

Rock 'N' Roll Summer Action

Variety; 60 min; ABC 7/17/85 to 8/28/85

A blend of music and stand-up comedy from a beach party setting with host Christopher Atkins, the music of David Russo, and the announcing of Charlie O'Donnell. Produced by Dick Clark.

Rock 'N' Roll: The First 25 Years

Music Documentary; 60 min; Syn. 7/82

A six-part series that traces the history of rock and roll music through interviews, film clips, and live-on-tape performances.

Hosts: Patrick Simmons and Michael McDonald ("The Groups of Rock and Roll"), Tina Turner ("The Women of Rock and Roll"), Alice Cooper ("The Theatrics of Rock and Roll"), Toni Tennille, Daryl Dragon ("The Geography of Rock and Roll"), William "Smokey" Robinson ("The Idols of Rock and Roll"), Pat Boone ("The Birth of Rock and Roll")

Announcer-Narrator: Robert W. Morgan

Producer: Matthew Herman, Jerry Harrison

The Rock Rainbow

Drama Pilot; 60 min; ABC 7/15/78

The story of three young women (Jess, Lil, and Catherine) and their struggles to succeed as a rock group in the highly competitive music world. Based on the British series "The Rock Follies."

Jess	Ellen Greene	Jim Rockford	James Garner
Lil	Louisa Flaningam	Joseph "Rocky"	
Catherine	Susan Bigelow	Rockford	Noah Beery Jr.
Speed	John Shea		Robert Noah*
Mr. Malone	Robert Alda	Beth Davenport	Gretchen Corbett
Jim	Kenneth Tigar	Sgt. Dennis Becker	Joe Santos
David	Scott Porter	Angel Martin	Stuart Margolin
Mack	John Aprea	Peggy Becker	Pat Finley

Producer: Martin Starger, Diana Gould, Robert Scheerer

Rockabye the Infantry

Comedy Pilot; 30 min; Unaired; Produced in 1963

The misadventures of Gifford Tyler, a private with the 1st Battle Group, 317th Infantry of Camp Hayworth, as he attempts to run a business (Tyler Enterprises; which caters to the families of soldiers) and become a soldier.

Pvt. Gifford Tyler	Bobby Rydell
Col. Irwin Tyler	Fred Clark
Hortense Tyler	Nancy Carroll
Sgt. Frank Mahoney	William Bendix
Alice Mahoney	Florence Sundstrom
Connie Mahoney	Lynda Day
Max	Jan Conaway
Gen. Ingram	Roy Roberts
Dudley	Jimmy Bates

Theme Vocal ("Rockabye the Infantry"): Bobby Rydell

Producer: Harry Ackerman, Winston O'Keefe

The Rockford Files

Crime Drama; 60 min; NBC 9/13/74 to 7/25/80

The exploits of Jim Rockford, an ex-con turned private investigator (owner of the Rockford Detective Agency) as he attempts to solve criminal cases that are considered unsolvable and labelled inactive by police.

Megan Dougherty	Kathryn Harrold
Lance White	Tom Selleck
Rita Capkovic	Rita Moreno
Richie Brockelman	Dennis Dugan
John Cooper	Bo Hopkins
Capt. McEnroe	Jack Garner
Lt. Alex Deih	Tom Atkins
Lt. Chapman	James Luisi

Music: Mike Post, Pete Carpenter

Producer: Meta Rosenberg, Stephen J. Cannell, Juanita Bartlett

*TV movie role (3/27/74).

Rockhopper

Comedy Pilot; 30 min; CBS 7/9/85

The comical exploits of Nick Larabee, code name Rockhopper, a U.S. government secret agent for the National Security Agency (whose front is the Flightless Bird Society). (The Rockhopper is a penguin that hops around, like Nick.)

Nick Larabee	Parker Stevenson
Carl Seldon	Oliver Clark
Beth Johnson	Gina Hecht
Alice Selvy	Jessica Nelson
Mildred Voitlander	Pat Carroll
Joe Larabee	Robert Wuhl
Helen Larabee	Janis Paige
Bill Larabee	Fred Burrell
Sonia Petrova	Amy Yasbeck

Producer: Mitch Ackerman, Jeff Freilich, Karen Mack

Rocket Robin Hood

Cartoon; 30 min; Syn. 1967

The futuristic exploits of Robin Hood as he battles the forces of injustice in the year 3000. Produced by Steve Krantz.

Rocky and His Friends

Cartoon; 30 min; ABC 11/19/59 to 9/23/61

Segments: "Rocky & Bullwinkle" (adventures of Rocky the Flying Squirrel and his dim-witted friend, Bullwinkle J. Moose, as they battle the evil Boris Badenov); "Peabody's Improbable History" (Mr. Peabody the dog, and Sherman the boy travel back in time to help people); "Dudley Do-Right" (a dim-witted Mountie's efforts to apprehend the villainous Snidley Whiplash); "Fractured Fairy Tales," and "Aesop's Fables."

Rocky	June Foray
Bullwinkle	Bill Scott
Boris Badenov	Paul Frees
Natasha Fataly	June Foray
Aesop	Charlie Ruggles
Mr. Peabody	Bill Scott
Sherman	June Foray
Dudley Do-Right	Bill Scott
Nell Fenwick	June Foray
Snidley Whiplash	Hans Conried

Narrators: Paul Frees and William Conrad ("Rocky & Bullwinkle"); Edward Everett Horton ("Fractured Fairy Tales")

Producer: Jay Ward, Bill Scott

Rocky Jones, Space Ranger

Adventure; 30 min; Syn. 1954

The interplanetary exploits of Rocky Jones, chief of the Space Rangers, as he struggles to protect the planets of a united solar system from evil.

Rocky Jones	Richard Crane
Vena Ray	Sally Mansfield
Winky	Scott Beckett
	Bill Lechner
Bobby	Robert Lyden
Prof. Newton	Maurice Cass
Yarra	Dian Fauntelle
Biff	Jimmy Lydon
Clark	William Hudson

Producer: Roland Reed

Rocky King, Inside Detective

Crime Drama; 30 min; DuMont 1/14/50 to 12/26/54

The exploits of Rocky King, a plainclothes detective with the Homicide Division of the Manhattan 24th Precinct.

Rocky King	Roscoe Karns
Mabel King	Grace Carney
Sgt. Hart	Todd Karns
Sgt. Lane	Earl Hammond

Producer: Lawrence Menkin, Charles Spear, Jerry Layton

Rod Brown of the Rocket Rangers

Adventure; 30 min; CBS 4/18/53 to 5/29/54

The battle against interplanetary evil as seen through the exploits of Rod Brown, a member of the Rocket Rangers (22nd-century defense organization), as he explores the unknown realms of outer space.

Ranger Rod Brown	Cliff Robertson
Ranger Frank Boyle	Bruce Hall
Commander Swift	John Boruff
Ranger Wilbur Wormser	Jack Weston
Ranger	Shirley Standlee

Producer: John Haggott, William Dozier

Rod Serling's Night Gallery

See "Night Gallery."

Roger Doesn't Live Here Anymore

Comedy; 30 min; TEC 10/82 to 3/83

The tragic and humorous sides of divorce as seen through Roger Flower, an impoverished composer who divorces his acrimonious wife (Emma), for the arms of a flaky girlfriend (Rose) who prefers married men. The somewhat unusual British comedy, which also relates Roger's attempts to win back the affections of his children (Arabella and Charles), is presented like a play without a studio audience.

Roger Flower	Jonathan Pryce
Emma Flower	Diane Fletcher
Arabella Flower	Alice Berry
Charles Flower	Benjamin Taylor
Rose	Kate Fahy

Producer: Dennie Main Wilson

The Roger Miller Show

Variety; 30 min; NBC 9/12/66 to 1/3/67

A program of music and songs with singer Roger Miller, regulars Arthur Godfrey and the Doodletown Pipers, and the orchestra of Eddie Karam. Produced by Gary Smith and Dwight Hemion.

Roger Ramjet

Cartoon; 5 min; Syn. 1965

While scientist Roger Ramjet is experimenting, he discovers a power pill that endows him with the power of twenty atom bombs for twenty seconds. Stories relate his battle against evil.

Roger Ramjet   Gary Owens

The Rogues

Drama; 60 min; NBC 9/13/64 to 9/5/65

The activities of the Fleming-St. Clairs, a family of con artists who steal treasures from those who can afford to be robbed, or deserve to be.

Alec Fleming	David Niven
Marcel St. Clair	Charles Boyer
Tony Fleming	Gig Young
Timmy Fleming	Robert Coote
Margaret Fleming	Gladys Cooper
Insp. Briscoe	John Williams

"The Rogues Theme" by Nelson Riddle

Producer: Collier Young

Roll Out!

Comedy; 30 min; CBS 10/5/73 to 1/4/74

The World War II adventures of the 5050th Quartermaster Trucking Company of the U.S. Third Army's Red Ball Express, a mostly black-staffed company that delivers supplies to the front lines.

Cpl. Carter "Sweet" Williams	Stu Gilliam
Pvt. Jed Brooks	Hilly Hicks
Sgt. B. J. Bryant	Mel Stewart
	Richard Ward*
Capt. Rocco Calvelli	Val Bisoglio
Lt. Robert Chapman	Ed Begley Jr.
Capt. Henry Aldrich	Jimmy Lydon
Wheels Dawson	Garrett Morris
High Strung	Theodore Wilson
Phone Booth	Rod Gist
Sgt. Grease	Sam Laws
Madame Delacourt	Penny Santon
	Fifi D'Orsay*
Dominique Delacourt	Dana Brady

Producer: Gene Reynolds, Larry Gelbart, James Lydon

*Pilot episode roles (6/5/73).

The Rollergirls

Comedy; 30 min; NBC 4/24/78 to 5/10/78

The antics of the Pittsburgh Pitts, a five-woman roller derby team based in Pennsylvania.

Selma "Books" Cassidy	Joanna Cassidy
Mongo Sue Lampert	Rhonda Bates
Honey Bee Novack	Marcie Hanson
Shana "Pipeline" Akira	Marilyn Tokuda
J. B. Johnson	Candy Ann Brown
Don Mitchell (team owner)	Terry Kiser
Howard Divine (rink announcer)	James Murtaugh

"Rollergirls" Theme Vocal: Shari Saba

Producer: James Komack, Stan Cutler

Rollin' on the River

Variety; 30 min; Syn. 1971

Music, songs, and comedy set on the Mississippi River Boat, "River Queen." Also known as "Rollin' with Kenny Rogers and the First Edition."

Host: Kenny Rogers

Regulars: Mary Arnold, Mickey Jones, Kin Vassey, Terry Williams

Orchestra: Larry Cansler

Producer: Burt Rosen, David Winters

The Roman Holidays

Cartoon; 30 min; NBC 9/9/72 to 9/1/73

Twentieth-century life is depicted in ancient Rome (A.D. 63) where the adventures of Gus Holiday, an engineer for the Forum Construction Company, are depicted as he struggles to cope with the endless problems of a changing world.

Gus Holiday	Dave Willock
Laurie Holiday	Shirley Mitchell
Precocia Holiday	Pamelyn Ferdin
Happius "Happy" Holiday	Stanley Livingston
Mr. Evictus	Dom DeLuise
Mr. Tycoonius	Hal Smith
Groovia	Judy Strangis
Herman	Hal Peary
Henrietta	Janet Waldo
Brutus	Daws Butler

Producer: William Hanna, Joseph Barbera

Romance

Anthology; 30 min; CBS 11/3/49 to 12/29/49

A live series of dramas based on popular love stories. Produced by Robert Stevens.

Romance Theatre

Anthology; 30 min; Syn. 9/82

Louis Jourdan as the host of a daily series that dramatizes romance stories. Produced by Bill Glenn, Charlotte Savitz, and Ed Lammi.

Romper Room and Friends

Children; 30 min; Syn. 1981

Music, songs, games and related entertainment geared to pre-school children. The only syndicated version of a locally produced format that was first presented to stations in 1953.

Miss Molly	Molly McCloskey
Kimble/Up Up Do Bee/Paddington	Bruce Edward Hall
Bear	Candy Claster
Granny Cat	Molly McCloskey
Story Song Man	Carmine Ravosa

Producer: Sally Claster Gelbard, John Claster

Rona Barrett's Hollywood

A syndicated (1969) two-and-one-half minute filler program of Hollywood gossip with Rona Barrett.

The Rookies

Crime Drama; 60 min; ABC 9/11/72 to 6/15/76

The exploits of a group of rookie officers (Station Number 7 of the Southern California Police Department) as they attempt to implement a nonviolent approach to crime control.

Lt. Ed Ryker	Gerald S. O'Loughlin Darren McGavin*
Off. William Gillis	Michael Ontkean
Off. Terry Webster	Georg Stanford Brown
Off. Michael Danko	Sam Melville
Jill Danko	Kate Jackson Jennifer Billingsley*
Off. Chris Owens	Bruce Fairbairn
Police Radio Dispatcher	Darlyn Ann Lindley
Chris's Sister Kim	Season Hubley
Jill's Sister Amanda	Elinor Donahue
Jill's Niece Tori	Kamme Hartling

Producer: Aaron Spelling, Leonard Goldberg

*TV Movie roles (3/7/72).

Room For One More

Comedy; 30 min; ABC 1/27/62 to 9/22/62

Incidents in the lives of the Rose family: George, an engineer; his wife, Anna, and their children Laurie and Flip (natural), and Mary and Jeff (adopted).

George Rose	Andrew Duggan
Anna Rose	Peggy McCay
Laurie Rose	Carol Nicholsen
Flip Rose	Ronnie Dapo
Jeff Rose	Tim Rooney
Mary Rose	Anna Capri
Walter Burton	Jack Albertson
Ruth Burton	Maxine Stuart
Elsie	Sara Seeger

Producer: William T. Orr, Ed Jurist

Room 222

Comedy-Drama; 30 min; ABC 9/17/69 to 1/11/74

Life at integrated Walt Whitman High School in Los Angeles as seen through the eyes of Pete Dixon, a black American history teacher whose classes are held in Room 222.

Pete Dixon	Lloyd Haynes
Seymour Kaufman (principal)	Michael Constantine
Liz Macintyre	Denise Nicholas
Alice Johnson	Karen Valentine
Miss Evans	Hollis Irving
Miss Hogarth	Patsy Garrett
Miss Portnoy	Carol Worthington
Ken Dragon	Ivor Francis
Richie Lane*	Howard Rice
Jason Allen*	Heshimu
Bonnie*	Jane Actman
Helen Loomis*	Judy Strangis
Pamela*	Ta Tanisha
Larry*	Eric Laneuville
Bernie*	David Jolliffe
Laura*	Pamela Peters

Producer: William P. D'Angelo, Gene Reynolds

*Students; prior cast are teachers

Roomies

Comedy; 30 min; NBC 3/19/87 to 5/15/87

Seeking to better his life and acquire the college education he never achieved, twenty-year Marine veteran Nick Chase resigns and enters Saginaw University, where he becomes the roommate of Matthew Wiggins, a 14-year-old whiz kid interested in fish. Stories relate an odd couple's misadventures in college.

Nick Chase	Burt Young
Matthew Wiggins	Cory Haim
Jason (student)	Michael Horton
Sheldon (student)	Joshua Nelson
Elsa (student)	Bee Bee Smith
Kate Adler (teacher)	Jane Daly
Suzy (student)	Suzanne Blinkoff
Carl (student)	Sean Gregory Sullivan
Singing Freshmen	Michael Lesco
	Larry Wray
	Robert Reams

Producer: Chick Mitchell, Geoff Neigher, Sy Rosen

Roosevelt and Truman

Comedy Pilot; 30 min; CBS 4/29/77

The misadventures of Roosevelt and Truman, the trouble-prone owners of the R&T Bail Bond and Security Guard Agency.

Roosevelt	Art Evans
Truman	Philip Michael Thomas
Juanita	Ilka Payan
Richie	Richard Karron
Rev. Davis	Hank Rolike
Mrs. Tilsen	Minnie S. Lindsey
Quinn	Michael Keaton

Producer: Norman Steinberg

Rootie Kazootie

Children; 30 min; NBC 12/9/50 to 11/1/52
ABC 12/22/52 to 5/7/54

Music, songs, and puppet antics set against the background of the Rootie Kazootie Club.

Host: Todd Russell

Mr. Deetle Doodle	John Schoepperle John Lee
Voice of Rootie Kazootie	Naomi Lewis
Voice of Polka Dottie/El Squeako	Naomi Lewis
Voice of Gala Poochie Pup/ Nipper/Poison Zoomack	Frank Milano

Producer: Steve Carlin

The Roots of Rock 'N' Roll

Music Documentary; 60 min; Syn. 7/81

A six-part series that traces the history of rock and roll music from 1955 to 1981 through rare film clips, live interviews, and performances staged especially for the program.

Hosts: Frankie Avalon ("The Early Years, 1955–58"), Paul Anka ("The Teen Idol Years, 1959–63"), Neil Sedaka ("A Farewell to Innocence, 1963–66"), Rod Stewart ("The Psychedelic Years, 1967–70"), Elton John ("A Time of Change, 1971–75"), Michael McDonald and Patrick Simmons ("Every Which Way, 1976–81")

Narrator: David McQueen

Producer: Hal Cerra, Roy Nevins, Malcolm Gold

The Ropers

Comedy; 30 min; ABC 3/13/79 to 5/22/80

A spin-off from "Three's Company," but based on the British series "George and Mildred" (which see). Following the sale of his Santa Monica apartment house, Stanley Roper and his wife, Helen, move to the plush Royal Dale Condo Town House in Chevia Hills, California. Stories relate the Ropers efforts to become a part of their new social circle and find their long-sought life of peace and quiet.

Stanley Roper	Norman Fell
Helen Roper	Audra Lindley
Jeffrey P. Brookes III	Jeffrey Tambor
Anne Brookes	Patricia McCormack
David Brookes	Evan Cohan
Debbie Hopper	Lois Areno
Jenny Ballinger	Louise Vallance
Ethel Armbruster	Dena Dietrich
Hubert Armbruster	Rod Colbin
Helen's Mother	Lucille Benson
Hilda	Dulcie Pullman

Music: Joe Raposo

Producer: Don Nicholl, Michael Ross, Bernie West

Rose Petal Place

Cartoon Pilot; 30 min; Syn. 4/85

The story, set in Rose Petal Place, a magical land where beautiful flowers (who resemble girls) live, relates incidents in the lives of its residents, especially Rose Petal, the most beautiful of flowers, as she battles Nastina, an evil caterpillar who yearns to take over the garden.

Rose Petal	Marie Osmond
Nastina	Susan Blu
Violet	Marilyn Schreffler

Additional Voices: Renae Jacobs, Stacy McLaughlin, Frank Welker

Producer: Joe Ruby, Ken Spears

The Rosemary Clooney Show

Variety; 30 min; Syn. 1956

Music and songs with singer Rosemary Clooney, the Hi-Lo's and the orchestra of Nelson Riddle. Produced by Joseph Shibeman.

The Rosemary Clooney Show

Variety; 30 min; NBC 9/26/57 to 6/19/58

A weekly series of music and songs that is also known as "The Lux Show Starring Rosemary Clooney" (when sponsored by Lux detergent).

Hostess: Rosemary Clooney

Regulars: Paula Kelly and the Modernaires, The Jones Boys

Orchestra: Frank DeVol

Producer: Dick Darley, Joseph Shibeman

Rosenthal and Jones

Comedy Pilot; 30 min; CBS 4/11/75

The comic adventures of two retired widowers (Nate and Henry) who share a low-rent apartment as the only alternative to living a miserable existence with their grown children.

Nate Rosenthal	Ned Glass
Henry Jones	George Kirby
David Rosenthal	Jerry Fogel
Marge Rosenthal	Nedra Deen
Lucille Jones	Lucille Timberlake

Theme Vocal ("All Kinds of People"): Phyllis McGuire

Producer: Ira Barmak

Rosetti and Ryan

Crime Drama; 60 min; NBC 9/22/77 to 11/10/77

The exploits of Joseph Rosetti and Frank Ryan, free-wheeling, girl-chasing criminal attorneys based in Los Angeles.

Joseph Rosetti	Tony Roberts
Frank Ryan	Squire Fridell
Assistant D.A. Jessica Hornesby	Jane Elliot
Rocky (Joe's secretary)	Randi Oakes
Emma (Joe's receptionist)	Ruth Manning
Judge Marcus T. Block	Dick O'Neill
Judge Praetor Hardcastle	William Marshall
Rosa Rosetti (Joe's mother)	Penny Santon

Producer: Leonard B. Stern, Jerry Davis

The Rosey Grier Show

A syndicated (1969) program of music, talk, and interviews with host Rosey Grier.

The Rough Riders

Western; 30 min; ABC 10/2/58 to 9/24/59

Following the surrender at Appomattox, two Union officers (Flagg and Sinclair) and a Confederate lieutenant (Kirby) team, and journey West to begin new lives. Stories, set in various areas between the Great Smokies and the High Sierras, relate their adventures as they seek a place to call home.

Capt. Jim Flagg	Kent Taylor
Lt. Colin Kirby	Jan Merlin
Sgt. Buck Sinclair	Peter Whitney

Producer: ZIV-TV

Roughcuts

Variety Pilot; 30 min; Syn. 4/84

A potpourri of film footage, behind-the-scenes reports, outtakes, and celebrity profiles.

Host: Stuart Whitman

Music: Mike Post

Producer: John Joslyn, Doug Llewellyn

The Rounders

Comedy; 30 min; ABC 9/6/66 to 1/3/67

The saga of Ben Jones and Howdy Lewis, two dim-witted cowboys who work as hired hands for Jim Ed Love, the owner of the J.L. Cattle Ranch in Texas. Based on the feature film.

Jim Ed Love	Chill Wills
Howdy Lewis	Patrick Wayne
Ben Jones	Ron Hays
Sally (Ben's girlfriend)	Janis Hansen
Ada (Howdy's girlfriend)	Bobbi Jordan
Vince (Love's assistant)	J. Pat O'Malley
Shorty Davis (ranch hand)	Jason Wingreen

"The Rounders Theme" by Jeff Alexander

Producer: Burt Kennedy, Ed Adamson

The Rousters

Adventure; 60 min; NBC 10/1/83 to 7/21/84

The exploits of Wyatt Earp III, a descendant of the famous lawman, and a bouncer for the Sladetown Carnival; his bounty-hunting mother, Amanda; and his self-styled mechanical genius brother, Evan—the Rousters of the title.

Wyatt Earp III	Chad Everett
Amanda Earp	Maxine Stuart
Evan Earp	Jim Varney
Michael Earp	Timothy Gibbs
Cactus Jack Slade	Hoyt Axton
Ellen Slade	Mimi Rogers
Lt. Bart Aaronson	Ken Swofford
Rowena Slade	Ruta Lee

Theme Vocal ("Tough Enough"): Ronnie Milsap

Producer: Stephen J. Cannell, Jo Swerling Jr., Babs Greyhosky

Route 66

Adventure; 60 min; CBS 10/7/60 to 9/18/64

The exploits of Tod Stiles and Buzz Murdock, two young men who wander along the highway of Route 66, seeking work and eventually a place to settle down.

Tod Stiles	Martin Milner
Buzz Murdock	George Maharis
Linc Case (replaced Buzz)	Glenn Corbett

"Route 66" Theme Song by Nelson Riddle

Producer: Herbert B. Leonard, Jerry Thomas, Sam Manners

Rowan and Martin's Laugh-In

Variety Pilot; 60 min; NBC 9/9/67

The pilot for the series; an hour of satirical sketches.

Host: Dan Rowan and Dick Martin

Regulars: Barbara Feldon, Ken Berry, Pamela Austin, Judy Carne, Ruth Buzzi, Henry Gibson, Larry Hovis, Arte Johnson, Monty Landis, Jo Anne Worley

Producer: George Schlatter

Rowan and Martin's Laugh-In

Variety; 60 min; NBC 1/22/68 to 5/7/73

A satirization of the contemporary scene through music, song, dance, and comedy. Also known as "Laugh-In."

Hosts: Dan Rowan and Dick Martin

Regulars: Judy Carne, Goldie Hawn, Pamela Rogers, Teresa Graves, Arte Johnson, Jeremy Lloyd, Byron Gilliam, Dennis Allen, Eileen Brennan, Roddy Maude-Roxby, Barbara Sharma, Ann Elder, Richard Dawson, Harvey Jason, Jo Anne Worley, Alan Sues, Henry Gibson, Betty Ann Carr, Patty Deutsch, Sarah Kennedy, Donna Jean Young, Jud Strunk, Dave Madden, Ruth Buzzi, Lily Tomlin, Chelsea Brown, Larry Hovis, Nancy Phillips, Pigmeat Markham, Charlie Brill, Mitzi McCall, Willie Taylor, Muriel Landers, Moosie Drier, Janice Whitby, Rosetta Cox, Adele Yosioka, Kyra Carlton, Joy Robiero, Meredith Bernhardt

Announcer: Gary Owens

Orchestra: Ian Bernard

Producer: George Schlatter, Paul W. Keyes, Carolyn Raskin

The Rowan and Martin Report

Comedy Pilot; 30 min; ABC 11/5/75

A satirization of TV news shows and news reporters.

Anchorman: Dan Rowan and Dick Martin

Reporters: Judy Pace, Cyndi Haynie, Carolyn Calcote, Jim Connell, Robbie Rist, Dick Stewart, Ed Monaghan

Producer: Paul W. Keyes

The Rowan and Martin Show

Variety; 60 min; NBC 6/16/66 to 9/8/66

Music and comedy with comedians Rowan and Martin.

Hosts: Dan Rowan, Dick Martin

Regulars: Lainie Kazan, Frankie Randall, Judi Rolin, The Wisa D'Orso Dancers

Orchestra: Les Brown

Producer: Hal Kemp, Greg Garrison

The Rowdies

Comedy-Drama Pilot; 60 min; ABC 8/8/86

The exploits of Calvin T. "Rowdy" Harlan, the head of Harlan Home Security, a protection service whose officers deal their own brand of justice to evil doers.

Calvin T. Harlan	Pat Harrington Jr.
Rhonda Harlan	Connie Stevens
"Beef" McCullough	Dennis Burkley
George Modell	Sam Anderson
Bill Stokes	John Scott Clough
Irene "Patches" Brady	Kitty Moffat
Wilson Tarbuck	Tommy Swerdlow
Capt. John Jackson	Jonathan Banks
Calvin Harlan Jr.	Corey Feldman

Producer: Richard Chapman, Bill Dial

Roxie

Comedy; 30 min; CBS 4/1/87 to 4/8/87

The misadventures of Roxanne "Roxie" Brinkerhoff, the program director of WNYV-TV, Channel 66, in New York City, a financially troubled UHF station whose slogan is "Pictures That Fly Through the Air," as she struggles to "program average programs for the average viewer." Originally titled "Andrea Spinelli-Brinkerhoff."

Roxie Brinkerhoff	Andrea Martin
Marcie McKinley	Teresa Ganzel
Leon Buchannan	Jerry Stiller*
	Jack Riley
Michael Brinkerhoff	Mitchell Laurance
Vito	Ernie Sabella
Yetta	Deborah Lacey
Randy	Jerry Pavlon
Vito's Uncle Emilio	Ralph Manza

Producer: Allan Katz, Liz Sage, Bill Richmond

*Role in the unaired pilot version.

Roxy Page

Comedy Pilot; 30 min; NBC 9/6/76

The comic adventures of Roxy Hagopian, an ambitious young singer working as a page at the Roxy Theatre who is determined to make it to the Broadway stage.

Roxy Hagopian	Janice Lynde
Sylvia Hagopian	Leslie Ackerman
Anna Hagopian	Rhoda Gimignani
Alex Hagopian	Jeff Corey
Charlie Martin	Jim Catusi
Director	Ken Olfson

Producer: Don Kirshner, Allan Manings

The Roy Rogers and Dale Evans Show

Variety; 60 min; ABC 9/29/62 to 12/29/62

A weekly series of music and songs featuring country and western entertainers.

Hosts: Roy Rogers and Dale Evans

Regulars: Pat Brady, Kathy Taylor, Kirby Buchanon, The Sons of the Pioneers, and Roy and Dale's children (Dodie, Debbie, Dusty, and Sandy Rogers)

Orchestra: Ralph Carmichael

Producer: Ralph Wonders, Bob Henry

The Roy Rogers Show

Western; 30 min; CBS 10/4/51 to 9/19/64

A modern-era western that relates the adventures of Roy Rogers and Dale Evans, ranchers and owners of a diner, as they strive to maintain law and order.

Roy Rogers	Himself
Dale Evans	Herself
Pat Brady	Himself
Mayor Ralph Cotton	Harry Lauter
Sheriff Potter	Harry Harvey Sr.

Various Roles: Ruta Lee, Gloria Talbot, Denver Pyle, Minerva Urecal, Dub Taylor, Wally West, Troy Melton, Russ Scott

Regulars: The Sons of the Pioneers

Theme Vocal ("Happy Trails to You"): Roy Rogers, Dale Evans

Producer: Jack Lacey, Bob Henry, Roy Rogers, Leslie H. Martinson

Royal Canadian Mounted Police

Adventure; 30 min; Syn. 1960

The series, set in Shamattawa, Canada, relates the exploits of three Canadian Mounted

Policeman and the methods they use to battle crime.

Cpl. Jacques Gagnier	Gilles Pelletier
Constable Scott	John Perkins
Constable Mitchell	Don Francks

Royal Match

Comedy Pilot; 60 min; CBS 8/2/85

The story, set in the mythical kingdom of Crescenda, relates incidents in the lives of its royal family: Edmond, its king; Susan, his American wife; Estelle, his mother, the queen; and Duke Alford, his uncle.

King Edmond	John Moulder-Brown
Susan	Haviland Morris
Queen Estelle	Tammy Grimes
Duke Alford	Ian Abercrombie
Prime Minister	
Weyback	Clive Revill
Princess Katerina	Jean Smart
Butler Deevers	Ivor Barry
Becky Buxton	Leslie Ackerman

Producer: Leonard Goldberg, Deborah Aal, Michele Rappaport

Royal Playhouse

A DuMont series of retitled episode originally shown on "Fireside Theatre." The 52-episodes were broadcast from 4/12/51 to 7/12/51 and 4/3/52 to 6/26/52.

Royal Showcase

Variety; 30 min; Syn. 1952

George Abbott as the host of a show that spotlights an up and coming comic, movie figure, or recording personality. Music by Gordon Jenkins. Announcing by Ben Grauer.

Royce

Western Pilot; 60 min; CBS 5/21/76

The exploits of Royce, a strong, silent man who lived with the Commanche Indians and learned well how to deal with the harsh realities of 1870 frontier life.

Royce	Robert Forster
Susan Mabry	Maybeth Hurt
Heather Mabry	Terri Lynn Wood
Stephen Mabry	Moosie Drier
Blair Mabry	Michael Parks
White Bull	Eddie Little Sky

Producer: Jim Byrnes

The Rubber Gun Squad

Comedy Pilot; 30 min; NBC 9/1/77

The misadventures of two misfit policemen (Chopper and Eddie) working out of New York's Central Park precinct.

Chopper	Andy Romano
Eddie	Lenny Baker
Sgt. O'Leary	Tom Signorelli
Rosie	Betty Buckley
Jerome	Alan Weeks
Capt. Egan	Kenneth McMillan
Austin	Paul Jabara

Producer: Philip D'Antoni, Sonny Grosso

Rubik, The Amazing Cube

Cartoon; 30 min; ABC 9/10/83 to 9/1/84

The adventures of Rubik, the amazing puzzle cube, and its human friends, Lisa, Renaldo, and Carlos, as they battle evil. Based on the Rubik's Cube puzzle created by Enro Rubik.

Rubik	Ron Palillo

Additional Voices: Jennifer Ann Fajardo, Michael Bell, Angela Moya, Michael Saucedo

Producer: Joe Ruby, Ken Spears

The Ruff and Reddy Show

Cartoon; 30 min; NBC 12/14/57 to 9/26/64

Serial-like stories about the adventures of Ruff the cat and Reddy the dog.

Capt. Bob Cottle (host)	Bob Cottle
Voice of Ruff	Don Messick
Voice of Reddy	Daws Butler

Producer: Bob Cottle, William Hanna, Joseph Barbera

The Ruggles

Comedy; 30 min; ABC 11/3/49 to 6/19/52

A simplistic comedy series that relates the everyday events in the lives of the Ruggles family: Charlie, the father; his wife, Margaret; and their children Sharon, Chuck, Donna, and Donald.

Charlie Ruggles	Himself
Margaret Ruggles	Erin O'Brien Moore
Sharon Ruggles	Margaret Kerry
Donna Ruggles	Judy Nugent
Chuck Ruggles	Tommy Bernard
Donald Ruggles	Jimmy Hawkins

Producer: Bob Raisbeck

Run, Buddy, Run

Comedy; 30 min; CBS 9/12/66 to 1/2/67

In a cloudy steam room, mild-mannered accountant Buddy Overstreet overhears gangsters plotting the murder of "The Man in Chicago," and the mysterious words "Chicken Little." Buddy is spotted and chased by the hoods (who believe he is onto them) but escapes. Fearful that Buddy will talk, syndicate leader Devere orders Buddy's murder. Stories relate Buddy's efforts to escape capture and resolve the differences between himself and Mr. Devere.

Buddy Overstreet	Jack Sheldon
Mr. Devere	Bruce Gordon
Junior Devere	Jim Connell
Harry (hood)	Gregg Palmer
Wendell (hood)	Nicholas Georgiade
Miss Oglethorpe (Devere's secretary)	Jackie Joseph
Susan (Buddy's sister)	Laurel Goodwin

"Run, Buddy, Run Theme" by Jerry Fielding

Producer: David Susskind, Dan Melnick, Leonard B. Stern, Jack Elinson

Run For Your Life

Adventure; 60 min; NBC 9/13/65 to 9/11/68

When a medical report reveals that he is dying of incurable chronic myelocytic leukemia, attorney Paul Bryan decides to cram a lifetime of living into his remaining one or two years.

Stories relate his adventures as he involves himself in the problems of others. The pilot episode, "Rapture at Two-Forty," aired on "The Kraft Suspense Theatre" on 4/15/65.

Paul Bryan	Ben Gazzara
Doctor (in open)	John Hoyt

Producer: Roy Huggins, Jo Swerling Jr., Paul Freeman

Run Jack Run

Comedy Pilot; 30 min; NBC 7/20/70

During a retirement party for underworld figure Smiley John Grazioni, a girl, posing as a newspaper photographer, pays hotel waiters Chester and Jack $50 to take a picture of the gangster. When Chester presses the shutter button, a bullet is fired and wounds Smiley. The unsold series was to relate Chester and Jack's efforts to escape from Grazioi's hit men.

Jack Perry	Dave Astor
Chester Blinsol	Adam Keefe
Smiley John Grazioni	Robert Middleton
Lefty	Anthony Caruso
Girl	Marilyn Hanold

Run, Joe, Run

Adventure; 30 min; NBC 9/7/74 to 9/4/76

Falsely accused of attacking his master, an Army-trained German Shepherd (Joe) is declared a fugitive when he escapes before being destroyed. Stories relate the efforts of Joe's master (William Corey) to find Joe and clear his name. Second season stories relate Joe's adventures when he teams with a backpacker (Josh McCoy) traveling across the U.S.

Sgt. William Corey	Arch Whiting
Josh McCoy	Chad States
Joe	Heinrich of Midvale

Producer: William P. D'Angelo, Norm Prescott, Lou Scheimer

Runaround

Game; 30 min; NBC 9/9/72 to 9/1/73

A question is read and three possible answers appear on stage. Each of the nine children who compete chooses one answer. Correct players receive one token. The player with the most tokens is the winner and receives merchandise prizes.

Host: Paul Winchell (with dummy friends Jerry Mahoney and Knucklehead Smiff)

Announcer: Kenny Williams

Runaway with the Rich and Famous

Human Interest; 30 min; Syn. 2/87

A spin-off from "Lifestyles of the Rich and Famous" that travels to different world-wide locations to visit vacationing celebrities.

Host: Robin Leach

Narrator: David Perry

Theme Music ("Runaway"): Bill Conti

Producer: Robin Leach, Robert Hess

The Runaways

Drama; 60 min; NBC 5/29/79 to 9/4/79

A revised version of "Operation: Runaway," which relates the exploits of Steve Arizzio, a Los Angeles-based psychologist who specializes in tracking down runaways.

Steve Arizzio	Alan Feinstein
Karen Wingate	Karen Machon
Debbi Shaw	Patti Cohoon
Mark Johnson	Michael Biehn
Det. Hal Grady	James Callahan

Producer: William Robert Yates, Quinn Martin

The Russ Morgan Show

Variety; 60 min; CBS 7/7/56 to 9/1/56

Music and songs with bandleader Russ Morgan, vocalist Helen O'Connell, and announcer Hal Simms.

Russell

Drama Pilot; 30 min; Unaired; Produced in 1961

An authentic view of the Old West as seen through the eyes of Charles Russell, an artist, sculptor, writer, and cowboy who helps peo-

ple in trouble. The unsold series was to have been based on the paintings and sculptors Russell Created.

Charles M. Russell	Fess Parker
Bonnie	Beverly Garland
Windy	Jay C. Flippen
Tracey Blue	Paul Carr

Producer: Gordon Kay, Frank O'Connor

Ruth Lyons 50 Club

Women; 60 min; Syn. 1951

Music, songs, interviews, and household tips with hostess Ruth Lyons, regulars Dick Noel and Bill Thall, and the orchestra of Bert Farber. Produced by Gene Walz.

Ruthie on the Telephone

Comedy; 5 min; CBS 8/7/49 to 11/5/49

The story of a young lady (Ruthie) and her efforts to impress a man (Richard) she loves, but who wants nothing to do with her. The live program features one of the first uses of the split screen effect (via mirrors) to allow the viewer to see Ruthie in her home while she talks to Richard at the office.

Ruthie	Ruth Gilbert
Richard	Philip Reed

Producer: Goodman Ace

Rx for the Defense

Crime Drama Pilot; 60 min; ABC 4/15/73

The story of Zach Clinton, a doctor turned attorney who works for a firm that specializes in cases associated with the medical world.

Zach Clinton	Tim O'Connor
Laura Masters	Nancy Malone
Al Moore	Ronny Cox
Daniel Kemper	Fritz Weaver
Hilda Kemper	Kathryn Walker
D. A. Horn	Charles Durning
Dr. Packer	Kevin Conway

Producer: Herbert Brodkin

Ryan's Four

Drama; 60 min; ABC 4/5/83 to 4/27/83

The experiences of Thomas Ryan, the director of interns at Wilshire Memorial Hospital in Los Angeles.

Dr. Thomas Ryan	Tom Skerritt
Dr. Ingrid Sorenson	Lisa Eilbacher
Dr. Edward Gillian	Timothy Daly
Dr. Terry Wilson	Albert Hall
Dr Norman Rostov	Dirk Blocker
Dr. Morris Wilford	Nicholas Coster
Nurse Springfield	Helena Carroll
Nurse Florence	
Hudson	Hannah Hertelendy
Nurse Downey	Cheryl Francis
Nurse Rose	Lilyan Chauvan
Nurse Bonnie	Dorothy Meyer

Producer: Henry Winkler, David Victor

Saber of London

Crime Drama; 30 min; NBC 10/13/57 to 5/15/60

A revised version of "Mark Saber," which, set in England, relates the exploits of Mark Saber, a one-armed chief inspector of Scotland Yard.

Mark Saber	Donald Gray
Barney O'Keefe	Michael Balfour
Judy	Teresa Thorne
Stephanie Ames	Diane Decker
Peter Paulson	Neil McCallum
Insp. Parker	Colin Tapley
Bob Page	Robert Arden

Producer: J. Donald Wilson, Roland Reed, Edward J. and Harry Lee Danziger

Sable

Adventure; 60 min; ABC 11/7/87 to 1/2/88

The series, set in Chicago, relates the exploits of Nicholas Flemming, a children's book author ("The Adventures of B.B. Flynn") who battles evil as Jon Sable, a mysterious figure who helps people in trouble. Based on the comic strip, "Jon Sable, Freelance."

Nicholas Flemming/ Jon Sable	Lewis Van Bergen
Eden Kendall	Rene Russo
Cheesecake (Ernest Tyson)	Ken Page
Cynthia	Marge Kotlisky
Michele "Myke" Blackman	Holly Fulger

Producer: Dick Rosetti, Steve Feke

Sabrina, The Teenage Witch

Cartoon; 30 min; CBS 9/11/71 to 9/1/73

The misadventures of Sabrina, a high school student and apprentice witch whose efforts to perfect her craft cause problems for all concerned.

Sabrina	Jane Webb

Producer: Norm Prescott, Lou Scheimer

Safari

Adventure Pilot; 60 min; NBC 4/3/62

A proposed series based on "The African Queen" film. The story, set in a German occupied colony in Africa just before World War I, relates the adventures of Charlie Allnot, a gin-soaked riverboat captain, and Rosie Sayer, the missionary who tries to reform him. See also "The African Queen." Aired on "The Dick Powell Show."

Charlie Allnot	James Coburn
Rosie Sayer	Glynis Johns
Poke	Juan Hernandez
Capt. Kramer	Oscar Beregi
Mrs. Butterworth	Ellen Corby

Producer: Dick Powell

Sailor of Fortune

Adventure; 30 min; Syn. 1957

The exploits of Grant Mitchell, captain of an American motor freighter, as he roams the Mediterranean.

Grant Mitchell	Lorne Greene
His Assistant	Jack McGowran

Producer: Leon Fromkees

The Saint

Adventure; 60 min; Syn. 1963–1966
NBC 5/21/67 to 9/2/67
2/18/68 to 9/14/68
4/11/69 to 9/12/69

The exploits of Simon Templar, alias The Saint, a dashing, free-lance troubleshooter who helps people in distress. See also "Return of the Saint."

Simon Templar	Roger Moore
Claude Eustace Teal	Winsley Pithey
	Norman Pitt
	Ivor Dean

"The Saint" Theme Song: Leslie Charteris (also the series creator)

Producer: Robert S. Baker

St. Elsewhere

Drama; 60 min; NBC 10/26/82 (Premiere)

A realistic portrayal of the medical profession as seen through the experiences of the staff of St. Eligius Hospital in Boston. (Because of its understaffing and decrepit condition, it has become a dumping ground for patients with no place else to go and thus named St. Elsewhere.)

Dr. Mark Craig	William Daniels
Dr. Ben Samuels	David Birney
Dr. Annie Cavanero	Cynthia Sikes
Nurse Helen Rosenthal	Christina Pickles
Dr. Jack Morrison	David Morse
Dr. Peter White	Terence Knox
Dr. Victor Erlich	Ed Begley Jr.
Dr. V.J. Kochar	Kavi Raz
Dr. Hugh Beale	G.W. Bailey
Dr. Wayne Fiscus	Howie Mandel
Dr. Cathy Martin	Barbara Whinnery
Dr. Donald Westphall	Ed Flanders
Dr. Wendy Armstrong	Kim Miyori
Nurse Shirley Daniels	Ellen Bry
Orderly Luther Hawkins	Eric Laneuville
Dr. Philip Chandler	Denzel Washington
Dr. Daniel Auschlander	Norman Lloyd
Dr. Robert Caldwell	Mark Harmon

Nurse Lucy Papandrao	Jennifer Savidge
Nurse Sandy Burns	Jane Kaczmarek
Dr. Jacqueline Wade	Sagan Lewis
Dr. Mary Woodley	Karen Austin
Nurse Julie McPhail	Melinda Culea
Dr. Susan Birch	Jamie Rose
Orderly Sean Rooney	Lance Guest
Ellen Craig	Bonnie Bartlett
Deborah White	Karen Landry
Roberta Sloan	Jean Bruce Scott
Dr. Elliott Axelrod	Stephen Furst
Katherine Auschlander	Jane Wyatt
Clancy Williams	Helen Hunt
Dr. Roxanne Turner	Alfre Woodard
Nurse Peggy Shotwell	Saundra Sharpe
Nurse Lynn Thornton	Mary Margaret Lewis
Paramedic Faith Yee	Christine Kukubo
Dr. Simon Weiss	Philip Sterling
Orderly Warren Coolidge	Byron Stewart

"St. Elsewhere" Theme Song: Dave Grusin

Producer: Bruce Paltrow, Mark Tinker, Joshua Brand, John Falsey

Saint Peter

Comedy Pilot; 30 min; NBC 3/8/81

The story of Father Peter Matthews, a young Episcopalian priest, as he begins his duties at the 4th Street Church in Manhattan.

Father Peter Matthews	Fred McCarren
Sheila Haynes	Susan Blanchard
Max	Lou Jacobi
Hank Chin	Benson Fong
Martha Chin	Beulah Quo
Cynthia Kreole	Clarice Stellar
Mrs. Grueneuv	Pearl Shear

Producer: Reinhold Weege

Saints and Sinners

Drama; 60 min; NBC 9/18/62 to 1/28/63

A behind-the-scenes look at the work of newspaper men and women as seen through the experiences of Nick Alexander, a reporter for the New York "Record" (later, the "Bulletin"). See also "Savage Sunday."

Nick Alexander	Nick Adams
Mark Grainger	John Larkin
Dave Toback	Robert F. Simon
Liz Hogan	Barbara Rush
Polly Holleran	Sharon Farrell
Klugie	Richard Erdman

Producer: Marc Daniels

Sale of the Century

Game; 30 min; NBC 9/29/69 to 7/13/73

Object: For players to answer general knowledge questions and build a bank account to purchase expensive merchandise items at bargain prices. Correct answers add $5 to a player's starting cash of $25; incorrect answers deduct $5.

Host: Jack Kelly, Joe Garagiola

Announcer: Bill Wendell

Producer: Al Howard

Sale of the Century

Game; 30 min; NBC 1/3/83 (Premiere)
Syn. 2/85

Three contestants compete, each of whom receives $25 starting money. A rapid-fire question-and-answer round is played wherein players win $5 per correct response, but lose that amount if they incorrectly answer. The person with the highest cash score is the winner and receives the chance to buy expensive prizes at a fraction of their cost—but only with money earned on the program.

Host: Jim Perry

Co-Host: Sally Julian, Summer Bartholomew

Announcer: Jay Stewart

Producer: Al Howard, Robert Noah

Sally

Comedy; 30 min; NBC 9/15/57 to 2/9/58

The global adventures of Myrtle Banford, a rich, elderly widow (part owner of the Banford and Bascomb Dept. Store), and Sally Truesdale, her young traveling companion. See the following title also.

Sally Truesdale	Joan Caulfield
Myrtle Banford	Marion Lorne

Producer: Frank Ross

Sally

Comedy; 30 min; NBC 2/16/58 to 3/30/58

A revised version of the prior title. Following her duties as Mrs. Banford's traveling companion, Sally begins work as a salesgirl in the Banford-Bleacher Dept. Store. Stories relate Sally's experiences.

Sally Truesdale	Joan Caulfield
Myrtle Banford	Marion Lorne
Bascomb Bleacher Sr.	Gale Gordon
Jim Kendall	Johnny Desmond
Junior Bleacher	Arte Johnson

Producer: Frank Ross

Sally and Sam

Comedy Pilot; 30 min; CBS 7/5/65

Sally Marten, a beautiful young career woman, and Sam Cody, a medical student at Johns Hopkins, are strangers who meet and fall in love during a weekend in Manhattan. The unsold series was to relate their romantic misadventures.

Sally Marten	Cynthia Pepper
Sam Cody	Gary Lockwood
Glen	Bernie Kopell
Nurse	Phyllis Douglas
Joy	Nancy Jeris
Phil	Jay Strong

Producer: Hal Kanter

The Sally Jessy Raphael Show

A syndicated (1985) topical-issues discussion series with hostess Sally Jessy Raphael.

Salt and Pepe

Comedy Pilot; 30 min; CBS 4/18/75

The misadventures of a prejudiced black businessman (Salt) and his son-in-law and employee, Pepe, a Puerto Rican.

Jeremiah Salt	Mel Stewart
Pepe	Frank LaLoggia
Abigail Salt	Dorothy Meyer
Yolanda Salt	Diane Sommerfield
Millie	Clarice Taylor
Nadine	Sharon Brown

Producer: E. Duke Vincent

Salty

Adventure; 30 min; Syn. 9/74

When their parents are killed during a hurricane in the Bahamas, Taylor and his brother Tim are unofficially adopted by Clancy Ames, their rescuer, a retired lawyer who runs the Cove Marina in Nassau. Stories relate their experiences, and the adventures shared by Tim and his pet sea lion, Salty.

Clancy Ames	Julius Harris
Taylor Reed	Mark Slade
Tim Reed	Johnny Doran
Rod Porterfield	Vincent Dale

Producer: Kobi Jaeger

Salvage 1

Adventure; 60 min; ABC 1/29/79 to 11/11/79

The exploits of Harry Broderick, owner of the Jettison Salvage Company, as he and his partners, Melanie and Skip, use a homemade rocketship ("The Vulture") to recover the unrecoverable.

Harry Broderick	Andy Griffith
Melanie Solzar	Trish Stewart
Addison "Skip" Carmichael	Joel Higgins
Mack	J. Jay Saunders
Jack Klinger	Richard Jaeckel
Michele Ryan	Heather McAdam

Producer: Harve Bennett, Harris Katleman

Sam

Crime Drama; 30 min; CBS 3/14/78 to 4/18/78

The story of Mike Breen, a Los Angeles police officer, and Sam, his partner, a specially trained Labrador Retriever; an experimental man-and-dog patrol car unit designated Two-Henry-Six.

Off. Mike Breen	Mark Harmon
Capt. Tom Clagett	Len Wayland
Capt. Gene Cody	Gary Crosby

Producer: Jack Webb, Paul Donnelly

Sam

Comedy Pilot; 30 min; ABC 6/11/85

The misadventures of Samantha "Sam" Flynn, a beautiful working mother (managing editor of the Raleigh Publishing Company) as she attempts to cope with life at work and at home.

Samantha Flynn	Loretta Swit
Megan Flynn	Keri Houlihan
George Kosovich	Barney Martin
Valerie	Kit McDonough
Susan	Cathy Silvers
Barry Suckerman	Stephen Godwin
Mrs. Petrovitch	Dorothy Neuman

Producer: Allan Katz

Sam Benedict

Drama; 60 min; NBC 9/15/62 to 9/7/63

The story of Sam Benedict, a defense attorney working out of San Francisco. See also "333 Montgomery."

Sam Benedict	Edmond O'Brien
Hank Tabor	Richard Rust
Trudy Wagner	Joan Tompkins

"Sam Benedict" Theme: Nelson Riddle

Producer: E. Jack Newman

Sam Hill

Western Pilot; 60 min; NBC 6/3/61

The adventures of Sam Hill, a traveling blacksmith who roams throughout the West of 1864 with only a knife and a hammer. Aired on "Bonanza."

Sam Hill	Claude Akins
John Henry Hill	Edgar Buchanan
Billy Joe	Robert Ridgely
Colonel Tyson	Ford Rainey
Saloon Girl	Caroline Richter

Producer: David Dortort

The Sam Levenson Show

Comedy; 30 min; CBS 1/27/51 to 6/10/52

The humor of school teacher-turned-TV star Sam Levenson coupled with a discussion segment wherein celebrities appear with their children to discuss their problems.

Host: Sam Levenson

Orchestra: Henry Sylvern

Producer: Irving Mansfield

Sam Penny and Associate

Crime Drama Pilot; 60 min; CBS 11/14/85

The exploits of Sam Penny, a hard-boiled private detective one step away from bankruptcy, and his beautiful assistant, Elizabeth Charles. Aired on "Simon and Simon."

Sam Penny	Robert Lansing
Elizabeth Charles	Caren Kaye
Ron Lottick	Vincent Baggetta
Warden Latham	Barry Jenner
Roger Brunswick	James Widdoes
Toni Myers	Virginia Vincent

Producer: John G. Stephens, Richard Chapman

Sammy and Company

Variety; 90 min; Syn. 9/75

Sammy Davis Jr. as the host of a weekly program of music and comedy with regulars Avery Schreiber, Joyce Jillson, Johnny Brown, and Kay Dingle. With the orchestra of George Rhodes and the announcing of William B. Williams. Produced by Pierre Cossette.

The Sammy Davis Jr. Show

Variety; 60 min; NBC 1/7/66 to 4/22/66

Sammy Davis Jr. as the host of a weekly program of music and songs. With the Lester Wilson Dancers and the orchestra of George Rhodes. Produced by Joe Hamilton.

The Sammy Kaye Show

See "So You Want to Lead a Band."

Sammy Kaye's Music from Manhattan

Variety; 30 min; ABC 9/20/58 to 6/13/59

A program of music and songs with bandleader Sammy Kaye.

Host: Sammy Kaye

Regulars: Lynn Roberts, Janice Jones, Jack Jennings, Harry Reser, Joe Mack, Larry O'Brien, Ray Michaels, Larry Ellis, Toby Wright, J. Blasingame Bond, Charles Roder, The Dixieland Quartet, The Kaydettes

Orchestra: Sammy Kaye

Producer: Coby Ruskin

Sampson and Goliath

Cartoon; 30 min; NBC 9/9/67 to 9/7/68

A battle against crime as seen through the exploits of a young boy who possesses the ability to become the mighty Sampson and transform his dog into the lion Goliath.

Sampson	Tim Matthieson
	(Tim Matheson)

Producer: William Hanna, Joseph Barbera

San Francisco Beat

The syndicated title for "Line-Up."

San Francisco International Airport

Drama; 60 min; NBC 10/28/70 to 8/25/71

A "Four-In-One" series that presents a behind-the-scenes look at the problems that plague a large airport.

Jim Conrad	Lloyd Bridges
	Pernell Roberts*
Bob Hatten	Clu Gulager
Suzie Conrad	Barbara Sigel
June	Barbara Werle

Producer: Richard Irving

*TV Movie role (9/29/70)

The San Pedro Beach Bums

Comedy-Drama; 60 min; ABC 9/19/77 to 12/19/77

The misadventures of five knockabout young men (Buddy, Boychick, Dancer, Stuf, and Moose) who live on "Our Boat," an old fishing boat docked in San Pedro, California.

Buddy Binder	Christopher Murney
Boychick	Chris DeRose
	Jeff Druce*
Edward "Dancer" McClory	John Mark Robinson
Anthony "Stuf" Danelli	Stuart Pankin
Moose Maslosky	Darryl McCullough
Suzy Camelli	Susan Mullen
Louise	Louise Hoven
Marge	Lisa Reeves
Julie	Nancy Morgan
Ralph	Christoff St. John

Producer: Aaron Spelling, Douglas S. Cramer, E. Duke Vincent

*TV Movie roles ("The San Pedro Bums" 5/13/77).

Sandy Dreams

Children; 30 min; ABC 10/7/50 to 12/2/50

A live series that transports viewers to the dream world of an 8-year-old girl named Sandy. As Sandy drifts off to sleep, her dreams of a magical land where children sing, dance, and perform in sketches are shared with the audience. Originally a local Los Angeles show (1948) and the first scripted program on the West Coast.

Sandy	Rose Marie Iannone
Candy	Patty Iannone
Stuffy	Stuffy Singer
Alicia	Alice Adams

Producer: Klaus Landsberg, Bud Stefan, Gladys Ruben

The Sandy Duncan Show

Comedy; 30 min; CBS 9/17/72 to 12/31/72

A spin-off from "Funny Face" that relates the comic adventures of Sandy Stockton as a student teacher at U.C.L.A. and a part-time secretary at the Quinn and Cohen Advertising Agency.

Sandy Stockton	Sandy Duncan
Bert Quinn	Tom Bosley
Kay Fox	Marian Mercer
Hilary	Pamela Zarit
Leonard Cohen	Alfie Wise
Ben Hamilton	Eric Christmas

Music: Patrick Williams

Producer: Arne Sultan

Sandy Strong

Children; 15 min; ABC 9/25/50 to 3/23/51

A marionette series about the adventures of Sandy Strong.

Host (Mr. Mack)	Ray Suber
	Forrest Lewis

Producer: George Anderson

Sanford

Comedy; 30 min; NBC 3/15/80 to 9/10/80
                         1/9/81 to 7/10/81

A continuation of "Sanford and Son," which relates the adventures of Fred Sanford, the irascible Watts junkman, as he resumes his business with Cal Pettie, a not-too-bright friend of Lamont's (who is working on the Alaska pipeline).

Fred G. Sanford	Redd Foxx
Cal Pettie	Dennis Burkley
Evelyn Lewis	Marguerite Ray
Rollo Larson	Nathaniel Taylor
Cissy Lewis	Suzanne Stone
Winston	Percy Rodrigues
Clara	Cathy Cooper
Esther Anderson	LaWanda Page
Cliff Anderson	Clinton Derricks-Carroll
Officer Smitty	Hal Williams
Officer Hoppy	Howard Platt
Grady Wilson	Whitman Mayo

Producer: Mort Lachman, Sy Rosen

Sanford and Son

Comedy; 30 min; NBC 1/14/72 to 9/2/77

The story of Fred G. Sanford, a 65-year-old black junk dealer, and his 34-year-old son and partner, Lamont, a bachelor who longs to quit the business and begin a life of his own. Spin-offs: "Grady," "Sanford," and "Sanford Arms."

Fred G. Sanford	Redd Foxx
Lamont Sanford	Demond Wilson
Grady Wilson	Whitman Mayo
Esther Anderson	LaWanda Page
Woody Anderson	Raymond Allen
Daniel Anderson	Eric Laneuville
Rollo Larson	Nathaniel Taylor
Julio Fuentas	Gregory Sierra
Melvin	Slappy White
Off. Swanhauser	Noam Pitlik
Off. Smitty	Hal Williams
Off. "Hoppy"	
Hopkins	Howard Platt
Bubba	Don Bexley
Donna Harris	Lynn Hamilton
Leroy	Leroy Daniels
May Hopkins	Nancy Kulp
Janet	Marianne Clark
Ah Chu	Pat Morita

"Sanford and Son" Theme Song: Quincy Jones

Producer: Norman Lear, Bud Yorkin, Bernie Orenstein, Saul Turteltaub

Sanford Arms

Comedy; 30 min; NBC 9/16/77 to 10/14/77

Following the death of his wife, retired Army man Phil Wheeler purchases the Sanford and Son junkyard and turns it into a rooming house called Sanford Arms. Stories relate Phil and his children's efforts to run the rooming house.

Phil Wheeler	Theodore Wilson
Angie Wheeler	Tina Andrews
Nat Wheeler	John Earl
Esther Anderson	LaWanda Page
Woody Anderson	Raymond Allen
Jeannie	Bebe Drake-Hooks
Grady Wilson	Whitman Mayo
Bubba	Don Bexley

Music: Henry Mancini

Producer: Bud Yorkin, Saul Turteltaub, Bernie Orenstein

Sara

Western; 60 min; CBS 2/13/76 to 7/30/76

Dissatisfied with her life in Philadelphia, Sara Yarnell, a pretty school teacher, leaves what she considers to be a dull existence to teach school out west. Stories, set in Independence, Colorado, in 1870, relate Sara's experiences as a school teacher.

Sara Yarnell	Brenda Vaccaro
Emmett Ferguson	Bert Kramer
Martin Pope	Albert Stratton
Julia Bailey	Mariclare Costello
George Bailey	William Wintersole
Martha Higgins	Louise Latham
Emma Higgins	Hallie Morgan
Deborah Higgins	Debbie Leyton
Samuel Higgins	Al Henderson
Georgie Bailey	Kraig Metzinger
Claranet	Silvia Soares
Mayor Claude	
Barstow	William Edward
	Phipps
Jimmy Wiggins	Stephen Manley

"Sara's Theme" Song by Lee Holdridge

Producer: George Eckstein, Richard Collins

Sara

Comedy; 30 min; NBC 1/23/85 to 5/29/85

The joys, sorrows, and romantic misadventures of Sara McKenna, a beautiful idealistic attorney working for the Bay Area Legal Group (later Cooper & Associates).

Sara McKenna	Geena Davis
Roz Dupree	Alfre Woodard
Helen Newcomb	Ronnie Clare
	Edwards
Marty Lang	Bill Maher
Dennis Kemper	Bronson Pinchot
Stewart Webber	David Rasche
Jesse Webber	Matthew Lawrence
Michael Cooper	Richard Venture
Claire McKenna	K Callan
Sara's Cousin Emily	Jill Schoelen

Producer: Gary David Goldberg, Ruth Bennett

The Sarah Churchill Show

A CBS series (10/7/51 to 12/30/51) of interviews with hostess Sarah Churchill.

Sarge

Drama; 60 min; NBC 9/21/71 to 1/11/72

Shattered emotionally after his wife is killed by an assassin's bullet that was meant for him, veteran detective Sarge Swanson enters the priesthood. Three years later he is ordained as Father Samuel Patrick Cavanaugh and assigned to San Diego's St. Aloysius Parish. Stories relate Father Cavanaugh's experiences, still referred to as "Sarge," as he struggles to solve the problems of his urban community.

Father Samuel	
Cavanaugh	George Kennedy
Valerie	Sallie Shockley
Lt. Barney Verick	Ramon Bieri
Kenji Takichi	Harold Sakata
Father Terrence	Stewart Moss
Bishop Andrade	Henry Wilcoxon

Producer: David Levy, David Levinson

Satan's Waitin'

Comedy-Drama Pilot; 30 min; CBS 9/12/64

The story of a nameless, mysterious stranger, assumed to be Satan, who intervenes in people's lives to give them the opportunity to become a candidate for Hell.

The Stranger	Ray Walston
Velma Clarke	Jo Van Fleet
Walter Leighton	Lee Philips
Linda	Sue Randall
Minister	Simon Twigg

Producer: Joel Malone

The Saturday Night Dance Party

Variety; 60 min; NBC 6/7/52 to 8/30/52

A program of music and comedy that replaced "Your Show of Shows" for the Summer of 1952. Hosted by Jerry Lester.

Saturday Night Jamboree

Variety; 60 min; NBC 12/4/48 to 7/2/49

Elton Britt and Boyd Heath as hosts of a program of country and western music. With Ted Grant, Edwin Smith, Eddy Howard, Gabe Drake, and Johnny Havens.

Saturday Night Live

Variety; 90 min; NBC 10/11/75 (Premiere)

Topical comedy sketches are coupled with performances by guest rock groups. Broadcast live from New York (11:30 p.m. to 1:00 a.m.).

Cast (9/75–5/80): Chevy Chase, Gilda Radner, John Belushi, Jane Curtin, Laraine Newman, Dan Aykroyd, Garrett Morris, Bill Murray

Cast (11/80–3/81): Denny Dillon, Gilbert Gotfried, Joe Piscopo, Gail Matthius, Ann Risley, Charles Rocket, Yvonne Hudson, Eddie Murphy, Tony Rosato, Robin Duke, Laurie Metcalfe

Cast (10/81–9/82): Joe Piscopo, Eddie Murphy, Mary Gross, Christine Ebersole, Tim Kazurinsky, Robin Duke, Brad Hall, Brian Doyle-Murray

Cast (9/82–5/84): Joe Piscopo, Brad Hall, Tim Kazurinsky, Robin Duke, Julia Louis-Dreyfus, Gary Kroeger, Mary Gross, Jim Belushi

Cast (10/84–5/85): Jim Belushi, Billy Crystal, Rich Hall, Pamela Stephenson, Christopher Guest, Martin Short, Harry J. Shearer, Gary Kroeger

Cast (10/85–5/86): Anthony Michael Hall, Randy Quaid, Joan Cusack, Robert Downer, Nora Dunn, Terry Sweeney, John Lovitz, Danita Vance, Dennis Wilson

Cast (l0/86-): Dana Carvey, Phil Hartman, Jan Hooks, Victoria Jackson, A. Whitney Brown, Kevin Nealon, Jon Lovitz, Dennis Miller, Nora Dunn

Saturday Night Live with Howard Cosell

Variety; 60 min; ABC 9/20/75 to 1/17/76

A live series (from the Ed Sullivan Theatre in New York) that features performances by major guest stars.

Host: Howard Cosell

Regulars: The Peter Gennaro Dancers

Announcer: John Bartholomew Tucker

Orchestra: Elliot Lawrence

Producer: Roone Arledge, Rupert Hitzig

The Saturday Night Revue

Variety; 60 min; NBC 6/6/53 to 9/5/53
                    6/12/54 to 9/18/54

Name bands, filmed European variety acts, and performances by show business personalities.

New York Host: Sid Caesar

Chicago Host: Jack Carter

Additional Hosts: Eddie Albert, Hoagy Carmichael, Alan Young, Ben Blue

Regulars: Pat Carroll, Jackie Kannon, Hy Averback, Susan Stewart, Jackie Lockridge, Donald Richards, Betty Bruce, The Bill Callahan Dance Troupe

Orchestra: Lou Breese, Ed Sauter

Producer: Ernest D. Glucksman

Savage: In the Orient

Crime Drama Pilot; 60 min; CBS 6/21/83

The exploits of Peter Savage, a wealthy private detective and antique shop owner based in Manila.

Peter Savage	Joe Penny
Major (his assistant)	Leif Erickson
Nick Costa	John Saxon
Leslie	Heather McNair
Julia Clydesdale	Gayle Hunnicutt
Allan Clydesdale	Lew Ayres

Producer: Terry Becker

Savage Sunday

Drama Pilot; 60 min; NBC 5/1/62

The pilot for "Saints and Sinners." The story of Nick Phillips and Albert King, rival reporters for a Manhattan daily newspaper. Aired on "The Dick Powell Show."

Nick Phillips	Nick Adams
Albert King	Russell Thorson
Lizzie Hogan	Ann Blyth
Mark Grainger	John Larkin
Marilee Ledbetter	Carolyn Kearney

Producer: Dick Powell

Sawyer and Finn

Adventure Pilot; 60 min; NBC 4/22/83

When the river life no longer excites him, Tom Sawyer heads west. He unexpectedly encounters his old friend, Huck Finn, and the two join forces to seek adventure. The unsold series was to relate their adventures in the Old West.

Tom Sawyer	Peter Horton
Huck Finn	Michael Dudikoff
Goldie Malloy	P.J. Soles
Marshal	Don "Red" Barry
Sheriff	Slim Pickens
Boot McGraw	Jack Elam

Producer: George Schenck, Frank Cardea

Sawyer Views Hollywood

Interview; 30 min; ABC 6/29/51 to 8/31/51

A program of celebrity interviews with host Hal Sawyer and the music of the Gaylord Carter Trio.

Say It with Acting

Game; 30 min; DuMont 2/20/49 to 8/7/49
                NBC 8/14/49 to 9/24/50
                ABC 9/7/51 to 2/22/52

The original format features two celebrity teams in a game of charades with the team performing in the least amount of time winning. Later, following a cast performing a scene that can be described by a single word, a telephone call would be placed to a home viewer. If the viewer could guess the word, he received a merchandise prize. Originally aired locally in New York as "Look Ma, I'm Acting" and later "Act It Out."

Hosts: Bill Cullen, Maggi McNellis, Bud Collyer

Regulars: Robert Alda, Patty Adair, Monty Banks Jr., Ed Casey, Leon Kay

Producer: West Hooker

Say When

Game; 30 min; NBC 1/2/61 to 3/26/65

A specific money amount is established, and various merchandise items are displayed on stage. The object is for each of the two players who compete to select items (whose prices are not known) that add up to, but do not surpass the established amount. The player who comes closest wins those items.

Host: Art James

Assistant: Ruth Hasely

Producer: Robert Kweskin, Rupert S. Rowe

Scalpels

Comedy Pilot; 30 min; NBC 10/26/80

The comical escapades of a group of less-than-believable San Francisco doctors.

Dr. Carl Jerrett	Rene Auberjonois
Dr. Betty Hacker	Marilyn Sokol
Dr. Nicole Tessier	Livia Genise
Dr. Lawrence Hacker	Charles Haid
Nurse Connie Primble	Kimberly Beck
Dr. Robert Hobart	Simon MacCorkindale

Producer: Steve Zacharias, Bruce Johnson

Scamps

Comedy Pilot; 30 min; NBC 6/3/82

In an attempt to earn the extra money he needs to pay his bills, a struggling writer (Oliver Hopkins) turns a spare room in his home into a day-care center for children. The unsold series was to relate Oliver's efforts to care for a group of mischievous kids.

Oliver Hopkins	Bob Denver
Mandy (his friend)	Dreama Denver
Miss Pitts (his neighbor)	Dena Dietrich
Princess*	Jennifer George
Cricket*	Erin Nicole Brown
Casey*	Damon Hines
Tank*	Matt Connors
Daisy*	Marissa Mendenhall
Scooter*	Scooter Cohen
Buttons*	Shannon Izuchara
Sparky*	Joey Lawrence
Jinx*	Petter Jacobs

Theme Vocal ("Scamps"): Robert Jason

Producer: Sherwood Schwartz

*The kids.

Scarecrow and Mrs. King

Adventure; 60 min; CBS 10/3/83 (Premiere)

While being pursued by enemy agents, secret agent Lee Stetson (code name "Scarecrow") runs into a beautiful housewife (Amanda King) and gives her a package to deliver. Amanda takes the package, which is being sought by the enemy agents, and leaves. Later, Lee tracks down Amanda and with her help, plugs a security leak in his organization, The Agency. Because Lee is a professional, and Amanda is an anonymous amateur, she finds work as Lee's partner. Stories relate the exploits of the Scarecrow and Mrs. King (divorced) as they perform missions for the U.S. government.

Amanda King	Kate Jackson
Lee Stetson	Bruce Boxleitner
Dorothea "Dotty" West	Beverly Garland
Billy Melrose	Mel Stewart
Francine Desmond	Martha Smith
Philip King	Paul Stout
Jamie King	Greg Morton
Emily Farnsworth	Jean Stapleton
Dirk Fredericks	John Saxon
Mrs. Marston	Shirley Anthony
Henry "Buck" O'Connell	Frank Bonner

"Scarecrow and Mrs. King" Theme Song: Arthur B. Rubinstein

Producer: Eugenie Ross-Leming, Brad Buckner, Juanita Bartlett, Michael McLean

Scared Silly

Comedy Pilot; 30 min; ABC 9/2/82

The ghost-busting exploits of Skip Midler and Harold Van Couver, investigators for B.O.O.O. (The Beardsley Office of Occult Occurances).

Skip Midler	Jeff Altman
Harold Van Couver	Donovan Scott
Darcy & Marie Winfield	Lisa Hartman
Bryce Needles	Steve Franken
Edgar	Fred Stuthman

Producer: Aaron Spelling, Douglas S. Cramer

The Scarlet Letter

Drama; 60 min; PBS 3/2/79 to 3/5/79

An adaptation of Nathaniel Hawthorne's 1850 novel about Hester Prynne, a seamstress in 1600s Boston who, convicted of adultry, must wear a scarlet letter "A"—for adultress—on her dress forever as a badge of shame.

Hester Prynne	Meg Foster
Roger	
Chillingsworth	Kevin Conway
Arthur Dimsdale	John Heard
Pearl (infant)	Alexandra Smets
Pearl (age 3)	Danielle Hoebeke
Pearl (age 5)	Jessica Ruth Olin
Pearl (age 7)	Elisa Erali
Nathaniel	
Hawthorne (host)	Josef Sommer

Producer: Herbert Hirschman

The Scarlet Pimpernel

See "The Adventures of the Scarlet Pimpernel."

Scary Tales

Anthology Pilot; 30 min; Syn. 10/86

A proposed series of horror yarns. In the pilot, titled "Night Elevator," a beautiful girl (Molly) schemes to get rich by tricking her boyfriend into stealing valuable computer data.

Host: Mario Ruccuzio

Molly	Justine Bateman
Howard	Marc McClure
Sean	Michael Tulin

Producer: Jerry Golod, T.J. Castronova

Scene of the Crime

Mystery; 60 min; NBC 4/14/85 to 5/26/85

A mystery in which a crime is committed is shown. The viewer sees all the suspects and is given all the clues. The viewer is then challenged to identify the culprit before the police arrive. After a given amount of time, the culprit is revealed and the crime reenacted. Each episode contains a second, thirty-minute suspense story that is complete in itself. The pilot aired 9/30/84.

Host: Orson Welles

Producer: Jon Epstein, Leonard Kaufman, George Crosby

Scene 70

A syndicated program (1970) of performances by rock and roll stars with host Jay Reynolds. With the Scene 70 Action Dancers.

Scenes from a Marriage

Drama; 60 min; PBS 3/9/77 to 4/20/77

A study of the incidents that break up and lead to a couple divorcing after ten years of marriage. Produced in Sweden.

Marianne (wife)	Liv Ullmann
Johan (husband)	Eriand Josephson

Hostess: Liv Ullmann

Producer: Lars-Owen Carlberg, Paulette Rubinstein

The Schaefer Century Theatre

A 14-episode syndicated (1952) series of dramatic stories under the sponsorship of Schaefer Beer. Performers include Bonita Granville, Natalie Wood, Randy Stuart, Lynn Bari, Garry Moore, Billy Gray, Lynn Roberts, Robert Hutton, Alan Mowbray, and John Qualen.

Schlitz Playhouse of Stars

Anthology; CBS 10/5/51 to 5/16/52 (60 min)
               5/23/52 to 6/19/59 (30 min)

A series of live and filmed dramas under the sponsorship of Schlitz Beer.

Hostess (1952): Irene Dunne

Producer: Joseph T. Naar, William Self, Edward Lewis, Felix Jackson, Jules Bricken

School House

Variety; 30 min; DuMont 1/18/49 to 4/12/49

The series, set in a school house with a "teacher" as host, relates vaudeville like music, songs, and comedy sketches, all performed by undiscovered talent.

Teacher: Kenny Delmar

Regulars: Arnold Stang, Maureen Cannon, Ann Morgan, Wally Cox, Mary Ann Reeves, Tommy Dix

Producer: Robert Gordon

Science Fiction Theatre

Anthology; 30 min; Syn. 1955

Dramas that present an insight into the problems man will face as he ventures forth to unravel the mysteries of science and nature.

Host-Narrator: Truman Bradley

Producer: Ivan Tors

Scooby-Doo and Scrappy-Doo

Cartoon; 30 min; ABC 9/22/79 to 12/15/79

A spin-off from "Scooby-Doo, Where Are You?," which see, and which adds the new character of Scooby's nephew, Scrappy-Doo.

Scooby-Doo	Don Messick
Scrappy-Doo	Lennie Weinrib
Shaggy	Casey Kasem
Velma	Patricia Stevens
	Marla Frumkin
Freddy	Frank Welker
Daphne	Heather North

Producer: William Hanna, Joseph Barbera

The Scooby-Doo and Scrappy-Doo Show

Cartoon; 30 min; ABC 11/8/80 to 9/18/82

The antics of cowardly dogs Scooby and Scrappy-Doo, and their human friend, Shaggy, as they become involved with strange phenomena.

Scooby and Scrappy	Don Messick
Shaggy	Casey Kasem

Producer: William Hanna, Joseph Barbera

The Scooby-Doo/Dynomutt Hour

Cartoon; 60 min; ABC 9/11/76 to 9/3/77

Segments: "Scooby-Doo, Where Are You?" (which see for case and storyline); and "The Blue Falcon" (about a daring crime fighter and his assistant, Dynomutt).

Blue Falcon	Gary Owens
Dynomutt	Frank Welker
Narrator	Ron Feinberg

Producer: William Hanna, Joseph Barbera

Scooby-Doo, Where Are You?

Cartoon; ABC 9/13/69 to 9/2/72 (30 min)
9/9/72 to 8/31/74 (60 min)

The exploits of Freddy, Daphne, Velma, and Shaggy, the members of a crime club, and their Great Dane, Scooby-Doo, as they attempt to solve supernatural-based crimes.

Scooby-Doo	Don Messick
Freddy	Frank Welker
Daphne	Heather North
Shaggy	Casey Kasem
Velma	Nicole Jaffe

Producer: William Hanna, Joseph Barbera

Scooby's All-Star Laff-A-Lympics

Cartoon; 2 hrs; ABC 9/10/77 to 9/2/78

An elaborate cartoon about various Hanna-Barbera characters competing in wild Olympic-like games throughout the world.

Snagglepuss/ Huckleberry Hound/Hokey Wolf/Wally Gator/ Yogi Bear/ Blabber/Snooper/ Doggie Daddy/ Quick Draw McGraw/Mr. Jinks/Scooby-Dum/Dastardly Dalton	Daws Butler
Yakky Doodle/ Tinker/Sooey Pig/ Magic Rabbit	Frank Welker
Boo Boo Bear/Pixie/ Scooby-Doo/ Creepy Son/ Mumbly/Dirty Dalton	Don Messick
Grape Ape/Orful Octopus/Dinky	Bob Holt
Cindy Bear	Julie Bennett
Hong Kong Phooey	Scatman Crothers
Jeannie	Julie McWhirter

Blue Falcon	Gary Owens
Dee Dee	Vernee Watson
Brenda/Daisy	
Mayhem	Marilyn Schreffler
Captain Caveman	Mel Blanc
Babu	Joe Besser
Taffy/Creepy Wife	Laurel Page

Producer: William Hanna, Joseph Barbera

Scooby's Mystery Funhouse

Cartoon; 30 min; ABC 9/7/85 to 2/22/86

New and repeat episodes about the adventures of a cowardly Great Dane (Scooby-Doo) and his human friends (Shaggy and Daphne) as they attempt to solve mysterious crimes.

Scooby-Doo	Don Messick
Shaggy	Casey Kasem

Additional Voices: Adrienne Alexander, Peggy Webber, Rene Auberjonois, Jennifer Darling, Dena Dietrich, Jack Angel

Producer: William Hanna, Joseph Barbera

Scott Island

See "Harbourmaster."

The Scott Music Hall

Variety; 30 min; CBS 7/15/52 to 9/25/52

A program of music and songs sponsored by the Scott Paper Company.

Hostess: Patti Page

Substitute Host: Eddie Fisher, Les Paul and Mary Ford

Orchestra: Carl Hoff

Producer: Buzz Kulik

Scotland Yard

Crime Drama; 30 min Syn. 1955
ABC 11/17/57 to 4/6/58

Dramas based on the files of the Criminal Investigation Division of Scotland Yard in London.

Host-Narrator: Edgar Lustgarten

Insp. Duggan	Russell Napier
Insp. Ross	Ken Henry
Sgt. Mason	Arthur Mason

Producer: Alex Snowden

Scrabble

Game; 30 min; NBC 7/2/84 (Premiere)

A large scrabble board with one word is revealed. A clue, based on one letter of that word, is read. One player (of two who compete) selects one letter of the alphabet. If the letter is contained in the unknown word, it appears on the board. The player continues to select letters until he misses (thus allowing the opponent a turn) or guesses the word (thus beginning a new round). The first player to guess three words wins $500.

Host: Chuck Wollery

Announcer: Jay Stewart

Producer: Robert Noah, Gary Johnson

Screen Director's Playhouse

Anthology; 30 min; NBC 10/5/55 to 6/27/56
ABC 7/4/56 to 9/26/56

A series of original half-hour programs featuring well-known screen directors, writers, and Hollywood stars. The program, created by the Directors Guild, deliberately has no producer as the directors were in charge. See the following titles for information on the pilot films that aired: "Arroyo," "It's Always Sunday," "The Life of Vernon Hathaway," "Meet the Governor," and "Tom and Jerry."

Directors Include: Leo McCarey, John Brahm, Andrew Stone, Stuart Heisler, John Ford, George Marshall, Tay Garnett, Allan Dwan, Ida Lupino, David Butler, Ted Post, Lewis Allen, and John Rich

The Sea Hawk

See "Adventures of the Sea Hawk."

Sea Hunt

Adventure; 30 min; Syn. 1957

The story of Mike Nelson, an ex-Navy frog-man turned underwater troubleshooter.

Mike Nelson	Lloyd Bridges
Various kid roles	Beau Bridges

"Sea Hunt" Theme by Ray Llewellyn

Producer: Ivan Tors, Leon Benson, John Florea

Sea Hunt

Adventure; 30 min; Syn. 9/87

The exploits of Mike Nelson, a former Navy frogman turned troubleshooter and owner of a boat called the "Sea Hunt," and his beautiful daughter, Jennifer, a marine biologist, as they help people in need. A revised version of the Lloyd Bridges series of the same title.

Mike Nelson	Ron Ely
Jennifer Nelson	Melissa Sue Anderson*
	Kimber Sissons

Narrator: Ron Ely

Producer: Len Kaufman, Myles Wilder

*Originally cast in the role and later dropped.

Seabert

Cartoon; 25 min; HBO 4/5/87 (Premiere)

While vacationing in Greenland, a young boy (Tommy) befriends a playful baby seal he names Seabert, and a young Eskimo girl (Aura). After the trio helps to protect baby seals from hunters, they make a pact to protect endangered wildlife. Stories relate their adventures.

Voices: Diana Ellington, Melissa Freeman, Ron Knight, Bruce Robertson, Morgan Upton

Producer: Freddy Monnickendam, Joop Visch

The Seal

Adventure Pilot; 60 min; NBC 11/27/81

The exploits of a man known only as "The Seal," a former mercenary turned free agent who tackles dangerous, high risk cases.

The Seal	Ron Ely
Stephanie Thayer	Jenny Sullivan
Bill Thayer	Lee DeBroux
Lily Thayer	Kyle Richards
Paula	Karen Machon
Hutchins	Denny Miller
Jennings	Gerald McRaney

Producer: James D. Parriott, Richard Chapman

Sealab 2020

Cartoon; 30 min; NBC 9/9/72 to 9/1/73

The struggles of 250 pioneering men, women, and children, as they attempt to maintain Sealab 2020, an experimental underwater city.

Capt. Mike Murphy	John Stephenson
Dr. Paul Williams	Ross Martin
Sally Murphy	Pamelyn Ferdin
Bobby Murphy	Joshua Albee
Gail	Ann Jillian
Hal	Jerry Dexter
Sparks	Bill Callaway
Jamie	Gary Shapiro
Ed	Ron Pinkard

Producer: William Hanna, Joseph Barbera

Seaway

Adventure; 60 min; Syn. 1965

The exploits of Nick King, an agent for the Montreal-based Ship Owners Association, an organization that is responsible for security along the St. Lawrence Seaway.

Nick King	Stephen Young
Admiral Fox	Austin Willis

The Search

Crime Drama Pilot; 60 min; CBS 7/29/68

The exploits of Paul Cannon, a London-based detective who helps American travelers in trouble.

Paul Cannon	Mark Miller
Martin Purcell	Michael Rennie
Insp. Sheppard	Barry Foster
Molly	Julie Sommars
Ingersoll	Ryan O'Neal

Producer: Stanley Rubin

Search

Adventure; 60 min NBC 9/12/72 to 8/29/73

The exploits of Hugh Lockwood, Probe One; Nick Bianco, Omega Probe; and Christopher Grover, Standby Probe, three skilled investigators for Probe, a computerized detective agency that operates out of the World Securities Corporation in Washington, D.C.

Hugh Lockwood	Hugh O'Brian
Nick Bianco	Tony Franciosa
Christopher R. Grover	Doug McClure
B.G. Cameron (head of Probe)	Burgess Meredith
Dr. Barnett (senior director)	Ford Rainey
Gloria Harding*	Angel Tompkins
Kuroda*	Byron Chung
Miss Keach*	Ginny Golden
Amy*	Cheryl Ladd
Griffin*	Albert Popwell
Ann Mulligan*	Ann Prentiss
Miss James*	Pamela Jones
Harris*	Tom Hallick

Producer: Leslie Stevens

*Probe Control Agents.

Search and Rescue: The Alpha Team

Adventure; 30 min; NBC 9/10/77 to 1/28/78

The series, set at the Alpha Ranch in Canada, relates the exploits of widower Bob Donell and his two children, Kate and Jim, as they train wild animals for difficult rescue assignments.

Bob Donell	Michael J. Reynolds
Kate Donell	Donann Calvin
Jim Donell	Michael Tough
Dr. Liz Warren	Helen Shaver

Producer: Seymour Berns, Will Lorin

Second Chance

Drama Pilot; 60 min; ABC 3/13/62

The pilot for "Wide Country" that relates the adventures of Mitch Guthrie, a champion rodeo rider. Aired on "Alcoa Premiere."

Mitch Guthrie	Earl Holliman
Andy Guthrie	Andrew Prine
Hoby Dunlap	Cliff Robertson
Oralee Dunlap	Jacqueline Scott
Hebert Greshon	John Anderson
Wes Holbrook	Donald Barry
Lonnie Dunlap	Roger Mobley

Producer: Frank Telford

Second Chance

Game; 30 min; ABC 3/7/77 to 7/15/77

Three players write their answers to a question that is read. Players are permitted to keep their own answer or choose one of three that now appears on a board. An unchanged answer that is correct scores three points; a second chance correct answer scores one point. After three such rounds, players use their points for spins on a large electronic game board. The object is to build a large cash and merchandise total without hitting a devil (which erases all earnings). The highest cash value scorer is the winner.

Host: Jim Peck

Announcer: Jay Stewart, Jack Clark

Producer: Bill Carruthers, Joel Stein

Second Chance

Comedy; 30 min; FOX 9/26/87 to 1/9/88

On July 29, 2011, Charles Russell is killed in a car crash and sent to St. Peter's office. When Charles is judged unfit for either Heaven or Hell, he is sent back to earth to relive his own past and right his wrongs. Charles arrives at his childhood home in Venice, California on September 26, 1987. There he meets his own self (15-year-old Chazz) and his mother (Helen). Charles introduces himself as Charles Time and rents a room his mother has for rent. Stories relate Charles's efforts to keep his young self on the straight and narrow.

Charles Time	Kiel Martin
Chazz Russell	Matthew Perry
Helen Russell	Randee Heller
Eugene Blooberman	Demian Slade
Booch	William Galo
St. Peter	Joseph Maher

Producer: Gary Menteer, David W. Dulcon

Second City Television

Comedy; Syn. 1977–81 (30 min)
     NBC 5/15/81 to 6/24/83 (90 min)
     Cinemax 11/22/83 to 1/17/84 (45 min)

The program, set at the mythical Second City Television Station, Channel 109, in Mellonville, Canada, satirizes life at a "typical" station by spoofing, via sketches, the programs broadcast throughout the day.

Cast: John Candy, Joe Flaherty, Eugene Levy, Andrea Martin, Catherine O'Hara, Harold Ramis, Dave Thomas, Martin Short, Rick Moranis, Tony Rosato, Robin Duke

Producer: Andrew Alexander, Doug Holt, Jack Rhodes, Bernard Shalins, Miland Bessada, Carol Henson, Pamela Roberts

Second Edition

Comedy Pilot; 30 min; CBS 7/17/84

Events in the life of Cliff Penrose, the editor of "Columbus Life," an Ohio magazine he is struggling to save.

Cliff Penrose	Hal Linden
Ruth Reynolds	Sharon Spelman
Carson Barrett	Emory Bass
Ric Williams	Lou Richards
Fred Lewicki	Gordon Jump
Jaime Scott	Isabel Grandin
Mr. Antoine	Don Diamond
Denise	Alley Mills
Dr. Emily Maxwell	Jane Hallaren
Ida Antoine	Edie McClurg

Producer: John Rappaport

The Second Hundred Years

Comedy; 30 min; ABC 9/6/67 to 9/19/68

While searching for gold in Alaska in 1900, 33-year-old prospector Luke Carpenter is caught in an avalanche and buried alive. In Woodland Oakes, California, in 1967, 67-year-old retired businessman and widower Edwin Carpenter learns from the air force that a recent avalanche in Alaska has uncovered his father—who is alive, and though chronologically one hundred years old, physically and mentally unchanged since 1900. Stories relate the misadventures of a turn-of-the-century prospector as he attempts to adjust to life in the late 1960s.

Luke Carpenter/Ken Carpenter (Luke's 33-year-old grandson)	Monte Markham
Edwin Carpenter	Arthur O'Connell
Erica	Kay Reynolds
Col. Garroway	Frank Maxwell
Mr. Tolliver	Don Beddoe

Producer: Harry Ackerman

The Second Time Around

Comedy Pilot; 30 min; ABC 7/24/79

The story of Joanne and David Norman, a husband and wife team of marriage counselors who, after two years of separation, decide to live together again.

Joanne Norman	Mariette Hartley
David Norman	Edward Winter
Mark Norman	Brad Savage
Bert	Jim Staahl

Theme Vocal ("The Second Time Around"): Steve Lawrence

Producer: Jerry Tokofsky

Secret Agent

Adventure; 60 min; CBS 4/4/65 to 9/10/68

The exploits of John Drake, a British Intelligence Agent. See also "Danger Man" and "The Prisoner."

John Drake	Patrick McGoohan

Theme Vocal ("Secret Agent Man"): Johnny Rivers

Producer: Sidney Cole, Ralph Smart

Secret Army

Drama; 60 min; TEC 7/82 to 11/82

The World War II exploits of the men and women of Lifeline, a Belgium organization that helps Allied servicemen to escape from the Germans and return to the fighting.

Albert Foiret	Bernard Hepton
Lisa Colbert	Jan Francis
John Curtis	Christopher Neame
Maj. Ludwig Kessler	Clifford Rose
Monique Duchamps	Angela Richards
Maj. Brandt	Michael Culver
Natalie	Julie Hill

Producer: Gerard Glaister

The Secret Empire

Adventure; 15 min; NBC 2/27/79 to 5/1/79

While investigating a series of gold robberies from the Aurora Mining Company in Wyoming (1880), Marshal Jim Donner discovers Chimera, a futuristic society of aliens who fled their world of oppression to live inside the earth. Stories relate Jim's efforts to thwart the evil Thorval's plans to conquer the surface world. Aired on "Cliffhangers."

Jim Donner	Geoffrey Scott
Millie Thomas	Carlene Watkins
Billy	Tiger Williams
Thorval	Mark Lenard
Princess Tara	Diane Markoff
Princess Maya	Pamela Brull
Demeter	Jay Robinson
Yannuck	Sean Garrison
Jess Keller	Peter Breck

Producer: Kenneth Johnson, B.W. Sandefur

Secret File, U.S.A.

Adventure; 30 min; Syn. 1954

The exploits of American espionage agent Bill Morgan and Colonel Custer, his female assistant, as they investigate situations that pose a threat to the safety of the U.S.

Bill Morgan	Robert Alda
Col. Custer	Lois Hensen
Jane Morgan	Kay Callard

Producer: Arthur Dreifuss

The Secret Files of Captain Video

See "Captain Video."

The Secret Jury

Drama; 30 min; Syn. 10/59

A little-known series about the exploits of a big city grand jury. With Ross Martin as the Prosecutor. Produced by Charles Irving.

The Secret Life of John Monroe

Comedy Pilot; 30 min; NBC 6/8/59

The story of John Monroe, a magazine writer who lives in two worlds: the one which everyone faces, and his secret world of the imagination. Broadcast as "Christabel" on "Goodyear Theatre." See also "My World and Welcome to It."

John Monroe	Arthur O'Connell
Ellen Monroe	Georgann Johnson
Lydia Monroe	Susan Gordon
Charley	Charles Herbert
Cop	Dabbs Greer

Producer: Jules Goldstone

The Secret Lives of Waldo Kitty

Comedy; 30 min; NBC 9/6/75 to 9/4/76

The program begins with three live-action animals: Waldo, a cat; Felicia, his girlfriend cat; and Tyrone, the mean bulldog. When Tyrone becomes a threat to Felicia, Waldo envisions himself as her heroic savior. Animation takes over, and each week features Waldo as a different hero out to protect Felicia.

Waldo Kitty	Howard Morris
Felicia	Jane Webb
Tyrone	Allan Melvin

Producer: Lou Scheimer, Norm Prescott

The Secret of Mystery Lake

Drama; 30 min; ABC 9/16/57 to 9/24/57

A "Mickey Mouse Club" serial about a naturalist's (Bill Richards) efforts to explore the wonders of Nature as it abounds at Real Foot Lake in Tennessee.

| Bill Richards | George Fenneman |
| Lanie Thorne (guide) | Gloria Marshall |

Producer: Walt Disney, Bill Walsh

Secret Squirrel

See "The Atom Ant/Secret Squirrel Show."

The Secrets of Isis

See "Isis."

The Secrets of Midland Heights

Drama; 60 min; CBS 12/6/80 to 1/24/81

The dreams, frustrations, and hidden secrets of the people who live and work in Midland Heights, a small midwestern college town.

Margaret Millington	Martha Scott
Dorothy Wheeler	Bibi Besch
Guy Millington	Jordan Christopher
Holly Wheeler	Linda Grovernor
	Marilyn Jones
Ann Dulles	Doran Clark
Nathan Welsh	Robert Hogan
Teddy Welsh	Daniel Zippi
Burt Carroll	Lorenzo Lamas
Lisa Rogers	Linda Hamilton
Micki Carroll	Melora Hardin
John Grey	Jim Youngs
Calvin Richardson	Mark Pinter
Lucy Dexter	Jenny O'Hara
Mrs. Grey	Arlene Golonka
Sue	Irene Arranga

"The Secrets of Midland Heights" Theme Song: Jerrold Immel

Producer: Lee Rich, Michael Filerman, David Jacobs

Sectaurs—Warriors of Symbion

Cartoon; 30 min; Syn. 3/86

On the utopian planet Symbion, a secret biological experiment goes awry and creates a mutant life form that begins to ravage the planet. The new evil is controlled by Spirdax and his Terror Troops of the Dark Realm. To battle Spirdax, a humanoid force called Sectaurs are created. Stories relate the Sectaurs battle to defeat Spirdax and regain control of their planet.

Voices: Dan Gilvezan, Peter Renaday, Peter Cullen, Laurie Faso, Arthur Burghardt, Frank Welker, B.J. Ward, Neil Ross

Producer: Joe Ruby, Ken Spears

See How They Rock!

Variety Pilot; 30 min; Syn. 8/85

Boy George as the host of a proposed series of interviews and features on rock personalities. Produced by John Pattyson and Scott McVeigh.

Seeing Stars

Interview; 30 min; Syn. 4/85

Jim Finnerty as the host of a program of celebrity interviews. Produced by Dick Crew and Joe Tobin.

Seeing Things

Comical Mystery; 60 min; Syn. 11/83

The series, set in Canada, relates the adventures of Louis Ciconne, a newspaper reporter for the "Toronto Gazette," who possesses "second sight"—a gift to see the past and future which he uses to solve crimes.

Louie Ciconne	Louis Del Grande
Marge Ciconne	Martha Gibson
Jason Ciconne	Ivan Beaulieu
Heather Medford	Janet Lainie Green
Max Spencer	Cec Linder
Alberto Ciconne	Al Bernardo
Anna Ciconne	Lynne Gordon

Producer: Robert Allen

Theme Vocal ("Seeing Things"): Philip Schreibman

The Seekers

Crime Drama Pilot; 60 min; ABC 11/20/62

The cases of Agatha Stewart, a lieutenant with the Chicago Police Department's Bureau of Missing Persons during the 1930s. The first pilot, broadcast as "Elegy" on "The Untouchables," relates Agatha's attempts to find a dying mobster's missing daughter. See next title also.

Lt. Agatha Stewart	Barbara Stanwyck
Lt. Harrison	Bill Sargent
Margaret	Peggy Ann Garner
Charlie Radick	John Larch

Producer: Jerry Thorpe, Leonard Freeman

The Seekers

Crime Drama Pilot; 60 min; ABC 1/1/63

A second pilot (see prior title) about Agatha Stewart, a lieutenant with the Chicago Police Department's Bureau of Missing Persons during the 1930s. The second pilot, broadcast as "Search for a Dead Man" on "The Untouchables," relates Agatha's efforts to identify a body found in Lake Michigan.

Lt. Agatha Stewart	Barbara Stanwyck
Benson	Edward Asner
Off. Harrison	Jerry Douglas
June	Virginia Capers
Claire Simmons	Sheree North
Sonny Dale	Tom Reese

Producer: Leonard Freeman

Semi-Tough

Comedy; 30 min; ABC 5/29/80 to 6/19/80

The comic adventures of Billy Clyde Puckett and Marvin "Shake" Tiller, two womanizing pro football players for the seldom-winning New York Bulls.

Billy Clyde Puckett	Bruce McGill
	Douglas Barr*
Marvin Tiller	David Hasselhoff
	Josh Taylor*
Barbara Jane Bookman	Markie Post
	Mary Louise Weller*
Big Ed Bookman	Hugh Gillin
Big Barbara Bookman	Mary Jo Catlett
Puddin	Bubba Smith
T.J.	Carlos Brown
Michele	Michele Leon
Pearly	Chuck McCann
Hal	Jim MacGeorge
Bert Turnbee	Jim McKrell
Coach Harry Cooper	Ed Peck
Story Time	Freeman King

Producer: David Merrick, Jerry Davis

*Pilot episode role (1/6/80).

The Senator

Drama; 60 min; NBC 9/13/70 to 8/22/71

A "Bold Ones" segment about Senator Hays Stowe, a progressive California politician, who attempts to meet and understand the needs of the people he represents.

Hays Stowe	Hal Holbrook
Ellen Stowe	Sharon Acker
Norma Stowe	Cynthia Eilbacher
Jordon Boyle	Michael Tolan
Governor	John Randolph
Mayor	John Marley

Producer: William Sackheim

Sense and Nonsense

Game; 30 min; NBC 11/24/52 to 4/5/53

Two three member teams compete in a series of games based on the five senses (sight, hearing, touch, taste, and smell). Each player competes in one round designed to test one sense without the aid of the others. Points are awarded for each problem that is solved by each sense. Winners are the highest scorers.

Host: Bob Kennedy, Ralph Paul

Assistant: Vivian Farrar

The Sentimental Agent

Adventure; 60 min; Syn. 1962

The exploits of Carlos Borella, a troubleshooter for an import-export company. Starring Carlos Thompson as Carlos Borella.

Serenade

Variety; 15 min; ABC 1/23/49 to 10/30/49

Dolores Marshall as the host of a series of music and songs with the music of the George Barnes Trio.

Sergeant Bilko

See "The Phil Silvers Show."

Sergeant Dekker

See "Not For Hire."

Sergeant Preston of the Yukon

Adventure; 30 min; Syn. 1955

The adventures of Sergeant William Preston of the Northwest Canadian Mounted Police as he attempts to maintain law and order in the early Gold Rush days of the Yukon (1890s).

Sgt. William Preston   Richard Simmons

Producer: Tom R. Curtis, Charles E. Skinner

Sergeant T.K. Yu

Crime Drama Pilot; 60 min; NBC 4/19/79

As part of an exchange program, Korean detective T.K. Yu is assigned to the L.A.P.D. to study American crime detection methods. The unsold series was to relate Yu's experiences with the L.A.P.D.

Sgt. T.K. Yu	Johnny Yune
Lt. Robert Ridge	John Lehne
Sam Palfy	Marty Brill

Producer: Joseph Barbera

Serpico

Crime Drama; 60 min; NBC 9/24/76 to 1/28/77

The exploits of Frank Serpico, an undercover patrolman with the 22nd Precinct in New York City.

Off. Frank Serpico	David Birney
Lt. Sullivan	Tom Atkins

Producer: Emmet G. Lavery Jr.

Sesame Street

Children; 60 min; PBS 11/10/69 (Premiere)

Various entertainment geared to teach children reading skills, the alphabet, counting, and the ability to solve problems.

Bob	Bob McGrath
Susan	Loretta Long
David	Northern J. Callaway
Maria	Sonia Manzano
Gordon	Roscoe Orman
Luis	Emilio Delgado
Linda	Linda Bove
Olivia	Alaina Reed
Samantha	Cara Buono
Mr. Hooper	Will Lee
Big Bird	Carroll Spinney

Regulars: Charlotte Rae, Matt Robinson, Clarice Taylor, Anne Revere, Larry Block, Paul Brice, Jim Henson's Muppets

Producer: Jon Stone, Dulcy Singer

Seven Against the Sea

Comedy Drama Pilot; 60 min; ABC 4/3/62

The pilot for "McHale's Navy," which relates the adventures of Quinton McHale, the commander of a P.T. boat during World War II. In the pilot, broadcast on "Alcoa Premiere," McHale's carefree lifestyle is threatened when a hard-nosed lieutenant arrives to whip him and his crew back in shape.

Lt. Quinton McHale	Ernest Borgnine
Lt. Durham	Ron Foster
Bosun Gallagher	William Bramley
Crew members	Bobby Wright
	Juan Hernandez

Producer: John Champion

Seven at Eleven

Variety; 60 min; NBC 5/23/51 to 6/27/51

A live program of music and songs from New York City (broadcast at eleven p.m. and on an alternating basis with "Broadway Open House").

Host: George DeWitt

Regulars: Denise Lor, Buddy Lester, Sid Gould, Milton DeLugg, Jack Stanton

Orchestra: Milton DeLugg

Seven Brides for Seven Brothers

Drama; 60 min; CBS 9/19/82 to 7/2/83

The adventures of the seven parentless, but self-sufficient McFadden Brothers, owners of the Circle Bar 7 Ranch in California: Adam, the eldest (married to Hannah Moss), Brian (25), Crane (21), Daniel (18), Evan (16), Ford (15), and Guthrie (12). Based on the feature film.

Adam McFadden	Richard Dean Anderson	Stuart Bailey	Efrem Zimbalist Jr.
		Jeff Spencer	Roger Smith
Hannah Moss-McFadden	Terri Treas	Gerald Lloyd Kookson III (Kookie)	Edd Byrnes
Brian McFadden	Drake Hogestyn	Rex Randolph	Richard Long
Crane McFadden	Peter Horton	Suzanne Fabray	Jacqueline Beer
Daniel McFadden	Roger Wilson	Roscoe	Louis Quinn
Evan McFadden	Tim Topper	J.R. Hale	Robert Logan
Ford McFadden	Brian Utman	Lt. Gilmore	Byron Keith
Guthrie McFadden	River Phoenix	Hannah	Joan Staley
Marie (town bartender)	Joan Kjar	Various "Red Herring" Roles	Nora Hayden
Cooper Johnson (rodeo star)	Hoyt Axton		
Sally Listen (Cooper's daughter)	Susan Swift		

Theme Vocal ("Seven Brides for Seven Brothers"): Phil Silas

Producer: David Gerber, James H. Brown

Seven Keys

Game; 30 min; ABC 4/3/61 to 3/27/64

A picture, which represents a person, place, or event, is flashed on a screen. The first player (of two who compete) to identify the picture scores one point. The player with the highest score receives merchandise prizes and one key. The player vies to win seven straight games to acquire the seven keys needed to open a valuable showcase.

Host: Jack Narz

Producer: Carol Jampel, Bobbie John

The Seven Lively Arts

Anthology; 60 min; CBS 11/3/57 to 2/16/58

John Crosby as the host of a cultural program that explores the arts of music, song, and literature. Produced by Robert Herridge.

77 Sunset Strip

Mystery; 60 min; ABC 10/10/58 to 2/26/64

The exploits of Stuart Bailey and Jeff Spencer, private detectives who operate out of plush offices at 77 Sunset Strip in Hollywood, California. See also "Anything for Money" and "Girl on the Run."

Producer: William T. Orr, Jack Webb, William Conrad, Roy Huggins, Howie Horwitz, Fenton Earnshaw, Harry Tatelman, Joel Rogosin

Seymour Presents

Comedy; 1 min; Syn. 1974

A 60-second program designed to be inserted into horror films (to provide a comical touch between commercial breaks).

Seymour	Larry Vincent

Producer: Gary Blair

Sha Na Na

Variety; 30 min; Syn. 9/77

Music and comedy set against the background of a city neighborhood in the 1950s.

Sha Na Na: Jon "Bowzer" Bauman, Lennie Baker, Johnny Contardo, Denny Greene, Dan McBride, John Marcellino, Scott "Santini" Powell, David "Chico" Ryan, "Screamin'" Scott Simon, Donny York

Regulars: Avery Schreiber, Ken Mars, Soupy Sales, Pamela Myers, Jane Dulo, Phil Roth, Jack Wohl, June Gable

Announcer: Pamela Myers

Orchestra: Ray Charles

Producer: Pierre Cossette, Bernard Rothman, Walter C. Miller, Jack Wohl

Shadow Chasers

Adventure; 60 min; ABC 11/14/85 to 1/16/86

The exploits of Edgar "Benny" Benedek, an

occult book writer and reporter for the "National Register," and Jonathon MacKenzie, an anthropologist with the Georgetown Institute for Science in Washington, as they team to solve mysterious happenings that are attributed to the supernatural.

Edgar "Benny" Benedek	Dennis Dugan
Jonathon MacKenzie	Trevor Eve
Dr. Juliana Moorhouse	Nina Foch

"Shadow Chasers" Theme: Mark Tanner, John Reed

Producer: Kenneth Johnson, Harry & Renee Longstreet

The Shadow of Sam Penny

Crime Drama Pilot; 60 min; CBS 11/3/83

The exploits of Sam Penny, an aging San Francisco-based private detective who, in the pilot, attempts to recover diamonds that were stolen in 1953. Aired on "Simon and Simon."

Sam Penny	Robert Lansing
Angel Barkley	Anne Francis
Toni Myers	Joan Leslie
Dutch Silver	Elisha Cook
Del Mooney	Dane Clark
Alex Kidd	Scott Brady
Wally Kaper	Phil Bruns

Producer: Philip DeGuere

Shadow of the Cloak

Adventure; 30 min; DuMont 6/6/51 to 3/20/52

The exploits of Peter House, the chief agent of International Security Intelligence, a U.S. government organization that battles espionage rings.

Peter House	Helmut Dantine

Producer: Roger Gerry

Shaft

Crime Drama; 90 min; CBS 10/9/73 to 9/3/74

The cases of John Shaft, a black New York detective who strives to solve complex and baffling crimes.

John Shaft	Richard Roundtree
Lt. Al Rossi	Ed Barth

"Shaft" Theme: Isaac Hayes

Producer: Allan Balter, Willian Reed Woodfield

The Shameful Secrets of Hastings Corners

Comedy Pilot; 30 min; NBC 1/14/70

A spoof of TV serials as seen through the activities of the Honker and Fandango families, residents of Hastings Corners, and their continual feud.

Dr. Byron Dorman	Alan Oppenheimer
Ta Ta Honker	Woodrow Parfrey
Corey and Morey Honker	Hal Linden
Jenny Honker	Karen Black
Charlotte Honker	Ann Willis
Pa Fandango	Hoke Howell
Brett Fandango	Peter Brocco
Tina Fandango	Stefani Warren
Junior Fandango	Barry Williams
Frieda Bindel	Madge Blake
Stacy Bindel	Robyn Millan

Producer: Harry Ackerman, Lawrence J. Cohen, Fred Freeman

Shane

Western; 60 min; ABC 9/10/66 to 12/31/66

The series, set in Wyoming during the late 1800s, relates the adventures of Shane, a mysterious wandering ex-gunman who, for unknown reasons, sides with homesteaders against the cattlemen in the bloodthirsty quest for land.

Shane	David Carradine
Marian Starrett	Jill Ireland
Joey Starrett	Christopher Shea
Tom Starrett	Tom Tully
Rufe Ryker	Bert Freed
Sam Grafton	Sam Gilman

"Shane" Theme Song: Victor Young

Producer: David Shaw, Herbert Brodkin

Shannon

Adventure; 30 min; Syn. 9/61

The exploits of Joe Shannon, an insurance investigator for the Transport Bonding and Surety Company.

Joe Shannon	George Nader
Bill Cochran	Regis Toomey

Producer: Jerry Briskin

Shannon

Crime Drama; 60 min; CBS
11/11/81 to 12/2/81
3/17/82 to 3/31/82

The story of Jack Shannon, a detective lieutenant with the S-Squad, an elite group of special assignment agents with the San Francisco Police Department.

Lt. Jack Shannon	Kevin Dobson
John Shannon	Charlie Fields
Irene Lokatelli	Karen Kondazian
Paul Lokatelli	Al Ruscio
Lt. Rudy Moraga	Michael Durrell
Det. Norm White	William Lucking
Det. Schmidt	Bruce Kirby
Sally Reynolds	Joan Pringle

Producer: Alvin Sapinsley, James Aubrey, James McAdams

The Shape of Things

Variety; 60 min; NBC 4/6/82 to 4/27/82

Music and songs coupled with comedy sketches that present a view of the world as seen through the eyes of women.

Host (Program 1): Morgan Fairchild, Lynn Redgrave, Sarah Purcell, Betty White

Host (Program 2): Susan Anton, Juliet Prowse, Ruth Buzzi, Isabel Sanford

Host (Program 3): Eileen Brennan, Donna Dixon, Nancy Dussault, Rita Moreno

Regulars: Rhonda Bates, Elayne Boosler, Judy Carter, Maureen Murphy, Debbie Archibald, Alvernette Jimenez, Howie Mandel, The Chippendale Dancers

Orchestra: Lenny Stack

Producer: George Schlatter, Bob Wynn

Shaping Up

Comedy; 30 min; ABC 3/20/84 to 4/17/84

The experiences of Buddy Fox, the owner-operator of the Los Angeles-based Buddy Fox's Health Spa.

Buddy Fox	Leslie Nielsen
Ben Zachary	Michael Fontaine
Shannon Winters	Jennifer Tilly
Melissa McDonald	Shawn Weatherly
Zonya Antonova	Catherine Shirriff
Shirley	Judy Pioli
Jerry	Jake Steinfeld

Producer: Ken Estin, Sam Simon

The Shari Lewis Show

Children; 30 min; NBC 10/1/60 to 9/28/63

Music, song, and comedy with ventriloquist Shari Lewis and her puppets Lamb Chop, Hush Puppy, and Charlie Horse.

Shari	Shari Lewis
Mr. Goodfellow	Ronald Radd
Jump Pup	Jackie Warner

Producer: E. Roger Muir, Robert Scheerer

The Shari Lewis Show

Children; 30 min; Syn. 1975

The program, set at the puppet-operated Bearly Broadcasting Company, relates ventriloquist Shari Lewis's experiences as the human assistant station manager. Situations are designed to relate a problem and its solution to children.

Shari	Shari Lewis

Voices: Shari Lewis, Mallory Tarcher, Ron Martin

Music: Bob Alberti

Producer: Florence Small

The Sharpshooter

Western Pilot; 30 min; CBS 3/7/58

The pilot for "The Rifleman," which aired on "Zane Grey Theatre." Following the death of his wife, Lucas McCain, alias "The Rifleman," and his young son, Mark, arrive in North Fork, New Mexico, seeking to begin new lives as ranchers. The story relates how Lucas enters a turkey shoot to win the money he needs to buy a ranch, and how he defeats a crooked town boss (Jim Lewis) to make North Fork a decent place to live.

Lucas McCain	Chuck Connors
Mark McCain	Johnny Crawford
Jim Lewis	Leif Erickson
Vern	Dennis Hopper
Judge Hanovan	Sidney Blackmer
Sheriff Fred Thompson	R.G. Armstrong

Producer: Hal Hudson

Shaughnessey

Comedy Pilot; 30 min; NBC 9/6/76

The antics of the drivers and crew of the Morgan Cab Company in Chicago.

Eddie Shaughnessey	Pat McCormick
Doris Shaughnessey	Nita Talbot
Mona Phillips	Sally Kirkland
Banners	Warren Berlinger
Steve Williams	Jack Mullaney
Phil Jenkins	Ralph Wilcox
Clyde Hawkins	David Hinton
Dominic Mazaracio	Tom Fuccello
Mr. Morgan	David Doyle

Producer: Elliott Kozak

Shazam!

Adventure; 30 min; CBS 9/7/74 to 9/3/77

Seeking a human to battle injustice, the immortal elders Mercury, Zeus, Achilles, and Atlas, endow radio broadcaster Billy Batson with the ability to transform himself into the daring crime fighter Captain Marvel. Stories relate Billy and his assistant, Mentor's, battle against evil.

Billy Batson	Michael Gray
Mentor	Les Tremayne
Captain Marvel	Jackson Bostwick
	John Davey

Producer: Norm Prescott, Lou Scheimer

Shazzan!

Cartoon; 30 min; CBS 9/9/67 to 9/6/69

When twins Nancy and Chuck find two ancient ring halves and place them together (spelling the word "Shazzan") they are transported to the age of the Arabian Knights and become the masters of Shazzan, a powerful sixty-foot genie. Stories relate their adventures.

Shazzan	Barney Phillips
Nancy	Janet Waldo
Chuck	Jerry Dexter

Producer: William Hanna, Joseph Barbera

Sheehy and the Supreme Machine

Comedy Pilot; 30 min; ABC 8/22/77

The story of an ex-marine (Jack Sheehy) turned apartment building manager. (The title refers to a group of teenagers, the Supreme Machine, who hang out in the building's basement.)

Jack Sheehy	John Byner
Mr. Cagle	Tige Andrews
Dirt	John Cassisi
Bogen	Jimmy Baio
Teddy	Pierre Daniel
Evel	Moosie Drier
Pantsface	David Arnott
Loretta Bogen	Gwynne Gilford

Producer: Harry Colomby, Bernie Kukoff, Jeff Harris

Sheena, Queen of the Jungle

Adventure; 30 min; Syn. 1955

A young American girl, orphaned in Africa, is raised by a noble tribe. The girl, named Sheena, grows into a beautiful woman and becomes known as a white jungle goddess who battles evil. Stories relate Sheena's exploits as she and her white trader friend, Bob Rayburn*, battle the unscrupulous characters who invade her homeland.

Sheena	Irish McCalla
Bob Rayburn	Christian Drake

Producer: Don Sharpe, William Nassour

*Befriended Sheena when she rescued him from impending doom.

Sheila

Comedy Pilot; 30 min; CBS 8/29/77

Comical incidents in the life of a single girl as seen through the experiences of Sheila Levine, an attractive Girl Friday for Marty Rose, a lady-chasing Broadway producer.

Sheila Levine	Dori Brenner
Marty Rose	Milton Berle
Kate	Barbara Trentham
Stewart Rose	George Wyner
Joshua	Larry Breeding

Producer: Gail Parent

The Sheila Graham Show

Sheila Graham as host of an NBC series of celebrity interviews (1/20/51 to 7/14/51).

The Sheila MacRae Show

A syndicated (1971) series of interviews with guests on topical issues with hostess Sheila MacRae and her daughters Meredith and Heather MacRae.

Shell Game

Crime Drama; 60 min; CBS 1/8/87 to 2/12/87

When a con by Jennie Jerome goes awry, her former partner, now TV producer John Reid, helps her by hiding her out. In return, Jennie helps John acquire a story for his consumer show ("Solutions" over KJME-TV, Ch. 6 in Santa Ana, Calif.). The two become partners again and stories relate their adventures as they use their skills to acquire stories.

Jennie Jerome (a.k.a. Pocket)	Margot Kidder
John Reid (a.k.a. Riley)	James Read
Natalie Thayer	Marg Helgenberger
William Bauer	Rod McCary
Bert Luna	Chip Zien
Jason Starr (Jennie's father)	Gene Barry
Vince Vanneman	Fred McCarren

Producer: Michele Rappaport, Lou Antonio

Shelley Duvall's Tall Tales and Legends

Anthology; 60 min; SHO 12/20/85 (Premiere)

Adaptations of well known folk tales and legends. Stories include "Annie Oakley" (with Jamie Lee Curtis, Brian Dennehy, Cliff De-Young), "Casey at the Bat" (Elliott Gould, Carol Kane), "Pecos Bill, King of the Cowboys" (Rebecca Morney, Martin Mull), "Johnny Appleseed" (Martin Short, Molly Ringwald, Rob Reiner), and "The Legend of Sleepy Hollow" (Beverly D'Angelo, Ed Begley Jr.).

Hostess: Shelley Duvall

Producer: Shelley Duvall, Fredric S. Ruchs, Bridget Terry

Shenanagans

Game; 30 min; ABC 9/26/64 to 3/20/65

Two children compete and begin on the start position of a large electronic game board. Players move the amount of spaces determined by the roll of two dice and must answer a question or perform the stunt that is printed on the square on which they land. Each correct answer or performed stunt awards Shenanagans play money. The first player to complete the game board wins and trades his money for prizes.

Host: Stubby Kaye

Announcer: Kenny Williams

Shepherd's Flock

Comedy Pilot; 30 min; CBS 8/29/71

Following his retirement from football, Jack Shepherd becomes a minister and is assigned to Cypress Bay Union Church. The unsold series was to relate Jack's attempts to adjust to a new life and new responsibilities.

Jack Shepherd	Kenneth Mars
Abby Scoffield	Jill Jaress
Dr. Hewitt	Don Ameche
Ralph Williams	Walter Hackett

Producer: David Davis

She-Ra: Princess of Power

Cartoon; 30 min; Syn. 9/85

A spin-off from "He Man and the Masters of the Universe." The exploits of Adora, twin sister of He Man, a beautiful princess who uses her amazing powers to defend the planet Eternia from the evils of the Horda, an evil creature who seeks to rule it.

She-Ra .... Melendy Britt

Additional Voices: George DiCenzo, Linda Gary, John Erwin, Alan Oppenheimer, Erica Scheimer

Producer: Lou Scheimer, Arthur H. Nadel

The Sheriff and the Astronaut

Crime Drama; 60 min; CBS 5/24/84

The work of Ed Cassaday, a frontier-style sheriff in Carrow County, and Dr. Ellen Vale, his girlfriend, an astronaut at the NASA Dwight D. Eisenhower Space Center.

Ed Cassaday	Alec Baldwin
Ellen Vale	Ann Gillespie
Deputy Tom Cassaday	Don Hood
Al Stark	Kene Holliday
John Fitch	Gregg Berger
Billy LaPantier	Tuck Milligan
Robert Malfi	Scott Paulin
Felice Winter	Ruth Britt
Agent Henley	Steve Franken
Hank Bashaw	John Randolph

Producer: Gerald Dipego, Robert Lovenheim

Sheriff of Cochise

Crime Drama; 30 min; Syn. 1956–58

The exploits of Frank Morgan, the modern-day Sheriff of Cochise, Arizona. See also "U.S. Marshal."

Sheriff Frank Morgan	John Bromfield
Deputy Rafe Patterson	Stan Jones

Producer: Mort Briskin

Sheriff Who?

Comedy Pilot; 30 min; NBC 9/5/67

A spoof of westerns, which, set in Blood, Texas, relates the exploits of Roy Slade, an evil outlaw who rules the town and its cowardly citizens. The title is derived from the citizens' efforts to find a sheriff who can live long enough to bring law and order to Blood.

Roy Slade	John Astin
Crawford Offwhite	Dick Shawn
Betsy	Jeannine Riley
Whittler	Dick Stahl
Judge Grant	Hal Smith

Producer: Garry K. Marshall, Jerry Belson

Sherlock Holmes

Mystery; 30 min; Syn. 1954

The series, set in 1890s London, England, relates the exploits of Sherlock Holmes, a consulting detective who intervenes in baffling police matters, and his roommate and biographer, Dr. John H. Watson. Based on characters created by Sir Arthur Conan Doyle. Filmed in France and also known as "The Adventures of Sherlock Holmes."

Sherlock Holmes	Ronald Howard
John H. Watson	H. Marion Crawford
Insp. Lestrade	Archie Duncan

Narrator: H. Marion Crawford

Producer: Sheldon Reynolds

Sherlock Jones and Proctor Watson

Children; 30 min; PBS Syn. 10/86

In London during the 1890s, the famed Sherlock Holmes attempts to duplicate himself, but fails when a three foot version of himself appears (Sherlock Jones). Holmes crates his creation and ships him to the FBI in New York. En route, however, the crate is rerouted and sent to a woman in Texas. She places the crate in her attic and forgets about it. Many years later (1986), young Brian Hudson hears voices coming from the attic of that home and investigates. He discovers that his dog, Proctor, has befriended the diminutive Sherlock Jones. Stories relate Brian's efforts to solve crimes with the help of Sherlock and Proctor (both puppets).

Sherlock Jones	Mark Ritts
Proctor Watson	Graham Beach
Brian Hudson	Chad Sheets
Lynn Hudson	Julie Atkin
Ben Hudson	Michael Costello
Anne Hudson	Mona Lee Fultz
Teddy	Jason Smith
Uncle Doyle	Mark Evers
Mrs. Munson	Diana Perella

Producer: Leo Eaton, Dick Peterson, S. Bryan Hickox

She's the Sheriff

Comedy; 30 min; Syn. 9/87

Following the death of Jim Granger, the sheriff of Lakes County, Nevada, Hildy Granger, his widow and the mother of two children (Allison and Kenny) replaces him as the new sheriff. Stories relate Hildy's efforts to run the sheriff's department and contend with Max Rubin, a deputy who is seeking her job. See also "Cass Malloy."

Hildy Granger	Priscilla Barnes
	Suzanne Somers
Gussie Holt	Pat Carroll
Allison Granger	Nicky Rose
Kenny Granger	Taliesin Jaffe
Max Rubin	George Wyner
Dennis Putnam	Lou Richards
Hugh Mulcahy	Guich Koock
Alvin Wiggins	Leonard Lightfoot

Producer: Mark Rothman, David Goldsmith

She's With Me

Comedy Pilot; 30 min; CBS 8/24/82

The ups and downs of two pretty sisters (Bonnie and Ellen) working and living in San Francisco.

Ellen Madison	Gloria Gifford
Bonnie Madison	Deborah Pratt
Mr. Chatfield	Patrick J. Cronin
Mr. Rogers	Greg Mullavey
Mr. Meltzer	Howard Morton
Tugboat Captain	Barry Hope

Producer: Mort Lachman, Sy Rosen

She's With Me

Comedy Pilot; 30 min; NBC 7/19/86

While selling New Beginning Cosmetics, Edie Gruber, an attractive divorcee, meets Maris McKay, a beautiful fashion model who finds a true friend in Edie when she helps her solve a romantic problem. So greatful for her help, Maris offers Edie a job as her Girl Friday, which she accepts. The unsold series was to relate the misadventures of two friends sharing each other's joys and sorrows.

Edie Gruber	Dinah Manoff
Maris McKay	Jerry Hall
Alma Alderman	Candice Azzara
Yetta	Carol Helvey
Hedda	Jean Sincere
Cubby Lyons	Christopher Rich
Mark Denton	Charles R. Cooper
Ray	Michael Sabatino
Greta	Beatrice Colen

Producer: John Maxwell Anderson

Shields and Yarnell

Variety; 30 min; CBS 6/13/77 to 7/25/77
1/31/78 to 3/28/78

A weekly program of music, songs, and comedy.

Hosts: Robert Shields, Lorene Yarnell

Regulars: Joanna Cassidy, Ted Zeigler, Gailard Sartain, Philip Reade

Orchestra: Norman Mamey

Producer: Steve Binder, Frank Peppiatt, John Aylesworth

Shindig

Variety; 60 min; ABC 9/16/64 to 1/5/66

A weekly program of performances by the top names in music.

Host: Jimmy O'Neal

Regulars: Bobby Sherman, Glen Campbell, Donna Loren, The Righteous Brothers, The Shindig Dancers

Music: The Ray Pohlman Band, The Shindogs

Producer: Selig Seligman, Leon Mirell, Dean Whitmore

Shipshape

Comedy Pilot; 30 min; CBS 8/1/78

The story of Leslie O'Hara, a pretty Navy ensign, as she attempts to train a group of misfit sailors.

Leslie O'Hara	Deborah Ryan
Capt. Latch	Earl Boen
Yeoman Rita Sweetzer	Shell Kepler
Seaman Howard Beltzman	Andrew Bloch
Seaman House	Lorenzo Lamas
Seaman Howard Kozak	Demetre Phillips
Seaman Watkins	Gary Veney
Mr. Nelson	Ted Hartley
Mrs. Nelson	Kristin Larkin

Producer: James Komack

Shirley

Comedy-Drama; 60 min; NBC 10/26/79 to 1/25/80

Following her husband, Jake's, death, Shirley Miller and her four children (Debra, Bill, Michele, and Hemm) move from the conjestion of New York to the peaceful shores of Placer County, Lake Tahoe, Nevada, to begin a new life. Stories relate their experiences.

Shirley Miller	Shirley Jones
Debra Miller	Rosanna Arquette
Bill Miller	Peter Barton
Michele Miller	Tracey Gold
Hemm Miller	Bret Shryer
Charlotte McHenry	Ann Doran
Ethan "Dutch" McHenry	John McIntire
Lew Armitage	Patrick Wayne
Tracy	Cynthia Eilbacher

Producer: Greg Strangis, William Hogan, Paul Dubov, Gwen Bagni

The Shirley MacLaine Show

See "Shirley's World."

Shirley Temple's Storybook

Anthology; 60 min; NBC 1/12/58 to 12/21/58 ABC 9/18/60 to 3/19/61

Entertaining adaptations of fairy tales and classic stories. Broadcast on ABC as "The Shirley Temple Theatre." The episode of 3/5/58, "The Legend of Sleepy Hollow" marked Miss Temple's dramatic acting debut on TV (in the role of Katrina Van Tassel).

Hostess: Shirley Temple

Theme Vocalist (NBC, "Dreams Are Made for Children"): Shirley Temple

Theme (ABC, "The Enchanted Melody"): Vic Mizzy

Producer: William H. Brown Jr., William Asher, Henry Jaffe, Alvin Cooperman

Shirley's World

Comedy; 30 min; ABC 9/15/71 to 1/5/72

The assignments of Shirley Logan, a beautiful photojournalist with "World Illustrated" magazine, who possesses an insatiable curiosity and a warm-hearted nature that involves her in other peoples problems.

Shirley Logan	Shirley MacLaine
Dennis Croft	John Gregson

"Shirley's World" Theme Song: John Barry

Producer: Sheldon Leonard, Ray Austin

The Shirt Tales

Cartoon; 30 min; NBC 9/18/83 to 9/7/84

The exploits of five animals who battle crime in a large city. Based on the Hallmark greeting card characters.

Rick Raccoon	Ronnie Schell
Tyg Tiger	Steve Schatzberg
Pammy Panda	Pat Parris
Digger Mole	Bob Ogle
Bogey Orangutan	Fred Travalena
Mr. Dinkel	Herb Vigran
Commissioner	William Woodson

Producer: William Hanna, Joseph Barbera

Shivaree

A syndicated (1965) variety series that spotlights rock performers. Hosted by Gene Weed and featuring the Shivaree Dancers.

Shoestring

Crime Drama; 60 min; TEC 9/4/82 to 12/30/82

The exploits of Eddie Shoestring, an unconventional private detective working for England's Radio West, who acquires his cases from the listeners who phone in with their problems.

Eddie Shoestring	Trevor Eve
Erica Bayliss	Doran Godwin
Dona Satchley	Michael Medwin
Sonia Price	Liz Crowther

Producer: Robert Banks Stewart

Shoestring Safari

Comedy Pilot; 30 min; Unaired (Produced for CBS in 1967)

A proposed series about a famous African hunter (Colonel Hazeltine) who runs a misguided safari service for visiting hunters.

Colonel Hazeltine	Andy Devine
Cindy Hazeltine	Kelly Jean Peters
Tricker Bailey	Jeff DeGenning
The Inspector	James Millhollin

Producer: Bob Sweeney

Shoot for the Stars

Game; 30 min; NBC 1/3/77 to 9/30/77

One member of a two member team selects a clue from a large board (e.g., "Clever as a lash"). The player has to unscramble the first half of the phrase by providing a synonym for the first word (e.g., smart for clever) and his partner has to unravel the second half (whip for lash). Two teams compete and the team with the most correct responses is the winner.

Host: Geoff Edwards

Announcer: Bob Clayton

Producer: Bob Stewart

Shore Leave

Comedy Pilot; 30 min; NBC 8/18/61

The misadventures of Goobie Jones and Joe Baker, two trouble-prone sailors.

Goobie Jones	Paul Gilbert
Joe Baker	Peter Marshall
Big Mike Fogarty	Henry Kulky

Short, Short Drama

Anthology; 15 min; NBC 9/30/52 to 4/9/53

A series of fifteen minute dramatic productions.

Hostess: Ruth Warrick

Producer: Bernard Prockter

The Short Story Theatre

Anthology; 15 min; Syn. 1952

A series of one-act plays made especially for syndication.

Hostess: Mary Kay

Producer: Ted Mills, Renee Williams

Shorty

Comedy Pilot; 10 min; CBS 9/8/46

A brief children's program revolving around the antics of Shorty and his friend Patty.

Shorty	Syd Hoft
Patty	Patty Foster

Producer-Director: Philip Booth

Shotgun Slade

Western; 30 min; Syn. 1959

The exploits of Shotgun Slade, a detective who possesses a unique two-barreled shotgun, as he strives to maintain peace on the lawless frontier of the 1860s.

Shotgun Slade	Scott Brady
Monica	Monica Lewis
Alice Barton	Marie Windsor

Theme Vocal ("Shotgun Slade of the Two-Barreled Gun"): Monica Lewis

Producer: Nat Holt, Frank Gruber

Show Business

Magazine Pilot; 60 min; ABC 3/30/81

An inside look at the entertainment industry with hosts David Frost and Sandy Hill. Produced by Bernie Brillstein.

Show Business, Inc.

Variety; 30 min; NBC 3/10/49 to 9/4/49

A live series that features highlights of Broadway shows with performances by original cast members. Also known as "Broadway Spotlight" and "Dayton Walker's Broadway Scrapbook."

Host: Dayton Walker, Richard Kollmar

Regulars: Joey Faye, The June Taylor Dancers

Orchestra: Ving Merlin

Producer: Martin Jones

The Show Goes On

Variety; 60 min; CBS 1/19/50 to 2/16/52

Undiscovered professional talent performs with the hope of receiving bookings from the talent buyers who are present during the broadcast.

Host: Robert Q. Lewis

Producer: Lester Gottlieb, Lou Melamed

The Show Must Go On

Variety Pilot; 60 min; NBC 4/12/82

An imaginative pilot about a group of performers attempting to stage a variety show that is plagued by numerous difficulties.

Host: E.G. Marshall

Regulars: Wendy Goldman, Susan Edwards, Bernadette Burgette, Rick Overton, Melody Rogers, Donovan Scott, Jim Varney

Announcer: Art James

Orchestra: Peter Matz

Producer: Bernie Kukoff, Jeff Harris

Show Street

Phyllis Diller as host of a syndicated (1964) program of performances by undiscovered talent.

Showcase '68

Variety; 60 min; NBC 6/11/68 to 9/3/68

Performances by undiscovered professional talent with host Lloyd Thaxton.

Showdown

Game; 30 min; NBC 7/4/66 to 10/4/66

A general-knowledge question-and-answer game show wherein players with the most correct answers receive merchandise prizes.

Host: Joe Pyne

Producer: Merrill Heatter, Bob Quigley

Showoffs

Game; 30 min; ABC 6/30/75 to 12/26/75

Two three-member teams compete. One team is placed in an isolation booth. One player of the other team becomes the guesser; the other two members, the actors. The actors pantomime as many words as possible within sixty seconds. Each word that the guesser identifies scores one point. At the end of the time, the other team is brought out and they compete with the same words. The highest scoring team is the winner.

Host: Bobby Van

Announcer: Gene Wood

Producer: Mark Goodson, Bill Todman

Showtime

Variety; 60 min; CBS 6/11/68 to 9/17/68

A series of entertainment acts, produced in England, and hosted by American guests (e.g., Juliet Prowse, Liberace, Bill Dana, and Phyllis Diller). With the orchestra of Jack Parnell and The Mike Sammes Singers and The London Line Dancers.

Showtime at the Apollo

Willie Bryant as the host of a syndicated (1954) variety series that features performances by black entertainers (including Nat King Cole, Dinah Washington, Nipsey Russell, Sarah Vaughan, Cab Calloway, Count

Basie, and Martha Davis). Taped at Harlem's Apollo Theatre.

Showtime, U.S.A.

Variety; 30 min; ABC 10/1/50 to 6/24/51

Scenes from Broadway plays are presented and performed by original cast members.

Host: Vinton Freedley

Announcer: Tom Gilbert

Producer: Vinton Freedley, Bernard Gerstein, Winston O'Keefe

Sid Caesar Invites You

Comedy; 30 min; ABC 1/20/58 to 5/25/58

A weekly series of comedy sketches.

Host: Sid Caesar

Regulars: Carl Reiner, Howard Morris, Jeanne Bal, Paul Reed, Milt Kamen, The Kirby Stone Four

Orchestra: Paul Weston

Producer: Hal Janis

Sid Caesar Presents Comedy Preview

Comedy; 60 min; NBC 7/4/55 to 9/12/55

A weekly series of comedy sketches that replaced "Caesar's Hour" during the Summer of 1955.

Host: Phil Foster, Bobby Sherwood

Regulars: Barbara Nichols, Cliff Norton, Sid Gould, The Ted Cappy Dancers

Music: Bill Hayes, Judy Tyler

The Sid Caesar Show

Variety; 30 min; ABC 9/19/63 to 3/16/64

A weekly series of music and comedy.

Host: Sid Caesar

Regulars: Gisele MacKenzie, Charlotte Rae, Joey Forman

Orchestra: Peter Matz

Producer: Greg Garrison

Side by Side

Comedy Pilot; 30 min; CBS 7/27/76

The misadventures of four couples boxed together in a housing development: Charlie and Connie, a conservative couple; Carmine and Luis, a Latin Duo; Sally and Dick, young liberals; and Billy Joe and Hadley, a transplanted southern couple.

Charlie Ryan	Stubby Kaye
Connie Ryan	Peggy Pope
Carmine Rivera	Barbara Luna
Luis Rivera	Luis Avalos
Sally Stern	Janie Sell
Dick Stern	Keith Charles
Hadley Pearson	Diane Stilwell
Billy Joe Pearson	Don Scardino

Producer: Darryl Hickman

Side by Side

Comedy Pilot; 30 min; ABC 7/6/84

Events in the lives of Harry Deegan, a shipping affairs supervisor and his longtime friend, Joey Caruso, a shipping clerk.

Harry Deegan	Charles Durning
Joey Caruso	Ron Leibman
Mildred Deegan	Katherine Helmond
Deborah Kazinsky	Caren Kaye
Peter Wagner	Joseph Mascolo
Moose	Justin Lord
Hernandez	Dick Balduzzi
George McCloskey	Charles Lane

Producer: Marc Merson, Bob Schiller, Bob Weiskopf

Sidekicks

Crime Drama; 30 min; ABC 9/18/86 to 3/14/87

When an aging Chinese grandfather (Sabasan) fears that when he is gone there will be no one around to care for his ten-year-old grandson, Ernie, he convinces Jake Rizzo, an unmarried cop to care for him. Stories relate their exploits as Ernie, a Karate master, helps Jake solve crimes. The pilot episode, "The Last Electric Knight," aired 2/26/86.

Jake Rizzo	Gil Gerard
Ernie	Ernie Reyes Jr.
Patricia Blake	Nancy Stafford
Grandfather Sabasan	Keye Luke
Det. Marty Mooney	Frank Bonner
Capt. Blanks	Vinny Argiro
Randy	Joy Garrett
Jake's mother	Magda Harout

Theme Vocal ("Side By Side"): Kip Lennon

Producer: Richard Chapman, Bill Dial, Michael Weisbarth

Sierra

Drama; 60 min; NBC 9/12/74 to 12/12/74

The series, set in the fictional Sierra National Park, depicts the rescue operations of the National Park Rangers, the men and women who risk their lives to protect people from nature and nature from people.

Ranger Tim Cassidy	James Richardson
Ranger Julie Beck	Susan Foster
Ranger Jack Moore	Robert Hogan
	Jim B. Smith*
Ranger Matt Harper	Ernest Thompson
	Colby Chester*
Ranger P.J. Lewis	Michael Warren

Producer: Robert A. Cinader

*TV Movie roles ("The Rangers," 12/14/74).

Sigmund and the Sea Monsters

Comedy; 30 min; NBC 9/8/73 to 10/18/75

When a sea monster (Sigmund) is disowned by his family for his inability to scare humans, he leaves home and begins to wander on a beach. He is found and "adopted" by two brothers (Johnny and Scott) who hide him in their clubhouse. Stories relate Johnny and Scott's efforts to keep Sigmund's presence a secret and protect him from his family, who deviously scheme to retrieve him when emergencies arrive that require his presence at home.

Sigmund Ooz	Billy Barty
Johnny Stuart	Johnny Whitaker
Scott Stuart	Scott Kolden
Zelda Marshall	Mary Wickes
Sheriff Chuck Bevins	Joe Higgins
Miss Eddels	Margaret Hamilton
Sheldon the Sea Genie	Rip Taylor
Shelby	Sparky Marcus
Gertrude Gouch	Fran Ryan
Sweet Mama Ooz	Sharon Baird
Big Daddy Ooz	Van Snowden
Blurp Ooz	Paul Gale
Slurp Ooz	Larry Larson

Producer: Sid and Marty Krofft

Sign-On

Variety Pilot; 30 min; CBS 2/3/81

Music, drama, comedy, consumer information, and reviews of the arts interwoven into a magazine-like program (which also features a continuing vignette called "Welcome to Twin Oakes." The story of Trish Carlon, A divorcee, and her teenage daughter, Jenny).

Hosts: Susan Spilker, Steve McNaughton.

Trish Carlon	Elinor Donahue
Jenny Carlon	Michelle Downey
Voice of Eugene Harold (the CBS guard dog)	Jim Thurman

Narrator: Christopher Glenn

Music: John Rodby and His Rascals of Rhythm

Producer: David Connell

The Silent Force

Crime Drama; 30 min; ABC 9/21/70 to 1/11/71

The exploits of the Silent Force, a Washington, D.C.-based, secret government organization that is designed to disrupt the inner workings of organized crime.

Amelia Cole	Lynda Day
Jason Hart	Percy Rodrigues
Ward Fuller	Ed Nelson

Producer: Walter Grauman

The Silent Service

Anthology; 30 min; Syn. 1957

Dramas based on the lives of the officers and men of the U.S. Navy's submarine division.

Host-Narrator: Rear Admiral Thomas Dykers

Producer: Darrell McGowan, George M. Cahan, Thomas Dykers

Silents, Please

Documentary; 30 min; ABC 8/4/60 to 10/13/60
3/23/61 to 10/5/61

A history of the silent era of motion pictures.

Host-Narrator: Ernie Kovacs

Producer: Paul Killiam

Silver Spoons

Comedy; 30 min; NBC 9/25/82 to 9/7/86
Syn. First Run 11/86

The story of Edward Stratton III, a divorced, eccentric millionaire who loves toys and heads the Eddie Toys Company, and his son, Ricky, a computer genius, who lives with him in a mansion at 123 Mockingbird Lane on Long Island.

Edward Stratton	Joel Higgins
Ricky Stratton	Ricky Schroder
Kate Sommers	Erin Gray
Leonard	Leonard Lightfoot
Dexter Stuffins	Franklyn Seales
Edward Stratton II	John Houseman
Alfonso Spears	Alfonso Ribeiro
Evelyn Stratton	Christine Belford
Derek Taylor	Jason Bateman
Harry Summers	Ray Walston
Freddy Lippincotterman	Corky Pigeon
Leslie	Georgi Irene
Lulu Baker	Pearl Bailey
Marjorie Sommers	Georgann Johnson
	Gloria Henry
Kate's father	John Inge
Ruth Taylor	Holland Taylor
Myrna Lippincotterman	Miriam Flynn
Marie (Edward's housekeeper)	Jo Marie Payton-France
Kate's Grandmother Pearl	Billie Bird

Producer: David Duclon, Robert Illes, James Stein

Note: Kate and Edward married on 2/10/85

Silver Theatre

Anthology; 30 min; CBS 10/3/49 to 6/26/50

A series of mostly live programs that emphasize both the comedic and dramatic sides of romance. Sponsored by the International Sterling Company.

Host: Conrad Nagel

Producer: Frank Telford

The Silverhawks

Cartoon; 30 min; Syn. 2/86

In the year 2839, Monstar, the most evil of beings, escapes from a prison in the distant galaxy, Limbo. Star Glazer, leader of Limbo, requests help from the Earth to stop Monstar, who is bent on destroying the universe. Five people are chosen to assist: Jonathan Quick, Twins Emily and Will Hart, Bluegrass, and the Copper Kid. To withstand the enormous pressures of space, the team is transformed into the Silverhawks, beings who are part metal, part human, and possess the wings of hawks. Stories relate their efforts to stop Monstar and his evil army from destroying the universe.

Voices: Robert McFadden, Earl Hammond, Larry Kenny, Maggie Jakobson, Peter Newman

Producer: Arthur Rankin Jr., Jules Bass

Simon and Simon

Crime Drama; 60 min; CBS 11/24/81 (Premiere)

The exploits of A.J. and Rick Simon, mismatched brothers who operate Simon & Simon, a freewheeling, but near-bankrupt private detective organization at 3461 LaCosta Road in San Diego.

Andrew "A.J."
Simon   Jameson Parker
Richard "Rick"
Simon   Gerald McRaney
Cecilia Simon   Mary Carver
Det. Marcel
"Downtown"
Brown   Tim Reid
Myron Flower   Ed Barth
Janet Flower   Jeannie Wilson
Elizabeth Charles
(Simon's cousin)   Caren Kaye
Bud Krelman
(Simon's uncle)   Jack Elam
Roy Simon (Simon's
uncle)   John Astin

Producer: Philip DeGuere, John G. Stevens, Chas. Floyd Johnson, Richard Chapman

First Season Theme Vocal ("Theme from Simon & Simon"): The Thrasher Bros.

Remainder Series Theme ("Simon & Simon Theme"): Barry DeVorzon

Simon Lash

Crime Drama Pilot; 30 min; Unaired (Produced in 1960)

A never-televised pilot about Simon Lash, a two-fisted private detective.

Simon Lash   Jock Mahoney
Janie   Elaine Edwards
Slocum   Walter Sande
Lt. Wile   Gregory Walcott
Joe   Edward Kemmer
Mavis   Ann McCrea
Paletti   Warren Stevens

Producer: Sidney Salkow

Sinbad

Adventure Pilot; 60 min; Unaired (Produced for CBS in 1967)

The exploits of Sinbad, "The Ulysses of Persia," as he sails the Arabian Seas seeking adventure.

Sinbad   Michael Stefan
Galgo   Abraham Sofaer
Shalu   Cal Bolder
Shizzan   Sammy Ross
Sultan   Victor Buono

Producer: Frank King

Sing Along

Variety; 30 min; CBS 6/4/58 to 7/16/58

The lyrics to songs are rolled across the bottom of the screen to allow home viewers to singalong with the regular cast.

Host: Jim Lowe

Regulars: Florence Henderson, Tina Robin, June Roselle, Somethin' Smith and the Redheads

Orchestra: Harry Sosnik

Sing Along with Mitch

Variety; 60 min; NBC 1/27/61 to 4/21/61
            9/28/61 to 9/21/64

The lyrics of familiar songs are rolled across the bottom of the screen to allow home viewers to "Sing Along with Mitch" and his TV family.

Host: Mitch Miller

Regulars: Leslie Uggams, Gloria Lambert, Louise O'Brien, Victor Griffin, Gloria Chu, Bob McGrath, Mary Lou Rhyal, Bill Ventura, Phil Okon, Frank Raye, Len Stokes, Tommy Nordon, Stan Carlson, Diana Trask, Jack Brown, Rita McLaughlin, Sam Carter, The James Starbuck Singers

Orchestra: Jimmy Carroll

Producer: Bill Hobin, Gordon Cotler

Note: The pilot aired on NBC on 5/24/60 and featured Diana Trask, Leslie Uggams, and The Brothers Four as guests. Tutti Camarata provided the music and Hubbell Robinson produced it.

Sing-Co-Pation

Dolores Marshall and Joanelle Jones as host of a musical interlude ABC series from Chicago (1/23/49 to 10/30/49).

Sing it Again

Game; 60 min; CBS 10/7/50 to 6/23/51

Object: For players to identify song titles from either several notes of music or from a line from the song itself. Players with the most correct answers receive merchandise prizes.

Host: Dan Seymour, Jan Murray

Regulars: Judy Lynn, Alan Dale, Patti Clayton, Larry Douglas, Bob Howard, The Riddlers

Orchestra: Ray Bloch

Producer: Lester Gottlieb, Louis Cowan, Herb Moss

The Singers

Variety Pilot; 60 min; CBS 9/8/69

An unsold series that was to spotlight performances by the top names in show business.

Hostess: Michele Lee

Producer: Mel Torme, Bill Foster

The Singing Lady

Children; 30 min; ABC 8/12/48 to 8/6/50
9/27/53 to 3/21/54

A program of music, songs, and fairy tales with Ireene Wicker, the Singing Lady. Also known as "Ireene Wicker Story Time" (1953–54).

The Singing Lady: Ireene Wicker

Featured: The Suzari Marionettes

Music: Allen Grant

Producer: Balir Walliser

The Single Life

Comedy Pilot; 30 min; NBC 8/21/80

The life of Barrie Shepherd, a beautiful writer for "The Single Life," a lonely-hearts column for "Manhattanite" magazine.

Barrie Shepherd	Barrie Youngfellow
Stephanie	Celia Weston
Rocky	Paul Regina
Doris	Joyce Reehling
John Muller	Fred McCarren

Theme Vocal ("The Single Life"): Phyllis Brown

Singles

Comedy Pilot; 30 min; CBS 3/17/72

The misadventures of Michele and Ruth, working girls in a greeting card company who are also best friends and roommates.

Michele	Michele Lee
Ruth	Ruth Buzzi
Sidney	Henry Jones
Freddy	John Byner
Cop	Jerry Fogel

Producer-Director: Sheldon Leonard

Sir Francis Drake

See "The Adventures of Sir Francis Drake."

Sirota's Court

Comedy; 30 min; NBC 12/1/76 to 4/13/77

A comical look at life in a night court as seen through the hectic experiences of Matthew J. Sirota, a compassionate judge.

Matthew Sirota	Michael Constantine
Maureen O'Connor	Cynthia Harris
Gail Goodman	Kathleen Miller
Sawyer Dabney	Ted Ross
H.R. Bud Nugent	Fred Willard
John Belson	Owen Bush

Producer: Harvey Miller, Peter Miller

Siskel & Ebert at the Movies

Movie critics Gene Siskel and Roger Ebert review first-run feature films and movies available on video cassette. The thirty minute series was syndicated in September of 1986. Produced by Donna La Pietra.

Sister Terri

Comedy Pilot; 30 min; ABC 5/27/78

The story of Terri Morgan, a former gang leader (as Terri the Terror of the Velvet Knuckles Gang) who becomes a Catholic nun. The unsold series was to relate Terri's experiences teaching youngsters at a grammar school.

Sister Terri	Pam Dawber
Mother Superior	
Helen	Allyn Ann McLerie
Sister Agatha	Amy Johnson
Samantha	Robbie Lee
Angel	Scott Colomby
Jenny	Kimberly LaPage

Theme Vocal ("Sister Terri"): Shelby Flint

Producer: Bob Brunner, Arthur Silver

Sit or Miss

Game; 30 min; ABC 8/6/50 to 10/29/50

Five players compete and each walks around four chairs. When a musical selection stops, each has to grab a chair and sit down. Players who are sitting each receive $10. The standing player is asked a question. If he answers it correctly, he receives $10. If not, he receives one more chance to win the money by performing a stunt.

Hostess: Kay Westfall

Assistant: George Sotos

Sitcom

Comedy Pilot; 30 min; HBO 10/2/83

A spoof of TV sitcoms as seen through the eyes of the Gooseberry's, a less-than-intelligent American family fraught with problems.

Bronco Gooseberry	Alan Young
Betty Gooseberry	Alice Hirson
Sis Gooseberry	Dey Young
Junior Gooseberry	John Calvin
Chip Gooseberry	W.H. Macy
Al Slavedriver	Hansford Rowe

Producer: Bernie Brillstein, Jay Tarses

The Six Million Dollar Man

Adventure; 60 min; ABC 10/20/73 to 2/27/78

When civilian astronaut Steve Austin is seriously injured during a test flight, Oscar Goldman (of the Office of Scientific Intelligence) arranges a six million dollar bionic operation to save Steve's life (replacing both legs, his right arm and eye with synthetic, nuclear-powered mechanisms that produce superhuman abilities). Stories relate Steve's assignments on behalf of the O.S.I. See also "The Bionic Woman."

Steve Austin	Lee Majors
Oscar Goldman	Richard Anderson
Dr. Rudy Wells	Alan Oppenheimer
	Martin E. Brooks
Janet (a.k.a.Peggy)	
Callahan	Jennifer Darling
Miss Johnson	Susan Keller
Jaime Sommers	Lindsay Wagner
Kelly Wood and	
Victoria Webster	
(Steve's friends)	Farrah Fawcett
Shalon (alien)	Stefanie Powers
Aploy (alien)	Severn Darden
Big Foot	Andre the Giant
	Ted Cassidy
Kuroda (Japanese	
soldier Steve	
found in a jungle)	John Fujioka

Theme Vocal ("The Six Million Dollar Man"): Dusty Springfield

Producer: Harve Bennett, Allan Balter, Kenneth Johnson, Glen A. Larson

The Six O'Clock Follies

Comedy; 30 min; NBC 4/24/80 to 4/26/80
8/2/80 (1 episode)
9/13/80 (1 episode)

The series, set in wartime Saigon (1967) relates the antics of the staff of "The AFVN (Armed Forces Vietnam Network) News and Sports," a six o'clock news program that is known as "The Follies."

Col. Harvey Marvin	Joby Baker
Candi LeRoy	Aarika Wells
Sam Paige	A.C. Weary
Cpl. Don Robinson	Laurence Fishburne
Lt. Vaughn Beuhler	Randall Carver
Midas Metcovitch	Philip Charles
	MacKenzie
Ho	George Kee Cheung
Percy Wiggins	David Hubbard
Lou Roskoe	Howard Witt
Marcel Valjean	Byron Webster
Voice of Lyndon B.	
Johnson	Fred Travalena

Theme Vocal ("Home"): Joe Crocker

Producer: Marvin Kupfer, Norman Steinberg

The Six of Us

Drama Pilot; 60 min; NBC 6/13/82

A story of two broken families struggling to become one as seen through the marriage of Sally Benjamin and Kevin Tree, divorced parents with children from their previous marriages. See also "Family Tree."

Sally Benjamin-Tree	Gail Strickland
Tessa Benjamin	Susan Swift
Sam Benjamin	Lee Montgomery
Toby Benjamin	Jonathan Hall
	Kovacs
Kevin Tree	Marco St. John
Jake Tree	Patrick Cassidy
Robert Benjamin	Philip R. Allen

Producer: Nigel Mackeand, Deanne Berkley

Six Pack

Drama Pilot; 60 min; NBC 7/24/83

When stock car racer Brewster Baker catches the five Akins children attempting to strip his car, he takes them under his wing when he learns they are orphans (their parents killed in an auto crash). The unsold series was to relate Brewster's everyday problems as he attempts to care for his new family.

Brewster Baker	Don Johnson
Sally Leadbetter	Markie Post
Heather "Breezy"	
Akins	Jennifer Runyon
Duffy Akins	Billy Warlock
Rebel Akins	Bubba Dean
Hank Akins	Con Martin
Tad Akins	Leaf Phoenix
Sybil Cadbury	Mae Marmy

Producer: Gy Waldron, Rod Amateau

The Sixth Sense

Drama; 60 min; ABC 1/15/72 to 12/30/72

The investigations of Michael Rhodes, a professor of parapsychology at the University School in Los Angeles, as he helps people threatened by "ghosts" and solves crimes that are linked to supernatural occurances.

Michael Rhodes	Gary Collins
Nancy Murphy	Catherine Farrar

Producer: Stan Sheptner

The $64,000 Challenge

Game; 30 min; CBS 4/8/56 to 9/7/58

An extension series based on "The $64,000 Question." Three players compete: one "Question" champion and two challengers. Contestants, placed in separate isolation booths, answers questions based on a category chosen by the champion. Incorrect answers defeat a player and money doubles as in "The $64,000 Question."

Host: Sonny Fox, Ralph Story

Announcer: Bill Rogers

Producer: Merrill Heatter

The $64,000 Question

Game; 30 min; CBS 6/7/55 to 11/2/58

Players, who possess knowledge in at least one specific field, compete. The player begins by answering one question, which is worth one dollar. Each additional question doubles the previous amount of money; however, an incorrect response defeats a player who loses everything he has won up to that point. A player's winnings are based on either his ability to correctly answer the $64,000 question, or at what money point he decided to quit.

Host: Hal March

Assistant: Lynn Dollar

Announcer: Wayne Howell

Producer: Merrill Heatter, Mert Hoplin, Joseph Cates

Revlon Spokeswoman: Barbara Britton

Skag

Drama; 60 min; NBC 1/6/80 to 2/21/80

The story of Peter "Skag" Skagska, a steel mill foreman (for East Pittsurgh Steel, Local 1602), a loving husband, and father of four troubled children.

Peter Skagska	Karl Malden
Jo Skagska	Piper Laurie
Patricia Skagska	Kathryn Holcomb
Barbara Skagska	Leslie Ackerman
John Skagska	Peter Gallagher
David Skagska	Craig Wasson
Petar Skagska	George Voskovec
Audrey	Gwen Humble
Jim Whalen	Powers Boothe
Zanski	R.G. Armstrong
Packa	Frank Campanella
Madman Meissik	Richard Bright

Producer: Abby Mann, Lee Rich

The Skatebirds

Cartoon; 60 min; CBS 9/10/77 to 1/21/78

Segments: "The Skatebirds" (three rollerskating birds, Knock-Knock, Scooter, and Satchel, plagued by the mischievous Scat Cat); "The Robonic Stooges" (antics of a space age Moe, Larry, and Curly); "Wonder Wheels" (story of Wheelie, the owner of a motorcycle he uses to battle crime); "Woofer and Wimper" (adventures of two detective dogs); and "Mystery Island" (a live-action segment about the evil Dr. Strenge's efforts to control the world).

Scooter	Joe Giamalva
Knock-Knock	Bruce Hoy
Satchel	Ken Means
Scat Cat	Maurice Cook
Moe	Paul Winchell
Larry	Joe Baker
Curly	Frank Welker
Triple O	Ross Martin
Wheelie	Mickey Dolenz
Dooley	Susan Lawrence
Woofer & Wimper	Paul Winchell

Live Action Cast:

Chuck Kelly	Stephen Parr
Sue Corwin	Lynne Marie Johnson
Sandy Corwin	Larry Vouk
Dr. Strenge	Michael Kermotan
Voice of POPS	Frank Welker

Producer: William Hanna, Joseph Barbera, Terry Morse Jr.

Sketchbook

Anthology Pilot; 30 min; ABC 5/24/53

A proposed series of vignettes based on stories by famous authors.

Host: Sir Cedric Hardwicke

Producer Herbert Brodkin

The Skip Farrell Show

Variety; 15 min; ABC 1/17/49 to 8/28/49

A program of music and songs from Chicago.

Host: Skip Farrell

Regulars: Joanelle James, The Adele Scott Trio, The George Baines Trio

Announcer: Jack Lester

Music Director: Bill Moss

Skip Taylor

Crime Drama Pilot; 30 min; Syn. 1953

A little-known, syndicated pilot about the exploits of Skip Taylor, a rugged private detective.

Skip Taylor   Mark Andrews

Also: James Best, Joe Corey, Ralph Hodges, Bobby Ellis

Producer: Stuart Reynolds

Skippy, The Bush Kangaroo

Adventure; 30 min; Syn. 1969

The series, set at the Waratah National Park in Australia, relates the adventures of Sonny Hammond, son of the park ranger (Matt), as he and his pet kangaroo, Skippy, help to protect the game preserve.

Matt Hammond	Ed Devereaux
Sonny Hammond	Garry Pankhurst
Matt Hammond	Ken James
Jerry King	Tony Bonner
Clarissa "Clancy" Merrick	Liza Goddard
Dr. Anna Steiner	Elke Neidhardt

Producer: John McCallum, Bud Austin

Sky King

Adventure; 30 min; CBS 9/16/51 to 9/3/66

The exploits of Sky King, a former naval aviator turned rancher, as he struggles to maintain law and order in the Arizona ranching area of Grover City (near which he maintains the Flying Crown Ranch).

Sky King	Kirby Grant
Penny King	Gloria Winters
Clipper King	Ron Hagerthy
Mitch	Ewing Mitchell

Producer: Darrell McGowan, Clark Playlow, Jack Chertok

Skyhawks

Cartoon; 30 min; ABC 9/6/69 to 9/4/71

The story of the Wilson family, the owners of Skyhawks, Inc., a daredevil air transport and rescue service.

Mike Wilson	Michael Rye
Caroline Wilson	Iris Rainer
Steve Wilson	Casey Kasem
Pappy Wilson	Dick Curtis
Cynthia Hughes	Melinda Casey
Red Hughes	Dick Curtis
Maggie McNally	Joan Gerber
Buck Devlin	Bob Arbogast

"Skyhawks" Theme Vocal: Mike Curb and the Curbstones

Producer: Ken Snyder

The Sky's the Limit

Game; CBS 11/1/54 to 8/19/55 (15 min)
8/22/55 to 6/1/56 (30 min)

Selected studio audience members compete in various contests in return for prizes.

Host: Gene Rayburn

Assistants: Hope Lange, Marilyn Cantor

The Sky's the Limit

Comedy Pilot; 30 min; CBS 8/16/60

The escapades of three trainees at a Naval air base in Pensacola, Florida.

John Holt	Doug McClure
Danny Wallace	Ross Martin
Pete Peterson	Joey Forman
Admiral	Ralph Dumke

Producer: Charles Weintraub

The "Slap" Maxwell Story

Comedy; 30 min; ABC 9/23/87 (Premiere)

The story of Slap Maxwell, a 50-year-old, abrasive and crusty sports writer ("Slap Shots" column) for the "Ledger," a second-rate, Midwest newspaper.

Slap Maxwell	Dabney Coleman
Nelson Kruger	Brian Smiar
Annie Maxwell	Susan Anspach
Judy	Megan Gallagher
Dutchman	Bill Cobbs
Charlie	Bill Calvert
Elliot Maxwell	Joseph Brutsman

Producer: Bernie Brillstein, Roz Doyle

Slattery's People

Drama; 60 min; CBS 9/21/64 to 11/26/65

The story of James Slattery, politician, lawyer, and minority leader in the state legislature who crusades against the injustices of government.

James Slattery	Richard Crenna
Liz Andrews	Kathie Brown
Mike Valera	Alejandro Rey
B.J. Clawson	Maxine Stewart
Wendy Wendkoski	Francine York
Bert Metcaff ·	Tol Avery
Johnny Ramos	Paul Geary
Frank Radcliffe	Edward Asner

Producer: Matthew Rapf

Sledge Hammer

Comedy; 30 min; ABC 9/23/86 to 4/28/87

The exploits of Sledge Hammer, an unorthodox cop who dispenses his own brand of justice to evil doers.

Off. Sledge Hammer	David Rasche
Off. Dori Doreau	Ann-Marie Martin
Capt. Trunk	Harrison Page
Off. Grace	Toni Attell
Off. Woebegone	Duane Tucker
Off. Mayjoy	Leslie Morris
Mrs. Steinberg (Sledge's landlady)	Mei Hunt

Producer: Robert Lovenheim, William P. D'Angelo, Alan Spencer

Sleepy Joe

Children; 15 min; ABC 10/3/49 to 10/28/49
Syn. 1951

A puppet series in which Sleepy Joe, an "Uncle Remus" type of character, tells stories to a young girl.

| Sleepy Joe | Jimmy Scribner |
| Girl | Gayle Scribner |

Slezak and Son

Comedy Pilot; 30 min; CBS 9/5/60

The story of Count Von Slezak, a boastful European nobleman, and his son, Leo, as they attempt to parlay a title into a life of royalty in the U.S.

Count Von Slezak	Walter Slezak
Leo Von Slezak	Leo Slezak
Hotel manager	Norman Lloyd
Hotel guest	Neva Patterson

Producer-Director: John Rich

The Slightly Fallen Angel

Comedy Pilot; 30 min; NBC 5/4/59

The story of Finch, a disreputable soul who enters Heaven and becomes an angel through a clerical error. The unsold series was to relate Finch's efforts to live up to that honor by performing good deeds on earth. Aired on "Alcoa Theatre."

Finch	Walter Slezak
Mills	David White
Stan Gorman	Lee Bergere
Mrs. Edwards	Elizabeth Watts

Producer: William Sackheim

Slither

Comedy Pilot; 30 min; CBS 3/21/74

The hectic misadventures of Dick Kanipsia, a likeable young man who gets involved in unusual situations.

| Dick Kanipsia | Barry Bostwick |
| Ruthie (his girlfriend) | Patti Deutsch |

Producer: Jack Shea

Small and Frye

Comedy; 30 min; CBS 3/7/83 to 3/21/83
6/1/83 to 6/14/83

The exploits of Nick Small, an ex-cop turned owner of Small & Frye Investigations, and his partner Chip Frye, who possesses the ability to reduce his height to six inches (the result of a lab accident), thus making him a master of diminutive undercover work.

Nick Small	Darren McGavin
Chip Frye	Jack Blessing
Phoebe Small (Nick's daughter)	Debbie Zipp
Dr. Henry Hanratty (police chemist)	Bill Daily
Eddie Fitzsimmons (bar owner)	Warren Berlinger
Vicki (waitress at Eddie's Bar)	Victoria Carroll
The Bar Drunk	Dick Wilson

Narrator: Darren McGavin

Producer: William Robert Yates, Nick Arnold, Jan Williams

The Small Fry Club

Children; 30 min; DuMont 3/11/47 to 6/15/51

Bob Emery as the host and producer of a program of stories, game contests, magic tricks, audience participation, and other related entertainment geared to children.

Small Wonder

Comedy; 30 min; Syn. 9/85

In an attempt to help handicapped children, computer engineer Ted Lawson (of United Robotronics) creates Voice Imput Child Identicate, Vicki for short, a very pretty ten-year-old girl who happens to be an experimental robot. Stories relate Vicki's attempts to learn about life; and Ted's efforts to guide her progress and keep her secret until he can perfect her.

Vicki	Tiffany Brissette
Ted Lawson	Dick Christie
Joan Lawson	Marla Pennington
Jamie Lawson	Jerry Supiran
Harriet Brendl	Emily Schulman
Bonnie Brendl	Edie McClurg
Brandon Brendl	William Bogert
Reggie	Paul C. Scott
Harriet's Cousin	
Mary	Leslie Bega
Ted's father (Bill)	Jack Manning
Ted's mother	
(Evelyn)	Peggy Converse

Theme Song ("She's a Small Wonder"): Rod Alexander, Howard Leeds

Producer: Howard Leeds, Budd Grossman

The Smith Family

Comedy-Drama; 30 min; ABC
1/20/71 to 9/8/71
4/12/72 to 6/14/72

Events in the lives of the Smith family: Chad, a detective sergeant with the L.A.P.D., his wife, Betty, and their children, Cindy, Bob, and Brian.

Chad Smith	Henry Fonda
Betty Smith	Janet Blair
Cindy Smith	Darleen Carr
Bob Smith	Ron Howard
Brian Smith	James-Michael Wixted
Ray Martin	John Carter
Capt. Hughes	Charles McGraw

Theme Vocal ("Primrose Lane"): Mike Minor

Producer: Don Fedderson, Edmund Hartmann

The Smothers Brothers Comedy Hour

Variety; 60 min; CBS 2/5/67 to 6/8/69

A controversial (for the time) series of music, songs, and topical skits.

Hosts: Tom and Dick Smothers

Regulars: Pat Paulsen, Jennifer Warren, Leigh French, Bob Einstein, John Hartford, Cathy Cahill, Carl Gotlieb, Jessica Myerson, The Jimmy Joyce Singers, The Anita Kerr Singers, The Ron Poindexter Dancers, The Louis DaPron Dancers

Announcer: Roger Carroll

Orchestra: Nelson Riddle

Producer: Saul Ilson, Ernest Chambers, Chris Bearde, Allan Blye

The Smothers Brothers Show

Comedy; 30 min; CBS 9/17/65 to 9/9/66

Tom Smothers, who drowned at sea many years ago, returns to earth as an apprentice angel and takes up residence in the bachelor apartment of his brother, Dick. Stories relate Tom's efforts to acquire full angel status by helping people in trouble.

Tom Smothers	Himself
Dick Smothers	Himself
Leonard J. Costello	Roland Winters
Harriet Costello	Harriet MacGibbon
Diane Costello	Marilyn Scott
Janet	Ann Elder

"Theme Vocal ("The Smothers Brothers Theme"): Tom and Dick Smothers

Producer: Fred DeCordova

The Smothers Brothers Show

Variety; 60 min; ABC 7/15/70 to 9/16/70

A weekly series of music, songs, and topical humor.

Hosts: Tom and Dick Smothers

Regulars: Sally Struthers, Spencer Quinn

Announcer: Roger Carroll

Orchestra: Denny Vaughn

Producer: Norman Sedawie

The Smothers Brothers Show

Variety; 60 min; ABC 1/3/75 to 5/26/75

A weekly program of music, comedy, and songs.

Hosts: Tom and Dick Smothers

Regulars: Pat Paulsen, Leigh French, Don Novello, Pete Smith, Bob Einstein, Betty Aberlin, Evelyn Russell

Orchestra: Marty Paich

Producer: Joe Hamilton, Gail Parent, Kenny Solms

The Smothers Organic Prime Time Space Ride

Variety; 30 min; Syn. 9/71

A series of off-beat, controversial comedy. (The Space Ride refers to new talent discoveries.)

Host: Tom Smothers

Occasional Co-Host: Dick Smothers

Producer: John Barrett, Norman Sedawie

The Smokey the Bear Show

Cartoon; 30 min; ABC 9/6/69 to 9/12/71

The adventures of Smokey the Bear as both a bear and a cub, as he struggles to protect forests from fire. Produced by Arthur Rankin Jr. and Jules Bass.

The Smurfs

Cartoon; Various (60, 90 & 120 min) NBC 9/12/81 (Premiere)

The adventures of the Smurfs, small blue people who live in a mushroom village concealed in a medieval woods, as they battle Gargamel, an evil wizard who seeks to destroy them.

Gargamel	Paul Winchell
Papa Smurf/Azrael	
the Cat	Don Messick
Brainy Smurf	Danny Goldman
Clumsy Smurf	Bill Callaway
Hefty Smurf/Pee	
Wee Smurf	Frank Welker
Jokey Smurf	June Foray
Smurfette	Lucille Bliss
Vanity Smurf	Alan Oppenheimer
Greedy Smurf	Hamilton Camp
Lazy, Handy, and	
Grouchy Smurf	Michael Bell
Harmony Smurf	Hamilton Camp
King	Bob Holt
Sabina	Jennifer Darling

Producer: William Hanna, Joseph Barbera

Snafu

Comedy Pilot; 30 min; NBC 8/23/76

A humorous look at the insanity of combat as seen through the eyes of battle-weary G.I.'s spending World War II in the muddy trenches of Italy. (The title refers to Situation Normal, All Fouled Up.)

Sgt. Mike Conroy	Tony Roberts
Capt. Bill Kaminski	James Cromwell
Lt. Hemsley Hauser	Kip Niven
Pvt. Wiggins	Fred Fate
Pvt. Crosetti	Joey Aresco
Pvt. Hinkley	Wally Dalton
Capt. Robinson	Phillip R. Allen
Pvt. Lockwood	Terry Hinz
Pvt. Braverman	Jay Leno
Pvt. Fowler	Rick Podell

Producer: Leonard B. Stern

Snap Judgement

Game; 30 min; NBC 9/17/65 to 3/28/69

One player of each two-member team is given a concealed word. Through one-word clues he must relate its meaning to his partner. Words start at ten points and diminish by one point until identified. The player with the highest score wins merchandise prizes.

Host: Ed McMahon, Gene Rayburn

Announcer: Johnny Olsen

Snavely

Comedy Pilot; 30 min; ABC 6/24/78

The story of Henry Snavely, the loud-mouthed and totally incompetent proprietor of Snavely Manor, a resort hotel. Based on the British series "Fawlty Towers."

Henry Snavely	Harvey Korman
Gladys Snavely	Betty White
Connie	Deborah Zon
Petro	Frank LaLoggia
Mr. Bishop	Jack Dodson

Producer: Rod Parker

Sneak Previews

Movie Reviews; 30 min; PBS 1978 (Premiere)

In depth reviews and analysis of current motion pictures.

Host (1978–82): Gene Siskel, Roger Ebert

Host (1982–86): Jeffrey Lyons, Neal Gabler

Host (1986–): Jeffrey Lyons, Michael Medved

The Snooky Lanson Show

Variety; 15 min; NBC 7/17/56 to 9/1/56

Snooky Lanson as the host of a program of music and songs. With the Mellolarks vocal group and the announcing of Bill Wendell.

The Snoop Sisters

Crime Drama; 90 min; NBC 1/29/74 to 8/26/74

The exploits of sisters Ernestine and Gwendolyn Snoop, eccentric mystery writers who solve crimes to acquire story material.

Ernestine Snoop	Helen Hayes
Gwendolyn Snoop	Mildred Natwick
Lt. Steve Ostrowski	Bert Convy
Barney	Art Carney
	Lou Antonio

Producer: Leonard B. Stern

Snorks

Cartoon; 30 min; NBC 9/15/84 to 9/6/86

The misadventures of the Snorks, multi-colored creatures with built-in snorkels, who live beneath the sea.

Voices: Michael Bell, Nancy Cartwright, Peter Cullen, Joan Gardner, Barry Gordon, Gail Matthius, Mitzi McCall, Edie McClurg, Frank Nelson, Robert Ridgely, Frank Welker

Producer: William Hanna, Joseph Barbera

So This Is Hollywood

Comedy; 30 min; NBC 1/1/55 to 8/19/55

The hopes and heartaches of Kim Tarcy, an aspiring actress, and her roommate Queenie Dugan, a stunt girl, as they struggle to make their mark on the movie capital.

Queenie Dugan	Mitzi Green
Kim Tracy	Virginia Gibson
Hubie Dodd	Gordon Jones
Andy Boone	James Lydon
April Adams	Peggy Knudsen
Mr. Snead	Charles Lane
Queenie's stand-in	Shirley Lucas

Narrator: Virginia Gibson

Producer: Edmund Beloin

So You Think You Got Troubles?!

Human Interest; 30 min; Syn. 9/82

People with real-life problems are interviewed then offered advice by a professional guest panel.

Host: Jay Johnson (with his dummy Bob)

Announcer: Rod Roddy

Producer: Ralph Edwards, Stu Billett

So You Want to Lead a Band

Variety; 30 min; NBC 6/11/50 to 7/21/51
CBS 7/28/51 to 7/19/52
NBC 8/8/53 to 9/5/53

Music, songs, comedy vignettes, and a quiz segment wherein studio audience members are selected to lead the orchestra. The best conductor, as determined by audience applause, receives a prize. Also known as "The Sammy Kaye Show."

Host: Sammy Kaye

Band Boy: Chubby Silvers

Regulars: Barbara Benson, Tony Alamo, Jeffrey Clay, The Kaydettes, The Kay Choir

Orchestra: Sammy Kaye

Producer: Jim Lichtman, Vic McLeod, Coby Ruskin

Soap

Satire; 30 min; ABC 9/13/77 to 4/20/81

A spoof of afternoon soap operas as depicted through the lives of two sisters: the wealthy Jessica Tate, and the not-so-rich Mary Campbell. Stories also focus on the outlandish activities of both families, residents of Dunns River, Connecticut.

Jessica Tate	Katherine Helmond
Mary Campbell	Cathryn Damon
Chester Tate	Robert Mandan
Burt Campbell	Richard Mulligan
Corinne Tate	Diana Canova
Eunice Tate	Jennifer Salt
Billy Tate	Jimmy Baio
Danny Dallas	Ted Wass
Jodie Dallas	Billy Crystal
Benson DuBois	Robert Guillaume
Sanders	Roscoe Lee Browne
The Major	Arthur Peterson
Chuck Campbell	Jay Johnson
Tim Flosky	Sal Viscuso
Peter Campbell	Robert Urich
Carol Darwin	Udana Power
Walter McCallam	Edward Winter
Marilyn McCallam	Judith-Marie Bergan
Ingrid Svenson	Ingred Swenson
Randolph Svenson	Bernard Fox
E. Ronald Mallu	Eugene Roche
Mr. Lefkowitz	Sorrell Booke
Elaine Lefkowitz	Dinah Manoff
Carol David	Rebecca Balding
Sheriff Tinkler	Gordon Jump
George Donehue	John Byner
Dutch Lightner	Donnelly Rhodes
Polly Dawson	Lynne Moody
Lorelene David	Peggy Pope
Sol	Jack Gilford
Millie	Candice Azzara
Leslie Walker	Marla Pennington
Sally	Caroline McWilliams
Alice	Randee Heller
Maggie Chandler	Barbara Rhoades
Carlos El Puerco	
Valdez	Gregory Sierra
Gwen	Jesse Wells

Producer: Paul Junger Witt, Tony Thomas, Susan Harris

Announcer: Rod Roddy

Soap Factory Disco

Variety; 30 min; Syn. 1978

The program, taped in Palisades Park, New Jersey, features young adults dancing to disco music. Hosted by Paul Harriss and produced by David Bergman.

Soap World

Magazine; 30 min; Syn. 9/82

A look at the world of TV soap operas via interviews and behind-the-scenes reports.

Host: Michael Young

Reporters: Chantal Westerman, Richard Bey

Producer: Richard S. Kline, Bill Hillier

The Soft Touch

Comedy Pilot; 30 min; CBS 7/3/62

The story of Ernestine McDougal, the beautiful but slightly dizzy daughter of a loan company officer (Charles) who believes her intuition is better than collateral in determining the recipients of loans.

Ernestine McDougal	Marie Wilson
Charles McDougal	Charlie Ruggles
Mrs. Munson	Madge Blake
Mr. Martin	Charles Lane
Woman	Nancy Kulp

Producer: William Harmon

Soldier Parade

Variety; 30 min; NBC 6/25/55 to 9/3/55

Performances by Army talent.

Hosts: Gisele MacKenzie, Arlene Francis, Martha Wright, Richard Hayes

Producer: Dave Nyren

The Soldiers

Comedy; 30 min; NBC 6/25/55 to 9/3/55

The misadventures of two reluctant privates (Hal and Tom) who find nothing but trouble while attempting to complete their hitch with the Army.

Hal	Hal March
Tom	Tom D'Andrea
Captain	John Dehner
Sergeant	Red Pearson

Producer: Bud Yorkin

Soldiers of Fortune

Adventure; 30 min; Syn. 1955

The exploits of Tim Kelly and Toubo Smith, American soldiers of fortune, as they battle the forces of injustice throughout the world.

Tim Kelly   John Russell
Toubo Smith   Chick Chandler

Producer: John English

Solid Gold

Variety; 60 min; Syn. 9/80

Live performances by the top names in music.

Hostess: Dionne Warwick, Marilyn McCoo

Hosts: Rex Smith, Rick Dees

Regulars: Wayland Flowers, Marty Cohen, Steve Allen, Arsenio Hall, Nina Blackwood, The Solid Gold Dancers (Beverly Jeanne, Jamilah Lucas, Darcel, Pamela Rossi, Eileen Fairbanks, Derek Jackson, Nicole Romine, Mark Sellers)

Announcer: Robert W. Morgan

Orchestra: Michael Miller

Producer: Bob Banner, Brad Lachman

Solid Gold Hits

Variety; 30 min; Syn. 6/84

A daily extension series based on the weekly "Solid Gold" series that features the latest in music videos.

Host: Grant Goodeve

Announcer: Robert W. Morgan

Producer: Brad Lachman

Solo

Comedy; 30 min; Syn. 2/87

The story of Gemma Palmer, a beautiful, unmarried thirty-year-old woman, as she struggles to cope with life on her own.

Gemma Palmer   Felicity Kendal
Danny   Stephen Moore
Mrs. Palmer   Elspet Gray
Bernadette   Stella Goodier
Josie   Debbie Wheeler

Producer: Gareth Gwenlan

The Somerset Maugham Theatre

See "Teller of Tales."

Something Special

A syndicated (1966) series of variety programs tailored to the talents of its guest hosts (Barbara McNair, Patti Page, Pearl Bailey, Julie London, Ethel Waters, Allan Sherman, Peggy Lee, The New Christy Minstrels, and The Young Americans). Produced by Stewart Moss.

Something Else

Variety; 30 min; Syn. 1969

Performances by the recording industry's top stars. Hosted by John Byner and featuring the Action Faction Dancers. Produced by Robert Dellinger.

Somewhere in Italy . . . Company B

Comedy Pilot; 60 min; ABC 8/21/66

The World War II antics of a foul-up infantry squadron cut off from its battalion command.

Lt. John Leahy   Robert Reed
Sgt. Willie Krantz   Harold J. Stone
Selena   Barbara Shelley
Paulo Pietri   Vassill Lambrinos

Producer-Writer-Director: Danny Arnold

Song and Dance Time

Variety; 15 min; NBC 12/17/48 to 6/21/49

A live program of music, song, and dance.

Hosts: Roberta Quinlan, Barbara Marshall

Dancers: Ellsworth and Fairchild

Music: The Tony Mottola Trio

Song Snapshots on a Summer Holiday

Variety; 15 min; CBS 6/24/54 to 9/9/54

A Summer series of music and song with singers Merv Griffin and Betty Ann Grove. With The Peter Birch Dancers and the orchestra of Henry Sylvern. Produced by Byron Paul.

Songs at Twilight

An NBC series (7/3/51 to 8/31/51) of music and songs with Bob Carroll, Buddy Greco, and Johnny Andrews.

Songs for Sale

Variety; 30 min; CBS 7/7/50 to 6/28/52

The material of four songwriters (per show) is performed, then judged and evaluated by a professional panel.

Host: Jan Murray, Steve Allen

Vocalists: Margaret Whiting, Rosemary Clooney, Richard Hayes, Toni Arden, Betty Clooney, Bob Carroll, Martha Stewart, Don Cherry, Eileen Burton, Helen Forrest, Joan Edwards, Johnny Johnston, Tony Bennett, Richard Himber, The Four Aces

Judges: Mitch Miller, Morey Amsterdam, Bob Hilliard, Martin Block, Duke Ellington, Dorothy Loudon

Orchestra: Ray Bloch

Producer: Al Span, Herb Morse, Bob Bleyer

The Son-in-Law

Comedy Pilot; 30 min; NBC 10/26/80

The story of an American girl (Cindy) who marries an unemployed Korean comic (Johnny) and the misadventures that ensue when they move in with her disapproving father (Manny) and mother (Charlotte).

Cindy Quan	Judith-Marie Bergan
Johnny Quan	Johnny Yune
Charlotte Sugarman	Rue McClanahan
Manny Sugarman	Pat Cooper
Mr. Muirfield	Bernard Fox

Producer: Martin Starger, Arthur Julian

The Sonny and Cher Comedy Hour

Variety; 60 min; CBS 8/1/71 to 5/29/74

A weekly program of music, songs, and comedy.

Hosts: Sonny Bono and Cher

Regulars: Chastity Bono, Peter Cullen, Ted Zeigler, Clive Clerk, Murray Riff, Teri Garr, Freeman King, Billy Van, Murray Langston, Steve Parker, The Jaime Rogers Dancers, The Tony Mordente Dancers, The Earl Brown Singers

Announcer: Peter Cullen

Orchestra: Jimmy Dale, Marty Paich

Producer: Allan Blye, Chris Bearde

The Sonny and Cher Show

Variety; 60 min; CBS 2/1/76 to 3/18/77

A revised version of the previous title, which features music, songs, and comedy sketches.

Hosts: Sonny Bono and Cher

Regulars: Ted Zeigler, Billy Van, Peter Cullen, Jack Harnell, Richard Lewis, Felix Silla

Orchestra: Harold Battiste

Producer: Nick Vanoff

Sonny Boy

Comedy Pilot; 30 min; CBS 5/16/74

The story of Gregory "Sonny" Waller, a 35-year-old frustrated mama's boy.

Sonny Waller	Allen Garfield
Marjorie Waller	Florence Stanley
Lorraine	Yvonne Wilder
Uncle Ralph	Joshua Shelley
Doris	Beverly Carter

Producer: Robert Precht, Rob Reiner, Phil Mishkin

The Sonny Comedy Revue

Variety; 60 min; ABC 9/22/74 to 12/29/74

A weekly program of music and comedy.

Host: Sonny Bono

Regulars: Teri Garr, Ted Zeigler, Freeman King, Peter Cullen, Billy Van, Murray Langston

Announcer: Peter Cullen

Orchestra: Lex DeAvezedo

Producer: Allan Blye, Chris Bearde

The Sonny Kendis Show

Variety; 15 min; CBS 4/18/49 to 1/6/50

An interlude series of music and songs with host Sonny Kendis and singer Gigi Durston. Produced by Barry Wood.

Sons and Daughters

Drama; 60 min; CBS 9/12/74 to 11/6/74

A depiction of the last innocence of American youth as seen through the eyes of Anita Cramer and Jeff Reed, seniors at Southwest High School in Stockton, California, during the 1950s.

Anita Cramer	Glynnis O'Connor
Jeff Reed	Gary Frank
Ruth Cramer	Jan Shutan
Walter Cramer	John S. Ragin
Lucille Reed	Jay W. McIntosh
Danny Reed	Michael Morgan
Evie Martinson	Debralee Scott
Murray "Moose" Kerner	Barry Livingston
Mary Anne	Laura Siegel
Stash	Scott Colomby
Charlie	Lionel Johnston
Lisa	Chris Nelson
Tina	Randi Kallan
Marylou	Teresa Medaris
Dana	Cheryl Linde
Angie	Bonnie Van Dyke

Producer: David Levinson, Michael Gleason

Sorority '62

Comedy Pilot; 30 min; Syn. 1/78

The experiences of four Gamma Phi sorority sisters at Stafford College in Northern Indiana in 1962.

Vickie	Marcie Hanson
Cindy	Karen Bercovici
Sheila	Myra Small
Gloria	Suzanne Wishner
Miss Fletcher	Marj Dusay
Coach	Joey Bishop
Roger	John Torp

Producer: Dick Clark, Jerry Frank

Soul Train

A syndicated (1971) series, hosted by Don Cornelius, and featuring performances by soul stars. Produced by Don Cornelius.

Sound Off Time

Variety; 60 min; NBC 10/14/51 to 1/6/52

A short-lived series of programs tailored to the talents of its rotating hosts and their guests.

Rotating Hosts: Fred Allen, Bob Hope, Jerry Lester

Announcer: Hy Averback

Orchestra: Al Goodman, Les Brown

Producer: Doug Coulter, Monroe Hack, Jack Hope

The Soupy Sales Show

Comedy; 30 min; ABC 7/4/55 to 8/26/55
10/3/59 to 4/1/61
Syn. 1966 to 1968

The slapstick antics of Soupy Sales, a comedian who seems to attract misadventure. Puppet characters include White Fang, Black Tooth, Pookie the Lion, and Hippie the Hippo.

Host: Soupy Sales

Regulars: Clyde Adler, Frank Nastagia

Southern Fried

Comedy Pilot; 30 min; NBC 8/3/70

The misadventures of Lonnie Allen, a stock car racer who, in the pilot, gets duped into running moonshine.

Lonnie Allen	John Neilson
Wilma	Dorra Cook
Lamaar	Ramon Bieri
Alvin	Jerry Lanning

Producer-Director: Gene Reynolds

Space Academy

Adventure; 25 min; CBS 9/10/77 to 9/8/79

The exploits of the Nova Blue Team, a futuristic group of young cadets assigned for training on the man-made planetoid Space Academy, as they patrol, protect, and explore the universe in the year 3732.

Cmdr. Gampu	Jonathan Harris
Cadet Laura Gentry	Pamelyn Ferdin
Cadet Adrian	Maggie Cooper
Capt. Chris Gentry	Ric Carrott
Lt. Paul Jerome	Ty Henderson
Cadet Tee Gar	Brian Tochi
Loki (alien ally)	Eric Greene

Producer: Norm Prescott, Lou Scheimer

Space Angel

Cartoon; 5 min; Syn. 2/62

The exploits of Scott McCloud, alias Space Angel, an agent for the Interplanetary Space Force, as he battles evil in outer space.

Scott McCloud	Ned Lefebver

Producer: Dick Brown

Space Force

Comedy Pilot; 30 min; NBC 4/28/78

The comic adventures of a crew of astronauts assigned to a remote military space station.

Cmdr. Irving Hinkley	William Edward Phipps
Capt. Thomas Woods	Fred Willard
Pvt. Arnold Fleck	Larry Block
Capt. Leon Stoner	Jimmy Boyd
Capt. Robert Milford	Hilly Hicks
Sgt. Eve Bailey	Maureen Mooney

Producer: John Boni, Norman Stiles

Space Ghost

Cartoon; 30 min; CBS 9/10/66 to 9/7/68

Segments: "Space Ghost" (about an interplanetary crime fighter) and "Dino Boy" (prehistoric adventures with Tag and Ugh as they battle evil).

Space Ghost	Gary Owens
Jan	Ginny Tyler
Tad	John E. Carson
Ugh	Mike Road

Producer: William Hanna, Joseph Barbera

Space Giants

Adventure; 30 min; Syn. 1969

When the evil alien scientist Rodak begins his invasion of the planet Earth, the Earth responds by constructing Goldar, a 50-foot gold robot, Silva, its silver wife, and Gam, their gold son. Stories relate the robots efforts to defend the Earth against Rodak's creatures of destruction. Produced in Japan; dubbed in English.

Tomoko Mura	Mayako Yashiro
Mikko Mura	Toshio Egi
Itomura	Masumi Okada
Gam	Hideki Ninomiya

Space Kiddettes

Cartoon; 30 min; NBC 9/10/66 to 9/2/67

The battle against celestial evil as seen through the exploits of the Space Kiddettes, a group of space-age youngsters.

Scooter	Chris Allen
Snoopy	Lucille Bliss
Countdown	Don Messick
Jenny	Janet Waldo
Capt. Skyhook	Daws Butler
Pupstar	Don Messick

Producer: William Hanna, Joseph Barbera

Space: 1999

Science Fiction; 60 min; Syn. 9/75

In the year 1999, shortly after an early warning system is established to repel alien invaders, a radioactive chain reaction blasts the moon out of its Earth orbit. Three hundred men and women are marooned as the moon slowly begins to drift in space, seeking a new planet to which to affix itself. Stories relate the marooned Earthlings' adventures in the far regions of outer space.

Cmdr. John Koenig	Martin Landau
Dr. Helena Russell	Barbara Bain
Maya	Catherine Schell
Prof. Victor Bergman	Barry Morse
Tony Verdeschi	Tony Anholt
Sandra Benes	Zienia Merton
Yasko	Yasuko Nagazumi
Dr. Bob Mathias	Anton Phillips
Dr. Ben Vincent	Jeffrey Kisson
Bill Frazer	John Hug
David Kano	Prentiss Hancock
Dr. Ed Spencer	Sam Destor

Producer: Gerry Anderson, Sylvia Anderson, Fred Freiberger

Space Patrol

Adventure; ABC 3/13/50 to 7/2/54 (15 min)
9/11/50 to 2/26/55 (30 min)

The battle against celestial dangers as seen through the assignments of Buzz Corey, the commander-in-chief of the Space Patrol, a 21st-century organization that is responsible for the safety of the United Planets (Earth, Mars, Venus, Jupiter, and Mercury).

Cmdr. Buzz Corey	Ed Kemmer
Cadet Happy	Lyn Osborn
Carol Carlisle	Virginia Hewitt
Tonga	Nina Bara
Dr. Von Meter	Rudolph Anders
Maj. Robbie Robertson	Ken Mayer
Kitt Corey*	Glen Denning
Evil Prince Bacarrati	Bela Kovacs
Secretary General	Hal Forrest
	Paul Cavanaugh
Mr. Proteus	Marvin Miller
Major Sova	Jack McHugh

Announcer: Jack Narz

Producer: Dick Darley, Bela Kovacs

*In March of 1950, when the series was local over KECA-TV in Los Angeles, Kitt (Buzz's brother) was the original patrol leader.

Space Stars

Cartoon; 60 min; NBC 9/12/81 to 9/11/82

Segments: "Space Ghost" (exploits of Space Ghost, Blip, and Jan and Jace as they battle evil); "Teen Force" (futuristic adventures with Kid Comet and the Teen Force: Elektra, Moleculad, Plutem, Glax, and Uglor); "The Herculoids" (a group of space creatures struggling to protect their planet from alien invaders); and "Astro and the Space Mutts" (comedy about the futuristic detective Space Ace and three space mutts: Astro, Cosmo, and Dipper).

Space Ghost	Gary Owens
Jan	Alexandra Stoddard
Jace	Steve Spears
Blip	Frank Welker
Kid Comet	Darryl Hickman
Elektra	B.J. Ward
Moleculad	David Hubbard
Plutem/Glax	Mike Winslow
Uglor	Alan Lurie
Zandor/Zok/Igoo/ Thundro	Mike Road
Gleep/Gloop	Don Messick
Tara	Virginia Gregg
Dorno	Sparky Marcus
Space Ace	Michael Bell
Dipper	Lennie Weinrib
Astro	Don Messick

Producer: William Hanna, Joseph Barbera

Sparring Partners

Game; 30 min; CBS 4/8/49 to 5/6/49

Male vs. female teams compete in a question-and-answer session with the highest scorers receiving prizes.

Host: Walter Kiernan

Producer: Sean Dillon

Sparrow

Crime Drama Pilot; 60 min; CBS 1/12/78

The story of Jerry Sparrow, a mailroom clerk turned detective. In the first pilot (see next title) Sparrow attempts to solve a series of senseless and unrelated crimes.

Jerry Sparrow	Randy Herman
Mr. Medwick (employer)	Don Gordon
Tammy (Medwick's secretary)	Beverly Sanders
Harriet (Jerry's girlfriend)	Karen Sedgley
Karen	Dori Brenner
Marty	Lenny Baker
Bruce	Jeff Holland

Producer: Herbert B. Leonard

Sparrow

Crime Drama Pilot; 60 min; CBS 8/11/78

The exploits of Jerry Sparrow, an investigator with a large New Orleans detective agency. The second story relates Jerry's efforts to recover a valuable missing bird.

Jerry Sparrow	Randy Herman
Mr. Medwick (employer)	Gerald S. O'Loughlin
Valerie (Jerry's girlfriend)	Catherine Hicks
Mrs. Benet	Lillian Gish
Landon	Dolph Sweet
Dory	Jonelle Allen

"Sparrow" Theme Song: Paul Williams

Producer: Herbert B. Leonard

Speak Up America

Human Interest; 60 min; NBC
4/22/80 to 4/29/80
8/1/80 to 10/10/80

People speak directly to the camera and relate their thoughts concerning the issues that affect their daily lives

Hosts: Marjoe Gortner, Jayne Kennedy, Rhonda Bates, Herb Brooks, Felicia Jeter, Magic Johnson

Theme Vocal: Jim Kirk and the TM Singers

Producer: George Schlatter, John Barbour, Bob Wynn

Special Agent 7

Drama; 30 min; Syn. 1958

The exploits of Philip Conroy, a U.S. Treasury Agent, as he investigates crimes against the IRS. Starring Lloyd Nolan as Agent Philip Conroy.

Special Edition

Barbara Feldon as host of a syndicated (1977) series of filmed versions of magazine stories. Produced by Alan P. Sloan.

Speed Buggy

Cartoon; 30 min; CBS 9/8/73 to 8/31/74

The story of a talking car (Speed Buggy) and its three human friends (Debbie, Tinker, and Mark) and their adventures as they travel around the country.

Speed Buggy	Mel Blanc
Debbie	Arlene Golonka
Mark	Michael Bell
Tinker	Phil Luther

Producer: William Hanna, Joseph Barbera

Speed Racer

Cartoon; 30 min; Syn. 9/67

A Japanese produced series about a daring young racing car driver named Speed Racer.

Speed Racer	Jack Grimes
Trixie/Spridal/Mrs. Racer	Corinne Orr
Racer X/Pops Racer	Jack Curtis

Producer: Tatsuo Yoshida

Spencer

Comedy; 30 min; NBC 12/1/84 to 1/12/85

The adventures of Spencer Winger, a slightly offbeat, girl-crazy 16-year-old high school student who excels in finding trouble. See also "Under One Roof."

Spencer Winger	Chad Lowe
Doris Winger	Mimi Kennedy
George Winger	Ronny Cox
Andrea Winger	Amy Locane
Benjamin Beanley	Richard Sanders
Miss Speer	Beverly Archer
Wayne	Grant Heslov
Herbie	David Greenlee
	Dean Cameron

Producer: Mort Lachman, Sy Rosen

Spencer's Pilots

Adventure; 60 min; CBS 9/17/76 to 11/19/76

The exploits of Cass Garrett and Stan Lewis, charter pilots for Spencer Aviation, a California-based organization that tackles hazardous assignments. The pilot aired 4/9/76.

Cass Garrett	Christopher Stone
Stan Lewis	Todd Susman
Spencer Parish	Gene Evans
Linda Dann	Margie Impert
Mickey "Wig"	
Wiggins	Britt Leach

Producer: Bob Sweeney, Edward H. Feldman, Larry Rosen

Spenser: For Hire

Crime Drama; 60 min; ABC 9/20/85 (Premiere)

The exploits of Sam Spenser, a Boston-Based private detective who helps people in deep trouble.

Sam Spenser	Robert Urich
Susan Silverman (his	
love interest)	Barbara Stock
Rita Fiori (love	
interest, later)	Carolyn McCormick
Hawk (Sam's friend)	Avery Brooks
Lt. Martin Quirk	Richard Jaeckel
Sgt. Frank Belson	Ron McLarty

Producer: John Wilder, William Robert Yates

Spider-Man

Cartoon; 30 min; ABC 8/30/69 to 9/9/72

While attending a demonstration of radioactivity, New York Central High School student Peter Parker is bitten by a spider that had been exposed to radiation. Later, Peter realizes that the spider's venom has become a part of his bloodstream and that he has absorbed the proportionate power and ability of a living spider. Developing a special costume, and acquiring a job as a reporter for the "Daily Bugle," Peter wages a war on crime, dispensing justice as the mysterious Spider-Man. See also "The Amazing Spider-Man."

Peter/Spider-Man	Bernard Cowan
	Peter Soles
Betty Brandt	Peg Dixon
J. Jonah Jameson	Paul Kligman

Producer: Robert L. Lawrence

Spider-Man

See "The Amazing Spider-Man."

Spider-Woman

Cartoon; 30 min; ABC 9/22/79 to 3/1/80

While in her father's lab, Jessica Drew is bitten by a poisonous spider. With only one hope of saving his daughter's life, Dr. Drew injects her with an experimental spider serum. The serum saves her life and endows her with extraordinary powers. Stories depict Jessica's exploits as she battles evil as Spider-Woman.

Jessica/Spider-	
Woman	Joan Van Ark
Jeff Hunt	Bruce Miller
Billy Drew	Byron Scott

Announcer: Dick Tufeld

Producer: David DePatie, Friz Freleng

Spies

Adventure; 60 min; CBS 3/3/87 (Premiere)

Rather than fire Ian Stone, a master spy for The Company who defies rules and regulations, "C of B" Brady, head of the U.S. government agency, decides to give him a second chance if he will mend his ways and train Ben Smythe, an idealistic new agent. Stories relate Ian's adventures as he tries to live by the rules, yet break them when he finds it is the only way he can complete an assignment. See the following title also.

Ian Stone	George Hamilton
Ben Smythe	Gary Kroeger
"C of B" Brady	Barry Corbin

Theme Vocal ("Someone's Gotta Do It"): Deborah Davis

Producer: Jordan Moffet

Spies

Adventure Pilot; 60 min; Unaired (Produced for CBS in 1986)

The original pilot for the above series which relates the adventures of master spy Ian Stone. Exactly the same storyline as the above title, but with a different cast and a different theme song.

Ian Stone	Tony Curtis
Ben Smythe	Gary Kroeger
Thomas Brady	Kevin McCarthy

Producer: Jordan Moffet

The Spike Jones Show

Variety; 60 min; NBC 1/2/54 to 5/8/54

Music, song, and outlandish comedy with bandleader Spike Jones and regulars Helen Grayco, Jan Peerce, George Rock, Freddie Morgan, Sir Frederick Gar, and the Wayne Marlin Trio. Music by the City Slickers.

The Spike Jones Show

Variety 30 min; CBS 4/2/57 to 8/27/57

A weekly series of music, song, and comedy.

Host: Spike Jones

Regulars: Helen Grayco, Billy Barty

Announcer: Jack Narz

Music: The City Slickers

Producer: Tom Waldman, Dick Darley

The Spike Jones Show

Variety; 60 min; CBS 8/1/60 to 9/19/60
                         7/17/61 to 9/25/61

Spike Jones as the host of a Summer series of music and comedy with vocalist Helen Grayco and the music of the City Slickers.

Spin and Marty

Comedy; 30 min; ABC 11/7/55 to 12/9/55

A "Mickey Mouse Club" serial about two boys, Spin and Marty, and their experiences at the Triple R Summer Boys Camp. See also "The Further Adventures of Spin and Marty" and "The New Adventures of Spin and Marty."

Spin Evans	Tim Considine
Marty Markham	David Stollery
Jim Logan	Roy Barcroft
Bill Burnett	Harry Carey Jr.
Perkins	J. Pat O'Malley
Sam	Sammee Tong
Ambitious	B.G. Norman
Joe	Sammy Ogg
Speckle	Tim Hartnagle

Producer: Walt Disney, Bill Walsh

Spin-Off

Game; 30 min; CBS 6/16/75 to 9/5/75

Placed before two husband-and-wife couples are five numbered wheels (1 to 6) that spin at the rate of 17 numbers per second. When a team correctly answers a question, a number is revealed. The team can keep the number or spin it off for another number. Five questions are played and the team with the highest number values (as in poker) is the winner.

Host: Jim Lange

Producer: Nick Nicholson, E. Roger Muir

Spin the Picture

Game; 60 min; DuMont 6/18/49 to 2/4/50

A rapidly spun picture is flashed on the screen, followed by a verbal clue. A telephone call is placed to a home viewer (post card selection) who is asked to identify the picture. A prize is awarded if he can; a consolation prize if he is unable.

Host: Carl Caruso, Eddie Dunn, Kathi Norris

Regulars: Shaye Coogan, Bob Dunn

Spitting Image

Satire Pilot; 30 min; NBC 8/30 & 9/6/86 (1st
                                  pilot)
                         1/14/87 (2nd pilot)

A would-be American series in which life size puppets (from England's Spitting Image Workshop) lampoon famous celebrities. In the first pilot, "Down and Out in the White House," celebrities who secretly control the U.S., attempt to elect Sylvester Stallone as the next President. The second story, "The Ronnie and Nancy Show," relates Nancy efforts to throw a surprise anniversary party for hubby Ron, depicted as the senile President of the U.S.

Host (1st Pilot Only): David Frost

Voices: Chris Barrie, Louise Duart, Jon Glover, Jessica Martin, John Sessions, Harry Shearer, Pamela Stephenson, Frank Welker

Producer: John Lloyd, Jon Blair, David Frost

Split Personality

Game; 30 min; NBC 9/28/59 to 2/5/60

Two sets of clues, each of which depicts one facet of a celebrity's life, are relayed to two players. The first player to identify the celebrity scores one point. The highest scorer receives merchandise prizes.

Host: Tom Poston

Producer: Mark Goodson, Bill Todman

Split Second

Game; 30 min; Syn. 9/86

Three subjects are revealed on a screen. Each of the three players who compete must give an answer that corresponds to one of the subjects. Money is scored for each correct answer, and the highest money scorer is the winner.

Host: Monty Hall

Producer: Stefan Hatos, Monty Hall

Split Second

Game; 30 min; ABC 3/20/72 to 6/27/75

Three topics are displayed (e.g., Mad, Playboy, and People magazines) and a question is read that refers to them. Players sound a bell and give their answers as they are recognized. If all three players choose the same answer, and are correct, each receives $5; if two choose the same correct response, $10 is awarded; a single player with the correct answer wins $25. Several such rounds are played and the player with the highest score is the winner.

Host: Tom Kennedy

Announcer: Jack Clark

Producer: Stu Billett

Sport Billy

Cartoon; 30 min; Syn. 6/82

When Sporticus XI, ruler of the planet Olmpus, discovers that the evil Queen Vanda is responsible for ruining sports throughout the universe, he assigns Sport Billy, Sport Lilly, and Willie (a dog) to end Vanda's reign of terror. Stories relate their efforts to keep sporting events legitimate.

Sport Billy	Lane Scheimer
Sport Lilly	Joyce Bulifant
Willie	Frank Welker
Queen Vanda	Joyce Bulifant
Sporticus XI	Frank Welker

Producer: Norm Prescott, Lou Scheimer

Spotlight

Variety; 60 min; CBS 7/4/67 to 8/29/67

A weekly music and comedy series from England that features celebrities as guest hosts. With the Lionel Blair Dancers and the orchestra of Jack Parnell. Produced by Ian Scofield.

Spotlight Playhouse

Anita Louise as the host of a CBS Summer series (7/1/58 to 9/23/58) of repeat episodes from "The Loretta Young Theatre."

Spunky and Tadpole

Cartoon; 3½ min; Syn. 9/58

The fantasy-like adventures of a little boy (Spunky) and his come-to-life teddy bear (Tadpole).

Spunky	Joan Gardner
Tadpole	Don Messick
	Ed Janis

Square Pegs

Comedy; 30 min; CBS 9/27/82 to 9/12/83

Events in the lives of Patty Greene and Lauren Hutchinson, students at Weemawee Central High School (in the small town of Weemawee Heights).

Patty Greene	Sarah Jessica Parker
Lauren Hutchinson	Amy Linker
Jennifer DiNuccio	Tracy Nelson
Muffy Tupperman	Jami Gertz
Johnny "Slash"	
Lashawich	Merritt Butrick
Marshall Blechtman	John Femina
LaDonna Fredericks	Claudette Wells
Vinnie Pasetta	Jon Caliri
Larry Simpson	Ben Marley
Steve Griffin	David Hubbard
Principal Winfrop	
Dingelman	Basil Hoffman
Allison Loomis	Caitlin Adams
Rob Donovan	Steven Peterman
Beverly Tupperman	Marj Dusay

"Square Pegs" Theme Vocal: The Waitresses

Producer: Ronald Frazier, Anne Beatts

The Square World of Ed Butler

Ed Butler as the host of a syndicated (1970) discussion series. Produced by Phil Paladino and Portia Nelson.

The S.S. Holiday

Variety; 60 & 120 min; DuMont 4/9/50 to 11/26/50

The program, also known as "Starlit Time" spotlights the performances of a regular cast and acts culled from various New York clubs.

Host: Bill Williams, Phil Hanna

Regulars: Ralph Stanley, Holly Harris, Bibi Osterwald, Minnie Joe Curtis, Allan Prescott, Sam Steen, Eddie Holmes, The Reggie Beane Dancers

Music: The Reggie Beane Trio, The Cy Coleman Trio

Producer: Bob Lowei

The S.S. Telecruise

Variety; 1 hr. 45 min; ABC 4/28/51 to 6/2/51

A program of music and songs set in a different tropical port each week (accomplished via photographic backgrounds).

Host: Jack Steck

Regulars: Carol Wynne, Eddie Roecker, The Crewmen, The Thomas Cannon Ballet

Music: The Dave Appel Trio

The Staff of Life

Comedy Pilot; 30 min; ABC 5/17/85

A comical behind-the-scenes look at "Life," a TV soap opera, as seen through the eyes of its head writers, Barry Cooper and his ex-wife, Joanna.

Barry Cooper	Granville Van Dusen
Joanna Cooper	Anne Twomey
Cindy	Deborah Burrell
Roland	Richard McKenzie
Shirley	Doris Belack
Alexis	Jeanne Elias
Marshall Durkee	Howard George
Rebecca	Barbara Barnett
Craig	Scott McGinnis

Producer: Arne Sultan, Earl Barrett

Stage a Number

Variety; 30 min; DuMont 9/10/52 to 5/20/53

The program spotlights the talents of fledging comedians, writers, directors, singers, musicians, magicians, and other show business people.

Host: Bill Wendell

Producer: Roger Gerry

Stage Door

Drama; 30 min; CBS 2/7/50 to 3/28/50

Life in and around the Broadway theatre as seen through the eyes of Celia Knox and Hank Merlin, lovers who are also aspiring actors. Based on the play by George S. Kaufman and Edna Ferber.

Celia Knox	Louise Albritton
Hank Merlin	Scott McKay

Producer: Carol Irwin

Stage Entrance

Variety; 15 min; DuMont 5/2/51 to 3/9/52

Earl Wilson as the host of a program that features performances by undiscovered talent.

Stage 7

Anthology; 30 min; CBS 1/30/55 to 9/25/55

A series of filmed dramas from Hollywood that feature such stars as Phyllis Coates, Vanessa Brown, Dan O'Herlihy, George Nader, Charles Bronson, Frank Lovejoy, Stephen McNally, Peggy Ann Garner, Neville Brand, Angela Lansbury, George Montgomery, and Claire Trevor.

Producer: Warren Lewis

Stage Show

Variety; 60 min; CBS 7/3/54 to 9/18/54
                        10/1/55 to 9/22/56

Performances by guest entertainers. Most notable of those who appeared was Elvis Presley, who emceed on 1/28/56, 2/4, 11, and 18/56, and on 3/17 and 24/56.

Hosts: Tommy and Jimmy Dorsey

Regulars: The June Taylor Dancers

Music: The Dorsey Orchestra

Producer: Al Span

Stage 13

Anthology; 30 min; CBS 5/3/50 to 6/28/50

A series of mystery and suspense stories, broadcast live from New York City, that are situated around the number 13. Produced by Wyllis Cooper.

Stage Two Revue

Variety; 60 min; ABC 7/30/50 to 9/24/50

Georgia Lee as the host of a program of music and song with regulars Arlene Harris and Bob Harris, and the orchestra of Buzz Adlam.

Stagecoach West

Western; 60 min; ABC 10/4/60 to 9/26/61

The experiences of Luke Perry and Simon Kane, drivers for the Overland Stage Coach Lines during the 1860s.

Luke Perry	Wayne Rogers
Simon Kane	Robert Bray
David Kane	Richard Eyer
Zeke Bonner	James Burke
Kathleen Kane	Jane Greer

Producer: Vincent M. Fennelly

Stand Up and Be Counted

Advice; 30 min; CBS 5/28/56 to 9/6/57

Bob Russell as host of a show that offers advice to people with problems. At a later date, the person returns to tell if the advice was helpful or not. Produced by Richard Brill.

Stand Up and Cheer

Variety Pilot; 60 min; ABC 2/16/71

The pilot for "Johnny Mann's Stand Up and Cheer." A musical salute to America.

Host: Johnny Mann

With: The Johnny Mann Singers and Orchestra

Guests: Henry Fonda, Pearl Bailey

Producer: Pierre Cossette, Burt Sugarman

Stand By for Crime

Crime Drama; 30 min; ABC 1/11/49 to 8/27/49

The program, which relates the exploits of Inspector Webb, presents the viewer and a guest with all the clues to a crime. Before the culprit is revealed, the action is stopped and the guest is asked to name the killer. The drama is continued to reveal the culprit.

Insp. Webb	Boris Aplon
Sgt. Kramer	George Cisar
Lt. Anthony Kidd	Myron Wallace

Producer: Greg Garrison

Stanley

Comedy; 30 min; NBC 9/24/56 to 3/11/57

The story of Stanley Peck, the sloppy, nonaggressive proprietor of a New York hotel lobby newsstand.

Stanley Peck   Buddy Hackett
Celia   Carol Burnett
Horace Fenton   Paul Lynde
George Phillips   Frederic Tozere
Jane   Jane Connell

Producer: Max Liebman

The Stanley Siegel Show

Talk; 30 min; Syn. 6/81

Celebrity interviews and discussions on controversial issues with appropriate guests.

Host: Stanley Siegel

Producer: Chris Bearde, Nancy Haas

Star Chart

Variety; 30 min; Syn. 9/80

Terry David Mulligan as host of a weekly series that charts the progress of music stars (who also perform live). Produced by Doug Hutton, Ken Gibson.

Star for Today

A syndicated (1963) series of "Telephone Time" repeats with hosts John Nesbitt and Dr. Frank Baxter.

Star Games

Game; 60 min; Syn. 9/85

Three celebrity teams compete in various athletic events for cash and prizes.

Hostess (1985): Pamela Sue Martin

Hostess (1986): Morgan Brittany

Host: Bruce Jenner

Regular: Flip Wilson

Commissioner: Dick Butkus

Producer: Carolyn Raskin, Bill Garnett

Star Maidens

Science Fiction; 30 min; Syn. 9/77

Following a disaster that causes the female-run planet Medusa to drift through outer space, the planet locks itself onto a solar system in which another life-supporting planet—the Earth—is discovered. The Earth, however, contradicts the Medusians' programmed society and is declared off limits to its citizens. As with all laws, it too is broken when two Medusian men, Adam and Shem, escape to Earth and open the doorway for the inhabitants of both worlds to meet. Stories depict incidents in the lives of the Earthlings and Medusians as they meet and interact for the first time.

Fulvia (Medusian)   Judy Geeson
Octavia (Medusian)   Christine Kruger
Liz Baker   Liz Harrow
Clara (Medusian)   Dawn Addams
Shem (Medusian)   Gareth Thomas
Adam (Medusian)   Pierre Brice
Prof. Evans   Derek Farr
Kate Moss   Jenny Morgan
Rudi Schmitt   Christian Quadflieg
Andrea (Medusian)   Uschi Mellin
Medusian Girl   Penelope Horner

"The Star Maidens Theme" by Patrick Aulton

Producer: James Gatward

Star of the Family

Variety; 60 min; CBS 9/22/50 to 6/26/52

Performances by selected members of American families (preselected by letters written to the program by members of the individual's family).

Hosts: Peter Lind Hayes, Mary Healy, Morton Downey

Featured: The Beatrice Kroft Dancers

Announcer: Frank Waldecker

Orchestra: Carl Hoff

Producer: Perry Lafferty, Coby Ruskin

Star of the Family

Comedy; 30 min; ABC 9/30/82 to 12/23/82

The life of Jennie Lee Krebs, the beautiful daughter of a fire captain, as she struggles up the rocky road to stardom as a teenage singer.

Jennie Lee Krebs	Kathy Maisnik
Leslie "Buddy" Krebs (her father)	Brian Dennehy
Douggie Krebs (her brother)	Michael Dudikoff
Judy "Moose" Wells (her manager)	Judy Pioli
Leo Feldman (fireman)	Todd Susman
Max Hernandez (fireman)	Danny Mora
Frank Rosetti (fireman)	George Deloy
Tiffany (Jennie's friend)	Amanda Wyss

Theme Vocal ("Movin' Along"): Kathy Maisnik

Producer: Charles H. Joffe, Buddy Morra

Star Route

Variety; 30 min; Syn. 1964

Performances by country and western entertainers who have achieved a gold record.

Host: Rod Cameron

Regulars: Glen Campbell, Lorrie Collins, The Collins Kids

Orchestra: Gene Davis

Star Search

Variety; 60 min; Syn. 9/83

The program spotlights talented amateurs who compete in eight categories vying for the top prize of $100,000 and a chance at a professional show business career.

Host: Ed McMahon

Assistant: Marla Heasley

Pilot Host (4/83): John Schneider

Producer: Bob Banner, Sam Riddle

Star Theatre

A syndicated (1963) series of repeat dramas from various anthology series.

Star Tonight

Anthology; 30 min; ABC 2/3/55 to 8/9/56

Dramatic presentations that each week teams an unknown performer with an established professional. Produced by Harry Herrmann.

Star Trek

Science Fiction; 60 min; NBC 9/8/66 to 9/9/69

The voyages of the starship U.S.S. Enterprise, representing the United Federation of Planets, as it explores the endless universe, seeking new life, new worlds, and new civilizations. See the following two titles also.

Capt. James T. Kirk	William Shatner
Mr. Spock	Leonard Nimoy
Dr. Leonard "Bones" McCoy	DeForest Kelley
Lt. Uhura	Nichelle Nichols
Lt. Montgomery Scott	James Doohan
Yeoman Janice Rand	Grace Lee Whitney
Ensign Paval Chekov	Walter Koenig
Mr. Sulu	George Takei
Transporter Chief Kyle	John Winston
Mr. DePaul	Sean Kenny
Nurse Christine Chapel	Majel Barrett
Lt. Starnes	James Wellman
Lt. John Farrell	Jim Goodwin
Lt. Palmer	Elizabeth Rogers
Robert Fox (Ambassador of the United Planets)	Gene Lyons
Harry Mudd	Roger C. Carmel
Amanda (Spock's Earth mother)	Jane Wyatt
Sarek (Spock's Vulcan father)	Mark Lenard

Producer: Gene Roddenberry, John Meredyth Lucas, Gene L. Coon, Fred Freiberger

Star Trek

Science Fiction Pilot; 60 min; Unaired (Produced in 1964)

The original pilot that combines footage from the color "Menagerie" episode with black and white footage from "The Cage" pilot, wherein Captain Pike, captain of the Enterprise, attempts to rescue an Earth crew stranded on a distant planet for 18 years.

Capt. Christopher	
Pike	Jeffrey Hunter
Mr. Spock	Leonard Nimoy
First Officer Number	
1	Majel Barrett
Dr. Philip Boyce	John Hoyt
Vena	Susan Oliver
Navigator Jose	Joe Tyler
Navigator Taylor	Peter Duryea
Jose Mendez	Malachi Throne
Yeoman J.M. Colt	Laurel Goodwin

Producer-Writer-Creator: Gene Roddenberry

Star Trek

Cartoon; 30 min; NBC 9/8/73 to 8/30/75

A continuation of the "Star Trek" series, which relates the further explorations of the starship U.S.S. Enterprise.

Capt. James T. Kirk	William Shatner
Mr. Spock	Leonard Nimoy
Dr. Leonard McCoy	DeForest Kelley
Lt. Uhura	Nichelle Nichols
Lt. Montgomery	
Scott	James Doohan
Nurse Christine	
Chapel	Majel Barrett
Mr. Sulu	George Takei
Ensign Paval Chekov	James Doohan

Producer: Norm Prescott, Lou Scheimer

Star Trek: The Next Generation

Science Fiction; 60 min; Syn 9/87

A revised version of the "Star Trek" series which, set 78 years later, follows the adventures of Jean-Luc Picard, the captain of a redesigned Star Ship "Enterprise," as he and his crew explore the endless galaxy.

Capt. Jean-Luc	
Picard	Patrick Stewart
Cmdr. Natasha Yur	Denise Crosby
Cmdr. William (No.	
1) Riker	Jonathan Frakes
Lt. Geodi La Forge	LeVar Burton
Dr. Beverly Crusher	Gates McFadden
Deanna Troi	Marina Sirtis
Lt. Cmdr. Data	Brent Spiner
Wesley Crusher	Will Wheaton
Klingon Lt. Worf	Michael Dorn

Producer: Gene Roddenberry

The Starland Vocal Band

Variety; 30 min; CBS 7/31/77 to 9/2/77

A weekly program of music, songs, and comedy with the Starland Vocal Band singing group.

Starland Vocal Band: Bill and Taffy Danoff, Margot Chapman, Jon Carroll

Regulars: Mark Russell, David Letterman, Jeff Altman, Peter Bergman

Announcer: David Letterman

Orchestra: Milt Okin

Producer: Jerry Weintraub, Al Rogers

Starlight Theatre

Anthology; 30 min; CBS 4/2/50 to 10/4/51

A series of romance stories that feature well-known actors (e.g., Cara Williams, Leslie Nielsen, Barry Nelson, Meg Mundy, Mildred Natwick, George Reeves, Dorothy Gish, Wally Cox, John Forsythe, Julie Harris, and Jackie Cooper). Produced by Robert Stevens.

The Starlost

Science Fiction; 60 min; Syn. 1973

When he is deemed unsuitable to marry the wealthy Rachel, Devon, a poor farmer who loves her, speaks in protest. Devon, who is ordered to die for his actions, escapes from his captors and runs into a forbidden cave where he finds the Earth Ship Ark. While exploring, he learns that in the year 2290 all life was threatened with extinction and the Ark was built to save selected Earthlings (who are suspended in biospheres) by transporting them to a Class Six star. For some unknown reason, the Ark never made its destination. Stories relate Devon's adventures as he and Rachel* explore the Ark and attempt to save the remains of Earth life by finding the class six star—the Starlost. Produced in Canada.

Devon	Keir Dullea
Rachel	Gay Rowan
Garth	Robin Ward
Mulander 165	William Osler
Oro	Walter Koenig

Producer: Doug Trumbull, Jerry Zeitman, Robert Kline

*Rachel later joins Devon when he returns for her.

Starr, First Baseman

Comedy Pilot; 30 min; CBS 7/23/65

The misadventures of Joe Starr, a rookie with the New York Yankees baseball team.

Joe Starr	Martin Milner
Freddie Gordon	Stuart Whitman
Eddie Ryan	David Thurshy

Producer: Vernon E. Clark

Starring Boris Karloff

See "The Boris Karloff Mystery Playhouse."

Stars in Khaki and Blue

Variety; 30 min; NBC 9/13/52 to 9/27/52

Wendy Barrie as host of a program that features performances by members of the armed services. Produced by Craig G. Allen.

Stars on Parade

Variety; 30 min; DuMont 11/4/53 to 6/30/54

Performances by both military and civilian talent. Hosted by Bobby Sherwood and Don Russell with the orchestra of Elliot Lawrence.

Stars Over Hollywood

Anthology; 30 min; NBC 9/27/50 to 5/16/51

A Hollywood-based series of dramas that feature such stars as Cameron Mitchell, Raymond Burr, Buddy Ebsen, Anita Louise, Gloria Saunders, Bruce Cabot, Mary Stuart, Ellen Corby, Frances Rafferty, Leon Ames, Adele Jergens, Cliff Arquette, Gerald Mohr, and Maria Palmer.

Starman

Adventure; 60 min; ABC 9/19/86 (Premiere)

On a visit to the planet Earth, an alien Starman meets and befriends Jenny Hayden, a woman with whom he has an affair. When federal authorities become suspicious of the alien, he escapes capture and returns to his planet. Nine months later, Jenny gives birth to a son she names Scott.

Fourteen years later, when the Starman believes his son is in trouble, he begins a journey back to Earth. When the helicopter on which photographer Paul Forrester is traveling crashes and kills Paul, the Starman assumes Paul's identity. The Starman finds Scott and, after winning Scott's trust, he and Scott join forces to help each other and find Jenny (who was forced to give Scott up for adoption eleven years ago). Stories relate their search and attempts to avoid George Fox, a Federal Security Agency agent who believes Paul is an alien and seeks to capture him. Based on the feature film.

Paul Forrester	Robert Hays
Scott Hayden	C.B. Barnes
George Fox	Michael Cavanaugh
Stella Forrester (real Paul's mother)	Jane Wyatt
Jenny Hayden	Erin Gray

Producer: James Henerson, James Hirsch, Michael Douglas

Starsky and Hutch

Crime Drama; 60 min; ABC 9/10/75 to 8/28/79

The exploits of Dave Starsky and Ken "Hutch" Hutchinson, plainclothes detectives with the Metropolitan Division of the L.A.P.D.

Det. Dave Starsky	Paul Michael Glaser
Det. Ken Hutchinson	David Soul
Capt. Harold Dobey	Richard Ward*
	Bernie Hamilton
Huggy Bear	Antonio Fargas
Fat Rollo	Michael Lerner

Producer: Aaron Spelling, Leonard Goldberg

*TV Movie role (4/30/75).

Starstruck

Comedy Pilot; 30 min; CBS 6/9/79

The futuristic adventures of the McCallister family, the owners of The Midway Inn, a hotel-restaurant-saloon on an orbiting way station somewhere between Earth and Pluto.

Ben McCallister	Beeson Carroll
Kate McCallister	Tania Myren
Mark McCallister	Meegan King
Rupert McCallister	Kevin Brando
Ezra McCallister	Guy Raymond
Abigail McCallister	Elvia Allman
Amber LaRue	Lynne Lipton
Delight	Sarah Kennedy

Producer: Herbert B. Leonard

The Start of Something Big

Human Interest; 60 min; Syn. 4/85

The program features celebrity guests discussing their beginnings in show business; the secrets of successful people who made it big; and the fascinating origins of everyday people and events.

Host: Steve Allen

Narrator: Michael Carroll

Theme ("This Could Be the Start of Something Big"): Steve Allen

Producer: Robin Leach, Jim Masini

Startime

Variety; 60 min; DuMont 10/6/50 to 2/5/51

A weekly series of music, songs, and comedy.

Hosts: Frances Langford and Don Ameche

Regulars: Lew Parker, Ben Blue, Phil Regan, Kathryn Lee, The Benny Goodman Sextet, The Don Liberti Chorus

Producer: Hubbell Robinson, Robert Wright

Starting Fresh

Comedy Pilot; 30 min; NBC 6/27/79

The story of Maggie Harris, a beautiful 36-year-old divorcee who enrolls at the same college as her 17-year-old daughter, Stephanie, and the mild misadventures that occur when they both share the same classes.

Maggie Harris	Lynnette Mettey
Stephanie Harris	Kimberly Beck
Phoebe Johnson	Janie Sell
Judy	Susan Duvall
Cliffie	Ike Eisenmann

Producer: Danny Thomas, Ronald Jacobs

Stat!

Drama Pilot; 30 min; CBS 7/31/73

The story of a harried medical staff that is forced to cope with a physically and emotionally exhausting daily routine.

Dr. Ben Voorhees	Frank Converse
Dr. Nick Candros	Michael Delano
Nurse Ellen Quayle	Marian Collier
Dr. Juan Cavanaugh	Casey MacDonald
Dr. Neil Patricks	Henry Brown
Mary Ann Murphy	Monika Heinreid
Dolores Payne	Marcy Lafferty

Producer: E. Jack Neuman

State Trooper

Crime Drama; 30 min; Syn. 1957

The exploits of Rod Blake, chief of the Nevade State Troopers.

Rod Blake	Rod Cameron

Producer: Richard Irving

Steambath

Comedy; 30 min; SHO 1984–85

An allegorical series about life in the hereafter. Stories, set in a Sauna, relate the experiences of four souls who are placed on a waiting list between this world and the next. Based on the off-Broadway play.

God (who appears as
  Morty, the
  washroom
  attendant)   Jose Perez
Meredith (sexy
  female soul)   Janis Ward
Rod Tandy (P.R.
  man)   Robert Picardo
Blanche (sensuous
  female soul)   Rita Taggart
Davinci (cab driver)   Al Ruscio

Producer: Jeb Rosenbrook, David Pollock,
  Elias Davis

Steel Collar Man

Adventure Pilot; 60 min; CBS 8/7/85

Dr. Constance Fletcher, a robotics designer
for Ultra Intelligent Machines, develops D-5-
B, a superhuman android for the military.
When the government learns that the android
can think and learn from experience, they fear
intelligent humanoids in the armed forces and
order J. G. Willis to destroy D-5-B and retrieve its computer brain. Unwilling to see her
creation destroyed, Constance allows D-5-B
to escape. The unsold series was to relate
D-5-B's adventures as he attempts to escape
from his relentless pursuer (Willis).

Robot D-5-B   Charles Rocket
Constance Fletcher   Dorian Lopinto
Red   Hoyt Axton
J.G. Willis   Chuck Connors
Don Liddle   Paul Dooley
Big Jake   Chuck Mitchell
Johnny   Robert O'Reilly
General   John Brandon

Producer: Dave Thomas, Gerald W. Abrams

Steeltown

Drama Pilot; 60 min; CBS 5/19/79

The story of Modge Modgelewsky, a steel-
worker with the Riverbend Steel Company in
Pennsylvania.

Modge
  Modgelewsky   Frank Converse
Aggie Modgelewsky   Mare Winningham
Stevie Modgelewsky   Justin Randi

Chris Modgelewsky   Kraig Cassity
Bill Anderson   James Carroll Jordan
Janet Anderson   Bibi Besch
Gibby Anderson   Michael Biehn
Terri   Wendy Rastatter
Alma   Anna Garduno

Producer: Gerald W. Abrams

Step This Way

Dance Contest; 30 min; NBC 7/9/55 to 4/14/56

The program features couples competing in
several phases of a dance contest: their own
specialty and a dance of the week selection.
The couples are judged by a guest panel and
the winners receive merchandise prizes.

Host: Bobby Sherwood

Judges: Dancers Zedan and Carol

Orchestra: Nat Brandywyne, Buddy Weed

Step This Way

Dance Contest; 30 min; Syn. 1966

A revised version of the prior title, which see
for format.

Host: Gretchen Wyler

Announcer: Jim Lucas

Music: The Warren Covington Band, The Ray
  McKinley Band

Stephanie

Comedy Pilot; 30 min; CBS 9/8/81

The misadventures of Stephanie Burke, reporter and hostess of "L.A.L.A.," a local
Los Angeles (KXLA) TV magazine program.

Stephanie Burke   Stephanie Faracy
Agnes Dewey   Betty White
Harry Babcock   Robert Hitt
Rita Melvoin   Jeanetta Arnette
Claude Pomerantz   Alvy Moore
Sonny Brazil   Kent Perkins
Anatole Pinsky   Steve Landesberg

Music: Patrick Williams

Producer: Alan Uger, Michael Kagan

The Steve Allen Comedy Hour

Variety; 60 min; CBS 6/14/67 to 8/16/67

A weekly program of music and comedy.

Host: Steve Allen

Regulars: Jayne Meadows, Louis Nye, Ruth Briggs, The David Winters Dancers

Music: The Terry Gibbs Band

The Steve Allen Comedy Hour

Variety; 60 min; NBC 10/18/80 to 1/10/81

A weekly series of comedy sketches.

Host: Steve Allen

Regulars: Catherine O'Hara, Bill Saluga, Helen Brooks, Kaye Ballard, Carol Donnelly, Joey Forman, Fred Smoot, Nancy Steen, Dorothy Hess

Orchestra: Terry Gibbs

Producer: Frank Peppiatt, William O. Harbach

The Steve Allen Show

Variety; 60 min; NBC 6/24/56 to 5/3/59

A weekly program of music, song, and comedy.

Host: Steve Allen

Regulars: Don Knotts (Nervous Man), Louis Nye (Gordon Hathaway), Tom Poston (Amnesiac), Skitch Henderson (Man from the Bronx), Dayton Allen (Why Not Man), Bill Dana (Jose Jimenez), Pat Harrington Jr., Gabriel Dell

Commercial Spokesman: John Cameron Swayze, Erin O'Brien

Announcer: Gene Rayburn

Orchestra: Skitch Henderson

Producer: Bill Harbach, Jules Green

The Steve Allen Show

Variety; 60 min; NBC 9/28/59 to 6/6/60

A weekly series of music and comedy that was an unsuccessful attempt to duplicate the prior Allen program.

Host: Steve Allen

Regulars: Don Knotts, Louis Nye, Gabriel Dell, Pat Harrington Jr., Johnny Carson, Andy Griffith, Martha Raye

Orchestra: Les Brown

Producer: Bill Harbach

The Steve Allen Show

Variety; 90 min; Syn. 1962

A daily series of music, celebrity interviews, and outlandish comedy.

Host: Steve Allen

Announcer: Johnny Jacobs

Orchestra: Don Trenner

Producer: Allan Sherman, Milt Hoffman

The Steve Allen Show

Variety; 60 & 90 min; Syn. 1968

A daily series of music, comedy, and celebrity interviews.

Host: Steve Allen

Orchestra: Paul Smith

Producer: Jeff Harris

Steve Allen's Laugh-Back

Comedy; 90 min; Syn. 6/76

Highlights of Steve Allen's TV career via film clips from his various series.

Host: Steve Allen

Regulars: Jayne Meadows, Louis Nye, Bill Dana, Martha Raye, Don Knotts, Skitch Henderson, Pat Harrington Jr.

Music: Terry Gibbs

Producer: Jerry Harrison, Roger Ailes

Steve Allen's Music Room

Music; 60 min; DISNEY 4/84

The program features well-known composers and lyricists in musical performances and conversation in a relaxed atmosphere.

Host: Steve Allen

Music: Terry Gibbs

Producer: Steve Allen, Fred Tatashore

Steve Canyon

Adventure; 30 min; NBC 9/13/58 to 9/7/59

Originally, the exploits of Steve Canyon as a troubleshooter for the U.S. Air Force; later, Steve's adventures as a commanding officer at Big Thunder Air Force Base.

Col. Steve Canyon	Dean Fredericks
Maj. Willie Willston	Jerry Paris
Police Chief	
Hagedorn	Ted DeCorsia
Airman Abel	
Featherstone	Abel Fernandez
Sgt. Charlie Berger	Robert Hoy
Ingrid (Steve's	
secretary)	Ingrid Goude

Producer: David Haft

Steve Donovan, Western Marshal

Western; 30 min; Syn. 1955

The exploits of a marshal (Steve) and his deputy (Rusty) as they maintain the law on the ruthless frontier of the late 19th-century.

Marshal Steve	
Donovan	Douglas Kennedy
Deputy Rusty Lee	Eddy Waller

Producer: Jack Chertok

The Steve Landesberg Television Show

Comedy Pilot; 30 min; NBC 4/14/83

Various sketches that highlight the talents of comedian Steve Landesberg.

Host: Steve Landesberg

Regulars: Lisa Sutton, Jimmy Martinez, Laurie Faso, Gailard Sartain

Orchestra: Marvin Laird

Producer: Rick Bernstein, Alan Uger, Michael Kagan

The Steve Lawrence and Eydie Gorme Show

Variety; 60 min; NBC 7/13/58 to 8/31/58

A weekly program of music and songs.

Hosts: Steve Lawrence and Eydie Gorme

Featured: The Artie Malvin Singers

Announcer: Gene Rayburn

Orchestra: Jack Kane

The Steve Lawrence Show

Variety; 60 min; CBS 9/13/65 to 12/13/65

Music, songs, and comedy with singer Steve Lawrence and regulars Donna Mills, Charles Nelson Reilly, Betty Walker, and The Pussycat Dancers. Orchestrations by Joseph Guerico and produced by George Schlatter.

Stick Around

Comedy Pilot; 30 min; ABC 5/30/77

The comic adventures of Elaine and Vance Keefer, a space-age husband-and-wife attempting to cope with life's everyday problems.

Elaine Keefer	Nancy New
Vance Keefer	Fred McCarren
Andy the Robot	Andy Kaufman
Joe Burkus	Cliff Norton
Earl the Robot	
Butler	Craig Richard Nelson
Lisa	Liberty Williams
Ed	Jeffrey Kramer

Producer: Fred Freeman, Lawrence J. Cohen

Still the Beaver

Comedy; 30 min; DISNEY 10/84 (Premiere)

The update of the "Leave It to Beaver" series, which, set twenty years later in Mayfield, finds June Cleaver, a widow since 1977; Wally, married (to Mary Ellen) and a lawyer; and Theodore ("Beaver"), married (to Kimberly), the father of two boys (Corey and Oliver), out of work and on the verge of divorce. Stories relate Theodore's efforts to turn his life around despite the fact that he feels he's still the Beaver and plagued by life's misfortune. See also "The New Leave It to Beaver."

June Cleaver	Barbara Billingsley
Wally Cleaver	Tony Dow
Beaver Cleaver	Jerry Mathers
Kimberly Cleaver	Joanna Gleason
Mary Ellen Cleaver	Janice Kent
Corey Cleaver	Corey Feldman
Oliver Cleaver	John Snee
Eddie Haskell	Ken Osmond
Clarence "Lumpy" Rutherford	Frank Bank
Fred Rutherford	Richard Deacon
Eddie Haskell Jr.	Eric Osmond
Larry Mondello	Rusty Stevens
Richard Rockover	Richard Correll

Producer: Bud Austin, Nick Abdo

The Stiller and Meara Show

Comedy Pilot; 30 min; NBC 6/9/86

Incidents in the lives of Anne Bender, a commercials actress, and Jerry Bender, her husband, a New York Assistant Deputy Mayor; a couple married thirty years, the parents of three children—and a family fraught with problems.

Anne Bender	Anne Meara
Jerry Bender	Jerry Stiller
Daniel Bender	Todd Waring
Chrissie Bender Marino	Laura Innes
Max Bender	Peter Smith
Lt. Langston	Bill Cobbs

Producer: Mort Lachman

Stingray

Marionette Adventure; 30 min; Syn. 1965

The exploits of Troy Tempest, a member of the World Aquanaut Security Patrol, and captain of the submarine Stingray, as he battles injustice throughout the world.

Troy Tempest	Don Mason
Atlanta	Lois Maxwell
Cmdr. Sam Shore/ Titan	Ray Barrett
Phones/X-20	Robert Easton

Producer: Gerry and Sylvia Anderson

Stingray

Adventure; 60 min; NBC 3/11/86 to 8/8/86
1/9/87 (Premiere)

The story of a mysterious man, known only as Stingray (by the '65 black Corvette Stingray he drives) who helps people in deep trouble and asks only to repay him with a favor when the time arises.

| Stingray | Nick Mancuso |
| The Man (his advisary) | Robert Vaughn |

Music: Mike Post and Pete Carpenter

Producer: Stephen J. Cannell, Lawrence Hertzog, Jo Swerling Jr.

Stir Crazy

Comedy; 60 min; CBS 9/18/85 to 10/23/85

Millionaire P.K. Hunter is murdered by a man wearing a tattoo (reading 4LU) and placed in a cab owned by two friends (Harry and Skip). When Skip and Harry discover the body and report it to the police, they are accused of murder and later sentenced to 132 years in prison. Shortly after, during a prison riot, Skip and Harry escape, but are relentlessly pursued by Captain Betty and her deputy, Crawford. Stories relate Skip and Harry's efforts to find the tattooed man and clear their names.

Skip Harrington	Joseph Guzaldo
Harry Fletcher	Larry Riley
Kathryn D'Angelo	Cynthia Sikes
Capt. Bettina "Betty" Phillips	Polly Holliday Jeannie Wilson
Deputy Crawford	Royce Applegate Marc Singer
Tattooed Man (Marty Duran)	M.C. Gainey
Skip's Aunt Doris	Alice Ghostley
P.K. Hunter (first episode)	Charles Davis

Theme Vocal ("Theme from Stir Crazy"): Paulette McWilliams

Producer: Larry Rosen, Larry Tucker

Stockard Channing in Just Friends

Comedy; 30 min; CBS 3/4/79 to 8/11/79

The story of Susan Hughes, a girl on the rebound from a broken marriage, and her experiences as the assistant manager of the Beverly Hills Fountain of Youth Health Spa.

Susan Hughes	Stockard Channing
Victoria Chasen	Mimi Kennedy
Milt DeAngelo	Lou Criscuolo
Miranda DeAngelo	Liz Torres
Angelo DeAngelo	Albert Insinnia
Coral	Sydney Goldsmith
Leonard Scribner	Garret Graham
Mrs. Fisher	Joan Toletino
Frank Hughes	Lawrence Pressman

"Stockard's Theme" by Delaney Bramlett

Producer: David Debin, Peter Locke, Al Rogers

The Stockard Channing Show

Comedy; 30 min; CBS 3/24/80 to 6/28/80

Following her divorce, Susan Goodenow acquires a job as assistant to Brad Gabriel, a consumer advocate who hosts "The Big Rip-off" on West Hollywood's KXLA-TV. Stories relate Susan's antics as she dons various disguises to expose rip-off artists.

Susan Goodenow	Stockard Channing
Brad Gabriel	Ron Silver
Earline Cunningham	Sydney Goldsmith
Gus Clyde	Max Showalter
Mr. Cramer	Jack Somack
Alf	Bruce Baum
Lisa Cartwright	Maureen Arthur
Barton Blair	Marty Cohen
Bonnie	Marcie Barkin
Wendy Simon	Wendie Jo Sperber

Theme Vocalist ("Stockard's Theme"): Delaney Bramlett

Producer: Aaron Ruben, George Yanok

The Stockers

Comedy Pilot; 30 min; NBC 4/24/81

The adventures of J.J. Spangler, a stock car racer, and his mechanic, Curtis Witlock, as they compete in various races seeking to qualify for the Daytona 500.

J.J. Spangler	Terry Bradshaw
Curtis Witlock	Mel Tillis
Crusher	Robert Tessier
Joanie Fisk	Samantha Harper
Lee Weldon	Archie Hahn
Mr. Fisk	R.G. Armstrong

Producer: John J. McMahon

Stone

Crime Drama; 60 min; ABC 1/14/80 to 3/17/80

The exploits of Dan Stone, a novelist and homicide detective with the Metropolitan Division of the L.A.P.D.

Sgt. Dan Stone	Dennis Weaver
Diane Stone	Beth Brickell
	Mariette Hartley*
Jill Stone	Nancy McKeon
Chief Gene Paulton	Pat Hingle
Britte Martin	Barbara Rhoades
Off. Buck Rogers	Robby Weaver
Murray Weinstock	Joby Baker

"Stone" Theme Song: Dennis Weaver, Nancy Adams

Producer: Stephen J. Cannell, Donald P. Bellisario

*TV Movie role (8/26/79).

Stoney Burke

Adventure; 60 min; ABC 10/1/62 to 9/2/63

The story of champion rodeo rider Stoney Burke as he travels from one rodeo to another seeking to secure the Gold Buckle, the trophy that is awarded to the world's best saddle bronco buster.

Stoney Burke	Jack Lord
E.J. Stocker	Bruce Dern
Wes Painter	Warren Oates
Cody Bristal	Robert Dowdell
Red	Bill Hart

Producer: Leslie Stevens

Stop Me If You Heard This One

Game; 30 min; NBC 3/5/48 to 4/22/49

The host reads an incomplete joke submitted by a home viewer. A panel of three comedians have to complete it with an original punch line. The sender receives $5 for submitting the joke, and an additional $5 if the panel fails to complete it. Originally aired locally in Los Angeles in 1945, and the first TV series to be broadcast with a live studio audience.

Host: Ted Brown, Roger Bower, Leon Janney

Panelists: Morey Amsterdam, Cal Tinney, Mae Questel, Lew Lehr, Benny Rubin

Producer: Irving Mansfield, Barry Wood, Larry Schwab

Stop Susan Williams

Drama; 20 min; NBC 2/27/79 to 5/1/79

A "Cliffhangers" segment about Susan Williams, a beautiful photographer for the "New York Dispatch," as she attempts to expose a group of conspirators who are planning a mission that could start World War III.

Susan Williams	Susan Anton
Bob Richard	Ray Walston
Jennifer	Marj Dusay
Jack Schoengarth	Michael Swan
Anthony Korf	Albert Paulsen

Narrator: Brad Crandall

Producer: Kenneth Johnson, B.W. Sandefur

Stop the Music

Game; 60 min; ABC 5/5/49 to 4/24/52
9/7/54 to 6/14/56

As the orchestra plays a song, three girls place telephone calls to possible viewers. When a call is completed, she yells "Stop the Music" and the host picks up the phone. If the viewer can identify the song that had been playing, he wins a merchandise jackpot; if not, a consolation prize is awarded. The game also involves studio audience members attempting to identify song titles for prizes.

Host: Bert Parks, Jimmy Blaine

Regulars: Jaye P. Morgan, Betty Ann Grove, Jack Haskell, Estelle Loring, Martin Croft, Kay Armen, Maureen Palmer, Charles Luchsinger, June Valli, Harriet Roeder

Announcer: Jack Haskell, Don Hancock, Kenny Williams, Dennis James, Sidney Smith

Orchestra: Harry Sosnik

Producer: Louis Cowan, Mark Goodson, Joseph Cates, Steve Carlin

Stopwatch: 30 Minutes of Investigative Ticking

Comedy Pilot; 30 min; HBO 9/3/83

A lampoon of TV news magazine series.

Chris Mantock	Alan Oppenheimer
Ron Ramsgate	Michael G. Kelly
Angry Arnie	Bill Kirchenbauer

Producer: Rudy DeLuca, Barry Levinson

The Storefront Lawyers

Crime Drama; 60 min; CBS 9/16/70 to 1/13/71

The cases of a group of attorneys attached to the Neighborhood Legal Services in Century City, Los Angeles. See also "Men at Law."

David Hansen	Robert Foxworth
Deborah Sullivan	Sheila Larken
Gabriel Kay	David Arkin
Roberto Barelli	A Martinez
Mr. Thatcher	Gerald S.
	O'Loughlin
Rachel	Royce Wallace

Producer: Robert Stivers, Roland Kibbee, Harold Gast

Stories in One Camera

Anthology Pilot; 20 min; DuMont 8/14/46

An unsold series of one-act plays presented in a simplistic style with the use of only one TV camera. The pilot tells the story of a detective who will tackle any case if the price is high enough.

Detective	Mel Brandt

Also: Betty Williams, Ogden Miles

Producer-Director: David P. Lewis

Stories of the Century

Western; 30 min; Syn. 1956

The series, set over a thirty-year period (1870s through 1890s) relates the exploits of Southwestern Railroad detectives Matt Clark and Frankie Adams (later Jonesy Jones) as they attempt to track down notorious outlaws.

Matt Clark   Jim Davis
Frankie Adams   Mary Castle
Jonesy Jones   Kristine Miller

Included Outlaws: Belle Starr (Marie Windsor), Billy the Kid (Richard Jaeckel), Frank and Jesse James (Lee Van Cleef, Richard Travis), Cattle Kate (Jean Parker), Sam Bass (Don Haggerty), Johnny Ringo (Donald Curtis), Doc Holliday (Kim Spaulding), John Wesley Hardin (Richard Webb), Black Bart (Arthur Space), and Kate Bender (Veda Ann Borg)

Narrator: Marvin Miller

Producer: Rudy Ralston

The Stork Club

Interview; 15 & 30 min;
CBS 7/7/50 to 10/31/53
ABC 9/11/54 to 7/24/55

Celebrity interviews are conducted against the background of the Stork Club.

Interviewer: Sherman Billingsley

Hostesses: Betty Ann Grove, Virginia Peine

Regulars: Peter Lind Hayes, Mary Healy, Johnny Johnston

Announcer: George Bryan

Producer: Irving Mansfield, Mike Dutton, Sherman Billingsley

Story for Americans

Anthology; 30 min; CBS 7/6/52 to 11/2/52

Carmen Andrews and Eugene Lee perform in dramas based on past American history.

The Story Of—

John Willis as the host of a syndicated (1962) series of dramas based on the lives of interesting people. Produced by Mel Stuart.

Story Theatre

Anthology; 30 min; Syn 1/49

The first syndicated anthology series. Quality dramas that feature such stars as Marjorie Lord, Phyllis Coates, Eva Gabor, Jeanne Cagney, Melville Cooper, Evelyn Ankers, Stanley Holloway, Fay Baker, Jan Clayton, Kirby Grant, and Elisabeth Fraser. Produced by Stanley Rubin, Louis Lantz, Eugene Lorie, and Elihu Winer.

Story Theatre

Fables; 30 min; Syn. 1971

Stories, based on tales by Aesop and the Brothers Grimm, are performed in an improvisational theatre with actors speaking their lines (as if reading from a book) and providing their own narration.

Host: Paul Sills

Performers: Bob Dishy, Mina Kolb, Peter Bonerz, Judy Graubart, Melinda Dillon, Richard Libertini, Paul Sand, Hamilton Camp, Severn Darden, Ann Sweeny, Jeff Brownstein

Producer: Burt Rosen, David Winters

The Storybook Squares

Game; 30 min; NBC 1/4/69 to 8/30/69

A children's version of "The Hollywood Squares." Nine celebrity guests, dressed as storybook characters, appear in a large tic tac toe board. One child player (two compete) chooses a celebrity and must either agree or disagree with the answer he will give to a question. A correct guess awards him that square, while an incorrect guess means a square for his opponent. The first player to acquire three squares in a row wins.

Host: Peter Marshall

Announcer: Kenny Williams

Producer: Merrill Heatter, Bob Quigley

The Storyteller

Fantasy Pilot; 30 min; NBC 1/31/87

A proposed series of dramas based on European folk and fairy tales that are related by a medieval storyteller and presented through the creations of Jim Henson. The pilot, "Hans My Hedgehog," tells of a young man, half-human, half-hedgehog, who marries a beautiful young princess.

Storyteller	John Hurd
His Dog	Brian Henson
Princess	Abigail Cruttenden
Hedgehog	Ailsa Berk
King	David Swift
Queen	Helen Lindsay

Producer: Jim Henson, Mark Shivas

Straightaway

Adventure; 30 min; ABC 10/6/61 to 7/4/62

The exploits of Scott Ross and Clipper Hamilton, the owners of the Straightaway Garage, as they become involved with professional drivers and races. Originally titled "The Racers."

| Scott Ross | Brian Kelly |
| Clipper Hamilton | John Ashley |

Producer: Josef Shaftel

Stranded

Adventure Pilot; 60 min; Unaired; Produced in 1966

While enroute from Florida to Mexico City, the passengers of Maridian Flight 603 are marooned on a deserted island when their plane crashes. The unsold series was to relate their struggle for survival. The pilot, with added footage (with Lois Nettleton) was released as the 1967 feature film, "Valley of Mystery."

Wade Cochrane	Richard Egan
Ben Barstow	Peter Graves
Connie Lane	Karen Sharpe
Pete Patton	Joby Baker
Joey O'Neill	Harry Guardino
Joan Simon	Julie Adams
Francisco Rivera	Fernando Lamas
Dino Doretti	Lee Patterson
Ann Dickson	Barbara Werle
Spence Atherton	Leonard Nimoy
Dr. John Quincy	Otis Young

Producer: Frank P. Rosenberg

Stranded

Drama Pilot; 60 min; CBS 5/26/76

The story, set on an isolated South Pacific island, relates the hardships faced by the survivors of an Australian-bound airplane that crashed.

Rafe Harder	Kevin Dobson
Crystal Norton	Lara Parker
Rose Orselli	Marie Windsor
Julie Blake	Devon Ericson
Tim Blake	Jimmy McNichol
John Rados	Rex Everhart
Ali Baba	Erin Blunt
Jerry Holmes	James Cromwell
Charley Lee	John Fujioka

Music: Gordon Jenkins

Producer: David Victor

Strange Paradise

Serial; 30 min; Syn. 9/69

The series, set on the forbidding Caribbean island of Maljardan, tells of a man (Jean Paul) and his efforts to restore the life of his dead wife (Erica) by summoning the powers of darkness; and his efforts to destroy those forces when Erica is brought back to life as an evil woman who seeks only to kill.

Jean Paul Desmond	Colin Fox
Erica Desmond	Tudi Wiggins
Holly Marshall	Sylvia Feigel
Alison Kerr	Dawn Greenhalgh
Raxil	Cosette Lee
Quito	Kurt Dchiegl
Elizabeth Marshall	Paisley Maxwell
Vangie	Angela Roland
Dan Forrest	John Granik
Matthew Dawson	Dan McDonald
Emily	Lucy Warner
Cort	David Wells
Tim Stanton	Bruce Gray

Producer: Selig Alkon

The Strange Report

Mystery; 60 min; NBC 1/8/71 to 9/12/71

The story of Adam Strange, a London-based criminologist who intervenes in domestic and international crises to help the police solve baffling crimes.

Adam Strange	Anthony Quayle
Evelyn McLean	Anneke Wells
Ham Gynt	Kaz Garas

Producer: Norman Felton

Strange Stories

A syndicated (1956) anthology series, hosted by Edward Arnold, and featuring tales of the supernatural.

Strange True Stories

Anthology Pilot; 30 min; Syn. 1/82

Dramatic recreations of strange but true stories of mystical experiences and parapsychology.

Host: Alexander Scourby

Producer: Don Carmody, Jim Hanley

The Stranger

Drama; 30 min; DuMont 6/25/54 to 2/11/55

The story of the Stranger, an unknown man who mysteriously appears to help people who are threatened by unscrupulous characters.

The Stranger	Robert Carroll

Producer: Frank Telford

Strawhat Matinee

Variety; NBC 6/27/51 to 9/7/51 (30 min)
5/27/53 to 9/8/54 (60 min)

A program of music, songs, variety acts, and fashion previews. Also titled "Strawhat Theatre" in 1953.

Hosts: Mel Martin, Rosemary Olberding

Regulars: June Pickens, Lee Jones, Marian Spellman, The Log Jammers, The Pine Mountain Boys

Orchestra: Ernie Lee

The Strawhatters

Variety; 30 min; DuMont 5/27/53 to 9/9/53
6/23/54 to 9/8/54

Performances by undiscovered talent, country and western artists, guest bands, vocalists, and acrobats.

Hosts: Johnny Olsen, Virginia Graham

Producer: Roger Gerry

Street Hawk

Adventure; 60 min; ABC 1/4/85 to 3/8/85

When Jesse Mach, an L.A.P.D. motorcycle cop, is injured and regulated to an office, he is recruited by federal agent Norman Tuttle to ride Street Hawk, a highly sophisticated motorcycle designed to battle crime. Stories relate Mach's battle against crime as the mysterious Street Hawk.

Off. Jesse Mach	Rex Smith
Norman Tuttle	Joe Regalbuto
Sandy McCoy	Jayne Modean
Rachel Adams	Jeannie Wilson
Cmdr. Leo Altobelli	Richard Venture

Producer: Paul Belous, Robert Wolterstoff, Bruce Lansbury

The Streets

Crime Drama Pilot; 60 min; NBC 9/2/84

The exploits of Danny Wreade and Max Grozzo, undercover detectives with the N.Y.P.D. Originally titled "Street Heat."

Sgt. Danny Wreade	Michael Beck
Sgt. Max Grozzo	Jerry Orbach
Jeannie	Dana Delany
Whitcomb	Val Avery
Morrison	Jerry Strivelli

Producer: Lawrence and Charles Gordon

Streets of Danger

See "The Lone Wolf."

The Streets of San Francisco

Crime Drama; 60 min; ABC 9/16/72 to 6/23/77

The exploits of Mike Stone and Steve Keller, homicide detectives with the San Francisco Police Department.

Lt. Mike Stone	Karl Malden
Det. Steve Keller	Michael Douglas
Jean Stone	Darleen Carr
Insp. Dan Robbins	Richard Hatch
Off. Haseejian	Vic Tayback
Lt. Lessing	Lee Harris
Sgt. Sekulovich	Art Passarella

Producer Quinn Martin

Strictly for Laughs

Comedy; 15 min; CBS 11/8/49 to 6/23/50

The humorous music of the Kirby Stone Quintet. Produced by Barry Wood and directed by Leonard Valenta.

Strike Force

Crime Drama; 60 min; ABC 11/13/81 to 9/24/82

The cases of the Strike Force, a special unit of the L.A.P.D. that tackles the crimes considered too dangerous for ordinary police officers.

Capt. Frank Murphy	Robert Stack
Sgt. Rosie Johnson	Trisha Noble
Sgt. Charlie Gunzer	Richard Romanus
Sgt. Paul Strobber	Dorian Harewood
Sgt. Mark Osborn	Michael Goodwin
Cmdr. Herbert Klein	Herb Edelman
Loraine Klein	Lynn Carlin
Eve Murphy	Joanna Cassidy

Producer: Aaron Spelling, Douglas S. Cramer

Strike it Rich

Game; 30 min; CBS 5/7/51 to 1/3/58

Contestants stand before the studio audience and relate their hard-luck stories. The saddest storytellers, as determined by studio audience applause, receives a cash bonanza.

Host: Warren Hull

Substitute Host: Monty Hall

Assistant: Jack Carson

Announcer: Ralph Paul

Commercial Spokeswoman: Virginia Graham

Producer: Walt Framer

Strike it Rich

Game; 30 min; Syn. 9/86

A category topic is revealed and each two-member team selects the number of questions to answer (1–3). If they answer the questions, they move that many spaces across an eight step arch. Each step wins them a prize; however, secretly hidden among the prizes is the "Bandit," who reclaims prizes if he appears.

The first team to cross the arch wins the prizes they have accumulated.

Host: Joe Garagiola

Announcer: Bob Hilton

Model: Theresa Ring

Producer: Richard S. Kline, Gary Cox

Struck by Lightning

Comedy; 30 min; CBS 9/19/79 to 10/3/79

Shortly after inheriting the Bridgewater Inn, a decrepit Victorian Lodge in Maine, Ted Stein, a science teacher and descendant of the famous Dr. Frankenstein, discovers that Frank, the caretaker, is the 230-year-old creation of his great grandfather. Stories relate Ted's efforts to run the inn and develop the special serum Frank needs every fifty years to survive.

Frank	Jack Elam
Ted Stein	Jeffrey Kramer
Nora	Millie Slavin
Glenn Hillman	Bill Erwin
Brian	Jeff Cotler
Walt	Richard Stahl

Producer: Arthur Fellows, Terry Keegan

Stryker of Scotland Yard

Crime Drama; 30 min; Syn. 1957

The exploits of Robert Stryker, chief inspector of Scotland Yard, as he investigates cases wherein innocent people have become the pawns of master criminals.

Robert Stryker	Clifford Evans
Sgt. Sam Hawker	George Woodbridge

Producer: William N. Boyle

The Stu Erwin Show

See "Trouble with Father."

Stud's Place

Comedy; 15 min; NBC 11/26/49 to 8/24/50
                         ABC 10/13/50 to 12/24/51

The misadventures of Studs Turkel, the owner of the Chicago-based Stud's Place restaurant-bar, as he becomes involved with staff and customer problems.

Studs Turkel	Himself
Grace (waitress)	Beverly Younger
Carolyn (pianist)	Carolyn Gilbert
Pianist (later)	Chet Robel
Handyman	Win Strackle

Producer: Norman Felton, Biggie Levin, Daniel Petrie, Ben Park

Studio One

Anthology; 60 min; CBS 11/7/48 to 9/2/57
1/6/58 to 9/29/58

A series of quality dramatic productions. Also titled "Studio One in Hollywood" (1958) and "Studio One Summer Theatre" (which replaced "Studio One" during the Summer).

Producer: Herbert Brodkin, Worthington Miner, Fletcher Markle, Felix Jackson, Norman Felton, Gordon Duff, William Brown, Paul Nickell, Franklin Schaffner, Charles H. Schulz

Stump the Authors

Game Pilot; 30 min; NBC 9/13/46

Object: For three guests to weave a plot around props that have been suggested by the studio audience.

Host: Sydney Mason

Panelists: Jack Payne, Dorothy Day, Louis Zara

Producer: Richard Goggin

Stump the Stars

Game; 30 min; CBS 9/17/62 to 9/16/63

Two four-member celebrity teams compete. One member of one team is handed a charade, which he must perform to his team. The amount of time (up to two minutes) it takes the team to identify the charade is calculated. Each member of each team competes in the same manner. The team with the lowest performance time is the winner.

Host: Mike Stokey, Pat Harrington Jr.

Regulars: Beverly Garland, Diana Dors, Ruta Lee, Ross Martin, Hans Conried, Sebastian Cabot

Producer: Mike Stokey

Stump the Stars

Game; 30 min; Syn. 1969

A revised version of the prior title, which see for format.

Host: Mike Stokey

Regulars: Deanna Lund, Vera Miles, Roger C. Carmel, Dick Patterson

Producer: Mike Stokey, Burt Wenland

Stumpers

Game; 30 min; NBC 10/4/76 to 12/31/76

Object: For players to identify persons, places, or things within three clues. Fifteen points is awarded if the stumper is guessed on the first clue; ten points on the second clue, and five points if all three clues are needed. The highest scoring team (two of whom compete) is the winner.

Host: Allen Ludden

Producer: Lin Bolen, Walt Case, Noreen Colen

Suburban Beat

Crime Drama Pilot; 60 min; NBC 8/17/85

The story of four suburban housewives (Joanna, Mimi, Hope, and Rosemary) who form a committee to battle crime in their community of Jericho Downs. The pilot relates the girls efforts to solve the murders of two prostitutes.

Joanna	Dee Wallace
Mimi	Shelley Fabares
Hope Sherman	Heather Langenkamp
Rosemary	Patti Austin
Sgt. Mike DeSantis	Stephen Paar
Joanna's mother	Elena Verdugo
Charlie	Jeff Silverstein
Jennifer	Jenny Lewis
Eugene Moss	Jeff Pomerantz
Gaye Romanis	Sharon Spelman
Conchata	Sandy Martin
Sylvester Linus	Joe Santos

Producer: Brad Buckner, Eugenie Ross-Leming

Success: It Can Be Yours

Human Interest Pilot; 60 min; ABC 3/5/82

Gary Collins and Cyndy Garvey as the hosts of a program that recounts the stories of people who overcame adversity to achieve success. Produced by Alan Landsburg, Woody Fraser, and Kay Hoffman.

Sudden Silence

Western Pilot; 30 min; ABC 10/10/56

Incidents in the growth of an Old West town as seen through the eyes of Irene Frazier, the wife of a sheriff. Aired on "Ford Theatre."

Irene Frazier	Barbara Stanwyck
Sheriff Tom Frazier	Jeff Morrow
Deputy	Jim Hayward
Jordan	Trevor Bardette
Billy	Jimmy Baird
Mayor	Ralph Dumke

Producer: Jack Denove

Sugar Hill Times

Variety; 30 min; CBS 9/13/49 to 10/20/49

The program, also known as "Uptown Jubilee," spotlights black entertainers.

Host: Willie Bryant

Regulars: Harry Belafonte, Timmy Rogers, The Jubileers

Orchestra: Don Redmond

Producer: Barry Wood

Sugar Time

Comedy; 30 min; ABC 8/13/77 to 9/3/77
4/10/78 to 5/29/78

The heartaches, loves, struggles, and misadventures of Maxx, Diane, and Maggie, three beautiful starry-eyed rock singers who comprise the act "Sugar" and hope to make it to the big time.

Maxx Douglas	Barbi Benton
Diane Zuckerman	Didi Carr
Maggie Barton	Marianne Black
Al Marks	Wynn Irwin
Lightning Jack Rappaport	Charles Fleischer
Paul Landson	Mark Winkworth

Theme Vocal ("Girls, Girls, Girls"): Barbi Benton, Didi Carr, Marianne Black

Producer: James Komack

Sugarfoot

Western; 60 min; ABC 9/17/57 to 9/13/60

The exploits of Tom Brewster, a student of law who wanders across the frontier of the 1860s and, more often than not, helps people in distress. (The title refers to a cowboy one grade lower than a tenderfoot.)

Tom Brewster	Will Hutchins
Toothy Thompson	Jack Elam

Producer: William T. Orr, Harry Tatelman, Carroll Chase

Summer

Comedy Pilot; 30 min; CBS 7/14/84

The vacation activities of a group of spirited California high school students who live in an oceanfront community.

Melinda Danson	Jennifer Cooke
Alex Pierce	Gary Hershberger
Desmond Witherspoon	Tico Wells
Zack Stone	Johnny Timko
Erik Slade	Gerald Prendergast
Candy Barraro	Jill Carroll
Karen	Peggy Holmes
Justine	Nova Bell
Bobby Wilson	Ken Olandt
Mother (disco owner)	Sally Kirkland
Seaweed (surfer)	Cameron Thor
George Stone (Zack's father)	Robert Hogan

Producer: Don Reo, Judith Allison

Summer Fun

Pilot Films; 30 min; ABC 7/22/66 to 9/2/66

See the following titles for information: "Baby Crazy," "Little Leatherneck," "McNab's Lab," "Meet Me in St. Louis," "The Pirates of Flounder Bay," and "Thompson's Ghost."

Summer in the City

Variety; 30 min; CBS 8/18/51 to 8/25/51

A two-week Summer replacement for "Faye Emerson's Wonderful Town" with hosts Bob Sweeney and Hal March and regulars Nancy Kelly, Virginia Conwell, Gladys Swarthout, and Robert Scheerer.

The Summer Smothers Brothers Show

Variety; 60 min; CBS 6/23/68 to 9/8/68

A program of music and comedy that replaced "The Smothers Brothers Comedy Hour" for the Summer of 1968. Served as the basis for "The Glen Campbell Goodtime Hour."

Host: Glen Campbell

Regulars: Sally Struthers, Pat Paulsen, Jack Burns, John Hartford

Announcer: Roger Carroll

Orchestra: Nelson Riddle

Producer: George Sunga, Tom Smothers

Summer Theatre

Pilot Films; 30 min; NBC 7/8/69 to 9/1/69

See the following titles for information: "The Best Years," "Doc," "The Flim-Flam Man," "Harper Valley U.S.A.," and "Pioneer Spirit."

Summertime U.S.A.

Variety; 15 min; CBS 7/7/53 to 8/27/53

A twice-weekly program of music and songs.

Hosts: Teresa Brewer, Mel Torme

Vocalists: The Honeydreamers

Orchestra: Ray Bloch

Producer: Richard Lewin

Sunday Date

Variety; 15 min; NBC 8/21/49 to 10/9/49

Music and songs with singer Helen Lee and regulars Shirley Levitt, Paulette Seslan, Dick Style, and Joe E. Marks. Music by the Cavalier Trio.

Sunshine

Comedy-Drama; 30 min; NBC 3/16/75 to 6/19/75

The series, set in Vancouver, Canada, follows the life of Sam Hayden, a happy-go-lucky musician who is left in charge of his young daughter, Jill, after the death of his wife.

Sam Hayden	Cliff DeYoung
Jill Hayden	Elizabeth Cheshire
Nora	Meg Foster
Billy Weaver	Billy Mumy
Cory Givits	Corey Fischer
Ms. Cox	Barbara Bosson
Kate Hayden (Sam's wife)	Cristina Raines*
Jill Hayden	Lindsay and Sidney Green Bush*

Theme Song ("Sunshine"): John Denver, Dick Kniss, Mike Taylor

Producer: George Eckstein

*TV movie roles (11/9/73).

The Sunshine Boys

Comedy Pilot; 60 min; NBC 6/9/77

The misadventures of two retired vaudeville comics (Willie and Al) who share an apartment and struggle to get along with each other.

Willie Clark	Red Buttons
Al Lewis	Lionel Stander
Ben Clark	Michael Durrell
Myrna Navazio	Bobbi Mitchell
Muriel Green	Sarina Grant
Ray Banks	George Wyner
Anita DeVane	Ann Cooper
Julio	Danny Mora
Sylvia Banks	Barra Grant

Producer: Sam Denoff

The Super

Comedy; 30 min; ABC 6/21/72 to 8/23/72

The trials and tribulations of Joe Girelli, the superintendent of a less-than-fashionable apartment building in New York City.

Joe Girelli	Richard S. Castellano
Francesca Girelli	Ardell Sheridan
Joanne Girelli	Margaret E. Castellano
Anthony Girelli	B. Kirby Jr.
Frankie Girelli	Phil Mishkin
Officer Clark	Ed Peck
Dottie Clark	Virginia Vincent
Sylvia Stein	Janet Brandt
Janice Stein	Penny Marshall
Pizuti	Vic Tayback
Fritz	John Lawrence
Herbie	Wynn Irwin
Louie	Louis Basile

Producer: Gerald I. Isenberg

Super Circus

Variety; 60 min; ABC 11/6/49 to 6/3/56

Performances by circus variety acts.

Ringmaster	Claude Kirchner
	Jerry Colonna
Queen of the Super Circus	Mary Hartline
Cliffy the Clown	Cliff Sobier
Assistant Ringmaster	Sandy Wirth
Scampy the Clown	Brady Patton
	Sandy Dobritch
Nicky the Clown	Nicky Francis

Orchestra: Bruce Case

Producer: Jack Gibney, Phil Patton, Morton Stone

Super Cops

Crime Drama Pilot; 30 min; CBS 3/21/75

The exploits of Dave Greenberg and Bobby Hantz, two daring New York police officers known as "Batman and Robin" for their daring tactics and arrest and conviction record.

Dave Greenberg	Steven Keats
Bobby Hantz	Alan Feinstein
Capt. McLain	Dick O'Neill
Bessie	Peggy Rea
Lt. Gorney	Byron Morrow
Sgt. Falcone	Lou Tiano

Producer: Bruce Geller, James David Buchanan, Ronald Austin

Super Friends

Cartoon; ABC 9/8/73 to 9/5/80 (60 min)
9/12/80 to 9/3/83 (30 min)

The exploits of a group of super heroes who have united as the Justice League of America to battle evil.

Aquaman	Norman Alden
	Bill Callaway
Batman	Olan Soule
Robin	Casey Kasem
Superman	Danny Dark
Wonder Woman	Shannon Farnon
Marvin	Frank Welker
Wendy	Sherry Alberoni
Wonder Dog	Frank Welker
Janya	Liberty Williams
Zan	Michael Bell

Narrator: Ted Knight, William Woodson

Producer: William Hanna, Joseph Barbera

The Super Globetrotters

Cartoon; 30 min; NBC 9/22/79 to 12/1/79

The exploits of the Harlem Globetrotters basketball team as crime fighters dispensing justice throughout the world.

Curley Neal	Stu Gilliam
Geese Ausbie	John Williams
Sweet Lou Dunbar	Adam Wade
Nate Branch	Scatman Crothers
Twiggy Sander	Buster Jones
Crime Globe	Frank Welker

Announcer: Michael Rye

Producer: William Hanna, Joseph Barbera

Super Password

Game; 30 min; NBC 9/24/84 (Premiere)

A revised version of "Password." One member of each two-member team receives a password. Through one-word clues, the players must relate its meaning to their partners. Each word that is guessed becomes one of five clues to the identity of a mystery object (which scores a player $100 if he guesses it). The first team to score $350 or more receives the chance to play "Super Password" and win $10,000 by guessing ten passwords within sixty seconds.

Host: Bert Convy

Announcer: Rich Jeffries

Producer: Robert Sherman

Super Pay Cards

Game; 30 min; Syn. 9/81

A revised version of "Pay Cards," which see for format.

Host: Art James

Hostess: Mary Lou Basaraba

Producer: Nick Nicholson, E. Roger Muir

Super President

Cartoon; 30 min; NBC 9/9/67 to 12/28/68

Segments: "Super President" (the exploits of James Norcross, President of the U.S., as he uses the powers he acquired from a cosmic storm to battle evil) and "Spy Shadow" (the adventures of Richard Vance, a detective whose shadow is able to operate independently of himself).

James Norcross	Paul Frees
Richard Vance	Daws Butler

Producer: David DePatie, Friz Freleng

The Super Six

Cartoon; 30 min; NBC 9/10/66 to 8/31/69

The exploits of a group of crime fighters for Super Services, Inc.

Magneto Man	Daws Butler
Elevator Man	Paul Stewart
Super Scuba	Arte Johnson
Granite Man	Lyn Johnson
Captain Wammy	Paul Frees
Super Bwoing	Charles Smith

Producer: David DePatie, Friz Freleng

Super Witch

Cartoon; 30 min; NBC 11/19/77 to 1/28/78

The comic adventures of Sabrina, a beautiful but mischievous teenage witch.

Sabrina	Jane Webb

Producer: Norm Prescott, Lou Scheimer

Supercar

Marionette Adventure; 30 min; Syn. 1962

The battle against crime as seen through the adventures of Mike Mercury, an agent for Supercar, Inc., an anti-crime organization, and the pilot of Supercar, an indestructible car.

Voices: Paul Maxwell, David Graham, John Bluthal, Sylvia Anderson

Producer: Gerry and Sylvia Anderson

Supergran

Comedy; 30 min; Syn. 10/86

Yearning to see her grandson Willie play football, Granny Smith, a frail and elderly woman, journeys to Chileston Park. As Granny arrives at the park, Roderick Campbell, a thief who stole Professor Black's magic ray machine, sets the controls to make himself superhuman, but miscalculates and sends a magic ray flying out the window. The ray hits Granny Smith and transforms her into Supergran. Stories relate Supergran's comical exploits as she uses her amazing powers to battle evil. Produced in England.

Supergran	Gudrun Ure
Willie Smith	Ian Towell
Edison Faraday Black	Holly English
Professor Black	Bill Shine
Roderick Campbell	Ian Cuthberson
Tubb	Lee Marshall

Producer: Keith Richardson

Superior Court

Drama; 30 min; Syn. 9/86

Dramatizations based on criminal justice issues from current newspaper headlines.

Judge: William D. Burns

Producer: Stu Billet, Ralph Edwards, Jay Feldman, John William Corrigan, Joyce Corrigan

Superman

See "The Adventures of Superman."

Supermarket Sweep

Game; 30 min; ABC 12/20/65 to 7/17/67

The game is played in a supermarket where three husband-and-wife couples run up and down the isles and cram their shopping carts with food. The team with the highest grocery bill receives the items plus the chance to compete again.

Host: Bill Malone

Supertrain

Anthology; 60 min; NBC 2/7/79 to 3/14/79

Varying stories that relate brief incidents in the lives of passengers on the Supertrain, an ultra modern streamlined train, designed by the Trans-Allied Corporation, to improve passenger service. See the following title also.

Harry Flood (engineer)	Edward Andrews
Dave Noonan (social director)	Patrick Collins
Dr. Dan Lewis	Robert Alda
Nurse Rose Casey	Nita Talbot
George Boone (porter)	Harrison Page
Gilda (works in health spa)	Aarika Wells
Robert (beauty salon)	Charlie Brill
Sharon (gift shop)	Valorie Armstrong
Lou Atkins (bartender)	Michael DeLano
Maitre d'	Fritz Freed

Producer: Dan Curtis, Anthony Spinner, Rod Amateau

Supertrain

Anthology; 60 min; NBC 4/7/79 to 5/5/79

A revised version of the previous title, with an emphasis placed on character development and mystery and suspense stories.

Harry Flood (engineer)	Edward Andrews
George Boone (passenger relations)	Harrison Page
Dr. Dan Lewis	Robert Alda
Penny Whitaker (social director)	Ilene Graff
Wayne Randall (Harry's assistant)	Joey Aresco
Tex (Harry's assistant)	Ted Gehring
Supertrain Hostess	Rhonda Foxx

Producer: Robert Stambler

Sure as Fate

Anthology; 30 min; CBS 7/4/50 to 4/3/51

Dramas about people who are confronted with situations that are not of their own doing.

Host: Francis L. Sullivan

Narrator: Paul Lukas

Producer: Jerry Danzig

Surfside Six

Mystery; 60 min; ABC 9/3/60 to 9/24/62

The exploits of three private detectives (Dave, Ken, and Sandy) who operate out of a houseboat that is docked at Surfside 6 in Miami Beach, Florida.

Dave Thorne	Lee Patterson
Ken Madison	Van Williams
Sandy Winfield	Troy Donahue
Daphne DeWitt	Diane McBain
Cha Cha O'Brien	Margarita Sierra
Lt. Gene Plehan	Richard Crane
Lt. Snedigar	Donald Barry

Producer: William T. Orr, Jerry Davis, Charles Hoffman, Joel Rogosin

The Survivors

Drama; 60 min; ABC 9/22/69 to 9/17/70

The struggles and emotional problems of the rich as seen through the activities of the wealthy Carlyle family, the owners of a Wall Street banking empire. Also known as "Harold Robbins' The Survivors."

Baylor Carlyle	Ralph Bellamy
Tracy Carlyle	
Hastings	Lana Turner
Philip Hastings	Kevin McCarthy
Duncan Carlyle	George Hamilton
Jeffrey Carlyle	Jan-Michael Vincent
Jean Vale	Louise Sorel
Belle	Diana Muldaur
Riakos	Rossano Brazzi
Sheila	Katherine Cannon
Jonathan	Louis Hayward
Marguerita	Donna Baccalor
Rosemary	Pamela Tiffin
Corbett	Michael Bell

Producer: Walter Doniger, Richard Caffey

Susan and Sam

Comedy Pilot; 30 min; NBC 7/13/77

The misadventures of Susan and Sam, magazine writers who find their romance is floundering on the rocks of professional competition and vastly different tastes.

Susan Foster	Christine Belford
Sam Denton	Robert Foxworth
Doug Braden	Lee Bergere
Barbara	Christina Hart
Hilly	Alan Oppenheimer
Lionel	Rod McCary
Percy	Jack Bannon

Producer: Alan Alda (writer also) and Marc Merson

Susan Raye Time

Variety; 15 min; DuMont 10/2/50 to 11/20/50

A musical interlude series with singer-pianist Susan Raye.

Susan's Show

Children; 30 min; CBS 5/4/57 to 1/18/58

Twelve-year-old Susan Heinkel as host of a program of songs, stories, and "Popeye" cartoons. Produced by Frank Atlass, Paul Fromkin, and Barry McKinley.

Susie

See "Private Secretary."

Suspense

Anthology; 30 min; CBS 3/1/49 to 8/17/54

"Well calculated stories to keep you in . . . Suspense." Suspense dramas adapted from the radio series of the same title.

Voice of Suspense/Narrator: Paul Frees

Announcer: Larry Thor

Producer: Robert Stevens, David Herlwell, Martin Manulis

Suspense

Anthology; 30 min; CBS 3/25/64 to 9/16/64

A short-lived, revised version of the previous title that features average suspense stories.

Host: Sebastian Cabot

Producer: Gilbert A. Ralston, Fred Hendrickson

Suspense Playhouse

Pilot Films; 60 min; CBS 5/24/71 to 7/5/71

Repeats of unsold pilots that originally aired on "Premiere" (with the exception of "Lost Treasure," which replaced two half-hour comedies—"Operation: Greasepaint" and "Out of the Blue").

Suspense Theatre

A syndicated (1969) series of repeat dramas culled from "The Bob Hope Chrysler Theatre" and "The Kraft Suspense Theatre."

Suspense Theatre on the Air

Anthology Pilot; 30 min; Syn. 5/81

A proposed series of weekly suspense dramas. The pilot, "Till Death Do Us Part," tells of a young wife's efforts to kill her elderly husband.

Basil Bradford	Arthur Tracy
Sandra Bradford	Janet Bedlin
Andre	Everett MacLehman
Perkins	Tom Glennon

Producer: Victor Petrashevitch

Suspicion

Anthology; 60 min; NBC 9/30/57 to 9/22/58

Dramas that focus on people's fears and suspicions.

Host: Dennis O'Keefe, Walter Abel

Producer: Mort Abrahams, Alfred Hitchcock, Robert Fashko, Frank Rosenberg, Richard Lewis, William Frye, Allan Miller

Sutters Bay

Comedy Pilot; 30 min; CBS 8/15/83

Comical incidents in the lives of the people of a small American town (Sutters Bay).

Monnie	Susan Kellermann
Sheriff Ward	Dennis Burkley
Elfreda	Alice Ghostley
Jeff Hamner	Granville Van Dusen
Barbara Hamner	Linda Carlson
Doc Medford	Frank Cady
Mervyn	William Lanteau
Leroy	Bryan O'Byrne
Margaret Pierson	Meg Wyllie
Blake Simmons	Richard B. Shull
Ellen Simmons	Georgann Johnson
Edwin Simmons	Jay Johnson
April Hamner	Dana Kimmell
Emma Frye	Brandis Kemp
Mildred	Kathleen Freeman
Howard	Frank Bonner

Producer: Mort Lachman, Sy Rosen

Suzanne Pleshette Is Maggie Briggs

Comedy; 30 min; CBS 3/4/84 to 4/15/84

When financial problems threaten the "New York Examiner" with extinction, the management reassigns Maggie Briggs from hard news city reporter to feature writer for the paper's "Modern Living" section in hopes of improving circulation. Stories relate Maggie's efforts to adjust to her new position.

Maggie Briggs	Suzanne Pleshette
Walter Holden	Kenneth McMillan
Connie Piscipoli	Shera Danese
Melanie Bitterman	Alison LaPlaca
Donny Bauer	Roger Bowen
Sherman Milslagle	Stephen Lee
Geoff Bennett	John Getz
Leo Broadwater	Edward Edwards
Diana Barstow	Michele Nicasto

Music: Patrick Williams

Producer: Charlie Hauck, Deborah Leschin

Swamp Fox

Adventure; 60 min; ABC 10/23/59 to 1/22/60

A "Walt Disney Presents" series that, set during the American Revolution, relates the exploits of Francis Marion, an American General nicknamed "The Swamp Fox," as he attempts to thwart British advances in the South by striking from the glen.

Francis Marion	Leslie Nielsen
Maj. Peter Horry	Myron Healy
Gabriel Marion	Dick Foran
Gen. Lincoln	Wilson Graff
Dehlia	Louise Beavers
Mary Videaux	Barbara Eiler
Col. Tarleton	John Sutton

Producer: Walt Disney, James Pratt, Bill Anderson

S.W.A.T.

Crime Drama; 60 min; ABC 2/24/75 to 4/15/77

The exploits of the Special Weapons and Tactics Unit (SWAT) of the West California Police Department, a group of five men who tackle dangerous assignments.

Lt. Dan "Hondo" Harrelson	Steve Forrest
Sgt. David "Deacon" Kay	Rod Perry
Off. James Street	Robert Urich
Off. T.J. McCabe	James Coleman
Off. Dominic Luca	Mark Shera
Betty Harrelson	Ellen Weston
Matt Harrelson	Michael Harland
Kevin Harrelson	David Adams

Producer: Aaron Spelling, Leonard Goldberg

Sweepstakes

Anthology; 60 min; NBC 1/26/79 to 3/30/79

Comedy-dramas that relate incidents in the lives of million-dollar lottery finalists. Characters are followed from entry through the sweepstakes drawing (over KBEX-TV, Ch. 6 in Hollywood) to show how each copes with winning or losing.

Greg Harris (Lottery Show Host)	Edd Byrnes

Cindy, his assistant, played by: Sally Kim, Wendy Raebeck, Jo McDonnell, Blake Harris, Robin Evans, Katherine Greko

"Sweepstakes" Theme Vocal by Ron Dante

Producer: Robert Dozier

Sweet Surrender

Comedy; 30 min; NBC 4/18/87 to 5/16/87

Events in the hectic day-to-day lives of Georgia and Ken Holden, a young Philadelphia couple struggling to survive the difficult first years of marriage.

Georgia Holden	Dana Delany
Ken Holden	Mark Blum
Bart Holden (their son)	Edan Gross
Frank (Georgia's father)	David Doyle
Joyce (Ken's mother)	Marjorie Lord Jo deWinter
Cak (Georgia's friend)	Viveka Davis
Lyla (Georgia's friend)	Louise Williams
Marty (Lyla's husband)	Thom Sharp
Vaughn Parker (Ken's friend)	Christopher Rich

"Sweet Surrender" Theme: Ray Colcord

Producer: Deidre Fay, Stuart Wolpert

The Swift Home Service Show

See "Tex and Jinx."

The Swift Show

Variety; 30 min; NBC 4/1/48 to 8/4/49

Music, songs, and studio audience participation segments. Sponsored by Swift Foods.

Host: Lanny Ross

Regulars: Eileen Barton, Susan Shaw, Martha Wright, Frank Fontaine, Max Showalter, Ricki Hamilton, Sandra Gable, Dulcy Jordan

Commercial Spokeswoman: Martha Logan

Orchestra: Harry Simeone

Producer: Lee Cooley

The Swift Show Wagon

Variety; 30 min; NBC 1/8/55 to 10/1/55

Horace Heidt as the host of a program that salutes various American cities via music. With the orchestra of Frank DeVol. Produced by Jerry Brown.

Swingin' Together

Comedy Pilot; 30 min; CBS 8/26/63

The misadventrues of Bobby Day and the Four Knights, a small musical group struggling to make the big time.

Bobby Day	Bobby Rydell
Yogi	Peter Brooks
Skooby-Doo	Ben Bryant
Steve	Larry Merrill
Big D	Art Metrano
P.J. Cunningham	James Dunn
Linda Craig	Stefanie Powers

Producer: Howard B. Krcitsek

Swinging Country

Variety; 30 min; NBC 7/4/66 to 12/30/66

Performances by country and western artists.

Host: Roy Clark

Substitute Host: Minnie Pearl

Regulars: Molly Bee, Rusty Draper, The Swinging Countrymen, The Hometown Singers

Orchestra: Bill Walker

Producer: Rosalind Ross

Swiss Family Robinson

Adventure; 60 min; ABC 9/14/75 to 4/11/76

Following a fierce storm at sea, which ship-wrecks the Robinson family on a seemingly deserted tropical island, they discover that they are marooned with little chance for escape. Stories, set in the 1860s, relate the Robinsons struggle for survival and attempts to escape from the island. Based on the story by Johann Wyss.

Karl Robinson	Martin Milner
Lottie Robinson	Pat Delany
Fred Robinson	Willie Aames
	James-Michael Wixted*
Ernie Robinson	Eric Olson
Helga Wagner	Helen Hunt
	Cindy Fisher*
Jeremiah Worth	Cameron Mitchell

Producer: Irwin Allen

*TV movie role (4/15/75)

The Swiss Family Robinson

Adventure; 30 min; Syn. 9/76

The adventures of the Robinsons, a Swiss family who were marooned on a deserted tropical island when their ship was destroyed in a tropical storm, as they struggle for survival and seek a way off the island. The series, set in the year 1881, is produced in Canada.

Johann Robinson	Chris Wiggins
Elizabeth Robinson	Diana Leblanc
Marie Robinson	Heather Graham
Franz Robinson	Micky O'Neill
Ernest Robinson	Michael Duhig

Narrator: Chris Wiggins

Producer: Gerald Mayer

Switch

Crime Drama; 60 min; CBS 9/9/75 to 9/3/78

The story of a retired bunco cop (Frank Mac-Bride) and an ex-con (Pete Ryan) who team to become partners (The Ryan-MacBride Detective Organization), and their exploits as they attempt to beat swindlers at their own game.

Frank MacBride	Eddie Albert
Pete Ryan	Robert Wagner
Maggie Philbin	Sharon Gless
Malcolm Argos	Charlie Callas
Revel	Mindi Miller
Wang	James Hong
Lt. Schiller	William Bryant
Lt. Griffin	Ken Swofford
Lt. Modeen	Richard X. Slattery
Alice (Pete's con artist friend)	Jaclyn Smith
Pete's con artist friend	Anne Archer

Producer: Glen A. Larson, Matthew Rapf

The Sword

Adventure Pilot; 30 min; CBS 5/31/57

The story, set in 17th-century France, relates the adventures of Paul De La Force, a swash-buckler who helps people in distress. Aired on "Schlitz Playhouse of Stars."

Paul De La Force	Jacques Sernas
Cyrano de Bergerac	Fred Wayne
Marion	Nicola Michaels
Bouclet	John Doucette
Count Malvern	Henry Daniell

Producer: Richard Irving

The Sword of Freedom

Adventure; 30 min; Syn. 1957

The exploits of Marco Del Monte, a 15th-century Italian swordsman, as he attempts to defend the free republic against the iron-fisted rule of the Medici family.

Marco Del Monte	Edmund Purdom
Duke De Medici	Martin Benson
Angelica	Adrienne Corri
Machiavelli	Kenneth Hyde

Producer: Sidney Cole

Sword of Justice

Adventure; 60 min; NBC 10/7/78 to 12/31/78

Jack Cole, a wealthy playboy, is framed for a crime he did not commit (embezzling) and imprisoned. While in prison, Jack learns the tricks of the criminals' trade from his fellow inmates. When released, Jack and his cell-mate, Hector, team to battle injustice as mysterious crime fighters who help the federal authorities get the goods on white-collar criminals.

Jack Cole	Dack Rambo
Hector Ramirez	Bert Rosario
Arthur Woods	Alex Courtney

Producer: Glen A. Larson

Sybil

Comedy Pilot; 30 min; CBS 6/25/65

When it is ruled that a beautiful wood sprite (Sybil) has committed the sin of vanity, she is banished from her native habitat and sentenced to reside on Earth. The unsold series was to relate her attempts to atone for her sin by performing good deeds.

Sybil	Suzy Parker
Lionel	Wilfrid Hyde-White
Pete	John Ericson

Producer-Director: Hy Averback

Sylvan in Paradise

Comedy Pilot; 30 min; NBC 8/2/86

The misadventures of Sylvan Sprayberry, an inept bell captain at the Hotel Linalana in Hawaii.

Sylvan Sprayberry	Jim Nabors
Polly	Ann Wedgeworth
Clint C. Waddle	Brent Spiner
Sparky McMann	Glenn Withrow
Lucy	Courteney Cox
Vice Counsal	Michael Ensign
Roy Rogers	Pat McCormick
The Lady	Bunny Summers
Policeman	Clyde Kusatsu

Theme Vocal ("Sylvan in Paradise"): Thomas Bernfeld

Producer: Robert Illes, James Stein

Sylvester and Tweety

Cartoon; 30 min; CBS 9/11/76 to 9/3/77

Warner Brothers theatrical cartoons about Sylvester the Cat's relentless efforts to catch himself a decent meal: Tweety the canary.

Sylvester and Tweety	Mel Blanc

Producer: Warner Bros. TV

Szysznyk

Comedy; 30 min; CBS 8/1/77 to 8/29/77
12/7/77 to 1/27/78

The story of Nick Szysznyk (pronounced Ziznick), an ex-Marine sergeant turned playground supervisor, as he struggles to save the financially troubled Northeast Community Center in Washington, D.C.

Nick Szysznyk	Ned Beatty
Ms. Harrison	Olivia Cole
Sandi Chandler	Susan Lanier
Leonard Kreigler	Leonard Barr
Ray Gunn	Thomas Carter
Ralph	Jarrod Johnson
Tony LaPlaca	Scott Colomby
Bernard Fortwengler	Barry Miller

Producer: Jerry Weintraub, Rich Eustis, Michael Elias

The Tab Hunter Show

Comedy; 30 min; NBC 9/20/60 to 9/10/61

The misadventures of Paul Morgan, a playboy and creator-artist of the comic strip "Bachelor at Large" (published by Comics, Inc.).

Paul Morgan	Tab Hunter
Peter Fairfield III (Paul's friend)	Richard Erdman
John Larsen (Paul's publisher)	Jerome Cowan
Thelma (Paul's housekeeper)	Reta Shaw
Elaine (John's secretary)	Sharon Gibbs
John's mother	Ellen Corby
Joyce (model)	Della Sharmon
Paul's grandmother	Frieda Inescort

Producer: Norman Tokar

Tabitha

Comedy Pilot; 30 min; ABC 4/24/76

A spin-off from "Bewitched." The story of Tabitha Stevens, a beautiful 24-year-old witch (the daughter of Samantha), as she struggles to make it on her own as an editorial assistant at San Francisco's fashionable "Trend" magazine. See the following title also.

Tabitha Stevens	Liberty Williams
Adam Stevens	Bruce Kimmel
Roberta	Barbara Cason
Cliff	Archie Hahn
Bonnie	Cindi Haynie
Dinah	Barbara Rhoades
Leslie	Maria O'Brien

Producer-Director: William Asher

Tabitha

Comedy; 30 min; ABC 9/10/77 to 1/14/78

Events in the life of Tabitha Stevens, a beautiful witch (daughter of Samantha from "Bewitched"), who is employed as a production assistant at KXLA-TV in Los Angeles. The pilot aired on May 7, 1977.

Tabitha Stevens	Lisa Hartman
Adam Stevens	David Ankrum
Paul Thurston	Robert Urich
Marvin Decker	Mel Stewart
Tabitha's Aunt	
Minerva	Karen Morrow
Dr. Bombay	Bernard Fox

Theme Vocal ("It's Magic"): Lisa Hartman

Producer: Jerry Mayer, George Yanok, Robert Stambler

Tag the Gag

Game; 30 min; NBC 8/13/51 to 8/27/51

A group of actors pantomime a joke and stop before the punch line. Players have to supply an ending. The player who tags the gag (gives the funniest ending) receives a cash prize.

Host: Hal Block

Producer: Ray Buffum

Take a Good Look

Game; 30 min; ABC 10/22/59 to 7/21/60

A cast performs a dramatic sketch that relates clues to the identity of a mystery guest. The first celebrity panelist (three appear) to identify the guest receives one point. Winners are the highest scorers (prizes are awarded to the home viewers represented by the celebrities).

Host: Ernie Kovacs

Panelists: Edie Adams, Cesar Romero, Carl Reiner

Sketch Performers: Ernie Kovacs, Peggy Connelly, Bob Lauher

Announcer: Johnny Jacobs

Producer: Irving Mansfield, Peter Arnell

Take a Guess

Game; 30 min; CBS 6/18/53 to 9/10/53

Object: For players to indirectly question a celebrity panel and attempt to identify the mystery phrase that is known only to them.

Host: John K.M. McCaffery

Panelists: Ernie Kovacs, Dorothy Hart, Margaret Lindsey, John Crawford

Producer: Peter Arnell

Take Five

Comedy; 30 min; CBS 4/1/87 to 4/8/87

Events in the life of Andy Kooper, a divorced PR man (with Davis and Son) who finds solace in playing banjo with a Dixieland band (The Lenny Goodman Quartet). Originally titled "Kooper with a K."

Andy Kooper	George Segal
Dr. Noah Wolf	Severn Darden
Monty	Bruce Jarchow
Al	Derek McGrath
Kevin Davis	Todd Field
Laraine McDermott	Melanie Chartoff
Max Davis	Eugene Roche
Lenny Goodman	Jim Haynie

Producer: Brian Grazer, Ron Howard

Take Five with Stiller and Meara

A five-minute syndicated (1977) series of humorous blackouts that satirize everyday life. Starring Jerry Stiller and Anne Meara and produced by John Davis and William Watts.

Take It From Me

See "The Jean Carroll Show."

Take My Advice

Discussion; 30 min; NBC 1/5/76 to 6/11/76

Four celebrity guests discuss and suggest answers to problems submitted by viewers.

Hostess: Kelly Lange

Announcer: Bill Armstrong

Producer: Burt Sugarman

Take One Starring Jonathan Winters

Comedy Pilot; 30 min; NBC 5/1/81

An improvised program that features comedian Jonathan Winters in various situations without written dialogue. Hosted by Rich Little and produced by Paul W. Keyes.

Take Two

Game; 30 min; ABC 5/5/63 to 8/11/63

Four pictures are flashed on a screen (e.g., Marilyn Monroe, Jayne Mansfield, Mickey Mantle, and an apple). The first team (of the two celebrity teams who compete) who identify the related items (Marilyn and Jayne, actresses) score points. The highest scorers win prizes for the audience members they represent.

Host: Don McNeill

Producer: Fred Olsen

Taking It Home

Comedy Pilot; 30 min; NBC 9/12/86

After a twenty year absence, a free spirit (Nick) returns home, hoping to begin a new life. The unsold series was to relate his experiences when he joins the family business (Morelli Toys).

Nick Morelli	Scott Valentine
Papa Joe Morelli	Herschel Bernardi
Kitty DeLuca	Natalia Nogulich
Johnny DeLuca	Ray Baker
Franny DeLuca	Summer Phoenix
Lola	Liz Torres
Gino	Harry Basil
Sheila	Lisa Jane Persky

Producer: Ruth Bennett, Susan Seeger

A Tale of Wells Fargo

The pilot for "Tales of Wells Fargo" (which see).

Talent Jackpot

Variety; 30 min; DuMont; 7/19/49 to 8/23/49

Vinton Freedly and Bud Collyer as the host of a program that showcases undiscovered talent.

Talent Patrol

Variety; 30 min; ABC 1/19/53 to 9/8/55

The program features performances by non professional Army soldiers (original format) and budding civilian talent (revised format).

Hosts: Steve Allen, Bud Collyer, Richard Hayes

Hostess: Arlene Francis

Talent Scouts

See "Arthur Godfrey's Talent Scouts," "Celebrity Talent Scouts," and "Hollywood Talent Scouts."

Talent Varieties

Variety; 30 min; ABC 6/28/55 to 9/6/55

A program of country and western music with host Slim Pickens and The Tall Timber Trio and The Country Rhythm Boys. Produced by Bill Ring.

Tales from the Darkside

Anthology; 30 min; Syn. 9/84

Mystery and suspense stories about people who enter the opposite world of reality—a dark-sided world of evil and death.

Announcer: Paul Sparer

Producer: Rick Rubinstein, George A. Romero, Jerry Golod

Tales of the Apple Dumpling Gang

Comedy Pilot; 60 min; CBS 1/16/82

The basis for "Gun Shy." The story of Russell Donovan, a Gold Rush gambler who becomes the guardian of two orphans (Clovis and Celia) when he wins them in a poker game and can't get rid of them. Now, forced to care for them, Donovan settles down to a life of mining in Quake City, California (1880s). Meanwhile, Clovis and Celia team with Amos and Theodore, two hopeless outlaws, and form the Apple Dumpling Gang, a gang that performs good deads (as in the pilot, rescuing Donovan from bounty hunters).

Russell Donovan	John Bennett Perry
Clovis	Keith Mitchell
Celia	Sara Abeles
Millie Malloy	Sandra Kerns
Homer McCoy	Henry Jones
Amos Tucker	Ed Begley Jr.
Theodore	Arte Johnson
Monke Hardwicke	William Smith
Saloon Girl	Judith Baldwin

Producer: William Robert Yates

Tales of the Black Cat

Anthology; 30 min; Syn. 1950

James Monks as the host of a series of mystery and suspense stories. The title is derived from Thanatopsis, the black Siamese cat that assists the host. Produced by Bruce Anderson.

Tales of the City

See "Ben Hecht's Tales of the City."

Tales of the Gold Monkey

Adventure; 60 min; ABC 9/22/82 to 7/21/83

The series, set on the South Pacific island of Bora Bora in 1938, relates the exploits of Jake Cutler, pilot of the cargo plane Grumman Goose, as he becomes involved in various hair-raising adventures.

Jake Cutler	Stephen Collins
Sarah Stickney-	
White	Caitlin O'Heaney
Bon Chance Louie	Ron Moody
	Roddy McDowall
Corky	Jeff McKay
Princess Kogi	Marta DuBois
Todo	John Fujioka
Otto Wolfschmidt	Barrie Ingram
Rev. Willie Tenboom	John Calvin
Gouchie	Les Genky

"Tales of the Gold Monkey" Theme by Mike Post and Pete Carpenter

Producer: Donald P. Bellisario, John G. Stephens

Tales of the Haunted

Anthology Pilot; 30 min; Syn. 7/81

A proposed series of supernatural tales. Each story, which was to consist to five episodes (stripped Monday through Friday) was designed to be re-edited into a two-hour TV movie. The pilot, titled "Evil Stalks This House," tells of a lost traveler who becomes involved in witchcraft.

Host: Christopher Lee

Richard Stokes	Jack Palance
Maggie Simpson	Helen Hughes
Dodie Gaines	Frances Hyland
Tom	Michael Starr

Producer: Jack Barry, Dan Enright

Tales of the Red Caboose

Drama; 15 min; ABC 10/29/48 to 1/14/49

Stories of railroading lore which are depicted through the operation of Lionel "O" gauge electric trains on specially constructed pikes. Sponsored by Lionel Trains. See also "Roar of the Rails."

Host-Narrator: Dan Magee

Producer: J.E. Hanson

Tales of the 77th Bengal Lancers

Adventure; 30 min; NBC 10/21/56 to 6/2/57

The series, set in 19th-century India, relates the exploits of the 77th Bengal Lancers, a real unit of the British Cavalry, as they battle the constant native uprisings.

Lt. Michael Rhodes	Philip Carey
Lt. William Storm	Warren Stevens
Col. Standish	Pat Whyte
Capt. Scott Ellis	John Hubbard
Capt. Clary	Sean McClory

Producer: Herbert B. Leonard

Tales of the Texas Rangers

Western; 30 min; ABC 9/3/55 to 5/25/57

Dramas based on the files of the Texas Rangers, North America's oldest law enforcement organization.

Jace Pearson	Willard Parker
Clay Morgan	Harry Lauter

Producer: Fred Briskin, Colbert Clark, Harry Ackerman

Tales of Tomorrow

Anthology; 30 min; ABC 8/3/51 to 6/12/53

A series of science fiction stories culled from both classic and modern stories. Produced by Mort Abrahams and George Foley Jr.

Tales of the Unexpected

Anthology; 60 min; NBC 2/2/77 to 3/9/77

A series of mystery and suspense presentations.

Host: William Conrad

"Theme from Tales of the Unexpected" by David Shire

Producer: Quinn Martin, John Wilder, William Robert Yates

Tales of the Unexpected

Anthology; 30 min; Syn. 9/79

Dramas that depict how certain, unexpected events can alter the destinies of people. Originally titled "Roald Dahl's Tales of the Unexpected."

Host (1979–80): Roald Dahl

Host (1980–82): John Houseman

Theme Song ("Carrousel Theme from Tales of the Unexpected"): Ron Grainer

Producer: Sir John Woolf, John Fleming Ball

Tales of the Vikings

Adventure; 30 min; Syn. 1960

The series, set in Scandinavia in 1000 A.D., relates episodes of conquest and conflict in the lives of Leif Erickson and his sea raiders, the Vikings.

Leif Erickson	Jerome Courtland
Finn	Walter Barnes
Firebeard	Stefan Schnabel
Haldar	Peter Bull
Jessica	June Thorburn
Viking	Buddy Baer

Producer: George M. Cahan

Tales of Wells Fargo

Western; NBC 3/18/57 to 8/28/61 (30 min)
                   9/30/61 to 9/8/62 (60 min)

Originally, the exploits of Jim Hardie, an agent-troubleshooter for Wells Fargo, Inc., gold transporters, during the 1860s. In 1961, the format changed slightly to focus also on Jim's adventures as a rancher in San Francisco. The pilot episode, "A Tale of Wells Fargo," aired on Schlitz Playhouse of Stars" on 12/14/56.

Jim Hardie	Dale Robertson
Jeb Gane (ranch foreman)	William Demarest
Beau McCloud (Jim's assistant)	Jack Ging
Widow Ovie (Jim's neighbor)	Virginia Christine
Mary Gee (Ovie's daughter)	Mary Jane Saunders
Tina (Ovee's daughter)	Lory Patrick

Narrator: Dale Robertson

Producer: Nat Holt, Earl Lyon

The Tall Man

Western; 30 min; NBC 9/10/60 to 9/1/62

The series, set in 1870s Lincoln County, New Mexico, focuses on the relationship between

Sheriff Pat Garrett and his captor, William Bonney, alias Billy the Kid, who has been released in the custody of a rancher.

Pat Garrett   Barry Sullivan
William Bonney   Clu Gulager

"The Tall Man" Theme Song: Juan Esquivel

Producer: Nat Holt, Edward J. Montagne, Samuel A. Peeples, Frank Price

Tallahassee 7000

Crime Drama; 30 min; Syn. 1961

The exploits of Lex Rogers, a special agent and troubleshooter for the Florida Sheriff's Bureau (based in Miami Beach; the title refers to the bureau's telephone number).

Lex Rogers   Walter Matthau

Producer: Herbert B. Leonard

Tammy

Comedy; 30 min; ABC 9/17/65 to 7/15/66

Following the death of her parents, a young girl (Tammy) is raised by her grandfather (Mortecai) in the desolate Louisanna bayou. Many years later, after completing a special secretarial course, Tammy applies for a position with John Brent, a wealthy widower who hires her when she impresses him with her amazing typing abilities. Immediately, Tammy encounters the wrath of Lavinia Tate, an attractive widow who sought the job for her daughter, Gloria (thus allowing her a better chance to acquire John's long sought proposal of marriage). Stories relate Tammy's adventures as she struggles to overcome Lavinia's deceitful efforts to get her fired.

Tammy Tarleton   Debbie Watson
Mortecai Tarleton   Denver Pyle
Lucius Tarleton   Frank McGarth
John Brent   Donald Woods

Lavinia Tate   Dorothy Green
Gloria Tate   Linda Marshall
Dwayne DeWitt   George Furth
Peter Tate   David Macklin
Stephen Brent   Jay Sheffield
Cletus Tarleton   Dennis Robertson
Sheriff   Michael Ross
                                     Ross Elliott
Tammy's Aunt
  Hannah   Jeanette Nolan
Lavinia's Cousin
  Beauregard   Sal Ponti
Lavinia's Outcast
  Cousin Grundy   Jeff York
Grundy's Wife
  Sybelline   Bella Bruck

Producer: Dick Wesson

Note: The series is based on the novels "Tammy Out of Time" and "Tammy Tell Me True" by Ricketts Summer.

The Tammy Grimes Show

Comedy; 30 min; ABC 9/8/66 to 9/29/66

Following the death of a relative, Tamantha "Tammy" Ward, a beautiful, spendthrift young heiress, finds that she cannot claim her multimillion dollar inheritance until she becomes thirty. Stories relate Tammy's misadventures when she finds she cannot live on a restricted budget and devises elaborate schemes to finance her expensive tastes.

Tammy Ward   Tammy Grimes
Terence Ward   Dick Sargent
Uncle Simon
  Grimsley   Hiram Sherman
Mabel Ratchett   Maudie Prickett

Theme Song ("Theme from the Tammy Grimes Show"): Johnny Williams

Producer: William Dozier, Richard Whorf, Alex Gottlieb

Target

Anthology; 30 min; Syn. 1951

High-tension, impact dramas that depict the conflicting forces that drive men and women.

Host: Adolphe Menjou

Producer: Sutton Roley, Eddie Davis

Target

Crime Drama; 60 min; TEC 11/20/82 to 3/28/83

The exploits of Steve Hackett, the deputy superintendent of the 13 Regional Crime Squad, an elite team of police agents who tackle crimes in Hampshire, England.

Det. Steve Hackett	Patrick Mower
Det. Louise Colbert	Vivien Heilbroh
Det. Sup. Tate	Philip Madoc
Det. Frank Bonney	Brendan Price

Producer: Philip Hinchcliffe

Target: The Corrupters

Crime Drama; 60 min; ABC 9/21/61 to 9/21/62

The story of a racket reporter (Paul Marino) and a federal undercover agent (Jach Flood) who team to infiltrate the rackets and expose the methods of organized crime through the power of the press.

Paul Marino	Stephen McNally
Jach Flood	Robert Harland

Theme Song ("Target") by Rudy Schrager

Producer: Leonard Ackerman, John Burrows

Tarzan

Adventure; 60 min; NBC 9/8/66 to 9/13/68

One year after making Africa their home (put ashore by a mutinous crew and unable to escape) a son is born to Alice and John Greystoke. Shortly after, John and Alice are killed by Bull apes; and the baby taken by a female ape who raises him as Tarzan, Lord of the Jungle. Twenty years later, after a safari is marooned in Africa, Tarzan befriends a Frenchman who teaches him to speak English and persuades him to return to England. Although educated in the finest schools, Tarzan is unable to adjust and returns to Africa. Stories relate his battle against evil. Based on the characters created by Edgar Rice Burroughs.

Tarzan	Ron Ely
Jai (jungle boy)	Manuel Padilla Jr.
Jason Flood (Jai's tutor)	Alan Caillou
Rao (village vet)	Rockne Tarkington
Tall Boy (Rao's assistant)	Stewart Rafill

Producer: Jon Epstein, Maurice Unger

The Tarzan/Lone Ranger/Zorro Adventure Hour

Cartoon; 55 min; CBS 9/12/81 to 9/11/82

Segments: "Tarzan" (exploits of the Lord of the Jungle); "The Lone Ranger" (The Lone Ranger and Tonto's efforts to maintain law in the Old West); and "Zorro" (the adventures of Don Diego, alias Zorro, a mysterious freedom fighter of early California).

Tarzan	Robert Ridgely
Lone Ranger	William Conrad
Tonto	Ivan Naranjo
Don Diego	Henry Darrow
Maria	Christine Avila
Sgt. Gonzales	Don Diamond

Producer: Norm Prescott, Lou Scheimer

Tarzan: Lord of the Jungle

Cartoon; 30 min; CBS 9/11/76 to 9/2/78

The exploits of Tarzan, Lord of the African Jungle, as he battles the evils of man and beast.

Tarzan	Robert Ridgely

Additional Voices: Linda Gary, Joan Gerber Ted Cassidy, Jane Webb, Alan Oppenheimer

Producer: Norm Prescott, Lou Scheimer

Tarzan, The Ape Man

Adventure Pilot; 60 min; ABC 2/23/68 (filmed in 1959)

The first known pilot for a "Tarzan" series. The storyline follows the first title's recounting of how Tarzan came to be. His education, however, is different: While on a safari, Jane Parker wanders from its safety and is rescued from impending doom by Tarzan. Soon she befriends him and teaches him to speak English. Eventually, she decides to remain with him in Africa. The unsold series was to depict their adventures as they defend their jungle domain.

Tarzan	Denny Miller
Jane	Joanna Barnes
Colonel Parker	Robert Douglas
Holt	Cesare Danova
Riano	Thomas Yangha

Producer: Al Zimbalist, Donald Zimbalist

Tate

Western; 30 min; NBC 6/8/60 to 9/28/60

The saga of Tate, a wandering one-armed ex-gunfighter who sides with justice against criminal elements.

Tate	David McLean
Jessica Jackson (his friend)	Patricia Breslin

Producer: Shelly Hull

Tattletales

Game; 30 min; CBS 2/18/74 to 3/31/78
1/18/82 to 6/1/84

Three celebrity couples compete, each representing one third of the studio audience. The object is for the husbands to determine what their wives have said about their marriage, and vice versa. The team with the most correct answers wins $1,000, which is divided among the members of their section.

Host: Bert Convy

Announcer: Jack Clark, Johnny Olsen, Gene Wood

Producer: Mark Goodson, Bill Todman, Ira Skutch

Taxi

Comedy; 30 min; ABC 9/12/78 to 6/10/82
NBC 9/30/82 to 7/13/83

Incidents in the lives of the drivers and crew of the New York-based Sunshine Cab Company. See also "Shaughnessey."

Alex Reiger	Judd Hirsch
Elaine Nardo	Marilu Henner
Tony Banta	Tony Danza
Louie DePalma	Danny DeVito
Bobby Wheeler	Jeff Conaway
Latka Gravas	Andy Kaufman
Jim "Iggie" Ignatowski	Christopher Lloyd
Simka Gravas	Carol Kane
Jeff Bennett	Jeff Thomas
John Burns	Randall Carver
Suzanne Burns	Ellen Regan
Reverend Gorky	Vincent Schiavelli
Tommy (waiter at Mario's)	T.J. Castronova
Zena Sherman	Rhea Perlman
Jennifer Nardo	Melanie Gaffin
Jason Nardo	David Mendenhall
Alex's Daughter Cathy	Talia Balsam
Louie's Mother Gabriella	Julia DeVito
Tom Caldwell	Walter Olkewicz
Phyllis Reiger	Louise Lasser
Greta Gravas	Susan Kellerman
Monica Douglas	Julie Kavner
Mr. Caldwell (Jim's father)	Victor Buono
Simka's Cousin Zifka	Mark Blankfield

Theme Song ("Angela's Theme from Taxi"): Bob James

Producer: James L. Brooks, Stan Daniels, Ed Weinberger, David Davis, Glen Charles, Les Charles

Teachers Only

Comedy; 30 min; NBC 4/4/82 to 6/9/82

The experiences of Diana Swanson, an English teacher at the mythical Millard Fillmore High School in Los Angeles. See the following title also.

Diana Swanson	Lynn Redgrave
Ben Cooper	Norman Fell
Gwen Edwards	VanNessa Clarke
Michael Dreyfuss	Adam Arkin
Mr. Brody	Norman Bartold
Mr. Pafko	Richard Karron
David Lewis	Mark Metcalf
Lois McArdle	Kit McDonough
Amy Kelley	Amanda Wyss

Music: Earle Hagen

Producer: Aaron Ruben, George Yanok

Teachers Only

Comedy; 30 min; NBC 2/12/83 to 5/21/83

A revised version of the previous title. The misadventures of the faculty of the mythical Arnold Wilson High School in Brooklyn, N.Y.

Diana Swanson	Lynn Redgrave
Ben Cooper	Norman Fell
Samantha Keating	Teresa Ganzel
Shari	Jean Smart
Barney Baker	Joel Brooks
Michael Horn	Tim Reid
Spud LaBoone	Steve Ryan

Theme Vocal: The Commodores

Producer: Larry Rosen, Larry Tucker, April Kelly, Diana Kirgo

The Ted Bessell Show

Comedy Pilot; 30 min; CBS 5/8/73

The misadventures of Ted Harper, a married magazine editor who works in an office surrounded by a bevy of beautiful staff workers.

Ted Harper	Ted Bessell
Diane Harper	Barra Grant
Barney Raider	Robert Walden
Amy	Karen Jensen
Margaret	Beth Howland
Mario	Mark Gordon

Producer: Charles Jaffe

The Ted Knight Show

Comedy; 30 min; CBS 4/8/78 to 5/13/78

The comic adventures of Roger Dennis, the owner of the Mr. Dennis Escort Service in New York City.

Roger Dennis	Ted Knight
Dottie	Iris Adrian
Bert Dennis	Normann Burton
Winston Davis	Thomas Leopold
Joy	Deborah Harmon
Graziella	Cissy Colpitts
Irma	Ellen Regan
Cheryl	Janice Kent
Philadelphia Brown	Tanya Boyd
Honey	Fawne Harriman

Producer: Mark Rothman, Lowell Ganz

The Ted Knight Show

Comedy; 30 min; Syn. 4/86

A spin-off from "Too Close for Comfort." When their daughters Sarah and Jackie move, Henry and Muriel Rush decide to relocate to Marin County, California, where Henry buys half interest in the weekly newspaper, the "Marin Buglar." Stories relate Henry's misadventures as he attempts to adjust to life at home and at work.

Henry Rush	Ted Knight
Muriel Rush	Nancy Dussault
Monroe Ficus	JM J. Bullock
Hope Stinson	Pat Carroll
Lisa	Lisa Antelle
Andrew Rush	Joshua Goodwin
Hope's Niece Jennifer	Leah Ayres

Producer: Aaron Ruben, Volney Howard III, George Yanok

Ted Mack and the Original Amateur Hour

Variety; 30 min; DuMont 1/18/48 to 9/25/49
NBC 10/4/49 to 9/11/54
ABC 10/30/55 to 6/23/57
CBS 5/1/59 to 10/9/59
ABC 3/7/60 to 9/26/60
CBS 10/2/60 to 9/27/70

The series, adapted from the radio program "Major Bowes and His Original Amateur Hour," features performances by undiscovered talent.

Host: Ted Mack

Announcer: Dennis James, Roy Greece

Orchestra: Lloyd Marx

Producer: Ted Mack, Lou Goldberg

Ted Mack's Family Hour

Variety; 30 min; ABC 1/7/51 to 11/25/51

A Sunday evening program of music and songs.

Host: Ted Mack

Vocalist: Andy Roberts

Announcer: Dennis James

Orchestra: Lloyd Marx

Producer: Louis Graham

Ted Mack's Matinee

Variety; 30 min; NBC 4/4/55 to 10/28/55

A daily program of music and songs with host Ted Mack and regulars Elsie Rhodes, Dick Lee and the Honeydreamers. Produced by Louis Graham.

The Ted Steele Show

Variety; 30 min; NBC 9/29/48 to 10/29/48
                    DuMont 2/27/49 to 7/12/49
                    CBS 6/6/49 to 4/28/50

A program of music and songs with bandleader Ted Steele and regulars Helen Wood, Michael Rich, Mardi Bryant, and Charles Danford. Produced by Ken Redford.

Teen Wolf

Cartoon; 30 min; CBS 9/13/86 (Premiere)

The adventures of Scott Howard, a seemingly ordinary teenager who suffers from one slight disorder: he (and his family) become werewolves under the full moon. Based on the feature film.

Scott Howard	Coleman Townsend
Freida	Sheryl Bernstein
Boof	Jeannie Elias

Grandma	June Foray
Grandpa	Stacy Keach Sr.
Harold	James Hampton
Stiles	Donny Most
Mick	Craig Schafer
Chuck	Will Ryan

Producer: Buzz Potamkin, Jonathan Dana

Tele Pun

Game; 30 min; NBC 7/9/48 to 8/6/48

A player stands before the studio audience and performs a pun, which represents a person, place or thing. If the audience is satisfied, the player receives a prize; however, should he make a mistake, he is charged with "punning in public places" and arrested. The player is then defended by an attorney. When the judge dismisses the case, the player receives a consolation prize and the errant pun is performed in the correct manner.

Host-Judge: Johnny Bradford

Attorney-Announcer: Ray Michael

Producer: Vance Halleck

Tele-Varieties

Variety Pilot; 15 min; NBC 12/8/46

Performances by new talent discoveries.

Host: Tommy Farrell

Regulars: Betty Barto, Ann Crowley, Herb Howard

Producer: Wes McKee

The Telecomics

Children; 15 min; Syn. 1949
                    NBC 9/18/50 to 3/30/51

Nonanimated cartoon strips are viewed and narrated panel by panel. The syndicated version consists of "Brother Goose," "Joey and Jug," "Rick Rack, Special Agent," and "Sa-Lih." The network version, titled "NBC Comics," relates the adventures of "Danny March," "Johnny and Mr. Do-Right," "Kid Champion," and "Space Barton."

Telephone Time

Anthology; 30 min; CBS 4/8/56 to 3/3/57
             ABC 6/4/57 to 4/1/58

A series of historical dramas featuring well-known stars and quality productions.

Host-Narrator: John Nesbitt, Dr. Frank Baxter

Producer: Hal Roach Jr., Jerry Stagg

Teletips on Loveliness

Advice Pilot; 15 min; NBC 8/15/46

An unsold series of beauty tips and advice for women.

Hostess: Leona Woodworth

Guest: Mary Kelly

Producer: Harvey Marlowe

Television Fashion Fair

Experimental; 30 min; DuMont 12/15/46

A women's program of fashions and fashion news with the Conover Cover Girls.

Hostess: Florence Pritchett

Producer: Raymond E. Nelson

Television Inside and Out

Magazine; 60 min; NBC 12/5/81 to 1/2/82

A weekly look at the TV industry via interviews, investigative reporting, and nostalgic clips.

Hostess: Rona Barrett

Regulars: Sylvester "Pat" Weaver, Wil Shriner, Gary Deeb

Announcer: Tom Campbell

Producer: Bill Royce, Stu Bernstein

Television Roof

Experimental; 30 min; DuMont 9/38

The earliest known TV variety series. A weekly program that features performances by name entertainers at a time when only 300 TV sets were in existence.

Host: Dennis James

Producer: Dr. Allen B. DuMont

Television Screen Magazine

Variety; 30 min; NBC 11/17/46 to 7/23/49

Various features, including music, interviews, chatter, and songs.

Host: George Putnam

Regulars: Ray Forrest, Millicent Fenwick, John K.M. McCaffery, Alan Scott, William Berns

Tell It to Groucho

Quiz; 30 min; CBS 1/11/62 to 5/31/62

Two contestants are first interviewed, then compete in a quiz wherein they must identify persons, places, or objects from pictures that are rapidly flashed on a screen.

Host: Groucho Marx

Assistants: Patty Harmon, Jack Wheels

Announcer: George Fenneman

Producer: Bernie Smith

Tell It to the Camera

Comedy; 30 min; CBS 1/11/62 to 5/24/62

An extension based on "Candid Camera" wherein people, who are aware of a camera, speak directly into it and reveal their thoughts concerning themselves or wordly affairs.

Host: Red Rowe

Producer-Creator: Allen Funt

Tell Me, Dr. Brothers

A syndicated (1964) five-minute program of advice with Dr. Joyce Brothers.

The Teller and the Tale

Anthology Pilot; 60 min; Syn. 10/85

A proposed series that was to feature guests telling their favorite stories.

Hostess: Sally Struthers

Guests: Vincent Price, Hans Holzer, Jackie Torrance

Producer: Nelson Davis

Teller of Tales

Anthology; 30 min; CBS 10/18/50 to 3/28/51
                NBC 4/2/51 to 12/10/51

Dramas based on stories by William Somerset Maugham. Also known as "The Somerset Maugham Theatre."

Host: William Somerset Maugham

Producer: John Gibbs, Anne Marlowe, Marilyn Ritt, Daniel Mann

The Telltale Clue

Crime Drama; 30 min; CBS 7/8/54 to 9/23/54

The exploits of Richard Hale, a detective with the Metropolitan Homicide Division of the N.Y.P.D., as he attempts to solve crimes through one seemingly insignificant piece of evidence: The Telltale Clue.

Richard Hale   Anthony Ross

Producer: Charles Martin

Temperatures Rising

Comedy; 30 min; ABC 9/12/72 to 9/4/73

A comical portrait of life in a hospital as seen through the antics of Jerry Noland, a doctor assigned to Capitol General Hospital in Washington, D.C. See also "The New Temperatures Rising Show."

Dr. Vincent Campanelli	James Whitmore
Dr. Jerry Noland	Cleavon Little
Nurse Ann Carlisle	Joan Van Ark
Nurse Mildred MacInerney	Reva Rose
Nurse Ellen Turner	Nancy Fox
Miss Llewelleyn	Olive Dunbar

Producer: Harry Ackerman, William Asher

Temple Houston

Western; 60 min; NBC 9/19/63 to 9/17/64

The story of Temple Houston, a circuit-riding attorney, and his partner, George Taggert, an ex-gunfighter turned law enforcer, as they defend unjustly accused people before circuit-riding judges in the post-Civil War southwest. See also "The Man from Galveston."

Temple Houston	Jeffrey Hunter
George Taggert	Jack Elam

Producer: Joseph Dackow, Richard Bluel, Lawrence Dobkin, James Lydon

Temptation

Game; 30 min; ABC 10/2/67 to 7/2/68

Object: For three female players to select a merchandise showcase and identify its contents through a series of indirect probe rounds. The player who is first to identify the contents of the showcase wins.

Host: Art James

Producer: Merrill Heatter, Bob Quigley

Tenafly

Crime Drama; 90 min; NBC 10/2/73 to 8/26/74

The exploits of Harry Tenafly, a private detective with the Los Angeles-based Hightower Investigations.

Harry Tenafly	James McEachin
Ruth Tenafly	Lillian Lehman
Lorrie	Rosanna Huffman
Lt. Sam Church	David Huddleston
Mary Church	Mary Ann Gibson
Chief Vernon	Ford Rainey
Herb Tenafly	Paul Jackson

Producer-Creator: Richard Levinson, William Link

Tenko

Drama; 60 min; Syn. 9/85

The harsh and gruelling day-to-day lives of a group of British and Dutch women who are taken prisoner by the Japanese during World War II and placed in a decrepit camp on a hot and desolate island.

Blanche Simmons	Louise Jamison
Marian Jefferson	Ann Bell
Sylvia Ashburton	Renee Asherson
Rose Millar	Stephanie Beacham
Sister Ulrico	Patricia Lawrence
Beatrice Mason	Stephanie Cole
Nellie Keene	Jeannane Crowley
Kate Norris	Claire Oberman
Christina Campbell	Emily Bolton
Dorothy Bennett	Veronica Roberts
Sally Markham	Joanna Hole
Debbie Bowen	Karin Foley

Producer: Ken Riddington, Vere Lorrare

The Tennessee Ernie Ford Show

Variety; 30 min; NBC 1/3/55 to 6/28/57

A weekly program of music and songs with a country-western accent.

Host: Tennessee Ernie Ford

Regulars: Molly Bee, Reginald Gardiner, Doris Drew, The Voices of Walter Schumann

Announcer: Skip Farrell

Orchestra: Walter Schumann, Jack Fascinato

Producer: Milt Hoffman, Bud Yorkin

The Tennessee Ernie Ford Show

Variety; 30 min; ABC 4/2/62 to 3/26/65

A program of music and songs with host Tennessee Ernie Ford and regulars Anita Gordon, Dick Noel, and Billy Strange. With the music of Jack Fascinato and the announcing of Jim Lange.

Tennessee Tuxedo and His Tales

Cartoon; 30 min; Syn. 1963

Segments: "Tennessee Tuxedo" (antics of Tennessee Tuxedo, a penguin, and his friend, Chumley the walrus, as they attempt to improve living conditions at the Megapolis Zoo); "The King and Odie" (the attempts of villains Itchy Brother and Biggy Rat to dethrone Leonardo, the king of Bongo Congo); "Tutor the Turtle" (a turtle becomes what he wishes through Mr. Wizard the lizard).

Tennessee Tuxedo	Don Adams
Chumley	Bradley Bolke
Phineas J. Woopie	Larry Storch
King Leonardo/	
Biggy Rat	Jackson Beck
Odie Colognie/Itchy	
Brother/Tutor	Allen Swift
Mr. Wizard	Frank Milano

Producer: Peter Peach, Treadwell Covington

Tenspeed and Brown Shoe

Adventure; 60 min; ABC 1/27/80 to 7/11/80

The crime-solving exploits of a pair of unlikely detectives: E.L. "Tenspeed" Turner, a street-wise con artist; and Lionel Whitney, an avid mystery fan reader and demure stockbroker whom E.L. calls a "brown shoe" (a square).

E.L. Turner	Ben Vereen
Lionel Whitney	Jeff Goldblum
Mike Magill	James Sloyan
Sam Athena	James Beach
Tommy Tedesco	Richard Romanus
Bernice Coitney	Candice Azzara
Harriet Whitney	Dana Wynter
William Whitney	John Hillerman
John Dalem	Nicholas Coster
TV Newscaster	Tawny Little

Music: Mike Post and Pete Carpenter

Producer: Stephen J. Cannell, Alex Beaton, Chuck Bowman, Juanita Bartlett

Terrahawks

Marionette Adventure; 30 min; Syn. 12/84

The exploits of the Terrahawks, a secret organization of warriors who defend the Earth against alien invaders.

Voices: Denise Bryer, Windsor Davis, Jeremy Hitchen, Ann Ridler, Ben Stevens

Theme Vocal ("Living in the 21st Century"): Moya Griffiths

Producer: Gerry Anderson, Christopher Burr

Terry and the Pirates

Adventure; 30 min; Syn. 1952

The exploits of Terry Lee, Hot Shot Charlie, and Burma, pilots for Air Cathay, a small airline run by Chopstick Joe, as they battle the evils of Lai Choi San, alias The Dragon Lady, and her band of pirates as they wreck havoc in the Orient. Based on the comic strip by Milton Caniff.

Terry Lee	John Baer
Burma	Marie Blanchard
	Sandra Spence
Hot Shot Charlie	Walter Tracy
Chopstick Joe	Jack Reitzen
Dragon Lady	Gloria Saunders

Producer: Warren Lewis

Tex and Jinx

Variety; 30 min; NBC 4/1/48 to 8/4/49

A program of music, songs, fashion, cooking, and other items of interest to women. Also known as "The Tex and Jinx Swift Show." Sponsored by Swift Foods.

Host: Tex McCrary, Jinx Falkenberg

Regulars: Sandra Gable, Martha Logan, Helen Carroll and the Escorts

Announcer: Dan Seymour

Music: The Johnny Guarnieri Quintet

Producer: Lee Cooley

Texaco Star Theatre

Variety; 60 min; NBC 9/21/48 to 6/9/53

A program of music and outlandish slapstick comedy with Milton Berle, the comedian whose Tuesday night show drastically helped to boost the sale of TV sets at a time when the new medium was considered a vast wasteland. Sponsored by Texaco Gasoline.

Host: Milton Berle

Regulars: Arnold Stang, Sid Stone, Dolores Gray, Bobby Clark, Ruth Gilbert, Willie Field, The Merry Texaco Repairmen, The Dunhills, The Balicana Ivanko Troupe

Commercial Spokesman: Jimmy Nelson

Orchestra: Allen Roth

Producer: Ed Cashman, Milton Berle, Edward Sobol, Arthur Knorp

Texaco Star Theatre

Variety; 60 min; NBC 10/2/54 to 9/24/55

A weekly series of music, songs, and comedy under the sponsorship of Texaco Gasoline.

Host: Jimmy Durante

Regulars: Eddie Jackson, Jules Buffano, The Durante Girls

Orchestra: Allen Roth, Roy Bargy

Producer: Edward Buzzell

The Texan

Western; 30 min; CBS 9/29/58 to 9/12/60

The exploits of Bill Longley, a wandering ex-gunfighter who roams throughout the Texas of the 1870s to help people in distress.

Bill Longley	Rory Calhoun
Mac	Duncan Lamont

Narrator: Rory Calhoun

Producer: William T. Orr, Rory Calhoun, Vic Orsatti, Carroll Chase, Jerry Stagg

Texas John Slaughter

Western; 60 min; ABC 10/31/58 to 4/23/61

A "Walt Disney Presents" series about the exploits of John Slaughter, a Texas Ranger, then sheriff (of Friotown, Texas), as he attempts to maintain law and order.

John Slaughter	Tom Tyron
Viola Slaughter	Betty Lynn
Willie Slaughter	Brian Corcoran
Ranger Ben Jenkins	Harry Carey Jr.
Addie	Annette Gorman

Theme Vocal ("Texas John Slaughter"): Stan Jones

Producer: Walt Disney, James Pratt

The Texas Rangers

Crime Drama Pilot; 60 min; NBC 5/16/81

The exploits of Andy Bennett and Bill Cavanaugh, members of the Houston Division of the Texas Rangers, the country's oldest law enforcement organization.

Andy Bennett	Jeff Osterhage
Bill Cavanaugh	Larry Gilman
Ranger J.W. Stevens	Richard Farnsworth
Capt. Richard Barton	Arlen Dean Snyder
Blanche	Patricia Barry
Louise	Cis Rundle
Bobby Joe Ames	Michael Cavanaugh
Old Al	Paul Brinegar

Producer: Fran Von Zerneck, Robert Greenwald

The Texas Wheelers

Comedy; 30 min; ABC 9/13/74 to 10/4/74
6/26/75 to 7/24/75

The comic adventures of Zack Wheeler, a lazy, unemployed father, as he struggles to solve the problems that ensue from four children who can't wait to grow up.

Zack Wheeler	Jack Elam
Truckie Wheeler	Gary Busey
Doobie Wheeler	Mark Hamill
Boo Wheeler	Karen Oberdiear
B.J. Wheeler	Tony Becker
Sally	Lisa Eilbacher
Bud	Dennis Burkley
Sheriff	Noble Willingham

Producer: Dale McRaven, Chris Hayward

That Girl

Comedy; 30 min; ABC 9/8/66 to 9/10/71

Seeking to begin a career in show business, Ann Marie, a very pretty young actress, leaves her home in Brewster, New York, and heads for Manhattan, where her struggles to make her dreams become a reality are depicted. See the following title also.

Ann Marie	Marlo Thomas
Don Hollinger	Ted Bessell
Lou Marie	Lew Parker
Helen Marie	Rosemary DeCamp

Jules Benedict	Billy DeWolfe
Judy Bessimer	Bonnie Scott
Leon Bessimer	Dabney Coleman
Jerry Bauman	Bernie Kopell
Jerry Myer (before Bauman role)	Bernie Kopell
Margie Myer	Arlene Golonka
Ruth Bauman	Carolyn Daniels
	Alice Borden
Seymour Schwimmer	Don Penny
Harvey Peck	Ronnie Schell
Sandy Stone	Morty Gunty
George Lester	George Carlin
Bert Hollinger	Frank Faylen
Mildred Hollinger	Mabel Albertson
Jonathan Adams	Forrest Compton
	James Gregory
Agnes Adams	Phyllis Hill
Sandi Hollister	Cloris Leachman
Pete	Ruth Buzzi
Gloria	Bobo Lewis

Producer: Bill Persky, Sam Denoff, Bernie Orenstein, Saul Turteltaub

That Girl

Comedy Pilot; 30 min; Unaired (produced in 1965)

The original pilot for "That Girl," which follows the basic format of the aired series, with the exception being the role of Ted Bessell (who appeared as Don Hollinger, Ann's boyfriend and a writer for "Newsview" Magazine in the series; in the unaired pilot, he portrays Don Bluesky, Ann's agent).

Ann Marie	Marlo Thomas
Don Bluesky	Ted Bessell
Ann's father	Harold Gould
Ann's mother	Penny Santon
Sharon	Jackie Joseph
Charlotte	Shirley Bond
Chef	Cliff Norton

Producer: Jack Elinson

Director: Jerry Paris

Writer: Bill Persky, Sam Denoff

That Reminds Me

Game; 30 min; NBC 4/5/52 to 5/26/52

Object: For a celebrity panel to identify guests who appear in elaborate disguises.

Hostess: Arlene Francis

Panelists: Nina Foch, Roger Price, Robert Coates

That Teen Show

Magazine; 30 min; Syn. 9/81

Topics of interest geared to teenagers with guests providing information and possible solutions to the problems faced by teenagers. Also included is music, fashion, and opinions by teenagers across the country.

Hosts: Carolyn McCuen, Heywood Nelson, Tim Sloane

Producer: Charles Gerber, John DeWitt

That Was The Week That Was

Satire Pilot; 60 min; NBC 11/10/63

The pilot for the series. A satirization of news events via sketches, blackouts and commentary.

Host: Henry Fonda

Regulars: Henry Morgan, Nancy Ames, Charlie Mann

Orchestra: Billy Taylor

Producer: Leland Hayward

That Was The Week That Was

Satire; 30 min; NBC 1/10/64 to 5/4/65

A satirization of the prior week's news via sketches, blackouts, and commentary. Also known as "TW3."

Host: Elliott Reid

Regulars: Nancy Ames, Henry Morgan, Phyllis Newman, Pat Englund, David Frost, Doro Merande, Buck Henry, Burr Tillstrom, Bob Dishy

Music: Skitch Henderson, Billy Taylor

Producer: Leland Hayward, Marshall Jamison

That Was The Week That Was

Satire Pilot; 60 min; ABC 4/22/85

A satirical review of headline news stories that occurred one week prior to the show's air date.

Host: David Frost

Co-Host: Anne Bancroft

Regulars: Kimberly Beck, Jim Morris, Jan Hooks, Marcia Del Mar, Brian Bradley, Norman Lee Harris, Frank Welker, Ian Schoales, Julie McWhirter

Producer: David Frost, Woody Fraser

That Wonderful Guy

Comedy; 30 min; ABC 1/4/50 to 4/28/50

The misadventures of a would-be actor (Harold) who is employed by a drama critic (Franklin).

Harold	Jack Lemmon
His girlfriend	Cynthia Stone
Franklin Westbrook	Neil Hamilton

Producer: Charles Irving

That's Cat

Children; 30 min; Syn. 1977

A mixture of music, song, and comedy that attempts to explain various aspects of the world to children.

Alice	Alice Playten
Me	Frank Cala

Music: John Sebastain

Producer: Giovani Nigro-Chacon

That's Hollywood

Documentary; 30 min; Syn. 1977

Various aspects of films produced by 20th Century-Fox are showcased with on-camera performances and behind-the-scenes preparations.

Narrator: Tom Bosley

"That's Hollywood" Theme Music: Rudy Raksin

Producer: Jack Haley Jr., Aubrey Solomon, David Lawrence

That's Incredible

Human Interest; 60 min; ABC 3/3/80 to 4/30/84

Profiles of unusual people and strange phenomena.

Hosts: Cathy Lee Crosby, John Davidson, Fran Tarkenton

"That's Incredible" Theme Music: Jack Tillar, William Loose

Producer: Alan Landsburg, Merrill Grant, Woody Fraser

That's Life

Musical Comedy; 60 min; ABC 9/24/68 to 5/19/69

Stories, which combine the format of a serial, and the Broadway-paced blend of music and comedy, relate the meeting and courtship of Robert Dickson, a junior executive, and Gloria Quigley, a beautiful salesgirl, and their later marriage, struggle as newlyweds, and attempts to adjust to parenthood when their son is born.

Robert Dickson	Robert Morse
Gloria Quigley	E.J. Peaker
Mr. Quigley	Shelly Berman
Mrs. Quigley	Kay Medford

Featured: The Tony Mordente Dancers

Orchestra: Elliot Lawrence

Producer: Marvin Marx, Stan Harris

That's My Boy

Comedy; 30 min; CBS 4/19/54 to 1/1/55

Events in the lives of the Jackson family: "Jarrin" Jack, a former college athlete turned businessman; Alice, his wife, a former Olympic swimming champion; and their son, Jack Junior, a freshman at Rossmore (Ohio) College, who is near-sighted, a bookworm, adverse to sports, and prone to hayfever and sinus attacks.

Jack Jackson Sr.	Eddie Mayehoff
Alice Jackson	Rochelle Hudson
Jack Jackson Jr.	Gil Stratton Jr.
Sam Baker	Larry Blake
Henrietta Patterson	Mabel Albertson

Announcer: Bill Baldwin

Producer: Cy Howard

That's My Line

Human Interest; 60 min; CBS
8/9/80 to 8/23/80
2/3/81 to 4/11/81

The program spotlights the unusual occupations of ordinary people.

Host: Bob Barker

Assistants: Tiiu Leek, Suzanne Childs, Kerry Millerick

Announcer: Johnny Olsen

Producer: Mark Goodson, Bill Todman

That's My Mama

Comedy; 30 min; ABC 9/4/74 to 12/14/75

The story of Clifton Curtis, a 25-year-old bachelor who, while attempting to run his late father's business (Oscar's Barber Shop in Washington, D.C.) and live his own life, constantly finds his life being run by his meddling, well-meaning mother, Eloise. See also "The Furst Family of Washington."

Clifton Curtis	Clifton Davis
Eloise Curtis	Theresa Merrett
Tracy Taylor	Lynne Moody
	Joan Pringle
Leonard Taylor	Illunga Adell
Earl Chambers	Ed Bernard
	Theodore Wilson
Wildcat	Jester Hairson
Junior	Ted Lange
Josh	DeForest Covan
Laura	Helen Martin

Producer: Allan Blye, Chris Bearde

That's Our Sherman

Comedy Pilot; 15 min; NBC 5/3/48

A proposed series of comedy skits featuring the talents of comedian Hiram Sherman.

Star: Hiram Sherman

Regulars: Gloria Stroock, Meg Mundy, Marc Daniels, Billy Farrell

Producer: Ruth Wilk

That's TV

Comedy Pilot; 60 min; NBC 4/18/82

The program, set at an unidentified TV station, spoofs a day of typical programs through a series of skits and blackouts.

Regulars: Judy Landers, Maggie Roswell, Susan Elliot, Shon Vaughn, Terry Lester, Donovan Scott, Cindy Morgan, Charlie Dell, Carl Anderson

Guests: Susan Anton, Melissa Sue Anderson, Isabel Sanford, Mackenzie Phillips, Robert Conrad, Meadowlark Lemmon

Orchestra: Edward Gordon

Producer: Art Fisher, Frank Brill

T.H.E. Cat

Adventure; 30 min; NBC 9/16/66 to 9/1/67

The exploits of Thomas Hewitt Edward (T.H.E.) Cat, an aerialist-turned cat burglar-turned professional bodyguard.

T.H.E. Cat	Robert Loggia
Pepe	Robert Carricart
Maria	Norma Bengell
William McAllister	R.G. Armstrong
Lassiter	John Marley

Music: Lalo Schifrin

Producer: Boris Sagal

Theatre Macabre

Christopher Lee as host of a thirty minute syndicated (1970) series of horror yarns. Filmed in England and Poland.

Theatre '62

Anthology; 60 min; NBC 10/4/61 to 4/8/62

Jinx Falkenberg as the host of a seven episode series that commemorates the film legacy of David O. Selznick via adaptations of some of his best films: "The Farmer's Daughter," "Intermezzo," "Notorious," "The Paradine Case," "Rebecca," and "The Spiral Staircase."

Theatre Time

Anthology; 30 min; ABC 7/27/57 to 9/26/57

Anita Louise as host of a Summer series of repeat episodes from "Fireside Theatre" and "The G.E. Theatre."

Then Came Bronson

Drama; 60 min; NBC 9/17/69 to 9/9/70

The story of Jim Bronson, a young newspaperman who sets out on a cross-country quest to discover the meaning of life after his friend commits suicide.

Jim Bronson   Michael Parks

Producer: Herbert F. Solow, Robert Justman

There Goes the Neighborhood

Comedy Pilot; 30 min; NBC 6/4/83

Following the death of their wealthy friend, three hobos (Boxcar, Barney, and The Kid) inherit a vast wealth and a multimillion dollar estate in Bel Air, California. The unsold series was to relate the trios efforts to become a part of society.

Leonard "Boxcar" Mumfred	Buddy Hackett
Barney	G.W. Bailey
Kid Herbert	Patrick Collins
Philkins	William Glover
Milton Crocker	Graham Jarvis
Hortense Crocker	Sue Anne Gilfillan
Charles Hawthorne	Keene Curtis

Producer: Saul Ilson

There's Always Room

Comedy Pilot; 30 min; CBS 4/24/77

The story of Madelyn Fairchild, a middle-aged free spirit and the owner of a once-fashionable Los Angeles home that has become a haven for a variety of guests.

Madelyn Fairchild	Maureen Stapleton
Stewart Dennis	Conrad Janis
Annette Ederby	Debbie Zipp
Bob Ederby	Barry Nelson
Buck	Royce D. Applegate
McRaven	Woody Chambliss

Producer: Robert W. Christiansen, Rick Rosenberg

There's One in Every Family

Variety; 30 min; CBS 9/29/52 to 6/12/53

Members of a family who are outstandingly different appear and relate their stories to the studio audience. Applause determines the winner who can win prizes for his family by competing in a question-and-answer session.

Host: John Reed King, Dean Miller

Producer: Richard Levine, Stefan Hatos

These are the Days

Cartoon; 30 min; ABC 9/7/74 to 9/5/76

Life in America at the turn of the century as seen through the eyes of the Day family, residents of the town of Elmsville.

Martha Day	June Lockhart
Cathy Day	Pamelyn Ferdin
Danny Day	Jackie Earle Haley
Ben Day	Andrew Parks
Jeff Day	Henry Jones

Producer: William Hanna, Joseph Barbera

They Stand Accused

Drama; 60 min; DuMont 1/18/49 to 10/5/52

Dramas of actual courtroom cases with real lawyers and judges appearing as themselves. Broadcast live from Chicago, where it aired locally from April through September 1948. Produced by Richard Albrecht.

They Went Thataway

Comedy Pilot; 30 min; CBS 8/15/60

A satire on westerns as seen through the exploits of Black Ace Burton, "the meanest gunfighter in the Old West."

Black Ace Burton	James Westerfield
Sheriff Sam Claggert	Wayne Morris
Poison Pete	Ron Hagerthy

Producer: Robert J. Enders

They're Off

Game; 30 min; DuMont 6/30/49 to 8/18/49

A game show, about which very little is known, that features players attempting to answer questions based on newsreel footage of horse races.

Host: Tom Shirley

Announcer: Byron Field

Thicke of the Night

Variety; 90 min; Syn. 9/83

Celebrity interviews and offbeat comedy sketches.

Host: Alan Thicke.

Regulars: Fred Willard, Richard Belzer, Charles Fleischer, Isabel Grandin, Rick Ducommun, Mike McManus, Alvernette Jimenez, Gilbert Gottfried

Announcer: Charlie Tuna, Rick Ducommun

Orchestra: Tom Canning

Producer: Fred Silverman, Alan Thicke, Jeremy Stevens

Thicker Than Water

Comedy; 30 min; ABC 6/13/73 to 8/8/73

Fearing that he is soon to die, Jonas Paine, the aging founder of Paine's Pure Pickles, stipulates that for his two dislikeful of each other children (Nellie and Ernie) to inherit his money, they must live together for five years and operate the pickle factory. Stories relate Nellie and Ernie's misadventures as they struggle to live together, operate the family business, and care for a father who just won't kick the bucket.

Nellie Paine   Julie Harris
Ernie Paine   Richard Long
Jonas Paine   Malcolm Atterbury
Lily Paine   Jessica Myerson
Walter Paíne   Lou Fant
Bert Taylor   Pat Cranshaw
Lyle Woodstock   Jim Connell
Agnes Dorsel   Dolores Albin

Producer: Bob Banner

The Thin Man

Mystery; 30 min; NBC 9/20/57 to 6/26/59

Events in the lives of Nick Charles, a former
private detective turned mystery editor for a
publishing house, and Nora, his beautiful socialite wife, who possesses an uncanny knack
for stumbling upon and involving Nick in
crimes. Based on the characters created by
Dashiell Hammett. See also "Nick and
Nora."

Nick Charles   Peter Lawford
Nora Charles   Phyllis Kirk
Beatrice Dean (alias
  Blondie Collins)   Nita Talbot
Lt. Harry Evans   Jack Albertson
Lt.Ralph Raines   Stafford Repp
Lt. Steve King   Tol Avery
Mrs. Durkem   Blanche Sweet
Hazel   Patricia Donahue

Producer: Samuel Marx, Edmund Beloin

Things Are Looking Up

Comedy Pilot; 30 min; CBS 6/29/84

Events in the lives of a group of close-knit
students at John F. Kennedy High School in
Ventura, California.

Joanne Braithwaite   Gretchen Corbett
Mia Braithwaite   Beth Ehlers
Gisele Kraft   Tammy Lauren
Neil Troutman   Eric Stoltz
Dale Troutman   K.C. Martel
Clement McCallister   Clarence Gilyard Jr.
Joy Villafianco   Darvany Deal
Dionne McCallister   LaSaundra Hall
Ray Litertini   Mark Blum
Vice Principal
  Dougherty   Bill Cort
Mrs. Troutman   Virginia Morris
Selly Sanfillipo   Dean Cameron

Producer: Seth Freeman, Michele Gallery

The Third Man

Drama; 30 min; Syn. 1960

The exploits of Harry Lime, a London-based
business tycoon, troubleshooter, and private
detective, as he helps people in trouble.

Harry Lime   Michael Rennie
Bradford Webster   Jonathan Harris

Producer: Vernon Burns

The 13 Ghosts of Scooby-Doo

Cartoon; 30 min; ABC 9/14/85 to 2/22/86

When Scooby-Doo, the cowardly Great Dane,
opens a mysterious chest, he releases thirteen
of the most terrifying ghosts in the universe.
Stories relate Scooby's efforts to return the
ghosts to the Chest of Demons.

Vincent Van Ghoul   Vincent Price
Shaggy   Casey Kasem
Scooby-Doo   Don Messick
Scrappy-Doo   Lennie Weinrib
Daphne   Heather North

Producer: William Hanna, Joseph Barbera

13 Queens Boulevard

Comedy; 30 min; ABC 3/20/79 to 7/24/79

Events in the lives of Felicia and Steven Winters, an argumentative married couple who
reside at 13 Queens Boulevard in Queens,
N.Y. Originally titled "Queen's Court."

Felicia Winters   Eileen Brennan
Steven Winters   Jerry Van Dyke
Elaine Dowling   Marcia Rodd
Annie Dowling   Susan Elliot
Jill Capestro   Louise Williams
Millie Capestro   Helen Page Camp
Lois Sherman   Frances Lee McCain
Camile   Karen Rushmore
Laurie   Rachel Jacobs
Donny Sherman   Nicky Barton

Producer: Bud Yorkin, Bernie Orenstein,
  Saul Turteltaub

13 Thirteenth Avenue

Comedy Pilot; 30 min; CBS 8/15/83

The misadventures of the unusual residents who live like a family in an apartment house at 13 Thirteenth Avenue in New York City.

Melinda York (a witch)	Ilene Graff
Roland Keats (a vampire)	Paul Kreppel
Marv Hoberman (a werewolf)	Robert Harper
Vlastock Spoltechzep (a troll)	Ernie Sabella
Dr. Carey (their psychiatrist)	Clive Revill
Jack Gordon (a normal tenant)	A.C. Weary
Willie Gordon (his son)	Wil Wheton

Producer: Chris Thompson, Don Van Atta

Thirty Something

Comedy-Drama; 60 min; ABC 9/29/87 (Premiere)

A slice of Yuppie life as seen through the rather mundane experiences of Hope and Michael Steadman, young marrieds struggling to cope with life.

Hope Murdoch-Steadman	Mary Ellen "Mel" Harris
Michael Steadman	Ken Olin
Elliot	Timothy Busfield
Nancy	Patricia Wettig
Gary Shepherd	Peter Horton
Melissa	Melanie Mayron
Ellyn	Polly Draper
Jane Steadman	Jade & Lauren Mortimer
Ruth Murdoch	Shirley Knight
Ted Murdoch	George Coe

Producer: Marshal Herkovitz, Edward Zwick, Paul Haggis

This Better Be It

Comedy Pilot; 30 min; CBS 8/10/76

The story of Annie and Harry, two previously married, now divorced people who decide to marry and make a new life for themselves.

Annie Bell	Anne Meara
Harry Bell	Alex Rocco
Diana Bell (Harry's daughter)	Ballie Gersten
Flower (Annie's daughter)	Linda Conrad
Paul (Diana's fiance)	David Pollock

Producer: Charles Fries

This Is Alice

Comedy; 30 min; Syn. 1958

The series, set in River Glen, Georgia, relates the adventures of Alice Holliday, a pretty nine-year-old girl growing up in a small American town.

Alice Holliday	Patty Ann Gerrity
Clarissa Mae Holliday	Phyllis Coates
Chet Holliday	Tommy Farrell
Colonel Dixon	Lucien Littlefield
Soapie Weaver	Stephen Woolton

Producer: Sidney Salkow

This Is Charles Laughton

A syndicated (1952) program of readings from the Bible and classical and modern stories with Charles Laughton. Produced by Ernest Walling.

This Is Galen Drake

Variety; 30 min; ABC 1/12/57 to 5/11/57

Galen Drake as host of a program of music and songs for children. With Rita Ellis and Stuart Foster. Produced by Don Appel.

This Is Music

Variety; 30 min; DuMont 11/29/51 to 10/9/52

A regular cast perform the hits of recording artists through lip-synching.

Hostess: Alexandra Gray

Regulars: Nancy Carr, Lucille Reed, Jackie Van, Bruce Foote, Jacqueline James

This Is Music

Variety; 30 min; ABC 6/13/58 to 5/21/59

A revised version of the previous title which features a regular cast pantomiming the recordings of famous artists.

Host: Colin Male

Regulars: Wanda Lewis, Bud Chase, Bob Smith, Gail Johnson, Ramona Bennett, Paula Jane, Lee Fogel, Bob Shereve

This Is Show Business

Variety; 30 min; CBS 7/15/49 to 3/9/54
                      NBC 6/26/56 to 9/11/56

Celebrity guests first entertain, then discuss their problems with a celebrity panel (who in turn offer advice and possible solutions). Also known as "This Is Broadway."

Host: Clifton Fadiman

Panelists: Sam Levenson, Abe Burrows, Jacqueline Susann, Walter Slezak, George S. Kaufman

Announcer: Bern Bennett

Orchestra: Ray Bloch, Henry Sylvern

Producer: Irving Mansfield

This Is Tom Jones

Variety; 60 min; ABC 2/7/69 to 1/7/71

A weekly program of music, songs, and comedy.

Host: Tom Jones

Regulars: Big Jim Sullivan, The Mike Sammes Singers, The Norman Maen Dancers

Orchestra: Jack Parnell, Johnnie Spence

Producer: Jon Scoffield

This Week in Nemtin

Comedy Pilot; 30 min; CBS 4/14/72

A satirical survey of the events that occur in the fictional country of Nemtin.

Newscaster   Alex Drier
Wiseman   Carl Reiner

Producer: Saul Turteltab, Saul Ilson

This Is Your LIfe

Tribute; 30 min; NBC 10/1/52 to 9/3/61

The lives of well-known personalities are relived through the testimonies of friends and family.

Host: Ralph Edwards

Announcer: Bob Warren

Producer: Axel Greenberg, Al Pascholl, Richard Gottlieb, Bill Carruthers, Jim Washburn

This Is Your Life

Tribute; 30 min; Syn. 9/83

A semi-documentary presentation in which the lives of famous people, who appear as guests, are relived through the testimony of friends and family.

Host: Joseph Campanella

Producer: Ralph Edwards, Bob Parkinson, Andy Friendly

This Is Your Music

Variety; 30 min; Syn. 10/55

A weekly program of music and songs.

Host: Byron Palmer

Regulars: Erin Martin, Joan Weldon, Roy Fitzell, Jane Ekelund, Mary Margaret Gelden

Orchestra: Nelson Riddle

Producer: Jack Denove

This Man Dawson

Crime Drama; 30 min; Syn. 1959

The battle against crime as seen through the investigations of Colonel Frank Dawson, police chief of a large, unidentified community.

Frank Dawson   Keith Andes

Producer: William Conrad, Elliott Lewis

This Morning

Interview; 90 min; ABC 4/1/68 to 1/24/69

A mid-morning program of celebrity interviews.

Host: Dick Cavett

Announcer: Fred Foy

Orchestra: Bobby Rosengarden

Producer: Woody Fraser

This Old House

Restoration; 30 min; PBS Syn. 1978

The program features several major house renovations a year, each week depicting particular aspects of the work, problems, and cost of material involved.

Host: Bob Vila

Master Carpenter: Norm Abram

Producer: Russell Morash

This was America

Documentary; 30 min; Syn. 4/81

A sensitive, candid look at life in America at the turn of the century.

Host-Narrator: William Shatner

Producer: Claude Pelanne, Peter Fiedler

Thompson's Ghost

Comedy Pilot; 30 min; ABC 8/5/66

While experimenting with some formulas she finds in a book on Black Magic, ten-year-old Annabell Thompson accidentally conjures up the spirit of Henry Thompson, an ancestor who lived over 470 years ago. The unsold series was to have focused on Henry's adventures in the 1960s.

Henry Thompson	Bert Lahr
Annabell Thompson	Pamela Dapo
Milly Thompson	Phyllis Coates
Sam Thompson	Robert Rockwell
Eddie Thompson	Tim Matthieson
	(Tim Matheson)
Dr. Wheeler	Willard Waterman
Nurse	Trudy Howard
Chief Watson	Barry Kelly

The Thornton Show

Advice Pilot; 25 min; CBS 8/22/46

A proposed series of beauty tips and advice with demonstrations by models for the Thornton Agency.

Hostess: Judy Thornton

Producer: Ralph Warren

Those Amazing Animals

Human Interest; 60 min; ABC 8/24/80 to 8/16/81

A fascinating look at animals and the amazing things they do.

Hosts: Burgess Meredith, Priscilla Presley, Jim Stafford

Regulars: Jacques Costeau, Joan Embrey

Producer: Mel Stuart, Alan Landsburg, Woody Fraser, Merrill Grant

Those Endearing Young Charms

Comedy; 15 min; NBC 12/30/51 to 6/26/52

Events in the lives of the Charms, a not-so-typical American family who support themselves by running a mail order business that caters to collectors of household gadgets.

Ralph Charm	Maurice Copeland
Abby Charm	Fern Parsons
	Betty Arnold
Connie Charm	Pat Matthews
	Charon Follett
Clem Charm	Gerald Garvey
Uncle Duff Charm	Clarence Hartzell

Producer: Ben Park

Those Two

Variety; 15 min; NBC 11/26/51 to 4/24/53

A program of music and song built around the antics of an accompianist (Pinky) who is in love with a nightclub singer (Vivian) who has no interest in him.

Pinky	Pinky Lee
Vivian	Vivian Blaine
Martha (replaced Vivian)	Martha Stuart

Orchestra: Harry Lubin

Producer: Olive Barbour, Walter Craig

Those Whiting Girls

Comedy; 30 min; CBS 7/4/55 to 9/26/55

The adventures of the Whiting sisters: Margaret, a singer, and Barbara, a student at U.C.L.A. and a hopeful actress.

Margaret Whiting	Herself
Barbara Whiting	Herself
Eleanor Whiting (mother)	Mabel Albertson
Artie Grayson	Jerry Paris
Daisy Dunbar	Beverly Long
Penny	Kathleen Nolan

Producer: Samuel Marx

Three About Town

Variety; 15 min; ABC 8/11/48 to 10/27/48

Music and songs with Betsi Allison and her twin pianos (the three of the title).

Three Coins in the Fountain

Comedy Pilot; 30 min; NBC 8/10/70

The romantic misadventures of Maggie Wilson, an American girl living in Rome and working as a secretary. Based on the movie.

Maggie Wilson	Cynthia Pepper
Dorothy	Yvonne Craig
Ruth	Joanna Moore
Gino	Antony Alda
Count Giorgio	Nino Castelnuovo

Theme Vocal ("Three Coins in the Fountain"): Trini Lopez

Producer: Hal Kanter, Robert L. Jacks

Three Eyes

Crime Drama Pilot; 60 min; NBC 6/27/82

The exploits of Tony, Buzz, and Cowboy, three private investigators who own The Three Eyes, a night club and detective organization, and who will to any lengths to solve a case.

Tony Rossi	Ed Marinaro
Buzz	Michael Horton
Cowboy	Robin Strand
Francis	Allan Miller
Ace	Peter Barton
Barbara Harmon	Kim Lankford
James Bemmelman	Peter Brown
Vincent	Larry Manetti

Producer: Robert Singer, Daniel H. Blatt

The Three Flames Show

Variety; 30 min; NBC 6/13/49 to 8/20/49

A live series of music and songs with the Three Flames (Tiger Haynes, Roy Testamark, Bill Pollard), a popular black trio of the 1940s.

Three for Danger

Adventure Pilot; 30 min; NBC 9/8/67

The exploits of three soldiers of fortune (Chris, Alan, Simon) who hire out their expertise for a price.

Chris	Larry Pennell
Alan	Alejandro Rey
Simon	Charles Carlson
Serena	Joanna Pettet
Kirk	Jason Evers

Producer: Warren Duff

Three for Tahiti

Comedy Pilot; 30 min; ABC 8/19/70

Three men (Kelly, Muk, and Jay) plagued by life's endless problems, decide to get away from it all and purchase, sight unseen, a hotel in Tahiti. The unsold series was to relate their efforts to run a hotel fraught with problems.

Kelly	Robert Hogan
Muk	Bob Einstein
Jay	Steve Franken
Cecil Barrett	Alan Oppenheimer
Chief Longet	Marcel Hillaire

Producer: Bill Persky, Ken Kragen, E.W. Swackhamer

Three for the Money

Game; 30 min; NBC 9/29/75 to 11/28/75

Three categories, each containing three questions, are revealed. A question, chosen by one team (two three-member teams compete) is read and clues appear on an electronic board. The first player to sound a buzzer stops the clues and receives a chance to answer. A correct answer awards money; an incorrect response allows the opposing team a free chance to win the money. The team with the highest score wins.

Host: Dick Enberg

Model: Jane Nelson

Announcer: Jack Clark

Producer: Stefan Hatos

Three for the Road

Drama; 60 min; CBS 9/14/75 to 11/30/75

The experiences of photographer Pete Karris and his sons John and Endy, as they travel across the country seeking story material.

Pete Karris	Alex Rocco
John Karris	Vincent Van Patten
Endy Karris	Leif Garrett

Producer: Jerry NcNeely, John G. Stephens

Three Girls Three

Variety; 60 min; NBC 3/30/77 (1 episode)
6/15/77 to 6/29/77

A musical comedy that spotlights the talents of three unknown "but terribly talented girls doing a variety series about three unknown but terribly talented girls."

Hosts: Debbie Allen, Mimi Kennedy, Ellen Foley

Regulars: Warren Burton, Oliver Clark, Richard Byrd

Orchestra: Marvin Laird

Producer: Gary Smith, Dwight Hemion

The Three Musketeers

Adventure; 30 min; Syn. 1956

The exploits of the Three Musketeers (D'Artagnan, Porthos, and Aramis) as they struggle to protect the throne of France (1620s) from the evil Richlieu.

D'Artagnan	Jeffrey Stone
Porthos	Peter Trent
Aramis	Paul Campbell
Jacqueline	Martina Berti
Capt. DeTreville	George Conneaur
Sasquinet	Alan Furlan

Producer: George Fass

Three on an Island

Comedy Pilot; 30 min; CBS 8/27/65

When a sculptress (Taffy) accepts half the contract of a prize fighter (Bulldog) as payment for a job, she and her two roommates (Kris and Andrea) suddenly become involved in the world of boxing. The unsold series was to relate their attempts to launch their glass-jawed boxer on a winning career.

Taffy Warren	Pamela Tiffin
Kris Meeker	Julie Newmar
Andrea Franks	Monica Moran
Julius "Bulldog" Sweetley	Jody McCrea
Martha Sweetley	Sheila Bromley
Perry	Rhodes Reason
Riley	Ned Glass
Glen	Ron Husmann

Producer-Writer: Hal Kanter

Three on a Match

Game; 30 min; NBC 8/2/71 to 6/28/74

Three category topics are revealed. Each of the three players who compete secretly choose a category and the number of questions (1 to 4) they wish to answer. Players answer questions accordingly and score money for each correct response. When a player scores at least $150 he plays "Three on a Match." A twelve-square board is revealed that contains three vertical rows of money amounts and four horizontal rows of colors. A prize is revealed. The player must match that prize with two identical prizes to win.

Host: Bill Cullen

Announcer: Roger Tuttle, Don Pardo

The Three Robonic Stooges

Cartoon; 25 min; CBS 1/28/78 to 9/2/78

The antics of a space age Moe, Larry, and Curly (robots constructed from the finest parts available) as they battle evil. Adapted from the 1940s theatrical series, "The Three Stooges."

Moe	Paul Winchell
Larry	Joe Baker
Curly	Frank Welker
Triple O	Ross Martin

Producer: William Hanna, Joseph Barbera

330 Independence S.W.

Drama Pilot; 60 min; NBC 3/20/62

The story of Jim Corcoran, an investigator for the Department of Health, Education and Welfare. Aired on "The Dick Powell Show." During the spring of 1963, a series was set by Four Star and was to be titled "The Robert Taylor Show." While shooting the fifth episode, HEW withdrew its approval and the series was canceled. The four never-telecast episodes were produced by Bruce Geller and Bernard L. Kowalski.

Jim Corcoran	David McLean
Robin	Julie Adams
Guts Finney	William Bendix
Guy Vista	Alan Reed
Jeff	Yale Summers
Mac	Ed Kemmer
Connie	Adrienne Ellis
Joe Vista	Bert Freed

Producer: Dick Powell, E.J Rosenberg

333 Montgomery

Crime Drama Pilot; 60 min; NBC 6/13/60

The pilot for "Sam Benedict," which relates the exploits of Jake Brittin, a criminal attorney who resides at 333 Montgomery in San Francisco. Aired on "Alcoa Hour."

Jake Brittin	DeForest Kelley
Jake's secretary	Joanne Davis
Police captain	Tom Greenway
Eva Fremont	Joanna Barnes
Liz	Midge Ware
Frank Piper	Steve Peck

Producer: Robert Sparks, Gene Roddenberry

Three Times Daley

Comedy Pilot; 30 min; CBS 8/3/76

The comic adventures of Bob Daley, a divorced newspaper columnist, his son, Wes, and his father, Alex—three generations of one family trying to live together under one roof.

Bob Daley	Don Adams
Wes Daley	Jerry Houser
Alex Daley	Liam Dunn
Stacy	Bibi Besch
Janny	Ayn Ruyman

Producer: Leonard B. Stern

Three Wishes

Comedy Pilot; 30 min; CBS 7/29/63

While in the basement of her uncle's antique shop, Annie Brenner accidentally locks herself in. Seeking a way out, she stumbles upon a dusty old lamp, which when rubbed, produces a puff of smoke that materializes into a genie. Having released the genie from 1,000 years of imprisonment, she becomes his master. The unsold series was to relate Annie's adventures as the master of a genie who can grant her any wish.

Annie Brenner	Diane Jergens
Genie	Gustavo Rojo
Uncle Jonas	Wallace Ford
Henry	George Grizzard
Miles Bunker	Gage Clark
John Bunker	Dan Tobin

Producer: Robert Welch

The Three Wives of David Wheeler

Comedy Pilot; 30 min; NBC 8/1/79

The story of David Wheeler, owner of Wheeler Graphic Arts, and a man with three wives: Ginger, his first ex-wife and still his business partner; Bibi, his second ex-wife, a model he still employs; and Julia, his current wife, a girl who understands—usually.

David Wheeler	Art Hindle
Ginger Wheeler	Cathy Lee Crosby
Bibi Wheeler	Sherilynn Katzman
Julia Wheeler	Nancy Grigor
Vinnie	Archie Hahn
Debbie	Susan Tolsky

Producer: Norman S. Powell

Three's a Crowd

Game; 30 min; Syn. 9/79

Three husbands are asked three questions relating to either his wife or his secretary. The secretaries join their employers and are asked the same questions. Each time a secretary matches her boss, she scores one point. The wives are then brought out and asked the same questions; but in order to score points, the wife must match both her husband's and his secretary's answers. The team (secretary or wife) that scores highest, splits $1,000.

Host: Jim Peck

Announcer: Johnny Jacobs

Producer: Chuck Barris

Three's a Crowd

Comedy; 30 min; ABC 9/18/84 to 9/17/85

A spin-off from "Three's Company," but based on the British series "Robin's Nest" (which see). After eight years, the curtain comes down on "Three's Company": Jack falls in love with Vicky Bradford, a pretty stewardess; Janet announces her plans to marry Philip Dawson (an art dealer played by David Ruprecht), and Terri is transferred to Hawaii. As Janet and Terri depart, Jack and Vicky move into an apartment above Jack's restaurant, Jack's Bistro. Stories relate their courtship (and eventual marriage) and their efforts to run the bistro.

Jack Tripper	John Ritter
Vicky Bradford	Mary Cadorette
James Bradford	Robert Mandan
Claudia Bradford	Jessica Walter
E.Z. Taylor	Alan Campbell
Jack's Aunt Mae	Billie Bird

Producer: Michael Ross, Bernie West, Paul Nicholl

Three's Company

Variety; 15 min; CBS 5/18/50 to 9/29/50

A twice-weekly program of music, songs, and comedy with host Cy Walter, regulars Stan Freeman, Judy Lynn, and Martha Wright, and the music of the Cy Coleman Trio.

Three's Company

Comedy; 30 min; ABC 3/15/77 to 4/21/77
8/11/77 to 9/18/84

When the high cost of living prevents them from living comfortably, Janet Wood and Chrissy Snow resolve their problem by taking in a male roommate—Jack Tripper, a culinary student they find sleeping in their bathtub after a wild party. Stories relate their misadventures as they struggle to live their own lives while attempting to maintain a strictly platonic relationship. See also "Three's a Crowd" (comedy version). Based on the British series, "Man About the House" (which see).

Jack Tripper	John Ritter
Janet Wood	Joyce DeWitt
Christmas "Chrissy" Snow	Suzanne Somers
Cindy Snow	Jenilee Harrison
Terri Alden	Priscilla Barnes
Larry Dallas	Richard Kline
Stanley Roper	Norman Fell
Helen Roper	Audra Lindley
Ralph Furley	Don Knotts
Lana Shields	Ann Wedgeworth
Regal Beagle Bartender	Paul Ainsley
Rev. Luther Snow	Peter Mark Richman
Dean Travers	William Pierson
Frank Angelino	Jordan Charney
Bart Furley	Hamilton Camp
Felipe Gomez	Gino Conforti
Larry's Sister Diane	Lucinda Dooling
Cindy's Aunt Rebecca	Sue Ane Langdon
Janet's Sister Jenny	Devon Ericson
Terri's Sister Samantha	Jennifer Walker
Ralph's Niece Veronica	Robin G. Eisenman
Stanley's Niece Karen	Cristina Hart
Jack's Mother	Georgann Johnson
Terri's Mother	Mina Kolb
Janet's Mother (Ruth)	Paula Shaw
Janet's Father (Roland)	Macon McCalman
Greedy Gretchen (Jack's dream date)	Teresa Ganzel

Theme Vocal ("Three's Company"): Julia Rinker, Ray Charles

Producer: Don Nicholl, Michael Ross, Bernie West, Budd Grossman

Thriller

Anthology; 60 min; NBC 9/13/60 to 7/9/62

Mystery and suspense stories of people trapped in unexpected situations that are fostered through greed, emotion, or the threat of crime.

Host: Boris Karloff

Producer: Hubbell Robinson, Fletcher Markle, William Frye, Maxwell Shane

Throb

Comedy; 30 min; Syn. 9/86

Following her divorce, Sandy Beatty moves from Buffalo, N.Y. to Manhattan, where she acquires a job as the administrative assistant to Zachary Armstrong, the president of Throb Records. Stories relate Sandy's misadventures as she struggles to support herself and her young son (Jeremy).

Sandy Beatty	Diana Canova
Jeremy Beatty	Paul W. Cooper
Zachary Armstrong	Jonathan Prince
Meredith	Maryedith Burrell
Blue	Jane Leeves
Phil	Richard Cummings Jr.

Theme Vocal ("Throb"): Diana Canova and the Nylons

Producer: Sy Rosen, Fredi Towbin

Through the Crystal Ball

Children; 30 min; CBS 4/18/49 to 7/4/49

A series of live dramas based on popular children's fables.

Hosts: Anita Alvarez, Jimmy Salvo

Producer: Paul Belanger

Through Wendy's Window

Interview; 15 min; NBC 12/22/49 to 2/16/50

A program of celebrity interviews with hostess Wendy Barrie. Produced by Martin Goodman.

Thru the Crystal Ball

Variety Pilot; 60 min; CBS 6/20/49

An hour of music and songs with hostess Ethel Merman and her guest star, Gil Lamb. Produced by Barry Wood.

Thundarr the Barbarian

Cartoon; 25 min; ABC 10/4/80 to 9/12/82

In the year 1994, a runaway planet crosses between the Earth and the moon and destroys both worlds. Two thousand years later, the Earth is reborn, but a strange new world emerges from the old: a world of savagery, super science, sorcery, and evil beings. Stories relate the adventures of Thundarr, a slave who broke his bonds and now battles the evils that exist on Earth.

Thundarr	Robert Ridgely
Princess Ariel	Nellie Bellflower
Oukla	Henry Corden

Producer: Joe Ruby, Ken Spears

Thunder

Adventure; 30 min; NBC 9/10/77 to 9/2/78

The story of Thunder, a semi-wild black stallion, and the adventures of the young girl, Cindy, who befriends him.

Cindy Prescott	Melora Hardin
Bill Prescott	Clint Ritchie
Ann Prescott	Melissa Converse
Willie Williams	Justin Randi
Sam Williams	Ray Girardin

Producer: Irving Cummings, Charles Mason

Thunderbirds

Marionette Adventure; 30 min; Syn. 1968

The exploits of the men and women of International Rescue, a global organization that uses highly skilled equipment (the Thunderbirds) to rescue people trapped in unusual predicaments.

Jeff Tracy	Peter Dyneley
Scott Tracy	Shane Rimmer
Virgil Tracy	David Holliday
Alan Tracy	Matt Zimmerman
Gordon Tracy/Prof.	
Brains/Kyrano	David Graham
John Tracy/The	
Hood	Ray Barrett
Lady Penelope	
Creighton-Ward	Sylvia Anderson
Tin Tin Kyrano	Christine Finn

Producer: Gerry Anderson, Reg Hill

Thunderbirds: 2086

Cartoon; 30 min; Syn. 9/85

A revised version of the previous title, which continues to depict the work of International Rescue, an organization of sophisticated machines and equipment that is used to rescue people trapped in unusual situations.

Voices: Joan Audiberti, Paollo Audiberti, Earl Hammond, Ira Lewis, Keith Mandell, Alexander Marshall, Terry Vantell

Producer: Banjiro Uemura, Shinji Nakagawa

Thundercats

Cartoon; 30 min; Syn. 2/85

The exploits of the Thundercats, survivors of a doomed world, who use their amazing powers to battle evil throughout the universe.

Voices: Robert McFadden, Earl Hammond, Larry Kenny, Lynne Lipton, Peter Newman

Producer: Arthur Rankin Jr, Jules Bass

Tic Tac Dough

Game; 30 min; NBC 7/30/56 to 10/30/59

Object: For two contestants (Player X and Player O) to answer questions and acquire the three squares necessary to win tic tac toe.

Host: Jack Barry, Gene Rayburn, Bill Wendell, Jay Jackson

Producer: Stan Greene, Robert Noah, Howard Felsher, Hudson Fausett

Tic Tac Dough

Game; 30 min; CBS 7/3/78 to 9/1/78
Syn. 9/78

A revised version of the previous title, which see for format.

Host: Wink Martindale, Jim Caldwell

Announcer: Jay Stewart, Charlie O'Donnell

Producer: Ron Greenberg, Jack Barry, Dan Enright

Tiger! Tiger!

Comedy Pilot; 60 min; NBC 8/18/69

The story of Don MacMasters, an animal behaviorist in the town of Kingsview.

Don MacMasters	Peter Jason
Louise MacMasters	Marilyn Devin
Dr. Fred Bentley	J. Pat O'Malley
Doug Rowe	Otis Day
Sheriff Wade	Phil Dean

Producer: Ivan Tors, Andy White

Writer: Earl Hamner

Tightrope

Crime Drama; 30 min; CBS 9/8/59 to 9/13/60

The exploits of Nick Stone, an undercover police agent, as he attempts to infiltrate and expose the ranks of organized crime.

Nick Stone*   Mike Connors

*In some sources he is referred to as "The Unnamed Agent" or "The Undercover Agent."

The Tim Conway Comedy Hour

Variety; 60 min; CBS 9/20/70 to 12/28/70

A weekly program of music, songs, and comedy.

Host: Tim Conway

Regulars: Sally Struthers, McLean Stevenson, Art Metrano, Bonnie Boland, The Tom Hanson Dancers

Orchestra: Nelson Riddle

Producer: Bill Hobin, Ron Clark, Sam Bobrick

The Tim Conway Show

Comedy; 30 min; CBS 1/30/70 to 6/19/70

The misadventures of an inept pilot (Spud) and his equally inept executive officer (Herbert) as they struggle to make a success of the Lucky Linda, a decrepit plane that comprises Triple A Airlines.

Timothy "Spud" Barrett	Tim Conway
Herbert Kenworth	Joe Flynn
Mrs. Crawford	Anne Seymour
Ronnie Crawford	Johnnie Collins III
Becky	Emily Banks
Sherman	Dennis Robertson
Harry	Fabian Dean

Producer: Burt Nodella

The Tim Conway Show

Variety; CBS 3/22/80 to 5/17/80 (60 min)
              8/30/80 to 3/7/81 (30 min)

A weekly program of music and comedy.

Host: Tim Conway

Regulars: Harvey Korman, Maggie Roswell, Kelly Garrett, Jack Riley, Dick Orkin, Miriam Flynn, Eric Boardman, The Don Crichton Dancers

Orchestra: Peter Matz

Producer: Joe Hamilton, Bill Richmond, Gene Perret

Time for Beany

Puppet Adventure; 15 min; Syn. 1950

The misadventures of a small boy named Beany, his pet sea serpent, Cecil, and Horatio K. Huffenpuff, captain of a boat called "The Leakin' Lena." See also "The Beany and Cecil Show."

Voices: Stan Freberg, Daws Butler, Jerry Colonna, Scatman Crothers

Producer: Stan Freberg, Bob Clampett

The Time Element

Drama Pilot; 60 min; CBS 11/24/58

The pilot for "The Twilight Zone." The story of a man, sent back in time to December 5, 1941, and his frantic efforts to warn military officials of the approaching bombing of Pearl Harbor. Aired on "Desilu Playhouse."

Peter Jenson	William Bendix
Dr. Gillespie	Martin Balsam
Maid	Jesslyn Fax
Bartender	Jesse White

Producer: Bert Grante

Writer: Rod Serling

Time Express

Anthology; 60 min; CBS 4/26/79 to 5/17/79

Stories about people who board the Time Express, a special train that takes them back in time in order to alter important moments in their pasts.

Jason Winters (Time Express host)	Vincent Price
Margaret Winters (his wife)	Coral Browne
Richard Walker (porter)	James Reynolds
E. Patrick Callahan (engineer)	William Edward Phipps
Ticket Agent	Woodrow Parfrey

Producer: Ivan Goff, Ben Roberts

Time Machine

Game; 30 min; NBC 1/7/85 to 4/26/85

Three players compete in various games based on events of the past. The highest scoring player competes in the time capsule segment wherein he must answer difficult questions associated with a particular year. Cash is awarded depending on the number of correct answers given.

Host: John Davidson

Announcer: Charlie O'Donnell

Producer: Robert Noah, Caryn Lucas

The Time Tunnel

Adventure; 60 min; ABC 9/9/66 to 9/1/67

When scientist Tony Newman discovers that the government is considering scraping the Time Tunnel, a $7.5 billion project concerned with time displacement, because they have not yet sent a man back in time, he decides to take matters into his own hands. Tony enters the tunnel's chamber and vanishes. Because he had previously taken a radioactive bath, engineers are able to pinpoint his whereabouts and receive his voice and image. However, their ability to control his destiny or return him to the present has not been mastered. When it is learned that Tony has become an unregistered passenger on the Titanic, scientist Doug Phillips enters the tunnel in an attempt to save him. When Doug finds Tony, the two are removed from danger and sent into time. Stories relate the experiences of two travelers lost in time.

Tony Newman	James Darren
Doug Phillips	Robert Colbert
Gen. Heywood Kirk	Whit Bissell
Dr. Ann McGregor	Lee Meriwether
Dr. Raymond Swain	John Zaremba
Sgt. Jiggs	Wesley Lau
Jerry	Sam Groom

Producer: Irwin Allen

Time Will Tell

Comedy; 30 min; DuMont 9/3/54 to 10/15/54

A comical game wherein players compete in a series of question-and-answer rounds that are interspersed with the clowning of Ernie Kovacs.

Host: Ernie Kovacs

Announcer: Bob Russell

Orchestra: Eddie Hatrak

Times Square Playhouse

A syndicated (1963) series of repeat dramas from other anthology programs with Herbert Marshall as host.

The Timid Soul

Comedy Pilot; 30 min; NBC 1/29/49

The story of Casper Milquetoast, a timid man who is constantly plagued by life's misfortune.

Casper Milquetoast	Ernest Truex
His wife	Sylvia Field

Producer: James L. Caddigan, Lawrence Menkin

Timmy and Lassie

Drama; 30 min; CBS 9/8/57 to 8/30/64

A continuation of the "Jeff's Collie" Lassie series. Shortly after the death of Gramps, Ellen, who is unable to run the farm, sells it to Paul and Ruth Martin, a childless couple who later adopt Timmy, the orphan she had been caring for. Jeff, who is unable to take Lassie to the city with him, leaves her with her new master, Timmy. Stories relate the adventures shared by a boy and his dog. "Timmy and Lassie" is the syndicated title for the 1957–64 episodes of "Lassie."

Timmy Martin	Jon Provost
Ruth Martin	Cloris Leachman
	June Lockhart
Paul Martin	Jon Shepodd
	Hugh Riley
Petrie Martin	George Chandler
Boomer Bates	Todd Farrell
Dr. Frank Weaver	Arthur Space
Sheriff Harry Miller	Robert Foulk
Cully Wilson	Andy Clyde
Scott	Ricky Allen

Producer: Jack Wrather, Robert Golden, Bonita Granville, William Beaudine Jr., Rudy E. Abel

Tin Pan Alley TV

Variety; 30 min; ABC 4/28/50 to 9/29/50

The program spotlights the work of guest composers.

Host: Johnny Desmond

Regulars: Gloria Van, Chet Roble, The Visionaires

Orchestra: Rex Maupin

Producer: Frank Killan, Tim Morrow

Tin Tin

Cartoon; 5½ min; Syn. 1/71

The adventures of Tin Tin, a 12-year-old boy, and his dog, Snowy. Based on the comic strip by Herge (Georges Remi). Produced in France and dubbed in English.

T.J. Hooker

Crime Drama; 60 min; ABC 3/13/82 to 5/4/85
CBS 9/25/85 (Premiere)

The exploits of T.J. Hooker, a veteran police officer, hardened by divorce and the shooting death of his partner, as he fights for justice.

Sgt. T.J. Hooker	William Shatner
Off. Vince Romano	Adrian Zmed
Off. Stacey Sheridan	Heather Locklear
Off. Victoria Taylor	April Clough
Off. Jim Corrigan	James Darren
Capt. Dennis Sheridan	Richard Herd
Fran Hooker (T.J.'s ex-wife)	Lee Bryant
	Leigh Christian
Chrissy Hooker (T.J.'s daughter)	Nicole Eggert
	Jennifer Beck
Cathy Hooker (T.J.'s daughter)	Susan McClung
Tommy Hooker (T.J.'s son)	Andre Gower
Lt. O'Brien	Hugh Farrington
Off. Lisa Christopher	Debra Blee
Sherry (bartender)	Pamela Brull
Claudia (T.J.'s friend)	Shawn Weatherly
John Hooker (T.J.'s father)	John McLiam

Producer: Aaron Spelling, Leonard Goldberg, Rick Husky

T.L.C.

Comedy Pilot; 30 min; NBC 8/8/84

The misadventures of Danny Martin and Pete Hamlin, roommates and the only male students at the prior all-female Philadelphia Nursing Academy.

Jessica Craigmont	Jessica Walter
Danny Martin	Jonathan Schmock
Pete Hamlin	James Vallely
Liz Hunter	Cathy Silvers
Debbie Fisher	Stacy Nelkin
Claudia	Rosalind Ingledew
Judy	Mary Garripoli
Beth	Jere Fields
Rhonda	Judy Walton
Kitty	Wendy Levin

Theme Song: "Here We Go" by Bruce Taylor, Kathy & Steve Coon

TMT

Magazine; 30 min; Syn. 6/83

The program, which refers to "Tomorrow's Music Today," spotlights rock stars and their music.

Hostess: Toni Tennille

Host: Bob Travis

Producer: Tim Iacofano, Elizabeth Eden, Dan Keefe

To Rome with Love

Comedy; 30 min; CBS 9/28/69 to 9/1/71

The trials and tribulations of Michael Endicott, an Iowa school professor hired to teach at the American School in Rome, Italy, as he and his family struggle to adjust to a new homeland.

Michael Endicott	John Forsythe
Alison Endicott	Joyce Menges
Penny Endicott	Susan Neher
Jane "Pokey" Endicott	Melanie Fullerton
Andy Pruitt	Walter Brennan
Harriet Endicott	Kay Medford
Gino Mancini	Vito Scotti
Mama Vitale	Peggy Mondo
Nico	Gerald Michenaud
Margot	Brioni Farrell
Tina	Brenda Benet

Producer: Don Fedderson, Edmund Hartmann

To Say the Least

Game; 30 min; NBC 10/3/77 to 4/21/78

Two three-member teams compete. Two players on each team are isolated backstage. A phrase is shown to the two on-stage players (e.g. "She followed Mary to school one day"). On an alternating basis, the players eliminate words from it. At any time the contestant at play can take out a word or challenge. When a challenge is made, the backstage players are brought out and the challenged player's teammates must identify the meaning of the phrase from the remaining words ("lamb" in the example). If they identify it, they score one point; if not, the opponents score the point. The highest scoring team wins.

Host: Tom Kennedy

Announcer: Kenny Williams

Producer: Merrill Heatter, Bob Quigley, Robert Noah

To Sir, with Love

Comedy Pilot; 30 min; CBS 4/19/74

The story of Paul Cameron, an idealistic American exchange teacher at a London high school. Adapted from the feature film.

Paul Cameron	Hari Rhodes
Headmaster	
Hawthorne	James Grout
Philippa	Rosemary Leach
Walter	Roddy Maude-Roxby
Cheryl	Jane Anthony
Ruby	Jane Carr
Trevor	Marc Harris
Terry	Leonard Brockwell
Charles	Brinsley Forde

Producer: David Gerber

To Tell the Truth

Game; 30 min; CBS 12/18/56 to 5/22/67 (evening run)
12/18/62 to 9/6/68 (daytime run)

Through a series of question-and-answer rounds, a celebrity panel of four must determine which of three guests, each claiming to be the same person, is telling the truth.

Host: Bud Collyer

Panelists: Sally Ann Howes, Polly Bergen, Dick Van Dyke, Phyllis Newman, Peggy Cass, Tom Poston, Orson Bean, Kitty Carlisle, Milt Kamen, Joan Fontaine, Sam Levenson, Dr. Joyce Brothers, Hildy Parks, John Cameron Swayze

Announcer: Johnny Olsen

Producer: Mark Goodson, Bill Todman

To Tell the Truth

Game; 30 min; Syn. 9/69

A revised version of the prior title, which see for format.

Host: Garry Moore, Joe Garagiola

Panelists: Bill Cullen, Orson Bean, Kitty Carlisle, Peggy Cass

Announcer: Johnny Olsen, Bill Wendell, Alan Calter

Producer: Mark Goodson, Bill Todman

To Tell the Truth

Game; 30 min; Syn. 9/80

An updated version of the first title, which see for format.

Host: Robin Ward

Panelists: Soupy Sales, Peggy Cass

Announcer: Alan Calter

Producer: Gil Fates, Mimi O'Brien

To the Manor Born

Comedy; 30 min; Syn. 1/82

The story of Audrey Forbes-Hamilton, a widow left bankrupt after the death of her husband, as she struggles to once again gain control of Grantleigh Manor, the 400-year-old family estate she was forced to sell to pay off debts. Produced in England.

Audrey Forbes-Hamilton	Penelope Keith
Richard DeVere	Peter Bowles
Marjorie Frobisher	Angela Thorne
Brabinger	John Rudling

Producer: Gareth Gwenlan

To the Queen's Taste

See "Dionne Lucas' Cooking School."

Toast of the Town

See "The Ed Sullivan Show."

Today's FBI

Crime Drama; 60 min; ABC 10/25/81 to 8/14/82

The exploits of Ben Slater, a dedicated government agent who heads an elite team of federal investigators. Based on actual files.

Ben Slater	Mike Connors
Maggie Clinton	Carol Potter
Al Gordean	Richard Hill
Nick Frazier	Joseph Cali
Dwayne Thompson	Charles Brown
	Harold Sylvester
Phyllis Slater	Roberta Maxwell
George Shannon	Lawrence Haddon

Theme Song ("The FBI"): Elmer Bernstein

Producer: David Gerber, Christopher Morgan

Together Again

Comedy Pilot; 26 min; Unaired (Produced in 12/86)

By chance two former high school sweethearts (Andrea, a divorced mother with two children who runs the Maple Travel Agency, and Michael, a divorced contractor) meet in Las Vegas 17 years after graduation. Andrea and Michael, who had drifted apart, find that they still love each other and marry. The unsold series was to relate their marital misadventures.

Andrea	Caren Kaye
Michael	Richard Kline
Terry (Andrea's daughter)	Kelli Martin
Brad (Andrea's son)	Justin Gocke
Betty (Andrea's mother)	Carole Cook
Andrea's assistant	Jesse Welles

"Together Again" Theme Vocal: Jennifer Taylor Green

Producer: Neil Rosen, George Tricker

Together We Stand

Comedy; 30 min; CBS 9/22/86 to 10/29/86

Events in the lives of David and Lori Randall, a loving husband and wife with one natural child (Jack) and three adopted children (Amy, Sam, and Sally). Based on the "Kelly's Kids" episode of "The Brady Bunch." See "Kelly's Kids" for information. See also "Nothing Is Easy."

David Randall	Elliott Gould
Lori Randall	Dee Wallace
Amy Randall	Katie O'Neill
Jack Randall	Scott Grimes
Sam	Ke Huy Quan
Sally	Natasha Bobo

Producer: Sherwood Schwartz, Al Burton

Tom and Jerry

Comedy Pilot; 30 min; NBC 11/30/55

The romantic misadventures of newlyweds Tom and Jerry Macy. Aired on "Screen Director's Playhouse."

Tom Macy	Peter Lawford
Jerry Macy	Nancy Gates
Father O'Dowd	Frank Fay
Lola	Marie Windsor
Garrity	Charles Lane

Writer-Director: Leo McCarey

The Tom and Jerry Comedy Show

Cartoon; 25 min; CBS 9/6/80 to 9/12/81

The escapades of mischief makers Tom (cat) and Jerry (mouse).

Voices: Frank Welker

Producer: Norm Prescott, Lou Scheimer

The Tom and Jerry Show

Cartoon; 30 min; CBS 9/10/66 to 9/17/72

Theatrical and made-for-TV cartoons about the antics of two non-talking animals: Tom the cat and Jerry the mouse.

Vocal Effects: Paul Frees, June Foray, Mel Blanc, Allen Swift

Producer: Fred Quimby, Chuck Jones, William Hanna, Joseph Barbera

Tom and Joann

Drama Pilot; 60 min; CBS 7/5/78

The story of Tom and Joann, a divorced couple who explore new relationships while maintaining their mutual affection a year after their 16-year marriage has ended.

Joann Hammil	Elizabeth Ashley
Tom Hammil	Joel Fabiani
Amy Hammil	Jennifer Cook
T.C. Hammil	Colin McKenna
Louise	Bibi Besch
Gabe	David Ackroyd
Helene	Brenda Donohue

Producer: David Susskind, Diana Kerew

Tom Corbett, Space Cadet

Adventure; 15 & 30 min;
    CBS 10/2/50 to 12/29/50
    ABC 1/1/51 to 9/26/52
    NBC 7/7/51 to 9/8/51
    DuMont 8/29/53 to 5/22/54
    NBC 12/11/54 to 6/25/55

The exploits of Tom Corbett, a cadet at Space Academy, U.S.A., an Earth-based West Point wherein young men and women train to become Solar Guards, the agents of a celestial police force that has been established to protect the planets of the Solar Alliance (Earth, Mars, Venus, and Jupiter).

Tom Corbett	Frankie Thomas
Cadet Roger	
Manning	Jan Merlin
Astro	Al Markhim
Capt. Larry Strong	Michael Harvey
	Edward Bryce
Dr. Joan Dale	Patricia Ferris
	Margaret Garland
Cadet T.J. Fissell	Jack Grimes
Commander	
Arkwright	Carter Blake
Betty	Beryl Berney
Gloria	Marian Brash

Announcer: Jackson Beck

Producer: Allen Ducovny, Leonard Carlton

Tom Cottle: Up Close

A syndicated (1982) series of personal one-on-one interviews with Tom Cottle. Produced by Claude Pelanne and Merrill Mauzer.

Tom, Dick, and Harry

Comedy Pilot; 30 min; CBS 9/20/60

The story of three former army buddies (Tom, Dick, and Harry) who pool their resources and rent a restaurant. The unsold series was to relate their attempts to make a success of their business venture.

Tom Fellows	Gene Nelson
Dick Rawlings	Joe Mantell
Harry Murphy	Marvin Kaplan
Shirley Fellows	Cheryl Callaway
Pamela Rawlings	Pamela Dean

Producer: Fred Briskin, Ben Starr

Tom, Dick, and Mary

Comedy; 30 min; NBC 10/5/64 to 1/4/65

Unable to afford their own apartment, a young intern (Tom) and his wife (Mary) solve their problem by sharing an apartment and expenses with their bachelor intern friend (Dick). Stories relate the trio's misadventures as they attempt to share an apartment. Aired on "90 Bristol Court."

Tom Gentry	Tom Galloway
Mary Gentry	Joyce Bulifant
Dick Moran	Steve Franken
Dr. Kievoy	John Hoyt
Cliff Murdock	Guy Raymond

Producer: Les Colodny

The Tom Ewell Show

Comedy; 30 min; CBS 9/27/60 to 7/18/61

Events in the lives of the Potter family: Tom, an easy-going real estate salesman; his wife, Frances; their children, Debbie, Carol, and Cissy; and Frances's mother, Irene.

Tom Potter	Tom Ewell
Frances Potter	Marilyn Erskine
Debbie Potter	Sherry Alberoni
Carol Potter	Cindy Robbins
Cissy Potter	Eileen Chesis
Irene Brady	Mabel Alberston

Theme Song ("Theme from the Tom Ewell Show"): Jerry Fielding

Producer: Hy Averback

Tom Snyder's Celebrity Spotlight

Interview Pilot; 60 min; NBC 1/21/80, 3/17/80, 6/23/80

An unsold series of celebrity interviews.

Host: Tom Snyder

First Pilot Guests: Bo Derek, Clint Eastwood, Barry Manilow, Gary Coleman

Second Pilot Guests: Loni Anderson, Cher, Jack Lemmon, Chevy Chase

Third Pilot Guests: James Cagney, Priscilla Presley, Carroll O'Connor, Erik Estrada

Producer: Andy Friendly

The Tom Swift and Linda Craig Mystery Hour

Mystery Pilot; 60 min; ABC 7/3/83

The exploits of Tom Swift, a scientific genius, and his cousin, Linda Craig, a beautiful young detective.

Tom Swift	Willie Aames
Linda Craig	Lori Loughlin
Kathy Hamilton	Amanda Wyss
Rad Gorman	Christopher Blande
Bronco Mallory	William Windom
Grandma Mallory	Carmen Zapata
Mrs. Gorman	Ja'net DuBois
Father Simon	Leonard J. Stone
Rudolph Ulmer	George DiCenzo

Producer: Joseph Stern, Angelo Pizzo, Harry Harris

Tom Terrific

Cartoon; 5 min; CBS 6/10/57 to 9/21/61

The exploits of Tom Terrific, a small boy who acquires amazing powers from a funnel-like hat that he wears.

Tom Terrific/Mighty Manfred	Lionel Wilson

Producer: Bill Weiss

Toma

Crime Drama; 60 min; ABC 10/4/73 to 9/6/74

The exploits of David Toma, an undercover agent with the Newark, New Jersey Police Department.

Det. David Toma	Tony Musante
Patty Toma	Susan Strasberg
Donna Toma	Michele Livingston
Jimmy Toma	Sean Mannering
Insp. Spooner	Simon Oakland
Various Roles	David Toma

Music: Mike Post, Pete Carpenter

Producer: Roy Huggins, Stephen J. Cannell, Jo Swerling Jr.

Tomahawk

Adventure; 30 min; Syn. 1957

The series, set in America's Northwest during the 1700s, relates the exploits of Pierre Radisson and his partner, Medard, as they assist the pioneers who are attempting to settle in a new and unexplored territory.

Pierre Radisson	Jacques Godin
Medard	Rene Caron

Tombstone Territory

Western; 30 min; ABC 10/16/57 to 10/9/59

The exploits of Harris Clayton, editor of the Tombstone, Arizona "Epitaph," as he struggles to establish peace through the power of the press in "the town too tough to die."

Harris Clayton (a.k.a. Harris Clayborne)	Richard Eastham
Sheriff Clay Hollister	Pat Conway
Deputy Charlie Riggs	Gil Rankin

Theme Vocal ("Take Me Back to Tombstone Territory"): William Backer

Producer: Frank Pittman, Andy White

Tomfoolery

Cartoon; 30 min; NBC 9/12/70 to 9/4/71

Sketches, songs, and poetry based on children's literature. Produced by Arthur Rankin Jr., Jules Bass, John Halas, and Joy Batchelor.

The Tomorrow Show

Discussion; NBC 10/15/73 to 9/15/80 (60 min)
9/16/80 to 1/28/82 (90 min)

Interviews with people rarely seen on TV and for the most part non-show business who have a story to tell.

Host: Tom Snyder

Co-Host: Rona Barrett

Announcer: Frank Barton, Bill Wendell

Producer: Joel Tator, Pamela Burke, Bruce McKay

The Toni Tennille Show

Variety; 60 min; Syn. 9/80

A relaxed, enjoyable program of music and songs.

Hostess: Toni Tennille

Regulars: Daryl Dragon, Melissa Tennille

Orchestra: Ira Newborn

Producer: Bob Eubanks, Michael Hill, Walt Case

Toni Twin Time

Variety; 30 min; CBS 4/5/50 to 9/20/50

A program of music and song (including undiscovered talent) with Arlene and Ardelle Terry, the singing teenage twins. Sponsored by Toni hair care products.

Host: Jack Lemmon

Regulars: Arlene and Ardell Terry, Jim Kirkwood, Lee Goodwin, Ann Koesun, Jack Kriza

Orchestra: Ray Bloch

Producer: Sherman Marks

Toni's Boys

Crime Drama Pilot; 60 min; ABC 4/2/80

A "Charlie's Angels" spin-off about Antonia "Toni" Blake, a private detective agency owner, who solves crimes with the assist of three handsome operatives (Bob, Cotton, Matt) and a butler (Rolph).

Toni Blake	Barbara Stanwyck
Bob Sorensen	Bob Seagren
Cotton Harper	Stephen Shortridge
Matt Parrish	Bruce Jenner
Rolph	James E. Broadhead
Michael Durano	Robert Loggia

Producer: Aaron Spelling, Leonard Goldberg

Tonight! America After Dark

Variety; 105 min; NBC 1/28/57 to 7/26/57

Live interviews coupled with on-the-spot news coverage.

Host: Jack Lescoulie, Al Collins

Vocalist: Judy Johnson

Newscaster: Earl Wilson, Bob Considine, Hy Gardner, Vernon Scott, Paul Coates, Irv Kupcinet, Lee Giroux

Music: The Lou Stein Trio, The Mort Lindsey Quartet

Tonight on Broadway

Variety; 30 min; CBS 4/6/48 to 5/23/48

Excerpts from Broadway shows coupled by interviews with their stars.

Host: Martin Gosch, James Mason Brown

Producer: Martin Gosch

The Tonight Show

Variety; 90 min; NBC 9/27/54 to 1/25/57

A late-night program of music, comedy, and celebrity interviews. Aired originally in New York from 7/27/53 to 9/24/54.

Host: Steve Allen

Regulars: Steve Lawrence, Eydie Gorme, Pat Marshall, Andy Williams, Helen Dixon

Announcer: Gene Rayburn

Orchestra: Skitch Henderson

The Tonight Show

Variety; 105 min; NBC 10/1/56 to 1/22/57

A program of music and comedy that preempted the prior title twice a week for four months.

Host: Ernie Kovacs

Vocalist: Maureen Arthur, Pete Hanley

Announcer: Bill Wendell

Orchestra: Leroy Holmes

The Tonight Show

Variety; 105 min; NBC 7/29/57 to 3/30/62

The revised version of "The Tonight Show" following the demise of "Tonight! America After Dark." A nightly series of music and chatter.

Host: Jack Paar

Regulars: Cliff Arquette, Pat Harrington Jr., Peggy Cass, Alexander King, Mary Margaret McBride, Dody Goodman, Betty Johnson, Elsa Maxwell, Tedi Thurman, The Bil and Cora Baird Puppets

Announcer: Hugh Downs, Art James

Orchestra: Jose Melis

The Tonight Show Starring Johnny Carson

Variety; NBC 10/2/62 to 9/15/80 (90 min)
9/16/80 (60 min. Premiere)

A nightly series of music, comedy, and celebrity interviews.

Host: Johnny Carson

Regulars: Carol Wayne, Teresa Ganzel

Announcer: Jack Haskell, Durward Kirby, Ed McMahon

Orchestra: Skitch Henderson, Milton De-Lugg, Doc Severinsen

Substitute Conductor: Tommy Newson

Producer: Fred DeCordova

The Tony Bennett Show

Variety; 60 min; NBC 8/11/56 to 9/8/56

A weekly program of music and songs with singer Tony Bennett and regulars The Spellbinders and The Frank Lewis Dancers.

The Tony Martin Show

Variety; 15 min; NBC 4/26/54 to 2/26/56

Tony Martin as the host of a weekly program of music and songs with The Interludes and the Hal Bourne (and later David Rose) Orchestra. Produced by Bud Yorkin.

Tony Orlando and Dawn

Variety; 60 min; CBS 7/3/74 to 7/24/74
12/4/74 to 12/28/76

A weekly hour of music and song with the singing group Tony Orlando and Dawn. Also titled "The Tony Orlando and Dawn Rainbow Hour."

Host: Tony Orlando

Dawn: Joyce Vincent Wilson, Telma Hopkins

Regulars: Susan Tolsky, George Carlin, Steve Franken, Jimmy Martinez, Edie McClurg, Adam Wade, Susan Lancer

Announcer: Roger Carroll, Dick Tufeld

Orchestra: Bob Rozario

Producer: Saul Islon, Ernest Chambers

The Tony Randall Show

Comedy; 30 min; ABC 9/23/76 to 3/10/77
CBS 9/24/77 to 3/25/78

The home and working life of Walter O. Franklin, a less-than-magisterial judge of the Court of Common Pleas in Philadelphia.

Walter Franklin	Tony Randall
Roberta Franklin	Devon Scott
	Penny Peyser
Oliver Franklin Jr.	Brad Savage
Janet Reubner	Allyn Ann McLerie
Bonnie McClellan	Rachel Roberts
Jack Terwilliger	Barney Martin
Judy Trowbridge	Brooke Adams
Mario Lanza	Zane Lasky
Wyatt Franklin	Hans Conried
Judge Eleanor Hooper	Diana Muldaur
Tanya Terwilliger	Helen Page Camp
Bailiff	Steve Hershaw

Music: Patrick Williams

Producer: Tom Patchett, Jay Tarses, Hugh Wilson, Gary David Goldberg

Tony the Pony

Children; 30 min; Syn. 9/79

When the "Book of Magic" declares that a colt named Tony be endowed with magical powers, a young boy (Jonathan) is chosen to become its owner. Stories relate their adventures as they help children in trouble.

Jonathan	Poindexter Yothers
G.G. the Wizard	Sterling Holloway
Agnes the Witch	Barbara Cason

Theme Vocal ("Tony the Pony"): Jill Jackson

Producer: James Lowe

Too Close for Comfort

Comedy; 30 min; ABC 11/11/80 to 9/15/83
　　　　　Syn. 4/84 to 3/86

The misadventures of Henry Rush, an over-protective father, as he struggles to keep tabs on his two beautiful daughters, Jackie and Sarah, who have moved out on their own—and into the funky downstairs apartment of the Rushes' San Francisco duplex. Based on the British series, "Keep It in the Family." See also "The Ted Knight Show" (1986 version).

Henry Rush	Ted Knight
Muriel Rush	Nancy Dussault
Jackie Rush	Deborah Van Valkenburg
Sarah Rush	Lydia Cornell
Monroe Ficus	JM J. Bullock
April Rush	Deena Freeman
Iris Martin	Audrey Meadows
Arthur Wainwright	Hamilton Camp
Regis	Inga Neilson
	Marta Ferguson
Mildred Rafkin	Selma Diamond
Huey Rush	Ray Middleton
Wendell Balaban	Bill Dana
Baby Andrew Rush	William & Michael Cannon
	Joshua Goodwin
	Eric & Jason Willis
Voice of Andrew (baby talk)	Sunni Walton
Voice of Andrew (thoughts)	Frank Welker
Monroe's father (Ben)	Pat Paulsen
Muriel's mother Betty	Priscilla Pointer
Dr. Connelly (Muriel's pediatrician)	Paddi Edwards

"Too Close for Comfort" Theme: Johnny Mandel

Producer: Arne Sultan, Earl Barrett, Austin & Irma Kalish

Too Good to be True

Comedy Pilot; 30 min; ABC 8/5/83

The misadventures that occur when the Pepperidge Prepatory School for Girls changes its policy to accept male students.

Principal Claire Shelton	Diana Muldaur
Gerald Whitworth	Reid Shelton
Mona Rainey	Beah Richards
Cassie	Diane Franklin
Rhonda	Sarah Buxton
Nance Mayberry	Allison Roth
Camille	Cindy Herron
Mick	John Stockwell
Ditto	Moosie Drier
Joey	Patrick Laborteaux
Eliot Zinberg	Brian Backer

Theme Vocal ("Too Good to Be True"): Robert Leischman

Producer: Gary Adelson, Karen Mack Goldsmith

Too Young to Go Steady

Comedy; 30 min; NBC 5/14/59 to 6/25/59

The innocent romantic misadventures of Pamela Blake, a pretty 15-year-old girl who is struggling to make the transition from tomboy to young lady.

Pamela Blake	Brigid Bazlen
Tom Blake	Don Ameche
Mary Blake	Joan Bennett
John Blake	Martin Houston
Timmie	Lorna Gillam

Producer: David Susskind, Ronald Alexander

Tootsie Hippodrome

Variety; 30 min; ABC 2/3/52 to 1/30/54

A program of entertainment geared to children: circus acts, western entertainers, and telephone quizzes (which awards a child a prize if he correctly answers a question).

Host: John Reed King, Whitey Carson, Boyd Heath

Assistant (Judy Ann): Mary Reynolds

Producer: Vernon P. Becker, Eli Broidy, Whitey Carson, Milton Stanson

Top Cat

Cartoon; 30 min; ABC 9/27/61 to 3/30/62

The adventures of Top Cat, a master con artist, as he attempts to enjoy a carefree life. Based on characters from "The Phil Silvers Show."

Top Cat	Arnold Stang
Choo Choo	Marvin Kaplan
Benny the Ball	Maurice Gosfield
Spook	Leo DeLyon
Goldie	Jean VarderPyl
Fancy Fancy/Pierre	John Stephenson
Officer Dibble	Allen Jenkins

Producer: William Hanna, Joseph Barbera

Top Dollar

Game; 30 min; CBS 3/29/58 to 8/30/58 (evening run)
9/1/58 to 10/23/59 (daytime run)

A line that contains blank spaces, and refers to an unknown word, is displayed. Each of the three players who compete suggest a letter that may be contained in the word. $100 is earned for each letter a player suggests that is contained in the word. Suggesting the last letter disqualifies a player. The highest scoring player is the winner.

Host: Toby Reed

Judge: Dr. Bergen Evans

Producer: Steve Carlin

Top 40 Videos

Music; 30 min; Syn. 1/84

A visual radio series that showcases the latest rock videos.

Video D.J.: Barbara Barrett, Kenny Noble

Producer: Gary Hunt, Barry Jaffe

Top of the Month

Variety; 30 min; Syn. 1972

Highlights of each month of the year are saluted via music and comedy.

Hosts: Tony Randall, E.J. Peaker

Regulars: Anson Williams, Tina Andrews, The Anita Mann Dancers, The Alan Copeland Singers

Orchestra: Alan Copeland

Producer: Perry Cross

Top of the Pops

Music; 60 min; CBS 9/25/87 to 3/18/88

Performances by both American and British (via satellite) singers. Based on the long-running British series of the same title (which premiered in England on January 1, 1964).

Host: Nia Peeples, Gary Davies

Producer: Drew S. Levin, Joel Gallen

Top of the World

Game; 30 min; Syn. 6/82

Each of the three contestants who compete, representing the U.S., the U.K., and Australia, answer four questions based on his challenger's countries. A second round quizzes each player on a subject of his own choosing; and a final round tests world knowledge. The player with the most correct answers is the winner. The program is based in England and uses satellite transmission to pick up players in Europe, Australia, and America.

Host: Eamonn Andrews

Producer: Shep Morgan

Top Plays of 1954

An NBC Summer series (6/1/54 to 8/24/54) of repeat dramas from "Ford Theatre."

Top Secret U.S.A.

Drama; 30 min; Syn. 1954

The exploits of Brand and Powell, undercover agents with the Bureau of Scientific Information.

Brand	Paul Stewart
Powell	Gena Rowlands

Topper

Comedy; 30 min; CBS 10/3/53 to 9/30/55

Shortly after purchasing a home, henpecked banker Cosmo Topper discovers that he has inherited three ghosts—its previous owners, George and Marian Kerby (a man and wife who were killed while skiing in Switzerland) and Neil, a liquor-consuming St. Bernard dog, who was also the victim of the avalanche. Stories relate George and Marian's efforts to bring some fun into Topper's dull life; and Topper's efforts to cope with three mischievous ghosts.

Cosmo Topper	Leo G. Carroll
Marian Kerby	Anne Jeffreys
George Kerby	Robert Sterling
Henrietta Topper	Lee Patrick
Katie	Kathleen Freeman
Maggie	Edna Skinner
Thelma Gibney	Mary Field
Humphrey Schuyler	Thurston Hall
Elsie Worble	Elvia Allman
Neil	Buck

Producer: John W. Loveton, Bernard L. Schubert

Topper Returns

Comedy Pilot; 30 min; NBC 3/19/73

An update of the Topper story in which Cosmo Topper Jr., the nephew of the late Cosmo Topper, finds his life plagued when he inherits his uncle's possessions, including the spirits of George and Marian Kerby. The ghosts who appeared and spoke only to his uncle now appear and speak only to him in an attempt to bring some cheer into his dull life.

Cosmo Topper Jr.	Roddy McDowall
Marian Kerby	Stefanie Powers
George Kerby	John Fink
Jones (Cosmo's butler)	Reginald Owen

Music: Patrick Williams

Producer: Arthur Jacobs

The Tortellis

Comedy; 30 min; NBC 1/22/87 to 5/5/87

A spin-off from "Cheers." When the somewhat spacey Loretta Tortelli catches her low-life husband, Nick, cheating on her, she decides to leave him and heads for her sister, Charlotte's home in Las Vegas. Shortly after, a reformed Nick arrives and receives Loretta's forgiveness. Stories relate Nick's misadventures as a TV repairman and Loretta's experiences as a hopeful singer.

Nick Tortelli	Dan Hedaya
Loretta Tortelli	Jean Kasem
Charlotte Cooper	Carlene Watkins
Anthony Tortelli (Nick's son)	Timothy Williams
Annie Tortelli (Anthony's wife)	Mandy Ingber
Mark Cooper (Charlotte's son)	Aaron Moffatt

Producer: Ken Estin, Tim Berry, Kimberly Hill

Total Eclipse

Experimental; 8 min; NBC 9/5/39

A short program of music and songs with Howard Reed. Produced by Edward Sobol.

A Touch of Grace

Comedy; 30 min; ABC 1/20/73 to 6/16/73

Events in the life of Grace Sherwood, a 65-year-old widow who is struggling to make a life for herself at the home of her married daughter (Myra) and her husband (Walter).

Grace Sherwood
  (a.k.a. Grace
  Simpson)   Shirley Booth
Herbert Morrison   J. Pat O'Malley
Myra Bradley   Marian Mercer
Walter Bradley   Warren Berlinger

Producer: Sal Turteltaub, Bernie Orenstein

Touche Turtle

Cartoon; 5 min; Syn. 1962

The exploits of Touche Turtle, a modern-day knight who helps people in trouble.

Touche Turtle   Bill Thompson
Dumm Dumm   Alan Reed

Producer: William Hanna, Joseph Barbera

Tough Cookies

Action Comedy; 30 min; CBS 3/6/86 to 4/23/86

The comical exploits of Cliff Brady, a detective with the Chicago Police Department, who patrols his old neighborhood; an area "full of tough cookies."

Det. Cliff Brady   Robby Benson
Lt. Iverson   Art Metrano
Rita   Lainie Kazan
Danny Polchek   Adam Arkin
Richie Messina   Matt Craven
Connie Rivera   Elizabeth Pena
Father McCaskey   Alan North
Diane Taylor   Gail Edwards
Ruthie   Peggy Pope
Cliff's Sister Jennie   Wendy Goldman
Arthur (Jennie's
  husband)   Archie Hahn

Producer: Paul Junger Witt, Tony Thomas, Amy Heckerling

Tour of Duty

Drama; 60 min; CBS 9/24/87 (Premiere)

The experiences of a group of young soldiers with Bravo Company who are serving their twelve month tour of duty in Vietnam in 1967. The series, quite different for broadcast television, is a gruelling portrait of the horrors of war.

Sgt. Zeke Anderson   Terence Knox
Pvt. Alberto Ruiz   Ramon Franco
Cpl. Danny Percell   Tony Becker
Pvt. Marvin Johnson   Stan Foster
Lt. Myron Goldman   Stephen Caffrey
Pvt. Roger Horn   Joshua Mauer
Cpl. Rusty Wallace   Kevin Conroy
Pvt. Scott Baker   Eric Bruskotter
Pvt. Marcus Taylor   Miguel A. Nunez Jr.

Producer: Zev Braun, Bill Norton

Toyland Express

Children; 30 min; ABC 11/7/55 to 12/12/55

A program of music and comedy with ventriloquist Paul Winchell and his dummy friends, Jerry Mahoney and Knucklehead Smiff. Music by Ralph Herman and produced by Paul Winchell.

The Tracer

Drama; 30 min; Syn. 1957

The series, based on the files of the Tracers Company, relates the adventures of Regan, as he attempts to locate missing heirs and beneficiaries.

Regan   James Chandler

Producer: Ben Parker

The Tracey Ullman Show

Comedy; 30 min; FOX; 4/5/87 (Premiere)

Various sketches (presented in a situation comedy format) that features British singer Tracey Ullman in a variety of situations.

Hostess: Tracey Ullman

Regulars: Julie Kavner, Dan Castellaneta, Daniel Rosen, Mitchell Lester, Jamey Turner

Producer: James L. Brooks, Ken Estin, Heidi Perlman, Jerry Belson

Trackdown

Western; 30 min; CBS 10/4/57 to 9/23/59

The exploits of Hoby Gilman, a Texas Ranger, as he attempts to apprehend outlaws in the west of the 1870s.

Hoby Gilman   Robert Culp

Producer: Vincent M. Fennelly

Traffic Court

Drama; 30 min; ABC 6/18/58 to 10/2/59

Reenactments of actual traffic court cases.

Judge   Edgar Allan Jones
                                           Jr.
Court Clerk   Samuel Whitson
Bailiff   Frank McClure

Producer: Lou Brott

The Trailblazers

Adventure Pilot; 30 min; Unaired; Produced
  in 1952

The exploits of Roger Stone, the director of
the North Oaks Boys Camp. In the pilot episode, titled "The Fugitive," Roger and his
campers attempt to capture an escaped murderer.

Roger Stone   Alan Hale Jr.
Spike   Dick Tyler
Jim   Henry Blair
Feathers   Bobby Hiatt
Ben   Harry McCormick
Pudge   Jim Flowers
Joe McClain   Lyle Talbot
Dan Angus   Duke York

Producer: William F. Broidy, Wesley Barry,
  Bob Nunes

Trails West

Ray Milland as the host of a syndicated (1958)
series of western dramas that originally aired
on "Death Valley Days."

Training Camp: The Bulls are Back

Comedy; 30 min; HBO 8/19/86 to 9/23/86

A sequel to "First and Ten," which continues
to depict the misadventures of Diane Barrow,
the beautiful owner of a rowdy football team
called the California Bulls. See also "First
and Ten: The Championships."

Diane Barrow   Delta Burke
Ernie Denardo   Reid Shelton
T.D. Parker   O.J. Simpson
Tom Yinessa   Jason Beghe
Mad Dog   Tony Longo
Jamie Waldron   Jeff Kaate
Bubba Kincaid   Prince Hughes
Rick Lambert   Sam Jones
Fred Grier   Stan Kamber
Jethro   Marcus Allen
Dr. Death   Donald Gibb
Max Greene   Mark Lonow

Producer: Peter Locke, Donald Kushner,
  Jonathan Debin

The Transformers

Cartoon; 30 min; Syn. 9/84

The battle for good over evil as seen through
the exploits of the Autobots, residents of the
planet Zobitron, as they attempt to stop the
Deceptitrons, a race of deadly robots who
seek to control the universe.

Voices: Michael Bell, Peter Cullen, Casey
  Kasem, Don Messick, Scatman Crothers,
  Ken Samson, John Stephenson, Cory Bur-
  ton, Chris Latta

Producer: Lee Gunther, Joe Bacal, Margaret
  Loesch, Tom Griffin

The Trap

Anthology; 30 min; CBS 4/29/50 to 6/24/50

Live dramas about people who are suddenly
confronted with uncertain situations.

Narrator: Joe DeSantis

Producer: Franklin Heller

Trapper John, M.D.

Drama; 60 min; CBS 9/23/79 to 9/4/86

A M*A*S*H spin-off, that set in present
times, relates incidents in the life of Dr. John
McIntyre (nicknamed Trapper John), a chief
surgeon at San Francisco Memorial Hospital.

Dr. John McIntyre	Pernell Roberts	Dr. Michael	
Dr. G. Alonzo		"Cutter" Royce	James Naughton
"Gonzo" Gates	Gregory Harrison	John Six	Lou Ferrigno
Nurse Gloria		Dr. Nate "Skate"	
"Ripples"		Baylor	Dorian Harewood
Brancusi	Christopher Norris	Buck Williams	Jack Bannon
Dr. Stanley		Dr. Brigitte Blaine	Wendie Malick
Riverside II	Charles Siebert	Nurse Jane Hooter	Jayne Modean
Dr. Justin "Jackpot"		Nurse Agnes Decker	Eileen Heckart
Jackson	Brian Mitchell	Sidney "Hatter"	
Melanie McIntyre	Jessica Walter	Petchelli	Alfie Wise
Nurse Clara		Dr. Chas	
"Starch"		Sternhauser	Arlen Dean Snyder
Willoughby	Mary McCarty	Dr. "Beaver"	
Nurse Ernestine		Bouvee	Bill Randolph
Shoop	Madge Sinclair	Chas's secretary	Marla Adams
Arnold Slocum	Simon Scott	Nurse	Marion Yume
E.J. Riverside	Marcia Rodd		Deborah Greene
John T. McIntyre Jr.	Timothy Busfield		
Andrea Brancusi	Tanya Fenmore		
Nurse Libby Kegler	Lorna Luft		
Catherine Hackett	Janis Paige		
Nurse Barbara			
Andrews	Sarah Cunningham		
Dr. Andy Pagano	Beau Gravitte		
Dr. Fran Brennan	Andrea Marcovicci		
Stanley Riverside Sr.	David Wayne		
Dr. Francis McDuffy	John Randolph		

"Trauma Center" Theme Song: James DiPasquale

Producer: Frank Glicksman, Don Brinkley

Producer: Glen A. Larson, Harry & Renee Longstreet

Trash or Treasure

Human Interest; 30 min; DuMont 10/1/52 to 9/27/53

Nelson Case as the host of a program that features appraisals of antiques and works of art (by Sigmund Rotschild) that are brought to the studio by ordinary people.

Traveling Man

Drama Pilot; 60 min; CBS 9/11/87

When he feels that there is no sense, no justice or no reward as a hospital trauma surgeon, Dr. John "Doc" Dockery quits and takes to the road seeking adventure. The unsold series was to relate his adventures with the people he meets. In the pilot, Doc becomes involved with a beautiful girl (Raylene) and her estranged father (Carl).

Trauma Center

Drama; 60 min; ABC 9/22/83 to 12/8/83

The work of the doctors, nurses, and paramedics attached to the Medstar Trauma Center of the McKee General Hospital in Los Angeles.

Dr. John Dockery	James Naughton
Raylene Lipscomb	Kay Lenz
Carl Lipscomb	Richard Farnsworth
Matt	Matt Clark
Max	Frank Ferris
Annie Dockery	Leslie Wing
Dudan	Dennis Letts
Brad Buckner	Sean McGraw

Producer: Robert Singer

The Travels of Jaimie McPheeters

Adventure; 60 min; ABC 9/15/63 to 3/15/64

The hardships encountered by the Beaver Patrol, a wagon train of settlers destined for the California of 1849. Their experiences are seen through the eyes of Jaimie McPheeters, a 12-year-old boy.

Doc Sardius
McPheeters — Dan O'Herlihy
Jaimie McPheeters — Kurt Russell
Buck Coulter — Michael Witney
Linc Murdock — Charles Bronson
Henry T. Coe — Hadley Mattingley
Othello — Vernett Allen III
Dick McBride — John Chandler
Matt Kissel — Marl Allen
Mrs. Kissel — Meg Wyllie
The Kissel Children — The Osmond Brothers
John Murrell — James Westerfield
Hard Luck Slater — Robert Carriort
Shep Bagott — Sandy Kenyon
Jenny — Jean Engstrom
Donna Anderson

Producer: Robert Thompson, Robert Sparks, Don Ingalls

Treasure Hunt

Game; 30 min; ABC 9/7/56 to 5/24/57
NBC 8/12/57 to 12/4/59

Two players compete in a question-and-answer session wherein the highest-scoring player chooses one of thirty treasure chests. The contents of the chest, from a head of cabbage to $25,000 in cash, becomes his prize.

Host: Jan Murray

Assistants: Marian Stafford, Greta Tyssen

Treasure Hunt

Game; 30 min; Syn. 9/81

A female player, chosen from the studio audience, receives the chance to select one box from sixty-six boxes that are displayed on stage. The player can receive either the contents of the box (zonks to $20,000 in cash) or a cash bribe (up to $2,000) not to take the box. See also "The New Treasure Hunt."

Host: Geoff Edwards

Announcer: Johnny Jacobs

Producer: Chuck Barris, Budd Granoff

Treasure Isle

Game; 30 min; ABC 12/18/67 to 12/27/68

An elaborate outdoor game show in which three married couples compete in various contests seeking to acquire the most points and win the opportunity to hunt for buried treasure chests. The winning couple receives a series of clues and within a three minute time limit, must unscramble them and dig for the buried chests. The players receive what prizes the chests contain (printed on small cards).

Host: John Bartholomew Tucker

Assistants: Renee Hampton, Bonnie Maudsley

Producer: Paul Alter

Treasury Men in Action

Crime Drama; 30 min; ABC 9/11/50 to 12/4/50
NBC 4/5/51 to 4/1/54
ABC 10/7/54 to 9/20/55

Dramas based on the files of the U.S. Customs and Treasury departments. Also known as "Federal Men."

Chief — Walter Greaza

Announcer: Durward Kirby, Carl Frank, Murray Golden

Producer: Everett Rosenthal, Robert Sloane, Bernard Prockter

The Trials of O'Brien

Drama; 60 min; CBS 9/18/65 to 5/27/66

The story of Daniel J. O'Brien, an untidy and disorganized criminal attorney working in New York City.

Daniel J. O'Brien — Peter Falk
Katie O'Brien — Joanna Barnes
The Great
McGonigle — David Burns
Margaret — Ilka Chase
Miss G — Elaine Stritch
Lt. Garrison — Dolph Sweet

Theme Song ("Theme from the Trials of O'Brien"): Sid Ramin

Producer: Richard Alan Simmons, Gene Wang

Trivia Trap

Game; 30 min; ABC 10/15/84 to 4/5/85

Two rows of four answers are revealed. A question that relates to one row is read. One team, of the two three-member teams who compete, must eliminate the wrong answers contained in the row. $50 is scored per correct elimination; $300 if all the incorrect answers are selected. If the correct answer is chosen, the team loses its turn and their opponents play. The first team to score $1,000 is the winner.

Host: Bob Eubanks

Announcer: Gene Wood, Bob Hilton

Producer: Chester Feldman

Trollkins

Cartoon; 25 min; CBS 9/12/81 to 9/11/82

The misadventures of the Trollkins, wee green and blue people who live in a woodland city called Trolltown.

Pudge Trollsom	Alan Oppenheimer
Pixlee Trollsom	Jennifer Darling
Blitz Plumkin	Steve Spears
Flooky	Frank Welker
Grubb Trollmaine	Michael Bell
Dolly Durkle	Jennifer Darling
DepuTroll Flake	Marshall Efron
Mayor Lumpkin	Paul Winchell

Producer: William Hanna, Joseph Barbera

Trouble, Inc.

Crime Drama Pilot; 30 min; DuMont 7/27/49

The story of Jason and Jane Meadows, an adventuresome couple who operate Trouble, Inc., a detective organization that tackles any job—anywhere, anytime.

Jason Meadows	Earl Hammond
Jane Meadows	Carol Hill
Singer	Elaine Williams
Thug	Maurice Gosfield

Producer: Elwood Hoffman

Trouble with Father

Comedy; 30 min; ABC 10/21/50 to 4/13/55

Events in the lives of the Erwins: Stu, the principal of Hamilton High School; his wife, June; and their children Joyce and Jackie. Also known as "Life with the Erwins" and "The Stu Erwin Show."

Stu Erwin	Himself
June Erwin	June Collyer
Joyce Erwin	Ann Todd
	Merry Anders
Jackie Erwin	Sheila James
Willie	Willie Best
Jimmy Clark	Martin Milner
Harry	Harry Hayden

Producer: Hal Roach Jr., Roland Reed

Trouble with Richard

Comedy Pilot; 30 min; CBS 8/22/60

The misadventures of Richard Abernathy, a disorganized bank teller.

Richard Abernathy	Dick Van Dyke
Harold Martin	Howard Smith
Gramps	Parker Fennelly
Aunt Julia	Doro Merande

Producer: Aaron Ruben

Trouble with Tracy

Comedy; 30 min; Syn. 1971

Events in the lives of the newlywed Youngs: Douglas, an executive with the advertising firm of Hutton, Dutton & Norris; and his well-meaning but scatterbrained wife, Tracy. Produced in Canada.

Tracy Young	Diane Nyland
Douglas Young	Steve Weston
Sally Anderson	Bonnie Brooks
Paul Sherwood	Franz Russell
Jonathan Norris	Ben Lennick
Margaret Norris	Sandra Scott

Producer: Seymour Berns

The Troubleshooters

Adventure; 30 min; NBC 9/11/59 to 6/17/60

The exploits of Kodiak and Dugan, construction supervisors for the Stenrud Corporation, as they intervene in construction-site difficulties and attempt to return the job to normal.

Kodiak	Keenan Wynn
Frank Dugan	Bob Mathias
Loft	Eddie Firestone
Slats	Chet Allen
Jim	Bob Harris
Skinner	Carey Loftin
Scotty	Bob Fortier

Producer: Frank Rosenberg, John Gibbs

Try and Do It

Game; 30 min; NBC 7/4/48 to 9/5/48

Object: For contestants to perform stunts in return for prizes.

Host: Jack Bright

Producer: Herb Leder

True

See "G.E. True."

True Confessions

Anthology; 30 min; Syn. 9/86

Dramatizations based on stories appearing in "True Confessions" magazine.

Host: Bill Bixby

Producer: Alan Landsburg, Barbara Lewis, Kay Hoffman

True Life Stories

Anthology Pilot; 60 min; ABC 9/13/81

The program recreates the trials and tribulations of real life people. The pilot tells the stories of Charlie Steen, a geologist who made and lost millions; and of Barbara Hallberg and of her search to find her real mother.

Hosts: Regis Philbin, Mary Hart

Charlie Steen	Dick Van Dyke
Minnie Lee Steen	Lisa Blake Richards
Barbara Hallberg	Marion Ross

Producer: Louis Rudolph

True Story

Anthology; 30 min; NBC 3/16/57 to 12/20/58

Dramatic presentations with hostess Kathy Norris. Produced by Wilbur Stark.

Truth or Consequences

Game; 30 min; CBS 9/7/50 to 6/7/51
NBC 1/14/52 to 9/24/65

Selected contestants are first interviewed, then asked to answer a nonsense riddle. If they are unable to answer it, they have to pay the consequences by performing stunts. Prizes are awarded based on the success of their performances.

Host: Ralph Edwards, Jack Bailey, Bob Barker

Announcer: Ken Carpenter

Producer: Ralph Edwards, Ed Bailey

Truth or Consequences

Game; 30 min; Syn. 1967

A revised version of the prior title, which see for format.

Host: Bob Barker

Announcer: Charles Lyon

Producer: Ralph Edwards

Tucker's Witch

Crime Drama; 60 min; CBS
10/6/82 to 11/10/82
3/31/83 to 5/5/83

The story of Amanda and Rick Tucker, husband and wife owners of Tucker & Tucker, a private detective organization. The twist: Amanda is a beautiful witch, still in the process of developing her craft, who uses her powers to solve crimes.

Amanda Tucker	Catherine Hicks
	Kim Cattrall*
Rick Tucker	Tim Matheson
	Art Hindle*
Ellen Hobbs	Barbara Barrie
Marsha Fulbright	Alfre Woodard
Lt. Sean Fisk	Bill Morey
Fred Sandrich	Charles Parks

Producer: Philip Mandelker, Leonard Hill, Bernie Kukoff

*Cast in the filmed, but not televised pilot, "The Good Witch of Laurel Canyon."

Tugboat Annie

Comedy; 30 min; Syn. 1957

The misadventures of Annie Brennan, the middle-aged, sympathetic, and often troubled skipper of the tugboat "Narcissus." Based on the stories by Norman Reilly Raine. Also known as "The Adventures of Tugboat Annie."

Annie Brennan	Minerva Urecal
Horatio Bullwinkle	Walter Sande
Murdoch McArdle	Stan Francis

Producer: Anthony Veiller

Turbo-Teen

Cartoon; 30 min; ABC 9/8/84 to 9/7/85

While driving through a storm, a bolt of lightning causes a car being driven by Bret Matthews to crash through the wall of a building in which a secret experiment is being conducted. A ray from the machine strikes Bret, causing him and his car to become one (when the temperature rises, Bret becomes the car; when he feels cool, he is a normal teenager). Stories relate Bret's misadventures.

Voices: T.K. Carter, Pamela Hayden, Frank Welker, Pat Fraley, Clive Revill

Producer: Joe Ruby, Ken Spears

Turnabout

Comedy; 30 min; NBC 1/29/79 to 3/30/79

When Penny Alston, a vice president with Aura Cosmetics, believes her husband Sam's life (a writer for "Sports Life" magazine) is better than hers and idly wishes they could trade places, her wish is granted by an impish statue she purchased from a gypsy. Stories relate their comic adventures as Penny, with Sam's personality, and Sam, with Penny's personality, struggle to adjust—and live as the other.

Penny Alston	Sharon Gless
Sam Alston	John Schuck
Judy Overmeyer	Bobbi Jordan
Jack Overmeyer	Richard Stahl
Al Brennan	Bruce Kirby
Geoffrey St. James	James B. Sikking

Narrator: Sterling Holloway

Producer: Sam Denoff

Turn of Fate

Anthology; 30 min; NBC 9/30/57 to 6/30/58

Dramas of people who are suddenly propelled into unexpected and perilous situations.

Regulars: Robert Ryan, Jane Powell, Jack Lemmon, David Niven, Charles Boyer

Producer: Robert Fillous

Turn On

Variety; 30 min; ABC 2/5/69

Visual fast-paced comedy coupled with electronic distortion and stop-action photography. Because of its risque material, the program was cancelled the same night it premiered.

Guest Host: Tim Conway

Regulars: Chuck McCann, Bonnie Boland, Hamilton Camp, Teresa Graves, Maura McGiveney, Debbie Macomber, Mel Stewart, Ken Greenwald, Alice MaVega, Maxine Green, Alma Murphy

Announcer: Chuck McCann

Producer: George Schlatter, Digby Wolfe

Turn to a Friend

Game; 30 min; ABC 10/5/53 to 12/31/53

Contestants stand before the studio audience and bear their souls, stating their single most needed possession. Studio audience applause determine the saddest story teller, who in return receives the help requested.

Host: Dennis James

TV Auction

Game; 15 min; ABC 7/10/54 to 8/28/54

Various merchandise items are displayed on stage. The limit price of each item is stated. Via wire or mail, the items are sold to the home viewers whose bids are found to be acceptable.

Auctioneer: Sid Stone

TV Funnies

Comedy Pilot; 30 min; NBC 6/18/82

Fast-paced comedy sketches based on the funnies found in daily newspapers. Mythical strips are used and live actors perform in cartoon-like sets designed to give the illusion of a comic strip come to life.

Host: Conrad Bain

Regulars: Jacqueline Scott, Jerry Marin, Robert Sparr, Kip King, Charlie Dell, Vic Dunlop, Reece Clark, Deena Crowder, C.W. Metcalf, Princess O'Mahoney, Wynn Irwin, Julie Brown, Jeffrey Barron, Sandra Gould, Marcy Vosburgh, Lou Cutell

Music: Bob Rozario

Producer: Saul Ilson

TV General Store

Game; 60 min; ABC 6/14/53 to 7/12/53

Various merchandise items are displayed on stage and the limit price of each item is stated. Home viewers bid on items via wire or mail. The viewer whose bid is highest is able to purchase that particular item. Hosted by Dave and Judy Clark.

TV Readers Digest

Anthology; 30 min; ABC 1/17/55 to 7/9/56

Dramas based on stories that appear in "Readers Digest" magazine.

Host: Hugh Riley, Gene Raymond

Producer: Chester Erskine

TV Screen Magazine

Variety; 30 min; NBC 1/8/48 to 4/30/49

A program of music, songs, chatter, and fashion previews.

Host: John K.M. McCaffery

Regulars: Millicent Fenwick, Ray Forrest

TV Shopper

Women; 15 min; DuMont 11/1/48 to 12/1/50

Shopping hints, fashion tips, marketing advice, consumer reports, and other topics of interest to women.

Hostess: Kathi Norris

The TV Show

Comedy Pilot; 70 min; ABC 7/24/79

A satirization of TV and its programs via comedy sketches.

Cast: Rob Reiner, Billy Crystal, Martin Mull, Christopher Guest, Johnny Brown, Deborah Harmon, Harry J. Shearer, Michael McKean

Music: Steve Cagan

Producer: Rob Reiner, Phil Mishkin

TV 2000

Music: 60 min; Syn. 7/85

A weekly series of rock videos, interviews, and industry news.

Host: Lisa Robinson, John Kassir

Producer: Jeff Franklin, Alan Zaretsky

The TV TV Show

Comedy Pilot; 90 min; NBC 5/1/77

A satirization of local TV newscasts and newscasters via comedy skits.

Ralph Buckler (anchor) — Howard Hesseman
Mary Kay (co-anchor) — Mary Frann
News editor — Rene Auberjonois

Regulars: Annie Roth, Carl Gotlieb, Gary Goodrow, Mina Kolb, Garret Graham

Producer: Michael Shamberg

TV's Bloopers and Practical Jokes

Comedy; 60 min; NBC 1/9/83 to 9/14/86

A weekly program of outtakes from TV programs, movies, and commercials. The show also stages very elaborate practical jokes, which it pulls on famous celebrities.

Host: Dick Clark, Ed McMahon

Blooper Awards Girl: Deborah Ray, Diana Merritt, Linda Weistmeyer, Barbara Edwards, Kim Hopkins, K.C. Winkler

Regulars: Rick Dees, Tom Sharp, Robert Klein

Producer: Dick Clark, John J. McMahon, Lee Miller, Al Schwartz

TV's Top Tunes

Variety; 15 min; CBS 7/2/51 to 8/17/51

Renditions of popular songs.

Hosts: Peggy Lee, Mel Torme

Vocalists: The Skylarks

Orchestra: Mitchell Ayres

Producer: Lee Cooley

TV's Top Tunes

Variety; 30 min; CBS 6/28/54 to 8/24/54
7/9/55 to 9/3/55

A revised version of the prior title, which again features renditions of popular songs.

Host: Julius LaRosa

Regulars: Helen O'Connell, Marcie Miller, Bob Eberly, Tommy Mercer, The Ray Anthony Chorus

Orchestra: Ray Anthony

Announcer: Tony Marvin

Producer: Lee Cooley

12 O'Clock High

Drama; 60 min; ABC 9/18/64 to 1/13/67

The World War II adventures of the men and officers of the 918th Bombardment Squadron of the U.S. 8th Air Force.

Gen. Frank Savage	Robert Lansing
Gen. Wiley Crowe	John Larkin
Maj. Harvey Stovall	Frank Overton
	Lew Gallow
Maj. Doc Kaiser	Barney Phillips
Col. Joe Gallagher	Paul Burke
Sgt. Sandy	
Komansky	Chris Robinson
Gen. Edward Britt	Andrew Duggan

Producer: Quinn Martin

20 Minute Workout

Exercise; 30 min; Syn. 6/83

The benefits of aerobic exercise are demonstrated by a bevy of beautiful girls.

Exercise Girls: Sharon Bisset, Laurie Briscoe, Holly Butler, Sue Carter, Bess Motta, Nicole Nardini, Anne Schumacher, Leslie Smith, Arlaine Wright

Producer: Jamie Kellner, Ian McDougall

20 Questions

Game; 30 min; NBC 11/26/49 to 12/24/49
ABC 3/17/50 to 6/29/51
DuMont 7/6/51 to 4/5/54

A subject, which is either vegetable, animal, or mineral, is revealed. Four panelists (three regulars and one contestant) have to identify it by asking questions, twenty being the maximum. If the contestant can identify the subject before the panel, he receives a prize.

Host: Bill Slater, Jay Jackson

Panelists: Bobby McGuire, Fred Von Deventer, Florence Rinard, Herb Palesie, Johnny McFee

Announcer: John Gregson, Frank Waldecker

Producer: Gary Stevens, George Elbes

The $20,000 Pyramid

Game; 30 min; CBS 3/26/73 to 3/29/74
ABC 5/6/74 to 6/27/80

One team (two teams compete) chooses one subject from six that are displayed on a board. Each subject contains seven related objects. One player must use one-word clues and relate the meaning of each object to his partner. Each correct guess scores one ponit. Each team plays three rounds. The highest scoring team receives the chance to win $20,000 by identifying six subjects within sixty seconds.

Host: Dick Clark

Announcer: Bob Clayton, Steve O'Brien

Producer: Bob Stewart, Anne Marie Schmitt

The 20th Century

Documentary; 30 min; CBS 10/20/57 to 8/28/66

Events of the 20th century are recounted via newsreel footage.

Host-Narrator: Walter Cronkite

Producer: Burton Benjamin, Al Wasserman, Marshall Flaum, Isaac Kleinerman

20th Century Follies

Variety Pilot; 60 min; ABC 2/16/72

An unsold weekly series of music, songs, and comedy sketches.

Host: Alan King

Regulars: Julie Amato, Ron Carey, Nell Carter, Fay DeWitt, Joy Harmon, Jerry Lacy, Barry Livingston, Carol Worthington

Producer: Saul Ilson, Ernest Chambers

The 20th Century-Fox Hour

Anthology; 60 min; CBS 10/5/55 to 9/18/57

Television adaptations of theatrical films produced by 20th Century-Fox. Produced by Jules Bricken, Ben Feiner Jr., Samuel Marx, Otto Lang, and Peter Packer.

Twenty-One

Game; 30 min; NBC 9/12/56 to 10/16/58

Two players compete and choose questions to answer by their point value (1 to 11). The first player to score exactly twenty-one is the winner and receives $500 per point difference between his score and his opponent's score.

Host: Jack Barry

Announcer: Bill McCord

Producer: Robert Noah, Albert Freeman

21 Beacon Street

Crime Drama; 30 min; NBC 7/2/59 to 9/24/59
12/27/59 to 3/20/60

The story of David Chase, a private detective who incorporates scientific principals to solve baffling crimes. (The title refers to the Boston address of the David Chase Detective Agency.)

David Chase	Dennis Morgan
Lola	Joanna Barnes
Brian	Brian Kelly
Jim	James Maloney

Producer: Al Simon

21 Jump Street

Crime Drama; 60 min; FOX 4/12/87 (Premiere)

In an attempt to curtail the rising crime rate in high schools, a secret undercover unit called Jump Street Chapel (located in an abandoned chapel at 21 Jump Street) is established by the Metropolitan Police Department. Stories detail the work of five such police officers as they infiltrate high schools to battle juvenile crime.

Off. Tom Hanson	Johnny Depp
Off. Judy Hoffs	Holly Robinson
Capt. Richard Jenko	Frederic Forrest
Off. H.T. (Harry Truman) Ioki	Dustin Nguyen
Off. Doug Penhall	Peter DeLuise

Producer: Stephen J. Cannell, Jo Swerling Jr.

The 25th Man (Ms)

Crime Drama Pilot; 60 min; NBC 8/15/82

The exploits of a group of L.A.P.D. rookie cops. The title refers to Lynn Taylor, the police academy's only female recruit.

Lynn Taylor	Ellen Regan
Capt. Mike Houston	Edward Winter
Sgt. Bill "Cigar" Seeger	Michael Bell
T.J. Putnam	Michael Andrew
Billy Dodge	Justin Lord
Ted Masters	Stephen Farr
Joe Montoya	Pepe Serna
Bob Purvis	Robert Jarvis
Mrs. Taylor	Virginia Gregg
Bobby Taylor	Marty Gold

Producer: Jack Webb, William Stark

The $25,000 Pyramid

Game; 30 min; Syn. 1974

A syndicated version of "The $20,000 Pyramid" (which see for format) and which increases the final prize from $20,000 to $25,000.

Host: Bill Cullen

Announcer: Bob Clayton

Producer: Bob Stewart

26 Men

Western; 30 min; Syn. 1957

The exploits of the Arizona Rangers, men, limited by law to twenty-six, who dispensed justice in the final days of the Old West.

| Capt. Tom Rynning | Tris Coffin |
| Ranger Clint Travis | Kelo Henderson |

Producer: Russell Hayden

Twiggy's Juke Box

A syndicated (1978) variety series in which Twiggy presents performances by guest rock stars. Produced by Malcolm Gold. See also "Britt Ekland's Juke Box."

The Twilight Zone

Anthology; CBS 10/2/59 to 9/14/62 (30 min)
9/27/63 to 9/18/64 (30 min)
1/3/63 to 9/19/63 (60 min)

Tales of people confronted with the mysterious unexplored regions of the fifth dimension; an area that is everywhere, yet nowhere; the area between what is known and what is beyond understanding—the "Twilight Zone." See also "Time Element."

Host: Rod Serling

Producer: Rod Serling, Buck Houghton, William Froug, Herbert Hirschman

The Twilight Zone

Anthology; CBS 9/27/85 to 4/11/86 (60 min)
6/13/86 to 10/18/86 (60 min)
12/4/86 to 12/18/86 (30 min)

A revised version of the prior title. Eerie tales (most original) of the uncharted dimensions of the mind.

Narrator: Charles Aidman

Producer: Philip DeGuere, Harvey Frand, James Heinz

Twin Time

See "Toni Twin Time."

Two Faces West

Western; 30 min; Syn. 1960

The series, set in the town of Gunnison during the 1860s, relates the adventures of the twin January brothers, Ben, a doctor, and Rick, a trail bum.

Ben and Rick	
January	Charles Bateman
Julie Greer	Joyce Meadows
Stacy	June Blair
Sheriff Maddox	Francis DeSales
Deputy Johnny Evans	Paul Comi

Producer: Matthew Rapf

Two for the Money

Game; 30 min; NBC 9/30/52 to 8/11/53
CBS 8/15/53 to 9/22/56
CBS 3/23/57 to 9/7/57

Three players compete in a series of general knowledge question-and-answer rounds. The highest scoring player competes in a second round where for each correct answer he receives the amount of money he won in round one. In the final round, the player wins the total earnings of rounds one and two for each correct answer.

Host (pilot): Fred Allen

Host (Series): Herb Shriner, Walter O'Keefe, Dennis James, Sam Levenson

Announcer: Dennis James

Producer: Mark Goodson, Bill Todman, Gil Fates

Two in Love

Game; 30 min; CBS 6/19/54 to 9/11/54

Friends and family of newly married or engaged couples appear to answer questions. For each question that is asked, a cash prize is put in a nest egg. Each of the couples must predict (in seconds) the time it will take them to answer a question. The couple who come closest to their predicted time wins the nest egg.

Host: Bert Parks

Two Girls Named Smith

Comedy; 30 min; ABC 1/20/51 to 10/13/51

The misadventures of Babs and Peggy Smith, two small town girls who come to New York to further their careers as fashion models.

Babs Smith	Peggy Ann Garner
	Marcia Henderson
Peggy Smith	Peggy French
Babs's boyfriend	Richard Hayes
Landlady	Adeline Klein

Producer: Richard Lewis

Two Guys from Muck

Comedy Pilot; 30 min; NBC 3/29/82

The misadventures of Louie and Buzz, photo-journalists for "Muck," a cheap, Los Angeles-based weekly magazine whose policy is not only to inform, but give readers what they want—muck.

Louie	Alan Arkin
Buzz	Rick Casorla
Mr. Davis	Graham Jarvis
Sybil Sanders	Gwen Humble
Miss DeMandt	Jill St. John
Mr. Big	Victor Buono
Casey Muir	Larry Storch
Thug	Sid Haig
Birdie Muir	Beverly Sanders

Producer: Lee Rich, Philip Capice

Two Marriages

Drama; 60 min; ABC 4/23/83 to 9/14/83
3/8/84 to 4/26/84

The trials and tribulations of two suburban Iowa couples: Ann and Jim Daley, who are struggling to balance their careers with the responsibility of raising three children (Kim, Scott, Willie), and their neighbors Art and Nancy Armstrong, a married couple with a rocky marriage but a strong common love for their children (Shelby and Eric).

Ann Daley	Karen Carlson
Jim Daley	Tom Mason
Kim Daley	Tiffany Toyoshima
Scott Thompson	C. Thomas Howell
Willie Daley	Ian Fried
Nancy Armstrong	Janet Eilber
Art Armstrong	Michael Murphy
Shelby Armstrong	Louanne
Eric Armstrong	Kirk Cameron
Woody Daley (Jim's father)	John McLiam
Kate (Scott's girlfriend)	Melora Hardin
Jeff Daley (Jim's brother)	Nicholas Hammond

Theme Vocal ("Home Here"): Jerry Fuller

Producer: Philip Capice

The Two of Us

Comedy Pilot; 30 min; CBS 8/29/66

The story of a seven-year-old boy (Chris) who prefers the world of fantasy he created from his mother's book illustrations to that of making real friends.

Elizabeth Williams	Patricia Crowley
Chris Williams	Billy Mumy
Helen	Mary Jane Croft
Roger	Barry Livingston
Captain Gibson	Russ Brown

Producer: Elliott Lewis, Arthur Julian

The Two of Us

Comedy; 30 min; CBS 4/6/81 to 4/27/81
9/15/81 to 8/10/82

Following her divorce, Nan Gallagher, the disorganized host of the New York-based "Mid-Morning Manhattan" TV show, hires Robert Brentwood, a spit-and-polish British butler, to organize her life. Stories relate Brentwood's misadventures as he attempts to care for the untidy Ms. Gallagher and her daughter, Gabrielle.

Robert Brentwood	Peter Cook	Deputy Kestenbaum	Steve Tanner
Nan Gallagher	Mimi Kennedy	Dispatcher Kam	Margie Foster
Gabrielle "Gabby"		Deputy Hamilton	Rene LeVant
Gallagher	Dana Hill	Deputy Bottendott	Brant Van Hoffman
Cubby Royce	Oliver Clark	Deputy Price	Jeff Bannister
Reggie Cavanaugh	Tim Thomerson	Deputy DeVito	Jeff Gallucci
Shirley Havelmeyer	Candice Azzara	Captain Berman	Taylor Lacher
		Sheriff	Peter J. Pitchess

Music: Patrick Williams

Producer: Martin Starger, Charlie Hauck

"240-Robert" Theme: Mike Post, Pete Carpenter

Producer: Rick Rosner, Chuck Bowman

240-Robert

Adventure; 60 min; ABC 9/3/79 to 12/10/79

The search and rescue operations of three L.A. County Sheriff's Emergency Service Department deputies (Dwayne, Morgan, and T.R.) who operate under the code name 240-Robert. See the following title also.

Deputy Dwayne	
Thibideaux	Mark Harmon
Deputy Morgan	
Wainwright	Joanna Cassidy
Deputy T.R.	
Applegate	John Bennett Perry
Deputy C.B. Harris	Lew Saunders
Deputy Roverino	JoeAl Nicassio
Deputy Terry Caster	Thomas Babson
Deputy Kestenbaum	Steve Tanner
Sheriff	Peter J. Pitchess

Music: Mike Post, Pete Carpenter

Producer: Rick Rosner, Richard M. Rosenbloom

240-Robert

Adventure; 60 min; ABC 3/7/81 to 3/21/81

A revised version of the previous title, which relates the exploits of Trap, Sandy, and Brett, the new members of the 240-Robert rescue team.

Deputy T.R.	
Applegate	John Bennett Perry
Deputy Sandy	
Harper	Pamela Hensley
Deputy Brett Cueva	Stephan Burns

Two the Hard Way

Comedy Pilot; 30 min; CBS 8/11/81

The misadventures of Walter Chester and Richard Mallory, the writers of the fictional TV soap opera "Paradise Lost."

Walter Chester	Eugene Roche
Richard Mallory	Fred McCarren
Augusta Sedwell	Mary Jackson
Rodney West	Lyle Waggoner
Veronica Moorehead	Marlyn Mason
Penny	Loyita Chapel

Producer: Bill Brademan, Ed Self

2½ Dads

Comedy Pilot; 60 min; ABC 2/16/86

The story follows the ups and downs of two fathers (Peter, divorced, and Frank, a widower) and a bachelor (Chick) who decide to pool their resources and live together to cut down on expenses.

Peter Seltzer	George Dzundza
Frank Manley	Richard Young
Chick Leoni	Sal Viscuso
Danny Seltzer	Billy Warlock
Dorothy Seltzer	Lenore Kasdorf
Rosie Seltzer	Shana O'Neil
Kathleen Manley	Mary Kohnert
Frank Manley Jr.	Rickey Stout
Arlene	Marissa Mendenhall

Producer: Fred Silverman, Gordon Farr

227

Comedy; 30 min; NBC 9/14/85 (Premiere)

Comic incidents in the life of Mary Jenkins, a housewife and busybody who resides in a tenement at 227 in Washington, D.C.

Mary Jenkins	Marla Gibbs
Lester Jenkins	Hal Williams
Brenda Jenkins	Regina King
Tiffany Jenkins	Kia Goodwin
Rose Holloway	Alaina Reed
Sandra Clark	Jackee Harry
Pearl Shay	Helen Martin
Calvin	Curtis Baldwin
Henry Hurley (Mary's father)	Whitman Mayo
Carolyn Hurley (Mary's mother)	Beah Richards

Producer: Jack Elinson, Dick Bensfield, Perry Grant

Two's Company

Comedy Pilot; 30 min; CBS 5/8/73

The misadventures of Charlie Travis, a running back for the Chicago Cherokees football team. See also "The Living End."

Charlie Travis	John Amos
Diana Travis	Diana Sands
Bullets	Vic Tayback

Producer: Hy Averback

The Tycoon

Comedy; 30 min; ABC 9/15/64 to 9/6/65

Events in the life of Walter Andrews, the 65-year-old head of the Thunder Holding Corporation in Los Angeles.

Walter Andrews	Walter Brennan
Herbert Wilson	Jerome Cowan
Pat Burns	Van Williams
Betty Franklin	Janet Lake
Martha Keane	Patricia McNulty
Tom Keane	George Lindsey
Louise Wilson	Grace Albertson
Una Fields	Monty Margetts

Producer: Danny Thomas, Charles Isaacs

The Tyrees of Capitol Hill

Drama Pilot; 30 min; CBS 4/9/63

The adventures of Andrew Jackson Tyree, the grandson of Andrew Jackson, and his son, Boford, as Senate page boys in Washington, D.C.

Andrew Jackson Tyree	Edgar Buchanan
Boford Tyree	Phil Alford
Senator Guthrie	Lloyd Bridges

U.F.O.

Science Fiction; 60 min; Syn. 1972

As unidentified flying objects become established and are believed to be a threat to the Earth, world governments unite to construct S.H.A.D.O. (Supreme Headquarters, Alien Defense Organization). Stories relate S.H.A.D.O.'s battle against alien invaders as it attempts to discover who they are, where they come from, and what they want.

Cmdr. Edward Stryker	Ed Bishop
Col. Alec Freeman	George Sewell
Lt. Gay Ellis	Gabrielle Drake
Col. Paul Foster	Michael Billington
Lt. Nina Barry	Dolores Mantez
Lt. Joan Harrington	Antoni Ellis
Col. Virginia Lake	Wanda Ventham
Capt. Peter Karlin	Peter Gordeno
Miss Eland	Norma Roland
Douglas Jackson	Valdek Sheybol
Lt. Keith Ford	Keith Alexander
Gen. James Henderson	Grant Taylor
Miss Scott	Louise Pajd
Miss Holland	Lois Maxwell
Lew Waterman	Garry Myers
Moon Base Operator	Andrea Allan
Mark Bradley	Harry Baird
Radio Operator Turner	Patrick Allen

Producer: Reg Hill, Gerry Anderson

The Ugily Family

Comedy Pilot; 30 min; ABC 7/26/80

The story of Sal Ugily (pronounced U-giel-ie), a Global Can Company employee who receives a promotion and moves from New Jersey to southern California where he and his family struggle to adjust to their new surroundings.

Sal Ugily	Al Molinaro
Verna Ugily	Mimi Hines
Susan Ugily	Susan Elliot
Bradley Ugily	Stephen Myers
Tillie Brock	Bella Bruck
Kenny Bing	Lyle Waggoner
Babs Bing	Elaine Joyce
Bambi Bing	Lory Walsh
Jeffrey	Bumper Yothers

Producer: Walter Kempley

The Ugliest Girl in Town

Comedy; 30 min; ABC 9/26/68 to 1/30/69

To help his heartbroken brother Tim forget his girlfriend (Julie, who moved to London) photographer Gene Blair persuades him to pose as a girl for some hippie pictures. When Gene is later commissioned to shoot a layout in London using the same "girl," Tim finds a way to be with Julie and agrees to continue with the masquerade. Stories relate Tim's attempts to lead a dual life: modeling by day as Timmie; and dating Julie by night as Tim.

Tim/Timmie Blair	Peter Kastner
Gene Blair	Gary Marshall
Julie Renfield	Patricia Brake
Mr. Courtney	Nicholas Parsons

Producer: Harry Ackerman

Ukulele Ike

A fifteen minute program of music and songs with Cliff "Ukulele" Ike, singer Beverly Fite and the music of the Slim Jackson Quartet. Produced by Barry Wood and broadcast on CBS in 1950.

Ultra Quiz

Game Pilot; 60 min; NBC 11/10/81 (Part 1)
                               11/17/81 (Part 2)

The program begins in Dodger Stadium where 932 contestants compete in several games that are designed to eliminate all but 84 players. These players compete in a series of contests that are conducted in various cities around the world. When two players remain, they return to the U.S. and compete in the final competition for $100,000.

Host: Dan Rowan, Dick Martin

Co-Host: Jayne Kennedy, Richard Simmons

Producer: Dick Clark, George Paris, Bill Carruthers

Ulysses 31

Cartoon; 30 min; Syn. 4/86

The series, inspired by Homer's "Odyssey," relates the adventures of a futuristic Ulysses as he battles evil throughout the universe in the 31st century. Produced by Jean Chalopin and Yutaka Fujioka.

The Uncle Al Show

Children; 60 min; ABC 10/18/58 to 9/19/59

Music, songs, puppet antics, and adventure stories for children.

Uncle Al	Al Lewis
Cinderella	Janet Green
Captain Windy	Wanda Lewis

Voices/Puppeteer: Larry Smith

Uncle Croc's Block

Children; ABC 9/6/75 to 10/18/75 (60 min)
                    10/25/75 to 2/14/76 (30 min)

A spoof of children's programs as seen through the antics of Uncle Croc, the crocodile-costumed host of "Uncle Croc's Block," a kids' show he hates doing.

Uncle Croc	Charles Nelson Reilly
Basil Bitterbottom	Jonathan Harris
Rabbit Ears	Johnny Silver
	Alfie Wise
Steve Exhaustion, the $6.95 Man	Robert Ridgely
Mr. Mean Jeans	Huntz Hall
Captain Klangaroo	Robert Ridgely

Producer: Mack Bing, Don Christensen, Lou Scheimer, Norm Prescott

The Uncle Floyd Show

Comedy; 30 min; Syn. 6/82

A program of outlandish comedy sketches. Broadcast locally in the New York area from 1/74 to 11/86.

Host: Floyd Vivino

Regulars: Pat Cupo, Scott Gordon, Marc Nathan, Tony Petrillo, Lydia Sue Abrahms, Skip Rooney, Charlie Stoddard (and, as known) Netto, Mugsy, and Weenie

Producer: Floyd Vivino, Mark Chalom

Uncle Johnny Coons

Children; 30 min; CBS 9/4/54 to 12/3/55
NBC 3/3/56 to 12/1/56

Stories, silent films, and sketches that relate good habits to children with ventriloquist Johnny Coons and his dummy George. Produced by James Green.

Uncle Mistletoe and His Adventures

Children; 30 min; Syn. 1952

The lives of the magic little people (puppets) who live on Candy Cane Lane, a magic street in Wonderland where dreams come true.

Cast: Jennifer Holt, Doris Larson, Elmira Roessler, Johnny Coons, Pat Percy, Helen York, Skeets Morton, Sam Singer

Producer: Stefan Hatos, Fred Niles

Uncovered

See "Mark Saber."

Under One Roof

Comedy; 30 min; NBC 3/23/85 to 5/11/85

A revised version of "Spencer," which begins when George Winger, the father, runs off with his 23-year-old bookkeeper and leaves his wife, Doris, and their two children, Spencer and Andrea, to fend for themselves. To fill the void left by George's departure, Doris's parents, Ben and Millie, decide to move in and help raise the children. Stories relate the misadventures that occur as three generations of one family strive to live together under one roof.

Doris Winger	Mimi Kennedy
Spencer Winger	Ross Harris
Andrea Winger	Amy Locane
Ben Sprague	Harold Gould
Millie Sprague	Frances Sternhagen
Wayne Westin	Grant Heslov
Benjamin Beanly	Richard Sanders
Bailey	Dean Cameron
Amy	Dana Anderson
Miss Spier	Beverly Archer
Heidi	Julie Ann Haddock
Kay	Cheryl Anderson
Donna Urnst	Karen Bercovici
Wayne's mother	Beverly Sanders
Wayne's father	Michael Alaimo

Producer: Mort Lachman

Under the Yum Yum Tree

Comedy Pilot; 60 min; NBC 9/2/69

The misadventures of Charlie Procter, an unemployed writer who suddenly finds a wealth of story material when he inherits an apartment building for singles in Los Angeles. The unsold series was to relate incidents in the lives of the tenants as seen through Charlie's eyes.

Charlie Procter	Jack Sheldon
Thelma	Nita Talbot
Mike	Ryan O'Neal
Jennifer Hunnicutt	Leigh Taylor-Young
Mr. Hunnicutt	Harold Gould

Producer: Harry Ackerman, E.W. Swackhamer

Undercurrent

Retitled episodes of "The Web" that ran on CBS from 7/1/55 to 9/23/55.

Underdog

Cartoon; 30 min; NBC 10/3/64 to 9/3/66

Segments: "Underdog" (the exploits of Shoeshine Boy, a humble dog who becomes a daring crime fighter known as Underdog); "The Hunter" (a bloodhound's efforts to apprehend the notorious Fox); "The Go Go Gophers" (two gophers, Ruffled Feathers and Running Bored, attempt to capture an Old West fort guarded over by Col. Kit Coyote).

Underdog	Wally Cox
Sweet Polly	
Purebred	Norma McMillan
Hunter/Kit Coyote	Kenny Delmar
Fox	Ben Stone
Sergeant/Ruffled	
Feathers	Sandy Becker
Running Bored	George S. Irving

The Unexpected

Anthology; 30 min; Syn. 1952

Dramas that depict the plight of people who are trapped in unexpected situations.

Host-Narrator: Herbert Marshall

The Unexplained

Anthology Pilot; 30 min; NBC 7/10/56

The episode for an unsold series of chilling fantasy stories. The pilot tells of a deserted carnival merry-go-round whose forward motion advances age while its reverse motion decreases age. The story itself tells of a disreputable man who uses the carousel to become a boy and commit a robbery—and what happens when he is pursued by two other boys who break the carousel mechanism and jam it into the forward position.

First Boy	Peter Votrian
Second Boy	Barry Froner
Pursued Boy	Whitey Hautt
Man	Leo Gordon
Father	Whit Bissell
Mother	Virginia Christine

Producer: Samuel Goldwyn Jr.

Union Pacific

Adventure; 30 min; Syn. 1958

The saga of the final linking between East and West (Omaha to Cheyenne) of the Union Pacific Railroad as seen through the experiences of Bart McClelland, the operations head (based in Dale, Wyoming).

Bart McClelland	Jeff Morrow
Bill Kincaid	Judd Pratt
Georgia	Susan Cummings

Producer: George M. Cahan

Unit 4

Adventure Pilot; 60 min; CBS 9/29/81

With the growth of terrorist activities, the U.S. government recruits the best commandos from its military forces and divides them into small, anti-terrorist strike forces. The unsold series was to relate the exploits of one such strike force—Unit 4.

Max Catlin	Nick Mancuso
Martin Farnum	Ben Murphy
Zina Brandt	Tori Lysdahl
Deke Thomas	William Allen Young
Jordan Harrower	Keene Curtis
Jimmy Yew	Keye Luke
Tracey Phillips	Dominique Dunne
Liz Phillips	Jane Merrow
Dwight Phillips	Linwood McCarthy

Producer: Philip Saltzman, Cliff Gould

United States

Comedy-Drama; 30 min; NBC 3/11/80 to 4/29/80

Incidents in the day-to-day lives of marrieds Richard and Libby Chapin and their children Dylan and Nicky.

Richard Chapin	Beau Bridges
Libby Chapin	Helen Shaver
Dylan Chapin	Rosie Harris
Nicky Chapin	Justin Dana

Producer: Larry Gelbart

Universal Star Time

A syndicated (1971) series of repeat dramas from "The Bob Hope Chrysler Theatre."

Unk and Andy

Children; 15 min; Syn. 1950

The program attempts to explain facts about wildlife to children via animals drawn from letters of the alphabet. With Jack Kenaston as the host (Uncle Jack) and the voice of the animated Andy Auk. Produced, written, and directed by Jack Kenaston.

The Unknown

Anthology Pilot; 60 min; ABC 5/6/64

A proposed but unsold series of lavish science fiction stories. The pilot, titled "The Form of Things Unknown," tells of Tone Hobart, a man of the future who travels through time. Aired on "The Outer Limits."

Tone Hobart	David McCallum
Andre Pavan	Scott Marlowe
Kassia Paine	Vera Miles
Leonora Edmond	Barbara Rush
Colas	Sir Cedric Hardwicke

Producer: Joseph Stefano

The Untouchables

Crime Drama Pilot; 60 min; CBS 4/20/59 (Part 1) 4/27/59 (Part 2)

The original pilot for the series, which, broadcast on "The Desilu Playhouse," relates Eliot Ness's attempts to break up Al Capone's gang.

Eliot Ness	Robert Stack
Agent Martin Flattery	Bill Williams
Agent William Longfellow	Abel Fernandez
Agent Tony Ligari	Paul Picerni
Al Capone	Neville Brand
Betty Anderson	Patricia Crowley
Brandy LaFrance	Barbara Nichols

Producer: Bert Granet

The Untouchables

Crime Drama; 60 min; ABC 10/15/59 to 9/10/63

The exploits of the Federal Special Squad, an elite team of U.S. Treasury agents known as the Untouchables, as they battle the forces of underworld corruption of Chicago in the 1930s.

Eliot Ness	Robert Stack
Martin Flaherty	Jerry Paris
William Longfellow	Abel Fernandez
Jack Rossman	Steve London
Enrico Rossi	Nicholas Georgiade
Cam Allison	Anthony George
Lee Hobson	Paul Picerni
Mobster Frank Nitti	Bruce Gordon
Mobster Al Capone	Neville Brand
Mobster George "Bugs" Moran	Lloyd Nolan
Mobster Dutch Schultz	Lawrence Dobkin
Mobster Vincent "Mad Dog" Coll	Clu Gulager

Narrator: Walter Winchell

"The Untouchables" Theme: Nelson Riddle

Producer: Jerry Thorpe, Leonard Freeman, Howard Hoffman, Alan A. Armer, Alvin Cooperman, Fred Freiberger, Charles Russell

Up Front

A syndicated (6/86) series of one on one celebrity interviews with Greg Jackson. Produced by Dolores Danska.

Up to Paar

Game; 30 min; NBC 7/28/52 to 9/26/52

Object: For players to answer questions based on current newspaper stories.

Host: Jack Paar

Uptown Saturday Night

Comedy Pilot; 30 min; NBC 6/28/79

The misadventures of two Harlem go-getters (Wardell and Monroe).

Wardell Washington	Cleavon Little
Monroe Hoover	Adam Wade
Sarah Washington	Starletta DuPois
Greecy Dan	Julius Harris
Janitor	Don Bexley

Producer: Eric Cohen

U.S. Border Patrol

Drama; 30 min; Syn. 1958

Dramas based on the Department of Justice files concerning the activities of the U.S. Border Patrol.

Deputy Chief Don Jagger	Richard Webb

Producer: Sam Gallu

U.S. Marshal

Crime Drama; 30 min; Syn. 1958

A spin-off from "The Sheriff of Cochise," which relates the exploits of Frank Morgan, a U.S. Marshal working in Arizona.

Frank Morgan	John Bromfield
Deputy Blake	Robert Brubaker
Deputy Tom Ferguson	James Griffith

Producer: John Auer, Mort Briskin

The U.S. of Archie

Cartoon; 30 min; CBS 9/7/74 to 9/5/76

The series features the Archie Gang as great American heroes in stories that detail their achievements throughout history.

Archie Andrews/ Reggie Mantle	Dallas McKennon
Betty Cooper/ Veronica Lodge	Jane Webb
Jughead Jones	Howard Morris

Producer: Norm Prescott, Lou Scheimer

U.S. Royal Showcase

Variety; 30 min; NBC 1/13/52 to 6/29/52

Performances by singers, comedians, and undiscovered professional talent. Sponsored by the U.S. Rubber Company.

Host: George Abbott, Jack Carson

Producer: George Abbott

The U.S. Steel Hour

Anthology; 60 min; ABC 10/27/53 to 6/21/55
CBS 7/6/55 to 6/12/63

A series of quality dramatic productions featuring well-known performers and talented writers and directors. Produced by Norman Felton, David Alexander, George Kondolf.

Used Cars

Comedy Pilot; 30 min; CBS 5/15/84

An unsold series about Barbara Fuchs, the owner of the New Deal Used Car lot in Las Vegas, and Roy L. Fuchs, her uncle, the owner of Roy Fuchs Auto Emporium, and his devious attempts to buy Barbara out and acquire a monopoly on used car lots in the area.

Barbara Fuchs	Deborah Harmon
Roy L. Fuchs	Pat Corley
Rudy Russo	Fred McCarren
Jeff Kirkwood	Clayton Landey
Jim	Frank McRae
Mickey	Michael Talbott

Theme Vocal ("Used Cars"): Roy Clark

Producer: Barbara Corday, Bob Gale

V

Science Fiction; 60 min; NBC 10/26/84 to 3/22/85

Desperately in need of food and water, aliens from the planet Sirius begin an invasion of Earth. At first the aliens (The Visitors) are thought to be friendly and have come here to seek our help in producing a chemical they need to survive. As their true natures become known (evil reptilian lizards who falsely resemble humans), small bands of resistance fighters begin to form. Stories relate their battle against the Visitors, in particular the beautiful alien leader, Diana.

Stories especially feature Mike Donovan, a TV newsman and leader of a Los Angeles resistance group; Juliette (Julie) Parrish, a doctor with Science Frontiers, who helps to develop Red Dust, a biological germ that is capable of destroying the Visitors; Willie, an alien who joins Donovan's resistance fighters; and Elizabeth Maxwell, the Star Child, the daughter of an Earth mother (Robin) and an alien (Brian, played by Peter Nelson), who grows rapidly from infant to child; then becomes a woman through metamorphis. It is Elizabeth, possessing amazing abilities, who becomes the hope of the world. Adapted from two ministeries: "V" (5/1 & 5/2/83) and "V: The Final Battle" (5/6 to 5/8/84).

Mike Donovan
Julie Parrish
Diana*
Lydia*
Elizabeth Maxwell

Robin Maxwell
William*
Ham Tyler
Nathan Bates
Elias Taylor
Kyle Bates
Sean Donovan
Chiang
Chris Farber
Charles*
John Langley
Lt. James*
Martin and Phillip*
Thelma*
Freedom Network
  Newscaster

Marc Singer
Faye Grant
Jane Badler
June Chadwick
Jenny Beck
Jennifer Cooke
Blair Tefkin
Robert Englund
Michael Ironside
Lane Smith
Michael Wright
Jeff Yagher
Nicky Katt
Aki Aleong
Mickey Jones
Duncan Regehr
Bruce Davison
Judson Scott
Frank Ashmore
Marilyn Jones

Howard K. Smith

Producer: Daniel H. Blatt, Robert Singer

*Aliens.

VTV

Variety; 60 min; Syn. 1/87

Celebrity interviews, audience participation, and a shopping club (Value Television) wherein viewers can purchase merchandise at greatly reduced prices via a toll-free number and their credit card.

Hosts: Alex Trebek, Meredith MacRae, Richard Simmons

Announcer: Bob Braun

Producer: E.V. DiMassa Jr.

The Val Doonican Show

Variety; 60 min; ABC 6/5/71 to 8/14/71

A summer program of music, songs, and comedy sketches.

Host: Val Doonican

Regulars: Bob Todd, Bernard Cribbins, The Norman Maen Dancers, The Mike Sammes Singers

Announcer: Paul Griffith

Orchestra: Jack Parnell, Kenny Woods

Producer: Bill Hitchcock

Valentine's Day

Comedy; 30 min; ABC 9/18/64 to 9/10/65

The life and times of New York Playboy Valentine Farrow, the nonfiction editor for Brackett and Dunstall, a Park Avenue publishing house.

Valentine Farrow   Anthony Franciosa
Rockwell "Rocky"
  Sin   Jack Soo
Libby Freeman   Janet Waldo
O.D. Dunstall   Jerry Hausner
Molly   Mimi Dillard
Mr. Fipple   Eddie Quillan
Muriel Farrow (Val's
  mother)   Helen Traubel

"Valentine's Day" Theme: Jeff Alexander

Producer: Hal Kanter

Valentino

Women; 30 min; ABC 12/18/52 to 3/5/53

Barry Valentino as host of a program of soft music, poetry readings, and romantic monologues.

Valerie

Comedy; 30 min; NBC 3/1/86 (Premiere)

The story of Valerie Hogan, a working mother of three boys whose husband, Michael, an airline pilot, is away most of the time. Her efforts to raise her sons, run a household, and hold down a job (manager of Forman-Lydell Antiques) is the focal point of each episode.

Valerie Hogan	Valerie Harper
Michael Hogan	Josh Taylor
David Hogan	Jason Bateman
Willie Hogan	Danny Ponce
Mark Hogan	Jeremy Licht
Barbara Goodwin	Christine Ebersole
Annie	Judith Kahan
Patty Poole	Edie McClurg
Michael's Sister	
Caroline	Francine Tacker
Valerie's Aunt	
Josephine	Nan Martin

Theme Vocal ("Together Through the Years"): Roberta Flack

Producer: Charlie Hauck, Robert L. Boyett, Charles Miller

Valerie's Family: The Hogans

Comedy; 30 min; NBC 9/21/87 (Premiere)

A revised version of "Valerie"*. Six months after the tragic death of Valerie Hogan in a traffic accident, Michael Hogan arranges for his sister, Sandy, recently divorced and living in Minneapolis, to move in with him and help him raise his kids. Stories relate Sandy's misadventures as she helps Mike raise three mischievous boys (David, Willie, and Mark).

Sandy Hogan	Sandy Duncan
Michael Hogan	Josh Taylor
David Hogan	Jason Bateman
Willie Hogan	Danny Ponce
Mark Hogan	Jeremy Licht
Patty Poole	Edie McClurg
Peter Poole	Willard Scott
Rich	Tom Hodges
Bert	Steve Whitting

Producer: Judy Pioli, Chip Keyes, Doug Keyes

*A salary dispute between Valerie Harper and the producers caused Miss Harper to quit. Although she agreed to return to work, she was unexpectedly fired by the producers and replaced by Sandy Duncan.

The Valiant Years

Documentary; 30 min; ABC 11/27/60 to 6/11/61

The life of Sir Winston Churchill is recalled through interviews, stills, and films. Also known as "Winston Churchill."

Host-Narrator: Gary Merrill

Music: Richard Rodgers

Producer: Ben Feiner Jr., Robert D. Grafe

Valley of the Dinosaurs

Cartoon; 30 min; CBS 9/7/74 to 9/4/76

While exploring an uncharted river canyon in Africa, the 20th-century Butler family is engulfed by a whirlpool, propelled through an underground cavern, and transported to the prehistoric era, where they befriend their cave family counterparts. Stories relate the efforts of both families to work in harmony and ensure their survival.

John Butler	Mike Road
Kim Butler	Shannon Farnon
Katie Butler	Margene Fudenna
Greg Butler	Jackie Earle Haley
Gorak	Alan Oppenheimer
Gera	Joan Gardner
Tanya	Melanie Baker
Lock	Stacey Bertheau

Producer: William Hanna, Joseph Barbera

Van Camp's Little Show

See "John Conte's Little Show."

Van Dyke and Company

Variety; 60 min; NBC 9/20/76 to 12/30/76

A weekly hour of music and comedy. The pilot episode, with guests Mary Tyler Moore, Carl Reiner, Ken Mars, Lynne Lipton, Richard Kiel, and Tina Turner, aired on 10/30/75.

Host: Dick Van Dyke

Regulars: Marilyn Sokol, Lois January, Pat Proft, Andy Kaufman, Mickey Rose, Al Bloomfield, Bob Einstein, Chuck McCann, Barry Van Dyke, Michael Wheeler, Tom Kelly

Orchestra: Lex DeAvezedo

Producer: Byron Paul, Allan Blye, Chris Bearde

Vanity Fair

Women; 30 min; CBS 10/12/48 to 11/2/51

Interviews, beauty tips and advice, and other topics of interest to women.

Hostess: Robin Chandler, Dorothy Doan

Regulars: The Lily Dache Models

Announcer: Tony Marvin

Orchestra: Johnny Green

Producer: John Cazabon, Gil Fates, Frances Buss

Vaudeo Varieties

Variety; 60 min; ABC 1/14/49 to 4/15/49

Eddie Hubbard as host of a live program from Chicago that features different entertainment acts each week.

Vaudeville

Variety; 60 min; Syn. 1975

The program features performances by vaudeville comedians and a recreation of vaudeville routines by new talent discoveries.

Card Girl: Donna Jean Young

Orchestra: George Wyle

Producer: Burt Rosen, Mort Green

Vaudeville Show

A four-week ABC interim show (12/9/53 to 12/30/53) in which guests recreate vaudeville routines.

The Vaughn Monroe Show

Variety; 30 min; CBS 10/10/50 to 7/3/51

A program of music and song with band-leader Vaughn Monroe and regulars Shaye Cogan, Ada Lynne, Henry Davis, Olga Suarey, Ziggy Latent, and The Moon Maidens. Produced by Don Appel.

The Vaughn Monroe Show

Variety; 15 min; NBC 8/31/54 to 9/30/54
6/28/55 to 9/8/55

A weekly program of music and songs.

Host: Vaughn Monroe

Regulars: The Satisfiers, The Tunesmiths

Orchestra: Richard Hayman, Richard Maltby

Producer: Bill Stuart

Vegas

Crime Drama; 60 min; ABC 9/20/78 to 9/16/81

The exploits of Dan Tanna, a macho private detective working out of Las Vegas, Nevada.

Dan Tanna	Robert Urich
Bea Travis	Phyllis Davis
Angie Turner	Judy Landers
Robert "Binzer" Borseau	Bart Braverman
Lt. Dave Nelson	Greg Morris
Sgt. Bella Archer	Naomi Stevens
Philip "Slick" Roth	Tony Curtis
Harlan Two Leaf	Will Sampson
Julie Travis	Heather Hobbs
Diamond Jim	Victor Buono
Burt M. Cohen	Himself
Various Roles	Heather Menzies

"Vegas" theme by Dominic Frontiere

Producer: Aaron Spelling, Douglas S. Cramer, E. Duke Vincent

The Veil

Anthology; 30 min; Syn. 1958

Dramas based on incredible but true phenomena.

Host-Performer: Boris Karloff

Producer: Hal Roach Jr., Frank P. Bibas

Venice Medical

Comedy Pilot; 30 min; ABC 7/29/83

The antics of the doctors and nurses attached to the Venice (California) Medical Clinic.

Dr. Pete Marcus	Michael Brandon
Nurse Ruth	
O'Malley	Barbara Rhoades
Dr. Becky Warfield	Clara Perryman
Dr. Randy Young	Brian Keeler
Nurse Abby McGee	D.D. Howard
Mrs. Baker	Carol Arthur
Gwen Marcus	Elaine Giftos

Producer: Aaron Spelling, Douglas S. Cramer, E. Duke Vincent

The Verdict Is Yours

Drama; 30 min; CBS 7/3/58 to 9/22/58
           (evening run)
           9/2/57 to 9/28/62
           (daytime run)

Dramas based on actual courtroom cases. Guests appear as judges, witnesses, and plaintiffs, practicing attorneys portray defense counselors.

Court Reporter: Jim McKay, Bill Stout

Versatile Varieties

Variety; 30 min; NBC 8/26/49 to 1/19/51
           CBS 1/28/51 to 7/22/51
           ABC 9/21/51 to 12/14/51

Originally, performances by guest acts; later, a children's program of songs, stories, and performances by juvenile talent. Sponsored by Bonny Maid products.

Host: George Givot (1949), Harold Barry (1949–50), Bob Russell (1950–51), Lady Iris Mountbatten (1951).

Regulars: Anne Francis, Janis Paige, Eva Marie Saint, Edie Adams, The Delmars

Orchestra: Jerry Jerome, Bernie Sands, Mark Towers

Producer: Charles Basch, Frances Scott

The Vic Damone Show

Variety; 30 min; CBS 7/2/56 to 9/24/56
           7/3/57 to 9/11/57

A weekly program of music and songs.

Host: Vic Damone

Regulars: Peggy King, The Spellbinders

Announcer: Rex Marshall, Johnny Olsen

Orchestra: Tutti Camarata, Bert Farber

Producer: Don Appel

The Vic Damone Show

Variety; 60 min; NBC 7/8/71 to 8/19/71

Vic Damone as host of a program of music and songs with Carol Lawrence and Gail Martin, and the orchestra of Les Brown. Produced by Greg Garrison.

The Victor Borge Show

Variety; 30 min; NBC 2/3/51 to 6/30/51

A program of music and comedy with Victor Borge, the comical wizard of the keyboard. With the orchestra of Phil Ingallis. Produced by Perry Lafferty.

Victory at Sea

Documentary; 30 min; NBC 10/16/52 to 4/19/53

Films that detail the U.S. Naval operations during World War II.

Narrator: Leonard Graves

Music: Richard Rodgers

Producer: Henry Salomon

The Video Game

Game; 30 min; Syn. 10/84

Object: For contestants to play various video arcade games in return for prizes.

Host: Greg Winfield

Assistant: Karen Lea

Announcer: Chris Creasis

Producer: James Caruso, Mavis Arthur

Video Village

Game; 30 min; CBS 7/1/60 to 9/23/60 (evening run)
           7/11/60 to 6/15/62 (daytime run)
           9/30/61 to 6/16/62 (children's version, "Video Village Jr.")

Two players compete in a game that is played on a large board with numerous squares of instructions (e.g., "Move ahead one space," "Go to jail"). Players moves are determined by the roll of two dice and the first person to reach the finish line is the winner.

Host (The Mayor): Jack Narz, Monty Hall

Assistant: Eileen Burton, Joanne Copeland

Announcer: Kenny Williams

Producer: Merrill Heatter, Bob Quigley

Village Barn

Variety; 30 min; NBC 5/17/48 to 5/29/50

Music and songs from the Village Barn, a nightclub in New York's Greenwich Village.

Host: Piute Pete

Regulars: Dick Thomas, Charlie Althoff, Ray Forrest, Dick Dudley, Bob Stanton, Zebe Carver

Music: Pappy Howard and His Tumbleweed Gang, Bill Long and His Ranch Girls

Producer: Hal Keith

The Vin Scully Show

Variety; 30 min; CBS 1/15/73 to 3/23/73

Music, songs, and celebrity interviews.

Host: Vin Scully

Announcer: Harry Blackstone Jr.

Orchestra: H.B. Barnum

Producer: Paul W. Keyes, Armand Grant

The Vincent Lopez Show

Variety; 30 min; CBS 10/13/56 to 4/27/57

A program of music and songs with bandleader Vincent Lopez and regulars Judy Lynn, Teddy Norman, Eddie O'Connor, Danny Davis, Johnny Messner, and Johnny Amorosa.

The Virginia Graham Show

Virginia Graham as host of a daily, syndicated (1970) series of talk and interviews. Music by the Ellie Frankel Quintet and the Jimmy Rowles Quartet. Produced by Forrest Fraser.

The Virginian

Western Pilot; 30 min; NBC 7/6/58

The original pilot for "The Virginian." In an attempt to acquire help for his ranch (bookkeeping and new methods of caring for stock), Judge Henry sends to Virginia for the son of an old friend. When the unnamed man arrives in Wyoming, he becomes involved in a plot to stop the judge from building a railroad spur to his ranch. When the Virginian exposes the ranch foreman (Ben) as the culprit, he becomes Judge Henry's new foreman. The unsold version was to relate the Virginian's efforts to help Judge Henry turn an unsettled region into a booming town.

The Virginian	James Drury
Judge Henry	Robert Barton
Ben Stocker	Andrew Duggan
Dora	Jeanette Nolan
Salem	Dan Blocker
Dawes	Robert Gist
Steven Henry	Stephen Joyce

Producer: Winston O'Keefe

The Virginian

Western; 90 min; NBC 9/19/62 to 9/9/70

Events in the shaping of Wyoming during the 1880s as seen through the eyes of the Virginian, the foreman of the Shiloh Ranch in Medicine Bow. See also the prior title and "The Men from Shiloh."

The Virginian	James Drury
Judge Henry Garth	Lee J. Cobb
Morgan Starr	John Dehner
John Grainger	Charles Bickford
Clay Grainger	John McIntire
Trampas	Doug McClure
Molly Wood	Pippa Scott
Betsy Garth	Roberta Shore
Steve Hill	Gary Clarke
Deputy Emmett Ryker	Clu Gulager
Randy Garth	Randy Boone
Belden	L.Q. Jones
Jennifer Garth	Diane Roter
Sheriff Mark Abbott	Ross Elliott
Elizabeth Grainger	Sara Lane
Stacy Grainger	Don Quine
Holly Grainger	Jeanette Nolan
David Sutton	David Hartman

Jim Horn   Tim Matheson
Sheriff Brannon   Harlan Warde
Gene   Jean Peloquin

"The Virginian" Theme: Percy Faith

Producer: Leslie Stevens, Norman Mac-
Dowell, Herbert Hirschman, James
McAdams, Howard Christie, Roy Huggins,
Richard Irving, Winston Miller

The Vise

Drama; 30 min; ABC 10/1/54 to 12/16/55 (anthology version)
12/23/55 to 10/12/56
("Mark Saber" ver-
sion)

Originally, a series of dramas that depict the
plight of people who are caught in a web of
their own misdeeds; later, the adventures of
Mark Saber, a former Scotland Yard inspector turned private detective. Host (Anthology
Version): Ron Rondell.

Mark Saber   Donald Gray

Producer: Edward J. and Harry Lee Danziger

Visual Girl

Advice; 30 min; Syn. 1971

The program, geared to teenage girls, presents ideas and suggestions concerning exercise, fashion, makeup, and skin care. Hosted
by Ron Russell and Lois Rose.

Viva Valdez

Comedy; 30 min; ABC 5/13/76 to 9/6/76

The trials and tribulations of the Valdezes, a
Mexican-American family living in east Los
Angeles, as they strive to maintain their tradi-
tional values in a rapidly changing world.

Sophie Valdez   Carmen Zapata
Luis Valdez   Rodolfo Hoyos
Connie Valdez   Lisa Mordente
Victor Valdez   James Victor
Ernesto Valdez   Nelson D. Cuevas
Pepe Valdez   Claudio Martinez
Jerry Ramerez   Jorge Cervera Jr.

Producer: Stan Jacobson, Bernard Rothman

Voice of Firestone

Music; 60 min; NBC 9/5/49 to 6/7/54
ABC 6/14/54 to 6/16/63

A series of classical and semiclassical concerts sponsored by the Firestone Tire and
Rubber Company. The program actually began on November 29, 1943 as "Voice of Firestone Televues" wherein ten-to-fifteen minute
documentaries were shown.

Host-Narrator: John Daly

Vocalists: The Howard Barlow Chorus

Announcer: Hugh James

Orchestra: Howard Barlow

Producer: Charles Polachek, Herbert Swope
Jr., Frederick Heider

Voltron—Defender of the Universe

Cartoon; 30 min; Syn. 9/84

The exploits of Voltron, a super-powered
robot and member of the Space Explorers, as
he defends outer space from the evils of King
Zarcer, ruler of the planet of Doom, who
seeks to control the universe.

Voices: Jack Angel, Michael Bell, Peter
Cullen, Neil Ross, B.J. Ward, Lennie
Weinrib

Producer: Peter Keefe

Volume One

Anthology; 30 min; ABC 6/16/49 to 7/21/49

Eerie stories of horror and suspense. The title
refers to the titles given to each story (e.g.,
the first episode is "Volume One, Number
One." The second episode is "Volume One,
Number Two"). Originally titled "Quiet
Please."

Host-Narrator: Ernest Chappel

Announcer: Ed Michael

Producer: Wyllis Cooper

Voyage to the Bottom of the Sea

Adventure; 60 min; ABC 9/14/64 to 9/15/68

The experiences of the men and officers of the
atomic-powered submarine "Seaview," as

they explore and battle the sinister elements of the ocean floor.

Adm. Harriman Nelson	Richard Basehart
Cmdr. Lee Crane	David Hedison
CPO Curley Jones	Henry Kulky
Chief Francis Sharkey	Terry Becker
Cmdr. Chip Morton	Bob Dowdell
Crewman Ski Kowalski	Del Moore
Crewman Sparks	Arch Whiting
Doc	Richard Bull
	Wright King
	Wayne Heffley
Crewman Patterson	Paul Trinka
Crewman Stu Riley	Allan Hunt
Crewman Malone	Mark Slade

"Voyage to the Bottom of the Sea" Theme: Paul Sawtell

Producer: Irwin Allen

Voyagers!

Fantasy; 60 min; NBC 10/3/82 to 3/27/83
6/12/83 to 8/7/83

While on a mission to 1492 to help Christopher Columbus, Voyager Phineas Bogg (a traveler in time who helps history along), "falls to earth" in 1982 when his Omni (compass-like traveling device) malfunctions. When Bogg finds himself on a building ledge, he breaks a window and enters the bedroom of an 11-year-old orphan (Jeffrey). When Jeffrey's dog grabs Bogg's guidebook, a struggle ensues and Jeffrey falls backward out the window. In an attempt to save the boy, Bogg jumps out the window, touches Jeffrey, and activates his Omni*. The two are transported to another time (1450 B.C. Egypt) and safety. With Bogg unable to return Jeffrey to his time (his Omni had only been programmed up to 1970), the two become partners. Stories relate their exploits as they monitor history through Bogg's Omni, seeking to return the flashing red lights (indicating history is wrong) to the everything is normal green light.

Phineas Bogg	Jon-Erik Hexum
Jeffrey Jones	Meeno Peluce
Olivia Dunn (a Voyager)	Tracy Brooks Swope
Drake (renegade Voyager)	Stephen Liska
Amy Jones (Jeffrey's great grandmother)	Anne Lockhart
Steven Jones (Jeffrey's great grandfather)	John O'Connell

"Voyagers" theme: Jerrold Immel

Producer: James D. Parriott, Alan J. Levi, Robert Janes

*When Bogg touches someone, they become part of the Omni's transmission field. The Omni is engraved with the words "Time Waits For No Man."

The Wackiest Ship in the Army

Adventure; 60 min; NBC 9/19/65 to 9/4/66

The World War II adventures of the USS "Kiwi", a two-mastered 1871 schooner that has been incorporated by U.S. Army Intelligence to pose as a Swedish vessel and roam the South Pacific to observe Japanese movements, assist allies, and inform officials of enemy strategy. Based on the feature film.

Maj. Simon Butcher	Jack Warden
Lt. Richard "Rip" Riddle	Gary Collins
Chief Willie Miller	Mike Kellin
Machinist's Mate Seymour Trivers	Fred Smoot
Charles Tyler (cook)	Don Penny
Radioman Patrick Hollis	Mark Slade
Crewman Nagurski	Rudy Solari
Crewman Finch	Duke Hobbie
Gen. Cross	Bill Zuckert
Adm. Vincent Beckett	Charles Irving

Producer: Herbert Hirschman

Wacko

Comedy; 30 min; CBS 9/17/77 to 11/12/77

A series of unrelated, outlandish comedy and musical skits geared to children.

Cast: Julie McWhirter, Bo Kaprall, Charles Flescher, Millicent Crisp, Doug Cox, Bob Comfort, Rick Kellard

Orchestra: Stu Gardner

Producer: Chris Bearde, Bob Wood

The Wacky Races

Cartoon; 30 min; CBS 9/14/68 to 9/5/70

The saga of a cross-country auto race in which the evil Dick Dastardly schemes to secure the title of "The World's Wackiest Racer."

Dick Dastardly	Paul Winchell
Penelope Pitstop	Janet Waldo
Muttley	Don Messick
Red Max/Rufus Rufcut/Rock and Gravel Slag/Peter Perfect	Daws Butler
Luke and Blubber Bear/The General	John Stephenson
The Ant Hill Mob	Mel Blanc

Narrator: Dave Willock

Producer: William Hanna, Joseph Barbera

The Wacky World of Jonathan Winters

Comedy; 30 min; Syn. 1972

Unrehearsed comedy sketches that utilize Jonathan Winter's greatest gift: his ability to improvise.

Host: Jonathan Winters

Regulars: Marian Mercer, Mary Gregory, Ronnie Graham, The Soul Sisters

Orchestra: Van Alexander

Producer: Hal Pareta

Wagon Train

Western; 60 & 90 min; NBC 9/18/57 to 9/12/62
ABC 9/19/62 to 9/5/65

The saga of a wagon train's journey from the midwest to California in the 1800s. Stories relate incidents in the lives of the passengers who have booked passage.

Wagon Master Seth Adams	Ward Bond
Wagon Master Chris Hale	John McIntire
Trail Scout Flint McCullough	Robert Horton
Charlie Wooster (cook)	Frank McGrath
Trail Scout Bill Hawks	Terry Wilson
Trail Scout Cooper Smith	Robert Fuller
Trail Scout Duke Shannon	Denny Miller
Barnaby West (Hale's ward)	Michael Burns
Kate Crowley (Hale's romantic interest)	Barbara Stanwyck

Producer: Howard Christie, Richard Lewis

Wait Til Your Father Gets Home

Cartoon; 30 min; Syn. 1972

The story of Harry and Irma Boyle, an old-fashioned couple struggling to close the generation gap that exists between them and their three modern and progressive children (Alice, Chet, and Jaimie).

Harry Boyle	Tom Bosley
Irma Boyle	Joan Gerber
Alice Boyle	Kristina Holland
Chet Boyle	David Hayward
Jaimie Boyle	Jackie Haley
Ralph (neighbor)	Jack Burns

Producer: William Hanna, Joseph Barbera

Wake Up

Children; 30 min; CBS 9/28/81 to 1/15/82

Songs, sketches, and musical numbers geared for children. The briefly revised title for "Captain Kangaroo."

Host: Bob Keeshan

Picture Pages Host: Bill Cosby

Regulars: Lumpy Brannum, Cosmo F. Allegretti, Carolyn Migini

Producer: Bob Keeshan, Richard Sloa, Joel Kosofky

Waldo

Comedy Pilot; 30 min; CBS 9/19/60

The story of Rashford Wallingford III, an anthropologist who is attempting to civilize a talented but headstrong chimpanzee named Waldo.

Rashford Wallington	
III	Gil Stratton
His father	Emory Parnell
His aunt	Eleanor Odley
His girlfriend	Virginia Wells
Cop	Frank Jenks
Judge	Robert Griffin

Producer: Rudy E. Abel

Wally Gator

Cartoon; 5 min; Syn. 1962

The adventures of a bon vivant alligator-about-town.

Wally Gator	Daws Butler
Twiddles	Don Messick

Producer: William Hanna, Joseph Barbera

Wally Western

Children; 12½ min; Syn. 1962

Edited theatrical western stories hosted by the animated Wally Western and his pal, Skeets.

Wally's Workshop

A syndicated (1972) program of home repair and advice with Wally and Natalie Bruner. Announcing by Johnny Olsen.

A Walk in the Night

Adventure Pilot; 60 min; CBS 7/15/68

The story of James Van Ducci, the head of the Great Lakes Interstate Bureau, a Chicago-based investigative organization. The pilot relates Van Ducci's efforts to find a Swedish sailor who jumped ship and is unaware that he is carrying a live bomb.

James Van Ducci	Carroll O'Connor
Owen Kerr	Andrew Duggan
William Smith	Michael Murphey
Ellie Van Ducci	Jacqueline Betton
Granstrom	Gunnar Hellstrom
Linde	Albert Paulsen
Kathryn	Linda Wallenberg
Erickson	Karl Swenson

Producer: Robert Altman, Raymond Wagner

Walkin' Walter

Comedy Pilot; 30 min; ABC 6/13/77

The story of Walkin' Walter, a free-spirited ex-vaudevillian songwriter who moves in with and freeloads off of his long-lost brother's wife and her two foster children.

Walkin' Walter	Spo-De-Odee
Roseabell "Mama"	
Hoxie	Madge Sinclair
Booker Brown	Christoff St. John
Jackie Onassis	
Orlando	Denise Marcia
Loud Leon	David Yanez
Wendell Henderson	Jack Dodson
Rev. Tucker Tooley	Theodore Wilson

Producer: Garry Marshall, Thomas L. Miller, Edward K. Milkis

Walking Tall

Crime Drama; 60 min; NBC 1/17/81 to 6/13/81

The exploits of Buford Pusser, the heroic sheriff of NcNeal County, Tennessee, as he battles lawlessness with his own brand of justice: fearless determination and a large club.

Sheriff Buford	
Pusser	Bo Svenson
Carl Pusser	Walter Barnes
Dwana Pusser	Heather McAdam
Michael Pusser	Rad Daly
Deputy Joan Litton	Courtney Pledger
Deputy Aaron	
Fairfax	Harold Sylvester
Deputy Grady	
Spooner	Jeff Lester
Judge Hines	Ivan Bonar

Theme Vocal ("Walking Tall"): Victor Sondor

Producer: David Gerber, Mel Swope

Walt Disney

A series of programs designed for family viewing (nature films, cartoons, dramas, comedies, Disney theatrical films, and documentaries). Hosted by Walt Disney from 1954 to 1966 and broadcast as: "Disneyland" (ABC, 10/27/54 to 12/28/55); "Walt Disney Presents" (ABC, 1/4/56 to 5/28/61), "Walt Disney's Wonderful World of Color (NBC, 9/24/61 to 4/15/79), "Disney's Wonderful World" (NBC, 9/9/79 to 9/7/80), "Disney's Wonderful World" (CBS, 9/14/80 to 5/1/82), and "The Disney Sunday Movie" (ABC, 2/16/86 to   ).

W*A*L*T*E*R

Comedy Pilot; 30 min; CBS 7/17/84

A proposed spin-off from "M*A*S*H*." Following his release from the Army in 1954, Walter "Radar" O'Reilly, returns to his home in Iowa with hopes of working the family farm. When he is unable to make the farm pay for itself, Walter departs for St. Louis, where he becomes a police officer. The unsold series was to relate Walter's experiences as a rookie cop.

Walter O'Reilly	Gary Burghoff
Off. Wendell Mikeljohn	Ray Buktenica
Sgt. Sowell	Noble Willingham
Victoria Peterson	Victoria Jackson
Sgt. Bigelow	Lyman Ward
Judith Crane	Sarah Abrell
Bubbles Sincere	Victoria Carroll
Dixie Devoe	June Berry
Interviewer	Clete Roberts

Music: Patrick Williams

Producer: Bob Schiller, Bob Weiskopf, Michael Zinberg

Walter of the Jungle

Comedy Pilot; 30 min; Unaired (Produced for CBS in 1967)

An unsold and unaired spoof of "Tarzan" which relates the not-so-heroic exploits of Walter, a clumsy, mother-dominated jungle king.

Walter	Jonathan Daly
Mama	Rose Marie
Sidney	Nipsey Russell
Reginald Stanhope	Bernard Fox
Gillian Stanhope	Vikki Harrington

Producer: Joe Connelly

Walter Cronkite's Universe

Magazine; 30 min; CBS 7/12/80 to 8/2/80
6/15/82 to 9/4/82

A technical look at the complexities of modern-day life.

Host: Walter Cronkite

Producer: Jonathan Ward, Brian Ellis

Walter Fortune

Drama; 30 min; Syn. 4/50

The story of Walter Fortune, a man with a shady past who opens a pawn shop in San Francisco. Episodes relate his efforts to help the troubled people he meets.

Walter Fortune	Howard DaSilva

Producer: Howard DaSilva, Bernard Girard, Joe Landon

The Walter Winchell File

Anthology; 30 min; ABC 10/2/57 to 3/28/58

Dramas based on the stories covered by newspaper columnist Walter Winchell (who serves as host) when he covered the police beat for the New York "Daily Mirror."

Walter Winchell	Himself
Lt. Michaels	John Larch
Lt. Hauser	Harold J. Stone
Lt. Rizzo	Ed Nelson

The Walter Winchell Show

Variety; 30 min; NBC 10/5/56 to 3/4/57

Performances by top name entertainers.

Host: Walter Winchell

Orchestra: Carl Hoff

Producer: Alan Handley

The Waltons

Drama; 60 min; CBS 9/14/72 to 8/20/81

The series, set in Jefferson County, Virginia, during the 1930s and 40s, depicts events in the lives of the Waltons, a poor rural family and operators of a sawmill. Stories are seen through the sentimental eyes of John-Boy, the eldest son and hopeful writer whose fond memories of his youth extoll the simple virtues of chastity, honesty, thrift, family virtue, and love.

John Walton	Ralph Waite
	Andrew Duggan*
Olivia Walton	Michael Learned
	Patricia Neal*
Grandpa Zeb Walton	Will Geer
	Edgar Bergen*
Grandma Esther Walton	Ellen Corby
John-Boy Walton	Richard Thomas
	Robert Wightman
Mary Ellen Walton	Judy Norton-Taylor
Jason Walton	Jon Walmsley
Erin Walton	Mary Elizabeth McDonough
Ben Walton	Eric Scott
Elizabeth Walton	Kami Cotler
Jim-Bob Walton	David S. Harper
Dr. Curtis Willard	Tom Bower
	Scott Hylands
Cindy Brunson	Leslie Winston
John Curtis Walton Willard	Marshall & Michael Reed
Ike Godsey	Joe Conley
Corabeth Godsey	Ronnie Claire Edwards
Aimee Godsey	Rachel Longaker
Mamie Baldwin	Helen Kleeb
	Josephine Hutchinson*
Emily Baldwin	Mary Jackson
	Dorothy Stickorey*
Rev. Matthew Fordwicke	John Ritter
Rosemary Fordwicke	Mariclare Costello
Sheriff Ep Bridges	John Crawford
Yancy Tucker	Robert Donner
Sissy Tucker	Cissy Williams
Flossie Brimmer	Nora Marlowe
Vernon Rutley	George Tobias
Rose Burton	Peggy Rea
Serena	Martha Nix
Jeffrey	Keith Mitchell
Patsy Brimmer	Eileen McDonough
Fannie Tatum	Sheila Allen
Prof. Parks	Paul Jenkins
J.D. Pickett	Lewis Arquette
Daisy Garner	Deirdre Lenihan
G.W. Haines	David Doremus
Verdie Foster	Lynn Hamilton
Harley Foster	Hal Williams
Rev. Andrew March	Sean Roche

Narrator: Earl Hamner Jr.

Producer: Lee Rich, Earl Hamner Jr., Robert L. Jacks, Andy White

*TV Movie roles ("The Homecoming" 12/19/71). Three TV Movies were also produced for NBC: "A Day for Thanks on Walton's Mountain" (11/22/82), "Mother's Day on Walton's Mountain" (5/9/82), and "Wedding on Walton's Mountain" (2/22/82).

Wanted

Documentary; 30 min; CBS 10/20/55 to 1/5/56

Walter McGraw as the host and narrator of dramas based on incidents in the lives of criminals wanted by the FBI.

Wanted: Dead or Alive

Western; 30 min; CBS 9/6/58 to 9/14/61

The exploits of Josh Randall, an 1870s bounty hunter who tracks wanted men and women for their offered rewards. Though filmed in black and white, the series has been computer colored for syndication beginning in 1987. See also "The Bounty Man."

Josh Randall	Steve McQueen
Jason Nichols	Wright King

Various Roles: Gloria Talbot, Warren Oates

"Wanted: Dead or Alive" Theme Song: Rudy Schrager

Producer: John Robinson, Ed Adamson, Harry Harris

Warner Brothers Presents

Drama; 60 min; ABC 9/13/55 to 9/10/57

The title for four series, which see: "Casablanca" (1955 version), "Cheyenne," "Conflict," and "King's Row." Hosted by Gig Young.

The Warren Hull Show

Interview; 30 min; CBS 1/12/49 to 6/3/49
           2/27/50 to 6/26/50

Interviews with people from all walks of life with Warren Hull. Produced by Ken Redford.

Washington Square

Variety; 60 min; NBC 10/21/56 to 6/13/57

Music, songs, dances, and comedy sketches set against the background of New York's Greenwich Village.

Host: Ray Bolger

Regulars: Kay Armen, Rusty Draper, Arnold Stang, Elaine Stritch, The Bil and Cora Baird Puppets, The Danny Daniels Singers

Orchestra: Charles Sanford

Producer: William Bacher

Washingtoon

Comedy; 30 min; SHO 10/15/84 (Premiere)

A satirization on the personalities and politics of Capitol Hill as seen through the adventures of Bob Forehead, a TV announcer turned political candidate seeking a congressional seat.

Bob Forehead	Thomas Calloway
Ginger Forehead	Anne Lockhart
Sally Forehead	Christina Applegate
Robert Forehead	Jason Naylor
Gerard Oxboggle	Stanley Kamel

Producer: Michael Lepiner, Marcia Lewis, Kenneth Kaufman

Watch Me

Human Interest; 30 min; Syn. 1980

Robert King as the host of a program that focuses on ordinary people as they appear on camera and display some hidden talent. Produced by Bob Schwartz and John Horvath.

Waterfront

Adventure; 30 min; Syn. 1954

The adventures of John Herrick, captain of the tugboat "Cheryl Ann."

Capt. John Herrick	Preston Foster
May Herrick	Lois Moran
Jim Herrick	Harry Lauter
Nancy Herrick	Dian Fauntelle
Teddy Herrick	Billy Chapin
Capt. Dan Cord	Ramon Vallo
Tip Hubbard	Pinky Tomlin
Capt. Lars Swenson	Walter Sande
Billy Slocum	Willie Best

"Waterfront" Theme Song: Alexander Laszlo

Producer: Guy V. Thayer, Arthur Pierson

The Waverly Wonders

Comedy; 30 min; NBC 9/22/78 to 10/6/78

The story of Joe Casey, a washed-up professional football player who now coaches basketball and teaches history at Waverly High School.

Joe Casey	Joe Namath
Linda Harris	Gwynne Gilford
George Benton	Ben Piazza
Connie Rafkin	Kim Lankford
Tony Faguzzi	Joshua Grenrock
Hatsy	Tierre Turner
John Pate	Charles Bloom

Producer: Lee Rich, Marc Merson

Way of the World

Anthology; 15 min; NBC 1/3/55 to 10/7/55

Adaptations of stories that appear in leading women's magazines. Hosted by Gloria Lucas (who appears as Linda Porter).

Way Out

Anthology; 30 min; CBS 3/31/61 to 7/14/61

Roald Dahl as the host of a series of supernatural-based tales. Produced by David Susskind and Jacqueline Babbin.

Way Out Games

Game; 25 min; CBS 9/11/76 to 9/3/77

Two three-member teams of junior high school students compete in various contests of skill, seeking to complete stunts in the quickest time.

Host: Sonny Fox

Assistant: Mark Smith

Producer: Jack Barry, Dan Enright

Wayne and Shuster Take an Affectionate Look At . . .

Documentary; 60 min; CBS 6/17/66 to 7/29/66

The comic movie trends of the past and the lives of individual comedians are recalled through film clips.

Hosts: Johnny Wayne and Frank Shuster

Producer: Gil Rodin, Bob Jarvis

The Wayne King Show

Variety; 30 min; NBC 9/29/49 to 6/26/52

A live program of music and songs from Chicago.

Host: Wayne King

Regulars: Gloria Van, Nancy Evans, Barbara Becker, Jackie Jones, Harry Hall, The Don Large Chorus

Orchestra: Wayne King

Producer: Harry Christian, Ken Craig

We Dare You!

Comedy Pilot; 30 min; ABC 4/5/82

The program recruits people to play practical jokes on unsuspecting friends and family members.

Host: Terrence McGovern, Jon Bauman

Guests: Paul Williams, Pat McCormick

Producer: George Tompkins, Tom Walsh, Michael Hill

We Got It Made

Comedy; 30 min; NBC 9/8/83 to 3/10/84

The misadventures of Mickey McKenzie, the beautiful live-in maid to two New York bachelors (David and Jay) who share a messy apartment. Focal point of the series is the efforts of David and Jay to convince their girlfriends (Claudia and Beth) that they share a platonic relationship with Mickey.

Mickey McKenzie	Teri Copley
David Tucker	Matt McCoy
Jay Bostwick	Tom Villard
Claudia	Stepfanie Kramer
Beth Sorenson	Bonnie Urseth
Arlene (Mickey's mother)	Elaine Joyce
Rick (David's brother)	David Knell

Theme Song ("We Got It Made"): Tom Wells

Producer: Fred Silverman, Gordon and Lynn Farr

We Got It Made

Comedy; 30 min; Syn. 9/87

A revised version of the NBC series of the same title which continues to depict the misadventures of Mickey MacKenzie, the beautiful live-in maid to two sloppy New York bachelors (Jay and David).

Mickey MacKenzie	Teri Copley
Jay Bostwick	Tom Villard
David Tucker	John Hillner
Max Papavasilios Sr.	Ron Karabatsos
Max Papavasilios Jr.	Lance Wilson-White

Producer: Gordon Farr, Fred Silverman

We Take Your Word

Game; 30 min; CBS 4/1/50 to 6/1/51

Object: For a celebrity panel to supply definitions of words submitted by home viewers. Words that stump the panel award the sender a cash prize.

Host: John Daly, John K.M. McCaffery

Panelists: Ilka Chase, Cornelia Otis Skinner, Abe Burrows

Weapons Man

Crime Drama Pilot; 60 min; ABC 4/8/63

The exploits of Mark Vickers, a weapons expert who assists the police in unusual cases in which a weapon was used to commit a crime. Aired on "Stoney Burke."

Mark Vickers	J.D. Cannon
Matt Elder	Henry Silva
Margo Tecas	Pilar Seurat

Producer: Leslie Stevens

The Web

Anthology; 30 min; CBS 7/24/50 to 9/27/54

Dramas of people who are suddenly trapped in perilous situations.

Host-Narrator: Jonathan Drake

Producer: Franklin Heller, Mark Goodson, Bill Todman

The Web

Anthology; 30 min; NBC 7/7/57 to 10/6/57

Stories of people who attempt to overcome problems that were caused by their own doing. Produced by Charles H. Schner and Vincent McConnor.

W.E.B.

Drama; 60 min; NBC 9/13/78 to 10/5/78

A behind-the-scenes look at the world of TV as seen through the experiences of Ellen Cunningham, an up-and-coming programming executive with the Trans-Atlantic Broadcasting Company in New York City. (In the 2-hour pilot episode, the network is Trans-American Broadcasting.)

Ellen Cunningham	Pamela Bellwood
Jack Kiley	Alex Cord
Dan Costello	Andrew Prine
Gus Dunlap	Richard Basehart
Harry Brooks	John Colicos
	Stephen McNally
Walter Matthews	Howard Witt
Harvey Pearlstein	Lee Wilkof
Christine Nichols	Tisch Raye
Kevin	Peter Coffield

Producer: Lin Bolen, Christopher Morgan

Webster

Comedy; 30 min; ABC 9/16/83 (Premiere)

When his friends, Travis and Gert Long, are killed in a car crash, sportscaster George Papadopolis becomes the legal guardian of their son (and his godchild) Webster. Stories relate Webster's misadventures as he attempts to adjust to a new life; and George and his wife, Katherine's efforts to adjust to parenthood.

Katherine Papadopolis	Susan Clark
George Papadopolis	Alex Karris
Webster Long	Emmanuel Lewis
Cassie Parker	Cathryn Damon
Bill Parker	Eugene Roche
Maggie Parker	Jennifer Holmes
Jerry Silver	Henry Polic II
Philip Long	Ben Vereen
Maurice	Richard Karron
Harry	Billy Sands
Peanut Butter	Art LaFleur
George Papadopolis Sr.	Jack Kruschen
Melanie	Heather O'Rourke
Kathy	Tiffany Brissette
Curtis	Bumper Robinson
Emily Calder-Young	Neva Patterson
Ms. Oliver	Sheila DeWindt
Samantha	Pila Gray
Katherine's Aunt Charlotte	Gwen Verdon

Producer: Stu Silver, William P. D'Angelo, Bruce Johnson, Steve Sunshine, Madeline Sunshine

Wedding Day

Human Interest Pilot; 30 min; NBC 6/8/81 to 6/12/81

A five-part pilot for a potential series of daily weddings (wherein real life couples are married on the air).

Hosts: Mary Ann Mobley, Huell Howser

Producer: Deanne Barkley, Bill Anderson

Wedding Party

Game; 30 min; ABC 4/1/68 to 7/1/68

Three husband and wife couples compete. The wives are isolated backstage while the husbands select three prizes from items that appear on stage. The husbands are then isolated and the wives brought on stage to select three items. The couples are then united on stage and receive as their prizes any items that both selected.

Host: Al Hamel

Producer: Al Stark, Roy Kammerman, Fred Tatashore

Wednesday Night Out

Comedy Pilot; 30 min; NBC 4/24/72

The story, set in the town of Bryer Crest, focuses on three suburban couples and a divorcee who take turns inviting one another to theme parties on Wednesday evenings.

Jim Warren	Jim Hutton
Tess Warren	Kathleen Nolan
Paula (the divorcee)	Gloria DeHaven
Frank Bonio	Pat Harrington Jr.
Anna Maria Bonio	Brenda Benet
David Goldberg	Greg Mullavey
Sandy Goldberg	Marcia Strassman

Producer: Douglas S. Cramer, Larry Rosen

Weekend

Comedy Pilot; 30 min; NBC 9/9/67

The adventures of a group of high school kids who flock to the beach in southern California each weekend for two days of fun and sun.

Eunice	Lori Martin
Randy	Tim Matthieson (Tim Matheson)
Eldon	Rick Kellman
Norm	Tony Dow

Producer: Norman Henry

Welcome Aboard

Variety; 30 min; NBC 10/3/48 to 2/20/49

A live program of music and song set against the background of a cruise ship, that features top-name singers and comedians as guest hosts.

Regulars: The Four Step Brothers

Orchestra: Russ Morgan

Producer: Vic McLeod

Welcome Back, Kotter

Comedy; 30 min; ABC 9/9/75 to 8/3/79

Ten years after he graduates from Brooklyn's James Buchanan High School, Gabe Kotter returns to teach Special Guidance Remedial Academics to a group of incorrigible students known as "Sweathogs." Stories relate his efforts to teach the students, who are very much like the way he was when he attended the school.

Gabe Kotter	Gabriel Kaplan
Julie Kotter	Marcia Strassman
Vice Principal Michael Woodman	John Sylvester White
Voice of Principal John Lazarus	James Komack
Vinnie Barbarino	John Travolta
Juan Epstein	Robert Hegyes
Frederick "Boom Boom" Washington	Lawrence-Hilton Jacobs
Arnold Horshack	Ron Palillo
Rosalie "Hotsie" Totzi	Debralee Scott
Vernajean Williams	Vernee Watson
Angie Graboski	Melonie Haller
Carvelli	Charles Fleischer
Beau DeLabarre	Stephen Shortridge
Wilbur Murray	Bob Harcum
Bambi Foster	Susan Lanier
Jean Tremaine	Della Reese
Judy Borden	Helaine Lembeck
Todd Ludlow	Dennis Bowen
Arnold's mother	Ellen Travolta
Sally (Vinnie's girlfriend)	Linda McCullough
Mo Epstein (Juan's uncle)	Herb Edelman
Mary Johnson (Arnold's girlfriend)	Irene Arranga
Jenny Henson (Julie's sister)	Susan Pratt
Carmine (Juan's sister)	Lisa Mordente

Theme Vocal ("Welcome Back"): John B. Sebastian

Producer: James Komack, Ed Simmons, Nick Arnold, George Yanok

Welcome to Paradise

Adventure Pilot; 60 min; CBS 6/12/84

The exploits of three adventurers (Andy, Felicity, and Bo) as they roam the South Pacific in their boat, the "Paradise."

Andy Coles	Woody Brown
Felicity Ryan	Kelbe Nugent
Bo Wallace	Jerry Dinome
Henderson	Norman Forsey
Hunemoa	Carmen Heta
Koro	James Cross

Music: Mike Post, Pete Carpenter

Producer: Stirling Silliphant, Joel Rogosin

Welcome to Washington

See "The Claudette Colbert Show."

Welcome Travelers

Interview; 30 min; NBC 9/8/52 to 5/2/54
               CBS   7/5/54   to
               10/21/55

Travelers, met at bus, plane, and railroad terminals, are invited to the studio where they relate their experiences and impressions of Chicago.

Hosts: Tony Bartlett, Bob Cunningham

Announcer: William T. Lazar

Producer: Tom Hicks, Charles Powers, Don Meier

We'll Get By

Comedy; 30 min; CBS 3/6/75 to 5/30/75

Events in the lives of the Platt family: George, a lawyer; his wife, Liz; and their three bright children, Michael, Andrea, and Kenny.

George Platt	Paul Sorvino
Liz Platt	Mitzi Hoag
Michael "Muff"	
Platt	Jerry Houser
Andrea Platt	Devon Scott
Kenny Platt	Willie Aames
Liz's father	Henry Jones

Producer: Marc Merson, Alan Alda

We'll Take Manhattan

Comedy Pilot; 30 min; CBS 9/3/68

Just as tycoon Harrison Conroy is to begin construction on a New York Skyscraper, Chief Irontail, a 149-year-old Indian and the last of the Manhattan Tribe, lays claim to the property, declaring that it is legally his. Through Lucas Greystone, Irontail's attorney, it is discovered that over 100 years ago the original buyer failed to pay the chief for the property and it has since reverted back to him. The unsold series was to focus on Conroy's attempts to evict the chief and construct Conroy Towers.

Lucas Greystone	Dwayne Hickman
Chief Irontail	Ben Blue
Eagle Eye	Allan Melvin
Laughing Brook	Leslie Perkins
Harrison Conroy	Walter Woolf King

Producer: Larry Markes, Michael Morris

Wendy and Me

Comedy; 30 min; ABC 9/14/64 to 9/6/65

The marital misadventures of the Conways: Jeff, an airline pilot, and his beautiful but scatterbrained wife, Wendy.

George Burns	
(landlord)	Himself
Wendy Conway	Connie Stevens
Jeff Conway	Ron Harper
Danny Adams	James Callahan
Mr. Bundy	J. Pat O'Malley
Catherine	Robyn Grace
Mr. Norton	Bartlett Robinson
Mrs. Norton	Jane Morgan
Jeff's Aunt Harriet	Sheila Bromley

"Wendy and Me" Theme Song: Ervin Drake

Producer: Herm Saunders, George Burns

The Wendy Barrie Show

See "Through Wendy's Window."

Wendy Hooper—U.S. Army

Comedy Pilot; 30 min; NBC 8/14/81

Hoping to further her career as a country and western singer, a pretty but naive Alabama girl (Wendy Hooper) joins the Army, believing that the communications center will help her. Stories relate Wendy's misadventures when the truth finally dawns on her and she strives to do her best as a private at Fort Waco.

Pvt. Wendy Hooper	Wendy Holcombe
Sgt. Michael Bruno	Michael Pataki
Pvt. Diane Simpson	VanNessa Clarke
Pvt. Theresa Pelligrini	Carol Ann Susi
Col. Alfred Hubik	Dana Elcar
Mrs. Hubik	Helen Page Camp
Bruno's girlfriend	Kathy Shea

Music: Earle Hagen

Producer: Aaron Ruben, Gene Marcione

We're Dancin'

Music; 30 min; Syn. 3/83

A teenage audience dances to the hits of guest performers.

Host: Townsend Coleman

Producer: Syd Vinnedge, Tony Scotti, Ron Kantor

We're Movin'

Magazine; 30 min; Syn. 11/81

The program spotlights the usual and unusual activities of ordinary people (basically geared to children).

Host: Scott Baio, Willie Aames

Producer: Nancy Hamilton, Jim Crum

We're Puttin' on the Ritz

Comedy Pilot; 60 min; CBS 7/26/86

While working for John Barry, a never-seen, recluse millionaire, Max Montana, his chauffeur, finds a discarded black tie party invitation and convinces Barry's secretary, Mickey Kline, to attend the charity affair with him. There, they pretend to be Max and Mickey Sterling, a wealthy brother and sister. Later, when Max and Mickey expose the charity affair as the front for a bunco operation, they become the hit of society and the most sought after guests. The unsold series was to relate their misadventures as they put on the ritz.

Mickey Kline	Leah Ayres
Max Montana	Matt McCoy
Mr. Mao	Kim Chan
Mr. Duvall	George Martin
Thomas	John Bedford-Lloyd
Alberta Livingstone	Rosalyn Landor
Dolly Chambers	Jane Hoffman
Jean Paul Lumiere	Philippe Benichou

Producer: Merrill Grant, Alan Wagner

Werewolf

Thriller; 30 min; FOX 7/11/87 (Premiere)

While working on the fishing boat of Captain Janos Skorzeny, Ted Nichols is bitten by a werewolf (Janos) and cursed to become a murderous creature by the light of the full moon. Hoping to end his curse, Ted approaches his friend, Eric, tells him what has happened, and gives him a gun loaded with silver bullets. A disbelieving Eric witnesses Ted's transformation; but before he is able to do anything, he is attacked and bitten by Ted. Now, himself cursed, Eric begins a quest to find and kill Janos (to sever the original bloodline and end the curse). Stories relate Eric's search, helping people along the way, and his efforts to avoid Alamo Joe, a bounty hunter who has seen his transformation and now seeks to kill him.

Eric Cord	John J. York
Alamo Joe Rogan	Lance LeGault
Janos Skorzeny	Chuck Connors
Ted (first episode)	Raphael Sbarge

Producer: Frank Lupo, John Ashley

Wesley

Comedy; 30 min; CBS 5/8/49 to 8/30/49

The misadventures of Wesley Eggleston, a mischievous 12-year-old boy living in a small, rural community.

Wesley Eggleston	Donald Devlin
	Johnny Stewart
Wesley's father	Frankie Thomas Sr.
Wesley's mother	Mona Thomas
Elizabeth Eggleston	Joy Reese
Alvin	Bill Nevard
Wesley's grandfather	Joseph Sweeney
Elizabeth's boyfriend	Jack Ayres

Producer: Worthington Miner

The West Point Story

Anthology; 30 min; CBS 10/5/56 to 9/27/57
                    ABC 10/8/57 to 7/1/58

Dramas based on incidents in the training periods of West Point Academy cadets.

Cadet Charles C.
  Thompson   Donald May
Various Roles   Clint Eastwood

Theme Song ("The West Point March"): Philip Egner, Alfred Parham

Producer: Maurice Unger, James Sheldon, Leon Benson, Henry Kessler

Western Hour

Chuck Connors as host of a syndicated (1963) program of repeat episodes of "The Rifleman" and "Zane Grey Theatre."

Western Star Theatre

A syndicated (1963) series of repeat episodes from "Death Valley Days" with Rory Calhoun as host.

The Westerner

Western Pilot; 30 min; Syn. 11/53

A not widely syndicated pilot about a sheriff in a small California town.

Cast: James Craig (as the Sheriff), Kathleen Crowley, Sandy Saunders, William Phipps, and James Millican

Writer: Sloan Nibley

Director: Robert G. Walker

The Westerner

Western; 30 min; NBC 9/30/60 to 12/30/60

The exploits of Dave Blassingame, a wandering cowboy of the 1890s who helps people in trouble. See also "The Losers" and "Winchester."

Dave Blassingame   Brian Keith
Burgundy Smith   John Dehner

Producer: Hal Hudson, Sam Peckinpah

The Westerners

Anthology; 30 min; Syn. 1965

The syndicated title for selected episodes of "Black Saddle," "Johnny Ringo," "The Law of the Plainsman," "The Westerner," and "Zane Grey Theatre." Hosted by Keenan Wynn. The program uses the "Black Saddle" theme as its opening theme.

Westinghouse Desilu Playhouse

See "Desilu Playhouse."

Westinghouse Playhouse

See "Yes Yes Nanette."

Westinghouse Summer Theatre

Anthology; 30 min; CBS 6/18/51 to 9/10/51
                              6/23/52 to 9/15/52

A Summer series of dramatic productions under the sponsorship of the Westinghouse Corporation. Produced by Jerry Danzig and William Spier.

Westside Medical

Drama; 60 min; ABC 3/15/77 to 4/14/77

The personal and professional lives of the physicians at California's Westside Memorial Hospital.

Dr. Sam Lanagan   James Sloyan
Dr. Janet Cottrell   Linda Carlson
Dr. Phil Parker   Ernest Thompson
Carrie   Alice Nunn

Producer: Martin Starger, Alan A. Armer

The Westwind

Adventure; 30 min; NBC 9/6/75 to 9/4/76

The adventures of Steve Andrews, an underwater photographer, and his wife, Kate, a marine biologist, as they explore the various Hawaiian islands on their yacht, the Westwind.

Steve Andrews						Van Williams
Kate Andrews						Niki Dantine
Robin Andrews						Kimberly Beck
Tom Andrews						Steve Burns

Producer: William P. D'Angelo, Norm Prescott, Lou Scheimer

We've Got Each Other

Comedy; 30 min; CBS 10/1/77 to 1/7/78

The misadventures of the Hibbards: Judy, a not-so-attractive, lanky photographer's assistant, and her husband, Stuart, a copywriter for bizarre devices advertised in the Herman Gutman Mail Order Catalogue.

Judy Hibbard						Beverly Archer
Stuart Hibbard						Oliver Clark
Damon Jerome						Tom Poston
Dee Dee Baldwin					Joan Van Ark
Donna							Ren Woods
Ken Redford						Martin Kove
Belinda Baldwin					Jennifer McAllister
Judy's Mother
 McCree							Ann Doran
Anitra							Anitra Ford
Reba							Reba Waters

Theme Vocal ("We've Got Each Other"): Nino Candido

Producer: Tom Patchett, Jay Tarses, Jack Burns

Whacked Out

Comedy Pilot; 30 min; NBC 9/26/81

The antics of the staff of "Whacked Out," a far-out news magazine published by the Van Gordon Gordon Communications Corporation.

Jack Ferguson					Desi Arnaz Jr.
Trish Van Gordon
 Gordon						Melinda Culea
Sarah							Susanna Dalton
Hini							Richard Dimitri
Bud Dugen						Howard Witt
Simon							Dana Carvey
Mr. Van Gordon
 Gordon						Hansford Rowe
Louis							Tom Villard
Mrs. Dumont						Helene Winston

Theme Vocal ("Whacked Out"): Ronald M. Cohan

Producer: Nick Arnold, Eric Cohen

What a Country

Comedy; 30 min; Syn. 9/86

The misadventures of a group of foreign students studying for their citizenship tests in a Los Angeles high school. Based on the British series "Mind Your Manners."

Taylor Brown
 (teacher)						Garrett M. Brown
Principal Courtney					Gail Strickland
Principal F. Jerry
 "Bud" McPherson					Don Knotts
Dani (owner of the
 hangout, Dani's
 Diner)						Elaine Giftos
Nikolai Rostopovitz					Yakov Smirnoff
Maria Lopez						Ada Maris
Yung Hee						Leila Hee Olsen
Laslo Garbo						George Murdock
Victor Ortega						Julian Reges
Robert Moboto						Harry Waters Jr.
Ali							Vijay Amritraj

Theme Vocal ("I Want to Be an American"): Richard DeBenedictis

Producer: Martin Ripps, Eric Cohen, Lenny Ripps

What Do You Have in Common?

Game; 30 min; CBS 7/1/54 to 9/23/54

Object: For three specially selected players, who each possess something in common (but are unknown to each other) to discover what the common denominator is.

Host: Ralph Story

What Happened?

Game; 30 min; Syn. 1952

A person, who performed some unique act for which he received newspaper headlines appears. A panel of celebrities must determine what he did via a series of indirect question-and-answer rounds.

Host: Ben Grauer

Panelists: Lisa Ferraday, Maureen Stapleton, Roger Price, Frank Gallop

What Have You Got to Lose?

Game; 30 min; ABC 5/25/53 to 8/7/53

Object: For players to question the host and determine the identity of white-elephant objects that have been submitted by home viewers.

Host: John Reed King

What Really Happened to the Class of '65?

Anthology; 60 min; NBC 12/8/77 to 7/27/78

Dramas that update the lives of the 1965 graduating class of the fictitious Bret Harte High School in Los Angeles. Stories open with a commentary by Sam Ashley, a '65 grad who now teaches at the school, as he recalls his fellow classmates. The program then chronicles the life of a particular grad from 1965 to 1977.

Sam Ashley   Tony Bill

Producer: Richard Irving, Rick Husky, Jack Laird, Ron Satlof

What Will They Think of Next?

Comedy; 30 min; NBC 9/18/48 to 10/9/48

Inventors of clever gadgets appear and demonstrate their creations to a panel of three comedians who, in turn, appraise it. Inventors appear with the hope of interesting a manufacturer in their product.

Host: Ed Herlihy

Panelists: Arthur Q. Bryan, Janet Graham, Harry Hirsh

Producer: Lawrence Schwab

Whatever Happened to Dobie Gillis?

Comedy Pilot; 30 min; CBS 5/10/77

An update of "Dobie Gillis," which reunites the original cast in an unsold pilot that was to relate events in the life of Dobie, now married to Zelda, the father of a teenage son (George) and partners with his father (Herbert) in an expanded Gillis Grocery Store. The story finds Maynard, now an entrepreneur, returning to help Dobie celebrate his 40th birthday.

Dobie Gillis	Dwayne Hickman
Maynard G. Krebs	Bob Denver
Herbert T. Gillis	Frank Faylen
Zelda Gillis	Sheila James
George Gillis	Steven Paul
Lucky	Lorenzo Lamas
Mrs. Tucker	Susan Davis
Mrs. Lazlo	Alice Backes
Henshaw	Wynn Irwin

Producer: James Komack, Paul Mason

What's Going On?

Game; 30 min; CBS 7/22/54 to 12/26/54

Two three-member teams compete: The Insiders and The Outsiders. The Outsiders are brought to a remote location and asked to perform certain activities. Through a series of question-and-answer probe rounds with the host, The Insiders have to discover where the other team is and what they are doing.

Host: Lee Bowman

Regulars: Kitty Carlisle, Jayne Meadows, Susan Oakland, Hy Gardner, Gene Raymond

Announcer: Jimmy Blaine

What's Happened to Elaine?

Comedy Pilot; 30 min; Unaired; Produced in 1973

The story of a deceased wife (Elaine) who comes back to earth as a ghost to help her husband (Richard) raise their young son (Nicky).

Elaine	Michele Carey
Richard	Richard Mulligan
Nicky	Larry Wilson
Mr. Wilson	Richard Stahl
Wilson's secretary	Shirley Mitchell

Producer: Neil T. Maffeo

What's Happening!!

Comedy; 30 min; ABC 8/5/76 to 8/26/76
11/13/76 to 4/28/79

The antics of three black teenagers: Roger "Raj" Thomas, Dwayne Clemens, and Freddie "Rerun" Stubbs. See also "What's Happening Now!!"

Roger Thomas	Ernest Thomas
Dwayne Clemens	Haywood Nelson
Freddie Stubbs	Fred Berry
Mabel Thomas	Mabel King
Dee Thomas	Danielle Spencer
Bill Thomas	Thalmus Rasulala
Lee Thomas	Lee Chamberlain
Shirley Wilson	Shirley Hemphill
Rob (owner of Rob's Place)	Earl Billings
Martin (school paper reporter)	Bryan O'Dell
Donna (Roger's sister)	Chip Fields
Ike (Donna's husband)	Nathaniel Taylor
Larry Clemens (Dwayne's father)	Greg Morris

Music: Henry Mancini

Producer: Saul Turteltaub, Bernie Orenstein, Bud Yorkin, William S. Bickley, Michael Warren

What's Happening Now!!

Comedy; 30 min; Syn. 9/85

A continuation of the prior title which updates the lives of Roger (Raj), Dwayne, and Rerun, three high school friends who parted company after graduation. The new version begins with Roger and his beautiful wife (Nadine) returning to live in his former home (his mother has since remarried and moved to Arizona). Soon after, he meets Dwayne, now in computers, and Rerun, a salesman for K Doe's Used Cars. When Roger discovers that Rob's Place, their former hangout, has been shut down, he becomes partners with Shirley (the former waitress) and together they re-open the diner. Stories relate the misadventures that befall Roger, Nadine, Dwayne, Rerun, and Shirley.

Roger Thomas	Ernest Thomas
Nadine Thomas	Anne-Marie Johnson
Dwayne Clemens	Haywood Nelson
Freddie "Rerun" Stubbs	Fred Berry
Shirley Wilson	Shirley Hemphill
Dee Thomas (Roger's sister)	Danielle Spencer
Yvonne Hudson (Nadine's mother)	Lillian Lehman
Carolyn (orphan adopted by Roger & Nadine)	Reina King

Producer: Jay Morarity, Mike Mulligan

What's Hot, What's Not

Magazine; 30 min; Syn. 10/85

The series, aimed at women, reports on current trends.

Host: Fred Willard, Melanie Chartoff

Co-Host: Ken Minyard

Producer: Bill Hillier, E.V. DiMassa Jr.

What's in a Word

Game; 30 min; ABC 7/22/54 to 9/9/54

A contestant presents a single rhyme to the host (e.g., "Red Bed"). Through one-word clues provided by the host, a celebrity panel has to identify it. For each clue that is used, the player receives $5.

Host: Mike Wallace, Clifton Fadiman

Panelists: Audrey Meadows, Faye Emerson, Carl Reiner, Jim Moran

Producer: Peter Arnell

What's It all About World?

Variety; 60 min; ABC 2/6/69 to 5/1/69

Music, songs, and comedy sketches that satirize everyday life.

Host: Dean Jones

Regulars: Dick Clair, Jenna McMahon, Byan Johnson, Gerri Granger, Scoey Mitchlll, Maureen Arthur, Ron Price, Dennis Allen, The Kevin Carlisle Three

Announcer: Roger Carroll

Orchestra: Denny Vaughn

Producer: Saul Ilson, Ernest Chambers

What's It For?

Game; 30 min; NBC 10/12/57 to 1/4/58

Object: For a celebrity panel to identify the purposes of thingamajigs registered by the U.S. Patent Office since 1800.

Host: Hal March

Panelists: Hans Conried, Betsy Palmer, Cornelia Otis Skinner, Abe Burrows

Producer: Ed Jurist

What's It Worth?

Human Interest; 30 min;
   CBS 5/21/48 to 3/28/49
   DuMont 10/21/52 to 10/11/53

A panel of experts appraise the paintings and objects d'art that are brought to the show each week by their owners.

Host: Gil Fates, Nelson Case, Bill Wendell

Appraiser: Sigmund Rothschild

Producer: Frances Buss

What's My Line?

Game; 30 min; CBS 2/16/50 to 9/3/67

Object: for a celebrity panel to question a guest and discover the nature of his occupation.

Host: John Daly

Panelists: Arlene Francis, Dorothy Kilgallen, Bennett Cerf, Fred Allen, Steve Allen, Hal Block, Harold Hoffman, Louis Untermeyer

Announcer: John Briggs, Johnny Olsen

What's My Line?

Game; 30 min; Syn. 1968

A revised version of the prior title, which see for format.

Host: Wally Bruner, Larry Blyden

Panelists: Arlene Francis, Soupy Sales, Jack Cassidy, Kaye Ballard, Anita Gillette, Gene Rayburn, Alan Alda, Nancy Dussault, Joanna Barnes, Bennett Cerf, Bert Convy

Announcer: Johnny Olsen, Chet Gould

Producer: Gil Fates, Lloyd Gross

What's New Mr. Magoo?

Cartoon; 30 min; CBS 9/10/77 to 9/2/78

The adventures of the nearsighted Quincy Magoo and his equally nearsighted dog, McBarker.

Quincy Magoo   Jim Backus
McBarker   Frank Welker

Producer: David DePatie, Friz Freleng

What's On

Magazine Pilot; 30 min; Syn. 4/86

An in-depth analysis of TV programs, specials, and telefilms.

Hostess: Pat Collins

Critics: Tom Curley, Rick Brown

Producer: Alan Lubell, Gary Cohen, Jeff Scott

What's the Story?

Game; 30 min; DuMont 9/11/51 to 9/23/55

Object: For a panel of journalists to identify famous news events from sketches that are performed on stage.

Host: Walter Raney, Walter Kiernan, Al Capp, John K.M. McCaffery

Panelists: Jimmy Cannon, Harriet Van Horne, Robert Sullivan

Producer: Gil Fates, David Lowe

What's This Song?

Game; 30 min; NBC 10/26/64 to 9/24/65

Object: For players to identify song titles from brief musical selections. Additional points can be won if a player can sing the opening four bars.

Host: Wink Martindale

Orchestra: Bobby Hammack

Producer: Stuart W. Phelps

What's Up?

Comedy Pilot; 30 min; NBC 8/26/71

A satirization of the contemporary scene via sketches, interviews, and newsreel footage.

Host: Jackie Cooper

Guests: John Ritter, Tom Bosley, Marian Mercer, Phil Leeds, Lee H. Montgomery, Bill Zuckert

Producer: Ed Weinberger

What's Up Doc

Comedy Pilot; 30 min; ABC 5/27/78

The romantic misadventures of Howard Bannister, a professor of music at the Claunch Polytechnic Institute, and Judy Maxwell, a student who falls madly in love with him.

Howard Bannister	Barry Van Dyke
Judy Maxwell	Harriet Hall
Claudia	Caroline McWilliams
Urban Wyatt	Don Porter
Amanda Wyatt	Neva Patterson
Fabian Leek	Jeffrey Kramer

Producer: Hal Kanter, Charles B. Fitzsimons

What's Your Bid?

Game; 30 min; ABC 2/14/53 to 4/11/53
DuMont 5/3/53 to 6/28/53

Studio audience members use their own money to bid for merchandise items. The highest bidder receives the item, which he donates to charity. For his generosity, the program awards him a duplicate item plus additional gifts for his kindness.

Host: John Reed King (ABC), Robert Alda (DuMont)

Auctioneer: Leonard Rosen

Announcer: Dick Shepard

Wheel of Fortune

Testimonial; 30 min; CBS 10/2/52 to 12/25/53

Good samaritans are honored and awarded prizes for their unselfish acts of kindness to other people.

Host: Todd Russell

Wheel of Fortune

Game; 30 min; NBC 1/6/75 (Premiere)
Syn. 9/85

One of three players spins a large wheel that pinpoints a money amount. The player suggests a letter that might be contained in a mystery name, place, or event that is displayed on stage and represented by a number of blank spaces. If a correct letter is given, it appears in its appropriate space and the player scores the money. When an incorrect letter is given, the next player receives a turn. The player who is first to identify the mystery receives the money he has accumulated, which he uses to purchase items from a merchandise showcase.

Host: Chuck Woolery, Pat Sajak

Hostess: Susan Stafford, Vanna White

Announcer: Charlie O'Donnell

Producer: Nancy Jones, David Williger, Paul Gilbert

Wheelie and the Chopper Bunch

Cartoon; 30 min; NBC 9/7/74 to 8/30/75

The adventures of Wheelie, an almost human Volkswagen, and his girlfriend, Rota Ree, and their efforts to overcome the evils of the Chopper Bunch, daredevil motorcycles led by Chopper, who plots to acquire Rota's affections.

Wheelie	Frank Welker
Rota Ree	Judy Strangis
Chopper	Frank Welker
Revs	Paul Winchell
Hi Riser	Lennie Weinrib

Producer: William Hanna, Joseph Barbera

When Television Was Live

Nostalgia; 30 min; PBS 8/6/75 to 9/17/75

The TV careers of Peter Lind Hayes and Mary Healy (who host) are recalled via kinescopes of their various series. Produced by Peter Lind Hayes.

When the Nightingale Sang in Berkeley Square

Experimental; 65 min; NBC 9/28/39

A TV adaptation of the Michael Arlen story about an ex-con, trying to go straight, who is duped into robbing a bank.

Cast: John Moore, Patricia Clayert, Lionel Glenister, J. Malcolm Dunn, Bruce Evans, Matthew Smith

Producer-Writer-Director: Thomas Riley

When the Whistle Blows

Comedy; 60 min; ABC 3/14/80 to 7/27/80

The antics of a group of hard-living construction workers for the Tri-State Construction Company in Los Angeles.

Darlene Ridgeway	Sue Ane Langdon
Big Buzz Dillard	Douglas Barr
Lucy Davis	Susan Buckner
Norm Jenkins	Dolph Sweet
Randy Harford	Philip Brown
Martin "Hunk" Kincaid	Tim Rossovich
Bulldog	Noble Willingham
Ted Hanrahan	Gary Allen
Dottie Jenkins	Alice Hirson
Sharon Jenkins	Talia Balsam
Jill Macklin	Stacey Kuhne

Theme Vocal ("When the Whistle Blows"): Jerry Whitman

Producer: Leonard Goldberg, Jerry Weintraub, Rick Husky

When Things Were Rotten

Comedy; 30 min; ABC 9/10/75 to 12/14/75

A satire based on the legend of Robin Hood, which depicts Robin, the man who stole from the rich to give to the poor, as a birdbrain; his Merry Men, free-born Englishmen loyal to the king, as klutzes; and Maid Marian, Robin's romantic interest, as a sexy dumb blonde.

Robin Hood	Dick Gautier
Maid Marian	Misty Rowe
Alan-A-Dale	Bernie Kopell
Friar Tuck	Dick Van Patten
Renaldo/Bertram	Richard Dimitri
Little John	David Sabin
Lord Hubert	Henry Polic II
Prince John	Ron Rifkin
Princess Isabelle	Jane Johnston
Sylvester	Jimmy Martinez

Producer: Mel Brooks, Norman Steinberg

Creator: Mel Brooks, Buck Henry

Where the Action Is

Variety; 30 min; ABC 7/5/65 to 4/14/67

A daily program of music and songs featuring performances by guest rock stars.

Host: Dick Clark

Regulars: Linda Scott, Steve Alaimo, Paul Revere and the Raiders

Theme Vocal ("Action"): Freddy Cannon

Producer: Dick Glasser, Jerry Bresler

Where There's Smokey

Comedy Pilot; 30 min; CBS 8/1/66

The story of an ineffectual but eager fireman (Smokey) who lives with his sister (Blossom) and her husband (Warren), the fire chief. Subplot of the unsold series was Warren's efforts to find Smokey a wife and get him out of his home.

Fireman Smokey	Soupy Sales
Chief Warren Packard	Gale Gordon
Blossom Packard	Hollis Irving
Richie Packard	Ricky Allen
Maggie Dennison	Louise Glenn
Fireman Hogan	Jack Weston

Producer: Sid Dorfman

Where Was I?

Game; 30 min; DuMont 9/2/52 to 10/6/53

Originally, panelists had to guess where contestants had been at certain times; later, a panel of four celebrities had to locate hidden objects in photographs.

Host: Dan Seymour, Ken Roberts, John Reed King

Panelists: Bill Cullen, Peter Donald, Skitch Henderson, Nancy Guild, David Ross, Samuel Graffin

Announcer: Bob Williams

Where Were You?

Anthology; 30 min; Syn. 1954

The program recreates incidents in the lives of famous people.

Host: Ken Murray

Regulars: Barbara Eiler, Bette Lou Murray, Dan Tobin

Producer: Ken Murray

Where's Everett?

Comedy Pilot; 30 min; CBS 4/18/66

Early one morning a spaceship lands in a small suburban town. Its inhabitants place a seemingly empty basket on the doorstep of a home owned by Arnold and Sylvia Barker and leave. Moments later, a baby's cries awaken the Barkers—who discover an invisible baby named Everett and a note asking them to care for it. The unsold series was to focus on the Barkers as they attempt to raise and keep secret the existence of an invisible baby.

Arnold Barker	Alan Alda
Sylvia Barker	Patricia Smith
Lizzie Barker	Doreen Miller
Dr. Paul Jellicoe	Nicholas Coster
Murdock	Frank DeVol
Milkman	Robert Cleaves

Producer: Ed Simmons

Where's Huddles

Cartoon; 30 min; CBS 7/1/70 to 9/10/70

The misadventures of Ed Huddles and Bubba McCoy, quarterback and team center for the Rhinos, a disorganized professional football team.

Ed Huddles	Cliff Norton
Bubba McCoy	Mel Blanc
Marge Huddles	Jean VanderPyl
Penny McCoy	Marie Wilson
Claude Pertwee	Paul Lynde
Coach	Alan Reed
Freight Train	Herb Jeffries

Producer: William Hanna, Joseph Barbera

Where's Poppa?

Comedy Pilot; 30 min; ABC 7/17/79

The story of a senile widow whose demands are wrecking havoc on her son's social life and law practice.

Momma Hockheiser	Elsa Lanchester
Gordon Hockheiser	Steven Keats
Louise Hamelin	Judith-Marie Bergan
Sid Hockheiser	Allan Miller

Producer: Robert Klane, Marvin Worth

Where's Raymond?

Comedy; 30 min; ABC 10/8/53 to 6/10/55

The story of Raymond Wallace, a professional song and dance man with a habit of arriving for a performance at the very last minute (hence the title). After one season, the title changed to "The Ray Bolger Show" and focused also on Ray's relationship with Susan, a young woman who had come to New York to further her writing career.

Raymond Wallace	Ray Bolger
Jonathan Wallace	Allyn Joslyn
Pete Morrisey	Richard Erdman
June	Betty Lynn
Farley	Charles Smith
Ruth Farley	Gloria Winters
Ruth's mother	Verna Felton
Susan	Margie Millar
Katie	Chris Nelson
Artie Herman	Charlie Cantor
Ray's dancing partner	Sylvia Lewis

Orchestra: Al Goodwin, Herbert Spencer, Earle Hagen

Producer: Stanley Shapiro, Paul Henning, Jerry Bresler

Where's the Fire?

Comedy Pilot; 30 min; ABC 5/17/75

The antics of the firefighters of Engine Company 22. The pilot story relates their attempts to stage a beauty contest to attract beautiful girls to the stationhouse.

Captain O'Hara	Dave Ketchum
Fire Chief	Roger Bowen
Fireman Rosco	Johnny Brown
Fireman Buck	John Fink
Fireman Stanley	Danny Fortus
Fireman Renaldo	Gregory Sierra
Skipper	J. Pat O'Malley
Angelina	Leigh French
Acropolis	Carl Ballantine
Trusdale	Edward Andrews

Producer: Douglas S. Cramer

Whew!

Game; 30 min; CBS 4/23/79 to 5/30/80

Two players compete, the Charger and the Blocker. While the Charger is offstage, the Blocker selects six boxes from a board of 28 boxes. The Charger is brought out and begins the game by calling a box. A blooper is read that the Charger must correct. Each correct response wins him money. The object is for the Charger to call and correct six bloopers within a 60-second time limit (if one of the blocked boxes is called, it deducts five seconds from the 60 seconds). The Blocker wins the round if the Charger fails to correct six bloopers. Players alternate turns and the first contestant who wins two games is the champion.

Host: Tom Kennedy

Announcer: Rod Roddy

Producer: Bud Austin, Burt Sugarman

Whiplash

Adventure; 30 min; Syn. 1961

The story of Chris Cobb, the American owner of the Cobb and Company Stage Coach Lines, as he attempts to maintain Australia's first stage route (1850s).

Chris Cobb	Peter Graves
Dan	Anthony Wickert

Producer: Ben Fox

Whirlybirds

Adventure; 30 min; Syn. 1954

The exploits of Chuck Martin and P.T. Moore, the owner-operators of Whirlybirds, Inc., a helicopter charter service based at Longwood Field in California.

Chuck Martin	Kenneth Tobey
P.T. Moore	Craig Hill
Helen Carter	Nancy Hale
Al	Joe Perry
P.T.'s girlfriend	Sandra Spence
Sheriff Rollo Brice	Robert B. Williams

Producer: N. Gayle Gitterman, John Auer

Whispering Smith

Crime Drama; 30 min; NBC 5/8/61 to 9/18/61

The series, set in Denver during the 1870's, relates the adventures of Tom "Whispering" Smith, the first police detective to incorporate modern methods of analysis and apprehension in the practice of law enforcement in the West.

Det. Tom Smith	Audie Murphy
Det. George Romack	Guy Mitchell
Chief John Richards	Sam Buffington

Producer: Richard Lewis

The Whistling Wizard

Puppet Adventure; 15 min; CBS 10/15/51 to 9/20/52

While looking into an enchanted well, young J. P. loses his balance and falls in. He reappears in the fantasy kingdom of the Land of Beyond. Stories relate his adventures in the bewitched kingdom.

Voices/Puppeteers: Bil and Cora Baird

Producer: Bil Baird

White and Reno

Comedy Pilot; 30 min; NBC 5/31/81

The misadventures of Steve White and Danny Reno, a struggling comedy team. In the pilot, White, who is black, and Reno, who is white, take a booking sight unseen—only to later discover that it is a Ku Klux Klan association dinner.

Steve White	William Allen Young
Danny Reno	Martin Short
Benjamin White	Slappy White
Bunny Holly	Judy Landers
Karen Holly	Audrey Landers
Bernie Starker	Bobby Ramsen
KKK Member	William Bronder

Producer: Don Reo, Judith Allison, Charles Raymond

The White Avengers

Adventure Pilot; 30 min; Unaired; Produced in 1951

The exploits of Bob and Billy White, brothers known as the White Avengers, as they crusade for justice in the West of the 1800s. In the pilot, titled "The Fangs of Justice," Bob and Billy attempt to stop a swindler from cheating Indians out of their land.

Bob White	Clint Swanstrom
Billy White	Bill Dix
Badger MacGregor	Warren MacGregor
Ray Dobbs	Clint Johnson

Producer: Carl Swanstrom

White Hunter

Adventure; 30 min; Syn. 10/57

The exploits of John A. Hunter, a game hunter and trapper based in Africa.

John A. Hunter	Rhodes Reason
Game Commissioner	Tim Turner

Producer: Sydney Box, Bernard L. Schubert

The White Shadow

Drama; 60 min; CBS 11/27/78 to 8/12/81

The story of Ken Reeves, a former pro football player who acquires a job as basketball coach for Carver High School in Los Angeles.

Ken Reeves	Ken Howard
Principal Jim Willis	Jason Bernard
	Ed Bernard
Vice Principal Sybil Buchanan	Joan Pringle

Katie Donahue (Ken's sister)	Robin Rose
Bill Donahue (Katie's husband)	Jerry Fogel
Harold Witherspoon (reporter)	David Hubbard
Referee	Dick Baker
Phil Jeffries (team manager)	Russell Philip Robinson
School PA Announcer	Billy Crawford

The High School Team:	
Morris Thorpe	Kevin Hooks
Warren Coolidge	Byron Stewart
Curtis Jackson	Eric Kilpatrick
Mario "Salami" Petrino	Timothy Van Patten
Milton Reese	Nathan Cook
James Hayward	Thomas Carter
Ricardo Gomez	Ira Augustain
Abner Goldstein	Ken Michaelman
Nick Vitaglia	John Mengatti
Jessie Mitchell	Stoney Jackson
Wardell Stone	Larry Flash Jenkins
Patrick Falahey	John Laughlin
Eddie Franklin	Art Holliday
Teddy Rutherford	Wolfe Perry

Music: Mike Post, Pete Carpenter

Producer: Bruce Paltrow, Mark Tinker

Whitney and the Robot

Children; 30 min; Syn. 9/79

An unusual series in which aspects of the adult world are explained to children via the adventures of Whitney, a cab driver, and 4-U-2, a robot from the planet Zeda who was sent to Earth to study our ways.

Whitney	Whitney Rydbeck
4-U-2	Buddy Douglas
Corky	Corky Greene

Producer: Stephanie Gray

The Whiz Kids

Adventure; 60 min; CBS 10/5/83 to 6/2/84

The adventures of Richie Adler, a teenage computer genius, and his friends, Alice, Ham, and Jeremy, as they become involved with and attempt to solve baffling crimes.

Richie Adler	Matthew Laborteaux
Alice Tyler	Andrea Elson
Hamilton "Ham" Parker	Todd Porter
Jeremy Saldino	Jeffrey Jacquet
Irene Adler	Madelyn Cain
Cheryl Adler	Melanie Gaffin
Lew Farley	Max Gail
Lt. Neil Quinn	A Martinez
Carson Marsh	Dan O'Herlihy
Ms. Vance	Linda Scruggs
Don Adler (Richie's father)	Jim McMullan
Aggie (Ham's mother)	Barbara Brownell
Lee (Ham's father)	Wayne Norton
Dave (Alice's father)	Michael Boyle
Lew's editor	Reid Shelton

Producer: Philip DeGuere, John G. Stephens, Bob Shayne

Who Do You Trust?

Game; 30 min; CBS 1/3/56 to 3/26/57
ABC 7/14/58 to 12/23/63

Married couples, chosen for their unusual backgrounds, compete. The host asks each couple four sets of questions for a total of $1200. The husband may answer himself or trust his wife to do so. Money is awarded based on the number of correct answers. Originally aired on CBS as "Do You Trust Your Wife?"

Host: Edgar Bergen (CBS), Johnny Carson (ABC), and Woody Woodbury (replaced Carson)

Announcer: Ed Reimers, Del Sharbutt, Ed McMahon

Producer: Joe Landis, Art Stark, Jim Morgan, Don Fedderson

Who Pays?

Game; 30 min; NBC 7/2/59 to 9/24/59

Object: For a celebrity panel to identify mystery guests by indirectly questioning two of his or her employees.

Host: Mike Wallace

Panelists: Celeste Holm, Sir Cedric Hardwicke, Gene Klavin

Producer: Jerome Schnur

Who Said That?

Game; 30 min; NBC 12/19/48 to 2/18/51
NBC 4/5/52 to 4/26/52
NBC 4/13/53 to 7/5/54
ABC 2/2/55 to 7/26/55

Object: For a celebrity panel to identify news stories from which quotations are taken.

Host: Robert Trout, Walter Kiernan, John Daly

Panelist: June Lockhart, John Cameron Swayze, Morey Amsterdam, Bob Considine, H. V. Kaltenborn, John Mason Brown, Bill Henry

Announcer: Peter Roberts

Producer: Fred W. Friendly, Anne Gillis, Herb Leder

The Who, What or Where Game

Game; 30 min; NBC 12/29/69 to 1/4/74

A category topic is revealed followed by three questions: the Who (even money), the What (two to one), and the Where (three to one). Each player selects a W and wagers a cash amount on his ability to answer the questions. Correct responses score money accordingly; incorrect answers deduct the bet amount (from the $125 starting money each player receives). The highest scoring player is the winner.

Host: Art James

Announcer: Mike Darrow

Producer: Ron Greenberg

Whodunit?

Game; 30 min; NBC 4/12/79 to 5/17/79

Following a vignette in which a murder is committed, the suspects are brought on stage and cross-examined by three celebrity guests. Three contestants compete and each must determine which suspect is the killer. Money is awarded to the player who solves the crime.

Host: Ed McMahon

Regular: F. Lee Bailey

Producer: Martin Starger, Bill Carruthers, Doris Quinlan, Joel Stein

Who's On Call?

Comedy Pilot; 30 min; ABC 12/16/79

The antics of a group of medical students at New York's Manhattan General Hospital.

Dr. Liz Spencer	Forbesy Russell
Dr. Leland Forsythe	Jim McKrell
Nurse Bremmer	Fran Ryan
Marsha Stone	Melissa Steinberg
Eddie Grado	Matt Landers
Neil Goggini	Frank Covsentino

Producer: Coleman Mitchell, Geoffrey Neigher

Who's the Boss?

Game; 30 min; ABC 2/19/54 to 8/20/54

Object: For a celebrity panel to identify an employer through a series of probe rounds with his secretary. Secretaries receive $100 if the panel fails to identify her boss.

Host: Walter Kiernan

Panelists: Peggy McCay, Polly Rowles, Sylvia Lyons, Mike Wallace, Horace Sutton, Dick Kollman

Who's the Boss?

Comedy; 30 min; ABC 9/20/84 (Premiere)

Dissatisfied with life in Brooklyn, and his inability to properly raise his daughter, Samantha, fish truck driver Tony Micelli seeks to better his life by applying for a building manager's position in Connecticut. There he meets Mona Robinson, a glamorous widow, who is seeking a housekeeper for her divorced daughter Angela (president of the Wallace & McQuade Ad Agency) and her son, Jonathan. Though reluctant at first, Angela hires Tony as her housekeeper. Stories relate Tony's misadventures as he attempts to run Angela's household.

Tony Micelli	Tony Danza
Angela Bower	Judith Light
Mona Robinson	Katherine Helmond
Samantha Micelli	Alyssa Milano
Jonathan Bower	Danny Pintauro
Michael Bower	James Naughton
Jim Peterson	Earl Boen
Nick Malano	James Coco
Rosie	Diane Robin
Wendy Wittener	Dori Brenner
Young Angela (flashbacks)	Lani Golay
Young Tony (flashbacks)	Danny Geuis
Heather Bower	Suzanne Barnes
Marci Ferguson	Nicole Eggert
Robin Fraser	Tonya Crowe
Julia	Angela Lee
Bonnie	Shanna Lane-Block

Producer: Blake Hunter, Martin Cohan, Bud Wiser

Who's There?

Game; 30 min; CBS 7/14/52 to 9/15/52

Object: For panelists to identify a mystery guest through props, personal items, and apparel clues.

Hostess: Arlene Francis

Panelists: Bill Cullen, Paula Stone, Robert Coote, Roger Price

Announcer: Rex Marshall

Producer: Richard Lewis

Who's Watching the Kids?

Comedy; 30 min; NBC 9/22/78 to 12/15/78

The story of two beautiful showgirls (Stacy and Angie) at the seedy Club Sand Pile in Las Vegas. The girls share an apartment with Angie's mischievous brother (Frankie) and Stacy's know-it-all sister (Melissa). The title relates Angie and Stacy's problem: who can watch their kids when they are working? Their solution: Larry, A KVGS-TV newscaster, and Burt, his cameraman, neighbors who, to impress the girls, babysit when they can.

Stacy Turner	Caren Kaye
Angie Vitola	Lynda Goodfriend
Melissa Turner	Tammy Lauren
Frankie Vitola	Scott Baio
Larry Parnell	Larry Breeding
Burt Gunkel	Jim Belushi
Mitzi Logan	Marcia Lewis
Memphis	Lorrie Mahaffey
Cochise	Shirley Kirkes
Bridget	Elaine Bolton

Producer: Garry K. Marshall, Tony Marshall, Don Silverman

Who's Whose?

Game Pilot; 30 min; CBS 6/25/51

Three men and three women sit opposite a celebrity panel. Through a series of probe rounds, the panelists have to discover who is married to whom.

Host: Phil Baker

Panelists: Robin Chandler, Art Ford, Basil Davenport

Producer: Lester Lewis

Why?

Game: 30 min; ABC 12/29/52 to 4/20/53

Players, who are given the Who, What, When, and Where of a situation must determine the Why through a series of question-and-answer rounds with the host.

Host: John Reed King

Assistant (and producer): Bill Cullen

Why Us?

Comedy Pilot; 30 min; NBC 8/21/81

The problems of an unlikely marriage as seen through the experiences of Geri Sanborn, a female auto mechanic, and her husband, Jules, a college professor at U.C.L.A.

Geri Sanborn	Joanna Gleason
Jules Sanborn	John Lawlor
Holly Sanborn	Kim Richards
Zoey Sanborn	Lauri Hendler
Hugh Whitaker	Lance Guest

Producer: John J. McMahon, Eugenie Ross-Leming, Brad Buckner

Wichita Town

Western; 30 min; NBC 9/30/59 to 4/4/60

The exploits of Marshal Mike Dunbar as he attempts to maintain law and order in Wichita Town, Kansas, during the 1870s.

Marshal Mike Dunbar	Joel McCrea
Deputy Ben Matheson	Jody McCrea
Deputy Rico Rodriguez	Carlos Romero
Joe Kingston	Robert Foulk
Dr. Nat Wyndham	George Neise

Producer: Frank Baur

Wide Country

Adventure; 60 min; NBC 9/20/62 to 9/12/63

The story of Mitch Guthrie, a champion rodeo rider, as he travels from rodeo to rodeo seeking the Gold Buckle, the trophy that is awarded to the world's best bronco buster. See also "Second Chance."

Mitch Guthrie	Earl Holliman
Andy Guthrie	Andrew Prine

"Wide Country" Theme Song: Stanley Wilson

Producer: Ralph Edwards, Frank Telford

The Wil Shriner Show

Variety; 60 min; Syn. 9/87

A daily series of celebrity interviews, segments on fitness and health, and discussions with various experts and authors.

Host: Wil Shriner

Producer: Charles Colarusso, Paul Block

Wild About Harry

Comedy Pilot; 30 min; NBC 5/26/78

The romantic misadventures of Harry Baxter, a 45-year-old architect, and Vickie Knowles, the 20-year-old girl he falls in love with.

Harry Baxter	Efrem Zimbalist Jr.
Vickie Knowles	Andrea Howard
Molly Knowles	Emmaline Henry
Jennie	Stephanie Zimbalist
Frank Knowles	Dick Yarmy
Maggie	Elaine Giftos
Don	Bernie Kopell
Delia	Reva Rose
Sophie	Ruth Manning
Sheila Marshall	Gloria Stroock

Producer: George Eckstein, Leonard B. Stern

Wild Bill Hickok

Western; 30 min; Syn. 1951

The exploits of U.S. Marshal James Butler (Wild Bill) Hickok and his partner, Jingles P. Jones, as they battle injustice throughout the West of the 1870s.

Wild Bill Hickok	Guy Madison
Jingles P. Jones	Andy Devine

Announcer: John Cannon, Charles Lyon

Producer: William F. Broidy

The Wild Wild West

Western; 60 min; CBS 9/17/65 to 9/19/69

The exploits of James West and Artemus Gordon, U.S. government Secret Service agents (of the 1870s) as they use ingenious scientific weapons to battle diabolical villains. Originally titled "The Wild West."
Series stars Robert Conrad and Ross Martin continued their roles as agents James T. West and Artemus Gordon in two CBS TV movies ("The Wild Wild West Revisited" [5/9/79] and "More Wild Wild West" [10/7 and 10/8/80]) that updated the series to the 1890s and pitted them against two new enemies: Michelito Loveless Jr. (Paul Williams) and Prof. Albert Paradine (Jonathan Winters).

James T. West	Robert Conrad
Artemus Gordon	Ross Martin
Jeremy Pike	Charles Aidman
Pres. Ulysses S. Grant	James Gregory
	Roy Engle
Dr. Miguelito Loveless	Michael Dunn
Count Manzeppi	Victor Buono
Colonel Richmond	Douglas Henderson
President Juarez	Walter Sorello
Colonel Crockett	Walter Sande
Tennison	Charles Davis
Voltaire	Richard Kiel
Antoinette	Phoebe Dorin
Prof. Montague	Arthur Malet
Frank Harper	William Schallert
Bosley Cranston	Pat Paulsen

Producer: Philip Leacock, Michael Garrison, Fred Freiberger, Gene L. Coon

Wilder and Wilder

Comedy Pilot; 30 min; CBS 8/26/78

The comic adventures of marrieds Steffi and Sam Wilder, a TV writing team often plagued by a clash of identical careers.

Steffi Wilder	Meredith McRae
Sam Wilder	Greg Mullavey
Tina Chambers	Susan Lanier
Al Meredith	Lou Criscuolo
Roger Bacon	Lonnie Shorr
Phil Crawford	Warren Burton
Jason	T. K. Carter

Producer: Mark Carliner, Austin & Irma Kalish

Wildfire

Cartoon; 30 min; CBS 9/13/86 (Premiere)

When the evil witch Diabolyn threatens to kill the infant daughter (Sara) of the dying queen of Darshad, a powerful and magical stallion (Wildfire) takes Sara to America, where she is raised by Mr. Cavanaugh. Twelve years later, when Diabolyn begins her takeover of Darshad, Wildfire returns for Sara, now a beautiful young girl, and takes her back to her kingdom. Stories relate Princess Sara's efforts to defeat Diabolyn's evil attempts to become queen.

Princess Sara	Georgi Irene
Diabolyn	Jessica Walter
Wildfire	John Vernon
Doran	Bobby Jacoby
Alvanor	Rene Auberjonois
John	David Ackroyd

Producer: William Hanna, Joseph Barbera

The Wilds of Ten Thousand Islands

Drama Pilot; 60 min; CBS 2/24/78

The story of the Wilds, a contemporary family of animal behaviorists working in the wilderness wetlands (the Ten Thousand Islands) of Western Florida along the Gulf of Mexico.

Dr. Jeff Wild	Chris Robinson
Dr. Barbara Wild	Julie Gregg
Sara Wild	Mary Ellen McKeon
Jeff Wild	Charles Aiken
Clara Mooney	Rachel Roberts
Miss Kathy	Monica Gayle
Orville	John Ashton

Producer: Lee Rich, Philip Capice, Andy White

Wildside

Western; 60 min; ABC 3/21/85 to 4/25/85

The series, set in Wildside County, California, during the late 1800s, relates the exploits of five men who combine their unique skills to form the Chamber of Commerce, an elite law enforcement team.

Brodie Hollister	William Smith
Sutton Hollister	J. Eddie Peck
Bannister Sparks	Howard E. Rollins Jr.
Vargas de la Costa	John Di Aquino
Prometheus Jones	Terry Funk
Alice Freeze	Robin Hoff
Cally Oaks	Meg Ryan
Zeke	Jason Hervey
Elliot Throckmorton	Kurt Fuller
G. W. Summerhays	Sandy McPeak
Pete Montana	Patrick Culliton
Keye Ahn	Jon Fong

Producer: Tom Greene, E. Arthur Keane

Will the Real Jerry Lewis Please Sit Down

Cartoon; 30 min; ABC 9/12/70 to 9/2/72

The antics of comedian Jerry Lewis as a fumbling janitor for the Odd Job Employment Agency.

| Jerry Lewis | David L. Lander |

Producer: Lou Scheimer, Norm Prescott

Creator: Jerry Lewis

Willow B: Women in Prison

Drama Pilot; 60 min; ABC 6/29/80

Life in the El Camino Institution for Women as seen through the eyes of Kim Cavanaugh, a socialite, convicted of felony manslaughter, and confined to section Willow B. Based on the Australian series, "Prisoner: Cell Block H" (which see).

Kim Cavanaugh	Debra Clinger
Chris Bricker	Trisha Noble
Claire Hastings	Carol Lynley
Kate Stewart	Sally Kirkland
Sabrina Reynolds	Sarah Kennedy
Trini Santos	Liz Torres
T. J.	Susan Tyrrell
Eloise Baker	Virginia Capers
Lynn	Lynne Moody
Prison Governor McCallister	Norma Donaldson
Sgt. Pritchett	Ruth Roman
Guard Dave Tyree	Jared Martin
Guard Canady	John P. Ryan

Producer: Lee Rich, Michael Filerman

Willy

Comedy; 30 min; CBS 9/18/54 to 3/31/55

Following her passing of the bar exam, Willy Dodger returns to her home town of Renfrew, New Hampshire, to begin her law practice. Stories relate her adventures as she attempts to acquire clients in a town that is distrustful of female lawyers. See the following title also.

Willy Dodger	June Havoc
Mr. Dodger	Wheaton Chambers
Charlie Bush	Whitfield Connor
Emily	Mary Treen
Franklin Sanders	Danny Richards Jr.

Producer: William Spier

Willy

Comedy; 30 min; CBS 4/7/55 to 7/7/55

A revised version of the previous title that, set in New York City, relates Willy's adventures as the legal counselor for the Bannister Vaudeville Company.

Willy Dodger	June Havoc
Perry Bannister	Hal Peary
Harvey Evelyn	Sterling Holloway

Producer: William Spier

Win, Lose or Draw

Game; 30 min; NBC 9/7/87 (Premiere)
Syn. 9/87

Two three-member teams compete (two celebrities, one contestant). One member of one team receives a secret name or saying and must convey it to his team by drawing clues to it on a large paper pad. $200 is awarded for each puzzle that is guessed. Each member of each team receives a chance to draw and the team with the highest score is the winner. Created by Burt Reynolds.

Host (NBC): Vickie Lawrence

Host (Syn.): Bert Convy

Announcer: Bob Hilton

Producer: Burt Reynolds, Bert Convy, Richard S. Kline

Win With a Winner

Game; 30 min; NBC 6/24/58 to 9/9/58

Five players compete and stand before a numbered post (as in a horse race). The object calls for players to reach the finish line by answering questions. Also known as "Winner's Circle."

Host: Sandy Becker, Win Elliott

Assistant: Marilyn Toomey, Rita Hayes

Announcer: Bill Wendell

Win With the Stars

Game; 30 min; Syn. 1968

Two two-member teams compete in a series of 45-second rounds in which they must identify as many song titles as possible from brief selections that are played. The highest scoring team receives merchandise prizes.

Host: Allen Ludden

Announcer: Jay Stewart

Orchestra: Bobby Hammack

Winchester

Western Pilot; 30 min; CBS 3/26/59

The story of Dave Blassingame, a wandering cowboy of the Old West. Aired as "Trouble at Tres Cruces" on "Zane Grey Theatre."

Dave Blassingame	Brian Keith
Tyrant	Neville Brand

Producer: Hal Hudson

Window on Main Street

Comedy-Drama; 30 min; CBS 10/2/61 to 9/12/62

Life in a small American town (Millsburg) as seen through the eyes of Cameron Garrett Brooks, a novelist who, after the death of his wife, returns to his home town to write about its people.

Cameron Brooks	Robert Young
Lloyd Ramsey	Ford Rainey
Chris Logan	Constance Moore
Wally Evans	James Byron
Peggy Evans	Carol Byron
Henry McGill	Warner Jones
Arnie Logan	Brad Berwick

Producer: Eugene B. Rodney

Window Shopping

Game; 30 min; ABC 4/2/62 to 6/29/62

A photograph is briefly flashed on a screen. Each of the three players who compete states the items he believes were depicted in the photo. For each correct identification, he receives one point. The highest scorer receives his score transferred into seconds. For that amount of time he is allowed to window shop by looking at numerous merchandise items on stage. The items that he is able to recall become his prize.

Host: Bob Kennedy

Judge: William Wood

Producer: Alan Gilbert

Windows

Anthology; 30 min; CBS 7/8/55 to 8/26/55

A short-lived series of dramas about people confronting real problems. Produced by Leonard Valenta, Mort Abrahams, and Shelly Hull.

Windows, Doors, and Keyholes

Variety Pilot; 60 min; NBC 5/16/78

Various adult-oriented sketches that satirize topical issues.

Hosts: Lindsay Wagner, Telly Savalas, Bill Dana

Regulars: John Schuck, Hamilton Camp, Patrick J. Cronin, McIntyre Dixon, Dee Dee Rescher, Linda Redford, Joy Garrett, Hilary Beane, Trisha Hart, Mickey Deems

Producer: Leonard B. Stern, Arne Sultan

Windy City Jamboree

Variety; 60 min; DuMont 3/26/50 to 6/18/50

An hour of music and songs from Chicago.

Host: Danny O'Neal

Regulars: Gloria Van, Jane Brockman, Jimmy McPartland, Dick Edwards, Paula Raye, Bud Tygett

Orchestra: Julian Stockdale

Wingo

Game; 30 min; CBS 4/1/58 to 5/6/58

Two players compete in a series of very difficult question-and-answer rounds. Players with the highest scores are the winners and receive $1000.

Host: Bob Kennedy

Producer: Dave Brown

Winky Dink and You

Children; 30 min; CBS 10/10/53 to 4/27/57

The adventures of Winky Dink, an animated cartoon boy, and his animated friend, Woofer the dog. Children are encouraged to participate via Winky Dink home kits (wherein a plastic screen is placed over the TV screen and with crayons, children draw the essentials to help the characters out of dangerous situations).

Host: Jack Barry

Assistants: Dayton Allen (as Mr. Bungle), Mike McBean

Producer: Jack Barry, Dan Enright

Winky Dink and You

Cartoon; 5 min; Syn. 1969

A syndicated version of the previous title, which relates the adventures of Winky Dink (a young boy) and his dog, Woofer. Children participate via Winky Dink home kits.

Winky Dink	Mae Questel
Woofer	Dayton Allen

Producer: Fred Calvert

Winner Take All

Game; 30 min; CBS 6/15/48 to 10/3/50
                      1/12/51 to 4/20/51
                      2/25/52 to 10/5/52

Object: For players to answer questions based on sketches that are performed on stage.

Host: Bud Collyer, Bill Cullen

Assistant: Sheila Connolly

Regulars: Betty Watson, Jerry Austen, Howard Malone, Barry Gray

Producer: Mark Goodson, Bill Todman, Gil Fates

Winner Take All

Crime Drama Pilot; 60 min; CBS 4/1/77

The story of a stunning insurance investigator (Allison) and an L.A.P.D. lieutenant (Charlie) who are often pitted against each other, but work in tandem to solve crimes.

Allison Nash — Joanna Pettet
Lt. Charlie Quigley — Michael Murphy
E. P. Woodhouse — Clive Revill
Mo Rellis — Mark Gordon
Swenson — Loni Anderson
Solange — Martine Beswick
Hiram Yarby — David Huddleston
Maria — Signe Hasso
Clarence Woo — James Hong

Producer: Quinn Martin, John Wilder

Winning Streak

Game; 30 min; NBC 7/1/74 to 1/3/75

One player (of two who compete) chooses one letter from sixteen that are displayed on a board. To score points, the player must correctly answer a question that corresponds to that letter (e.g., if letter A is chosen, the answer will begin with an A). The highest scoring player is the winner.

Host: Bill Cullen

Announcer: Don Pardo

Producer: Bob Stewart

Wire Service

Adventure; 60 min; ABC 10/4/56 to 9/23/57

The rotational exploits of Dean Evans, Katherine Wells, and Dan Miller, Wire Service reporters for Trans Globe News.

Dean Evans — George Brent
Katherine Wells — Mercerdes McCambridge
Dan Miller — Dane Clark

Producer: Don Sharpe, Warren Lewis

Wiseguy

Crime Drama; 60 min; CBS 9/16/87 (Premiere)

In an attempt to infiltrate the mob, the Organized Crime and Task Force unit of the FBI arranges for an agent (Vinnie Terranova) to serve time in the Newark (N.J.) State pen to help establish his cover. Shortly after his release, Vinnie infiltrates the mob "family" of Sonny Steelgrave, a powerful figure in organized crime. The series relates Vinnie's exploits as a "Wiseguy" (a member of the mob)

and an undercover agent. (Vinnie's experiences with Steelgrave ran until the episode of November 12, 1987, at which time his cover was blown and Sonny killed. With the episode of January 4, 1988, Vinnie infiltrates the mob of Susan and Mel Profitt, powerful underworld sister and brother figures; stories relate his experiences.)

Vinnie Terranova — Ken Wahl
Frank McPike — Jonathan Banks
Lifeguard — Jim Byrnes
Father Peter Terranova — Gerald Anthony
Carlotta Terranova — Elsa Raven
Sonny Steelgrave — Ray Sharkey
Tracy Steelgrave — Jessica Steen
Dave Steelgrave — Gianni Russo
Susan Profitt — Joan Severance
Mel Profitt — Kevin Spacey
Roger Lococco — William Russ

Producer: Stephen J. Cannell, Les Sheldon

Wishman

Fantasy Pilot; 60 min; ABC 6/23/83

In an attempt to create a biological worker, Dr. Alex MacGregor produces Wishman, a playful little creature that fails to respond to commands during testing. When Wishman is ordered to be destroyed, Alex decides to save him. Suddenly, Alex and his wife, Mattie, find themselves on the run when Galen Reed, security chief of the Cromogene Corporation, is ordered to recapture Wishman. The unsold series was to relate Alex and Mattie's efforts to elude Reed and safeguard Wishman.

Alex MacGregor — Joseph Bottoms
Mattie MacGregor — Linda Hamilton
Galen Reed — James Keach
Wishman — Margarita Fernandez
Karen Kaleb — Jean Bruce Scott
Sam — John Reilly
Nat Kaleb — Sam Weisman

Producer: Terry Morse Jr.

Witness

Crime Drama; 30 min; CBS 9/29/60 to 1/26/61

People who have witnessed or become innocently involved in a crime relate their experiences to a panel of defense attorneys.

Narrator: Verne Collett

Panelists: Richard Steele, Richard Geoghan, Benedict Ginsberg, Charles Hayden

Producer: David Susskind, Murray Suskind, Nick Mayo

Wives

Comedy Pilot; 30 min; CBS 3/21/75

The daily routines and misadventures of five married women.

Connie	Penny Marshall
Doris	Phyllis Davis
Mary Margaret	Candice Azzara
Francine	Janie Sell
Lillian	Jacque Lynn Colton
Miss Chin	Barbara Luna
Waiter	Pat Morita

Producer: Garry K. Marshall

The Wizard

Adventure; 60 min; CBS 9/9/86 to 4/30/87

Deprived of a normal childhood by his parents, the now adult Simon McKay decides to devote his life to keeping magic alive by creating ingenious toys for children. Soon, Simon is nicknamed "The Wizard" and comes to the attention of the U.S. government who recruit him for special assignments. Stories relate Simon's exploits as he uses his amazing inventions to battle evil. Originally titled "The Wizard of Elm Street."

Simon McKay	David Rappaport
Alex Jaeger	Douglas Barr
Darcy Stafford	Cheryl McFadden
Tillie	Fran Ryan
Mr. Linder	Macom McCalman
Jack Brooks	Billy Jacoby

Producer: Paul Radin, Rick Middleton, Douglas Schwartz, Michael Berke

The Wizard of Odds

Game; 30 min; NBC 6/17/73 to 6/28/74

Selected members of the studio audience compete in greatly varying games designed to test their knowledge of national odds and averages and bring forth a "Wizard's Champion." The player with the overall highest score is the winner and receives merchandise prizes.

Host: Alex Trebek

Assistant: Mary Pom

Announcer: Owen Spam, Charlie O'Donnell

Producer: Burt Sugarman, Alan Thicke, Perry Cross

Wizards and Warriors

Fantasy; 60 min; CBS 2/26/83 to 5/14/83

The exploits of Erik Greystone, a dashing prince, as he battles the evils of Dirk Blackpool, a prince who seeks to gain control of Camarand (a mythical medieval kingdom).

Erik Greystone	Jeff Conaway
Marko	Walter Olkewicz
Dirk Blackpool	Duncan Regehr
Bethel	Randi Brooks
King Edwin Baaldorf	Thomas Hill
Princess Ariel Baaldorf	Julia Duffy
Queen Lattinia Baaldorf	Julie Payne
Vector	Clive Revill
Traquill	Ian Wolfe
Justin Greystone	Jay Kerr
Geoffrey Blackpool	Tim Dunigan
Cassandra	Phyllis Katz

Producer: Don Reo, Judith Allison

WKRP in Cincinnati

Comedy; 30 min; CBS 9/17/78 to 11/6/78
1/15/79 to 9/20/82

The antics of the staff and management of WKRP, a 5000 watt, hard-rock format AM radio station in Cincinnati, Ohio.

Andy Travis	Gary Sandy
Jennifer Marlowe	Loni Anderson
Arthur Carlson	Gordon Jump
Bailey Quarters	Jan Smithers
Dr. Johnny Fever	
(Johnny Caravella)	Howard Hesseman
Herb Tarlek	Frank Bonner
Les Nessman	Richard Sanders
Venus Flytrap	
(Gordon Simms)	Tim Reid
Lillian Carlson	
(Arthur's mother)	Sylvia Sidney
	Carol Bruce
Carmen Carlson	
(Arthur's wife)	Allyn Ann McLerie
Arthur Carlson Jr.	Sparky Marcus
Lucille Tarlek	
(Herb's wife)	Edie McClurg
Herb Tarlek Sr.	Bert Parks
Bunny Tarlek	
(Herb's daughter)	Stacy Heather Tolkin
Lori Caravella	
(Johnny's daughter)	Patrie Allen
Carol Travis (Andy's sister)	Allison Argo
Hirsch (Lillian's butler)	Ian Wolfe

Producer: Hugh Wilson, Rod Daniel, Bill Dial, Peter Torokvei, Steven Kampmann

Wolf Rock TV

Cartoon; 30 min; ABC 9/8/84 to 9/7/85

Music videos are combined with the antics of Wolfman Jack and a group of kids (Sarah, Sunni, Ricardo) who run a music video TV station owned by Mr. Morris.

Wolfman Jack	Himself
Sunni	Si Ming Carson
Sarah	Noelle North
Ricardo	Robert Vega
Mr. Morris	William Calloway

Producer: Jean Chalopin, Dick Clark, Andy Heyward

The Wolfman Jack Show

Variety; 30 min; Syn. 10/77

A weekly series of music, songs, and comedy sketches.

Host: Wolfman Jack

Regulars: Peter Cullen, Murray Langston, John Harris

Orchestra: Jimmy Dale

Producer: Don Kelly, Riff Markowitz

The Wolfman Jack Radio Show

Music Pilot; 60 min; Syn. 6/80

Performances by guest recording artists with host Wolfman Jack. Produced by Jerry Harrison and Joe Siegman.

Woman on the Run

Drama Pilot; 60 min; CBS 12/17/77

After three years of marriage, Laura Frazier discovers that her husband, Daniel, is a foreign spy. Fearing for her life, Laura flees. The unsold series was to depict Laura's efforts to elude her husband and his organization who seek to silence her—by killing her.

Laura Frazier	Donna Mills
Daniel Frazier	Edward Winter
Owen	Bo Hopkins
Crandell	Dan O'Herlihy
Ed Miles	David Opatoshu

Producer: Frank Glicksman

A Woman to Remember

Drama; 15 min; DuMont 2/21/49 to 7/15/49

The series, set in an AM radio station where a daily serial is produced, relates the conflicts and tensions of its cast, in particular Carol Winstead, an unknown actress who is hired to replace the leading star.

Carol Winstead	Joan Castle
Christine Baker	Patricia Wheel
Steve Hammond	John Raby
Charlie Anderson	Frankie Thomas
Bessie Thatcher	Ruth McDevitt

Producer: Bob Steele

Woman with a Past

Drama; 15 min; CBS 2/1/54 to 7/2/54

The dramatic story of Lynn Sherwood, a fashion designer.

Lynn Sherwood	Constance Ford
Peggy Sherwood	Anne Hegira
Diane Sherwood	Barbara Ellen Myers
Gwen	Jean Stapleton

Producer: Richard Bill

Woman's Page

Magazine; 30 min; Syn. 9/81

Beauty, health and consumer information for women.

Host: Larry Freeman

Consumer Editor: Jo Giese Brown

Fashion Editor: Alanna Davis

Hair Care Editor: John & Suzanne Chadwick

Medical Editor: Dr. Walter Dishell

Financial Editor: Bob Roseki

Cooking Editor: Claude Gobet

Seafood Editor: Michele Wetmore

Gourmet Editor: Dennis Overstreet

There's Got to Be a Better Way Editor: Rita Davenport

Producer: Fred Tatashore

Women in Prison

Comedy; 30 min; FOX 10/11/87 (Premiere)

A comical view of prison life as seen through the experiences of Vicki Springer, a beautiful, pampered, and naive girl who is set up on a shoplifting charge and sentenced to Cell Block J of the Bass Women's Prison in Wisconsin.

Vicki Springer	Julia Campbell
Eve Shipley	Peggy Cass
Bonnie Harper	Antoinette Byron
Pam Norwell	Wendie Jo Sperber
Dawn Murphy	C.C.H. Pounder
Clint Rafferty (warden)	Blake Clark
Meg Brando (guard)	Denny Dillon

Producer: Katherine Greene, Richard Gurman

Wonder Woman

Adventure Pilot; 90 min; ABC 3/12/74

On an island of superhuman women (Paradise Island), the beautiful Diana is instructed by her Queen Mother to assist the world in its battle against evil. Shortly after leaving the island, Diana adopts the guise of Diana Prince, and acquires a job as secretary to U.S. government agent Steve Trevor. The unsold series was to relate Diana's exploits as she uses her amazing powers to battle evil.

Diana/Wonder Woman	Cathy Lee Crosby
Steve Trevor	Kaz Garas
Queen Mother	Charlene Holt
Ahnjayla	Anitra Ford
Abner Smith	Ricardo Montalban
George Calvin	Andrew Prine
Cass	Donna Garrett
Colonel	Richard X. Slattery
Joey	Robert Porter

Producer: John D. F. Black, John G. Stephens

Wonder Woman

Adventure Pilot; 90 min; ABC 11/7/75

The setting is World War II. A plane, flown by U.S. fighter pilot Steve Trevor, is hit by gunfire and crash lands on Paradise Island, an uncharted land mass that is inhabited by a race of Amazons. Steve is found by the beautiful Princess Diana and nursed back to health. When Diana learns of the war, she receives permission from her Queen Mother to use her unique powers to help America in its battle against Naziism. Later, after returning Steve to Washington D.C., the princess adopts the guise of Diana Prince. She becomes a Navy Yeoman and is assigned to the War Department as Steve's secretary. The pilot relates Diana's efforts to foil a German plot to destroy an American bombsite.

Diana/Wonder Woman	Lynda Carter
Maj. Steve Trevor	Lyle Waggoner
Gen. Philip Blankenship	John Randolph
Queen Mother	Cloris Leachman
Marcia	Stella Stevens
Ashley Norman	Red Buttons
Col. Von Balasko	Ken Mars
Amazon Doctor	Fannie Flagg
Nicholas	Henry Gibson
Kapitan Drangel	Eric Braeden

Producer: Douglas S. Cramer

Wonder Woman

Adventure; 60 min; ABC 3/31/76 to 7/30/77

The exploits of Diana Prince, an Amazon from Paradise Island, who journeys to America to assist the U.S. in its battle against Naziism as the mysterious Wonder Woman. See the prior title for additional information. Originally titled "The New, Original Wonder Woman."

Diana/Wonder Woman	Lynda Carter
Maj. Steve Trevor	Lyle Waggoner
Gen. Philip Blankenship	Richard Eastman
Yeoman Etta Candy	Beatrice Colen
Drusilla/Wonder Girl	Debra Winger
Queen Mother	Carolyn Jones
Madga (Amazon)	Pamela Susan Shoop
Dalma (Amazon)	Erica Hagen

Producer: Douglas S. Cramer, Wilfred Lloyd Baumes

Wonder Woman

Adventure; 60 min; CBS 9/23/77 to 9/11/79

A revised version of the prior title that is set in modern times. When the tranquality of Paradise Island is shattered and the Princess Diana learns that the world is still threatened by evil, she receives permission to once again become Wonder Woman and assist the outside world in its battle for justice. She again adopts the alias of Diana Prince and returns to Washington, D.C., where she becomes the assistant to Steve Trevor Jr. Stories relate Diana's exploits as an agent for the I.A.D.C.

(Inter Agency Defense Command). Originally titled "The New Adventures of Wonder Woman."

Diana/Wonder Woman	Lynda Carter
Steve Trevor Jr.	Lyle Waggoner
Joe Atkinson	Normann Burton
Queen Mother	Beatrice Straight
Eve	Saundra Sharp
Harold Farnum	Ed Begley Jr.
Voice of IRA (I.A.D.C. Computer)	Tom Kratochzil

Producer: Douglas S. Cramer, Wilfred Lloyd Baumes

Wonderbug

Comedy; 15 min; ABC 9/11/76 to 9/2/78

While seeking a used car, three teenagers (Susan, Barry, and C. C.) find Schlep Car, a conglomeration of several wrecked cars. When Susan places what turns out to be a magic horn on the car, it becomes Wonderbug, a car that is capable of amazing feats. Stories relate the quartet's battle against evil. Aired on "The Krofft Supershow."

Susan	Carol Anne Seflinger
Barry	David Levy
C. C.	John Anthony Bailey
Voice of Wonderbug	Frank Welker

Producer: Sid and Marty Krofft

Wonderful John Acton

Comedy; 30 min; ABC 7/12/53 to 10/6/53

Events in the lives of the Actons, an Irish-American family living in Ludlow, Kentucky, as seen through the eyes of Kevin, the family's son, as he reminisces about his childhood.

John Acton	Harry Holcombe
Julia Acton	Virginia Dwyer
Kevin Acton	Ronnie Walker
Terence Acton	Ian Martain
Perry Bodkin Jr.	Pat Harrington
Bessie Acton	Jane Rose
Birdie Bodkin	Mary Michael

Producer: Edward Byron

The Wonderful World of Philip Malley

Comedy-Drama Pilot; 60 min; CBS 5/18/81

The misadventures of Philip Malley, a bright science professor at Rutledge University in Riverside County.

Philip Malley	Stephen Nathan
Dean Frederick Carswell	William Daniels
Meredith Carswell	Lori Lethin
Ben Grady	Stubby Kaye
Rodney "Mongo" Bronson	John Calvin
Francine Grady	Bibi Osterwald
Lyle Floon	Stuart Pankin

Producer: David Gerber, Charles B. Fitzsimons

Woobinda—Animal Doctor

Adventure; 30 min; Syn. 1978

An Australian series about Dr. John Stevens, a veterinary surgeon in the town of Gottens Creek.

Dr. John Stevens	Don Pascoe
Tiggie Stevens	Sonia Hofmann
Kevin Stevens	Bindi Williams
Jack Johnson	Slim Degrey

Producer: Roger Mirams

The Woody Woodbury Show

A syndicated (1967) program of celebrity interviews with host Woody Woodbury and the music of the Michael Melvin Combo.

The Woody Woodpecker Show

Cartoon; 30 min; ABC 10/3/57 to 9/25/58

A series of theatrical cartoons, including "Woody Woodpecker," "Andy Panda," "Space Mouse," "Charley Beary," and "Gabby Gator."

Host: Walter Lantz

Woody's Voice: Grace Lantz

Additional Voices: Paul Frees, June Foray, Walter Tetley, Daws Butler

Producer: Walter Lantz

Word for Word

Game; 30 min; NBC 9/30/63 to 10/23/64

Object: For players to make as many three-and-four letter words as possible from larger words. Each acceptable word scores a player one point. The winner receives his score transferred into seconds, which he uses against the electronic Word-O-Meter. If the player can unscramble a jumbled word before the machine, he wins a cash prize.

Host: Merv Griffin

Announcer: Frank Simms

Producer: Peter Lane

Word Play

Game; 30 min; NBC 12/29/86 (Premiere)

A board with nine words is displayed. One player (two compete) selects one word. Three celebrity guests each define the meaning of the word. The player must determine the correct definition of the word. A correct choice awards a money amount; an incorrect guess allows the opponent a chance. The player with the highest score after six words is the winner.

Host: Tom Kennedy

Announcer: Charlie O'Donnell

Producer: Syd Vinnedge, Tony Scotti

Words and Music

Variety; 15 min; NBC 8/2/49 to 9/8/49

A twice weekly program of music and songs with hostess Barbara Marshall and the music of the Jerry Jerome Trio.

Words and Music

Game; 30 min; NBC 9/28/70 to 2/12/71

One player (three compete) selects one of sixteen squares that are displayed on a board. A clue that relates to a particular word in a song is read. An accompanying song is sung and the first player to associate the clue with the word scores one point and selects the next clue. The highest scorer wins a cash prize.

Host: Wink Martindale

Vocalists: Peggy Connelly, Katie Grant, Pat Henderson, Bob Marlo, Don Minter

Announcer: Johnny Gilbert

Orchestra: Bobby Hammack

Producer: Armand Grant

Working Stiffs

Comedy; 30 min; CBS 9/15/79 to 10/6/79

The story of two incompetent brothers (Ernie and Mike) and their misadventures as janitors in the O'Rourke Building, a Chicago establishment owned by the only man who will hire them—their Uncle Harry.

Ernie O'Rourke	Jim Belushi
Mike O'Rourke	Michael Keaton
Harry O'Rourke	Michael Conrad
Charles Pressman (manager, 1st ep.)	Neil Thompson
Al Steckler (manager, 2nd ep.)	Val Bisoglio
Frank Falzone (manager, 3rd & 4th episodes)	Phil Rubinstein
Mitch Hannigan	Allan Arbus
Nikki Evashevsky	Lorna Patterson
Ralph Evashevsky	Thomas Calloway

Producer: Arthur Silver, Bob Brunner

The World Beyond

Thriller Pilot; 60 min; CBS 1/27/78

The story of Paul Taylor, a sportswriter who dies on the operating table and is brought back from the brink of death. Though in a world of the living, Paul still holds a connection to the world beyond, one that commands him to help people threatened by the occult. The story finds Paul battling a Golem, an evil creature who seeks only to kill. See the following title also.

Paul Taylor	Granville Van Dusen
Marian Faber	JoBeth Williams
Frank Faber	Richard Fitzpatrick
Andy Borchard	Barnard Hughes
Sam Barker	Jan Van Evera

Producer: David Susskind

The World of Darkness

Thriller Pilot; 60 min; CBS 4/17/77

The story of a sportswriter (Paul Taylor) who is brought back from the brink of death, but still holds a connection to the world beyond. In the story, an inner voice brings Paul to New England to help a girl (Clara) threatened by an evil presence.

Paul Taylor	Granville Van Dusen
Clara Sanford	Tovah Feldshuh
Joanna Sanford	Beatrice Straight
Thomas Madsen	Gary Merrill
John Sanford	James Austin
Helen	Jayne Eastwood

Producer: David Susskind, Diana Kerew

The World of Entertainment

Variety Pilot; 60 min; Syn. 4/25/82

Performances by personalities from around the world (linked via satellite). An attempt to recreate the "The Ed Sullivan Show," which brought international acts to TV.

Host: Gene Kelly

Guests: Patricia Crowley, Mary Ann Mobley, Joe Montanna

Producer: Bob Finkel, Andy Friendly

World of Giants

Adventure; 30 min; Syn. 1959

In an attempt to expose criminal organizations, an experiment is conducted wherein American counterespionage agent Mel Hunter is reduced to a height of six inches, thus enabling him to do things normal agents cannot. Stories relate his adventures as he and his normal-sized partner, Bill Winters, carry out dangerous assignments for the government. Originally made for CBS in 1957.

Mel Hunter	Marshall Thompson
Bill Winters	Arthur Franz

Producer: Edgar Peterson, Ralph Smart, Otto Lang

The World of Mr. Sweeny

Comedy; 15 min; NBC 6/30/54 to 12/30/55

A daily series about the lighthearted adventures of Cicero P. Sweeny, the owner of a general store in the small town of Mapleton.

Cicero P. Sweeny	Charlie Ruggles
Marge Franklin	Helen Wagner
Kippie Franklin	Glen Walker
Tom Millikan	Harry Gresham
Abigail Millikan	Betty Garde
Henrietta	Janet Fox
Molly	Jane Cleveland
Little Eva	Lydia Reed

Producer: Sam Schiff

The World of People

Human Interest; 30 min; Syn. 8/81

The program spotlights the usual and unusual activities of people.

Host: Sarah Edwards, Steve Adelman, Jan D'Atry, Nigel Bulard, David Sisson, Sharon Anderson, Mark Shaw

Producer: Bill Hillier, Mary Ann Welker

World War I

Documentary; 30 min; CBS 9/22/64 to 9/5/65

Robert Ryan as the host and narrator of a series that uses films to recall the key events and battles of the first world war. Produced by Burton Benjamin.

World's Fair Beauty Show

Experimental; 60 min; NBC 6/21/39

Television's first beauty contest, which was broadcast live from the New York World's Fair. As a tie-in with RCA's demonstration of home TV sets, one girl, chosen from the ranks of the Fair Girls, was crowned "The Fair's Television Girl."

Host: Ernest Chappell

Commentator: Jack Frazier

Producer: Edward Sobol

The World's Greatest Super Heroes

Cartoon; 55 min; ABC 9/9/78 to 9/5/80

A spin-off from "The Super Friends," which finds the mighty heroes battling the evil Legion of Doom.

Wonder Woman	Shannon Farnon
Superman	Danny Dark
Batman	Olan Soule
Robin	Casey Kasem
Aquaman	Bill Callaway
Hawkman/Samurai/ Flash	Jack Angel
Green Lantern/ Apache Chief	Michael Rye
Jana	Louise Williams
Brainic/Black Manta	Ted Cassidy
Toyman	Frank Welker
Riddler/Zan/Gleek	Michael Bell
Captain Gold	Dick Ryal
Sinestro	Vic Perrin
Giganta	Ruth Forman
Scarecrow	Don Messick

Producer: William Hanna, Joseph Barbera

Wrangler

Western; 30 min; NBC 8/4/60 to 9/15/60

The exploits of Pitcarin, a wandering, two-fisted cowboy of the 1880s, who helps people he finds in trouble. The first videotaped western series.

Pitcarin	Jason Evers

Producer: Paul Harrison

Wren's Nest

Comedy; 15 min; ABC 1/13/49 to 4/30/49

Events in the lives of a young newlywed couple (Sam and Virginia) as they struggle to survive the difficult first years of marriage.

Sam Wren	Himself
Virginia Wren	Herself

Producer: Sherling Oliver

The Wuzzles

Cartoon; 30 min; CBS 9/14/85 to 9/6/86

The misadventures of the Wuzzles, hybrid creatures who are two animals in one and who reside on the isolated isle of Wuz.

Voices: Brian Cummings, Henry Gibson, Kathleen Helppie, Alan Oppenheimer, Bill Scott, Jo Anne Worley

Producer: Fred Wolf

Wyatt Earp

See "The Life and Legend of Wyatt Earp."

The Xavier Cugat Show

Variety; 15 min; NBC 2/27/57 to 5/22/57

A twice weekly program of music and song featuring the Continental sound.

Host: Xavier Cugat

Vocalist: Abbe Lane

Orchestra: Xavier Cugat

Producer: Barry Shear

Yancy Derringer

Adventure; 30 min; CBS 10/2/58 to 9/24/59

The series, set in New Orleans during the 1800s, relates the exploits of Yancy Derringer, a roguish riverboat gambler, as he struggles to institute a system of law and order in a city overrun with corruption.

Yancy Derringer	Jock Mahoney
Pahoo-Ka-Ta-Wha ("Wolf Who Stands in the Water")	X Brands
John Colton	Kevin Hagen
Mme. Francine	Frances Bergen

Producer: Don Sharpe, Warren Lewis

The Yeagers

Drama; 60 min; ABC 6/1/80 to 6/8/80

The series, set in Mackenzie County, Washington, follows the life of Carroll Yeager, the owner of the Yeager Logging and Mining Company, and his family, as they struggle to maintain the family business.

Carroll Yeager	Andy Griffith
	Eddie Albert*
Willie Yeager	James Whitmore Jr.
	Martin Kove*
John David Yeager	David Ackroyd
	James Sloyan*
Joanna Yeager	Deborah Shelton
	Robin Dearden*
Carrie Yeager	Molly Cheek
	Belinda J. Montgomery*
Tony Yeager	Kevin Brophy
Kyle Yeager	Gregg Henry
	Steve Doubet*
Scotty Yeager	Jimmy Mayer
Timmy Yeager	Bob Olidi
Lisa Yeager	Joan Goodfellow
Sheriff	William Stratton
	John Lupton*
Roy	John Quade

Producer: Paul Junger Witt, Tony Thomas

*TV Movie roles ("Trouble in High Timber Country," 6/27/80).

A Year at the Top

Comedy; 30 min; CBS 8/5/77 to 9/4/77

The story of two unknown songwriters (Greg and Paul) who sell their souls to Paragon Records president Frederick J. Hanover (the Devil's son) in return for a year at the top in the music world. See the following title also.

Greg	Greg Evigan
Paul	Paul Shaffer
Mickey Durbin	Mickey Rooney
Frederick J. Hanover	Gabriel Dell
Linda	Priscilla Lopez
Miss Worley	Priscilla Morrill
Dee Dee	Kelly Bishop
Bell Durbin	Nedra Volz

Producer: Norman Lear, Darryl Hickman, Patricia Fass Palmer

A Year at the Top

Comedy; 30 min; Unaired (Produced in 1976)

The original, unaired version of the prior title. The story of three aging performers (Lillian, Cliff, and Studly) who sell their souls to the Devil for youth (30 years younger) and a year at the top in the music world. See also "Hereafter."

Elder Lillian	Vivian Blaine
Young Lillian	Judith Cohen
Elder Cliff	Robert Alda
Young Cliff	Greg Evigan
Elder Studly	Phil Leeds
Young Studly	Paul Shaffer
Dee Dee (Devil's daughter)	Kelly Bishop
Mickey	Mickey Rooney

Producer: Norman Lear, Darryl Hickman

A Year in the Life

Drama; 60 min; NBC 9/16/87 (Premiere)

A sentimental series that relates daily incidents in the lives of the Gardners, a troubled family living in Seattle, Washington. Adapted from the miniseries of the same title.

Joe Gardner	Richard Kiley
Ruth Gardner	Eva Marie Saint*
Jack Gardner	Morgan Stevens
Sam Gardner	David Oliver
Anne Gardner-Maxwell	Wendy Phillips
Kay	Sarah Jessica Parker
Sunny Maxwell	Amanda Peterson
Lindley Gardner-Eisenberg	Jayne Atkinson
Jim Eisenberg	Adam Arkin
Dr. Alice Foley	Diana Muldaur
David Maxwell	Trey Ames
Glenn Maxwell	Scott Paulin
Marvin Eisenberg	Alan Arkin
Billy Putsy	Brian Benben

Producer: Joshua Brand, John Falsey

*Role in the miniseries as Joe's wife (12/15 to 12/17/86)

The Yellow Rose

Drama; 60 min; NBC 10/2/83 to 5/12/84

The lives of the Champions, modern-day ranchers as they struggle to safeguard their 200,000 acre west Texas Ranch, the Yellow Rose. Focal point is the efforts of Jeb Hollister to regain control of the Yellow Rose—which he lost over a bet with its late owner, Wade Champion.

Roy Champion	David Soul
Colleen Champion	Cybill Shepherd
Quisto Champion	Edward Albert
Chance MacKenzie	Sam Elliott
L. C. "Love Child" Champion	Michelle Bennett
Whit Champion	Tom Schanley
Grace MacKenzie	Susan Anspach
Jeb Hollister	Chuck Connors
Rose Hollister	Jane Russell
Luther Dillard	Noah Beery Jr.
Hoyt Coryell	Ken Curtis
Juliette Hollister	Deborah Shelton
Lenny Hollister	Steve Sandor
Caryn Cabrera	Teri Keane
John Stronghart	Will Sampson
Marlene Champion	Karen Carlson
Trey Champion	Greg Evigan

Theme Vocal ("The Yellow Rose"): Johnny Lee, Lane Brody

Producer: Michael Zinberg, John Wilder

Yes Yes Nanette

Comedy; 30 min; NBC 1/6/61 to 7/7/61

Events in the lives of the McGovern family: Dan, a Hollywood writer; Nanette, his wife, a former Broadway actress; and their children, Nancy and Buddy. Stories are based on real-life incidents drawn from the lives of Nanette Fabray and her husband, writer Ranald MacDougall. Also known as "The Nanette Fabray Show" and "Westinghouse Playhouse."

Nanette McGovern	Nanette Fabray
Dan McGovern	Wendell Corey
Nancy McGovern	Jacklyn O'Donnell
Buddy McGovern	Bobby Diamond
Mrs. Harper (housekeeper)	Doris Kemper

Producer: Larry Berns

The Yesterday Show

Comedy Pilot; 30 min; HBO 4/6/83

A spoof of TV newsmagazine shows wherein each program is devoted to a specific time, and through news footage and sketches, events of that time are satirized.

Jane Lawlor	Ann Ryerson
Nick Spangler III	Eric Boardman
Tony Burrell	Jim Staahl

Regulars: Rick Thomas, Megan Faye, Fran Guinan, Mike Hagarty, Joe Keefe, Lance Kinsey, Jeanette Schwaba, Lucy D'Alliso

Producer: Bernard and Jane Shalins

Yogi Bear

Cartoon; 30 min; Syn. 1958

Segments: "Yogi Bear" (the antics of Yogi, a Jellystone National Park bear); "Snagglepuss" (misadventures of a trouble-prone lion); and "Yakky Doodle Duck" (adventures of a mischievous duckling).

Yogi Bear/ Snagglepuss	Daws Butler
Boo Boo Bear/ Ranger Smith	Don Messick
Yakky Doodle	Jimmy Weldon

Producer: William Hanna, Joseph Barbera

Yogi's Gang

Cartoon; 30 min; ABC 9/8/73 to 8/30/75

As living conditions become intolerable, Yogi Bear and his friends hire inventor Noah Smith to build a flying ark. Stories relate the efforts of Yogi and his gang to battle the enemies of man and nature—polluters.

Yogi Bear/Augie Doggie/ Huckleberry Hound/ Snagglepuss/ Quick Draw McGraw/Peter Potamus/Wally Gator	Daws Butler
Boo Boo Bear/ Touche Turtle/ Atom Ant	Don Messick
Magilla Gorilla	Allan Melvin
Doggie Daddy	John Stephenson

Producer: William Hanna, Joseph Barbera

Yogi's Space Race

Cartoon; NBC 9/9/78 to 10/28/78 (90 min)
11/4/78 to 1/27/79 (60 min)

The format finds Yogi Bear and his friend, Scarebear, as astronauts who compete in various space races for prizes.

Yogi Bear/ Huckleberry Hound	Daws Butler
Scarebear	Joe Besser
Jabberjaw/Buford/ Captain Good/ Kleen Cat/ Phantom Phink/ Sludge	Frank Welker
Rita	Pat Parris
Wendy	Marilyn Schreffler
Quackup	Mel Blanc
Announcer	Gary Owens

Producer: William Hanna, Joseph Barbera

Yogi's Treasure Hunt

Cartoon; 30 min; Syn. 9/85

The series features many Hanna-Barbera characters joining forces to recover lost treasures.

Yogi Bear/ Huckleberry Hound/Quick Draw McGraw/ Snagglepuss/Wally Gator	Daws Butler
Boo Boo Bear/ Touche Turtle	Don Messick
Top Cat	Arnold Stang
Dick Dastardly	Paul Winchell

Producer: William Hanna, Joseph Barbera

You Again?

Comedy; 30 min; NBC 2/27/86 to 1/7/87

When his wife runs off with another man, and his ten-year-old son decides to go with his mother, middle-aged businessman Henry Willows files for divorce. Seven years later, Henry's son, Matthew, returns home to live with his father when he can no longer get along with his step-father. Stories relate the misadventures of a conservative, loudmouthed father and his liberal-minded son.

Henry Willows — Jack Klugman
Matthew Willows — John Stamos
Enid Tompkins
  (housekeeper) — Elizabeth Bennett
Wendy (Henry's
  secretary) — Valorie Armstrong
Pam (replaced
  Wendy) — Valerie Landsburg
Maggie Davis
  (Henry's boss) — Barbara Rhoades
Randy Willows
  (Henry's brother) — George Grizzard
Sue (Henry's ex-
  wife) — Anita Gillette
Mabel (Enid's
  friend) — Fritzi Burr
Jim Berry
  (accountant)* — Armin Shimmerman

Producer: Sarah Lawson, Ronny Hallin, Rick Mintz

*At Global Markets, where Henry is an assistant buyer.

You Are the Jury

Drama Pilot; 60 min; NBC 5/5/84 (1st pilot)
        5/26/86 (2nd pilot)
        11/25/86 (3rd pilot)

A proposed series that allows viewers to determine the guilt or innocence of a defendant in a crime. The program begins in a courtroom and flashbacks are used to recall the crime. Special 900 telephone numbers are given (one for guilty; one for innocent) and the viewer results are given at the end of the drama. In the first pilot, "The Case of the People vs. Joseph Landrum," viewers found the defendant innocent of murdering his wife's lover (the actual jury found him guilty); viewers found the defendant in the second pilot ("The State of Arizona vs. Dr. Evan Blake") guilty, while the actual jury found him innocent of killing his wife. In the final pilot, "The State of Ohio vs. James Wolsky," viewers found the defendant guilty of killing his girlfriend—as did the real jury.

Host (Pilots 1&3): Efrem Zimablist Jr.

Host (Pilot 2): Robert Vaughn

Joseph Landrum — Joseph Regalbuto
Dorothy Landrum — Cindy Fisher
Sara Dabney — Nita Talbot
Elizabeth Hardy — Judith Light
Dr. Evan Blake — Wayne Northrop
Susan Grant — Constance McCashin
James Wolsky — Pat O'Bryan
Philip Lombardo — Vince Edwards

Producer: Dick Clark, Al Schwartz, Mary Jo Blue

You Are There

Anthology; 30 min; CBS 11/4/53 to 10/13/57

Through reenactments and present-day interviews, people and situations that affected world events are brought to life through eyewitness accounts.

Host-Narrator: Walter Cronkite

Reporters: Harry Marble, Winston Burdett, Bill Leonard, Dick Joy, Todd Hunter, William Kenneally, Clete Roberts, Harlow Wilcox, Grant Sewell, Lou Cioffi

Regulars: DeForest Kelley, Paul Birch, Barry Atwater, Claude Akins, John Larch, Whit Bissell

Producer: Charles Russell, James Fonda

You Are There

Anthology; 30 min; CBS 9/11/71 to 9/2/72

A revised version of the prior title (which see for format) with Walter Cronkite again serving as the host and narrator. Produced by Burton Benjamin, Vern Diamond, and Barbara Schwartz.

You Asked For It

Human Interest; 30 min; DuMont 12/29/50 to
           12/3/51
         ABC 12/10/51 to
           9/2/59

The program attempts to answer viewers' requests (through films) for unusual sights or entertainment acts. Also titled "The Art Baker Show."

Host: Art Baker, Jack Smith

Producer: Cran Chamberlain, Tommy

Tomlilson, Steve Carlin, Wayne Steffner, Rick Mittleman

You Asked For It

Human Interest; 30 min; Syn. 9/81

Videotaped segments that fulfill viewers' requests to see unusual or bizarre events.

Host: Rich Little, Jack Smith

Hostess: Janet Langhart, Dale Harimoto

Field Reporters: Toni Thomas, Kathy Cronkite, Desaree Goyette, Danielle Folquet, Alan Erickson, Alanna Davis, Adrienne Allen, Delvene Delaney

Announcer: John Harlan, Paul Kirby

Producer: Sandy Frank, Lee Mendelson, Robert Guenette, Chris Pye

You Bet Your Life

Game; 30 min; NBC 9/5/50 to 9/21/61

Two players, working as a team, compete. Contestants are first interviewed, then must answer a series of questions based on a category they chose. Correct answers score money (according to the money value of the question chosen) while incorrect responses cuts any cash total they may have in half. The team with the highest score receives the money they have won, plus the chance to win additional cash by answering a difficult general knowledge question.

Host: Groucho Marx

Announcer-Assistant: George Fenneman

Secret Word Girl: Marilyn Burtis

Theme Song ("Hooray for Captain Spaulding"): Bert Kalmar, Harry Ruby

Producer: John Guedel

You Bet Your Life

Game; 30 min; Syn. 9/80

A revised version of the prior title, which see for format.

Host: Buddy Hackett

Assistant: Ron Husmann

Music: The Robert Ivie Organization

Producer: Bob Eubanks, Michael Hill

You Can't Take It with You

Comedy; 30 min; Syn. 9/87

Events in the day-to-day lives of an eccentric Staten Island (N.Y.) family: Martin Vanderhoff, a retired advertising man; Penelope "Penny" Sycamore, his married daughter, a writer; Paul, Penny's husband, a wacky toy inventor; and Penny's two daughters, Alice and Essie.

Martin Vanderhoff	Harry Morgan
Penny Sycamore	Lois Nettleton
Paul Sycamore	Richard Sanders
Alice Sycamore	Lisa Aliff
Essie Sycamore	Elizabeth Townsend*
	Heather Blodgett
Durward Pinner (Paul's assistant)	Teddy Wilson
Mr. DePinna	Teddy Wilson*

Producer: Pamela Rosser, Chris Peterson, Larry Hart, Sid Smith

*Role in the never-telecast, original pilot

You Don't Say

Game; 30 min; NBC 4/1/63 to 9/26/69

One member (of each two member team) receives the name of a famous person or place. This player makes up and relates a sentence to his partner wherein he leaves the last word, which sounds like part of the name, blank. If the player guesses the name, the team scores one point; if not, the opponents receive a turn. A two-out-of-three match competition is played with the winners receiving $100. See next title also.

Host: Tom Kennedy

Announcer: John Harlan

Producer: Ralph Andrews, Bill Yageman

You Don't Say

Game; 30 min; ABC 7/7/75 to 11/26/75

Four celebrities are given the name of a famous person or place. One player (two compete) selects one celebrity, who in turn gives him a clue by making up a sentence and leaving the last word, which sounds like a part of the name, blank. If the player identifies the name or place within five seconds, he scores $200; if not, his opponent receives a chance (a second clue decreases money to $150; a third clue to $100; and a final clue to $50). The first player to score $600 is the winner.

Host: Tom Kennedy

Announcer: John Harlan

Producer: Bill Carruthers

You Don't Say

Game; 30 min; Syn. 9/78

A syndicated version of the prior title, which see for format.

Host: Jim Peck

Announcer: John Harlan

Producer: Ralph Edwards

You Should Meet My Sister

Comedy Pilot; 30 min; NBC 5/16/60

The pilot for "My Sister Eileen" (which aired on "Goodyear Theatre"). The story of two pretty sisters who leave Ohio and head for New York to further their careers: Ruth as a writer, and Eileen as an actress.

Ruth Sherwood	Elaine Stritch
Eileen Sherwood	Anne Helm
Mr. Spivak	Henry Corden
The Wreck	Tom Reese
Helen	Pattie Chapman

You Write the Songs

Contest; 30 min; Syn. 9/86

Aspiring songwriters compete for the opportunity to win $100,000. The original compositions of three songwriters, which are performed by a resident company of singers and dancers, are judged by a celebrity panel who rate it from 1 to 10 (based on hit potential). The weekly winners receive $1,000 and return the following week to compete again. The five best songs in a twelve week period are judged in a final competition with the best songwriter receiving $100,000.

Host: Ben Vereen

Regulars: Sam Harris, Catte Adams, Kenny James, Monica Page, Terry Gregory, Derrell Coleman

Producer: Bob Banner, Sam Riddle

Young Dan'l Boone

Adventure; 60 min; CBS 9/12/77 to 10/4/77

The series, set in Kentucky during the 19th-century, details the exploits of Daniel Boone, the frontiersman-pioneer, as a young man (age 25) before he became a legend.

Daniel Boone	Rick Moses
Rebecca Bryan	Devon Ericson
Peter Dawes	John Joseph Thomas
Hawk	Ji-Tu Cumbuka
Tsiskwa	Eloy Phil Casados

Theme Vocal ("Young Dan'l Boone"): The Mike Curb Congregation

Producer: Ernie Frankel, Jimmy Sangster

Young Dr. Kildare

Drama; 30 min; Syn. 1972

An updated version of "Doctor Kildare," which continues to depict the victories and defeats of James Kildare, a young resident intern at Blair General Hospital.

Dr. James Kildare	Mark Jenkins
Dr. Leonard Gillespie	Gary Merrill
Nurse Marsha Lord	Marsha Mason
Nurse Ferris	Dixie Marquis
Nurse Newell	Olga James
Orderly	Dennis Robinson

Producer: Joseph Gantman

Young Guy Christian

Comedy Pilot; 30 min; ABC 5/24/79

A spoof a superspy dramas as seen through the exploits of Guy Christian, a playboy who combats international evil in his spare time.

Guy Christian	Barry Bostwick
Prof. Mishugi	Pat Morita
Mia Mishugi	Shelley Long
Junkman	Richard Karron

Producer: Jerry Belson, Michael Leeson

Young Hearts

Comedy Pilot; 30 min; NBC 3/18/84

The misadventures of a group of middle-class St. Louis teenagers who find fun and romance at the local shopping mall.

Doug Fettis	Jeffrey Rogers
Karen Fettis	Anne Howard
Larry Fettis	Jerry Supiran
Wendy Fettis	Patricia Harty
Carl Fettis	Michael Callan
Kate	Michelle Downey
Bernie	Anthony Holland
Eddie	Charles Zucker
Beef	Michael Zorek
Jeanie Grousley	Janeen Best
Keith	Michael Dudikoff

Theme Vocal ("Young Hearts"): Donna McDaniel

Producer: Jeff Franklin, Howard West

Young In Heart

Comedy Pilot; 30 min; CBS 8/16/65

The story of Margaret Malloy, the house-mother at Kappa Phi, a college sorority house.

Margaret Malloy	Mercedes McCambridge
Gerry Hart	Barbara Bain
Evelyn Winters	Kay Stewart
Ted Halsey	Lin Foster
Liz Prescott	Nancy Marshall
Charles Prescott	Charles Watt

Producer: Fletcher Markle

The Young Lawyers

Drama; 60 min; ABC 9/21/70 to 5/5/71

The experiences of Aaron Silverman and Pat Walters, Bercol University law students, who work part time for the Neighborhood Law Office, a legal-aid service in Boston, Mass.

David Barrett (senior lawyer)	Lee J. Cobb
Michael Cannon (senior lawyer)	Jason Evers*
Aaron Silverman	Zalman King
Pat Walters	Judy Pace
Ann Fielding	Judy Pace*
Lawyer Chris Blake	Philip Clark

Producer: Matthew Rapf

*TV Movie roles (10/28/69).

Young Maverick

Western; 60 min; CBS 11/28/79 to 1/16/80

A continuation of the "Maverick" series, which details the exploits of Ben Maverick (Beau's son), a suave, fast-talking gambler who roams throughout the west seeking rich prey. See also "Bret Maverick" and "Maverick."

Ben Maverick	Charles Frank
Neil McGarrahan	Susan Blanchard
Marshal Edge Troy	John Dehner

Producer: Robert Van Scoyk, Andy White, Chuck Bowman

Young Mr. Bobbin

Comedy; 30 min; NBC 8/26/51 to 5/18/52

The story of Alexander Bobbin, a recent high school graduate, as he struggles to establish himself in the business world.

Alexander Bobbin	Jackie Kelk
Nancy (his girlfriend)	Pat Hosley
Susie (Nancy's sister)	Laura Webber
Aunt Birdie	Jane Seymour
Aunt Bertha	Nydia Westman

Producer: Jack Scibetta

The Young Pioneers

Drama; 60 min; ABC 4/2/78 to 4/16/78

The series, set in Dakota during the 1870s, relates the enduring hardships of Molly and David Beaton, young newlyweds who are struggling to make a new life for themselves on the hostile frontier. Based on the "The Young Pioneer" books by Rose Wilder Lane.

Molly Beaton	Linda Purl
David Beaton	Roger Kern
Dan Gray	Robert Hays
Mr. Peters	Robert Donner
Nettie Peters	Mare Winningham
	Shelley Jutner*
	Kay Kimler**
Flora Peters	Michelle Stacy
	Sherri Wagner**
Charlie Peters	Jeff Cotler
	Brian Melrose**

Narrator: Linda Purl

Producer: Earl Hamner, Lee Rich, Ed Friendly

*TV Movie role ("The Young Pioneers," 3/1/76).
**TV Movie role ("The Young Pioneers' Christmas," 12/17/76).

The Young Rebels

Adventure; 60 min; ABC 9/20/70 to 1/15/71

The series, set in Chester, Pennsylvania, in 1777, follows the exploits of the Yankee Doodle Society, a secret organization that struggles to foil British advances on the Colonies.

Jeremy Larkin	Rick Ely
Isak Poole	Lou Gossett
Elizabeth Coates	Hilary Thompson
Henry Abington	Alex Henteloff
Gen. Lafayette	Philippe Forquet

Producer: Aaron Spelling, Jon Epstein

The Young Sentinels

Cartoon; 30 min; NBC 9/10/77 to 9/2/78

At a time when the Earth was young, three people (Hercules, Astria, and Mercury) are chosen by an alien life force (Sentinel One) for a special mission: to battle evil. The Earthlings, specially trained and instructed, are returned to their planet. Stories relate their efforts watch over the human race and help the good flourish.

Hercules	Geroge DiCenzo
Astria	Dee Timberlake
Mercury	Evan Kim

Producer: Norm Prescott, Lou Scheimer

The Young Set

Discussion; 60 min; ABC 9/6/65 to 12/17/65

Phyllis Kirk as the host of a daily series of discussions on topical issues. "The Young Set" theme song by Ray Martin.

Your All American College Show

Variety; 30 min; Syn. 1968

Performances by college entertainment acts (four per show). The winners, determined by guest judges, receive $1000.

Host: Dennis James, Rich Little, Arthur Godfrey

Producer: Arthur Godfrey

Your Chevrolet Showroom

Variety; 60 min; ABC 11/20/53 to 2/12/54

Cesar Romero as the host of a variety showcase that spotlights lesser known performers. Sponsored by Chevrolet.

Your Favorite Story

Anthology; 30 min; Syn. 1/53

Dramas based on stories selected by guests. Hosted by Adolphe Menjou and produced by Frederic A. Ziv.

Your First Impression

Game; 30 min; NBC 1/2/62 to 4/27/64

Object: For a celebrity panel to identify mystery guests through a series of indirect question-and-answer rounds.

Host: Dennis James, Bill Leyden

Producer: Monty Hall

Your Funny Funny Films

Comedy; 30 min; ABC 7/8/63 to 9/9/63

Amateur home movies, which have been professionally edited for laughs, are showcased.

Host: George Fenneman

Producer: Hy Freedman, Albert Z. Freedman

Your Hit Parade

Variety; 30 min; NBC 7/10/50 to 6/17/58

America's taste in popular music is dramatized via musical sketches. See also the following two titles.

Cast: June Valli, Eileen Wilson, Dorothy Collins, Snooky Lanson, Gisele MacKenzie, Russell Arms, Tommy Leonetti, Jill Corey, Virginia Gibson, Alan Copeland

Regulars: Niles & Fosse, The Hit Parade Singers & Dancers

Orchestra: Raymond Scott, Peter Van Steeden, Dick Jacobs, Harry Sosnik

Announcer: Andre Baruch, John Laing

Producer: Dan Lounsberry, Ted Fetter

Your Hit Parade

Variety; 30 min; CBS 10/10/58 to 4/24/59

A revised version of the prior title, which continues to dramatize America's taste in popular music.

Cast: Dorothy Collins, Jill Corey, Virginia Gibson, Johnny Desmond

Regulars: Chuck Cassey, Sara Jane Tallman, Ken Bridges, Bob Sands, Marilyn Jackson, Ray Cooke, Dean Parker, Lia Farmer

Orchestra: Harry Sosnik

Announcer: Art Gilmore

Producer: Perry Lafferty

Your Hit Parade

Variety; 30 min; CBS 8/2/74 to 8/30/74

A revised version of the previous title, which see for format.

Regulars: Kelly Garrett, Sheralee, Chuck Woolery, The Tom Hanson Dancers

Announcer: Art Gilmore

Orchestra: Milton DeLugg

Producer: Chuck Barris, Budd Granoff

Your Jeweler's Showcase

Anthology; 30 min; CBS 11/11/52 to 6/9/53

Dramatizations produced by Gilbert A. Ralston and directed by Arthur Ripley. Featuring such stars as Phyllis Coates, Celeste Holm, Sheldon Leonard, Jan Clayton, Barbara Whiting, Martha Hayer, Ellen Corby, and Ruth Warrick.

Your Lucky Clue

Game; 30 min; CBS 7/1/52 to 8/31/52

A dramatic sketch, which outlines the facts of a criminal case, is enacted on stage. The first player to solve the case is the winner and receives merchandise prizes.

Host: Basil Rathbone

Announcer: Andre Baruch

Your Luncheon Date

Variety; 30 min; DuMont 11/9/51 to 1/5/52

An afternoon program of music and songs with Hugh Downs and Nancy Wright. Music by the Art Van Damme Quintet.

Your New Day

Variety; 30 min; Syn. 9/80

A daily series of consumer tips, beauty advice, exercise, and related entertainment geared to women.

Host: Vidal Sassoon

Regulars: Suzy Prudden, Nina Blanchard

Announcer: John Harlan

Producer: John E. Ringel, Stanley H. Moger

Your Number's Up

Game; 30 min; NBC 9/23/85 to 12/20/85

Three players compete and answer questions based on numbers that appear on a spinning wheel. A correct response scores the player one diamond and the number in play is placed on a large board. Prior to the game, studio audience members were asked to write down the last four digits of their phone numbers. When a studio member matches his phone number with the numbers that appear on the board, he chooses the player he feels will be the winner. The first player to score six diamonds is the winner and receives $500. If the studio audience player is correct, he wins a prize.

Host: Nipsey Russell

Hostess: Lee Minney

Announcer: Gene Wood, John Harlan

Producer: Sande Stewart

Your Place or Mine?

Comedy Pilot; 30 min; CBS 5/27/78

Kelly, an attractive editorial assistant for a Manhattan magazine, lives in Queens. Jeff, a young writer, lives in Manhattan, but longs for the tranquility of the country. The unsold series was to relate their misadventures when they meet, fall in love, and decide to swap residences to be closer to what they each require.

Kelly Barnes	Jane Actman
Jeff Burrell	Stuart Gillard
Frances Barnes	Alice Hirson
Ernie Barnes	Peter Hobbs
Linda Heller	Judy Graubart
Mrs. Hicks	Elizabeth Kerr
Harold	George Pentecost
Carol	Elizabeth Halliday

Producer: Bob Ellison, David Lloyd

Your Show of Shows

Variety; 90 min; NBC 2/25/50 to 6/5/54

A weekly series of music, songs, and comedy featuring high quality material and an outstanding cast of comedians.

Host: Sid Caesar

Regulars: Imogene Coca, Carl Reiner, Howard Morris, Cliff Norton, Judy Johnson, Robert Merrill, Marguerite Piazza, Bill Hayes, Nellie Fisher, Virginia Curtis, Roy Drakely, Rod Alexander, The Bob Hamilton Trio, The Billy Williams Quartet, The Chandra Kay Dancers

Orchestra: Charles Sanford, Tony Romano, Irwin Kostal

Announcer: Vaughn Monroe

Producer: Max Liebman

Creator: Sylvestor "Pat" Weaver

Your Show Time

Anthology; 30 min; NBC 1/21/49 to 7/15/49

An early series of filmed dramas with Arthur Fields as host.

Your Star Showcase

A syndicated (1953) series of retitled episodes of "The G.E. Theatre" with Edward Arnold as host.

Your Surprise Package

Game; 30 min; CBS 3/13/61 to 2/23/62

A large box, which contains merchandise items, is displayed. The value of the box, but not its contents is revealed to three players. The first player who correctly answers a question receives cash and a chance to purchase time with which to question the host concerning the contents of the box. The game continues until one player identifies the contents (which become his prize).

Host: George Fenneman

Announcer: Bern Bennett

Producer: Al Singer, Allan Sherman

Your Surprise Store

Game; 30 min; CBS 5/12/52 to 6/27/52

Selected players compete in either question-and-answer rounds or by performing stunts. The most successful player receives a chance to select items from a "Surprise Store" that is constructed on stage.

Host: Lew Parker

Co-Host: Jacqueline Susann

Announcer: Bern Bennett

Producer: Hal Frimberg

You're Gonna Love It Here

Comedy Pilot; 30 min; CBS 6/1/77

The story of Lolly Rogers, a Broadway star who is suddenly saddled with the temporary care of her 11-year-old grandson, Peter, when the boy's parents are jailed for tax evasion.

Lolly Rogers	Ethel Merman	Harry Toffler Sr.	Dick Shawn
Peter Rogers	Christopher Barnes	Harry Toffler Jr.	Barry Gordon
Harry Rogers		Cheryl Toffler	Nellie Bellflower
(Lolly's son)	Austin Pendleton	Claudine	Maureen Arthur

Theme Vocal ("You're Gonna Love It Here"): Ethel Merman

Producer: Frank Konigsberg

You're in the Picture

Game; 30 min; CBS 1/20/61 (as above title) 1/27/61 to 3/24/61 (as "The Jackie Gleason Show")

Each of the four celebrities who appear stand behind large picture scenes with their heads through appropriate cutouts. Players, who are unable to see the celebrities, had to identify their situations through a question-and-answer session with the host. After the first telecast, the format was dropped (as host Jackie Gleason felt the idea was just so bad) and Jackie appeared the following week to apologize for the initial episode. The remainder of the series became a talk show with Jackie interviewing guests and talking about his career.

Host: Jackie Gleason

Panelists: Keenan Wynn, Pat Carroll, Jan Sterling, Arthur Treacher

Producer: Steve Carlin, Jack Philbin

You're Invited

Variety; 30 min; ABC 7/1/48 to 9/20/48

Ralph Vincent as the host of a program that spotlights performances by guests.

You're Just Like Your Father

Comedy Pilot; 30 min; CBS 8/13/76

The comic adventures of a father (Harry Sr.) who believes in the great American Dream that success is just around the corner, and his son (Harry Jr.) and partner in the near-bankrupt Toffler Enterprises, who is following in his misguided footsteps.

Producer: Lee Rich, Lawrence Marks

You're On Your Own

Game; 30 min; CBS 12/22/56 to 3/10/57

Three players compete in a question-and-answer session wherein correct answers score points, while incorrect answers force players to perform humiliating stunts. The highest scoring player is the winner.

Host: Steve Dunne

Producer: Jack Barry, Dan Enright

You're Only Young Once

Comedy Pilot; 30 min; CBS 9/11/62

The trials and tribulations of Casey and Liz McDermott, newlyweds who are also students at the University of Southern California.

Casey McDermott	Jim Hutton
Liz McDermott	Patricia Blair
Mildred Offenbach	Dorothy Provine
Piggy Burke	Charlie Briggs
Midge Burke	Lynn Alden
Connie Fletcher	Ann Morgan Guilbert

Producer: Richard L. Bare

You're Only Young Twice

Comedy Pilot; 30 min; CBS 8/1/60

The story of a middle-aged couple (Charles and Kit) who, after their children marry, decide to rediscover life.

Charles Tyler	George Murphy
Kit Tyler	Martha Scott
Lois	Sue Randall
Arthur	Roger Perry
Olga	Jane Darwell

Producer: Desi Arnaz, Ed Jurist

You're Only Young Twice

Comedy Pilot; 30 min; CBS 7/3/67

The story of Hubert Abernathy, a scientist who invents a rejuvenation pill that makes people ten years younger—but only for a short period of time.

Prof. Hubert	
Abernathy	Ed Wynn
Carrie	Ethel Waters
Betsy Fleming	Kathryn Hays
George Fleming	Andrew Duggan
Andy	Andy Devine
Charlie	Steve Dunn
George	Jerry Van Dyke
Joan	Patricia Crowley
Lennie	Dwayne Hickman

Producer: Stan Shpetner

You're Putting Me On

Game; 30 min; NBC 7/3/69 to 12/26/69

One member of each two-member team is given the name of a celebrity. By assuming that celebrity's identity, he must get his partner to guess who he is. Correct answers score points, and the highest scoring team wins.

Host: Bill Cullen, Larry Blyden

Panelists: Anne Meara, Peggy Cass

Announcer: Jack Clark

Yours For a Song

Game; 30 min; ABC 11/14/61 to 9/18/63 (evening run)
12/4/61 to 3/19/63 (daytime run)

The lyrics to a popular song, which contain certain word omissions, are flashed on a screen. The first player (two compete) who is able to fill in the missing words receives $20. Winners, who receive their earnings, are the highest cash scorers.

Host: Bert Parks

Model: Michaelina Martel

Announcer: Johnny Gilbert

Zane Grey Theatre

Anthology; 30 min; CBS 10/5/56 to 9/20/62

An above average series of western dramas that feature top-name guest stars and well-written and directed stories. Also known as "Dick Powell's Zane Grey Theatre."

Host: Dick Powell

Producer: Hal Hudson, Aaron Spelling, Stephen Lord

Zero Intelligence

Comedy Pilot; 30 min; ABC 8/10/76

A lighter side of the Cold War as seen through the activities of a group of servicemen stationed at a top-secret radar station in Alaska in 1959.

Higgins	Don Galloway
Deerfield	Sorrell Booke
Fred	Tom Rosqui
Arnold	Michael Huddleston
Ruben	Chu Chu Malave
Mo	Clyde Kusatsu

Producer: Saul Ilson, Ernest Chambers

Zero One

Adventure; 30 min; Syn. 1962

The exploits of Alan Garrett, the head of Airline Security International, a London-based airline crime detection team.

Alan Garrett	Nigel Patrick
Maya	Katya Douglas
Jim Delaney	William Smith

The Zoo Gang

Crime Drama; 60 min; NBC 7/6/75 to 8/6/75

The story of four World War II resistance fighters, known as the Zoo Gang, who reunite twenty-eight years later to battle crime in Europe.

Steven Halliday (the	
Fox)	Brian Keith
Monouche Roget	
(the Leopard)	Lilli Palmer
Tom Devon (the	
Elephant)	John Mills
Alec Marlowe (the	
Tiger)	Barry Morse
Lt. Georges Roget	Michael Petrovitch
Jill Barton (Tom's	
niece)	Seretta Wilson

Theme Song ("The Zoo Gang"): Paul & Linda McCartney

Producer: Herbert Hirschman

Zoobilee Zoo

Children; 30 min; Syn. 9/86

A musical variety series that spotlights the talents of the Zoobles, the magical animals of Zoobilee Zoo.

Mayor Ben	Ben Vereen
Wazzat Kangaroo	Louise Vallance
Bill Der Beaver	Sandy Grinn
	Michael Sheehan
Lookout Bear	Michael D.
	Monyahan
Van Go Lion	Forrest Gardner
Bravo Fox	Gary Schwartz
Talkatoo Cockatoo	Karen Hartman

Producer: Steve Binder, Andy Heyward, Jean Chalopin

Zorro

Adventure; 30 min; ABC 9/19/57 to 9/24/59

When Enrique Monastario, an evil Spanish captain establishes himself as commandant of Old Los Angeles (Monterey, 1820s), the wealthy Don Diego de la Vega poses as a lazy man-about-town as a cover for his secret alias of El Zorro (The Fox), a mysterious nobleman who crusades against injustice. Stories relate Don Diego's efforts to end Monastario's reign. See also "Zorro and Son."

Don Diego/Zorro	Guy Williams
Capt. Enrique	
Monastario	Britt Lomond
Bernardo	Gene Sheldon

Sgt. Garcia	Henry Calvin
Nacho Torres	Jan Arvan
Elena Torres	Eugenia Paul
Anita Cabrillo	Annette Funicello
Ricardo Del Amo	Richard Anderson
Anna Maria	Jolene Brand
Magistrate Galindo	Vinton Hayworth
Cpl. Reyes	Don Diamond

Producer: Walt Disney, William H. Anderson

Zorro and Son

Comedy; 30 min; CBS 4/6/83 to 6/1/83

A satirical version of the prior title. When Bernardo, Don Diego's faithful servant, realizes that Diego is aging and unable to perform as Zorro should, he sends to Spain for Diego's son, Don Carlos. When Don Carlos arrives in Old California and discovers that the new commandante, Paco Pico, is unfairly posing his law on the citizens, he is instilled with a desire to help them. Seeing this, Don Diego reveals to his son his other identity—and begins a quest to train his son as the new Zorro. Stories depict the comical exploits of Zorro and Son as they struggle to protect the oppressed.

Don Diego	Henry Darrow
Don Carlos	Paul Regina
Bernardo	Bill Dana
Commandante Paco	
Pico	Gregory Sierra
Sgt. Sepulveda	Richard Beauchamp
Cpl. Cassette	John Moschitta Jr.
Brothers Napa and	
Sonoma	Barney Martin
Senorita Anita	Catherine Parks

Producer: William Robert Yates, Eric Cohen, Kevin Corcoran

Performers Index

The following selective index lists performers followed by the programs on which they worked. Page or program numbers have been omitted. Further information can be found by looking up the desired program. Because of the unusual nature of this index, please keep in mind that the credits listed are for series and pilot film work only; individual episode or TV movie appearances are not included.

Show—Hot Off the Wire, Mr. Magoo, New Adventures of Gilligan, What's New Mr. Magoo?

Baddeley, Hermione: Call Holme, Camp Runamuck, Cara Williams Show, Good Life, Maude

Badler, Jane: Riptide, V

Baer, Max: Asphalt Cowboy, Beverly Hillbillies, Circle Family

Baer, Parley: Addams Family, Adventures of Ozzie and Harriet, Andy Griffith Show, Carolyn, Doc, Don Rickles Show, Double Life of Henry Phyfe, Hello Larry, Marriage Broker

Baggetta, Vincent: Chicago Story, Eddie Capra Mysteries, Jack and Mike, Lou Grant, Sam Penny and Associate

Bailey, G.W.: Earthlings, Goodnight Beantown, Hardcase, M*A*S*H, On Our Way, Second Edition, St. Elsewhere, There Goes the Neighborhood

Bailey, Pearl: Pearl Bailey Show, Silver Spoons

Bailey, Raymond: Beverly Hillbillies, Dear Mom, Dear Dad, Dobie Gillis, Life of Vernon Hathaway, My Sister Eileen

Bain, Barbara: Mission: Impossible, Richard Diamond Private Detective, Space: 1999, Young in Heart

Bain, Conrad: Diff'rent Strokes, Maude, Mr. President

Baio, Jimmy: Academy, Family Business, Freeman, Joe and Sons, Sheehy and the Supreme Machine, Soap

Baio, Scott: Blansky's Beauties, Charles in Charge (two titles), Happy Days, Joanie Loves Chachi, Legs, We're Movin', Who's Watching the Kids?

Baird, Bil and Cora: Bil Baird Show, Life with Snarky Parker, Whistling Wizard

Baird, Sharon: Annette, Bay City Rollers Show, Bugaloos, Donny and Marie, Land of the Lost, Lidsville, Mickey Mouse Club, New Zoo Revue, Sigmund and the Sea Monsters

Bakalyan, Dick: Bobby Darin Amusement Company, Border Pals, Bunco

Baker, Art: End of the Rainbow, You Asked for It

Baker, Diane: Here We Go Again, Kojak

Baker, Joby: Good Morning, World, Six O'Clock Follies, Stone

Baker, Joe: Big Show, Cheap Show, Des O'Connor Show, Fred and Barney Meet the Thing, Kopycats, No Soap Radio, Off the Wall, Plasticman, Rich Little Show, Skatebirds, Steve Allen Comedy Hour, Three Robonic Stooges

Baker, Joe Don: Eischied

Baker, Tom: Doctor Who

Bal, Jeanne: Bachelor Father, Mr. Novak, NBC Playhouse

Baldavin, Barbara: Adam-12, Medical Center, Star Trek

Balding, Rebecca: Family Ties, Lou Grant, Makin' It, Mr. & Mrs. & Mr., Soap

Balduzzi, Dick: Heaven on Earth, Mary Tyler Moore Show, Pete 'N' Tittie, Susan and Sam

Baldwin, Alec: Cutter to Houston, Sheriff and the Astronaut

Baldwin, Bill: Andy Griffith Show, Leave It to Beaver, Mayor of Hollywood, Sawyer and Finn

Baldwin, Judith: Gilligan's Island, Tales of the Apple Dumpling Gang

Ball, Lucille: Here's Lucy, I Love Lucy, Life with Lucy, Lucille Ball-Desi Arnaz Show, Lucy Show, Music Mart

Ballard, Kaye: Colgate Comedy Hour, Doris Day Show, Henry Morgan's Great Talent Hunt, Irene, Mothers-in-Law, Steve Allen Comedy Hour

Balsam, Martin: Archie Bunker's Place, Defender, Time Element

Balsam, Talia: Fit for a King, Punky Brewster, Taxi, When the Whistle Blows

Balson, Allison: Life and Times of Eddie Roberts, Little House on the Prairie

Baltzell, Deborah: I'm a Big Girl Now, Love at First Sight

Bancroft, Anne: That Was the Week That Was (pilot)

Bankhead, Tallulah: Big Party for Revlon

Banks, Jonathan: Boys in Blue, Fighting Nightingales, G.I.'s, Gangster Chronicles, Report to Murphy, Rowdies

Bannon, Jack: Lou Grant, Maureen, Susan and Sam, Trauma Center

Barash, Olivia: Daughters, In the Beginning, Out of the Blue

Barbeau, Adrienne: Fighting Nightingales, Maude

Barber, Glynis: Blake's 7, Dempsey and Makepeace

Bari, Lynn: Arroyo, Boss Lady, Detective's Wife

Barker, Bob: End of the Rainbow, Family Game, New Price Is Right, Price Is Right, That's My Line, Truth Or Consequences

Barnes, Joanna: Anything for Money, Betty White Show, Dateline: Hollywood, Executive Suite, Patrick Stone, Tarzan the Ape Man, Trials of O'Brien, 21 Beacon Street, 333 Montgomery

Barnes, Priscilla: American Girls, She's the Sheriff, Three's Company

Baron, Sandy: Della, Hey Landlord

Barr, Douglas (Doug): Fall Guy, Semi-Tough, When the Whistle Blows, Wizard

Barrett, Majel: Leave It to Beaver, Star Trek (three titles)

Barrett, Rona: Dateline: Hollywood, Television Inside and Out

Barrie, Barbara: All Together Now, Barney Miller, Breaking Away, Decoy, Diana, Double Trouble, Late Bloomer, Phil Silvers Show, Private Benjamin, Reggie, Tucker's Witch

Barrie, Wendy: Adventures of Oky Doky, Stars in Khaki and Blue, Through Wendy's Window

Barris, Chuck: Chuck Barris Rah-Rah Show, Gong Show

Barry, Gene: Adventurer, Amos Burke, Secret Agent, Bat Masterson, Burke's Law, Name of the Game, Our Miss Brooks, Shell Game

Barry, Jack: Big Surprise, Break the Bank, Concentration, Generation Gap, High Low, Joe Di-Maggio Show, Joker! Joker!! Joker!!!, Joker's Wild, Juvenile Jury, Life Begins at 80, Oh Baby, $100,000 Big Surprise, Reel Game, Tic Tac Dough, Twenty-One, Winky Dink and You

Barry, Patricia: Eddie, First Love, Freewheelers, Harris Against the World, Texas Rangers

Barrymore, Drew: Adventures of Con Sawyer and Hucklemary Finn, Amazing Stories, Ray Bradbury Theatre

Barrymore, Ethel: Ethel Barrymore Theatre

Bartlett, Bonnie: Little House on the Prairie, St. Elsewhere, V

Barton, Peter: Powers of Matthew Star, Shirley, Three Eyes

Barty, Billy: Ace Crawford Private Eye, Bay City Rollers Show, Bugaloos, Captain and Tennille, Circus Boy, Club Oasis, Doctor Shrinker, Don't Call Us, Great Day, Life and Times of Eddie Roberts, Peter Gunn, Red Skelton Show, Sigmund and the Sea Monsters, Spike Jones Show

Basehart, Richard: Judge, Knight Rider, Voyage to the Bottom of the Sea, W.E.B.

Basinger, Kim: Dog and Cat, From Here to Eternity

Bastedo, Alexandra: Champions

Bateman, Charles: Hazel, Two Faces West

Bateman, Jason: It's Your Move, Little House on the Prairie, Silver Spoons, Valerie, Valerie's Family

Bateman, Justine: Family Ties, Scary Tales

Bates, Rhonda: Blansky's Beauties, Isabel Sanford's Honeymoon Hotel, Keep on Truckin', Shape of Things, Speak Up America

Bauman, Jon: All Night Radio, Bowzer, Match Game-Hollywood Squares Hour, Pop 'N' Rocker Game

Baumann, Katherine: Border Pals, Harry O, Keep on Truckin'

Bavier, Frances: Andy Griffith Show, Eve Arden Show, If You Knew Tomorrow, It's a Great Life, Mayberry R.F.D.

Baxley, Barbara: All That Glitters, Home

Baxter, Anne: Batman, Hotel, Marcus Welby, M.D.

Baxter, Meredith Birney: See Birney, Meredith Baxter

Bean, Orson: Arthur Godfrey Show, Bean Show, Blue Angel, Chamber Music Society of Lower Basin Street, Dunniger Show, Forever Fernwood, Mr. Bevis, To Tell the Truth

Beasley, Allyce: Cheers, Moonlighting

Beatty, Ned: Szysznky

Beatty, Warren: Dobie Gillis

Beauchamp, Richard: Angie, C.P.O. Sharkey, Cheap Detective, Jackie and Darlene, Zorro and Son

Beaudine, Deka: Paper Chase

Beaumont, Hugh: Alias Mike Hercules, Fireside Theatre, Leave It to Beaver

Beavers, Louise: Beulah, Make Room for Daddy

Beck, Jackson: Jet Fighter, King Leonardo, Popeye the Sailor, Tennessee Tuxedo

Beck, John: Buffalo Soldiers, Crazy Dan, Dallas, Flamingo Road, Nichols

Beck, Kimberly: Eight Is Enough, Lucas Tanner, Peyton Place, Rich Man Poor Man, Scalpels, Starting Fresh, Westwind

Becker, Sandy: Go Go Gophers, Underdog, Win With a Winner

Beckman, Henry: Bronk, Family Holvak, Funny Face, Here Come the Brides, I'm Dickens . . . He's Fenster, McHale's Navy, My Living Doll

Bedelia, Bonnie: New Land

Beery Jr., Noah: Asphalt Cowboy, Beyond Witch Mountain, Circus Boy, Doc Elliot, Hondo, Murdocks and the McClays, Powers Play, Quest, Revenge of the Gray Gang, Riverboat, Rockford Files, Yellow Rose

Begley, Ed: Leave It to Larry

Begley Jr., Ed: Battlestar Galactica, Bobby Jo and the Big Apple Goodtime Band, Making It, Mary Hartman, Mixed Nuts, Roll Out, Shelley Duvall's Tall Tales and Legends, St. Elsewhere, Tales of the Apple Dumpling Gang, Wonder Woman (last title)

Bel Geddes, Barbara: Dallas

Belafonte-Harper, Shari: Hotel

Belford, Christine (Christina): Banacek, Colorado C.I., Dynasty, Empire, It's Not Easy, Married: The First Year, 100 Centre Street, Silver Spoons, Susan and Sam

Bell, Michael: Barkleys, Batman and the Super 7, C.B. Bears, Charlie's Angels, Dallas, Devlin, Egan, Flo's Place, Godzilla, Inhumanoids, Kwicky Koala Show, New Super Friends Hour, Petrocelli, Plasticman, Speed Buggy, Super Friends, Survivors, Trollkins, World's Greatest Super Heroes

Bellamy, Ralph: Defender, Eleventh Hour, Hotel, Hunter, Immortal, Man Against Crime, Most Deadly Game, Survivors

Bellaver, Harry: Billy Bean Show, Mr. Belvedere (first title), Naked City

Beller, Kathleen: At Ease, Bronx Zoo, Dynasty

Bellini, Cal: Asphalt Cowboy, Diagnosis: Unknown, In the Dead of Night, Matt Houston

Bellwood, Pamela: Dynasty, W.E.B.

Belushi, Jim: Saturday Night Live, Who's Watching the Kids?, Working Stiffs

Belushi, John: Saturday Night Live

Benaderet, Bea: All About Barbara, Beverly Hillbillies, Flintstones, George Burns and Gracie Allen Show, Life of Riley, Peter Loves Mary, Petticoat Junction

Benben, Brian: Gangster Chronicles, Kay O'Brien, Mr. Sunshine

Bendix, William: Ivy League, Life of Riley (third title), Overland Trail, Pine Lake Lodge, Rockabye the Infantry, Time Element, 330 Independence S.W.

Benedict, Dirk: A-Team, Battlestar Galactica,

Braverman, Bart: Fang Face, Harvey Korman Show, Krofft Komedy Hour Look Out World, Magic Mongo, New Odd Couple, Plasticman, Vegas

Bray, Thom: Breaking Away, Concrete Beat, Four Eyes, Harry, One Day at a Time, Prime Times, Riptide

Brazzi, Rosanno: Survivors

Breck, Peter: Big Valley, Black Saddle, Secret Empire

Breeding, Larry: Last Resort, Sheila, Who's Watching the Kids?

Brennan, Eileen: New Kind of Family, Private Benjamin, Rowan and Martin's Laugh-In, Shape of Things, Taxi, 13 Queens Boulevard

Brennan, Walter: Alias Smith and Jones, Guns of Will Sonnett, Mr. Tutt, Real McCoys, To Rome with Love, Tycoon

Brenner, Dori: Brothers, Cassie and Company, Charmings, Friends, Sheila, Sparrow, Who's the Boss? (second title)

Breslin, Patricia: People's Choice, Peyton Place, Tate

Brewster, Diane: Fugitive, Islanders, Maverick, Michael Shayne, Detective

Brian, David: Mr. District Attorney

Brickell, Beth: Gentle Ben, Stone

Bridges, Beau: Ensign O'Toole, Frank Merriwell, Lloyd Bridges Show, Sea Hunt, United States

Bridges, Lloyd: Joe Forrester, Lloyd Bridges Show, Lloyd Bridges Water World, Loner, Paper Dolls, San Francisco International Airport, Sea Hunt

Bridges, Todd: Diff'rent Strokes, High School U.S.A., Orphan and the Dude

Brill, Marty: All in the Family (second title), Archie Bunker's Place, New Dick Van Dyke Show, New Soupy Sales Show, Sergeant T.K. Yu

Brimley, Wilford: Firm, Our House

Brisebois, Danielle: All in the Family (second title), Knots Landing

Brisette, Tiffany: Small Wonder, Webster

Brittany, Morgan (aka, Suzanne Cupito): Dallas, Glitter, Meet Me in St. Louis, On Top All Over the World, Richard Boone Show, Star Games

Britton, Barbara: Big Party for Revlon, Climax, Date with Life, Fabulous Sycamores, Head of the Family, Mr. and Mrs. North, Revlon Revue

Britton, Pamela: Blondie (two titles), Life of Riley, My Favorite Martian

Broderick, James: Brenner, Family

Brolin, James: Hotel, Marcus Welby, M.D., Monroes

Bromley, Sheila: Bachelor Father, Hank, I Married Joan, Ivy League, Life of Riley, Three on an Island, Wendy and Me

Bronson, Charles: Empire, Luke and the Tenderfoot, Man with a Camera, Travels of Jaimie McPheeters

Brooke, Hillary: Abbott and Costello Show, My Little Margie

Brooks, Foster: Dean Martin Celebrity Roast,

Dean's Place, Mork and Mindy, New Bill Cosby Show, Real Tom Kennedy Show

Brooks, Geraldine: Bonanza, Colossus, Dumplings, Executive Suite, Faraday and Company

Brooks, Joel: After George, Facts of Life, Hail to the Chief, Just Married, My Sister Sam, Private Benjamin, Teachers Only

Brooks, Martin E.: Bionic Woman, Medical Center, Six Million Dollar Man

Brooks, Randi: Herndon and Me, Last Precinct, Wizards and Warriors

Brophy, Kevin: Lucan, Yeagers

Brosnan, Pierce: Remington Steele

Brough, Candi and Randi: B. J. and the Bear, Branagan and Mapes

Brown, Blair: Days and Nights of Molly Dodd, Faculty, Oregon Trail

Brown, Georg Stanford: The City, Rookies

Brown, Joe E.: Arthur Godfrey's Talent Scouts, Buick Circus Hour, Five's a Family

Brown, Johnny: Good Times, Leslie Uggams Show, Plasticman, Rowan and Martin's Laugh-In, Sammy and Company, Where's the Fire?

Brown, Peter: Lawman

Brown, Ted: Across the Board, Greatest Man on Earth, Happy Birthday, Howdy Doody, Joe Dimaggio Show, Stop Me If You Heard This One

Brown, Vanessa: All That Glitters, My Favorite Husband, Walter Fortune

Browne, Roscoe Lee: High Five, McCoy, Miss Winslow and Son, Soap

Bruce, Carol: WKRP in Cincinnati

Brull, Pamela: Off the Rack, Secret Empire, T. J. Hooker

Bruns, Philip: But Mother, Chopped Liver Brothers, Forever Fernwood, Great Day, Jackie Gleason and His American Scene Magazine, Mary Hartman, Shadow of Sam Penny

Bry, Ellen: Amazing Spider-Man, St. Elsewhere

Bryan, Arthur Q.: Halls of Ivy, Hank McCune Show, Meet the Governor, Movieland Quiz, Professional Father, Tom and Jerry

Brynner, Yul: Anna and the King

Buchanan, Edgar: Cade's County, Green Acres, Hopalong Cassidy, Judge Roy Bean, Leave It to Beaver, Luke and the Tenderfoot, National Velvet, Petticoat Junction, Rifleman, Tyrees of Capitol Hill

Buckley, Betty: Eight Is Enough, Rubber Gun Squad

Buckman, Tara: Lobo, The Master

Buckner, Susan: Friends, Nancy Drew Mysteries, When the Whistle Blows

Buktenica, Ray: Bumpers, Cousins, Goodbye Charlie, House Calls, Rhoda, W*A*L*T*E*R

Bulifant, Joyce: Arnold's Closet Revue, Arthur Murray's Dance Party, Bad News Bears, Big John, Little John, Bill Cosby Show, First Hundred Years, Flo, It's a Man's World, Love Thy Neighbor, Mary Tyler Moore Show, Michele Lee Show, Sport Billy, Tom, Dick, and Mary

Bullock, JM J.: Animal Crack-Ups, Ted Knight Show, Too Close for Comfort

Bundy, Brooke: Best Years, Holloway's Daughters, Kelly's Kids, McClain's Law, Mr. Novak

Buono, Victor: Batman, Brenda Starr, Judgement Day, Man from Atlantis, Rita Moreno Show, Sinbad, Taxi, Two Guys from Muck, Vegas, Wild Wild West

Burgess, Bobby: Lawrence Welk Show, Memories with Lawrence Welk, Mickey Mouse Club

Burghoff, Gary: Don Knotts Show, M*A*S*H, W*A*L*T*E*R

Burke, Billie: Doc Corkle, Eddie Cantor Comedy Theatre

Burke, Delta: Chisholms, Designing Women, Filthy Rich, First and 10: The Championships, Home Front, Johnny Blue, Training Camp: The Bulls Are Back

Burke, Paul: Dynasty, Five Fingers, Harbourmaster, Hot Shots, Naked City, Noah's Ark, Twelve O'Clock High

Burkley, Dennis: B. J. and the Bear, Book of Lists, Forever Fernwood, Hanging In, Mary Hartman, Mr. Dugan, Rowdies, Sanford, Sutters Bay, Texas Wheelers

Burnett, Carol: Carol Burnett and Company, Carol Burnett Show, Entertainers, Garry Moore Show, Li'l Abner, Mama's Family (first title), Pantomime Quiz, Stanley

Burns, George: George Burns and Gracie Allen Show, George Burns Comedy Week, George Burns Show, Wendy and Me

Burns, Jack: Andy Griffith Show, Bonkers, Burns and Schreiber Comedy Hour, Entertainers, Getting Together, Operation Greasepaint, Our Place, Summer Smothers Brothers Show, Wait Til Your Father Gets Home

Burns, Michael: Gidget Gets Married, Harry's Business, It's a Man's World, Off We Go, Wagon Train

Burr, Raymond: Eischied, Ironside, Kingston: Confidential, Perry Mason

Burrell, Maryedith: Family Ties, Fridays, Remington Steele, Throb

Burstyn, Ellen (aka, Ellen McRae): Big Brain, Ellen Burstyn Show, Harry's Girls (second title), Iron Horse

Busey, Gary: Texas Wheelers

Butkus, Dick: Blue Thunder, Cass Malloy, Half Nelson, My Two Dads

Butler, Dean: Gidget's Summer Reunion, Little House on the Prairie, Little House: A New Beginning, New Gidget

Buttons, Red: Dean Martin's Celebrity Roast, Double Life of Henry Phyfe, Flannery and Quilt, Red Buttons Show, Sunshine Boys, Wonder Woman (second title)

Buttram, Pat: Down Home, Gene Autry Show, Green Acres, Howdy

Buzzi, Ruth: Alice, Baggy Pants and the Nitwits, Berenstain Bears, Dean Martin's Celebrity Roast, Lost Saucer, Rowan and Martin's Laugh-In, Shape of Things, Singles, That Girl (first title)

Byington, Spring: December Bride, Here Comes Melinda, Laramie

Byner, John: Bizarre, Garry Moore Show, McNamara's Band (two titles) Nancy Dussault Show, Practice, Sheehy and the Supreme Machine, Soap, Something Else

Byrd, Ralph: Dick Tracy

Byrnes, Edd (Edward): Girl on the Run, 77 Sunset Strip, Sweepstakes

Byron, Jean: Batman, Dobie Gillis, Mayor of the Town, Pat Paulsen's Half a Comedy Hour, Patty Duke Show

Cabot, Sebastian: Beachcomber, Bravo Duke, Checkmate, Family Affair, Ghost Story, Jack the Ripper, Stump the Stars, Suspense, Three Musketeers

Cadorette, Mary: Three's a Crowd

Caesar, Sid: Admiral Broadway Revue, America 2100, Caesar's Hour, Pink Lady, Sid Caesar Show, Your Show of Shows

Calhoun, Rory: Pottsville, Texan, Western Star Theatre

Callahan, James: Charles in Charge (second title), Convoy, Governor and J. J., Hercule Poirot, McNaughton's Daughter, Runaways, Wendy and Me

Callan, K: Cutter to Houston, Day to Day, Four of Us, James at 15, Joe's World, Married: The First Year, One Day at a Time, Private Benjamin, Sara (1985)

Callan, Michael: Occasional Wife, Young Hearts

Callas, Charlie: Andy Williams Show, Bungle Abbey, Des O'Connor Show, Kopycats, Switch, Take One Starring Jonathan Winters

Calvin, John: Living End, Paul Lynde Show, Sitcom, Tales of the Gold Monkey, Wonderful World of Philip Malley

Cameron, JoAnna: Isis

Cameron, Kirk: Growing Pains, Two Marriages

Cameron, Rod: City Detective, Coronado 9, Star Route, State Trooper

Camp, Hamilton: Chameleon, Dog's Life, Family in Blue, Flintstone Kids, Foofur, He and She, Just Our Luck, Nashville Palace, Pottsville, Prime Times, Smurfs, Story Theatre, Too Close for Comfort, Windows, Doors and Keyholes

Campanella, Frank: Decoy, Gibbsville, Skag

Campanella, Joseph: Colbys Expose, Lawyers, Mannix, Nurses, One Day at a Time, Police Woman: The Gamble, This Is Your Life

Campbell, Glen: Glen Campbell Goodtime Hour, Glen Campbell Music Show, Summer Smothers Brothers Show

Campbell, Nicholas: Diamonds, Hitchhiker, Insiders

Campbell, William: Cannonball, Dynasty, Mr. & Mrs. Cop

Candy, John: Big City Comedy, Second City Television, Welcome to the Fun Zone

Canfield, Mary Grace: Bewitched, Family, Green Acres, Hathaways, Heaven Help Us

Cannon, J. D.: Alias Smith and Jones, Beyond Witch Mountain, Call to Glory, Lady Luck, McCloud, Misadventures of Sheriff Lobo, Weapons Man

Canova, Diana: Dinah and Her New Best Friends, Foot in the Door, I'm a Big Girl Now, No Complaints, Soap, Throb

Canova, Judy: Cap'n Ahab, Colgate Comedy Hour, Li'l Abner

Carey, Macdonald: Doctor Christian, Gidget Gets Married, Lock Up

Caridi, Carmine: Alice, Charlie and Company, Fame, Good Penny, Pete 'N' Tillie, Phyllis

Carlisle, Kitty: Celebrity Time, To Tell the Truth, What's Going On?

Carlson, Karen: American Dream, Two Marriages, Yellow Rose

Carlson, Linda: Kaz, Newhart, Pals, Sutters Bay, Westside Medical

Carlson, Richard: Eye Witness, I Led Three Lives, Mackenzie's Raiders

Carmel, Richard C.: Batman, Eyes of Texas, Fitz and Bones, Mothers-in-law, Stump the Stars

Carne, Judy: Baileys of Balboa, Fair Exchange, Kraft Music Hall Presents Sandler and Young, Love on a Rooftop, Rowan and Martin's Laugh-In

Carney, Art: Batman, Henry Morgan's Great Talent Hunt, Honeymooners, Jackie Gleason Show, Lanigan's Rabbi, Morey Amsterdam Show

Caroleo, Dina: Girl of My Dreams

Carr, Darlene: Bret Maverick, Dean Martin Presents the Golddiggers, John Forsythe Show, Miss Winslow and Son, Oregon Trail, Smith Family, Streets of San Francisco

Carradine, David: Kung Fu, Shane

Carradine, John: Adventures of Dr. Fu Manchu, Branded, Munsters, My Friend Irma

Carradine, Robert: Cowboys, Faerie Tale Theatre

Carroll, Diahann: Diahann Carroll Show, Dynasty, Julia

Carroll, Leo G.: Channing, Girl from UNCLE, Going My Way, Man from UNCLE, Moonglow Affair, Topper

Carroll, Pat: Busting Loose, Crazy Dan, Galaxy High School, Getting Together, Make Room for Daddy, Oh Nurse, Pandora and Friend, Rockhopper, Saturday Night Revue, She's the Sheriff, Ted Knight Show (1986)

Carroll, Victoria: Alice, Foofur, Life and Times of Eddie Roberts, No Soap Radio, Small and Frye, W*A*L*T*E*R

Carson, Jack: All-Star Revue, Another Day Another Dollar; Arroyo, How's Business?, Jack Carson Show, Johnny Come Lately, Strike It Rich

Carson, Johnny: Carson's Comedy Classics, Earn Your Vacation, Tonight Show, Who Do You Trust?

Carson, Mindy: Club Embassy, Ford Star Revue, Mindy Carson Sings Perry Como Show

Carter, Dixie: Designing Women, Diff'rent Strokes, Filthy Rich, On Our Own, Out of the Blue

Carter, Jack: Jack Carter and Company, Jack Carter Show, Saturday Night Revue

Carter, Lynda: Partners in Crime (first title), Wonder Woman

Carter, Nell: Gimme a Break, Lobo, 20th Century Follies

Cartwright, Angela: Everything Happens to Me, High School U.S.A., Lost in Space, Make Room for Daddy, Make Room for Grandaddy, Mr. and Ms.

Case, Allen: Apartment in Rome, Arthur Godfrey and Friends, Deputy, Legend of Jesse James, Life and Times of Eddie Roberts, Riding High

Casey, Bernie: Bay City Blues, Harris and Company, Pros and Cons

Cash, Johnny: Johnny Cash and Friends, Johnny Cash Show

Cason, Barbara: Brady Brides, Brady Girls Get Married, Carter Country, Comedy Tonight, Hollywood Beat, Madame's Place, New Temperatures Rising Show, Tabitha, Tony the Pony

Cass, Peggy: Everything's Relative, Hathaways, Jack Paar Tonight, Ladies in Blue, To Tell the Truth, Tonight Show, Women in Prison

Cassavetes, John: Alexander the Great, Fliers, Johnny Staccato

Cassidy, David: David Cassidy—Man Undercover, Partridge Family

Cassidy, Jack: Dean's Place, He and She

Cassidy, Joanna: Buffalo Bill, Code Name: Foxfire, Falcon Crest Family Tree, Rollergirls, Shields and Yarnell, Strike Force, 240 Robert

Cassidy, Shaun: Breaking Away, Hardy Boys Mysteries

Cassidy, Ted: Addams Family, Birdman, Fantastic Four, Frankenstein Jr. and the Impossibles, I Dream of Jeannie, New Adventures of Huckleberry Finn, World's Greatest Super Heroes

Cast, Tricia: Bad News Bears, It's a Living, It's Your Move, Mr. Belvedere (second title)

Cattrall, Kim: Night Rider, Tucker's Witch

Caulfield, Joan: High Chaparral, My Favorite Husband, Sally (2 titles)

Cavanaugh, Michael: Joe Bash, Starman, Texas Rangers

Cavett, Dick: Dick Cavett Show, Grand Tour, This Morning

Cesana, Renzo: Continental

Chadwick, June: Riptide, V

Chamberlain, Richard: Doctor Kildare

Champion, Marge and Gower: Admiral Broadway Revue, Marge and Gower Champion Show

Chandler, Chick: It's Always Sunday, One Happy Family, Soldiers of Fortune

Chandler, George: Abbott and Costello Show, Ichabod and Me, Indemnity, McGhee, Timmy and

Crane, Richard: Commando Cody, Mysteries of Chinatown, Rocky Jones Space Ranger, Surfside Six

Crawford, Broderick: Highway Patrol, Hunter, Interns, King of Diamonds

Crawford, Joan: Batman, Talent Scouts Program, Talent Search

Crenna, Richard: All's Fair, It Takes Two, Joshua's World, London and Davis in New York, Look at Us, Our Miss Brooks, Real McCoys, Slattery's People

Crewson, Wendy: Call Holme, High Chaparral

Croft, Mary Jane: Adventures of Ozzie and Harriet, Here's Lucy, I Love Lucy, Life of Riley, Lucy Show, People's Choice, Two of Us

Cromwell, James: All in the Family (second title), Earthlings, Easy Street, Eddie and Herbert, Hot 1 Baltimore, Last Precinct, Little House on the Prairie, Nancy Walker Show, Pottsville, Snafu, Stranded

Crosby, Bing: Bing Crosby Show

Crosby, Cathy Lee: Hotel, That's Incredible, Three Wives of David Wheeler, Wonder Woman (first title)

Crosby, Mary: Big Easy, Brothers and Sisters, Crazy Dan, Dallas

Crosby, Norm: Beautiful Phyllis Diller Show, Comedy Shop, Everything Goes

Cross, Murphy: Maximum Security, Phyl and Mikhy

Crothers, Scatman: Casablanca, Chico and the Man, Harlem Globetrotters, Hong Kong Phooey, Morning Star/Evening Star, One of the Boys, Paw Paws, Revenge of the Gray Gang, Scooby's All-Star Laff-a-Lympics, Super Globetrotters, Time for Beany

Crowley, Patricia (Pat): All in the Family (first title), Date with Judy, I Remember Caviar, Joe Forrester, Please Don't Eat the Daisies, Two of Us, You're Only Young Twice

Crystal, Billy: Billy Crystal Comedy Hour, Soap

Culea, Melinda: A-Team, Dear Penelope and Peter, Dear Teacher, Family Ties, Glitter, Whacked Out

Cullen, Bill: Bank on the Stars, Bill Cullen Show, Blankety Blanks, Chain Reaction, Child's Play, Down You Go, Eye Guess, Give and Take, Hot Potato, I've Got a Secret, Joker's Wild, Love Experts, Name That Tune, Pass the Buck, Password Plus, Place the Face, Price Is Right, Say It with Acting, Three on a Match, To Tell the Truth, $25,000 Pyramid, Why? Winner Take All, Winning Streak, You're Putting Me On

Culp, Robert: Bounty Hunter, Greatest American Hero, I Spy, Now Is Tomorrow, Trackdown

Cummings, Bob: Bob Cummings Show, Gidget Grows Up, Love That Bob, My Living Doll

Cummings, Quinn: Big Eddie, Family, Hail to the Chief, Jerimiah of Jacob's Neck, Remington Steele

Cupito, Suzanne: See Brittany, Morgan

Curtin, Jane: Comedy Zone, Coneheads, Kate and Allie, Saturday Night Live

Curtin, Valerie: Jim Stafford Show, 9 to 5 (two titles), Primary English Class

Curtis, Jamie Lee: Callahan, Operation Petticoat, Shelley Duvall's Tall Tales and Legends

Curtis, Keene: Amanda's, Empire, Magician, Modesty Blaise, One in a Million, There Goes the Neighborhood, Unit 4

Curtis, Ken: Gunsmoke, Ripcord, Yellow Rose

Curtis, Tony: McCoy, Persuaders, Spies (pilot), Vegas

Dailey, Dan: Faraday and Company, Four Just Men, Governor and J.J., Low Man on the Totem Pole, Papa G.I.

Daily, Bill: Aloha Paradise, Alone at Last, Bob Newhart Show, I Dream of Jeannie, Inside O.U.T., Small and Frye

Dalton, Abby: Adams of Eagle Lake, Anderson and Company, Barney Miller, Belle Starr, Falcon Crest, Hennessey, Joey Bishop Show (second title), Jonathan Winters Show, Rifleman

Daly, John: Celebrity Time, It's News to Me, March of Time, We Take Your Word, What's My Line?, Who Said That?

Daly, Jonathan: C.P.O. Sharkey, Jimmy Stewart Show, O.K. Crackerby, Walter of the Jungle

Daly, Tyne: Cagney and Lacey, Medical Center

Damon, Cathryn: Getting There, Soap, Webster

Damon, Stuart: Adventurer, America, Champions

Damone, Vic: Dean Martin Presents the Vic Damone Show, Lively Ones, Morey Amsterdam Show, Vic Damone Show

Dana, Bill: Bill Dana Show, Las Vegas Show, Make Room for Daddy, New Steve Allen Show, No Soap Radio, Steve Allen Show, Too Close for Comfort, Windows, Doors and Keyholes, Zorro and Son

Daniels, William: Captain Nice, Fabulous Dr. Fable, Freebie and the Bean, Heaven on Earth, Instant Family, Knight Rider, Nancy Walker Show, Nuts and Bolts, One of Our Own, Private Benjamin, St. Elsewhere, Wonderful World of Philip Malley

Danner, Blythe: Adam's Rib

Danova, Cesare: Border Town, Garrison's Gorillas, Police Woman: The Gamble, Tarzan the Ape Man

Danson, Ted: Allison Sidney Harrison, Benson, Cheers, Dear Teacher

Danton, Ray: Alaskans, Our Man Flint

Danza, Tony: Taxi, Who's the Boss? (second title)

Darden, Severn: Beyond Westworld, Forever Fernwood, Home Room, Story Theatre

Darin, Bobby: Bobby Darin Amusement Company

Darling, Jennifer: Bionic Woman, Centurions, Eight Is Enough, Galaxy High School, Gary Coleman Show, Goltar and the Golden Lance, New Temperatures Rising Show, Six Million Dollar Man, Smurfs, Trollkins

Diamond, Selma: Night Court, Too Close for Comfort

Dickinson, Angie: Cassie and Company, Men Into Space, Police Woman, Police Woman: The Gamble

Diller, Phyllis: Beautiful Phyllis Diller Show, Pruitts of Southampton, Show Street

Dillman, Bradford: Case Aganist Paul Ryker, Court-Martial, Hot Pursuit, King's Crossing, Longstreet

Dillon, Melinda: Enigma, Freeman, Hellinger's Law, Story Theatre

Dixon, Donna: Berringer's, Bosom Buddies, Charmed Lives, Shape of Things

Dobkin, Lawrence: I Was a Bloodhound, Lady Died at Midnight, Mr. Adams and Eve, Untouchables

Dobson, Kevin: Knots Landing, Kojak, Shannon, Stranded

Dodd, Jimmie: Mickey Mouse Club

Dodson, Jack: All's Fair, Andy Griffith Show, Happy Days (second title), In the Beginning, Mayberry R.F.D., Phyl and Mikhy, Snavely, Walkin' Walter

Doherty, Shannen: His and Hers, Little House: A New Beginning, Our House

Dolenz, Mickey (aka Mickey Braddock): Circus Boy, Devlin, Funky Phantom, Monkees, Skatebirds

Donahue, Elinor: Andy Griffith Show, Calling Miss Peters, Dennis the Menace, Father Knows Best, Gidget Gets Married, Grady Nutt Show, High School U.S.A., If I Love You Am I Trapped Forever?, Many Happy Returns, Mulligan's Stew, One Day at a Time, New Adventures of Beans Baxter, Please Stand By, Rookies, Sign-On

Donahue, Phil: Phil Donahue Show

Donahue, Troy: Hawaiian Eye, Surfside 6

Donnell, Jeff: George Gobel Show, Matt Helm, Spider-Man

Dooley, Paul: Dom DeLuise Show, Firm, Momma the Detective

Dors, Diana: Stump the Stars

Douglas, Diana: Cowboys, Dirty Work

Douglas, Donna: Bachelor Father, Beverly Hillbillies

Douglas, Mike: Club 60, Kay Kyser's Kollege of Musical Knowledge, Mike Douglas Show, Music Show

Douglass, Robyn: Galactica 1980, Houston Knights

Dow, Tony: High School U.S.A., Leave It to Beaver, Mr. Novak, New Leave It to Beaver, Still the Beaver

Doyle, David: Bridget Loves Bernie, Charlie's Angels, Invisible Woman, New Dick Van Dyke Show, Ozzie's Girls, Patty Duke Show, Shaughnessey, Sweet Surrender

Drier, Moosie: Barbara Eden Show, Bob Newhart Show, Doc, Executive Suite, Kids Incorporated, Rowan and Martin's Laugh-In, Royce, Sheehy

and the Supreme Machine, Too Good to Be True

Dru, Joanne: Adventures of a Model, Guestward Ho (first title)

Drury, James: Alias Smith and Jones, Firehouse, Men from Shiloh, Virginian (2 titles)

Dryer, Fred: Force 7, Girl's Life, Hunter (last title)

DuBois, Ja'net: Big Easy, Good Times, Hellinger's Law, Tom Swift and Linda Craig Mystery Hour

Duff, Howard: Batman, Felony Squad, Flamingo Road, Knots Landing, Mr. Adams and Eve

Duffy, Julia: Irene, Newhart, Wizards and Warriors

Duffy, Patrick: Dallas, Man from Atlantis

Dugan, Dennis: Did You Hear About Josh and Kelly, Empire (second title), Father O Father, Full House, Making a Living, Richie Brockelman Private Eye, Rockford Files, Shadow Chasers

Duggan, Andrew: Bourbon Street Beat, Down Home, Jake's Way, Lancer, Markham, Momma the Detective, Room for One More, Twelve O'Clock High, Virginian (first title), A Walk in the Night, Waltons, You're Only Young Twice

Duke, Patty (aka, Astin, Patty Duke): Comedy Zone, Hail to the Chief, It Takes Two, Karen's Song, Patty Duke Show, Phillip and Barbara

Dullea, Keir: Channing, Starlost

Duncan, Sandy: Act II, Funny Face, Funny World of Fred and Bunni, Sandy Duncan Show, Six Million Dollar Man, Valerie's Family

Dunn, James: Ben Casey, It's a Great Life

Dunne, Dominique: Breaking Away, Unit 4

Durant, Don: Johnny Ringo, Loner, Macreedy's Woman, Ray Anthony Show

Durante, Jimmy: All-Star Revue, Colgate Comedy Hour, Jimmy Durante Presents the Lennon Sisters Hour, Jimmy Durante Show, Lennon Sisters Show, Texaco Star Theatre

Durning, Charles: Cop and the Kid, Eye to Eye, P.O.P., Rx for the Defense, Side by Side

Duryea, Dan: Affairs of China Smith, Confidentially Yours, Justice of the Peace, Peyton Place, Riverboat

Dusay, Marj: Blondie, Bobby Parker and Company, Bret Maverick, Facts of Life, In the Dead of Night, Sorority '62, Square Pegs, Stop Susan Williams

Dusenberry, Ann: Family Tree, Fraud Squad, Life with Lucy, Little Women

Dussault, Nancy: Nancy Dussault Show, New Dick Van Dyke Show, Shape of Things, Ted Knight Show (1986), Too Close for Comfort

Duvall, Shelley: Faerie Tale Theatre, Lily, Shelley Duvall's Tall Tales and Legends

Dzundza, George: Open All Night, 2½ Dads

Eastwood, Clint: Navy Log, Rawhide, West Point Story

Ebersole, Christine: Cavanaughs, Saturday Night Live, Valerie

Ebsen, Buddy: Barnaby Jones, Beverly Hillbillies, Corky and White Shadow, Davy Crockett, Graduation Dress, Matt Houston, Northwest Passage

Fairbanks Jr., Douglas: Douglas Fairbanks Jr. Presents

Fairchild, Morgan: Escapade, Flamingo Road, Mork and Mindy (first title), On Top All Over the World, Our Planet Tonight, Paper Dolls, Shape of Things

Falk, Peter: Columbo, Trials of O'Brien

Faracy, Stephanie: Bumpers, Eye to Eye, Fighting Nightingales, Goldie and the Bears, Goodnight Beantown, Last Resort, Private Benjamin, Stephanie

Farentino, James: Blue Thunder, Cool Million, Dynasty, Lawyers, Mary, My Wife Next Door

Farnsworth, Richard: Anne of Green Gables, Cherokee Trail, Texas Rangers

Farr, Jamie: AfterMash, Celebrity Charades, Chicago Teddy Bears, Class of 55, Dear Phoebe, Dhondo, Las Vegas Beat, M*A*S*H, Rhyme and Reason

Farrell, Mike: Amanda Fallon, Interns, Man and the City, M*A*S*H

Farrell, Sharon: Hawaii Five-O, Lassiter, Rituals, Saints and Sinners

Farrow, Mia: Peyton Place

Fawcett, Farrah: Charlie's Angels, Harry O, Inside O.U.T., Six Million Dollar Man

Faye, Joey: Candid Camera, Dagmar's Canteen, Ethel Waters Show, 54th Street Revue, Guess Again, Joey Faye's Frolics, Mack and Myer for Hire, New Treasure Hunt, Off the Record, Show Business, Inc.

Faylen, Frank: Dobie Gillis, Eddie, That Girl (first title), Whatever Happened to Dobie Gillis?

Fee, Melinda: Invisible Man (second title)

Feldman, Corey: Another Man's Shoes, Bad News Bears, Cass Malloy, Love Natalie, Madame's Place, Mork and Mindy (first title)

Feldman, Marty: Golddiggers in London, Marty Feldman Comedy Machine

Feldon, Barbara: Dean Martin's Comedy World, Father on Trial, Four of Us, Get Smart, Marty Feldman Comedy Machine, Natural Look, Real Life Stories, Rowan and Martin's Laugh-In, Special Edition

Feldshuh, Tovah: Mariah, Murder Ink, World of Darkness

Fell, Norman: Dan August, 87th Precinct, Executive Suite, Getting There, Ghostbreaker, Going Places, Look What They've Done to My Song, Moonglow Affair, Needles and Pins, Risko, Ropers, Teachers Only, Three's Company

Fenneman, George: Anybody Can Play, You Bet Your Life, Your Funny Funny Films, Your Surprise Package

Ferdin, Pamelyn: Baby Crazy, Blondie, Curiosity Shop, Flying Nun, Guess What I Did Today, John Forsythe Show, Lassie, Odd Couple, Paul Lynde Show, Roman Holidays, Sealab 2020, Space Academy, These Are the Days

Ferrell, Conchata: B.J. and the Bear, E/R, Hot l Baltimore, McClain's Law, Mixed Nuts, Rag Business

Ferrer, Jose: Good Heavens, Newhart, Return of Captain Nemo

Ferrer, Mel: Behind the Screen, Dallas, Falcon Crest

Ferringo, Lou: Incredible Hulk, Trauma Center

Field, Sally: Alias Smith and Jones, Flying Nun, Gidget, Girl with Something Extra, Hey Landlord

Fields, Chip: Amazing Spider-Man, Brothers, Change at 125th Street, What's Happening

Fields, Kim: Baby, I'm Back, Facts of Life

Fields, Sidney: Abbott and Costello Show, Jackie Gleason and His American Scene Magazine

Finley, Pat: Bob Newhart Show, Flannery & Quilt, From a Bird's Eye View, Funny Side, Keeping Up with the Joneses, Over and Out, Rockford Files

Fisher, Carrie: The Couch

Fisher, Cindy: Hellinger's Law, Swiss Family Robinson, You Are the Jury

Fisher, Eddie: Coke Time with Eddie Fisher, Eddie Fisher Show, George Gobel Show

Flagg, Fannie: Candid Camera, Harper Valley, Harper Valley PTA, Home Cookin', New Dick Van Dyke Show

Flaherty, Joe: Really Weird Tales, Second City Television

Flanagan, Fionnula: Hard Copy, How the West Was Won

Fleischer, Charles: Aloha Paradise, Blue Jeans, Keep on Truckin', Richard Pryor Show, Sugar Time, Wacko, Welcome Back, Kotter

Fleming, Art: Californians, Doctor I.Q., International Detective, Jeopardy, Major Dell Conway of the Flying Tigers, Man Against Crime, NBC Adventure Theatre

Fleming, Eric: Major Dell Conway of the Flying Tigers, Rawhide

Flippen, Jay C.: Dean Jones Show, Ensign O'Toole, Gentry's People

Flippen, Lucy Lee: Flo, Little House on the Prairie

Flynn, Errol: Errol Flynn Theatre

Flynn, Joe: Adventure of Ozzie and Harriet, Amateur's Guide to Love, Barbara Eden Show, Joey Bishop Show, Let's Join Joanie, McHale's Navy, Ready and Willing, Tim Conway Show

Foch, Nina: Chameleon, Gidget Grows Up, Hercule Poirot, Pottsville, Shadow Chasers

Foley, Ellen: Night Court, Three Girls Three

Follows, Megan: Anne of Green Gables, Baxters, Domestic Life, Faculty

Fonda, Henry: Deputy, Family, Henry Fonda Presents the Star and Story, Howdy, Smith Family, That Was the Week That Was

Fonda, Jane: 9 to 5 (first title)

Fontaine, Frank: Jackie Gleason and His American Scene Magazine, Scott Music Hall, Swift Show

Foran, Dick: Five's a Family, Forest Ranger, O.K. Crackerby, Off We Go

Forbes, Scott: Adventures of Jim Bowie, Loner (first title)

Ford, Faith: Popcorn Kid

Ford, Glenn: Cade's County, Family Holvak, Howdy, My Town

Ford, Paul: Aunt Jenny's Real Life Stories, Baileys of Balboa, Norby, Phil Silvers Show

Ford, Tennessee Ernie: Kay Kyster's Kollege of Musical Knowledge, Tennessee Ernie Ford Show

Forman, Joey: Barney and Me, Get Smart, Hey Mulligan, Joey Bishop Show, New Steve Allen Show, Sky's the Limit, Steve Allen Comedy Hour

Forrest, Steve: Baron, S.W.A.T.

Forster, Robert: Banyon, Higher and Higher Attorneys at Law, Nakia, Once a Hero, Royce

Forsyth, Rosemary: Defenders, Is There a Doctor in the House?, Sam Penny and Associate

Forsythe, John: Bachelor Father, Belle Starr, Charlie's Angels, Dynasty, John Forsythe Show, Miss and the Missiles, New Girl in His Life, To Rome with Love

Foster, Jodie: Addams Family (second title), Amazing Chan and the Chan Clan, Bob & Carol & Ted & Alice, Courtship of Eddie's Father, My Sister Hank, My Three Sons, Paper Moon, Partridge Family

Foster, Meg: Cagney and Lacey, Scarlet Letter, Sunshine

Foster, Phil: All-Star Revue, Laverne and Shirley

Fowley, Douglas V: Detective School, Father on Trial, Life and Legend of Wyatt Earp, Nuts and Bolts, Oregon Trail, Pistols and Petticoats (two titles)

Fox, Bernard: Andy Griffith Show, Bewitched, Hogan's Heroes, Intertect, Make Room for Daddy, Soap, Son-in-Law, Tabitha, Walter of the Jungle

Fox, Michael J.: Family Ties, High School U.S.A., Palmerstown U.S.A.

Fox, Sonny: Let's Take a Trip, Movie Game, On Your Mark, $64,000 Challenge, Way Out Games

Foxworth, Robert: Falcon Crest, Men at Law, Storefront Lawyers, Susan and Sam

Foxx, Redd: My Buddy, Redd Foxx Comedy Hour, Redd Foxx Show, Sanford, Sanford and Son

Foy Jr., Eddie: Fair Exchange, King of the Road, Rear Guard, Seven Little Foys

Franciosa, Tony (Anthony): Finder of Lost Loves, Matt Helm, Name of the Game, Search, Valentine's Day

Francis, Anne: Dallas, Honey West, My Three Sons, O'Malley, Riptide, Shadow of Sam Penny, Versatile Varieties

Francis, Arlene: Arlene Francis Show, Blind Date, By Popular Demand, Fashion Magic, Home, Soldier Parade, Talent Patrol, That Reminds Me, Who's There?

Francis, Connie: Big Beat, Dick Clark Presents the Rock and Roll Years, Jimmie Rodgers Show

Francis, Genie: Bare Essence, Murder, She Wrote

Franciscus, James: Doc Elliot, Hunter (1977), Investigators, Longstreet, Mr. Novak, Naked City

Frank, Charles: Annie Flynn, Chisholms, Emerald Point N.A.S., Filthy Rich, Riding High, Young Maverick

Frank, Gary: Family, Norma Rae, Remington Steele, Sons and Daughters

Franken, Steve: Dobie Gillis, High School U.S.A., Lieutenant, Scared Silly, Sheriff and the Astronaut, Three for Tahiti, Tom, Dick and Mary

Franklin, Bonnie: Comedy Zone, Gidget, Love Boat, On Top All Over the World, One Day at a Time

Frann, Mary: First Time Second Time, Gidget's Summer Reunion, Harry, King's Crossing, Newhart

Franz, Arthur: Doc Holliday, Nurses, World of Giants

Fraser, Sally: Annie Oakley, Father Knows Best (pilot)

Frawley, William: I Love Lucy, Lucille Ball-Desi Arnaz Show, My Three Sons

Freberg, Stan: Chevy Summer Show, Chris and the Magical Drip, Comedy News, Time for Beany, Willie Wonderful

Freeman, Damita Jo: Hot W.A.C.S., Look What They've Done to My Song, Private Benjamin, Redd Foxx Comedy Hour

Freeman, Deena: In Trouble, Too Close for Comfort

Freeman, Joan: Bus Stop, Code R, Four Eyes

Freeman, Kathleen: Donna Reed Show, Father O Father, Freewheelers, Funny Face, Good Old Days, Hogan's Heroes, It's About Time, Mayor of the Town, Miss and the Missiles, Ready and Willing, Sutters Bay, Topper

French, Victor: Carter Country, Cherokee Trail, Get Smart, Hero, Highway to Heaven, Little House on the Prairie, Little House: A New Beginning, Riding for the Pony Express

Frey, Leonard: Best of the West, Earthlings, Fit for a King, Mr. Smith, Mr. Sunshine, Phillip and Barbara

Frizzell, Lou: Chopper One, Colorado C.I., Forever Fernwood, Jackie and Darlene, New Land

Frost, David: David Frost Revue, David Frost Show, Headliners with David Frost, Spitting Image, That Was the Week That Was (two titles)

Frye, Soleil Moon: Little Shots, Punky Brewster (two titles)

Fuller, Penny: Ann in Blue, Bare Essence, Fortune Dane

Fuller, Robert: Emergency, Jake's Way, Laramie, Wagon Train

Funicello, Annette: Adventures in Dairyland, Annette, Easy Does It, Frankie and Annette, Further Adventures of Spin and Marty, Make Room for Daddy, Mickey Mouse Club, New Adventures of Spin and Marty, Zorro

Funt, Allen: Candid Camera, Candid Kids, It's

a Summer Holiday, Word for Word

Griffith, Andy: Adams of Eagle Lake, Andy Griffith Show, Best of the West, Headmaster, Matlock, New Andy Griffith Show, Salvage 1, Yeagers

Grimes, Tammy: Royal Match, Tammy Grimes Show

Grizzard, George: Night Rider, You Again

Groh, David: Another Day, Rhoda

Groom, Sam: Doctor Simon Locke, Otherworld, Police Surgeon, Time Tunnel

Guardino, Harry: Bender, Get Christie Love, Monty Nash, On Our Way, Reporter, Stranded

Gudegast, Hans: See Braeden, Eric

Guillaume, Robert: Benson, Soap

Gulager, Clu: MacKenzies of Paradise Cove, San Francisco International Airport, Tall Man, Virginian

Gunn, Moses: Contender, Cowboys, Father Murphy

Gwynne, Fred: Anderson and Company, Car 54, Where are You?, Guess What I Did Today?, Munsters

Hack, Shelley: Charlie's Angels, Cutter to Houston, Jack and Mike

Hackett, Buddy: Jackie Gleason Show, Stanley, There Goes the Neighborhood, You Bet Your Life (second Title)

Hackett, Joan: Another Day, Girl's Life, Paper Dolls

Haddock, Julie Anne: Facts of Life, Mulligan's Stew, Under One Roof

Hagen, Jean: Make Room for Daddy

Hagen, Kevin: Land of the Giants, Little House on the Prairie, Little House: A New Beginning, Man from Gavelston, Yancy Derringer

Haggerty, Dan: Life and Times of Grizzly Adams

Haggerty, Don: Alias Mike Hercules, Cases of Eddie Drake, Files of Jeffrey Jones, Life and Legend of Wyatt Earp

Hagitay, Mariska: Downtown

Hagman, Larry: Dallas, Detective, Good Life, Here We Go Again, I Dream of Jeannie

Hahn, Archie: Ghost of a Chance, Manhattan Transfer, Mary Hartman, Stockers, Tabitha, Three Wives of David Wheeler, Tough Cookies

Haid, Charles: Delvecchio, Hill Street Blues, Kate McShane, Scalpels

Hale Jr., Alan: Biff Baker U.S.A., Casey Jones, Gilligan's Island, Gilligan's Planet, Good Guys, Johnny Risk, Mighty O, New Adventures of Gilligan, Trail Blazers

Hale, Barbara: Meet the Governor, Perry Mason

Hall, Deidre: Electra Woman and Dyna Girl, Emergency, Hot Pursuit, Our House

Hall, Huntz: Chicago Teddy Bears, Uncle Croc's Block

Hall, Monty: Beat the Clock, Cowboy Theatre, It's Anybody's Guess, Keep Talking, Let's Make a Deal, Split Second, Strike It Rich, Video Village

Halop, Billy: All in the Family, Bracken's World, Papa G.I., Unexpected

Halop, Florence: Allan, Alone at Last, Betty White Show, Harry's Battles, Joanna, Meet Millie, St. Elsewhere

Halsey, Brett: Brock Callahan, Follow the Sun

Hamel, Al: Anniversary Game, Mantrap, Wedding Party

Hamel, Veronica: City of Angels, Hill Street Blues

Hamer, Rusty: Make Room for Daddy, Make Room for Granddaddy

Hamill, Mark: Eight Is Enough, Texas Wheelers

Hamilton, Alexa: Hail to the Chief, Invisible Woman

Hamilton, George: Hellcats, Paris 7000, Poor Richard, Spies, Survivors

Hamilton, Linda: Beauty and the Beast, Hill Street Blues, King's Crossing, Secrets of Midland Heights, Wishman

Hamilton, Margaret: Addams Family, Ethel and Albert, Ghostbreaker, Is There a Doctor in the House, Life with Virginia, Patty Duke Show, Sigmund and the Sea Monsters

Hamilton, Murray: B.J. and the Bear, Boys in Blue, Cheap Detective, Hail to the Chief, Man Who Never Was

Hamlin, Harry: L.A. Law

Hampton, James: Bravo Two, Doris Day Show, Dukes of Hazzard, F Troop, Houston Knights, Kudzu, Maggie, Mary, Teen Wolf

Hanks, Tom: Bosom Buddies, Family Ties

Hanley, Bridget: Bell, Book and Candle, Gidget, Guess What I Did Today?, Harper Valley, Harper Valley PTA, Here Come the Brides, Pirates of Flounder Bay

Hardin, Melora: Best Times, Catalina C-Lab, Cliffwood Avenue Kids, Family Tree, Little House on the Prairie, Secrets of Midland Heights, Thunder, Two Marriages

Hardin, Ty: Bronco, Hunter's Moon, Riptide (1965)

Harewood, Dorian: Dirty Work, Glitter, Kingpins, Strike Force, Trauma Center

Harmon, Deborah: Comedy of Horrors, Day to Day, Fun Factory, Leo and Liz in Beverly Hills, M*A*S*H, Ted Knight Show (first title), Used Cars

Harmon, Mark: Flamingo Road, Sam, St. Elsewhere, 240-Robert

Harper, Ron: 87th Precinct, Garrison's Gorillas, Jean Arthur Show, Land of the Lost, Planet of the Apes, Wendy and Me

Harper, Valerie: Mary Tyler Moore Show, Rhoda, Valerie

Harrington Jr., Pat: Another Man's Shoes, Bobby Jo and the Big Apple Goodtime Band, Couple of Joes, Funny World of Fred and Bunni, Journey to the Center of the Earth, Make Room for Daddy, Max and Me, Mr. Deeds Goes to Town, New Steve Allen Show, One Day at a Time, Owen Marshall, Rhyme and Reason, Rowdies, Steve Allen Show, Steve Allen's Laugh Back, Stump the Stars, Tonight Show, Wednesday Night Out

Hurst, Rick: Amanda's, Dukes of Hazzard, From Here to Eternity, I'll Never Forget What's Her Name, On the Rocks

Hurd, John: Storyteller

Hutchins, Will: Blondie, Hey Landlord, Sugarfoot

Hutton, Betty: Betty Hutton Show

Hutton, Gunilla: Hee Haw, Higher and Higher Attorneys at Law, Petticoat Junction

Hutton, Jim: Butterflies (second title), Call Holme, Everything's Relative, Wednesday Night Out, You're Only Young Once

Hutton, Lauren: Paper Dolls

Hyde-White, Wilfrid: Associates, Buck Rogers (1979), Sybil

Hyland, Diana: Eight Is Enough, Guilty or Not Guilty, Hercules, Peyton Place

Impert, Margie: Maggie, Magnum P.I., Spencer's Pilots

Ingber, Mandy: Charles in Charge (first title), Tortellis

Ingels, Marty: Always April, Cattanoga Cats, Dick Van Dyke Show, Great Grape Ape Show, I'm Dickens . . . He's Fenster, Motor Mouse, Pac-Man, Pruitts of Southampton

Ireland, Jill: Shane

Ireland, John: Cassie and Company, Cheaters, Rawhide

Irene, Georgi: Barbara Mandrell and the Mandrell Sisters, Galactica 1980, Silver Spoons, Wildfire

Irving, Amy: Amazing Stories

Irving, Hollis: Blondie, Five's a Family, Margie, Room 222, Where There's Smokey

Irwin, Wynn: Corey: For the People, Hart to Hart, Home Cookin', Laverne and Shirley, Sugar Time, Super

Isacksen, Peter: C.P.O. Sharkey, Half-Hour Comedy Hour, Jessie, Piper's Pets

Ito, Robert: Amazing Chan and the Chan Clan, Burns and Schreiber Comedy Hour, Eyes of Texas, Quincy, M.E.

Ives, Burl: Alias Smith and Jones, Daniel Boone, Lawyers, O.K. Crackerby

Jackson, Janet: Diff'rent Strokes, Good Times, Jacksons, New Kind of Family

Jackson, Kate: Charlie's Angels, Movin' On, New Healers, Rookies, Scarecrow and Mrs. King

Jackson, Mary: City, Hardcastle and McCormick, Inspector Perez, My Town, Open All Night, Two the Hard Way, Waltons

Jackson, Sammy: Code of Jonathan West, Li'l Abner, No Time for Sergeants

Jackson, Sherry: Brenda Starr Reporter, Come a Running, Enigma, Make Room for Daddy, Make Room for Granddaddy

Jackson, Victoria: Half-Hour Comedy Hour, Half Nelson, W*A*L*T*E*R

Jacobi, Lou: Allan, Arena, Dean Martin Show, Happeners, Ivan the Terrible, Joanna, Kibbee Hates Fitch, Melba, Rear Guard, Saint Peter

Jacobs, Rachel: Dear Teacher, It's Not Easy, Maggie, 13 Queens Boulevard

Jacoby, Billy: Bad News Bears, It's Not Easy, Maggie

Jaeckel, Richard: At Ease, Banyon, Firehouse, Frontier Circus, Hot W.A.C.S., Luke and the Tenderfoot, Mighty O, Salvage 1, Spenser: For Hire

Jaffe, Sam: Ben Casey

Jagger, Dean: Matt Lincoln, Mr. Novak

James, Art: Blank Check, Catch Phrase, Concentration, Fractured Phrases, Magnificent Marble Machine, Matches 'N' Mates, Pay Cards, Say When, Super Pay Cards

James, Dennis: Cash and Carry, Chance of a Lifetime, Club 60, Dennis James Show, Dennis James Sports Parade, Dennis James Carnival, Haggis Baggis, High Finance, Judge for Yourself, Name That Tune, Name's the Same, Okay Mother, On Your Account, P.D.Q., People Will Talk, Price Is Right, Television Roof, Turn to a Friend, Two for the Money, Your All American College Show, Your First Impression

James, John: Colbys, Dynasty

James, Sheila: Broadside, Dobie Gillis, Trouble with Father, Whatever Happened to Dobie Gillis?

Janis, Conrad: Bonino, Danny and the Mermaid, Full Speed Anywhere, Jimmy Hughes, Rookie Cop, Mork and Mindy (two titles), Quark, Rear Guard, There's Always Room

Janssen, David: Fugitive, Harry O, O'Hara: U.S. Treasury, Richard Diamond, Private Detective

Jarrett, Renne: Nancy

Jarvis, Graham: Border Pals, Bungle Abbey, Forever Fernwood, Making the Grade, Mary Hartman, Number 96, There Goes the Neighborhood, Two Guys from Muck

Jason, Rick: Case of the Dangerous Robin, Combat, Prudence and the Chief

Jeffreys, Anne: Delphi Bureau, Finder of Lost Loves, Ghostbreaker, Love That Jill, Topper

Jenkins, Allen: Duke, Forest Ranger, Hey Jeannie, Top Cat

Jenks, Frank: Adventures of Colonel Flack, Eddie Cantor Comedy Theatre, Front Page Detective, Make Room for Daddy, Waldo

Jens, Salome: All's Fair, From Here to Eternity, Mary Hartman

Jensen, Karen: Bracken's World, Ted Bessell Show

Jensen, Maren: Battlestar Galactica

Jergens, Diane: It's Always Sunday, Love That Bob, McGonigle, Three Wishes

Jessel, George: All-Star Revue, Comeback Story, George Jessel's Show Business, Here Come the Stars

Jillian, Ann: Dean Jones Show, Hazel, It's a Living (two titles), Jennifer Slept Here, Making a Living, Off We Go, Rainbow Girl, Sealab 2020

Johns, Glynis: Batman, Cheers, Glynis, Hide and Seek, Safari

Johnson, Ann-Marie: Double Trouble, High School

U.S.A., What's Happening Now

Johnson, Arch: Asphalt Jungle, Camp Runamuck, It's Always Jan, Peter Loves Mary

Johnson, Arte: Arnold's Closet Revue, B.B. Beegle Show, Baggy Pants and the Nitwits, Bobby Vinton Show, Bunco, Call Holme, Don't Call Me Charlie, Glitter, Hennessey, Houndcats, Ivy League, Knockout, Rowan and Martin's Laugh-In, Sally, Super Six, Tales of the Apple Dumpling Gang

Johnson, Georgann: Archie Bunker's Place, Cutter to Houston, Larry Storch Show, Living in Paradise, Mr. Peepers, Our Family Honor, Secret Life of John Monroe, Silver Spoons, Sutters Bay, Three's Company

Johnson, Janet Louise (aka, Julian, Janet): B.J. and the Bear, Battlestar Galactica, Key Tortuga, Nancy Drew Mysteries

Johnson, Jay: Celebrity Charades, So You Think You Got Troubles, Soap, Sutters Bay

Johnson, Kathie Lee: Hee Haw, Hee Haw Honeys (two titles)

Johnson, Lynn-Holly: Chips

Johnson, Melodie: Enigma, Ready and Willing

Johnson, Russell: Black Saddle, Gilligan's Island, Gilligan's Planet New Adventures of Gilligan, Owen Marshall: Counselor at Law

Johnson, Van: At Your Service, Batman, Glitter, One Day at a Time, Rich Man, Poor Man

Jones, Carolyn: Addams Family, Batman, Wonder Woman (second title)

Jones, Davy: Monkees

Jones, Dean: Chicago Teddy Bears, Dean Jones Show, Ensign O'Toole, Herbie the Love Bug, I Love Her Anyway, What's It All About World

Jones, Gordon: Abbott and Costello Show, Dobie Gillis, Meet Mr. McNutly, So This Is Hollywood

Jones, Henry: B.J. and the Bear, Chameleon, Channing, Code Name: Foxfire, Girl with Something Extra, Gun Shy, Honestly Celeste, I Married Dora, Kate Loves a Mystery, Last Chance Cafe, Lost in Space, Mrs. Columbo, Of This Time, Of That Place, Phyllis, Quick and Quiet, Singles, Tales of the Apple Dumpling Gang, These Are the Days

Jones, James Earl: Faerie Tale Theatre, Me and Mom, Paris

Jones, L.Q.: Buffalo Soldiers, Colorado—C.I., Klondike, Rawhide, Virginian (second title)

Jones, Marilyn: King's Crossing, MacGyver, V

Jones, Mickey: Down Home, Dukes of Hazzard, Goober and the Truckers' Paradise, Norma Rae, Rollin' On the River, V

Jones, Shirley: Adventures of Pollyana, Big Show, For the Love of Mike, Out of the Blue (first title), Partridge Family, Shirley

Jones, Spike: All-Star Revue, Club Oasis, Spike Jones Show

Jory, Victor: King's Row, Manhunt, Nakia

Joseph, Jackie: All-New Popeye Hour, Barbara Mandrell and the Mandrell Sisters, Bob Newhart Show, Doris Day Show, Josie and the Pussycats, Kelly's Kids, Run Buddy Run, That Girl (pilot)

Joslyn, Allyn: Addams Family, Eve Arden Show, Heave Ho Harrigan, McKeever and the Colonel (two titles), Where's Raymond

Jourdan, Louis: Paris Precinct

Joyce, Elaine: Allison Sidney Harrison, Alone at Last, Carol, City of Angels, Don Knotts Show, Fashion Story, I've Got a Secret, Mr. Merlin, Ugily Family, We Got It Made

Julian, Janet: See Johnson, Janet Louise

Jump, Gordon: Archie, Archie Situation Comedy Show, Great Day, McDuff the Talking Dog, Second Edition, Soap, WKRP in Cincinnati

Kaczmarek, Jane: Hill Street Blues, Hometown, Paper Chase: The Second Year, St. Elsewhere

Kahan, Judith (Judy): All's Fair, Branagan and Mapes, Doc, Forever Fernwood, Free Country, Love Natalie, Mary, Mo and Jo, Valerie

Kahn, Madeline: Chameleon, Comedy Tonight, Oh Madeline

Kalember, Patricia: Kay O'Brien

Kanaly, Steve: Dallas

Kane, Carol: All Is Forgiven, Shelley Duvall's Tall Tales and Legends, Taxi

Kaplan, Gabriel (Gabe): Lewis and Clark, Welcome Back, Kotter

Kaplan, Marvin: Alice, C.B. Bears, Chicago Teddy Bears, Hooray for Hollywood, Maggie Brown, Meet Millie, Out of the Blue, Top Cat

Karabatsos, Ron: Dreams, Joanna, Our Family Honor

Karen, James: Cheers, Eight Is Enough, Me and Ducky, Melba, Powers of Matthew Star

Karlen, John: Cagney and Lacey, Colorado C.I.

Karloff, Boris: Boris Karloff Mystery Theatre, Colonel March of Scotland Yard, Veil

Karron, Richard: Charlie and Company, Further Adventures of Wally Brown, Good Time Harry, Mixed Nuts, Pen 'N' Inc., Roosevelt and Truman, Teachers Only, Young Guy Christian

Kastner, Peter: Delta House, Ugliest Girl in Town

Kasznar, Kurt: Land of the Giants

Katt, William: Greatest American Hero

Kaufman, Andy: Lisa Hartman Show, Stick Around, Taxi, Van Dyke and Company

Kavner, Julie: Fine Romance, Rhoda, Taxi, Tracey Ullman Show

Kay, Dianne: Cass Malloy, Eight Is Enough, Flamingo Road, Glitter, Once a Hero, Reggie

Kaye, Caren: Betty White Show, Blansky's Beauties, Empire (second title), It's Your Move, Legs, Natural Look, Sam Penny and Associate, Simon and Simon, Together Again, Who's Watching the Kids?

Kaye, Danny: Danny Kaye Show

Kaye, Stubby: Full Speed Anywhere, My Sister Eileen, Pantomime Quiz, Shenanagans, Side By Side, Wonderful World of Philip Malley

Kazan, Lainie: Family Business, Karen's Song,

Rowan and Martin Show, Tough Cookies

Keach, Stacy: Caribe, Harry, Mickey Spillane's Mike Hammer, New Mike Hammer

Keane, James: In Security, Paper Chase, Paper Chase: Graduation, Paper Chase: Second Year, Paper Chase: Third Year

Keane, Teri: Dirty Work, Hot Pursuit, Yellow Rose

Kearns, Joseph: Adventures of Ozzie and Harriet, Alan Young Show, Dennis the Menace, It's a Small World, Our Miss Brooks, Professional Father

Keeshan, Bob: Captain Kangaroo, CBS Storybreak, Howdy Doody, Mr. Mayor, Wake Up

Keith, Brian: Archer, Crusader, Family Affair, Hardcastle and McCormick, Little People, Pursuit of Happiness, Seekers, Westerner, Winchester

Keller, Mary Page: Duet

Kellerman, Susan: At Your Service, Hail to the Chief, Sutters Bay, Taxi

Kelley, DeForest; Johnny Risk, Star Trek, 333 Montgomery, You Are There

Kellin, Mike: Bonino, Fitz and Bones, Honestly Celeste, Nightside, Wackiest Ship in the Army

Kelly, Gene: Big Show, Funny Side, Going My Way

Kelly, Jack: Get Christie Love, Hardy Boys Mysteries, King's Row, Maverick, NBC Comedy Theatre, Palms Precinct, Sale of the Century

Kelly, Roz: Happy Days (second title), New Lorenzo Music Show

Kelsey, Linda: Doc, Lou Grant, M*A*S*H

Kendal, Felicity: Good Neighbors, Solo

Kennedy, George: Bliss, Blue Knight, Counterattack: Crime in America, Never Say Never, Phil Silvers Show, Sarge

Kennedy, Jayne: Mitchell and Woods, Speak Up America

Kennedy, Mimi: Big Show, I've Had It Up to Here, Mr. Boogedy, Spencer, Stockard Channing in Just Friends, Three Girls Three, Two of Us, Under One Roof

Kennedy, Tom: Big Game, Body Language, Break the Bank, Doctor I.Q., 50 Grand Slam, It's Your Bet, $100,000 Name That Tune, Name That Tune, Password Plus, Real Tom Kennedy Show, Split Second, To Say the Least, Whew, Word Play, You Don't Say

Kercheval, Ken: Dallas, You Are the Jury

Kerns, Joanna: Four Seasons, Growing Pains

Kerns, Sandra: Charles in Charles (second title), Flamingo Road

Kerwin, Brian: B.J. and the Bear, Busters, Chisholms, James Boys, Lobo, Misadventures of Sheriff Lobo

Kerwin, Lance: Family Holvak, James at 15

Ketchum, Dave: Call Holme, Camp Runamuck, Get Smart, I'm Dickens . . . He's Fenster, Legs, Where's the Fire

Khambatta, Persis: Exciting People, Exotic Places

Kidder, Margot: Nichols, Shell Game

Kiel, Richard: Barbary Coast, Land of the Lost,

Van Dyke and Company, Wild Wild West

Kiff, Kaleena: Love Sidney, New Leave it to Beaver

King, Alan: Alan King Show

King, John Reed: Battle of the Ages, Chance of a Lifetime, Give and Take, Have a Heart, It's a Gift, Missus Goes a Shopping, On Your Way, There's One in Every Family, Tootsie Hippodrome, What Have You Got to Lose?, What's Your Bid?, Where Was I?, Why?

Kirby, Durward: Candid Camera, G.E. Guest House, Garry Moore Show

Kirk, Phyllis: Red Buttons Show, Thin Man, Young Set

Kirkland, Sally: Shaughnessey, Summer, Willow B: Women in Prison

Kiser, Terry: Bay City Amusement Company, Change at 125th Street, Crazy Dan, Night Court, Off the Wall, Rollergirls

Klein, Robert: Comedy Tonight, Comedy Zone, Father's Day, Klein Time, TV's Bloopers and Practical Jokes

Kline, Richard: His and Hers, It's a Living (second title), Second Time Around, Three's Company, Together Again

Klous, Patricia (Pat): Aloha Paradise, Flying High, Johnny Blue, Love Boat

Klugman, Jack: Captain Video, Harris Against the World, Odd Couple, Quincy, M.E., You Again

Knight, Ted: Aquaman, Fantastic Voyage, Journey to the Center of the Earth, Lassie's Rescue Rangers, Mary Tyler Moore Show, New Adventures of Superman, Super Friends, Ted Knight Show (2 titles), Too Close for Comfort

Knotts, Don: Andy Griffith Show, Don Knotts Show, Harry and Maggie, Howdy Doody, Piper's Pets, Steve Allen Show, Steve Allen's Laugh-Back, Three's Company, What a Country

Komack, James: Charlie Angelo, Courtship of Eddie's Father, 9 to 5 (first title), Welcome Back, Kotter

Kopell, Bernie: Bewitched, Diana Rigg Show, Doris Day Show, Flo's Place, Love Boat, Needles and Pins, Sally and Sam, That Girl, When Things Were Rotten, Wild About Harry

Kopins, Karen: Heart Beat, Riptide

Korman, Harvey: Carol Burnett Show, Couch, Cracker Brothers, Danny Kaye Show, Harvey Korman Show (2 titles), Invisible Woman, Leo and Liz in Beverly Hills, Mama's Family (first title), Snavely, Tim Conway Show

Kovacs, Ernie: Ernie in Kovacsland, Ernie Kovacs Show, Gamble on Love, I Was a Bloodhound, It's Time for Ernie, Kovacs on the Corner, Kovacs Unlimited, New Ernie Kovacs Show, Silents Please, Take a Good Look, Time Will Tell, Tonight Show

Kove, Martin: Cagney and Lacey, Code R, We've Got Each Other, Yeagers

Kruschen, Jack: Busting Loose, E/R, Emergency, Hong Kong, Nick and Nora, No Soap Radio,

Rifleman, Webster

Kulp, Nancy: Adventures of a Model, Beverly Hillbillies, Fountain of Youth, Freewheelers, Little People, Love That Bob, Pine Lake Lodge, Sanford and Son, Soft Touch

Kurtz, Swoosie: Love Sidney, Mary

Kurtzman, Katy: Allison Sidney Harrison, Dynasty, Mulligan's Stew

Kusatsu, Clyde: Bring 'Em Back Alive, Sylvan in Paradise, Zero Intelligence

Ladd, Cheryl: Charlie's Angels, Harry O, Josie and the Pussycats, Ken Berry Wow Show, Search

Lahr, Bert: Mr. O'Malley, Thompson's Ghost

Lamas, Fernando: Stranded

Lamas, Lorenzo: California Fever, Dancin' to the Hits, Falcon Crest, Secrets of Midland Heights, Shipshape, Whatever Happened to Dobie Gillis

Lampert, Zohra: Comedy Zone, Doctors Hospital, Girl With Something Extra, Mixed Nuts

Lanchester, Elsa: Nanny and the Professor

Landau, Martin: Buffalo Bill, Mission: Impossible, Space: 1999

Lander, David L.: Laverne and Shirley, Rock Candy, Will the Real Jerry Lewis Please Sit Down

Landers, Audrey: Archie, Archie Situation Comedy Show, Dallas, Fit for a King, Goober and the Trucker's Paradise, Highcliffe Manor, Rock Candy, White and Reno

Landers, Judy: B.J. and the Bear, Celebrity Charades, Charlie's Angels, Daughters, Four in Love, Gossip, Here's Richard, Madame's Place, Rock Candy, That's TV, Vegas, White and Reno

Landesberg, Steve: Barney Miller, Black Bart, Bobby Darin Amusement Company, Comedy Zone, Don Rickles Show, Paul Sand in Friends and Lovers, Stephanie, Steve Landesberg TV Show

Landon, Michael: Belle Starr, Bonanza, Highway to Heaven, Johnny Risk, Little House on the Prairie

Lane, Charles: Bewitched, Dear Phoebe, Dennis the Menace, Karen (second title), Love Nest, Love on a Rooftop, Lucy Show, Mr. Bevis, Petticoat Junction, Real McCoys, Side By Side, So This Is Hollywood, Soft Touch, Tom and Jerry

Lane, Nancy: Angie, Between the Lines, Duck Factory, Moscow Bureau, Rhoda

Laneuville, Eric: Cop and the Kid, Flo's Place, Furst Family of Washington, St. Elsewhere

Langdon, Sue Ane: All in the Family (first title), Andy Griffith Show, Apartment House, Arnie, Bachelor Father, Grandpa Goes to Washington, Happy Days (second title), Jackie Gleason and His American Scene Magazine, Little Leatherneck, When the Whistle Blows

Lange, Hope: Back the Fact, Ghost and Mrs. Muir, Hazard's People, New Dick Van Dyke Show, Sky's the Limit

Lange, Jim: Bullseye, Dating Game, Give-N-Take,

Hollywood Connection, New $100,000 Name That Tune, New Newlywed Game, Operation: Entertainment, Spin-Off

Lankford, Kim: Hollywood High, Knots Landing, Three Eyes, Waverly Wonders

Lansbury, Angela: Murder, She Wrote, Pantomime Quiz

Lansing, Joi: Beverly Hillbillies, Fountain of Youth, Jones Boys, Klondike, Love That Bob

Lansing, Robert: Assignment: Earth, 87th Precinct, Man Who Never Was, Sam Penny & Associate, Shadow of Sam Penny, Twelve O'Clock High

Larroquette, John: Black Sheep Squadron, Doctors Hospital, 416th, Night Court

Larsen, Keith: Brave Eagle, Hunter (first title), Northwest Passage

Lasser, Louise: Class of 55, Making a Living, Mary Hartman, Mo and Jo, St. Elsewhere, Taxi

Lauren, Tammy: Angie, Best Times, Mork and Mindy, Morning Star Evening Star, Out of the Blue (second title), Things Are Looking Up, Who's Watching the Kids?

Lavin, Linda: Alice

Lawford, Peter: Dear Phoebe, Doris Day Show, Thin Man, Tom and Jerry

Lawrence, Vicki: Anything for Love, Carol Burnett and Company, Carol Burnett Show, Funny World of Fred and Bunni, Jimmie Rodgers Show, Laverne and Shirley, Mama's Family (2 titles), Win, Lose or Draw

Leachman, Cloris: Bob and Ray Show, Book of Lists, Charlie Wild Private Detective, Ernie Madge and Artie, Facts of Life, Mary Tyler Moore Show, Pete 'N' Tillie, Phyllis, Timmy and Lassie, Wonder Woman

Learned, Michael: Nurse, Waltons

Leary, Brianne: Astronauts, Black Sheep Squadron, Chips, No Soap Radio, Pen 'N' Inc.

Lee, Christopher: Aggie, Tales of the Haunted

Lee, Gypsy Rose: Gypsy, Gypsy Rose Lee Show, Pruitts of Southampton

Lee, Jonna: Hail to the Chief, Otherworld

Lee, Michele: Alias Smith and Jones, Knots Landing, Michele Lee Show, Singles

Lee, Pinky: Gumby, Pinky and Company, Pinky Lee Show, Those Two

Lee, Ruta: First and 10, Flintstone Family Adventures, Flintstone Funnies, High Rollers, Line-Up, Man from Everywhere, Rousters, Roy Rogers Show, Stump the Stars

Leibman, Ron: Kaz, Side by Side

Leigh, Janet: My Wives Jane, On Our Way

Lembeck, Harvey: Ensign O'Toole, Goldbergs, Hathaways, Mother, Juggs and Speed, Phil Silvers Show

Lembeck, Michael: Flannery and Quilt, Foley Square, Funny Side, Gidget Grows Up, Goodbye Doesn't Mean Forever, Krofft Supershow, Mary Hartman, One Day at a Time

Lemmon, Christopher: Brothers and Sisters, Duet

Lemmon, Jack: Ad-Libbers, Frances Langford-

Don Ameche Show, Heaven for Betsy, I Remember Mama, That Wonderful Guy, Toni Twin Time

Lenska, Rula: Rock Follies

Lenz, Kay: Fall Guy, Heart of the City, Rich Man, Poor Man, Travelling Man

Leonard, Sheldon: Big Eddie, Dick Van Dyke Show, Duke (first title), It's Always Sunday, Linus the Lionhearted, Make Room for Daddy

Lerman, April: Charles in Charge (first title), Rita

Leslie, Bethel: The Girls, Richard Boone Show

Lester, Jerry: Broadway Open House, Candid Camera, Jerry Lester Show, Jerry Lester's Blind Date, Li'l Abner, Saturday Night Dance Party, Sound Off Time

Lester, Ketty: Adventuring with the Chopper, Handsome Harry's, Little House on the Prairie, Little House: A New Beginning, Morning Star Evening Star, Rituals

Lethin, Lori: Dukes of Hazzard, Matlock, Wonderful World of Philip Malley

Letterman, David: David Letterman Show, Late Night with David Letterman, Mary, Starland Vocal Band

Lewis, Emmanuel: Webster

Lewis, Jerry: Jerry Lewis Show

Lewis, Robert Q.: Get the Message, Hidden Treasure, Make Me Laugh, Masquerade Party, Names the Same, Play Your Hunch, Robert Q's Matinee, Show Goes On

Lewis, Shari: Hi Mom, Shari Lewis Show

Leyden, Bill: Call My Bluff, It Could Be You, Musical Chairs

Liberace: Batman, Liberace Show

Light, Judith: Charmed Lives, Family Ties, Who's the Boss?, You Are The Jury

Linden, Hal: Barney Miller, Blacke's Magic, Second Edition, Shameful Secrets of Hastings Corners

Lindley, Audra: Bridget Loves Bernie, Doc, Fay, Ropers, Three's Company

Lindsey, George: Andy Griffith Show, Goober and the Truckers' Paradise, Hee Haw, Mayberry R.F.D., Nashville Palace, Take One Starring Jonathan Winters, Tycoon

Linkletter, Art: Art Linkletter Show, Art Linkletter's House Party, Hollywood Talent Scouts, Life with Linkletter, People Are Funny

Linn-Baker, Mark: Comedy Zone, O'Malley, Perfect Strangers, Recovery Room

Linville, Larry: Calling Dr. Storm, Checking In, Grandpa Goes to Washington, Herbie the Love Bug, M*A*S*H, Paper Dolls

Lipton, Peggy: John Forsythe Show, Mod Squad

Lithgow, John: Faerie Tale Theatre

Little, Cleavon: David Frost Revue, Komedy Tonite, Mr. Dugan, New Temperatures Rising Show, Now We're Cookin', Temperatures Rising

Little, Rich: Dean Martin Celebrity Roast, Flying Nun, John Davidson Show, Julie Andrews Hour, Kopycats, Love on a Rooftop, Pioneer Spirit,

Rich Little Show, You Asked for It

Lloyd, Christopher: Best of the West, Old Friends, Taxi

Lloyd, Kathleen: Amazing Stories, Call to Glory, Gangster Chronicles, Harry O, Magnum P.I., Owen Marshall: Counselor at Law

Lockhart, Anne: B.J. and the Bear, Battlestar Galactica, Gidget's Summer Reunion, Last Chance Cafe, Washingtoon

Lockhart, June: Colbys, Greatest American Hero, Knots Landing, Lost in Space, Petticoat Junction, These Are the Days, Timmy and Lassie

Locklear, Heather: Dynasty, T.J. Hooker

Lockwood, Gary: Follow the Sun, Lieutenant, Sally and Sam

Loggia, Robert: Elfego Baca, Emerald Point N.A.S., T.H.E. Cat, Toni's Boys

Lollobrigida, Gina: Falcon Crest

Long, Richard: Big Valley, Bourbon Street Beat, Maverick, Nanny and the Professor, Rimfire, 77 Sunset Strip, Thicker Than Water

Long, Shelley: Cheers, Dooley Brothers, Ghost of a Chance, Young Guy Christian

Longo, Tony: Best of Times, First and 10, First and 10: The Championships, Heart of the City, Just Married, Training Camp: The Bulls Are Back

Lord, Jack: Border Town, Hawaii Five-O, Stoney Burke

Lord, Marjorie: Make More Room for Daddy, Make Room for Daddy, Make Room for Granddaddy, Sweet Surrender

Loring, Lynn: Baby Crazy, Dobie Gillis, Fair Exchange, FBI, Jean Carroll Show

Lorne, Marion: Bewitched, Garry Moore Show, Mr. Peepers, Sally

Loudon, Dorothy: Dorothy, Garry Moore Show, It's a Business, Ma and Pa

Louise, Tina: Call to Danger, Don't Call Us, Gilligan's Island, Jan Murray Show, Rituals

Lovejoy, Frank: Chicago 212, County General, Man Against Crime, Meet McGraw (2 titles)

Luckinbill, Laurence: Delphi Bureau, Momma the Detective, One More Try

Ludden, Allen: Allen Ludden's Gallery, G.E. College Bowl, Liar's Club, Password, Password Plus, Stumpers, Win with the Stars

Luke, Keye: Amazing Chan and the Chan Clan, Anna and the King, Battle of the Planets, Brothers, Harry O, King Fu, Sidekicks, Unit 4

Lupino, Ida: Batman, Ida Lupino Theatre, Mr. Adams and Eve

Lupton, John: Broken Arrow, Me and Benjy

Lydon, Jimmy: Ellery Queen, First Hundred Years, Life of Riley (1949), Love That Jill, Real McCoys, Roll Out, So This Is Hollywood

Lyman, Dorothy: Hearts Island, Mama's Family (two titles)

Lynch, Richard: Galactica 1980, Once a Hero, Phoenix

Lynde, Paul: Bewitched, Cattanoga Cats, Dean Martin Presents the Golddiggers, Donny and

Marie, Flying Nun, Gidget Gets Married, Gidget Grows Up, Hollywood Squares, Motor Mouse, Munsters, New Temperatures Rising Show, Paul Lynde Show, Perils of Penelope Pitstop, Red Buttons Show, Stanley, Where's Huddles

Lynley, Carol: Fliers, Immortal, Judgement Day, Willow B: Women in Prison

Lynn, Betty: Andy Griffith Show, Love That Jill, Matlock, Texas John Slaughter, Where's Raymond?

McAdam, Heather: Facts of Life, Rags to Riches, Salvage 1, Walking Tall

McCallum, David: Invisible Man (2nd title), Man from UNCLE, The Unknown

McCann, Chuck: All That Glitters, Arnold's Closet Revue, C.B. Bears, Cool McCool, Drak Pack, Far Out Space Nuts, Happy Days (first title), New Kind of Family, New Shmoo, One Day at a Time, Pac-Man, Semi-Tough, Turn On, Van Dyke and Company

McCardle, Andrea: Mo and Jo

McCarthy, Kevin: Amanda's, Flamingo Road, Ghostbreaker, Home, Spies (pilot), Survivors

McCashin, Constance: Knots Landing, Many Loves of Arthur, Married: The First Year, You Are the Jury

McCay, Peggy: Gibbsville, Lazarus Syndrome, Lou Grant, Love at First Sight, Room for One More

McClanahan, Rue: And They All Lived Happily Ever After, Apple Pie, Charles in Charge (first title), Gimme a Break, Golden Girls, Mama's Family (first title), Maude, Mother and Me, M.D., Son-in-Law

McClure, Doug: Barbary Coast, Checkmate, Ivy League, Master, Men from Shiloh, Out of This World, Overland Trail, Search, Sky's the Limit, Virginian

McClure, Marc: California Fever, James at 15, Scary Tales

McCook, John: Code Name: Foxfire, Our House, Rainbow Girl, Rear Guard

McCord, Kent: Adam-12, Adventures of Ozzie and Harriet, Galactica 1980

MacCorkindale, Simon: Falcon Crest, Manimal, Scalpels

McCormack, Patricia: Emergency (second title), I Remember Mama, Mr. Sunshine, Peck's Bad Girl, Ropers

McCormick, Maureen: Brady Brides, Brady Bunch, Brady Bunch Hour, Brady Girls Get Married, Brady Kids

McCormick, Pat: Bay City Amusement Company, Cracker Brothers, Gun Shy, Shaughnessey, Sylvan in Paradise, We Dare You

McCoy, Matt: Hot Hero Sandwich, Pen 'N' Inc., We Got It Made, We're Puttin' on the Ritz

McCullough, Linda: B.J. and the Bear, Welcome Back, Kotter

McDonough, Kit: Angie, Fast Times, Rita Moreno Show, Sam (1986), Teachers Only

McDowall, Roddy: Batman, Fantastic Journey, Fantasy Island, Judgement Day, London and Davis in New York, Planet of the Apes, Tales of the Gold Monkey, Topper Returns

McGavin, Darren: Crime Photographer, Day to Day, Father on Trial, Mike Hammer Detective, Night Stalker, Old Nickerbocker Music Hall, Outsider, Riverboat, Rookies, Small and Frye

McGiver, John: Boston Terrier, Jimmy Stewart Show, Low Man on the Totem Pole, Many Happy Returns, Miss and the Missiles, Mr. Terrific, Patty Duke Show, Pruitts of Southampton

McGoohan, Patrick: Danger Man, Prisoner, Rafferty, Secret Agent

McIntire, John: American Dream, Americans, Naked City, Shirley, Virginian, Wagon Train

McKay, Gardner: Adventures in Paradise, Boots and Saddles, Ginger Rogers Show

McKeon, Nancy: Dusty, Facts of Life, High School U.S.A., Stone

MacLachlan, Janet: Archie Bunker's Place, Friends, Love Thy Neighbor

MacLaine, Shirley: Shirley's World

MacLeod, Gavin: Baby Crazy, Big Show, Love Boat, Mary Tyler Moore Show, McHale's Navy, My Favorite Martian

McLerie, Allyn Ann: After George, Days and Nights of Molly Dodd, Duck Factory, Faculty, Sister Terri, Tony Randall Show, WKRP in Cincinnati

McMahon, Ed: Big Top, Carson's Comedy Classics, Concentration, Missing Links, NBC Adventure Theatre, Snap Judgement, Star Search, Tonight Show, TV's Bloopers and Practical Jokes

McMahon, Horace: Make Room for Daddy, Martin Kane, Mr. Bevis, Mr. Broadway, Naked City

MacMurray, Fred: Apartment House, My Three Sons

McNichol, Kristy: Apple's Way, Family

McPherson, Patricia: Concrete Beat, Knight Rider

McQueen, Steve: Bounty Hunter, Defender, Wanted: Dead Or Alive

McRae, Ellen: See, Burstyn, Ellen

MacRae, Meredith: Fantasy, Hollywood Reporter, My Three Sons, Petticoat Junction, Sheila MacRae Show, VTV, Wilder and Wilder

McWilliams, Caroline: Benson, Cass Malloy, Many Loves of Arthur, Maximum Security, Moscow Bureau, Soap, St. Elsewhere, What's Up Doc?

Mack, Ted: Ted Mack and the Original Amateur Hour, Ted Mack's Family Hour, Ted Mack's Matinee

Macnee, Patrick: Avengers, Battlestar Galactica, Comedy of Horrors, Empire (second title), Gavilan, Lime Street, New Avengers

Macy, Bill: All in the Family (second title), Hanging In, Maude, Nothing in Common

Maharis, George: Most Deadly Game, Route 66

Mahoney, Jock: B.J. and the Bear, Range Rider, Simon Lash, Yancy Derringer

Majors, Lee: Big Valley, Bionic Woman, Fall Guy,

bassy, Honeymooners, Jackie Gleason Show, Too Close for Comfort

Meadows, Jayne: It's Not Easy, Man and the Challenge, Medical Center, Rise and Shine, Steve Allen Comedy Hour, Steve Allen's Laugh-Back, What's Going On?

Meara, Anne: Archie Bunker's Place, Corner Bar, Kate McShane, Paul Lynde Show, Rhoda, Stiller and Meara Show, Take Five with Stiller and Meara, This Better Be It

Mekka, Eddie: Blansky's Beauties, Laverne and Shirley

Melton, Sid: Bachelor Father, Captain Midnight, Green Acres, It's Always Jan, Make Room for Daddy, Make Room for Granddaddy

Melville, Sam: Is There a Doctor in the House?, Rookies

Menzies, Heather: Bob Newhart Show, Captain America, Doctor Dan, Logan's Run, Man in the Middle

Mercer, Marian: Calling Dr. Storm, Dean Martin Show, Dom DeLuise Show, Forever Fernwood, It's a Living (2 titles), King of the Road, Making a Living, Mary Hartman, Sandy Duncan Show, St. Elsewhere, Touch of Grace, Wacky World of Jonathan Winters

Meredith, Burgess: Batman, Big Story, Blinkins, Gloria, Mr. Novak, Return of Captain Nemo, Search, Those Amazing Animals

Meriwether, Lee: Barnaby Jones, Mission: Impossible, New Andy Griffith Show, Time Tunnel

Merman, Ethel: Batman, Love Boat, Maggie Brown, You're Gonna Love It Here

Merrill, Dina: Alan King Show, Hot Pursuit, Hotel

Merrill, Gary: Justice, Lady Died at Midnight, Mask, Reporter, World of Darkness

Metrano, Art: Amy Prentiss, Baretta, Barney Miller, Chicago Teddy Bears, Flo's Place, Fred and Barney, Joanie Loves Chachi, Loves Me Loves Me Not, Movin' On, Rise and Shine, Soupy Sales Show, Swingin' Together, Tim Conway Comedy Hour, Tough Cookies

Mettey, Lynnette: Amanda Fallon, Fitz and Bones, Kibbee Hates Fitch Fitch Hates Kibbee, M*A*S*H, Quincy, M.E., Starting Fresh.

Milano, Alyssa: Animal Crack-Ups, Who's the Boss?

Milland, Ray: Hart to Hart, Markham (two titles), Meet Mr. McNutley, Ray Milland Show, Trails West

Miller, Denise: Archie Bunker's Place, Every Stray Dog and Kid, Fish, Makin' It

Miller, Denny: Keeper of the Wild, Life of Riley (third title), Mona McCluskey, Nick and Nora, Seal, Tarzan the Ape Man, V, Wagon Train

Miller, Mark: Guestward Ho (first title), Man from Denver, Name of the Game, Please Don't Eat the Daisies, Search

Miller, Marvin: Aquaman, Famous Adventures of Mr. Magoo, Fantastic Voyage, FBI, Gerald McBoing-Boing, Lone Ranger, Maya, Mil-

lionaire, Mysteries of Chinatown, New Adventures of Huckleberry Finn, Space Patrol, Stories of the Century

Mills, Alley: Associates, Hill Street Blues, I Married Dora, Maggie (pilot), Making the Grade, Poor Richard, Second Edition

Mills, Donna: Bunco, Good Life, Knots Landing, Steve Lawrence Show, Woman on the Run

Mills, John: Dundee and the Culhane, Zoo Gang

Mills, Juliet: Nanny and the Professor

Milner, Martin: Adam-12, Gidget, Life of Riley (third title), Route 66, Seekers, Starr First Baseman, Swiss Family Robinson, Trouble with Father

Mimieux, Yvette: Bell, Book and Candle, Berringer's, Most Deadly Game

Mitchell, Cameron: Beachcomber, Empire (second title), High Chaparral, Lassiter, Meeting at Apalachin, Partners in Crime (first title), Swiss Family Robinson

Mitchell, Shirley: All About Barbara, Bachelor Father, Behind the Screen, Doctor Was a Lady, Good Life, Great Gildersleeve, I Was a Bloodhound, Marie, Pete and Gladys, Petticoat Junction, Please Don't Eat the Daisies, Real McCoys, Rita Moreno Show, Roman Holidays

Mitchlll, Scoey: Barefoot in the Park, Cops, Fog, Handsome Harry's, Me and Mrs. C., New Kind of Family, Rhoda, What's It All About World?

Mobley, Mary Ann: Be Our Guest, Moonglow Affair, Wedding Day, World of Entertainment

Modean, Jayne: Man About Town, Me and Ducky, Street Hawk, Trauma Center

Moffat, Donald: Chisholms, Lily, Logan's Run, New Land

Moffat, Kitty (Katherine): Boone, Rowdies

Mohr, Gerald: Bravo Duke, Fantastic Four, Foreign Intrigue: Cross Current, My Friend Irma

Molinaro, Al: Anson and Lorrie, Great Day, Happy Days (second title), Joanie Loves Chachi, Odd Couple, Ugily Family

Moll, Richard: Night Court

Montalban, Ricardo: Colbys, Executive Suite, Fantasy Island, McNaughton's Daughter, Wonder Woman (first title)

Montgomery, Belinda J.: Dynasty, Man from Atlantis, Miami Vice, Murder She Wrote, Yeagers

Montgomery, Elizabeth: Bewitched, Boston Terrier, Montgomery's Summer Stock

Moody, Lynne: Benson, E/R, Foofur, Now We're Cookin', Redd Foxx Show, That's My Mama, Willow B: Women in Prison

Moody, Ron: Nobody's Perfect, Tales of the Gold Monkey

Moore, Clayton: Lone Ranger

Moore, Garry: Garry Moore Show, I've Got a Secret, To Tell the Truth

Moore, Mary Tyler: Adventures of Ozzie and Harriet, Bachelor Father, Dick Van Dyke Show, Ivy League, Mary, Mary Tyler Moore Comedy Hour, Mary Tyler Moore Show, Richard Diamond, Private Detective

Moore, Melba: Flamingo Road, Melba, Melba Moore-Clifton Davis Jr. Show, Melba Moore's Collection of Love Songs

Moore, Roger: Alaskans, Ivanhoe, Maverick, On Top All Over the World, Persuaders, Saint

Moorehead, Agnes: Bewitched, My Sister Eileen

Moran, Erin: Daktari, Don Rickles Show (second title), Happy Days (second title), Joanie Loves Chachi

Moreno, Rita: Dominic's Dream, I'll Never Forget What's Her Name, 9 to 5 (first title), Rita, Rita Moreno Show, Rockford Files, Shape of Things

Morgan, Harry: AfterMash, Arena, Blacke's Magic, Cat Ballou, D.A., December Bride, Dragnet, Hec Ramsey, Kentucky Jones, Marriage Broker, M*A*S*H, Oh Those Bells, Pete and Gladys, Richard Boone Show, You Can't Take It with You

Morgan, Henry: Draw to Win, Henry Morgan's Great Talent Hunt, I've Got a Secret, My World . . . And Welcome to It, On the Corner, That Was the Week That Was

Morita, Pat: Barbara Eden Show, Blansky's Beauties, Cops, Crash Island, Happy Days (second title), Mr. T. and Tina, Ohara, Queen and I, Sanford and Son, Young Guy Christian

Morrill, Priscilla: Baby Makes Five, Bret Maverick, Chameleon, Dorothy, Family, In the Beginning, Mary Tyler Moore Show, Mork and Mindy, Newhart, One Day at a Time, Stick Around, Year at the Top

Morris, Chester: Captured, Diagnosis: Unknown, Gangbusters

Morris, Garrett: At Your Service, Change at 125th Street, Hunter, Invisible Woman, It's Your Move, Roll Out, Saturday Night Live

Morris, Greg: Mission: Impossible, Vegas, What's Happening

Morris, Howard: Andy Griffith Show, Archie Comedy Hour, Archie's TV Funnies, Atom Ant/Secret Squirrel Show, Bang Shang Lalapalooza Show, Caesar's Hour, Everything's Archie, Famous Adventures of Mr. Magoo, Flintstone Kids, Galaxy High School, Jetsons, King Features Trilogy, Magilla Gorilla Show, Mission Magic, Pantomime Quiz, Paw Paws, Peter Potamus Show, Secret Lives of Waldo Kitty, U.S. of Archie, Your Show of Shows

Morrow, Vic: B.A.D. Cats, Combat

Morse, Barry: Adventurer, Fugitive, Higher and Higher Attorneys at Law, Space: 1999, Zoo Gang

Morse, Robert: That's Life

Moses, William R (Billy): Falcon Crest

Most, Donny: Dungeons and Dragons, Fonz and the Happy Days Gang, Happy Days (second title), Teen Wolf

Mostel, Zero: Off the Record

Mowbray, Alan: Adventures of Colonel Flack, Best in Mystery, Dante, Hey Mulligan

Mr. T (Lawrence Tero): A-Team, Mr. T

Muldaur, Diana: Born Free, Call to Danger, Fitz and Bones, Hizzoner, McCloud, Quincy, M.E., Survivors, Tony Randall Show, Too Good to Be True, A Year in the Life

Mulgrew, Kate: Kate Loves a Mystery, Mrs. Columbo, My Town

Mulhare, Edward: Ghost and Mrs. Muir, Gidget Grows Up, Knight Rider

Mull, Martin: America 2-Night, Domestic Life, Fernwood 2-Night, Mary Hartman, Shelley Duvall's Tall Tales and Legends

Mullavey, Greg: Crash Island, Forever Fernwood, Mary Hartman, Number 96, Rituals, She's with Me, Wednesday Night Out, Wilder and Wilder

Mulligan, Richard: Hero, Reggie, Soap

Murphy, Ben: Alias Smith and Jones, Berringer's, Chisholms, Gemini Man, Gidget's Summer Reunion, Griff, Lottery, Name of the Game, Unit 4

Murphy, Eddie: Saturday Night Live

Murray, Jan: Blind Date, Chain Letter, Charge Account, Dollar a Second, Go Lucky, Jan Murray Show, Meet Your Match, Sing It Again, Songs for Sale, Treasure Hunt

Murray, Ken: Ken Murray Show

Murrow, Edward R.: Person to Person

Musante, Tony: Toma

Music, Lorenzo: Carlton Your Doorman, Disney's Adventures of the Gummi Bears, Lorenzo and Henrietta Music Show, New Lorenzo Music Show, Real Ghostbusters, Rhoda

Myerson, Bess: Big Payoff, Candid Camera, Jacques Fray's Music Room

Nabors, Jim: Andy Griffith Show, Gomer Pyle USMC, Jim Nabors Hour, Jim Nabors Show, Lost Saucer, Sylvan in Paradise

Nash, J. Carrol: Guestward Ho, Life with Luigi, New Adventures of Charlie Chan

Napier, Charles: A-Team, B.J. and the Bear, Oregon Trail, Outlaws

Narz, Jack: Beat the Clock, Dotto, Life with Elizabeth, Now You See It, Seven Keys, Video Village

Natwick, Mildred: Alice, Hardcastle and McCormick, McMillan and Wife, Snoop Sisters

Naud, Melinda: Cracker Brothers, Detective School, New Operation Petticoat, Nightside, Operation Petticoat

Naughton, David: At Ease, Makin' It, My Sister Sam

Navin Jr., John P.: Academy, Jennifer Slept Here, Mr. Sunshine

Neal, Patricia: Waltons

Nelkin, Stacey: Adventures of Pollyana, Chisholms, T.L.C.

Nelson, Barry: Is There a Doctor in the House?, Heaven Help Us, Hunter (first title), Mason, My Favorite Husband, My Wives Jane, There's Always Room

Nelson, David: Adventures of Ozzie and Harriet, High School U.S.A.

O'Neill, Jennifer: Bare Essence, Cover Up

Oakes, Randi: Battlestar Galactica, Chips, Lovers and Other Strangers, Rosetti and Ryan

Oakland, Simon; Alexander the Great, Black Sheep Squadron, David Cassidy—Man Undercover, Decoy, Night Stalker, Toma

Oates, Warren: African Queen, Stoney Burke, Wanted: Dead or Alive

Oh, Soon-Teck: Charlie's Angels, Enigma, Magnum P.I.

Oliver, Susan: Apartment in Rome, Peyton Place

Olkewicz, Walter: Comedy of Horrors, Duck Factory, Family Ties, I Had Three Wives, Last Resort, Partners in Crime (first title), Taxi, Wizards and Warriors

Olsen, Johnny: Doorway to Fame, Fun for the Money, Johnny Olsen's Rumpus Room, Kids and Company

Olsen, Merlin: Father Murphy, Fathers and Sons, Little House on the Prairie

Opatoshu, David: Bonino, Man Against Crime, Woman on the Run

Osmond, Ken: Happy Days (second title), High School U.S.A. (2 titles), Leave It to Beaver, New Leave It to Beaver, Still the Beaver

Osmond, Marie: Big Show, Donny and Marie, Marie (2 titles), Osmond Family Show, Ripley's Believe It or Not, Rose Petal Place

Owens, Gary: Gong Show, Green Hornet, Hudson Brothers Show, Letters to Laugh-In, No Soap Radio, Perils of Penelope Pitstop, Roger Ramjet, Rowan and Martin's Laugh-In, Space Ghost

Paar, Jack: Bank on the Stars, Jack Paar Show, Place the Face, Tonight Show, Up to Paar

Page, LaWanda: B.A.D. Cats, Brothers and Sisters, Dean Martin's Celebrity Roast, Detective School, Redd Foxx Comedy Hour, Sanford, Sanford and Son, Sanford Arms

Page, Patti: Big Record, Patti Page Show, Scott Music Hall

Paige, Janis: Baby Makes Five, Betty White Show, Eight Is Enough, Gun Shy, Horray for Love, It's Always Jan, Lanigan's Rabbi, Maisie, No Man's Land, Rockhopper

Palance, Jack: Bronk, Greatest Show on Earth, Ripley's Believe It or Not, Rivak the Barbarian, Tales of the Haunted

Pankin, Stuart: Car Wash, Eyes of Texas, No Soap Radio, Not Necessarily the News, San Pedro Beach Bums, Wonderful World of Philip Malley

Pare, Michael: Greatest American Hero, Houston Knights

Paris, Jerry: Dick Van Dyke Show, Michael Shayne Private Detective, Steve Canyon, Those Whiting Girls, Untouchables

Parker, Eleanor: Bracken's World, Guess Who's Coming to Dinner?, Knight's Gambit

Parker, Fess: Annie Oakley, Code of Jonathan West, Daniel Boone, Davy Crockett, Fess Parker Show, Mr. Smith Goes to Washington, Russell

Parker, Jameson: Simon and Simon

Parker, Penny: Make Room for Daddy, Margie

Parker, Sarah Jessica: Alan King Show, Square Pegs, A Year in the Life

Parker, Suzy: Sybil

Parkins, Barbara: Peyton Place

Parks, Bert: Balance Your Budget, Bandstand, Bert Parks Show, Bid 'N' Buy, Big Payoff, Break the Bank, Break the $250,000 Bank, County Fair, Double or Nothing, Giant Step, Haggis Baggis, Hold That Note, Masquerade Party, Stop the Music, Two in Love, Yours for a Song

Parks, Michael: Colbys, Diagnosis: Danger, Royce, Then Came Bronson

Parsons, Estelle: All in the Family (second title), Home

Parton, Dolly: Dolly, Porter Waggoner Show

Pataki, Michael: Amazing Spider-Man, Chopped Liver Brothers, Eyes of Texas, Flying Nun, Friends and Lovers, Get Christie Love, Paul Sand in Friends and Lovers, Phyl and Mikhy, Wendy Hooper—U.S. Army

Patterson, Lorna: Beane's of Boston, Book of Lists, Goodtime Girls, Lovebirds, Love Sidney, Private Benjamin, Working Stiffs

Paul, Richard: Carter Country, Hail to the Chief, Herbie the Love Bug, One in a Million, Space Force

Paulsen, Albert: Call to Danger, Doctors Hospital, Gypsy Warriors, McNamara's Band, Stop Susan Williams, Walk in the Night

Paulsen, Pat: Glen Campbell Goodtime Hour, Joey and Dad, Pat Paulsen's Half a Comedy Hour, Smothers Brothers Comedy Hour, Smothers Brothers Show, Summer Smothers Brothers Show, Wild Wild West

Payne, John: Call of the West, O'Connor's Ocean, Restless Gun

Payne, Julie: Duck Factory, Full House, Hot W.A.C.S., Joanna, Leo and Liz in Beverly Hills, Wizards and Warriors

Peaker, E.J.: Greatest American Hero, Madame's Place, That's Life, Top of the Month

Peary, Hal: Blondie, Buford and the Ghost, Fibber McGee and Molly, Pirates of Flounder Bay, Roman Holidays, Willy

Peck, Jim: Big Showdown, Hot Seat, Joker's Wild, Second Chance, Three's a Crowd (first title), You Don't Say

Peluce, Meeno: Bad News Bears, Best of the West, Detective in the House, Kangaroos in the Kitchen, Voyagers, W*A*L*T*E*R

Pennington, Marla: Buffalo Soldiers, Herndon and Me, Small Wonder, Soap

Penny, Joe: Forever Fernwood, Gangster Chronicles, Home Front, Jake and the Fatman, Mother, Juggs and Speed, Riptide

Penny, Sydney: Circle Family, Dear Teacher, Hearts Island, New Gidget, Night Rider

Peppard, George: A-Team, Banacek, Doctors Hospital

Family Adventures, Flintstone Funnies, Pee Wee's Playhouse

Rey, Alejandro: Flying Nun, Slattery's People, Three for Danger

Reynolds, Burt: Dan August, Gunsmoke, Hawk, Lassiter, Man from Everywhere, Out of This World, Riverboat

Reynolds, Debbie: Debbie Reynolds Show, Eddie Fisher Show, Jennifer Slept Here

Rhoades, Barbara: Blue Knight, Bureau, Busting Loose, Hanging In, Mr. Dugan, Soap, Tabitha, Venice Medical, You Again

Rhodes, Donnelly: Double Trouble (first title), Making a Living, Report to Murphy, Soap, Taxi

Rhue, Madlyn: Bracken's World, Dynasty, Executive Suite

Rich, Christopher: Charmings, Recovery Room, She's With Me, Sweet Surrender

Richards, Kim: Hello Larry, Here We Go Again, James at 15, Nanny and the Professor, Why Us?

Richards, Kyle: Father Knows Best Reunion, Good Time Harry, Hellinger's Law, Little House on the Prairie, Seal

Richardson, Susan: Eight Is Enough, One Day at a Time

Richman, Caryn: Gidget's Summer Reunion, New Gidget

Richman, Peter Mark: Cain's Hundred, Defenders of the Earth, Dynasty, Electra Woman and Dyna Girl, Ladies in Blue, Longstreet, Three's Company (second title)

Rickles, Don: C.P.O. Sharkey, Don Rickles Show (2 titles), Kibbee Hates Fitch, Max

Rifkin, Ron: Adam's Rib, Bachelor at Law, Gidget, Husbands, Wives and Lovers, Mary Tyler Moore Comedy Hour, One Day at a Time, When Things Were Rotten

Rigg, Diana: Avengers, Diana, Diana Rigg Show

Riley, Jack: All Night Radio, Bob Newhart Show, Bumpers, Facts of Life, Joe and Valerie, Keep on Truckin', Mother and Me, M.D., One Day at a Time, Roxie, Tim Conway Show

Riley, Jeannine: Dusty's Trail, Harper Valley U.S.A., Hee Haw, Li'l Abner, Petticoat Junction, Sheriff Who?

Ringwald, Molly: Facts of Life, Shelley Duvall's Tall Tales and Legends

Rist, Robbie: Big John Little John, Bionic Woman, Brady Bunch, Galactica 1980, Gossip, Instant Family, Kidd Video, Little Lulu, Lucas Tanner, Mary Tyler Moore Show

Ritter, John: Bachelor at Law, Hooperman, Three's a Crowd (second title), Three's Company (1977), Waltons

Rivers, Joan: Late Show Starring Joan Rivers, That Show Starring Joan Rivers

Roberts, Doris: Alice, Angie, Bell, Book and Candle, In Trouble, Maggie, Mary Tyler Moore Comedy Hour, Me and Mrs. C. (first title), Remington Steele, Soap

Roberts, Pernell: Bonanza, Night Rider, San Fran-cisco International Airport, Trapper John, M.D.

Roberts, Tanya: Charlie's Angels, Ladies in Blue

Roberts, Tony: Four Seasons, Lucie Arnaz Show, Rosetti and Ryan, Snafu

Robertson, Cliff: Batman, Falcon Crest, Rod Brown of the Rocket Rangers

Robertson, Dale: Big John, Death Valley Days, Dynasty, Frontier Adventures, Iron Horse, J.J. Starbuck, Tales of Wells Fargo

Rocco, Alex: Best of Times, Facts of Life, Husbands, Wives and Lovers, This Better Be It, Three for the Road

Roche, Eugene: Alone at Last, Corner Bar, Egan, For the People, Good Time Harry, Hart to Hart, Higher and Higher Attorneys at Law, Johnny Blue, Local 306, People Like Us, Soap, Take Five, Two the Hard Way, Webster

Rodd, Marcia: All in the Family (1971), Dumplings, Four Seasons, Pioneer Spirit, 13 Queens Boulevard, Trapper John, M.D.

Rodrigues, Percy: Cutter to Houston, Enigma, Executive Suite, Most Wanted, Night Rider, Peyton Place, Sanford, Silent Force

Rogers, Ginger: Ginger Rogers Show

Rogers, Mimi: Paper Dolls, Rousters

Rogers, Roy: Country Happening, Great Movie Cowboys, Roy Rogers and Dale Evans Show, Roy Rogers Show

Rogers, Wayne: City of Angels, House Calls, Long Hot Summer, M*A*S*H, Stagecoach West

Rolle, Esther: Good Times, Maude, Momma the Detective

Roman, Ruth: Long Hot Summer, Willow B: Women in Prison

Romero, Cesar: Batman, Berringer's, Cesar's World, Man from Everywhere, Passport to Danger, Rainbow Girl, Riptide, Your Chevrolet Showroom

Rooney, Mickey: Hey Mulligan, Mickey, Mickey Rooney Show, O'Malley, One of the Boys, Year at the Top

Rooney, Tim: Gidget, Human Comedy, Mickey, Room for One More

Rose, Jamie: Amazing Stories, Falcon Crest, Lady Blue, Never Again

Ross, Joe E.: C.B. Bears, Car 54 Where Are You, Help! It's the Hair Bear Bunch, Hong Kong Phooey, It's About Time, Phil Silvers Show

Ross, Katharine: Great Bible Adventures, Colbys

Ross, Marion: Alive and Well, Channing, Happy Days (second title), Life with Father, Mrs. G. Goes to College, True Life Stories, You Are the Jury

Ross, Ted: High Five, MacGruder and Loud, Sirota's Court

Rowan, Dan: Rowan Martin's Laugh-In, Rowan and Martin Show, Ultra Quiz

Rowe, Misty: Happy Days (second title), Hee Haw Honeys, Joe's World, When Things Were Rotten

Rubinstein, John: Crazy Like a Fox, Family, Mr. and Ms., Streets of San Francisco

Ruggles, Charlie: Adamsburg U.S.A., Beverly Hill-billies, Bullwinkle Show, Ginger Rogers Show, Here Comes Melinda, Rocky and His Friends, Ruggles, Soft Touch, World of Mr. Sweeny

Runyon, Jennifer: Charles in Charge (first title), Pros and Cons, Six Pack

Rush, Barbara: At Your Service, Barbara Rush Show, Batman, Flamingo Road, Fugitive, New Dick Van Dyke Show, Peyton Place, Saints and Sinners, Unknown

Russell, John: It Takes a Thief, Jason of Star Command, Lawman, Soldiers of Fortune

Russell, Kurt: New Land, Quest (first title), Travels of Jaimie McPheeters

Russell, Nipsey: Barefoot in the Park, Car 54 Where Are You?, Chain Reaction, Dean Martin's Comedy World, Masquerade Party, Walter of the Jungle, Your Number's Up

Ruttan, Susan: After George, Buffalo Bill, Empire (second title), L.A. Law

Ryan, Fran: Doris Day Show, Green Acres, Fuzz-bucket, Gunsmoke, New Zoo Revue, No Soap Radio, Odd Couple, Sigmund and the Sea Monsters, Wizard, Who's on Call?

Ryan, Irene: Beverly Hillbillies, Tom, Dick and Mary

Ryan, Meg: Charles in Charge (first title), Wildside

Ryan, Mitchell: Chase, Chisholms, Executive Suite, Fuzz Brothers, High Performance, Julie Farr M.D., King's Crossing

Sabella, Ernie: It's Your Move, 100 Center Street, Punky Brewster, Roxie, 13 Thirteenth Avenue

Sagal, Jean: Double Trouble (2 titles)

Sagal, Katey: Married . . . With Children, Mary (second title)

Sagal, Liz: Double Trouble (2 titles)

Saint, Eva Marie: How the West Was Won, Jamie, Moonlighting, One Man's Family, A Year in the Life

St. Jacques, Raymond: Eyes of Texas, 416th, Rawhide

Saint James, Susan: After George, It Takes a Thief, Kate and Allie, McMillan and Wife, Name of the Game

St. John, Jill: Brenda Starr, Emerald Point N.A.S., Two Guys from Muck

Sales, Soupy: Barney and Me, Chain Reaction, Hoofer, Junior Almost Anything Goes, New Soupy Sales Show, Soupy Sales Show, To Tell the Truth, Where There's Smokey

Salmi, Albert: Daniel Boone, Petrocelli

Samms, Emma: Colbys, Dynasty

Sand, Paul: Friends and Lovers, Gimme a Break, Lady Luck, Mona, Paul Sand in Friends and Lovers, St. Elsewhere

Sanders, George: Batman, George Sanders Mystery Theatre

Sanders, Richard: Berringer's, Inhumanoids, Invisible Woman, Spencer, Under One Roof, WKRP in Cincinnati, You Can't Take It with You

Sanderson, William: Newhart

Sandy, Gary: All Is Forgiven, All That Glitters, Hearts Island, WKRP in Cincinnati

Sanford, Isabel: All in the Family (1971), Isabel Sanford's Honeymoon Hotel, Shape of Things

Santos, Joe: A.K.A. Pablo, Me and Maxx, Rockford Files

Sarandon, Chris: Bliss, City

Sargent, Dick: Bewitched, Broadside, Dukes of Hazzard, Not Until Today, One Happy Family, Tammy Grimes Show

Saunders, Lori: Dusty's Trail, Oh Nurse, Petticoat Junction

Savalas, Telly: Acapulco, Kojak, Windows, Doors and Keyholes

Scalia, Jack: Berringer's, Devlin Connection, High Performance, Hollywood Beat, Remington Steele

Schaal, Wendy: AfterMash, Fantasy Island, It's a Living, Life and Times of Eddie Roberts

Schaeffer, Rebecca: My Sister Sam

Schallert, William: Adventures of Jim Bowie, Arroyo, Boys, Commando Cody, Dobie Gillis, Duck Factory, Get Smart, Gidget's Summer Reunion, Goltar and the Golden Lance, Here Come the Brides, Little Women, Lobo, Man from Denver, Nancy Drew Mysteries, New Gidget, Patty Duke Show, Waltons, Wild Wild West

Schedeen, Anne: ALF, Almost Heaven, Marcus Welby M.D., Never Say Never, Paper Dolls, Three's Company (1977)

Schell, Catherine: Adventurer, Space: 1999

Schell, Ronnie: Battle of the Planets, Flintstone Kids, Forever Fernwood, Gomer Pyle U.S.M.C., Goober and the Ghost Chasers, Good Morning World, Shirt Tales, That Girl (first title)

Schiavelli, Vincent: Comedy of Horrors, Corner Bar, Crazy Dan, Fast Times, Little Shots, Taxi

Schneider, John: Dukes, Dukes of Hazzard

Schreiber, Avery: Burns and Schreiber Comedy Hour, My Mother the Car, Operation Greasepaint, Our Place

Schroder, Ricky: Faerie Tale Theatre, Silver Spoons

Schuck, John: Holmes and Yogo, McMillan and Wife, New Odd Couple, Turnabout

Schulman, Emily: Small Wonder

Schultz, Dwight: A-Team

Scoggins, Tracy: Big John, Colbys, Hawaiian Heat, Renegades

Scolari, Peter: Baby Makes Five, Bosom Buddies, Further Adventures of Wally Brown, Goodtime Girls, Mr. Bill's Real Life Adventures, Newhart

Scott, Debralee: Angie, Chain Reaction, Forever Fernwood, Living in Paradise, Mary Hartman, Sons and Daughters, Welcome Back, Kotter

Scott, George C.: East Side/West Side, Mr. President

Scott, Jean Bruce: Airwolf, Magnum, P.I., St. Elsewhere, Wishman

Scott, Kathryn Leigh: Big Shamus Little Shamus, Boston and Kilbride, Gypsy Warriors, Philip

Marlowe Private Eye, Renegades

Scott, Pippa: Day by Day, Jigsaw John, Mr. Lucky, My Sister Hank, Virginian

Scotti, Vito: Andy's Gang, Barefoot in the Park, Campo 44, Flying Nun, Knight's Gambit, Life with Luigi, To Rome with Love

Segal, George: Take Five

Segall, Pamela: E/R, Facts of Life, Redd Foxx Show

Selby, David: Falcon Crest, Flamingo Road, Night Rider

Sellecca, Connie: Beyond Westworld, Captain America, Flying High, Greatest American Hero, Hotel

Selleck, Tom: Bunco, Gypsy Warriors, Magnum P.I., Rockford Files

Serling, Rod: Liar's Club, Night Gallery, Twilight Zone

Seymour, Carolyn: Adams Apple, Modesty Blaise

Seymour, Jane: On Top All Over the World, Onedin Line, Young Mr. Bobbin

Shackelford, Ted: Dallas, Knots Landing

Shandling, Gary: It's Gary Shandling's Show

Sharma, Barbara: Father O Father, Glitter, Ma and Pa, Masquerade (first title), Risko, Rhoda, Three for the Girls

Shatner, William: Alexander the Great, Barbary Coast, Colossus, Defender, For the People, Star Trek, T.J. Hooker, This Was America

Shaver, Helen: Amazing Stories, Hill Street Blues, Jessica Novak, Search and Rescue: The Alpha Team, United States

Shawn, Dick: Hail to the Chief, Mr. and Mrs. Dracula, Sheriff Who?, You're Just Like Your Father

Sheldon, Jack: Cara Williams Show, Girl with Something Extra, Merv Griffin Show, Nut House, Run Buddy Run, Under the Yum Yum Tree

Shelton, Reid: First and 10; First and 10: The Championships, Leo and Liz in Beverly Hills, Too Good to Be True, Training Camp: The Bulls Are Back, Whiz Kids

Shepherd, Cybill: Moonlighting, Yellow Rose

Shera, Mark: Adams House, Barnaby Jones, Blacke's Magic, S.W.A.T.

Sheridan, Ann: Calling Terry Conway, Pistols 'N' Petticoats (2 titles)

Sheridan, Nicolette: Knots Landing, Paper Dolls

Sherman, Bobby: Getting Together, Here Come the Brides, Knight in Shining Armour

Sherman, Ransom: And Here's the Show, Father of the Bride, Ransom Sherman Show

Shields, Brooke: Exciting People, Exotic Places

Shore, Dinah: Dinah and Her New Best Friends, Dinah Shore Chevy Show Dinah Shore Show, Dinah, Dinah's Place

Shriner, Herb: Herb Shriner Time, Meet the Governor, Two for the Money

Sidney, Sylvia: Maureen, Morning Star/Evening Star, WKRP in Cincinnati

Sikking, James B.: Calling Dr. Storm, Fugitive, Hill

Street Blues, Inside O.U.T., Mona, Turnabout

Silvers, Cathy: First and 10, Foley Square, Happy Days (second title), High School U.S.A., Sam (pilot), T.L.C.

Silvers, Phil: Beverly Hillbillies, Eddie, Happy Days (second title), New Phil Silvers Show, Phil Silvers Arrow Show, Phil Silvers Show

Simmons, Richard (actor): Sergeant Preston of the Yukon

Simmons, Richard (health expert): Here's Richard, Richard Simmons Show, Ultra Quiz, VTV

Simpson, O.J.: First and 10: The Championships, Training Camp: The Bulls Are Back

Sinatra, Frank: Frank Sinatra Show

Sinatra Jr., Frank: Clinic on 18th Street, Dean Martin Presents the Golddiggers

Sinclair, Madge: Down Home, Grandpa Goes to Washington, Guess Who's Coming to Dinner?, Ohara, Trappr John M.D., Walkin' Walter

Singer, Marc: Contender, Dallas, Paper Dolls, V

Skelton, Red: Red Skelton Show (2 titles)

Sladen, Elisabeth: Doctor Who, K-9 and Company

Slattery, Richard X.: C.P.O. Sharkey, Gallant Men, Mr. Roberts, Rich Man, Poor Man, Wonder Woman (first title)

Slavin, Millie: Black Bart, Landon Landon and Landon, Quick and Quiet, Rafferty, Struck By Lightning

Slezak, Walter: Batman, Chevy Mystery Show, Slezak and Son

Sloyan, James: Asphalt Cowboy, Oh Madeline, Pros and Cons, Tenspeed and Brown Shoe, Westside Medical

Smart, Jean: Designing Women, Maximum Security, Reggie, Royal Match, Teachers Only

Smith, Bob: Bob Smith Show, Chicagoland Mystery Players, Howdy Doody, New Howdy Doody Show

Smith, Bubba: Blue Thunder, Half Nelson, Open All Night, Semi-Tough

Smith, Cotter: D.C. Cop

Smith, Jack: Place the Face, You Asked for It

Smith, Jaclyn: Charlie's Angels, Switch

Smith, Kate: Kate Smith Evening Hour, Kate Smith Hour, Kate Smith Show

Smith, Lane: Big Easy, Hollywood Beat, Kay O'Brien, V

Smith, Paul: Doris Day Show, Fibber McGee and Molly, Inside O.U.T., McNab's Lab, Miss Pepperdine, Monster Squad, Mr. Terrific, Mrs. G. Goes to College, No Time for Sergeants

Smith, Rex: Dear Penelope and Peter, Street Hawk

Smith, Roger: Knight's Gambit, Mr. Roberts, 77 Sunset Strip

Smith, Samantha: Charles in Charge (first title), Lime Street

Smith, Shawnee: All Is Forgiven

Smith, Shelley: Associates, Charmed Lives, For Love and Honor, Phoenix

Smith, William: Hawaii Five-O, Laredo, Rich Man Poor Man, Rockford Files, Tales of the Apple

Dumpling Gang, Wildside

Smithers, Jan: Columnist, WKRP in Cincinnati

Smits, Jimmy: L.A. Law

Smothers, Dick: Fitz and Bones, Smothers Brothers Comedy Hour, Smothers Brothers Show, Smothers Organic Prime Time Space Ride

Smothers, Tom: See listing for Smothers, Dick

Snyder, Arlen Dean: Dear Detective, MacGruder and Loud, Texas Rangers, Trauma Center

Somers, Suzanne: Goodbye, Charlie, High Rollers, She's the Sheriff, Three's Company

Sommars, Julie: Governor and J.J., My Wife Next Door, Rituals, The Search

Sommer, Elke: Elke, Elke Sommer's World of Speed and Beauty, Forever Fernwood, Neat and Tidy, Painting with Elke Sommer

Sorel, Louise: Bewitched, Curse of Dracula, Knots Landing, Ladies' Man, One in a Million, Survivors

Sorvino, Paul: Bert D'Angelo/Superstar, Moonlighting, Oldest Rookie, We'll Get By

Sothern, Ann: Alias Smith and Jones, Ann Sothern Show, My Mother the Car, Private Secretary

Soul David: Casablanca (second title), Here Come the Brides, Intertect, Movin' On (first title), Starsky and Hutch, Yellow Rose

Spang, Laurette: B.J. and the Bear, Battlestar Galactica, Colorado C.I., McNamara's Band

Spelman, Sharon: Angie, Calling Dr. Storm, Cop and the Kid, Gimme a Break, Number 96, Paul Sand in Friends and Lovers, Second Edition, Suburban Beat

Spielberg, David: American Girls, Bob & Carol & Ted & Alice, From Here to Eternity, Jessica Novak, Operating Room, Practice, Stone

Stack, Robert: Floyd Gibbons Reporter, It's a Great Life (second title), Most Wanted, Name of the Game, Strike Force, Untouchables

Stamos, John: Dreams, Full House, You Again

Stang, Arnold: Billy Bean Show, Broadside, Bureau, December Bride, Doc Corkle, Top Cat

Stanwyck, Barbara: Barbara Stanwyck Theatre, Big Valley, Colbys, Josephine Little, Toni's Boys, Wagon Train

Stapleton, Jean: All in the Family (1971), Scarecrow and Mrs. King, Woman with a Past

Stephens, James: Paper Chase, Paper Chase: The Graduation, Paper Chase: Second Year, Paper Chase: Third Year

Stephens, Laraine: Bracken's World, Eischied, Matt Helm, O.K. Crackerby, Rich Man Poor Man, Risko

Sterling, Robert: Ichabod and Me, Love That Jill, Topper

Stevens, Andrew: Code Red, Emerald Point N.A.S., Oregon Trail

Stevens, Connie: Harry's Battles, Hawaiian Eye, Rowdies, Wendy and Me

Stevens, Craig: Best Years, Cabot Connection, Dallas, Home Front, Man of the World, Mighty O, Mr. Broadway, Nick and Nora, Peter Gunn

Stevens, Inger: Farmer's Daughter

Stevens, Mark: Big Town, Michael Shayne Detective, New Adventures of Martin Kane

Stevens, Stella: Ben Casey, Flamingo Road, Graduation Dress, Neat and Tidy

Stevens, Warren: Arena, Behind the Screen, Return of Captain Nemo, Simon Lash, Tales of the 77th Bengal Lancers

Stevenson, McLean: America, Astronauts, Condo, Doris Day Show, Hello Larry, In the Beginning, McLean Stevenson Show, M*A*S*H, My Wives Jane

Stevenson, Parker: Falcon Crest, Hardy Boys Mysteries, Rockhopper

Stewart, James: Hawkins, Jimmy Stewart Show

Stewart, Mel: All in the Family (1971), Freebie and the Bean, Good Ol' Boys, Invisible Woman, On the Rocks, One in a Million, Roll Out, Salt and Pepe, Scarecrow and Mrs. King, Tabitha

Stiller, Jerry: Archie Bunker's Place, Equalizer, Joe and Sons, Paul Lynde Show, Roxie, Stiller and Meara Show, Take Five with Stiller and Meara

Stilwell, Diane: Duck Factory, I Love Her Anyway, Man Called Sloane, Side By Side

Stockwell, Guy: Adventures in Paradise, Hell Town

Stokey, Mike: Pantomime Quiz, Stump the Stars

Stone, Christopher: Bionic Woman, Harper Valley, Interns, Spencer's Pilots

Stone, Harold J.: Bridget Loves Bernie, Goldbergs, Grand Jury, House Next Door, Joe and Sons, My World . . . And Welcome to It, Somewhere in Italy . . . Company B

Stone, Milburn: Gunsmoke

Storch, Larry: Brady Kids, Car 54 Where Are You, Charlie Angelo, Doris Day Show, F Troop, Ghost Busters, Larry Storch Show, Out of the Inkwell, Neat and Tidy, Queen and I, Tennessee Tuxedo, Two Guys from Muck

Storm, Gale: Gale Storm Show, My Little Margie, Mystery and Mrs, NBC Comedy Hour, Unexpected

Strange, Glenn: Gunsmoke, Lone Ranger, Man of the Comstock

Strangis, Judy: Electra Woman and Dyna Girl, Roman Holidays, Room 222, Wheelie and the Chopper Bunch

Strasberg, Susan: Marriage Broker, Toma

Strassman, Marcia: Brenda Starr, E/R, Good Time Harry, M*A*S*H, Nightengales, Wednesday Night Out, Welcome Back, Kotter

Strickland, Gail: Insiders, 9 to 5 (first title), Night Court, On Our Way, Six of Us, What a Country

Stritch, Elaine: Ellen Burstyn Show, Growing Paynes (first title), My Sister Eileen, Trials of O'Brien, You Should Meet My Sister

Stroud, Don: Gidget's Summer Reunion, Kate Loves a Mystery, Mickey Spillane's Mike Hammer, New Gidget, New Mike Hammer

Struthers, Sally: All in the Family (1971), Charmkins, Gloria, 9 to 5 (second title), Pebbles and Bamm Bamm, Teller and the Tale

Stuart, Barbara: Doctor Dan, George Burns Show, Gomer Pyle USMC, Great Gildersleeve, I and Claudie, Jones Boys, Mason, McLean Stevenson Show, Our Family Honor, Pete and Gladys, Queen and I

Stuart, Maxine: Fit for a King, Hail to the Chief, Margie, Norby, Revenge of the Gray Gang, Room for One More, Rousters, Slattery's People

Sullivan, Barry: Harbourmaster, Immortal, Judgement Day, Man Called X, Rich Man Poor Man, Road West, Tall Man

Sullivan: Ed Sullivan Show

Sullivan, Susan: Bell, Book and Candle, Falcon Crest, Incredible Hulk, Julie Farr M.D., Rich Man, Poor Man

Susann, Jacqueline: Jacqueline Susann Show, Morey Amsterdam Show, Your Surprise Store

Susman, Todd: Bob Crane Show, Ethel Is an Elephant, Flatfoots, Getting There, Going Places, Newhart, Number 96, Off the Wall, Spencer's Pilots, Star of the Family

Sutorius, James: Andros Targets, Bob Crane Show, Operating Room, No Complaints

Svenson, Bo: Here Come the Brides, I Do I Don't, Walking Tall

Swanson, Gloria: Crown Theatre with Gloria Swanson, Gloria Swanson Hour

Swayze, John Cameron: Chance for Romance, Guess What Happened?, It's a Wonderful World, Nothing But the Truth

Sweet, Dolph: Gimme a Break, Sparrow, Trials of O'Brien, When the Whistle Blows

Swit, Loretta: Cagney and Lacey, M*A*S*H, Sam (pilot)

Swofford, Ken: Eddie Capra Mysteries, Ellery Queen, Fame, Oregon Trail, Rich Man Poor Man, Rousters, Switch

Sylvester, Harold: Hearts of Steele, Today's FBI, Walking Tall

Tabori, Christopher: Between the Lines, Chicago Story, Home

Tacker, Francine: Associates, Bounder, Dallas, Empire (second title), Goodtime Girls, Oh Madeline, Paper Chase, Valerie

Talbot, Gloria: Annie Oakley, Life and Legend of Wyatt Earp, Mr. Novak, My Little Margie, Roy Rogers Show, Wanted: Dead or Alive

Talbot, Lyle: Adventures of Ozzie and Harriet, Commando Cody, Leave It to Beaver, Lone Ranger

Talbot, Nita: Bourbon Street Beat, Funny Face, Here We Go Again, Hogan's Heroes, Jim Backus Show—Hot Off the Wire, Joe and Mabel, Partridge Family, Shaughnessey, Soap, Supertrain, Thin Man, Under the Yum Yum Tree, You Are the Jury

Tambor, Jeffrey: Eddie and Herbert, Hill Street Blues, Max Headroom, Mr. Sunshine, Pals, Ropers

Tate, Sharon: Beverly Hillbillies

Tayback, Vic: Alice, Call Holme, Cops, Griff, Khan, Streets of San Francisco, Super, Two's Company

Taylor, Dub: Andy Griffith Show, Casey Jones, Dooley Brothers, Flim-Flam Man, Getting There, Great Day, Hazel, Murdocks and the McClays, Octavius and Me, Please Don't Eat the Daisies, Pumpboys and Dinettes on TV, Roy Rogers Show

Taylor, Elizabeth: On Top All Over the World

Taylor, Holland: Bosom Buddies, Harry, Me and Mom, Silver Spoons

Taylor, Renee: Forever Fernwood, Good Penny

Taylor, Rip: $1.98 Beauty Show, Here Comes the Grump, Sigmund and the Sea Monsters

Taylor, Robert: Colossus, Death Valley Days, Detectives, Dick Powell Show

Taylor, Rod: Bearcats, Hong Kong, Masquerade, Oregon Trail, Outlaws (second title)

Temple, Shirley: Shirley Temple's Storybook

Tennille, Toni: Captain and Tennille, Toni Tennille Show, TMT

Tewes, Lauren: Anything for Love, Love Boat

Thicke, Alan: Animal Crack-Ups, Growing Pains (second title), Thicke of the Night

Thinnes, Roy: Chicago 212, Falcon Crest, From Here to Eternity, Invaders, Long Hot Summer, Psychiatrist

Thomas, Betty: Hill Street Blues

Thomas, Danny: Danny Thomas Hour, I'm a Big Girl Now, Make More Room for Daddy, Make Room for Daddy, Make Room for Granddaddy, One Big Family

Thomas, Heather: Co-ed Fever, Eyes of Texas, Fall Guy

Thomas, Marlo: Donna Reed Show, Joey Bishop Show (first title), That Girl (2 titles)

Thomas, Richard: One, Two, Three-Go, Waltons

Thomerson, Tim: Angie, Associates, Down and Out in Beverly Hills, Getting There, Gun Shy, In Trouble, Quark, Two of Us

Thompson, Marshall: Angel, Daktari, Jambo, World of Giants

Thompson, Sada: Family

Thor, Jerome: Along the Barbary Coast, Foreign Intrigue: Dateline Europe, Great Merlini

Thorson, Linda: Avengers, Bronx Zoo, Marblehead Manor

Throne, Malachi: Batman, Electra Woman and Dyna Girl, It Takes a Thief, Star Trek (pilot)

Tigar, Kenneth: Dirty Work, Gangster Chronicles, Great Day, Gypsy Warriors, Love Natalie, Man from Atlantis, Rock Rainbow

Tillstrom, Burt: Kukla, Fran and Ollie

Tilton, Charlene: Dallas

Tobey, Kenneth: Adamsburg U.S.A., Clinic on 18th Street, Davy Crockett, Whirlybirds

Tobin, Michele: California Fever, Father on Trial, Fitzpatricks, Grandpa Goes to Washington

Tompkins, Joan: Father on Trial, My Three Sons, Rich Man Poor Man, Sam Benedict

Tone, Franchot: Ben Casey

Tong, Sammee: Bachelor Father, Mickey, New Girl in His Life, Spin and Marty

Toomey, Regis: Best in Mystery, Burke's Law, Hey Mulligan, Maggie Malone, Petticoat Junction, Richard Diamond Private Detective, Shannon

Torme, Mel: Mel Torme Show, TV's Top Tunes

Torres, Liz: All in the Family (1971), Checking In, New Odd Couple, Not in Front of the Kids, Phyllis, Popi, Stockard Channing in Just Friends, Taking It Home, Willow B: Women in Prison

Totter, Audrey: Cimarron City, Medical Center, Meet McGraw, My Darling Judge, Our Man Higgins

Tracy, Lee: Amazing Mr. Malone, Chalk One Up for Johnny, Martin Kane Private Eye, New York Confidential

Travalena, Fred: Anything for Money, Funny World of Fred and Bunni, Kopycats, Shirt Tales, Six O'Clock Follies

Travanti, Daniel J.: Call to Danger, Hill Street Blues

Travolta, Ellen: Allison Sidney Harrison, Happy Days (second title), Joanie Loves Chachi, Makin' It, Marie, Number 96, Welcome Back, Kotter

Travolta, Joey: Big John

Travolta, John: Welcome Back, Kotter

Trebek, Alex: Battlestars, Classic Concentration, High Rollers, Jeopardy, Pitfall, VTV, Wizard of Odds

Tripp, Paul: Dobie Gillis, It's Magic, Mr. I. Magination

Truex, Ernest: Ann Sothern Show, Jamie, Mr. Peepers, Timid Soul

Tucci, Michael: Friends, It's Gary Shandling's Show, On Our Own, Paper Chase: Second Year, Paper Chase: Third Year, Rainbow Girl

Tucker, Forrest: Alice, Bobby Jo and the Big Apple Goodtime Band, Cat Ballou, Crunch and Des, Doc, Dusty's Trail, F Troop, Filthy Rich, Flim-Flam Man, Ghost Busters, Pottsville

Turkel, Ann: Hollywood Beat, Matt Helm, Modesty Blaise

Turman, Glynn: Cass Malloy, Hail to the Chief, Manimal, Peyton Place

Tuttle, Lurene: All in the Family (first title), Apartment in Rome, Carlton Your Doorman, Father of the Bride, I Remember Caviar, Julia, Life with Father, Real McCoys

Tweed, Shannon: Crazy Dan, Falcon Crest

Twiggy: Twiggy's Juke Box

Tyrrell, Susan: MacGruder and Loud, Open All Night, Willow B: Women in Prison

Tyson, Cicely: East Side/West Side, Wednesday Night Out

Uggams, Leslie: Book of Lists, Fantasy, High Rollers, Leslie Uggams Show, Sing Along with Mitch

Ullman, Tracey: Tracey Ullman Show

Urecal, Minerva: Adventures of Jim Bowie, Human Comedy, Meet Mr. McNutley, Peter Gunn,

R.C.A. Victor Show, Roy Rogers Show, Tom and Jerry, Tugboat Annie

Urich, Robert: Bob & Carol & Ted & Alice, Bunco, Gavilan, Soap, Spenser: For Hire, S.W.A.T., Tabitha, Vegas

Urseth, Bonnie: We Got It Made

Ustinov, Peter: Doctor Snuggles, Omni: The New Frontier

Vaccaro, Brenda: Dear Detective, My Lucky Penny, Paper Dolls, Sara (first title)

Valentine, Karen: Adams House, America 2100, Gidget Grows Up, Girl's Life, Goodbye Doesn't Mean Forever, Karen (second title), Karen Valentine Show, Our Time, Room 222

Valentine, Scott: Family Ties, Taking It Home

Vallance, Louise: Dennis the Menace (1986), Lady Lovelylocks, Night Heat, Popples, Ropers, Zoo-bilee Zoo

Vallee, Rudy: Alias Smith and Jones, Batman, Matinee at the Bijou, On Broadway Tonight

Van Ark, Joan: Batman and the Super 7, Dallas, Knots Landing, Rhoda, Spider-Woman, Temperatures Rising, We've Got Each Other

Van Cleef, Lee: The Master

Van Doren, Mamie: Meet the Girls

Van Dusen, Granville: Allison Sidney Harrison, Astronauts, My Wife Next Door, Staff of Life, Sutters Bay, World Beyond, World of Darkness

Van Dyke, Barry: Airwolf (1987), Galactica 1980, Ghost of a Chance, Gun Shy, Harvey Korman Show (2 titles), Mr. Mom, Powers of Matthew Star, Redd Foxx Show, Tabitha, What's Up Doc?

Van Dyke, Dick: CBS Cartoon Theatre, Dick Van Dyke Show, Harry's Battles, Laugh Line, Mothers Day, New Dick Van Dyke Show (2 titles), Trouble with Richard, True Life Stories, Van Dyke and Company

Van Dyke, Jerry: Accidental Family, Dick Van Dyke Show, Headmaster, My Boy Googie, My Mother the Car, Picture This, 13 Queens Boulevard, You're Only Young Twice

Van Patten, Dick: Charo and the Sergeant, Eight Is Enough, Ernie Madge and Artie, Fit for a King, Grandpa Max, I Remember Mama, New Dick Van Dyke Show, Partners, Rock Candy, When Things Were Rotten

Van Patten, James: Chisholms, Love and Learn

Van Patten, Joyce: Bulba, Dobie Gillis, Don Rickles Show, Good Guys, Mary Tyler Moore Comedy Hour, Maureen, Plant Family

Vance, Vivian: Guestward Ho (second title), I Love Lucy, Lucille Ball-Desi Arnaz Show, Lucy Show

Varney, Jim: America 2-Night, New Operation Petticoat, Operation Petticoat, Rousters

Vaughn, Robert: A-Team, Boston Terrier (2 titles), Emerald Point N.A.S., Lieutenant, Man from UNCLE, Protectors, Stingray, You Are the Jury

Velez, Eddie: A-Team, Charlie and Company, For Love and Honor

Verdugo, Elena: Flim-Flam Man, Harry's Business,

Many Happy Returns Marcus Welby M.D., Meet Millie, Mona McCluskey, New Phil Silvers Show, Redigo, Suburban Beat

Vereen, Ben: Ben Vereen . . . Comin' At Ya, Charmkins, Tenspeed and Brown Shoe, Webster, You Write the Songs, Zobilee Zoo

Vernon, John: Delta House, Fuzzbucket, Hail to the Chief, Wildfire

Vigoda, Abe: Barney Miller, Fish

Villechiaze, Herve: Fantasy Island

Vincent, Jan-Michael: Airwolf (first title), Banana Splits Adventure Hour, Hardy Boys (1967), Survivors

Viscuso, Sal: M*A*S*H, Montefuscos, Soap, 2½ Dads

Visitor, Nana: Colbys, Fraud Squad

Vivyan, John: His Model Wife, Mr. Lucky

Voland, Herbert: Arnie, Love on a Rooftop, M*A*S*H, Mr. Deeds Goes to Town, Paul Lynde Show

Von Zell, Harry: Bachelor Father, George Burns and Gracie Allen Show, George Burns Show

Waggoner, Lyle: Barbara Eden Show, Carol Burnett Show, It's Your Bet, Rock Candy, Two the Hard Way, Ugily Family, Wonder Woman (second title)

Wagner, Lindsay: Bionic Woman, Jessie, Late Bloomer, Six Million Dollar Man, Windows, Doors and Keyholes

Wagner, Robert: Hart to Hart, It Takes a Thief, Lime Street, Switch

Wainwright, James: Beyond Westworld, Jigsaw

Waite, Ralph: Mississippi, Waltons

Walden, Robert: Bobby Jo and the Big Apple Goodtime Band, Brothers, Lou Grant, Ted Bissell Show

Walker, Clint: Cheyenne, Kodiak

Walker, Jimmie: At Ease, B.A.D. Cats, Bustin' Loose, Good Times

Walker, Nancy: Blansky's Beauties, Family Affair, Keep the Faith, Mama's Boy, Mary Tyler Moore Show, McMillan and Wife, Nancy Walker Show, Rhoda

Wallace, Dee: Dribble, Nothing Is Easy, 100 Centre Street, Suburban Beat, Together We Stand

Wallace, Marcia: Bewitched, Bob Newhart Show, Characters, New Love American Style, Rock Candy

Wallace, Mike: All Around Town, Big Surprise, Biography, Guess Again, I'll Buy That, Mike and Buff, $100,000 Big Surprise, What's in a Word, Who Pays?

Wallach, Eli: Batman, Our Family Honor

Walsh, Lory: Asphalt Cowboy, MacKenzies of Paradise Cove, Ugily Family

Walston, Ray: Amazing Stories, Danny and the Mermaid, Fast Times, Harry's Business, My Favorite Martian, Oh Madeline, Satan's Waitin', Stop Susan Williams

Walter, Jessica: All That Glitters, Amy Prentiss,

Bare Essence, For the People, Immortal, Mission: Impossible, Pursue and Destroy, T.L.C., Three's a Crowd (second title), Wildfire

Walters, Laurie: Eight Is Enough

Wanamaker, Sam: Berringer's

Ward, Burt: Batman, Batman and the Super 7, High School U.S.A., New Adventures of Batman

Warden, Jack: Asphalt Jungle, Bad News Bears, Blue Men, Crazy Like a Fox, Jigsaw John, N.Y.P.D., Renegade, Wackiest Ship in the Army

Warner, Malcolm-Jamal: Cosby Show

Warren, Jennifer: Butterflies, Paper Dolls

Warren, Lesley Ann: Cat Ballou, Faerie Tale Theatre, Mission: Impossible

Washburn, Beverly: Gidget, Loretta Young Show, Professional Father

Waterman, Willard: All About Barbara, Dennis the Menace, Dick Van Dyke Show, Great Gildersleeve, How to Marry a Millionaire, Pippi Longstocking (1961), Real McCoys, Thompson's Ghost

Waters, Ethel: Beulah, Ethel Waters Show, You're Only Young Twice

Watkins, Carlene: Best of the West, B.J. and the Bear, It's Not Easy, Mary, Secret Empire, Tortellis

Watson, Mills: B.J. and the Bear, Harper Valley, Lobo, Misadventures of Sheriff Lobo

Watson, Vernee: Benson, Captain Cavemen and the Teenangels, Carter Country, Dribble, Foley Square, London and Davis in New York, Welcome Back, Kotter

Wayne, Carol: Heaven on Earth, Tonight Show

Wayne, David: Batman, Dallas, Do Not Disturb, Ellery Queen, Family, Good Life, Holloway's Daughters, House Calls, Norby

Wayne, Patrick: Monte Carlo Show, Movin' On, Mr. Adams and Eve, Rounders, Shirley

Weatherly, Shawn: J.J. Starbuck, Ocean Quest, Shaping Up

Weaver, Dennis: Buck James, Emerald Point N.A.S., Gentle Ben, Gunsmoke, Kentucky Jones, McCloud, Stone

Weaver, Doodles: Day with Doodles, Doodles Weaver Show

Weaver, Fritz: The City, D.C. Cop, Momma the Detective, Rx for the Defense

Weaver, Lee: Bill Cosby Show, Easy Street, Guess Who's Coming to Dinner

Webb, Jack: Dragnet (2 titles), G.E. True

Webb, Lucy: Apartment 2-C, Not Necessarily the News, Private Benjamin

Webb, Richard: Anything for Money, Captain Midnight, U.S. Border Patrol

Wedgeworth, Ann: Filthy Rich, Sylvan in Paradise, Three's Company (1977)

Weitz, Bruce: Catalina C-Lab, Every Stray Dog and Kid, Hill Street Blues, Mama's Boy

Welch, Raquel: Hollywood Palace, On Top All Over the World

Weld, Tuesday: Dobie Gillis, Greatest Show on